W9-BSD-414

Oxford
Color French
Dictionary Plus

Revised second edition

FRENCH–ENGLISH
ENGLISH–FRENCH

FRANÇAIS–ANGLAIS
ANGLAIS–FRANÇAIS

OXFORD
UNIVERSITY PRESS

OXFORD

UNIVERSITY PRESS

Great Clarendon Street, Oxford ox2 6DP

Oxford University Press is a department of the University of Oxford.
It furthers the University's objective of excellence in research, scholarship,
and education by publishing worldwide in

Oxford New York

Auckland Bangkok Buenos Aires Cape Town Chennai
Dar es Salaam Delhi Hong Kong Istanbul Karachi Kolkata
Kuala Lumpur Madrid Melbourne Mexico City Mumbai Nairobi
São Paulo Shanghai Taipei Tokyo Toronto

Oxford is a registered trade mark of Oxford University Press
in the UK and in certain other countries

Published in the United States
by Oxford University Press Inc., New York

First published 1995 as the Oxford Colour French Dictionary
Revised edition published 1998
Second edition published 2001
Revised second edition published 2004

British Library Cataloguing in Publication Data

Data available

Library of Congress Cataloging in Publication Data

Data available

ISBN 978–0–19–860900–1
ISBN 0–19–860900–0
ISBN 978–0–19–860898–1
ISBN 0–19–860898–5 (US edition)

10 9 8 7 6 5 4 3

Typeset by Tradespools Ltd
Printed in Italy
by Legoprint S.p.A.

Contents

Preface

The *Oxford Color French Dictionary Plus* is a dictionary
designed primarily for students of French. The clear
presentation and color headwords make it easily accessible. It
contains completely new sections, not found in the *Oxford
Color French Dictionary*, on French life and culture,
letter-writing, and French grammar, making it even more
useful for students up to intermediate level.

List of contributors

Revised Second Edition

Marianne Chalmers

Second Edition

Editors:

Marianne Chalmers
Rosalind Combley
Catherine Roux
Laura Wedgeworth

Supplementary Material:

Marianne Chalmers
Martine Pierquin
Glynnis Chantrell
Valerie Grundy
Natalie Pomier

Proof-reading:

Andrew Hodgson

First Edition

Editors:

Michael Janes
Dora Latiri-Carpenter
Edwin Carpenter

Introduction

This dictionary is designed as an effective and practical reference tool for the student, adult learner, traveller, and business professional. It provides user-friendly treatment of core vocabulary across a broad spectrum of written and spoken language.

Enhanced coverage

The wordlist of the previous edition has been comprehensively revised to reflect recent additions to both languages and to cover such topics as **computing** and the **Internet**.

A further new feature of the dictionary is the special status given to more complex grammatical words which provide the basic structure of both languages. These *function words* are given a special layout to make them instantly accessible and offer clearly presented translation options and examples, with **short usage notes** to warn of possible pitfalls.

Coverage of verbs has been significantly extended so that all **French verbs** in the text are cross-referenced to the appropriate section of the expanded verb tables. Examples of the three main French verb groups, as well as *avoir* and *être*, are conjugated in the most commonly used tenses. A quick **reference guide** giving the English translation of an example verb in the principal tenses has been included, followed by exemplified guidance on **how to conjugate a reflexive verb**.

Easy reference

The dictionary layout has been designed to be **clear**, streamlined, and easy to consult. The wordlist has been fully **alphabetized**, with all English compounds and French hyphenated compounds in their correct alphabetical positions. **Bullet points** separate each new part of speech within an entry, making it easy to scan. Nuances of sense or usage are pinpointed by semantic indicators (in condensed type in round brackets) or by typical collocates (*in italics in round brackets*) with which the word frequently occurs, quickly guiding the user to the appropriate translation. Extra help is given in the form of **symbols** to mark the register of language unambiguously. An exclamation mark ⚠ indicates colloquial language and a cross ✖ indicates slang.

Each headword is followed by its **phonetic transcription** between slashes, except in the case of English compound headwords where the pronunciation can be derived from that of each of the component parts. The symbols used for the pronunciation are those of the International Phonetic Alphabet. Any unpredictable plural forms or irregular English conjugations, comparative and superlative forms are also given in brackets.

This dictionary is designed to present essential information in an accessible format, providing the user with a fast track to **clear and effective communication**.

Proprietary terms

This dictionary includes some words which are, or are asserted to be, proprietary terms or trademarks. The presence or absence of such assertions should not be regarded as affecting the legal status of any proprietary name or trademark.

The pronunciation of French

Vowels

a	*as in*	patte	/pat/		ɑ	*as in*	pâte	/pɑt/
ã		clan	/klã/		e		dé	/de/
ε		belle	/bεl/		ε̃		lin	/lε̃/
ə		demain	/dəmε̃/		i		gris	/gʀi/
o		gros	/gʀo/		ɔ		corps	/kɔʀ/
ɔ̃		long	/lɔ̃/		œ		leur	/lœʀ/
œ̃		brun	/bʀœ̃/		ø		deux	/dø/
u		fou	/fu/		y		pur	/pyʀ/

Semi-Vowels

j	*as in*	fille	/fij/
ɥ		huit	/ɥit/
w		oui	/wi/

Consonants

Aspiration of 'h'
Where it is impossible to make a liason this is indicated by /'/
immediately after the slash e.g. *haine* /'ɛn/.

b	*as in*	bal	/bal/		ŋ	*as in*	camping	/kɑ̃piŋ/
d		dent	/dã/		p		porte	/pɔʀt/
f		foire	/fwaʀ/		ʀ		rire	/ʀiʀ/
g		gomme	/gɔm/		s		sang	/sã/
k		clé	/kle/		ʃ		chien	/ʃjε̃/
l		lien	/ljε̃/		t		train	/tʀε̃/
m		mer	/mɛʀ/		v		voile	/vwal/
n		nage	/naʒ/		z		zèbre	/zɛbʀ/
ɲ		gnon	/ɲɔ̃/		ʒ		jeune	/ʒœn/

Glossary of grammatical terms

Abbreviation A shortened form of a word or phrase made by leaving out some letters or by using only the initial letter of each word: etc., DNA

Active In the active form the subject of the verb performs the action: **she whistled = elle a sifflé**

Adjective A word describing a noun: **a *red* pencil = un crayon *rouge***

Adverb A word that describes or changes the meaning of a verb, an adjective, or another adverb: **he drives *fast* = il conduit *vite*; *fairly* often = *assez* souvent**

Article The definite article, **the = le, la, l', les**, and indefinite article, **a/an = un, une**, are used in front of a noun

Attributive An adjective or noun is attributive when it is used directly before a noun: **the *big* dog = le *grand* chien; *birthday* card = carte d'anniversaire**

Auxiliary verb One of the verbs used to form the perfect, pluperfect, and future perfect tenses. In French the auxiliary verbs are **avoir** and **être**: **I have read the letter = j'*ai* lu la lettre; he had already gone = il *était* déjà parti**

Cardinal number A whole number representing a quantity: **one, two, three = un/une, deux, trois**

Clause A self-contained section of a sentence that contains a subject and a verb

Collective noun A noun that is singular in form but refers to a group of persons or things, e.g. **royalty, grain**

Collocate A word that regularly occurs with another; in French **livre** is a typical collocate of the verb **lire**

Comparative The form of an adjective or adverb for comparing two or more nouns or pronouns, often using **more, less** or **as** (**plus, moins, aussi**): **smaller = plus petit; more frequently = plus fréquemment; as intelligent = aussi intelligent**

Compound adjective An adjective formed from two separate words: **tout-puissant = all-powerful; nord-américain = North American**

Compound noun A noun formed from two or more separate words: **porte-clés = keyring**

Conditional tense A tense of a verb that expresses what would happen if something else occurred: **I would invite them = je les inviterais**

Conjugation Variation of the form of a verb to show tense, person, mood, etc.

Conjunction A word used to link clauses: **and = et, because = parce que**

Definite article: **the = le, la, l', les**

Demonstrative pronoun A pronoun indicating the person or thing referred to: *this one* is cheaper = *celui-ci* est moins cher

Determiner A word that comes before a noun to show how it is being used: **the = le, la, l', les; some = du/de l'/de la/des; my = mon/ma/mes**

Direct object the noun or pronoun directly affected by the verb: **she ate *the apple* = elle a mangé *la pomme***

Direct speech A speaker's actual words or the use of these in writing

Ending Letters added to the stem of verbs, as well as to nouns and adjectives, according to tense, number, gender

Exclamation A sound, word, or remark expressing a strong feeling such as anger, fear, or joy: **ouch! = aïe!**

Feminine One of the two noun genders in French: **la femme = the woman; la carte = the card**

Future tense The tense of a verb that refers to something that will happen in the future: **I will go = j'irai**

Gender One of the two groups of nouns in French: masculine and feminine

Imperative A form of a verb that expresses a command: **hurry up! = dépêche-toi!**

Imperfect tense The tense of a verb that refers to an uncompleted or a habitual action in the past: **I went there every day = j'y allais tous les jours**

Impersonal verb A verb used in English only with 'it' and in French only with 'il': **it is raining = il pleut**

Indefinite article: **a/an = un, une**

Indefinite pronoun A pronoun that does not identify a specific person or object: **one = on; something = quelque chose**

Indicative form The form of a verb used when making a statement of fact or asking questions of fact: **we like animals = nous aimons les animaux**

Indirect object The noun or pronoun indirectly affected by the verb, at which the direct object is aimed: **she gave *him* the key = elle *lui* a donné la clé**

Indirect speech A report of what someone has said which does not reproduce the exact words

Infinitive The basic part of a verb: **to play = jouer**

Inflect To change the ending or form of a word to show its tense or its grammatical relation to other words: **donne** and **donnez** are inflected forms of the verb **donner**

Interrogative pronoun A pronoun that asks a question: **who? = qui?**

Intransitive verb A verb that does not have a direct object: **he died yesterday = il est mort hier**

Invariable adjective An adjective that has the same form in the feminine as the masculine, as French **ivoire, transmanche**

Invariable noun A noun that has the same form in the plural as the singular as. English **sheep, species**, French **précis, rabais**

Irregular verb A verb that does not follow one of the set patterns and has its own individual forms, e.g. English **to be**, French **être**

Masculine One of the two noun genders in French: **le garçon = the boy; le livre = the book**

Modal verb A verb that is used with another verb to express permission, obligation, possibility, such as **might, should.** The French modal verbs are **devoir, pouvoir, savoir, vouloir, falloir**

Negative Expressing refusal or denial: **there aren't any = il n'y en a pas; he won't go = il ne veut pas partir**

Noun A word that names a person or thing

Number The state of being either singular or plural

Object The word or group of words which is immediately affected by the action indicated by the verb, as **livre** in **il a lu le livre**, or **voiture** in **elle lave la voiture**

Ordinal number A number that shows the position of a person or thing in a series: **the *third* time = la *troisième* fois, the *fourth* door on the left = la *quatrième* porte à gauche**

Part of speech A grammatical term for the function of a word; noun, verb, adjective, etc., are parts of speech

Passive In the passive form the subject of the verb experiences the action rather than performs it: **he was punished = il a été puni**

Past participle The part of a verb used to form past tenses: **she had *gone* = elle était *partie***

Perfect tense The tense of a verb that refers to an action that has taken place in a period of time that includes the present: **I have already eaten = j'ai déjà mangé; my bike has been stolen = on m'a volé mon vélo**

Person Any of the three groups of personal pronouns and forms taken by verbs. In the singular the **first person** (e.g. **I/je**) refers to the person speaking; **the second**

person (e.g. **you/tu**) refers to the person spoken to; the **third person** (e.g. **he, she, it/il, elle**) refers to the person spoken about. The corresponding plural forms are **we/nous, you/vous, they/ils, elles**

Personal pronoun A pronoun that refers to a person or thing

Phrasal verb A verb in English combined with a preposition or an adverb to have a particular meaning: **run away = se sauver**

Phrase A self-contained section of a sentence that does not contain a full verb

Pluperfect tense The tense of a verb that refers to something that happened before a particular point in the past: **when I arrived, he *had* already *left* = quand je suis arrivé, il *était* déjà *parti***

Plural Of nouns, etc., referring to more than one: **the children = les enfants**

Possessive adjective An adjective that shows possession, belonging to someone or something: **my = mon/ma/mes**

Possessive pronoun a pronoun that shows possession, belonging to someone or something: **mine = le mien/la mienne/les miens/les miennes**

Predicative An adjective is predicative when it comes after a verb such as **be** or **become** in English, or after **être** or **devenir** in French: **she is beautiful = elle est belle**

Prefix A group of letters added to the beginning of a word to change its meaning, e.g. **anti-, ultra-, non-**

Preposition A word that stands in front of a noun or pronoun, usually indicating movement, position or time: *on the chair* = *sur la chaise*; *towards* the car = *vers la voiture*

Present participle The part of a verb in English that ends in –ing; the corresponding ending in French is **-ant**

Present tense The tense of a verb that refers to something happening now: **I make = je fais**

Pronoun A word that stands instead of a noun: **he = il, she = elle, mine = le mien/la mienne/ les miens/les miennes**

Proper noun A name of a person, place, institution etc. written with a capital letter at the start; **France, the Alps, Madeleine, l'Europe** are all proper nouns

Reflexive pronoun A pronoun that goes with a reflexive verb: in French **me, te, se, nous, vous, se**

Reflexive verb a verb whose object is the same as its subject. In French it is used with a reflexive pronoun and conjugated with **être: you should wash yourself = tu devrais te laver**

Regular verb A verb that follows a set pattern in its different forms

Relative pronoun A pronoun that introduces a subordinate clause, relating to a person or thing mentioned in the main clause: **the book** *which* **I chose = le livre** *que* **j'ai choisi**

Reported speech Another name for **Indirect speech**

Sentence A sequence of words, with a subject and a verb, that can stand on their own to make a statement, ask a question, or give a command

Singular Of nouns, etc., referring to just one: **the tree = l'arbre**

Stem The part of a verb to which endings are added; **donn-** is the stem of **donner**

Subject In a clause or sentence, the noun or pronoun that causes the action of the verb: *he* **caught the ball =** *il* **a attrapé le ballon**

Subjunctive A verb form that is used to express doubt or uncertainty in English. It is more widely used in French, particularly after certain conjunctions and with verbs of wishing, fearing, ordering, forbidding followed by **que: I want you to be good = je veux que tu sois sage; you may be right = il est possible que tu aies raison**

Subordinate clause A clause which adds information to the main clause of a sentence, but cannot function as a sentence by itself, e.g. **when it rang** in **she answered the phone when it rang**

Suffix A group of letters joined to the end of a word to form another word, as **–eur** in **grandeur** or **–able** in **véritable**

Superlative The form of an adjective or adverb that makes it the 'most' or 'least': **the** *biggest* **house = *la plus grande* maison; the** *cheapest* **CD = le CD *le moins cher***

Tense The form of a verb that tells when the action takes place: present, future, imperfect, perfect, pluperfect are all tenses

Transitive verb A verb that is used with a direct object: **I wrote the letter = j'ai écrit la lettre**

Verb A word or group of words that describes an action: **the children are playing = les enfants jouent**

Abbreviations/Abréviations

adjective	*a*	adjectif
abbreviation	*abbr, abrév*	abréviation
adverb	*adv*	adverbe
anatomy	*Anat*	anatomie
archeology	*Archeol, Archéol*	archéologie
architecture	*Archit*	architecture
motoring	*Auto*	automobile
auxiliary	*aux*	auxiliaire
aviation	*Aviat*	aviation
botany	*Bot*	botanique
commerce	*Comm*	commerce
computing	*Comput*	informatique
conjunction	*conj*	conjonction
cookery	*Culin*	culinaire
determiner	*det, dét*	déterminant
electricity	*Electr, Électr*	électricité
figurative	*fig*	sens figuré
geography	*Geog, Géog*	géographie
geology	*Geol, Géol*	géologie
grammar	*Gram*	grammaire
humorous	*hum*	humoristique
interjection	*interj*	interjection
invariable	*inv*	invariable
law	*Jur*	droit
linguistics	*Ling*	linguistique
literal	*lit*	littéral
phrase	*loc*	locution
medicine	*Med, Méd*	médecine
military	*Mil*	armée
music	*Mus*	musique
noun	*n*	nom
nautical	*Naut*	nautisme
feminine noun	*nf*	nom féminin
masculine noun	*nm*	nom masculin
masculine and feminine noun	*nm,f* or *nmf* or *nm/f*	nom masculin et féminin
computing	*Ordinat*	informatique

pejorative	*pej, péj*	péjoratif
philosophy	*Phil*	philosophie
photography	*Photo*	photographie
plural	*pl*	pluriel
politics	*Pol*	politique
possessive	*poss*	possessif
past participle	*pp*	participe passé
prefix	*pref, préf*	préfixe
preposition	*prep, prép*	préposition
present participle	*pres p*	participe présent
pronoun	*pron*	pronom
psychology	*Psych*	psychologie
past	*pt*	prétérit
something	*qch*	quelque chose
somebody	*qn*	quelqu'un
railway	*Rail*	chemin de fer
relative pronoun	*rel pron, pron rel*	pronom relatif
religion	*Relig*	religion
somebody	*sb*	quelqu'un
school	*School, Scol*	scolaire
sport	*Sport*	sport
something	*sth*	quelque chose
technology	*Tech*	technologie
theatre	*Theat, Théât*	théâtre
television	*TV*	télévision
university	*Univ*	université
American English	*US*	anglais américain
auxiliary verb	*v aux*	verbe auxiliaire
intransitive verb	*vi*	verbe intransitif
reflexive verb	*vpr*	verbe pronominal
transitive verb	*vt*	verbe transitif
transitive and intransitive verb	*vt/i*	verbe transitif et intransitif
translation equivalent	≈	équivalent approximatif
trademark	®	marque déposée
colloquial	▣	familier
slang	▣	argot

a /a/ ⇒AVOIR [5].

- -

à /a/ *préposition*

  à+le = au
  à+les = aux

····➤ (avec verbe de mouvement) to.

····➤ (pour indiquer où l'on se trouve) ∼ **la maison** at home; ∼ **Nice** in Nice.

····➤ (âge, date, heure) ∼ **l'âge de...** at the age of...; **au XIXe siècle** in the 19th century; ∼ **deux heures** at two o'clock.

····➤ (description) with; **aux yeux verts** with green eyes.

····➤ (appartenance) ∼ **qui est ce stylo?** whose pen is this?; **c'est** ∼ **vous?** is this yours?

····➤ (avec nombre) ∼ **90 km/h** at 90 km per hour, ∼ **10 minutes d'ici** 10 minutes from here; **des tomates** ∼ **2 euros le kilo** tomatoes at 2 euros a kilo; **un timbre** ∼ **2 euros** a 2-euro stamp; **nous avons fait le travail** ∼ **deux** two of us did the work; **mener 5** ∼ **4** to lead 5 (to) 4.

····➤ (avec être) **c'est** ∼ **moi** it's my turn; **je suis** ∼ **vous tout de suite** I'll be with you in a minute; **c'est** ∼ **toi de décider** it's up to you to decide.

····➤ (hypothèse) ∼ **ce qu'il paraît** apparently; ∼ **t'entendre** to hear you talk.

····➤ (exclamatif) ∼ **ta santé!** cheers!; ∼ **demain/bientôt!** see you tomorrow/soon!

····➤ (moyen) ∼ **la main** by hand; ∼ **vélo** by bike; ∼ **pied** on foot; **chauffage au gaz** gas heating.

- -

abaissement /abɛsmɑ̃/ *nm* (de taux, de prix) cut; (de seuil) lowering.

abaisser /abese/ [1] *vt* lower; (*levier*) pull *ou* push down; (fig) humiliate. □ **s'**∼ *vpr* go down, drop; (fig) demean oneself; **s'**∼ **à** stoop to.

abandon /abɑ̃dɔ̃/ *nm* abandonment; (de personne) desertion; (de course) withdrawal; (naturel) abandon; **à l'**∼ in a state of neglect.

abandonner /abɑ̃dɔne/ [1] *vt* abandon; (*épouse, cause*) desert; (renoncer à) give up, abandon; (céder) give (**à** to); (*course*) withdraw from; (Ordinat) abort. □ **s'**∼ **à** *vpr* give oneself up to.

abasourdir /abazurdir/ [2] *vt* stun.

abat-jour /abaʒur/ *nm inv* lampshade.

abats /aba/ *nmpl* offal.

abattement /abatmɑ̃/ *nm* dejection; (faiblesse) exhaustion; (Comm) reduction; ∼ **fiscal** tax allowance.

abattre /abatr/ [11] *vt* knock down; (*arbre*) cut down; (*animal*) slaughter; (*avion*) shoot down; (affaiblir) weaken; (démoraliser) demoralize; **ne pas se laisser** ∼ not let things get one down. □ **s'**∼ *vpr* come down, fall (down).

abbaye /abei/ *nf* abbey.

abbé /abe/ *nm* priest; (supérieur d'une abbaye) abbot.

abcès /apsɛ/ *nm* abscess.

abdiquer /abdike/ [1] *vt/i* abdicate.

abdomen /abdɔmɛn/ *nm* abdomen.

abdominal (*pl* **-aux**) /abdɔminal/ *a* abdominal. **abdominaux** *nmpl* (Sport) stomach exercises.

abeille /abɛj/ *nf* bee.

aberrant, **~e** /abɛʀɑ̃, -t/ *a* absurd.

abêtir /abetiʀ/ [2] *vt* turn into a moron.

abîme /abim/ *nm* abyss.

abîmer /abime/ [1] *vt* damage, spoil. □ **s'~** *vpr* get damaged *ou* spoilt.

ablation /ablasjɔ̃/ *nf* removal.

aboiement /abwamɑ̃/ *nm* bark, barking; **~s** barking.

abolir /abɔliʀ/ [2] *vt* abolish.

abondance /abɔ̃dɑ̃s/ *nf* abundance; (*prospérité*) affluence. **abondant**, **~e** *a* abundant, plentiful.

abonder /abɔ̃de/ [1] *vi* abound (**en** in); **~ dans le sens de qn** agree wholeheartedly with sb.

abonné, **~e** /abɔne/ *nm, f* (*lecteur*) subscriber; (*voyageur, spectateur*) season-ticket holder.

abonnement /abɔnmɑ̃/ *nm* (à un journal) subscription; (de bus, Théât) season-ticket; (au gaz) standing charge.

abonner (**s'**) /(s)abɔne/ [1] *vpr* subscribe (**à** to).

abord /abɔʀ/ *nm* access; **~s** surroundings; **d'~** first.

abordable /abɔʀdabl/ *a* (*prix*) affordable; (*personne*) approachable; (*texte*) accessible.

aborder /abɔʀde/ [1] *vt* approach; (*lieu*) reach; (*problème*) tackle. ● *vi* reach land.

aborigène /abɔʀiʒɛn/ *nm* aborigine.

aboutir /abutiʀ/ [2] *vi* succeed, achieve a result; **~ à** end (up) in, lead to; **n'~ à rien** come to nothing.

aboutissement /abutismɑ̃/ *nm* outcome; (de carrière, d'évolution) culmination.

aboyer /abwaje/ [31] *vi* bark.

abrégé /abʀeʒe/ *nm* summary.

abréger /abʀeʒe/ [14] [40] *vt* (*texte*) shorten, abridge; (*mot*) abbreviate, shorten; (*visite*) cut short.

abreuver /abʀœve/ [1] *vt* water; (fig) overwhelm (**de** with). □ **s'~** *vpr* drink.

abréviation /abʀevjasjɔ̃/ *nf* abbreviation.

abri /abʀi/ *nm* shelter; **à l'~** under cover; (en lieu sûr) safe; **à l'~ de** sheltered from; **se mettre à l'~** take shelter.

abricot /abʀiko/ *nm* apricot.

abriter /abʀite/ [1] *vt* shelter; (recevoir) house. □ **s'~** *vpr* (take) shelter.

abrupt, **~e** /abʀypt/ *a* steep, sheer; (fig) abrupt.

abruti, **~e** /abʀyti/ *nm, f* 🔲 idiot.

absence /apsɑ̃s/ *nf* absence; **il a des ~s** sometimes his mind goes blank.

absent, **~e** /apsɑ̃, -t/ *a* (*personne*) absent, away; (*chose*) missing; **il est toujours ~** he's still away; **d'un air ~** absently. ● *nm, f* absentee.

absenter (**s'**) /(s)apsɑ̃te/ [1] *vpr* go *ou* be away; (sortir) go out, leave.

absolu, **~e** /apsɔly/ *a* absolute.

absorbant, **~e** /apsɔʀbɑ̃, -t/ *a* (travail) absorbing; (matière) absorbent.

absorber /apsɔʀbe/ [1] *vt* absorb;

être absorbé par qch be engrossed in sth.

abstenir (s') /(s)apstəniʀ/ [58] vpr abstain; **s'~ de** refrain from.

abstrait, ~e /apstʀɛ, -t/ a & nm abstract.

absurde /apsyʀd/ a absurd.

abus /aby/ nm abuse, misuse; (injustice) abuse; **~ de confiance** breach of trust.

abuser /abyze/ [1] vt deceive. ●vi go too far; **~ de** abuse, misuse; (profiter de) take advantage of; (alcool) overindulge in. □ **s'~** vpr be mistaken.

abusif, -ive /abyzif, -v/ a excessive; (impropre) wrong; (injuste) unfair.

académie /akademi/ nf academy; (circonscription) local education authority.

acajou /akaʒu/ nm mahogany.

accablant, ~e /akablã, -t/ a (chaleur) oppressive; (fait, témoignage) damning.

accabler /akable/ [1] vt overwhelm; **~ d'impôts** burden with taxes; **~ d'injures** heap insults upon.

accéder /aksede/ [14] vi **~ à** (lieu) reach; (pouvoir, trône) accede to; (requête) grant; (Ordinat) access; **~ à la propriété** become a homeowner.

accélérateur /akseleʀatœʀ/ nm accelerator.

accélérer /akseleʀe/ [14] vt/i accelerate. □ **s'~** vpr speed up.

accent /aksã/ nm accent; (sur une syllabe) stress, accent; **mettre l'~ sur** stress; **~ aigu/grave/ circonflexe** acute/grave/circumflex accent.

accentuer /aksãtɥe/ [1] vt (lettre, syllabe) accent; (fig) emphasize, accentuate. □ **s'~** vpr become more pronounced, increase.

accepter /aksɛpte/ [1] vt accept; **~ de faire** agree to do.

accès /aksɛ/ nm access; (porte) entrance; (de fièvre) bout; (de colère) fit; (d'enthousiasme) burst; (Ordinat) access; **les ~ de** (voies) the approaches to; **facile d'~** easy to get to.

accessoire /akseswaʀ/ a secondary, incidental. ●nm accessory; (Théât) prop.

accident /aksidã/ nm accident; **~ de train/d'avion** train/plane crash; **par ~** by accident.

accidenté, ~e a (personne) injured (in an accident); (voiture) damaged; (terrain) uneven, hilly.

accidentel, ~le a accidental.

acclamer /aklame/ [1] vt cheer, acclaim.

accommoder /akɔmɔde/ [1] vt adapt (à to); (cuisiner) prepare; (assaisonner) flavour. □ **s'~ de** vpr make the best of.

accompagnateur, -trice /akɔ̃paɲatœʀ, -tʀis/ nm, f (Mus) accompanist; (guide) guide; **~ d'enfants** accompanying adult.

accompagner /akɔ̃paɲe/ [1] vt accompany. □ **s'~ de** vpr be accompanied by.

accomplir /akɔ̃pliʀ/ [2] vt carry out, fulfil. □ **s'~** vpr take place, happen; (vœu) be fulfilled.

accord /akɔʀ/ nm agreement; (harmonie) harmony; (Mus) chord; **être d'~** agree (**pour** to); **se mettre d'~** come to an agreement, agree; **d'~!** all right!, OK!

accorder /akɔʀde/ [1] vt grant; (couleurs) match; (Mus) tune; (attribuer) (valeur, importance) assign. □ **s'~** vpr (se mettre d'accord) agree; (s'octroyer) allow oneself; **s'~ avec** (s'entendre avec) get on with.

accotement /akɔtmã/ nm verge; **~ non stabilisé** soft verge.

accouchement /akuʃmɑ̃/ *nm* childbirth; (*travail*) labour.

accoucher /akuʃe/ [1] *vi* give birth (**de** to); (*être en travail*) be in labour. ● *vt* deliver. **accoucheur** *nm* **médecin** ∼ obstetrician.

accoudoir /akudwaR/ *nm* arm-rest.

accoupler /akuple/ [1] *vt* (Tech) couple. □ **s'**∼ *vpr* mate.

accourir /akuRiR/ [20] *vi* run up.

accoutumance /akutymɑ̃s/ *nf* familiarization; (Méd) addiction.

accoutumer /akutyme/ [1] *vt* accustom. □ **s'**∼ *vpr* get accustomed.

accro /akRo/ *nmf* 🄸 (*drogué*) addict; (*amateur*) fan.

accroc /akRo/ *nm* tear, rip; (*fig*) hitch.

accrochage /akRɔʃaʒ/ *nm* hanging; hooking; (Auto) collision; (*dispute*) clash; (Mil) encounter.

accrocher /akRɔʃe/ [1] *vt* (*suspendre*) hang up; (*attacher*) hook, hitch; (*déchirer*) catch; (*heurter*) hit; (*attirer*) attract. □ **s'**∼ *vpr* cling, hang on (**à** to); (*se disputer*) clash.

accroissement /akRwasmɑ̃/ *nm* increase (**de** in).

accroître /akRwɑtR/ [24] *vt* increase. □ **s'**∼ *vpr* increase.

accroupir (s') /(s)akRupiR/ [2] *vpr* squat.

accru, ∼**e** /akRy/ *a* increased, greater.

accueil /akœj/ *nm* reception, welcome.

accueillant, ∼**e** /akœjɑ̃, -t/ *a* friendly, welcoming.

accueillir /akœjiR/ [25] *vt* receive; welcome; (*film, livre*) receive; (*prendre en charge*) (*réfugiés, patients*) take care of, cater for.

accumuler /akymyle/ [1] *vt* (*énergie*) store up; (*capital*) accumulate. □ **s'**∼ *vpr* (*neige, ordures*) pile up; (*dettes*) accrue.

accusation /akyzasjɔ̃/ *nf* accusation; (Jur) charge; **l'**∼ (*magistrat*) the prosecution.

accusé, ∼**e** /akyze/ *a* marked. ● *nm, f* defendant, accused.

accuser /akyze/ [1] *vt* accuse (**de** of); (*blâmer*) blame (**de** for); (Jur) charge (**de** with); (*fig*) emphasize; ∼ **réception de** acknowledge receipt of.

acharné, ∼**e** /aʃaRne/ *a* relentless, ferocious.

acharnement *nm* (*énergie*) furious energy; (*ténacité*) determination.

acharner (s') /(s)aʃaRne/ [1] *vpr* persevere; **s'**∼ **sur** set upon; (*poursuivre*) hound; **s'**∼ **à faire** (*s'évertuer*) try desperately; (*s'obstiner*) keep on doing.

achat /aʃa/ *nm* purchase; ∼**s** shopping; **faire l'**∼ **de** buy; **faire des** ∼**s** do some shopping.

acheminer /aʃ(ə)mine/ [1] *vt* dispatch, convey; (*courrier*) handle. □ **s'**∼ **vers** *vpr* head for.

acheter /aʃ(ə)te/ [6] *vt* buy; ∼ **qch à qn** (*pour lui*) buy sth for sb; (*chez lui*) buy sth from sb.

acheteur, -**euse** *nm, f* buyer; (*client de magasin*) shopper.

achèvement /aʃɛvmɑ̃/ *nm* completion.

achever /aʃ(ə)ve/ [6] *vt* finish (off). □ **s'**∼ *vpr* end.

acide /asid/ *a* acid, sharp. ● *nm* acid.

acier /asje/ *nm* steel.

acné /akne/ *nf* acne.

acompte /akɔ̃t/ *nm* deposit, part-payment.

à-côté (*pl* ∼**s**) /akote/ *nm* side issue; ∼**s** (*argent*) extras.

acoustique /akustik/ *nf* acoustics (+ *sg*). ● *a* acoustic.

acquéreur /akeRœR/ *nm* purchaser, buyer.

acquérir /akeʀiʀ/ [7] vt acquire, gain; (biens) purchase, acquire.

acquis, **~e** /aki, -z/ a acquired; (fait) established; **tenir qch pour ~** take sth for granted. ● nm experience. **acquisition** nf acquisition; purchase.

acquitter /akite/ [1] vt acquit; (dette) settle. □ **s'~ de** vpr (promesse) fulfil; (devoir) discharge.

âcre /ɑkʀ/ a acrid.

acrobatie /akʀɔbasi/ nf acrobatics (+ pl); **~ aérienne** aerobatics (+ pl).

acte /akt/ nm act, action, deed; (Théât) act; (Jur) deed; **~ de naissance/mariage** birth/marriage certificate; **~s** (compte rendu) proceedings; **prendre ~ de** note.

acteur /aktœʀ/ nm actor.

actif, **-ive** /aktif, -v/ a active; (population) working. ● nm (Comm) assets; **avoir à son ~** have to one's credit ou name.

action /aksjɔ̃/ nf action; (Comm) share; (Jur) action; (effet) effect; (initiative) initiative. **actionnaire** nmf shareholder.

activer /aktive/ [1] vt speed up; (feu) boost. □ **s'~** vpr hurry up; (s'affairer) be very busy.

activité /aktivite/ nf activity; **en ~** (volcan) active; (fonctionnaire) working; (usine) in operation.

actrice /aktʀis/ nf actress.

actualité /aktɥalite/ nf topicality; **l'~** current affairs; **les ~s** news; **d'~** topical.

actuel, **~le** /aktɥɛl/ a current, present; (d'actualité) topical. **actuellement** adv currently, at the present time.

acupuncture /akypɔ̃ktyʀ/ nf acupuncture.

adaptateur /adaptatœʀ/ nm (Électr) adapter.

adapter /adapte/ [1] vt adapt;

(fixer) fit. □ **s'~** vpr adapt (oneself); (Tech) fit.

additif /aditif/ nm (note) rider; (substance) additive.

addition /adisjɔ̃/ nf addition; (au café) bill; (US) check. **additionner** [1] vt add; (totaliser) add (up).

adepte /adɛpt/ nmf follower; (d'activité) enthusiast.

adéquat, **~e** /adekwa, -t/ a suitable; (suffisant) adequate.

adhérent, **~e** /adeʀɑ̃, -t/ nm, f member.

adhérer /adeʀe/ [14] vi adhere, stick (à to); **~ à** (club) be a member of; (s'inscrire à) join.

adhésif, **-ive** /adezif, -v/ a adhesive; **ruban ~** sticky tape.

adhésion /adezjɔ̃/ nf membership; (soutien) support.

adieu (pl **~x**) /adjø/ interj & nm goodbye, farewell.

adjectif /adʒɛktif/ nm adjective.

adjoint, **~e** /adʒwɛ̃, -t/ nm, f assistant; **~ au maire** deputy mayor. ● a assistant.

adjuger /adʒyʒe/ [40] vt award; (aux enchères) auction. □ **s'~** vpr take (for oneself).

admettre /admɛtʀ/ [42] vt let in, admit; (tolérer) allow; (reconnaître) admit, acknowledge; (candidat) pass.

administrateur, **-trice** /administʀatœʀ, -tʀis/ nm, f administrator, director; (Jur) trustee; **~ de site** Internet Webmaster.

administratif, **-ive** /administʀatif, -v/ a administrative; (document) official. **administration** nf administration; (gestion) management; **l'A~** Civil Service.

administrer /administʀe/ [1] vt run, manage; (justice, biens, antidote) administer.

admirateur, -trice /admiRatœR, -tRis/ *nm, f* admirer.

admiration /admiRasjɔ̃/ *nf* admiration.

admirer /admiRe/ [1] *vt* admire.

admission /admisjɔ̃/ *nf* admission.

ADN *abrév m* (**acide désoxyribonucléique**) DNA.

adolescence /adɔlesɑ̃s/ *nf* adolescence. **adolescent, ∼e** *nm, f* adolescent, teenager.

adopter /adɔpte/ [1] *vt* adopt. **adoptif, -ive** *a* (*enfant*) adopted; (*parents*) adoptive.

adorer /adɔRe/ [1] *vt* love; (*plus fort*) adore; (Relig) worship, adore.

adosser /adose/ [1] *vt* lean (**à**, **contre** against). □ **s'∼** *vpr* lean back (**à**, **contre** against).

adoucir /adusiR/ [2] *vt* soften; (*boisson*) sweeten; (*chagrin*) ease. □ **s'∼** *vpr* soften; (*chagrin*) ease; (*temps*) become milder. **adoucissant** *nm* (fabric) softener.

adresse /adRɛs/ *nf* address; (*habileté*) skill; **∼ électronique** e-mail address.

adresser /adRese/ [1] *vt* send; (*écrire l'adresse sur*) address; (*remarque*) address; **∼ la parole à** speak to. □ **s'∼ à** *vpr* address; (*aller voir*) (*personne*) go and ask *ou* see; (*bureau*) enquire at; (*viser, intéresser*) be directed at.

adroit, ∼e /adRwa, -t/ *a* skilful, clever.

adulte /adylt/ *nmf* adult. ● *a* adult; (*plante, animal*) fully-grown.

adultère /adyltɛR/ *a* adulterous. ● *nm* adultery.

adverbe /advɛRb/ *nm* adverb.

adversaire /advɛRsɛR/ *nmf* opponent, adversary.

aérer /aeRe/ [1] *vt* air; (*texte*) space out. □ **s'∼** *vpr* get some air.

aérien, ∼ne /aeRjɛ̃, -jɛn/ *a* air; (*photo*) aerial; (*câble*) overhead.

aérobic /aeRɔbik/ *nm* aerobics (+ *sg*).

aérogare /aeRɔgaR/ *nf* air terminal.

aéroglisseur /aeRɔglisœR/ *nm* hovercraft.

aérogramme /aeRɔgRam/ *nm* airmail letter; (US) aerogram.

aéronautique /aeRɔnotik/ *a* aeronautical. ● *nf* aeronautics (+ *sg*).

aéroport /aeRɔpɔR/ *nm* airport.

aérospatial, ∼e (*mpl* **-iaux**) /aeRɔspasjal, -jo/ *a* aerospace.

affaiblir /afebliR/ [2] *vt* weaken. □ **s'∼** *vpr* get weaker.

affaire /afɛR/ *nf* affair, matter; (Jur) case; (*histoire, aventure*) affair; (*occasion*) bargain; (*entreprise*) business; (*transaction*) deal; (*question, problème*) matter; **∼s** (Comm) business; (Pol) affairs; (*problèmes personnels*) business; (*effets personnels*) things; **c'est mon ∼** that's my business; **avoir ∼ à** deal with; **ça fera l'∼** that will do the job; **ça fera leur ∼** that's just what they need; **tirer qn d'∼** help sb out of a tight spot; **se tirer d'∼** get out of trouble.

affairé, ∼e /afeRe/ *a* busy.

affaisser (s') /(s)afese/ [1] *vpr* (*terrain, route*) sink, subside; (*poutre*) sag; (*personne*) collapse.

affamé, ∼e /afame/ *a* starving.

affectation /afɛktasjɔ̃/ *nf* (*nomination*) (à une fonction) appointment; (dans un lieu) posting; (de matériel, d'argent) allocation; (comportement) affectation.

affecter /afɛkte/ [1] *vt* (feindre) affect; (toucher, affliger) affect; (destiner) assign; (nommer) appoint, post.

affectif, -ive /afɛktif, -v/ *a* emotional.

affection /afɛksjɔ̃/ *nf* affection; (maladie) complaint.

affectueux, -euse /afɛktɥø, -z/ *a* affectionate.

affichage /afiʃaʒ/ *nm* billposting; (électronique) display.

affiche /afiʃ/ *nf* (public) notice; (publicité) poster; (Théât) bill; **être à l'~** (*film*) be showing; (*pièce*) be on.

afficher /afiʃe/ [1] *vt* (annonce) put up; (événement) announce; (sentiment) display; (Ordinat) display.

affirmatif, -ive /afiʀmatif, -v/ *a* affirmative. **affirmation** *nf* assertion.

affirmer /afiʀme/ [1] *vt* assert; (soutenir) maintain.

affligé, ~e /afliʒe/ *a* distressed; **~ de** afflicted with.

affluer /aflye/ [1] *vi* flood in; (sang) rush.

affolant, ~e /afɔlɑ̃, -t/ *a* alarming.

affoler /afɔle/ [1] *vt* throw into a panic. □ **s'~** *vpr* panic.

affranchir /afʀɑ̃ʃiʀ/ [2] *vt* stamp; (à la machine) frank; (esclave) emancipate; (fig) free. **affranchissement** *nm* (tarif) postage.

affreux, -euse /afʀø, -z/ *a* (laid) hideous; (mauvais) awful.

affrontement /afʀɔ̃tmɑ̃/ *nm* confrontation.

affronter /afʀɔ̃te/ [1] *vt* confront. □ **s'~** *vpr* confront each other.

affûter /afyte/ [1] *vt* sharpen.

afin /afɛ̃/ *prép & conj* **~ de faire** in order to do; **~ que** so that.

africain, ~e /afʀikɛ̃, -ɛn/ *a* African. **A~, ~e** *nm, f* African.

Afrique /afʀik/ *nf* Africa; **~ du Sud** South Africa.

agacer /agase/ [10] *vt* irritate, annoy.

âge /ɑʒ/ *nm* age; (vieillesse) (old)

age; **quel ~ avez-vous?** how old are you?; **~ adulte** adulthood; **~ mûr** maturity; **d'un certain ~** middle-aged.

âgé, ~e /ɑʒe/ *a* elderly; **~ de cinq ans** five years old.

agence /aʒɑ̃s/ *nf* agency, bureau, office; (succursale) branch; **~ d'interim** employment agency; **~ de voyages** travel agency; **~ publicitaire** advertising agency.

agenda /aʒɛ̃da/ *nm* diary; **~ électronique** electronic organizer.

agent /aʒɑ̃/ *nm* agent; (fonctionnaire) official; **~ (de police)** policeman; **~ de change** stockbroker; **~ commercial** sales representative.

agglomération /aglɔmeʀasjɔ̃/ *nf* town, built-up area.

aggraver /agʀave/ [1] *vt* aggravate, make worse. □ **s'~** *vpr* get worse.

agile /aʒil/ *a* agile, nimble.

agir /aʒiʀ/ [2] *vi* act; (se comporter) behave; (avoir un effet) work, take effect. □ **s'~ de** *vpr* (être nécessaire) **il s'agit de faire** we/you *etc.* must do; (être question de) **il s'agit de faire** it is a matter of doing; **dans ce livre il s'agit de** this book is about; **dont il s'agit** in question; **il s'agit de ton fils** it's about your son; **de quoi s'agit-il?** what is it about?

agitation /aʒitasjɔ̃/ *nf* bustle; (trouble) agitation; (malaise social) unrest.

agité, ~e /aʒite/ *a* restless, fidgety; (troublé) agitated; (mer) rough.

agiter /aʒite/ [1] *vt* (bras, mouchoir) wave; (liquide, boîte) shake; (troubler) agitate; (discuter) debate. □ **s'~** *vpr* bustle about; (enfant) fidget; (foule, pensées) stir.

agneau (*pl* **~x**) /aɲo/ *nm* lamb.

agrafe /agʀaf/ *nf* hook; (pour

papiers) staple. **agrafeuse** *nf*
stapler.

agrandir /agʀɑ̃diʀ/ [2] *vt* enlarge;
(*maison*) extend. □ **s'~** *vpr*
expand, grow. **agrandissement**
nm extension; (de photo)
enlargement.

agréable /agʀeabl/ *a* pleasant.

agréé, **~e** /agʀee/ *a* (*agence*)
authorized; (*nourrice, médecin*)
registered; (*matériel*) approved.

agréer /agʀee/ [15] *vt* accept; **~ à**
please; **veuillez ~, Monsieur, mes
salutations distinguées** (personne non
nommée) yours faithfully; (personne
nommée) yours sincerely.

agrégation /agʀegasjɔ̃/ *nf*
highest examination for
recruitment of teachers. **agrégé**,
~e *nm, f* teacher (*who has passed
the agrégation*).

agrément /agʀemɑ̃/ *nm* charm;
(plaisir) pleasure; (accord) assent.

agresser /agʀese/ [1] *vt* attack;
(pour voler) mug.

agressif, **-ive** /agʀesif, -v/ *a*
aggressive. **agression** *nf* attack;
(pour voler) mugging; (Mil)
aggression.

agricole /agʀikɔl/ *a* agricultural;
(*ouvrier, produit*) farm.
agriculteur *nm* farmer.
agriculture *nf* agriculture,
farming.

agripper /agʀipe/ [1] *vt* grab.
□ **s'~** *vpr* cling (**à** to).

agroalimentaire /agʀɔalimɑ̃tɛʀ/
nm food industry.

agrumes /agʀym/ *nmpl* citrus
fruit(s).

ai /e/ ⇒**avoir** [5].

aide /ɛd/ *nf* help, assistance; (en
argent) aid; **à l'~ de** with the help
of; **venir en ~ à** help; **~ à domicile**
home help; **~ familiale** mother's
help; **~ sociale** social security;
(US) welfare. ● *nmf* assistant.

aide-mémoire *nm inv* handbook
of key facts.

aider /ede/ [1] *vt/i* help, assist;
(subventionner) aid, give aid to; **~ à
faire** help to do. □ **s' ~ de** *vpr*
use.

aïeul, **~e** /ajœl/ *nm, f*
grandparent.

aigle /ɛgl/ *nm* eagle.

aigre /ɛgʀ/ *a* sour, sharp; (fig)
sharp.

aigrir /egʀiʀ/ [2] *vt* embitter.
□ **s'~** *vpr* turn sour; (*personne*)
become embittered.

aigu, **~ë** /egy/ *a* (*douleur,
problème*) acute; (*objet*) sharp;
(*voix*) shrill; (Mus) high(-pitched);
(*accent*) acute.

aiguille /eguij/ *nf* needle; (de
montre) hand; (de balance) pointer;
~ à tricoter knitting needle.

aiguilleur /eguijœʀ/ *nm*
pointsman; **~ du ciel** air traffic
controller.

aiguiser /eg(ɥ)ize/ [1] *vt*
sharpen; (fig) stimulate.

ail (*pl* **~s** *ou* **aulx**) /aj, o/ *nm*
garlic.

aile /ɛl/ *nf* wing.

ailier /elje/ *nm* winger; (US) end.

aille /aj/ ⇒**ALLER** [8].

ailleurs /ajœʀ/ *adv* elsewhere,
somewhere else; **d'~** besides,
moreover; **nulle part ~** nowhere
else; **par ~** moreover,
furthermore; **partout ~**
everywhere else.

aimable /ɛmabl/ *a* kind.

aimant /ɛmɑ̃/ *nm* magnet.

aimer /eme/ [1] *vt* like; (d'amour)
love; **j'aimerais faire** I'd like to do;
~ bien quite like; **~ mieux** *ou*
autant prefer.

aîné, **~e** /ene/ *a* eldest; (de deux)
elder. ● *nm, f* eldest (child);
(premier de deux) elder (child); **~s**
elders; **il est mon ~** he is older
than me *ou* my senior.

ainsi /ɛ̃si/ adv like this, thus; (donc) so; **et ~ de suite** and so on; **pour ~ dire** so to speak, as it were; **~ que** as well as; (comme) as.

air /ɛʀ/ nm air; (mine) look, air; (mélodie) tune; **~ conditionné** air-conditioning; **avoir l'~** look, appear; **avoir l'~ de** look like; **avoir l'~ de faire** appear to be doing; **en l'~** (up) in the air; (promesses) empty; **prendre l'~** get some fresh air.

aire /ɛʀ/ nf area; **~ d'atterrissage** landing-strip; **~ de pique-nique** picnic area; **~ de repas** rest area; **~ de services** (motorway) services.

aisance /ɛzɑ̃s/ nf ease; (richesse) affluence.

aise /ɛz/ nf joy; **à l'~** (sur un siège) comfortable; (pas gêné) at ease; (fortuné) comfortably off; **mal à l'~** uncomfortable; ill at ease; **aimer ses ~s** like one's creature comforts; **mettre qn à l'~** put sb at ease; **se mettre à l'~** make oneself comfortable.

aisé, **~e** /eze/ a easy; (fortuné) well-off.

aisselle /ɛsɛl/ nf armpit.

ait /ɛ/ ⇒AVOIR [5].

ajourner /aʒuʀne/ [1] vt postpone; (débat, procès) adjourn.

ajout /aʒu/ nm addition.

ajouter /aʒute/ [1] vt add (à to); **~ foi à** lend credence to. □ **s'~** vpr be added.

ajuster /aʒyste/ [1] vt adjust; (cible) aim at; (adapter) fit; **~ son coup** adjust one's aim.

alarme /alaʀm/ nf alarm; **donner l'~** raise the alarm.

alarmer /alaʀme/ [1] vt alarm. □ **s'~** vpr become alarmed (**de** at).

Albanie /albani/ nf Albania.

alcool /alkɔl/ nm alcohol; (eau de vie) brandy; **~ à brûler** methylated spirit. **alcoolique** a et nmf alcoholic. **alcoolisé**, **~e** a (boisson) alcoholic. **alcoolisme** nm alcoholism.

alcootest /alkɔtɛst/ nm breath test; (appareil) Breathalyser®.

aléa /alea/ nm hazard. **aléatoire** a unpredictable, uncertain; (Ordinat) random.

alentours /alɑ̃tuʀ/ nmpl surroundings; **aux ~ de** (de lieu) around; (de chiffre, date) about, around.

alerte /alɛʀt/ a (personne) alert; (vif) lively. ● nf alert; **~ à la bombe** bomb scare. **alerter** [1] vt alert.

algèbre /alʒɛbʀ/ nf algebra.

Algérie /alʒeʀi/ nf Algeria.

algue /alg/ nf seaweed; **les ~s** (Bot) algae.

aliéné, **~e** /aljene/ nm, f insane person.

aliéner /aljene/ [14] vt alienate; (céder) give up. □ **s'~** vpr alienate.

aligner /aliɲe/ [1] vt (objets) line up, make lines of; (chiffres) string together; **~ sur** bring into line with. □ **s'~** vpr line up; **s'~ sur** align oneself on.

aliment /alimɑ̃/ nm food. **alimentaire** /alimɑ̃tɛʀ/ a (industrie) food; (habitudes) dietary; **produits ~s** foodstuffs.

alimentation /alimɑ̃tasjɔ̃/ nf feeding, supply(ing); (régime) diet; (aliments) food; **magasin d'~** grocery shop ou store.

alimenter /alimɑ̃te/ [1] vt feed; (fournir) supply; (fig) sustain. □ **s'~** vpr eat.

allaiter /alete/ [1] vt (bébé) breast-feed; (US) nurse; (animal) suckle.

allée /ale/ nf path, lane; (menant à une maison) drive(way); (dans un cinéma, magasin) aisle; (rue) road; ~s **et venues** comings and goings.

allégé, **~e** /aleʒe/ a diet; (*beurre, yaourt*) low-fat.

alléger /aleʒe/ [14] [40] vt make lighter; (*fardeau, chargement*) lighten; (fig) (*souffrance*) alleviate.

allégresse /alegʀɛs/ nf gaiety, joy.

alléguer /alege/ [14] vt (*exemple*) invoke; (prétexter) allege.

Allemagne /almaɲ/ nf Germany.

allemand, **~e** /almã, -d/ a German. ●nm (Ling) German. **A~**, **~e** nm, f German.

....

aller /ale/ [8]

●*verbe auxiliaire*

••••▸ **je vais l'appeler** I'm going to call him; **j'allais partir** I was about to leave; **va savoir!** who knows?; **~ en s'améliorant** be improving.

●*verbe intransitif*

••••▸ (se déplacer) go; **allons-y!** let's go!; **allez!** come on!

••••▸ (se porter) **comment allez-vous?**, **comment ça va?** how are you?; **ça va (bien)** I'm fine; **qu'est-ce qui ne va pas?** what's the matter?; **ça ne va pas la tête?** 🄸 are you mad? 🄸.

••••▸ (mettre en valeur) **~ à qn** suit sb; **ça te va bien** it really suits you.

••••▸ (convenir) **ça va ma coiffure?** is my hair OK?; **ça ne va pas du tout** that's no good at all.

◻ **s'en aller** *verbe pronominal*

••••▸ go; **va-t'en!** go away!; **ça ne s'en va pas** (*tache*) it won't come out.

●*nom masculin*

••••▸ outward journey; **~** (**simple**) single (ticket); (US) one-way (ticket); **~ retour** return (ticket);

(US) round trip (ticket); **à l'~** on the way out.

....

allergie /alɛʀʒi/ nf allergy.
allergique a allergic (à to).

alliance /aljɑ̃s/ nf alliance; (bague) wedding-ring; (mariage) marriage.

allier /alje/ [45] vt combine; (Pol) ally. ◻ **s'~** vpr combine; (Pol) form an alliance; (*famille*) become related (à to).

allô /alo/ interj hallo, hello.

allocation /alɔkasjɔ̃/ nf allowance; **~ chômage** unemployment benefit; **~s familiales** family allowance.

allonger /alɔ̃ʒe/ [40] vt lengthen; (*bras, jambe*) stretch (out); (coucher) lay down. ◻ **s'~** vpr get longer; (s'étendre) lie down; (s'étirer) stretch (oneself) out.

allouer /alwe/ [1] vt allocate; (*prêt*) grant.

allumer /alyme/ [1] vt (*bougie, gaz*) light; (*lampe, appareil*) turn on; (*pièce*) switch the light(s) on in; (fig) arouse. ◻ **s'~** vpr (*lumière, appareil*) come on.

allumette /alymɛt/ nf match.

allure /alyʀ/ nf speed, pace; (démarche) walk; (apparence) appearance; **à toute ~** at full speed; **avoir de l'~** have style; **avoir des ~s de** look like; **avoir une drôle d'~** be funny-looking.

allusion /alyzjɔ̃/ nf allusion (à to); (implicite) hint (à at); **faire ~ à** allude to; hint at.

alors /alɔʀ/ adv (à ce moment-là) then; (de ce fait) so; (dans ce cas-là) then; **ça~!** well!; **et ~?** so what? ●conj **~ que** (pendant que) while; (tandis que) when, whereas.

alouette /alwɛt/ nf lark.

alourdir /aluʀdiʀ/ [2] vt weigh down; (rendre plus important) increase.

aloyau (*pl* ~**x**) /alwajo/ *nm* sirloin.

Alpes /alp/ *nfpl* **les** ~ the Alps.

alphabet /alfabɛ/ *nm* alphabet. **alphabétique** *a* alphabetical.

alphabétiser /alfabetize/ [1] *vt* teach to read and write.

alpinist /alpinist/ *nmf* mountaineer.

altérer /altere/ [14] *vt* (*fait, texte*) distort; (*abîmer*) spoil; (*donner soif à*) make thirsty. □ **s'**~ *vpr* deteriorate.

alternance /altɛrnɑ̃s/ *nf* alternation; **en** ~ alternately.

altitude /altityd/ *nf* altitude, height.

amabilité /amabilite/ *nf* kindness.

amaigrir /amegrir/ [2] *vt* make thin(ner).

amande /amɑ̃d/ *nf* almond; (*d'un fruit à noyau*) kernel.

amant /amɑ̃/ *nm* lover.

amarre /amar/ *nf* (mooring) rope; ~**s** moorings.

amas /amɑ/ *nm* heap, pile.

amasser /amase/ [1] *vt* amass, gather; (*empiler*) pile up. □ **s'**~ *vpr* pile up; (*gens*) gather.

amateur /amatœr/ *nm* amateur; ~ **de** lover of; **d'**~ amateur; (*péj*) amateurish.

ambassade /ɑ̃basad/ *nf* embassy. **ambassadeur, -drice** *nm, f* ambassador.

ambiance /ɑ̃bjɑ̃s/ *nf* atmosphere. **ambiant, ~e** *a* surrounding.

ambigu, ~ë /ɑ̃bigy/ *a* ambiguous.

ambitieux, -ieuse /ɑ̃bisjø, -z/ *a* ambitious. **ambition** *nf* ambition.

ambulance /ɑ̃bylɑ̃s/ *nf* ambulance.

ambulant, ~e /ɑ̃bylɑ̃, -t/ *a* itinerant, travelling.

âme /ɑm/ *nf* soul; ~ **sœur** soul mate.

amélioration /ameljɔrasjɔ̃/ *nf* improvement.

améliorer /ameljɔre/ [1] *vt* improve. □ **s'**~ *vpr* improve.

aménagement /amenaʒmɑ̃/ *nm* (*de magasin*) fitting out; (*de grenier*) conversion; (*de territoire*) development; (*de cuisine*) equipping.

aménager /amenaʒe/ [40] *vt* (*magasin*) fit out; (*transformer*) convert; (*territoire*) develop; (*cuisine*) equip.

amende /amɑ̃d/ *nf* fine; **faire** ~ **honorable** make amends.

amener /am(ə)ne/ [6] *vt* bring; (*causer*) bring about; ~ **qn à faire** cause sb to do. □ **s'**~ *vpr* 🄸 turn up.

amer, -ère /amɛr/ *a* bitter.

américain, ~e /amerikɛ̃, -ɛn/ *a* American. **A**~, ~**e** *nm, f* American.

Amérique /amerik/ *nf* America; ~ **centrale/latine** Central/Latin America; ~ **du Nord/Sud** North/South America.

amertume /amɛrtym/ *nf* bitterness.

ami, ~e /ami/ *nm, f* friend; (*amateur*) lover; **un** ~ **des bêtes** an animal lover. ● *a* friendly.

amiable /amjabl/ *a* amicable; **à l'**~ (*divorcer*) by mutual consent; (*se séparer*) on friendly terms; (*séparation*) amicable.

amical, ~e (*mpl* **-aux**) /amikal, -o/ *a* friendly.

amiral (*pl* **-aux**) /amiral, -o/ *nm* admiral.

amitié /amitje/ *nf* friendship; ~**s** (*en fin de lettre*) kind regards; **prendre qn en** ~ take a liking to sb.

amnistie /amnisti/ *nf* amnesty.

A

amoindrir /amwɛ̃dRiR/ [2] *vt* reduce.

amont: en ∼ /ɑ̃namɔ̃/ *loc* upstream.

amorcer /amɔRse/ [10] *vt* start; (*hameçon*) bait; (*pompe*) prime; (*arme à feu*) arm.

amortir /amɔRtiR/ [2] *vt* (*choc*) cushion; (*bruit*) deaden; (*dette*) pay off; ∼ **un achat** make a purchase pay for itself.

amortisseur /amɔRtisœR/ *nm* shock absorber.

amour /amuR/ *nm* love; **pour l'∼ de** for the sake of.

amoureux, -euse /amuRø, -z/ *a* (*personne*) in love; (*relation, regard*) loving; (*vie*) love; ∼ **de qn** in love with sb. ● *nm, f* lover.

amour-propre /amuRpRɔpR/ *nm* self-esteem.

amphithéâtre /ɑ̃fiteɑtR/ *nm* amphitheatre; (d'université) lecture hall.

ampleur /ɑ̃plœR/ *nf* extent, size; (de vêtement) fullness; **prendre de l'∼** spread, grow.

amplifier /ɑ̃plifje/ [45] *vt* amplify; (fig) expand, develop. □ **s'∼** *vpr* (son) grow; (scandale) intensify.

ampoule /ɑ̃pul/ *nf* (électrique) bulb; (sur la peau) blister; (Méd) phial, ampoule.

amusant, ∼e /amyzɑ̃, -t/ *a* (*blague*) funny; (*soirée*) enjoyable, entertaining.

amuse-gueule /amyzgœl/ *nm inv* cocktail snack.

amusement /amyzmɑ̃/ *nm* amusement; (passe-temps) entertainment.

amuser /amyze/ [1] *vt* amuse; (détourner l'attention de) distract. □ **s'∼** *vpr* enjoy oneself; (jouer) play.

amygdale /amidal/ *nf* tonsil.

an /ɑ̃/ *nm* year; **avoir dix ∼s** be ten years old; **un garçon de deux ∼s** a two-year-old boy; **à soixante ∼s** at the age of sixty; **les moins de dix-huit ∼s** under eighteens.

analogie /analɔʒi/ *nf* analogy.

analogue /analɔg/ *a* similar, analogous (**à** to).

analphabète /analfabɛt/ *a & nmf* illiterate.

analyse /analiz/ *nf* analysis; (Méd) test. **analyser** [1] *vt* analyse; (Méd) test.

ananas /anana(s)/ *nm* pineapple.

anarchie /anaRʃi/ *nf* anarchy.

anatomie /anatɔmi/ *nf* anatomy.

ancêtre /ɑ̃sɛtR/ *nm* ancestor.

anchois /ɑ̃ʃwa/ *nm* anchovy.

ancien, ∼ne /ɑ̃sjɛ̃, -jɛn/ *a* old; (de jadis) ancient; (meuble) antique; (précédent) former, ex-, old; (dans une fonction) senior; ∼ **combattant** veteran. ● *nm, f* senior; (par l'âge) elder. **anciennement** *adv* formerly. **ancienneté** *nf* age, seniority.

ancre /ɑ̃kR/ *nf* anchor; **jeter/lever l'∼** cast/weigh anchor.

andouille /ɑ̃duj/ *nf* sausage (filled with chitterlings); (idiot 🅸) fool; **faire l'∼** fool around.

âne /ɑn/ *nm* donkey, ass; (imbécile 🅸) dimwit 🅸.

anéantir /aneɑ̃tiR/ [2] *vt* destroy; (exterminer) annihilate; (accabler) overwhelm.

anémie /anemi/ *nf* anaemia.

ânerie /ɑnRi/ *nf* stupid remark.

anesthésie /anɛstezi/ *nf* (opération) anaesthetic.

ange /ɑ̃ʒ/ *nm* angel; **aux ∼s** in seventh heaven.

angine /ɑ̃ʒin/ *nf* throat infection.

anglais, ∼e /ɑ̃glɛ, -z/ *a* English. ● *nm* (Ling) English. **A∼, ∼e** *nm, f* Englishman, Englishwoman.

angle /ɑ̃gl/ *nm* angle; (coin) corner.

Angleterre /ɑ̃glətɛR/ *nf* England.

anglophone /ɑ̃glɔfɔn/ a English-speaking. ● *nmf* English speaker.

angoissant, ~e /ɑ̃gwasɑ̃, -t/ a alarming; (effrayant) harrowing.

angoisse /ɑ̃gwas/ *nf* anxiety. **angoissé**, ~e a anxious. **angoisser** [1] *vt* worry.

animal (*pl* -aux) /animal, -o/ *nm* animal; ~ **familier**, ~ **do compagnie** pet. ● a (*mpl* -aux) animal.

animateur, -trice /animatœʀ, -tʀis/ *nm, f* organizer, leader; (TV) host, hostess.

animation /animasjɔ̃/ *nf* liveliness; (affairement) activity; (au cinéma) animation; (activité dirigée) organized activity.

animé, ~e /anime/ a lively; (affairé) busy; (être) animate.

animer /anime/ [1] *vt* liven up; (débat, atelier) lead; (spectacle) host; (pousser) drive; (encourager) spur on. □ **s'~** *vpr* liven up.

anis /ani(s)/ *nm* (Culin) aniseed; (Bot) anise.

anneau (*pl* ~x) /ano/ *nm* ring; (de chaîne) link.

année /ane/ *nf* year; ~ **bissextile** leap year; ~ **civile** calendar year.

annexe /anɛks/ a (document) attached; (question) related; (bâtiment) adjoining. ● *nf* (bâtiment) annexe; (US) annex; (document) appendix; (électronique) attachment. **annexer** [1] *vt* annex; (document) attach.

anniversaire /anivɛʀsɛʀ/ *nm* birthday; (d'un événement) anniversary. ● a anniversary.

annonce /anɔ̃s/ *nf* announcement; (publicitaire) advertisement; (indice) sign.

annoncer /anɔ̃se/ [10] *vt* announce; (prédire) forecast; (être l'indice de) herald. □ **s'~** *vpr* (crise, tempête) be brewing; **s'~ bien/mal**

look good/bad. **annonceur** *nm* advertiser.

annuaire /anɥɛʀ/ *nm* year-book; ~ (**téléphonique**) (telephone) directory.

annuel, ~le /anɥɛl/ a annual, yearly.

annulation /anylasjɔ̃/ *nf* cancellation; (de sanction, loi) repeal; (de mesure) abolition.

annuler /anyle/ [1] *vt* cancel; (contrat) nullify; (jugement) quash; (loi) repeal. □ **s'~** *vpr* cancel each other out.

anodin, ~e /anɔdɛ̃, -in/ a insignificant; (sans risques) harmless, safe.

anonymat /anɔnima/ *nm* anonymity; **garder l'~** remain anonymous. **anonyme** a anonymous.

anorexie /anɔʀɛksi/ *nf* anorexia.

anormal, ~e (*mpl* -aux) /anɔʀmal, -o/ a abnormal.

anse /ɑ̃s/ *nf* handle; (baie) cove.

Antarctique /ɑ̃taʀktik/ *nm* Antarctic.

antenne /ɑ̃tɛn/ *nf* aerial; (US) antenna; (d'insecte) antenna; (succursale) agency; (Mil) outpost, **à l'~** on the air; ~ **chirurgicale** mobile emergency unit; ~ **parabolique** satellite dish.

antérieur, ~e /ɑ̃teʀjœʀ/ a previous, earlier; (placé devant) front; ~ **à** prior to.

antiaérien, ~ne /ɑ̃tiaeʀjɛ̃, -ɛn/ a anti-aircraft; **abri** ~ air-raid shelter.

antiatomique /ɑ̃tiatɔmik/ a **abri** ~ nuclear fall-out shelter.

antibiotique /ɑ̃tibjɔtik/ *nm* antibiotic.

anticipation /ɑ̃tisipasjɔ̃/ *nf* **d'~** (livre, film) science fiction; **par ~** in advance.

anticiper /ɑ̃tisipe/ [1] *vt* ~ (**sur**)

anticipate; (effectuer à l'avance) bring forward.

anticorps /ãtikɔʀ/ *nm* antibody.

antidater /ãtidate/ [1] *vt* backdate, antedate.

antigel /ãtiʒɛl/ *nm* antifreeze.

Antilles /ãtij/ *nfpl* **les ~** the West Indies.

antipathique /ãtipatik/ *a* unpleasant.

antiquaire /ãtikɛʀ/ *nmf* antique dealer.

antiquité /ãtikite/ *nf* (objet) antique; **l'A~** antiquity.

antisémite /ãtisemit/ *a* anti-Semitic.

antiseptique /ãtisɛptik/ *a & nm* antiseptic.

antivol /ãtivɔl/ *nm* anti-theft device; (Auto) steering lock.

anxiété /ãksjete/ *nf* anxiety.

anxieux, -ieuse /ãksjø, -z/ *a* anxious. ● *nm, f* worrier.

août /u(t)/ *nm* August.

apaiser /apeze/ [1] *vt* calm down; (colère, militant) appease; (douleur) soothe; (faim) satisfy. □ **s'~** *vpr* (tempête) die down.

apathie /apati/ *nf* apathy.

apathique *a* apathetic.

apercevoir /apɛʀsəvwaʀ/ [52] *vt* see. □ **s'~ de** *vpr* notice; **s'~ que** notice *ou* realize that.

aperçu /apɛʀsy/ *nm* (échantillon) glimpse, taste; (intuition) insight.

apéritif /apeʀitif/ *nm* aperitif, drink.

aphte /aft/ *nm* mouth ulcer.

apitoyer /apitwaje/ [31] *vt* move (to pity). □ **s'~** *vpr* **s'~ sur (le sort de) qn** feel sorry for sb.

aplanir /aplaniʀ/ [2] *vt* level; (fig) iron out.

aplatir /aplatiʀ/ [2] *vt* flatten (out). □ **s'~** *vpr* (s'immobiliser) flatten oneself.

aplomb /aplɔ̃/ *nm* balance; (fig) self-confidence; **d'~** (en équilibre)

steady; **je ne suis pas bien d'~** Ⅰ don't feel very well.

apogée /apoʒe/ *nm* peak.

apologie /apɔlɔʒi/ *nf* panegyric.

apostrophe /apɔstʀɔf/ *nf* apostrophe; (remarque) remark.

apothéose /apɔteoz/ *nf* high point; (d'événement) grand finale.

apparaître /apaʀɛtʀ/ [18] *vi* appear; **il apparaît que** it appears that.

appareil /apaʀɛj/ *nm* device; (électrique) appliance; (Anat) system; (téléphone) phone; (avion) plane; (Culin) mixture; (système administratif) apparatus; **~ (dentaire)** brace; (dentier) dentures; **~ (photo)** camera; **c'est Gabriel à l'~** it's Gabriel on the phone; **~ auditif** hearing aid; **~ électroménager** household electrical appliance.

appareiller /apaʀeje/ [1] *vi* (navire) cast off, put to sea.

apparemment /apaʀamã/ *adv* apparently.

apparence /apaʀãs/ *nf* appearance; **en ~** outwardly; (apparemment) apparently.

apparent, ~e /apaʀã, -t/ *a* apparent; (visible) conspicuous.

apparenté, ~e /apaʀãte/ *a* related; (semblable) similar.

apparition /apaʀisjɔ̃/ *nf* appearance; (spectre) apparition.

appartement /apaʀtəmã/ *nm* flat; (US) apartment.

appartenir /apaʀtəniʀ/ [58] *vi* belong (**à** to); **il lui appartient de** it is up to him to.

appât /apɑ/ *nm* bait; (fig) lure.

appauvrir /apovʀiʀ/ [2] *vt* impoverish. □ **s'~** *vpr* become impoverished.

appel /apɛl/ *nm* call; (Jur) appeal; (supplique) appeal, plea; (Mil) call-up; (US) draft; **faire ~** appeal; **faire ~ à** (recourir à) call on; (invoquer) appeal to; (évoquer) call up; (exiger) call for; **faire l'~** (Scol) call the register; (Mil) take a roll-call; **~ d'offres** (Comm) invitation to tender; **faire un ~ de phares** flash one's headlights.

appeler /aple/ [38] *vt* call; (téléphoner) phone, call; (nécessiter) call for; **en ~ à** appeal to; **appelé à** (destiné) destined for. □ **s'~** *vpr* be called; **il s'appelle Tim** his name is Tim *ou* he is called Tim.

appellation /apelasjɔ̃/ *nf* name, designation.

appendice /apɛdis/ *nm* appendix. **appendicite** *nf* appendicitis.

appesantir /apəzɑ̃tiʀ/ [2] *vt* weigh down. □ **s'~** *vpr* grow heavier; **s'~ sur** dwell upon.

appétissant, ~e /apetisɑ̃, -t/ *a* appetizing.

appétit /apeti/ *nm* appetite; **bon ~!** enjoy your meal!

applaudir /aplodiʀ/ [2] *vt/i* applaud. **applaudissements** *nmpl* applause.

application /aplikasjɔ̃/ *nf* (soin) care; (de loi) (respect) application; (mise en œuvre) implementation; (Ordinat) application program.

appliqué, ~e /aplike/ *a* (travail) painstaking; (sciences) applied; (élève) hard-working.

appliquer /aplike/ [1] *vt* apply; (loi) enforce. □ **s'~** *vpr* apply oneself (**à** to), take great care (**à faire** to do); **s'~ à** (concerner) apply to.

appoint /apwɛ̃/ *nm* support; **d'~** extra; **faire l'~** give the correct money.

apport /apɔʀ/ *nm* contribution.

apporter /apɔʀte/ [1] *vt* bring; (aide, précision) give; (causer) bring about.

appréciation /apʀesjasjɔ̃/ *nf* estimate, evaluation; (de monnaie)

appreciation; (jugement) assessment.

apprécier /apʀesje/ [45] *vt* appreciate; (évaluer) assess; (objet) value, appraise.

appréhender /apʀeɑ̃de/ [1] *vt* dread, fear; (arrêter) apprehend.

apprendre /apʀɑ̃dʀ/ [50] *vt* learn; (être informé de) hear, learn; (de façon indirecte) hear of; **~ qch à qn** (informer) tell sb sth; (enseigner) teach sb sth; **~ à faire** learn to do; **~ à qn à faire** teach sb to do; **~ que** learn that; (être informé) hear that.

apprenti, ~e /apʀɑ̃ti/ *nm,f* apprentice. **apprentissage** *nm* apprenticeship; (d'un sujet) learning.

apprêter /apʀete/ [1] *vt* prepare; (bois) prime; (mur) size. □ **s'~ à** *vpr* prepare to.

apprivoiser /apʀivwaze/ [1] *vt* tame.

approbation /apʀɔbasjɔ̃/ *nf* approval.

approchant, ~e /apʀɔʃɑ̃, -t/ *a* close, similar.

approcher /apʀɔʃe/ [1] *vt* (objet) move near(er) (**de** to); (personne) approach; **~ de** get nearer ou closer to. ●*vi* approach. □ **s'~ de** *vpr* approach, move near(er) to.

approfondir /apʀɔfɔ̃diʀ/ [2] *vt* deepen; (fig) (sujet) go into sth in depth; (connaissances) improve.

approprié, ~e /apʀɔpʀije/ *a* appropriate.

approprier (s') /(s)apʀɔpʀije/ [45] *vpr* appropriate.

approuver /apʀuve/ [1] *vt* approve; (trouver louable) approve of; (soutenir) agree with.

approvisionner /apʀɔvizjɔne/ [1] *vt* supply (**en** with); (compte en banque) pay money into. □ **s'~** *vpr* stock up.

approximatif, -ive /apʀɔksimatif, -v/ *a* approximate.

appui /apɥi/ *nm* support; (de fenêtre) sill; (pour objet) rest; **à l'~ de** in support of; **prendre ~ sur** lean on.

appui-tête (*pl* **appuis-tête**) /apɥitɛt/ *nm* headrest.

appuyer /apɥije/ [31] *vt* lean, rest; (presser) press; (soutenir) support, back. ● *vi* ~ **sur** press (on); (fig) stress. □ **s'~ sur** *vpr* lean on; (compter sur) rely on.

après /apʀɛ/ *prép* after; (au-delà de) after, beyond; ~ **avoir fait** after doing; ~ **tout** after all; ~ **coup** after the event; **d'~** (selon) according to; (en imitant) from; (adapté de) based on. ● *adv* after (wards); (plus tard) later; **le bus d'~** the next bus. ● *conj* ~ **qu'il est parti** after he left. **après-demain** *adv* the day after tomorrow. **après-guerre** (*pl* ~**s**) *nm ou f* postwar period. **après-midi** *nm ou f inv* afternoon. **après-rasage** (*pl* ~**s**) *nm* aftershave. **après-ski** *nm inv* moonboot. **après-vente** *a inv* after-sales.

a priori /apʀijɔʀi/ *adv* (à première vue) offhand, on the face of it; (sans réfléchir) out of hand. ● *nm* preconception.

à-propos /apʀopo/ *nm* timing, timeliness; (fig) presence of mind.

apte /apt/ *a* capable (**à** of); (ayant les qualités requises) suitable (**à** for); (en état) fit (**à** for).

aptitude /aptityd/ *nf* aptitude, ability.

aquarelle /akwaʀɛl/ *nf* watercolour.

aquatique /akwatik/ *a* aquatic; (Sport) water.

arabe /aʀab/ *a* Arab; (Ling) Arabic; (désert) Arabian. ● *nm* (Ling) Arabic. **A~** *nmf* Arab.

Arabie /aʀabi/ *nf* ~ **Saoudite** Saudi Arabia.

arachide /aʀaʃid/ *nf* groundnut; **huile d'~** groundnut oil.

araignée /aʀeɲe/ *nf* spider.

arbitraire /aʀbitʀɛʀ/ *a* arbitrary.

arbitre /aʀbitʀ/ *nm* referee; (au cricket, tennis) umpire; (expert) arbiter; (Jur) arbitrator. **arbitrer** [1] *vt* (match) referee, umpire; (Jur) arbitrate in.

arbre /aʀbʀ/ *nm* tree; (Tech) shaft.

arbuste /aʀbyst/ *nm* shrub.

arc /aʀk/ *nm* (arme) bow; (courbe) curve; (voûte) arch; ~ **de cercle** arc of a circle.

arc-en-ciel (*pl* **arcs-en-ciel**) /aʀkɑ̃sjɛl/ *nm* rainbow.

arche /aʀʃ/ *nf* arch; ~ **de Noé** Noah's ark.

archéologie /aʀkeɔlɔʒi/ *nf* archaeology.

archevêque /aʀʃəvɛk/ *nm* archbishop.

architecte /aʀʃitɛkt/ *nmf* architect. **architecture** *nf* architecture.

Arctique /aʀktik/ *nm* Arctic.

ardent, ~**e** /aʀdɑ̃, -t/ *a* burning; (passionné) ardent; (foi) fervent. **ardeur** *nf* ardour; (chaleur) heat.

ardoise /aʀdwaz/ *nf* slate; ~ **électronique** notepad computer.

arène /aʀɛn/ *nf* arena; ~**s** amphitheatre; (pour corridas) bullring.

arête /aʀɛt/ *nf* (de poisson) bone; (bord) ridge.

argent /aʀʒɑ̃/ *nm* money; (métal) silver; ~ **comptant** cash; **prendre pour ~ comptant** take at face value; ~ **de poche** pocket money. **argenté**, ~**e** /aʀʒɑ̃te/ *a* silver(y); (métal) (silver-)plated.

argenterie /aʀʒɑ̃tʀi/ *nf* silverware.

Argentine /aʀʒɑ̃tin/ *nf* Argentina.

argile /aʀʒil/ *nf* clay.

argot /aʀgo/ *nm* slang.

A

argument /aʀgymã/ nm
argument; ~ **de vente** selling
point. **argumenter** [1] vi argue.

aristocratie /aʀistɔkʀasi/ nf
aristocracy.

arithmétique /aʀitmetik/ nf
arithmetic. ● a arithmetical.

armature /aʀmatyʀ/ nf
framework; (de tente) frame.

arme /aʀm/ nf arm, weapon; ~ **à
feu** firearm; ~**s** (blason) coat of
arms.

armée /aʀme/ nf army; ~ **de l'air**
Air Force; ~ **de terre** Army.

armer /aʀme/ [1] vt arm; (fusil)
cock; (navire) equip; (renforcer)
reinforce; (Photo) wind on; □ **s'~
de** vpr arm oneself with.

armoire /aʀmwaʀ/ nf cupboard;
(penderie) wardrobe; (US) closet; ~
à pharmacie medicine cabinet.

armure /aʀmyʀ/ nf armour.

arnaque /aʀnak/ nf 🔟 swindling;
c'est de l'~ it's a swindle.

arobas(e) /aʀɔbas, aʀɔbz/ nm at
sign.

aromate /aʀɔmat/ nm herb,
spice.

aromatisé, ~**e** /aʀɔmatize/ a
flavoured.

arôme /aʀom/ nm aroma; (additif)
flavouring.

arpenter /aʀpɑ̃te/ [1] vt pace up
and down; (terrain) survey.

arqué, ~**e** /aʀke/ a arched;
(jambes) bandy.

arrache-pied: d'~ /daʀaʃpje/ loc
relentlessly.

arracher /aʀaʃe/ [1] vt pull out
ou off; (plante) pull ou dig up;
(cheveux, page) tear ou pull out;
(par une explosion) blow off; ~ **à**
(enlever à) snatch from; (fig) force
ou wrest from. □ **s'~ qch** vpr
fight over sth.

arranger /aʀɑ̃ʒe/ [40] vt arrange;
fix up; (réparer) put right; (régler)
sort out; (convenir à) suit. □ **s'~** vpr

(se mettre d'accord) come to an
arrangement; (se débrouiller)
manage (**pour** to).

arrestation /aʀɛstasjɔ̃/ nf arrest.

arrêt /aʀɛ/ nm stopping; (de
combats) cessation; (de production)
halt; (lieu) stop; (pause) pause; (Jur)
ruling; **aux ~s** (Mil) under arrest;
à l'~ (véhicule) stationary;
(machine) idle; **faire un ~** (make
a) stop; **sans ~** (sans escale)
nonstop; (sans interruption)
constantly; ~ **maladie** sick leave;
~ **de travail** (grève) stoppage; (Méd)
sick leave.

arrêté /aʀete/ nm order; ~
municipal bylaw.

arrêter /aʀete/ [1] vt stop; (date)
fix; (appareil) turn off; (renoncer à)
give up; (appréhender) arrest. ● vi
stop. □ **s'~** vpr stop; **s'~ de faire**
stop doing.

arrhes /aʀ/ nfpl deposit; **verser
des ~** pay a deposit.

arrière /aʀjɛʀ/ a inv back, rear.
● nm back, rear; (football) back; **à
l'~** in ou at the back; **en ~**
behind; (marcher, tomber)
backwards; **en ~ de** behind.

arrière-boutique (pl ~**s**) nf back
room (of the shop). **arrière-
garde** (pl ~**s**) nf rearguard.
arrière-goût (pl ~**s**) nm after-
taste. **arrière-grand-mère** (pl
arrière-grands-mères) nf great-
grandmother. **arrière-grand-
père** (pl **arrière-grands-pères**)
nm great-grandfather. **arrière-
pays** nm inv backcountry. **arrière-
pensée** (pl ~**s**) nf
ulterior motive. **arrière-plan** nm
(pl ~**s**) background.

arrimer /aʀime/ [1] vt secure;
(cargaison) stow.

arrivage /aʀivaʒ/ nm
consignment.

arrivée /aʀive/ nf arrival; (Sport)
finish.

arriver /aʀive/ [1] vi (aux être)

arrive, come; (*réussir*) succeed; (*se produire*) happen; ~ à (atteindre) reach; ~ à faire manage to do; je n'arrive pas à faire I can't do; en ~ à faire get to the stage of doing; il arrive que it happens that; il lui arrive de faire he (sometimes) does.

arriviste /aʀivist/ *nmf* go-getter, self-seeker.

arrondir /aʀɔ̃diʀ/ [2] *vt* (make) round; (*somme*) round off. □ s'~ *vpr* become round(ed).

arrondissement /aʀɔ̃dismɑ̃/ *nm* district.

arroser /aʀoze/ [1] *vt* water; (*repas*) wash down (with a drink); (*rôti*) baste; (*victoire*) drink to. **arrosoir** *nm* watering-can.

art /aʀ/ *nm* art; (*don*) knack (**de faire** of doing); ~s et métiers arts and crafts; ~s ménagers home economics (+ *sg*).

artère /aʀtɛʀ/ *nf* artery; (**grande**) ~ main road.

arthrite /aʀtʀit/ *nf* arthritis.

arthrose /aʀtʀoz/ *nf* osteoarthritis.

artichaut /aʀtiʃo/ *nm* artichoke.

article /aʀtikl/ *nm* article; (Comm) item, article; à l'~ de la mort at death's door; ~ de fond feature (article); ~s de voyage travel goods.

articulation /aʀtikylasjɔ̃/ *nf* articulation; (Anat) joint.

articuler /aʀtikyle/ [1] *vt* articulate; (*structurer*) structure; (*assembler*) connect (**sur** to).

artificiel, ~**le** /aʀtifisjɛl/ *a* artificial.

artisan /aʀtizɑ̃/ *nm* artisan, craftsman; l'~ de (fig) the architect of.

artisanal, ~**e** (*mpl* ~**aux**) /aʀtizanal/ *a* craft; (*méthode*) traditional; (*amateur*) home-made;

de fabrication ~e hand-made, hand-crafted.

artiste /aʀtist/ *nmf* artist. **artistique** *a* artistic.

as¹ /a/ ⇒AVOIR [5].

as² /ɑs/ *nm* ace.

ascenseur /asɑ̃sœʀ/ *nm* lift; (US) elevator.

ascension /asɑ̃sjɔ̃/ *nf* ascent; l'A~ Ascension.

aseptiser /asɛptize/ [1] *vt* disinfect; (*stériliser*) sterilize; **aseptisé** (péj) sanitized.

asiatique /azjatik/ *a* Asian. **A~** *nmf* Asian.

Asie /azi/ *nf* Asia.

asile /azil/ *nm* refuge; (Pol) asylum; (pour malades, vieillards) home; ~ de nuit night shelter.

aspect /aspɛ/ *nm* appearance; (facettes) aspect; (perspective) side; à l'~ de at the sight of.

asperge /aspɛʀʒ/ *nf* asparagus.

asperger /aspɛʀʒe/ [40] *vt* spray.

asphyxier /asfiksje/ [45] *vt* (*personne*) asphyxiate; (*entreprise, réseau*) paralyse. □ s'~ *vpr* suffocate; gas oneself; (*entreprise, réseau*) become paralysed.

aspirateur /aspiʀatœʀ/ *nm* vacuum cleaner.

aspirer /aspiʀe/ [1] *vt* inhale; (*liquide*) suck up. ● *vi* ~ à aspire to.

aspirine® /aspiʀin/ *nf* aspirin.

assainir /aseniʀ/ [2] *vt* clean up.

assaisonnement /asɛzɔnmɑ̃/ *nm* seasoning.

assassin /asasɛ̃/ *nm* murderer; (Pol) assassin. **assassiner** [1] *vt* murder; (Pol) assassinate.

assaut /aso/ *nm* assault, onslaught; **donner l'~ à, prendre d'~** storm.

assemblage /asɑ̃blaʒ/ *nm* assembly; (combinaison) collection; (Tech) joint.

assemblée /asãble/ *nf* meeting; (gens réunis) gathering; (Pol) assembly.

assembler /asãble/ [1] *vt* assemble, put together; (réunir) gather. □ **s'~** *vpr* gather, assemble.

asseoir /aswaʀ/ [9] *vt* sit (down), seat; (bébé, malade) sit up; (affermir) establish; (baser) base. □ **s'~** *vpr* sit (down).

assez /ase/ *adv* (suffisamment) enough; (plutôt) quite, fairly; **~ grand/rapide** big/fast enough (pour to); **~ de** enough; **j'en ai ~ (de)** I've had enough (of).

assidu, **~e** /asidy/ *a* (zélé) assiduous; (régulier) regular; **~ auprès de** attentive to. **assiduité** *nf* assiduousness, regularity.

assiéger /asjeʒe/ [14] [40] *vt* besiege.

assiette /asjɛt/ *nf* plate; (équilibre) seat; **~ anglaise** assorted cold meats; **~ creuse/plate** soup-/dinner-plate; **ne pas être dans son ~** feel out of sorts.

assigner /asiɲe/ [1] *vt* assign; (limite) fix.

assimilation /asimilasjõ/ *nf* assimilation; (comparaison) likening, comparison.

assimiler /asimile/ [1] *vt* **~ à** liken to; (classer) class as. □ **s'~** *vpr* assimilate; (être comparable) be comparable (à to).

assis, **~e** /asi, -z/ *a* sitting (down), seated. ●⇒ASSEOIR [9].

assise /asiz/ *nf* (base) foundation; **~s** (tribunal) assizes; (congrès) conference, congress.

assistance /asistãs/ *nf* audience; (aide) assistance; **l'A~ (publique)** welfare services.

assistant, **~e** /asistã, -t/ *nm,f* assistant; (Scol) foreign language assistant; **~s** (spectateurs) members of the audience; **~e sociale** social worker; **~ personnel numérique** personal digital assistant, PDA.

assister /asiste/ [1] *vt* assist; **~ à** attend, be (present) at; (accident) witness; **assisté par ordinateur** computer-assisted.

association /asɔsjasjõ/ *nf* association.

associé, **~e** /asɔsje/ *nm,f* partner, associate. ● *a* associate.

associer /asɔsje/ [45] *vt* associate; (mêler) combine (à with); **~ qn à** (projet) involve sb in; (bénéfices) give sb a share of. □ **s'~** *vpr* (sociétés, personnes) become associated, join forces (à with); (s'harmoniser) combine (à with); **s'~ à** (joie, opinion de qn) share; (projet) take part in.

assommer /asɔme/ [1] *vt* knock out; (animal) stun; (fig) overwhelm; (ennuyer 🔲) bore.

Assomption /asɔpsjõ/ *nf* Assumption.

assortiment /asɔʀtimã/ *nm* assortment.

assortir /asɔʀtiʀ/ [2] *vt* match (à with, to), **~ de** accompany with. □ **s'~** *vpr* match; **s'~ à qch** match sth.

assoupir (s') /(s)asupiʀ/ [2] *vpr* doze off; (s'apaiser) subside.

assouplir /asupliʀ/ [2] *vt* make supple; (fig) make flexible.

assourdir /asuʀdiʀ/ [2] *vt* (personne) deafen; (bruit) muffle.

assouvir /asuviʀ/ [2] *vt* satisfy.

assujettir /asyʒetiʀ/ [2] *vt* subjugate, subdue; **~ à** subject to.

assumer /asyme/ [1] *vt* assume; (coût) meet; (accepter) come to terms with, accept.

assurance /asyʀãs/ *nf* (self-) assurance; (garantie) assurance; (contrat) insurance; **~s sociales**

social insurance; ~ **automobile/ maladie** car/health insurance.

assuré, ~**e** /asyʀe/ a certain, assured; (*sûr de soi*) confident, assured. ●*nm, f* insured party.

assurer /asyʀe/ [1] *vt* ensure; (*fournir*) provide; (*exécuter*) carry out; (Comm) insure; (*stabiliser*) steady; (*frontières*) make secure; ~ **à qn que** assure sb that; ~ **qn de** assure sb of; ~ **la gestion/ défense de** manage/defend. □ **s'~** *vpr* take out insurance; **s'~ de/ que** make sure of/that; **s'~ qch** (*se procurer*) secure sth. **assureur** *nm* insurer.

astérisque /asteʀisk/ *nm* asterisk.

asthmatique /asmatik/ a & *nmf* asthmatic.

asthme /asm/ *nm* asthma.

asticot /astiko/ *nm* maggot.

astreindre /astʀɛ̃dʀ/ [22] *vt* ~ **qn à qch** force sth on sb; ~ **qn à faire** force sb to do.

astrologie /astʀɔlɔʒi/ *nf* astrology. **astrologue** *nmf* astrologer.

astronaute /astʀɔnot/ *nmf* astronaut.

astronomie /astʀɔnɔmi/ *nf* astronomy.

astuce /astys/ *nf* smartness; (*truc*) trick; (*plaisanterie*) wisecrack.

astucieux, **-ieuse** /astysjø, -z/ a smart, clever.

atelier /atəlje/ *nm* (*local*) workshop; (*de peintre*) studio; (*séance de travail*) workshop.

athée /ate/ *nmf* atheist. ●*a* atheistic.

athlète /atlɛt/ *nmf* athlete. **athlétisme** *nm* athletics.

Atlantique /atlɑ̃tik/ *nm* Atlantic (Ocean).

atmosphère /atmɔsfɛʀ/ *nf* atmosphere.

atomique /atɔmik/ a atomic; (*énergie, centrale*) nuclear.

atomiseur /atɔmizœʀ/ *nm* spray.

atout /atu/ *nm* trump (card); (*avantage*) asset.

atroce /atʀɔs/ a atrocious.

attabler (**s'**) /(s)atable/ [1] *vpr* sit down at table.

attachant, ~**e** /ataʃɑ̃, -t/ a charming.

attache /ataʃ/ *nf* (*agrafe*) fastener; (*lien*) tie.

attaché, ~**e** /ataʃe/ a **être** ~ **à** (*aimer*) be attached to. ●*nm, f* (Pol) attaché.

attacher /ataʃe/ [1] *vt* tie (up); (*ceinture, robe*) fasten; (*bicyclette*) lock; ~ **à** (*attribuer à*) attach to. ●*vi* (Culin) stick. □ **s'~** *vpr* fasten, do up; **s'~ à** (*se lier à*) become attached to; (*se consacrer à*) apply oneself to.

attaquant, ~**e** /atakɑ̃, -t/ *nm, f* attacker; (*au football*) striker; (*au football américain*) forward.

attaque /atak/ *nf* attack; ~ (**cérébrale**) stroke; **il va en faire une** ~ he'll have a fit; ~ **à main armée** armed attack.

attaquer /atake/ [1] *vt* attack; (*banque*) raid. ●*vi* attack. □ **s'~ à** *vpr* attack; (*problème, sujet*) tackle.

attardé, ~**e** /ataʀde/ a backward; (*idées*) outdated; (*en retard*) late.

attarder (**s'**) /(s)ataʀde/ [1] *vpr* linger.

atteindre /atɛ̃dʀ/ [22] *vt* reach; (*blesser*) hit; (*affecter*) affect.

atteint, ~**e** /atɛ̃, -t/ a ~ **de** suffering from.

atteinte /atɛ̃t/ *nf* attack (**à** on); **porter** ~ **à** attack; (*droit*) infringe.

atteler /atle/ [38] *vt* (*cheval*) harness; (*remorque*) couple. □ **s'~ à** *vpr* get down to.

attelle /atɛl/ *nf* splint.

attenant, **~e** /atnɑ̃, -t/ *a* **~** (**à**) adjoining.

attendant: **en ~** /ɑ̃natɑ̃dɑ̃/ *loc* meanwhile.

attendre /atɑ̃dʀ/ [3] *vt* wait for; (*bébé*) expect; (*être le sort de*) await; (*escompter*) expect; **~ que qn fasse** wait for sb to do. ● *vi* wait; (*au téléphone*) hold. □ **s'~ à** *vpr* expect.

attendrir /atɑ̃dʀiʀ/ [2] *vt* move (to pity). □ **s'~** *vpr* be moved to pity.

attendu¹ /atɑ̃dy/ *prép* given, considering; **~ que** considering that.

attendu², **~e** /atɑ̃dy/ *a* (*escompté*) expected; (*espéré*) long-awaited.

attentat /atɑ̃ta/ *nm* assassination attempt; **~** (**à la bombe**) (bomb) attack.

attente /atɑ̃t/ *nf* wait(ing); (*espoir*) expectations (+ *pl*).

attenter /atɑ̃te/ [1] *vi* **~ à** make an attempt on; (*fig*) violate.

attentif, **-ive** /atɑ̃tif, -v/ *a* attentive; (*scrupuleux*) careful; **~ à** mindful of; (*soucieux*) careful of.

attention /atɑ̃sjɔ̃/ *nf* attention; (*soin*) care; **~** (**à**)! watch out (for)!; **faire ~ à** (*écouter*) pay attention to, (*prendre garde à*) watch out for; (*prendre soin de*) take care of; **faire ~ à faire** be careful to do.

attentionné, **~e** *a* considerate.

attentisme /atɑ̃tism/ *nm* wait-and-see policy.

atténuer /atenɥe/ [1] *vt* (*violence*) reduce; (*critique*) tone down; (*douleur*) ease; (*faute*) mitigate. □ **s'~** *vpr* subside.

atterrir /ateʀiʀ/ [2] *vi* land.

atterrissage *nm* landing.

attestation /atɛstasjɔ̃/ *nf* certificate.

attester /atɛste/ [1] *vt* testify to; **~ que** testify that.

attirant, **~e** /atiʀɑ̃, -t/ *a* attractive.

attirer /atiʀe/ [1] *vt* draw, attract; (*causer*) bring. □ **s'~** *vpr* bring upon oneself; (*amis*) win.

attiser /atize/ [1] *vt* (*feu*) poke; (*sentiment*) stir up.

attitré, **~e** /atitʀe/ *a* accredited; (*habituel*) usual, regular.

attitude /atityd/ *nf* attitude; (*maintien*) bearing.

attraction /atʀaksjɔ̃/ *nf* attraction.

attrait /atʀɛ/ *nm* attraction.

attraper /atʀape/ [1] *vt* catch; (*corde, main*) catch hold of; (*habitude, accent*) pick up; (*maladie*) catch; **se faire ~** ▣ get told off.

attrayant, **~e** /atʀɛjɑ̃, -t/ *a* attractive.

attribuer /atʀibɥe/ [1] *vt* allocate; (*prix*) award; (*imputer*) attribute. □ **s'~** *vpr* claim (for oneself). **attribution** *nf* awarding, allocation.

attrouper (**s'**) /(s)atʀupe/ [1] *vpr* gather.

au /o/ ⇒**à**.

aubaine /obɛn/ *nf* godsend, opportunity.

aube /ob/ *nf* dawn, daybreak.

auberge /obɛʀʒ/ *nf* inn; **~ de jeunesse** youth hostel.

aubergine /obɛʀʒin/ *nf* aubergine; (*US*) eggplant.

aucun, **~e** /okœ̃, okyn/ *a* (*dans une phrase négative*) no, not any; (*positif*) any. ● *pron* (*dans une phrase négative*) none, not any; (*positif*) any; **~ des deux** neither of the two; **d'~s** some. **aucunement** *adv* not at all, in no way.

audace /odas/ *nf* daring; (*impudence*) audacity.

audacieux, **-ieuse** /odasjø, -z/ *a* daring.

au-delà /od(ə)la/ *adv* beyond. ● *prép* **~ de** beyond.

au-dessous /od(ə)su/ *adv* below.

●*prép* ~ **de** below; (couvert par) under.

au-dessus /od(ə)sy/ *adv* above.
●*prép* ~ **de** above.

au-devant /od(ə)vã/ *prép* **aller** ~ **de qn** go to meet sb; **aller** ~ **des désirs de qn** anticipate sb's wishes.

audience /odjãs/ *nf* audience; (d'un tribunal) hearing; (succès, attention) success.

audimat® /odimat/ *nm* **l'**~ the TV ratings.

audiovisuel, ~**le** /odjovizyɛl/ *a* audio-visual.

auditeur, **-trice** /oditœʀ, -tʀis/ *nm, f* listener.

audition /odisjõ/ *nf* hearing; (Théât, Mus) audition.

auditoire /oditwaʀ/ *nm* audience.

augmentation /ogmãtasjõ/ *nf* increase; ~ **(de salaire)** (pay) rise; (US) raise.

augmenter /ogmãte/ [1] *vt/i* increase; (*employé*) give a pay rise *ou* raise to.

augure /ogyʀ/ *nm* (devin) oracle; **être de bon/mauvais** ~ be a good/ bad sign.

aujourd'hui /oʒuʀdɥi/ *adv* today.

auparavant /opaʀavã/ *adv* (avant) before; (précédemment) previously; (en premier lieu) beforehand.

auprès /opʀɛ/ *prép* ~ **de** (à côté de) beside, next to; (comparé à) compared with; **s'excuser/se plaindre** ~ **de** apologize/complain to.

auquel /okɛl/ ⇒LEQUEL.

aura, **aurait** /oʀa, oʀɛ/ ⇒AVOIR [5].

aurore /oʀɔʀ/ *nf* dawn.

aussi /osi/ *adv* (également) too, also, as well; (dans une comparaison) as; (si, tellement) so; ~ **bien que** as well as. ●*conj* (donc) so, consequently.

aussitôt /osito/ *adv* immediately; ~ **que** as soon as, the moment; ~ **arrivé** as soon as he arrived.

austère /ostɛʀ/ *a* austere.

Australie /ɔstʀali/ *nf* Australia.

australien, ~**ne** /ɔstʀaljẽ, -ɛn/ *a* Australian. **A**~, ~**ne** *nm, f* Australian.

autant /otã/ *adv* (*travailler, manger*) as much (**que** as); ~ **(de)** (quantité) as much (**que** as); (nombre) as many (**que** as); (tant) so much, so many; ~ **faire** one had better do; **d'**~ **plus que** all the more than; **en faire** ~ do the same; **pour** ~ for all that.

autel /otɛl/ *nm* altar.

auteur /otœʀ/ *nm* author; **l'**~ **du crime** the perpetrator of the crime.

authentifier /otãtifje/ [45] *vt* authenticate.

authentique /otãtik/ *a* authentic.

auto /oto/ *nf* car; ~ **tamponneuse** dodgem, bumper car.

autobus /otobys/ *nm* bus.

autocar /otokaʀ/ *nm* coach.

autochtone /otɔktɔn/ *nmf* native.

autocollant, ~**e** /otɔkɔlã, -t/ *a* self-adhesive. ●*nm* sticker.

autodidacte /otɔdidakt/ *nmf* self-taught person.

auto-école (*pl* ~**s**) /otɔekɔl/ *nf* driving school.

automate /otɔmat/ *nm* automaton, robot.

automatique /otɔmatik/ *a* automatic.

automatisation /otɔmatizasjõ/ *nf* automation.

automne /otɔn/ *nm* autumn; (US) fall.

automobile /otɔmɔbil/ *a* motor, car; (US) automobile. ●*nf* (motor) car; **l'**~ the motor industry; (Sport) motoring. **automobiliste** *nmf* motorist.

autonome /otɔnɔm/ *a* autonomous; (Ordinat) stand-alone.

autoradio /otɔRadjo/ *nm* car radio.

autorisation /otɔRizasjɔ̃/ *nf* permission, authorization; (permis) permit.

autorisé, ~e /otɔRize/ *a* (*opinions*) authoritative; (approuvé) authorized.

autoriser /otɔRize/ [1] *vt* authorize, permit; (rendre possible) allow (of); (donner un droit) ~ **qn à faire** entitle sb to do.

autoritaire /otɔRitɛR/ *a* authoritarian.

autorité /otɔRite/ *nf* authority; **faire ~** be authoritative.

autoroute /otɔRut/ *nf* motorway; (US) highway; ~ **de l'information** (Ordinat) information superhighway.

auto-stop /otɔstɔp/ *nm* hitch-hiking; **faire de l'~** hitch-hike; **prendre qn en ~** give a lift to sb.

autour /otuR/ *adv* around; **tout ~** all around. ●*prép* ~ **de** around.

autre /otR/ *a* other; **un ~ jour/livre** another day/book; ~ **chose/part** something/somewhere else; **quelqu'un/rien d'~** somebody/ nothing else; **quoi d'~?** what else?; **d'~ part** on the other hand; (de plus) moreover, besides; **vous ~s Anglais** you English. ●*pron* **un ~, une ~** another (one); **l'~** the other (one); **les ~s** the others; (autrui) others; **d'~s** (some) others; **l'un l'~** each other; **l'un et l'~** both of them; **d'un jour à l'~** (bientôt) any day now; **entre ~s** among other things.

autrefois /otRəfwa/ *adv* in the past; (précédemment) formerly.

autrement /otRəmɑ̃/ *adv*

differently; (sinon) otherwise; (plus 🔲) far more; ~ **dit** in other words.

Autriche /otRiʃ/ *nf* Austria.

autrichien, ~ne /otRiʃjɛ̃, -jɛn/ *a* Austrian. **A~, ~ne** *nm, f* Austrian.

autruche /otRyʃ/ *nf* ostrich.

autrui /otRɥi/ *pron* others, other people.

aux /o/ ⇒À.

auxiliaire /oksiljɛR/ *a* auxiliary. ●*nmf* (assistant) auxiliary. ●*nm* (Gram) auxiliary.

auxquels, -quelles /okɛl/ ⇨LEQUEL.

aval: en ~ /ɑ̃naval/ *loc* downstream.

avaler /avale/ [1] *vt* swallow.

avance /avɑ̃s/ *nf* advance; (sur un concurrent) lead; ~ **(de fonds)** advance; **à l'~** in advance; **d'~** already; **en ~** early; (montre) fast; **en ~ (sur)** (menant) ahead (of).

avancement /avɑ̃smɑ̃/ *nm* promotion.

avancé, ~e /avɑ̃se/ *a* advanced.

avancer /avɑ̃se/ [10] *vi* move forward, advance; (travail) make progress; (montre) be fast; (faire saillie) jut out. ●*vt* move forward; (dans le temps) bring forward; (argent) advance; (montre) put forward. □ **s'~** *vpr* move forward, advance; (se hasarder) commit oneself.

avant /avɑ̃/ *nm* front; (Sport) forward. ●*a inv* front. ●*prép* before; ~ **de faire** before doing; **en ~ de** in front of; ~ **peu** shortly; ~ **tout** above all. ●*adv* (dans le temps) before, beforehand; (d'abord) first; **en ~** (dans l'espace) forward(s); (dans le temps) ahead; **le bus d'~** the previous bus. ●*conj* ~ **que** before; ~ **qu'il (ne) fasse** before he does.

avantage /avɑ̃taʒ/ *nm* advantage; (Comm) benefit.

avantager /avɑ̃taʒe/ [40] *vt* favour; (embellir) show off to advantage.

avantageux, -euse /avɑ̃taʒø, -z/ *a* advantageous, favourable; (*prix*) attractive.

avant-bras /avɑ̃bʀa/ *nm inv* forearm.

avant-centre (*pl* **avants-centres**) /avɑ̃sɑ̃tʀ/ *nm* centre forward.

avant-coureur (*pl* ∼s) /avɑ̃kuʀœʀ/ *a* precursory, foreshadowing.

avant-dernier, -ière (*pl* ∼s) /avɑ̃dɛʀnje, -jɛʀ/ *a & nm,f* last but one.

avant-goût (*pl* ∼s) /avɑ̃gu/ *nm* foretaste.

avant-hier /avɑ̃tjɛʀ/ *adv* the day before yesterday.

avant-poste (*pl* ∼s) /avɑ̃pɔst/ *nm* outpost.

avant-première (*pl* ∼s) /avɑ̃pʀəmjɛʀ/ *nf* preview.

avant-propos /avɑ̃pʀɔpo/ *nm inv* foreword.

avare /avaʀ/ *a* miserly; ∼ **de** sparing with. ● *nmf* miser.

avarié, ∼e /avaʀje/ *a* (*aliment*) spoiled.

avatar /avataʀ/ *nm* misfortune.

avec /avɛk/ *prép* with. ● *adv* ▣ with it *ou* them.

avènement /avɛnmɑ̃/ *nm* advent; (d'un roi) accession.

avenir /avniʀ/ *nm* future; **à l'**∼ in future; **d'**∼ with (future) prospects.

aventure /avɑ̃tyʀ/ *nf* adventure; (sentimentale) affair. **aventureux, -euse** *a* adventurous; (hasardeux) risky.

avérer (**s'**) /(s)aveʀe/ [14] *vpr* prove (to be).

averse /avɛʀs/ *nf* shower.

avertir /avɛʀtiʀ/ [2] *vt* inform; (mettre en garde, menacer) warn. **avertissement** *nm* warning.

avertisseur /avɛʀtisœʀ/ *nm* alarm; (Auto) horn; ∼ **d'incendie** fire-alarm; ∼ **lumineux** warning light.

aveu (*pl* ∼**x**) /avø/ *nm* confession; **de l'**∼ **de** by the admission of.

aveugle /avœgl/ *a* blind. ● *nmf* blind man, blind woman.

aviateur, -trice /avjatœʀ, -tʀis/ *nm, f* aviator.

aviation /avjasjɔ̃/ *nf* flying; (industrie) aviation; (Mil) air force.

avide /avid/ *a* greedy (**de** for); (anxieux) eager (**de** for); ∼ **de faire** eager to do.

avion /avjɔ̃/ *nm* plane, aeroplane, aircraft; (US) airplane; ∼ **à réaction** jet.

aviron /aviʀɔ̃/ *nm* oar; **l'**∼ (Sport) rowing.

avis /avi/ *nm* opinion; (conseil) advice; (renseignement) notification; (Comm) advice; **à mon** ∼ in my opinion; **changer d'**∼ change one's mind; **être d'**∼ **que** be of the opinion that; ∼ **au lecteur** foreword.

avisé, ∼e /avize/ *a* sensible; **être bien/mal** ∼ **de** be well-/ill-advised to.

aviser /avize/ [1] *vt* advise, notify. ● *vi* decide what to do. ▢ **s'**∼ **de** *vpr* suddenly realize; **s'**∼ **de faire** take it into one's head to do.

avocat, ∼e /avɔka, -t/ *nm, f* barrister; (US) attorney; (fig) advocate; ∼ **de la défense** counsel for the defence. ● *nm* (fruit) avocado (pear).

avoine /avwan/ *nf* oats (+ *pl*).

avoir /avwaʀ/ [5]

●*verbe auxiliaire*

····▸ have; **il nous a appelés hier** he called us yesterday.

●*verbe transitif*

····▸ (possession) have (got).

····▸ (obtenir) get; (au téléphone) get through to.

····▸ (duper) ▣ have; **on m'a eu!** I've been had!

····▸ ~ **chaud/faim** be hot/hungry.

····▸ ~ **dix ans** be ten years old.

●**avoir à** *verbe* + *préposition*

····▸ to have to; **j'ai beaucoup à faire** I have a lot to do; **tu n'as qu'à leur écrire** all you have to do is write to them.

●**en avoir pour** *verbe* + *préposition*

····▸ **j'en ai pour une minute** I will only be a minute; **j'en ai eu pour 100 euros** it cost me 100 euros.

●**il y a** *verbe impersonnel*

····▸ there is; (pluriel) there are; **qu'est-ce qu'il y a?** what's the matter?; **il est venu il y a cinq ans** he came here five years ago; **il y a au moins 5 km jusqu'à la gare** it's at least 5 km to the station.

●*nom masculin*

····▸ (dans un magasin) credit note.

····▸ (biens) asset (+ *pl*).

avortement /avɔʀtəmɑ̃/ *nm* (Méd) abortion.

avorter /avɔʀte/ [1] *vi* (*projet*) abort; (**se faire**) ~ have an abortion.

avoué, ~**e** /avwe/ *a* avowed. ●*nm* solicitor; (US) attorney.

avouer /avwe/ [1] *vt* (*amour, ignorance*) confess; (*crime*) confess to, admit. ●*vi* confess.

avril /avʀil/ *nm* April.

axe /aks/ *nm* axis; (essieu) axle; (d'une politique) main line(s), basis; ~ **(routier)** main road.

ayant /ɛjɑ̃/ ⇒AVOIR [5].

azote /azɔt/ *nm* nitrogen.

azur /azyʀ/ *nm* sky-blue.

baba /baba/ *nm* ~ **(au rhum)** (rum) baba; **en rester** ~ ▣ be flabbergasted.

babillard /babijaʀ/ *nm* ~ **électronique** (Internet) bulletin board system, BBS.

babines /babin/ *nfpl* **se lécher les** ~ lick one's chops.

babiole /babjɔl/ *nf* trinket.

bâbord /babɔʀ/ *nm* port (side).

baby-foot /babifut/ *nm inv* table football.

bac /bak/ *nm* (Scol) ⇒BACCALAURÉAT; (bateau) ferry; (récipient) tub; (plus petit) tray.

baccalauréat /bakalɔʀea/ *nm* school leaving certificate.

bâche /baʃ/ *nf* tarpaulin.

bachelier, -**ière** /baʃəlje, -jɛʀ/ *nm, f* holder of the *baccalauréat*.

bachoter /baʃɔte/ [1] *vi* cram (for an exam).

bâcler /bɑkle/ [1] *vt* botch (up).

bactérie /bakteʀi/ *nf* bacterium; ~**s** bacteria.

badaud, ~**e** /bado, -d/ *nm, f* onlooker.

badigeonner /badiʒɔne/ [1] *vt* whitewash; (barbouiller) daub.

badiner /badine/ [1] *vi* banter.

baffe /baf/ *nf* ▣ slap.

baffle /bafl/ *nm* speaker.

bafouiller /bafuje/ [1] vt/i stammer.

bagage /bagaʒ/ nm bag; (connaissances) knowledge; ~s luggage; ~ à main hand luggage.

bagarre /bagaʀ/ nf fight.

bagatelle /bagatɛl/ nf trifle; (somme) trifling amount.

bagnard /baɲaʀ/ nm convict.

bagnole /baɲɔl/ nf ▣ car.

bague /bag/ nf (bijou) ring.

baguette /bagɛt/ nf stick; (de chef d'orchestre) baton; (chinoise) chopstick; (pain) baguette; ~ magique magic wand; ~ de tambour drumstick.

baie /bɛ/ nf (Géog) bay; (fruit) berry; ~ (vitrée) picture window; (Ordinat) bay.

baignade /bɛɲad/ nf swimming.

baigner /beɲe/ [1] vt bathe; (enfant) bath. ●vi ~ dans l'huile swim in grease. □ se ~ vpr have a swim. **baigneur, -euse** nm, f swimmer.

baignoire /bɛɲwaʀ/ nf bath(tub).

bail (pl **baux**) /baj, bo/ nm lease.

bâiller /baje/ [1] vi yawn; (être ouvert) gape.

bailleur /bajœʀ/ nm ~ de fonds (Comm) sleeping partner.

bain /bɛ̃/ nm bath; (baignade) swim; prendre un ~ de soleil sunbathe; ~ de bouche mouthwash; être dans le ~ (fig) be in the swing of things; se remettre dans le ~ get back into the swing of things; prendre un ~ de foule mingle with the crowd.

bain-marie (pl **bains-marie**) /bɛ̃maʀi/ nm double boiler.

baiser /beze/ [1] vt (main) kiss; ▣ screw ▣. ●nm kiss.

baisse /bɛs/ nf fall, drop; être en ~ be going down.

baisser /bese/ [1] vt lower; (radio, lampe) turn down. ●vi (niveau) go down, fall; (santé, forces) fail. □ se ~ vpr bend down.

bal (pl ~s) /bal/ nm dance; (habillé) ball; (lieu) dance-hall; ~ costumé fancy-dress ball.

balade /balad/ nf stroll; (en auto) drive.

balader /balade/ [1] vt take for a stroll. □ se ~ vpr (à pied) (go for a) stroll; (en voiture) go for a drive; (voyager) travel.

baladeur /baladœʀ/ nm personal stereo.

balafre /balafʀ/ nf gash; (cicatrice) scar.

balai /balɛ/ nm broom.

balance /balɑ̃s/ nf scales (+ pl); la B~ Libra.

balancer /balɑ̃se/ [10] vt swing; (doucement) sway; (lancer ▣) chuck ▣; (se débarrasser de ▣) chuck out ▣. ●vi sway. □ se ~ vpr swing; sway; s'en ~ ▣ not to give a damn ▣.

balancier /balɑ̃sje/ nm (d'horloge) pendulum; (d'équilibriste) pole.

balançoire /balɑ̃swaʀ/ nf swing.

balayage /balejaʒ/ nm sweeping; (cheveux) highlights.

balayer /baleje/ [31] vt sweep (up); (vent) sweep away; (se débarrasser de) sweep aside.

balbutiement /balbysimɑ̃/ nm stammering; les ~s (fig) the first steps.

balcon /balkɔ̃/ nm balcony; (Théât) dress circle.

baleine /balɛn/ nf whale.

balise /baliz/ nf beacon; (bouée) buoy; (Auto) (road) sign. **baliser** [1] vt mark out (with beacons); (route) signpost; (sentier) mark out.

balivernes /balivɛʀn/ nfpl nonsense.

ballant, ~e /balɑ̃, -t/ a dangling.

balle /bal/ nf (projectile) bullet; (Sport) ball; (paquet) bale.

ballerine /balʀin/ *nf* (danseuse) ballerina; (chaussure) ballet pump.

ballet /balɛ/ *nm* ballet.

ballon /balɔ̃/ *nm* (Sport) ball; ~ (de baudruche) balloon; ~ de football football.

ballonné, ~e /balɔne/ *a* bloated.

balnéaire /balneɛʀ/ *a* seaside.

balourd, ~e /baluʀ, -d/ *nm, f* oaf. ● *a* uncouth.

balustrade /balystʀad/ *nf* railing.

ban /bɑ̃/ *nm* round of applause; ~s (de mariage) banns; **mettre au ~ de** cast out from.

banal, ~e (*mpl* ~s) /banal/ *a* commonplace, banal.

banane /banan/ *nf* banana.

banc /bɑ̃/ *nm* bench; (de poissons) shoal; ~ **des accusés** dock; ~ **d'essai** (test) testing ground.

bancaire /bɑ̃kɛʀ/ *a* (secteur) banking; (chèque) bank.

bancal, ~e (*mpl* ~s) /bɑ̃kal/ *a* wobbly; (solution) shaky.

bande /bɑ̃d/ *nf* (groupe) gang; (de papier) strip; (rayure) stripe; (de film) reel; (pansement) bandage; ~ **dessinée** comic strip; ~ **(magnétique)** tape; ~ **sonore** sound track.

bande-annonce (*pl* **bandes-annonces**) /bɑ̃danɔ̃s/ *nf* trailer.

bandeau (*pl* ~x) /bɑ̃do/ *nm* headband; (sur les yeux) blindfold; ~ **publicitaire** (Ordinat) banner.

bander /bɑ̃de/ [1] *vt* bandage; (arc) bend; (muscle) tense; ~ **les yeux à** blindfold.

banderole /bɑ̃dʀɔl/ *nf* banner.

bandit /bɑ̃di/ *nm* bandit. **banditisme** *nm* crime.

bandoulière: en ~ /ɑ̃buduljɛʀ/ *loc* across one's shoulder.

banlieue /bɑ̃ljø/ *nf* suburbs; **de ~** suburban. **banlieusard, ~e** *nm, f* (suburban) commuter.

bannir /baniʀ/ [2] *vt* banish.

banque /bɑ̃k/ *nf* bank; (activité) banking; ~ **de données** databank.

banqueroute /bɑ̃kʀut/ *nf* bankruptcy.

banquet /bɑ̃kɛ/ *nm* banquet.

banquette /bɑ̃kɛt/ *nf* seat.

banquier, -ière /bɑ̃kje, -jɛʀ/ *nm, f* banker.

baptême /batɛm/ *nm* baptism, christening. **baptiser** [1] *vt* baptize, christen; (nommer) call.

bar /baʀ/ *nm* (lieu) bar.

baragouiner /baʀagwine/ [1] *vt/i* gabble; (langue) speak a few words of.

baraque /baʀak/ *nf* hut, shed; (maison 🞑) house.

baratin /baʀatɛ̃/ *nm* 🞑 sweet *ou* smooth talk.

barbare /baʀbaʀ/ *a* barbaric. ● *nmf* barbarian.

barbe /baʀb/ *nf* beard; ~ **à papa** candy-floss; (US) cotton candy; **quelle ~!** 🞑 what a drag! 🞑.

barbelé /baʀbəle/ *a* **fil** ~ barbed wire.

barber /baʀbe/ [1] *vt* 🞑 bore.

barboter /baʀbɔte/ [1] *vi* (dans l'eau) paddle, splash. ● *vt* (voler 🞑) pinch.

barbouiller /baʀbuje/ [1] *vt* (souiller) smear (de with); **tu es tout barbouillé** your face is all dirty; **être barbouillé** feel queazy.

barbu, ~e /baʀby/ *a* bearded.

barème /baʀɛm/ *nm* list, table; (échelle) scale.

baril /baʀil/ *nm* barrel.

bariolé, ~e /baʀjɔle/ *a* multicoloured.

baromètre /baʀɔmɛtʀ/ *nm* barometer.

baron, ~ne /baʀɔ̃, -ɔn/ *nm, f* baron, baroness.

barque /baʀk/ *nf* (small) boat.

barrage /baʀaʒ/ *nm* dam; (sur route) roadblock.

barre /baʀ/ *nf* bar; (trait) line, stroke; (Naut) helm; ∼ **de boutons** (Ordinat) toolbar.

barreau (*pl* ∼**x**) /baʀo/ *nm* bar; (d'échelle) rung; **le** ∼ (Jur) the bar.

barrer /baʀe/ [1] *vt* block; (*porte*) bar; (rayer) cross out; (Naut) steer. □ **se** ∼ *vpr* 🎵 leave.

barrette /baʀɛt/ *nf* (hair) slide.

barrière /baʀjɛʀ/ *nf* (porte) gate; (clôture) fence; (obstacle) barrier.

bar-tabac (*pl* **bars-tabac**) /baʀtaba/ *nm* café (*selling stamps and cigarettes*).

bas, basse /bɑ, bɑs/ *a* (niveau, table) low; (*action*) base; **au** ∼ **mot** at the lowest estimate; **en** ∼ **âge** young; ∼ **morceaux** (viande) cheap cuts. ● *nm* bottom; (chaussette) stocking; ∼ **de laine** (fig) nest-egg. ● *adv* low; **en** ∼ down below; (dans une maison) downstairs; **en** ∼ **de la page** at the bottom of the page; **plus** ∼ further *ou* lower down; **mettre** ∼ give birth (to). **bas de casse** *nm inv* lower case. **bas-côté** (*pl* ∼**s**) *nm* (de route) verge; (US) shoulder.

bascule /baskyl/ *nf* (balance) scales (+ *pl*); **cheval/fauteuil à** ∼ rocking-horse/-chair.

basculer /baskyle/ [1] *vi* topple over; (*benne*) tip up.

base /bɑz/ *nf* base; (fondement) basis; (Pol) rank and file; **de** ∼ basic. **base de données** *nf* database.

baser /bɑze/ [1] *vt* base. □ **se** ∼ **sur** *vpr* go by.

bas-fonds /bafɔ̃/ *nmpl* (eau) shallows; (fig) dregs.

basilic /bazilik/ *nm* basil.

basilique /bazilik/ *nf* basilica.

basque /bask/ *a* Basque. **B**∼ *nmf* Basque.

basse /bɑs/ ⇒BAS.

basse-cour (*pl* **basses-cours**) /baskuʀ/ *nf* farmyard.

bassesse /bases/ *nf* baseness; (action) base act.

bassin /basɛ̃/ *nm* (pièce d'eau) pond; (de piscine) pool; (Géog) basin; (Anat) pelvis; (plat) bowl; ∼ **houiller** coalfield.

bassine /basin/ *nf* bowl.

basson /basɔ̃/ *nm* bassoon.

bas-ventre (*pl* ∼**s**) /bavɑ̃tʀ/ *nm* lower abdomen.

bat /ba/ ⇒BATTRE [11].

bataille /bataj/ *nf* battle; (fig) fight.

bâtard, ∼e /bɑtaʀ, -d/ *a* (solution) hybrid. ● *nm, f* bastard.

bateau (*pl* ∼**x**) /bato/ *nm* boat; ∼ **pneumatique** rubber dinghy. **bateau-mouche** (*pl* **bateaux-mouches**) *nm* sightseeing boat.

bâti, ∼e /bɑti/ *a* **bien** ∼ well-built.

bâtiment /bɑtimɑ̃/ *nm* building; (industrie) building trade; (navire) vessel.

bâtir /bɑtiʀ/ [2] *vt* build.

bâton /bɑtɔ̃/ *nm* stick; **conversation à** ∼**s rompus** rambling conversation; ∼ **de rouge** lipstick.

battant /batɑ̃/ *nm* (vantail) flap; **porte à deux** ∼**s** double door.

battement /batmɑ̃/ *nm* (de cœur) beat(ing); (temps) interval; (Mus) beat.

batterie /batʀi/ *nf* (Mil, Électr) battery; (Mus) drums; ∼ **de cuisine** pots and pans.

batteur /batœʀ/ *nm* (Mus) drummer; (Culin) whisk.

battre /batʀ/ [11] *vt/i* beat; (cartes) shuffle; (Culin) whisk; (l'emporter sur) beat; ∼ **des ailes** flap its wings; ∼ **des mains** clap; ∼ **des paupières** blink; ∼ **en retraite** beat a retreat; ∼ **la semelle** stamp one's feet; ∼ **son plein** be in full swing. □ **se** ∼ *vpr* fight.

baume /bom/ *nm* balm.

B

bavard, **~e** /bavaʀ, -d/ a talkative. ● nm, f chatterbox.

bavardage /bavaʀdaʒ/ nm chatter, gossip. **bavarder** [1] vi chat; (jacasser) chatter, gossip.

bave /bav/ nf dribble, slobber; (de limace) slime. **baver** [1] vi dribble, slobber. **baveux, -euse** a dribbling; (omelette) runny.

bavoir /bavwaʀ/ nm bib.

bavure /bavyʀ/ nf smudge; (erreur) blunder; **~ policière** police blunder.

bazar /bazaʀ/ nm bazaar; (objets 🄸) clutter.

BCBG abrév mf (**bon chic bon genre**) posh.

BD abrév f (**bande dessinée**) comic strip.

béant, **~e** /beɑ̃, -t/ a gaping.

béat, **~e** /bea, -t/ a (hum) blissful; **~ d'admiration** wide-eyed with admiration.

beau (**bel** before vowel or mute h), **belle** (mpl **~x**) /bo, bɛl/ a beautiful; (femme) beautiful; (homme) handsome; (temps) fine, nice. ● nm beauty. ● adv il fait **~** the weather is nice; **au ~ milieu** right in the middle; **bel et bien** well and truly; **de plus belle** more than ever; **faire le ~** sit up and beg; **on a ~ essayer/insister** however much one tries/insists.

beaucoup /boku/ adv a lot, very much; **~ de** (nombre) many; (quantité) a lot of; **pas ~ (de)** not many; (quantité) not much; **~ plus/mieux** much more/better; **~ trop** far too much; **de ~** by far.

beau-fils (pl **beaux-fils**) /bofis/ nm (remariage) stepson.

beau-frère (pl **beaux-frères**) /bofʀɛʀ/ nm brother-in-law.

beau-père (pl **beaux-pères**) /bopɛʀ/ nm father-in-law; (remariage) stepfather.

beauté /bote/ nf beauty; **finir en ~** end magnificently.

beaux-arts /bozaʀ/ nmpl fine arts.

beaux-parents /bopaʀɑ̃/ nmpl parents-in-law.

bébé /bebe/ nm baby. **bébé-éprouvette** (pl **bébés-éprouvette**) nm test-tube baby.

bec /bɛk/ nm beak; (de théière) spout; (de casserole) lip; (bouche 🄸) mouth; **~ de gaz** gas street-lamp.

bécane /bekan/ nf 🄸 bike.

bêche /bɛʃ/ nf spade.

bégayer /begeje/ [31] vt/i stammer.

bègue /bɛg/ nmf stammerer. ● a **être ~** stammer.

bégueule /begœl/ a prudish.

beige /bɛʒ/ a & nm beige.

beignet /bɛɲɛ/ nm fritter.

bel /bɛl/ ⇒BEAU.

bêler /bele/ [1] vi bleat.

belette /bəlɛt/ nf weasel.

belge /bɛlʒ/ a Belgian. **B~** nmf Belgian.

Belgique /bɛlʒik/ nf Belgium.

bélier /belje/ nm ram; **le B~** Aries.

belle /bɛl/ ⇒BEAU.

belle-fille (pl **belles-filles**) /bɛlfij/ nf daughter-in-law; (remariage) stepdaughter.

belle-mère (pl **belles-mères**) /bɛlmɛʀ/ nf mother-in-law; (remariage) stepmother.

belle-sœur (pl **belles-sœurs**) /bɛlsœʀ/ nf sister-in-law.

belliqueux, -euse /belikø, -z/ a warlike.

bémol /bemɔl/ nm (Mus) flat.

bénédiction /benediksjɔ̃/ nf blessing.

bénéfice /benefis/ nm (gain) profit; (avantage) benefit.

bénéficiaire /benefisjɛʀ/ nmf beneficiary.

bénéficier /benefisje/ [45] vi ~ de benefit from; (jouir de) enjoy, have.

bénéfique /benefik/ a beneficial.

Bénélux /benelyks/ nm Benelux.

bénévole /benevɔl/ a voluntary.

bénin, -igne /benɛ̃, -iɲ/ a minor; (tumeur) benign.

bénir /benir/ [2] vt bless. **bénit, ~e** a (eau) holy; (pain) consecrated.

benjamin, ~e /bɛ̃ʒamɛ̃, -in/ nm, f youngest child.

benne /bɛn/ nf (de grue) scoop; ~ à ordures (camion) waste disposal truck; (conteneur) skip; ~ (basculante) dump truck.

béquille /bekij/ nf crutch; (de moto) stand.

berceau (pl ~x) /bɛrso/ nm (de bébé, civilisation) cradle.

bercer /bɛrse/ [10] vt (balancer) rock; (apaiser) lull; (leurrer) delude.

béret /berɛ/ nm beret.

berge /bɛrʒ/ nf (bord) bank.

berger, -ère /bɛrʒe, -ɛr/ nm, f shepherd, shepherdess.

berne: en ~ /ãbɛrn/ loc at half-mast.

berner /bɛrne/ [1] vt fool.

besogne /bəzɔɲ/ nf task, job.

besoin /bəzwɛ̃/ nm need; **avoir ~ de** need; **au ~** if need be; **dans le ~** in need.

bestiole /bɛstjɔl/ nf 🔲 bug.

bétail /betaj/ nm livestock.

bête /bɛt/ a stupid. ● nf animal; ~ **noire** pet hate; ~ **sauvage** wild beast; **chercher la petite ~** be overfussy.

bêtise /betiz/ nf stupidity; (action) stupid thing.

béton /betɔ̃/ nm concrete; ~ **armé** reinforced concrete; **en ~** (mur) concrete; (argument 🔲) watertight. **bétonnière** nf concrete mixer.

betterave /bɛtrav/ nf beet; ~ **rouge** beetroot.

beugler /bøgle/ [1] vi bellow; (radio) blare out.

beur /bœr/ nmf & a 🔲 second-generation North African living in France.

beurre /bœr/ nm butter. **beurré, ~e** a buttered; 🔲 drunk. **beurrier** nm butter-dish.

bévue /bevy/ nf blunder.

biais /bjɛ/ nm (moyen) way; **par le ~ de** by means of; **de ~, en ~** at an angle.

bibelot /biblo/ nm ornament.

biberon /bibrɔ̃/ nm (feeding) bottle; **nourrir au ~** bottle-feed.

bible /bibl/ nf bible; **la B~** the Bible.

bibliographie /biblijɔgrafi/ nf bibliography.

bibliothécaire /biblijɔtekɛr/ nmf librarian.

bibliothèque /biblijɔtɛk/ nf library; (meuble) bookcase.

bic® /bik/ nm biro®.

bicarbonate /bikarbɔnat/ nm ~ **(de soude)** bicarbonate (of soda).

biceps /bisɛps/ nm biceps.

biche /biʃ/ nf doe; **ma ~** darling.

bichonner /biʃɔne/ [1] vt pamper.

bicyclette /bisiklɛt/ nf bicycle.

bide /bid/ nm (ventre 🔲) paunch; (échec 🔲) flop.

bidet /bidɛ/ nm bidet.

bidon /bidɔ̃/ nm can; (plus grand) drum; (ventre 🔲) belly; **c'est du ~** 🔲 it's a load of hogwash 🔲. ● a inv 🔲 phoney.

bidonville /bidɔ̃vil/ nf shanty town.

bidule /bidyl/ nm 🔲 thing.

Biélorussie /bjelɔrysi/ nf Byelorussia.

bien /bjɛ̃/ adv well; (très) quite, very; ~ **des** (nombre) many; **tu as**

∼ **de la chance** you are very lucky; **j'aimerais** ∼ I would like to; **ce n'est pas** ∼ **de** it is not nice to; ∼ **sûr** of course. ● *nm* good; (patrimoine) possession; ∼**s de consommation** consumer goods. ● *a inv* good; (passable) all right; (en forme) well; (à l'aise) comfortable; (beau) attractive; (respectable) nice, respectable. ● *conj* ∼ **que** (al-) though; ∼ **que ce soit** although it is. **bien-aimé,** ∼**e** *a & nm,f* beloved. **bien-être** *nm* well-being.

bienfaisance /bjɛ̃fəzɑ̃s/ *nf* charity; **fête de** ∼ charity event. **bienfaisant,** ∼**e** *a* beneficial.

bienfait /bjɛ̃fɛ/ *nm* (kind) favour; (avantage) beneficial effect. **bienfaiteur, -trice** *nm,f* benefactor.

bien-pensant, ∼**e** /bjɛ̃pɑ̃sɑ̃, -t/ *a* right-thinking.

bienséance /bjɛ̃seɑ̃s/ *nf* propriety.

bientôt /bjɛ̃to/ *adv* soon; **à** ∼ see you soon.

bienveillance /bjɛ̃vɛjɑ̃s/ *nf* kind-(li)ness.

bienvenu, ∼**e** /bjɛ̃vny/ *a* welcome. ● *nm,f* **être le** ∼, **être la** ∼**e** be welcome.

bienvenue /bjɛ̃vny/ *nf* welcome; **souhaiter la** ∼ **à** welcome.

bière /bjɛʀ/ *nf* beer; (cercueil) coffin; ∼ **blonde** lager; ∼ **brune** ≈ stout; ∼ **pression** draught beer.

bifteck /biftɛk/ *nm* steak.

bifurquer /bifyʀke/ [1] *vi* branch off, fork.

bigarré, ∼**e** /bigaʀe/ *a* motley.

bigoudi /bigudi/ *nm* curler.

bijou (*pl* ∼**x**) /biʒu/ *nm* jewel; ∼**x en or** gold jewellery. **bijouterie** *nf* (boutique) jewellery shop; (Comm) jewellery. **bijoutier, -ière** *nm,f* jeweller.

bilan /bilɑ̃/ *nm* outcome; (d'une catastrophe) (casualty) toll; (Comm) balance sheet; **faire le** ∼ **de** assess; ∼ **de santé** check-up.

bile /bil/ *nf* bile; **se faire de la** ∼ 🄸 worry.

bilingue /bilɛ̃g/ *a* bilingual.

billard /bijaʀ/ *nm* billiards (+ *pl*); (table) billiard-table.

bille /bij/ *nf* (d'enfant) marble; (de billard) billiard-ball.

billet /bijɛ/ *nm* ticket; (lettre) note; (article) column; ∼ **(de banque)** (bank) note; ∼ **de 50 euros** 50-euro note.

billetterie /bijɛtʀi/ *nf* cash dispenser.

billion /biljɔ̃/ *nm* billion; (US) trillion.

bimensuel, ∼**e** /bimɑ̃sɥɛl/ *a* fortnightly, bimonthly.

binette /binɛt/ *nf* hoe; (visage) face; (Internet) smiley.

biochimie /bjoʃimi/ *nf* biochemistry.

biodégradable /bjodegʀadabl/ *a* biodegradable.

biographie /bjɔgʀafi/ *nf* biography.

biologie /bjɔlɔʒi/ *nf* biology. **biologique** *a* biological; (produit) organic.

bioterrorisme /bjoteʀɔʀism/ *nm* bioterrorism.

bis /bis/ *nm & interj* encore.

biscornu, ∼**e** /biskɔʀny/ *a* crooked; (bizarre) cranky 🄸.

biscotte /biskɔt/ *nf* continental toast.

biscuit /biskɥi/ *nm* biscuit; (US) cookie; ∼ **salé** cracker; ∼ **de Savoie** sponge-cake.

bise /biz/ *nf* 🄸 kiss; (vent) north wind.

bison /bizɔ̃/ *nm* buffalo.

bisou /bizu/ *nm* 🄸 kiss.

bistro(t) /bistʀo/ *nm* 🄸 café, bar.

bit /bit/ *nm* (Ordinat) bit.

bitume /bitym/ *nm* asphalt.

bizarre /bizaʀ/ *a* odd, strange. **bizarrerie** *nf* peculiarity.

blafard, **~e** /blafaʀ, -d/ *a* pale.

blague /blag/ *nf* 🄸 joke; **sans ~!** no kidding! 🄸.

blaguer /blage/ [1] 🄸 *vi* joke.

blaireau (*pl* **~x**) /blɛʀo/ *nm* shaving-brush; (*animal*) badger.

blâmer /blame/ [1] *vt* criticize.

blanc, **blanche** /blɑ̃, blɑ̃ʃ/ *a* white; (*papier*, *page*) blank. ●*nm* white; (*espace*) blank; **~ d'œuf** egg white; **~ de poireau** white part of the leek; **~ (de poulet)** chicken breast; **le ~** (*linge*) whites; **laisser en ~** leave blank. **B~**, **Blanche** *nm, f* white man, white woman. **blanche** *nf* (Mus) minim.

blanchiment /blɑ̃ʃimɑ̃/ *nm* (d'argent) laundering.

blanchir /blɑ̃ʃiʀ/ [2] *vt* whiten; (*personne*) fig clear; (*argent*) launder; (Culin) blanch; **~ (à la chaux)** whitewash. ● *vi* turn white.

blanchisserie /blɑ̃ʃisʀi/ *nf* laundry.

blason /blazɔ̃/ *nm* coat of arms.

blasphème /blasfɛm/ *nm* blasphemy.

blé /ble/ *nm* wheat.

blême /blɛm/ *a* pallid.

blessant, **~e** /blesɑ̃, -t/ *a* hurtful.

blessé, **~e** /blese/ *nm, f* casualty, injured person.

blesser /blese/ [1] *vt* injure, hurt; (*par balle*) wound; (*offenser*) hurt. ◻ **se ~** *vpr* injure *ou* hurt oneself. **blessure** *nf* wound.

bleu, **~e** /blø/ *a* blue; (Culin) very rare; **~ marine/turquoise** navy blue/turquoise; **avoir une peur ~e** be scared stiff. ●*nm* blue; (*contusion*) bruise; **~ (de travail)** overalls (+ *pl*).

bleuet /bløɛ/ *nm* cornflower.

blindé, **~e** /blɛ̃de/ *a* armoured; (fig) immune (**contre** to); **porte ~e** security car. ●*nm* armoured car, tank.

blinder /blɛ̃de/ [1] *vt* armour; (fig) harden.

bloc /blɔk/ *nm* block; (de papier) pad; **serrer à ~** tighten hard; **en ~** (*matériau*) in a block; (nier) outright.

blocage /blɔkaʒ/ *nm* (des prix) freeze, freezing; (des roues) locking; (Psych) block.

bloc-notes (*pl* **blocs-notes**) /blɔknɔt/ *nm* note-pad.

blocus /blɔkys/ *nm* blockade.

blond, **~e** /blɔ̃, -d/ *a* fair, blond. ● *nm, f* fair-haired man, fair-haired woman.

bloquer /blɔke/ [1] *vt* block; (*porte*, *machine*) jam; (*roues*) lock; (*prix*, *crédits*) freeze. ◻ **se ~** *vpr* jam; (*roues*) lock; (*freins*) jam; (*ordinateur*) crash; **bloqué par la neige** snowbound.

blottir (se) /(sə)blɔtiʀ/ [2] *vpr* snuggle, huddle (**contre** against).

blouse /bluz/ *nf* overall. **blouse blanche** *nf* white coat.

blouson /bluzɔ̃/ *nm* jacket, blouson.

bluffer /blœfe/ [1] *vt/i* bluff.

bobine /bɔbin/ *nf* (de fil, film) reel; (Électr) coil.

bobo /bobo/ *nm* 🄸 sore, cut; **avoir ~** have a pain.

bocal (*pl* **-aux**) /bɔkal, -o/ *nm* jar.

bœuf (*pl* **~s**) /bœf, bø/ *nm* bullock; (US) steer; (viande) beef; **~s** oxen.

bogue /bɔg/ *nm* (Ordinat) bug.

bohème /bɔɛm/ *a & nmf* bohemian.

boire /bwaʀ/ [12] *vt/i* (*personne*, *plante*) drink; (*argile*) soak up; **~ un coup** 🄸 have a drink.

bois /bwa/ ⇒BOIRE [12]. ●*nm*

(matériau, forêt) wood; **de ~, en ~** wooden. ● *nmpl* (de cerf) antlers.

boiseries /bwazʀi/ *nfpl* panelling.

boisson /bwasɔ̃/ *nf* drink.

boit /bwa/ ⇒BOIRE [12].

boîte /bwat/ *nf* box; (de conserves) tin, can; (entreprise ⊞) firm; **en ~** tinned, canned; **~ à gants** glove compartment; **~ aux lettres** letter-box; **~ aux lettres électronique, blé** mailbox; **~ de nuit** night-club; **~ postale** post-office box; **~ de vitesses** gear box.

boiter /bwate/ [1] *vi* limp.

boiteux, -euse *a* lame; (*raisonnement*) shaky.

boîtier /bwatje/ *nm* case.

bol /bɔl/ *nm* bowl; **~ d'air** a breath of fresh air; **avoir du ~** ⊞ be lucky.

bolide /bɔlid/ *nm* racing car.

Bolivie /bɔlivi/ *nf* Bolivia.

bombardement /bɔ̃baʀdəmɑ̃/ *nm* bombing; shelling.

bombarder /bɔ̃baʀde/ [1] *vt* bomb; (par obus) shell; **~ qn de** (fig) bombard sb with. **bombardier** *nm* (Aviat) bomber.

bombe /bɔ̃b/ *nf* bomb; (atomiseur) spray, aerosol.

bombé, ~e /bɔ̃be/ *a* rounded; (*route*) cambered.

bon, bonne /bɔ̃, bɔn/ *a* good; (qui convient) right; **~ à/pour** (approprié) fit to/for; **bonne année** happy New Year; **~ anniversaire** happy birthday; **~ appétit/voyage** enjoy your meal/trip; **bonne chance/nuit** good luck/night; **~ sens** common sense; **bonne femme** (péj) woman; **de bonne heure** early; **à quoi ~?** what's the point? ● *adv* **sentir ~** smell nice; **tenir ~** stand firm; **il fait ~** the weather is mild. ● *interj* right, well. ● *nm* (billet) voucher, coupon; **~ de commande** order form; **pour de ~** for good.

bonne *nf* (domestique) maid.

bonbon /bɔ̃bɔ̃/ *nm* sweet; (US) candy.

bonbonne /bɔ̃bɔn/ *nf* demijohn; (de gaz) cylinder.

bond /bɔ̃/ *nm* leap; **faire un ~** (de surprise) jump.

bonde /bɔ̃d/ *nf* plug; (trou) plughole.

bondé, ~e /bɔ̃de/ *a* packed.

bondir /bɔ̃diʀ/ [2] *vi* leap; (de surprise) jump.

bonheur /bɔnœʀ/ *nm* happiness; (chance) (good) luck; **au petit ~** haphazardly; **par ~** luckily.

bonhomme (*pl* **bonshommes**) /bɔnɔm, bɔ̃zɔm/ *nm* fellow; **~ de neige** snowman. ● *a inv* good-hearted.

bonifier (se) /(sə)bɔnifje/ [45] *vpr* improve.

bonjour /bɔ̃ʒuʀ/ *nm & interj* hallo, hello, good morning *ou* afternoon.

bon marché /bɔ̃maʀʃe/ *a inv* cheap. ● *adv* cheap(ly).

bonne /bɔn/ ⇒BON.

bonne-maman (*pl* **bonnes-mamans**) /bɔnmamɑ̃/ *nf* ⊞ granny.

bonnement /bɔnmɑ̃/ *adv* **tout ~** quite simply.

bonnet /bɔnɛ/ *nm* hat; (de soutien-gorge) cup; **~ de bain** swimming cap. **bonneterie** *nf* hosiery.

bonsoir /bɔ̃swaʀ/ *nm* good evening; (en se couchant) good night.

bonté /bɔ̃te/ *nf* kindness.

bonus /bɔnys/ *nm* (Auto) no-claims bonus.

boots /buts/ *nmpl* ankle boots.

bord /bɔʀ/ *nm* edge; (rive) bank; **à ~ (de)** on board; **au ~ de la mer** at the seaside; **au ~ des larmes** on the verge of tears; **~ de la route** roadside.

bordeaux /bɔʀdo/ a inv maroon.
● nm inv Bordeaux.

bordel /bɔʀdɛl/ nm brothel;
(désordre 🔲) shambles.

border /bɔʀde/ [1] vt line, border;
(tissu) edge; (personne, lit) tuck
in.

bordereau (pl ~x) /bɔʀdəʀo/ nm
(document) slip.

bordure /bɔʀdyʀ/ nf border; en ~
de on the edge of.

borgne /bɔʀɲ/ a one-eyed.

borne /bɔʀn/ nf boundary
marker; (pour barrer le passage)
bollard; ~ (kilométrique) ≈
milestone; ~s limits.

borné, ~e /bɔʀne/ a (esprit)
narrow; (personne) narrow-
minded.

borner (se) /(sə)bɔʀne/ [1] vpr
confine oneself (à to).

bosniaque /bɔsnjak/ a Bosnian.
B~ nmf Bosnian.

Bosnie /bɔsni/ nf Bosnia.

bosse /bɔs/ nf bump; (de chameau)
hump; avoir la ~ de 🔲 have a gift
for; avoir roulé sa ~ have been
around. **bosselé**, ~e a dented;
(terrain) bumpy.

bosser /bɔse/ [1] vi 🔲 work
(hard).

bossu, ~e /bɔsy/ a
hunchbacked. ● nm, f hunchback.

botanique /bɔtanik/ nf botany.
● a botanical.

botte /bɔt/ nf boot; (de fleurs,
légumes) bunch; (de paille) bundle,
bale; ~s de caoutchouc
wellingtons.

botter /bɔte/ [1] vt 🔲 ça me botte
I like the idea.

bottin® /bɔtɛ̃/ nm phone book.

bouc /buk/ nm (billy-)goat; (barbe)
goatee; ~ émissaire scapegoat.

boucan /bukɑ̃/ nm 🔲 din.

bouche /buʃ/ nf mouth; (lèvres)
lips; ~ bée open-mouthed; ~
d'égout manhole; ~ d'incendie

(fire) hydrant; ~ de métro
entrance to the underground ou
subway (US). **bouche-à-bouche**
nm inv mouth-to-mouth
resuscitation. **bouche-à-oreille**
nm inv word of mouth.

bouché, ~e /buʃe/ a (profession,
avenir) oversubscribed; (stupide:
péj) stupid.

bouchée /buʃe/ nf mouthful.

boucher¹ /buʃe/ [1] vt block;
(bouteille) cork. □ se ~ vpr get
blocked; se ~ le nez hold one's
nose.

boucher², **-ère** /buʃe, -ɛʀ/ nm, f
butcher. **boucherie** nf butcher's
(shop); (carnage) butchery.

bouchon /buʃɔ̃/ nm stopper; (en
liège) cork; (de stylo, tube) cap; (de
pêcheur) float; (embouteillage) traffic
jam; ~ de cérumen plug of
earwax.

boucle /bukl/ nf (de ceinture)
buckle; (de cheveux) curl; (forme)
loop; ~ d'oreille earring. **bouclé**,
~e a (cheveux) curly.

boucler /bukle/ [1] vt fasten;
(enfermer 🔲) shut up; (encercler) seal
off; (budget) balance; (terminer)
finish off. ● vi curl.

bouclier /buklije/ nm shield.

bouddhiste /budist/ a & nmf
Buddhist.

bouder /bude/ [1] vi sulk. ● vt
stay away from.

boudin /budɛ̃/ nm black pudding.

boue /bu/ nf mud.

bouée /bwe/ nf buoy; ~ de sauvetage lifebuoy.

boueux, **-euse** /buø, -z/ a muddy.

bouffe /buf/ nf 🔲 food, grub.

bouffée /bufe/ nf puff, whiff;
(d'orgueil) fit; ~ de chaleur (Méd) hot
flush.

bouffi, ~e /bufi/ a bloated.

bouffon, ~ne /bufɔ̃, -ɔn/ a
farcical. ● nm buffoon.

B

bougeoir /buʒwaʀ/ *nm* candlestick.

bougeotte /buʒɔt/ *nf* **avoir la ~** 🔲 have the fidgets.

bouger /buʒe/ [40] *vt/i* move. □ **se ~** *vpr* 🔲 move.

bougie /buʒi/ *nf* candle; (Auto) spark(ing)-plug.

bouillant, ~e /bujɑ̃, -t/ *a* boiling; (très chaud) boiling hot.

bouillie /buji/ *nf* (pour bébé) baby cereal; (péj) mush; **en ~** crushed, mushy.

bouillir /bujiʀ/ [13] *vi* boil; (fig) seethe; **faire ~** boil.

bouilloire /bujwaʀ/ *nf* kettle.

bouillon /bujɔ̃/ *nm* (de cuisson) stock; (potage) broth.

bouillonner /bujɔne/ [1] *vi* bubble.

bouillotte /bujɔt/ *nf* hot-water bottle.

boulanger, -ère /bulɑ̃ʒe, -ɛʀ/ *nm, f* baker. **boulangerie** *nf* bakery. **boulangerie-pâtisserie** *nf* bakery (*selling cakes and pastries*).

boule /bul/ *nf* ball; **~s** (jeu) boules; **jouer aux ~s** play boules; **une ~ dans la gorge** a lump in one's throat; **~ de neige** snowball.

bouleau (*pl ~x*) /bulo/ *nm* (silver) birch.

boulet /bulɛ/ *nm* (de forçat) ball and chain; **~ (de canon)** cannonball; **~ de charbon** coal nut.

boulette /bulɛt/ *nf* (de pain, papier) pellet; (bévue) blunder; **~ de viande** meat ball.

boulevard /bulvaʀ/ *nm* boulevard.

bouleversant, ~e /bulvɛʀsɑ̃, -t/ *a* deeply moving. **bouleversement** *nm* upheaval. **bouleverser** [1] *vt* turn upside down; (*pays, plans*) disrupt; (émouvoir) upset.

boulimie /bulimi/ *nf* bulimia.

boulon /bulɔ̃/ *nm* bolt.

boulot, ~te /bulo, -ɔt/ *a* (rond 🔲) dumpy. ● *nm* (travail 🔲) work.

boum /bum/ *nm & interj* bang. ● *nf* (fête 🔲) party.

bouquet /bukɛ/ *nm* (de fleurs) bunch, bouquet; (d'arbres) clump; **c'est le ~!** 🔲 that's the last straw!

bouquin /bukɛ̃/ *nm* 🔲 book. **bouquiner** [1] *vt/i* 🔲 read. **bouquiniste** *nmf* second-hand bookseller.

bourbier /buʀbje/ *nm* mire; (fig) tangle.

bourde /buʀd/ *nf* blunder.

bourdon /buʀdɔ̃/ *nm* bumble-bee. **bourdonnement** *nm* buzzing.

bourg /buʀ/ *nm* (market) town (centre), village centre.

bourgeois, ~e /buʀʒwa, -z/ *a & nm,f* middle-class (person); (péj) bourgeois. **bourgeoisie** *nf* middle class(es).

bourgeon /buʀʒɔ̃/ *nm* bud.

bourgogne /buʀgɔɲ/ *nm* Burgundy.

bourlinguer /buʀlɛ̃ge/ [1] *vi* 🔲 travel about.

bourrage /buʀaʒ/ *nm* **~ de crâne** brainwashing.

bourratif, -ive /buʀatif, -v/ *a* stodgy.

bourreau (*pl ~x*) /buʀo/ *nm* executioner; **~ de travail** (fig) workaholic.

bourrelet /buʀlɛ/ *nm* weather-strip, draught excluder; (de chair) roll of fat.

bourrer /buʀe/ [1] *vt* cram (de with); (*pipe*) fill; **~ de** (*nourriture*) stuff with; **~ de coups** thrash; **~ le crâne à qn** brainwash sb.

bourrique /buʀik/ *nf* donkey; 🔲 pig-headed person.

bourru, ~e /buʀy/ *a* gruff.

bourse /buʀs/ *nf* purse;

(subvention) grant; **la B~** the Stock Exchange.

boursier, -ière /buʀsje, -jɛʀ/ a (valeurs) Stock Exchange. ● nm, f grant holder.

boursoufler /buʀsufle/ [1] vt (visage) cause to swell; (peinture) blister.

bousculade /buskylad/ nf crush; (précipitation) rush. **bousculer** [1] vt (pousser) jostle; (presser) rush; (renverser) knock over.

bousiller /buzije/ [1] vt ▣ wreck.

boussole /busɔl/ nf compass.

bout /bu/ nm end; (de langue, bâton) piece; (morceau) bit; **à ~** exhausted; **à ~ de souffle** out of breath; **à ~ portant** point-blank; **au ~ de** (après) after; **venir à ~ de** (finir) manage to finish; **d'un ~ à l'autre** throughout; **au ~ du compte** in the end; **~ filtre** filter-tip.

bouteille /butɛj/ nf bottle; **~ d'oxygène** oxygen cylinder.

boutique /butik/ nf shop; (de mode) boutique.

bouton /butɔ̃/ nm button; (sur la peau) spot, pimple; (pousse) bud; (de porte, radio) knob; **~ de manchette** cuff-link. **boutonner** [1] vt button (up). **boutonnière** nf buttonhole. **bouton-pression** (pl **boutons-pression**) nm press-stud; (US) snap.

bouture /butyʀ/ nf cutting.

bovin, ~e /bɔvɛ̃, -in/ a bovine. **bovins** nmpl cattle (pl).

box (pl **~ ou boxes**) /bɔks/ nm lock-up garage; (de dortoir) cubicle; (d'écurie) (loose) box; (Jur) dock.

boxe /bɔks/ nf boxing.

boyau (pl **~x**) /bwajo/ nm gut; (corde) catgut; (galerie) gallery; (de bicyclette) tyre; (US) tire.

boycotter /bɔjkɔte/ [1] vt boycott.

BP abrév f (**boîte postale**) PO Box.

bracelet /bʀaslɛ/ nm bracelet; (de montre) watchstrap.

braconnier /bʀakɔnje/ nm poacher.

brader /bʀade/ [1] vt sell off. **braderie** nf clearance sale.

braguette /bʀagɛt/ nf fly.

braille /bʀaj/ nm & a Braille.

brailler /bʀaje/ [1] vt/i bawl.

braise /bʀɛz/ nf embers (+ pl).

braiser /bʀeze/ [1] vt (Culin) braise.

brancard /bʀɑ̃kaʀ/ nm stretcher; (de charrette) shaft.

branche /bʀɑ̃ʃ/ nf branch.

branché, ~e /bʀɑ̃ʃe/ a ▣ trendy.

branchement /bʀɑ̃ʃmɑ̃/ nm connection. **brancher** [1] vt (prise) plug in; (à un réseau) connect.

brandir /bʀɑ̃diʀ/ [2] vt brandish.

branler /bʀɑ̃le/ [1] vi be shaky.

braquer /bʀake/ [1] vt (arme) aim; (regard) fix; (roue) turn; (banque: ▣) hold up; **~ qn contre** turn sb against. ● vi (Auto) turn (the wheel). □ **se ~** vpr dig one's heels in.

bras /bʀa/ nm arm; (de rivière) branch; (Tech) arm; **~ dessus ~ dessous** arm in arm; **~ droit** (fig) right hand man; **~ de mer** sound; **en ~ de chemise** in one's shirtsleeves. ● nmpl (fig) labour, hands.

brasier /bʀazje/ nm blaze.

brassard /bʀasaʀ/ nm armband.

brasse /bʀas/ nf breast-stroke; **~ papillon** butterfly (stroke).

brasser /bʀase/ [1] vt mix; (bière) brew; (affaires) handle a lot of. **brasserie** nf brewery; (café) brasserie.

brave /bʀav/ a (bon) good; (valeureux) brave. **braver** [1] vt defy.

bravo /bʀavo/ *interj* bravo. ● *nm* cheer.

bravoure /bʀavuʀ/ *nf* bravery.

break /bʀɛk/ *nm* estate car; (US) station-wagon.

brebis /bʀəbi/ *nf* ewe.

brèche /bʀɛʃ/ *nf* gap, breach; **être sur la ~** be on the go.

bredouille /bʀəduj/ *a* empty-handed.

bredouiller /bʀəduje/ [1] *vt/i* mumble.

bref, brève /bʀɛf, -v/ *a* short, brief. ● *adv* in short; **en ~** in short.

Brésil /bʀezil/ *nm* Brazil.

Bretagne /bʀətaɲ/ *nf* Brittany.

bretelle /bʀətɛl/ *nf* (de sac, maillot) strap; (d'autoroute) access road; **~s** (pour pantalon) braces; (US) suspenders.

breton, ~ne /bʀətɔ̃, -ɔn/ *a & nm* (Ling) Breton. **B~, ~ne** *nm, f* Breton.

breuvage /bʀœvaʒ/ *nm* beverage.

brève /bʀɛv/ ⇒BREF.

brevet /bʀəvɛ/ *nm* **~ (d'invention)** patent; (diplôme) diploma.

breveté, ~e /bʀəvəte/ *a* patented.

bribes /bʀib/ *nfpl* scraps.

bricolage /bʀikɔlaʒ/ *nm* do-it-yourself (jobs).

bricole /bʀikɔl/ *nf* trifle.

bricoler /bʀikɔle/ [1] *vi* do DIY; (US) fix things, tinker with.

bricoleur, -euse /bʀikɔlœʀ, -øz/ *nm, f* handyman, handywoman.

bride /bʀid/ *nf* bridle.

bridé, ~e /bʀide/ *a* **yeux ~s** slanting eyes.

brider /bʀide/ [1] *vt* (cheval) bridle; (fig) keep in check.

brièvement /bʀijɛvmɑ̃/ *adv* briefly.

brigade /bʀigad/ *nf* (de police) squad; (Mil) brigade; (fig) team.

brigadier *nm* (de gendarmerie) sergeant.

brigand /bʀigɑ̃/ *nm* robber.

brillant, ~e /bʀijɑ̃, -t/ *a* (couleur) bright; (luisant) shiny; (remarquable) brilliant. ● *nm* (éclat) shine; (diamant) diamond.

briller /bʀije/ [1] *vi* shine.

brimade /bʀimad/ *nf* vexation.

brimer /bʀime/ [1] *vt* bully, harass; **se sentir brimé** feel put down.

brin /bʀɛ̃/ *nm* (de muguet) sprig; (d'herbe) blade; (de paille) wisp; **un ~ de** (un peu) a bit of.

brindille /bʀɛ̃dij/ *nf* twig.

brioche /bʀijɔʃ/ *nf* brioche, sweet bun; (ventre 🗊) paunch.

brique /bʀik/ *nf* brick.

briquet /bʀikɛ/ *nm* (cigarette-) lighter.

brise /bʀiz/ *nf* breeze.

briser /bʀize/ [1] *vt* break. □ **se ~** *vpr* break.

britannique /bʀitanik/ *a* British. **B~** *nmf* Briton; **les B~s** the British.

brocante /bʀɔkɑ̃t/ *nf* bric-à-brac trade; (marché) flea market.

broche /bʀɔʃ/ *nf* brooch; (Culin) spit; **à la ~** spit-roasted.

broché, ~e /bʀɔʃe/ *a* paperback.

brochet /bʀɔʃɛ/ *nm* pike.

brochette /bʀɔʃɛt/ *nf* skewer.

brochure /bʀɔʃyʀ/ *nf* brochure, booklet.

broder /bʀɔde/ [1] *vt/i* embroider. **broderie** *nf* embroidery.

broncher /bʀɔ̃ʃe/ [1] *vi* **sans ~** without turning a hair.

bronchite /bʀɔ̃ʃit/ *nf* bronchitis.

bronze /bʀɔ̃z/ *nm* bronze.

bronzé, ~e /bʀɔ̃ze/ *a* (sun-)tanned.

bronzer /bʀɔ̃ze/ [1] *vi* (personne) get a (sun-)tan.

brosse /bʀɔs/ *nf* brush; **~ à dents** toothbrush; **~ à habits** clothes

brush; **en** ~ (*coiffure*) in a crew
cut.

brosser /bʀɔse/ [1] *vt* brush; (fig)
paint. □ **se** ~ *vpr* **se** ~ **les dents/
les cheveux** brush one's teeth/
hair.

brouette /bʀuɛt/ *nf*
wheelbarrow.

brouhaha /bʀuaa/ *nm* hubbub.

brouillard /bʀujaʀ/ *nm* fog.

brouille /bʀuj/ *nf* quarrel.

brouiller /bʀuje/ [1] *vt* (*vue*) blur;
(*œufs*) scramble; (*amis*) set at
odds; ~ **les pistes** cloud the issue.
□ **se** ~ *vpr* (*ciel*) cloud over;
(*amis*) fall out.

brouillon, ~**ne** /bʀujɔ̃, -ɔn/ *a*
untidy. ● *nm* (rough) draft.

brousse /bʀus/ *nf* **la** ~ the bush.

brouter /bʀute/ [1] *vt/i* graze.

broyer /bʀwaje/ [31] *vt* crush;
(*moudre*) grind.

bru /bʀy/ *nf* daughter-in-law.

bruine /bʀɥin/ *nf* drizzle.

bruissement /bʀɥismɑ̃/ *nm*
rustling.

bruit /bʀɥi/ *nm* noise; ~ **de
couloir** (fig) rumour.

bruitage /bʀɥitaʒ/ *nm* sound
effects.

brûlant, ~**e** /bʀylɑ̃, -t/ *a* burning
(hot); (*sujet*) red-hot; (*passion*)
fiery.

brûlé /bʀyle/ *nm* burning; **ça sent
le** ~ I can smell something
burning. ●⇒BRÛLER [1].

brûler /bʀyle/ [1] *vt/i* burn;
(*essence*) use (up); (*cierge*) light
(à to); ~ **un feu** (**rouge**) jump the
lights; ~ **d'envie de faire** be
longing to do. □ **se** ~ *vpr* burn
oneself.

brûlure /bʀylyʀ/ *nf* burn; ~**s
d'estomac** heartburn.

brume /bʀym/ *nf* mist. **brumeux,
-euse** *a* misty; (*esprit*) hazy.

brun, ~**e** /bʀœ̃, -yn/ *a* brown,
dark. ● *nm* brown. ● *nm, f* dark-

haired person. **brunir** [2] *vi* turn
brown; (*bronzer*) get a tan.

brushing /bʀœʃiŋ/ *nm* blow-dry.

brusque /bʀysk/ *a* (*personne*)
abrupt; (*geste*) violent; (*soudain*)
sudden.

brusquer /bʀyske/ [1] *vt* be
abrupt with; (*précipiter*) rush.

brut, ~**e** /bʀyt/ *a* (*diamant*)
rough; (*champagne*) dry; (*pétrole*)
crude; (Comm) gross.

brutal, ~**e** (*mpl* **-aux**) /bʀytal, -o/
a brutal. **brutalité** *nf* brutality.

brute /bʀyt/ *nf* brute.

Bruxelles /bʀysɛl/ *npr* Brussels.

bruyant, ~**e** /bʀɥijɑ̃, -t/ *a* noisy.

bruyère /bʀyjɛʀ/ *nf* heather.

bu /by/ ⇒BOIRE [12].

bûche /byʃ/ *nf* log; ~ **de Noël**
Christmas log; **ramasser une** ~ 🄳
fall.

bûcher /byʃe/ [1] *vt/i* 🄳 slog
away (at) 🄳. ● *nm* (*supplice*) stake.

bûcheron /byʃʀɔ̃/ *nm*
lumberjack.

budget /bydʒɛ/ *nm* budget.
budgétaire *a* budgetary.

buée /bɥe/ *nf* condensation.

buffet /byfɛ/ *nm* sideboard; (table
garnie) buffet.

buffle /byfl/ *nm* buffalo.

buisson /bɥisɔ̃/ *nm* bush.

buissonnière /bɥisɔnjɛʀ/ *af* **faire
l'école** ~ play truant.

bulbe /bylb/ *nm* bulb.

bulgare /bylgaʀ/ *a* & *nm*
Bulgarian. **B**~ *nmf* Bulgarian.

Bulgarie /bylgaʀi/ *nf* Bulgaria.

bulldozer /byldozɛʀ/ *nm*
bulldozer.

bulle /byl/ *nf* bubble.

bulletin /byltɛ̃/ *nm* bulletin,
report; (Scol) report; ~
d'information news bulletin; ~
météorologique weather report; ~
(**de vote**) ballot-paper; ~ **de
salaire** pay-slip.

buraliste /byʀalist/ *nmf* tobacconist.

bureau (*pl* ~x) /byʀo/ *nm* office; (*meuble*) desk; (*comité*) board; ~ d'études design office; ~ de poste post office; ~ de tabac tobacconist's (shop); ~ de vote polling station.

bureaucrate /byʀokʀat/ *nmf* bureaucrat. **bureaucratie** *nf* bureaucracy. **bureaucratique** *a* bureaucratic.

bureautique /byʀotik/ *nf* office automation.

burlesque /byʀlɛsk/ *a* (*histoire*) ludicrous; (*film*) farcical.

bus /bys/ *nm* bus.

buste /byst/ *nm* bust.

but /by(t)/ *nm* target; (*dessein*) aim, goal; (*football*) goal; **avoir pour** ~ **de** aim to; **de** ~ **en blanc** point-blank; **dans le** ~ **de** with the intention of; **aller droit au** ~ go straight to the point.

butane /bytan/ *nm* butane, Calor gas®.

buté,~e /byte/ *a* obstinate.

buter /byte/ [1] *vi* ~ **contre** knock against; (*problème*) come up against. ●*vt* antagonize. □ **se** ~ *vpr* (s'entêter) become obstinate.

buteur /bytœʀ/ *nm* (au football) striker.

butin /bytɛ̃/ *nm* booty, loot.

butte /byt/ *nf* mound; **en** ~ **à** exposed to.

buvard /byvaʀ/ *nm* blotting-paper.

buvette /byvɛt/ *nf* (refreshment) bar.

buveur, -euse /byvœʀ, -øz/ *nm, f* drinker.

c' /s/ ⇒CE.

ça /sa/
●*pronom démonstratif*
····▶ (sujet) it; that; ~ **flotte** it floats; ~ **suffit!** that's enough!; ~ **y est!** that's it!; ~ **sent le brûlé** there's a smell of burning; ~ **va?** how are things?
····▶ (objet) (proche) this; (plus éloigné) that; **c'est** ~ that's right.
····▶ (dans expressions) **où** ~? where?; **quand** ~? when?; **et avec** ~? anything else?

çà /sa/ *adv* ~ **et là** here and there.

cabane /kaban/ *nf* hut; (à outils) shed.

cabaret /kabaʀɛ/ *nm* cabaret.

cabillaud /kabijo/ *nm* cod.

cabine /kabin/ *nf* (à la piscine) cubicle; (de bateau) cabin; (de camion) cab; (d'ascenseur) cage; ~ **d'essayage** fitting room; ~ **de pilotage** cockpit; ~ **de plage** beach hut; ~ (téléphonique) phone booth, phone box.

cabinet /kabinɛ/ *nm* (de médecin) surgery; (US) office; (d'avocat) office; (clientèle) practice; (cabinet collectif) firm; (Pol) Cabinet; (pièce) room; ~s (toilettes) toilet; (US) bathroom; ~ **de toilette** bathroom.

câble /kɑbl/ *nm* cable; (corde) rope; (TV) cable TV. **câbler** *vt* [1] cable; (TV) install cable television in.

cabosser /kabɔse/ [1] vt dent.

cabotage /kabɔtaʒ/ nm coastal navigation.

cabrer (se) /(sə)kabʀe/ [1] vpr (cheval) rear; **se ~ contre** rebel against.

cabriole /kabʀijɔl/ nf **faire des ~s** caper about.

cacahuète /kakawɛt/ nf peanut.

cacao /kakao/ nm cocoa.

cachalot /kaʃalo/ nm sperm whale.

cache /kaʃ/ nm mask. ● nf hiding place; **~ d'armes** arms cache.

cache-cache /kaʃkaʃ/ nm inv hide-and-seek.

cache-nez /kaʃne/ nm inv scarf.

cacher /kaʃe/ [1] vt hide, conceal (à from). □ **se ~** vpr hide; (se trouver caché) be hidden.

cachet /kaʃɛ/ nm (de cire) seal; (à l'encre) stamp; (de la poste) postmark; (comprimé) tablet; (d'artiste) fee; (chic) style, cachet.

cachette /kaʃɛt/ nf hiding-place; **en ~** in secret.

cachot /kaʃo/ nm dungeon.

cachottier, -ière /kaʃɔtje, -jɛʀ/ a secretive.

cacophonie /kakɔfɔni/ nf cacophony.

cactus /kaktys/ nm cactus.

cadavérique /kadaveʀik/ a (teint) deathly pale.

cadavre /kadavʀ/ nm corpse; (de victime) body.

caddie /kadi/ nm (de supermarché)® trolley; (au golf) caddie.

cadeau (pl ~x) /kado/ nm present, gift; **faire un ~ à qn** give sb a present.

cadenas /kadna/ nm padlock.

cadence /kadɑ̃s/ nf rhythm, cadence; (de travail) rate; **en ~** in time; (marcher) in step.

cadet, ~te /kadɛ, -t/ a youngest; (entre deux) younger. ● nm, f youngest (child); younger (child).

cadran /kadʀɑ̃/ nm dial; **~ solaire** sundial.

cadre /kadʀ/ nm frame; (lieu) setting; (milieu) surroundings; (limites) scope; (contexte) framework; **dans le ~ de** (à l'occasion de) on the occasion of; (dans le contexte de) in the framework of. ● nm (personne) executive; **les ~s** the managerial staff.

cadrer /kadʀe/ [1] vi **~ avec** tally with. ● vt (photo) centre.

cafard /kafaʀ/ nm (insecte) cockroach; **avoir le ~** ⚅ be down in the dumps.

café /kafe/ nm coffee; (bar) café; **~ crème** espresso with milk; **~ en grains** coffee beans; **~ au lait** white coffee.

cafetière /kaftjɛʀ/ nf coffee-pot; **~ électrique** coffee machine.

cage /kaʒ/ nf cage; **~ d'ascenseur** lift shaft; **~ d'escalier** stairwell; **~ thoracique** rib cage.

cageot /kaʒo/ nm crate.

cagibi /kaʒibi/ nm storage room.

cagneux, -euse /kaɲø, -z/ a **avoir les genoux ~** be knock-kneed.

cagnotte /kaɲɔt/ nf kitty.

cagoule /kagul/ nf hood; (passe-montagne) balaclava.

cahier /kaje/ nm notebook; (Scol) exercise book; **~ de textes** homework notebook; **~ des charges** (Tech) specifications (+ pl).

cahot /kao/ nm bump, jolt.

cahoteux, -euse a bumpy.

caïd /kaid/ nm ⚅ big shot.

caille /kaj/ nf quail.

cailler /kaje/ [1] vi curdle; **ça caille** ⚅ it's freezing. □ **se ~** vpr (sang) clot; (lait) curdle. **caillot** nm (blood) clot.

caillou (pl ~**x**) /kaju/ nm stone; (galet) pebble.

caisse /kɛs/ nf crate, case; (tiroir, machine) till; (guichet) cash desk; (au supermarché) check-out; (bureau) office; (Mus) drum; ~ **enregistreuse** cash register; ~ **d'épargne** savings bank; ~ **de retraite** pension fund. **caissier, -ière** nm, f cashier.

cajoler /kaʒɔle/ [1] vt coax.

calcaire /kalkɛR/ a (sol) chalky; (eau) hard.

calciné, ~e /kalsine/ a charred.

calcul /kalkyl/ nm calculation; (Scol) arithmetic; (différentiel) calculus; ~ **biliaire** gallstone.

calculatrice /kalkylatRis/ nf calculator. **calculer** [1] vt calculate. **calculette** nf (pocket) calculator.

cale /kal/ nf wedge; (pour roue) chock; (de navire) hold; ~ **sèche** dry dock.

calé, ~e /kale/ a ▣ clever.

caleçon /kalsɔ̃/ nm boxer shorts (+ pl); underpants (+ pl); (de femme) leggings.

calembour /kalɑ̃buR/ nm pun.

calendrier /kalɑ̃dRije/ nm calendar; (fig) schedule, timetable.

calepin /kalpɛ̃/ nm notebook.

caler /kale/ [1] vt wedge. ● vi stall; (abandonner ▣) give up.

calfeutrer /kalføtRe/ [1] vt (fissure) stop up; (porte) draught proof.

calibre /kalibR/ nm calibre; (d'un œuf, fruit) grade.

calice /kalis/ nm (Relig) chalice; (Bot) calyx.

califourchon: à ~ /akalifuRʃɔ̃/ loc astride.

câlin, ~e /kɑlɛ̃, -in/ a (regard, ton) affectionate; (personne) cuddly.

calmant /kalmɑ̃/ nm sedative.

calme /kalm/ a calm. ● nm peace; calm; (maîtrise de soi) composure; **du ~**! calm down!

calmer /kalme/ [1] vt (personne) calm down; (situation) defuse; (douleur) ease; (soif) quench. □ **se ~** vpr (personne, situation) calm down; (agitation, tempête) die down; (douleur) ease.

calomnie /kalɔmni/ nf (orale) slander; (écrite) libel. **calomnier** [45] vt slander; libel. **calomnieux, -ieuse** a slanderous; libellous.

calorie /kalɔRi/ nf calorie.

calque /kalk/ nm tracing; (papier) ~ tracing paper; (fig) exact copy. **calquer** /kalke/ [1] vt trace; (fig) copy; ~ **qch sur** model sth on.

calvaire /kalvɛR/ nm (croix) Calvary; (fig) suffering.

calvitie /kalvisi/ nf baldness.

camarade /kamaRad/ nmf friend; (Pol) comrade; ~ **de jeu** playmate. **camaraderie** nf friendship.

cambouis /kɑ̃bwi/ nm dirty oil.

cambrer /kɑ̃bRe/ [1] vt arch. □ **se ~** vpr arch one's back.

cambriolage /kɑ̃bRijɔlaʒ/ nm burglary. **cambrioler** [1] vt burgle. **cambrioleur, -euse** nm, f burglar.

camelot /kamlo/ nm ▣ street vendor.

camelote /kamlɔt/ nf ▣ junk.

caméra /kameRa/ nf (cinéma, télévision) camera.

caméscope® /kameskɔp/ nm camcorder.

camion /kamjɔ̃/ nm lorry, truck. **camion-citerne** (pl **camions-citernes**) nm tanker. **camionnage** nm haulage. **camionnette** nf van. **camionneur** nm lorry ou truck driver; (entrepreneur) haulage contractor.

camisole /kamizɔl/ *nf* ~ (de force) straitjacket.

camoufler /kamufle/ [1] *vt* camouflage.

camp /kɑ̃/ *nm* camp; (Sport, Pol) side.

campagnard, ~e /kɑ̃paɲaʀ, -d/ *a* country. ● *nm, f* countryman, countrywoman.

campagne /kɑ̃paɲ/ *nf* country; countryside; (Mil, Pol) campaign.

campement /kɑ̃pmɑ̃/ *nm* camp, encampment.

camper /kɑ̃pe/ [1] *vi* camp. ● *vt* (esquisser) sketch. □ se ~ *vpr* plant oneself. **campeur, -euse** *nm, f* camper.

camping /kɑ̃piŋ/ *nm* camping; **faire du** ~ go camping; (**terrain de**) ~ campsite. **camping-car** (*pl* ~s) *nm* camper-van; (US) motorhome. **camping-gaz®** *nm inv* (réchaud) camping stove.

Canada /kanada/ *nm* Canada.

canadien, ~ne /kanadjɛ̃, -ɛn/ *a* Canadian. **C~**, ~ne *nm, f* Canadian. **canadienne** *nf* (veste) fur-lined jacket; (tente) ridge tent.

canaille /kanɑj/ *nf* rogue.

canal (*pl* **-aux**) /kanal, -o/ *nm* (artificiel) canal; (bras de mer) channel; (Tech, TV) channel; (moyen) channel; **par le** ~ **de** through. **canalisation** *nf* (tuyaux) mains (+ *pl*). **canaliser** [1] *vt* (eau) canalize; (fig) channel.

canapé /kanape/ *nm* sofa.

canard /kanaʀ/ *nm* duck; (journal 🔲) rag.

canari /kanaʀi/ *nm* canary.

cancans /kɑ̃kɑ̃/ *nmpl* 🔲 gossip.

cancer /kɑ̃sɛʀ/ *nm* cancer; **le C~** Cancer. **cancéreux, -euse** *a* cancerous. **cancérigène** *a* carcinogenic.

cancre /kɑ̃kʀ/ *nm* dunce.

candeur /kɑ̃dœʀ/ *nf* ingenuousness.

candidat, ~e /kɑ̃dida, -t/ *nm, f* (à un examen, Pol) candidate; (à un poste) applicant, candidate (**à** for).

candidature /kɑ̃didatyʀ/ *nf* application; (Pol) candidacy; **poser sa** ~ **à un poste** apply for a job.

candide /kɑ̃did/ *a* ingenuous.

cane /kan/ *nf* (female) duck. **caneton** *nm* duckling.

canette /kanɛt/ *nf* (bouteille) bottle; (boîte) can.

canevas /kanva/ *nm* canvas; (ouvrage) tapestry; (plan) framework, outline.

caniche /kaniʃ/ *nm* poodle.

canicule /kanikyl/ *nf* scorching heat; (vague de chaleur) heatwave.

canif /kanif/ *nm* penknife.

canine /kanin/ *nf* canine (tooth).

caniveau (*pl* ~**x**) /kanivo/ *nm* gutter.

cannabis /kanabis/ *nm* cannabis.

canne /kan/ *nf* (walking) stick; ~ **à pêche** fishing rod; ~ **à sucre** sugar cane.

cannelle /kanɛl/ *nf* cinnamon.

cannibale /kanibal/ *a & nmf* cannibal.

canoë /kanɔe/ *nm* canoe; (Sport) canoeing.

canon /kanɔ̃/ *nm* (big) gun; (ancien) cannon; (d'une arme) barrel; (principe, règle) canon.

canot /kano/ *nm* dinghy, (small) boat; ~ **de sauvetage** lifeboat; ~ **pneumatique** rubber dinghy. **canotier** *nm* boater.

cantatrice /kɑ̃tatʀis/ *nf* opera singer.

cantine /kɑ̃tin/ *nf* canteen.

cantique /kɑ̃tik/ *nm* hymn.

cantonner /kɑ̃tɔne/ [1] *vt* (Mil) billet. □ se ~ **dans** *vpr* confine oneself to.

canular /kanylaʀ/ *nm* hoax.

caoutchouc /kautʃu/ *nm*

rubber; (élastique) rubber band; ~ **mousse** foam rubber.

cap /kap/ *nm* cape, headland; (direction) course; (obstacle) hurdle; **franchir le ~ de la cinquantaine** pass the fifty mark; **mettre le ~ sur** steer a course for.

capable /kapabl/ *a* capable (**de** of); ~ **de faire** able to do, capable of doing.

capacité /kapasite/ *nf* ability; (contenance, potentiel) capacity.

cape /kap/ *nf* cape; **rire sous ~** laugh up one's sleeve.

capillaire /kapilɛʀ/ *a* (lotion, soins) hair; (vaisseau) ~ capillary.

capitaine /kapitɛn/ *nm* captain.

capital, ~e (*mpl* **-aux**) /kapital, -o/ *a* key, crucial, fundamental; (peine, lettre) capital. ● *nm* (*pl* **-aux**) (Comm) capital; (fig) stock; **capitaux** (Comm) capital; ~**-risque** venture capital; ~**-risqueur** venture capitalist. **capitale** *nf* (ville, lettre) capital.

capitalisme /kapitalism/ *nm* capitalism.

capitonné, ~e /kapitɔne/ *a* padded.

capituler /kapityle/ [1] *vi* capitulate.

caporal (*pl* **-aux**) /kapɔʀal, -o/ *nm* corporal.

capot /kapo/ *nm* (Auto) bonnet; (US) hood.

capote /kapɔt/ *nf* (Auto) hood; (US) top; (préservatif 🛈) condom.

capoter /kapɔte/ [1] *vi* overturn; (fig) collapse.

câpre /kɑpʀ/ *nf* (Culin) caper.

caprice /kapʀis/ *nm* whim; (colère) tantrum; **faire un ~** throw a tantrum. **capricieux, -ieuse** *a* capricious; (appareil) temperamental.

Capricorne /kapʀikɔʀn/ *nm* **le ~** Capricorn.

capsule /kapsyl/ *nf* capsule; (de bouteille) cap.

capter /kapte/ [1] *vt* (eau) collect; (émission) get; (signal) pick up; (fig) win, capture.

captif, -ive /kaptif, -v/ *a* & *nm,f* captive.

captiver /kaptive/ [1] *vt* captivate.

capturer /kaptyʀe/ [1] *vt* capture.

capuche /kapyʃ/ *nf* hood. **capuchon** *nm* hood; (de stylo) cap.

car /kaʀ/ *conj* because, for. ● *nm* coach; (US) bus.

carabine /kaʀabin/ *nf* rifle.

caractère /kaʀaktɛʀ/ *nm* (lettre) character; (nature) nature; ~**s d'imprimerie** block letters; **avoir bon/mauvais ~** be good-natured/bad-tempered; **avoir du ~** have character.

caractériel, ~le /kaʀaktɛʀjɛl/ *a* (trait) character; (enfant) disturbed.

caractériser /kaʀaktɛʀize/ [1] *vt* characterize. ▢ **se ~ par** *vpr* be characterized by.

caractéristique *a* & *nf* characteristic.

carafe /kaʀaf/ *nf* carafe.

Caraïbes /kaʀaib/ *nfpl* **les ~** the Caribbean.

carambolage /kaʀɑ̃bɔlaʒ/ *nm* pile-up.

caramel /kaʀamɛl/ *nm* caramel; (bonbon) toffee.

carapace /kaʀapas/ *nf* shell.

caravane /kaʀavan/ *nf* (Auto) caravan; (US) trailer; (convoi) caravan.

carbone /kaʀbɔn/ *nm* carbon; (papier) ~ carbon (paper). **carboniser** [1] *vt* burn (to ashes).

carburant /kaʀbyʀɑ̃/ *nm* (motor) fuel.

carburateur /kaʀbyʀatœʀ/ *nm* carburettor; (US) carburetor.

carcan /kaʀkɑ̃/ *nm* constraints (+ *pl*).

C

carcasse /kaʀkas/ *nf* (squelette) carcass; (armature) frame; (de voiture) shell.

cardiaque /kaʀdjak/ *a* heart. ●*nmf* heart patient.

cardinal, ~e (*mpl* **-aux**) /kaʀdinal, -o/ *a & nm* cardinal.

Carême /kaʀɛm/ *nm* le ~ Lent.

carence /kaʀɑ̃s/ *nf* shortcomings (+ *pl*); inadequacy; (Méd) deficiency; (absence) lack.

caresse /kaʀɛs/ *nf* caress; (à un animal) stroke. **caresser** [1] *vt* caress, stroke; (*espoir*) cherish.

cargaison /kaʀgɛzɔ̃/ *nf* cargo.

cargo /kaʀgo/ *nm* cargo boat.

caricature /kaʀikatyʀ/ *nf* caricature.

carie /kaʀi/ *nf* (trou) cavity; la ~ (dentaire) tooth decay.

carillon /kaʀijɔ̃/ *nm* chimes (+ *pl*); (horloge) chiming clock.

caritatif, -ive /kaʀitatif, -v/ *a* **association caritative** charity.

carnage /kaʀnaʒ/ *nm* carnage.

carnassier, -ière /kaʀnasje, -jɛʀ/ *a* carnivorous.

carnaval (*pl* **~s**) /kaʀnaval/ *nm* carnival.

carnet /kaʀnɛ/ *nm* notebook; (de tickets, timbres) book; ~ **d'adresses** address book; ~ **de chèques** chequebook.

carotte /kaʀɔt/ *nf* carrot.

carpe /kaʀp/ *nf* carp.

carré, ~e /kaʀe/ *a* (forme, mesure) square; (fig) straightforward; **un mètre ~** one square metre. ●*nm* square; (de terrain) patch.

carreau (*pl* **~x**) /kaʀo/ *nm* (window) pane; (par terre, au mur) tile; (dessin) check; (aux cartes) diamonds (+ *pl*); **à ~x** (*tissu*) check(ed); (*papier*) squared.

carrefour /kaʀfuʀ/ *nm* crossroads (+ *sg*).

carrelage /kaʀlaʒ/ *nm* tiling; (sol) tiles.

carrément /kaʀemɑ̃/ *adv* (complètement) completely; (*stupide, dangereux*) downright; (*dire*) straight out; **elle a ~ démissionné** she went straight ahead and resigned.

carrière /kaʀjɛʀ/ *nf* career; (terrain) quarry.

carrossable /kaʀɔsabl/ *a* suitable for vehicles.

carrosse /kaʀɔs/ *nm* (horse-drawn) coach.

carrosserie /kaʀɔsʀi/ *nf* (Auto) body(work).

carrure /kaʀyʀ/ *nf* shoulders; (fig) necessary qualities, calibre.

cartable /kaʀtabl/ *nm* satchel.

carte /kaʀt/ *nf* card; (Géog) map; (Naut) chart; (au restaurant) menu; **~s** (jeu) cards; **à la ~** (*manger*) à la carte; (*horaire*) personalized; **donner ~ blanche à** give a free hand to; ~ **de crédit** credit card; ~ **de fidélité** loyalty card; ~ **grise** (car) registration document; ~ **d'identité** identity card; ~ **magnétique** swipe card; ~ **de paiement** debit card; ~ **postale** postcard; ~ **à puce** smart card; ~ **de séjour** resident's permit; ~ **des vins** wine list; ~ **de visite** (business) card.

cartilage /kaʀtilaʒ/ *nm* cartilage.

carton /kaʀtɔ̃/ *nm* cardboard; (boîte) (cardboard) box; ~ **à dessin** portfolio; **faire un ~** 🔳 do well.

cartonné, ~e /kaʀtɔne/ *a* **livre ~** hardback.

cartouche /kaʀtuʃ/ *nf* cartridge; (de cigarettes) carton. **cartouchière** *nf* cartridge-belt.

cas /kɑ/ *nm* case; **au ~ où** in case; ~ **urgent** emergency; **en aucun ~** on no account; **en ~ de** in the event of, in case of; **en tout ~** in any case; (du moins) at least; **faire ~ de** set great store by; ~ **de conscience** moral dilemma.

casanier, -ière /kazanje, -jɛʀ/ a home-loving.

cascade /kaskad/ nf waterfall; (au cinéma) stunt; (fig) spate, series (+ sg).

cascadeur, -euse /kaskadœʀ, -øz/ nm, f stuntman, stuntwoman.

case /kaz/ nf hut; (de damier) square; (compartiment) pigeon-hole; (sur un formulaire) box.

caser /kaze/ [1] vt ▯ (mettre) put; (loger) put up; (dans un travail) find a job for; (marier: péj) marry off.

caserne /kazɛʀn/ nf barracks; ~ de sapeurs-pompiers fire station.

casier /kazje/ nm pigeon-hole, compartment; (à bouteilles, chaussures) rack; ~ **judiciaire** criminal record.

casque /kask/ nm (de motard) crash helmet; (de cycliste) cycle helmet; (chez le coiffeur) (hair-) drier; ~ (à écouteurs) headphones; ~ **anti-bruit** ear defenders; ~ **de protection** safety helmet.

casquette /kaskɛt/ nf cap.

cassant, ~e /kasɑ̃, -t/ a brittle; (brusque) curt.

cassation /kasasjɔ̃/ nf **cour de ~ appeal court**.

casse /kas/ nf (objets) breakages; (lieu) breaker's yard; **mettre à la ~** scrap.

casse-cou /kasku/ nmf inv daredevil.

casse-croûte /kaskʀut/ nm inv snack.

casse-noix /kasnwa/ nm inv nutcrackers (+ pl).

casse-pieds /kaspje/ nmf inv ▯ pain (in the neck) ▯.

casser /kase/ [1] vt break; (annuler) annul; ~ **les pieds à qn** ▯ annoy sb. ● vi break. □ **se ~ vpr** break; (partir ▯) be off ▯.

casserole /kasʀɔl/ nf saucepan.

casse-tête /kastɛt/ nm inv (problème) headache; (jeu) brain teaser.

cassette /kasɛt/ nf casket; (de magnétophone) cassette, tape; (de vidéo) video tape; ~ **audionumérique** digital audio tape.

cassis /kasi(s)/ nm inv blackcurrant.

cassure /kasyʀ/ nf break.

castor /kastɔʀ/ nm beaver.

castration /kastʀasjɔ̃/ nf castration.

catalogue /katalɔg/ nm catalogue.

catalyseur /katalizœʀ/ nm catalyst; (Auto) catalytic convertor.

catastrophe /katastʀɔf/ nf disaster, catastrophe.

catastrophique a catastrophic.

catch /katʃ/ nm (all-in) wrestling.

catéchisme /kateʃism/ nm catechism.

catégorie /kategɔʀi/ nf category.

catégorique a categorical.

cathédrale /katedʀal/ nf cathedral.

catholique /katɔlik/ a Catholic; **pas très ~** a bit fishy.

catimini: en ~ /katimini/ loc on the sly.

cauchemar /koʃmaʀ/ nm nightmare.

cause /koz/ nf cause; (raison) reason; (Jur) case; **à ~ de** because of; **en ~** (en jeu, concerné) involved; **pour ~ de** on account of; **mettre en ~** implicate; **remettre en ~** call into question.

causer /koze/ [1] vt cause; (discuter de ▯) ~ **travail** talk shop; ~ **de** talk about. ● vi chat.

causerie nf talk.

causette /kozɛt/ nf (Internet) chat; **faire la ~** chat.

caution /kosjɔ̃/ nf surety; (Jur) bail; (appui) backing; (garantie) deposit; **libéré sous** ∼ released on bail. **cautionner** [1] *vt* guarantee; (soutenir) back.

cavalcade /kavalkad/ *nf* stampede, rush.

cavalier, -ière /kavalje, -jɛʀ/ *a* offhand; **allée cavalière** bridle path. ●*nm, f* rider; (pour danser) partner. ●*nm* (aux échecs) knight.

cave /kav/ *nf* cellar. ●*a* sunken.

caveau (*pl* ∼**x**) /kavo/ *nm* vault.

caverne /kavɛʀn/ *nf* cave.

CCP *abrév m* (**compte chèque postal**) post office account.

CD *abrév m* (**compact disc**) CD.

CD-ROM *abrév m inv* (**compact disc read only memory**) CD-ROM.

∙∙∙∙∙∙∙∙∙∙∙∙∙∙∙∙∙∙∙∙∙∙∙∙∙∙∙∙∙∙∙∙

ce, c', cet, cette (*pl* **ces**) /sə, s, sɛt, sɛt/

c' before e. cet before vowel or mute h.

●**ce, cet, cette** (*pl* **ces**) *adjectif démonstratif*
∙∙∙▶ this; (plus éloigné) that; **ces** these; (plus éloigné) those; **cette nuit** (passée) last night; (à venir) tonight.

●**ce, c'** *pronom démonstratif*
∙∙∙▶ **c'est** it's *ou* it is; **c'est un policier** he's a policeman; ∼ **sont eux qui l'ont fait** THEY did it; **qui est-**∼**?** who is it?
∙∙∙▶ **ce que/qui** what; ∼ **que je ne comprends pas** what I don't understand; **elle est venue,** ∼ **qui est étonnant** she came, which is surprising; **que tu as de la chance!** how lucky you are!; **tout** ∼ **que je sais** all I know; **tout** ∼ **qu'elle trouve/peut** everything she finds/can.
∙∙∙∙∙∙∙∙∙∙∙∙∙∙∙∙∙∙∙∙∙∙∙∙∙∙∙∙∙∙∙∙

CE *abrév f* (**Communauté européenne**) EC.

ceci /səsi/ *pron* this.

cécité /sesite/ *nf* blindness.

céder /sede/ [14] *vt* give up; ∼ **le passage** give way; (vendre) sell. ●*vi* (se rompre) give way; (se soumettre) give in.

cédérom /sederɔm/ *nm* CD-ROM.

cédille /sedij/ *nf* cedilla.

cèdre /sɛdʀ/ *nm* cedar.

CEI *abrév f* (**Communauté des États indépendants**) CIS.

ceinture /sɛ̃tyʀ/ *nf* belt; (taille) waist; ∼ **de sauvetage** lifebelt; ∼ **de sécurité** seatbelt.

cela /səla/ *pron* it, that; (pour désigner) that; ∼ **va de soi** it is obvious; ∼ **dit/fait** having said/done that.

célèbre /selɛbʀ/ *a* famous.

célébrer [14] *vt* celebrate. **célébrité** *nf* fame; (personne) celebrity.

céleri /sɛlʀi/ *nm* (en branches) celery. **céleri-rave** (*pl* **céleris-raves**) *nm* celeriac.

célibat /seliba/ *nm* celibacy; (état) single status.

célibataire /selibatɛʀ/ *a* single. ●*nm* bachelor. ●*nf* single woman.

celle, celles /sɛl/ ⇒CELUI.

cellulaire /selylɛʀ/ *a* cell; **emprisonnement** ∼ solitary confinement; **fourgon** *ou* **voiture** ∼ prison van; **téléphone** ∼ cellular phone.

cellule /selyl/ *nf* cell; ∼ **souche** stem cell.

celui, celle (*pl* **ceux, celles**) /səlɥi, sɛl, sø/ *pron* the one; ∼ **de mon ami** my friend's; ∼**-ci** this (one); ∼**-là** that (one); **ceux-ci** these (ones); **ceux-là** those (ones).

cendre /sɑ̃dʀ/ *nf* ash.

cendrier /sɑ̃dʀije/ *nm* ashtray.

censé, ∼**e** /sɑ̃se/ *a* **être** ∼ **faire** be supposed to do.

censeur /sɑ̃sœʀ/ nm censor;
(Scol) administrator in charge of
discipline.

censure /sɑ̃syʀ/ nf censorship.
censurer [1] vt censor; (critiquer)
censure.

cent /sɑ̃/ a (a) hundred; **20 pour
~** 20 per cent. ● n (quantité)
hundred; **~ un** a hundred and
one; (centième d'euro) cent.

centaine /sɑ̃tɛn/ nf hundred; **une
~ (de)** (about) a hundred.

centenaire /sɑ̃tnɛʀ/ nm
(anniversaire) centenary.

centième /sɑ̃tjɛm/ a & nmf
hundredth.

centimètre /sɑ̃timɛtʀ/ nm
centimetre; (ruban) tape-measure.

central, ~e (mpl -aux) /sɑ̃tʀal,
-o/ a central. ● nm (pl -aux) **~
(téléphonique)** (telephone)
exchange. **centrale** nf power-
station.

centre /sɑ̃tʀ/ nm centre; **~
d'appel** call centre; **~ commercial**
shopping centre; (US) mall; **~ de
formation** training centre; **~
hospitalier** hospital. **centrer** [1] vt
centre. **centre-ville** (pl **centres-
villes**) nm town centre.

centuple /sɑ̃typl/ nm **le ~ de** a
hundred times; **au ~** a
hundredfold.

cep /sɛp/ nm vine stock.
cépage /sepaʒ/ nm grape variety.
cèpe /sɛp/ nm cep.

cependant /səpɑ̃dɑ̃/ adv
however.

céramique /seʀamik/ nf
ceramic; (art) ceramics (+ sg).

cercle /sɛʀkl/ nm circle; (cerceau)
hoop; (association) society, club; **~
vicieux** vicious circle.

cercueil /sɛʀkœj/ nm coffin.
céréale /seʀeal/ nf cereal; **~s**
(Culin) (breakfast) cereal.

cérébral, ~e (mpl -aux)
/seʀebʀal, -o/ a cerebral.

cérémonie /seʀemɔni/ nf
ceremony; **sans ~s** (repas)
informal; (recevoir) informally.

cerf /sɛʀ/ nm stag.
cerfeuil /sɛʀfœj/ nm chervil.
cerf-volant (pl **cerfs-volants**)
/sɛʀvɔlɑ̃/ nm kite.

cerise /s(ə)ʀiz/ nf cherry.
cerisier nm cherry tree.

cerner /sɛʀne/ [1] vt surround;
(question) define; **avoir les yeux
cernés** have rings under one's
eyes.

certain, ~e /sɛʀtɛ̃, -ɛn/ a certain;
(sûr) certain, sure (de of; que
that); **d'un ~ âge** no longer
young; **un ~ temps** some time.
certainement adv (probablement)
most probably; (avec certitude)
certainly. **certains, -es** pron
some people.

certes /sɛʀt/ adv (sans doute)
admittedly; (bien sûr) of course.

certificat /sɛʀtifika/ nm
certificate.

certifier /sɛʀtifje/ [45] vt certify;
~ qch à qn assure sb of sth; **copie
certifiée conforme** certified true
copy.

certitude /sɛʀtityd/ nf certainty.

cerveau (pl **~x**) /sɛʀvo/ nm
brain.

cervelle /sɛʀvɛl/ nf (Anat) brain;
(Culin) brains.

ces /se/ ⇒CE.

césarienne /sezaʀjɛn/ nf
Caesarean (section).

cesse /sɛs/ nf **n'avoir de ~ que**
have no rest until; **sans ~**
constantly, incessantly.

cesser /sese/ [1] vt stop; **~ de
faire** stop doing. ● vi cease; **faire
~** put an end to.

cessez-le-feu /seselfø/ nm inv
ceasefire.

cession /sesjɔ̃/ nf transfer.

c'est-à-dire /setadiʀ/ *conj* that is (to say).

cet, **cette** /sɛt/ ⇒CE.

ceux /sø/ ⇒CELUI.

chacun, **~e** /ʃakœ̃, -yn/ *pron* each (one), every one; (tout le monde) everyone; **~ d'entre nous** each (one) of us.

chagrin /ʃagʀɛ̃/ *nm* sorrow; **avoir du ~** be sad.

chahut /ʃay/ *nm* row, din.

chahuter /ʃayte/ [1] *vi* make a row. ●*vt* (*enseignant*) be rowdy with; (*orateur*) heckle.

chaîne /ʃɛn/ *nf* chain; (de télévision) channel; **~ (d'assemblage)** assembly line; **~s** (Auto) snow chains; **~ de montagnes** mountain range; **~ de montage/fabrication** assembly/ production line; **~ hi-fi** hi-fi system; **~ laser** CD player; **en ~** (*accidents*) multiple; (*réaction*) chain. **chaînette** *nf* (small) chain. **chaînon** *nm* link.

chair /ʃɛʀ/ *nf* flesh; **bien en ~** plump; **en ~ et en os** in the flesh; **~ à saucisses** sausage meat; **la ~ de poule** goose pimples. ●*a inv* (couleur) ~ flesh-coloured.

chaire /ʃɛʀ/ *nf* (d'église) pulpit; (Univ) chair.

chaise /ʃɛz/ *nf* chair; **~ longue** deckchair.

châle /ʃɑl/ *nm* shawl.

chaleur /ʃalœʀ/ *nf* heat; (moins intense) warmth; (d'un accueil, d'une couleur) warmth. **chaleureux**, **-euse** *a* warm.

chalumeau (*pl* **~x**) /ʃalymo/ *nm* blowtorch.

chalutier /ʃalytje/ *nm* trawler.

chamailler (**se**) /(sə)ʃamɑje/ [1] *vpr* squabble.

chambre /ʃɑ̃bʀ/ *nf* (bed)room; (Pol, Jur) chamber; **faire ~ à part** sleep in separate rooms; **~ à air** inner tube; **~ d'amis** spare *ou* guest room; **~ de commerce (et d'industrie)** Chamber of Commerce; **~ à coucher** bedroom; **~ à un lit/deux lits** single/twin room; **~ pour deux personnes** double room; **~ forte** strong-room; **~ d'hôte** bed and breakfast, B and B. **chambrer** [1] *vt* (vin) bring to room temperature.

chameau (*pl* **~x**) /ʃamo/ *nm* camel.

chamois /ʃamwa/ *nm* chamois.

champ /ʃɑ̃/ *nm* field; **~ de bataille** battlefield; **~ de courses** racecourse; **~ de tir** firing range.

champêtre /ʃɑ̃pɛtʀ/ *a* rural.

champignon /ʃɑ̃piɲɔ̃/ *nm* mushroom; (moisissure) fungus; **~ de Paris** button mushroom.

champion, **~ne** /ʃɑ̃pjɔ̃, -on/ *nm,f* champion. **championnat** *nm* championship.

chance /ʃɑ̃s/ *nf* (good) luck; (possibilité) chance; **avoir de la ~** be lucky; **quelle ~!** what luck!

chanceler /ʃɑ̃sle/ [38] *vi* stagger; (fig) falter, waver.

chancelier /ʃɑ̃səlje/ *nm* chancellor.

chanceux, **-euse** /ʃɑ̃sø, -z/ *a* lucky.

chandail /ʃɑ̃daj/ *nm* sweater.

chandelier /ʃɑ̃dəlje/ *nm* candlestick.

chandelle /ʃɑ̃dɛl/ *nf* candle; **dîner aux ~s** candlelight dinner.

change /ʃɑ̃ʒ/ *nm* (foreign) exchange; (taux) exchange rate.

changement /ʃɑ̃ʒmɑ̃/ *nm* change; **~ de vitesse** (dispositif) gears.

changer /ʃɑ̃ʒe/ [40] *vt* change; **~ qch de place** move sth; (échanger) change (pour, contre for); **~ de nom/voiture** change one's name/ car; **~ de place/train** change places/trains; **~ de direction**

change direction; ~ **d'avis** *ou* **d'idée** change one's mind; ~ **de vitesse** change gear. □ **se** ~ *vpr* change, get changed.

chanson /ʃɑ̃sɔ̃/ *nf* song.

chant /ʃɑ̃/ *nm* singing; (chanson) song; (Relig) hymn.

chantage /ʃɑ̃taʒ/ *nm* blackmail.

chanter /ʃɑ̃te/ [1] *vt* sing; **si cela vous chante** 🄳 if you feel like it. ● *vi* sing; **faire** ~ (délit) blackmail.

chanteur, -euse *nm, f* singer.

chantier /ʃɑ̃tje/ *nm* building site; ~ **naval** shipyard; **mettre en** ~ get under way, start.

chaos /kao/ *nm* chaos.

chaparder /ʃaparde/ [1] *vt* 🄳 pinch 🄳, filch.

chapeau (*pl* ~**x**) /ʃapo/ *nm* hat; ~**!** well done!

chapelet /ʃaplɛ/ *nm* rosary; (fig) string.

chapelle /ʃapɛl/ *nf* chapel.

chapelure /ʃaplyʀ/ *nf* (Culin) breadcrumbs.

chaperonner /ʃapʀɔne/ [1] *vt* chaperone.

chapiteau (*pl* ~**x**) /ʃapito/ *nm* marquee; (de cirque) big top; (de colonne) capital.

chapitre /ʃapitʀ/ *nm* chapter; (fig) subject.

chaque /ʃak/ *a* every, each.

char /ʃaʀ/ *nm* (Mil) tank; (de carnaval) float; (charrette) cart; (dans l'antiquité) chariot.

charabia /ʃaʀabja/ *nm* 🄳 gibberish.

charade /ʃaʀad/ *nf* riddle.

charbon /ʃaʀbɔ̃/ *nm* coal; (Méd) anthrax; ~ **de bois** charcoal.

charcuterie /ʃaʀkytʀi/ *nf* pork butcher's shop; (aliments) (cooked) pork meats. **charcutier, -ière** *nm, f* pork butcher.

chardon /ʃaʀdɔ̃/ *nm* thistle.

charge /ʃaʀʒ/ *nf* load, burden;

(Mil, Électr, Jur) charge; (responsabilité) responsibility; **avoir qn à** ~ be responsible for; ~**s** expenses; (de locataire) service charges; **être à la** ~ **de** (*personne*) be the responsibility of; (*frais*) be payable by; ~**s sociales** social security contributions; **prendre en** ~ take charge of.

chargé, ~e /ʃaʀʒe/ *a* (*véhicule*) loaded; (*journée, emploi du temps*) busy; (*langue*) coated. ● *nm, f* ~ **de mission** head of mission; ~ **d'affaires** chargé d'affaires, ~ **de cours** lecturer.

chargement /ʃaʀʒəmɑ̃/ *nm* loading; (objets) load.

charger /ʃaʀʒe/ [40] *vt* load; (Ordinat, Photo) load; (attaquer) charge; (*batterie*) charge; ~ **qn de** (*fardeau*) weigh sb down with; (*tâche*) entrust sb with; ~ **qn de faire** make sb responsible for doing. ● *vi* (attaquer) charge. □ **se** ~ **de** *vpr* take charge *ou* care of.

chariot /ʃaʀjo/ *nm* (à roulettes) trolley; (US) cart; (charrette) cart.

charitable /ʃaʀitabl/ *a* charitable.

charité /ʃaʀite/ *nf* charity; **faire la** ~ **à** give (money) to.

charlatan /ʃaʀlatɑ̃/ *nm* charlatan.

charmant, ~e /ʃaʀmɑ̃, -t/ *a* charming.

charme /ʃaʀm/ *nm* charm; (qui envoûte) spell. **charmer** [1] *vt* charm. **charmeur, -euse** *nm, f* charmer.

charnel, ~le /ʃaʀnɛl/ *a* carnal.

charnière /ʃaʀnjɛʀ/ *nf* hinge; **à la** ~ **de** at the meeting point between.

charnu, ~e /ʃaʀny/ *a* plump, fleshy.

charpente /ʃaʀpɑ̃t/ *nf* framework; (carrure) build.

charpentier /ʃaʀpɑ̃tje/ nm carpenter.

charrette /ʃaʀɛt/ nf cart.

charrue /ʃaʀy/ nf plough.

chasse /ʃas/ nf hunting; (au fusil) shooting; (poursuite) chase; (recherche) hunt(ing); ~ (d'eau) (toilet) flush; ~ **sous-marine** harpoon fishing.

chasse-neige /ʃasnɛʒ/ nm inv snowplough.

chasser /ʃase/ [1] vt hunt; (au fusil) shoot; (faire partir) chase away; (odeur, employé) get rid of. ● vi go hunting; (au fusil) go shooting.

chasseur, -euse /ʃasœʀ, -øz/ nm, f hunter. ● nm bellboy; (US) bellhop; (avion) fighter plane.

châssis /ʃasi/ nm frame; (Auto) chassis.

chasteté /ʃastəte/ nf chastity.

chat¹ /ʃa/ nm cat; (mâle) tomcat.

chat² /tʃæt/ nm (Internet) chat.

châtaigne /ʃatɛɲ/ nf chestnut. **châtaignier** nm chestnut tree. **châtain** a inv chestnut (brown).

château (pl ~x) /ʃato/ nm castle; (manoir) manor; ~ **d'eau** water tower; ~ **fort** fortified castle.

châtiment /ʃatimɑ̃/ nm punishment.

chaton /ʃatɔ̃/ nm (chat) kitten.

chatouillement /ʃatujmɑ̃/ nm tickling. **chatouiller** [1] vt tickle. **chatouilleux, -euse** a ticklish; (susceptible) touchy.

châtrer /ʃatʀe/ [1] vt castrate; (chat) neuter.

chatte /ʃat/ nf female cat.

chaud, ~e /ʃo, -d/ a warm; (brûlant) hot; (vif: fig) warm. ● nm heat; **au** ~ in the warm(th); **avoir** ~ be warm; be hot; **il fait** ~ it is warm; it is hot; **pour te tenir** ~ to keep you warm. **chaudement** adv warmly; (disputé) hotly.

chaudière /ʃodjɛʀ/ nf boiler.

chaudron /ʃodʀɔ̃/ nm cauldron.

chauffage /ʃofaʒ/ nm heating; ~ **central** central heating.

chauffard /ʃofaʀ/ nm (péj) reckless driver.

chauffer /ʃofe/ [1] vt/i heat (up); (moteur, appareil) overheat. □ **se** ~ vpr warm oneself (up).

chauffeur /ʃofœʀ/ nm driver; (aux gages de qn) chauffeur.

chaume /ʃom/ nm (de toit) thatch.

chaussée /ʃose/ nf road(way).

chausse-pied (pl ~s) /ʃospje/ nm shoehorn.

chausser /ʃose/ [1] vt (chaussures) put on; (enfant) put shoes on (to). ● vi ~ **bien** (aller) fit well; ~ **du 35** take a size 35 shoe. □ **se** ~ vpr put one's shoes on.

chaussette /ʃosɛt/ nf sock.

chausson /ʃosɔ̃/ nm slipper; (de bébé) bootee; ~ **de danse** ballet shoe; ~ **aux pommes** apple turnover.

chaussure /ʃosyʀ/ nf shoe; ~ **de ski** ski boot; ~ **de marche** hiking boot.

chauve /ʃov/ a bald.

chauve-souris (pl **chauves-souris**) /ʃovsuʀi/ nf bat.

chauvin, ~e /ʃovɛ̃, -in/ a chauvinistic. ● nm, f chauvinist.

chavirer /ʃaviʀe/ [1] vt (bateau) capsize; (objets) tip over.

chef /ʃɛf/ nm leader, head; (supérieur) boss, superior; (Culin) chef; (de tribu) chief; **architecte en** ~ chief ou head architect; ~ **d'accusation** (Jur) charge; ~ **d'équipe** foreman; (Sport) captain; ~ **d'État** head of State; ~ **de famille** head of the family; ~ **de file** (Pol) leader; ~ **de gare** stationmaster; ~ **d'orchestre** conductor; ~ **de service**

department head; ~ **de train**
guard; (US) conductor.

chef-d'œuvre (pl **chefs-d'œuvre**) /ʃɛdœvʀ/ nm
masterpiece.

chef-lieu (pl **chefs-lieux**) /ʃɛfljø/
nm county town, administrative
centre.

chemin /ʃəmɛ̃/ nm road; (étroit)
lane; (de terre) track; (pour piétons)
path; (passage) way; (direction, trajet)
way; **avoir du ~ à faire** have a
long way to go; ~ **de fer** railway;
par ~ de fer by rail; ~ **de halage**
towpath; ~ **vicinal** country lane.

cheminée /ʃəmine/ nf chimney;
(intérieure) fireplace; (encadrement)
mantelpiece; (de bateau) funnel.

cheminot /ʃəmino/ nm
railwayman; (US) railroad man.

chemise /ʃəmiz/ nf shirt; (dossier)
folder; (de livre) jacket; ~ **de nuit**
nightdress. **chemisette** nf short-
sleeved shirt. **chemisier** nm
blouse.

chêne /ʃɛn/ nm oak.

chenil /ʃəni(l)/ nm (pension)
kennels (+ sg).

chenille /ʃənij/ nf caterpillar;
véhicule à ~s tracked vehicle.

cheptel /ʃɛptɛl/ nm livestock.

chèque /ʃɛk/ nm cheque; ~ **sans
provision** bad cheque; ~ **de
voyage** traveller's cheque.
chéquier nm chequebook.

cher, chère /ʃɛʀ/ a (coûteux) dear,
expensive; (aimé) dear; (dans la
correspondance) dear. ●adv (coûter,
payer) a lot (of money); (en importance) dearly. ●nm, f **mon ~, ma
chère** my dear.

chercher /ʃɛʀʃe/ [1] vt look for;
(aide, paix, gloire) seek; **aller ~**
go and get ou fetch, go for; ~ **à
faire** attempt to do; ~ **la petite bête**
be finicky.

chercheur, -euse /ʃɛʀʃœʀ, -øz/
nm, f research worker.

chèrement /ʃɛʀmɑ̃/ adv dearly.

chéri, ~e /ʃeʀi/ a beloved.
●nm, f darling.

chérir /ʃeʀiʀ/ [2] vt cherish.

chétif, -ive /ʃetif, -v/ a puny.

cheval (pl **-aux**) /ʃəval, -o/ nm
horse; **à ~** on horseback; **à ~ sur**
astride, straddling; **faire du ~**
ride, go horse-riding.

chevalerie /ʃəvalʀi/ nf chivalry.

chevalet /ʃəvalɛ/ nm easel; (de
menuisier) trestle.

chevalier /ʃəvalje/ nm knight.

chevalière /ʃəvaljɛʀ/ nf signet
ring.

cheval-vapeur (pl **chevaux-
vapeur**) /ʃəvalvapœʀ/ nm
horsepower.

chevaucher /ʃəvoʃe/ [1] vt sit
astride. □ **se ~** vpr overlap.

chevelu, ~e /ʃəvly/ a (péj) long-
haired; (Bot) hairy.

chevelure /ʃəvlyʀ/ nf hair.

chevet /ʃəvɛ/ nm **au ~ de** at the
bedside of; **livre de ~** bedside
book.

cheveu (pl **~x**) /ʃəvø/ nm (poil)
hair; **~x** (chevelure) hair; **avoir les
~x longs** have long hair.

cheville /ʃəvij/ nf ankle; (fiche)
peg, pin; (pour mur) (wall) plug.

chèvre /ʃɛvʀ/ nf goat.

chevreuil /ʃəvʀœj/ nm roe
(deer); (Culin) venison.

chevron /ʃəvʀɔ̃/ nm (poutre)
rafter; **à ~s** herringbone.

chez /ʃe/ prép (au domicile de) at
the house of; (parmi) among; (dans
le caractère ou l'œuvre de) in; **aller ~
qn** go to sb's house; ~ **le boucher**
at ou to the butcher's; ~ **soi** at
home; **rentrer ~ soi** go home.
chez-soi nm inv home.

chic /ʃik/ a inv smart; (gentil)
kind. ●nm style; **avoir le ~ pour**
have a knack for; ~ **(alors)!** great!

chicane /ʃikan/ nf double bend;

chercher ~ à qn pick a quarrel with sb.

chiche /ʃiʃ/ *a* mean (**de** with); **~ que je le fais!** 🄸 I bet you I can do it.

chichis /ʃiʃi/ *nmpl* 🄸 fuss.

chicorée /ʃikɔʀe/ *nf* (frisée) endive; (à café) chicory.

chien /ʃjɛ̃/ *nm* dog; **~ d'aveugle** guide dog; **~ de garde** watch-dog. **chienne** *nf* dog, bitch.

chiffon /ʃifɔ̃/ *nm* rag; (pour nettoyer) duster; **~ humide** damp cloth. **chiffonner** [1] *vt* crumple; (préoccuper 🄸) bother.

chiffre /ʃifʀ/ *nm* figure; (numéro) number; (code) code; **~s arabes/ romains** Arabic/Roman numerals; **~s (statistiques)** statistics; **~ d'affaires** turnover. **chiffrer** /ʃifʀe/ [1] *vt* put a figure on, assess; (texte) encode. □ **se ~ à** *vpr* come to.

chignon /ʃiɲɔ̃/ *nm* bun, chignon.

Chili /ʃili/ *nm* Chile.

chimère /ʃimɛʀ/ *nf* fantasy.

chimie /ʃimi/ *nf* chemistry. **chimique** *a* chemical. **chimiste** *nmf* chemist.

chimpanzé /ʃɛ̃pɑ̃ze/ *nm* chimpanzee.

Chine /ʃin/ *nf* China.

chinois, ~e /ʃinwa, -z/ *a* Chinese. ●*nm* (Ling) Chinese. **C~, ~e** *nm, f* Chinese.

chiot /ʃjo/ *nm* pup(py).

chipoter /ʃipɔte/ [1] *vi* (manger) pick at one's food; (discuter) quibble.

chips /ʃips/ *nf inv* crisp; (US) chip.

chirurgie /ʃiʀyʀʒi/ *nf* surgery; **~ esthétique** plastic surgery. **chirurgien** *nm* surgeon.

chlore /klɔʀ/ *nm* chlorine.

choc /ʃɔk/ *nm* (heurt) impact, shock; (émotion) shock; (collision)

crash; (affrontement) clash; (Méd) shock; **sous le ~** in shock.

chocolat /ʃɔkɔla/ *nm* chocolate; (à boire) drinking chocolate; **~ au lait** milk chocolate; **~ chaud** hot chocolate; **~ noir** plain *ou* dark chocolate.

chœur /kœʀ/ *nm* (antique) chorus; (chanteurs, nef) choir; **en ~** in chorus.

choisir /ʃwaziʀ/ [2] *vt* choose, select.

choix /ʃwa/ *nm* choice, selection; **fromage ou dessert au ~** a choice of cheese or dessert; **de ~** choice; **de premier ~** top quality.

chômage /ʃomaʒ/ *nm* unemployment; **au ~, en ~** unemployed; **mettre en ~ technique** lay off.

chômeur, -euse /ʃomœʀ, -øz/ *nm, f* unemployed person; **les ~s** the unemployed.

choquer /ʃɔke/ [1] *vt* shock; (commotionner) shake.

choral, ~e (*mpl* **~s**) /kɔʀal/ *a* choral. **chorale** *nf* choir, choral society.

chorégraphie /kɔʀegʀafi/ *nf* choreography.

choriste /kɔʀist/ *nmf* (à l'église) chorister; (à l'opéra) member of the chorus *ou* choir.

chose /ʃoz/ *nf* thing; (très) **peu de ~** nothing much; **pas grand ~** not much.

chou (*pl* **~x**) /ʃu/ *nm* cabbage; **~** (à la crème) cream puff; **~ de Bruxelles** Brussels sprout; **mon petit ~** 🄸 my dear.

chouchou, ~te /ʃuʃu, -t/ *nm, f* (de professeur) pet; (du public) darling.

choucroute /ʃukʀut/ *nf* sauerkraut.

chouette /ʃwɛt/ *nf* owl. ●*a* 🄸 super.

chou-fleur (*pl* **choux-fleurs**) /ʃuflœʀ/ *nm* cauliflower.

choyer /ʃwaje/ [31] *vt* pamper.

chrétien, ~ne /kʀetjɛ̃, -jɛn/ *a & nm,f* Christian.

Christ /kʀist/ *nm* le ~ Christ.

chrome /kʀom/ *nm* chromium, chrome.

chromosome /kʀomozom/ *nm* chromosome.

chronique /kʀɔnik/ *a* chronic. ● *nf* (rubrique) column; (nouvelles) news; (annales) chronicle.

chronologique /kʀɔnɔlɔʒik/ *a* chronological.

chronomètre /kʀɔnɔmɛtʀ/ *nm* stopwatch. **chronométrer** [14] *vt* time.

chrysanthème /kʀizɑ̃tɛm/ *nm* chrysanthemum.

chuchoter /ʃyʃɔte/ [1] *vt/i* whisper.

chut /ʃyt/ *interj* shh, hush.

chute /ʃyt/ *nf* fall; (déchet) offcut; ~ (d'eau) waterfall; ~ de pluie rainfall; ~ des cheveux hair loss; ~ des ventes drop in sales; ~ de 5% 5% drop. **chuter** [1] *vi* fall.

Chypre /ʃipʀ/ *nf* Cyprus.

ci /si/ *adv* here; ~-gît here lies; **cet homme-~** this man; **ces maisons-~** these houses.

ci-après /siapʀɛ/ *adv* below.

cible /sibl/ *nf* target.

ciboulette /sibulɛt/ *nf* (Culin) chives (+ *pl*).

cicatrice /sikatʀis/ *nf* scar.

cicatriser /sikatʀize/ [1] *vt* heal. □ **se** ~ *vpr* heal.

ci-dessous /sidəsu/ *adv* below.

ci-dessus /sidəsy/ *adv* above.

cidre /sidʀ/ *nm* cider.

ciel (*pl* **cieux, ciels**) /sjɛl, sjø/ *nm* sky; (Relig) heaven; **cieux** (Relig) heaven.

cierge /sjɛʀʒ/ *nm* (church) candle.

cigale /sigal/ *nf* cicada.

cigare /sigaʀ/ *nm* cigar.

cigarette /sigaʀɛt/ *nf* cigarette.

cigogne /sigɔɲ/ *nf* stork.

ci-joint /sijwɛ̃/ *adv* enclosed.

cil /sil/ *nm* eyelash.

cime /sim/ *nf* peak, tip.

ciment /simɑ̃/ *nm* cement.

cimetière /simtjɛʀ/ *nm* cemetery, graveyard; ~ **de voitures** breaker's yard.

cinéaste /sineast/ *nmf* film-maker.

cinéma /sinema/ *nm* cinema; (US) movie theater. **cinémathèque** *nf* film archive; (salle) film theatre. **cinématographique** *a* cinema.

cinéphile /sinefil/ *nmf* film lover.

cinglant, ~e /sɛ̃glɑ̃, -t/ *a* (vent) biting; (remarque) scathing.

cinglé, ~e /sɛ̃gle/ *a* 🄳 crazy.

cinq /sɛ̃k/ *a & nm* five.

cinquante /sɛ̃kɑ̃t/ *a & nm* fifty.

cinquième /sɛ̃kjɛm/ *a & nmf* fifth.

cintre /sɛ̃tʀ/ *nm* coat-hanger; (Archit) curve.

cirage /siʀaʒ/ *nm* polish.

circoncision /siʀkɔ̃sizjɔ̃/ *nf* circumcision.

circonflexe /siʀkɔ̃flɛks/ *a* circumflex.

circonscription /siʀkɔ̃skʀipsjɔ̃/ *nf* district; ~ **électorale** constituency; (US) district; (de conseiller, maire) ward.

circonscrire /siʀkɔ̃skʀiʀ/ [30] *vt* (incendie, épidémie) contain; (sujet) define.

circonspect, ~e /siʀkɔ̃spɛkt/ *a* circumspect.

circonstance /siʀkɔ̃stɑ̃s/ *nf* circumstance; (situation) situation; (occasion) occasion; ~**s atténuantes** mitigating circumstances.

circuit /siʀkɥi/ nm circuit; (trajet) tour, trip.

circulaire /siʀkylɛʀ/ a & nf circular.

circulation /siʀkylasjɔ̃/ nf circulation; (de véhicules) traffic.

circuler /siʀkyle/ [1] vi (se répandre, être distribué) circulate; (aller d'un lieu à un autre) get around; (en voiture) travel; (piéton) walk; (être en service) (bus, train) run; **faire ~** (badauds) move on; (rumeur) spread.

cire /siʀ/ nf wax.

ciré /siʀe/ nm oilskin.

cirer /siʀe/ [1] vt polish.

cirque /siʀk/ nm circus; (arène) amphitheatre; (désordre: fig) chaos; **faire le ~** ▣ make a racket ▣.

ciseau (pl ~**x**) /sizo/ nm chisel; ~**x** scissors.

ciseler /sizle/ [6] vt chisel.

citadelle /sitadɛl/ nf citadel.

citadin, ~**e** /sitadɛ̃, -in/ nm, f city-dweller. ●a city.

citation /sitasjɔ̃/ nf quotation; (Jur) summons.

cité /site/ nf city; (logements) housing estate; ~ **universitaire** (university) halls of residence.

citer /site/ [1] vt quote, cite; (Jur) summon.

citerne /sitɛʀn/ nf tank.

citoyen, ~**ne** /sitwajɛ̃, -ɛn/ nm, f citizen.

citron /sitʀɔ̃/ nm lemon; ~ **vert** lime. **citronnade** nf lemon squash, (still) lemonade.

citrouille /sitʀuj/ nf pumpkin.

civet /sivɛ/ nm stew; ~ **de lièvre** jugged hare.

civière /sivjɛʀ/ nf stretcher.

civil, ~**e** /sivil/ a civil; (non militaire) civilian; (poli) civil. ●nm civilian; **dans le ~** in civilian life; **en ~** in plain clothes.

civilisation /sivilizasjɔ̃/ nf civilization.

civiliser /sivilize/ [1] vt civilize. □ **se ~** vpr become civilized.

civique /sivik/ a civic.

clair, ~**e** /klɛʀ/ a clear; (éclairé) light, bright; (couleur) light; **le plus ~ de** most of. ●adv clearly; **il faisait ~** it was already light. ●nm ~ **de lune** moonlight; **tirer une histoire au ~** get to the bottom of things. **clairement** adv clearly.

clairière /klɛʀjɛʀ/ nf clearing.

clairsemé, ~**e** /klɛʀsəme/ a sparse.

clamer /klame/ [1] vt proclaim.

clameur /klamœʀ/ nf clamour.

clan /klɑ̃/ nm clan.

clandestin, ~**e** /klɑ̃dɛstɛ̃, -in/ a secret; (journal) underground; (immigration, travail) illegal; **passager ~** stowaway.

clapier /klapje/ nm (rabbit) hutch.

clapoter /klapɔte/ [1] vi lap.

claquage /klakaʒ/ nm strained muscle; **se faire un ~** pull a muscle.

claque /klak/ nf slap.

claquer /klake/ [1] vi bang; (porte) slam, bang; (fouet) crack; (se casser ▣) conk out; (mourir ▣) snuff it ▣; ~ **des doigts** snap one's fingers; ~ **des mains** clap one's hands; **il claque des dents** his teeth are chattering. ●vt (porte) slam, bang; (dépenser ▣) blow; (fatiguer ▣) tire out.

claquettes /klakɛt/ nfpl tap dancing.

clarifier /klaʀifje/ [45] vt clarify.

clarinette /klaʀinɛt/ nf clarinet.

clarté /klaʀte/ nf light, brightness; (netteté) clarity.

classe /klas/ nf class; (salle: Scol) classroom; (cours) class, lesson; **aller en ~** go to school; **faire la ~**

teach; ~ **ouvrière/moyenne**
working/middle class.

classement /klasmã/ *nm*
classification; (d'élèves) grading;
(de documents) filing; (rang) place,
grade; (de coureur) placing.

classer /klase/ [1] *vt* classify; (par
mérite) grade; (*papiers*) file; (Jur)
(*affaire*) close. □ se ~ *vpr* rank.

classeur /klasœR/ *nm* (meuble)
filing cabinet; (chemise) file; (à
anneaux) ring binder.

classification /klasifikasjõ/ *nf*
classification.

classique /klasik/ *a* classical; (de
qualité) classic; (habituel) classic,
standard. ● *nm* classic; (auteur)
classical author.

clavecin /klavsẽ/ *nm*
harpsichord.

clavicule /klavikyl/ *nf*
collarbone.

clavier /klavje/ *nm* keyboard; ~
numérique keypad.

clé, clef /kle/ *nf* key; (outil)
spanner; (Mus) clef; ~ **anglaise**
(monkey-)wrench; ~ **de contact**
ignition key; ~ **à molette**
adjustable spanner; ~ **de voûte**
keystone. ● *a inv* key.

clémence /klemãs/ *nf* (de climat)
mildness; (indulgence) leniency.

clergé /klɛRʒe/ *nm* clergy.

clérical, ~e (*mpl* **-aux**)
/kleRikal, -o/ *a* clerical.

clic /klik/ *nm* (Ordinat) click.

cliché /kliʃe/ *nm* cliché; (Photo)
negative.

client, ~e /klijã, -t/ *nm, f*
customer; (d'un avocat) client; (d'un
médecin) patient; (d'hôtel) guest; (de
taxi) passenger.

clientèle /klijãtɛl/ *nf* customers,
clientele; (d'un avocat) clients,
practice; (d'un médecin) patients,
practice; (soutien) custom.

cligner /kliɲe/ [1] *vi* ~ **des yeux**
blink; ~ **de l'œil** wink.

clignotant /kliɲɔtã/ *nm* (Auto)
indicator, turn.

clignoter /kliɲɔte/ [1] *vi* blink;
(*lumière*) flicker; (comme signal)
flash.

climat /klima/ *nm* climate.

climatisation /klimatizasjõ/ *nf*
air-conditioning.

clin d'œil /klɛ̃dœj/ *nm* wink; **en
un ~** in a flash.

clinique /klinik/ *a* clinical. ● *nf*
(private) clinic.

clinquant, ~e /klɛ̃kã, -t/ *a*
showy.

clip /klip/ *nm* video.

cliquer /klike/ [1] *vi* (Ordinat) click
(**sur** on).

cliqueter /klikte/ [38] *vi*
(couverts) clink; (clés, monnaie)
jingle; (ferraille) rattle. **cliquetis**
nm clink(ing), jingle, rattle.

clivage /klivaʒ/ *nm* divide.

clochard, ~e /klɔʃaR, -d/ *nm, f*
tramp.

cloche /klɔʃ/ *nf* bell; (imbécile 🄓)
idiot; ~ **à fromage** cheese-cover.

cloche-pied: à ~ /aklɔʃpje/ *loc*
sauter à ~ hop on one leg.

clocher /klɔʃe/ *nm* bell-tower;
(pointu) steeple; **de ~** parochial.

cloison /klwazõ/ *nf* partition; (fig)
barrier.

cloître /klwatR/ *nm* cloister.

cloîtrer (se) [1] *vpr* shut oneself
away.

clonage /klonaʒ/ *nm* cloning.

cloner /klone/ [1] *vt* clone.

cloque /klɔk/ *nf* blister.

clos, ~e /klo, -z/ *a* closed.

clôture /klotyR/ *nf* fence;
(fermeture) closure; (de magasin,
bureau) closing; (de débat, liste) close;
(en Bourse) close of trading.

clôturer [1] *vt* enclose, fence in;
(festival, séance) close.

clou /klu/ *nm* nail; (furoncle) boil;
(de spectacle) star attraction; **les ~s**

(passage) pedestrian crossing; (US) crosswalk.

clouer /klue/ [1] vt nail down; (fig) pin down; **être cloué au lit** be confined to one's bed; **~ le bec à qn** shut sb up.

clouté, ~e /klute/ a studded; **passage ~** pedestrian crossing; (US) crosswalk.

coaliser (se) /(sə)kɔalize/ [1] vpr join forces.

coalition /kɔalisjɔ̃/ nf coalition.

cobaye /kɔbaj/ nm guinea-pig.

cocaïne /kɔkain/ nf cocaine.

cocasse /kɔkas/ a comical.

coccinelle /kɔksinɛl/ nf ladybird; (US) ladybug.

cocher /kɔʃe/ [1] vt tick (off), check. ● nm coachman.

cochon, ~ne /kɔʃɔ̃, -ɔn/ nm, f (personne 🔲) pig. ● a 🔲 filthy. ● nm pig. **cochonnerie** nf (saleté 🔲) filth; (marchandise 🔲) rubbish, junk.

cocon /kɔkɔ̃/ nm cocoon.

cocorico /kɔkɔriko/ nm cock-a-doodle-doo.

cocotier /kɔkɔtje/ nm coconut palm.

cocotte /kɔkɔt/ nf (marmite) casserole; **~ minute®** pressure-cooker; **ma ~** 🔲 my dear.

cocu, ~e /kɔky/ nm, f 🔲 deceived husband, deceived wife.

code /kɔd/ nm code; **~s** dipped headlights; **se mettre en ~s** dip one's headlights; **~ (à) barres** bar code; **~ confidentiel (d'identification)** PIN number; **~ postal** post code; (US) zip code; **~ de la route** Highway Code. **coder** [1] vt code, encode.

coéquipier, -ière /kɔekipje, -jɛr/ nm, f team mate.

cœur /kœr/ nm heart; (aux cartes) hearts (+ pl); **~ d'artichaut** artichoke heart; **~ de palmier** palm heart; **à ~ ouvert**

(opération) open-heart; (parler) freely; **avoir bon ~** be kind-hearted; **de bon ~** willingly; (rire) heartily; **par ~** by heart; **avoir mal au ~** feel sick ou nauseous; **je veux en avoir le ~ net** I want to be clear in my own mind (about it).

coffre /kɔfr/ nm chest; (pour argent) safe; (Auto) boot; (US) trunk.

coffre-fort (pl **coffres-forts**) nm safe.

coffret /kɔfrɛ/ nm casket, box; (de livres, cassettes) boxed set.

cogner /kɔɲe/ [1] vt/i knock. □ se **~** vpr knock oneself; **se ~ la tête** bump one's head.

cohabitater /kɔabite/ [1] vi live together.

cohérent, ~e /kɔerɑ̃, -t/ a coherent; (homogène) consistent.

cohue /kɔy/ nf crowd.

coi, ~te /kwa, -t/ a silent.

coiffe /kwaf/ nf headgear.

coiffer /kwafe/ [1] vt do the hair of; (chapeau) put on; (surmonter) cap; **~ qn d'un chapeau** put a hat on sb; **coiffé de** wearing; **être bien/ mal coiffé** have tidy/untidy hair. □ se **~** vpr do one's hair.

coiffeur, -euse /kwafœr, -øz/ nm, f hairdresser. **coiffeuse** nf dressing-table.

coiffure /kwafyr/ nf hairstyle; (métier) hairdressing; (chapeau) hat.

coin /kwɛ̃/ nm corner; (endroit) spot; (cale) wedge; **au ~ du feu** by the fireside; **dans le ~** locally; **du ~** local.

coincer /kwɛ̃se/ [10] vt jam; (caler) wedge; (attraper 🔲) catch. □ se **~** vpr get jammed.

coïncidence /kɔɛ̃sidɑ̃s/ nf coincidence.

coing /kwɛ̃/ nm quince.

coït /kɔit/ nm intercourse.

col /kɔl/ nm collar; (de bouteille) neck; (de montagne) pass; **~ blanc** white-collar worker; **~ roulé**

polo-neck; (US) turtle-neck; ~ de l'utérus cervix; se casser le ~ du fémur break one's hip.

colère /kɔlɛʀ/ *nf* anger; (accès) fit of anger; en ~ angry; se mettre en ~ lose one's temper; faire une ~ throw a tantrum.

coléreux, -euse /kɔleʀø, -z/ *a* quick-tempered.

colin /kɔlɛ̃/ *nm* (merlu) hake; (lieu noir) coley.

colique /kɔlik/ *nf* diarrhoea; (Méd) colic.

colis /kɔli/ *nm* parcel.

collaborateur, -trice /kɔlabɔʀatœʀ, -tʀis/ *nm, f* collaborator; (journaliste) contributor; (collègue) colleague.

collaboration /kɔlabɔʀasjɔ̃/ *nf* collaboration (à on); (à ouvrage, projet) contribution (à to).

collaborer /kɔlabɔʀe/ [1] *vi* collaborate (à on); ~ à (journal) contribute to.

collant, ~e /kɔlɑ̃, -t/ *a* (moulant) skin-tight; (poisseux) sticky. ● *nm* (bas) tights; (US) panty hose.

colle /kɔl/ *nf* glue; (en pâte) paste; (problème 🄸) poser; (Scol 🄸) detention.

collecter /kɔlɛkte/ [1] *vt* collect.

collectif, -ive /kɔlɛktif, -v/ *a* collective; (billet, voyage) group.

collection /kɔlɛksjɔ̃/ *nf* collection; (ouvrages) series (+ *sg*); (du même auteur) set. **collectionner** [1] *vt* collect. **collectionneur, -euse** *nm, f* collector.

collectivité /kɔlɛktivite/ *nf* community; ~ locale local authority.

collège /kɔlɛʒ/ *nm* secondary school (up to age 15); (US) junior high school; (assemblée) college. **collégien, ~ne** *nm, f* schoolboy, schoolgirl.

collègue /kɔlɛg/ *nmf* colleague.

coller /kɔle/ [1] *vt* stick; (avec colle liquide) glue; (affiche) stick up; (mettre 🄸) stick; (par une question 🄸) stump; (Scol 🄸) se faire ~ get a detention; je me suis fait ~ en maths I failed *ou* flunked maths. ● *vi* stick (à to); (être collant) be sticky; ~ à (convenir à) fit, correspond to.

collet /kɔlɛ/ *nm* (piège) snare; ~ monté prim and proper; mettre la main au ~ de qn collar sb.

collier /kɔlje/ *nm* necklace; (de chien) collar.

colline /kɔlin/ *nf* hill.

collision /kɔlizjɔ̃/ *nf* (choc) collision; (lutte) clash; entrer en ~ (avec) collide (with).

collyre /kɔliʀ/ *nm* eye drops (+ *pl*).

colmater /kɔlmate/ [1] *vt* plug, seal.

colombe /kɔlɔ̃b/ *nf* dove.

Colombie /kɔlɔ̃bi/ *nf* Colombia.

colon /kɔlɔ̃/ *nm* settler.

colonel /kɔlɔnɛl/ *nm* colonel.

colonie /kɔlɔni/ *nf* colony; ~ de vacances children's holiday camp.

colonne /kɔlɔn/ *nf* column; ~ vertébrale spine; en ~ par deux in double file.

colorant /kɔlɔʀɑ̃/ *nm* colouring.

colorier /kɔlɔʀje/ [45] *vt* colour (in).

colosse /kɔlɔs/ *nm* giant.

colza /kɔlza/ *nm* rape(-seed).

coma /kɔma/ *nm* coma; dans le ~ in a coma.

combat /kɔ̃ba/ *nm* fight; (Sport) match; ~s fighting. **combatif, -ive** *a* eager to fight; (esprit) fighting.

combattre /kɔ̃batʀ/ [11] *vt/i* fight.

combien /kɔ̃bjɛ̃/ *adv* ~ (de) (quantité) how much; (nombre) how many; (temps) how long; ~ il a changé! (comme) how he has changed!; ~ y a-t-il d'ici à ...? how far is it to …?; **on est le ~ aujourd'hui?** what's the date today?

combinaison /kɔ̃binɛzɔ̃/ *nf* combination; (de femme) slip; (bleu de travail) boiler suit; (US) overalls; **~ d'aviateur** flying-suit; **~ de plongée** wetsuit.

combine /kɔ̃bin/ *nf* trick; (fraude) fiddle; (intrigue) scheme.

combiné /kɔ̃bine/ *nm* (de téléphone) receiver, handset.

combiner /kɔ̃bine/ [1] *vt* (réunir) combine; (calculer) devise; **~ de faire** plan to do.

comble /kɔ̃bl/ *a* packed. ●*nm* height; **~s** (mansarde) attic, loft; **c'est le ~!** that's the (absolute) limit!

combler /kɔ̃ble/ [1] *vt* fill; (perte, déficit) make good; (désir) fulfil; **~ qn de cadeaux** lavish gifts on sb.

combustible /kɔ̃bystibl/ *nm* fuel.

comédie /kɔmedi/ *nf* comedy; (histoire 🔢) fuss; **~ musicale** musical; **jouer la ~** put on an act. **comédien, ~ne** *nm, f* actor, actress.

comestible /kɔmɛstibl/ *a* edible.

comète /kɔmɛt/ *nf* comet.

comique /kɔmik/ *a* comical, funny; (genre) comic. ●*nm* (acteur) comic; (comédie) comedy; (côté drôle) comical aspect.

commandant /kɔmɑ̃dɑ̃/ *nm* commander; (dans l'armée de terre) major; **~ (de bord)** captain; **~ en chef** Commander-in-Chief.

commande /kɔmɑ̃d/ *nf* (Comm) order; (Tech) control; **~s** (d'avion) controls.

commandement /kɔmɑ̃dmɑ̃/ *nm* command; (Relig) commandment.

commander /kɔmɑ̃de/ [1] *vt* command; (acheter) order; (étude,

œuvre d'art) commission; **~ à** (maîtriser) control; **~ à qn de** command sb to. ●*vi* be in command.

comme /kɔm/ *adv* **~ c'est bon!** it's so good!; **~ il est mignon!** isn't he sweet! ●*conj* (dans une comparaison) as; (dans une équivalence, illustration) like; (en tant que) as; (puisque) as, since; (au moment où) as; **vif ~ l'éclair** as quick as a flash; **travailler ~ sage-femme** work as a midwife; **~ ci ~ ça** so-so; **~ il faut** properly; **~ pour faire** as if to do; **jolie ~ tout** as pretty as anything; **qu'est-ce qu'il y a ~ légumes?** what is there in the way of vegetables?

commencer /kɔmɑ̃se/ [10] *vt/i* begin, start; **~ à faire** begin *ou* start to do.

comment /kɔmɑ̃/ *adv* how; **~?** (répétition) pardon?; (surprise) what?; **~ est-il?** what is he like?; **le ~ et le pourquoi** the whys and wherefores.

commentaire /kɔmɑ̃tɛr/ *nm* comment; (d'un texte, événement) commentary. **commentateur, -trice** *nm, f* commentator.

commenter /kɔmɑ̃te/ [1] *vt* comment on; (film, visite) provide a commentary for; (radio, TV) commentate.

commérages /kɔmeraʒ/ *nmpl* gossip.

commerçant, ~e /kɔmɛrsɑ̃, -t/ *a* (rue) shopping; (personne) business-minded. ●*nm, f* shopkeeper.

commerce /kɔmɛrs/ *nm* trade, commerce; (magasin) business; **faire du ~** be in business; **~ électronique** e-commerce.

commercial, ~e (mpl **-iaux**) /kɔmɛrsjal, -jo/ *a* commercial. **commercialiser** [1] *vt* market.

commettre /kɔmɛtr/ [42] *vt* commit.

commis /kɔmi/ *nm* (de magasin) assistant; (de bureau) clerk.

commissaire /kɔmisɛR/ *nm* commissioner; (Sport) steward; ~ (de police) (police) superintendent. **commissaire-priseur** (*pl* **commissaires-priseurs**) *nm* auctioneer.

commissariat /kɔmisaRja/ *nm* ~ (de police) police station.

commission /kɔmisjɔ̃/ *nf* commission; (course) errand; (message) message; ~s shopping.

commode /kɔmɔd/ *a* handy, convenient; (*facile*) easy; **il n'est pas** ~ he's a difficult customer. ●*nf* chest (of drawers). **commodité** *nf* convenience.

commotion /kɔmosjɔ̃/ *nf* ~ (**cérébrale**) concussion.

commun, ~**e** /kɔmœ̃, -yn/ *a* common; (*effort, action*) joint; (*frais, pièce*) shared; **en** ~ jointly; **avoir** *ou* **mettre en** ~ share; **le** ~ **des mortels** ordinary mortals.

communal, ~**e** (*mpl* **-aux**) *a* of the commune, local.

communauté /kɔmynote/ *nf* community.

commune /kɔmyn/ *nf* (circonscription, collectivité) commune.

communicatif, **-ive** /kɔmynikatif, -v/ *a* (*personne*) talkative; (*gaieté*) infectious.

communication /kɔmynikasjɔ̃/ *nf* communication; (téléphonique) call; ~s (relations) communications (+ *pl*); **voies** *ou* **moyens de** ~ communications (+ *pl*).

communier /kɔmynje/ [45] *vi* (Relig) receive communion; (fig) commune.

communiqué /kɔmynike/ *nm* statement; (de presse) communiqué.

communiquer /kɔmynike/ [1] *vt* pass on, communicate; (*date, décision*) announce. ●*vi* communicate. □ **se** ~ **à** *vpr* spread to.

communiste /kɔmynist/ *a & nmf* communist.

commutateur /kɔmytatœR/ *nm* (Électr) switch.

compagne /kɔ̃paɲ/ *nf* companion.

compagnie /kɔ̃paɲi/ *nf* company; **tenir** ~ **à** keep company; **en** ~ **de** together with; ~ **aérienne** airline.

compagnon /kɔ̃paɲɔ̃/ *nm* companion.

comparable /kɔ̃paRabl/ *a* comparable (à to). **comparaison** *nf* comparison; (littéraire) simile.

comparaître /kɔ̃paRɛtR/ [18] *vi* (Jur) appear (**devant** before).

comparatif, **-ive** /kɔ̃paRatif, -v/ *a & nm* comparative.

comparer /kɔ̃paRe/ [1] *vt* compare (à with). □ **se** ~ *vpr* compare oneself; (être comparable) be comparable.

compartiment /kɔ̃paRtimɑ̃/ *nm* compartment.

comparution /kɔ̃paRysjɔ̃/ *nf* (Jur) appearance.

compas /kɔ̃pa/ *nm* (pair of) compasses; (boussole) compass.

compassion /kɔ̃pasjɔ̃/ *nf* compassion.

compatible /kɔ̃patibl/ *a* compatible.

compatir /kɔ̃patiR/ [2] *vi* sympathize; ~ **à** share in.

compatriote /kɔ̃patRijɔt/ *nmf* compatriot.

compensation /kɔ̃pɑ̃sasjɔ̃/ *nf* compensation. **compenser** [1] *vt* compensate for, make up for.

compère /kɔ̃pɛR/ *nm* accomplice.

compétence /kɔpetɑ̃s/ *nf* competence; (fonction) domain, sphere; **entrer dans les ~s de qn** be in sb's domain. **compétent, ~e** a competent.

compétition /kɔ̃petisjɔ̃/ nf competition; (sportive) event; **de ~** competitive.

complaire (se) /(sə)kɔ̃plɛR/ [47] vpr **se ~ dans** delight in.

complaisance /kɔ̃plɛzɑ̃s/ nf kindness; (indulgence) indulgence.

complément /kɔ̃plemɑ̃/ nm supplement; (Gram) complement; **~ (d'objet)** (Gram) object; **~ d'information** further information. **complémentaire** a complementary; (renseignements) supplementary.

complet, -ète /kɔ̃plɛ, -t/ a complete; (train, hôtel) full. ● nm suit.

compléter /kɔ̃plete/ [14] vt complete; (agrémenter) complement. □ **se ~** vpr complement each other.

complexe /kɔ̃plɛks/ a complex. ● nm (sentiment, bâtiments) complex. **complexé, ~e** /kɔ̃plekse/ a **être ~** have a lot of hang-ups.

complice /kɔ̃plis/ nm accomplice.

compliment /kɔ̃plimɑ̃/ nm compliment; **~s** (félicitations) compliments, congratulations.

compliquer /kɔ̃plike/ [1] vt complicate. □ **se ~** vpr become complicated.

complot /kɔ̃plo/ nm plot.

comportement /kɔ̃pɔRtəmɑ̃/ nm behaviour; (de joueur, voiture) performance.

comporter /kɔ̃pɔRte/ [1] vt (être composé de) comprise; (inclure) include; (risque) entail. □ **se ~** vpr behave; (joueur, voiture) perform.

composant /kɔ̃pozɑ̃/ nm component.

composé, ~e /kɔ̃poze/ a

composite; (salade) mixed; (guindé) affected. ● nm compound.

composer /kɔ̃poze/ [1] vt make up, compose; (chanson, visage) compose; (numéro) dial; (page) typeset. ● vi (transiger) compromise. □ **se ~ de** vpr be made up ou composed of.

compositeur, -trice nm, f (Mus) composer.

composter /kɔ̃pɔste/ [1] vt (billet) punch.

compote /kɔ̃pɔt/ nf stewed fruit; **~ de pommes** stewed apples.

compréhensible /kɔ̃pReɑ̃sibl/ a understandable; (intelligible) comprehensible.

compréhensif, -ive /kɔ̃pReɑ̃sif, -v/ a understanding.

compréhension /kɔ̃pReɑ̃sjɔ̃/ nf understanding, comprehension.

comprendre /kɔ̃pRɑ̃dR/ [50] vt understand; (comporter) comprise, be made up of. □ **se ~** vpr (personnes) understand each other; **ça se comprend** that is understandable.

compresse /kɔ̃pRɛs/ nf compress.

comprimé /kɔ̃pRime/ nm tablet.

comprimer /kɔ̃pRime/ [1] vt compress; (réduire) reduce.

compris, ~e /kɔ̃pRi, -z/ a included; (d'accord) agreed; **~ entre** (contained) between; **service (non) ~** service (not) included; **tout ~** (all) inclusive; **y ~** including.

compromettre /kɔ̃pRɔmɛtR/ [42] vt compromise. **compromis** nm compromise.

comptabilité /kɔ̃patibilite/ nf accountancy; (comptes) accounts; (service) accounts department.

comptable /kɔ̃tabl/ a accounting. ● nmf accountant.

comptant /kɔ̃tɑ̃/ adv (payer) (in) cash; (acheter) for cash.

compte /kɔ̃t/ nm count; (facture,

comptabilité) account; (nombre exact) right number; $\sim$ **bancaire**, $\sim$ **en banque** bank account; **prendre qch en** $\sim$, **tenir** $\sim$ **de qch** take sth into account; **se rendre** $\sim$ **de** realize; **demander/rendre des** $\sim$**s** ask for/ give an explanation; **à bon** $\sim$ cheaply; **s'en tirer à bon** $\sim$ get off lightly; **travailler à son** $\sim$ be self-employed; **faire le** $\sim$ **de** count; **pour le** $\sim$ **de** on behalf of; **sur le** $\sim$ **de** about; **au bout du** $\sim$ all things considered; $\sim$ **à rebours** countdown.

compte-gouttes /kɔ̃tgut/ *nm inv* (Méd) dropper; **au** $\sim$ (fig) in dribs and drabs.

compter /kɔ̃te/ [1] *vt* count; (prévoir) allow, reckon on; (facturer) charge for; (avoir) have; (classer) consider; $\sim$ **faire** intend to do. ● *vi* (calculer, importer) count; $\sim$ **avec** reckon with; $\sim$ **parmi** (figurer) be considered among; $\sim$ **sur** rely on, count on.

compte(-)rendu /kɔ̃tʀɑ̃dy/ *nm* report; (de film, livre) review.

compteur /kɔ̃tœʀ/ *nm* meter; $\sim$ **de vitesse** speedometer.

comptine /kɔ̃tin/ *nf* nursery rhyme.

comptoir /kɔ̃twaʀ/ *nm* counter; (de café) bar.

comte /kɔ̃t/ *nm* count.

comté /kɔ̃te/ *nm* county.

comtesse /kɔ̃tɛs/ *nf* countess.

con, $\sim$**ne** /kɔ̃, kɔn/ *a* ▣ bloody stupid ▣. ● *nm*, *f* ▣ bloody fool ▣.

concentrer /kɔ̃sɑ̃tʀe/ [1] *vt* concentrate. □ **se** $\sim$ *vpr* be concentrated.

concept /kɔ̃sɛpt/ *nm* concept.

concerner /kɔ̃sɛʀne/ [1] *vt* concern; **en ce qui me concerne** as far as I am concerned.

concert /kɔ̃sɛʀ/ *nm* concert; **de** $\sim$ in unison.

concerter /kɔ̃sɛʀte/ [1] *vt* organize, prepare. □ **se** $\sim$ *vpr* confer.

concession /kɔ̃sesjɔ̃/ *nf* concession; (terrain) plot.

concevoir /kɔ̃svwaʀ/ [52] *vt* (imaginer, engendrer) conceive; (comprendre) understand; (élaborer) design.

concierge /kɔ̃sjɛʀʒ/ *nmf* caretaker.

concilier /kɔ̃silje/ [45] *vt* reconcile. □ **se** $\sim$ *vpr* (s'attirer) win (over).

concis, $\sim$**e** /kɔ̃si, -z/ *a* concise.

conclure /kɔ̃klyʀ/ [16] *vt* conclude; $\sim$ **à** conclude in favour of. ● *vi* $\sim$ **en faveur de/contre** find in favour of/against. **conclusion** *nf* conclusion.

concombre /kɔ̃kɔ̃bʀ/ *nm* cucumber.

concordance /kɔ̃kɔʀdɑ̃s/ *nf* agreement.

concourir /kɔ̃kuʀiʀ/ [20] *vi* compete. ● *vt* $\sim$ **à** contribute towards.

concours /kɔ̃kuʀ/ *nm* competition; (examen) competitive examination; (aide) help; (de circonstances) combination.

concret, **-ète** /kɔ̃kʀɛ, -t/ *a* concrete.

concrétiser /kɔ̃kʀetize/ [1] *vt* give concrete form to. □ **se** $\sim$ *vpr* materialize.

conçu, $\sim$**e** /kɔ̃sy/ *a* **bien/mal** $\sim$ well/badly designed.

concubinage /kɔ̃kybinaʒ/ *nm* cohabitation; **vivre en** $\sim$ live together, cohabit.

concurrence /kɔ̃kyʀɑ̃s/ *nf* competition; **faire** $\sim$ **à** compete with; **jusqu'à** $\sim$ **de** up to a limit of.

concurrencer /kɔ̃kyʀɑ̃se/ [10] *vt* compete with.

concurrent, $\sim$**e** /kɔ̃kyʀɑ̃, -t/

nm, f competitor; (Scol) candidate.
● *a* rival.

condamnation /kɔ̃danasjɔ̃/ *nf*
condemnation; (peine) sentence;
~ **centralisée des portières** central
locking. **condamné**, ~**e** *nm, f*
condemned man, condemned
woman. **condamner** [1] *vt*
(censurer, obliger) condemn; (Jur)
sentence; (porte) block up.

condition /kɔ̃disjɔ̃/ *nf* condition;
~**s** (prix) terms; **à** ~ **de** *ou* **que**
provided (that); **sans** ~
unconditional(ly); **sous** ~
conditionally.

conditionnel, ~**le** /kɔ̃disjɔnɛl/
a conditional. ● *nm* conditional
(tense).

conditionnement /kɔ̃disjɔnmɑ̃/
nm conditioning; (emballage)
packaging.

condoléances /kɔ̃dɔleɑ̃s/ *nfpl*
condolences.

conducteur, -trice /kɔ̃dyktœʀ,
-tʀis/ *nm, f* driver.

conduire /kɔ̃dɥiʀ/ [17] *vt* take (à
to); (guider) lead; (Auto) drive;
(affaire) conduct; ~ **à** (faire aboutir)
lead to. ● *vi* drive. □ **se** ~ *vpr*
behave.

conduit /kɔ̃dɥi/ *nm* duct.

conduite /kɔ̃dɥit/ *nf* conduct,
behaviour; (Auto) driving; (tuyau)
pipe; **voiture avec** ~ **à droite** right-
hand drive car.

confection /kɔ̃fɛksjɔ̃/ *nf* making;
de ~ ready-made; **la** ~ the
clothing industry.

conférence /kɔ̃feʀɑ̃s/ *nf*
conference; (exposé) lecture; ~ **au**
sommet summit meeting.
conférencier, -ière *nm, f*
lecturer.

confesser /kɔ̃fese/ [1] *vt* confess.
□ **se** ~ *vpr* go to confession.

confiance /kɔ̃fjɑ̃s/ *nf* trust; **avoir**
~ **en** trust.

confiant, ~**e** /kɔ̃fjɑ̃, -t/ *a* (assuré)
confident; (sans défiance) trusting.

confidence /kɔ̃fidɑ̃s/ *nf*
confidence.

confidentiel, ~**le** /kɔ̃fidɑ̃sjɛl/ *a*
confidential.

confier /kɔ̃fje/ [45] *vt* ~ **à qn**
entrust sb with; ~ **un secret à qn**
tell sb a secret. □ **se** ~ **à** *vpr*
confide in.

confiner /kɔ̃fine/ [1] *vt* confine;
~ **à** border on. □ **se** ~ *vpr*
confine oneself (à, dans to).

confirmation /kɔ̃fiʀmasjɔ̃/ *nf*
confirmation. **confirmer** [1] *vt*
confirm.

confiserie /kɔ̃fizʀi/ *nf* sweet
shop; ~**s** confectionery.

confisquer /kɔ̃fiske/ [1] *vt*
confiscate.

confit, ~**e** /kɔ̃fi, -t/ *a* candied;
(fruits) crystallized. ● *nm* ~ **de**
canard confit of duck.

confiture /kɔ̃fityʀ/ *nf* jam.

conflit /kɔ̃fli/ *nm* conflict.

confondre /kɔ̃fɔ̃dʀ/ [3] *vt*
confuse, mix up; (étonner)
confound. □ **se** ~ *vpr* merge; **se**
~ **en excuses** apologize profusely.

conforme /kɔ̃fɔʀm/ *a* **être** ~ **à**
comply with; (être en accord) be in
keeping with.

conformer /kɔ̃fɔʀme/ [1] *vt*
adapt. □ **se** ~ **à** *vpr* conform to.

conformité /kɔ̃fɔʀmite/ *nf*
compliance, conformity; **agir en** ~
avec act in accordance with.

confort /kɔ̃fɔʀ/ *nm* comfort; **tout**
~ with all mod cons.
confortable *a* comfortable.

confrère /kɔ̃fʀɛʀ/ *nm* colleague.

confronter /kɔ̃fʀɔ̃te/ [1] *vt*
confront; (textes) compare. □ **se**
~ **à** *vpr* be confronted with.

confus, ~**e** /kɔ̃fy, -z/ *a* confused;
(gêné) embarrassed.

congé /kɔ̃ʒe/ *nm* holiday; (arrêt
momentané) time off, leave; (avis de

C

départ) notice; **en ~** on holiday *ou* leave; **~ de maladie/maternité** sick/maternity leave; **jour de ~** day off; **prendre ~ de** take one's leave of.

congédier /kɔ̃ʒedje/ [45] *vt* dismiss.

congélateur /kɔ̃ʒelatœʀ/ *nm* freezer.

congeler /kɔ̃ʒle/ [6] *vt* freeze.

congère /kɔ̃ʒɛʀ/ *nf* snowdrift.

congrès /kɔ̃gʀɛ/ *nm* conference; (Pol) congress.

conjoint, ~e /kɔ̃ʒwɛ̃, -t/ *nm, f* spouse. ● *a* joint.

conjonctivite /kɔ̃ʒɔ̃ktivit/ *nf* conjunctivitis.

conjoncture /kɔ̃ʒɔ̃ktyʀ/ *nf* situation; (économique) economic climate.

conjugaison /kɔ̃ʒygɛzɔ̃/ *nf* conjugation.

conjugal, ~e (*mpl* **-aux**) /kɔ̃ʒygal, -o/ *a* conjugal, married.

conjuguer /kɔ̃ʒyge/ [1] *vt* (Gram) conjugate; (*efforts*) combine. □ **se ~** *vpr* (Gram) be conjugated; (*facteurs*) be combined.

conjurer /kɔ̃ʒyʀe/ [1] *vt* (éviter) avert; (implorer) beg.

connaissance /kɔnɛsɑ̃s/ *nf* knowledge; (personne) acquaintance; **~s** (science) knowledge; **faire la ~ de** meet; (apprécier une personne) get to know; **perdre/reprendre ~** lose/regain consciousness; **sans ~** unconscious.

connaisseur /kɔnɛsœʀ/ *nm* expert, connoisseur.

connaître /kɔnɛtʀ/ [18] *vt* know; (*difficultés, faim, succès*) experience; **faire ~** make known. □ **se ~** *vpr* (se rencontrer) meet; **s'y ~ en** know (all) about.

connecter /kɔnɛkte/ [1] *vt* connect; **être/ne pas être connecté** be on-/off-line. □ **se ~ à** *vpr* (Ordinat) log on to.

connerie /kɔnʀi/ *nf* ▣ **faire une ~** do something stupid; **dire des ~s** talk rubbish.

connu, ~e /kɔny/ *a* well-known.

conquérant, ~e /kɔ̃keʀɑ̃, -t/ *nm, f* conqueror.

conquête /kɔ̃kɛt/ *nf* conquest.

consacrer /kɔ̃sakʀe/ [1] *vt* devote; (Relig) consecrate; (sanctionner) sanction. □ **se ~ à** *vpr* devote oneself to.

conscience /kɔ̃sjɑ̃s/ *nf* conscience; (perception) awareness; (de collectivité) consciousness; **avoir/ prendre ~ de** be/become aware of; **perdre/reprendre ~** lose/regain consciousness; **avoir bonne/ mauvaise ~** have a clear/guilty conscience.

conscient, ~e /kɔ̃sjɑ̃, -t/ *a* conscious; **~ de** aware *ou* conscious of.

conseil /kɔ̃sɛj/ *nm* (piece of) advice; (assemblée) council, committee; (séance) meeting; (personne) consultant; **~ d'administration** board of directors; **~ en gestion** management consultant; **~ des ministres** Cabinet; **~ municipal** town council.

conseiller[1] /kɔ̃seje/ [1] *vt* advise; **~ à qn** advise sb to; **~ qch à qn** recommend sth to sb.

conseiller[2], **-ère** /kɔ̃seje, -jɛʀ/ *nm, f* adviser, counsellor; **~ municipal** town councillor; **~ d'orientation** careers adviser.

consentement /kɔ̃sɑ̃tmɑ̃/ *nm* consent.

conséquence /kɔ̃sekɑ̃s/ *nf* consequence; **en ~** (comme il convient) accordingly; **en ~ (de quoi)** as a result of which.

conséquent, ~e /kɔ̃sekɑ̃, -t/ *a* consistent, logical; (important)

substantial; **par** ∼ consequently,
therefore.
conservateur, **-trice** /kɔ̃sɛʀ-
vatœʀ, -tʀis/ a conservative.
● nm, f (Pol) conservative; (de musée) curator. ● nm preservative.
conservation /kɔ̃sɛʀvasjɔ̃/ nf
preservation; (d'espèce, patrimoine)
conservation.
conservatoire /kɔ̃sɛʀvatwaʀ/
nm academy.
conserve /kɔ̃sɛʀv/ nf tinned ou
canned food; **en** ∼ tinned,
canned; **boîte de** ∼ tin, can.
conserver /kɔ̃sɛʀve/ [1] vt keep;
(en bon état) preserve; (Culin)
preserve. ▫ **se** ∼ vpr (Culin) keep.
considérer /kɔ̃sideʀe/ [14] vt
consider; (respecter) esteem; ∼
comme consider to be.
consigne /kɔ̃siɲ/ nf (de gare) left-
luggage office; (US) baggage
checkroom; (somme) deposit;
(ordres) orders; ∼ **automatique**
left-luggage lockers; (US) baggage
lockers.
consistance /kɔ̃sistɑ̃s/ nf
consistency; (fig) substance,
weight. **consistant**, ∼**e** a solid;
(épais) thick.
consister /kɔ̃siste/ [1] vi ∼ **en**/
dans consist of/in; ∼ **à faire**
consist in doing.
consoler /kɔ̃sɔle/ [1] vt console.
▫ **se** ∼ vpr find consolation; **se** ∼
de qch get over sth.
consolider /kɔ̃sɔlide/ [1] vt
strengthen; (fig) consolidate.
consommateur, **-trice** /kɔ̃sɔ-
matœʀ, -tʀis/ nm, f (Comm)
consumer; (dans un café) customer.
consommation /kɔ̃sɔmasjɔ̃/ nf
consumption; (accomplissement)
consummation; (boisson) drink; **de**
∼ (Comm) consumer.
consommer /kɔ̃sɔme/ [1] vt
consume, use; (manger) eat; (boire)
drink; (mariage) consummate.

▫ **se** ∼ vpr (être mangé) be eaten;
(être utilisé) be used.
consonne /kɔ̃sɔn/ nf consonant.
constat /kɔ̃sta/ nm (official)
report; ∼ **(à l')amiable** accident
report drawn up by those
involved.
constatation /kɔ̃statasjɔ̃/ nf
observation, statement of fact.
constater /kɔ̃state/ [1] vt note, notice;
(certifier) certify.
consternation /kɔ̃stɛʀnasjɔ̃/ nf
dismay.
constipé, ∼**e** /kɔ̃stipe/ a
constipated; (fig) uptight.
constituer /kɔ̃stitɥe/ [1] vt
(composer) make up, constitute;
(organiser) form; (être) constitute;
constitué de made up of. ▫ **se** ∼
vpr **se** ∼ **prisonnier** give oneself
up.
constitution /kɔ̃stitysjɔ̃/ nf
formation, setting up; (Pol, Méd)
constitution.
constructeur /kɔ̃stʀyktœʀ/ nm
manufacturer, builder.
construction /kɔ̃stʀyksjɔ̃/ nf
building; (structure, secteur)
construction; (fabrication)
manufacture.
construire /kɔ̃stʀɥiʀ/ [17] vt
build; (système, phrase)
construct.
consulat /kɔ̃syla/ nm consulate.
consultation /kɔ̃syltasjɔ̃/ nf
consultation; (réception: Méd)
surgery; (US) office; **heures de** ∼
surgery ou office (US) hours.
consulter /kɔ̃sylte/ [1] vt
consult. ● vi (médecin) hold
surgery, see patients. ▫ **se** ∼ vpr
consult together.
contact /kɔ̃takt/ nm contact;
(toucher) touch; **au** ∼ **de** on contact
with; (personne) by contact with,
by seeing; **mettre/couper le** ∼
(Auto) switch on/off the ignition;

prendre ∼ **avec** get in touch with.
contacter [1] *vt* contact.

contagieux, -ieuse /kɔ̃taʒjø, -z/
a contagious.

conte /kɔ̃t/ *nm* tale; ∼ **de fées**
fairy tale.

contempler /kɔ̃tɑ̃ple/ [1] *vt*
contemplate.

contemporain, ∼e /kɔ̃tɑ̃pɔRɛ̃,
-ɛn/ *a & nm,f* contemporary.

contenance /kɔ̃t(ə)nɑ̃s/ *nf*
(volume) capacity; (allure) bearing;
perdre ∼ lose one's composure.

contenir /kɔ̃t(ə)niR/ [58] *vt*
contain; (avoir une capacité de) hold.
□ **se ∼** *vpr* contain oneself.

content, ∼e /kɔ̃tɑ̃, -t/ *a* pleased,
happy (**de** with); ∼ **de faire**
pleased *ou* happy to do.

contenter /kɔ̃tɑ̃te/ [1] *vt* satisfy.
□ **se ∼ de** *vpr* content oneself
with.

contenu /kɔ̃t(ə)ny/ *nm* (de
récipient) contents (+ *pl*); (de texte)
content.

conter /kɔ̃te/ [1] *vt* tell, relate.

contestation /kɔ̃tɛstasjɔ̃/ *nf*
dispute; (opposition) protest.

contester /kɔ̃tɛste/ [1] *vt*
question, dispute; (s'opposer)
protest against. ● *vi* protest.

conteur, -euse /kɔ̃tœR, -øz/ *nm,f*
storyteller.

contigu, ∼ë /kɔ̃tigy/ *a* adjacent
(**à** to).

continent /kɔ̃tinɑ̃/ *nm* continent.

continu, ∼e /kɔ̃tiny/ *a*
continuous.

continuer /kɔ̃tinɥe/ [1] *vt*
continue. ● *vi* continue, go on; ∼
à *ou* **de faire** carry on *ou* go on *ou*
continue doing.

contorsionner (se) /(sə)kɔ̃tɔR-
sjɔne/ [1] *vpr* wriggle.

contour /kɔ̃tuR/ *nm* outline,
contour; ∼**s** (d'une route) twists and
turns, bends.

contourner /kɔ̃tuRne/ [1] *vt* go

round, by-pass; (difficulté) get
round.

contraceptif, -ive /kɔ̃tRasɛptif,
-v/ *a* contraceptive. ● *nm*
contraceptive. **contraception** *nf*
contraception.

contracter /kɔ̃tRakte/ [1] *vt* (maladie) contract; (dette) incur;
(muscle) tense; (assurance) take
out. □ **se ∼** *vpr* contract.

contractuel, ∼le /kɔ̃tRaktɥɛl/
nm,f (agent) traffic warden.

contradictoire /kɔ̃tRadiktwaR/ *a*
contradictory; (débat) open.

contraignant, ∼e /kɔ̃tRɛɲɑ̃, -t/ *a*
restricting.

contraindre /kɔ̃tRɛ̃dR/ [22] *vt*
force, compel (**à faire** to do).

contrainte /kɔ̃tRɛ̃t/ *nf* constraint.

contraire /kɔ̃tRɛR/ *a* opposite; ∼
à contrary to. ● *nm* opposite; **au**
∼ on the contrary; **au ∼ de**
unlike.

contrarier /kɔ̃tRaRje/ [45] *vt*
annoy; (projet, volonté) frustrate;
(chagriner) upset.

contraste /kɔ̃tRast/ *nm* contrast.

contrat /kɔ̃tRa/ *nm* contract.

contravention /kɔ̃tRavɑ̃sjɔ̃/ *nf*
(parking) ticket; **en ∼** in breach
(**à** of).

contre /kɔ̃tR(ə)/ *prép* against; (en
échange de) for; **par ∼** on the other
hand; **tout ∼** close by. **contre-
attaque** (*pl* ∼**s**) *nf* counter-
attack. **contre-attaquer** [1] *vt*
counter-attack. **contre-balancer**
[10] *vt* counterbalance.

contrebande /kɔ̃tRəbɑ̃d/ *nf*
contraband; **faire la ∼ de** smuggle.

contrebas: en ∼ /ɑ̃kɔ̃tRəba/ *loc*
below.

contrebasse /kɔ̃tRəbas/ *nf*
double bass.

contrecœur: à ∼ /akɔ̃tRəkœR/
loc reluctantly.

contrecoup /kɔ̃tRəku/ *nm*
effects, repercussions.

contredire /kɔ̃tʀədiʀ/ [37] *vt* contradict. □ **se** ~ *vpr* contradict oneself.

contrée /kɔ̃tʀe/ *nf* region; (pays) land.

contrefaçon /kɔ̃tʀəfasɔ̃/ *nf* (objet imité, action) forgery.

contre-indiqué, ~**e** /kɔ̃tʀɛ̃dike/ *a* (Méd) contra-indicated; (déconseillé) not recommended.

contre-jour: **à** ~ /akɔ̃tʀəʒuʀ/ *loc* against the light.

contrepartie /kɔ̃tʀəpaʀti/ *nf* compensation; **en** ~ in exchange, in return.

contreplaqué /kɔ̃tʀəplake/ *nm* plywood.

contresens /kɔ̃tʀəsɑ̃s/ *nm* misinterpretation; (absurdité) nonsense; **à** ~ the wrong way.

contretemps /kɔ̃tʀətɑ̃/ *nm* hitch; **à** ~ (fig) at the wrong time.

contribuable /kɔ̃tʀibɥabl/ *nmf* taxpayer.

contribuer /kɔ̃tʀibɥe/ [1] *vt* contribute (**à** to, towards).

contrôle /kɔ̃tʀol/ *nm* (maîtrise) control; (vérification) check; (des prix) control; (poinçon) hallmark; (Scol) test; ~ **continu** continuous assessment; ~ **des changes** exchange control; ~ **des naissances** birth control; ~ **de soi-même** self-control; ~ **technique** (des véhicules) MOT (test).

contrôler /kɔ̃tʀole/ [1] *vt* (vérifier) check; (surveiller, maîtriser) control. □ **se** ~ *vpr* control oneself.

contrôleur, **-euse** /kɔ̃tʀolœʀ, -øz/ *nm, f* inspector.

convaincre /kɔ̃vɛ̃kʀ/ [59] *vt* convince; ~ **qn de faire** persuade sb to do.

convalescence /kɔ̃valesɑ̃s/ *nf* convalescence; **être en** ~ be convalescing.

convenable /kɔ̃vnabl/ *a* (correct) decent, proper; (approprié) suitable; (acceptable) reasonable, acceptable.

convenance /kɔ̃vnɑ̃s/ *nf* **à ma** ~ to my satisfaction; **les** ~**s** convention.

convenir /kɔ̃vniʀ/ [58] *vt/i* be suitable; ~ **à** suit; ~ **que** admit that; ~ **de qch** (avouer) admit sth; (s'accorder sur) agree on sth; ~ **de faire** agree to do; **il convient de** it is advisable to; (selon les bienséances) it would be right to.

convention /kɔ̃vɑ̃sjɔ̃/ *nf* agreement, convention; (clause) article, clause; ~**s** (convenances) convention; **de** ~ conventional; ~ **collective** industrial agreement.

convenu, ~**e** /kɔ̃vny/ *a* agreed.

conversation /kɔ̃vɛʀsasjɔ̃/ *nf* conversation.

convertir /kɔ̃vɛʀtiʀ/ [2] *vt* convert (**à** to; **en** into). □ **se** ~ *vpr* be converted, convert.

conviction /kɔ̃viksjɔ̃/ *nf* conviction; **avoir la** ~ **que** be convinced that.

convivial, ~**e** (*mpl* **-iaux**) /kɔ̃vivjal, -jo/ *a* convivial; (Ordinat) user-friendly.

convocation /kɔ̃vɔkasjɔ̃/ *nf* (Jur) summons; (d'une assemblée) convening; (document) notification to attend.

convoi /kɔ̃vwa/ *nm* convoy; (train) train; ~ (**funèbre**) funeral procession.

convoquer /kɔ̃vɔke/ [1] *vt* (assemblée) convene; (personne) summon; **être convoqué pour un entretien** be called for interview.

coopération /kɔɔpeʀasjɔ̃/ *nf* cooperation; (Mil) civilian national service abroad.

coordination /kɔɔʀdinasjɔ̃/ *nf* coordination. **coordonnées** *nfpl* coordinates; (adresse) address and telephone number.

copain /kɔpɛ̃/ *nm* friend; (petit ami) boyfriend.

copie /kɔpi/ *nf* copy; (Scol) paper; ~ **d'examen** exam paper *ou* script; ~ **de sauvegarde** back-up copy.

copier /kɔpje/ [45] *vt/i* copy; ~ **sur** (Scol) copy *ou* crib from.

copieux, -ieuse /kɔpjø, -z/ *a* copious.

copine /kɔpin/ *nf* friend; (petite amie) girlfriend.

coq /kɔk/ *nm* cockerel.

coque /kɔk/ *nf* shell; (de bateau) hull.

coquelicot /kɔkliko/ *nm* poppy.

coqueluche /kɔklyʃ/ *nf* whooping cough.

coquet, ~te /kɔkɛ, -t/ *a* flirtatious; (élégant) pretty; (somme 𝔼) tidy.

coquetier /kɔktje/ *nm* eggcup.

coquillage /kɔkijaʒ/ *nm* shellfish; (coquille) shell.

coquille /kɔkij/ *nf* shell; (faute) misprint; ~ **Saint-Jacques** scallop.

coquin, ~e /kɔkɛ̃, -in/ *a* mischievous. ● *nm, f* rascal.

cor /kɔr/ *nm* (Mus) horn; (au pied) corn.

corail (*pl* **-aux**) /kɔraj, -o/ *nm* coral.

corbeau (*pl* **~x**) /kɔrbo/ *nm* (oiseau) crow.

corbeille /kɔrbɛj/ *nf* basket; ~ **à papier** waste-paper basket.

corbillard /kɔrbijar/ *nm* hearse.

cordage /kɔrdaʒ/ *nm* rope; ~s (Naut) rigging.

corde /kɔrd/ *nf* rope; (d'arc, de violon) string; ~ **à linge** washing line; ~ **à sauter** skipping-rope; ~ **raide** tightrope; ~s **vocales** vocal cords.

cordon /kɔrdõ/ *nm* string, cord; ~ **de police** police cordon.

cordonnier /kɔrdɔnje/ *nm* cobbler.

Corée /kɔre/ *nf* Korea.

coriace /kɔrjas/ *a* tough.

corne /kɔrn/ *nf* horn.

corneille /kɔrnɛj/ *nf* crow.

cornemuse /kɔrnəmyz/ *nf* bagpipes (+ *pl*).

corner /kɔrne/ [1] *vt* (*page*) turn down the corner of; **page cornée** dog-eared page. ● *vi* (Auto) hoot, honk.

cornet /kɔrnɛ/ *nm* (paper) cone; (crème glacée) cornet, cone.

corniche /kɔrniʃ/ *nf* cornice; (*route*) cliff road.

cornichon /kɔrniʃõ/ *nm* gherkin.

corporel, ~le /kɔrpɔrɛl/ *a* bodily; (*châtiment*) corporal.

corps /kɔr/ *nm* body; (Mil) corps; **combat** ~ **à** ~ hand-to-hand combat; ~ **électoral** electorate; ~ **enseignant** teaching profession.

correct, ~e /kɔrɛkt/ *a* proper, correct; (exact) correct.

correcteur, -trice /kɔrɛktœr, -tris/ *nm, f* (d'épreuves) proofreader; (Scol) examiner; ~ **liquide** correction fluid; ~ **d'orthographe** spell-checker.

correction /kɔrɛksjõ/ *nf* correction; (d'examen) marking, grading; (punition) beating.

correspondance /kɔrɛspõdãs/ *nf* correspondence; (de train, d'autobus) connection; **vente par** ~ mail order; **faire des études par** ~ do a correspondence course.

correspondant, ~e /kɔrɛspõdã, -t/ *a* corresponding. ● *nm, f* correspondent; penfriend; (au téléphone) **votre** ~ the person you are calling.

correspondre /kɔrɛspõdr/ [3] *vi* (s'accorder, écrire) correspond; (*chambres*) communicate. ● *v + prép* ~ **à** (être approprié à) match, suit; (équivaloir à) correspond to. □ **se** ~ *vpr* correspond.

corrida /kɔrida/ *nf* bullfight.

corriger /kɔʀiʒe/ [40] vt correct; (devoir) mark, grade, correct; (punir) beat; (guérir) cure.

corsage /kɔʀsaʒ/ nm bodice; (chemisier) blouse.

corsaire /kɔʀsɛʀ/ nm pirate.

Corse /kɔʀs/ nf Corsica. ● nmf Corsican. **corse** a Corsican.

corsé, ~e /kɔʀse/ a (vin) full-bodied; (café) strong; (scabreux) racy; (problème) tough.

cortège /kɔʀtɛʒ/ nm procession; ~ **funèbre** funeral procession.

corvée /kɔʀve/ nf chore.

cosmonaute /kɔsmɔnot/ nmf cosmonaut.

cosmopolite /kɔsmɔpɔlit/ a cosmopolitan.

cosse /kɔs/ nf (de pois) pod.

cossu, ~e /kɔsy/ a (gens) well-to-do; (demeure) opulent.

costaud, ~e /kɔsto, -d/ 🄵 a strong. ● nm strong man.

costume /kɔstym/ nm suit; (Théât) costume.

cote /kɔt/ nf (classification) mark; (en Bourse) quotation; (de cheval) odds (de on); (de candidat, acteur) rating; ~ **d'alerte** danger level; **avoir la** ~ be popular.

côte /kot/ nf (littoral) coast; (pente) hill; (Anat) rib; (Culin) chop; ~ **à** ~ side by side; **la C**~ **d'Azur** the (French) Riviera.

côté /kote/ nm side; (direction) way; **à** ~ nearby; **voisin d'à** ~ next-door neighbour; **à** ~ **de** next to; (comparé à) compared to; **à** ~ **de la cible** wide of the target; **aux** ~**s de** by the side of; **de** ~ (regarder) sideways; (sauter) to one side; **mettre de** ~ put aside; **de ce** ~ this way; **de chaque** ~ on each side; **de tous les** ~**s** on every side; (partout) everywhere; **du** ~ **de** (vers) towards; (dans les environs de) near.

côtelette /kotlɛt/ nf chop.

coter /kɔte/ [1] vt (Comm) quote;

coté en Bourse listed on the Stock Exchange; **très coté** highly rated.

cotiser /kɔtize/ [1] vi pay one's contributions (**à** to); (à un club) pay one's subscription. ☐ **se** ~ vpr club together.

coton /kɔtɔ̃/ nm cotton; ~ **hydrophile** cotton wool.

cou /ku/ nm neck.

couchant /kuʃɑ̃/ nm sunset.

couche /kuʃ/ nf layer; (de peinture) coat; (de bébé) nappy; (US) diaper; ~**s** (Méd) childbirth; ~**s sociales** social strata.

coucher /kuʃe/ [1] vt put to bed; (loger) put up; (étendre) lay down; ~ (**par écrit**) set down. ● vi sleep. ☐ **se** ~ vpr go to bed; (s'étendre) lie down; (soleil) set. ● nm ~ (**de soleil**) sunset; **au** ~ **du soleil** at sunset.

couchette /kuʃɛt/ nf (de train) couchette; (Naut) berth.

coude /kud/ nm elbow; (de rivière, chemin) bend; ~ **à** ~ side by side.

cou-de-pied (pl **cous-de-pied**) /kudpje/ nm instep.

coudre /kudʀ/ [19] vt/i sew.

couette /kwɛt/ nf duvet, continental quilt.

couler /kule/ [1] vi flow, run; (fromage, nez) run; (fuir) leak; (bateau) sink; (entreprise) go under; **faire** ~ **un bain** run a bath. ● vt (bateau) sink; (sculpture, métal) cast. ☐ **se** ~ vpr slip (**dans** into).

couleur /kulœʀ/ nf colour; (peinture) paint; (aux cartes) suit; ~**s** (teint) colour; **de** ~ (homme, femme) coloured; **en** ~**s** (télévision, film) colour.

couleuvre /kulœvʀ/ nf grass snake.

coulisse /kulis/ nf (de tiroir) runner; **à** ~ (porte, fenêtre) sliding;

∼s (Théât) wings; **dans les** ∼s (fig) behind the scenes.

couloir /kulwaʀ/ *nm* corridor; (Sport) lane; ∼ **de bus** bus lane.

coup /ku/ *nm* blow; (choc) knock; (Sport) stroke; (de crayon, chance, cloche) stroke; (de fusil, pistolet) shot; (fois) time; (aux échecs) move; **donner un** ∼ **de pied/poing à** kick/ punch; **à** ∼ **sûr** definitely; **après** ∼ after the event; **boire un** ∼ 🔲 have a drink; ∼ **sur** ∼ in rapid succession; **du** ∼ as a result; **d'un seul** ∼ in one go; **du premier** ∼ first go; **sale** ∼ dirty trick; **sous le** ∼ **de la fatigue/colère** out of tiredness/anger; **sur le** ∼ instantly; **tenir le** ∼ hold out; **manquer son** ∼ 🔲 blow it 🔲; ∼ **de chiffon** wipe (with a rag); ∼ **de coude** nudge; ∼ **de couteau** stab; ∼ **d'envoi** kick-off; ∼ **d'État** (Pol) coup; ∼ **de feu** shot; ∼ **de fil** 🔲 phone call; ∼ **de filet** haul, (fig) police raid; ∼ **de foudre** love at first sight; ∼ **franc** free kick; ∼ **de frein** sudden braking; ∼ **de grâce** coup de grâce; ∼ **de main** helping hand; ∼ **d'œil** glance; ∼ **de pied** kick; ∼ **de poing** punch; ∼ **de soleil** sunburn; ∼ **de sonnette** ring (on a bell); ∼ **de téléphone** (tele-) phone call; ∼ **de tête** wild impulse; ∼ **de théâtre** dramatic event; ∼ **de tonnerre** thunderclap; ∼ **de vent** gust of wind.

coupable /kupabl/ *a* guilty. ● *nmf* culprit.

coupe /kup/ *nf* cup; (de champagne) goblet; (à fruits) dish; (de vêtement) cut; (dessin) section; ∼ **de cheveux** haircut.

couper /kupe/ [1] *vt* cut; (arbre) cut down; (arrêter) cut off; (voyage) break up; (appétit) take away; (vin) water down; ∼ **par** take a short cut via; ∼ **la parole à qn** cut sb short. ● *vi* cut. □ **se** ∼ *vpr* cut oneself; **se** ∼ **le doigt** cut one's

finger; (routes) intersect; **se** ∼ **de** cut oneself off from.

couple /kupl/ *nm* couple; (d'animaux) pair.

coupure /kupyʀ/ *nf* cut; (billet de banque) note; (de presse) cutting; (pause, rupture) break; ∼ **(de courant)** power cut.

cour /kuʀ/ *nf* (court)yard; (du roi) court; (tribunal) court; ∼ **(de récréation)** playground; ∼ **martiale** court-martial; **faire la** ∼ **à** court.

courageux, -euse /kuʀaʒø, -z/ *a* courageous.

couramment /kuʀamɑ̃/ *adv* frequently; (parler) fluently.

courant, -e /kuʀɑ̃, -t/ *a* standard, ordinary; (en cours) current. ● *nm* current; (de mode, d'idées) trend; ∼ **d'air** draught; **dans le** ∼ **de** in the course of; **être/mettre au** ∼ **de** know/tell about; (à jour) be/bring up to date on.

courbature /kuʀbatyʀ/ *nf* ache; **avoir des** ∼s be stiff, ache.

courber /kuʀbe/ [1] *vt* bend.

coureur, -euse /kuʀœʀ, -øz/ *nm, f* (Sport) runner; ∼ **automobile** racing driver; ∼ **cycliste** racing cyclist. ● *nm* womanizer.

courgette /kuʀʒɛt/ *nf* courgette; (US) zucchini.

courir /kuʀiʀ/ [20] *vi* run; (se hâter) rush; (nouvelles) go round; ∼ **après qn/qch** chase after sb/ sth. ● *vt* (risque) run; (danger) face; (épreuve sportive) run *ou* compete in; (fréquenter) do the rounds of; (filles) chase (after).

couronne /kuʀɔn/ *nf* crown; (de fleurs) wreath.

couronnement /kuʀɔnmɑ̃/ *nm* coronation, crowning; (fig) crowning achievement.

courrier /kuʀje/ *nm* post, mail; (à écrire) letters; ∼ **du cœur** problem page; ∼ **électronique** e-mail.

cours /kuʀ/ *nm* (leçon) class; (série de leçons) course; (prix) price; (cote) (de valeur, denrée) price; (de devises) exchange rate; (déroulement, d'une rivière) course; (allée) avenue; **au ~ de** in the course of; **avoir ~** (*monnaie*) be legal tender; (fig) current; (Scol) have a lesson; **~ d'eau** river, stream; **~ du soir** evening class; **~ particulier** private lesson; **~ magistral** (Univ) lecture; **en ~** current; (*travail*) in progress; **en ~ de route** along the way.

course /kuʀs/ *nf* running; (épreuve de vitesse) race; (activité) racing; (entre rivaux: fig) race; (de projectile) flight; (voyage) journey; (commission) errand; **~s** (achats) shopping; (de chevaux) races; **faire la ~ avec qn** race sb.

coursier, -ière /kuʀsje, -jɛʀ/ *nm, f* messenger.

court, ~e /kuʀ, -t/ *a* short. ● *adv* short; **à ~ de** short of; **pris de ~** caught unawares. ● *nm* **~ (de tennis)** (tennis) court.

courtier, -ière /kuʀtje, -jɛʀ/ *nm, f* broker.

courtiser /kuʀtize/ [1] *vt* woo, court.

courtois, ~e /kuʀtwa, -z/ *a* courteous. **courtoisie** *nf* courtesy.

cousin, ~e /kuzɛ̃, -in/ *nm, f* cousin; **~ germain** first cousin.

coussin /kusɛ̃/ *nm* cushion.

coût /ku/ *nm* cost; **le ~ de la vie** the cost of living.

couteau (*pl* **~x**) /kuto/ *nm* knife; **~ à cran d'arrêt** flick knife.

coûter /kute/ [1] *vt/i* cost; **coûte que coûte** at all costs; **au prix coûtant** at cost (price).

coutume /kutym/ *nf* custom.

couture /kutyʀ/ *nf* sewing; (métier) dressmaking; (points) seam.

couturier *nm* fashion designer. **couturière** *nf* dressmaker.

couvée /kuve/ *nf* brood.

couvent /kuvã/ *nm* convent.

couver /kuve/ [1] *vt* (œufs) hatch; (*personne*) overprotect, pamper; (*maladie*) be coming down with, be sickening for. ● *vi* (*feu*) smoulder; (*mal*) be brewing.

couvercle /kuvɛʀkl/ *nm* (de marmite, boîte) lid; (qui se visse) screwtop.

couvert, ~e /kuvɛʀ, -t/ *a* covered (**de** with); (habillé) covered up; (*ciel*) overcast. ● *nm* (à table) place setting; (prix) cover charge; **~s** (couteaux etc.) cutlery; **mettre le ~** lay the table; (abri) cover; **à ~** (Mil) under cover; **à ~ de** (fig) safe from.

couverture /kuvɛʀtyʀ/ *nf* cover; (de lit) blanket; (toit) roofing; (dans la presse) coverage; **~ chauffante** electric blanket.

couvre-feu (*pl* **~x**) /kuvʀəfø/ *nm* curfew.

couvre-lit (*pl* **~s**) /kuvʀəli/ *nm* bedspread.

couvrir /kuvʀiʀ/ [21] *vt* cover. □ **se ~** *vpr* (s'habiller) wrap up; (se coiffer) put one's hat on; (*ciel*) become overcast.

covoiturage /kɔvwatyʀaʒ/ *nm* car sharing.

cracher /kʀaʃe/ [1] *vi* spit; (*radio*) crackle. ● *vt* spit (out); (*fumée*) belch out.

crachin /kʀaʃɛ̃/ *nm* drizzle.

craie /kʀɛ/ *nf* chalk.

craindre /kʀɛ̃dʀ/ [22] *vt* be afraid of, fear; (être sensible à) be easily damaged by.

crainte /kʀɛ̃t/ *nf* fear (**pour** for); **de ~ de/que** for fear of/that. **craintif, -ive** *a* timid.

crampon /kʀɑ̃pɔ̃/ *nm* (de chaussure) stud.

cramponner (se) /(sə)kʀɑ̃pɔne/ [1] *vpr se ~ à* cling to.

cran /kʀɑ̃/ *nm* (entaille) notch; (trou) hole; (courage 🔲) guts 🔲, courage; **~ de sûreté** safety catch.

crâne /kʀɑn/ *nm* skull.

crapaud /kʀapo/ *nm* toad.

craquer /kʀake/ [1] *vi* crack, snap; (*plancher*) creak; (*couture*) split; (fig) (*personne*) break down; (céder) give way. ● *vt* (*allumette*) strike; (*vêtement*) split.

crasse /kʀɑs/ *nf* grime.

cravache /kʀavaʃ/ *nf* (horse) whip.

cravate /kʀavat/ *nf* tie.

crayon /kʀejɔ̃/ *nm* pencil; **~ de couleur** coloured pencil; **~ à bille** ballpoint pen; **~ optique** light pen.

créateur, -trice /kʀeatœʀ, -tʀis/ *a* creative. ● *nm, f* creator, designer.

crèche /kʀɛʃ/ *nf* day nursery, crèche; (Relig) crib.

crédit /kʀedi/ *nm* credit; (somme allouée) funds; **à ~** on credit; **faire ~** give credit (à to).

créer /kʀee/ [15] *vt* create; (*produit*) design; (*société*) set up.

crémaillère /kʀemajɛʀ/ *nf* **pendre la ~** have a house-warming party.

crème /kʀɛm/ *a inv* cream. ● *nm* (café) **~** espresso with milk. ● *nf* cream; (dessert) cream dessert; **~ anglaise** egg custard; **~ fouettée** whipped cream; **~ pâtissière** confectioner's custard. **crémerie** *nf* dairy. **crémeux, -euse** *a* creamy. **crémier, -ière** *nm, f* dairyman, dairywoman.

créneau (*pl* **~x**) /kʀeno/ *nm* (trou, moment) slot, window; (dans le marché) gap; **faire un ~** parallel-park.

crêpe /kʀɛp/ *nf* (galette) pancake.

● *nm* (tissu) crêpe; (matière) crêpe (rubber).

crépitement /kʀepitmɑ̃/ *nm* crackling; (d'huile) sizzling.

crépuscule /kʀepyskyl/ *nm* twilight, dusk.

cresson /kʀesɔ̃/ *nm* (water)cress.

crête /kʀɛt/ *nf* crest; (de coq) comb.

crétin, ~e /kʀetɛ̃, -in/ *nm, f* 🔲 moron 🔲.

creuser /kʀøze/ [1] *vt* dig; (évider) hollow out; (fig) go into in depth. □ *vpr* (écart) widen; **se ~ (la cervelle)** 🔲 rack one's brains.

creux, -euse /kʀø, -z/ *a* hollow; (heures) off-peak. ● *nm* hollow; (de l'estomac) pit; **dans le ~ de la main** in the palm of the hand.

crevaison /kʀəvezɔ̃/ *nf* puncture.

crevasse /kʀəvas/ *nf* crack; (de glacier) crevasse; (de la peau) chap.

crevé, ~e /kʀəve/ *a* 🔲 worn out.

crever /kʀəve/ [1] *vt* burst; (*pneu*) puncture, burst; (exténuer 🔲) exhaust; (œil) put out. ● *vi* (*pneu, sac*) burst; (mourir 🔲) die.

crevette /kʀəvɛt/ *nf* **~ grise** shrimp; **~ rose** prawn.

cri /kʀi/ *nm* ⏥ (de douleur) scream, cry; **pousser un ~** cry out, scream.

criard, ~e /kʀijaʀ, -d/ *a* (couleur) garish; (voix) shrill.

crier /kʀije/ [45] *vi* (fort) shout, cry (out); (de douleur) scream; (grincer) creak. ● *vt* (ordre) shout (out).

crime /kʀim/ *nm* crime; (meurtre) murder.

criminel, ~le /kʀiminɛl/ *a* criminal. ● *nm, f* criminal; (assassin) murderer.

crinière /kʀinjɛʀ/ *nf* mane.

crise /kʀiz/ *nf* crisis; (Méd) attack; (de colère) fit; **~ cardiaque** heart attack; **~ de foie** bilious attack; **~ de nerfs** hysterics (+ *pl*).

crisper /kʀispe/ [1] *vt* tense; (énerver 🔲) irritate. □ **se** ~ *vpr* tense; (*mains*) clench.

critère /kʀitɛʀ/ *nm* criterion.

critique /kʀitik/ *a* critical. ● *nf* criticism; (*article*) review; (*commentateur*) critic; **la** ~ (*personnes*) the critics. **critiquer** [1] *vt* criticize.

Croate /kʀɔat/ *a* Croatian. **C**~ *nmf* Croatian.

Croatie /kʀɔasi/ *nf* Croatia.

croche /kʀɔʃ/ *nf* quaver.

croche-pied (*pl* ~**s**) /kʀɔʃpje/ *nm* **faire un** ~ **à** trip up.

crochet /kʀɔʃɛ/ *nm* hook; (détour) detour; (signe) (square) bracket; (tricot) crochet; **faire au** ~ crochet.

crochu, ~**e** /kʀɔʃy/ *a* hooked.

crocodile /kʀɔkɔdil/ *nm* crocodile.

croire /kʀwaʀ/ [23] *vt* believe (**à**, **en** in); (*estimer*) think, believe (**que** that). ● *vi* believe.

croisade /kʀwazad/ *nf* crusade.

croisement /kʀwazmɑ̃/ *nm* crossing; (fait de passer à côté de) passing; (carrefour) crossroads.

croiser /kʀwaze/ [1] *vi* (*bateau*) cruise. ● *vt* cross; (*passant*, *véhicule*) pass; ~ **les bras** fold one's arms; ~ **les jambes** cross one's legs; (*animaux*) crossbreed. □ **se** ~ *vpr* (*véhicules*, *piétons*) pass each other; (*lignes*) cross. **croisière** *nf* cruise.

croissance /kʀwasɑ̃s/ *nf* growth.

croissant, ~**e** /kʀwasɑ̃, -t/ *a* growing. ● *nm* crescent; (pâtisserie) croissant.

croix /kʀwa/ *nf* cross; ~ **gammée** swastika; **C**~**-Rouge** Red Cross.

croquant, ~**e** /kʀɔkɑ̃, -t/ *a* crunchy.

croque-monsieur /kʀɔkməsjø/ *nm inv* toasted ham and cheese sandwich.

croque-mort (*pl* ~**s**) /kʀɔkmɔʀ/ *nm* 🔲 undertaker.

croquer /kʀɔke/ [1] *vt* crunch; (dessiner) sketch; **chocolat à** ~ plain chocolate. ● *vi* be crunchy.

croquis /kʀɔki/ *nm* sketch.

crotte /kʀɔt/ *nf* dropping.

crotté, ~**e** /kʀɔte/ *a* muddy.

crottin /kʀɔtɛ̃/ *nm* (horse) dropping.

croupir /kʀupiʀ/ [2] *vi* stagnate.

croustillant, ~**e** /kʀustijɑ̃, -t/ *a* crispy; (*pain*) crusty; (fig) spicy.

croûte /kʀut/ *nf* crust; (de fromage) rind; (de plaie) scab; **en** ~ (Culin) in pastry.

croûton /kʀutɔ̃/ *nm* (bout de pain) crust; (avec potage) croûton.

CRS *abrév m* (**Compagnie républicaine de sécurité**) French riot police; **un** ~ *a member of the French riot police.*

cru[1] /kʀy/ ⇒CROIRE [23].

cru[2], ~**e** /kʀy/ *a* raw; (*lumière*) harsh; (*propos*) crude. ● *nm* vineyard; (vin) vintage wine.

crû /kʀy/ ⇒CROÎTRE [24].

cruauté /kʀyote/ *nf* cruelty.

cruche /kʀyʃ/ *nf* jug, pitcher.

crucial, ~**e** (*mpl* **-iaux**) /kʀysjal, -jo/ *a* crucial.

crudité /kʀydite/ *nf* (de langage) crudeness; ~**s** (Culin) raw vegetables.

crue /kʀy/ *nf* rise in water level; **en** ~ in spate.

crustacé /kʀystase/ *nm* shellfish.

cube /kyb/ *nm* cube. ● *a* (*mètre*) cubic.

cueillir /kœjiʀ/ [25] *vt* pick, gather; (*personne* 🔲) pick up.

cuiller, cuillère /kɥijɛʀ/ *nf* spoon; ~ **à soupe** soup spoon; (mesure) tablespoonful.

cuir /kɥiʀ/ *nm* leather; ~ **chevelu** scalp.

cuire /kɥiʀ/ [17] *vt* cook; ~ (**au**

four) bake. ●*vi* cook; **faire ~** cook.

cuisine /kɥizin/ *nf* kitchen; (art) cookery, cooking; (aliments) food; **faire la ~** cook.

cuisiner /kɥizine/ [1] *vt* cook; (interroger 🗊) grill. ●*vi* cook.

cuisinier, -ière /kɥizinje, -jɛʀ/ *nm, f* cook. **cuisinière** *nf* (appareil) cooker, stove.

cuisse /kɥis/ *nf* thigh; (de poulet) thigh; (de grenouille) leg.

cuisson /kɥisɔ̃/ *nf* cooking.

cuit ~**e** /kɥi, -t/ *a* cooked; **bien ~** well done *ou* cooked; **trop ~** overdone.

cuivre /kɥivʀ/ *nm* copper; ~ **(jaune)** brass; ~**s** (Mus) brass.

cul /ky/ *nm* (derrière 🖩) backside, bottom, arse 🖩.

culbuter /kylbyte/ [1] *vi* (personne) tumble; (objet) topple (over). ●*vt* knock over.

culminer /kylmine/ [1] *vi* reach its highest point *ou* peak.

culot /kylo/ *nm* (audace 🗊) nerve, cheek; (Tech) base.

culotte /kylɔt/ *nf* (de femme) pants (+ *pl*), knickers (+ *pl*); (US) panties (+ *pl*); ~ **de cheval** riding breeches; **en ~ courte** in short trousers.

culpabilité /kylpabilite/ *nf* guilt.

culte /kylt/ *nm* cult, worship; (religion) religion; (office protestant) service.

cultivateur, -trice /kyltivatœʀ, -tʀis/ *nm, f* farmer.

cultiver /kyltive/ [1] *vt* cultivate; (plantes) grow.

culture /kyltyʀ/ *nf* cultivation; (de plantes) growing; (agriculture) farming; (éducation) culture; (connaissances) knowledge; ~**s** (terrains) lands under cultivation; ~ **physique** physical training.

culturel, ~le /kyltyʀɛl/ *a* cultural.

cumuler /kymyle/ [1] *vt* accumulate; (fonctions) hold concurrently.

cure /kyʀ/ *nf* (course of) treatment.

curé /kyʀe/ *nm* (parish) priest.

cure-dent (*pl* ~**s**) /kyʀdɑ̃/ *nm* toothpick.

curer /kyʀe/ [1] *vt* clean. □ **se ~** *vpr* **se ~ les dents/ongles** clean one's teeth/nails.

curieux, -ieuse /kyʀjø, -z/ *a* curious. ●*nm, f* (badaud) onlooker.

curiosité /kyʀjozite/ *nf* curiosity; (objet) curio; (spectacle) unusual sight.

curriculum vitae /kyʀikylɔm vite/ *nm inv* curriculum vitae; (US) résumé.

curseur /kyʀsœʀ/ *nm* cursor.

cutané, ~e /kytane/ *a* skin.

cuve /kyv/ *nf* vat; (à mazout, eau) tank.

cuvée /kyve/ *nf* (de vin) vintage.

cuvette /kyvɛt/ *nf* bowl; (de lavabo) (wash)basin; (des cabinets) pan, bowl.

CV *abrév m* (**curriculum vitae**) CV.

cyberbranché, ~e /sibɛʀbʀɑ̃ʃe/ *a* cyberwired.

cybercafé /sibɛʀkafe/ *nm* cybercafe.

cyberespace /sibɛʀsɛpas/ *nm* cyberspace.

cybernaute /sibɛʀnot/ *nmf* Netsurfer.

cybernétique /sibɛʀnetik/ *nf* cybernetics (+ *pl*).

cyclisme /siklism/ *nm* cycling.

cycliste /siklist/ *nmf* cyclist. ●*nm* cycling shorts. ●*a* cycle.

cyclone /siklon/ *nm* cyclone.

cygne /siɲ/ *nm* swan.

cynique /sinik/ *a* cynical. ●*nm* cynic.

d' /d/ ⇒DE.

d'abord /dabɔʀ/ *adv* first; (au début) at first.

dactylo /daktilo/ *nf* typist. **dactylographier** [45] *vt* type.

dada /dada/ *nm* hobby-horse.

daim /dɛ̃/ *nm* (fallow) deer; (cuir) suede.

dallage /dalaʒ/ *nm* paving. **dalle** *nf* slab.

daltonien, ∼ne /daltɔnjɛ̃, -ɛn/ *a* colour-blind.

dame /dam/ *nf* lady; (cartes, échecs) queen; **∼s** (jeu) draughts; (US) checkers.

damier /damje/ *nm* draught-board; (US) checker-board; **à ∼** chequered.

damner /dane/ [1] *vt* damn.

dandiner (se) /(sə)dɑ̃dine/ [1] *vpr* waddle.

Danemark /danmaʀk/ *nm* Denmark.

danger /dɑ̃ʒe/ *nm* danger; **en ∼** in danger; **mettre en ∼** endanger.

dangereux, -euse /dɑ̃ʒ(ə)ʀø, -z/ *a* dangerous.

danois, ∼e /danwa, -z/ *a* Danish. ●*nm* (Ling) Danish. **D∼, ∼e** *nm, f* Dane.

dans /dɑ̃/ *prép* in; (mouvement) into; (à l'intérieur de) inside, in; **être ∼ un avion** be on a plane; **∼ dix jours** in ten days' time; **boire ∼ un verre** drink out of a glass; **∼ les 10 francs** about 10 francs.

danse /dɑ̃s/ *nf* dance; (art) dancing.

danser /dɑ̃se/ [1] *vt/i* dance. **danseur, -euse** *nm, f* dancer.

darne /daʀn/ *nf* steak (of fish).

date /dat/ *nf* date; **∼ limite** deadline; **∼ limite de vente** sell-by date; **∼ de péremption** use-by date.

dater /date/ [1] *vt/i* date; **à ∼ de** as from.

datte /dat/ *nf* (fruit) date.

daube /dob/ *nf* casserole.

dauphin /dofɛ̃/ *nm* (animal) dolphin.

davantage /davɑ̃taʒ/ *adv* more; (plus longtemps) longer; **∼ de** more; **je n'en sais pas ∼** that's as much as I know.

....

de, d' /də, d/

d' before vowel or mute h.

●*préposition*

····▸ of; **le livre ∼ mon ami** my friend's book; **un pont ∼ fer** an iron bridge.

····▸ (provenance) from.

····▸ (temporel) from; **∼ 8 heures à 10 heures** from 8 till 10.

····▸ (mesure, manière) **dix mètres ∼ haut** ten metres high; **pleurer ∼ rage** cry with rage.

····▸ (agent) by; **un livre ∼ Marcel Aymé** a book by Marcel Aymé.

●**de, de l', de la, du,** (*pl* **des**) *déterminant*

····▸ some; **du pain** (some) bread; **des fleurs** (some) flowers; **je ne bois jamais ∼ vin** I never drink wine.

de + le = du
de + les = des

....

dé /de/ *nm* (à jouer) dice; (à coudre) thimble; **∼s** (jeu) dice.

débâcle /debɑkl/ *nf* (Géog) breaking up; (Mil) rout.

déballer /debale/ [1] *vt* unpack;
(*révéler*) spill out.

débarbouiller /debaʀbuje/ *vt*
wash the face of. □ **se ~** *vpr*
wash one's face.

débarcadère /debaʀkadɛʀ/ *nm*
landing-stage.

débardeur /debaʀdœʀ/ *nm*
(*vêtement*) tank top.

débarquement /debaʀkəmɑ̃/ *nm*
disembarkation. **débarquer** [1]
vt/i disembark, land; (*arriver* 🔲)
turn up.

débarras /debaʀa/ *nm* junk
room; **bon ~!** good riddance!

débarrasser /debaʀase/ [1] *vt*
clear (**de** of); **~ qn de** relieve sb
of; (*défaut, ennemi*) rid sb of. □ **se
~ de** *vpr* get rid of.

débat /deba/ *nm* debate.

débattre /debatʀ/ [11] *vt* debate.
●*vi* **~ de** discuss. □ **se ~** *vpr*
struggle (to get free).

débauche /deboʃ/ *nf*
debauchery; (fig) profusion.

débaucher /deboʃe/ [1] *vt*
(*licencier*) lay off; (*distraire*) tempt
away.

débile /debil/ *a* weak; 🔲 stupid.
●*nmf* moron 🔲.

débit /debi/ *nm* (rate of) flow;
(*élocution*) delivery; (*de compte*)
debit; **~ de tabac** tobacconist's
shop; **~ de boissons** bar.

débiter /debite/ [1] *vt* (*compte*)
debit; (*fournir*) produce; (*vendre*)
sell; (*dire*: péj) spout; (*couper*) cut
up.

débiteur, -trice /debitœʀ, -tʀis/
nm, f debtor. ●*a* (*compte*) in
debit.

déblayer /debleje/ [31] *vt* clear.

déblocage /deblɔkaʒ/ *nm* (de prix)
deregulating. **débloquer** [1] *vt*
(*prix, salaires*) unfreeze.

déboiser /debwaze/ [1] *vt* clear
(of trees).

déboîter /debwate/ [1] *vi*
(*véhicule*) pull out. ●*vt* (*membre*)
dislocate.

débordement /debɔʀdəmɑ̃/ *nm*
(de joie) excess.

déborder /debɔʀde/ [1] *vi*
overflow. ●*vt* (*dépasser*) extend
beyond; **~ de** (*joie etc.*) be
brimming over with.

débouché /debuʃe/ *nm* opening;
(*carrière*) prospect; (Comm) outlet;
(*sortie*) end, exit.

déboucher /debuʃe/ [1] *vt*
(*bouteille*) uncork; (*évier*)
unblock. ●*vi* come out (**de** from);
~ sur (*rue*) lead into.

débourser /debuʀse/ [1] *vt* pay
out.

debout /dəbu/ *adv* standing; (levé,
éveillé) up; **être ~, se tenir ~** be
standing, stand; **se mettre ~**
stand up.

déboutonner /debutɔne/ [1] *vt*
unbutton. □ **se ~** *vpr* unbutton
oneself; (*vêtement*) come undone.

débrancher /debʀɑ̃ʃe/ [1] *vt*
(*prise*) unplug; (*système*)
disconnect.

débrayer /debʀeje/ [31] *vi* (Auto)
declutch; (faire grève) stop work.

debris /debʀi/ *nmpl* fragments;
(*détritus*) rubbish (+ *sg*); debris.

débrouillard, ~e /debʀujaʀ, -d/
a 🔲 resourceful.

débrouiller /debʀuje/ [1] *vt*
disentangle; (*problème*) solve.
□ **se ~** *vpr* manage.

début /deby/ *nm* beginning; **faire
ses ~s** (en public) make one's
début; **à mes ~s** when I started
out. **débutant, ~e** *nm, f*
beginner. **débuter** [1] *vi* begin;
(dans un métier etc.) start out.

déca /deka/ *nm* 🔲 decaf.

deçà /dəsa/ **~ de** /ɑ̃dəsa/ *loc* this side.
●*prép* **en ~ de** this side of.

décacheter /dekaʃte/ [6] *vt*
open.

D

décade /dekad/ *nf* ten days; (décennie) decade.

décadent, ~e /dekadɑ̃, -t/ *a* decadent.

décalage /dekalaʒ/ *nm* (écart) gap; ~ **horaire** time difference.
décaler [1] *vt* shift.

décalquer /dekalke/ [1] *vt* trace.

décamper /dekɑ̃pe/ [1] *vi* clear off.

décanter /dekɑ̃te/ *vt* allow to settle. □ **se ~** *vpr* settle.

décapant /dekapɑ̃/ *nm* chemical agent; (pour peinture) paint stripper.
● *a* (humour) caustic.

décapotable /dekapɔtabl/ *a* convertible.

décapsuleur /dekapsylœr/ *nm* bottle-opener.

décédé, ~e /desede/ *a* deceased.
décéder [14] *vi* die.

déceler /desle/ [6] *vt* detect; (démontrer) reveal.

décembre /desɑ̃br/ *nm* December.

décemment /desamɑ̃/ *adv* decently. **décence** *nf* decency.
décent, ~e *a* decent.

décennie /deseni/ *nf* decade.

décentralisation /desɑ̃tralizasjɔ̃/ *nf* decentralization. **décentraliser** [1] *vt* decentralize.

déception /desɛpsjɔ̃/ *nf* disappointment.

décerner /desɛrne/ [1] *vt* award.

décès /desɛ/ *nm* death.

décevant, ~e /des(ə)vɑ̃, -t/ *a* disappointing. **décevoir** [52] *vt* disappoint.

déchaîner /deʃene/ [1] *vt* (enthousiasme) rouse. □ **se ~** *vpr* go wild.

décharge /deʃarʒ/ *nf* (de fusil) discharge; ~ **électrique** electric shock; ~ **publique** municipal dump.

décharger /deʃarʒe/ [40] *vt*

unload; ~ **qn de** relieve sb from.
□ **se ~** *vpr* (batterie, pile) go flat.

déchausser (se) /(sə)deʃose/ [1] *vpr* take off one's shoes; (dent) work loose.

dèche /dɛʃ/ *nf* 🔲 **dans la ~** broke.

déchéance /deʃeɑ̃s/ *nf* decay.

déchet /deʃɛ/ *nm* (reste) scrap; (perte) waste; ~**s** (ordures) refuse.

déchiffrer /deʃifre/ [1] *vt* decipher.

déchiqueter /deʃikte/ [38] *vt* tear to shreds.

déchirement /deʃirmɑ̃/ *nm* heartbreak; (conflit) split.

déchirer /deʃire/ [1] *vt* (par accident) tear; (lacérer) tear up; (arracher) tear off *ou* out; (diviser) tear apart. □ **se ~** *vpr* tear.
déchirure *nf* tear.

décibel /desibɛl/ *nm* decibel.

décidément /desidemɑ̃/ *adv* really.

décider /deside/ [1] *vt* decide on; (persuader) persuade; ~ **que**/**de** decide that/to; ~ **de qch** decide on sth. □ **se ~** *vpr* make up one's mind (**à** to).

décimal, ~e (*mpl* ~**aux**) /desimal, -o/ *a* & *nf* decimal.

décisif, -ive /desizif, -v/ *a* decisive.

décision /desizjɔ̃/ *nf* decision.

déclaration /deklarasjɔ̃/ *nf* declaration; (commentaire politique) statement; ~ **d'impôts** tax return.

déclarer /deklare/ [1] *vt* declare; (naissance) register; **déclaré coupable** found guilty; ~ **forfait** (Sport) withdraw. □ **se ~** *vpr* (feu) break out.

déclencher /deklɑ̃ʃe/ [1] *vt* (Tech) set off; (conflit) spark off; (avalanche) start; (rire) provoke.
□ **se ~** *vpr* (Tech) go off.
déclencheur *nm* (Photo) shutter release.

déclic /deklik/ *nm* click.

déclin /deklɛ̃/ nm decline.

déclinaison /deklinɛzɔ̃/ nf (Ling) declension.

décliner /dekline/ [1] vt (refuser) decline; (dire) state; (Ling) decline.

décocher /dekɔʃe/ [1] vt (coup) fling; (regard) shoot.

décollage /dekɔlaʒ/ nm take-off.

décoller /dekɔle/ [1] vt unstick. ● vi (avion) take off. □ se ~ vpr come off.

décolleté, **~e** /dekɔlte/ a low-cut. ● nm low neckline.

décolorer /dekɔlɔre/ [1] vt fade; (cheveux) bleach. □ se ~ vpr fade.

décombres /dekɔ̃bR/ nmpl rubble.

décommander /dekɔmɑ̃de/ [1] vt cancel.

décomposer /dekɔ̃poze/ [1] vt break up; (substance) decompose. □ se ~ vpr decompose.

décompte /dekɔ̃t/ nm deduction; (détail) breakdown.

décongeler /dekɔ̃ʒle/ [6] vt thaw.

déconseillé, **~e** /dekɔ̃sɛje/ a not recommended, inadvisable.

déconseiller /dekɔ̃sɛje/ [1] vt ~ qch à qn advise sb against sth.

décontracté, **~e** /dekɔ̃trakte/ a relaxed.

déconvenue /dekɔ̃vny/ nf disappointment.

décor /dekɔR/ nm (paysage) scenery; (de cinéma, théâtre) set; (cadre) setting; (de maison) décor.

décoratif, **-ive** /dekɔratif, -v/ a decorative.

décorateur, **-trice** /dekɔratœr, -tris/ nm, f (de cinéma) set designer. **décoration** nf decoration. **décorer** [1] vt decorate.

décortiquer /dekɔrtike/ [1] vt shell; (fig) dissect.

découdre (se) /(sə)dekudR/ [19] vpr come unstitched.

découler /dekule/ [1] vi ~ de follow from.

découper /dekupe/ [1] vt cut up; (viande) carve; (détacher) cut out.

découragement /dekuraʒmɑ̃/ nm discouragement.

décourager /dekuraʒe/ [40] vt discourage. □ se ~ vpr become discouraged.

décousu, **~e** /dekuzy/ a (vêtement) which has come unstitched; (idées) disjointed.

découvert, **~e** /dekuvɛR, -t/ a (tête) bare; (terrain) open. ● nm (de compte) overdraft; **à ~** exposed; (fig) openly.

découverte /dekuvɛRt/ nf discovery; **à la ~ de** in search of.

découvrir /dekuvriR/ [21] vt discover; (voir) see; (montrer) reveal. □ se ~ vpr (se décoiffer) take one's hat off; (ciel) clear.

décrasser /dekRase/ [1] vt clean.

décrépit, **~e** /dekRepi, -t/ a decrepit. **décrépitude** nf decay.

décret /dekRɛ/ nm decree.

décréter [14] vt order; (dire) declare.

décrié, **~e** /dekRije/ a criticized.

décrire /dekRiR/ [30] vt describe.

décroché, **~e** /dekRɔʃe/ a (téléphone) off the hook.

décrocher /dekRɔʃe/ [1] vt unhook; (obtenir 🔟) get. ● vi (abandonner 🔟) give up; ~ (le téléphone) pick up the phone.

décroître /dekRwatR/ [24] vi decrease.

déçu, **~e** /desy/ a disappointed.

décupler /dekyple/ [1] vt/i increase tenfold.

dédaigner /dedene/ [1] vt scorn.

dédain /dedɛ̃/ nm scorn.

dédale /dedal/ nm maze.

dedans /dədɑ̃/ adv & nm inside; **en ~** on the inside.

dédicacer /dedikase/ [10] *vt* dedicate; (signer) sign.

dédier /dedje/ [45] *vt* dedicate.

dédommagement /dedɔmaʒmɑ̃/ *nm* compensation. **dédommager** [40] *vt* compensate (**de** for).

déduction /dedyksjɔ̃/ *nf* deduction; ~ **d'impôts** tax deduction.

déduire /dedɥiʀ/ [17] *vt* deduct; (conclure) deduce.

déesse /dees/ *nf* goddess.

défaillance /defajɑ̃s/ *nf* (panne) failure; (évanouissement) blackout. **défaillant**, ~**e** *a* (système) faulty; (personne) faint.

défaire /defɛʀ/ [33] *vt* undo; (valise) unpack; (démonter) take down. □ **se** ~ *vpr* come undone; **se** ~ **de** rid oneself of.

défait, ~**e** /defɛ, -t/ *a* (cheveux) ruffled; (visage) haggard; (nœud) undone. **défaite** *nf* defeat.

défaitiste /defetist/ *a* & *nmf* defeatist.

défalquer /defalke/ [1] *vt* (somme) deduct.

défaut /defo/ *nm* fault, defect; (d'un verre, diamant, etc.) flaw; (pénurie) shortage; **à** ~ **de** for lack of; **pris en** ~ caught out; **faire** ~ (argent etc.) be lacking; **par** ~ (Jur) in one's absence; ~ **de paiement** non-payment.

défavorable /defavɔʀabl/ *a* unfavourable.

défavoriser /defavɔʀize/ [1] *vt* discriminate against.

défectueux, -euse /defɛktɥø, -z/ *a* faulty, defective.

défendre /defɑ̃dʀ/ [3] *vt* defend; (interdire) forbid; ~ **à qn de** forbid sb to. □ **se** ~ *vpr* defend oneself; (se protéger) protect oneself; (se débrouiller) manage; **se** ~ **de** (refuser) refrain from.

défense /defɑ̃s/ *nf* defence; ~ **de fumer** no smoking; (d'éléphant) tusk.

défenseur *nm* defender.
défensif, -ive *a* defensive.

déferler /defɛʀle/ [1] *vi* (vagues) break; (violence) erupt.

défi /defi/ *nm* challenge; (provocation) defiance; **mettre au** ~ challenge.

déficience /defisjɑ̃s/ *nf* deficiency. **déficient**, ~**e** *a* deficient.

déficit /defisit/ *nm* deficit. **déficitaire** *a* in deficit.

défier /defje/ [45] *vt* challenge; (braver) defy.

défilé /defile/ *nm* procession; (Mil) parade; (fig) (continual) stream; (Géog) gorge; ~ **de mode** fashion parade.

défiler /defile/ [1] *vi* march; (visiteurs) stream; (images) flash by; (chiffres, minutes) add up. □ **se** ~ *vpr* 🗆 sneak off.

défini, ~**e** /defini/ *a* (Ling) definite.

définir /definiʀ/ [2] *vt* define.

définitif, -ive /definitif, -v/ *a* final, definitive; **en définitive** in the end.

définition /definisjɔ̃/ *nf* definition; (de mots croisés) clue.

définitivement /definitivmɑ̃/ *adv* definitively, permanently.

déflagration /deflagʀasjɔ̃/ *nf* explosion.

déflation /deflasjɔ̃/ *nf* deflation. **déflationniste** *a* deflationary.

défoncé, ~**e** /defɔ̃se/ *a* (terrain) full of potholes; (siège) broken; (drogué: 🗆) high.

défoncer /defɔ̃se/ [10] *vt* (porte) break down; (mâchoire) break. □ **se** ~ *vpr* 🗆 to give one's all.

déformation /defɔʀmasjɔ̃/ *nf* distortion. **déformer** [1] *vt* put out of shape; (faits, pensée) distort.

défouler (se) /(sə)defule/ [1] *vpr* let off steam.

défrayer /defʀeje/ [31] *vt* (payer) pay the expenses of; ~ **la chronique** be the talk of the town.

défricher /defʀiʃe/ [1] *vt* clear.

défroisser /defʀwase/ [1] *vt* smooth out.

défunt, ~**e** /defœ̃, -t/ *a* (mort) late. ● *nm, f* deceased.

dégagé, ~**e** /degaʒe/ *a* (ciel) clear; (front) bare; **d'un ton** ~ casually.

dégagement /degaʒmɑ̃/ *nm* clearing; (football) clearance.

dégager /degaʒe/ [40] *vt* (exhaler) give off; (désencombrer) clear; (faire ressortir) bring out; (ballon) clear. □ **se** ~ *vpr* free oneself; (ciel, rue) clear; (odeur) emanate.

dégarnir (se) /(sə)degaʀniʀ/ [2] *vpr* clear, empty; (personne) be going bald.

dégâts /dega/ *nmpl* damage (+ sg).

dégel /deʒɛl/ *nm* thaw. **dégeler** [6] *vi* thaw (out).

dégénéré, ~**e** /deʒeneʀe/ *a & nm,f* degenerate.

dégivrer /deʒivʀe/ [1] *vt* (Auto) de-ice; (réfrigérateur) defrost.

déglinguer /deglɛ̃ge/ 🄴 [1] *vt* bust. □ **se** ~ *vpr* break down.

dégonflé, ~**e** /degõfle/ *a* (pneu) flat; (lâche 🄴) yellow 🄴.

dégonfler /degõfle/ [1] *vt* deflate. ● *vi* (blessure) go down. □ **se** ~ *vpr* 🄴 chicken out.

dégouliner /deguline/ [1] *vi* trickle.

dégourdi, ~**e** /deguʀdi/ *a* smart.

dégourdir /deguʀdiʀ/ [2] *vt* (membre, liquide) warm up. □ **se** ~ *vpr* **se** ~ **les jambes** stretch one's legs.

dégoût /degu/ *nm* disgust.

dégoûtant, ~**e** /degutɑ̃, -t/ *a* disgusting.

dégoûter /degute/ [1] *vt* disgust; ~ **qn de qch** put sb off sth.

dégradant, ~**e** /degʀadɑ̃, -t/ *a* degrading.

dégradation /degʀadasjõ/ *nf* damage; **commettre des** ~**s** cause damage.

dégrader /degʀade/ [1] *vt* (abîmer) damage. □ **se** ~ *vpr* (se détériorer) deteriorate.

dégrafer /degʀafe/ [1] *vt* unhook.

degré /dəgʀe/ *nm* degree; (d'escalier) step.

dégressif, -**ive** /degʀesif, -v/ *a* graded; **tarif** ~ tapering charge.

dégrèvement /degʀɛvmɑ̃/ *nm* ~ **fiscal** *ou* **d'impôts** tax reduction.

dégringolade /degʀɛ̃gɔlad/ *nf* tumble.

dégrossir /degʀosiʀ/ [2] *vt* (bois) trim; (projet) rough out.

déguerpir /degɛʀpiʀ/ [2] *vi* clear off.

dégueulasse /degœlas/ *a* 🄴 disgusting, lousy.

dégueuler /degœle/ [1] *vt* 🄴 throw up.

déguisement /degizmɑ̃/ *nm* (de carnaval) fancy dress; (pour duper) disguise.

déguiser /degize/ [1] *vt* dress up; (pour duper) disguise. □ **se** ~ *vpr* (au carnaval etc.) dress up; (pour duper) disguise oneself.

déguster /degyste/ [1] *vt* taste, sample; (savourer) enjoy.

dehors /dəɔʀ/ *adv* **en** ~ **de** outside; (hormis) apart from; **jeter/ mettre** ~ throw/put out. ● *nm* outside.

● *nmpl* (aspect de qn) exterior.

déjà /deʒa/ *adv* already; (avant) before, already.

déjeuner /deʒœne/ [1] *vi* have lunch; (le matin) have breakfast. ● *nm* lunch; **petit** ~ breakfast.

delà /dəla/ *adv & prép* **au** ~ **(de)**, **par** ~ beyond.

délai /delɛ/ *nm* time-limit; (attente) wait; (sursis) extension (of time);

sans ~ immediately; **dans un** ~
de 2 jours within 2 days; **finir dans
les** ~**s** finish within the deadline;
dans les plus brefs ~**s** as soon as
possible.

délaisser /delese/ [1] *vt* (*négliger*)
neglect.

délassement /delasmã/ *nm*
relaxation.

délation /delasjõ/ *nf* informing.

délavé, ~**e** /delave/ *a* faded.

délayer /deleje/ [31] *vt* mix (with
liquid); (*idée*) drag out.

délecter (se) /(sə)delɛkte/ [1]
vpr **se** ~ **de** delight in.

délégué, ~**e** /delege/ *nm, f*
delegate.

délibéré, ~**e** /delibeʀe/ *a*
deliberate; (*résolu*) determined.

délicat, ~**e** /delika, -t/ *a*
delicate; (plein de tact) tactful.
délicatesse *nf* delicacy; (tact)
tact. **délicatesses** *nfpl* (kind)
attentions.

délice /delis/ *nm* delight.
délicieux, **-ieuse** *a* (au goût)
delicious; (*charmant*) delightful.

délier /delje/ [45] *vt* untie;
(délivrer) free. □ **se** ~ *vpr* come
untied.

délimiter /delimite/ [1] *vt*
determine, demarcate.

délinquance /delɛ̃kɑ̃s/ *nf*
delinquency. **délinquant**, ~**e** *a &
nm, f* delinquent.

délirant, ~**e** /deliʀɑ̃, -t/ *a*
delirious; (frénétique) frenzied; Ⅱ
wild.

délire /deliʀ/ *nm* delirium; (fig)
frenzy. **délirer** [1] *vi* be delirious
(**de** with); Ⅱ be off one's rocker
Ⅱ.

délit /deli/ *nm* offence.

délivrance /delivʀɑ̃s/ *nf* release;
(soulagement) relief; (remise) issue.
délivrer [1] *vt* free, release;
(pays) liberate; (remettre) issue.

déloyal, ~**e** (*mpl* **-aux**)
/delwajal, -jo/ *a* disloyal;
(procédé) unfair.

deltaplane /dɛltaplan/ *nm* hang-
glider.

déluge /delyʒ/ *nm* downpour; **le
D**~ the Flood.

démagogie /demagɔʒi/ *nm*
demagogy. **démagogue** *nmf*
demagogue.

demain /dəmɛ̃/ *adv* tomorrow.

demande /dəmɑ̃d/ *nf* request; ~
d'emploi job application; ~ **en
mariage** marriage proposal.

demander /dəmɑ̃de/ [1] *vt* ask
for; (chemin, heure) ask;
(nécessiter) require; ~ **que/si** ask
that/if; ~ **qch à qn** ask sb sth; ~ **à
qn de** ask sb to; ~ **en mariage**
propose to. □ **se** ~ *vpr* **se** ~ **si/où**
wonder if/where.

demandeur, **-euse** /dəmɑ̃dœʀ,
-øz/ *nm, f* ~ **d'emploi** job seeker;
~ **d'asile** asylum-seeker.

démangeaison /demɑ̃ʒɛzõ/ *nf*
itch(ing).

démanteler /demɑ̃tle/ [6] *vt*
break up.

démaquillant /demakijɑ̃/ *nm*
make-up remover. **démaquiller
(se)** [1] *vpr* remove one's
make-up.

démarchage /demaʀʃaʒ/ *nm*
door-to-door selling.

démarche /demaʀʃ/ *nf* walk,
gait; (procédé) step.

démarcheur, **-euse** /demaʀʃœʀ,
-øz/ *nm, f* (door-to-door)
canvasser.

démarrage /demaʀaʒ/ *nm* start.

démarrer /demaʀe/ [1] *vi*
(moteur) start (up); (partir) move
off; (fig) get moving. ● *vt* Ⅱ get
moving.

démarreur /demaʀœʀ/ *nm*
starter.

démêlant /demelɑ̃/ *nm*

conditioner. **démêler** [1] *vt* disentangle.

déménagement /demenaʒmɑ̃/ *nm* move; (transport) removal.

déménager /demenaʒe/ [40] *vi* move (house). ● *vt* (*meubles*) remove.

déménageur /demenaʒœR/ *nm* removal man.

démence /demɑ̃s/ *nf* insanity.

démener (se) /(sə)demne/ [6] *vpr* move about wildly; (fig) put oneself out.

dément, **~e** /demɑ̃, -t/ *a* insane. ● *nm, f* lunatic.

démenti /demɑ̃ti/ *nm* denial.

démentir /demɑ̃tiR/ [46] *vt* deny; (contredire) refute; **~ que** deny that.

démerder (se) /(sə)demɛRde/ [1] *vpr* ⊠ manage.

démettre /demɛtR/ [42] *vt* (*poignet etc.*) dislocate; **~ qn de** relieve sb of. □ **se ~** *vpr* resign (de from).

demeure /dəmœR/ *nf* residence; **mettre en ~ de** order to.

demeurer /dəmœre/ [1] *vi* live; (rester) remain.

demi, **~e** /dəmi/ *a* half(-). ● *nm, f* half. ● *nm* (bière) (half pint) glass of beer; (football) half-back. ● *adv* **à ~** half; (*ouvrir, fermer*) half-way; **à la ~e** at half past; **une heure et ~e** an hour and a half; (à l'horloge) half past one; **une ~-journée/-livre** half a day/pound. **demi-cercle** (*pl* **~s**) *nm* semicircle. **demi-finale** (*pl* **~s**) *nf* semifinal. **demi-frère** (*pl* **~s**) *nm* half-brother, stepbrother. **demi-heure** (*pl* **~s**) *nf* half-hour, half an hour. **demi-litre** (*pl* **~s**) *nm* half a litre. **demi-mesure** (*pl* **~s**) *nf* half-measure. **à demi-mot** *adv* without having to express every word. **demi-pension** *nf* half-board. **demi-queue** *nm* boudoir grand piano.

demi-sel *a inv* slightly salted.

demi-sœur (*pl* **~s**) *nf* half-sister, stepsister.

démission /demisjɔ̃/ *nf* resignation.

demi-tarif (*pl* **~s**) /dəmitaRif/ *nm* half-fare.

demi-tour (*pl* **~s**) /dəmituR/ *nm* about turn; (Auto) U-turn; **faire ~** turn back.

démocrate /demɔkRat/ *nmf* democrat. ● *a* democratic. **démocratie** *nf* democracy.

démodé, **~e** /demɔde/ *a* old-fashioned.

demoiselle /dəmwazɛl/ *nf* young lady; (célibataire) single lady; **~ d'honneur** bridesmaid.

démolir /demɔliR/ [2] *vt* demolish.

démon /demɔ̃/ *nm* demon; **le D~** the Devil. **démoniaque** *a* fiendish.

démonstration /demɔ̃stRasjɔ̃/ *nf* demonstration; (de force) show.

démonter /demɔ̃te/ [1] *vt* take apart, dismantle; (*installation*) take down; (fig) disconcert. □ **se ~** *vpr* come apart.

démontrer /demɔ̃tRe/ [1] *vt* demonstrate; (indiquer) show.

démoraliser /demɔRalize/ [1] *vt* demoralize.

démuni, **~e** /demyni/ *a* impoverished; **~ de** without.

démunir /demyniR/ [2] *vt* **~ de** deprive of. □ **se ~ de** *vpr* part with.

dénaturer /denatyRe/ [1] *vt* (*faits*) distort.

dénigrement /denigRəmɑ̃/ *nm* denigration.

dénivellation /denivɛlasjɔ̃/ *nf* (pente) slope.

dénombrer /denɔ̃bRe/ [1] *vt* count.

dénomination /denɔminasjɔ̃/ *nf* designation.

dénommé, ~e /denɔme/ *nm, f* le ~ **X** the said X.

dénoncer /denɔ̃se/ [10] *vt* denounce. □ se ~ *vpr* give oneself up. **dénonciateur, -trice** *nm, f* informer.

dénouement /denumɑ̃/ *nm* outcome; (Théât) dénouement.

dénouer /denwe/ [1] *vt* undo. □ se ~ *vpr* (*nœud*) come undone.

dénoyauter /denwajote/ [1] *vt* stone.

denrée /dɑ̃ʀe/ *nf* ~ **alimentaire** foodstuff.

dense /dɑ̃s/ *a* dense. **densité** *nf* density.

dent /dɑ̃/ *nf* tooth; **faire ses ~s** teethe; ~ **de lait** milk tooth; ~ **de sagesse** wisdom tooth; (de roue) cog. **dentaire** *a* dental.

denté, ~e /dɑ̃te/ *a* (*roue*) toothed

dentelé, ~e /dɑ̃tle/ *a* jagged.

dentelle /dɑ̃tɛl/ *nf* lace.

dentier /dɑ̃tje/ *nm* dentures (+ *pl*), false teeth (+ *pl*).

dentifrice /dɑ̃tifʀis/ *nm* toothpaste.

dentiste /dɑ̃tist/ *nmf* dentist.

dentition /dɑ̃tisjɔ̃/ *nf* teeth, dentition.

dénudé, ~e /denyde/ *a* bare.

dénué, ~e /denɥe/ *a* ~ **de** devoid of.

dénuement /denymɑ̃/ *nm* destitution.

déodorant /deɔdɔʀɑ̃/ *nm* deodorant.

dépannage /depanaʒ/ *nm* repair; (Ordinat) troubleshooting. **dépanner** [1] *vt* repair; (fig) help out. **dépanneuse** *nf* breakdown lorry.

dépareillé, ~e /depaʀeje/ *a* odd, not matching.

départ /depaʀ/ *nm* departure; (Sport) start; **au ~ de Nice** from Nice; **au ~** (d'abord) at first.

département /depaʀtəmɑ̃/ *nm* department.

dépassé, ~e /depɑse/ *a* outdated.

dépasser /depɑse/ [1] *vt* go past, pass; (*véhicule*) overtake; (excéder) exceed; (*rival*) surpass; **ça me dépasse** Ⓘ it's beyond me. ● *vi* stick out.

dépaysement /depeizmɑ̃/ *nm* change of scenery; (désagréable) disorientation.

dépêche /depɛʃ/ *nf* dispatch.

dépêcher /depɛʃe/ [1] *vt* dispatch. □ se ~ *vpr* hurry (up).

dépendance /depɑ̃dɑ̃s/ *nf* dependence; (à une drogue) dependency; (bâtiment) outbuilding.

dépendre /depɑ̃dʀ/ [3] *vt* take down. ● *vi* depend (de on); ~ de (appartenir à) belong to.

dépens /depɑ̃/ *nmpl* **aux ~ de** at the expense of.

dépense /depɑ̃s/ *nf* expense; expenditure.

dépenser /depɑ̃se/ [1] *vt/i* spend; (*énergie etc.*) use up. □ se ~ *vpr* get some exercise.

dépérir /depeʀiʀ/ [2] *vi* wither.

dépêtrer (se) /(sə)depetʀe/ [1] *vpr* get oneself out (de of).

dépeupler /depœple/ [1] *vt* depopulate. □ se ~ *vpr* become depopulated.

déphasé, ~e /defaze/ *a* Ⓘ out of step.

dépilatoire /depilatwaʀ/ *a & nm* depilatory.

dépistage /depistaʒ/ *nm* screening. **dépister** [1] *vt* detect; (*criminel*) track down.

dépit /depi/ *nm* resentment; **par ~** out of pique; **en ~ de** despite; **en ~ du bon sens** in a very illogical way. **dépité**, ~e *a* vexed.

déplacé, ~**e** /deplase/ *a*
(*remarque*) uncalled for.

déplacement /deplasmɑ̃/ *nm*
(*voyage*) trip.

déplacer /deplase/ [10] *vt* move.
□ **se** ~ *vpr* move; (*voyager*) travel.

déplaire /deplɛʀ/ [47] *vi* ~ **à**
(*irriter*) displease; **ça me déplaît** I
don't like it.

déplaisant, ~**e** /deplɛzɑ̃, -t/ *a*
unpleasant, disagreeable.

dépliant /deplijɑ̃/ *nm* leaflet.

déplier /deplije/ [45] *vt* unfold.

déploiement /deplwamɑ̃/ *nm*
(*démonstration*) display; (*militaire*)
deployment.

déplorable /deplɔʀabl/ *a*
deplorable. **déplorer** [1] *vt* (*trouver
regrettable*) deplore; (*mort*) lament.

déployer /deplwaje/ [31] *vt*
(*ailes, carte*) spread; (*courage*)
display; (*armée*) deploy.

déportation /depɔʀtasjɔ̃/ *nf* (en
1940) internment in a
concentration camp.

déposer /depoze/ [1] *vt* put
down; (*laisser*) leave; (*passager*)
drop; (*argent*) deposit; (*plainte*)
lodge; (*armes*) lay down. ●*vi* (Jur)
testify. □ **se** ~ *vpr* settle.

dépositaire /depozitɛʀ/ *nmf*
(Comm) agent.

déposition /depozisjɔ̃/ *nf* (Jur)
statement.

dépôt /depo/ *nm* (*entrepôt*)
warehouse; (*d'autobus*) depot;
(*particules*) deposit; (*garantie*)
deposit; **laisser en** ~ give for safe
keeping; ~ **légal** formal deposit
of a publication with an
institution.

dépouille /depuj/ *nf* skin, hide;
~ (**mortelle**) mortal remains.

dépouiller /depuje/ [1] *vt*
(*courrier*) open; (*scrutin*) count;
(*écorcher*) skin; ~ **qn de** strip sb of.

dépourvu, ~**e** /depuʀvy/ *a* ~ **de**

devoid of; **prendre au** ~ catch
unawares.

déprécier /depʀesje/ [45] *vt*
depreciate. □ **se** ~ *vpr*
depreciate.

déprédations /depʀedasjɔ̃/ *nfpl*
damage (+ *sg*).

dépression /depʀesjɔ̃/ *nf*
depression; ~ **nerveuse** nervous
breakdown.

déprimer /depʀime/ [1] *vt*
depress.

....

depuis /dəpɥi/

●*préposition*

····▸ (*point de départ*) since; ~ **quand
attendez-vous?** how long have
you been waiting?

····▸ (*durée*) for; ~ **toujours** always;
~ **peu** recently.

●*adverbe*

····▸ since; **il a eu une attaque le
mois dernier,** ~ **nous sommes
inquiets** he had a stroke last
month and we've been worried
ever since.

●**depuis que** *conjonction*

····▸ since, ever since: **Sophie a
beaucoup changé depuis que
Camille est née** Sophie has
changed a lot since Camille was
born.

....

député /depyte/ *nm* ≈ Member
of Parliament.

déraciné, -**e** /deʀasine/ *nm, f*
rootless person.

déraillement /deʀajmɑ̃/ *nm*
derailment.

dérailler /deʀaje/ [1] *vi* be
derailed; (fig 🄓) be talking
nonsense; **faire** ~ derail.
dérailleur *nm* (de vélo) derailleur.

déraisonnable /deʀɛzɔnabl/ *a*
unreasonable.

dérangement /deʀɑ̃ʒmɑ̃/ *nm*

bother; (*désordre*) disorder, upset; **en** ~ out of order; **les** ~**s** the fault reporting service.

déranger /deʀɑ̃ʒe/ [40] vt (*gêner*) bother, disturb; (*dérégler*) upset, disrupt. □ **se** ~ vpr (aller) go; (fig) put oneself out; **ça te dérangerait de...?** would you mind...?

dérapage /deʀapaʒ/ nm skid. **déraper** [1] vi skid; (fig) (*prix*) get out of control.

déréglé, ~**e** /deʀegle/ a (*vie*) dissolute; (*estomac*) upset; (*mécanisme*) (that is) not running properly.

dérégler /deʀegle/ [14] vt make go wrong. □ **se** ~ vpr go wrong.

dérision /deʀizjɔ̃/ nf mockery; **tourner en** ~ ridicule.

dérive /deʀiv/ nf **aller à la** ~ drift.

dérivé /deʀive/ nm by-product.

dériver /deʀive/ [1] vi (*bateau*) drift; ~ **de** stem from.

dermatologie /dɛʀmatɔlɔʒi/ nf dermatology.

dernier, -ière /dɛʀnje, -jɛʀ/ a last; (*nouvelles, mode*) latest; (*étage*) top. ● nm, f last (one); **ce** ~ the latter; **le** ~ **de mes soucis** the least of my worries.

dernièrement /dɛʀnjɛʀmɑ̃/ adv recently.

dérober /deʀɔbe/ [1] vt steal. □ **se** ~ vpr slip away; **se** ~ **à** (*obligation*) shy away from.

dérogation /deʀɔgasjɔ̃/ nf special authorization.

déroger /deʀɔʒe/ [40] vi ~ **à** depart from.

déroulement /deʀulmɑ̃/ nm (d'une action) development.

dérouler /deʀule/ [1] vt (*fil etc.*) unwind. □ **se** ~ vpr unwind; (avoir lieu) take place; (*récit, paysage*) unfold.

déroute /deʀut/ nf (Mil) rout.

dérouter /deʀute/ [1] vt disconcert.

derrière /dɛʀjɛʀ/ prép & adv behind. ● nm back, rear; (*postérieur* ⊞) behind ⊞; **de** ~ (*fenêtre*) back, rear; (*pattes*) hind.

des /de/ ⇒DE.

dès /dɛ/ prép (right) from; ~ **lors** from then on; ~ **que** as soon as.

désabusé, ~**e** /dezabyze/ a disillusioned.

désaccord /dezakɔʀ/ nm disagreement.

désaffecté, ~**e** /dezafɛkte/ a disused.

désagréable /dezagʀeabl/ a unpleasant.

désagrément /dezagʀemɑ̃/ nm annoyance, inconvenience.

désaltérer (se) /(sə)dezalteʀe/ [14] vpr quench one's thirst.

désamorcer /dezamɔʀse/ [10] vt (*situation, obus*) defuse.

désapprobation /dezapʀɔbasjɔ̃/ nf disapproval. **désapprouver** [1] vt disapprove of.

désarçonner /dezaʀsɔne/ [1] vt throw.

désarmement /dezaʀməmɑ̃/ nm (Pol) disarmament.

désarroi /dezaʀwa/ nm distress.

désastre /dezastʀ/ nm disaster. **désastreux, -euse** a disastrous.

désavantage /dezavɑ̃taʒ/ nm disadvantage. **désavantager** [40] vt put at a disadvantage.

désaveu (*pl* ~**x**) /dezavø/ nm denial. **désavouer** [1] vt deny.

descendance /dɛsɑ̃dɑ̃s/ nf descent; (enfants) descendants (+ *pl*). **descendant**, ~**e** nm, f descendant.

descendre /desɑ̃dʀ/ [3] vi (aux être) go down; (venir) come down; (*passager*) get off *ou* out; (*nuit*) fall; ~ **à pied** walk down; ~ **par l'ascenseur** take the lift down; ~ **de** (être issu de) be descended from; ~ **à l'hôtel** go to a hotel; ~ **dans la rue** (Pol) take to the streets. ● *vt* (*aux avoir*) (*escalier etc.*) take down; (*abattre* 🄳) shoot down.

descente /desɑ̃t/ *nf* descent; (à ski) downhill; (raid) raid; **dans la ~** going downhill; **~ de lit** bedside rug.

descriptif, -ive /dɛskʀiptif, -v/ *a* descriptive. **description** *nf* description.

désemparé, ~e /dezɑ̃paʀe/ *a* distraught.

désendettement /dezɑ̃dɛtmɑ̃/ *nm* reduction of the debt.

déséquilibré, ~e /dezekilibʀe/ *a* unbalanced; 🄳 crazy. ● *nm, f* lunatic. **déséquilibrer** [1] *vt* throw off balance.

désert, ~e /dezɛʀ, -t/ *a* deserted. ● *nm* desert.

déserter /dezɛʀte/ [1] *vt/i* desert. **déserteur** *nm* deserter.

désertique /dezɛʀtik/ *a* desert.

désespérant, ~e /dezɛspeʀɑ̃, -t/ *a* utterly disheartening.

désespéré, ~e /dezɛspeʀe/ *a* in despair; (*état, cas*) hopeless; (*effort*) desperate.

désespérer /dezɛspeʀe/ [14] *vt* drive to despair. ● *vi* despair, lose hope; **~ de** despair of. □ se **~** *vpr* despair.

désespoir /dezɛspwaʀ/ *nm* despair; **en ~ de cause** as a last resort.

déshabillé, ~e /dezabije/ *a* undressed. ● *nm* négligee.

déshabiller /dezabije/ [1] *vt* undress. □ se **~** *vpr* get undressed.

désherbant /dezɛʀbɑ̃/ *nm* weed-killer.

déshérité, ~e /dezeʀite/ *a* (*région*) deprived; (*personne*) the underprivileged.

déshériter /dezeʀite/ [1] *vt* disinherit.

déshonneur /dezɔnœʀ/ *nm* disgrace.

déshonorer /dezɔnɔʀe/ [1] *vt* dishonour.

déshydrater /dezidʀate/ [1] *vt* dehydrate. □ se **~** *vpr* get dehydrated.

désigner /dezine/ [1] *vt* (*montrer*) point to *ou* out; (*élire*) appoint; (*signifier*) designate.

désillusion /dezilyzjɔ̃/ *nf* disillusionment.

désinence /dezinɑ̃s/ *nf* (Gram) ending.

désinfectant /dezɛ̃fɛktɑ̃/ *nm* disinfectant. **désinfecter** [1] *vt* disinfect.

désintéressé, ~e /dezɛ̃teʀese/ *a* (*personne, acte*) selfless.

désintéresser (se) /(sə)dezɛ̃teʀese/ [1] *vpr* se **~ de** lose interest in.

désintoxiquer /dezɛ̃tɔksike/ [1] *vt* detoxify; **se faire ~** to undergo detoxification.

désinvolte /dezɛ̃vɔlt/ *a* casual. **désinvolture** *nf* casualness.

désir /deziʀ/ *nm* wish, desire; (*convoitise*) desire.

désirer /deziʀe/ [1] *vt* want; (*sexuellement*) desire; **vous désirez?** what would you like?

désireux, -euse /deziʀø, -z/ *a* **~ de faire** anxious to do.

désistement /dezistəmɑ̃/ *nm* withdrawal.

désobéir /dezɔbeiʀ/ [2] *vi* **~ (à)** disobey. **désobéissant, ~e** *a* disobedient.

désobligeant, ~e /dezɔbliʒɑ̃, -t/ *a* disagreeable, unkind.

désodorisant /dezɔdɔʀizɑ̃/ *nm* air freshener.

désodoriser /dezɔdɔʀize/ [1] *vt* freshen up.

désœuvré, ~e /dezœvʀe/ *a* at a loose end. **désœuvrement** *nm* lack of anything to do.

désolation /dezɔlasjɔ̃/ *nf* distress.

désolé, ~e /dezɔle/ *a* (au regret) sorry; (*région*) desolate.

désoler /dezɔle/ [1] *vt* distress. □ **se ~** *vpr* be upset (**de qch** about sth).

désopilant, ~e /dezɔpilɑ̃, -t/ *a* hilarious.

désordonné, ~e /dezɔRdɔne/ *a* untidy; (*mouvements*) uncoordinated.

désordre /dezɔRdR/ *nm* untidiness; (Pol) disorder; **en ~** untidy.

désorganiser /dezɔRganize/ [1] *vt* disorganize.

désorienter /dezɔRjɑ̃te/ [1] *vt* disorient.

désormais /dezɔRmɛ/ *adv* from now on.

desquels, desquelles /dekɛl/ ⇒LEQUEL.

dessécher /deseʃe/ [1] *vt* dry out. □ **se ~** *vpr* dry out, become dry; (*plante*) wither.

dessein /desɛ̃/ *nm* intention; **à ~** intentionally.

desserrer /deseRe/ [1] *vt* loosen; **il n'a pas desserré les dents** he never once opened his mouth. □ **se ~** *vpr* come loose.

dessert /deseR/ *nm* dessert; **en ~** for dessert.

desservir /deseRviR/ [46] *vt/i* (*débarrasser*) clear away; (*autobus*) serve.

dessin /desɛ̃/ *nm* drawing; (motif) design; (discipline) art; (contour) outline; **professeur de ~** art teacher; **~ animé** (cinéma) cartoon; **~ humoristique** cartoon.

dessinateur, -trice /desinatœR, -tRis/ *nm, f* artist; (industriel) draughtsman.

dessiner /desine/ [1] *vt/i* draw; (fig) outline. □ **se ~** *vpr* appear, take shape.

dessoûler /desule/ [1] *vt/i* sober up.

dessous /dəsu/ *adv* underneath. ● *nm* underside, underneath. ● *nmpl* underwear; **les ~ d'une histoire** what is behind a story; **du ~ bottom;** (*voisins*) downstairs; **en ~, par-~** underneath. **dessous-de-plat** *nm inv* (heat-resistant) table-mat. **dessous-de-table** *nm inv* backhander. **dessous-de-verre** *nm inv* coaster.

dessus /dəsy/ *adv* on top (of it), on it. ● *nm* top; **du ~** top; (*voisins*) upstairs; **avoir le ~** get the upper hand. **dessus-de-lit** *nm inv* bedspread.

destabiliser /destabilize/ [1] *vt* destabilize, unsettle.

destin /destɛ̃/ *nm* (sort) fate; (avenir) destiny.

destinataire /destinatɛR/ *nmf* addressee.

destination /destinasjɔ̃/ *nf* destination; (fonction) purpose; **vol à ~ de** flight to.

destinée /destine/ *nf* destiny.

destiner /destine/ [1] *vt* **~ à** intend for; (vouer) destine for; **le commentaire m'est destiné** this comment is aimed at me; **être destiné à faire** be intended to do; (obligé) be destined to do. □ **se ~ à** *vpr* (*carrière*) intend to take up.

destituer /destitɥe/ [1] *vt* discharge.

destructeur, -trice /destRyktœR, -tRis/ *a* destructive. **destruction** *nf* destruction.

désuet, -ète /dezɥɛ, -t/ *a* outdated.

détachant /detaʃɑ̃/ *nm* stain remover.

détacher /detaʃe/ [1] *vt* untie; (ôter) remove, detach; (déléguer) second. □ **se ~** *vpr* come off,

break away; (*nœud etc.*) come
undone; (ressortir) stand out.
détail /detaj/ *nm* detail; (de
compte) breakdown; (Comm) retail;
au ~ (*vendre etc.*) retail; **de ~**
(*prix etc.*) retail; **en ~** in detail;
entrer dans les ~s go into detail.
détaillant, ~e /detajã, -t/ *nm, f*
retailer.
détaillé, ~e /detaje/ *a* detailed.
détailler /detaje/ [1] *vt* (*rapport*)
detail; **~ ce que qn fait** scrutinize
what sb does.
détaler /detale/ [1] *vi* 🔟 bolt.
détartrant /detartrã/ *nm*
descaler.
détecter /detɛkte/ [1] *vt* detect.
détecteur *nm* detector.
détective /detɛktiv/ *nm*
detective.
déteindre /detɛ̃dr/ [22] *vi* (dans
l'eau) fade; (au soleil)
fade; **~ sur** (fig) rub off on.
détendre /detɑ̃dr/ [3] *vt* slacken;
(*ressort*) release; (*personne*)
relax. □ **se ~** *vpr* (*ressort*)
slacken; (*personne*) relax.
détendu, ~e *a* (calme) relaxed.
détenir /det(ə)nir/ [58] *vt* hold;
(*secret, fortune*) possess.
détente /detɑ̃t/ *nf* relaxation;
(Pol) détente; (saut) spring;
(gâchette) trigger; **être lent à la ~** 🔟
be slow on the uptake.
détenteur, -trice /detɑ̃tœr, -tris/
nm, f holder.
détention /detɑ̃sjɔ̃/ *nf* detention;
~ provisoire custody.
détenu, ~e /detny/ *nm, f*
prisoner.
détergent /detɛrʒɑ̃/ *nm*
detergent.
détérioration /deterjɔrasjɔ̃/ *nf*
deterioration; (dégât) damage.
détériorer /deterjɔre/ [1] *vt*
damage. □ **se ~** *vpr* deteriorate.
détermination /detɛrminasjɔ̃/
nf determination. **déterminé, ~e**

a (résolu) determined; (précis)
definite. **déterminer** [1] *vt*
determine.
déterrer /detere/ [1] *vt* dig up.
détestable /detɛstabl/ *a*
(*caractère, temps*) foul.
détester /detɛste/ [1] *vt* hate.
□ **se ~** *vpr* hate each other.
détonation /detɔnasjɔ̃/ *nf*
explosion, detonation.
détour /detur/ *nm* (crochet)
detour; (fig) roundabout means;
(virage) bend.
détournement /deturnəmɑ̃/ *nm*
hijack(ing); (de fonds)
embezzlement.
détourner /deturne/ [1] *vt*
(*attention*) divert; (*tête, yeux*) turn
away; (*avion*) hijack; (*argent*)
embezzle. □ **se ~ de** *vpr* stray
from.
détraquer /detrake/ [1] *vt* make
go wrong; (*estomac*) upset. □ **se
~** *vpr* (*machine*) go wrong.
détresse /detrɛs/ *nf* distress;
dans la ~, en ~ in distress.
détritus /detrity(s)/ *nmpl*
rubbish (+ *sg*).
détroit /detrwa/ *nm* strait.
détromper /detrɔ̃pe/ [1] *vt* set
straight. □ **se ~** *vpr* **détrompe-toi!**
you'd better think again!
détruire /detrɥir/ [17] *vt*
destroy.
dette /dɛt/ *nf* debt.
deuil /dœj/ *nm* (période) mourning;
(décès) bereavement; **porter le ~**
be in mourning; **faire son ~ de**
qch give sth up as lost.
deux /dø/ *a & nm* two; **~ fois**
twice; **tous (les) ~** both.
deuxième *a & nmf* second.
deux-pièces *nm inv* (maillot de
bain) two-piece; (logement) two-
room flat. **deux-points** *nm inv*
(Gram) colon. **deux-roues** *nm inv*
two-wheeled vehicle.

dévaliser /devalize/ [1] vt rob, clean out.

dévalorisant, ~e /devalɔʀizã, -t/ a demeaning.

dévaloriser /devalɔʀize/ [1] vt (*monnaie*) devalue. □ **se** ~ vpr (*personne*) put oneself down.

dévaluation /devalɥasjɔ̃/ nf devaluation.

dévaluer /devalɥe/ [1] vt devalue. □ **se** ~ vpr devalue.

devancer /dəvɑ̃se/ [10] vt be *ou* go ahead of; (*arriver*) arrive ahead of; (*prévenir*) anticipate.

devant /d(ə)vɑ̃/ prép in front of; (*distance*) ahead of; (*avec mouvement*) past; (*en présence de*) in front of; (*face à*) in the face of; **avoir du temps** ~ **soi** have plenty of time. ● adv in front; (*à distance*) ahead; **de** ~ front. ● nm front; **prendre les** ~**s** take the initiative.

devanture /dəvɑ̃tyʀ/ nf shop front; (*vitrine*) shop window.

développement /devlɔpmɑ̃/ nm development; (*de photos*) developing.

développer /devlɔpe/ [1] vt develop. □ **se** ~ vpr (*corps, talent*) develop; (*entreprise*) grow, expand.

devenir /dəvniʀ/ [58] vi (*aux être*) become; **qu'est-il devenu?** what has become of him?

dévergondé, ~e /devɛʀɡɔ̃de/ a & nm,f shameless (person).

déverser /devɛʀse/ [1] vt (*liquide*) pour; (*ordures, pétrole*) dump. □ **se** ~ vpr (*rivière*) flow; (*égout, foule*) pour.

dévêtir /devetiʀ/ [61] vt undress. □ **se** ~ vpr get undressed.

déviation /devjasjɔ̃/ nf diversion.

dévier /devje/ [45] vt divert; (*coup*) deflect. ● vi (*ballon, balle*) veer; (*personne*) deviate.

devin /dəvɛ̃/ nm soothsayer.

deviner /dəvine/ [1] vt guess; (*apercevoir*) distinguish.

devinette /dəvinɛt/ nf riddle.

devis /dəvi/ nm estimate, quote.

dévisager /devizaʒe/ [40] vt stare at.

devise /dəviz/ nf motto; ~**s** (*monnaie*) (foreign) currency.

dévisser /devise/ [1] vt unscrew.

dévitaliser /devitalize/ [1] vt (*dent*) carry out root canal treatment on.

dévoiler /devwale/ [1] vt reveal.

....

devoir /dəvwaʀ/ [26]

● *verbe auxiliaire*

····▸ ~ **faire** (obligation, hypothèse) must do; (nécessité) have got to do; **je dois dire que...** I have to say that...; **il a dû partir** (nécessité) he had to leave; (hypothèse) he must have left.

····▸ (prévision) **je devais lui dire** I was to tell her; **elle doit rentrer bientôt** she's due back soon.

····▸ (conseil) **tu devrais** you should.

● *verbe transitif*

····▸ (argent, excuses) owe; **combien je vous dois?** (en achetant) how much is it?

□ **se devoir** *verbe pronominal*

····▸ **je me dois de le faire** it's my duty to do it.

● *nom masculin*

····▸ duty; **faire son** ~ do one's duty.

····▸ (Scol) ~ (**surveillé**) test; **les** ~**s** homework (+ sg); **faire ses** ~**s** do one's homework.

....

dévorer /devɔʀe/ [1] vt devour.

dévot, ~e /devo, -ɔt/ a devout.

dévoué, ~e /devwe/ a devoted. **dévouement** nm devotion.

dévouer (se) /(sə)devwe/ [1] vpr

devote oneself (**à** to); (**se sacrifier**) sacrifice oneself.

dextérité /dɛksteʀite/ *nf* skill.

diabète /djabɛt/ *nm* diabetes. **diabétique** *a & nmf* diabetic.

diable /djɑbl/ *nm* devil.

diagnostic /djagnɔstik/ *nm* diagnosis. **diagnostiquer** [1] *vt* diagnose.

diagonal, **∼e** (*mpl* **-aux**) /djagɔnal, -o/ *a* diagonal. **diagonale** *nf* diagonal; **en ∼e** diagonally.

diagramme /djagʀam/ *nm* diagram; (*graphique*) graph.

dialecte /djalɛkt/ *nm* dialect.

dialogue /djalɔg/ *nm* dialogue. **dialoguer** [1] *vi* have talks, enter into a dialogue.

diamant /djamɑ̃/ *nm* diamond.

diamètre /djamɛtʀ/ *nm* diameter.

diapositive /djapozitiv/ *nf* slide.

diarrhée /djaʀe/ *nf* diarrhoea.

dictateur /diktatœʀ/ *nm* dictator.

dicter /dikte/ [1] *vt* dictate. **dictée** *nf* dictation.

dictionnaire /diksjɔnɛʀ/ *nm* dictionary.

dicton /diktɔ̃/ *nm* saying.

dièse /djɛz/ *nm* (Mus) sharp.

diesel /djezɛl/ *nm & a inv* diesel.

diète /djɛt/ *nf* restricted diet.

diététicien, **∼ne** /djetetisjɛ̃, -ɛn/ *nm,f* dietician.

diététique /djetetik/ *nf* dietetics. ● *a* **produit** *ou* **aliment ∼** dietary product; **magasin ∼** health food shop *ou* store.

dieu (*pl* **∼x**) /djø/ *nm* god; **D∼** God.

diffamation /difamasjɔ̃/ *nf* slander; (par écrit) libel. **diffamer** [1] *vt* slander; (par écrit) libel.

différé: **en ∼** /ɑ̃difeʀe/ *loc* (*émission*) pre-recorded.

différemment /difeʀamɑ̃/ *adv* differently.

différence /difeʀɑ̃s/ *nf* difference; **à la ∼ de** unlike.

différencier /difeʀɑ̃sje/ [45] *vt* differentiate. □ **se ∼** *vpr* differentiate oneself; **se ∼ de** (différer de) differ from.

différend /difeʀɑ̃/ *nm* difference (of opinion).

différent, **∼e** /difeʀɑ̃, -t/ *a* different (**de** from).

différer /difeʀe/ [14] *vt* postpone. ● *vi* differ (**de** from).

difficile /difisil/ *a* difficult; (exigeant) fussy. **difficilement** *adv* with difficulty.

difficulté /difikylte/ *nf* difficulty; **faire des ∼s** raise objections.

diffus, **∼e** /dify, -z/ *a* diffuse.

diffuser /difyze/ [1] *vt* (*émission*) broadcast; (*nouvelle*) spread; (*lumière, chaleur*) diffuse; (Comm) distribute. **diffusion** *nf* broadcasting; diffusion; distribution.

digérer /diʒeʀe/ [14] *vt* digest; (endurer 🔲) stomach. **digeste** *a* digestible.

digestif, **-ive** /diʒɛstif, -v/ *a* digestive. ● *nm* after-dinner liqueur.

digital, **∼e** (*mpl* **-aux**) /diʒital, -o/ *a* digital.

digne /diɲ/ *a* (noble) dignified; (approprié) worthy; **∼ de** worthy of; **∼ de foi** trustworthy.

digue /dig/ *nf* dyke; (US) dike.

dilater /dilate/ [1] *vt* dilate. □ **se ∼** *vpr* dilate; (*estomac*) distend.

dilemme /dilɛm/ *nm* dilemma.

dilettante /diletɑ̃t/ *nmf* amateur.

diluant /dilɥɑ̃/ *nm* thinner.

diluer /dilɥe/ [1] *vt* dilute.

dimanche /dimɑ̃ʃ/ *nm* Sunday.

dimension /dimɑ̃sjɔ̃/ *nf* (taille) size; (mesure) dimension; (aspect) dimension.

diminuer /diminɥe/ [1] *vt* reduce, decrease; (*plaisir,* *courage)* dampen; (dénigrer) diminish. ● *vi* (se réduire) decrease; (faiblir) *(bruit, flamme)* die down; *(ardeur)* cool. **diminutif** *nm* diminutive; (surnom) pet name. **diminution** *nf* decrease (**de** in); (réduction) reduction; (affaiblissement) diminishing.

dinde /dɛ̃d/ *nf* turkey.

dîner /dine/ [1] *vi* have dinner. ● *nm* dinner.

dingue /dɛ̃g/ *a* 🔲 crazy.

dinosaure /dinozɔʀ/ *nm* dinosaur.

diphtongue /diftɔ̃g/ *nf* diphthong.

diplomate /diplɔmat/ *nmf* diplomat. ● *a* diplomatic. **diplomatique** *a* diplomatic.

diplôme /diplom/ *nm* certificate, diploma; (Univ) degree. **diplômé, ~e** *a* qualified.

dire /diʀ/ [27] *vt* say; *(secret, vérité, heure)* tell; (penser) think; **~ que** say that; **~ à qn que** tell sb that; **~ à qn de** tell sb to; **ça me dit de faire** I feel like doing; **on dirait que** it would seem that, it seems that; **dis/dites donc!** hey! □ **se ~** *vpr* (mot) be said; (penser) tell oneself; (se prétendre) claim to be. ● *nm* **au ~ de, selon les ~s de** according to.

direct, ~e /diʀɛkt/ *a* direct. ● *nm* (train) express train; **en ~** *(émission)* live.

directeur, -trice /diʀɛktœʀ, -tʀis/ *nm, f* director; (chef de service) manager, manageress; (de journal) editor; (d'école) headteacher; (US) principal; **~ de banque** bank manager; **~ commercial** sales manager; **~ des ressources humaines** human resources manager.

direction /diʀɛksjɔ̃/ *nf* (sens) direction; (de société) management; (Auto) steering; **en ~ de** (going) to.

dirigeant, ~e /diʀiʒɑ̃, -t/ *nm, f* (Pol) leader; (Comm) manager. ● *a* (classe) ruling.

diriger /diʀiʒe/ [40] *vt* *(service, école, parti, pays)* run; *(entreprise, usine)* manage; *(travaux)* supervise; *(véhicule)* steer; *(orchestre)* conduct; (braquer) aim; (tourner) turn. □ **se ~** *vpr* (s'orienter) find one's way; **se ~ vers** head for, make for.

dis /di/ ⇒DIRE [27].

discernement /disɛʀnəmɑ̃/ *nm* discernment.

disciplinaire *a* disciplinary. **discipline** *nf* discipline.

discontinu, ~e /diskɔ̃tiny/ *a* intermittent.

discordant, ~e /diskɔʀdɑ̃, -t/ *a* discordant.

discothèque /diskɔtɛk/ *nf* record library; (boîte de nuit) disco (thèque).

discours /diskuʀ/ *nm* speech; (propos) views.

discret, -ète /diskʀɛ, -t/ *a* discreet.

discrétion /diskʀesjɔ̃/ *nf* discretion; **à ~** (vin) unlimited; *(manger, boire)* as much as one desires.

discrimination /diskʀiminasjɔ̃/ *nf* discrimination. **discriminatoire** *a* discriminatory.

disculper /diskylpe/ [1] *vt* exonerate. □ **se ~** *vpr* vindicate oneself.

discussion /diskysjɔ̃/ *nf* discussion; (querelle) argument.

discutable /diskytabl/ *a* debatable; (critiquable) questionable.

discuter /diskyte/ [1] *vt* discuss; (contester) question. ● *vi* (parler) talk; (répliquer) argue; **~ de** discuss.

disette /dizɛt/ *nf* food shortage.

disgrâce /disgrɑs/ nf disgrace.

disgracieux, -ieuse /disgrasjø, -z/ a ugly, unsightly.

disjoindre /disʒwɛ̃dʀ/ [22] vt take apart. □ se ~ vpr come apart.

disloquer /dislɔke/ [1] vt (membre) dislocate; (machine) break (apart). □ se ~ vpr (parti, cortège) break up; (meuble) come apart.

disparaître /disparɛtʀ/ [18] vi disappear; (mourir) die; **faire** ~ get rid of. **disparition** nf disappearance; (mort) death.

disparate /disparat/ a ill-assorted.

disparu, ~e /dispary/ a missing. ● nm, f missing person; (mort) dead person.

dispensaire /dispɑ̃sɛʀ/ nm clinic.

dispense /dispɑ̃s/ nf exemption.

dispenser /dispɑ̃se/ [1] vt exempt (de from). □ se ~ de vpr avoid.

disperser /dispɛʀse/ [1] vt (éparpiller) scatter; (répartir) disperse. □ se ~ vpr disperse.

disponibilité /dispɔnibilite/ nf availability. **disponible** a available.

dispos, ~e /dispo, -z/ a frais et ~ fresh and alert.

disposé, ~e /dispoze/ a bien/mal ~ in a good/bad mood; ~ à prepared to; ~ envers disposed towards.

disposer /dispoze/ [1] vt arrange; ~ à (engager à) incline to. ● vi ~ de have at one's disposal. □ se ~ à vpr prepare to.

dispositif /dispozitif/ nm device; (ensemble de mesures) operation.

disposition /dispozisjɔ̃/ nf arrangement, layout; (tendance) tendency; ~**s** (humeur) mood; (préparatifs) arrangements; (mesures) measures; (aptitude) aptitude; **mettre à la ~ de** place ou put at the disposal of.

disproportionné, ~e /dispʀopɔʀsjɔne/ a disproportionate; ~ à out of proportion with.

dispute /dispyt/ nf quarrel.

disputer /dispyte/ [1] vt (match) play; (course) run in; (prix) fight for; (gronder 🛈) tell off. □ se ~ vpr quarrel; (se battre pour) fight over; (match) be played.

disquaire /diskɛʀ/ nmf record dealer.

disque /disk/ nm (Mus) record; (Sport) discus; (cercle) disc, disk; (Ordinat) disk; ~ **compact** compact disc; ~ **dur** hard disk; ~ **optique compact** CD-ROM; ~ **souple** floppy disk.

disquette /diskɛt/ nf floppy disk, diskette; ~ **de sauvegarde** back-up disk.

disséminer /disemine/ [1] vt spread, scatter.

dissertation /disɛʀtasjɔ̃/ nf essay, paper.

disserter /disɛʀte/ [1] vi ~ **sur** speak about; (par écrit) write about.

dissident, ~e /disidɑ̃, -t/ a & nm, f dissident.

dissimulation /disimylasjɔ̃/ nf concealment; (fig) deceit.

dissimuler /disimyle/ [1] vt conceal (à from). □ se ~ vpr conceal oneself.

dissipé, ~e /disipe/ a (élève) unruly.

dissiper /disipe/ [1] vt (fumée, crainte) dispel; (fortune) squander; (personne) distract. □ se ~ vpr disappear; (élève) grow restless.

dissolvant /disɔlvɑ̃/ nm solvent; (pour ongles) nail polish remover.

dissoudre /disudʀ/ [53] vt dissolve. □ se ~ vpr dissolve.

dissuader /disɥade/ [1] vt
dissuade (de from).

dissuasion /disɥazjɔ̃/ nf
dissuasion; **force de** ~ deterrent
force.

distance /distɑ̃s/ nf distance;
(écart) gap; **à** ~ at ou from a
distance.

distancer /distɑ̃se/ [10] vt
outdistance.

distendre /distɑ̃dʀ/ [3] vt
(estomac) distend; (corde) stretch.

distinct, ~**e** /distɛ̃(kt), -ɛ̃kt/ a
distinct.

distinctif, **-ive** /distɛ̃ktif, -v/ a
(trait) distinctive; (signe,
caractère) distinguishing.

distinction /distɛ̃ksjɔ̃/ nf
distinction; (récompense) honour.

distinguer /distɛ̃ge/ [1] vt
distinguish.

distraction /distʀaksjɔ̃/ nf
absent-mindedness; (passe-temps)
entertainment, leisure; (détente)
recreation.

distraire /distʀɛʀ/ [29] vt amuse;
(rendre inattentif) distract; ~ **qn de
qch** take sb's mind off sth. □ **se**
~ vpr amuse oneself.

distrait, ~**e** /distʀɛ, -t/ a absent-
minded; (élève) inattentive.

distrayant, ~**e** /distʀɛjɑ̃, -t/ a
entertaining.

distribuer /distʀibɥe/ [1] vt hand
out, distribute; (répartir) distribute;
(tâches, rôles) allocate; (cartes)
deal; (courrier) deliver.

distributeur /distʀibytœʀ/ nm
(Auto, Comm) distributor; ~
(**automatique**) vending-machine;
~ **de billets** (**de banque**) cash
dispenser. **distribution** nf
distribution; (du courrier) delivery;
(acteurs) cast; (secteur) retailing.

district /distʀikt/ nm district.

dit[1], **dites** /di, dit/ ⇒DIRE [27].

dit[2], ~**e** /di, dit/ a (décidé) agreed;
(surnommé) known as.

diurne /djyʀn/ a diurnal;
(activité) daytime.

divagations /divagasjɔ̃/ nfpl
ravings.

divergence /divɛʀʒɑ̃s/ nf
divergence. **divergent**, ~**e** a
divergent. **diverger** [40] vi
diverge.

divers, ~**e** /divɛʀ, -s/ a (varié)
diverse; (différent) various; (frais)
miscellaneous; **dépenses** ~**es**
sundries. **diversifier** [45] vt
diversify.

diversité /divɛʀsite/ nf diversity,
variety.

divertir /divɛʀtiʀ/ [2] vt amuse,
entertain. □ **se** ~ vpr amuse
oneself; (passer du bon temps) enjoy
oneself. **divertissement** nm
amusement, entertainment.

dividende /dividɑ̃d/ nm
dividend.

divin, ~**e** /divɛ̃, -in/ a divine.
divinité nf divinity.

diviser /divize/ [1] vt divide. □ **se**
~ vpr become divisible; **se** ~ **par
sept** be divisible by seven. **division** nf division.

divorce /divɔʀs/ nm divorce.

divorcé, ~**e** /divɔʀse/ a
divorced. ● nm, f divorcee.

divorcer /divɔʀse/ [10] vi ~
(**d'avec**) divorce.

dix /dis/ (/di/ before consonant,
/diz/ before vowel) a & nm ten.

dix-huit /dizɥit/ a & nm eighteen.

dixième /dizjɛm/ a & nmf tenth.

dix-neuf /diznœf/ a & nm
nineteen.

dix-sept /disɛt/ a & nm
seventeen.

docile /dɔsil/ a docile.

docteur /dɔktœʀ/ nm doctor.

doctorat /dɔktɔʀa/ nm doctorate,
PhD.

document /dɔkymɑ̃/ nm
document. **documentaire** a &
nm documentary.

documentaliste /dɔkymɑ̃talist/ *nmf* information officer; (Scol) librarian.

documentation /dɔkymɑ̃tasjɔ̃/ *nf* information, literature; **centre de ~** resource centre.

documenté, ~e /dɔkymɑ̃te/ *a* well-documented.

documenter /dɔkymɑ̃te/ [1] *vt* provide with information. □ **se ~** *vpr* collect information.

dodo /dodo/ *nm* faire **~** (langage enfantin) sleep.

dodu, ~e /dɔdy/ *a* plump.

dogmatique /dɔgmatik/ *a* dogmatic. **dogme** *nm* dogma.

doigt /dwa/ *nm* finger; **un ~ de** a drop of; **montrer qch du ~** point at sth; **à deux ~s de** a hair's breadth away from; **~ de pied** toe. **doigté** *nm* (Mus) fingering, touch; (diplomatie) tact.

dois, doit /dwa/ ⇒DEVOIR [26].

doléances /dɔleɑ̃s/ *nfpl* grievances.

dollar /dɔlaʀ/ *nm* dollar.

domaine /dɔmɛn/ *nm* estate, domain; (fig) domain, field.

domestique /dɔmɛstik/ *a* domestic. ● *nmf* servant. **domestiquer** [1] *vt* domesticate.

domicile /dɔmisil/ *nm* home; **à ~** at home; (livrer) to the home.

domicilié, ~e /dɔmisilje/ *a* resident; **être ~ à Paris** live *ou* be resident in Paris.

dominant, ~e /dɔminɑ̃, -t/ *a* dominant. **dominante** *nf* dominant feature.

dominer /dɔmine/ [1] *vt* dominate; (surplomber) tower over, dominate; (sujet) master; (peur) overcome. ● *vi* dominate; (équipe) be in the lead; (prévaloir) stand out.

domino /dɔmino/ *nm* domino.

dommage /dɔmaʒ/ *nm* (tort) harm; **~(s)** (dégâts) damage; **c'est**

~ it's a pity *ou* shame; **quel ~** what a pity *ou* shame.

dommages-intérêts *nmpl* (Jur) damages.

dompter /dɔ̃te/ [1] *vt* tame.

dompteur, -euse *nm, f* tamer.

DOM-TOM /dɔmtɔm/ *abrév mpl* (**départements et territoires d'outre-mer**) French overseas departments and territories.

don /dɔ̃/ *nm* (cadeau, aptitude) gift.

donateur, -trice *nm, f* donor.

donation *nf* donation.

donc /dɔ̃k/ *conj* so, then; (par conséquent) so, therefore; **quoi ~?** what did you say?; **tiens ~!** fancy that!

donjon /dɔ̃ʒɔ̃/ *nm* (tour) keep.

donné, ~e /dɔne/ *a* (fixé) given; (pas cher 🏛) dirt cheap; **étant ~ que** given that.

donnée /dɔne/ *nf* (élément d'information) fact; **~s** data.

donner /dɔne/ [1] *vt* give; (vieilles affaires) give away; (distribuer) give out; (fruits, résultats) produce; (film) show; (pièce) put on; **ça donne soif/faim** it makes one thirsty/hungry; **~ qch à réparer** take sth to be repaired; **~ lieu à** give rise to. ● *vi* **~ sur** look out on to; **~ dans** tend towards. □ **se ~ à** *vpr* devote oneself to; **se ~ du mal** go to a lot of trouble (**pour faire** to do).

dont /dɔ̃/

● *pronom*

····▶ (personne) **la fille ~ je te parlais** the girl I was telling you about; **l'homme ~ la fille a dit...** the man whose daughter said...

····▶ (chose) which, **l'affaire ~ il parle** the matter which he is referring to; **la manière ~ elle parle** the way she speaks; **ce ~ il parle** what he's talking about.

D

····▸ (provenance) from which.

····▸ (parmi lesquels) **deux personnes ~ toi** two people, one of whom is you; **plusieurs thèmes ~ l'identité et le racisme** several topics including identity and racism.

dopage /dɔpaʒ/ *nm* (de cheval) doping; (d'athlète) illegal drug-use.

doper /dɔpe/ [1] *vt* dope. □ **se ~** *vpr* take drugs.

doré, ~e /dɔʀe/ *a* (couleur d'or) golden; (qui rappelle de l'or) gold; (avec de l'or) gilt; **la jeunesse ~e** gilded youth.

dorénavant /dɔʀenavɑ̃/ *adv* henceforth.

dorer /dɔʀe/ [1] *vt* gild; (Culin) brown.

dormir /dɔʀmiʀ/ [46] *vi* sleep; (être endormi) be asleep; **~ debout** be asleep on one's feet; **une histoire à ~ debout** a cock-and-bull story.

dortoir /dɔʀtwaʀ/ *nm* dormitory.

dorure /dɔʀyʀ/ *nf* gilding.

dos /do/ *nm* back; (de livre) spine; **à ~ de** riding on; **au ~ de** (chèque) on the back of; **de ~** from behind; **~ crawlé** backstroke.

dosage /dozaʒ/ *nm* (mélange) mixture; (quantité) amount, proportions. **dose** *nf* dose. **doser** [1] *vt* measure out; (contrôler) use in a controlled way.

dossier /dɔsje/ *nm* (documents) file; (Jur) case; (de chaise) back; (TV, presse) special feature.

dot /dɔt/ *nf* dowry.

douane /dwan/ *nf* customs.

douanier, -ière /dwanje, -jɛʀ/ *a* customs. ● *nm* customs officer.

double /dubl/ *a & adv* double. ● *nm* (copie) duplicate; (sosie) double; **le ~ (de)** twice as much

ou as many (as); **le ~ messieurs** the men's doubles.

double-cliquer /dublklike/ [1] *vt* double-click.

doubler /duble/ [1] *vt* double; (dépasser) overtake; (vêtement) line; (film) dub; (classe) repeat; (cap) round. ● *vi* double.

doublure /dublyʀ/ *nf* (étoffe) lining; (acteur) understudy.

douce /dus/ ⇒DOUX.

doucement /dusmɑ̃/ *adv* gently; (sans bruit) quietly; (lentement) slowly.

douceur /dusœʀ/ *nf* (mollesse) softness; (de climat) mildness; (de personne) gentleness; (friandise) sweet; (US) candy; **en ~** smoothly.

douche /duʃ/ *nf* shower.

doucher (se) /duʃe/ [1] **~** *vpr* have *ou* take a shower.

doudoune /dudun/ *nf* 🄁 down jacket.

doué, ~e /dwe/ *a* gifted; **~ de** endowed with.

douille /duj/ *nf* (Électr) socket.

douillet, ~te /dujɛ, -t/ *a* cosy, comfortable; (personne: péj) soft.

douleur /dulœʀ/ *nf* pain; (chagrin) sorrow, grief. **douloureux, -euse** *a* painful.

doute /dut/ *nm* doubt; **sans ~** no doubt; **sans aucun ~** without doubt.

douter /dute/ [1] *vt* **~ de** doubt; **~ que** doubt that. ● *vi* doubt. □ **se ~ de** *vpr* suspect; **je m'en doutais** I thought so.

douteux, -euse /dutø, -z/ *a* dubious, doubtful.

Douvres /duvʀ/ *npr* Dover.

doux, douce /du, dus/ *a* (moelleux) soft; (sucré) sweet; (clément, pas fort) mild; (pas brusque, bienveillant) gentle.

douzaine /duzɛn/ *nf* about twelve; (douze) dozen; **une ~ d'œufs** a dozen eggs.

douze /duz/ *a & nm* twelve.
douzième *a & nmf* twelfth.

doyen, **~ne** /dwajɛ̃, -ɛn/ *nm, f*
dean; (en âge) most senior person.

dragée /dʁaʒe/ *nf* sugared
almond.

draguer /dʁage/ [1] *vt* (rivière)
dredge; (filles 🔲) chat up.

drainer /dʁene/ [1] *vt* drain.

dramatique /dʁamatik/ *a*
dramatic; (tragique) tragic. ● *nf*
(television) drama.

dramatiser /dʁamatize/ [1] *vt*
dramatize.

dramaturge /dʁamatyʁʒ/ *nmf*
dramatist.

drame /dʁam/ *nm* (genre) drama;
(pièce) play; (événement tragique)
tragedy.

drap /dʁa/ *nm* sheet; (tissu)
(woollen) cloth.

drapeau (*pl* ~x) /dʁapo/ *nm*
flag.

drap-housse (*pl* **draps-
housses**) /dʁaus/ *nm* fitted
sheet.

dressage /dʁesaʒ/ *nm* training;
(compétition équestre) dressage.

dresser /dʁese/ [1] *vt* put up,
erect; (tête) raise; (animal) train;
(liste, plan) draw up; ~ l'oreille
prick up one's ears. □ se ~ *vpr*
(bâtiment) stand; (personne) draw
oneself up. **dresseur**, **-euse** *nm, f*
trainer.

dribbler /dʁible/ [1] *vi* (Sport)
dribble.

drive /dʁajv/ *nm* (Ordinat) drive.

drogue /dʁɔg/ *nf* drug; la ~
drugs.

drogué, **~e** /dʁɔge/ *nm, f* drug
addict.

droguer /dʁɔge/ [1] *vt* (malade)
drug heavily; (victime) drug. □ se
~ *vpr* take drugs.

droguerie /dʁɔgʁi/ *nf* hardware

shop. **droguiste** *nmf* owner of a
hardware shop.

droit, **~e** /dʁwa, -t/ *a* (contraire de
gauche) right; (non courbe) straight;
(loyal) upright; **angle** ~ right
angle. ● *adv* straight. ● *nm* right;
~(s) (taxe) duty; **le** ~ (Jur) law;
avoir ~ **à** be entitled to; **avoir le** ~
de be allowed to; **être dans son** ~
be in the right; ~ **d'auteur**
copyright; ~ **d'inscription**
registration fee; ~s **d'auteur**
royalties.

droite /dʁwat/ *nf* (contraire de
gauche) right; **à** ~ on the right;
(direction) (to the) right; **la** ~ the
right (side); (Pol) the right (wing);
(ligne) straight line. **droitier**,
-ière *a* right-handed.

drôle /dʁol/ *a* (amusant) funny;
(bizarre) funny, odd. **drôlement**
adv funnily; (très 🔲) really.

dru, **~e** /dʁy/ *a* thick; **tomber** ~
fall thick and fast.

drugstore /dʁœgstɔʁ/ *nm*
drugstore.

du /dy/ ⇒DE.

dû, **due** /dy/ *a* due. ● *nm* due;
(argent) dues; ~ **à** is due to.
● ⇒DEVOIR [26].

duc, **duchesse** /dyk, dyʃɛs/ *nm, f*
duke, duchess.

duo /dɥo/ *nm* (Mus) duet; (fig) duo.

dupe /dyp/ *nf* dupe.

duplex /dyplɛks/ *nm* split-level
apartment; (US) duplex; (émission)
link-up.

duplicata /dyplikata/ *nm inv*
duplicate.

duquel /dykɛl/ ⇒LEQUEL.

dur, **~e** /dyʁ/ *a* hard; (sévère)
harsh, hard; (viande) tough; (col,
brosse) stiff; ~ **d'oreille** hard of
hearing. ● *adv* hard. ● *nm, f*
tough nut 🔲; (Pol) hardliner.

durable /dyʁabl/ *a* lasting.

durant /dyʁɑ̃/ *prép* (au cours de)
during; (avec mesure de temps) for;

~ des heures for hours; **des heures ~** for hours and hours.

durcir /dyʀsiʀ/ [2] *vt* harden. ● *vi* (*terre*) harden; (*ciment*) set; (*pain*) go hard. □ **se ~** *vpr* harden.

durée /dyʀe/ *nf* length; (*période*) duration; **de courte ~** short-lived; **pile longue ~** long-life battery.

durer /dyʀe/ [1] *vi* last.

dureté /dyʀte/ *nf* hardness; (*sévérité*) harshness.

duvet /dyvɛ/ *nm* down; (*sac*) sleeping-bag.

dynamique /dinamik/ *a* dynamic.

dynamite /dinamit/ *nf* dynamite.

dynamo /dinamo/ *nf* dynamo.

eau (*pl* **~x**) /o/ *nf* water; **~ courante** running water; **~ de mer** seawater; **~ de source** spring water; **~ douce/salée** fresh/salt water; **~ de pluie** rainwater; **~ potable** drinking water; **~ de Javel** bleach; **~ minérale** mineral water; **~ gazeuse** sparkling water; **~ plate** still water; **~ de toilette** eau de toilette; **~x usées** dirty water; **~x et forêts** forestry commission (+ *sg*); **tomber à l'~** (fig) fall through; **prendre l'~** take in water. **eau-de-vie** (*pl* **eaux-de-vie**) *nf* brandy.

ébahi, **~e** /ebai/ *a* dumbfounded.

ébauche /eboʃ/ *nf* (*dessin*) sketch; (fig) attempt.

ébéniste /ebenist/ *nm* cabinet-maker.

éblouir /ebluiʀ/ [2] *vt* dazzle.

éboueur /ebwœʀ/ *nm* dustman.

ébouillanter /ebujɑ̃te/ [1] *vt* scald.

éboulement /ebulmɑ̃/ *nm* landslide.

ébouriffé, **~e** /eburife/ *a* dishevelled.

ébrécher /ebʀeʃe/ [14] *vt* chip.

ébruiter /ebʀɥite/ [1] *vt* spread about. □ **s'~** *vpr* get out.

ébullition /ebylisjɔ̃/ *nf* boiling; **en ~** boiling.

écaille /ekaj/ *nf* (de poisson) scale; (de peinture, roc) flake; (matière) tortoiseshell.

écarlate /ekaʀlat/ *a* scarlet.

écarquiller /ekaʀkije/ [1] *vt* **~ les yeux** open one's eyes wide.

écart /ekaʀ/ *nm* gap; (de prix) difference; (embardée) swerve; **~ de conduite** lapse in behaviour; **être à l'~** be isolated; **se tenir à l'~ de** stand apart from; (fig) keep out of the way of.

écarté, **~e** /ekaʀte/ *a* (*lieu*) remote; **les jambes ~es** (with) legs apart; **les bras ~s** with one's arms out.

écarter /ekaʀte/ [1] *vt* (séparer) move apart; (*membres*) spread; (*branches*) part; (éliminer) dismiss; **~ qch de** move sth away from; **~ qn de** keep sb away from. □ **s'~** *vpr* (s'éloigner) move away; (quitter son chemin) move aside; **s'~ de** stray from.

ecchymose /ekimoz/ *nf* bruise.

écervelé, **~e** /esɛʀvəle/ *a* scatterbrained. ● *nm, f* scatterbrain.

échafaudage /eʃafodaʒ/ *nm* scaffolding; (amas) heap.

échalote /eʃalɔt/ *nf* shallot.

échancré, **~e** /eʃɑ̃kʀe/ *a* low-cut.

échange /eʃɑ̃ʒ/ *nm* exchange; **en ~ (de)** in exchange (for).

échanger [40] *vt* exchange (**contre** for).

échangeur /eʃɑ̃ʒœʀ/ *nm* (Auto) interchange.

échantillon /eʃɑ̃tijɔ̃/ *nm* sample.

échappatoire /eʃapatwaʀ/ *nf* way out.

échappement /eʃapmɑ̃/ *nm* exhaust.

échapper /eʃape/ [1] *vi* ~ **à** escape; (en fuyant) escape (from); ~ **des mains de** slip out of the hands of; **ça m'a échappé** (fig) it just slipped out!; **l'~ belle** have a narrow *ou* lucky escape. □ **s'~** *vpr* escape.

écharde /eʃaʀd/ *nf* splinter.

écharpe /eʃaʀp/ *nf* scarf; (de maire) sash; **en ~** (*bras*) in a sling.

échasse /eʃɑs/ *nf* stilt.

échauffement /eʃofmɑ̃/ *nm* (Sport) warm-up.

échauffer /eʃofe/ [1] *vt* heat; (fig) excite. □ **s'~** *vpr* warm up.

échéance /eʃeɑ̃s/ *nf* due date (for payment); (délai) deadline; (obligation) (financial) commitment.

échéant: le cas ~ /ləkazeʃeɑ̃/ *loc* if need be.

échec /eʃɛk/ *nm* failure; ~**s** (jeu) chess; ~ **et mat** checkmate.

échelle /eʃɛl/ *nf* ladder; (dimension) scale.

échelon /eʃlɔ̃/ *nm* rung; (hiérarchique) grade; (niveau) level.

échevelé, ~e /eʃəvle/ *a* dishevelled.

écho /eko/ *nm* echo; ~**s** (dans la presse) gossip.

échographie /ekɔgʀafi/ *nf* (ultrasound) scan.

échouer /eʃwe/ [1] *vi* (bateau) run aground; (ne pas réussir) fail; ~ **à un examen** fail an exam. ● *vt* (bateau) ground. □ **s'~** *vpr* run aground.

échu, ~e /eʃy/ *a* (délai) expired.

éclabousser /eklabuse/ [1] *vt* splash.

éclair /eklɛʀ/ *nm* (flash of) lightning; (fig) flash; (gâteau) éclair. ● *a inv* (visite) brief.

éclairage /eklɛʀaʒ/ *nm* lighting.

éclaircie /eklɛʀsi/ *nf* sunny interval.

éclaircir /eklɛʀsiʀ/ [2] *vt* lighten; (mystère) clear up. □ **s'~** *vpr* (ciel) clear; (mystère) become clearer. **éclaircissement** *nm* clarification.

éclairer /eklɛʀe/ [1] *vt* light (up); (personne) (fig) enlighten; (situation) throw light on. ● *vi* give light. □ **s'~** *vpr* become clearer.

éclaireur, -euse /eklɛʀœʀ, -øz/ *nm, f* (boy) scout, (girl) guide.

éclat /ekla/ *nm* fragment; (de lumière) brightness; (splendeur) brilliance; ~ **de rire** burst of laughter.

éclatant, ~e /eklatɑ̃, -t/ *a* brilliant; (soleil) dazzling.

éclater /eklate/ [1] *vi* burst; (exploser) go off; (verre) shatter; (guerre) break out; (groupe) split up; ~ **de rire** burst out laughing.

éclipse /eklips/ *nf* eclipse.

éclosion /eklozjɔ̃/ *nf* hatching, opening.

écluse /eklyz/ *nf* (de canal) lock.

écœurant, ~e /ekœrɑ̃, -t/ *a* (gâteau) sickly; (fig) disgusting.

écœurer [1] *vt* sicken.

éco-guerrier, -ière (pl **éco-guerriers, ières**) /ekogɛʀie, ɛʀ/ *nmf* eco-warrior.

école /ekɔl/ *nf* school; ~ **maternelle/primaire/secondaire** nursery/primary/secondary school; ~ **normale** teachers' training college. **écolier, -ière** *nm, f* schoolboy, schoolgirl.

écologie /ekɔlɔʒi/ *nf* ecology.

écologique *a* ecological, green.

écologiste *nmf* (chercheur)

ecologist; (dans l'âme) environmentalist; (Pol) Green.

économie /ekɔnɔmi/ nf economy; (discipline) economics; ∼s (argent) savings; **une ∼ de** (gain) a saving of. **économique** a (Pol) economic; (bon marché) economical.

économiser /ekɔnɔmize/ [1] vt/i save.

écorce /ekɔʀs/ nf bark; (de fruit) peel.

écorcher /ekɔʀʃe/ [1] vt (genou) graze; (animal) skin. □ s'∼ vpr graze oneself. **écorchure** nf graze.

écossais, ∼**e** /ekɔsɛ, -z/ a Scottish. **É∼**, ∼**e** nm, f Scot.

Écosse /ekɔs/ nf Scotland.

écoulement /ekulmã/ nm flow.

écouler /ekule/ [1] vt dispose of, sell. □ s'∼ vpr (liquide) flow; (temps) pass.

écourter /ekuʀte/ [1] vt shorten.

écoute /ekut/ nf listening; **à l'∼ (de)** listening in (to); **heures de grande ∼** prime time; **∼s téléphoniques** phone tapping.

écouter /ekute/ [1] vt listen to. ● vi listen; ∼ **aux portes** eavesdrop. **écouteur** nm earphones (+ pl); (de téléphone) receiver.

écran /ekʀã/ nm screen; ∼ **total** sun-block.

écraser /ekʀaze/ [1] vt crush; (piéton) run over; (cigarette) stub out. □ s'∼ vpr crash (**contre** into).

écrémé, ∼**e** /ekʀeme/ a skimmed; **demi-∼** semi-skimmed.

écrevisse /ekʀəvis/ nf crayfish.

écrier (s') /(s)ekʀije/ [45] vpr exclaim.

écrin /ekʀɛ̃/ nm case.

écrire /ekʀiʀ/ [30] vt/i write; (orthographier) spell. □ s'∼ vpr (mot) be spelt.

écrit /ekʀi/ nm document;

(examen) written paper; **par ∼** in writing.

écriteau (pl ∼x) /ekʀito/ nm notice.

écriture /ekʀityʀ/ nf writing; ∼s (Comm) accounts.

écrivain /ekʀivɛ̃/ nm writer.

écrou /ekʀu/ nm (Tech) nut.

écrouler (s') /(s)ekʀule/ [1] vpr collapse.

écru, ∼**e** /ekʀy/ a (couleur) natural; (tissu) raw.

écueil /ekœj/ nm reef; (fig) danger.

éculé, ∼**e** /ekyle/ a (soulier) worn at the heel; (fig) well-worn.

écume /ekym/ nf foam; (Culin) scum.

écumer /ekyme/ [1] vt skim. ● vi foam.

écureuil /ekyʀœj/ nm squirrel.

écurie /ekyʀi/ nf stable.

écuyer, **-ère** /ekɥije, -jɛʀ/ nm, f (horse) rider.

eczéma /ɛgzema/ nm eczema.

EDF abrév f (**Électricité de France**) French electricity board.

édifice /edifis/ nm building.

édifier /edifje/ [45] vt construct; (porter à la vertu) edify.

Édimbourg /edɛ̃buʀ/ npr Edinburgh.

édit /edi/ nm edict.

éditer /edite/ [1] vt publish; (annoter) edit. **éditeur**, **-trice** nm, f publisher; (réviseur) editor.

édition /edisjɔ̃/ nf (activité) publishing; (livre, disque) edition.

éditique /editik/ nf electronic publishing.

éditorial, ∼**e** (pl **-iaux**) /editɔʀjal, -jo/ a & nm editorial.

édredon /edʀədɔ̃/ nm eiderdown.

éducateur, **-trice** /edykatœʀ, -tʀis/ nm, f youth worker.

éducatif, -ive /edykatif, -v/ *a* educational.

éducation /edykasjɔ̃/ *nf* (façon d'élever) upbringing; (enseignement) education; (manières) manners; ~ **physique** physical education.

éduquer /edyke/ [1] *vt* (élever) bring up; (former) educate.

effacé, ~e /efase/ *a* (modeste) unassuming.

effacer /efase/ [10] *vt* (gommer) rub out; (à l'écran) delete; (souvenir) erase. □ **s'~** *vpr* fade; (s'écarter) step aside.

effarer /efaʀe/ [1] *vt* alarm; **être effaré** be astounded.

effaroucher /efaʀuʃe/ [1] *vt* scare away.

effectif, -ive /efɛktif, -v/ *a* effective. ● *nm* (d'école) number of pupils; ~**s** numbers.
effectivement *adv* effectively; (en effet) indeed.

effectuer /efɛktɥe/ [1] *vt* carry out, make.

efféminé, ~e /efemine/ *a* effeminate.

effervescent, ~e /efɛʀvesã, -t/ *a* **comprimé ~** effervescent tablet.

effet /efɛ/ *nm* effect; (impression) impression; ~**s** (habits) clothes, things; **sous l'~ d'une drogue** under the influence of drugs; **en ~** indeed; **faire de l'~** have an effect, be effective; **faire bon/ mauvais ~** make a good/bad impression; **ça fait un drôle d'~** it feels strange.

efficace /efikas/ *a* effective; (personne) efficient. **efficacité** *nf* effectiveness; (de personne) efficiency.

effleurer /eflœʀe/ [1] *vt* touch lightly; (sujet) touch on; **ça ne m'a pas effleuré** it did not cross my mind.

effondrement /efɔ̃dʀəmã/ *nm* collapse. **effondrer** (**s'**) [1] *vpr* collapse.

efforcer (**s'**) /(s)efɔʀse/ [10] *vpr* try (hard) (**de** to).

effort /efɔʀ/ *nm* effort.

effraction /efʀaksjɔ̃/ *nf* **entrer par ~** break in.

effrayant, ~e /efʀejã, -t/ *a* frightening; (fig) frightful.

effrayer /efʀeje/ [31] *vt* frighten; (décourager) put off. □ **s'~** *vpr* be frightened.

effréné, ~e /efʀene/ *a* wild.

effriter (**s'**) /(s)efʀite/ [1] *vpr* crumble.

effroi /efʀwa/ *nm* dread.

effronté, ~e /efʀɔ̃te/ *a* cheeky. ● *nm, f* cheeky boy, cheeky girl.

effroyable /efʀwajabl/ *a* dreadful.

égal, ~e (*mpl* **-aux**) /egal, -o/ *a* equal; (surface, vitesse) even. ● *nm, f* equal; **ça m'est/lui est ~** it is all the same to me/him; **sans ~** matchless; **d'~ à ~** between equals. **également** *adv* equally; (aussi) as well. **égaler** [1] *vt* equal.

égaliser /egalize/ [1] *vt/i* (Sport) equalize; (niveler) level out; (cheveux) trim.

égalitaire /egaliteʀ/ *a* egalitarian.

égalité /egalite/ *nf* equality; (de surface) evenness; **être à ~** be level.

égard /egaʀ/ *nm* consideration; ~**s** respect (+ *sg*); **par ~ pour** out of consideration for; **à cet ~** in this respect; **à l'~ de** with regard to; (envers) towards.

égarer /egaʀe/ [1] *vt* mislay; (tromper) lead astray. □ **s'~** *vpr* get lost; (se tromper) go astray.

égayer /egeje/ [31] *vt* (personne) cheer up; (pièce) brighten up.

église /egliz/ *nf* church.

E

égoïsme /egɔism/ *nm*
selfishness, egoism.

égoïste /egɔist/ *a* selfish. ● *nmf*
egoist.

égorger /egɔRʒe/ [40] *vt* slit the
throat of.

égout /egu/ *nm* sewer.

égoutter /egute/ [1] *vt* drain.
□ **s'~** *vpr* (*vaisselle*) drain;
(*lessive*) drip dry. **égouttoir** *nm*
draining-board.

égratigner /egRatiɲe/ [1] *vt*
scratch. **égratignure** *nf* scratch.

Égypte /eʒipt/ *nf* Egypt.

éjecter /eʒɛkte/ [1] *vt* eject.

élaboration /elabɔRasjɔ̃/ *nf*
elaboration. **élaborer** [1] *vt*
elaborate.

élan /elɑ̃/ *nm* (*animal*) moose;
(Sport) run-up; (*vitesse*)
momentum; (*fig*) surge.

élancé, **~e** /elɑ̃se/ *a* slender.

élancement /elɑ̃smɑ̃/ *nm*
twinge.

élancer (**s'**) /(s)elɑ̃se/ [10] *vpr*
leap forward, dash; (*arbre,
édifice*) soar.

élargir /elaRʒiR/ [2] *vt* (*route*)
widen; (*connaissances*) broaden.
□ **s'~** *vpr* (*famille*) expand;
(*route*) widen; (*écart*) increase;
(*vêtement*) stretch.

élastique /elastik/ *a* elastic.
● *nm* elastic band; (*tissu*) elastic.

électeur, **-trice** /elɛktœR, -tRis/
nm, f voter. **élection** *nf* election.

électoral, **~e** (*mpl* **-aux**) *a*
(*réunion*) election. **électorat** *nm*
electorate, voters (+ *pl*).

électricien, **~ne** /elɛktRisjɛ̃, ɛn/
nm, f electrician. **électricité** *nf*
electricity.

électrifier /elɛktRifje/ [45] *vt*
electrify.

électrique /elɛktRik/ *a* electric;
(*installation*) electrical.

électrocuter /elɛktRɔkyte/ [1] *vt*
electrocute.

électroménager
/elɛktRɔmenaʒe/ *nm* **l'~**
household appliances (+ *pl*).

électron /elɛktRɔ̃/ *nm* electron.
électronicien, **~ne** *nm, f*
electronics engineer.

électronique /elɛktRɔnik/ *a*
electronic. ● *nf* electronics.

élégance /elegɑ̃s/ *nf* elegance.
élégant, **~e** *a* elegant.

élément /elemɑ̃/ *nm* element;
(*meuble*) unit. **élémentaire** *a*
elementary.

éléphant /elefɑ̃/ *nm* elephant.

élevage /ɛlvaʒ/ *nm* (stock-)
breeding.

élévation /elevasjɔ̃/ *nf* rise;
(*hausse*) rise; (*plan*) elevation; **~ de
terrain** rise in the ground.

élève /elɛv/ *nmf* pupil.

élevé, **~e** /ɛlve/ *a* high; (*noble*)
elevated; **bien ~** well-mannered.

élever /ɛlve/ [6] *vt* (*lever*) raise;
(*enfants*) bring up, raise; (*animal*)
breed. □ **s'~** *vpr* rise; (*dans le ciel*)
soar up; **s'~ à** amount to.
éleveur, **-euse** *nm, f* (stock-)
breeder.

éligible /eliʒibl/ *a* eligible.

élimination /eliminasjɔ̃/ *nf*
elimination.

éliminatoire /eliminatwaR/ *a*
qualifying. ● *nf* (Sport) heat.

éliminer /elimine/ [1] *vt*
eliminate.

élire /eliR/ [39] *vt* elect.

elle /ɛl/ *pron* she; (*complément*) her;
(*chose*) it. **elle-même** *pron*
herself; itself. **elles** *pron* they;
(*complément*) them. **elles-mêmes**
pron themselves.

élocution /elɔkysjɔ̃/ *nf* diction.

éloge /elɔʒ/ *nm* praise; **faire l'~
de** praise; **~s** praise (+ *sg*).

éloigné, **~e** /elwaɲe/ *a* distant;
~ de far away from; **parent ~**
distant relative.

éloigner /elwaɲe/ [1] *vt* take

away *ou* remove (**de** from); (*danger*) ward off; (*visite*) put off. □ **s'~** *vpr* go *ou* move away (**de** from); (*affectivement*) become estranged (**de** from).

élongation /elɔ̃gasjɔ̃/ *nf* strained muscle.

éloquent, **~e** /elɔkɑ̃, -t/ *a* eloquent.

élu, **~e** /ely/ *a* elected. ● *nm, f* (Pol) elected representative.

élucider /elyside/ [1] *vt* elucidate.

éluder /elyde/ [1] *vt* evade.

émacié, **~e** /emasje/ *a* emaciated.

e-mail /imɛl/ *nm* e-mail; **envoyer un ~ à qn** e-mail sb.

émail (*pl* **-aux**) /emaj, -o/ *nm* enamel.

émanciper /emɑ̃sipe/ [1] *vt* emancipate. □ **s'~** *vpr* become emancipated.

émaner /emane/ [1] *vi* emanate.

emballage /ɑ̃balaʒ/ *nm* (dur) packaging; (souple) wrapping.

emballer /ɑ̃bale/ [1] *vt* pack; (en papier) wrap; **ça ne m'emballe pas** Ⓘ I'm not taken by it. □ **s'~** *vpr* (*moteur*) race; (*cheval*) bolt; (*personne*) get carried away; (*prices*) shoot up.

embarcadère /ɑ̃baRkadɛR/ *nm* landing-stage.

embarcation /ɑ̃baRkasjɔ̃/ *nf* boat.

embardée /ɑ̃baRde/ *nf* swerve.

embarquement /ɑ̃baRkəmɑ̃/ *nm* (de passagers) boarding; (de fret) loading.

embarquer /ɑ̃baRke/ [1] *vt* take on board; (*frêt*) load; (emporter Ⓘ) cart off. ● *vi* board. □ **s'~** *vpr* board; **s'~ dans** embark upon.

embarras /ɑ̃baRa/ *nm* (gêne) embarrassment; (difficulté) difficulty.

embarrasser /ɑ̃baRase/ [1] *vt* (encombrer) clutter (up); (fig) embarrass. □ **s'~ de** *vpr* burden oneself with.

embauche /ɑ̃boʃ/ *nf* hiring.

embaucher [1] *vt* hire, take on.

embaumer /ɑ̃bome/ [1] *vt* (*pièce*) fill; (*cadavre*) embalm. ● *vi* be fragrant.

embellir /ɑ̃beliR/ [2] *vt* make more attractive; (*récit*) embellish.

embêtant, **~e** /ɑ̃bɛtɑ̃, -t/ *a* Ⓘ annoying.

embêter /ɑ̃bete/ [1] *vt* bother. □ **s'~** *vpr* be bored.

emblée: **d'~** /dɑ̃ble/ *loc* right away.

emblème /ɑ̃blɛm/ *nm* emblem.

emboîter /ɑ̃bwate/ [1] *vt* fit together; **~ le pas à qn** (imiter) follow suit. □ **s'~** *vpr* fit together; (**s'**)**~ dans** fit into.

embonpoint /ɑ̃bɔ̃pwɛ̃/ *nm* stoutness.

embourber (**s'**) /(s)ɑ̃buRbe/ [1] *vpr* get stuck in the mud; (fig) get bogged down.

embouteillage /ɑ̃butɛjaʒ/ *nm* traffic jam.

emboutir /ɑ̃butiR/ [2] *vt* (Auto) crash into.

embraser (**s'**) /(s)ɑ̃bRaze/ [1] *vpr* catch fire.

embrasser /ɑ̃bRase/ [1] *vt* kiss; (adopter, contenir) embrace. □ **s'~** *vpr* kiss.

embrayage /ɑ̃bRɛjaʒ/ *nm* clutch.

embrayer [31] *vi* engage the clutch.

embrouiller /ɑ̃bRuje/ [1] *vt* confuse; (*fils*) tangle. □ **s'~** *vpr* become confused.

embryon /ɑ̃bRijɔ̃/ *nm* embryo.

embûches /ɑ̃byʃ/ *nfpl* traps.

embuer (**s'**) /(s)ɑ̃bɥe/ [1] *vpr* mist up.

embuscade /ɑ̃byskad/ *nf* ambush.

E

émeraude /ɛmʀod/ *nf* emerald.

émerger /emɛʀʒe/ [40] *vi* emerge; (fig) stand out.

émeri /ɛmʀi/ *nm* emery.

émerveillement /emɛʀvɛjmɑ̃/ *nm* amazement, wonder.

émerveiller /emɛʀveje/ [1] *vt* fill with wonder. □ **s'~** *vpr* marvel at.

émetteur /emɛtœʀ/ *nm* transmitter.

émettre /emɛtʀ/ [42] *vt* (*son*) produce; (*message*) send out; (*timbre, billet*) issue; (*opinion*) express.

émeute /emœt/ *nf* riot.

émietter /emjete/ [1] *vt* crumble. □ **s'~** *vpr* crumble.

émigrant, ~e /emigʀɑ̃, -t/ *nm, f* emigrant. **émigration** *nf* emigration. **émigrer** [1] *vi* emigrate.

émincer /emɛ̃se/ [10] *vt* cut into thin slices.

éminent, ~e /eminɑ̃, -t/ *a* eminent.

émissaire /emisɛʀ/ *nm* emissary.

émission /emisjɔ̃/ *nf* (programme) programme; (de chaleur, gaz) emission; (de timbre) issue.

emmagasiner /ɑ̃magazine/ [1] *vt* store.

emmanchure /ɑ̃mɑ̃ʃyʀ/ *nf* armhole.

emmêler /ɑ̃mele/ [1] *vt* tangle. □ **s'~** *vpr* get mixed up.

emménager /ɑ̃menaʒe/ [40] *vi* move in; **~ dans** move into.

emmener /ɑ̃mne/ [6] *vt* take; (comme prisonnier) take away.

emmerder /ɑ̃mɛʀde/ [1] ▣ *vt* **~ qn** get on sb's nerves. □ **s'~** *vpr* be bored.

emmitoufler /ɑ̃mitufle/ [1] *vt* wrap up warmly. □ **s'~** *vpr* wrap oneself up warmly.

émoi /emwa/ *nm* turmoil; (plaisir) excitement.

émotif, -ive /emɔtif, -v/ *a* emotional. **émotion** *nf* emotion; (peur) fright. **émotionnel, ~le** *a* emotional.

émousser /emuse/ [1] *vt* blunt.

émouvant, ~e /emuvɑ̃, -t/ *a* moving.

empailler /ɑ̃paje/ [1] *vt* stuff.

empaqueter /ɑ̃pakte/ [38] *vt* package.

emparer (s') /(s)ɑ̃paʀe/ [1] *vpr* **s'~ de** get hold of.

empêchement /ɑ̃pɛʃmɑ̃/ *nm* **avoir un ~** to be held up.

empêcher /ɑ̃pɛʃe/ [1] *vt* prevent; **~ de faire** prevent *ou* stop (from) doing; (il) **n'empêche que** still. □ **s'~** *vpr* **il ne peut pas s'en ~** he cannot help it.

empereur /ɑ̃pʀœʀ/ *nm* emperor.

empester /ɑ̃pɛste/ [1] *vt* stink out; (*essence*) stink of. ● *vi* stink.

empêtrer (s') /(s)ɑ̃petʀe/ [1] *vpr* become entangled.

empiéter /ɑ̃pjete/ [14] *vi* **~ sur** encroach upon.

empiffrer (s') /(s)ɑ̃pifʀe/ [1] *vpr* ▣ stuff oneself.

empiler /ɑ̃pile/ [1] *vt* pile up. □ **s'~** *vpr* pile up.

empire /ɑ̃piʀ/ *nm* empire.

emplacement /ɑ̃plasmɑ̃/ *nm* site.

emplâtre /ɑ̃plɑtʀ/ *nm* (Méd) plaster.

emploi /ɑ̃plwa/ *nm* (travail) job; (embauche) employment; (utilisation) use; **un ~ de chauffeur** a job as a driver; **~ du temps** timetable. **employé, ~e** *nm, f* employee.

employer /ɑ̃plwaje/ [31] *vt* (*personne*) employ; (utiliser) use. □ **s'~** *vpr* be used; **s'~ à** devote oneself to. **employeur, -euse** *nm, f* employer.

empoigner /ɑ̃pwaɲe/ [1] *vt* grab. □ **s'~** *vpr* come to blows.

empoisonnement /ɑ̃pwazɔnmɑ̃/ *nm* poisoning.

empoisonner /ɑ̃pwazɔne/ [1] *vt* poison; (embêter 🗓) annoy. □ **s'~** *vpr* to poison oneself.

emporter /ɑ̃pɔʀte/ [1] *vt* take (away); (entraîner) sweep away; (arracher) tear off. □ **s'~** *vpr* lose one's temper; **l'~** get the upper hand (**sur** de); **plat à ~** take-away.

empoté, **~e** /ɑ̃pɔte/ *a* clumsy.

empreinte /ɑ̃pʀɛ̃t/ *nf* mark; ~ (**digitale**) fingerprint; ~ **de pas** footprint.

empressé, **~e** /ɑ̃pʀese/ *a* eager, attentive.

empresser (**s'**) /(s)ɑ̃pʀese/ [1] *vpr* **s'~ de** hasten to; **s'~ auprès de** be attentive to.

emprise /ɑ̃pʀiz/ *nf* influence.

emprisonnement /ɑ̃pʀizɔnmɑ̃/ *nm* imprisonment. **emprisonner** [1] *vt* imprison.

emprunt /ɑ̃pʀœ̃/ *nm* loan; **faire un ~** take out a loan.

emprunté, **~e** /ɑ̃pʀœ̃te/ *a* awkward.

emprunter /ɑ̃pʀœ̃te/ [1] *vt* borrow (**à** from); (*route*) take; (fig) assume. **emprunteur**, **-euse** *nm, f* borrower.

ému, **~e** /emy/ *a* moved; (intimidé) nervous.

émule /emyl/ *nmf* imitator.

....

en /ɑ̃/

➡ Pour les expressions comme **en principe**, **en train de**, **s'en aller**, etc. ⇒**principe**, **train**, **aller**, etc.

● *préposition*

····▸ (lieu) in.

····▸ (avec mouvement) to.

····▸ (temps) in.

····▸ (manière, état) in; ~ **faisant** by *ou* while doing; **je t'appelle ~ rentrant** I will call you when I get back.

····▸ (en qualité de) as.

····▸ (transport) by.

····▸ (composition) made of; **table ~ bois** wooden table.

● *pronom*

····▸ ~ **avoir/vouloir** have/want some; **ne pas ~ avoir/vouloir** not have/want any; **j'~ ai deux** I've got two; **prends-~ plusieurs** take several; **il m'~ reste un** I have one left; **j'~ suis content** I am pleased with him/her/it/them; **je m'~ souviens** I remember it.

····▸ ~ **êtes-vous sûr?** are you sure?

....

encadrement /ɑ̃kadʀəmɑ̃/ *nm* framing; (de porte) frame. **encadrer** [1] *vt* frame; (entourer d'un trait) circle; (superviser) supervise.

encaisser /ɑ̃kese/ [1] *vt* (*argent*) collect; (*chèque*) cash; (*coups* 🗓) take.

encart /ɑ̃kaʀ/ *nm* ~ **publicitaire** (advertising) insert.

en-cas /ɑ̃kɑ/ *nm* (stand-by) snack.

encastré, **-e** /ɑ̃kastʀe/ *a* built-in.

encaustique /ɑ̃kɔstik/ *nf* wax polish.

enceinte /ɑ̃sɛ̃t/ *af* pregnant; ~ **de 3 mois** 3 months pregnant. ● *nf* enclosure; ~ (**acoustique**) speaker.

encens /ɑ̃sɑ̃/ *nm* incense.

encercler /ɑ̃sɛʀkle/ [1] *vt* surround.

enchaînement /ɑ̃ʃɛnmɑ̃/ *nm* (suite) chain; (d'idées) sequence.

enchaîner /ɑ̃ʃene/ [1] *vt* chain (up); (*phrases*) link (up). ● *vi* continue. □ **s'~** *vpr* follow on.

enchanté, **~e** /ɑ̃ʃɑ̃te/ *a* (ravi) delighted. **enchanter** [1] *vt* delight; (ensorceler) enchant.

E

enchère /ɑ̃ʃɛʀ/ *nf* bid; **mettre** *ou* **vendre aux ~s** sell by auction.

enchevêtrer /ɑ̃ʃəvetʀe/ [1] *vt* tangle. □ **s'~** *vpr* become tangled.

enclave /ɑ̃klav/ *nf* enclave.

enclencher /ɑ̃klɑ̃ʃe/ [1] *vt* engage.

enclin, ~e /ɑ̃klɛ̃, -in/ *a* **à** inclined to.

enclos /ɑ̃klo/ *nm* enclosure.

enclume /ɑ̃klym/ *nf* anvil.

encoche /ɑ̃kɔʃ/ *nf* notch.

encolure /ɑ̃kɔlyʀ/ *nf* neck.

encombrant, ~e /ɑ̃kɔ̃bʀɑ̃, -t/ *a* cumbersome.

encombre /ɑ̃kɔ̃bʀ/ *nm* **sans ~** without any problems.

encombrement /ɑ̃kɔ̃bʀəmɑ̃/ *nm* (Auto) traffic congestion; (volume) bulk.

encombrer /ɑ̃kɔ̃bʀe/ [1] *vt* clutter (up); (obstruer) obstruct. □ **s'~ de** *vpr* burden oneself with.

encontre: à l'~ de /alɑ̃kɔ̃tʀədə/ *loc* against.

encore /ɑ̃kɔʀ/ *adv* (toujours) still; (de nouveau) again; (de plus) more; (aussi) also; **~ plus grand** even larger; **~ un café** another coffee; **pas ~** not yet; **si ~** if only; **et puis quoi ~?** 🗨 what next?

encouragement /ɑ̃kuʀaʒmɑ̃/ *nm* encouragement. **encourager** [40] *vt* encourage.

encourir /ɑ̃kuʀiʀ/ [20] *vt* incur.

encrasser /ɑ̃kʀase/ [1] *vt* clog up (with dirt).

encre /ɑ̃kʀ/ *nf* ink. **encrier** *nm* ink-well.

encyclopédie /ɑ̃siklɔpedi/ *nf* encyclopaedia.

endettement /ɑ̃dɛtmɑ̃/ *nm* debt.

endetter /ɑ̃dete/ [1] *vt* put into debt. □ **s'~** *vpr* get into debt.

endiguer /ɑ̃dige/ [1] *vt* dam; (fig) curb.

endimanché, ~e /ɑ̃dimɑ̃ʃe/ *a* in one's Sunday best.

endive /ɑ̃div/ *nf* chicory.

endoctriner /ɑ̃dɔktʀine/ [1] *vt* indoctrinate.

endommager /ɑ̃dɔmaʒe/ [40] *vt* damage.

endormi, ~e /ɑ̃dɔʀmi/ *a* asleep; (apathique) sleepy.

endormir /ɑ̃dɔʀmiʀ/ [46] *vt* send to sleep; (médicalement) put to sleep; (duper) dupe (**avec** with). □ **s'~** *vpr* fall asleep.

endosser /ɑ̃dose/ [1] *vt* (vêtement) put on; (assumer) take on; (Comm) endorse.

endroit /ɑ̃dʀwa/ *nm* place; (de tissu) right side; **à l'~** the right way round; **par ~s** in places.

enduire /ɑ̃dɥiʀ/ [17] *vt* coat. **enduit** *nm* coating.

endurance /ɑ̃dyʀɑ̃s/ *nf* endurance. **endurant, ~e** *a* tough.

endurcir /ɑ̃dyʀsiʀ/ [2] *vt* strengthen. □ **s'~** *vpr* become hard(ened).

endurer /ɑ̃dyʀe/ [1] *vt* endure.

énergétique /enɛʀʒetik/ *a* energy; (food) high-calorie. **énergie** *nf* energy; (Tech) power. **énergique** *a* energetic.

énervant, ~e /enɛʀvɑ̃, -t/ *a* irritating, annoying.

énerver /enɛʀve/ [1] *vt* irritate. □ **s'~** *vpr* get worked up.

enfance /ɑ̃fɑ̃s/ *nf* childhood; **la petite ~** infancy.

enfant /ɑ̃fɑ̃/ *nmf* child. **enfantillage** *nm* childishness. **enfantin, ~e** *a* simple, easy; (puéril) childish; (jeu, langage) children's.

enfer /ɑ̃fɛʀ/ *nm* (Relig) Hell; (fig) hell.

enfermer /ɑ̃fɛʀme/ [1] *vt* shut up. □ **s'~** *vpr* shut oneself up.

enfiler /ɑ̃file/ [1] *vt* (aiguille)

thread; (*vêtement*) slip on; (*rue*) take.

enfin /ɑ̃fɛ̃/ *adv* (de soulagement) at last; (en dernier lieu) finally; (résignation, conclusion) well; ~ **presque** well nearly.

enflammé, ~**e** /ɑ̃flame/ *a* (Méd) inflamed; (*discours*) fiery; (*lettre*) passionate.

enflammer /ɑ̃flame/ [1] *vt* set fire to. □ **s'~** *vpr* catch fire.

enfler /ɑ̃fle/ [1] *vt* (*histoire*) exaggerate. ● *vi* (*partie du corps*) swell (up); (*mer*) swell; (*rumeur, colère*) spread. □ **s'~** *vpr* (*colère*) mount; (*rumeur*) grow.

enfoncer /ɑ̃fɔ̃se/ [10] *vt* (*épingle*) push *ou* drive in; (*chapeau*) push down; (*porte*) break down. ● *vi* sink. □ **s'~** *vpr* sink (**dans** into).

enfouir /ɑ̃fwiʀ/ [2] *vt* bury.

enfourcher /ɑ̃fuʀʃe/ [1] *vt* mount.

enfreindre /ɑ̃fʀɛ̃dʀ/ [22] *vt* infringe, break.

enfuir (s') /(s)ɑ̃fɥiʀ/ [35] *vpr* run away.

enfumé, ~**e** /ɑ̃fyme/ *a* filled with smoke.

engagé, ~**e** /ɑ̃ɡaʒe/ *a* committed.

engagement /ɑ̃ɡaʒmɑ̃/ *nm* (promesse) promise; (Pol, Comm) commitment.

engager /ɑ̃ɡaʒe/ [40] *vt* (lier) bind, commit; (embaucher) take on; (commencer) start; (introduire) insert; (investir) invest. □ **s'~** *vpr* (promettre) commit oneself; (commencer) start; (*soldat*) enlist; (concurrent) enter; **s'~ à faire** undertake to do; **s'~ dans** (*voie*) enter.

engelure /ɑ̃ʒlyʀ/ *nf* chilblain.

engendrer /ɑ̃ʒɑ̃dʀe/ [1] *vt* (causer) generate.

engin /ɑ̃ʒɛ̃/ *nm* device; (véhicule) vehicle; (missile) missile.

engloutir /ɑ̃ɡlutiʀ/ [2] *vt* swallow (up).

engouement /ɑ̃ɡumɑ̃/ *nm* passion.

engouffrer /ɑ̃ɡufʀe/ [1] *vt* ▣ gobble up. □ **s'~ dans** *vpr* rush in.

engourdir /ɑ̃ɡuʀdiʀ/ [2] *vt* numb. □ **s'~** *vpr* go numb.

engrais /ɑ̃ɡʀɛ/ *nm* manure; (chimique) fertilizer.

engrenage /ɑ̃ɡʀənaʒ/ *nm* gears (+ *pl*); (fig) spiral.

engueuler /ɑ̃ɡœle/ [1] ▣ *vt* shout at. □ **s'~** *vpr* have a row.

enhardir (s') /(s)ɑ̃aʀdiʀ/ [2] *vpr* become bolder.

énième /ɛnjɛm/ *a* umpteenth.

énigmatique /enigmatik/ *a* enigmatic. **énigme** *nf* enigma; (devinette) riddle.

enivrer /ɑ̃nivʀe/ [1] *vt* intoxicate. □ **s'~** *vpr* get intoxicated.

enjambée /ɑ̃ʒɑ̃be/ *nf* stride. **enjamber** [1] *vt* step over; (*pont*) span.

enjeu (*pl* ~**x**) /ɑ̃ʒø/ *nm* stake.

enjoué, ~**e** /ɑ̃ʒwe/ *a* cheerful.

enlacer /ɑ̃lase/ [10] *vt* entwine.

enlèvement /ɑ̃lɛvmɑ̃/ *nm* (de colis) removal; (d'ordures) collection; (rapt) kidnapping.

enlever /ɑ̃lve/ [6] *vt* remove (**à** from); (*vêtement*) take off; (*tache, organe*) take out, remove; (kidnapper) kidnap; (gagner) win.

enliser (s') /(s)ɑ̃lize/ [1] *vpr* get bogged down.

enneigé, ~**e** /ɑ̃neʒe/ *a* snow-covered.

ennemi, ~**e** /ɛnmi/ *a & nm* enemy; ~ **de** (fig) hostile to.

ennui /ɑ̃nɥi/ *nm* problem; (tracas) boredom; **s'attirer des ~s** run into trouble.

ennuyer /ɑ̃nɥije/ [31] *vt* bore; (irriter) annoy; (préoccuper) worry; **si**

cela ne t'ennuie pas if you don't mind. □ s'~ *vpr* get bored.

ennuyeux, -euse /ɑ̃nɥijø, -z/ *a* boring; (fâcheux) annoying.

énoncé /enɔ̃se/ *nm* wording, text; (Gram) utterance.

énoncer /enɔ̃se/ [10] *vt* express, state.

enorgueillir (s') /(s)ɑ̃nɔʀgœjiʀ/ [2] *vpr* s'~ de pride oneself on.

énorme /enɔʀm/ *a* enormous.

enquête /ɑ̃kɛt/ *nf* (Jur) investigation, inquiry; (sondage) survey; **mener l'~** lead the inquiry. **enquêter** [1] *vi* ~ (**sur**) investigate. **enquêteur, -euse** *nm, f* investigator.

enquiquinant, ~e /ɑ̃kikinɑ̃, -t/ *a* 🗊 irritating.

enraciné, ~e /ɑ̃ʀasine/ *a* deep-rooted.

enragé, ~e /ɑ̃ʀaʒe/ *a* furious; (chien) rabid; (fig) fanatical.

enrager /ɑ̃ʀaʒe/ [40] *vi* be furious; **faire ~ qn** annoy sb.

enregistrement /ɑ̃ʀ(ə)ʒistʀəmɑ̃/ *nm* recording; (des bagages) check-in. **enregistrer** [1] *vt* (Mus, TV) record; (mémoriser) take in; (bagages) check in.

enrhumer (s') /(s)ɑ̃ʀyme/ [1] *vpr* catch a cold.

enrichir /ɑ̃ʀiʃiʀ/ [2] *vt* enrich. □ s'~ *vpr* grow rich(er). **enrichissant, ~e** *a* (expérience) rewarding.

enrober /ɑ̃ʀɔbe/ [1] *vt* coat (**de** with).

enrôler /ɑ̃ʀole/ [1] *vt* recruit. □ s'~ *vpr* enlist, enrol.

enroué, ~e /ɑ̃ʀwe/ *a* hoarse.

enrouler /ɑ̃ʀule/ [1] *vt* wind, wrap. □ s'~ *vpr* wind; **s'~ dans une couverture** roll oneself up in a blanket.

ensanglanté, ~e /ɑ̃sɑ̃glɑ̃te/ *a* bloodstained.

enseignant, ~e /ɑ̃sɛɲɑ̃, -t/ *nm, f* teacher. ●*a* teaching.

enseigne /ɑ̃sɛɲ/ *nf* sign.

enseignement /ɑ̃sɛɲəmɑ̃/ *nm* (profession) teaching; (instruction) education.

enseigner /ɑ̃sɛɲe/ [1] *vt/i* teach; ~ **qch à qn** teach sb sth.

ensemble /ɑ̃sɑ̃bl/ *adv* together. ●*nm* group; (Mus) ensemble; (vêtements) outfit; (cohésion) unity; (maths) set; **dans l'~** on the whole; **d'~** (idée) general; **l'~ de** (totalité) all of, the whole of.

ensevelir /ɑ̃səvliʀ/ [2] *vt* bury.

ensoleillé, ~e /ɑ̃sɔleje/ *a* sunny.

ensorceler /ɑ̃sɔʀsəle/ [38] *vt* bewitch.

ensuite /ɑ̃sɥit/ *adv* next, then; (plus tard) later.

ensuivre (s') /(s)ɑ̃sɥivʀ/ [57] *vpr* follow; **et tout ce qui s'ensuit** and all the rest of it.

entaille /ɑ̃taj/ *nf* cut; (profonde) gash; (encoche) notch.

entamer /ɑ̃tame/ [1] *vt* start; (inciser) cut into; (ébranler) shake.

entasser /ɑ̃tase/ [1] *vt* (livres) pile; (argent) hoard; (personnes) cram (**dans** into). □ s'~ *vpr* (objets) pile up (**dans** into); (personnes) squeeze (**dans** into).

entendement /ɑ̃tɑ̃dmɑ̃/ *nm* understanding; **ça dépasse l'~** it's beyond belief.

entendre /ɑ̃tɑ̃dʀ/ [3] *vt* hear; (comprendre) understand; (vouloir dire) mean; ~ **parler de** hear of; ~ **dire que** hear that. □ s'~ *vpr* (être d'accord) agree; **s'~ (bien)** get on (**avec** with); **cela s'entend** of course.

entendu, ~e /ɑ̃tɑ̃dy/ *a* (convenu) agreed; (sourire, air) knowing; **bien ~** of course; **(c'est) ~!** all right!

entente /ɑ̃tɑ̃t/ *nf* understanding; **bonne ~** good relationship.

enterrement /ɑ̃tɛʀmɑ̃/ *nm* funeral.

enterrer /ɑ̃tɛʀe/ [1] *vt* bury.

en-tête /ɑ̃tɛt/ *nm* heading; **à ~** headed.

entêté, ~e /ɑ̃tete/ *a* stubborn. **entêtement** *nm* stubbornness. **entêter (s')** [1] *vpr* persist (**à**, **dans** in).

enthousiasme /ɑ̃tuzjasm/ *nm* enthusiasm. **enthousiasmer** [1] *vt* fill with enthusiasm. **enthousiaste** *a* enthusiastic.

enticher (s') /(s)ɑ̃tiʃe/ [1] *vpr* **s'~ de** become infatuated with.

entier, -ière /ɑ̃tje, -jɛʀ/ *a* whole; (absolu) absolute; (entêté) unyielding. ●*nm* whole; **en ~** entirely.

entonnoir /ɑ̃tɔnwaʀ/ *nm* funnel; (trou) crater.

entorse /ɑ̃tɔʀs/ *nf* sprain; (fig) **~ à** (loi) infringement of.

entortiller /ɑ̃tɔʀtije/ [1] *vt* wind, wrap (**autour** around); (duper 𝕀) get round.

entourage /ɑ̃tuʀaʒ/ *nm* circle of family and friends; (bordure) surround.

entouré ~e /ɑ̃tuʀe/ *a* (personne) supported.

entourer /ɑ̃tuʀe/ [1] *vt* surround (**de** with); (réconforter) rally round; **~ qch de mystère** shroud sth in mystery.

entracte /ɑ̃tʀakt/ *nm* interval.

entraide /ɑ̃tʀɛd/ *nf* mutual aid. **entraider (s')** [1] *vpr* help each other.

entrain /ɑ̃tʀɛ̃/ *nm* zest, spirit.

entraînement /ɑ̃tʀɛnmɑ̃/ *nm* (Sport) training.

entraîner /ɑ̃tʀene/ [1] *vt* (emporter) carry away; (provoquer) lead to; (Sport) train; (actionner) drive. □ **s'~** *vpr* train. **entraîneur** *nm* trainer.

entrave /ɑ̃tʀav/ *nf* hindrance. **entraver** [1] *vt* hinder.

entre /ɑ̃tʀ(ə)/ *prép* between; (parmi) among(st); **~ autres** among other things; **l'un d'~ nous/eux** one of us/them.

entrebâillé, ~e /ɑ̃tʀəbaje/ *a* ajar, half-open.

entrechoquer (s') /(s)ɑ̃tʀəʃɔke/ [1] *vpr* knock against each other.

entrecôte /ɑ̃tʀəkot/ *nf* rib steak.

entrecouper /ɑ̃tʀəkupe/ [1] *vt* **~ de** intersperse with.

entrecroiser (s') /(s)ɑ̃tʀəkʀwa-ze/ [1] *vpr* (routes) intertwine.

entrée /ɑ̃tʀe/ *nf* entrance; (vestibule) hall; (accès) admission, entry; (billet) ticket; (Culin) starter; (Ordinat) **tapez sur E~** press Enter; '**~ interdite**' 'no entry'.

entrejambes /ɑ̃tʀəʒɑ̃b/ *nm* crotch.

entremets /ɑ̃tʀəmɛ/ *nm* dessert.

entremise /ɑ̃tʀəmiz/ *nf* intervention; **par l'~ de** through.

entreposer /ɑ̃tʀəpoze/ [1] *vt* store.

entrepôt /ɑ̃tʀəpo/ *nm* warehouse.

entreprenant, ~e /ɑ̃tʀəpʀənɑ̃, -t/ *a* (actif) enterprising; (séducteur) forward.

entreprendre /ɑ̃tʀəpʀɑ̃dʀ/ [50] *vt* start on, undertake; (personne) buttonhole; **~ de faire** undertake to do.

entrepreneur /ɑ̃tʀəpʀənœʀ/ *nm* (de bâtiment) contractor; (chef d'entreprise) firm manager.

entreprise /ɑ̃tʀəpʀiz/ *nf* (projet) undertaking; (société) firm, business, company.

entrer /ɑ̃tʀe/ [1] *vi* (aux être) go in, enter; (venir) come in, enter; **~ dans** go ou come into, enter; (club) join; **~ en collision** collide (**avec** with); **faire ~** (personne) show in; **laisser ~** let in; **~ en guerre** go to war. ●*vt* (données) enter.

E

entre-temps /ɑ̃tRətɑ̃/ *adv* meanwhile.

entretenir /ɑ̃tRət(ə)niR/ [58] *vt* (*appareil*) maintain; (*vêtement*) look after; (*alimenter*) (*feu*) keep going; (*amitié*) keep alive; (*amitié*) **~ qn de** converse with sb about. □ **s'~** *vpr* speak (**de** about; **avec** to).

entretien *nm* maintenance; (*discussion*) talk; (*pour un emploi*) interview.

entrevoir /ɑ̃tRəvwaR/ [63] *vt* make out; (*brièvement*) glimpse.

entrevue /ɑ̃tRəvy/ *nf* meeting.

entrouvert, ~e /ɑ̃tRuvɛR, -t/ *a* ajar, half-open.

énumération /enymeRasjɔ̃/ *nf* enumeration. **énumérer** [14] *vt* enumerate.

envahir /ɑ̃vaiR/ [2] *vt* invade, overrun; (*douleur, peur*) overcome.

enveloppe /ɑ̃vlɔp/ *nf* envelope; (*emballage*) wrapping; **~ budgétaire** budget. **envelopper** [1] *vt* wrap (up); (*fig*) envelop.

envergure /ɑ̃vɛRgyR/ *nf* wingspan; (*importance*) scope; (*qualité*) calibre.

envers /ɑ̃vɛR/ *prép* toward(s), to. ● *nm* (*de tissu*) wrong side; **à l'~** (*tableau*) upside down; (*devant derrière*) back to front; (*chaussette*) inside out.

envie /ɑ̃vi/ *nf* urge; (*jalousie*) envy; **avoir ~ de qch** feel like sth; **avoir ~ de faire** want to do; (*moins urgent*) feel like doing; **faire ~ à qn** make sb envious.

envier /ɑ̃vje/ [45] *vt* envy. **envieux, -ieuse** *a* envious.

environ /ɑ̃viRɔ̃/ *adv* about.

environnant, ~e /ɑ̃viRɔnɑ̃, -t/ *a* surrounding.

environnement /ɑ̃viRɔnmɑ̃/ *nm* environment.

environs /ɑ̃viRɔ̃/ *nmpl* vicinity;

aux ~ de (*lieu*) in the vicinity of; (*heure*) round about.

envisager /ɑ̃vizaʒe/ [40] *vt* consider; (*imaginer*) envisage; **~ de faire** consider doing.

envoi /ɑ̃vwa/ *nm* dispatch; (*paquet*) consignment; **faire un ~** send; **coup d'~** (Sport) kick-off.

envoler (s') /(s)ɑ̃vɔle/ [1] *vpr* fly away; (*avion*) take off; (*papiers*) blow away.

envoyé, ~e /ɑ̃vwaje/ *nm, f* envoy; **~ spécial** special correspondent.

envoyer /ɑ̃vwaje/ [32] *vt* send; (*lancer*) throw.

éolienne /eɔljɛn/ *nf* windmill; **ferme d'~s** wind farm.

épais, ~se /epɛ, -s/ *a* thick. **épaisseur** *nf* thickness.

épaissir /epesiR/ [2] *vt/i* thicken. □ **s'~** *vpr* thicken; (*mystère*) deepen.

épanoui, ~e /epanwi/ *a* (*personne*) beaming, radiant.

épanouir (s') /(s)epanwiR/ [2] *vpr* (*fleur*) open out; (*visage*) beam; (*personne*) blossom.

épanouissement *nm* (*éclat*) blossoming, full bloom.

épargne /epaRɲ/ *nf* savings.

épargner /epaRɲe/ [1] *vt/i* save; (*ne pas tuer*) spare; **~ qch à qn** spare sb sth.

éparpiller /epaRpije/ [1] *vt* scatter. □ **s'~** *vpr* scatter.

épars, ~e /epaR, -s/ *a* scattered.

épatant, ~e /epatɑ̃, -t/ *a* 🄳 amazing.

épaule /epol/ *nf* shoulder.

épave /epav/ *nf* wreck.

épée /epe/ *nf* sword.

épeler /ɛple/ [6] *vt* spell.

éperdu, ~e /epɛRdy/ *a* wild, frantic.

éperon /epRɔ̃/ *nm* spur.

éphémère /efemɛR/ *a* ephemeral.

épi /epi/ *nm* (de blé) ear; (mèche) tuft of hair; ~ **de maïs** corn cob.

épice /epis/ *nf* spice. **épicé**, ~**e** *a* spicy.

épicerie /episʀi/ *nf* grocery shop; (produits) groceries. **épicier, -ière** *nm,f* grocer.

épidémie /epidemi/ *nf* epidemic.

épiderme /epidɛʀm/ *nm* skin.

épier /epje/ [45] *vt* spy on.

épilepsie /epilɛpsi/ *nf* epilepsy. **épileptique** *a* & *nmf* epileptic.

épiler /epile/ [1] *vt* remove unwanted hair from; (sourcils) pluck.

épilogue /epilɔg/ *nm* epilogue; (fig) outcome.

épinard /epinaʀ/ *nm* ~**s** spinach (+ *sg*).

épine /epin/ *nf* thorn, prickle; (d'animal) prickle, spine; ~ **dorsale** backbone. **épineux, -euse** *a* thorny.

épingle /epɛ̃gl/ *nf* pin; ~ **de nourrice**, ~ **de sûreté** safety-pin.

épisode /epizɔd/ *nm* episode; à ~**s** serialized.

épitaphe /epitaf/ *nf* epitaph.

épluche-légumes /eplyʃlegym/ *nm inv* (potato) peeler.

éplucher /eplyʃe/ [1] *vt* peel; (examiner: fig) scrutinize.

épluchure /eplyʃyʀ/ *nf* ~**s** peelings.

éponge /epɔ̃ʒ/ *nf* sponge.

éponger [40] *vt* (liquide) mop up; (surface, front) mop; (fig) (dettes) wipe out.

épopée /epɔpe/ *nf* epic.

époque /epɔk/ *nf* time, period; à l'~ at the time; d'~ period.

épouse /epuz/ *nf* wife.

épouser /epuze/ [1] *vt* marry; (forme, idée) adopt.

épousseter /epuste/ [38] *vt* dust.

épouvantable /epuvɑ̃tabl/ *a* appalling.

épouvantail /epuvɑ̃taj/ *nm* scarecrow.

épouvante /epuvɑ̃t/ *nf* terror. **épouvanter** [1] *vt* terrify.

époux /epu/ *nm* husband; **les** ~ the married couple.

éprendre (**s'**) /(s)epʀɑ̃dʀ/ [50] *vpr* **s'**~ **de** fall in love with.

épreuve /epʀœv/ *nf* test; (Sport) event; (malheur) ordeal; (Photo, d'imprimerie) proof; **mettre à l'**~ put to the test.

éprouver /epʀuve/ [1] *vt* (ressentir) experience; (affliger) distress; (tester) test.

éprouvette /epʀuvɛt/ *nf* test-tube.

EPS *abrév f* (**éducation physique et sportive**) PE.

épuisé, ~**e** /epɥize/ *a* exhausted; (livre) out of print. **épuisement** *nm* exhaustion.

épuiser /epɥize/ [1] *vt* (fatiguer, user) exhaust. □ **s'**~ *vpr* become exhausted.

épuration /epyʀasjɔ̃/ *nf* purification; (Pol) purge. **épurer** [1] *vt* purify; (Pol) purge.

équateur /ekwatœʀ/ *nm* equator.

équilibre /ekilibʀ/ *nm* balance; **être** *ou* **se tenir en** ~ (personne) balance; (objet) be balanced. **équilibré**, ~**e** *a* well-balanced.

équilibrer /ekilibʀe/ [1] *vt* balance. □ **s'**~ *vpr* balance each other.

équilibriste /ekilibʀist/ *nmf* acrobat.

équipage /ekipaʒ/ *nm* crew.

équipe /ekip/ *nf* team; ~ **de nuit/ jour** night/day shift.

équipé, ~**e** /ekipe/ *a* equipped; **cuisine** ~**e** fitted kitchen.

équipement /ekipmɑ̃/ *nm* equipment; ~**s** (installations) amenities, facilities.

équiper /ekipe/ [1] *vt* equip (**de** with). □ **s'**~ *vpr* equip oneself.

équipier, -ière /ekipje, -jɛʀ/ *nm, f* team member.

équitable /ekitabl/ *a* fair.

équitation /ekitasjɔ̃/ *nf* (horse-) riding.

équivalence /ekivalɑ̃s/ *nf* equivalence. **équivalent, ~e** *a* equivalent.

équivaloir /ekivalwaʀ/ [60] *vi* ~ à be equivalent to.

équivoque /ekivɔk/ *a* equivocal; (louche) questionable. ● *nf* ambiguity.

érable /eʀabl/ *nm* maple.

érafler /eʀafle/ [1] *vt* scratch. **éraflure** *nf* scratch.

éraillé, ~e /eʀaje/ *a* (voix) raucous.

ère /ɛʀ/ *nf* era.

éreintant, ~e /eʀɛ̃tɑ̃, -t/ *a* exhausting. **éreinter (s')** [1] *vpr* wear oneself out.

ériger /eʀiʒe/ [40] *vt* erect. □ s'~ en *vpr* set (oneself) up as.

éroder /eʀɔde/ [1] *vt* erode. **érosion** *nf* erosion.

errer /eʀe/ [1] *vi* wander.

erreur /eʀœʀ/ *nf* mistake, error; **dans l'~** mistaken; **par ~** by mistake; **~ judiciaire** miscarriage of justice.

erroné, ~e /eʀɔne/ *a* erroneous.

érudit, ~e /eʀydi, -t/ *a* scholarly. ● *nm, f* scholar.

éruption /eʀypsjɔ̃/ *nf* eruption; (Méd) rash.

es /ɛ/ ⇒ÊTRE [4].

escabeau (*pl* ~x) /ɛskabo/ *nm* step-ladder.

escadron /ɛskadʀɔ̃/ *nm* (Mil) company.

escalade /ɛskalad/ *nf* climbing; (Pol, Comm) escalation. **escalader** [1] *vt* climb.

escale /ɛskal/ *nf* (d'avion) stopover; (port) port of call; **faire ~ à** (avion, passager) stop over at; (navire, passager) put in at.

escalier /ɛskalje/ *nm* stairs (+ *pl*); ~ **mécanique** *ou* **roulant** escalator.

escalope /ɛskalɔp/ *nf* escalope.

escargot /ɛskaʀgo/ *nm* snail.

escarpé, ~e /ɛskaʀpe/ *a* steep.

escarpin /ɛskaʀpɛ̃/ *nm* court shoe; (US) pump.

escient: **à bon ~** /abɔnesjɑ̃/ *loc* wisely.

esclandre /ɛsklɑ̃dʀ/ *nm* scene.

esclavage /ɛsklavaʒ/ *nm* slavery. **esclave** *nmf* slave.

escompte /ɛskɔ̃t/ *nm* discount. **escompter** [1] *vt* expect; (Comm) discount.

escorte /ɛskɔʀt/ *nf* escort.

escrime /ɛskʀim/ *nf* fencing.

escroc /ɛskʀo/ *nm* swindler.

escroquer /ɛskʀɔke/ [1] *vt* swindle; ~ **qch à qn** swindle sb out of sth. **escroquerie** *nf* swindle.

espace /ɛspas/ *nm* space; ~s **verts** gardens and parks.

espacer /ɛspase/ [10] *vt* space out. □ s'~ *vpr* become less frequent.

espadrille /ɛspadʀij/ *nf* rope sandal.

Espagne /ɛspaɲ/ *nf* Spain.

espagnol, ~e /ɛspaɲɔl/ *a* Spanish. ● *nm* (Ling) Spanish. **E~, ~e** *nm, f* Spaniard.

espèce /ɛspɛs/ *nf* kind, sort; (race) species; **en ~s** (argent) in cash; ~ **d'idiot!** 🄳 you idiot! 🄳.

espérance /ɛspeʀɑ̃s/ *nf* hope.

espérer /ɛspeʀe/ [14] *vt* hope for; ~ **faire/que** hope to do/that. ● *vi* hope.

espiègle /ɛspjɛgl/ *a* mischievous.

espion, ~ne /ɛspjɔ̃, -ɔn/ *nm, f* spy. **espionnage** *nm* espionage, spying. **espionner** [1] *vt* spy (on).

espoir /ɛspwaʀ/ *nm* hope; **reprendre ~** feel hopeful again.

esprit /ɛspri/ *nm* (intellect) mind; (humour) wit; (fantôme) spirit; (ambiance) atmosphere; **perdre l'~** lose one's mind; **reprendre ses ~s** come to; **faire de l'~** try to be witty.

esquimau, ~de (*mpl* ~**x**) /ɛskimo, -d/ *nm, f* Eskimo.

esquinter /ɛskɛ̃te/ [1] *vt* 🗊 ruin.

esquisse /ɛskis/ *nf* sketch; (fig) outline.

esquiver /ɛskive/ [1] *vt* dodge. □ **s'~** *vpr* slip away.

essai /esɛ/ *nm* (épreuve) test, trial; (tentative) try; (article) essay; (au rugby) try; ~**s** (Auto) qualifying round (+ *sg*); **à l'~** on trial.

essaim /esɛ̃/ *nm* swarm.

essayage /esɛjaʒ/ *nm* fitting; **salon d'~** fitting room.

essayer /eseje/ [31] *vt/i* try; (*vêtement*) try (on); (*voiture*) try (out); ~ **de faire** try to do.

essence /esɑ̃s/ *nf* (carburant) petrol; (nature, extrait) essence; ~ **sans plomb** unleaded petrol.

essentiel, ~le /esɑ̃sjɛl/ *a* essential. ● *nm* **l'~** the main thing; (quantité) the main part.

essieu (*pl* ~**x**) /esjø/ *nm* axle.

essor /esɔR/ *nm* expansion; **prendre son ~** expand.

essorage /esɔRaʒ/ *nm* spin-drying.

essorer [1] *vt* (*linge*) spin-dry; (en tordant) wring.

essoreuse /esɔRøz/ *nf* spin-drier; ~ **à salade** salad spinner.

essoufflé, ~e /esufle/ *a* out of breath.

essuie-glace /esɥiglas/ *nm inv* windscreen wiper.

essuie-mains /esɥimɛ̃/ *nm inv* hand-towel.

essuie-tout /esɥitu/ *nm inv* kitchen paper.

essuyer /esɥije/ [31] *vt* wipe; (subir) suffer. □ **s'~** *vpr* dry *ou* wipe oneself.

est¹ /ɛ/ ⇒ÊTRE [4].

est² /ɛst/ *nm* east. ● *a inv* east; (partie) eastern; (direction) easterly.

estampe /ɛstɑ̃p/ *nf* print.

esthète /ɛstɛt/ *nmf* aesthete.

esthéticienne /ɛstetisjɛn/ *nf* beautician.

esthétique /ɛstetik/ *a* aesthetic.

estimation /ɛstimasjɔ̃/ *nf* (de coûts) estimate; (valeur) valuation.

estime /ɛstim/ *nf* esteem.

estimer /ɛstime/ [1] *vt* (*tableau*) value; (calculer) estimate; (respecter) esteem; (considérer) consider (**que** that).

estival, ~e (*mpl* **-aux**) /ɛstival, -o/ *a* summer. **estivant, ~e** *nm, f* summer visitor.

estomac /ɛstɔma/ *nm* stomach.

estomaqué, ~e /ɛstɔmake/ *a* 🗊 stunned.

Estonie /ɛstɔni/ *nf* Estonia.

estrade /ɛstRad/ *nf* platform.

estragon /ɛstRagɔ̃/ *nm* tarragon.

estropié, ~e /ɛstRɔpje/ *nm, f* cripple. ● *a* crippled.

estuaire /ɛstɥɛR/ *nm* estuary.

et /e/ *conj* and; ~ **moi?** what about me?; ~ **alors?** so what?

étable /etabl/ *nf* cow-shed.

établi, ~e /etabli/ *a* established; **un fait bien ~** a well-established fact. ● *nm* work-bench.

établir /etabliR/ [2] *vt* establish; (*liste, facture*) draw up; (*personne, camp, record*) set up. □ **s'~** *vpr* (*personne*) settle; **s'~ à son compte** set up on one's own.

établissement /etablismɑ̃/ *nm* (entreprise) organization; (institution) establishment; ~ **scolaire** school.

étage /etaʒ/ *nm* floor, storey; (de fusée) stage; **à l'~** upstairs; **au premier ~** on the first floor.

étagère /etaʒɛR/ *nf* shelf; (meuble) shelving unit.

étain /etɛ̃/ *nm* pewter.

E

étais, **était** /etɛ/ ⇒ÊTRE [4].

étalage /etalaʒ/ *nm* display; (vitrine) shop-window; **faire ~ de** flaunt. **étalagiste** *nmf* window-dresser.

étaler /etale/ [1] *vt* spread; (*journal*) spread (out); (*pâte*) roll out; (exposer) display; (*richesse*) flaunt. □ **s'~** *vpr* (prendre de la place) spread out; (tomber 🇫) fall flat; **s'~ sur** (*paiement*) be spread over.

étalon /etalɔ̃/ *nm* (cheval) stallion; (modèle) standard.

étanche /etɑ̃ʃ/ *a* watertight; (*montre*) waterproof.

étancher /etɑ̃ʃe/ [1] *vt* (*soif*) quench.

étang /etɑ̃/ *nm* pond.

étant /etɑ̃/ ⇒ÊTRE [4].

étape /etap/ *nf* stage; (lieu d'arrêt) stopover; (fig) stage.

état /eta/ *nm* state; (liste) statement; (métier) profession; **en bon/mauvais ~** in good/bad condition; **en ~ de** in a position to; **en ~ de marche** in working order; **faire ~ de** (citer) mention; **être dans tous ses ~s** be in a state; **~ civil** civil status; **~ des lieux** inventory of fixtures. **État** *nm* State.

état-major (*pl* **états-majors**) /etamaʒɔr/ *nm* (officiers) staff (+ *pl*).

États-Unis /etazyni/ *nmpl* **~** (d'Amérique) United States (of America).

étau (*pl* **~x**) /eto/ *nm* vice.

étayer /eteje/ [31] *vt* prop up.

été¹ /ete/ ⇒ÊTRE [4].

été² /ete/ *nm* summer.

éteindre /etɛ̃dr/ [22] *vt* (*feu*) put out; (*lumière, radio*) turn off. □ **s'~** *vpr* (*feu, lumière*) go out; (*appareil*) go off; (*mourir*) die. **éteint**, **~e** *a* (*feu*) out; (*volcan*) extinct.

étendard /etɑ̃dar/ *nm* standard.

étendre /etɑ̃dr/ [3] *vt* (*nappe*) spread (out); (*bras, jambes*) stretch (out); (*linge*) hang out; (agrandir) extend. □ **s'~** *vpr* (s'allonger) lie down; (se propager) spread; (*plaine*) stretch; **s'~ sur** (*sujet*) dwell on.

étendu, **~e** /etɑ̃dy/ *a* extensive. **étendue** *nf* area; (d'eau) stretch; (importance) extent.

éternel, **~le** /etɛrnɛl/ *a* (*vie*) eternal; (fig) endless.

éterniser (**s'**) /(s)etɛrnize/ [1] *vpr* (durer) drag on.

éternité /etɛrnite/ *nf* eternity.

éternuement /etɛrnymɑ̃/ *nm* sneeze. **éternuer** [1] *vi* sneeze.

êtes /ɛt/ ⇒ÊTRE [4].

éthique /etik/ *a* ethical. ● *nf* ethics (+ *sg*).

ethnie /ɛtni/ *nf* ethnic group. **ethnique** *a* ethnic.

étincelant, **~e** /etɛ̃slɑ̃, -t/ *a* sparkling. **étinceler** [38] *vi* sparkle. **étincelle** *nf* spark.

étiqueter /etikte/ [38] *vt* label. **étiquette** *nf* label; (protocole) etiquette.

étirer /etire/ [1] *vt* stretch. □ **s'~** *vpr* stretch.

étoffe /etɔf/ *nf* fabric.

étoffer /etɔfe/ [1] *vt* expand. □ **s'~** *vpr* fill out.

étoile /etwal/ *nf* star; **à la belle ~** in the open; **~ filante** shooting star; **~ de mer** starfish.

étonnant, **~e** /etɔnɑ̃, -t/ *a* (curieux) surprising; (formidable) amazing. **étonnement** *nm* surprise; (plus fort) amazement.

étonner /etɔne/ [1] *vt* amaze. □ **s'~** *vpr* be amazed (**de** at).

étouffant, **~e** /etufɑ̃, -t/ *a* stifling.

étouffer /etufe/ [1] *vt/i* suffocate; (*sentiment, révolte*) stifle; (*feu*) smother; (*bruit*) muffle; **on étouffe**

it is stifling. □ **s'∼** *vpr* suffocate; (en mangeant) choke.

étourderie /etuʀdəʀi/ *nf* thoughtlessness; (acte) careless mistake.

étourdi, ∼e /etuʀdi/ *a* absent-minded. ● *nm, f* scatterbrain.

étourdir /etuʀdiʀ/ [2] *vt* stun; (fatiguer) make sb's head spin. **étourdissant, ∼e** *a* stunning.

étourneau (*pl* ∼**x**) /etuʀno/ *nm* starling.

étrange /etʀɑ̃ʒ/ *a* strange.

étranger, -ère /etʀɑ̃ʒe, -ɛʀ/ *a* (inconnu) strange, unfamiliar; (d'un autre pays) foreign. ● *nm, f* foreigner; (inconnu) stranger; **à l'∼** abroad; **de l'∼** from abroad.

étrangler /etʀɑ̃gle/ [1] *vt* strangle; (col) throttle. □ **s'∼** *vpr* choke.

··

être /ɛtʀ/ [4]

● *verbe auxiliaire*

····▶ (du passé) have; **elle est partie/ venue hier** she left/came yesterday.

····▶ (de la voix passive) be.

● *verbe intransitif (aux avoir)*

····▶ be; ∼ **médecin** be a doctor; **je suis à vous** I'm all yours; **j'en suis à me demander si...** I'm beginning to wonder whether...; **qu'en est-il de...?** what's the news about...?

····▶ (appartenance) be, belong to.

····▶ (heure, date) be; **nous sommes le 3 mars** it's March 3.

····▶ (aller) be; **je n'y ai jamais été** I've never been; **il a été le voir** he went to see him.

····▶ **c'est** it is *or* it's; **c'est moi qui l'ai fait** I did it; **est-ce que tu veux du thé?** do you want some tea?

● *nom masculin*

····▶ being; ∼ **humain** human being.

····▶ (personne) person; **un ∼ cher** a loved one.

··

étreindre /etʀɛ̃dʀ/ [22] *vt* embrace. **étreinte** *nf* embrace.

étrennes /etʀɛn/ *nfpl* (New Year's) gift (+ *sg*); (argent) money.

étrier /etʀije/ *nm* stirrup.

étriqué, ∼e /etʀike/ *a* tight.

étroit, ∼e /etʀwa, -t/ *a* narrow; (vêtement) tight; (liens, surveillance) close; **à l'∼** cramped. **étroitement** *adv* closely. **étroitesse** *nf* narrowness.

étude /etyd/ *nf* study; (enquête) survey; (bureau) office; (salle d')∼ (Scol) prep room; **à l'∼** under consideration; **faire des ∼s (de)** study; **il n'a pas fait d'∼s** he didn't go to university; ∼ **de marché** market research.

étudiant, ∼e /etydjɑ̃, -t/ *nm, f* student.

étudier /etydje/ [45] *vt/i* study.

étui /etyi/ *nm* case.

étuve /etyv/ *nf* steam room.

eu, ∼e /y/ ⇒AVOIR [5]

euro /øʀo/ *nm* euro.

Europe /øʀɔp/ *nf* Europe.

européen, ∼ne /øʀɔpeɛ̃, ɛn/ *a* European. **E∼, ∼ne** *nm, f* European.

euthanasie /øtanazi/ *nf* euthanasia.

eux /ø/ *pron* they; (complément) them. **eux-mêmes** *pron* themselves.

évacuation /evakɥasjɔ̃/ *nf* evacuation; (d'eaux usées) discharge. **évacuer** [1] *vt* evacuate.

évadé, ∼e /evade/ *a* escaped. ● *nm, f* escaped prisoner. **évader (s')** [1] *vpr* escape.

évaluation /evalɥasjɔ̃/ *nf*

assessment. **évaluer** [1] *vt* assess.

évangile /evɑ̃ʒil/ *nm* gospel; **l'É~** the Gospel.

évanouir (s') /(s)evanwiʀ/ [2] *vpr* faint; (disparaître) vanish.

évaporation /evapɔʀasjɔ̃/ *nf* evaporation. **évaporer (s')** [1] *vpr* evaporate.

évasif, -ive /evazif, -v/ *a* evasive.

évasion /evazjɔ̃/ *nf* escape.

éveil /evɛj/ *nm* awakening; **en ~** alert.

éveillé, ~e /eveje/ *a* awake; (intelligent) alert.

éveiller /eveje/ [1] *vt* awake(n); (susciter) arouse. □ **s'~** *vpr* awake.

événement /evɛnmɑ̃/ *nm* event.

éventail /evɑ̃taj/ *nm* fan; (gamme) range.

éventrer /evɑ̃tʀe/ [1] *vt* (*sac*) rip open.

éventualité /evɑ̃tɥalite/ *nf* possibility; **dans cette ~** in that event.

éventuel, ~le /evɑ̃tɥɛl/ *a* possible. **éventuellement** *adv* possibly.

évêque /evɛk/ *nm* bishop.

évertuer (s') /(s)evɛʀtɥe/ [1] *vpr* **s'~ à** struggle hard to.

éviction /eviksjɔ̃/ *nf* eviction.

évidemment /evidamɑ̃/ *adv* obviously; (bien sûr) of course.

évidence /evidɑ̃s/ *nf* obviousness; (fait) obvious fact; **être en ~** be conspicuous; **mettre en ~** (fait) highlight. **évident, ~e** *a* obvious, evident.

évier /evje/ *nm* sink.

évincer /evɛ̃se/ [10] *vt* oust.

éviter /evite/ [1] *vt* avoid (**de faire** doing); **~ qch à qn** (*dérangement*) save sb sth.

évocateur, -trice /evɔkatœʀ, -tʀis/ *a* evocative. **évocation** *nf* evocation.

évolué, ~e /evɔlɥe/ *a* highly developed.

évoluer /evɔlɥe/ [1] *vi* evolve; (*situation*) develop; (se déplacer) glide. **évolution** *nf* evolution; (d'une situation) development.

évoquer /evɔke/ [1] *vt* call to mind, evoke.

exacerber /ɛgzasɛʀbe/ [1] *vt* exacerbate.

exact, ~e /ɛgza(kt), -akt/ *a* (précis) exact, accurate; (juste) correct; (*personne*) punctual. **exactement** *adv* exactly. **exactitude** *nf* exactness; punctuality.

ex æquo /ɛgzeko/ *adv* **être ~** tie (**avec qn** with sb).

exagération /ɛgzaʒeʀasjɔ̃/ *nf* exaggeration. **exagéré, ~e** *a* excessive.

exagérer /ɛgzaʒeʀe/ [14] *vt/i* exaggerate; (abuser) go too far.

exalté, ~e /ɛgzalte/ *nm, f* fanatic. **exalter** [1] *vt* excite; (glorifier) exalt.

examen /ɛgzamɛ̃/ *nm* examination; (Scol) exam. **examinateur, -trice** *nm, f* examiner. **examiner** [1] *vt* examine.

exaspération /ɛgzaspeʀasjɔ̃/ *nf* exasperation. **exaspérer** [14] *vt* exasperate.

exaucer /ɛgzose/ [10] *vt* grant; (*personne*) grant the wish(es) of.

excédent /ɛksedɑ̃/ *nm* surplus; **~ de bagages** excess luggage; **~ de la balance commerciale** trade surplus. **excédentaire** *a* excess, surplus.

excéder /ɛksede/ [14] *vt* (dépasser) exceed; (agacer) irritate.

excellence /ɛksɛlɑ̃s/ *nf* excellence. **excellent, ~e** *a* excellent. **exceller** [1] *vi* excel (**dans** in).

excentricité /ɛksɑ̃tʀisite/ *nf*

eccentricity. **excentrique** *a* & *nmf* eccentric.

excepté, ~**e** /ɛksɛpte/ *a* & *prép* except.

excepter /ɛksɛpte/ [1] *vt* except.

exception /ɛksɛpsjɔ̃/ *nf* exception; **à l'~** de except for; **d'~** exceptional; **faire ~** be an exception. **exceptionnel**, ~**le** *a* exceptional. **exceptionnellement** *adv* exceptionally.

excès /ɛksɛ/ *nm* excess; ~ **de vitesse** speeding.

excessif, -**ive** /ɛksesif, -v/ *a* excessive.

excitant, ~**e** /ɛksitɑ̃, -t/ *a* stimulating; (*palpitant*) exciting. ● *nm* stimulant.

exciter /ɛksite/ [1] *vt* excite; (*irriter*) get excited. □ **s'~** *vpr* get excited.

exclamer (**s'**) /(s)ɛksklame/ [1] *vpr* exclaim.

exclure /ɛksklyʀ/ [16] *vt* exclude; (*expulser*) expel; (*empêcher*) preclude.

exclusif, -**ive** /ɛksklyzif, -v/ *a* exclusive.

exclusion /ɛksklyzjɔ̃/ *nf* exclusion.

exclusivité /ɛksklyzivite/ *nf* (Comm) exclusive rights (+ *pl*); **projeter en ~** show exclusively.

excursion /ɛkskyʀsjɔ̃/ *nf* excursion; (à pied) hike.

excuse /ɛkskyz/ *nf* excuse; ~**s** apology (+ *sg*); **faire des** ~**s** apologize.

excuser /ɛkskyze/ [1] *vt* excuse; **excusez-moi** excuse me. □ **s'~** *vpr* apologize (**de** for).

exécrable /ɛgzekʀabl/ *a* dreadful. **exécrer** [14] *vt* loathe.

exécuter /ɛgzekyte/ [1] *vt* carry out, execute; (Mus) perform; (tuer) execute.

exécutif, -**ive** /ɛgzekytif, -v/ *a* & *nm* (Pol) executive.

exécution /ɛgzekysjɔ̃/ *nf* execution; (Mus) performance.

exemplaire /ɛgzɑ̃plɛʀ/ *a* exemplary. ● *nm* copy.

exemple /ɛgzɑ̃pl/ *nm* example; **par ~** for example; **donner l'~** set an example.

exempt, ~**e** /ɛgzɑ̃, -t/ *a* ~ **de** exempt (**de** from).

exempter /ɛgzɑ̃te/ [1] *vt* exempt (**de** from). **exemption** *nf* exemption.

exercer /ɛgzɛʀse/ [10] *vt* exercise; (*influence, contrôle*) exert; (*former*) train, exercise; ~ **un métier** have a job; ~ **le métier de...** work as a... □ **s'~** *vpr* practise.

exercice /ɛgzɛʀsis/ *nm* exercise; (de métier) practice; **en ~** in office; (*médecin*) in practice.

exhaler /ɛgzale/ [1] *vt* emit.

exhaustif, -**ive** /ɛgzostif, -v/ *a* exhaustive.

exhiber /ɛgzibe/ [1] *vt* exhibit.

exhorter /ɛgzɔʀte/ [1] *vt* exhort (à to).

exigeant, ~**e** /ɛgziʒɑ̃, -t/ *a* demanding; **être ~ avec qn** demand a lot of sb. **exigence** *nf* demand. **exiger** [40] *vt* demand.

exigu, ~**ë** /ɛgzigy/ *a* tiny.

exil /ɛgzil/ *nm* exile. **exilé**, ~**e** *nm, f* exile.

exiler /ɛgzile/ [1] *vt* exile. □ **s'~** *vpr* go into exile.

existence /ɛgzistɑ̃s/ *nf* existence. **exister** [1] *vi* exist.

exode /ɛgzɔd/ *nm* exodus.

exonérer /ɛgzɔneʀe/ [14] *vt* exempt (**de** from).

exorbitant, ~**e** /ɛgzɔʀbitɑ̃, -t/ *a* exorbitant.

exorciser /ɛgzɔʀsize/ [1] *vt* exorcize.

exotique /ɛgzɔtik/ *a* exotic.

expansé, ~e /ɛkspɑ̃se/ a (Tech) expanded.

expansif, -ive /ɛkspɑ̃sif, -v/ a expansive. **expansion** nf expansion.

expatrié, ~e /ɛkspatʀije/ nm, f expatriate.

expectative /ɛkspɛktativ/ nf être dans l'~ wait and see.

expédient /ɛkspedjɑ̃/ nm expedient; **vivre d'~s** live by one's wits; **user d'~s** resort to expedients.

expédier /ɛkspedje/ [45] vt send, dispatch; (tâche 🔲) polish off. **expéditeur, -trice** nm, f sender.

expéditif, -ive /ɛkspeditif, -v/ a quick.

expédition /ɛkspedisjɔ̃/ nf (envoi) dispatching; (voyage) expedition.

expérience /ɛkspeʀjɑ̃s/ nf experience; (scientifique) experiment.

expérimental, ~e (mpl -aux) /ɛkspeʀimɑ̃tal, o/ a experimental. **expérimentation** nf experimentation.

expérimenté, ~e a experienced. **expérimenter** [1] vt test, experiment with.

expert, ~e /ɛkspɛʀ, -t/ a expert. ● nm expert; (d'assurances) adjuster. **expert-comptable** (pl **experts-comptables**) nm accountant.

expertise /ɛkspɛʀtiz/ nf valuation; (de dégâts) assessment. **expertiser** [1] vt value; (dégâts) assess.

expier /ɛkspje/ [45] vt atone for. **expiration** /ɛkspiʀasjɔ̃/ nf expiry.

expirer /ɛkspiʀe/ [1] vi breathe out; (finir, mourir) expire.

explicatif, -ive /ɛksplikatif, -v/ a explanatory.

explication /ɛksplikasjɔ̃/ nf explanation; (fig) discussion; ~ **de texte** (Scol) literary commentary.

explicite /ɛksplisit/ a explicit.

expliquer /ɛksplike/ [1] vt explain. □ s'~ vpr explain oneself; (discuter) discuss things; (être explicable) be understandable.

exploit /ɛksplwa/ nm exploit.

exploitant, ~e /ɛksplwatɑ̃, -t/ nm, f ~ (**agricole**) farmer.

exploitation /ɛksplwatasjɔ̃/ nf exploitation; (d'entreprise) running; (ferme) farm.

exploiter /ɛksplwate/ [1] vt exploit; (ferme) run; (mine) work.

explorateur, -trice /ɛksplɔʀatœʀ, -tʀis/ nm, f explorer. **exploration** nf exploration. **explorer** [1] vt explore.

exploser /ɛksploze/ [1] vi explode; **faire ~** explode; (bâtiment) blow up.

explosif, -ive /ɛksplozif, -v/ a & nm explosive. **explosion** nf explosion.

exportateur, -trice /ɛkspɔʀtatœʀ, -tʀis/ nm, f exporter. ● a exporting. **exportation** nf export. **exporter** [1] vt export.

exposant, ~e /ɛkspozɑ̃, -t/ nm, f exhibitor.

exposé, ~e /ɛkspoze/ nm talk (sur on); (d'une action) account; **faire l'~ de la situation** give an account of the situation. ● a ~ **au nord** facing north.

exposer /ɛkspoze/ [1] vt display, show; (expliquer) explain; (soumettre, mettre en danger) expose (à to); (vie) endanger. □ s'~ à vpr expose oneself to.

exposition /ɛkspozisjɔ̃/ nf (d'art) exhibition; (de faits) exposition; (géographique) aspect.

exprès¹ /ɛkspʀɛ/ adv specially; (délibérément) on purpose.

exprès², -esse /ɛkspRɛs/ a
express.

express /ɛkspRɛs/ a & nm inv
(**café**) ~ espresso; (**train**) ~ fast
train.

expressif, -ive /ɛkspresif, -v/ a
expressive. **expression** nf
expression.

exprimer /ɛkspRime/ [1] vt
express. □ **s'**~ vpr express
oneself.

expulser /ɛkspylse/ [1] vt expel;
(locataire) evict; (joueur) send
off. **expulsion** nf (d'élève)
expulsion; (de locataire) eviction;
(d'immigré) deportation.

exquis, ~e /ɛkski, -z/ a
exquisite.

extase /ɛkstɑz/ nf ecstasy.

extasier (s') /(s)ɛkstɑzje/ [45]
vpr **s'**~ **sur** be ecstatic about.

extensible /ɛkstɑ̃sibl/ a (tissu)
stretch.

extension /ɛkstɑ̃sjɔ̃/ nf
extension; (expansion) expansion.

exténuer /ɛkstenɥe/ [1] vt
exhaust.

extérieur, ~e /ɛksteRjœR/ a
outside; (signe, gaieté) outward;
(politique) foreign. ● nm outside,
exterior; (de personne) exterior; **à**
l'~ (**de**) outside. **extérioriser** [1]
vt show, externalize.

extermination /ɛkstɛRminasjɔ̃/
nf extermination. **exterminer** [1]
vt exterminate.

externe /ɛkstɛRn/ a external.
● nmf (Scol) day pupil.

extincteur /ɛkstɛ̃ktœR/ nm fire
extinguisher.

extinction /ɛkstɛ̃ksjɔ̃/ nf
extinction; **avoir une** ~ **de voix**
have lost one's voice.

extorquer /ɛkstɔRke/ [1] vt
extort.

extra /ɛkstRa/ a inv first-rate.
● nm inv (repas) (special) treat.

extraction /ɛkstRaksjɔ̃/ nf
extraction.

extrader /ɛkstRade/ [1] vt
extradite.

extraire /ɛkstRɛR/ [29] vt extract.
extrait nm extract.

extraordinaire /ɛkstRaɔRdinɛR/
a extraordinary.

extravagance /ɛkstRavagɑ̃s/ nf
extravagance. **extravagant, ~e**
a extravagant.

extraverti, ~e /ɛkstRavɛRti/
nm, f extrovert.

extrême /ɛkstRɛm/ a & nm
extreme. **extrêmement** adv
extremely.

Extrême-Orient /ɛkstRɛmɔRjɑ̃/
nm Far East.

extrémiste /ɛkstRemist/ nmf
extremist.

extrémité /ɛkstRemite/ nf end;
(mains, pieds) extremity.

exubérance /ɛgzyberɑ̃s/ nf
exuberance. **exubérant, ~e** a
exuberant.

F abrév f (**franc, francs**) franc,
francs.

fabricant, ~e /fabRikɑ̃, -t/ nm, f
manufacturer. **fabrication** nf
making; manufacture.

fabrique /fabRik/ nf factory.
fabriquer [1] vt make;
(industriellement) manufacture; (fig)
make up.

fabuler /fabyle/ [1] vi fantasize.

fabuleux, -euse /fabylø, -z/ a
fabulous.

fac /fak/ nf ▢ university.

façade /fasad/ *nf* front; (fig) façade.

face /fas/ *nf* face; (d'un objet) side; **en ~ (de), d'en ~** opposite; **en ~ de** (fig) faced with; **~ à** facing; (fig) faced with; **faire ~ à** face. **face-à-face** *nm inv* (débat) one-to-one debate.

fâcher /faʃe/ [1] *vt* anger; **fâché** angry; (désolé) sorry. □ **se ~** *vpr* get angry; (se brouiller) fall out.

facile /fasil/ *a* easy; (caractère) easygoing.

facilité /fasilite/ *nf* easiness; (aisance) ease; (aptitude) ability; **~s** (possibilités) facilities, opportunities; **~s d'importation** import opportunities; **~s de paiement** easy terms.

faciliter /fasilite/ [1] *vt* facilitate, make easier.

façon /fasɔ̃/ *nf* way; (de vêtement) cut; **de cette ~** in this way; **de ~ à** so as to; **de toute ~** anyway; **~s** (chichis) fuss; **faire des ~s** stand on ceremony; **sans ~s** (repas) informal; (personne) unpretentious. **façonner** [1] *vt* shape; (faire) make.

fac-similé (*pl* **~s**) /faksimile/ *nm* facsimile.

facteur, -trice /faktœʀ, -tʀis/ *nm, f* postman, postwoman. ● *nm* (élément) factor.

facture /faktyʀ/ *nf* bill; (Comm) invoice; **~ détaillée** itemized bill. **facturer** [1] *vt* invoice. **facturette** *nf* credit card slip.

facultatif, -ive /fakyltatif, -v/ *a* optional.

faculté /fakylte/ *nf* faculty; (possibilité) power; (Univ) faculty.

fade /fad/ *a* insipid.

faible /fɛbl/ *a* weak; (espoir, quantité, écart) slight; (revenu, intensité) low; **~ d'esprit** feeble-minded. ● *nm* (personne) weakling;

(penchant) weakness. **faiblesse** *nf* weakness. **faiblir** [2] *vi* weaken.

faïence /fajɑ̃s/ *nf* earthenware.

faillir /fajiʀ/ [2] *vi* **j'ai failli acheter** I almost bought.

faillite /fajit/ *nf* bankruptcy; (fig) collapse.

faim /fɛ̃/ *nf* hunger; **avoir ~** be hungry; **rester sur sa ~** (fig) be left wanting more.

fainéant, ~e /feneɑ̃, -t/ *a* idle. ● *nm, f* idler.

....

faire /fɛʀ/ [33]

➡ Pour les expressions comme **faire attention, faire la cuisine**, etc. ⇒**attention, cuisine**, etc.

● *verbe transitif*

····▸ (préparer, créer) make; **~ une tarte/une erreur** make a tart/a mistake.

····▸ (se livrer à une activité) do; **~ du droit** do law; **~ du foot/du violon** play football/the violin; **qu'est-ce qu'elle fait?** (dans la vie) what does she do?; (en ce moment précis) what is she doing?

····▸ (dans les calculs, mesures, etc.) **10 et 10 font 20** 10 and 10 make 20; **ça fait 25 euros** that's 25 euros; **~ 60 kilos** weigh 60 kilos; **il fait 1,75 m** he's 1.75 m tall.

····▸ (dans les expressions de temps) **ça fait une heure que j'attends** I have been waiting for an hour.

····▸ (imiter) **~ le clown** act the clown; **faire le malade** pretend to be ill.

····▸ (parcourir) **~ 10 km** do *ou* cover 10 km; **~ les musées** go round the museums.

····▸ (entraîner, causer) **ça ne fait rien** it doesn't matter; **l'accident a fait 8 morts** 8 people died in the accident.

····➤ (dire) say; **'excusez-moi', fit-elle** 'excuse me', she said.

● *verbe auxiliaire*

····➤ **(faire + infinitif + qn) make;** ~ **pleurer qn** make sb cry.

····➤ **(faire + infinitif + qch) have, get;** ~ **réparer sa voiture** have *ou* get one's car mended.

····➤ **(ne faire que + infinitif)** (continuellement) **ne ~ que pleurer** do nothing but cry; (*seulement*) **je ne fais qu'obéir** I'm only following orders.

● *verbe intransitif*

····➤ (agir) do, act; ~ **vite** act quickly; **fais comme tu veux** do as you please; **fais comme chez toi** make yourself at home.

····➤ (paraître) look; ~ **joli** look pretty; **ça fait cher** it's expensive.

····➤ (en parlant du temps) **il fait chaud/gris** it's hot/overcast.

□ **se faire** *verbe pronominal*

····➤ (obtenir, confectionner) make; **se** ~ **des amis** make friends; **se** ~ **un thé** make (oneself) a cup of tea.

····➤ **(se faire + infinitif) se** ~ **gronder** be scolded; **se ~ couper les cheveux** have one's hair cut.

····➤ (devenir) **il se fait tard** it's getting late.

····➤ (être d'usage) **ça ne se fait pas** it's not the done thing.

····➤ (emploi impersonnel) **comment se fait-il que tu sois ici?** how come you're here?

····➤ □ **se faire à** get used to; **je ne m'y fais pas** I can't get used to it.

····➤ □ **s'en faire** worry; **ne t'en fais pas** don't worry.

❗ Lorsque **faire** remplace un verbe plus précis, on traduira quelquefois par ce dernier: **faire une visite** *pay*

a visit, **faire un nid** *build a nest*.

faire-part /fɛʀpaʀ/ *nm inv* announcement.

fais /fɛ/ ⇒FAIRE [33].

faisan /fəzɑ̃/ *nm* pheasant.

faisceau (*pl* ~**x**) /fɛso/ *nm* (rayon) beam; (fagot) bundle.

fait, ~e /fɛ, fɛt/ *a* done; (*fromage*) ripe; ~ **pour** made for; **tout** ~ ready made; **c'est bien** ~ **pour toi** it serves you right. ● *nm* fact; (événement) event; **au** ~ **(de)** informed (of); **de ce** ~ therefore; **du** ~ **de** on account of; ~ **divers** (trivial) news item; ~ **nouveau** new development; **prendre qn sur le** ~ catch sb in the act.
● ⇒FAIRE [33].

faîte /fɛt/ *nm* top; (fig) peak.

faites /fɛt/ ⇒FAIRE [33].

falaise /falɛz/ *nf* cliff.

falloir /falwaʀ/ [34] *vi* **il faut qch/qn** we/you *etc.* need sth/so; **il lui faut du pain** he needs bread; **il faut rester** we/you *etc.* have to *ou* must stay; **il faut que j'y aille** I have to *ou* must go; **il faudrait que tu partes** you should leave; **il aurait fallu le faire** we/you *etc.* should have done it; **comme il faut** (*manger, se tenir*) properly; (*personne*) respectable, proper.
□ **s'en** ~ *vpr* **il s'en est fallu de peu qu'il gagne** he nearly won; **il s'en faut de beaucoup que je sois** I am far from being.

falsifier /falsifje/ [45] *vt* falsify; (*signature, monnaie*) forge.

famé, ~e /fame/ *a* **mal** ~ disreputable, seedy.

fameux, -euse /famø, -z/ *a* famous; (excellent Ⅰ) first-rate.

familial, ~e (*mpl* **-iaux**) /familjal, -jo/ *a* family.

familiale /familjal/ *nf* estate car; (US) station wagon.

familiariser /familjaʀize/ [1] vt familiarize (**avec** with). □ **se ~** vpr familiarize oneself.

familier, -ière /familje, -jɛʀ/ a familiar; (amical) informal.

famille /famij/ nf family; **en ~** with one's family.

famine /famin/ nf famine.

fanatique /fanatik/ a fanatical. ● nmf fanatic.

fanfare /fɑ̃faʀ/ nf brass band; (musique) fanfare.

fantaisie /fɑ̃tezi/ nf imagination, fantasy; (caprice) whim; (**de**) ~ (boutons etc.) fancy. **fantaisiste** a unorthodox; (personne) eccentric.

fantasme /fɑ̃tasm/ nm fantasy.

fantastique /fɑ̃tastik/ a fantastic.

fantôme /fɑ̃tom/ nm ghost; **cabinet(-)~** (Pol) shadow cabinet.

faon /fɑ̃/ nm fawn.

FAQ abrév f (**Foire aux questions**) (Internet) FAQ, Frequently Asked Questions.

farce /faʀs/ nf (practical) joke; (Théât) farce; (hachis) stuffing.

farcir /faʀsiʀ/ [2] vt stuff.

fard /faʀ/ nm make-up; ~ **à paupières** eye-shadow; **piquer un ~** blush.

fardeau (pl ~x) /faʀdo/ nm burden.

farfelu, ~e /faʀfəly/ a & nm,f eccentric.

farine /faʀin/ nf flour. **farineux, -euse** a floury. **farineux** nmpl starchy food.

farouche /faʀuʃ/ a shy; (peu sociable) unsociable; (violent) fierce.

fascicule /fasikyl/ nm (brochure) booklet; (partie d'un ouvrage) fascicule.

fasciner /fasine/ [1] vt fascinate.

fascisme /faʃism/ nm fascism.

fasse /fas/ ⇒FAIRE [33].

fast-food /fastfud/ nm fast-food place.

fastidieux, -ieuse /fastidjø, -z/ a tedious.

fatal, ~e (mpl ~s) /fatal/ a inevitable; (mortel) fatal. **fatalité** nf (destin) fate.

fatigant, ~e /fatigɑ̃, -t/ a tiring; (ennuyeux) tiresome.

fatigue /fatig/ nf fatigue, tiredness.

fatigué, ~e /fatige/ a tired.

fatiguer /fatige/ [1] vt tire; (yeux, moteur) strain. ● vi (moteur) labour. □ **se ~** vpr get tired, tire (**de** of).

faubourg /fobuʀ/ nm suburb.

faucher /foʃe/ [1] vt (herbe) mow; (voler 囲) pinch; ~ **qn** (véhicule, tir) mow sb down.

faucon /fokɔ̃/ nm falcon, hawk.

faudra, faudrait /fodʀa, fodʀɛ/ ⇒FALLOIR [34].

faufiler (se) /(sə)fofile/ [1] vpr edge one's way, squeeze.

faune /fon/ nf wildlife, fauna.

faussaire /fosɛʀ/ nmf forger.

fausse /fos/ ⇒FAUX².

fausser /fose/ [1] vt buckle; (fig) distort; ~ **compagnie à qn** give sb the slip.

faut /fo/ ⇒FALLOIR [34].

faute /fot/ nf mistake; (responsabilité) fault; (délit) offence; (péché) sin; **en ~** at fault; ~ **de** for want of; ~ **de quoi** failing which; **sans ~** without fail; ~ **de frappe** typing error; ~ **de goût** bad taste; ~ **professionnelle** professional misconduct.

fauteuil /fotœj/ nm armchair; (de président) chair; (Théât) seat; ~ **roulant** wheelchair.

fautif, -ive /fotif, -v/ a guilty; (faux) faulty. ● nm,f guilty party.

fauve /fov/ a (couleur) fawn, tawny. ● nm wild cat.

faux¹ /fo/ nf scythe.

faux², **fausse** /fo, fos/ a false; (falsifié) fake, forged; (numéro, calcul) wrong; (voix) out of tune; **c'est ∼!** that is wrong!; **∼ témoignage** perjury; **faire ∼ bond à qn** stand sb up; **fausse couche** miscarriage; **∼ frais** incidental expenses. ● adv (chanter) out of tune. ● nm forgery. **faux-filet** (pl **∼s**) nm sirloin.

faveur /favœʀ/ nf favour; **de ∼** (régime) preferential; **en ∼ de** in favour of.

favorable /favɔʀabl/ a favourable.

favori, **∼te** /favɔʀi, -t/ a & nm,f favourite. **favoriser** [1] vt favour.

fax /faks/ nm fax. **faxer** [1] vt fax.

fébrile /febʀil/ a feverish.

fécond, **∼e** /fekɔ̃, -d/ a fertile. **féconder** [1] vt fertilize. **fécondité** nf fertility.

fédéral, **∼e** (mpl **-aux**) /fedeʀal, -o/ a federal. **fédération** nf federation.

fée /fe/ nf fairy. **féerie** nf magical spectacle. **féerique** a magical.

feindre /fɛ̃dʀ/ [22] vt feign; **∼ de** pretend to.

fêler /fele/ [1] vt crack. □ **se ∼** vpr crack.

félicitations /felisitasjɔ̃/ nfpl congratulations (**pour** on). **féliciter** [1] vt congratulate (**de** on).

félin, **∼e** /felɛ̃, -in/ a & nm feline.

femelle /fəmɛl/ a & nf female.

féminin, **∼e** /feminɛ̃, -in/ a feminine; (sexe) female; (mode, équipe) women's. ● nm feminine. **féministe** nmf feminist.

femme /fam/ nf woman; (épouse) wife; **∼ au foyer** housewife; **∼ de chambre** chambermaid; **∼ de ménage** cleaning lady.

fémur /femyʀ/ nm thigh-bone.

fendre /fɑ̃dʀ/ [3] vt (couper) split; (fissurer) crack. □ **se ∼** vpr crack.

fenêtre /fənɛtʀ/ nf window.

fenouil /fənuj/ nm fennel.

fente /fɑ̃t/ nf (ouverture) slit, slot; (fissure) crack.

féodal, **∼e** (mpl **-aux**) /feodal, -o/ a feudal.

fer /fɛʀ/ nm iron; **∼ (à repasser)** iron; **∼ à cheval** horseshoe; **∼ de lance** spearhead; **∼ forgé** wrought iron.

fera, **ferait** /fəʀa, fəʀɛ/ ⇒FAIRE [33].

férié, **∼e** /feʀje/ a **jour ∼** public holiday.

ferme /fɛʀm/ nf farm; (maison) farm(house). ● a firm. ● adv (travailler) hard.

fermé, **∼e** /fɛʀme/ a closed; (gaz, radio) off.

fermenter /fɛʀmɑ̃te/ [1] vi ferment.

fermer /fɛʀme/ [1] vt/i close, shut; (cesser d'exploiter) close ou shut down; (gaz, robinet) turn off. □ **se ∼** vpr close, shut.

fermeté /fɛʀməte/ nf firmness.

fermeture /fɛʀmətyʀ/ nf closing; (dispositif) catch; **∼ annuelle** annual closure; **∼ éclair®** zip(-fastener); (US) zipper.

fermier, **-ière** /fɛʀmje, -jɛʀ/ a farm. ● nm farmer. **fermière** nf farmer's wife.

féroce /feʀɔs/ a ferocious.

ferraille /feʀaj/ nf scrap-iron.

ferrer /feʀe/ [1] vt (cheval) shoe.

ferroviaire /feʀɔvjɛʀ/ a rail(way).

ferry /feʀi/ nm ferry.

fertile /fɛʀtil/ a fertile; **∼ en** (fig) rich in. **fertiliser** [1] vt fertilize. **fertilité** nf fertility.

fervent, **∼e** /fɛʀvɑ̃, -t/ a fervent. ● nm,f enthusiast (**de** of).

fesse /fɛs/ nf buttock. **fessée** nf spanking, smack.

festin /fɛstɛ̃/ nm feast.

festival (pl **∼s**) /fɛstival/ nm festival.

F

fêtard, ~e /fɛtaʀ, -d/ *nm, f* 🔲 party animal.

fête /fɛt/ *nf* holiday; (religieuse) feast; (du nom) name-day; (réception) party; (en famille) celebration; (foire) fair; (folklorique) festival; ~ **des Mères** Mother's Day; ~ **foraine** fun-fair; **faire la** ~ live it up; **les** ~**s** (**de fin d'année**) the Christmas season. **fêter** [1] *vt* celebrate; (*personne*) give a celebration for.

fétiche /fetiʃ/ *nm* fetish; (fig) mascot.

feu[1] (*pl* ~**x**) /fø/ *nm* fire; (lumière) light; (de réchaud) burner; **à** ~ **doux/vif** on a low/high heat; ~ **rouge/vert/orange** red/green/ amber light; **aux** ~**x, tournez à droite** turn right at the traffic lights; **avez-vous du** ~? (pour cigarette) have you got a light?; **au** ~! fire!; **mettre le** ~ **à** set fire to; **prendre** ~ catch fire; **jouer avec le** ~ play with fire; **ne pas faire long** ~ not last; ~ **d'artifice** firework display; ~ **de joie** bonfire; ~ **de position** sidelight.

feu[2] /fø/ *a inv* (mort) late.

feuillage /fœjaʒ/ *nm* foliage.

feuille /fœj/ *nf* leaf; (de papier) sheet; (formulaire) form; ~ **d'impôts** tax return; ~ **de paie** payslip.

feuilleté, ~e /fœjte/ *a* **pâte** ~e puff pastry. ● *nm* savoury pasty.

feuilleter /fœjte/ [1] *vt* leaf through.

feuilleton /fœjtɔ̃/ *nm* (à suivre) serial; (histoire complète) series.

feutre /føtʀ/ *nm* felt; (chapeau) felt hat; (crayon) felt-tip (pen).

fève /fɛv/ *nf* broad bean.

février /fevʀije/ *nm* February.

fiable /fjabl/ *a* reliable.

fiançailles /fjɑ̃saj/ *nfpl* engagement.

fiancé, ~e /fjɑ̃se/ *a* engaged. ● *nm* fiancé. **fiancée** *nf* fiancée.

fiancer (**se**) [10] *vpr* become engaged (**avec** to).

fibre /fibʀ/ *nf* fibre; ~ **de verre** fibreglass.

ficeler /fisle/ [38] *vt* tie up.

ficelle /fisɛl/ *nf* string.

fiche /fiʃ/ *nf* (index) card; (formulaire) form, slip; (Électr) plug.

ficher[1] /fiʃe/ [1] *vt* (enfoncer) drive (**dans** into).

ficher[2] /fiʃe/ [1] 🔲 *vt* (faire) do; (donner) give; (mettre) put; ~ **le camp** clear off. □ **se** ~ **de** *vpr* make fun of; **il s'en fiche** he couldn't care less.

fichier /fiʃje/ *nm* file.

fichu, ~e /fiʃy/ *a* 🔲 (mauvais) rotten; (raté) done for; **mal** ~ terrible.

fictif, **-ive** /fiktif, -v/ *a* fictitious.

fiction *nf* fiction.

fidèle /fidɛl/ *a* faithful. ● *nmf* (client) regular; (Relig) believer; ~**s** (à l'église) congregation. **fidélité** *nf* fidelity.

fier[1], **fière** /fjɛʀ/ *a* proud (**de** of).

fier[2] (**se**) /(sə)fje/ [45] *vpr* **se** ~ **à** trust.

fierté /fjɛʀte/ *nf* pride.

fièvre /fjɛvʀ/ *nf* fever; **avoir de la** ~ have a temperature; ~ **aphteuse** foot-and-mouth disease. **fiévreux**, **-euse** *a* feverish.

figer /fiʒe/ [40] *vi* (graisse) congeal; (sang) clot; **figé sur place** frozen to the spot. □ **se** ~ *vpr* (personne, sourire) freeze; (graisse) congeal; (sang) clot.

figue /fig/ *nf* fig.

figurant, ~e /figyʀɑ̃, -t/ *nm, f* (au cinéma) extra.

figure /figyʀ/ *nf* face; (forme, personnage) figure; (illustration) picture.

figuré, ~e /figyʀe/ *a* (sens) figurative.

figurer /figyʀe/ [1] *vi* appear. ● *vt* represent. □ **se** ~ *vpr* imagine.

fil /fil/ *nm* thread; (métallique,

électrique) wire; (de couteau) edge; (à coudre) cotton; **au ~ de** with the passing of; **au ~ de l'eau** with the current; **~ de fer** wire; **au bout du ~** 🕾 on the phone.

file /fil/ *nf* line; (voie: Auto) lane; **~ (d'attente)** queue; (US) line; **en ~ indienne** in single file.

filer /file/ [1] *vt* spin; (suivre) shadow; **~ qch à qn** 🕾 slip sb sth. ● *vi* (bas) ladder, run; (liquide) run; (aller vite 🕾) speed along, fly by; (partir 🕾) dash off; (disparaître 🕾) **~ entre les mains** slip through one's fingers; **~ doux** do as one's told.

filet /filε/ *nm* net; (d'eau) trickle; (de viande) fillet; **~** (luggage) rack; **~ à provisions** string bag (*for shopping*).

filiale /filjal/ *nf* subsidiary (company).

filière /filjεʀ/ *nf* (official) channels; (de trafiquants) network; **passer par** *ou* **suivre la ~** (employé) work one's way up.

fille /fij/ *nf* girl; (opposé à fils) daughter. **fillette** *nf* little girl.

filleul /fijœl/ *nm* godson.

filleule /fijœl/ *nf* god-daughter.

film /film/ *nm* film; **~ d'épouvante/muet/parlant** horror/silent/talking film; **~ dramatique** drama. **filmer** [1] *vt* film.

filon /filɔ̃/ *nm* (Géol) seam; (travail lucratif 🕾) money spinner; **avoir trouvé le bon ~** be onto a good thing.

fils /fis/ *nm* son.

filtre /filtʀ/ *nm* filter. **filtrer** [1] *vt/i* filter; (personne) screen.

fin¹ /fɛ̃/ *nf* end; **à la ~** finally; **en ~ de compte** all things considered; **~ de semaine** weekend; **mettre ~ à** put an end to; **prendre ~** come to an end.

fin², **~e** /fɛ̃, in/ *a* fine; (tranche,

couche) thin; (taille) slim; (plat) exquisite; (esprit, vue) sharp; **~es herbes** mixed herbs. ● *adv* (couper) finely.

final, **~e** (*mpl* **-aux**) /final, -o/ *a* final.

finale /final/ *nm* (Mus) finale. ● *nf* (Sport) final; (Gram) final syllable.

finalement *adv* finally; (somme toute) after all. **finaliste** *nmf* finalist.

finance /finɑ̃s/ *nf* finance.

financer [10] *vt* finance.

financier, **-ière** /finɑ̃sje, -jεʀ/ *a* financial. ● *nm* financier.

finesse /finεs/ *nf* fineness; (de taille) slimness; (acuité) sharpness; **~s** (de langue) niceties.

finir /finiʀ/ [2] *vt/i* finish, end; (arrêter) stop; (manger) finish (up); **en ~ avec** have done with; **~ par faire** end up doing; **ça va mal ~** it will turn out badly.

finlandais, **~e** /fɛ̃lɑ̃dε, -z/ *a* Finnish. **F~**, **~e** *nm, f* Finn.

Finlande /fɛ̃lɑ̃d/ *nf* Finland.

finnois, **~e** /finwa/ *a* Finnish. ● *nm* (Ling) Finnish.

firme /fiʀm/ *nf* firm.

fisc /fisk/ *nm* tax authorities. **fiscal**, **~e** (*mpl* **-aux**) *a* tax, fiscal. **fiscalité** *nf* tax system.

fissure /fisyʀ/ *nf* crack.

fixe /fiks/ *a* fixed; (stable) steady; **à heure ~** at a set time; **menu à prix ~** set menu. ● *nm* basic pay.

fixer /fikse/ [1] *vt* fix; **~** (du regard) stare at; **être fixé** (personne) have made up one's mind. □ **se ~** *vpr* (s'attacher) be attached; (s'installer) settle down.

flacon /flakɔ̃/ *nm* bottle.

flagrant, **~e** /flagʀɑ̃, -t/ *a* flagrant, blatant; **en ~ délit** in the act.

flair /flεʀ/ *nm* (sense of) smell; (fig) intuition.

flamand, **~e** /flamɑ̃, -d/ *a*

Flemish. ● *nm* (Ling) Flemish. **F~, ~e** *nm, f* Fleming.

flamant /flamã/ *nm* flamingo.

flambeau (*pl* ~**x**) /flãbo/ *nm* torch.

flambée /flãbe/ *nf* blaze; (fig) explosion.

flamber /flãbe/ [1] *vi* blaze; (*prix*) shoot up. ● *vt* (*aiguille*) sterilize; (*volaille*) singe.

flamme /flam/ *nf* flame; (fig) ardour; **en ~s** ablaze.

flan /flã/ *nm* custard tart.

flanc /flã/ *nm* side; (d'animal, d'armée) flank.

flâner /flane/ [1] *vi* stroll. **flânerie** *nf* stroll.

flanquer /flãke/ [1] *vt* flank; (jeter □) chuck; (donner □) give; **~ à la porte** kick out.

flaque /flak/ *nf* (d'eau) puddle; (de sang) pool.

flash (*pl* ~**es**) /flaʃ/ *nm* (Photo) flash; (information) news flash; **~ publicitaire** commercial.

flatter /flate/ [1] *vt* flatter. □ **se ~ de** *vpr* pride oneself on.

flatteur, -euse /flatœR, -øz/ *a* flattering. ● *nm, f* flatterer.

fléau (*pl* ~**x**) /fleo/ *nm* (désastre) scourge; (personne) pest.

flèche /flɛʃ/ *nf* arrow; (de clocher) spire; **monter en ~** spiral; **partir en ~** shoot off.

flécher /fleʃe/ [14] *vt* mark *ou* signpost (with arrows). **fléchette** *nf* dart.

fléchir /fleʃiR/ [2] *vt* bend; (*personne*) move, sway. ● *vi* (faiblir) weaken; (*prix*) fall; (*poutre*) sag, bend.

flemme /flɛm/ *nf* □ laziness; **j'ai la ~ de faire** I can't be bothered doing.

flétrir (**se**) /(sə)fletRiR/ [2] *vpr* (*plante*) wither; (*fruit*) shrivel; (*beauté*) fade.

fleur /flœR/ *nf* flower; **à ~ de**

terre/d'eau just above the ground/ water; **à ~s** flowery; **~ de l'âge** prime of life; **en ~s** in flower.

fleurir /flœRiR/ [2] *vi* flower; (*arbre*) blossom; (fig) flourish. ● *vt* decorate with flowers. **fleuriste** *nmf* florist.

fleuve /flœv/ *nm* river.

flic /flik/ *nm* □ cop.

flipper /flipœR/ *nm* pinball (machine).

flirter /flœRte/ [1] *vi* flirt.

flocon /flɔkɔ̃/ *nm* flake.

flore /flɔR/ *nf* flora.

florissant, ~e /flɔRisã, -t/ *a* flourishing.

flot /flo/ *nm* flood, stream; **être à ~** be afloat; **les ~s** the waves.

flottant, ~e /flɔtã, -t/ *a* (*vêtement*) loose; (indécis) indecisive.

flotte /flɔt/ *nf* fleet; (pluie □) rain; (eau □) water.

flottement /flɔtmã/ *nm* (incertitude) indecision.

flotter /flɔte/ [1] *vi* float; (*drapeau*) flutter; (*nuage, parfum, pensées*) drift; (pleuvoir □) rain. **flotteur** *nm* float.

flou, ~e /flu/ *a* out of focus; (fig) vague.

fluctuer /flyktɥe/ [1] *vi* fluctuate.

fluet, ~te /flyɛ, -t/ *a* thin.

fluide /flɥid/ *a & nm* fluid.

fluor /flyɔR/ *nm* (pour les dents) fluoride.

fluorescent, ~e /flyɔResã, -t/ *a* fluorescent.

flûte /flyt/ *nf* flute; (verre) champagne glass.

fluvial, ~e (*mpl* -**iaux**) /flyvjal, -jo/ *a* river.

flux /fly/ *nm* flow; **~ et reflux** ebb and flow.

FM *abrév f* (**frequency modulation**) FM.

fœtus /fetys/ *nm* foetus.

foi /fwa/ *nf* faith; **être de bonne/ mauvaise ~** be acting in good/bad faith; **ma ~**! well (indeed)!

foie /fwa/ *nm* liver.

foin /fwɛ̃/ *nm* hay.

foire /fwaʀ/ *nf* fair; **faire la ~** ▣ live it up.

fois /fwa/ *nf* time; **une ~** once; **deux ~** twice; **à la ~** at the same time; **des ~** (parfois) sometimes; **une ~ pour toutes** once and for all.

fol /fɔl/ ⇒FOU.

folie /fɔli/ *nf* madness; (bêtise) foolish thing, folly; **faire une ~**, **faire des ~s** be extravagant.

folklore /fɔlklɔʀ/ *nm* folklore. **folklorique** *a* folk; ▣ eccentric.

folle /fɔl/ ⇒FOU.

foncé, ~e /fɔ̃se/ *a* dark.

foncer /fɔ̃se/ [10] *vt* darken. ● *vi* (s'assombrir) darken; (aller vite ▣) dash along; **~ sur** ▣ charge at.

foncier, -ière /fɔ̃sje, -jɛʀ/ *a* fundamental; (Comm) real estate.

fonction /fɔ̃ksjɔ̃/ *nf* function; (emploi) position; **~s** (obligations) duties; **en ~ de** according to; **~ publique** civil service; **voiture de ~** company car. **fonctionnaire** *nmf* civil servant. **fonctionnement** *nm* working.

fonctionner /fɔ̃ksjɔne/ [1] *vi* work; **faire ~** work.

fond /fɔ̃/ *nm* bottom; (de salle, magasin, etc.) back; (essentiel) basis; (contenu) content; (plan) background; (Sport) long-distance running; **à ~** thoroughly; **au ~** basically; **de ~** (bruit) background; **de ~ en comble** from top to bottom; **au** *ou* **dans le ~** really; **~ de teint** foundation, make-up base.

fondamental, ~e (*mpl* **-aux**) /fɔ̃damɑ̃tal, -o/ *a* fundamental.

fondateur, -trice /fɔ̃datœʀ, -tʀis/ *nm, f* founder. **fondation** *nf* foundation.

fonder /fɔ̃de/ [1] *vt* found; (baser) base (**sur** on); (**bien**) **fondé** well-founded. □ **se ~ sur** *vpr* be guided by, be based on.

fonderie /fɔ̃dʀi/ *nf* foundry.

fondre /fɔ̃dʀ/ [3] *vt/i* melt; (dans l'eau) dissolve; (mélanger) merge; **faire ~** melt; dissolve; **~ en larmes** burst into tears; **~ sur** swoop on. □ **se ~** *vpr* merge.

fonds /fɔ̃/ *nm* fund; **~ de commerce** business. ● *nmpl* (capitaux) funds.

fondu, ~e /fɔ̃dy/ *a* melted; (métal) molten.

font /fɔ̃/ ⇒FAIRE [33].

fontaine /fɔ̃tɛn/ *nf* fountain; (source) spring.

fonte /fɔ̃t/ *nf* melting; (fer) cast iron; **~ des neiges** thaw.

foot /fut/ *nm* ▣ football.

football /futbol/ *nm* football.

footing /futiŋ/ *nm* jogging.

forain /fɔʀɛ̃/ *nm* fairground entertainer; **marchand ~** stall-holder.

forçat /fɔʀsa/ *nm* convict.

force /fɔʀs/ *nf* force; (physique) strength; (hydraulique etc.) power; **~s** (physiques) strength; **à ~ de** by sheer force of; **de ~, par la ~** by force; **~ de dissuasion** deterrent; **~ de frappe** strike force, deterrent; **~ de l'âge** prime of life; **~s de l'ordre** police (force); **~s de marché** market forces.

forcé, ~e /fɔʀse/ *a* forced; (inévitable) inevitable; **c'est ~ qu'il fasse** ▣ he's bound to do. **forcément** *adv* necessarily; (évidemment) obviously.

forcené, ~e /fɔʀsəne/ *a* frenzied. ● *nm, f* maniac.

forcer /fɔʀse/ [10] *vt* force (**à faire** to do); (*voix*) strain; **~ la dose** ▣ overdo it. ● *vi* force; (exagérer) overdo it. □ se ∼ vpr force oneself.

forer /fɔʀe/ [1] vt drill.

forestier, -ière /fɔʀɛstje, -jɛʀ/ a forest. ● nm, f forestry worker.

forêt /fɔʀɛ/ nf forest.

forfait /fɔʀfɛ/ nm (Comm) (prix fixe) fixed price; (offre promotionnelle) package. **forfaitaire** a (prix) fixed.

forger /fɔʀʒe/ [40] vt forge; (inventer) make up.

forgeron /fɔʀʒəʀɔ̃/ nm blacksmith.

formaliser (se) /(sə)fɔʀmalize/ [1] vpr take offence (de at).

formalité /fɔʀmalite/ nf formality.

format /fɔʀma/ nm format. **formater** [1] vt (Ordinat) format.

formation /fɔʀmasjɔ̃/ nf formation; (professionnelle) training; (culture) education; ∼ **permanente** ou **continue** continuing education.

forme /fɔʀm/ nf form; (contour) shape, form; (de femme) figure; **être en** ∼ be in good shape, be on form; **en** ∼ **de** in the shape of; **en bonne et due** ∼ in due form.

formel, ∼le /fɔʀmɛl/ a formal; (catégorique) positive.

former /fɔʀme/ [1] vt form; (instruire) train. □ se ∼ vpr form.

formidable /fɔʀmidabl/ a fantastic.

formulaire /fɔʀmylɛʀ/ nm form.

formule /fɔʀmyl/ nf formula; (expression) expression; (feuille) form; ∼ **de politesse** polite phrase, letter ending. **formuler** [1] vt formulate.

fort, ∼e /fɔʀ, -t/ a strong; (grand) big; (pluie) heavy; (bruit) loud; (pente) steep; (élève) clever; **au plus** ∼ **de** at the height of; **c'est une** ∼**e tête** she/he's headstrong. ● adv (frapper) hard; (parler) loud; (très) very; (beaucoup) very

much. ● nm (atout) strong point; (Mil) fort.

fortifiant /fɔʀtifjɑ̃/ nm tonic.

fortifier [45] vt fortify.

fortune /fɔʀtyn/ nf fortune; **de** ∼ (improvisé) makeshift; **faire** ∼ make one's fortune.

forum /fɔʀɔm/ nm forum; ∼ **de discussion** (Internet) newsgroup.

fosse /fos/ nf (tombe) grave; ∼ **d'orchestre** orchestra pit; ∼ **septique** septic tank.

fossé /fose/ nm ditch; (fig) gulf; ∼ **numérique** digital divide.

fossette /fosɛt/ nf dimple.

fossile /fosil/ nm fossil.

fou (**fol** before vowel or mute h), **folle** /fu, fɔl/ a mad; (course, regard) wild; (énorme 🆘) tremendous; ∼ **de** crazy about; **le** ∼ **rire** the giggles. ● nm madman; (bouffon) jester. **folle** nf madwoman.

foudre /fudʀ/ nf lightning.

foudroyant, ∼e /fudʀwajɑ̃, -t/ a (mort, maladie) violent.

foudroyer /fudʀwaje/ [31] vt (orage) strike; (maladie etc.) strike down; ∼ **qn du regard** look daggers at sb.

fouet /fwɛ/ nm whip; (Culin) whisk.

fougère /fuʒɛʀ/ nf fern.

fougue /fug/ nf ardour. **fougueux, -euse** a ardent.

fouille /fuj/ nf search; (Archéol) excavation.

fouiller /fuje/ [1] vt/i search; (creuser) dig; ∼ **dans** (tiroir) rummage through.

fouillis /fuji/ nm jumble.

foulard /fulaʀ/ nm scarf.

foule /ful/ nf crowd; **une** ∼ **de** (fig) a mass of.

foulée /fule/ nf stride; **il l'a fait dans la** ∼ he did it while he was at ou about it.

fouler /fule/ [1] vt (raisin) press; (sol) set foot on; ∼ **qch aux pieds**

trample sth underfoot; (fig) ride roughshod over sth. □ **se ~** *vpr* **se ~ le poignet/le pied** sprain one's wrist/foot; **ne pas se ~** Ⓘ not strain oneself.

four /fuʀ/ *nm* oven; (de potier) kiln; (Théât) flop; **~ à micro-ondes** microwave oven; **~ crématoire** crematorium.

fourbe /fuʀb/ *a* deceitful.

fourche /fuʀʃ/ *nf* fork; (à foin) pitchfork. **fourchette** *nf* fork; (Comm) bracket, range.

fourgon /fuʀɡɔ̃/ *nm* van.

fourmi /fuʀmi/ *nf* ant; **avoir des ~s** have pins and needles.

fourmiller /fuʀmije/ [1] *vi* swarm (de with).

fourneau (*pl* **~x**) /fuʀno/ *nm* stove.

fourni, ~e /fuʀni/ *a* (épais) thick.

fournir /fuʀniʀ/ [2] *vt* supply, provide; (client) supply; (effort) put in; **~ à qn** supply sb with. □ **se ~ chez** *vpr* shop at.

fournisseur /fuʀnisœʀ/ *nm* supplier; **~ d'accès à l'Internet** Internet service provider.

fourniture /fuʀnityʀ/ *nf* supply.

fourrage /fuʀaʒ/ *nm* fodder.

fourré, ~e /fuʀe/ *a* (vêtement) fur-lined; (gâteau etc.) filled (with jam, cream, etc.). ● *nm* thicket.

fourre-tout /fuʀtu/ *nm inv* (sac) holdall.

fourreur /fuʀœʀ/ *nm* furrier.

fourrière /fuʀjɛʀ/ *nf* (lieu) pound.

fourrure /fuʀyʀ/ *nf* fur.

foutre /futʀ/ [3] *vt* Ⓧ = **ficher²** [1].

foutu, ~e /futy/ *a* Ⓧ = **fichu**.

foyer /fwaje/ *nm* home; (âtre) hearth; (club) club; (d'étudiants) hostel; (Théât) foyer; (Photo) focus; (centre) centre.

fracas /fʀaka/ *nm* din; (de train) roar; (d'objet qui tombe) crash.

fracassant, ~e *a* (bruyant) deafening; (violent) shattering.

fraction /fʀaksjɔ̃/ *nf* fraction.

fracture /fʀaktyʀ/ *nf* fracture; **~ du poignet** fractured wrist.

fragile /fʀaʒil/ *a* fragile; (peau) sensitive; (cœur) weak. **fragilité** *nf* fragility.

fragment /fʀaɡmɑ̃/ *nm* bit, fragment. **fragmenter** [1] *vt* split, fragment.

fraîchement /fʀɛʃmɑ̃/ *adv* (récemment) freshly; (avec froideur) coolly. **fraîcheur** *nf* coolness; (nouveauté) freshness. **fraîchir** [2] *vi* freshen, become colder.

frais¹, fraîche /fʀɛ, -ʃ/ *a* fresh; (temps, accueil) cool; (peinture) wet; **~ et dispos** fresh; **il fait ~** it is cool. ● *adv* (récemment) newly, freshly. ● *nm* **mettre au ~** put in a cool place; **prendre le ~** get some fresh air.

frais² /fʀɛ/ *nmpl* expenses; (droits) fees; **aux ~ de** at the expense of; **faire des ~** spend a lot of money; **~ généraux** (Comm) overheads, running expenses; **~ de scolarité** school fees.

fraise /fʀɛz/ *nf* strawberry.

fraisier *nm* strawberry plant; (gâteau) strawberry gateau.

framboise /fʀɑ̃bwaz/ *nf* raspberry. **framboisier** *nm* raspberry bush.

franc, franche /fʀɑ̃, -ʃ/ *a* frank; (regard) frank, candid; (cassure) clean; (net) clear; (libre) free; (véritable) downright. ● *nm* franc.

français, ~e /fʀɑ̃sɛ, -z/ *a* French. ● *nm* (Ling) French. **F~, ~e** *nm, f* Frenchman, Frenchwoman.

France /fʀɑ̃s/ *nf* France.

franchement /fʀɑ̃ʃmɑ̃/ *adv* frankly; (nettement) clearly; (tout à fait) really.

franchir /fʀɑ̃ʃiʀ/ [2] *vt* (obstacle)

get over; (*distance*) cover; (*limite*) exceed; (*traverser*) cross.

franchise /fʀɑ̃ʃiz/ *nf* (qualité) frankness; (Comm) franchise; (exemption) exemption; ~ **douanière** exemption from duties.

franc-maçon (*pl* **francs-maçons**) /fʀɑ̃masɔ̃/ *nm* Freemason. **franc-maçonnerie** *nf* Freemasonry.

franco /fʀɑ̃ko/ *adv* postage paid.

francophone /fʀɑ̃kɔfɔn/ *a* French-speaking. ● *nmf* French speaker.

franc-parler /fʀɑ̃paʀle/ *nm inv* outspokenness.

frange /fʀɑ̃ʒ/ *nf* fringe.

frappe /fʀap/ *nf* (de texte) typing.

frappé, ~**e** /fʀape/ *a* chilled.

frapper /fʀape/ [1] *vt/i* strike; (battre) hit, strike; (*monnaie*) mint; (à la porte) knock, bang; **frappé de panique** panic-stricken.

fraternel, ~**le** /fʀatɛʀnɛl/ *a* brotherly. **fraternité** *nf* brotherhood.

fraude /fʀod/ *nf* fraud; (à un examen) cheating; **passer qch en** ~ smuggle sth in. **frauder** [1] *vt/i* cheat. **frauduleux**, -**euse** *a* fraudulent.

frayer /fʀeje/ [31] *vt* open up. □ **se** ~ *vpr* se ~ **un passage** force one's way (à travers, dans through).

frayeur /fʀɛjœʀ/ *nf* fright.

fredonner /fʀədɔne/ [1] *vt* hum.

free-lance /fʀilɑ̃s/ *a* & *nmf* freelance.

freezer /fʀizœʀ/ *nm* freezer.

frein /fʀɛ̃/ *nm* brake; **mettre un** ~ **à** curb; ~ **à main** hand brake.

freiner /fʀene/ [1] *vt* slow down; (modérer, enrayer) curb. ● *vi* (Auto) brake.

frêle /fʀɛl/ *a* frail.

frelon /fʀəlɔ̃/ *nm* hornet.

frémir /fʀemiʀ/ [2] *vi* shudder, shake; (*feuille, eau*) quiver.

frêne /fʀɛn/ *nm* ash.

frénésie /fʀenezi/ *nf* frenzy. **frénétique** *a* frenzied.

fréquemment /fʀekamɑ̃/ *adv* frequently. **fréquence** *nf* frequency. **fréquent**, ~**e** *a* frequent. **fréquentation** *nf* frequenting.

fréquentations /fʀekɑ̃tasjɔ̃/ *nfpl* acquaintances; **avoir de mauvaises** ~ keep bad company.

fréquenter /fʀekɑ̃te/ [1] *vt* frequent; (*école*) attend; (*personne*) see.

frère /fʀɛʀ/ *nm* brother.

fret /fʀɛt/ *nm* freight.

friand, ~**e** /fʀijɑ̃, -d/ *a* ~ **de** very fond of.

friandise /fʀijɑ̃diz/ *nf* sweet; (US) candy; (*gâteau*) cake.

fric /fʀik/ *nm* Ⓕ money.

friction /fʀiksjɔ̃/ *nf* friction; (massage) rub-down.

frigidaire® /fʀiʒidɛʀ/ *nm* refrigerator.

frigo /fʀigo/ *nm* Ⓕ fridge. **frigorifique** *a* (*vitrine etc.*) refrigerated.

frileux, -**euse** /fʀilø, -z/ *a* sensitive to cold.

frime /fʀim/ *nf* Ⓕ **c'est de la** ~ it's all pretence; **pour la** ~ for show.

frimousse /fʀimus/ *nf* face.

fringale /fʀɛ̃gal/ *nf* Ⓕ ravenous appetite.

fringant, ~**e** /fʀɛ̃gɑ̃, -t/ *a* dashing.

fringues /fʀɛ̃g/ *nfpl* Ⓕ gear.

friper /fʀipe/ [1] *vt* crumple, crease. □ **se** ~ *vpr* crumple, crease.

fripon, ~**ne** /fʀipɔ̃, -ɔn/ *nm, f* rascal. ● *a* mischievous.

fripouille /fʀipuj/ *nf* rogue.

frire /fʀiʀ/ [56] *vt/i* fry; **faire** ~ fry.

frise /fʁiz/ nf frieze.

friser /fʁize/ [1] vt/i (cheveux) curl; (personne) curl the hair of; **frisé** curly.

frisson /fʁisɔ̃/ nm (de froid) shiver; (de peur) shudder. **frissonner** [1] vi shiver; shudder.

frit, **~e** /fʁi, -t/ a fried.

frite /fʁit/ nf chip; **avoir la ~** 🔲 feel good.

friteuse /fʁitøz/ nf chip pan; (électrique) (deep) fryer.

friture /fʁityʁ/ nf fried fish; (huile) (frying) oil ou fat.

frivole /fʁivɔl/ a frivolous.

froid, **~e** /fʁwa, -d/ a & nm cold; **avoir/prendre ~** be/catch cold; **il fait ~** it is cold. **froidement** adv coldly; (calculer) coolly. **froideur** nf coldness.

froisser /fʁwase/ [1] vt crumple; (fig) offend. □ **se ~** vpr crumple; (fig) take offence; **se ~ un muscle** strain a muscle.

frôler /fʁole/ [1] vt brush against, skim; (fig) come close to.

fromage /fʁɔmaʒ/ nm cheese.

fromager, **-ère** /fʁɔmaʒe, -ɛʁ/ a cheese. ● nm, f (fabricant) cheese-maker; (marchand) cheesemonger.

froment /fʁɔmɑ̃/ nm wheat.

froncer /fʁɔ̃se/ [10] vt gather; **~ les sourcils** frown.

front /fʁɔ̃/ nm forehead; (Mil, Pol) front; **de ~** at the same time; (de face) head-on; (côte à côte) abreast; **faire ~ à** face up to. **frontal**, **~e** (mpl -aux) a frontal; (Ordinat) front-end.

frontalier, **-ière** /fʁɔ̃talje, -jɛʁ/ a border; **travailleur ~** commuter from across the border.

frontière /fʁɔ̃tjɛʁ/ nf border, frontier.

frottement /fʁɔtmɑ̃/ nm rubbing; (Tech) friction. **frotter** [1] vt/i rub; (allumette) strike.

frottis /fʁɔti/ nm **~ vaginal** cervical smear.

frousse /fʁus/ nf 🔲 fear; **avoir la ~** 🔲 be scared.

fructifier /fʁyktifje/ [45] vi **faire ~** put to work.

fructueux, **-euse** /fʁyktɥø, -z/ a fruitful.

frugal, **~e** (mpl -aux) /fʁygal, -o/ a frugal.

fruit /fʁɥi/ nm fruit; **des ~s** (some) fruit; **~s de mer** seafood. **fruité**, **~e** a fruity.

frustrant, **~e** /fʁystʁɑ̃, -t / a frustrating. **frustrer** [1] vt frustrate.

fuel /fjul/ nm fuel oil.

fugitif, **-ive** /fyʒitif, -v/ a (passager) fleeting. ● nm, f fugitive.

fugue /fyg/ nf (Mus) fugue; **faire une ~** run away.

fuir /fɥiʁ/ [35] vi flee, run away; (eau, robinet, etc.) leak. ● vt (quitter) flee; (éviter) shun.

fuite /fɥit/ nf flight; (de liquide, d'une nouvelle) leak; **en ~** on the run; **mettre en ~** put to flight; **prendre la ~** take flight.

fulgurant, **~e** /fylgyʁɑ̃, -t/ a (vitesse) lightning.

fumé, **~e** /fyme/ a (poisson, verre) smoked.

fumée /fyme/ nf smoke; (vapeur) steam.

fumer /fyme/ [1] vt/i smoke.

fumeur, **-euse** /fymœʁ, -øz/ nm, f smoker; **zone non-~s** no smoking area.

fumier /fymje/ nm manure.

funambule /fynɑ̃byl/ nmf tightrope walker.

funèbre /fynɛbʁ/ a funeral; (fig) gloomy.

funérailles /fyneʁaj/ nfpl funeral.

funéraire /fyneʁɛʁ/ a funeral.

funeste /fynɛst/ a fatal.

F

fur: au ~ et à mesure /ofyʁea-
məzyʁ/ *loc* as one goes along,
progressively; **au ~ et à mesure
que** as.

furet /fyʁɛ/ *nm* ferret.

fureur /fyʁœʁ/ *nf* fury; (passion)
passion; **avec ~** furiously;
passionately; **mettre en ~**
infuriate; **faire ~** be all the rage.

furieux, -ieuse /fyʁjø, -z/ *a*
furious.

furoncle /fyʁɔ̃kl/ *nm* boil.

furtif, -ive /fyʁtif, -v/ *a* furtive.

fuseau (*pl* **~x**) /fyzo/ *nm* ski
trousers; (pour filer) spindle; **~
horaire** time zone.

fusée /fyze/ *nf* rocket.

fusible /fyzibl/ *nm* fuse.

fusil /fyzi/ *nm* rifle, gun; (de
chasse) shotgun; **~ mitrailleur**
machine-gun.

fusion /fyzjɔ̃/ *nf* fusion; (Comm)
merger. **fusionner** [1] *vt/i* merge.

fut /fy/ ⇒ÊTRE [5].

fût /fy/ *nm* (tonneau) barrel; (d'arbre)
trunk.

futé, ~e /fyte/ *a* cunning.

futile /fytil/ *a* futile.

futur, ~e /fytyʁ/ *a* future; **~e
femme/maman** wife-/
mother-to-be. ●*nm* future.

fuyant, ~e /fɥijɑ̃, -t/ *a* (front,
ligne) receding; (personne)
evasive.

fuyard, ~e /fɥijaʁ, -d/ *nm, f*
runaway.

gabardine /gabaʁdin/ *nf*
raincoat.

gabarit /gabaʁi/ *nm* size; (patron)
template; (fig) calibre.

gâcher /gɑʃe/ [1] *vt* (gâter) spoil;
(gaspiller) waste.

gâchette /gɑʃɛt/ *nf* trigger.

gâchis /gɑʃi/ *nm* waste.

gaffe /gaf/ *nf* 🄸 blunder; **faire ~**
be careful (à of).

gage /gaʒ/ *nm* security; (de bonne
foi) pledge; (de jeu) forfeit; **~s**
(salaire) wages; **en ~ de** as a token
of; **mettre en ~** pawn; **tueur à ~s**
hired killer.

gageure /gaʒyʁ/ *nf* challenge.

gagnant, ~e /gaɲɑ̃, -t/ *a*
winning. ●*nm, f* winner.

gagne-pain /gaɲpɛ̃/ *nm inv* job.

gagner /gaɲe/ [1] *vt* (match, prix)
win; (argent, pain) earn; (terrain)
gain; (temps) save; (atteindre)
reach; (convaincre) win over; **~ sa
vie** earn one's living. ●*vi* win;
(fig) gain.

gai, ~e /ge/ *a* cheerful; (ivre)
merry. **gaiement** *adv* cheerfully.
gaieté *nf* cheerfulness.

gain /gɛ̃/ *nm* (salaire) earnings;
(avantage) gain; (économie) saving;
~s (Comm) profits; (au jeu)
winnings.

gaine /gɛn/ *nf* (corset) girdle; (étui)
sheath.

galant, ~e /galɑ̃, -t/ *a* courteous;
(amoureux) romantic.

galaxie /galaksi/ *nf* galaxy.

gale /gal/ *nf* (de chat etc.) mange.

galère /galɛʀ/ *nf* (navire) galley; **c'est la ~!** ⊞ what an ordeal!

galérer /galeʀe/ [14] *vi* ⊞ (peiner) have a hard time.

galerie /galʀi/ *nf* gallery; (Théât) circle; (de voiture) roof-rack; **~ marchande** shopping arcade.

galet /galɛ/ *nm* pebble.

galette /galɛt/ *nf* flat cake; **~ des Rois** Twelfth Night cake.

Galles /gal/ *nfpl* **le pays de ~** Wales.

gallois, ~e /galwa, -z/ *a* Welsh. ●*nm* (Ling) Welsh. **G~, ~e** *nm, f* Welshman, Welshwoman.

galon /galɔ̃/ *nm* braid; (Mil) stripe; **prendre du ~** be promoted.

galop /galo/ *nm* canter; **aller au ~** canter; **grand ~** gallop; **~ d'essai** trial run. **galoper** [1] *vi* (*cheval*) canter; (*au grand galop*) gallop; (*personne*) run.

galopin /galopɛ̃/ *nm* ⊞ rascal.

gambader /gãbade/ [1] *vi* leap about.

gamelle /gamɛl/ *nf* (de soldat) mess kit; (d'ouvrier) lunch-box.

gamin, ~e /gamɛ̃, -in/ *a* childish; (*air*) youthful. ●*nm, f* ⊞ kid.

gamme /gam/ *nf* (Mus) scale; (série) range; **haut de ~** up-market, top of the range; **bas de ~** down-market, bottom of the range.

gang /gãg/ *nm* ⊞ gang.

ganglion /gãglijɔ̃/ *nm* ganglion.

gangster /gãgstɛʀ/ *nm* gangster; (escroc) crook.

gant /gã/ *nm* glove; **~ de ménage** rubber glove; **~ de toilette** face-flannel, face-cloth.

garage /gaʀaʒ/ *nm* garage. **garagiste** *nmf* garage owner; (employé) car mechanic.

garant, ~e /gaʀã, -t/ *nm, f* guarantor. ●*a* **se porter ~ de** vouch for.

garanti, ~e /gaʀãti/ *a* guaranteed.

garantie /gaʀãti/ *nf* guarantee; **~s** (de police d'assurance) cover.

garantir [2] *vt* guarantee; (protéger) protect (**de** from).

garçon /gaʀsɔ̃/ *nm* boy; (jeune homme) young man; (célibataire) bachelor; **~ (de café)** waiter; **~ d'honneur** best man. **garçonnière** *nf* bachelor flat.

garde¹ /gaʀd/ *nf* guard; (d'enfants, de bagages) care; (service) guard (duty); (infirmière) nurse; **de ~** on duty; **~ à vue** (police) custody; **mettre en ~** warn; **prendre ~** be careful (**à** of); **(droit de) ~** custody (**de** of).

garde² /gaʀd/ *nm* guard; (de propriété, parc) warden; **~ champêtre** village policeman; **~ du corps** bodyguard.

garde-à-vous /gaʀdavu/ *nm inv* (Mil) **se mettre au ~** stand to attention.

garde-chasse (*pl* **~s**) /gaʀdə-ʃas/ *nm* gamekeeper.

garde-manger /gaʀdmãʒe/ *nm inv* meat safe; (placard) larder.

garder /gaʀde/ [1] *vt* (conserver, maintenir) keep; (vêtement) keep on; (surveiller) look after; (défendre) guard; **~ le lit** stay in bed. □ **se ~** *vpr* (denrée) keep; **se ~ de faire** be careful not to do.

garderie /gaʀdəʀi/ *nf* day nursery.

garde-robe (*pl* **~s**) /gaʀdəʀɔb/ *nf* wardrobe.

gardien, ~ne /gaʀdjɛ̃, -ɛn/ *nm, f* (de locaux) security guard; (de prison, réserve) warden; (d'immeuble) caretaker; (de musée) attendant; (de zoo) keeper; (de traditions) guardian; **~ de but** goalkeeper; **~ de la paix** policeman; **~ de nuit** night watchman; **gardienne d'enfants** childminder.

G

gare /gaʀ/ nf (Rail) station; ~
routière coach station; (US) bus
station. ● interj ~ (**à toi**) watch
out!

garer /gaʀe/ [1] vt park. □ **se** ~
vpr park; (s'écarter) move out of
the way.

gargouille /gaʀguj/ nf water-
spout; (sculptée) gargoyle. **gargouiller** [1] vi gurgle; (stomach)
rumble.

garni, ~**e** /gaʀni/ a (plat) served
with vegetables; **bien** ~ (rempli)
well-filled.

garnir /gaʀniʀ/ [2] vt (remplir) fill;
(décorer) decorate; (couvrir) cover;
(doubler) line; (Culin) garnish.
garniture nf (légumes) vegetables;
(ornement) trimming; (de voiture)
trim.

gars /ga/ nm 🄴 lad; (adulte) guy,
bloke.

gas-oil /gazwal/ nm diesel (oil).

gaspillage /gaspijaʒ/ nm waste.
gaspiller [1] vt waste.

gastrique /gastʀik/ a gastric.

gastronome /gastʀɔnɔm/ nmf
gourmet.

gâteau (pl ~**x**) /gɑto/ nm cake;
~ **sec** biscuit; (US) cookie; **un
papa** ~ a doting dad.

gâter /gɑte/ [1] vt spoil. □ **se** ~
vpr (viande) go bad; (dent) rot;
(temps) get worse.

gâterie /gɑtʀi/ nf little treat.

gâteux, -**euse** /gɑtø, -z/ a senile.

gauche /goʃ/ a left; (maladroit)
awkward. ● nf left; **à** ~ on the
left; (direction) (to the) left; **la** ~
the left (side); (Pol) the left
(wing).

gaucher, -**ère** /goʃe, -ɛʀ/ a left-
handed.

gaufre /gofʀ/ nf waffle. **gaufrette**
nf wafer.

gaulois, ~**e** /golwa, -z/ a Gallic;
(fig) bawdy. **G**~, ~**e** nm, f Gaul.

gaver /gave/ [1] vt force-feed;

(fig) cram. □ **se** ~ **de** vpr gorge
oneself with; (fig) devour.

gaz /gaz/ nm inv gas; ~
d'échappement exhaust fumes; ~
lacrymogène tear-gas.

gaze /gaz/ nf gauze.

gazer /gaze/ [1] vi 🄴 **ça gaze?**
how's things?

gazette /gazɛt/ nf newspaper.

gazeux, -**euse** /gazø, -z/ a
(boisson) fizzy; (eau) sparkling.

gazoduc /gazɔdyk/ nm gas
pipeline.

gazon /gazɔ̃/ nm lawn, grass.

gazouiller /gazuje/ [1] vi (oiseau)
chirp; (bébé) babble.

GDF abrév m (**Gaz de France**)
French gas board.

géant, ~**e** /ʒeɑ̃, -t/ a giant. ● nm
giant. **géante** nf giantess.

geindre /ʒɛ̃dʀ/ [22] vi groan,
moan.

gel /ʒɛl/ nm frost; (produit) gel;
(Comm) freeze; ~ **coiffant** hair gel.

gelée /ʒ(ə)le/ nf frost; (Culin) jelly;
~ **blanche** hoarfrost.

geler /ʒəle/ [6] vt/i freeze; **on gèle**
(on a froid) it's freezing; **il** ou **ça
gèle** (il fait froid) it's freezing.

gélule /ʒelyl/ nf (Méd) capsule.

Gémeaux /ʒemo/ nmpl Gemini.

gémir /ʒemiʀ/ [2] vi groan.

gênant, ~**e** /ʒɛnɑ̃, -t/ a
embarrassing; (irritant) annoying;
(incommode) cumbersome.

gencive /ʒɑ̃siv/ nf gum.

gendarme /ʒɑ̃daʀm/ nm
policeman, gendarme.
gendarmerie nf police force;
(local) police station.

gendre /ʒɑ̃dʀ/ nm son-in-law.

gène /ʒɛn/ nm gene.

gêne /ʒɛn/ nf discomfort;
(confusion) embarrassment;
(dérangement) trouble,
inconvenience; (pauvreté) poverty.

gêné, ~**e** /ʒene/ a embarrassed;
(désargenté) short of money.

généalogie /ʒenealɔʒi/ *nf*
genealogy.

gêner /ʒene/ [1] *vt* bother,
disturb; (troubler) embarrass;
(entraver) block; (faire mal) hurt.

général, **~e** (*mpl* **-aux**) /ʒeneral,
-o/ *a* general; **en ~** in general.
● *nm* (*pl* **-aux**) general.

généralement /ʒeneralmã/ *adv*
generally.

généraliser /ʒeneralize/ [1] *vt*
make general. ● *vi* generalize.
□ **se ~** *vpr* become widespread
ou general.

généraliste /ʒeneralist/ *nmf*
general practitioner, GP.

généralité /ʒeneralite/ *nf*
general point.

génération /ʒenerasjɔ̃/ *nf*
generation.

généreux, **~euse** /ʒenerø, -z/ *a*
generous.

générique /ʒenerik/ *nm* (au
cinéma) credits. ● *a* generic.

générosité /ʒenerɔzite/ *nf*
generosity.

génétique /ʒenetik/ *a* genetic.
● *nf* genetics.

Genève /ʒənɛv/ *npr* Geneva.

génial, **~e** (*mpl* **-iaux**) /ʒenjal,
-jo/ *a* brilliant; (fantastique 🔲)
fantastic.

génie /ʒeni/ *nm* genius; **~ civil**
civil engineering.

génital, **~e** (*mpl* **-aux**) /ʒenital,
-o/ *a* genital.

génocide /ʒenɔsid/ *nm* genocide.

génoise /ʒenwaz/ *nf* sponge
(cake).

génome /ʒenom/ *nm* genome.

génothèque /ʒenɔtɛk/ *nf* gene
bank.

genou (*pl* **~x**) /ʒənu/ *nm* knee;
être à ~x be kneeling.

genre /ʒɑ̃R/ *nm* sort, kind; (Gram)
gender; (allure) **avoir bon/mauvais
~** to look nice/disreputable;
(comportement) **c'est bien son ~** it's

just like him/her.

gens /ʒɑ̃/ *nmpl* people.

gentil, **~le** /ʒɑ̃ti, -j/ *a* kind, nice;
(sage) good. **gentillesse** *nf*
kindness. **gentiment** *adv* kindly.

géographie /ʒeɔgrafi/ *nf*
geography.

geôlier, **-ière** /ʒolje, -jɛR/ *nm, f*
gaoler, jailer.

géologie /ʒeɔlɔʒi/ *nf* geology.

géomètre /ʒeɔmɛtR/ *nm*
surveyor.

géométrie /ʒeɔmetri/ *nf*
geometry. **géométrique** *a*
geometric.

gérance /ʒerɑ̃s/ *nf* management.

gérant, **~e** /ʒerɑ̃, -t/ *nm, f*
manager, manageress; **~
d'immeuble** landlord's agent.

gerbe /ʒɛRb/ *nf* (de fleurs) bunch,
bouquet; (d'eau) spray; (de blé)
sheaf.

gercer /ʒɛRse/ [10] *vt* chap; **avoir
les lèvres gercées** have chapped
lips. ● *vi* become chapped.
gerçure *nf* crack, chap.

gérer /ʒere/ [14] *vt* manage, run;
(traiter: fig) (*crise, situation*) handle.

germe /ʒɛRm/ *nm* germ; **~ de
soja** bean sprouts.

germer /ʒɛRme/ [1] *vi* germinate.

gestation /ʒɛstasjɔ̃/ *nf* gestation.

geste /ʒɛst/ *nm* gesture.

gesticuler /ʒɛstikyle/ [1] *vi*
gesticulate.

gestion /ʒɛstjɔ̃/ *nf* management.
gestionnaire *nmf* administrator.

ghetto /gɛto/ *nm* ghetto.

gibier /ʒibje/ *nm* (animaux) game.

giboulée /ʒibule/ *nf* shower.

gicler /ʒikle/ [1] *vi* squirt; **faire ~**
squirt.

gifle /ʒifl/ *nf* slap in the face.
gifler [1] *vt* slap.

gigantesque /ʒigɑ̃tɛsk/ *a*
gigantic.

G

gigot /ʒigo/ nm leg (of lamb).

gigoter /ʒigɔte/ [1] vi wriggle; (nerveusement) fidget.

gilet /ʒilɛ/ nm waistcoat; (cardigan) cardigan; ~ **de sauvetage** life-jacket.

gingembre /ʒɛ̃ʒɑ̃bʀ/ nm ginger.

girafe /ʒiʀaf/ nf giraffe.

giratoire /ʒiʀatwaʀ/ a **sens ~** roundabout.

girofle /ʒiʀɔfl/ nm **clou de ~** clove.

girouette /ʒiʀwɛt/ nf weathercock, weathervane.

gisement /ʒizmɑ̃/ nm deposit.

gitan, ~e /ʒitɑ̃, -an/ nm, f gypsy.

gîte /ʒit/ nm (maison) home; (abri) shelter; ~ **rural** holiday cottage.

givre /ʒivʀ/ nm frost; (sur pare-brise) ice.

givré, ~e /ʒivʀe/ a ▣ crazy.

glace /glas/ nf ice; (crème) ice-cream; (vitre) window; (miroir) mirror; (verre) glass.

glacé, ~e /glase/ a (vent, accueil) icy; (hands) frozen; (gâteau) iced.

glacer /glase/ [10] vt freeze; (gâteau, boisson) chill; (pétrifier) chill. ▢ se ~ vpr freeze.

glacier /glasje/ nm (Géog) glacier; (vendeur) ice-cream seller. **glacière** nf coolbox. **glaçon** nm ice-cube.

glaïeul /glajœl/ nm gladiolus.

glaise /glɛz/ nf clay.

gland /glɑ̃/ nm acorn; (ornement) tassel.

glande /glɑ̃d/ nf gland.

glander /glɑ̃de/ [1] vi ▣ laze around.

glaner /glane/ [1] vt glean.

glauque /glok/ a (fig) murky; (street) squalid.

glissade /glisad/ nf (jeu) slide; (dérapage) skid.

glissant, ~e /glisɑ̃, -t/ a slippery.

glissement /glismɑ̃/ nm sliding; gliding; (fig) shift; ~ **de terrain** landslide.

glisser /glise/ [1] vi slide; (être glissant) be slippery; (sur l'eau) glide; (déraper) slip; (véhicule) skid. ● vt (objet) slip (dans into); (remarque) slip in. ▢ se ~ vpr slip (dans into).

glissière /glisjɛʀ/ nf slide; **porte à ~** sliding door; ~ **de sécurité** (Auto) crash-barrier; **fermeture à ~** zip.

global, ~e (mpl -aux) /glɔbal, -o/ a (entier, général) overall.

globalement adv as a whole.

globe /glɔb/ nm globe; ~ **oculaire** eyeball; ~ **terrestre** globe.

globule /glɔbyl/ nm (du sang) corpuscle.

gloire /glwaʀ/ nf glory, fame.

glorieux, -ieuse a glorious. **glorifier** [45] vt glorify.

glose /gloz/ nf gloss.

glossaire /glɔsɛʀ/ nm glossary.

gloussement /glusmɑ̃/ nm chuckle; (de poule) cluck.

glouton, ~ne /glutɔ̃, -ɔn/ a gluttonous. ● nm, f glutton.

gluant, ~e /glyɑ̃, -t/ a sticky.

glucose /glykoz/ nm glucose.

glycérine /gliseʀin/ nf glycerin(e).

GO abrév fpl (**grandes ondes**) long wave.

goal /gol/ nm ▣ goalkeeper.

gobelet /gɔblɛ/ nm cup; (en verre) tumbler.

gober /gɔbe/ [1] vt swallow (whole); **je ne peux pas le ~** ▣ I can't stand him.

goéland /gɔelɑ̃/ nm (sea)gull.

gogo: à ~ /agogo/ loc ▣ galore, in abundance.

goinfre /gwɛ̃fʀ/ nm (glouton ▣) pig.

goinfrer (se) [1] vpr ▣ stuff oneself (de with).

golf /gɔlf/ nm golf; (terrain) golf course.

golfe /gɔlf/ nm gulf.

gomme /gɔm/ nf rubber; (US) eraser; (résine) gum. **gommer** [1] vt rub out.

gond /gɔ̃/ nm hinge; **sortir de ses ~s** ⊡ go mad.

gondoler (se) /(sə)gɔ̃dɔle/ [1] vpr (bois) warp; (métal) buckle.

gonflé, ~e /gɔ̃fle/ a swollen; **il est ~** ⊡ he's got a nerve.

gonflement /gɔ̃fləmɑ̃/ nm swelling.

gonfler /gɔ̃fle/ [1] vt (ballon, pneu) pump up, blow up; (augmenter) increase; (exagérer) inflate. ● vi swell.

gorge /gɔRʒ/ nf throat; (poitrine) breast; (vallée) gorge.

gorgée /gɔRʒe/ nf sip, gulp.

gorger /gɔRʒe/ [40] vt fill (de with); **gorgé de** full of. □ **se ~** vpr gorge oneself (de with).

gorille /gɔRij/ nm gorilla; (garde ⊡) bodyguard.

gosier /gozje/ nm throat.

gosse /gɔs/ nmf ⊡ kid.

gothique /gɔtik/ a Gothic.

goudron /gudRɔ̃/ nm tar. **goudronner** [1] vt tarmac.

gouffre /gufR/ nm abyss, gulf.

goujat /guʒa/ nm lout, boor.

goulot /gulo/ nm neck; **boire au ~** drink from the bottle.

goulu, ~e /guly/ a gluttonous. ● nm, f glutton.

gourde /guRd/ nf (à eau) flask; (idiot ⊡) fool.

gourer (se) /(sə)guRe/ [1] vpr ⊡ make a mistake.

gourmand, ~e /guRmɑ̃, -d/ a greedy.

gourmandise /guRmɑ̃diz/ nf greed; **~s** sweets.

gourmet /guRmɛ/ nm gourmet.

gourmette /guRmɛt/ nf chain bracelet.

gousse /gus/ nf **~ d'ail** clove of garlic.

goût /gu/ nm taste; (gré) liking; **prendre ~ à** develop a taste for; **avoir bon ~** (aliment) taste nice; (personne) have good taste; **donner du ~ à** give flavour.

goûter /gute/ [1] vt taste; (apprécier) enjoy; **~ à ou de** taste. ● vi have tea. ● nm tea, snack.

goutte /gut/ nf drop; (Méd) gout. **goutte-à-goutte** nm inv drip. **goutter** [1] vi drip.

gouttière /gutjɛR/ nf gutter.

gouvernail /guvɛRnaj/ nm rudder; (barre) helm.

gouvernement /guvɛRnəmɑ̃/ nm government.

gouverner /guvɛRne/ [1] vt/i govern; (dominer) control. **gouverneur** nm governor.

grâce /gRɑs/ nf (charme) grace; (faveur) favour; (volonté) grace; pardon; (Jur) pardon; (Relig) grace; **~ à** thanks to; **rendre ~(s) à** give thanks to.

gracier /gRasje/ [45] vt pardon.

gracieusement /gRasjøzmɑ̃/ adv gracefully; (gratuitement) free (of charge).

gracieux, -ieuse /gRasjø, -z/ a graceful.

grade /gRad/ nm rank; **monter en ~** be promoted.

gradin /gRadɛ̃/ nm tier, step; **en ~s** terraced; **les ~s** terraces.

gradué, ~e /gRadɥe/ a graded, graduated; **verre ~** measuring jug.

graffiti /gRafiti/ nmpl graffiti.

grain /gRɛ̃/ nm grain; (Naut) squall; **~ de beauté** beauty spot; **~ de café** coffee bean; **~ de poivre** pepper corn; **~ de raisin** grape.

graine /gRɛn/ nf seed.

graisse /gRɛs/ nf fat; (lubrifiant)

G

grease. **graisser** [1] *vt* grease.
graisseux, -euse *a* greasy.

grammaire /gʀam(m)ɛʀ/ *nf*
grammar.

gramme /gʀam/ *nm* gram.

grand, ~e /gʀɑ̃, -d/ *a* big, large;
(haut) tall; (intense, fort) great;
(brillant) great; (principal) main; (plus
âgé) big, elder; (adulte) grown-up;
au ~ air in the open air; **au ~ jour**
in broad daylight; (fig) in the
open; **en ~e partie** largely; **~e
banlieue** outer suburbs; **~
ensemble** housing estate; **~es
lignes** (Rail) main lines; **~ magasin**
department store; **~e personne**
grown-up; **~ public** general
public; **~ surface** hypermarket;
~es vacances summer holidays.
● *adv* (ouvrir) wide; **~ ouvert**
wide open; **voir ~** think big.
● *nm, f* (adulte) grown-up; (enfant)
big boy, big girl; (Scol) senior.

Grande-Bretagne /gʀɑ̃dbʀətaɲ/
nf Great Britain.

grand-chose /gʀɑ̃ʃoz/ *pron* **pas
~** not much, not a lot.

grandeur /gʀɑ̃dœʀ/ *nf* greatness;
(dimension) size; **folie des ~s**
delusions of grandeur.

grandir /gʀɑ̃diʀ/ [2] *vi* grow;
(bruit) grow louder. ● *vt* (talons)
make taller; (loupe) magnify.

grand-mère (*pl* **grands-mères**)
/gʀɑ̃mɛʀ/ *nf* grandmother.

grand-père (*pl* **grands-pères**)
/gʀɑ̃pɛʀ/ *nm* grandfather.

grands-parents /gʀɑ̃paʀɑ̃/ *nmpl*
grandparents.

grange /gʀɑ̃ʒ/ *nf* barn.

granulé /gʀanyle/ *nm* granule.

graphique /gʀafik/ *a* graphic;
(Ordinat) graphics; **informatique ~**
computer graphics. ● *nm* graph.

graphologie /gʀafɔlɔʒi/ *nf*
graphology.

grappe /gʀap/ *nf* cluster; **~ de
raisin** bunch of grapes.

gras, ~se /gʀɑ, -s/ *a* (gros) fat;
(aliment) fatty; (surface, peau,
cheveux) greasy; (épais) thick;
(caractères) bold; **faire la ~se
matinée** sleep late. ● *nm* (Culin) fat.

gratifiant, ~e /gʀatifjɑ̃, -t/ *a*
gratifying; (travail) rewarding.

gratifier /gʀatifje/ [45] *vt* favour,
reward (**de** with).

gratin /gʀatɛ̃/ *nm* gratin (baked
dish with cheese topping); (élite 🆃)
upper crust.

gratis /gʀatis/ *adv* free.

gratitude /gʀatityd/ *nf* gratitude.

gratte-ciel /gʀatsjɛl/ *nm inv*
skyscraper.

gratter /gʀate/ [1] *vt/i* scratch;
(avec un outil) scrape; **ça me gratte** 🆃
it itches. □ **se ~** *vpr* scratch
oneself; **se ~ la tête** scratch one's
head.

gratuiciel /gʀatɥisjɛl/ *nm*
(Internet) freeware.

gratuit, ~e /gʀatɥi, -t/ *a* free;
(acte) gratuitous. **gratuitement**
adv free (of charge).

grave /gʀav/ *a* (maladie, accident,
problème) serious; (solennel) grave;
(voix) deep; (accent) grave.

gravement *adv* seriously;
gravely.

graver /gʀave/ [1] *vt* engrave; (sur
bois) carve.

gravier /gʀavje/ *nm* **du ~** gravel.

gravité /gʀavite/ *nf* gravity.

graviter /gʀavite/ [1] *vi* revolve.

gravure /gʀavyʀ/ *nf* engraving;
(de tableau, photo) print, plate.

gré /gʀe/ *nm* (volonté) will; (goût)
taste; **à son ~** (agir) as one likes;
de bon ~ willingly; **bon ~ mal ~**
like it or not; **je vous en saurais ~**
I'd be grateful for that.

grec, ~que /gʀɛk/ *a* Greek. ● *nm*
(Ling) Greek. **G~, ~que** *nm, f*
Greek.

Grèce *nf* /gʀɛs/ Greece.

greffe /gʀɛf/ *nf* graft; (d'organe)

transplant. **greffer** [1] vt graft; transplant.

greffier, -ière /gʁefje, -jɛʁ/ nm, f clerk of the court.

grêle /gʁɛl/ a (maigre) spindly; (voix) shrill. ● nf hail.

grêler /gʁele/ [1] vi hail; **il grêle** it's hailing. **grêlon** nm hailstone.

grelot /gʁəlo/ nm (little) bell.

grelotter /gʁəlɔte/ [1] vi shiver.

grenade /gʁənad/ nf (fruit) pomegranate; (explosif) grenade.

grenat /gʁəna/ a inv dark red.

grenier /gʁənje/ nm attic; (pour grain) loft.

grenouille /gʁənuj/ nf frog.

grès /gʁɛ/ nm sandstone; (poterie) stoneware.

grésiller /gʁezije/ [1] vi sizzle; (radio) crackle.

grève /gʁɛv/ nf (rivage) shore; (cessation de travail) strike; **faire ~, être en ~** be on strike; **se mettre en ~** go on strike. **gréviste** nmf striker.

gribouiller /gʁibuje/ [1] vt/i scribble.

grief /gʁijɛf/ nm grievance.

grièvement /gʁijɛvmɑ̃/ adv seriously.

griffe /gʁif/ nf claw; (de couturier) label; **coup de ~** scratch.

griffé, ~e /gʁife/ a (vêtement, article) designer.

griffer /gʁife/ [1] vt scratch, claw.

grignoter /gʁiɲɔte/ [1] vt/i nibble.

gril /gʁil/ nm (de cuisinière) grill; (plaque) grill pan.

grillade /gʁijad/ nf (viande) grill.

grillage /gʁijaʒ/ nm wire netting.

grille /gʁij/ nf railings; (portail) (metal) gate; (de fenêtre) bars; (de cheminée) grate; (fig) grid. **grille-pain** nm inv toaster.

griller /gʁije/ [1] vt (pain) toast; (viande) grill; (ampoule) blow; (feu rouge) go through; (appareil) burn out. ● vi (ampoule) blow; (Culin) faire ~ (viande) grill; (pain) toast.

grillon /gʁijɔ̃/ nm cricket.

grimace /gʁimas/ nf (funny) face; (de douleur, dégoût) grimace; **faire des ~s** make faces; **faire la ~** pull a face, grimace.

grimper /gʁɛ̃pe/ [1] vt climb. ● vi climb; **~ sur** ou **dans un arbre** climb a tree.

grincement /gʁɛ̃smɑ̃/ nm creak (ing).

grincer /gʁɛ̃se/ [10] vi creak; **~ des dents** grind one's teeth.

grincheux, -euse /gʁɛ̃ʃø, -z/ a grumpy.

grippe /gʁip/ nf influenza, flu.

grippé, ~e /gʁipe/ a **être ~** have (the) flu; (mécanisme) be seized up ou jammed.

gris, ~e /gʁi, -z/ a grey; (saoul) tipsy.

grivois, ~e /gʁivwa, -z/ a bawdy.

grog /gʁɔg/ nm hot toddy.

grogner /gʁɔɲe/ [1] vi (animal) growl; (personne) grumble.

grognon /gʁɔɲɔ̃/ am grumpy.

groin /gʁwɛ̃/ nm snout.

gronder /gʁɔ̃de/ [1] vi (tonnerre, volcan) rumble; (chien) growl; (conflit) be brewing. ● vt scold.

groom /gʁum/ nm bellboy.

gros, ~se /gʁo, -s/ a big, large; (gras) fat; (important) big; (épais) thick; (lourd) heavy; (buveur, fumeur) heavy; **~ bonnet** 🅸 bigwig; **~ lot** jackpot; **~ mot** swear word; **~ plan** close-up; **~se caisse** bass drum; **~ titre** headline. ● nm, f fat man, fat woman. ● adv (écrire) big; (risquer, gagner) a lot. ● nm **le ~ de** the bulk of; **de ~** (Comm) wholesale; **en ~** roughly; (Comm) wholesale.

groseille /gʀozɛj/ *nf* redcurrant; **~ à maquereau** gooseberry.

grossesse /gʀosɛs/ *nf* pregnancy.

grosseur /gʀosœʀ/ *nf* (volume) size; (enflure) lump.

grossier, -ière /gʀosje, -jɛʀ/ *a* (sans finesse) coarse, rough; (rudimentaire) crude; (vulgaire) coarse; (impoli) rude; (erreur) gross. **grossièrement** *adv* (sommairement) roughly; (vulgairement) coarsely. **grossièreté** *nf* coarseness; crudeness; rudeness; (mot) rude word.

grossir /gʀosiʀ/ [2] *vt* (faire augmenter) increase, boost; (agrandir) enlarge; (exagérer) exaggerate; **~ les rangs** *ou* **la foule** swell the ranks. ● *vi* (personne) put on weight; (augmenter) grow.

grossiste /gʀosist/ *nmf* wholesaler.

grosso modo /gʀosomodo/ *adv* roughly.

grotesque /gʀotɛsk/ *a* grotesque; (ridicule) ludicrous.

grotte /gʀot/ *nf* cave; grotto.

grouiller /gʀuje/ [1] *vi* swarm; **~ de** be swarming with.

groupe /gʀup/ *nm* group; (Mus) group, band; **~ électrogène** generating set; **~ scolaire** school; **~ de travail** working party.

groupement /gʀupmɑ̃/ *nm* grouping.

grouper /gʀupe/ [1] *vt* put together. □ **se ~** *vpr* group (together).

grue /gʀy/ *nf* (machine, oiseau) crane.

gruyère /gʀyjɛʀ/ *nm* gruyère (cheese).

gué /ge/ *nm* ford; **passer** *ou* **traverser à ~** ford.

guenon /gənɔ̃/ *nf* female monkey.

guépard /gepaʀ/ *nm* cheetah.

guêpe /gɛp/ *nf* wasp.

guère /gɛʀ/ *adv* **ne ~** hardly; **il n'y a ~ d'espoir** there is no hope; **elle n'a ~ dormi** she didn't sleep much, she hardly slept.

guérilla /geʀija/ *nf* guerrilla warfare; (groupe) guerillas.

guérir /geʀiʀ/ [2] *vt* (personne, maladie, mal) cure (de of); (plaie, membre) heal. ● *vi* get better; (blessure) heal; **~ de** recover from. **guérison** *nf* curing; healing; (de personne) recovery.

guerre /gɛʀ/ *nf* war; **en ~** at war; **faire la ~** wage war (à against); **~ civile** civil war; **~ mondiale** world war.

guerrier, -ière /geʀje, -jɛʀ/ *a* warlike. ● *nm, f* warrior.

guet /gɛ/ *nm* watch; **faire le ~** be on the watch. **guet-apens** (*pl* **guets-apens**) *nm* ambush.

guetter /gete/ [1] *vt* watch; (attendre) watch out for.

gueule /gœl/ *nf* mouth; (figure 🖪) face; **ta ~!** 🖪 shut up!; **~ de bois** 🖪 hangover.

gueuleton /gœltɔ̃/ *nm* 🖪 blow-out, slap-up meal.

gui /gi/ *nm* mistletoe.

guichet /giʃɛ/ *nm* window, counter; (de gare) ticket-office; (Théât) box-office; **jouer à ~s fermés** (pièce) be sold out; **~ automatique** cash dispenser.

guide /gid/ *nm* guide. ● *nf* (fille scout) girl guide.

guider /gide/ [1] *vt* guide.

guidon /gidɔ̃/ *nm* handlebars.

guignol /giɲɔl/ *nm* puppet; (personne) clown; (spectacle) puppet-show.

guillemets /gijmɛ/ *nmpl* quotation marks, inverted

commas; **entre ~** in inverted commas.

guillotine /gijɔtin/ *nf* guillotine.

guimauve /gimov/ *nf* marshmallow; **c'est de la ~** 🔲 it's slushy *ou* schmaltzy 🔲.

guindé, ~e /gɛ̃de/ *a* stiff, formal; *(style)* stilted.

guirlande /giʀlɑ̃d/ *nf* garland; tinsel.

guitare /gitaʀ/ *nf* guitar.

gym /ʒim/ *nf* gymnastics; (Scol) physical education, PE.

gymnase /ʒimnɑz/ *nm* gym-(nasium). **gymnastique** *nf* gymnastics.

gynécologie /ʒinekɔlɔʒi/ *nf* gynaecology.

habile /abil/ *a* skilful, clever.

habillé, ~e /abije/ *a* *(vêtement)* smart; *(soirée)* formal.

habillement /abijmɑ̃/ *nm* clothing.

habiller /abije/ [1] *vt* dress (**de** in); *(équiper)* clothe; *(recouvrir)* cover (**de** with). □ **s'~** *vpr* get dressed; *(élégamment)* dress up.

habit /abi/ *nm* *(de personnage)* outfit; *(de cérémonie)* tails; **~s** clothes.

habitant, ~e /abitɑ̃, -t/ *nm, f* *(de maison, quartier)* resident; *(de pays)* inhabitant.

habitat /abita/ *nm* *(mode de peuplement)* settlement; *(conditions)* housing.

habitation /abitasjɔ̃/ *nf* *(logement)* house.

habité, ~e /abite/ *a* *(terre)* inhabited.

habiter /abite/ [1] *vi* live. ● *vt* live in.

habitude /abityd/ *nf* habit; **avoir l'~ de** be used to; **d'~** usually; **comme d'~** as usual.

habitué, ~e /abitɥe/ *nm, f* *(client)* regular.

habituel, ~le /abitɥɛl/ *a* usual. **habituellement** *adv* usually.

habituer /abitɥe/ [1] *vt* **~ qn à** get sb used to. □ **s'~ à** *vpr* get used to.

hache /'aʃ/ *nf* axe.

haché, ~e /'aʃe/ *a* *(viande)* minced; *(phrases)* jerky.

hacher /'aʃe/ [1] *vt* mince; *(au couteau)* chop.

hachis /'aʃi/ *nm* minced meat; (US) ground meat; **~ Parmentier** ≈ shepherd's pie.

hachisch /'aʃiʃ/ *nm* hashish.

hachoir /'aʃwaʀ/ *nm* *(appareil)* mincer; *(couteau)* chopper; *(planche)* chopping board.

haie /'ɛ/ *nf* hedge; *(de personnes)* line; **course de ~s** hurdle race.

haillon /'ɑjɔ̃/ *nm* rag.

haine /'ɛn/ *nf* hatred.

haïr /'aiʀ/ [36] *vt* hate.

hâlé, ~e /'ɑle/ *a* (sun-)tanned.

haleine /alɛn/ *nf* breath; **travail de longue ~** long job.

haleter /'alte/ [6] *vi* pant.

hall /'ol/ *nm* hall; *(de gare)* concourse.

halle /'al/ *nf* market hall; **~s** covered market.

halte /'alt/ *nf* stop; **faire ~** stop. ● *interj* stop; (Mil) halt.

haltère /altɛʀ/ *nm* dumbbell; **faire des ~s** to do weightlifting.

hameau *(pl ~x)* /'amo/ *nm* hamlet.

hameçon /amsɔ̃/ *nm* hook.

hanche /'ɑ̃ʃ/ *nf* hip.

handicap /'ãdikap/ *nm* handicap.
handicapé, ~e *a & nm,f* disabled (person).

hangar /'ãgaʀ/ *nm* shed; (pour avions) hangar.

hanter /'ãte/ [1] *vt* haunt.

hantise /'ãtiz/ *nf* dread; **avoir la ~ de** dread.

haras /'aʀɑ/ *nm* stud-farm.

harasser /'aʀase/ [1] *vt* exhaust.

harcèlement /'aʀsɛlmã/ *nm* ~ **sexuel** sexual harassment.

harceler /'aʀsəle/ [6] *vt* harass.

hardi, ~e /'aʀdi/ *a* bold.

hareng /'aʀã/ *nm* herring.

hargne /'aʀɲ/ *nf* (aggressive) bad temper.

haricot /'aʀiko/ *nm* bean; ~ **vert** French bean; (US) green bean.

harmonie /aʀmɔni/ *nf* harmony.
harmonieux, -ieuse *a* harmonious.

harmoniser /aʀmɔnize/ [1] *vt* harmonize. □ **s'~** *vpr* harmonize.

harnacher /'aʀnaʃe/ [1] *vt* harness.

harnais /'aʀnɛ/ *nm* harness.

harpe /'aʀp/ *nf* harp.

harpon /'aʀpɔ̃/ *nm* harpoon.

hasard /'azaʀ/ *nm* chance; (coïncidence) coincidence; **les ~s de** the fortunes of; **au ~** (choisir etc.) at random; (flâner) aimlessly.
hasardeux, -euse *a* risky.

hasarder /'azaʀde/ [1] *vt* risk; (remarque) venture.

hâte /'ɑt/ *nf* haste; **à la ~, en ~** hurriedly; **avoir ~ de** look forward to.

hâter /'ɑte/ [1] *vt* hasten. □ **se ~** *vpr* hurry (**de** to).

hâtif, -ive /'ɑtif, -v/ *a* hasty; (précoce) early.

hausse /'os/ *nf* rise (**de** in); ~ **des prix** price rise; **en ~** rising.

hausser /'ose/ [1] *vt* raise; (épaules) shrug.

haut, ~e /'o, 'ot/ *a* high; (de taille) tall; **à voix ~e** aloud; ~ **en couleur** colourful; **plus ~** higher up; (dans un texte) above; **en ~ lieu** in high places. ● *adv* high; **tout ~** out loud. ● *nm* top; **des ~s et des bas** ups and downs; **en ~** (regarder) up; (à l'étage) upstairs; **en ~ (de)** at the top (of).

hautbois /'obwa/ *nm* oboe.

haut-de-forme /'odfɔʀm/ (*pl* **hauts-de-forme**) *nm* top hat.

hauteur /'otœʀ/ *nf* height; (colline) hill; (arrogance) haughtiness; **être à la ~** be up to it; **à la ~ de** (ville) near; **être à la ~ de la situation** be equal to the situation.

haut-le-cœur /'olkœʀ/ *nm inv* nausea.

haut-parleur (*pl* ~**s**) /'opaʀlœʀ/ *nm* loudspeaker.

havre /'avʀ/ *nm* haven (**de** of).

hayon /'ajɔ̃/ *nm* (Auto) hatchback.

hebdomadaire /ɛbdɔmadɛʀ/ *a & nm* weekly.

hébergement /ebɛʀʒəmã/ *nm* accommodation.

héberger /ebɛʀʒe/ [40] *vt* (ami) put up; (réfugiés) take in.

hébreu (*pl* ~**x**) /ebʀø/ *am* Hebrew. ● *nm* (Ling) Hebrew; **c'est de l'~!** it's all Greek to me!

Hébreu (*pl* ~**x**) /ebʀø/ *nm* Hebrew; **les ~x** the Hebrews.

hécatombe /ekatɔ̃b/ *nf* slaughter.

hectare /ɛktaʀ/ *nm* hectare (= 10,000 square metres).

hélas /'elas/ *interj* alas. ● *adv* sadly.

hélice /elis/ *nf* propeller.

hélicoptère /elikɔptɛʀ/ *nm* helicopter.

helvétique /ɛlvetik/ *a* Swiss.

hématome /ematom/ *nm* bruise.

hémorragie /emɔʀaʒi/ *nf* haemorrhage.

hémorroïdes /emɔʀɔid/ *nfpl*
piles, haemorrhoids.

hennir /'eniʀ/ [2] *vi* neigh.

hépatite /epatit/ *nf* hepatitis.

herbe /ɛʀb/ *nf* grass; (Méd, Culin)
herb; **en ~** in the blade; (fig)
budding.

héréditaire /eʀeditɛʀ/ *a*
hereditary.

hérédité /eʀedite/ *nf* heredity.

hérisser /'eʀise/ [1] *vt* bristle; **~**
qn (fig) ruffle sb. □ **se ~** *vpr*
bristle.

hérisson /'eʀisɔ̃/ *nm* hedgehog.

héritage /eʀitaʒ/ *nm* inheritance;
(spirituel) heritage.

hériter /eʀite/ [1] *vt/i* inherit (**de**
from); **~ de qch** inherit sth.

héritier, -ière /eʀitje, -jɛʀ/ *nm, f* heir, heiress.

hermétique /ɛʀmetik/ *a* airtight;
(fig) unfathomable.

hernie /'ɛʀni/ *nf* hernia.

héroïne /eʀɔin/ *nf* (femme)
heroine; (drogue) heroin.

héroïque /eʀɔik/ *a* heroic.

héros /'eʀo/ *nm* hero.

hésiter /ezite/ [1] *vi* hesitate (**à**
to); **j'hésite** I'm not sure.

hétérogène /eteʀɔʒɛn/ *a*
heterogeneous.

hétérosexuel, ~le /eteʀɔsɛk-
sɥɛl/ *nm, f & a* heterosexual.

hêtre /'ɛtʀ/ *nm* beech.

heure /œʀ/ *nf* time; (soixante
minutes) hour; **quelle ~ est-il?** what
time is it?; **il est dix ~s** it is ten
o'clock; **à l'~** (*venir, être*) on
time; **d'~ en ~** by the hour;
toutes les deux ~s every two
hours; **~ de pointe** rush-hour; **~**
de cours (Scol) period; **~ indue**
ungodly hour; **~s creuses** off-
peak periods; **~s supplémentaires**
overtime.

heureusement /œʀøzmɑ̃/ *adv*
fortunately, luckily.

heureux, -euse /œʀø, -z/ *a*
happy; (chanceux) lucky, fortunate.

heurt /'œʀ/ *nm* collision; (conflit)
clash; **sans ~** smoothly.

heurter /'œʀte/ [1] *vt* (cogner) hit;
(*mur*) bump into, hit; (choquer)
offend. □ **se ~ à** *vpr* bump into,
hit; (fig) come up against.

hexagone /ɛgzagon/ *nm*
hexagon; **l'~** France.

hiberner /ibɛʀne/ [1] *vi*
hibernate.

hibou (*pl* **~x**) /'ibu/ *nm* owl.

hier /jɛʀ/ *adv* yesterday; **~ soir**
last night, yesterday evening.

hiérarchie /'jeʀaʀʃi/ *nf*
hierarchy.

hilare /ilaʀ/ *a* (*visage*) merry; **être**
~ be laughing.

hindou, ~e /ɛ̃du/ *a & nm, f*
Hindu. **H~, ~e** *nm, f* Hindu.

hippique /ipik/ *a* equestrian; **le**
concours ~ showjumping.

hippodrome /ipɔdʀom/ *nm*
racecourse.

hippopotame /ipɔpɔtam/ *nm*
hippopotamus.

hirondelle /iʀɔ̃dɛl/ *nf* swallow.

hisser /'ise/ [1] *vt* hoist, haul.
□ **se ~** *vpr* heave oneself up.

histoire /istwaʀ/ *nf* (récit) story;
(étude) history; (affaire) business;
~(s) (chichis) fuss; (ennuis) trouble.

historique *a* historical.

hiver /ivɛʀ/ *nm* winter. **hivernal,**
~e (*mpl* **-aux**) *a* winter; (glacial)
wintry.

H.L.M. *abbrév m ou f* (**habitation**
à loyer modéré) block of council
flats; (US) low-rent apartment
building.

hocher /'ɔʃe/ [1] *vt* **~ la tête** (pour
dire oui) nod; (pour dire non) shake
one's head.

hochet /'ɔʃɛ/ *nm* rattle.

hockey /'ɔkɛ/ *nm* hockey; **~ sur**
glace ice hockey.

hollandais, ~e /'ɔlɑ̃dɛ, -z/ *a*
Dutch. ●*nm* (Ling) Dutch. **H~,**

~**e** *nm, f* Dutchman,
Dutchwoman.
Hollande /'ɔlɑ̃d/ *nf* Holland.
homard /'ɔmaʀ/ *nm* lobster.
homéopathie /ɔmeɔpati/ *nf*
homoeopathy.
homicide /ɔmisid/ *nm* homicide;
~ **involontaire** manslaughter.
hommage /ɔmaʒ/ *nm* tribute; ~**s**
(salutations) respects; **rendre** ~ **à**
pay tribute to.
homme /ɔm/ *nm* man; (espèce)
man(kind); ~ **d'affaires**
businessman; ~ **de la rue** man in
the street; ~ **d'État** statesman; ~
politique politician.
homogène /ɔmɔʒɛn/ *a*
homogeneous.
homonyme /ɔmɔnim/ *nm*
(personne) namesake.
homosexualité /ɔmɔsɛksɥalite/
nf homosexuality.
homosexuel, ~**le** /ɔmɔsɛksɥɛl/
a & *nm,f* homosexual.
Hongrie /'ɔ̃gʀi/ *nf* Hungary.
hongrois, ~**e** /'ɔ̃gʀwa, -z/ *a*
Hungarian. ● *nm* (Ling)
Hungarian. **H**~, ~**e** *nm, f*
Hungarian.
honnête /ɔnɛt/ *a* honest; (juste)
fair. **honnêteté** *nf* honesty.
honneur /ɔnœʀ/ *nm* honour;
(mérite) credit; **d'**~ (invité, place)
of honour; **en l'**~ **de** in honour of;
en quel ~? 𝕀 why?; **faire** ~ **à**
(équipe, famille) bring credit to.
honorable /ɔnɔʀabl/ *a*
honourable; (convenable)
respectable.
honoraire /ɔnɔʀɛʀ/ *a* honorary.
honoraires *nmpl* fees.
honorer /ɔnɔʀe/ [1] *vt* honour;
(faire honneur à) do credit to.
honte /'ɔ̃t/ *nf* shame; **avoir** ~ be
ashamed (de of); **faire** ~ **à** make
ashamed. **honteux**, **-euse** *a*
(personne) ashamed (de of);
(action) shameful.

hôpital (*pl* **-aux**) /ɔpital, -o/ *nm*
hospital.
hoquet /'ɔkɛ/ *nm* **le** ~ (the)
hiccups.
horaire /ɔʀɛʀ/ *a* hourly. ● *nm*
timetable; ~**s libres** flexitime.
horizon /ɔʀizɔ̃/ *nm* horizon; (Fig)
outlook.
horizontal, ~**e** (*mpl* **-aux**) /ɔʀi-
zɔ̃tal, -o/ *a* horizontal.
horloge /ɔʀlɔʒ/ *nf* clock.
hormis /'ɔʀmi/ *prép* save.
hormonal, ~**e** (*mpl* **-aux**)
/ɔʀmɔnal, -o/ *a* hormonal,
hormone.
hormone /ɔʀmɔn/ *nf* hormone.
horreur /ɔʀœʀ/ *nf* horror; **avoir** ~
de hate.
horrible /ɔʀibl/ *a* horrible.
horrifier /ɔʀifje/ [45] *vt* horrify.
hors /'ɔʀ/ *prép* ~ **de** outside, (avec
mouvement) out of; ~ **d'atteinte** out
of reach; ~ **d'haleine** out of
breath; ~ **de prix** extremely
expensive; ~ **pair** outstanding; ~
de soi beside oneself. **hors-bord**
nm inv speedboat. **hors-d'œuvre**
nm inv hors-d'œuvre. **hors-jeu** *a
inv* offside. **hors-la-loi** *nm inv*
outlaw. **hors-piste** *nm* off-piste
skiing. **hors-taxe** *a inv* duty-free.
horticulteur, **-trice** /ɔʀtikyltœʀ,
-tʀis/ *nm, f* horticulturist.
hospice /ɔspis/ *nm* home.
hospitalier, **-ière** /ɔspitalje, -jɛʀ/
a hospitable; (Méd) hospital.
hospitaliser [1] *vt* take to
hospital. **hospitalité** *nf*
hospitality.
hostile /ɔstil/ *a* hostile. **hostilité**
nf hostility.
hôte /ot/ *nm* (maître) host; (invité)
guest.
hôtel /otɛl/ *nm* hotel; ~
(particulier) (private) mansion; ~
de ville town hall.
hôtelier, **-ière** /otəlje, -jɛʀ/ *a*

hotel. ● *nm, f* hotel keeper.
hôtellerie *nf* hotel business.
hôtesse /otɛs/ *nf* hostess; ~ **de l'air** stewardess.
hotte /'ɔt/ *nf* basket; ~ **aspirante** extractor (hood), (US) ventilator.
houblon /'ublɔ̃/ *nm* le ~ hops.
houille /'uj/ *nf* coal; ~ **blanche** hydroelectric power.
houle /'ul/ *nf* swell. **houleux, -euse** *a* (*mer*) rough; (*débat*) stormy.
housse /'us/ *nf* cover; ~ **de siège** seat cover.
houx /'u/ *nm* holly.
huées /'ɥe/ *nfpl* boos. **huer** [1] *vt* boo.
huile /ɥil/ *nf* oil; (personne 🄸) bigwig. **huiler** [1] *vt* oil. **huileux, -euse** *a* oily.
huis /'ɥi/ *nm* à ~ **clos** in camera.
huissier /ɥisje/ *nm* (Jur) bailiff; (portier) usher.
huit /'ɥi(t)/ *a* eight; ~ **jours** a week; **lundi en** ~ a week on Monday. ● *nm* eight. **huitième** *a* & *nmf* eighth.
huître /ɥitʀ/ *nf* oyster.
humain, ~e /ymɛ̃, -ɛn/ *a* human; (compatissant) humane.
humanitaire *a* humanitarian.
humanité *nf* humanity.
humble /œ̃bl/ *a* humble.
humeur /ymœʀ/ *nf* mood; (tempérament) temper; **de bonne/ mauvaise** ~ in a good/bad mood.
humide /ymid/ *a* damp; (*chaleur, climat*) humid; (*lèvres, yeux*) moist. **humidité** *nf* humidity.
humilier /ymilje/ [45] *vt* humiliate.
humoristique /ymɔʀistik/ *a* humorous.
humour /ymuʀ/ *nm* humour; **avoir de l'**~ have a sense of humour.
hurlement /'yʀləmɑ̃/ *nm* howl (ing). **hurler** [1] *vt/i* howl.

hutte /'yt/ *nf* hut.
hydratant, ~e /idʀatɑ̃, -t/ *a* (lotion) moisturizing.
hydravion /idʀavjɔ̃/ *nm* seaplane.
hydroélectrique /idʀɔelɛktʀik/ *a* hydroelectric.
hydrogène /idʀɔʒɛn/ *nm* hydrogen.
hygiène /iʒjɛn/ *nf* hygiene.
hygiénique *a* hygienic.
hymne /imn/ *nm* hymn; ~ **national** national anthem.
hyperlien /ipɛʀljɛ̃/ *nm* (Internet) hyperlink.
hypermarché /ipɛʀmaʀʃe/ *nm* (supermarché) hypermarket.
hypertension /ipɛʀtɑ̃sjɔ̃/ *nf* high blood-pressure.
hypertexte /ipɛʀtɛkst/ *nm* (Internet) hypertext.
hypnotiser /ipnɔtize/ [1] *vt* hypnotize.
hypocrisie /ipɔkʀizi/ *nf* hypocrisy.
hypocrite /ipɔkʀit/ *a* hypocritical. ● *nmf* hypocrite.
hypothèque /ipɔtɛk/ *nf* mortgage.
hypothèse /ipɔtɛz/ *nf* hypothesis.
hystérie /isteʀi/ *nf* hysteria.

ici /isi/ *adv* (dans l'espace) here; (dans le temps) now; **d'**~ **demain** by tomorrow; **d'**~ **là** in the meantime; **d'**~ **peu** shortly; ~ **même** in this very place; **jusqu'**~

until now; (dans le passé) until
then.

idéal, ~**e** (*mpl* -**aux**) /ideal, -o/ *a*
& *nm* ideal. **idéaliser** [1] *vt*
idealize.

idée /ide/ *nf* idea; (esprit) mind;
avoir dans l'~ de faire plan to do;
il ne me viendrait jamais à l'~ de
faire it would never occur to me
to do; ~ **fixe** obsession; ~ **reçue**
conventional opinion.

identification /idãtifikasjõ/ *nf*
identification. **identifier** [45] *vt*,
s'identifier *vpr* identify (à with).

identique /idãtik/ *a* identical.

identité /idãtite/ *nf* identity.

idéologie /ideɔlɔʒi/ *nf* ideology.

idiome /idjom/ *nm* idiom.

idiot, ~**e** /idjo, -ɔt/ *a* idiotic.
● *nm*, *f* idiot. **idiotie** *nf* idiocy;
(acte, parole) idiotic thing.

idole /idɔl/ *nf* idol.

if /if/ *nm* yew.

ignare /iɲaʀ/ *a* ignorant. ● *nmf*
ignoramus.

ignoble /iɲɔbl/ *a* vile.

ignorance /iɲɔʀãs/ *nf* ignorance.

ignorant, ~**e** /iɲɔʀã, -t/ *a*
ignorant. ● *nm*, *f* ignoramus.

ignorer /iɲɔʀe/ [1] *vt* not know;
je l'ignore I don't know;
(personne) ignore.

il /il/ *pron* (personne, animal familier)
he; (chose, animal) it; (impersonnel) it;
~ **est vrai que** it is true that; ~
neige/pleut it is snowing/raining;
~ **y a** there is; (pluriel) there are;
(temps) ago; (durée) for; ~ **y a 2 ans**
2 years ago; ~ **y a plus d'une
heure que j'attends** I've been
waiting for over an hour.

île /il/ *nf* island; ~ **déserte** desert
island; ~**s anglo-normandes**
Channel Islands; ~**s Britanniques**
British Isles.

illégal, ~**e** (*mpl* ~**aux**) /ilegal,
-o/ *a* illegal.

illégitime /ileʒitim/ *a*
illegitimate.

illettré, ~**e** /iletʀe/ *a* & *nm,f*
illiterate.

illicite /ilisit/ *a* illicit; (Jur)
unlawful.

illimité, ~**e** /ilimite/ *a* unlimited.

illisible /ilizibl/ *a* illegible; (livre)
unreadable.

illogique /ilɔʒik/ *a* illogical.

illuminé, ~**e** /ilymine/ *a* lit up;
(monument) floodlit.

illusion /ilyzjõ/ *nf* illusion; se
faire des ~**s** delude oneself.
illusoire *a* illusory.

illustre /ilystʀ/ *a* illustrious.

illustré, ~**e** /ilystʀe/ *a*
illustrated. ● *nm* comic.

illustrer /ilystʀe/ [1] *vt* illustrate.
□ **s'**~ *vpr* become famous.

îlot /ilo/ *nm* islet; (de maisons)
block.

ils /il/ *pron* they.

image /imaʒ/ *nf* picture;
(métaphore) image; (reflet) reflection.
imagé, ~**e** *a* full of imagery.

imaginaire /imaʒinɛʀ/ *a*
imaginary. **imaginatif**, -**ive** *a*
imaginative. **imagination** *nf*
imagination.

imaginer /imaʒine/ [1] *vt*
imagine; (inventer) think up. □ **s'**~
vpr (se représenter) imagine (que
that); (croire) think (que that).

imbécile /ɛ̃besil/ *a* idiotic. ● *nmf*
idiot.

imbiber /ɛ̃bibe/ [1] *vt* soak (de
with). □ **s'**~ *vpr* become soaked
(de with).

imbriqué, ~**e** /ɛ̃bʀike/ *a* (lié)
interlinked, interlocking; (tuiles)
overlapping.

imbu, ~**e** /ɛ̃by/ *a* ~ **de** full of.

imitateur, -**trice** /imitatœr,
-tʀis/ *nm, f* imitator; (comédien)
impersonator. **imiter** [1] *vt*
imitate; (personnage)

impersonate; (*signature*) forge; (faire comme) do the same as.

immatriculation /imatrikylasjɔ̃/ nf registration.

immatriculer /imatrikyle/ [1] vt register; **se faire ~** register; **faire ~ une voiture** have a car registered.

immédiat, ~e /imedja, -t/ a immediate. ● nm **dans l'~** for the time being.

immense /imɑ̃s/ a huge, immense.

immerger /imɛrʒe/ [40] vt immerse. □ **s'~** vpr immerse oneself (**dans** in).

immeuble /imœbl/ nm block of flats, building; **~ de bureaux** office building *ou* block.

immigrant, ~e /imigrɑ̃, -t/ a & nm,f immigrant. **immigration** nf immigration. **immigré, ~e** a & nm,f immigrant. **immigrer** [1] vi immigrate.

imminent, ~e /iminɑ̃, -t/ a imminent.

immobile /imɔbil/ a still, motionless.

immobilier, -ière /imɔbilje, -jɛr/ a property; **agence immobilière** estate agent's office, (US) real estate office; **agent ~** estate agent; (US) real estate agent. ● nm **l'~** property; (US) real estate.

immobiliser /imɔbilize/ [1] vt immobilize; (stopper) stop. □ **s'~** vpr stop.

immonde /imɔ̃d/ a filthy.

immoral, ~e (mpl **-aux**) /imɔral, -o/ a immoral.

immortel, ~le /imɔrtɛl/ a immortal.

immuable /imɥabl/ a unchanging.

immuniser /imynize/ [1] vt immunize; **immunisé contre** (à l'abri de) immune to. **immunité** nf immunity.

impact /ɛ̃pakt/ nm impact.

impair, ~e /ɛ̃pɛr/ a (*numéro*) odd. ● nm blunder, faux pas.

imparfait, ~e /ɛ̃parfɛ, -t/ a & nm imperfect.

impasse /ɛ̃pɑs/ nf (rue) dead end; (situation) deadlock.

impatient, ~e /ɛ̃pasjɑ̃, -t/ a impatient.

impatienter /ɛ̃pasjɑ̃te/ [1] vt annoy. □ **s'~** vpr get impatient (**contre qn** with sb).

impayé, ~e /ɛ̃peje/ a unpaid.

impeccable /ɛ̃pekabl/ a (propre) impeccable, spotless; (soigné) perfect.

impensable /ɛ̃pɑ̃sabl/ a unthinkable.

impératif, -ive /ɛ̃peratif, -v/ a imperative. ● nm (Gram) imperative; (contrainte) imperative; **~s** (exigences) requirements, demands (**de** of).

impératrice /ɛ̃peratris/ nf empress.

impérial, ~e (mpl **-iaux**) /ɛ̃perjal, -jo/ a imperial.

impérieux, -ieuse /ɛ̃perjø, -z/ a imperious; (pressant) pressing.

imperméable /ɛ̃pɛrmeabl/ a impervious (**à** to); (*manteau, tissu*) waterproof. ● nm raincoat.

impersonnel, ~le /ɛ̃pɛrsɔnɛl/ a impersonal.

impertinent, ~e /ɛ̃pɛrtinɑ̃, -t/ a impertinent.

imperturbable /ɛ̃pɛrtyrbabl/ a unshakeable, unruffled.

impétueux, -euse /ɛ̃petɥø, -z/ a impetuous.

impitoyable /ɛ̃pitwajabl/ a merciless.

implant /ɛ̃plɑ̃/ nm implant.

implanter /ɛ̃plɑ̃te/ [1] vt establish, set up. □ **s'~** vpr become established.

I

implication /ɛ̃plikasjɔ̃/ nf
(conséquence) implication;
(participation) involvement.

impliquer /ɛ̃plike/ [1] vt (mêler)
implicate (dans in); (signifier)
imply, mean (que that); (nécessiter)
involve (de faire doing).

implorer /ɛ̃plɔʀe/ [1] vt implore,
beg for.

impoli, ~e /ɛ̃pɔli/ a impolite,
rude.

importance /ɛ̃pɔʀtɑ̃s/ nf
importance; (taille) size; (ampleur)
extent; **sans** ~ unimportant.

important, ~e /ɛ̃pɔʀtɑ̃, -t/ a
important; (en quantité)
considerable, sizeable, big; (air)
self-important. ● nm **l'**~ the
important thing.

importateur, -trice /ɛ̃pɔʀtatœʀ,
-tʀis/ nm, f importer. ● a
importing. **importation** nf
import.

importer /ɛ̃pɔʀte/ [1] vt (Comm)
import. ● vi matter, be important
(à to); **il importe que** it is
important that; **n'importe**, **peu
importe** it does not matter;
n'importe comment anyhow;
n'importe où anywhere; **n'importe
qui** anybody; **n'importe quoi**
anything.

importun, ~e /ɛ̃pɔʀtœ̃, -yn/ a
troublesome. ● nm, f nuisance.

imposer /ɛ̃poze/ [1] vt impose (à
on); (taxer) tax; **en** ~ **à qn** impress
sb. □ **s'**~ vpr (action) be
essential; (se faire reconnaître) stand
out; (s'astreindre à) **s'**~ **de faire**
force oneself to do.

imposition /ɛ̃pozisjɔ̃/ nf taxation;
~ **des mains** laying-on of hands.

impossible /ɛ̃posibl/ a
impossible. ● nm **faire l'**~ do
one's utmost.

impôt /ɛ̃po/ nm tax; ~**s**
(contributions) tax(ation), taxes; ~
sur le revenu income tax.

impotent, ~e /ɛ̃potɑ̃, -t/ a
disabled.

imprécis, ~e /ɛ̃presi, -z/ a
imprecise.

imprégner /ɛ̃preɲe/ [14] vt fill
(de with); (imbiber) impregnate (de
with). □ **s'**~ **de** vpr (fig) immerse
oneself in.

impression /ɛ̃presjɔ̃/ nf
impression; (de livre) printing.

impressionnant a impressive;
(choquant) disturbing.

impressionner [1] vt impress;
(choquer) disturb.

imprévisible /ɛ̃previzibl/ a
unpredictable.

imprévu, ~e /ɛ̃prevy/ a
unexpected. ● nm unexpected
incident; **sauf** ~ unless anything
unexpected happens.

imprimante /ɛ̃primɑ̃t/ nf (Ordinat)
printer; ~ **à jet d'encre** ink-jet
printer; ~ **(à) laser** laser printer.

imprimé, ~e /ɛ̃prime/ a printed.
● nm printed form.

imprimer /ɛ̃prime/ [1] vt print;
(marquer) imprint. **imprimerie** nf
(art) printing; (lieu) printing works.
imprimeur nm printer.

improbable /ɛ̃probabl/ a
unlikely, improbable.

impropre /ɛ̃propr/ a incorrect; ~
à unfit for.

improviste: à l'~ /alɛ̃provist/ loc
unexpectedly.

imprudence /ɛ̃prydɑ̃s/ nf
carelessness; (acte) careless
action.

imprudent, ~e /ɛ̃prydɑ̃, -t/ a
careless; **il est** ~ **de** it is unwise
to.

impudent, ~e /ɛ̃pydɑ̃, -t/ a
impudent.

impuissant, ~e /ɛ̃pɥisɑ̃, -t/ a
helpless; (Méd) impotent; ~ **à faire**
powerless to do.

impulsif, -ive /ɛ̃pylsif, -v/ a
impulsive. **impulsion** nf (poussée,

influence) impetus; (instinct, mouvement) impulse.

impur, ∼**e** /ɛ̃pyʀ/ a impure.

imputer /ɛ̃pyte/ [1] vt ∼ **à** attribute to, impute to.

inabordable /inabɔʀdabl/ a (prix) prohibitive.

inacceptable /inaksɛptabl/ a unacceptable.

inactif, -ive /inaktif, -v/ a inactive.

inadapté, ∼**e** /inadapte/ a maladjusted. ●nm, f (Psych) maladjusted person.

inadmissible /inadmisibl/ a unacceptable.

inadvertance /inadvɛʀtɑ̃s/ nf **par** ∼ by mistake.

inanimé, ∼**e** /inanime/ a (évanoui) unconscious; (mort) lifeless; (matière) inanimate.

inaperçu, ∼**e** /inapɛʀsy/ a unnoticed.

inapte /inapt/ a unsuited (à to); ∼ **à faire** incapable of doing; ∼ **au service militaire** unfit for military service.

inattendu, ∼**e** /inatɑ̃dy/ a unexpected.

inaugurer /inogyʀe/ [1] vt inaugurate.

incapable /ɛ̃kapabl/ a incapable (de qch of sth); ∼ **de faire** unable to do, incapable of doing. ●nmf incompetent.

incapacité /ɛ̃kapasite/ nf inability, incapacity; **être dans l'**∼ **de faire** be unable to do.

incarcérer /ɛ̃kaʀseʀe/ [14] vt imprison, incarcerate.

incarnation /ɛ̃kaʀnasjɔ̃/ nf embodiment, incarnation.

incarné, ∼**e** a (ongle) ingrowing.

incassable /ɛ̃kasabl/ a unbreakable.

incendiaire /ɛ̃sɑ̃djɛʀ/ a incendiary; (propos) inflammatory. ●nmf arsonist.

incendie /ɛ̃sɑ̃di/ nm fire; ∼ **criminel** arson. **incendier** [45] vt set fire to.

incertain, ∼**e** /ɛ̃sɛʀtɛ̃, -ɛn/ a uncertain; (contour) vague; (temps) unsettled. **incertitude** nf uncertainty.

inceste /ɛ̃sɛst/ nm incest

incidence /ɛ̃sidɑ̃s/ nf effect.

incident /ɛ̃sidɑ̃/ nm incident; ∼ **technique** technical hitch.

incinérer /ɛ̃sineʀe/ [14] vt incinerate; (mort) cremate.

inciser /ɛ̃size/ [1] vt make an incision in; (abcès) lance. **incisif, -ive** a incisive. **incision** nf incision; (d'abcès) lancing.

incitation /ɛ̃sitasjɔ̃/ nf incitement (à to); (encouragement) incentive. **inciter** [1] vt incite (à to); (encourager) encourage.

inclinaison /ɛ̃klinɛzɔ̃/ nf incline; (de la tête) tilt.

inclination /ɛ̃klinasjɔ̃/ nf (penchant) inclination; (geste) (du buste) bow; (de la tête) nod.

incliner /ɛ̃kline/ [1] vt tilt, lean; (courber) bend; (inciter) encourage (à to); ∼ **la tête** (approuver) nod; (révérence) bow. ●vi ∼ **à** be inclined to. □ **s'**∼ vpr lean forward; (se courber) bow down (devant before); (céder) give in, yield (devant to); (chemin) slope.

inclure /ɛ̃klyʀ/ [16] vt include; (enfermer) enclose; **jusqu'au lundi inclus** up to and including Monday.

incohérence /ɛ̃kɔeʀɑ̃s/ nf incoherence; (contradiction) discrepancy. **incohérent**, ∼**e** a incoherent, inconsistent.

incolore /ɛ̃kɔlɔʀ/ a colourless; (verre) clear.

incommoder /ɛ̃kɔmɔde/ [1] vt inconvenience, bother.

incompatible /ɛ̃kɔ̃patibl/ a incompatible.

incompétent, ~e /ɛ̃kɔ̃petɑ̃, -t/ a incompetent.

incomplet, -ète /ɛ̃kɔ̃plɛ, -t/ a incomplete.

incompréhension /ɛ̃kɔ̃preɑ̃sjɔ̃/ nf lack of understanding.

incompris, ~e /ɛ̃kɔ̃pri, -z/ a misunderstood.

inconcevable /ɛ̃kɔ̃svabl/ a inconceivable.

incongru, ~e /ɛ̃kɔ̃gry/ a unseemly.

inconnu, ~e /ɛ̃kɔny/ a unknown (à to). ●nm, f stranger. ●nm l'~ the unknown.

inconscience /ɛ̃kɔ̃sjɑ̃s/ nf unconsciousness; (folie) madness.

inconscient, ~e /ɛ̃kɔ̃sjɑ̃, -t/ a unconscious (de of); (fou) mad. ●nm (Psych) subconscious.

incontestable /ɛ̃kɔ̃tɛstabl/ a indisputable.

incontrôlable /ɛ̃kɔ̃tʀolabl/ a unverifiable; (non maîtrisé) uncontrollable.

inconvenant, ~e /ɛ̃kɔ̃vnɑ̃, -t/ a improper.

inconvénient /ɛ̃kɔ̃venjɑ̃/ nm disadvantage, drawback; (objection) objection.

incorporer /ɛ̃kɔʀpɔʀe/ [1] vt incorporate; (Culin) blend (à into); (Mil) enlist.

incorrect, ~e /ɛ̃kɔʀɛkt/ a (faux) incorrect; (malséant) improper; (impoli) impolite; (déloyal) unfair.

incrédule /ɛ̃kʀedyl/ a incredulous.

incriminer /ɛ̃kʀimine/ [1] vt (personne) incriminate; (conduite, action) attack.

incroyable /ɛ̃kʀwajabl/ a incredible.

incruster /ɛ̃kʀyste/ [1] vt inlay (de with).

incubateur /ɛ̃kybatœʀ/ nm incubator.

inculpation /ɛ̃kylpasjɔ̃/ nf charge (de, pour of). **inculpé**, ~e nm, f accused. **inculper** [1] vt charge (de with).

inculquer /ɛ̃kylke/ [1] vt instil (à into).

inculte /ɛ̃kylt/ a uncultivated; (personne) uneducated.

incurver /ɛ̃kyʀve/ [1] vt curve, bend. □ s'~ vpr curve, bend.

Inde /ɛ̃d/ nf India.

indécent, ~e /ɛ̃desɑ̃, -t/ a indecent.

indécis, ~e /ɛ̃desi, -z/ a (de nature) indecisive; (temporairement) undecided.

indéfini, ~e /ɛ̃defini/ a (Gram) indefinite; (vague) undefined; (sans limites) indeterminate.

indemne /ɛ̃dɛmn/ a unharmed.

indemniser /ɛ̃dɛmnize/ [1] vt compensate (de for).

indemnité /ɛ̃dɛmnite/ nf indemnity, compensation; (allocation) allowance; ~s de licenciement redundancy payment.

indépendance /ɛ̃depɑ̃dɑ̃s/ nf independence. **indépendant**, ~e a independent.

indéterminé, ~e /ɛ̃detɛʀmine/ a unspecified.

index /ɛ̃dɛks/ nm forefinger; (liste) index.

indicateur, -trice /ɛ̃dikatœʀ, -tʀis/ nm, f (police) informer. ●nm (livre) guide; (Tech) indicator.

indicatif, -ve /ɛ̃dikatif, -v/ a indicative (de of). ●nm (à la radio) signature tune; (téléphonique) dialling code; (Gram) indicative.

indication /ɛ̃dikasjɔ̃/ nf indication; (renseignement) information; (directive) instruction.

indice /ɛ̃dis/ nm sign; (dans une enquête) clue; (des prix) index; (évaluation) rating; ~ d'écoute audience ratings.

indifférence /ɛ̃difeʀɑ̃s/ nf
indifference.

indifférent, ~e /ɛ̃difeʀɑ̃, -t/ a
indifferent (à to); **ça m'est** ~ it
makes no difference to me.

indigène /ɛ̃diʒɛn/ a & nmf native,
indigenous; (du pays) local. ● nmf
native.

indigent, ~e /ɛ̃diʒɑ̃, -t/ a
destitute.

indigeste /ɛ̃diʒɛst/ a indigestible.
indigestion nf indigestion.

indigne /ɛ̃diɲ/ a unworthy (de
of); (acte) vile. **indigner (s')** [1]
vpr become indignant (de at).

indiqué, ~e /ɛ̃dike/ a (heure)
appointed; (opportun) appropriate;
(conseillé) recommended.

indiquer /ɛ̃dike/ [1] vt (montrer)
show, indicate; (renseigner sur)
point out, tell; (déterminer) give,
state, appoint; ~ **du doigt** point to
ou out ou à.

indirect, ~e /ɛ̃diʀɛkt/ a indirect.

indiscipliné, ~e /ɛ̃disipline/ a
unruly.

indiscret, **-ète** /ɛ̃diskʀɛ, -t/ a
(personne) inquisitive; (question)
indiscreet.

indiscutable /ɛ̃diskytabl/ a
unquestionable.

indispensable /ɛ̃dispɑ̃sabl/ a
indispensable; **il est** ~ **qu'il vienne**
it is essential that he comes.

individu /ɛ̃dividy/ nm individual.

individuel, ~le /ɛ̃dividɥɛl/ a
(pour une personne) individual; (qui
concerne l'individu) personal; **chambre**
~le single room; **maison** ~le
detached house.

indolore /ɛ̃dɔlɔʀ/ a painless.

Indonésie /ɛ̃dɔnezi/ nf
Indonesia.

indu, ~e /ɛ̃dy/ a **à une heure** ~e
at some ungodly hour.

induire /ɛ̃dɥiʀ/ [17] vt infer (de
from); (inciter) induce (à faire to
do); ~ **en erreur** mislead.

indulgence /ɛ̃dylʒɑ̃s/ nf
indulgence; (de jury) leniency.

indulgent, ~e /ɛ̃dylʒɑ̃/ a indulgent;
(clément) lenient.

industrialisé, ~e /ɛ̃dystʀijalize/
a industrialized.

industrie /ɛ̃dystʀi/ nf industry.

industriel, ~le /ɛ̃dystʀijɛl/ a
industrial. ● nm industrialist.

inédit, ~e /inedi, -t/ a
unpublished; (fig) original.

inefficace /inefikas/ a (remède,
mesure) ineffective; (appareil,
système) inefficient.

inégal, ~e (mpl **-aux**) /inegal, -o/
a unequal; (irrégulier) uneven.

inégalable a matchless.

inégalité nf (injustice) inequality;
(irrégularité) unevenness;
(disproportion) disparity.

inéluctable /inelyktabl/ a
inescapable.

inepte /inɛpt/ a inept, absurd.

inerte /inɛʀt/ a inert; (immobile)
lifeless; (sans énergie) apathetic.

inertie nf inertia; (fig) apathy.

inespéré, ~e /inɛspeʀe/ a
unhoped for.

inestimable /inɛstimabl/ a
priceless; (aide) invaluable.

inexact, ~e /inɛgza(kt), -kt/ a
(imprécis) inaccurate; (incorrect)
incorrect.

in extremis /inɛkstʀemis/ adv
(par nécessité) as a last resort; (au
dernier moment) at the last minute.
● a last-minute.

infaillible /ɛ̃fajibl/ a infallible.

infâme /ɛ̃fɑm/ a vile.

infantile /ɛ̃fɑ̃til/ a (puéril)
infantile; (maladie) childhood;
(mortalité) infant.

infarctus /ɛ̃faʀktys/ nm
coronary, heart attack.

infatigable /ɛ̃fatigabl/ a tireless.

infect, ~e /ɛ̃fɛkt/ a revolting.

infecter /ɛ̃fɛkte/ [1] vt infect.
□ **s'**~ vpr become infected.

infectieux, -ieuse *a* infectious.

infection *nf* infection.

inférieur, ~e /ɛ̃feʀjœʀ/ *a* (plus bas) lower; (moins bon) inferior (à to); ~ à (plus petit que) smaller than; (plus bas que) lower than. ● *nm, f* inferior. **infériorité** *nf* inferiority.

infernal, ~e (*mpl* **-aux**) /ɛ̃fɛʀnal, -o/ *a* infernal.

infester /ɛ̃feste/ [1] *vt* infest.

infidèle /ɛ̃fidɛl/ *a* unfaithful (à to). **infidélité** *nf* unfaithfulness; (acte) infidelity.

infiltrer (s') /sɛ̃filtʀe/ [1] *vpr* s'~ **(dans)** (*personnes, idées*) infiltrate; (*liquide*) seep through.

infime /ɛ̃fim/ *a* tiny, minute.

infini, ~e /ɛ̃fini/ *a* infinite. ● *nm* infinity; à l'~ endlessly.

infinité /ɛ̃finite/ *nf* l'~ infinity; une ~ de an endless number of.

infinitif /ɛ̃finitif/ *nm* infinitive.

infirme /ɛ̃fiʀm/ *a* disabled. ● *nmf* disabled person. **infirmerie** *nf* sickbay, infirmary. **infirmier** *nm* (male) nurse. **infirmière** *nf* nurse. **infirmité** *nf* disability.

inflammable /ɛ̃flamabl/ *a* inflammable.

inflation /ɛ̃flasjɔ̃/ *nf* inflation.

infliger /ɛ̃fliʒe/ [40] *vt* inflict; (*sanction*) impose.

influence /ɛ̃flyɑ̃s/ *nf* influence. **influencer** [10] *vt* influence. **influent, ~e** *a* influential.

influer /ɛ̃flye/ [1] *vi* ~ **sur** influence.

informateur, -trice /ɛ̃fɔʀmatœʀ, -tʀis/ *nm, f* informant; (pour la police) informer.

informaticien, ~ne /ɛ̃fɔʀmatisjɛ̃, -ɛn/ *nm, f* computer scientist.

information /ɛ̃fɔʀmasjɔ̃/ *nf* information; (Jur) inquiry; **une ~** (some) information; (nouvelle) (some) news; **les ~s** the news.

informatique /ɛ̃fɔʀmatik/ *nf* computer science; (techniques) information technology.

informatiser [1] *vt* computerize.

informer /ɛ̃fɔʀme/ [1] *vt* inform (de about, of). □ s'~ *vpr* enquire (de about).

inforoute /ɛ̃fɔʀut/ *nf* (Ordinat) information highway.

infortune /ɛ̃fɔʀtyn/ *nf* misfortune.

infraction /ɛ̃fʀaksjɔ̃/ *nf* offence; ~ **à** (*loi, règlement*) breach of.

infrastructure /ɛ̃fʀastʀyktyʀ/ *nf* infrastructure; (équipements) facilities.

infructueux, -euse /ɛ̃fʀyktɥø, -z/ *a* fruitless.

infuser /ɛ̃fyze/ [1] *vt/i* infuse, brew. **infusion** *nf* herbal tea, infusion.

ingénier (s') /(s)ɛ̃ʒenje/ [45] *vpr* s'~ **à** strive to.

ingénieur /ɛ̃ʒenjœʀ/ *nm* engineer.

ingénieux, -ieuse /ɛ̃ʒenjø, -z/ *a* ingenious. **ingéniosité** *nf* ingenuity.

ingénu, ~e /ɛ̃ʒeny/ *a* naïve.

ingérence /ɛ̃ʒeʀɑ̃s/ *nf* interference.

ingérer (s') /sɛ̃ʒeʀe/ [14] *vpr* s'~ **dans** interfere in.

ingrat, ~e /ɛ̃gʀa, -t/ *a* (*personne*) ungrateful; (*travail*) unrewarding, thankless; (*visage*) unattractive.

ingrédient /ɛ̃gʀedjɑ̃/ *nm* ingredient.

ingurgiter /ɛ̃gyʀʒite/ [1] *vt* swallow.

inhabité, ~e /inabite/ *a* uninhabited.

inhabituel, ~le /inabitɥɛl/ *a* unusual.

inhumain, ~e /inymɛ̃, -ɛn/ *a* inhuman.

inhumation /inymasjɔ̃/ *nf* burial.

initial, ~e (*mpl* **-iaux**) /inisjal, -jo/ *a* initial. **initiale** *nf* initial.

initialisation /inisjalizasjɔ̃/ *nf* (Ordinat) formatting. **initialiser** [1] *vt* format.

initiation /inisjasjɔ̃/ *nf* initiation; (formation) introduction (**à** to); **cours d'~** introductory course.

initiative /inisjativ/ *nf* initiative.

initier /inisje/ [45] *vt* initiate (**à** into); (faire découvrir) introduce (**à** to). □ **s'~** *vpr* **s'~ à qch** learn sth.

injecter /ɛ̃ʒɛkte/ [1] *vt* inject; **injecté de sang** bloodshot. **injection** *nf* injection.

injure /ɛ̃ʒyʀ/ *nf* insult. **injurier** [45] *vt* insult. **injurieux, -ieuse** *a* insulting.

injuste /ɛ̃ʒyst/ *a* unjust, unfair. **injustice** *nf* injustice.

inné, ~e /inne/ *a* innate, inborn.

innocence /inɔsɑ̃s/ *nf* innocence. **innocent, ~e** *a & nm,f* innocent. **innocenter** [1] *vt* clear, prove innocent.

innombrable /inɔ̃bʀabl/ *a* countless.

innovateur, -trice /inɔvatœʀ, -tʀis/ *nm, f* innovator. **innovation** *nf* innovation. **innover** [1] *vi* innovate.

inodore /inɔdɔʀ/ *a* odourless.

inoffensif, -ive /inɔfɑ̃sif, -v/ *a* harmless.

inondation /inɔ̃dasjɔ̃/ *nf* flood; (action) flooding.

inonder /inɔ̃de/ [1] *vt* flood; (mouiller) soak; (envahir) inundate (**de** with); **inondé de soleil** bathed in sunlight.

inopiné, ~e /inɔpine/ *a* unexpected; (mort) sudden.

inopportun, ~e /inɔpɔʀtœ̃, -yn/ *a* inopportune, ill-timed.

inoubliable /inublijabl/ *a* unforgettable.

inouï, ~e /inwi/ *a* incredible; (événement) unprecedented.

inox® /inɔks/ *nm* stainless steel.

inoxydable /inɔksidabl/ *a* **acier ~** stainless steel.

inqualifiable /ɛ̃kalifjabl/ *a* unspeakable.

inquiet, -iète /ɛ̃kjɛ, -t/ *a* worried. **inquiétant, ~e** *a* worrying.

inquiéter /ɛ̃kjete/ [14] *vt* worry. **inquiétude** *nf* anxiety, worry.

insaisissable /ɛ̃sezisabl/ *a* (personne) elusive; (nuance) indefinable.

insalubre /ɛ̃salybʀ/ *a* unhealthy.

insatisfaisant, ~e /ɛ̃satisfəzɑ̃, -t/ *a* unsatisfactory. **insatisfait, ~e** *a* (mécontent) dissatisfied; (frustré) unfulfilled.

inscription /ɛ̃skʀipsjɔ̃/ *nf* inscription; (immatriculation) enrolment.

inscrire /ɛ̃skʀiʀ/ [30] *vt* write (down); (graver, tracer) inscribe; (personne) enrol; (sur une liste) put down. □ **s'~** *vpr* put one's name down; **s'~ à** (école) enrol at; (club, parti) join; (examen) enter for.

insecte /ɛ̃sɛkt/ *nm* insect.

insécurité /ɛ̃sekyʀite/ *nf* insecurity.

insensé, ~e /ɛ̃sɑ̃se/ *a* mad.

insensibilité /ɛ̃sɑ̃sibilite/ *nf* insensitivity. **insensible** *a* insensitive (**à** to); (graduel) imperceptible.

insérer /ɛ̃seʀe/ [14] *vt* insert. □ **s'~** *vpr* be inserted; **s'~ dans** be part of.

insigne /ɛ̃siɲ/ *nm* badge; **~s** (d'une fonction) insignia.

insignifiant, ~e /ɛ̃siɲifjɑ̃, -t/ *a* insignificant.

insinuation /ɛ̃sinɥasjɔ̃/ *nf* insinuation.

insinuer /ɛ̃sinɥe/ [1] *vt* insinuate. □ **s'~** *vpr* (socialement) ingratiate oneself (**auprès de qn** with sb);

s'~ dans (se glisser) slip into; (*idée, nuance*) creep into.

insipide /ɛ̃sipid/ *a* insipid.

insistance /ɛ̃sistɑ̃s/ *nf* insistence. **insistant, ~e** *a* insistent.

insister /ɛ̃siste/ [1] *vi* insist (**pour faire** on doing); **~ sur** stress.

insolation /ɛ̃sɔlasjɔ̃/ *nf* (Méd) sunstroke.

insolent, ~e /ɛ̃sɔlɑ̃, -t/ *a* insolent.

insolite /ɛ̃sɔlit/ *a* unusual.

insolvable /ɛ̃sɔlvabl/ *a* insolvent.

insomnie /ɛ̃sɔmni/ *nf* insomnia.

insonoriser /ɛ̃sɔnɔʀize/ [1] *vt* soundproof.

insouciance /ɛ̃susjɑ̃s/ *nf* lack of concern. **insouciant, ~e** *a* carefree.

insoutenable /ɛ̃sutnabl/ *a* unbearable; (*argument*) untenable.

inspecter /ɛ̃spɛkte/ [1] *vt* inspect. **inspecteur, -trice** *nm, f* inspector. **inspection** *nf* inspection.

inspiration /ɛ̃spiʀasjɔ̃/ *nf* inspiration; (respiration) breath.

inspirer /ɛ̃spiʀe/ [1] *vt* inspire; **~ la méfiance à qn** inspire distrust in sb. ●*vi* breathe in. □ **s'~ de** *vpr* be inspired by.

instabilité /ɛ̃stabilite/ *nf* instability; unsteadiness. **instable** *a* unstable; (*temps*) unsettled.

installation /ɛ̃stalasjɔ̃/ *nf* installation; (de local) fitting out; (de locataire) settling in. **installations** *nfpl* facilities.

installer /ɛ̃stale/ [1] *vt* install; (*meuble*) put in; (*étagère*) put up; (*gaz, téléphone*) connect; (*équiper*) fit out. □ **s'~** *vpr* settle (down); (emménager) settle in; **s'~ comme** set oneself up as.

instance /ɛ̃stɑ̃s/ *nf* authority;

(prière) entreaty; **avec ~** with insistence; **en ~** pending; **en ~ de** in the course of, on the point of.

instant /ɛ̃stɑ̃/ *nm* moment, instant; **à l'~** this instant.

instantané, ~e /ɛ̃stɑ̃tane/ *a* instantaneous; (*café*) instant.

instar: à l'~ de /alɛ̃staʀdə/ *loc* like.

instaurer /ɛ̃stɔʀe/ [1] *vt* institute.

instigateur, -trice /ɛ̃stigatœʀ, -tʀis/ *nm, f* instigator.

instinct /ɛ̃stɛ̃/ *nm* instinct; **d'~** instinctively. **instinctif, -ive** *a* instinctive.

instituer /ɛ̃stitɥe/ [1] *vt* establish.

institut /ɛ̃stity/ *nm* institute; **~ de beauté** beauty parlour.

instituteur, -trice /ɛ̃stitytœʀ, -tʀis/ *nm, f* primary-school teacher.

institution /ɛ̃stitysjɔ̃/ *nf* institution; (école) private school.

instructif, -ive /ɛ̃stʀyktif, -v/ *a* instructive.

instruction /ɛ̃stʀyksjɔ̃/ *nf* (formation) education; (Mil) training; (document) directive; **~s** (ordres, mode d'emploi) instructions; (Ordinat) (énoncé) instruction; (pas de séquence) statement.

instruire /ɛ̃stʀɥiʀ/ [17] *vt* teach, educate; **~ de** inform of. □ **s'~** *vpr* learn, educate oneself; **s'~ de** enquire about. **instruit, ~e** *a* educated.

instrument /ɛ̃stʀymɑ̃/ *nm* instrument; (outil) tool; (moyen: fig) instrument; **~ de gestion** management tool; **~s de bord** (Aviat) controls.

insu: à l'~ de /alɛ̃sydə/ *loc* without the knowledge of.

insuffisance /ɛ̃syfizɑ̃s/ *nf* (pénurie) shortage; (médiocrité) inadequacy. **insuffisant, ~e** *a*

inadequate; (en nombre)
insufficient.

insulaire /ɛ̃sylɛR/ a island. ● nmf
islander.

insuline /ɛ̃sylin/ nf insulin.

insulte /ɛ̃sylt/ nf insult. **insulter**
[1] vt insult.

insupportable /ɛ̃sypɔRtabl/ a
unbearable.

insurger (s') /(s)ɛ̃syRʒe/ [40] vpr
rebel.

intact, ~e /ɛ̃takt/ a intact.

intangible /ɛ̃tɑ̃ʒibl/ a intangible;
(principe) inviolable.

intarissable /ɛ̃taRisabl/ a
inexhaustible.

intégral, ~e (mpl -aux) /ɛ̃tegRal,
-o/ a complete; (texte, édition)
unabridged; (paiement) full, in
full. **intégralement** adv in full.
intégralité nf whole.

intègre /ɛ̃tɛgR/ a upright.

intégrer /ɛ̃tegRe/ [14] vt
integrate. □ s'~ vpr (personne)
integrate; (maison) fit in.

intégriste /ɛ̃tegRist/ nmf
fundamentalist.

intégrité /ɛ̃tegRite/ nf integrity.

intellect /ɛ̃telɛkt/ nm intellect.
intellectuel, ~le a & nm,f
intellectual.

intelligence /ɛ̃teliʒɑ̃s/ nf
intelligence; (compréhension)
understanding; (complicité)
agreement; **agir d'~ avec qn** act in
agreement with sb. **intelligent,
~e** a intelligent.

intempéries /ɛ̃tɑ̃peRi/ nfpl
severe weather.

intempestif, -ive /ɛ̃tɑ̃pɛstif, -v/ a
untimely.

intenable /ɛ̃tnabl/ a unbearable;
(enfant) impossible.

intendance /ɛ̃tɑ̃dɑ̃s/ nf (Scol)
bursar's office.

intendant, ~e /ɛ̃tɑ̃dɑ̃, -t/ nm (Mil)
quartermaster. ● nm,f (Scol)
bursar.

intense /ɛ̃tɑ̃s/ a intense;
(circulation) heavy. **intensif, -ive**
a intensive. **intensité** nf
intensity.

intenter /ɛ̃tɑ̃te/ [1] vt ~ un
procès ou une action institute
proceedings (à, contre against).

intention /ɛ̃tɑ̃sjɔ̃/ nf intention (de
faire of doing); **à l'~ de qn** for sb.
intentionnel, ~le a intentional.

interactif, -ive /ɛ̃tɛRaktif, -v/ a
(TV, vidéo) interactive.

interaction /ɛ̃tɛRaksjɔ̃/ nf
interaction.

intercaler /ɛ̃tɛRkale/ [1] vt
insert.

intercéder /ɛ̃tɛRsede/ [14] vi
intercede (en faveur de on behalf
of).

intercepter /ɛ̃tɛRsɛpte/ [1] vt
intercept.

interdiction /ɛ̃tɛRdiksjɔ̃/ nf ban;
~ de fumer no smoking.

interdire /ɛ̃tɛRdiR/ [37] vt forbid;
(officiellement) ban, prohibit; ~ à qn
de faire forbid sb to do.

interdit, ~e /ɛ̃tɛRdi, -t/ a
prohibited, forbidden; (étonné)
dumbfounded.

intéressant, ~e /ɛ̃teResɑ̃, -t/ a
interesting; (avantageux) attractive.

intéressé, ~e /ɛ̃teRese/ a (en
cause) concerned; (pour profiter)
self-interested. ● nm, f person
concerned.

intéresser /ɛ̃teRese/ [1] vt
interest; (concerner) concern. □ s'~
à vpr be interested in.

intérêt /ɛ̃teRɛ/ nm interest;
(égoïsme) self-interest; ~(s) (Comm)
interest; **vous avez ~ à** it is in
your interest to.

interface /ɛ̃tɛRfas/ nf (Ordinat)
interface.

intérieur, ~e /ɛ̃teRjœR/ a inner,
inside; (mur, escalier) internal;
(vol, politique) domestic; (vie,
calme) inner. ● nm interior; (de

boîte, tiroir) inside; **à l'~ (de)** inside;
(fig) within. **intérieurement** *adv*
inwardly.

intérim /ɛ̃teʀim/ *nm* interim;
assurer l'~ deputize (**de** for); **par
~** on an interim basis; **président
par ~** acting president; **faire de
l'~** temp.

intérimaire /ɛ̃teʀimɛʀ/ *a*
temporary, interim. ● *nmf*
(secrétaire) temp; (médecin) locum.

interjection /ɛ̃tɛʀʒɛksjɔ̃/ *nf*
interjection.

interlocuteur, -trice
/ɛ̃tɛʀlɔkytœʀ, -tʀis/ *nm, f* **son ~**
the person one is speaking to.

interloqué, -e /ɛ̃tɛʀlɔke/ *a* **être
~** be taken aback.

intermède /ɛ̃tɛʀmɛd/ *nm*
interlude.

intermédiaire /ɛ̃tɛʀmedjɛʀ/ *a*
intermediate. ● *nmf*
intermediary. ● *nm* **sans ~**
without an intermediary, direct;
par l'~ de through.

interminable /ɛ̃tɛʀminabl/ *a*
endless.

intermittence /ɛ̃tɛʀmitɑ̃s/ *nf* **par
~** intermittently.

internat /ɛ̃tɛʀna/ *nm* boarding-
school.

international, ~e (*mpl* -**aux**)
/ɛ̃tɛʀnasjɔnal, -o/ *a* international.

internaute /ɛ̃tɛʀnot/ *nmf* (Ordinat)
Netsurfer, Internet user.

interne /ɛ̃tɛʀn/ *a* internal; (*cours,
formation*) in-house. ● *nmf* (Scol)
boarder; (Méd) house officer; (US)
intern.

internement /ɛ̃tɛʀnəmɑ̃/ *nm* (Pol)
internment. **interner** [1] *vt* (Pol)
intern; (Méd) commit.

Internet /ɛ̃tɛʀnɛt/ *nm* Internet;
sur ~ on the Internet.

interpellation /ɛ̃tɛʀpelasjɔ̃/ *nf*
(Pol) questioning. **interpeller** [1]
vt shout to; (apostropher) shout at;
(interroger) question.

interphone /ɛ̃tɛʀfɔn/ *nm*

intercom; (d'immeuble) entry
phone.

interposer (s') /(s)ɛ̃tɛʀpoze/ [1]
vpr intervene.

interprétariat /ɛ̃tɛʀpʀetaʀja/ *nm*
interpreting. **interprétation** *nf*
interpretation; (d'artiste)
performance. **interprète** *nmf*
interpreter; (artiste) performer.

interpréter [14] *vt* interpret;
(jouer) play; (chanter) sing.

interrogateur, -trice
/ɛ̃teʀɔgatœʀ, -tʀis/ *a* questioning.

interrogatif, -ive *a* interrogative.

interrogation *nf* question; (action)
questioning; (épreuve) test.

interrogatoire *nm* interrogation.

interroger [40] *vt* question;
(élève) test.

interrompre /ɛ̃teʀɔ̃pʀ/ [3] *vt*
break off, interrupt; (*personne*)
interrupt. □ **s'~** *vpr* break off.

interrupteur *nm* switch.

interruption *nf* interruption;
(arrêt) break.

interurbain, ~e /ɛ̃tɛʀyʀbɛ̃, -ɛn/ *a*
long-distance, trunk.

intervalle /ɛ̃tɛʀval/ *nm* space;
(temps) interval; **dans l'~** in the
meantime.

intervenir /ɛ̃tɛʀvəniʀ/ [58] *vi*
(agir) intervene (**auprès de qn** with
sb); (survenir) occur, take place;
(Méd) operate. **intervention** *nf*
intervention; (Méd) operation.

intervertir /ɛ̃tɛʀvɛʀtiʀ/ [2] *vt*
invert; (rôles) reverse.

interview /ɛ̃tɛʀvju/ *nf* interview.
interviewer [1] *vt* interview.

intestin /ɛ̃tɛstɛ̃/ *nm* intestine.

intime /ɛ̃tim/ *a* intimate; (*fête,
vie*) private; (*dîner*) quiet. ● *nmf*
intimate friend.

intimider /ɛ̃timide/ [1] *vt*
intimidate.

intimité /ɛ̃timite/ *nf* intimacy; (vie
privée) privacy.

intituler /ɛ̃tityle/ [1] *vt* call,

entitle. □ **s'~** *vpr* be called *ou*
entitled.
intolérable /ɛ̃tɔleʀabl/ *a*
intolerable. **intolérance** *nf*
intolerance. **intolérant, ~e** *a*
intolerant.
intonation /ɛ̃tɔnasjɔ̃/ *nf*
intonation.
intox /ɛ̃tɔks/ *nf* ▣ brainwashing.
intoxication /ɛ̃tɔksikasjɔ̃/ *nf*
poisoning; (fig) brainwashing; **~**
alimentaire food poisoning.
intoxiquer [1] *vt* poison; (fig)
brainwash.
intraitable /ɛ̃tʀɛtabl/ *a*
inflexible.
Intranet /ɛ̃tʀanɛt/ *nm* Intranet.
intransigeant, ~e /ɛ̃tʀɑ̃ziʒɑ̃, -t/
a intransigent.
intransitif, -ive /ɛ̃tʀɑ̃zitif, -v/ *a*
intransitive.
intraveineux, -euse /ɛ̃tʀavɛnø,
-z/ *a* intravenous.
intrépide /ɛ̃tʀepid/ *a* fearless.
intrigue /ɛ̃tʀig/ *nf* intrigue;
(scénario) plot.
intrinsèque /ɛ̃tʀɛ̃sɛk/ *a* intrinsic.
introduction /ɛ̃tʀɔdyksjɔ̃/ *nf*
introduction; (insertion) insertion.
introduire /ɛ̃tʀɔdɥiʀ/ [17] *vt*
introduce, bring in; (insérer) put
in, insert; **~ qn** show sb in. □ **s'~**
vpr get in; **s'~ dans** get into,
enter.
introuvable /ɛ̃tʀuvabl/ *a* that
cannot be found.
introverti, ~e /ɛ̃tʀɔvɛʀti/ *nm, f*
introvert. ●*a* introverted.
intrus, ~e /ɛ̃tʀy, -z/ *nm, f*
intruder. **intrusion** *nf* intrusion.
intuitif, -ive /ɛ̃tɥitif, -iv/ *a*
intuitive. **intuition** *nf* intuition.
inusable /inyzabl/ *a* hard-
wearing.
inusité, ~e /inyzite/ *a* little
used.
inutile /inytil/ *a* useless; (vain)

needless. **inutilement** *adv*
needlessly. **inutilisable** *a*
unusable.
invalide /ɛ̃valid/ *a & nmf*
disabled (person).
invariable /ɛ̃vaʀjabl/ *a*
invariable.
invasion /ɛ̃vazjɔ̃/ *nf* invasion.
invectiver /ɛ̃vɛktive/ [1] *vt*
abuse.
inventaire /ɛ̃vɑ̃tɛʀ/ *nm*
inventory; (Comm) stocklist; **faire**
l'~ draw up an inventory; (Comm)
do a stocktake.
inventer /ɛ̃vɑ̃te/ [1] *vt* invent.
inventeur, -trice *nm, f* inventor.
inventif, -ive *a* inventive.
invention *nf* invention.
inverse /ɛ̃vɛʀs/ *a* opposite;
(ordre) reverse; **en sens ~** in *ou*
from the opposite direction. ●*nm*
reverse; **c'est l'~** it's the other
way round. **inversement** *adv*
conversely. **inverser** [1] *vt*
reverse, invert.
investir /ɛ̃vɛstiʀ/ [2] *vt* invest.
investissement *nm* investment.
investiture /ɛ̃vɛstityʀ/ *nf* (de
candidat) nomination; (de président)
investiture.
invétéré, ~e /ɛ̃vetere/ *a*
inveterate; (menteur) compulsive;
(enraciné) deep-rooted.
invisible /ɛ̃vizibl/ *a* invisible.
invitation /ɛ̃vitasjɔ̃/ *nf* invitation.
invité, ~e *nm, f* guest. **inviter** [1]
vt invite (à to).
involontaire /ɛ̃vɔlɔ̃tɛʀ/ *a*
involuntary; (témoin, héros)
unwitting.
invoquer /ɛ̃vɔke/ [1] *vt* call upon,
invoke.
invraisemblable /ɛ̃vʀɛsɑ̃blabl/ *a*
improbable, unlikely; (incroyable)
incredible. **invraisemblance** *nf*
improbability.
iode /jɔd/ *nm* iodine.
ira, irait /iʀa, iʀɛ/ ⇒ALLER [8].

Irak /iʀak/ nm Iraq.

Iran /iʀɑ̃/ nm Iran.

iris /iʀis/ nm iris.

irlandais, ~e /iʀlɑ̃dɛ, -z/ a Irish. **I~, ~e** nm, f Irishman, Irishwoman.

Irlande /iʀlɑ̃d/ nf Ireland.

ironie /iʀɔni/ nf irony. **ironique** a ironic.

irrationnel, ~le /iʀasjɔnɛl/ a irrational.

irréalisable /iʀealizabl/ a (idée, rêve) unachievable; (projet) unworkable.

irrécupérable /iʀekypeʀabl/ a irretrievable; (capital) irrecoverable.

irréel, ~le /iʀeɛl/ a unreal.

irréfléchi, ~e /iʀefleʃi/ a thoughtless.

irrégulier, -ière /iʀegylje, -jɛʀ/ a irregular.

irrémédiable /iʀemedjabl/ a irreparable.

irremplaçable /iʀɑ̃plasabl/ a irreplaceable.

irréparable /iʀepaʀabl/ a (objet) beyond repair; (tort, dégâts) irreparable.

irréprochable /iʀepʀɔʃabl/ a flawless.

irrésistible /iʀezistibl/ a irresistible; (drôle) hilarious.

irrésolu, ~e /iʀezɔly/ a indecisive; (problème) unsolved.

irrespirable /iʀɛspiʀabl/ a stifling.

irresponsable /iʀɛspɔ̃sabl/ a irresponsible.

irrigation /iʀigasjɔ̃/ nf irrigation. **irriguer** [1] vt irrigate.

irritable /iʀitabl/ a irritable.

irriter /iʀite/ [1] vt irritate. □ **s'~** vpr get annoyed (de at).

irruption /iʀypsjɔ̃/ nf faire ~ dans burst into.

Islam /islam/ nm Islam. **islamique** a Islamic.

islandais, ~e /islɑ̃dɛ, -z/ a Icelandic. ● nm (Ling) Icelandic. **I~, ~e** nm, f Icelander.

Islande /islɑ̃d/ nf Iceland.

isolant /izɔlɑ̃/ nm insulating material. **isolation** nf insulation.

isolé, ~e /izɔle/ a isolated. **isolement** nm isolation.

isoler /izɔle/ [1] vt isolate; (Électr) insulate. □ **s'~** vpr isolate oneself.

isoloir /izɔlwaʀ/ nm polling booth.

Isorel® /izɔʀɛl/ nm hardboard.

Israël /isʀaɛl/ nm Israel. **israélien, ~ne** a Israeli.

israélite /isʀaelit/ a Jewish. ● nmf Jew.

issu, ~e /isy/ a être ~ de (personne) come from; (résulter de) result ou stem from.

issue /isy/ nf (sortie) exit; (résultat) outcome; (fig) solution; à l'~ de at the conclusion of; ~ de secours emergency exit; rue ou voie sans ~ dead end.

Italie /itali/ nf Italy.

italien, ~ne /italjɛ̃, -ɛn/ a Italian. ● nm (Ling) Italian. **I~, ~ne** nm, f Italian.

italique /italik/ nm italics.

itinéraire /itineʀɛʀ/ nm itinerary, route.

I.U.T. abrév m (Institut universitaire de technologie) university institute of technology.

I.V.G. abrév f (interruption volontaire de grossesse) abortion.

ivoire /ivwaʀ/ nm ivory.

ivre /ivʀ/ a drunk. **ivresse** nf drunkenness; (fig) exhilaration. **ivrogne** nmf drunk(ard).

j' /ʒ/ ⇒JE.

jacinthe /ʒasɛ̃t/ *nf* hyacinth.

jadis /ʒadis/ *adv* long ago.

jaillir /ʒajiʀ/ [2] *vi* (*liquide*) spurt (out); (*lumière*) stream out; (*apparaître*) burst forth, spring out.

jalonner /ʒalɔne/ [1] *vt* mark (out).

jalousie /ʒaluzi/ *nf* jealousy; (*store*) (venetian) blind. **jaloux, -ouse** *a* jealous.

jamais /ʒamɛ/ *adv* ever; **ne ~** never; **il ne boit ~** he never drinks; **à ~** for ever; **si ~** if ever.

jambe /ʒɑ̃b/ *nf* leg.

jambon /ʒɑ̃bɔ̃/ *nm* ham. **jambonneau** (*pl* **~x**) *nm* knuckle of ham.

janvier /ʒɑ̃vje/ *nm* January.

Japon /ʒapɔ̃/ *nm* Japan.

japonais, ~e /japɔnɛ, -z/ *a* Japanese. ●*nm* (Ling) Japanese. **J~, ~e** *nm, f* Japanese.

japper /ʒape/ [1] *vi* yap.

jaquette /ʒakɛt/ *nf* (de livre, femme) jacket; (d'homme) morning coat.

jardin /ʒaʀdɛ̃/ *nm* garden; **~ d'enfants** nursery (school); **~ public** public park. **jardinage** *nm* gardening. **jardiner** [1] *vi* do some gardening, garden. **jardinier, -ière** *nm, f* gardener.

jardinière /ʒaʀdinjɛʀ/ *nf* (meuble) plant-stand; **~ de légumes** mixed vegetables.

jarretelle /ʒaʀtɛl/ *nf* suspender; (US) garter.

jarretière /ʒaʀtjɛʀ/ *nf* garter.

jatte /ʒat/ *nf* bowl.

jauge /ʒoʒ/ *nf* capacity; (de navire) tonnage; (compteur) gauge; **~ d'huile** dipstick.

jaune /ʒon/ *a & nm* yellow; (péj) scab; **~ d'œuf** (egg) yolk; **rire ~** give a forced laugh. **jaunir** [2] *vt/ i* turn yellow. **jaunisse** *nf* jaundice.

javelot /ʒavlo/ *nm* javelin.

jazz /dʒaz/ *nm* jazz.

J.C. *abrév m* (**Jésus-Christ**) **500 avant/après ~** 500 B.C./A.D.

je, j' /ʒə, ʒ/ *pron* I.

jean /dʒin/ *nm* jeans; **un ~** a pair of jeans.

jet¹ /ʒɛ/ *nm* throw; (de liquide, vapeur) jet; **~ d'eau** fountain.

jet² /dʒɛt/ *nm* (avion) jet.

jetable /ʒətabl/ *a* disposable.

jetée /ʒəte/ *nf* pier.

jeter /ʒəte/ [38] *vt* throw; (au rebut) throw away; (regard, ancre, lumière) cast; (cri) utter; (bases) lay; **~ un coup d'œil** have *ou* take a look (**à** at). □ **se ~** *vpr* **se ~ contre** crash *ou* bash into; **se ~ dans** (*fleuve*) flow into; **se ~ sur** (se ruer sur) rush at.

jeton /ʒətɔ̃/ *nm* token; (pour compter) counter; (au casino) chip.

jeu (*pl* **~x**) /ʒø/ *nm* game; (amusement) play; (au casino) gambling; (Théât) acting; (série) set; (de lumière, ressort) play; **en ~** (honneur) at stake; (forces) at work; **~ de cartes** (paquet) pack of cards; **~ d'échecs** (boîte) chess set; **~ de mots** pun; **~ télévisé** television quiz; **~ vidéo** video game; **~x de grattage** scratch cards.

jeudi /ʒødi/ *nm* Thursday.

jeun: à ~ /aʒœ̃/ *loc* on an empty stomach.

jeune /ʒœn/ *a* young; **~ fille** girl; **~ pousse** (Comm) start-up; **~s mariés** newlyweds. ●*nmf* young person; **les ~s** young people.

jeûne /ʒøn/ *nm* fast.

J

jeunesse /ʒœnɛs/ *nf* youth;
(apparence) youthfulness; **la ~**
(jeunes) the young.

joaillerie /ʒɔajʀi/ *nf* jewellery;
(magasin) jeweller's shop.

joie /ʒwa/ *nf* joy.

joindre /ʒwɛ̃dʀ/ [22] *vt* join (à to);
(mains, pieds) put together;
(efforts) combine; (contacter)
contact; (dans une enveloppe)
enclose. □ **se ~ à** *vpr* join.

joint, ~e /ʒwɛ̃, -t/ *a* (efforts) joint;
(pieds) together. ● *nm* joint; (de
robinet) washer.

joli, ~e /ʒɔli/ *a* pretty, nice;
(somme, profit) nice; **c'est du ~!**
(ironique) charming! **c'est bien ~
mais** that is all very well but.

joncher /ʒɔ̃ʃe/ [1] *vt* litter, be
strewn over; **jonché de** littered
with.

jonction /ʒɔ̃ksjɔ̃/ *nf* junction.

jongleur, -euse /ʒɔ̃glœʀ, øz/ *nm, f*
juggler.

jonquille /ʒɔ̃kij/ *nf* daffodil.

joue /ʒu/ *nf* cheek.

jouer /ʒwe/ [1] *vt/i* play; (Théât)
act; (au casino) gamble; (fonctionner)
work; (film, pièce) put on;
(cheval) back; (être important) count;
~ à (jeu, Sport) play; **~ de** (Mus)
play; **~ la comédie** put on an act;
bien joué! well done!

jouet /ʒwɛ/ *nm* toy; (personne: fig)
plaything; (victime) victim.

joueur, -euse /ʒwœʀ, -øz/ *nm, f*
player; (parieur) gambler.

joufflu, ~e /ʒufly/ *a* chubby-
cheeked; (visage) chubby.

jouir /ʒwiʀ/ [2] *vi* (sexe) come; **~
de** (droit, avantage) enjoy; (bien,
concession) enjoy the use of.

jouissance *nf* pleasure; (usage)
use (de qch of sth).

joujou (pl ~x) /ʒuʒu/ *nm* 🔲 toy.

jour /ʒuʀ/ *nm* day; (opposé à nuit)
day(time); (lumière) daylight;
(aspect) light; (ouverture) gap; **de nos**

~s nowadays; **du ~ au lendemain**
overnight; **il fait ~** it is (day)light;
~ chômé ou férié public holiday;
~ de fête holiday; **~ ouvrable,
de travail** working day; **mettre à ~**
update; **mettre au ~** uncover; **au
grand ~** in the open; **donner le ~**
give birth; **voir le ~** be born; **vivre
au ~ le jour** live from day to day.

journal (pl **-aux**) /ʒuʀnal, -o/ *nm*
(news)paper; (spécialisé) journal;
(intime) diary; (à la radio) news; **~
de bord** log-book.

journalier, -ière /ʒuʀnalje, -jɛʀ/
a daily.

journalisme /ʒuʀnalism/ *nm*
journalism. **journaliste** *nmf*
journalist.

journée /ʒuʀne/ *nf* day.

jovial, ~e (mpl **-iaux**) /ʒɔvjal,
-jo/ *a* jovial.

joyau (pl **~x**) /ʒwajo/ *nm* gem.

joyeux, -euse /ʒwajø, -z/ *a*
merry, joyful; **~ anniversaire**
happy birthday.

jubiler /ʒybile/ [1] *vi* be jubilant.

jucher /ʒyʃe/ [1] *vt* perch. □ **se ~**
vpr perch.

judaïsme /ʒydaism/ *nm* Judaism.

judiciaire /ʒydisjɛʀ/ *a* judicial.

judicieux, -ieuse /ʒydisjø, -z/ *a*
judicious.

judo /ʒydo/ *nm* judo.

juge /ʒyʒ/ *nm* judge; (arbitre)
referee; **~ de paix** Justice of the
Peace; **~ de touche** linesman.

jugé: au ~ /oʒyʒe/ *loc* by
guesswork.

jugement /ʒyʒmɑ̃/ *nm*
judgement; (criminel) sentence.

juger /ʒyʒe/ [40] *vt/i* judge;
(estimer) consider (**que** that); **~ de**
judge.

juguler /ʒygyle/ [1] *vt* stamp out;
curb.

juif, -ive /ʒɥif, -v/ *a* Jewish.
● *nm, f* Jew.

juillet /ʒɥijɛ/ *nm* July.

juin /ʒyɛ̃/ nm June.

jumeau, -elle (mpl ~x) /ʒymo, -ɛl/ a & nm,f twin. **jumeler** [38] vt (villes) twin.

jumelles /ʒymɛl/ nfpl binoculars.

jument /ʒymɑ̃/ nf mare.

junior /ʒynjɔʀ/ a & nmf junior.

jupe /ʒyp/ nf skirt.

jupon /ʒypɔ̃/ nm slip, petticoat.

juré, ~e /ʒyʀe/ nm,f juror. ●a sworn.

jurer /ʒyʀe/ [1] vt swear (que that). ●vi (pester) swear; (contraster) clash (avec with).

juridiction /ʒyʀidiksjɔ̃/ nf jurisdiction; (tribunal) court of law.

juridique /ʒyʀidik/ a legal.

juriste /ʒyʀist/ nmf legal expert.

juron /ʒyʀɔ̃/ nm swear-word.

jury /ʒyʀi/ nm (Jur) jury; (examinateurs) panel of judges.

jus /ʒy/ nm juice; (de viande) gravy; ~ de fruit fruit juice.

jusque /ʒysk(ə)/ prép jusqu'à (up) to, as far as; (temps) until, till; (limite) up to; (y compris) even; jusqu'à ce que until; jusqu'à présent until now; jusqu'en until; jusqu'où? how far?; ~ dans, ~ sur as far as.

juste /ʒyst/ a fair, just; (légitime) just; (correct, exact) right; (vrai) true; (vêtement) tight; (quantité) on the short side; le ~ milieu the happy medium. ●adv rightly, correctly; (chanter) in tune; (seulement, exactement) just; (un peu) ~ (calculer, mesurer) a bit fine ou close; au ~ exactly; c'était ~ (presque raté) it was a close thing.

justement adv (précisément) precisely; (à l'instant) just; (avec justesse) correctly; (légitimement) justifiably.

justesse /ʒystɛs/ nf accuracy; de ~ just, narrowly.

justice /ʒystis/ nf justice; (autorités) law; (tribunal) court.

justifier /ʒystifje/ [45] vt justify.

●vi ~ de prove. □ se ~ vpr justify oneself.

juteux, -euse /ʒytø, -z/ a juicy.

juvénile /ʒyvenil/ a youthful; (délinquance, mortalité) juvenile.

kaki /kaki/ a inv & nm khaki.

kangourou /kɑ̃guʀu/ nm kangaroo.

karaté /kaʀate/ nm karate.

kart /kaʀt/ nm go-cart.

kascher /kaʃɛʀ/ a inv kosher.

kayak /kajak/ nm kayak.

képi /kepi/ nm kepi.

kermesse /kɛʀmɛs/ nf fête.

kidnapper /kidnape/ [1] vt kidnap.

kilo /kilo/ nm kilo.

kilogramme /kilɔgʀam/ nm kilogram.

kilométrage /kilɔmɛtʀaʒ/ nm ≈ mileage. **kilomètre** nm kilometre.

kinésithérapeute /kineziteʀapøt/ nmf physiotherapist. **kinésithérapie** nf physiotherapy.

kiosque /kjɔsk/ nm kiosk; ~ à musique bandstand.

kit /kit/ nm kit. ~ mains libres conducteur hands-free kit.

klaxon® /klaksɔn/ nm (Auto) horn. **klaxonner** [1] vi sound one's horn.

Ko abrév m (kilo-octet) (Ordinat) KB.

KO abrév m (knock-out) KO ▣.

K-way® /kawɛ/ nm inv windcheater.

kyste /kist/ nm cyst.

l', la /l, la/ ⇒LE.

là /la/

● *adverbe*

····▸ (dans ce lieu) there; (ici) here; (chez soi) in; **c'est ~ que** this is where; **~ où** where; **par ~** (dans cette direction) this way; (dans cette zone) around there; **de ~** hence.

····▸ (à ce moment) then; **c'est ~ que** that's when.

····▸ **cet homme-~** that man; **ces maisons-~** those houses.

● *interjection*

····▸ **~! c'est fini** there (now), it's all over!

là-bas /labɑ/ *adv* there; (à l'endroit que l'on indique) over there.

label /labɛl/ *nm* seal, label.

laboratoire /labɔʀatwaʀ/ *nm* laboratory.

laborieux, -ieuse /labɔʀjø, -z/ *a* laborious; (*personne*) industrious; **classes laborieuses** working classes.

labour /labuʀ/ *nm* ploughing; (US) plowing. **labourer** [1] *vt* plough; (US) plow; (*déchirer*) rip at.

labyrinthe /labiʀɛ̃t/ *nm* maze, labyrinth.

lac /lak/ *nm* lake.

lacer /lase/ [10] *vt* lace up.

lacet /lasɛ/ *nm* (de chaussure) (shoe-)lace; (de route) sharp bend.

lâche /lɑʃ/ *a* cowardly; (détendu) loose; (sans rigueur) lax. ● *nmf* coward.

lâcher /lɑʃe/ [1] *vt* let go of; (laisser tomber) drop; (abandonner) give up; (laisser) leave; (libérer) release; (*flèche, balle*) fire; (*juron, phrase*) come out with; (desserrer) loosen; **~ prise** let go. ● *vi* give way.

lâcheté /lɑʃte/ *nf* cowardice.

lacrymogène /lakʀimɔʒɛn/ *a* **gaz ~** tear gas.

lacune /lakyn/ *nf* gap.

là-dedans /lad(ə)dɑ̃/ *adv* (près) in here; (plus loin) in there.

là-dessous /lad(ə)su/ *adv* (près) under here; (plus loin) under there.

là-dessus /lad(ə)sy/ *adv* (sur une surface) on here; (plus loin) on there; (sur ce) with that; (quelque temps après) after that; **qu'avez-vous à dire ~?** what have you got to say about it?

ladite /ladit/ ⇒LEDIT.

lagune /lagyn/ *nf* lagoon.

là-haut /lao/ *adv* (en hauteur) up here; (plus loin) up there; (à l'étage) upstairs.

laïc /laik/ *nm* layman.

laid, ~e /lɛ, lɛd/ *a* ugly; (*action*) vile. **laideur** *nf* ugliness.

lainage /lɛnaʒ/ *nm* woollen garment.

laine /lɛn/ *nf* wool; **de ~** woollen.

laïque /laik/ *a* (*état, loi*) secular; (*habit, personne*) lay; (*école*) nondenominational. ● *nmf* layman, laywoman.

laisse /lɛs/ *nf* lead, leash; **tenir en ~** keep on a lead.

laisser /lese/ [1] *vt* (déposer) leave, drop off; (confier) leave (à **qn** with sb); (abandonner) leave; (rendre) **~ qn perplexe/froid** leave sb puzzled/cold; (*céder, prêter*) **~ qch à qn** let sb have sth; (donner) (*choix, temps*) give sb sth. □ **se ~**

vpr se ~ **persuader/insulter** let oneself be persuaded/insulted; **elle ne se laisse pas faire** she won't be pushed around; **laisse-toi faire** leave it to me/him/her *etc.*; **se ~ aller** let oneself go. ● *v aux* ~ **qn/ qch faire** let sb/sth do; **laisse-moi faire** (ne m'aide pas) let me do it; (je m'en occupe) leave it to me; **laisse faire!** so what! **laisser-aller** *nm inv* carelessness; (dans la tenue) scruffiness. **laissez-passer** *nm inv* pass.

lait /lɛ/ *nm* milk; ~ **longue conservation** long-life *ou* UHT milk; **frère/sœur de** ~ foster-brother/-sister. **laitage** *nm* milk product. **laiterie** *nf* dairy. **laiteux, -euse** *a* milky.

laitier, -ière /letje, -jɛʀ/ *a* dairy. ● *nm, f* (livreur) milkman, milkwoman.

laiton /lɛtɔ̃/ *nm* brass.

laitue /lety/ *nf* lettuce.

lama /lama/ *nm* llama.

lambeau (*pl* ~**x**) /lɑ̃bo/ *nm* shred; **en** ~**x** in shreds.

lame /lam/ *nf* blade; (lamelle) strip; (vague) wave; ~ **de fond** ground swell; ~ **de rasoir** razor blade.

lamentable /lamɑ̃tabl/ *a* deplorable. **lamenter (se)** [1] *vpr* moan (**sur** about, over).

lampadaire /lɑ̃padɛʀ/ *nm* standard lamp; (de rue) street lamp.

lampe /lɑ̃p/ *nf* lamp; (ampoule) bulb; (de radio) valve; ~ (**de poche**) torch; (US) flashlight; ~ **à souder** blowlamp; ~ **de chevet** bedside lamp; ~ **solaire**, ~ **à bronzer** sunlamp.

lance /lɑ̃s/ *nf* spear; (de tournoi) lance; (tuyau) hose; ~ **d'incendie** fire hose.

lancement /lɑ̃smɑ̃/ *nm* throwing; (de navire, de missile, mise sur le marché) launch.

lance-missiles /lɑ̃smisil/ *nm inv* missile launcher.

lance-pierres /lɑ̃spjɛʀ/ *nm inv* catapult.

lancer /lɑ̃se/ [10] *vt* throw; (avec force) hurl; (navire, idée, artiste) launch; (émettre) give out; (regard) cast; (moteur) start. □ **se** ~ *vpr* (Sport) gain momentum; (se précipiter) rush; **se** ~ **dans** (explication) launch into; (passe-temps) take up. ● *nm* throw; (action) throwing.

lancinant, ~e /lɑ̃sinɑ̃, -t/ *a* (douleur) shooting; (problème) nagging.

landau /lɑ̃do/ *nm* pram; (US) baby carriage.

lande /lɑ̃d/ *nf* heath, moor.

langage /lɑ̃gaʒ/ *nm* language; ~ **machine/de programmation** machine/programming language.

langouste /lɑ̃gust/ *nf* spiny lobster. **langoustine** *nf* Dublin Bay prawn.

langue /lɑ̃g/ *nf* (Anat) tongue; (Ling) language; **il m'a tiré la** ~ he stuck his tongue out at me; **de** ~ **anglaise** (personne) English-speaking, (journal) English-language; ~ **maternelle** mother tongue; ~ **vivante** modern language.

lanière /lanjɛʀ/ *nf* strap.

lanterne /lɑ̃tɛʀn/ *nf* lantern; (électrique) lamp; (de voiture) sidelight.

lapin /lapɛ̃/ *nm* rabbit; **poser un** ~ **à qn** ⊞ stand sb up; **le coup du** ~ rabbit punch; (en voiture) whiplash injury.

lapsus /lapsys/ *nm* slip (of the tongue).

laque /lak/ *nf* lacquer; (pour cheveux) hairspray; (peinture) gloss paint.

laquelle /lakɛl/ ⇒LEQUEL.

lard /laʀ/ *nm* streaky bacon.

L

large /laʀʒ/ a wide, broad; (grand) large; (généreux) generous; **avoir les idées ∼s** be broad-minded; **∼ d'esprit** broad-minded. ●adv (calculer, mesurer) on the generous side; **voir ∼** think big. ●nm **faire 10 cm de ∼** be 10 cm wide; **le ∼** (mer) the open sea; **au ∼ de** (Naut) off. **largement** adv widely; (ouvrir) wide; (amplement) amply; (généreusement) generously; (au moins) easily.

largesse /laʀʒɛs/ nf generous gift.

largeur /laʀʒœʀ/ nf width, breadth; **∼ d'esprit** broad-mindedness.

larguer /laʀge/ [1] vt drop; **∼ les amarres** cast off.

larme /laʀm/ nf tear; (goutte 🄵) drop; **en ∼s** in tears.

larmoyant, ∼e /laʀmwajɑ̃, -t/ a full of tears. **larmoyer** [31] vi (yeux) water; (pleurnicher) whine.

larynx /laʀɛ̃ks/ nm larynx.

las, ∼se /lɑ, lɑs/ a weary.

lasagnes /lazaɲ/ nfpl lasagna.

laser /lazɛʀ/ nm laser.

lasser /lɑse/ [1] vt weary. □ **se ∼** vpr grow tired, get tired (**de** of).

latéral, ∼e (mpl **-aux**) /lateʀal, -o/ a lateral.

latin, ∼e /latɛ̃, -in/ a Latin. ●nm (Ling) Latin.

latte /lat/ nf lath; (de plancher) board; (de siège) slat; (de mur, plafond) lath.

lauréat, ∼e /lɔʀea, -t/ a prize-winning. ●nm, f prize-winner.

laurier /lɔʀje/ nm (Bot) laurel; (Culin) bay-leaves.

lavable /lavabl/ a washable.

lavabo /lavabo/ nm wash-basin; **∼s** toilet(s).

lavage /lavaʒ/ nm washing; **∼ de cerveau** brainwashing.

lavande /lavɑ̃d/ nf lavender.

lave /lav/ nf lava.

lave-glace (pl **∼s**) /lavglas/ nm windscreen washer.

lave-linge /lavlɛ̃ʒ/ nm inv washing machine.

laver /lave/ [1] vt wash; **∼ qn de** (fig) clear sb of. □ **se ∼** vpr wash (oneself); **se ∼ les mains** wash one's hands.

laverie /lavʀi/ nf **∼ (automatique)** launderette; (US) laundromat.

lave-vaisselle /lavvɛsɛl/ nm inv dishwasher.

laxatif, -ive /laksatif, -v/ a & nm laxative.

layette /lɛjɛt/ nf baby clothes.

---

le, la, l' (pl **les**) /lə, la, l, le/ l' before vowel or mute h.

●déterminant

····▸ the.

····▸ (notion générale) **aimer la musique** like music; **l'amour** love.

····▸ (possession) **avoir les yeux verts** have green eyes; **il s'est cassé la jambe** he broke his leg.

····▸ (prix) **3 euros ∼ kilo** 3 euros a kilo.

····▸ (temps) **∼ lundi** on Mondays; **tous les mardis** every Tuesday.

····▸ (avec nom propre) **les Dury** the Durys; **la reine Margot** Queen Margot; **la Belgique** Belgium.

····▸ (avec adjectif) the; **je veux la rouge** I want the red one; **les riches** the rich.

●pronom

····▸ (homme) him; (femme) her; (chose, animal) it; (au pluriel) them.

····▸ (remplaçant une phrase) **je te l'avais bien dit** I told you so; **je ∼ croyais aussi** I thought so too.

lécher /leʃe/ [14] vt lick; (flamme) lick; (mer) lap.

lèche-vitrines /lɛʃvitrin/ *nm inv*
faire du ~ go window-shopping.
leçon /ləsɔ̃/ *nf* lesson; **faire la ~** à
lecture; **~ particulière** private
lesson; **~s de conduite** driving
lessons.
lecteur, -trice /lɛktœʀ, -tʀis/
nm, f reader; (Univ) foreign
language assistant; **~ de cassettes**
cassette player; **~ de disquettes**
(disk) drive; **~ laser** CD player;
~ optique optical scanner.
lecture /lɛktyʀ/ *nf* reading.
ledit, ladite (*pl* **lesdit(e)s**) /lədi,
ladit, ledi(t)/ *a* the
aforementioned.
légal, ~e (*mpl* **-aux**) /legal, -o/ *a*
legal. **légaliser** [1] *vt* legalize.
légalité *nf* legality; (loi) law.
légendaire /leʒɑ̃dɛʀ/ *a*
legendary. **légende** *nf* (histoire,
inscription) legend; (de carte) key;
(d'illustration) caption.
léger, -ère /leʒe, -ɛʀ/ *a* light;
(*bruit, faute, maladie*) slight;
(*café, argument*) weak; (*imprudent*)
thoughtless; (frivole) fickle; **à la
légère** thoughtlessly. **légèrement**
adv lightly; (*agir*) thoughtlessly;
(un peu) slightly. **légèreté** *nf*
lightness; thoughtlessness.
légion /leʒjɔ̃/ *nf* legion.
législatif, -ive /leʒislatif, -v/ *a*
legislative; **élections législatives**
general election.
législature /leʒislatyʀ/ *nf* term
of office.
légitime /leʒitim/ *a* (Jur)
legitimate; (fig) rightful; **agir en
état de ~ défense** act in self-
defence. **légitimité** *nf* legitimacy.
legs /lɛg/ *nm* legacy; (d'effets
personnels) bequest.
léguer /lege/ [14] *vt* bequeath.
légume /legym/ *nm* vegetable.
lendemain /lɑ̃dmɛ̃/ *nm* **le ~** the
next day; (fig) the future; **le ~ de**
the day after; **le ~ matin/soir** the

next morning/evening; **du jour au
~** from one day to the next.
lent, ~e /lɑ̃, -t/ *a* slow.
lentement *adv* slowly. **lenteur** *nf*
slowness.
lentille /lɑ̃tij/ *nf* (Culin) lentil;
(verre) lens; **~s de contact** contact
lenses.
léopard /leɔpaʀ/ *nm* leopard.
lèpre /lɛpʀ/ *nf* leprosy.

. . . .

lequel, laquelle (*pl* **les-quel**
(le)s), **auquel** (*pl* **auxquel(le)s**),
duquel (*pl* **desquel(le)s**) /ləkɛl,
lakɛl, lekɛl, ɔkɛl, dykɛl, dekɛl/

à + lequel	= auquel,
à + lesquel(le)s	= auxquel(le)s;
de + lequel	= duquel,
de + lesquel(le)s	= desquel(le)s

●*pronom*
····▶ (relatif) (personne) who;
(complément indirect) whom; (autres
cas) which; **l'ami auquel tu as écrit**
the friend to whom you wrote;
**les voisins chez lesquels Sophie
est allée** the neighbours whose
house Sophie went to.
····▶ (interrogatif) which; **~ tu veux?**
which one do you want?

●*adjectif*
····▶ **auquel cas** in which case.

. . . .

les /le/ ⇒LE.
lesbienne /lɛsbjɛn/ *nf* lesbian.
léser /leze/ [14] *vt* wrong.
lésiner /lezine/ [1] *vi* **ne pas ~
sur** not stint on.
lesquels, lesquelles /lekɛl/
⇒LEQUEL.
lessive /lesiv/ *nf* (poudre)
washing-powder; (liquide) washing
liquid; (linge, action) washing.
leste /lɛst/ *a* agile, nimble;
(grivois) coarse.
Lettonie /letɔni/ *nf* Latvia.

lettre /lɛtR/ *nf* letter; **à la ~, au pied de la ~** literally; **en toutes ~s** in full; **les ~s** (Univ) (the) arts.

leucémie /løsemi/ *nf* leukaemia.

....

leur (*pl* ~s) /lœR/

●*pronom personnel invariable*
····▸ them; **donne-le ~** give it to them; **je ~ fais confiance** I trust them.

●*adjectif possessif*
····▸ their; **~s enfants** their children; **à ~ arrivée** when they arrived.

●**le leur, la leur,** (*pl* **les leurs**) *pronom possessif*
····▸ theirs; **chacun le ~** one each; **je suis des ~s** I am one of them.

....

levain /ləvɛ̃/ *nm* leaven.

levé, ~e /ləve/ *a* (debout) up.

levée /ləve/ *nf* (de peine, de sanctions) lifting; (de courrier) collection; (de troupes, d'impôts) levying.

lever /ləve/ [6] *vt* lift (up), raise; (*interdiction*) lift; (*séance*) close; (*armée, impôts*) levy. ●*vi* (*pâte*) rise. □ **se ~** *vpr* get up; (*soleil, rideau*) rise; (*jour*) break. ●*nm* **au ~** on getting up; **~ du jour** daybreak; **~ de rideau** (Théât) curtain (up); **~ du soleil** sunrise.

levier /ləvje/ *nm* lever; **~ de changement de vitesse** gear lever.

lèvre /lɛvR/ *nf* lip.

lévrier /levRije/ *nm* greyhound.

levure /ləvyR/ *nf* yeast; **~ chimique** baking powder.

lexique /lɛksik/ *nm* vocabulary; (glossaire) lexicon.

lézard /lezaR/ *nm* lizard.

lézarde /lezaRd/ *nf* crack.

liaison /ljɛzõ/ *nf* connection; (transport, Ordinat) link; (contact) contact; (Gram, Mil) liaison;

(amoureuse) affair; **être en ~ avec** be in contact with; **assurer la ~ entre** liaise between.

liane /ljan/ *nf* creeper.

Liban /libã/ *nm* Lebanon.

libeller /libele/ [1] *vt* (*chèque*) write; (contrat) draw up; **libellé à l'ordre de** made out to.

libellule /libelyl/ *nf* dragonfly.

libéral, ~e (*mpl* -**aux**) /libeRal, -o/ *a* liberal; **les professions ~es** the professions.

libérateur, -trice /libeRatœR, -tRis/ *a* liberating. ●*nm, f* liberator. **libération** *nf* release; (de pays) liberation.

libérer /libeRe/ [14] *vt* (*personne*) free, release; (*pays*) liberate, free; (*bureau, lieux*) vacate; (*gaz*) release. □ **se ~** *vpr* free oneself.

liberté /libɛRte/ *nf* freedom, liberty; (loisir) free time; **être/ mettre en ~** be/set free; **~ conditionnelle** parole; **~ provisoire** provisional release (*pending trial*); **~ surveillée** probation; **~s publiques** civil liberties.

Libertel /libɛRtɛl/ *nm* (Internet) Freenet.

libraire /libRɛR/ *nmf* bookseller. **librairie** *nf* bookshop.

libre /libR/ *a* free; (*place, pièce*) vacant, free; (*passage*) clear; (*école*) private (*usually religious*); **~ de qch/de faire** free from sth/to do. **libre-échange** *nm* free trade. **libre-service** (*pl* **libres-services**) *nm* (magasin) self-service shop; (restaurant) self-service restaurant.

licence /lisãs/ *nf* licence; (Univ) degree.

licencié, ~e /lisãsje/ *nm, f* graduate; **~ ès lettres/sciences** Bachelor of Arts/Science.

licenciements /lisãsimã/ *nm* redundancy; (pour faute) dismissal.

licencier /45/ *vt* make
redundant; (*pour faute*) dismiss.

licorne /likɔʀn/ *nf* unicorn.

liège /liɛʒ/ *nm* cork.

lien /ljɛ̃/ *nm* (rapport) link; (attache)
bond, tie; (corde) rope; ~**s**
affectifs/de parenté emotional/
family ties.

lier /lje/ [45] *vt* tie (up), bind;
(rolier) link; (engager, unir) bind; ~
conversation strike up a
conversation; **ils sont très liés** they
are friends close. □ **se** ~ **avec** *vpr*
make friends with.

lierre /ljɛʀ/ *nm* ivy.

lieu (*pl* ~**x**) /ljø/ *nm* place; ~**x**
(locaux) premises; (d'un accident)
scene; **sur les** ~**x** at the scene; **au**
~ **de** instead of; **avoir** ~ take
place; **donner** ~ **à** give rise to;
tenir ~ **de** serve as; **s'il y a** ~ if
necessary; **en premier** ~ firstly; **en**
dernier ~ lastly; ~ **commun**
commonplace; ~ **de rencontre**
meeting place.

lièvre /ljɛvʀ/ *nm* hare.

lifting /liftiŋ/ *nm* face-lift.

ligne /liɲ/ *nf* line; (trajet) route; (de
métro, train) line; (formes) lines; (de
femme) figure; **en** ~ (joueurs) lined
up; (au téléphone) on the phone;
(Ordinat) on line; ~ **spécialisée**
(Internet) dedicated line.

ligoter /ligɔte/ [1] *vt* tie up.

ligue /lig/ *nf* league. **liguer (se)**
[1] *vpr* join forces (**contre**
against).

lilas /lila/ *nm & a inv* lilac.

limace /limas/ *nf* slug.

limande /limɑ̃d/ *nf* (poisson) dab.

lime /lim/ *nf* file; ~ **à ongles** nail
file.

limitation /limitasjɔ̃/ *nf*
limitation; ~ **de vitesse** speed
limit.

limite /limit/ *nf* limit; (de jardin,
champ) boundary; **à la** ~ **de** (fig)
verging on, bordering on; **à la** ~

if it comes to it, at a pinch; **dans**
une certaine ~ up to a point; **dans**
la ~ **du possible** as far as
possible. ● *a* (vitesse, âge)
maximum; **cas** ~ borderline case;
date ~ deadline; **date** ~ **de vente**
sell-by date.

limiter /limite/ [1] *vt* limit;
(délimiter) form the border of. □ **se**
~ *vpr* limit oneself (**à** to).

limonade /limɔnad/ *nf*
lemonade.

limpide /lɛ̃pid/ *a* limpid, clear.

lin /lɛ̃/ *nm* (tissu) linen.

linge /lɛ̃ʒ/ *nm* linen; (lessive)
washing; (torchon) cloth; ~ (**de**
corps) underwear. **lingerie** *nf*
underwear. **lingette** *nf* wipe.

lingot /lɛ̃go/ *nm* ingot.

linguistique /lɛ̃gɥistik/ *a*
linguistic. ● *nf* linguistics.

lion /ljɔ̃/ *nm* lion; **le L**~ Leo.
lionceau (*pl* ~**x**) *nm* lion cub.
lionne *nf* lioness.

liquidation /likidasjɔ̃/ *nf*
liquidation; (vente) (clearance)
sale; **entrer en** ~ go into
liquidation.

liquide /likid/ *a* liquid. ● *nm*
(argent) ~ ready money; **payer en**
~ pay cash; ~ **de frein** brake
fluid.

liquider /likide/ [1] *vt* liquidate;
(vendre) sell.

lire /liʀ/ [39] *vt/i* read. ● *nf* lira.

lis[1] /li/ ⇒LIRE[39].

lis[2] /lis/ *nm* (fleur) lily.

lisible /lizibl/ *a* legible; (roman)
readable.

lisière /lizjɛʀ/ *nf* edge.

lisse /lis/ *a* smooth.

liste /list/ *nf* list; ~ **d'attente**
waiting list; ~ **électorale** register
of voters; **être sur (la)** ~ **rouge** be
ex-directory.

listing /listiŋ/ *nm* printout.

lit /li/ *nm* bed; **se mettre au** ~ get
into bed; ~ **de camp** camp-bed;

L

~ **d'enfant** cot; ~ **d'une personne**
single bed; ~ **de deux personnes**,
grand ~ double bed.
literie /litʀi/ *nf* bedding.
litière /litjɛʀ/ *nf* litter.
litige /litiʒ/ *nm* dispute.
litre /litʀ/ *nm* litre.
littéraire /liteʀɛʀ/ *a* literary;
(*études, formation*) arts.
littéral, ~**e** (*mpl* -**aux**) /liteʀal,
-o/ *a* literal.
littérature /liteʀatyʀ/ *nf*
literature.
littoral (*pl* -**aux**) /litɔʀal, -o/ *nm*
coast.
Lituanie /lituani/ *nf* Lithuania.
livide /livid/ *a* deathly pale.
livraison /livʀɛzɔ̃/ *nf* delivery.
livre /livʀ/ *nf* (monnaie, poids)
pound. ● *nm* book; ~ **de bord**
log-book; ~ **de compte** books; ~
de poche paperback.
livrer /livʀe/ [1] *vt* (Comm) deliver;
(abandonner) give over (**à** to);
(remettre) (*coupable, document*)
hand over (**à** to); **livré à soi-même**
left to oneself. □ **se** ~ *vpr* (se
rendre) give oneself up (**à** to); **se** ~
à (*boisson, actes*) indulge in;
(ami) confide in.
livret /livʀɛ/ *nm* book; (Mus)
libretto; ~ **de caisse d'épargne**
savings book; ~ **scolaire** school
report (book).
livreur, -euse /livʀœʀ, -øz/ *nm, f*
delivery man, delivery woman.
local[1], ~**e** (*mpl* -**aux**) /lɔkal, -o/ *a*
local.
local[2] (*pl* -**aux**) /lɔkal, -o/ *nm*
premises; **locaux** premises.
localement /lɔkalmɑ̃/ *adv*
locally.
localiser /lɔkalize/ [1] *vt* (repérer)
locate; (circonscrire) localize.
locataire /lɔkatɛʀ/ *nmf* tenant;
(de chambre) lodger.
location /lɔkasjɔ̃/ *nf* (de maison)
renting; (de voiture, de matériel) hire,

rental; (de place) booking,
reservation; (par propriétaire) renting
out; hiring out; **en** ~ (*voiture*) on
hire, rented; (*habiter*) in rented
accommodation.
locomotive /lɔkɔmɔtiv/ *nf*
engine, locomotive.
locution /lɔkysjɔ̃/ *nf* phrase.
loft /lɔft/ *nm* loft (apartment).
loge /lɔʒ/ *nf* (de concierge, de franc-
maçons) lodge; (d'acteur) dressing-
room; (de spectateur) box.
logement /lɔʒmɑ̃/ *nm*
accommodation; (appartement) flat;
(habitat) housing.
loger /lɔʒe/ [40] *vt* (réfugié,
famille) house; (ami) put up;
(client) accommodate. ● *vi* live.
□ **se** ~ *vpr* live; **trouver à se** ~
find accommodation; **se** ~ **dans**
(balle) lodge itself in.
logiciel /lɔʒisjɛl/ *nm* software; ~
contributif shareware; ~
d'application application software;
~ **de groupe** groupware; ~ **de
jeux** games software; ~ **de
navigation** browser; ~ **public**
freeware.
logique /lɔʒik/ *a* logical. ● *nf*
logic.
logis /lɔʒi/ *nm* dwelling.
logistique /lɔʒistik/ *nf* logistics.
loi /lwa/ *nf* law.
loin /lwɛ̃/ *adv* far (away); **au** ~ far
away; **de** ~ from far away; (de
beaucoup) by far; ~ **de là** far from
it; **plus** ~ further; **il revient de** ~
(fig) he had a close shave.
lointain, ~**e** /lwɛ̃tɛ̃, -ɛn/ *a*
distant. ● *nm* distance; **dans le** ~
in the distance.
loisir /lwaziʀ/ *nm* (spare) time;
~**s** (temps libre) leisure, spare time;
(distractions) leisure activities; **à** ~
at one's leisure; **avoir le** ~ **de faire**
have time to do.
londonien, ~**ne** /lɔ̃dɔnjɛ̃, -ɛn/ *a*
London. **L**~, ~**e** *nm, f* Londoner.

Londres /lɔ̃dʀ/ npr London.

long, longue /lɔ̃, lɔ̃g/ a long; **à ~ terme** long-term; **être ~ à faire** be a long time doing. ● nm **de ~** (mesure) long; **de ~ en large** back and forth; **(tout) le ~ de** (all) along. ● adv **en dire ~ sur qn/qch** say a lot about sb/sth; **en savoir plus ~ sur** know more about.

longer /lɔ̃ʒe/ [40] vt go along; (limiter) border.

longitude /lɔ̃ʒityd/ nf longitude.

longtemps /lɔ̃tɑ̃/ adv a long time; **avant ~** before long; **trop ~** too long; **ça prendra ~** it will take a long time; **prendre plus ~ que prévu** take longer than anticipated.

longuement /lɔ̃gmɑ̃/ adv (longtemps) for a long time; (en détail) at length.

longueur /lɔ̃gœʀ/ nf length; **~s** (de texte) over-long parts; **à ~ de journée** all day long; **en ~** lengthwise; **~ d'onde** wavelength.

lopin /lɔpɛ̃/ nm **~ de terre** patch of land.

loque /lɔk/ nf **~s** rags; **~** (humaine) (human) wreck.

loquet /lɔkɛ/ nm latch.

lors de /lɔʀdə/ prép (au moment de) at the time of; (pendant) during.

lorsque /lɔʀsk(ə)/ conj when.

losange /lɔzɑ̃ʒ/ nm diamond.

lot /lo/ nm (portion) share; (aux enchères) lot; (Ordinat) batch; (destin) lot; **gagner le gros ~** hit the jackpot.

loterie /lɔtʀi/ nf lottery.

lotion /losjɔ̃/ nf lotion.

lotissement /lɔtismɑ̃/ nm (à construire) building plot; (construit) (housing) development.

louable /luabl/ a praiseworthy.

louange nf praise.

louche /luʃ/ a shady, dubious. ● nf ladle.

loucher /luʃe/ [1] vi squint.

louer /lwe/ [1] vt (approuver) praise (de for); (prendre en location) (maison) rent; (voiture, matériel) hire, rent; (place) book, reserve; (donner en location) (maison) rent out; (matériel) rent out, hire out; **à ~** to let, for rent (US).

loufoque /lufɔk/ a 🖪 crazy.

loup /lu/ nm wolf.

loupe /lup/ nf magnifying glass.

louper /lupe/ [1] vt 🖪 miss; (examen) flunk 🖪.

lourd, ~e /luʀ, -d/ a heavy; (faute) serious; **~ de dangers** fraught with danger; **il fait ~** it's close ou muggy.

loutre /lutʀ/ nf otter.

louveteau (pl **~x**) /luvto/ nm wolf cub; (scout) Cub (Scout).

loyal, ~e (mpl **-aux**) /lwajal, -o/ a loyal, faithful; (honnête) fair.

loyauté nf loyalty; fairness.

loyer /lwaje/ nm rent.

lu /ly/ ⇒LIRE [39].

lubrifiant /lybʀifjɑ̃/ nm lubricant.

lucide /lysid/ a lucid. **lucidité** nf lucidity.

lucratif, -ive /lykʀatif, -v/ a lucrative; **à but non ~** non-profit-making.

ludiciel /lydisjɛl/ nm (Ordinat) games software.

lueur /lɥœʀ/ nf (faint) light, glimmer; (fig) glimmer, gleam.

luge /lyʒ/ nf toboggan.

lugubre /lygybʀ/ a gloomy.

L

....

lui /lɥi/

●pronom

····▸ (masculin) (sujet) he; **~, il est à l'étranger** he's abroad; **c'est ~!** it's him!; (objet) him; (animal) it; **c'est à ~** it's his; **elle conduit mieux que ~** she's a better driver than he is.

····▸ (féminin) her; **je ~ ai annoncé** I told her.

·····► (masculin/féminin) **donne-le-∼**
: give it to him/her.

lui-même /lцimɛm/ *pron* himself;
(animal) itself.

luire /lцiʀ/ [17] *vi* shine; (reflet
humide) glisten; (reflet chaud, faible)
glow.

lumière /lymjɛʀ/ *nf* light; **∼s**
(connaissances) knowledge; **faire
(toute) la ∼ sur une affaire** clear a
matter up.

luminaire /lyminɛʀ/ *nm* lamp.

lumineux, -euse /lyminø, -z/ *a*
luminous; (éclairé) illuminated;
(*rayon*) of light; (radieux) radiant;
source lumineuse light source.

lunaire /lynɛʀ/ *a* lunar.

lunatique /lynatik/ *a*
temperamental.

lunch /lœnʃ/ *nm* buffet lunch.

lundi /lœdi/ *nm* Monday.

lune /lyn/ *nf* moon; **∼ de miel**
honeymoon.

lunettes /lynɛt/ *nfpl* glasses; (de
protection) goggles; **∼ de ski/
natation** ski/swimming goggles; **∼
noires** dark glasses; **∼ de soleil**
sun-glasses.

lustre /lystʀ/ *nm* (éclat) lustre;
(objet) chandelier.

lutin /lytɛ̃/ *nm* goblin.

lutte /lyt/ *nf* fight, struggle; (Sport)
wrestling. **lutter** [1] *vi* fight,
struggle; (Sport) wrestle. **lutteur,
-euse** *nm, f* fighter; (Sport)
wrestler.

luxe /lyks/ *nm* luxury; **de ∼**
luxury; (*produit*) de luxe.

Luxembourg /lyksãbuʀ/ *nm*
Luxembourg.

luxer (se) /(sə)lykse/ [1] *vpr* **se
∼ le genou** dislocate one's knee.

luxueux, -euse /lyksɥø, -z/ *a*
luxurious.

lycée /lise/ *nm* (secondary)
school. **lycéen, ∼ne** *nm, f* pupil
(at secondary school).

lyophilisé, ∼e /ljɔfilize/ *a*
freeze-dried.

lyrique /liʀik/ *a* (*poésie*) lyric;
(passionné) lyrical; **artiste/théâtre ∼**
opera singer/house.

lys /lis/ *nm* lily.

m' /m/ ⇒ME.

ma /ma/ ⇒MON.

macabre /makabʀ/ *a* macabre.

macadam /makadam/ *nm*
Tarmac®.

macaron /makaʀɔ̃/ *nm* (gâteau)
macaroon; (insigne) badge.

macédoine /masedwan/ *nf*
mixed diced vegetables; **∼ de
fruits** fruit salad.

macérer /maseʀe/ [14] *vt/i* soak;
(dans du vinaigre) pickle.

mâcher /mɑʃe/ [1] *vt* chew; **ne
pas ∼ ses mots** not mince one's
words.

machin /maʃɛ̃/ *nm* 🔲 (chose)
thing; (dont on ne trouve pas le nom)
whatsit 🔲.

machinal, ∼e (*mpl* **-aux**)
/maʃinal, -o/ *a* automatic.
machinalement *adv*
mechanically, automatically.

machination /maʃinasjɔ̃/ *nf*
plot; **des ∼s** machinations.

machine /maʃin/ *nf* machine;
(d'un train, navire) engine; **∼ à écrire**
typewriter; **∼ à laver/coudre**
washing-/sewing-machine; **∼ à
sous** fruit machine; (US) slot-
machine. **machine-outil** (*pl
machines-outils*) *nf* machine
tool. **machinerie** *nf* machinery.

machiniste /maʃinist/ *nm* (Théât)
stage-hand; (conducteur) driver.

mâchoire /maʃwaʀ/ *nf* jaw.

mâchonner /maʃɔne/ [1] *vt*
chew.

maçon /masɔ̃/ *nm* (entrepreneur)
builder; (poseur de briques)
bricklayer; (qui construit en pierre)
mason. **maçonnerie** *nf* (briques)
brickwork; (pierres) stonework,
masonry; (travaux) building.

madame (*pl* **mesdames**)
/madam, medam/ *nf* (à une
inconnue) (dans une lettre) **M~** Dear
Madam; **bonjour, ~** good
morning; **mesdames et messieurs**
ladies and gentlemen; (à une femme
dont on connaît le nom) (dans une lettre)
Chère M~ Dear Mrs *ou* Ms X;
bonjour, ~ good morning Mrs *ou*
Ms X; **oui M~ le Ministre** yes
Minister; (formule de respect) **oui M~**
yes madam.

mademoiselle (*pl*
mesdemoiselles) /madmwazɛl,
medmwazɛl/ *nf* (à une inconnue)
(dans une lettre) **M~** Dear Madam;
bonjour, ~ good morning; **entrez
mesdemoiselles** come in (ladies);
(à une jeune fille dont on connaît le nom)
(dans une lettre) **Chère M~** Dear Ms
ou Miss X; **bonjour, ~** good
morning Miss *ou* Ms X.

magasin /magazɛ̃/ *nm* shop,
store; (entrepôt) warehouse; (d'une
arme) magazine; **en ~** in stock.

magazine /magazin/ *nm*
magazine; (émission) programme.

Maghreb /magʀɛb/ *nm* North
Africa.

magicien, ~ne /maʒisjɛ̃, -ɛn/
nm, f magician.

magie /maʒi/ *nf* magic. **magique**
a magic; (mystérieux) magical.

magistral, ~e (*mpl* **-aux**)
/maʒistʀal, -o/ *a* masterly; (grand:
hum) tremendous; **cours ~**
lecture.

magistrat /maʒistʀa/ *nm*
magistrate.

magistrature /maʒistʀatyʀ/ *nf*
judiciary; (fonction) public office.

magner (se) /(sə)maɲe/ [1] *vpr*
🔲 get a move on.

magnétique /maɲetik/ *a*
magnetic. **magnétiser** [1] *vt*
magnetize. **magnétisme** *nm*
magnetism.

magnétophone /maɲetɔfɔn/ *nm*
tape recorder; (à cassettes) cassette
recorder.

magnétoscope /maɲetɔskɔp/
nm video recorder.

magnificence /maɲifisɑ̃s/ *nf*
magnificence. **magnifique** *a*
magnificent.

magot /mago/ *nm* 🔲 hoard (of
money).

magouille /maguj/ *nf* 🔲
scheming, skulduggery.

magret /magʀɛ/ *nm* **~ de canard**
duck breast.

mai /mɛ/ *nm* May.

maigre /mɛgʀ/ *a* thin; (viande)
lean; (yaourt) low-fat; (fig) poor,
meagre; **faire ~** abstain from
meat. **maigreur** *nf* thinness;
leanness; (fig) meagreness.

maigrir /megʀiʀ/ [2] *vi* get thin-
(ner); (en suivant un régime) slim.
● *vt* make thin(ner).

maille /maj/ *nf* stitch; (de filet)
mesh; **~ qui file** ladder, run; **avoir
~ à partir avec qn** have a brush
with sb.

maillet /majɛ/ *nm* mallet.

maillon /majɔ̃/ *nm* link.

maillot /majo/ *nm* (Sport) shirt,
jersey; **~ (de corps)** vest; (US)
undershirt; **~ (de bain)**
(swimming) costume.

main /mɛ̃/ *nf* hand; **donner la ~ à
qn** hold sb's hand; **se donner la ~**
hold hands; **en ~s propres** in
person; **en bonnes ~s** in good
hands; **~ courante** handrail; **se**

M

faire la ~ get the hang of it; **perdre la** ~ lose one's touch; **sous la** ~ to hand; **vol à** ~ **armée** armed robbery; **fait (à la)** ~ handmade; **haut les** ~**s!** hands up! **main-d'œuvre** (*pl* **mains-d'œuvre**) *nf* labour; (*ouvriers*) labour force.

main-forte /mɛ̃fɔʀt/ *nf inv* **prêter** ~ **à qn** come to sb's aid.

maint, ~**e** /mɛ̃, mɛ̃t/ *a* many a (+ *sg*); ~**s** many; **à** ~**es reprises** many times.

maintenant /mɛ̃t(ə)nɑ̃/ *adv* now; (*de nos jours*) nowadays; (*l'époque actuelle*) today.

maintenir /mɛ̃t(ə)niʀ/ [58] *vt* keep, maintain; (*soutenir*) support, hold up; (*affirmer*) maintain; (*decision*) stand by. □ **se** ~ *vpr* (*tendance*) persist; (*prix, malade*) remain stable.

maintien /mɛ̃tjɛ̃/ *nm* (*attitude*) bearing; (*conservation*) maintenance.

maire /mɛʀ/ *nm* mayor.

mairie /meʀi/ *nf* town hall; (*administration*) town council.

mais /mɛ/ *conj* but; ~ **oui** of course; ~ **non** of course not.

maïs /mais/ *nm* maize, corn; (*Culin*) sweetcorn.

maison /mɛzɔ̃/ *nf* house; (*foyer*) home; (*immeuble*) building; ~ (**de commerce**) firm; **à la** ~ at home; **rentrer** *ou* **aller à la** ~ go home; ~ **des jeunes (et de la culture)** youth club; ~ **de repos** rest home; ~ **de convalescence** convalescent home; ~ **de retraite** old people's home; ~ **mère** parent company. ● *a inv* (*Culin*) home-made.

maître, -**esse** /mɛtʀ, -ɛs/ *a* (*qui contrôle*) **être** ~ **de soi** be one's own master; ~ **de la situation** in control of the situation; (*principal*) (*idée, qualité*) key, main. ● *nm, f* (*Scol*) teacher; (*d'animal*) owner,

master. ● *nm* (*expert, guide*) master; (*dirigeant*) leader; ~ **de conférences** senior lecturer; ~ **d'hôtel** head waiter; (*domestique*) butler. **maître-assistant**, ~ **e** (*pl* **maîtres-assistants**) *nm, f* lecturer.

maître-chanteur (*pl* **maîtres-chanteurs**) *nm* blackmailer.

maître-nageur (*pl* **maîtres-nageurs**) *nm* swimming instructor. **maîtresse** *nf* (*amante*) mistress.

maîtrise /metʀiz/ *nf* mastery; (*contrôle*) control; (*Mil*) supremacy; (*Univ*) master's degree; ~ (**de soi**) self-control.

maîtriser /metʀize/ [1] *vt* (*sujet, technique*) master; (*incendie, sentiment, personne*) control. □ **se** ~ *vpr* have self-control.

maïzena® /maizena / *nf* cornflour.

majesté /maʒɛste/ *nf* majesty.

majestueux, -euse /maʒɛstɥø, z/ *a* majestic.

majeur, ~**e** /maʒœʀ/ *a* major, main; (*Jur*) of age; **en** ~**e partie** mostly; **la** ~**e partie de** most of. ● *nm* middle finger.

majoration /maʒɔʀasjɔ̃/ *nf* increase (**de** in). **majorer** [1] *vt* increase.

majoritaire /maʒɔʀitɛʀ/ *a* majority; **être** ~ be in the majority. **majorité** *nf* majority; **en** ~ chiefly.

Majorque /majɔʀk/ *nf* Majorca.

majuscule /maʒyskyl/ *a* capital. ● *nf* capital letter.

mal¹ /mal/ *adv* badly; (*incorrectement*) wrong(ly); **aller** ~ (*personne*) be unwell; (*affaires*) go badly; ~ **entendre/comprendre** not hear/understand properly; ~ **en point** in a bad state; **pas** ~ quite a lot. ● *a inv* bad, wrong; **c'est** ~ **de** it is wrong *ou* bad to; **ce n'est pas** ~ 🔲 it's not bad; **Nick**

n'est pas ~ ▣ Nick is not bad-looking.

mal² (pl maux) /mal, mo/ nm evil; (douleur) pain, ache; (maladie) disease; (effort) trouble; (dommage) harm; (malheur) misfortune; **avoir ~ à la tête/à la gorge** have a headache/a sore throat; **avoir le ~ de mer/du pays** be seasick/homesick; **faire ~** hurt; **se faire ~** hurt oneself; **j'ai ~** it hurts; **faire du ~ à** hurt, harm; **se donner du ~ pour faire qch** go to a lot of trouble to do sth.

malade /malad/ a sick, ill; (bras, œil) bad; (plante, poumons, côlon) diseased; **tomber ~** fall ill; (fou ▣) mad. ● nmf sick person; (d'un médecin) patient; **~ mental** mentally ill person.

maladie /maladi/ nf illness, disease; (manie ▣) mania.

maladif, -ive /maladif, -v/ a sickly; (jalousie, peur) pathological.

maladresse /maladrɛs/ nf clumsiness; (erreur) blunder.

maladroit, ~e /maladrwa, -t/ a clumsy; (sans tact) tactless.

malaise /malɛz/ nm feeling of faintness; (gêne) uneasiness; (état de crise) unrest.

malaisé, ~e /maleze/ a difficult.

Malaisie /malɛzi/ nf Malaysia.

malaria /malaRja/ nf malaria.

malaxer /malakse/ [1] vt (pétrir) knead; (mêler) mix.

malchance /malʃɑ̃s/ nf misfortune. **malchanceux, -euse** a unlucky.

mâle /mɑl/ a male; (viril) manly. ● nm male.

malédiction /malediksjɔ̃/ nf curse.

maléfice /malefis/ nm evil spell. **maléfique** a evil.

malentendant, ~e /malɑ̃tɑ̃dɑ̃, -t/ a hard of hearing.

malentendu /malɑ̃tɑ̃dy/ nm misunderstanding.

malfaçon /malfasɔ̃/ nf defect.

malfaisant, ~e /malfəzɑ̃, -t/ a harmful; (personne) evil.

malfaiteur /malfɛtœR/ nm criminal.

malformation /malfɔRmasjɔ̃/ nf malformation.

malgré /malgRe/ prép in spite of, despite; **~ tout** nevertheless.

malheur /malœR/ nm misfortune; (accident) accident; **par ~** unfortunately; **faire un ~** ▣ be a big hit; **porter ~** be ou bring bad luck.

malheureusement /malœRøzmɑ̃/ adv unfortunately.

malheureux, -euse /malœRø, -z/ a unhappy; (regrettable) unfortunate; (sans succès) unlucky; (insignifiant) paltry, pathetic. ● nm, f (poor) wretch.

malhonnête /malɔnɛt/ a dishonest. **malhonnêteté** nf dishonesty.

malice /malis/ nf mischief; **sans ~** harmless; **avec ~** mischievously. **malicieux, -ieuse** a mischievous.

malignité /maliɲite/ nf malignancy. **malin, -igne** a clever, smart; (méchant) malicious; (tumeur) malignant; (difficile ▣) difficult.

malingre /malɛ̃gR/ a puny.

malle /mal/ nf (valise) trunk; (Auto) boot; (US) trunk.

mallette /malɛt/ nf (small) suitcase; (pour le bureau) briefcase.

malmener /malməne/ [6] vt manhandle; (fig) give a rough ride to.

malnutrition /malnytRisjɔ̃/ nf malnutrition.

malodorant, ~e /malɔdɔRɑ̃, -t/ a smelly, foul-smelling.

M

malpoli, ~e /malpɔli/ a rude, impolite.

malpropre /malpRɔpR/ a dirty.

malsain, ~e /malsɛ̃, -ɛn/ a unhealthy.

malt /malt/ nm malt.

Malte /malt/ nf Malta.

maltraiter /maltRete/ [1] vt ill-treat.

malveillance /malvɛjɑ̃s/ nf malice. **malveillant**, ~e a malicious.

maman /mamɑ̃/ nf mum(my), mother; (US) mom(my).

mamelle /mamɛl/ nf teat.

mamelon /mamlɔ̃/ nm (Anat) nipple; (colline) hillock.

mamie /mami/ nf ▣ granny.

mammifère /mamifɛR/ nm mammal.

manche /mɑ̃ʃ/ nf sleeve; (Sport, Pol) round. ● nm (d'un instrument) handle; **~ à balai** broomstick; (Aviat) joystick. **M~ nf la M~** the Channel; **le tunnel sous la M~** the Channel tunnel.

manchette /mɑ̃ʃɛt/ nf cuff; (de journal) headline.

manchot, ~te /mɑ̃ʃo, -ɔt/ nm, f one-armed person; (sans bras) armless person. ● nm (oiseau) penguin.

mandarine /mɑ̃daRin/ nf tangerine, mandarin (orange).

mandat /mɑ̃da/ nm (postal) money order; (Pol) mandate; (procuration) proxy; (de police) warrant; **~ d'arrêt** arrest warrant.

mandataire /mɑ̃datɛR/ nm representative; (Jur) proxy.

manège /manɛʒ/ nm riding school; (à la foire) merry-go-round; (manœuvre) trick, ploy.

manette /manɛt/ nf lever; (de jeu) joystick.

mangeable /mɑ̃ʒabl/ a edible.

mangeoire /mɑ̃ʒwaR/ nf trough; (pour oiseaux) feeder.

manger /mɑ̃ʒe/ [40] vt eat; (fortune) go through; (profits) eat away at; (économies) use up; (ronger) eat into. ● vi eat; **donner à ~ à** feed. ● nm food.

mangue /mɑ̃g/ nf mango.

maniable /manjabl/ a easy to handle.

maniaque /manjak/ a fussy. ● nmf fusspot; (fou) maniac; (fanatique) fanatic; **un ~ de l'ordre** a stickler for tidiness.

manie /mani/ nf habit; (marotte) obsession.

maniement /manimɑ̃/ nm handling. **manier** [45] vt handle.

manière /manjɛR/ nf way, manner; ~s (politesse) manners; (chichis) fuss; **à la ~ de** in the style of; **de ~ à** so as to; **de toute ~** anyway, in any case.

maniéré, ~e /manjeRe/ a affected.

manif /manif/ nf ▣ demo.

manifestant, ~e /manifɛstɑ̃, -t/ nm, f demonstrator.

manifestation /manifɛstasjɔ̃/ nf expression, manifestation; (de maladie, phénomène) appearance; (Pol) demonstration; (événement) event; **~ culturelle** cultural event.

manifeste /manifɛst/ a obvious. ● nm manifesto.

manifester /manifɛste/ [1] vt show, manifest; (désir, crainte) express. ● vi (Pol) demonstrate. ☐ **se ~** vpr (sentiment) show itself; (apparaître) appear; (répondre à un appel) come forward.

manigance /manigɑ̃s/ nf little plot. **manigancer** [10] vt plot.

manipulation /manipylasjɔ̃/ nf handling; (péj) manipulation.

manivelle /manivɛl/ nf handle, crank.

mannequin /mankɛ̃/ nm (personne) model; (statue) dummy.

manœuvrer /manœvRe/ [1] vt

manoeuvre; (*machine*) operate.
● *vi* manoeuvre.

manoir /manwaʀ/ *nm* manor.

manque /mɑ̃k/ *nm* lack (**de** of);
(lacune) gap; ~ **à gagner** loss of
earnings; **en (état de)** ~ having
withdrawal symptoms.

manqué, ~**e** /mɑ̃ke/ *a* (*écrivain*)
failed; **garçon** ~ tomboy.

manquement /mɑ̃kmɑ̃/ *nm* ~ **à**
breach of.

manquer /mɑ̃ke/ [1] *vt* miss;
(gâcher) spoil; ~ **à** (*devoir*) fail in;
~ **de** be short of, lack; **il/ça lui
manque** he misses him/it; ~ (**de**)
faire (faillir) nearly do; **ne manquez
pas de** be sure to; ~ **à sa parole**
break one's word. ● *vi* be short
ou lacking; (être absent) be absent;
(en moins, disparu) be missing; **il me
manque 20 francs** I'm 20 francs
short.

mansarde /mɑ̃saʀd/ *nf* attic
(room).

manteau (*pl* ~**x**) /mɑ̃to/ *nm*
coat.

manucure /manykyʀ/ *nmf*
manicurist. ● *nf* (soins) manicure.

manuel, ~**le** /manɥɛl/ *a* manual.
● *nm* (livre) manual; (Scol)
textbook.

manufacture /manyfaktyʀ/ *nf*
factory; (fabrication) manufacture.
manufacturer [1] *vt*
manufacture.

manuscrit, ~**e** /manyskʀi, -t/ *a*
handwritten. ● *nm* manuscript.

mappemonde /mapmɔ̃d/ *nf*
world map; (sphère) globe.

maquereau (*pl* ~**x**) /makʀo/ *nm*
(poisson) mackerel; Ⓘ pimp.

maquette /makɛt/ *nf* (scale)
model; ~ (**de mise en page**)
paste-up.

maquillage /makijaʒ/ *nm*
make-up.

maquiller /makije/ [1] *vt* make

up; (truquer) doctor, fake. □ **se** ~
vpr make (oneself) up.

maquis /maki/ *nm* (paysage)
scrub; (Mil) Maquis, underground.

maraîcher, -**ère** /maʀeʃe, -ɛʀ/
nm, f market gardener; (US) truck
farmer.

marais /maʀɛ/ *nm* marsh.

marasme /maʀasm/ *nm* slump,
stagnation; **dans le** ~ in the
doldrums.

marbre /maʀbʀ/ *nm* marble.

marc /maʀ/ *nm* (eau-de-vie) marc;
~ **de café** coffee grounds.

marchand, ~**e** /maʀʃɑ̃, -d/ *a*
(valeur) market. ● *nm, f* trader;
(de charbon, vins) merchant; ~ **de
couleurs** ironmonger; (US)
hardware merchant; ~ **de
journaux** newsagent; ~ **de légumes**
greengrocer; ~ **de poissons**
fishmonger.

marchander /maʀʃɑ̃de/ [1] *vt*
haggle over. ● *vi* haggle.

marchandise /maʀʃɑ̃diz/ *nf*
goods.

marche /maʀʃ/ *nf* (démarche, trajet)
walk; (rythme) pace; (Mil, Mus, Pol)
march; (d'escalier) step; (Sport)
walking; (de machine) operation,
working; (de véhicule) running; **en**
~ (*train*) moving; (*moteur,
machine*) running; **faire** ~ **arrière**
(véhicule) reverse; **mettre en** ~
start (up); **se mettre en** ~ start
moving.

marché /maʀʃe/ *nm* market;
(contrat) deal; **faire son** ~ do one's
shopping; ~ **aux puces** flea
market; ~ **noir** black market.

marchepied /maʀʃəpje/ *nm* (de
train, camion) step.

marcher /maʀʃe/ [1] *vi* walk;
(poser le pied) tread (**sur** on); (aller)
go; (fonctionner) work, run;
(prospérer) go well; (*film, livre*) do
well; (consentir Ⓘ) agree; **faire** ~ **qn**
Ⓘ pull sb's leg.

mardi /maʀdi/ nm Tuesday; M~ gras Shrove Tuesday.

mare /maʀ/ nf (étang) pond; (flaque) pool.

marécage /maʀekaʒ/ nm marsh; (sous les tropiques) swamp.

maréchal (pl -aux) /maʀeʃal, -o/ nm field marshal.

maréchal-ferrant (pl -aux-ferrants /maʀeʃalferɑ̃/ nm blacksmith.

marée /maʀe/ nf tide; (poissons) fresh fish; ~ haute/basse high/ low tide; ~ noire oil slick.

marelle /maʀɛl/ nf hopscotch.

margarine /maʀgaʀin/ nf margarine.

marge /maʀʒ/ nf margin; en ~ de (à l'écart de) on the fringe(s) of; ~ bénéficiaire profit margin.

marginal, ~e (mpl -aux) /maʀʒinal, -o/ a marginal. ●nm, f drop-out.

marguerite /maʀgəʀit/ nf daisy; (qui imprime) daisy-wheel.

mari /maʀi/ nm husband.

mariage /maʀjaʒ/ nm marriage; (cérémonie) wedding.

marié, ~e /maʀje/ a married. ●nm, f (bride)groom, bride; les ~s the bride and groom.

marier /maʀje/ [45] vt marry. □ se ~ vpr get married, marry; se ~ avec marry, get married to.

marin, ~e /maʀɛ̃, -in/ a sea. ●nm sailor.

marine /maʀin/ nf navy; ~ marchande merchant navy. ●a inv navy (blue).

marionnette /maʀjɔnɛt/ nf puppet; (à fils) marionette.

maritalement /maʀitalmɑ̃/ adv (vivre) as husband and wife.

maritime /maʀitim/ a maritime, coastal; (agent, compagnie) shipping.

marmaille /maʀmaj/ nf ▣ brats.

marmelade /maʀməlad/ nf stewed fruit; ~ d'oranges (orange) marmalade.

marmite /maʀmit/ nf (cooking-) pot.

marmonner /maʀmɔne/ [1] vt mumble.

marmot /maʀmo/ nm ▣ kid.

Maroc /maʀɔk/ nm Morocco.

maroquinerie /maʀɔkinʀi/ nf (magasin) leather goods shop.

marquant, ~e /maʀkɑ̃, -t/ a (remarquable) outstanding; (qu'on n'oublie pas) memorable.

marque /maʀk/ nf mark; (de produits) brand, make; (décompte) score; à vos ~s! (Sport) on your marks!; de ~ (Comm) brand name; (fig) important; ~ de fabrique trademark; ~ déposée registered trademark.

marquer /maʀke/ [1] vt mark; (indiquer) show, say; (écrire) note down; (point, but) score; (joueur) mark; (influencer) leave its mark on; (exprimer) (volonté, sentiment) show. ●vi (laisser une trace) leave a mark; (événement) stand out; (Sport) score.

marquis, ~e /maʀki, -z/ nm, f marquis, marchioness.

marraine /maʀɛn/ nf godmother.

marrant, ~e /maʀɑ̃, -t/ a ▣ funny.

marre /maʀ/ adv en avoir ~ ▣ be fed up (de with).

marrer (se) /(sə)maʀe/ [1] vpr ▣ laugh, have a (good) laugh.

marron /maʀɔ̃/ nm chestnut; (couleur) brown; (coup ▣) thump; ~ d'Inde horse chestnut. ●a inv brown.

mars /maʀs/ nm March.

marteau (pl ~x) /maʀto/ nm hammer; ~ (de porte) (door) knocker; ~ piqueur ou pneumatique pneumatic drill; être ~ ▣ be mad.

marteler /maʀtəle/ [6] vt

hammer; (*poings, talons*) pound; (*scander*) rap out.

martial, ~e (*mpl* **-iaux**) /maʀsjal, -jo/ *a* military; (*art*) martial.

martien, ~ne /maʀsjɛ̃, -ɛn/ *a & nm, f* Martian.

martyr, ~e /maʀtiʀ/ *nm, f* martyr. ● *a* martyred; (*enfant*) battered.

martyre /maʀtiʀ/ *nm* (Relig) martyrdom; (fig) agony, suffering.

martyriser /maʀtiʀize/ [1] *vt* (Relig) martyr; (*torturer*) torture; (*enfant*) batter.

marxisme /maʀksism/ *nm* Marxism. **marxiste** *a & nmf* Marxist.

masculin, ~e /maskylɛ̃, -in/ *a* masculine; (*sexe*) male; (*mode, équipe*) men's. ● *nm* masculine.

masochisme /mazoʃism/ *nm* masochism.

masochiste /mazoʃist/ *nmf* masochist. ● *a* masochistic.

masque /mask/ *nm* mask; ~ **de beauté** face pack. **masquer** [1] *vt* (*cacher*) hide, conceal (**à** from); (*lumière*) block (off).

massacre /masakʀ/ *nm* massacre. **massacrer** [1] *vt* massacre; (*abîmer* 🔟) ruin.

massage /masaʒ/ *nm* massage.

masse /mas/ *nf* (*volume*) mass; (*gros morceau*) lump, mass; (*outil*) sledge-hammer; **en** ~ (*vendre*) in bulk; (*venir*) in force; **produire en** ~ mass-produce; **la** ~ (*foule*) the masses; **une** ~ **de** 🔟 masses of; **la** ~ **de** the majority of.

masser /mase/ [1] *vt* (*assembler*) assemble; (*pétrir*) massage. ◻ **se** ~ *vpr* (*gens, foule*) mass.

massif, **-ive** /masif, -v/ *a* massive; (*or, argent*) solid. ● *nm* (de fleurs) clump; (*parterre*) bed; (Géog) massif. **massivement** *adv* (*en masse*) in large numbers.

massue /masy/ *nf* club, bludgeon.

mastic /mastik/ *nm* putty; (*pour trous*) filler.

mastiquer /mastike/ [1] *vt* (*mâcher*) chew.

mat /mat/ *a* (*couleur*) matt; (*bruit*) dull; (*teint*) olive; **être** ~ (aux échecs) be in checkmate.

mât /mɑ/ *nm* mast; (*pylône*) pole; ~ **de drapeau** flagpole.

match /matʃ/ *nm* match; (US) game; **faire** ~ **nul** tie, draw; ~ **aller** first leg; ~ **retour** return match.

matelas /matla/ *nm* mattress; ~ **pneumatique** air bed.

matelassé, ~e /matlase/ *a* padded; (*tissu*) quilted.

matelot /matlo/ *nm* sailor.

mater /mate/ [1] *vt* (*révolte*) put down; (*personne*) bring into line.

matérialiser (se) /(sə)mateʀjalize/ [1] *vpr* materialize.

matérialiste /mateʀjalist/ *a* materialistic. ● *nmf* materialist.

matériau (*pl* ~**x**) /mateʀjo/ *nm* material.

matériel, ~**le** /mateʀjɛl/ *a* material. ● *nm* equipment, materials; ~ **informatique** hardware.

maternel, ~**le** /matɛʀnɛl/ *a* maternal; (*comme d'une mère*) motherly. **maternelle** *nf* nursery school.

maternité /matɛʀnite/ *nf* maternity hospital; (*état de mère*) motherhood; **de** ~ maternity.

mathématicien, ~**ne** /matematisjɛ̃, -ɛn/ *nm, f* mathematician.

mathématique /matematik/ *a* mathematical. **mathématiques** *nfpl* mathematics (+ *sg*).

maths /mat/ *nfpl* 🔟 maths (+ *sg*).

matière /matjɛʀ/ *nf* matter; (*produit*) material; (*sujet*) subject; **en**

∼ **de** as regards; ∼ **plastique** plastic; ∼**s grasses** fat content; ∼**s premières** raw materials.

matin /matɛ̃/ *nm* morning; **de bon** ∼ early in the morning.

matinal, ∼**e** (*mpl* **-aux**) /matinal, -o/ *a* morning; (*de bonne heure*) early; **être** ∼ **be** up early; (*d'habitude*) be an early riser.

matinée /matine/ *nf* morning; (*spectacle*) matinée.

matou /matu/ *nm* tomcat.

matraque /matrak/ *nf* (*de police*) truncheon; (US) billy (club). **matraquer** [1] *vt* club, beat; (*produit, chanson*) plug.

matrimonial, ∼**e** (*mpl* **-iaux**) /matrimɔnjal, -jo/ *a* matrimonial; **agence** ∼**e** marriage bureau.

maturité /matyrite/ *nf* maturity.

maudire /modir/ [41] *vt* curse.

maudit, ∼**e** /modi, -t/ *a* ⏢ blasted, damned.

maugréer /mogree/ [15] *vi* grumble.

mausolée /mozɔle/ *nm* mausoleum.

maussade /mosad/ *a* gloomy.

mauvais, ∼**e** /mɔvɛ, -z/ *a* bad; (*erroné*) wrong; (*malveillant*) evil; (*désagréable*) nasty, bad; (*mer*) rough; **le** ∼ **moment** the wrong time; ∼**e herbe** weed; ∼**e langue** gossip; ∼**e passe** tight spot; ∼ **traitements** ill-treatment. ●*adv* (*sentir*) bad; **il fait** ∼ the weather is bad. ●*nm* **le bon et le** ∼ the good and the bad.

mauve /mov/ *a* & *nm* mauve.

mauviette /movjɛt/ *nf* weakling, wimp.

maux /mo/ ⇨ MAL².

maximal, ∼**e** (*mpl* **-aux**) /maksimal, -o/ *a* maximum.

maxime /maksim/ *nf* maxim.

maximum /maksimɔm/ *a* maximum. ●*nm* maximum; **au** ∼ as much as possible; (*tout au plus*)

at most; **faire le** ∼ do one's utmost.

mazout /mazut/ *nm* (fuel) oil.

me, m' /mə, m/ *pron* me; (*indirect*) (to) me; (*réfléchi*) myself.

méandre /meɑ̃dr/ *nm* meander.

mec /mɛk/ *nm* ⏢ bloke, guy.

mécanicien, ∼**ne** /mekanisjɛ̃, -jɛn/ *nm, f* mechanic. ●*nm* train driver.

mécanique /mekanik/ *a* mechanical; (*jouet*) clockwork; **problème** ∼ engine trouble. ●*nf* mechanics (+ *sg*); (*mécanisme*) mechanism. **mécaniser** [1] *vt* mechanize.

mécanisme /mekanism/ *nm* mechanism.

méchamment /meʃamɑ̃/ *adv* spitefully. **méchanceté** *nf* nastiness; (*action*) wicked action.

méchant, ∼**e** /meʃɑ̃, -t/ *a* (*cruel*) wicked; (*désagréable, grave*) nasty; (*enfant*) naughty; (*chien*) vicious; (*sensationnel* ⏢) terrific. ●*nm, f* (*enfant*) naughty child.

mèche /mɛʃ/ *nf* (*de cheveux*) lock; (*de bougie*) wick; (*d'explosif*) fuse; (*outil*) drill bit; **de** ∼ **avec** in league with.

méconnaissable /mekɔnɛsabl/ *a* unrecognizable.

méconnaître /mekɔnɛtr/ [18] *vt* misunderstand, misread; (*mésestimer*) underestimate.

méconnu, ∼**e** /mekɔny/ *a* unrecognized; (*artiste*) neglected.

mécontent, ∼**e** /mekɔ̃tã, -t/ *a* dissatisfied (**de** with); (*irrité*) annoyed (**de** at, with). **mécontentement** *nm* dissatisfaction; annoyance. **mécontenter** [1] *vt* dissatisfy; (*irriter*) annoy.

médaille /medaj/ *nf* medal; (*insigne*) badge; (*bijou*) medallion. **médaillé**, ∼**e** *nm, f* medallist.

médaillon /medajɔ̃/ *nm* medallion; (bijou) locket.

médecin /mɛdsɛ̃/ *nm* doctor.

médecine /mɛdsin/ *nf* medicine.

média /medja/ *nm* medium; les ~s the media.

médiateur, -trice /medjatœr, -tris/ *nm, f* mediator.

médiatique /medjatik/ *a* (*événement, personnalité*) media.

médical, ~e (*mpl* -aux) /medikal, -o/ *a* medical.

médicament /medikamɑ̃/ *nm* medicine, drug.

médico-légal, ~e (*mpl* -aux) /medikɔlegal, -o/ *a* forensic.

médiéval, ~e (*mpl* -aux) /medjeval, -o/ *a* medieval.

médiocre /medjɔkr/ *a* mediocre, poor. **médiocrité** *nf* mediocrity.

médire /medir/ [37] *vi* ~ de speak ill of, malign.

médisance /medizɑ̃s/ *nf* ~(s) malicious gossip.

méditer /medite/ [1] *vi* meditate (**sur** on). ● *vt* contemplate; (*paroles, conseils*) mull over; ~ **de** plan to.

Méditerranée /mediterane/ *nf* la ~ the Mediterranean.

méditerranéen, ~ne /mediteraneɛ̃, -ɛn/ *a* Mediterranean.

médium /medjɔm/ *nm* (personne) medium.

méduse /medyz/ *nf* jellyfish.

meeting /mitin/ *nm* meeting.

méfait /mefɛ/ *nm* misdeed; les ~s de (conséquences) the ravages of.

méfiance /mefjɑ̃s/ *nf* suspicion, distrust. **méfiant, ~e** *a* suspicious, distrustful.

méfier (se) /(sə)mefje/ [45] *vpr* be wary *ou* careful; **se** ~ **de** distrust, be wary of.

mégaoctet /megaɔkte/ *nm* (Ordinat) megabyte.

mégère /meʒɛr/ *nf* (femme) shrew.

mégot /mego/ *nm* cigarette end.

meilleur, ~e /mɛjœr/ *a* (comparatif) better (**que** than); (superlatif) best; **le** ~ **livre** the best book; **mon** ~ **ami** my best friend; ~ **marché** cheaper. ● *nm, f* **le** ~, **la** ~**e** the best (one). ● *adv* (*sentir*) better; **il fait** ~ the weather is better.

mél /mel/ *nm* e-mail; **envoyer un** ~ send an e-mail.

mélancolie /melɑ̃kɔli/ *nf* melancholy.

mélange /melɑ̃ʒ/ *nm* mixture, blend.

mélanger /melɑ̃ʒe/ [40] *vt* mix; (*thés, parfums*) blend. □ **se** ~ *vpr* mix; (*thés, parfums*) blend; (*idées*) get mixed up.

mélasse /melas/ *nf* black treacle; (US) molasses.

mêlée /mele/ *nf* free for all; (au rugby) scrum.

mêler /mele/ [1] *vt* mix (**à** with); (*qualités*) combine; (embrouiller) mix up; ~ **qn à** (impliquer dans) involve sb in. □ **se** ~ *vpr* mix; combine; **se** ~ **à** (se joindre à) mingle with; (participer à) join in; **se** ~ **de** meddle in: **mêle-toi de ce qui te regarde** mind your own business.

méli-mélo (*pl* **mélis-mélos**) /melimelo/ *nm* jumble.

mélo /melo/ 🔲 *nm* melodrama. ● *a inv* slushy, schmaltzy 🔲.

mélodie /melɔdi/ *nf* melody. **mélodieux, -ieuse** *a* melodious. **mélodique** *a* melodic.

mélodramatique /melɔdramatik/ *a* melodramatic. **mélodrame** *nm* melodrama.

mélomane /melɔman/ *nmf* music lover.

melon /məlɔ̃/ *nm* melon; (chapeau) ~ bowler (hat).

membrane /mɑ̃bʀan/ *nf*
membrane.

membre /mɑ̃bʀ/ *nm* (Anat) limb;
(adhérent) member.

même /mɛm/ *a* same; **ce livre ~**
this very book; **la bonté ~**
kindness itself; **en ~ temps** at the
same time. ● *pron* **le ~, la ~** the
same (one). ● *adv* even; **à ~** (sur)
directly on; **à ~ de** in a position
to; **de ~** (aussi) too; (de la même
façon) likewise; **de ~ que** just as;
~si even if.

mémé /meme/ *nf* 🔲 granny.

mémo /memo/ *nm* note, memo.

mémoire /memwaʀ/ *nm* (rapport)
memorandum; (Univ) dissertation;
~s (souvenirs écrits) memoirs. ● *nf*
memory; **à la ~ de** to the memory
of; **de ~** from memory; **~ morte/**
vive (Ordinat) ROM/RAM.

mémorable /memɔʀabl/ *a*
memorable.

menace /mənas/ *nf* threat.
menacer [10] *vt* threaten (**de**
faire to do).

ménage /menaʒ/ *nm* (couple)
couple; (travail) housework; (famille)
household; **se mettre en ~** set up
house.

ménagement /menaʒmɑ̃/ *nm*
avec ~s gently; **sans ~s** (*dire*)
bluntly; (*jeter, pousser*) roughly.

ménager¹, -ère /menaʒe, -ɛʀ/ *a*
household, domestic; **travaux ~s**
housework.

ménager² /menaʒe/ [40] *vt* be
gentle with, handle carefully;
(utiliser) be careful with; (organiser)
prepare (carefully); **ne pas ~ ses**
efforts spare no effort.

ménagère /menaʒɛʀ/ *nf*
housewife.

ménagerie /menaʒʀi/ *nf*
menagerie.

mendiant, ~e /mɑ̃djɑ̃, -t/ *nm, f*
beggar.

mendier /mɑ̃dje/ [45] *vt* beg for.
● *vi* beg.

mener /məne/ [6] *vt* lead;
(*entreprise, pays*) run; (*étude,*
enquête) carry out; (*politique*)
pursue; **~ à** (accompagner à) take
to; (faire aboutir) lead to; **~ à bien**
see through. ● *vi* lead.

méningite /menɛ̃ʒit/ *nf*
meningitis.

menotte /mənɔt/ *nf* 🔲 hand; **~s**
handcuffs.

mensonge /mɑ̃sɔ̃ʒ/ *nm* lie; (action)
lying. **mensonger, -ère** *a* untrue,
false.

mensualité /mɑ̃sɥalite/ *nf*
monthly payment.

mensuel, ~le /mɑ̃sɥɛl/ *a*
monthly. ● *nm* monthly
(magazine). **mensuellement** *adv*
monthly.

mensurations /mɑ̃syʀasjɔ̃/ *nfpl*
measurements.

mental, ~e (*mpl* -**aux**) /mɑ̃tal,
-o/ *a* mental; **malade ~** mentally
ill person; **handicapé ~** mentally
handicapped person.

mentalité /mɑ̃talite/ *nf*
mentality.

menteur, -euse /mɑ̃tœʀ, -øz/
nm, f liar. ● *a* untruthful.

menthe /mɑ̃t/ *nf* mint.

mention /mɑ̃sjɔ̃/ *nf* mention;
(annotation) note; (Scol) grade; **rayer**
la ~ inutile delete as appropriate.
mentionner [1] *vt* mention.

mentir /mɑ̃tiʀ/ [46] *vi* lie.

menton /mɑ̃tɔ̃/ *nm* chin.

menu, ~e /məny/ *a* (petit) tiny;
(fin) fine; (insignifiant) minor. ● *adv*
(*couper*) fine. ● *nm* (carte) menu; ~
(repas) meal; (Ordinat) menu; **~**
déroulant pull-down menu.

menuiserie /mənɥizʀi/ *nf*
carpentry, joinery. **menuisier** *nm*
carpenter, joiner.

méprendre (se) /(sə)mepʀɑ̃dʀ/

[50] *vpr* **se ~ sur** be mistaken about.

mépris /mepʀi/ *nm* contempt, scorn (**de** for); **au ~ de** regardless of.

méprisable /mepʀizabl/ *a* contemptible, despicable.

méprise /mepʀiz/ *nf* mistake.

méprisant, ~e /mepʀizɑ̃, -t/ *a* scornful. **mépriser** [1] *vt* scorn, despise.

mer /mɛʀ/ *nf* sea; (marée) tide; **en pleine ~** out at sea.

mercenaire /mɛʀsənɛʀ/ *nm & a* mercenary.

mercerie /mɛʀs(ə)ʀi/ *nf* haberdashery; (US) notions store. **mercier, -ière** *nm, f* haberdasher; (US) notions seller.

merci /mɛʀsi/ *interj* thank you, thanks (**de, pour** for); **~ beaucoup, ~ bien** thank you very much. ● *nm* thank you. ● *nf* mercy.

mercredi /mɛʀkʀədi/ *nm* Wednesday; **~ des Cendres** Ash Wednesday.

merde /mɛʀd/ *nf* 🆇 shit 🆇.

mère /mɛʀ/ *nf* mother; **~ de famille** mother.

méridional, ~e (*mpl* **-aux**) /meʀidjɔnal, o/ *a* southern. ● *nm, f* Southerner.

mérite /meʀit/ *nm* merit; **avoir du ~ à faire** deserve credit for doing.

mériter /meʀite/ [1] *vt* deserve; **~ d'être lu** be worth reading.

méritoire /meʀitwaʀ/ *a* commendable.

merlan /mɛʀlɑ̃/ *nm* whiting.

merle /mɛʀl/ *nm* blackbird.

merveille /mɛʀvɛj/ *nf* wonder, marvel; **à ~** wonderfully; **faire des ~s** work wonders.

merveilleux, -euse /mɛʀvɛjø, -z/ *a* wonderful, marvellous.

mes /me/ ⇒MON.

mésange /mezɑ̃ʒ/ *nf* tit(mouse).

mésaventure /mezavɑ̃tyʀ/ *nf* misadventure; **par ~** by some misfortune.

mesdames /medam/ ⇒MADAME.

mesdemoiselles /medmwazɛl/ ⇒MADEMOISELLE.

mésentente /mezɑ̃tɑ̃t/ *nf* disagreement.

mesquin, ~e /mɛskɛ̃, -in/ *a* mean-minded, petty; (chiche) mean. **mesquinerie** *nf* meanness.

message /mesaʒ/ *nm* message; **un ~ électronique** an e-mail; **~ texte** text message.

messager, -ère /mesaze, -ɛʀ/ *nm, f* messenger. ● *nm* **~ de poche** pager.

messagerie /mesaʒʀi/ *nf* (transports) freight forwarding; (télécommunications) messaging; **~ électronique** electronic mail; **~ vocale** voice mail.

messe /mɛs/ *nf* (Relig) mass.

messieurs /mesjø/ ⇒MONSIEUR.

M

mesure /məzyʀ/ *nf* measurement; (quantité, unité) measure; (disposition) measure, step; (cadence) time; **en ~** in time; (modération) moderation; **à ~ que** as; **dans la ~ où** in so far as; **dans une certaine ~** to some extent; **en ~ de** in a position to; **sans ~** to excess; (fait) **sur ~** made-to-measure.

mesuré, ~e /məzyʀe/ *a* measured; (attitude) moderate.

mesurer /məzyʀe/ [1] *vt* measure; (juger) assess; (*argent, temps*) ration. ● *vi* **~ 15 mètres de long** be 15 metres long. □ **se ~ avec** *vpr* pit oneself against.

met /mɛ/ ⇒METTRE [42].

métal (*pl* **-aux**) /metal, -o/ *nm* metal. **métallique** *a* (objet) metal; (éclat) metallic.

métallurgie /metalyʀʒi/ *nf* (industrie) metalworking industry.

métamorphoser /metamɔʀfoze/

[1] *vt* transform. □ **se ~** *vpr* be transformed; **se ~ en** metamorphose into.

métaphore /metafɔʀ/ *nf* metaphor.

météo /meteo/ *nf* (bulletin) weather forecast.

météore /meteɔʀ/ *nm* meteor.

météorologie /meteɔʀɔlɔʒi/ *nf* meteorology.

météorologique /meteɔʀɔlɔʒik/ *a* meteorological; **conditions ~s** weather conditions.

méthode /metɔd/ *nf* method; (ouvrage) course, manual.

méthodique *a* methodical.

méticuleux, -euse /metikylø, -z/ *a* meticulous.

métier /metje/ *nm* job; (manuel) trade; (intellectuel) profession; (expérience) experience, skill; **~ (à tisser)** loom; **remettre qch sur le ~** rework sth.

métis, ~se /metis/ *a* mixed race. ● *nm, f* person of mixed race.

métrage /metʀaʒ/ *nm* length; **court ~** short (film); **long ~** feature-length film.

mètre /mɛtʀ/ *nm* metre; (règle) rule; **~ ruban** tape-measure.

métreur, -euse /metʀœʀ, -øz/ *nm, f* quantity surveyor.

métrique /metʀik/ *a* metric.

métro /metʀo/ *nm* underground; (US) subway.

métropole /metʀɔpɔl/ *nf* metropolis; (pays) mother country.

métropolitain, ~e *a* metropolitan.

mets /mɛ/ *nm* dish. ● ⇒METTRE [42].

mettable /mɛtabl/ *a* wearable.

metteur /mɛtœʀ/ *nm* **~ en scène** director.

mettre /mɛtʀ/ [42] *vt* put; (radio, chauffage) put *ou* switch on; (réveil) set; (installer) put in; (revêtir) put on; (porter habituellement)

(vêtement, lunettes) wear; (prendre) take; (investir, dépenser) put; (écrire) write, say; **elle a mis deux heures** it took her two hours; **~ la table** lay the table; **~ en question** question; **~ en valeur** highlight; (terrain) develop; **mettons que** let's suppose that. ● *vi* **~ bas** (animal) give birth. □ **se ~** *vpr* (vêtement, maquillage) put on; (se placer) (objet) go; (personne) (debout) stand; (assis) sit; (couché) lie; **se ~ en short** put shorts on; **se ~ debout** stand up; **se ~ au lit** go to bed; **se ~ à table** sit down at table; **se ~ en ligne** line up; **se ~ du sable dans les yeux** get sand in one's eyes; **se ~ au chinois/tennis** take up Chinese/tennis; **se ~ au travail** set to work; **se ~ à faire** start to do.

meuble /mœbl/ *nm* piece of furniture; **~s** furniture.

meublé /møble/ *nm* furnished flat.

meubler /møble/ [1] *vt* furnish; (fig) fill. □ **se ~** *vpr* buy furniture.

meugler /møgle/ [1] *vi* moo.

meule /møl/ *nf* millstone; **~ de foin** haystack.

meunier, -ière /mønje, -jɛʀ/ *nm, f* miller.

meurs, meurt /mœʀ/ ⇒MOURIR [43].

meurtre /mœʀtʀ/ *nm* murder.

meurtrier, -ière /mœʀtʀije, -jɛʀ/ *a* deadly. ● *nm, f* murderer, murderess.

meurtrir /mœʀtʀiʀ/ [2] *vt* bruise.

meute /møt/ *nf* pack of hounds.

Mexique /mɛksik/ *nm* Mexico.

mi- /mi/ *préf* mid-, half-; **à mi-chemin** half-way; **à mi-pente** half-way up the hill; **à la mi-juin** in mid-June.

miauler /mjole/ [1] *vi* miaow.

micro /mikʀo/ *nm* microphone, mike; (Ordinat) micro.

microbe /mikʀɔb/ *nm* germ.

microfilm /mikʀofilm/ *nm* microfilm.

micro-onde /mikʀɔɔ̃d/ *nf* microwave; **un four à ∼s** microwave (oven). **micro-ondes** *nm inv* microwave (oven).

micro-ordinateur (*pl* ∼s) /mikʀɔɔʀdinatœʀ/ *nm* personal computer.

microphone /mikʀofɔn/ *nm* microphone.

microprocesseur /mikʀopʀɔsɛsœʀ/ *nm* microprocessor.

microscope /mikʀoskɔp/ *nm* microscope.

midi /midi/ *nm* twelve o'clock, midday, noon; (déjeuner) lunch-time; (sud) south. **Midi** *nm* **le M∼** the South of France.

mie /mi/ *nf* soft part (of the loaf); **un pain de ∼** a sandwich loaf.

miel /mjɛl/ *nm* honey.

mielleux, -euse /mjɛlø, -z/ *a* unctuous.

mien, ∼ne /mjɛ̃, -ɛn/ *pron* **le ∼, la ∼ne, les ∼(ne)s** mine.

miette /mjɛt/ *nf* crumb; (fig) scrap; **en ∼s** in pieces.

mieux /mjø/ *a inv* better (**que** than); **le** *ou* **la** *ou* **les ∼** (the) best. ●*nm* best; (progrès) improvement; **faire de son ∼** do one's best; **le ∼ serait de** the best thing would be to. ●*adv* better; **le** *ou* **la** *ou* **les ∼** (de deux) the better; (de plusieurs) the best; **elle va ∼** she is better; **j'aime ∼ rester** I'd rather stay; **il vaudrait ∼ partir** it would be best to leave; **tu ferais ∼ de faire** you would be best to do.

mièvre /mjɛvʀ/ *a* insipid.

mignon, ∼ne /miɲɔ̃, -ɔn/ *a* cute; (gentil) kind.

migraine /migʀɛn/ *nf* headache; (plus fort) migraine.

migration /migʀasjɔ̃/ *nf* migration.

mijoter /miʒɔte/ [1] *vt/i* simmer; (tramer Ⓘ) cook up.

mil /mil/ *nm* a thousand.

milice /milis/ *nf* militia.

milieu (*pl* ∼x) /miljø/ *nm* middle; (environnement) environment; (appartenance sociale) background; (groupe) circle; (voie) middle way; (criminel) underworld; **au ∼ de** in the middle of; **en plein** *ou* **au beau ∼ de** right in the middle (of).

militaire /militɛʀ/ *a* military. ●*nm* soldier, serviceman.

militant, ∼e /militã, -t/ *nm, f* militant.

militer /milite/ [1] *vi* be a militant; **∼ pour** militate in favour of.

mille¹ /mil/ *a & nm inv* a thousand; **deux ∼** two thousand; **mettre dans le ∼** (fig) hit the nail on the head.

mille² /mil/ *nm* **∼ (marin)** (nautical) mile.

millénaire /milenɛʀ/ *nm* millennium. ●*a* a thousand years old.

mille-pattes /milpat/ *nm inv* centipede.

millésime /milezim/ *nm* date; (de vin) vintage.

millet /mijɛ/ *nm* millet.

milliard /miljaʀ/ *nm* thousand million, billion. **milliardaire** *nmf* multimillionaire.

millième /miljɛm/ *a & nmf* thousandth.

millier /milje/ *nm* thousand; **un ∼ (de)** about a thousand.

millimètre /milimɛtʀ/ *nm* millimetre.

million /miljɔ̃/ *nm* million; **deux ∼s (de)** two million. **millionnaire** *nmf* millionaire.

mime /mim/ *nmf* mime-artist.

M

● *nm* (art) mime. **mimer** [1] *vt*
mime; (imiter) mimic.

mimique /mimik/ *nf* expressions
and gestures.

minable /minabl/ *a* 🄐 (logement)
shabby; (médiocre) pathetic,
crummy.

minauder /minode/ [1] *vi*
simper.

mince /mɛ̃s/ *a* thin; (svelte) slim;
(faible) (espoir, majorité) slim.
● *interj* 🄐 blast 🄐, darn it 🄐.
minceur *nf* thinness; slimness.

mincir /mɛ̃siʀ/ [2] *vi* get slimmer;
ça te mincit it makes you look
slimmer.

mine /min/ *nf* expression; (allure)
appearance; **avoir bonne ~** look
well; **faire ~ de** make as if to;
(exploitation, explosif) mine; (de crayon)
lead; **~ de charbon** coal-mine.

miner /mine/ [1] *vt* (saper)
undermine; (garnir d'explosifs) mine.

minerai /minʀɛ/ *nm* ore.

minéral, **~e** (mpl **-aux**)
/mineʀal,o/ *a* mineral. ● *nm* (pl
-aux) mineral.

minéralogique /mineʀalɔʒik/ *a*
plaque ~ numberplate; (US)
license plate.

minet, **~te** /minɛ, -t/ *nm, f* (chat
🄐) pussy(cat).

mineur, **~e** /minœʀ/ *a* minor;
(Jur) under age. ● *nm, f* (Jur)
minor. ● *nm* (ouvrier) miner.

miniature /minjatyʀ/ *nf & a*
miniature.

minier, **-ière** /minje, -jɛʀ/ *a*
mining.

minimal, **~e** (mpl **-aux**)
/minimal,o/ *a* minimal,
minimum.

minime /minim/ *a* minimal,
minor. ● *nmf* (Sport) junior.

minimum /minimɔm/ *a*
minimum. ● *nm* minimum; **au ~**
(pour le moins) at the very least; **en
faire un ~** do as little as possible.

ministère /ministɛʀ/ *nm*
ministry; (gouvernement)
government; **~ public** public
prosecutor's office. **ministériel**,
~le *a* ministerial, government.

ministre /ministʀ/ *nm* minister;
(au Royaume-Uni) Secretary of State;
(US) Secretary.

Minitel® /minitɛl/ *nm* Minitel
(telephone videotext system).

minorer /minɔʀe/ [1] *vt* reduce.

minoritaire /minɔʀitɛʀ/ *a*
minority; **être ~** be in the
minority. **minorité** *nf* minority.

minuit /minɥi/ *nm* midnight.

minuscule /minyskyl/ *a* minute.
● *nf* (lettre) **~** lower case.

minute /minyt/ *nf* minute; **'talons
~'** 'heels repaired while you
wait'.

minuterie /minytʀi/ *nf* time-
switch.

minutie /minysi/ *nf*
meticulousness.

minutieux, **-ieuse** /minysjø, -z/ *a*
meticulous.

mioche /mjɔʃ/ *nm, f* 🄐 kid.

mirabelle /miʀabɛl/ *nf*
(mirabelle) plum.

miracle /miʀakl/ *nm* miracle; **par
~** miraculously.

miraculeux, **-euse** /miʀakylø,
-z/ *a* miraculous.

mirage /miʀaʒ/ *nm* mirage.

mire /miʀ/ *nf* (fig) centre of
attraction; (TV) test card.

mirobolant, **~e** /miʀɔbɔlɑ̃, -t/
🄐 marvellous.

miroir /miʀwaʀ/ *nm* mirror.

miroiter /miʀwate/ [1] *vi*
shimmer, sparkle.

mis, **~e** /mi, miz/ *a* **bien ~** well-
dressed. ● ⇒METTRE [42].

mise /miz/ *nf* (argent) stake; (tenue)
attire; **à feu** blast-off; **~ au
point** adjustment; (fig)
clarification; **~ de fonds** capital

outlay; ~ **en garde** warning; ~ **en plis** set; ~ **en scène** direction.

miser /mize/ [1] vt (argent) bet, stake (**sur** on). ● vi ~ **sur** (parier) place a bet on; (compter sur) bank on.

misérable /mizeʀabl/ a miserable, wretched; (indigent) destitute; (minable) seedy, squalid.

misère /mizɛʀ/ nf destitution; (malheur) trouble, woe. **miséreux, -euse** nm, f destitute person.

miséricorde /mizeʀikɔʀd/ nf mercy.

missel /misɛl/ nm missal.

missile /misil/ nm missile.

mission /misjɔ̃/ nm mission. **missionnaire** nmf missionary.

missive /misiv/ nf missive.

mistral /mistʀal/ nm (vent) mistral.

mitaine /mitɛn/ nf fingerless mitt.

mite /mit/ nf (clothes-)moth.

mi-temps /mitɑ̃/ nf inv (arrêt) half-time; (période) half. ● nm inv part-time work; **à** ~ part-time.

miteux, -euse /mitø, -z/ a shabby.

mitigé, ~**e** /mitiʒe/ a (modéré) lukewarm; (succès) qualified.

mitonner /mitɔne/ [1] vt cook slowly with care; (fig) cook up.

mitoyen, ~**ne** /mitwajɛ̃, -ɛn/ a **mur** ~ party wall.

mitrailler /mitʀaje/ [1] vt machine-gun; (fig) bombard.

mitraillette /mitʀajɛt/ nf submachine gun. **mitrailleuse** nf machine gun.

mi-voix: à ~ /amivwa/ loc in a low voice.

mixeur /miksœʀ/ nm liquidizer, blender; (batteur) mixer.

mixte /mikst/ a mixed; (commission) joint; (école) coeducational; (peau) combination.

mobile /mɔbil/ a mobile; (pièce) moving; (feuillet) loose. ● nm (art) mobile; (raison) motive.

mobilier /mɔbilje/ nm furniture.

mobilisation /mɔbilizasjɔ̃/ nf mobilization. **mobiliser** [1] vt mobilize.

mobilité /mɔbilite/ nf mobility.

mobylette® /mɔbilɛt/ nf moped.

moche /mɔʃ/ a ⚆ (laid) ugly; (mauvais) lousy.

modalités /mɔdalite/ nfpl (conditions) terms; (façon de fonctionner) practical details.

mode /mɔd/ nf fashion; (coutume) custom; **à la** ~ fashionable. ● nm method, mode; (genre) way; ~ **d'emploi** directions (for use).

modèle /mɔdɛl/ a model. ● nm model; (exemple) example; (Comm) (type) model; (taille) size; (style) style; ~ **familial** family size; ~ **réduit** (small-scale) model.

modeler /mɔdle/ [6] vt model (**sur** on). □ **se** ~ **sur** vpr model oneself on.

modem /mɔdɛm/ nm modem.

modérateur, -trice /mɔdeʀatœʀ, -tʀis/ a moderating. **modération** nf moderation.

modéré, ~**e** /mɔdeʀe/ a & nm. f moderate.

modérer /mɔdeʀe/ [14] vt (propos) moderate; (désirs, sentiments) curb. □ **se** ~ vpr restrain oneself.

moderne /mɔdɛʀn/ a modern. **moderniser** [1] vt modernize.

modeste /mɔdɛst/ a modest. **modestie** nf modesty.

modification /mɔdifikasjɔ̃/ nf modification.

modifier /mɔdifje/ [45] vt change, modify. □ **se** ~ vpr change, alter.

modique /mɔdik/ a modest.

modiste /mɔdist/ nf milliner.

M

moduler /mɔdyle/ [1] vt
modulate; (adapter) adjust.

moelle /mwal/ nf marrow; ~
épinière spinal cord; ~ **osseuse**
bone marrow.

moelleux, -euse /mwalø, -z/ a
soft; (onctueux) smooth.

mœurs /mœr(s)/ nfpl (morale)
morals; (usages) customs; (manières)
habits, ways.

moi /mwa/ pron me; (indirect) (to)
me; (sujet) I. ● nm self.

moignon /mwaɲɔ̃/ nm stump.

moi-même /mwamɛm/ pron
myself.

moindre /mwɛ̃dR/ a (moins grand)
lesser; **le** ou **la** ~, **les** ~**s** the
slightest, the least.

moine /mwan/ nm monk.

moineau (pl ~**x**) /mwano/ nm
sparrow.

moins /mwɛ̃/ prép minus; (pour
dire l'heure) to; **une heure** ~ **dix** ten
to one. ● adv less (que than); **le**
ou **la** ou **les** ~ the least; **le** ~
grand/haut the smallest/lowest; ~
de (avec un nom non dénombrable) less
(que than); ~ **de dix francs** less
than ten francs; ~ **de livres** fewer
books; **au** ~, **du** ~ at least; **à** ~
que unless; **de** ~ less; **de** ~ **en** ~
less and less; **en** ~ less; (manquant)
missing.

mois /mwa/ nm month.

moisi, ~e /mwazi/ a mouldy.
● nm mould; **de** ~ (odeur) musty.

moisir [2] vi go mouldy.
moisissure nf mould.

moisson /mwasɔ̃/ nf harvest.

moissonner /mwasɔne/ [1] vt
harvest, reap. **moissonneur,
-euse** nm, f harvester.

moite /mwat/ a sticky, clammy.

moitié /mwatje/ nf half; (milieu)
halfway mark; **s'arrêter à la** ~
stop halfway through; **à** ~ **vide**
half empty; **à** ~ **prix** (at) half-
price; **la** ~ **de** half (of). **moitié-
moitié** adv half-and-half.

mol /mɔl/ ⇒MOU.

molaire /mɔlɛR/ nf molar.

molécule /mɔlekyl/ nf molecule.

molester /mɔlɛste/ [1] vt
manhandle, rough up.

molle /mɔl/ ⇒MOU.

mollement /mɔlmɑ̃/ adv softly;
(faiblement) feebly. **mollesse** nf
softness; (faiblesse) feebleness;
(apathie) listlessness.

mollet /mɔlɛ/ nm (de jambe) calf.

mollir /mɔliR/ [2] vi soften; (céder)
yield.

môme /mom/ nmf 🄯 kid.

moment /mɔmɑ̃/ nm moment;
(période) time; (petit) ~ short
while; **au** ~ **où** when; **par** ~**s** now
and then; **du** ~ **où** ou **que** (pourvu
que) as long as, provided that;
(puisque) since; **en ce** ~ at the
moment.

momentané, ~e /mɔmɑ̃tane/ a
momentary. **momentanément**
adv momentarily; (en ce moment) at
present.

momie /mɔmi/ nf mummy.

mon, ma (**mon** before vowel or
mute h) (pl **mes**) /mɔ̃, ma, mɔ̃,
me/ a my.

Monaco /mɔnako/ npr Monaco.

monarchie /mɔnaRʃi/ nf
monarchy.

monarque /mɔnaRk/ nm
monarch.

monastère /mɔnastɛR/ nm
monastery.

monceau (pl ~**x**) /mɔ̃so/ nm
heap, pile.

mondain, ~e /mɔ̃dɛ̃, -ɛn/ a
society, social.

monde /mɔ̃d/ nm world; **du** ~ (a
lot of) people; (quelqu'un)
somebody; **le (grand)** ~ (high)
society; **se faire (tout) un** ~ **de qch**
make a great deal of fuss about

sth; **pas le moins du ～** not in the least.

mondial, **～s** *e* (*mpl* **-iaux**) /mɔ̃djal, -jo/ *a* world; (*influence*) worldwide. **mondialement** *adv* the world over. **mondialisation** /mɔ̃djalizasjɔ̃/ *nf* globalization.

monétaire /monetɛʀ/ *a* monetary.

moniteur, -trice /monitœʀ, -tʀis/ *nm, f* instructor; (de colonie de vacances) group leader; (US) (camp) counselor.

monnaie /monɛ/ *nf* currency; (pièce) coin; (appoint) change; **faire la ～ de** get change for; **faire de la ～ à qn** give sb change; **menue** *ou* **petite ～** small change.

monnayer /moneje/ [31] *vt* convert into cash.

monologue /monolog/ *nm* monologue.

monopole /monopol/ *nm* monopoly. **monopoliser** [1] *vt* monopolize.

monospace /monospas/ *nm* (Auto) people carrier.

monotone /monoton/ *a* monotonous. **monotonie** *nf* monotony.

Monseigneur (*pl* **Messeigneurs**) /mɔ̃sɛɲœʀ/ *nm* (à un duc, archevêque) Your Grace; (à un prince) Your Highness.

monsieur (*pl* **messieurs**) /məsjø, mesjø/ *nm* (à un inconnu) (dans une lettre) **M～** Dear Sir; **bonjour, ～** good morning; **mesdames et messieurs** ladies and gentlemen; (à un homme dont on connaît le nom) (dans une lettre) **Cher M～** Dear Mr X; **bonjour, ～** good morning Mr X; **M～ le curé** Father X; **oui M～ le ministre** yes Minister; (homme) man; (formule de respect) sir.

monstre /mɔ̃stʀ/ *nm* monster. ● *a* 🔲 colossal.

monstrueux, -euse /mɔ̃stʀyø, -z/

a monstrous. **monstruosité** *nf* monstrosity.

mont /mɔ̃/ *nm* mountain; **le ～ Everest** Mount Everest; **être toujours par ～s et par vaux** be always on the move.

montage /mɔ̃taʒ/ *nm* (assemblage) assembly; (au cinéma) editing.

montagne /mɔ̃taɲ/ *nf* mountain; (région) mountains; **～s russes** roller-coaster. **montagneux, -euse** *a* mountainous.

montant, ～e /mɔ̃tɑ̃, -t/ *a* rising; (col) high; (chemin) uphill. ● *nm* amount; (pièce de bois) upright.

mont-de-piété (*pl* **monts-de-piété**) /mɔ̃dpjete/ *nm* pawnshop.

monte-charge /mɔ̃tʃaʀʒ/ *nm inv* goods lift.

montée /mɔ̃te/ *nf* ascent, climb; (de prix) rise; (de coûts, risques) increase; (côte) hill.

monter /mɔ̃te/ [1] *vt* (aux. avoir) take up; (à l'étage) take upstairs; (escalier, rue, pente) go up; (assembler) assemble; (tente, échafaudage) put up; (col, manche) set in; (organiser) (pièce) stage; (société) set up; (attaque, garde) mount. ● *vi* (aux. être) *ou* come up; (à l'étage) go *ou* come upstairs; (avion) climb, (route) go uphill, climb; (augmenter) rise; (marée) come up; **～ sur** (trottoir, toit) get up on; (cheval, bicyclette) get on; **～ à l'échelle/l'arbre** climb the ladder/tree; **～ dans** (voiture) get in; (train, bus, avion) get on; **～ à bord** climb on board; **～ (à cheval)** ride; **～ à bicyclette/moto** ride a bike/motorbike.

monteur, -euse /mɔ̃tœʀ, -øz/ *nm, f* (Tech) fitter; (au cinéma) editor.

montre /mɔ̃tʀ/ *nf* watch; **faire ～ de** show.

montrer /mɔ̃tʀe/ [1] *vt* show (à to); **～ du doigt** point to. □ **se ～**

vpr show oneself; (être) be; (s'avérer) prove to be.

monture /mɔ̃tyʀ/ *nf* (cheval) mount; (de lunettes) frames (+ *pl*); (de bijou) setting.

monument /mɔnymɑ̃/ *nm* monument; ~ **aux morts** war memorial. **monumental** (*mpl* **-aux**) *a* monumental.

moquer (se) /(sə)mɔke/ [1] *vpr* **se** ~ **de** make fun of; **je m'en moque** Ⓘ I couldn't care less. **moquerie** *nf* mockery. **moqueur, -euse** *a* mocking.

moquette /mɔkɛt/ *nf* fitted carpet; (US) wall-to-wall carpeting.

moral, ~e (*mpl* **-aux**) /mɔʀal, -o/ *a* moral. ●*nm* (*pl* **-aux**) morale; **ne pas avoir le** ~ feel down; **avoir le** ~ be in good spirits; **ça m'a remonté le** ~ it gave me a boost. **morale** /mɔʀal/ *nf* moral code; (mœurs) morals; (de fable) moral; **faire la** ~ **à** lecture. **moralité** *nf* (de personne) morals (+ *pl*); (d'action, œuvre) morality; (de fable) moral.

moralisateur, -trice /mɔʀalizatœʀ, -tʀis/ *a* moralizing.

morbide /mɔʀbid/ *a* morbid.

morceau (*pl* **~x**) /mɔʀso/ *nm* piece, bit; (de sucre) lump; (de viande) cut; (passage) passage; **manger un** ~ Ⓘ have a bite to eat; **mettre en** ~**x** smash *ou* tear to bits.

morceler /mɔʀsəle/ [6] *vt* divide up.

mordant, ~e /mɔʀdɑ̃, -t/ *a* scathing; (froid) biting. ●*nm* vigour, energy.

mordiller /mɔʀdije/ [1] *vt* nibble at.

mordre /mɔʀdʀ/ [3] *vi* bite (**dans** into); ~ **sur** (ligne) go over; (territoire) encroach on; ~ **à l'hameçon** bite. ●*vt* bite.

mordu, ~e /mɔʀdy/ Ⓘ *nm, f* fan. ●*a* smitten; ~ **de** crazy about.

morfondre (se) /(sə)mɔʀfɔ̃dʀ/ [3] *vpr* wait anxiously; (languir) mope.

morgue /mɔʀg/ *nf* morgue, mortuary; (attitude) arrogance.

moribond, ~e /mɔʀibɔ̃, -d/ *a* dying.

morne /mɔʀn/ *a* dull.

morphine /mɔʀfin/ *nf* morphine.

mors /mɔʀ/ *nm* (de cheval) bit.

morse /mɔʀs/ *nm* (animal) walrus; (code) Morse code.

morsure /mɔʀsyʀ/ *nf* bite.

mort[1] /mɔʀ/ *nf* death.

mort[2], **~e** /mɔʀ, -t/ *a* dead; ~ **de fatigue** dead tired. ●*nm, f* dead man, dead woman; **les ~s** the dead.

mortalité /mɔʀtalite/ *nf* mortality; (**taux de**) ~ death rate.

mortel, ~le /mɔʀtɛl/ *a* mortal; (accident) fatal; (poison, silence) deadly. ● *nm, f* mortal. **mortellement** *adv* mortally.

mortifié, ~e /mɔʀtifje/ *a* mortified.

mort-né, ~e /mɔʀne/ *a* stillborn.

mortuaire /mɔʀtɥeʀ/ *a* (cérémonie) funeral.

morue /mɔʀy/ *nf* cod.

mosaïque /mɔzaik/ *nf* mosaic.

mosquée /mɔske/ *nf* mosque.

mot /mo/ *nm* word; (lettre, message) note; ~ **d'ordre** watchword; ~ **de passe** password; ~**s croisés** crossword (puzzle).

motard /mɔtaʀ/ *nm* biker; (policier) police motorcyclist.

moteur, -trice /mɔtœʀ, -tʀis/ *a* (Méd) motor; (force) driving; **à 4 roues motrices** 4-wheel drive. ●*nm* engine, motor; **barque à** ~ motor launch; ~ **de recherche** (Internet) search engine.

motif /mɔtif/ *nm* (raisons) grounds

(+ *pl*); (cause) reason; (Jur) motive; (dessin) pattern.

motion /mɔsjɔ̃/ *nf* motion.

motivation /mɔtivasjɔ̃/ *nf* motivation. **motiver** [1] *vt* motivate.

moto /mɔto/ *nf* motor cycle. **motocycliste** *nmf* motorcyclist.

motorisé, **~e** /mɔtɔʀize/ *a* motorized.

motrice /mɔtʀis/ ⇒MOTEUR.

motte /mɔt/ *nf* lump; (de beurre) slab; (de terre) clod; **~ de gazon** turf.

mou (**mol** *before vowel or mute h*), **molle** /mu, mɔl/ *a* soft; (*ventre*) flabby; (sans conviction) feeble; (apathique) sluggish, listless. ●*nm* slack; **avoir du ~** be slack.

mouchard, **~e** /muʃaʀ, -d/ *nm, f* informer; (Scol) sneak.

mouche /muʃ/ *nf* fly; (de cible) bull's eye.

moucher (se) /(sə)muʃe/ [1] *vpr* blow one's nose.

moucheron /muʃʀɔ̃/ *nm* midge.

moucheté, **~e** /muʃte/ *a* speckled.

mouchoir /muʃwaʀ/ *nm* handkerchief, hanky; **~ en papier** tissue.

moue /mu/ *nf* pout; **faire la ~** pout.

mouette /mwɛt/ *nf* (sea)gull.

moufle /mufl/ *nf* (gant) mitten.

mouillé, **~e** /muje/ *a* wet.

mouiller /muje/ [1] *vt* wet, make wet; **~ l'ancre** drop anchor. □ **se ~** *vpr* get (oneself) wet.

moulage /mulaʒ/ *nm* cast.

moule /mul/ *nf* (coquillage) mussel. ●*nm* mould; **~ à gâteau** cake tin; **~ à tarte** flan dish. **mouler** [1] *vt* mould; (*statue*) cast.

moulin /mulɛ̃/ *nm* mill; **~ à café** coffee grinder; **~ à poivre** pepper mill; **~ à vent** windmill.

moulinet /mulinɛ/ *nm* (de canne à pêche) reel; **faire des ~s avec qch** twirl sth around.

moulinette® /mulinɛt/ *nf* vegetable mill.

moulu, **~e** /muly/ *a* ground; (fatigué 🖩) worn out.

moulure /mulyʀ/ *nf* moulding.

mourant, **~e** /muʀɑ̃, -t/ *a* dying. ●*nm, f* dying person.

mourir /muʀiʀ/ [43] *vi* (*aux. être*) die; **~ d'envie de** be dying to; **~ de faim** be starving; **~ d'ennui** be dead bored.

mousquetaire /muskətɛʀ/ *nm* musketeer.

mousse /mus/ *nf* moss; (écume) froth, foam; (de savon) lather; (dessert) mousse; **~ à raser** shaving foam. ●*nm* ship's boy.

mousseline /muslin/ *nf* muslin; (de soie) chiffon.

mousser /muse/ [1] *vi* froth, foam; (*savon*) lather.

mousseux, **-euse** /musø, -z/ *a* frothy. ●*nm* sparkling wine.

mousson /musɔ̃/ *nf* monsoon.

moustache /mustaʃ/ *nf* moustache; **~s** (d'animal) whiskers.

moustique /mustik/ *nm* mosquito.

moutarde /mutaʀd/ *nf* mustard.

mouton /mutɔ̃/ *nm* sheep; (peau) sheepskin; (viande) mutton.

mouvant, **~e** /muvɑ̃, -t/ *a* changing; (*terrain*) shifting, unstable.

mouvement /muvmɑ̃/ *nm* movement; (agitation) bustle; (en gymnastique) exercise; (impulsion) impulse; (tendance) tend, tendency; **en ~** in motion.

mouvementé, **~e** /muvmɑ̃te/ *a* eventful.

moyen, **~ne** /mwajɛ̃, -ɛn/ *a* average; (médiocre) poor; **de taille moyenne** medium-sized. ●*nm* means, way; **~s** means; (dons)

M

ability; **au ~ de** by means of; **il n'y a pas ~ de** it is not possible to.
Moyen Âge *nm* Middle Ages (+ *pl*).

moyennant /mwajɛnɑ̃/ *prép* (pour) for; (grâce à) with.

moyenne /mwajɛn/ *nf* average; (Scol) pass-mark; **en ~** on average; **~ d'âge** average age.

moyennement *adv* moderately.

Moyen-Orient /mwajɛnɔrjɑ̃/ *nm* Middle East.

moyeu (*pl* **~x**) /mwajø/ *nm* hub.

mû, mue /my/ *a* driven (**par** by).

mucoviscidose /mykɔvisidoz/ *nf* cystic fibrosis.

mue /my/ *nf* moulting; (de voix) breaking of the voice.

muer /mɥe/ [1] *vi* moult; (voix) break. □ **se ~ en** *vpr* change into.

muet, ~te /mɥɛ, -t/ *a* (Méd) dumb; (fig) speechless (**de** with); (silencieux) silent. ● *nm, f* mute.

mufle /myfl/ *nm* nose, muzzle; (personne 🆒) boor, lout.

mugir /myʒir/ [2] *vi* (vache) moo; (bœuf) bellow; (fig) howl.

muguet /mygɛ/ *nm* lily of the valley.

mule /myl/ *nf* (female) mule; (pantoufle) mule.

mulet /mylɛ/ *nm* (male) mule.

multicolore /myltikɔlɔr/ *a* multicoloured.

multimédia /myltimedja/ *a & nm* multimedia.

multinational, ~e (*mpl* **-aux**) /myltinasjɔnal, -o/ *a* multinational. **multinationale** *nf* multinational (company).

multiple /myltipl/ *nm* multiple. ● *a* numerous, many; (naissances) multiple.

multiplication /myltiplikasjɔ̃/ *nf* multiplication.

multiplicité /myltiplisite/ *nf* multiplicity.

multiplier /myltiplije/ [45] *vt* multiply; (risques) increase. □ **se ~** *vpr* multiply; (accidents) be on the increase; (difficultés) increase.

multitude /myltityd/ *nf* multitude, mass.

municipal, ~e (*mpl* **-aux**) /mynisipal, -o/ *a* municipal; **conseil ~** town council.

municipalité *nf* (ville) municipality; (conseil) town council.

munir /mynir/ [2] *vt* **~ de** provide with. □ **se ~ de** *vpr* (apporter) bring; (emporter) take.

munitions /mynisjɔ̃/ *nfpl* ammunition.

mur /myr/ *nm* wall; **~ du son** sound barrier.

mûr, ~e /myr/ *a* ripe; (personne) mature.

muraille /myrɑj/ *nf* (high) wall.

mural, ~e (*mpl* **-aux**) /myral, -o/ *a* wall; **peinture ~e** mural.

mûre /myr/ *nf* blackberry.

mûrir /myrir/ [2] *vi* ripen; (abcès) come to a head; (personne, projet) mature. ● *vt* (fruit) ripen; (personne) mature.

murmure /myrmyr/ *nm* murmur.

muscade /myskad/ *nf* **noix ~** nutmeg.

muscle /myskl/ *nm* muscle. **musclé, ~e** *a* muscular.

musculaire *a* muscular.

musculation /myskylasjɔ̃/ *nf* bodybuilding.

musculature /myskylatyr/ *nf* muscles (+ *pl*).

museau (*pl* **~x**) /myzo/ *nm* muzzle; (de porc) snout.

musée /myze/ *nm* museum; (de peinture) art gallery.

muselière /myzəljɛr/ *nf* muzzle.

musette /myzɛt/ *nf* haversack.

muséum /myzeɔm/ *nm* natural history museum.

musical, ∼e (*mpl* **-aux**) /myzikal, -o/ *a* musical.

musicien, ∼ne /myzisjɛ̃, -ɛn/ *a* musical. ●*nm, f* musician.

musique /myzik/ *nf* music; (orchestre) band.

must /mœst/ *nm* 🇬🇧 must.

musulman, ∼e /myzylmɑ̃, -an/ *a* & *nm,f* Muslim.

mutation /mytasjɔ̃/ *nf* change; (biologique) mutation; (d'un employé) transfer.

muter /myte/ [1] *vt* transfer. ●*vi* mutate.

mutilation /mytilasjɔ̃/ *nf* mutilation. **mutiler** [1] *vt* mutilate. **mutilé**, ∼e *nm, f* disabled person.

mutin, ∼e /mytɛ̃, -in/ *a* mischievous. ●*nm* mutineer; (prisonnier) rioter.

mutinerie /mytinʀi/ *nf* mutiny; (de prisonniers) riot.

mutisme /mytism/ *nm* silence.

mutuel, ∼le /mytɥɛl/ *a* mutual. **mutuelle** *nf* mutual insurance company. **mutuellement** *adv* mutually; (l'un l'autre) each other.

myope /mjɔp/ *a* short-sighted. **myopie** *nf* short-sightedness.

myosotis /mjozotis/ *nm* forget-me-not.

myrtille /miʀtij/ *nf* bilberry, blueberry.

mystère /mistɛʀ/ *nm* mystery.

mystérieux, **-ieuse** /misteʀjø, -z/ *a* mysterious.

mystification /mistifikasjɔ̃/ *nf* hoax.

mysticisme /mistisism/ *nm* mysticism.

mystique /mistik/ *a* mystic(al). ●*nmf* mystic. ●*nf* mystique.

mythe /mit/ *nm* myth. **mythique** *a* mythical.

mythologie /mitɔlɔʒi/ *nf* mythology.

n' /n/ ⇒NE.

nacre /nakʀ/ *nf* mother-of-pearl.

nage /naʒ/ *nf* swimming; (manière) stroke; **traverser à la** ∼ swim across; **en** ∼ sweating.

nageoire /naʒwaʀ/ *nf* fin; (de mammifère) flipper.

nager /naʒe/ [40] *vt/i* swim. **nageur**, **-euse** *nm, f* swimmer.

naguère /nagɛʀ/ *adv* (autrefois) formerly.

naïf, **-ive** /naif, -v/ *a* naïve.

nain, ∼e /nɛ̃, nɛn/ *nm,f* & *a* dwarf.

naissance /nɛsɑ̃s/ *nf* birth; **donner** ∼ **à** give birth to; (fig) give rise to.

naître /nɛtʀ/ [44] *vi* be born; (résulter) arise (**de** from); **faire** ∼ (susciter) give rise to.

naïveté /naivte/ *nf* naïvety.

nappe /nap/ *nf* tablecloth; (de pétrole, gaz) layer; ∼ **phréatique** ground water.

napperon /napʀɔ̃/ *nm* (cloth) tablemat.

narco-dollars /naʀkodɔlaʀ/ *nmpl* drug money.

narcotique /naʀkɔtik/ *a* & *nm* narcotic. **narco(-)trafiquant**, ∼e (*pl* ∼s) *nm, f* drug trafficker.

narguer /naʀge/ [1] *vt* taunt; (autorité) flout.

narine /naʀin/ *nf* nostril.

nasal, ∼e (*mpl* **-aux**) /nazal, -o/ *a* nasal.

naseau (*pl* ∼x) /nazo/ *nm* nostril.

natal, ~e (*mpl* ~s) /natal/ *a* native.

natalité /natalite/ *nf* birth rate.

natation /natasjɔ̃/ *nf* swimming.

natif, -ive /natif, -v/ *a* native.

nation /nasjɔ̃/ *nf* nation.

national, ~e (*mpl* -aux) /nasjɔnal, -o/ *a* national. **nationale** *nf* A road; (US) highway. **nationaliser** [1] *vt* nationalize.

nationalité /nasjɔnalite/ *nf* nationality.

natte /nat/ *nf* (de cheveux) plait; (US) braid; (tapis de paille) mat.

nature /natyʀ/ *nf* nature; ~ **morte** still life; **de** ~ **à** likely to; **payer en** ~ pay in kind. ●*a inv* plain; (*yaourt*) natural; (*thé*) black.

naturel, ~le /natyʀɛl/ *a* natural. ●*nm* nature; (simplicité) naturalness; (Culin) au ~ plain; (*thon*) in brine. **naturellement** *adv* naturally; (bien sûr) of course.

naufrage /nofraʒ/ *nm* shipwreck; **faire** ~ be shipwrecked; (*bateau*) be wrecked.

nauséabond, ~e /nozeabɔ̃, -d/ *a* nauseating.

nausée /noze/ *nf* nausea.

nautique /notik/ *a* nautical; **sports** ~s water sports.

naval, ~e (*mpl* ~s) /naval/ *a* naval; **chantier** ~ shipyard.

navet /navɛ/ *nm* turnip; (film: péj) flop; (US) turkey.

navette /navɛt/ *nf* shuttle (service); **faire la** ~ shuttle back and forth.

navigateur, -trice /navigatœr, -tris/ *nm, f* sailor; (qui guide) navigator; (Internet) browser. **navigation** *nf* navigation; (trafic) shipping; (Internet) browsing.

naviguer /navige/ [1] *vi* sail; (piloter) navigate; (Internet) browse; ~ **dans l'Internet** surf the Internet.

navire /navir/ *nm* ship.

navré, ~e /navre/ *a* sorry (**de** to).

....

ne, n' /nə, n/

n' before vowel or mute h.

●*adverbe*

····▸ **je n'ai que 10 euros** I've only got 10 euros.

····▸ **tu n'avais qu'à le dire!** you only had to say so!

····▸ **je crains qu'il** ~ **parte** I am afraid he will leave.

┃ Pour les expressions
┃ comme **ne... guère, ne...**
┃ **jamais, ne... pas, ne... plus,**
┃ etc. ⇨**guère, jamais, pas,**
┃ **plus,** etc.
....

né, ~e /ne/ *a* born; ~e **Martin** née Martin; (dans composés) **dernier-**~ last-born. ●⇨NAÎTRE [44].

néanmoins /neɑ̃mwɛ̃/ *adv* nevertheless.

néant /neɑ̃/ *nm* nothingness; **réduire à** ~ (effet, efforts) negate, nullify; (espoir) dash; '**revenus:** ~' 'income: nil'.

nécessaire /neseser/ *a* necessary. ●*nm* (sac) bag; (trousse) kit; **le** ~ (l'indispensable) the necessities *ou* essentials; **faire le** ~ do what is necessary.

nécessité /nesesite/ *nf* necessity; **de première** ~ vital.

nécessiter /nesesite/ [1] *vt* necessitate.

néerlandais, ~e /neɛrlɑ̃dɛ, -z/ *a* Dutch. ●*nm* (Ling) Dutch. **N**~, ~e *nm, f* Dutchman, Dutchwoman.

néfaste /nefast/ *a* harmful (**à** to).

négatif, -ive /negatif, -v/ *a & nm* negative.

négligé, ~e /negliʒe/ *a* (travail)

careless; *(tenue)* scruffy. ●*nm*
(tenue) negligee.
négligent, ~e /negliʒɑ̃, -t/ *a*
careless, negligent.
négliger /negliʒe/ [40] *vt* neglect;
(ne pas tenir compte de) ignore,
disregard; ~ **de faire** fail to do.
□ **se** ~ *vpr* neglect oneself.
négoce /negɔs/ *nm* business,
trade. **négociant**, ~e *nm, f*
merchant.
négociation /negɔsjasjɔ̃/ *nf*
negotiation. **négocier** [45] *vt/i*
negotiate.
nègre /nɛgʀ/ *a (musique, art)*
Negro. ●*nm (écrivain)* ghost
writer.
neige /nɛʒ/ *nf* snow. **neiger** [40]
vi snow.
nénuphar /nenyfaʀ/ *nm* waterlily.
nerf /nɛʀ/ *nm* nerve; *(vigueur)*
stamina; **être sur les** ~**s** be on
edge.
nerveux, **-euse** /nɛʀvø, -z/ *a*
nervous; *(irritable)* nervy; *(centre,
cellule)* nerve; *(voiture)*
responsive. **nervosité** *nf*
nervousness; *(irritabilité)*
touchiness.
net, ~**te** /nɛt/ *a (clair, distinct)* clear;
(propre) clean; *(notable)* marked;
(soigné) neat; *(prix, poids)* net. ●
N~ *nm* (Ordinat) net. ●*adv*
(s'arrêter) dead; *(refuser)* flatly;
(parler) plainly; *(se casser)*
cleanly; *(tuer)* outright.
nettement *adv (expliquer)*
clearly; *(augmenter, se détériorer)*
markedly; *(indiscutablement)*
distinctly, decidedly. **netteté** *nf*
clearness.
netéconomie /nɛtekɔnɔmi/ *nf*
e-economy.
nétiquette /netikɛt/ *nf*
netiquette.
nettoyage /nɛtwajaʒ/ *nm*
cleaning; ~ **à sec** dry-cleaning;
produit de ~ cleaner; ~ **ethnique**
ethnic cleansing.

nettoyer /nɛtwaje/ [31] *vt* clean.
neuf[1] /nœf/ (/nœv/ *before vowels
and mute h*) *a inv* & *nm* nine.
neuf[2], **-euve** /nœf, -v/ *a* new; **tout**
~ brand new. ●*nm* new; **remettre
à** ~ brighten up; **du** ~ a new
development; **quoi de** ~? what's
new?
neutre /nøtʀ/ *a* neutral; (Gram)
neuter. ●*nm* (Gram) neuter.
neuve /nœv/ ⇒NEUF[2].
neuvième /nœvjɛm/ *a* & *nm, f*
ninth.
neveu (*pl* ~**x**) /nəvø/ *nm*
nephew.
névrose /nevʀoz/ *nf* neurosis.
névrosé, ~**e** *a* & *nm, f* neurotic.
nez /ne/ *nm* nose; ~ **à** ~ face to
face; ~ **retroussé** turned-up nose.
ni /ni/ *conj* neither, nor; ~ **grand**
~ **petit** neither big nor small; ~
l'un ~ **l'autre ne fument** neither
(one nor the other) smokes; **sortir
sans manteau** ~ **chapeau** go
without a coat or hat; **elle n'a dit**
~ **oui** ~ **non** she didn't say either
yes or no.
niais, ~**e** /njɛ, -z/ *a* silly.
niche /niʃ/ *nf (de chien)* kennel;
(cavité) niche.
nicher /niʃe/ [1] *vi* nest. □ **se** ~
vpr nest; *(se cacher)* hide.
nicotine /nikɔtin/ *nf* nicotine.
nid /ni/ *nm* nest; **faire un** ~ build
a nest. **nid-de-poule** (*pl* **nids-de-
poule**) *nm* pot-hole.
nièce /njɛs/ *nf* niece.
nier /nje/ [45] *vt* deny.
nigaud, ~**e** /nigo, -d/ *nm, f* fool.
nippon, ~**ne** /nipɔ̃, -ɔn/ *a*
Japanese. **N~**, ~**ne** *nm, f*
Japanese.
niveau (*pl* ~**x**) /nivo/ *nm* level;
(compétence) standard; *(étage)*
storey; (US) story; **au** ~ up to
standard; **mettre à** ~ (Ordinat)
upgrade; ~ **à bulle** (d'air) spirit-
level; ~ **de vie** standard of living.
niveler /nivle/ [6] *vt* level.

N

noble /nɔbl/ a noble. ●nm, f nobleman, noblewoman.
noblesse nf nobility.

noce /nɔs/ nf (fête 🏛) party; (invités) wedding guests; **~s** wedding; **faire la ~** 🏛 live it up.

nocif, -ive /nɔsif, -v/ a harmful.

nocturne /nɔktyʀn/ a nocturnal. ●nm (Mus) nocturne. ●nf (Sport) evening fixture; (de magasin) late-night opening.

Noël /nɔɛl/ nm Christmas.

nœud /nø/ nm (Naut) knot; (pour lier) knot; (pour orner) bow; **~s** (fig) ties; **~ coulant** slipknot, noose; **~ papillon** bow-tie.

noir, ~e /nwaʀ/ a black; (obscur, sombre) dark; (triste) gloomy. ●nm black; (obscurité) dark; **travail au ~** moonlighting. ●nm, f (personne) Black.

noircir /nwaʀsiʀ/ [2] vt blacken; **~ la situation** paint a black picture of the situation. ●vi (banane) go black; (mur) get dirty; (métal) tarnish. □ **se ~** vpr (ciel) darken.

noire /nwaʀ/ nf (Mus) crotchet.

noisette /nwazɛt/ nf hazelnut; (de beurre) knob.

noix /nwa/ nf nut; (du noyer) walnut; (de beurre) knob; **~ de cajou** cashew nut; **~ de coco** coconut; **à la ~** 🏛 useless.

nom /nɔ̃/ nm name; (Gram) noun; **au ~ de** on behalf of; **~ et prénom** full name; **~ déposé** registered trademark; **~ de famille** surname; **~ de jeune fille** maiden name; **~ de plume** pen name; **~ propre** proper noun.

nomade /nɔmad/ a nomadic; (Internet) mobile. ●nmf nomad.

nombre /nɔ̃bʀ/ nm number; **au ~ de** (parmi) among; (l'un de) one of;

en (grand) ~ in large numbers; **sans ~** countless.

nombreux, -euse /nɔ̃bʀø, -z/ a (en grand nombre) many, numerous; (important) large; **de ~ enfants** many children; **nous étions très ~** there were a great many of us.

nombril /nɔ̃bʀil/ nm navel.

nomination /nɔminasjɔ̃/ nf appointment.

nommer /nɔme/ [1] vt name; (élire) (à un poste) appoint; (à un lieu) post. □ **se ~** vpr (s'appeler) be called.

non /nɔ̃/ adv no; (pas) not; **~ (pas) que** not that; **il vient, ~?** he is coming, isn't he?; **moi ~ plus** neither am/do/can/etc. I. ●nm inv no.

non- /nɔ̃/ préf non-; **~-fumeur** non-smoker.

nonante /nɔnɑ̃t/ a & nm ninety.

non-sens /nɔ̃sɑ̃s/ nm inv absurdity.

nord /nɔʀ/ a inv (façade, côte) north; (frontière, zone) northern. ●nm north; **le ~ de l'Europe** northern Europe; **vent de ~** northerly (wind); **aller vers le ~** go north; **le Nord** the North; **du Nord** northern. **nord-est** nm north-east.

nordique /nɔʀdik/ a Scandinavian.

nord-ouest /nɔʀwɛst/ nm north-west.

normal, ~e (mpl **-aux**) /nɔʀmal, -o/ a normal. **normale** nf normality; (norme) norm; (moyenne) average.

normand, ~e /nɔʀmɑ̃, -d/ a Norman. **N~, ~e** nm, f Norman. **Normandie** /nɔʀmɑ̃di/ nf Normandy.

norme /nɔʀm/ nf norm; (de production) standard; **~s de sécurité** safety standards.

Norvège /nɔʀvɛʒ/ nf Norway.

norvégien, **~ne** /nɔʀveʒjɛ̃, -ɛn/ a Norwegian. **N~, ~ne** nm, f Norwegian.

nos /no/ ⇒NOTRE.

nostalgie /nɔstalʒi/ nf nostalgia; **avoir la ~ de son pays** be homesick. **nostalgique** a nostalgic.

notaire /nɔtɛʀ/ nm notary public.

notamment /nɔtamɑ̃/ adv notably.

note /nɔt/ nf (remarque) note; (chiffrée) mark, grade; (facture) bill; (Mus) note; **~ (de service)** memorandum.

noter /nɔte/ [1] vt note, notice; (écrire) note (down); (devoir) mark; (US) grade; **bien/mal noté** (employé) highly/poorly rated.

notice /nɔtis/ nf note; (mode d'emploi) instructions, directions.

notifier /nɔtifje/ [45] vt notify (à to).

notion /nɔsjɔ̃/ nf notion; **avoir des ~s de** have a basic knowledge of.

notoire /nɔtwaʀ/ a well-known; (criminel) notorious.

notre (pl **nos**) /nɔtʀ, no/ a our.

nôtre /notʀ/ pron **le** ou **la ~, les ~s** ours.

nouer /nwe/ [1] vt tie, knot; (relations) strike up.

nouille /nuj/ nf (Culin) noodle; **des ~s** noodles, pasta; (idiot Ⓘ) idiot.

nounours /nunuʀs/ nm Ⓘ teddy bear.

nourri, **~e** /nuʀi/ a **être logé ~** have bed and board; **~ au sein** breastfed.

nourrice /nuʀis/ nf childminder.

nourrir /nuʀiʀ/ [2] vt feed; (espoir, crainte) harbour; (projet) nurture; (passion) fuel. ●vi be nourishing. □ **se ~** vpr eat; **se ~ de** feed on. **nourrissant**, **~e** a nourishing.

nourrisson /nuʀisɔ̃/ nm infant.

nourriture /nuʀityʀ/ nf food.

nous /nu/ pron (sujet) we; (complément) us; (indirect) (to) us; (réfléchi) ourselves; (l'un l'autre) each other; **la voiture est à ~** the car is ours. **nous-mêmes** pron ourselves.

nouveau (**nouvel** before vowel or mute h), **nouvelle** (mpl **~x**) /nuvo, nuvɛl/ a new, **nouvel an** new year; **~x mariés** newly-weds; **~ venu, nouvelle venue** newcomer. ●nm, f (élève) new boy, new girl. ●nm **du ~** (fait nouveau) a new development; **de ~, à ~** again. **nouveau-né** (pl **~s**) nm newborn baby.

nouveauté /nuvote/ nf novelty; (chose) new thing; (livre) new publication; (disque) new release.

nouvelle /nuvɛl/ nf (pièce of) news; (récit) short story; **~s** news. **Nouvelle-Zélande** /nuvɛlzelɑ̃d/ nf New Zealand.

novembre /nɔvɑ̃bʀ/ nm November.

noyade /nwajad/ nf drowning.

noyau (pl **~x**) /nwajo/ nm (de fruit) stone; (US) pit; (de cellule) nucleus; (groupe) group; (centre, fig) core.

noyer /nwaje/ [31] vt drown; (inonder) flood. □ **se ~** vpr drown; (volontairement) drown oneself; **se ~ dans un verre d'eau** make a mountain out of a molehill. ●nm walnut-tree.

nu, **~e** /ny/ a (corps, personne) naked; (mains, mur, fil) bare; **à l'œil ~** to the naked eye. ●nm nude; **mettre à ~** expose.

nuage /nyaʒ/ nm cloud.

nuance /nyɑ̃s/ nf shade; (de sens) nuance; (différence) difference. **nuancer** [10] vt (opinion) qualify.

nucléaire /nykleɛʀ/ a nuclear. ●nm **le ~** nuclear energy.

nudisme /nydism/ nm nudism.

nudité /nydite/ *nf* nudity; (de lieu) bareness.

nuée /nɥe/ *nf* swarm, host.

nues /ny/ *nfpl* **tomber des ~** be amazed; **porter qn aux ~** praise sb to the skies.

nuire /nɥiʀ/ [17] *vi* **~ à** harm.

nuisible /nɥizibl/ *a* harmful (**à** to).

nuit /nɥi/ *nf* night; **cette ~** tonight; (hier) last night; **il fait ~** it is dark; **~ blanche** sleepless night; **la ~, de ~** at night; **~ de noces** wedding night.

nul, ~le /nyl/ *a* (aucun) no; (zéro) nil; (qui ne vaut rien) useless; (non valable) null; (*contrat*) void; (*testament*) invalid; **match ~** draw; **~ en sciences** no good at science; **nulle part** nowhere; **~ autre** no one else. ● *pron* no one.

nullement *adv* not at all. **nullité** *nf* uselessness; (personne) nonentity.

numérique /nymeʀik/ *a* numerical; (*montre, horloge*) digital.

numéro /nymeʀo/ *nm* number; (de journal) issue; (spectacle) act; **~ de téléphone** telephone number; **~ vert** freephone number. **numéroter** [1] *vt* number.

nuque /nyk/ *nf* nape (of the neck).

nurse /nœʀs/ *nf* nanny.

nutritif, -ive /nytʀitif, -v/ *a* nutritious; (*valeur*) nutritional.

oasis /ɔazis/ *nf* oasis.

obéir /ɔbeiʀ/ [2] *vt* **~ à** obey. ● *vi* obey. **obéissance** *nf* obedience. **obéissant, ~e** *a* obedient.

obèse /ɔbɛz/ *a* obese.

objecter /ɔbʒɛkte/ [1] *vt* object.

objectif, -ive /ɔbʒɛktif, -v/ *a* objective. ● *nm* objective; (Photo) lens.

objection /ɔbʒɛksjɔ̃/ *nf* objection; **soulever des ~s** raise objections.

objet /ɔbʒɛ/ *nm* (chose) object; (sujet) subject; (but) purpose, object; **être** *ou* **faire l'~ de** be the subject of; **~ d'art** objet d'art; **~s trouvés** lost property; (US) lost and found.

obligation /ɔbligasjɔ̃/ *nf* obligation; (Comm) bond; **être dans l'~ de** be under obligation to.

obligatoire /ɔbligatwaʀ/ *a* compulsory. **obligatoirement** *adv* (par règlement) of necessity; (inévitablement) inevitably.

obligeance /ɔbliʒɑ̃s/ *nf* **avoir l'~ de faire** be kind enough to do.

obliger /ɔbliʒe/ [40] *vt* compel, force (**à faire** to do); (aider) oblige; **être obligé de** have to (**de** for).

oblique /ɔblik/ *a* oblique; **regard ~** sidelong glance; **en ~** at an angle.

oblitérer /ɔblitere/ [14] *vt* (*timbre*) cancel.

obnubilé, ~e /ɔbnybile/ *a* obsessed.

obscène /ɔpsɛn/ *a* obscene.

obscur, ~e /ɔpskyʀ/ *a* dark;

(confus, humble) obscure; (vague) vague.

obscurcir /ɔpskyʀsiʀ/ [2] *vt* make dark; (fig) obscure. □ **s'~** *vpr* (ciel) darken.

obscurité /ɔpskyʀite/ *nf* darkness; (de passage, situation) obscurity.

obsédant, ~e /ɔpsedɑ̃, -t/ *a* (problème) nagging; (musique, souvenir) haunting.

obsédé, ~e /ɔpsede/ *nm, f* ~ (sexuel) sex maniac; ~ du ski/jazz ski/jazz freak.

obséder /ɔpsede/ [14] *vt* obsess.

obsèques /ɔpsɛk/ *nfpl* funeral.

observateur, -trice /ɔpsɛʀvatœʀ, -tʀis/ *a* observant. ●*nm, f* observer.

observation /ɔpsɛʀvasjɔ̃/ *nf* observation; (remarque) remark, comment; (reproche) criticism; (obéissance) observance; **en ~** under observation.

observer /ɔpsɛʀve/ [1] *vt* (regarder) observe; (surveiller) watch, observe; (remarquer) notice, observe; **faire ~ qch** point sth out (à to).

obsession /ɔpsesjɔ̃/ *nf* obsession.

obstacle /ɔpstakl/ *nm* obstacle; (pour cheval) fence, jump; (pour athlète) hurdle; **faire ~ à** stand in the way of, obstruct.

obstétrique /ɔpstetʀik/ *nf* obstetrics (+ *sg*).

obstiné, ~e /ɔpstine/ *a* stubborn, obstinate.

obstiner (s') /(s)ɔpstine/ [1] *vpr* persist (à in).

obstruction /ɔpstʀyksjɔ̃/ *nf* obstruction; (de conduit) blockage.

obstruer /ɔpstʀye/ [1] *vt* obstruct, block.

obtenir /ɔptəniʀ/ [58] *vt* get, obtain. **obtention** *nf* obtaining.

obus /ɔby/ *nm* shell.

occasion /ɔkazjɔ̃/ *nf* opportunity (de faire of doing); (circonstance) occasion; (achat) bargain; (article non neuf) second-hand buy; **à l'~** sometimes; **d'~** second-hand.

occasionnel, ~le *a* occasional.

occasionner /ɔkazjɔne/ [1] *vt* cause.

occident /ɔksidɑ̃/ *nm* (direction) west; **l'O~** the West.

occidental, ~e (*mpl* -aux) /ɔksidɑ̃tal, -o/ *a* western. **O~, ~e** (*mpl* -aux) *nm, f* westerner.

occulte /ɔkylt/ *a* occult.

occupant, ~e /ɔkypɑ̃, -t/ *nm, f* occupant. ●*nm* (Mil) forces of occupation.

occupation /ɔkypasjɔ̃/ *nf* occupation.

occupé, ~e /ɔkype/ *a* busy; (place, pays) occupied; (téléphone) engaged, busy; (toilettes) engaged.

occuper /ɔkype/ [1] *vt* occupy; (poste) hold; (espace, temps) take up. □ **s'~** *vpr* (s'affairer) keep busy (à faire doing); **s'~ de** (personne, problème) take care of; (bureau, firme) be in charge of; (se mêler) **occupe-toi de tes affaires** mind your own business.

occurrence: en l'~ /ɑ̃lɔkyʀɑ̃s/ *loc* in this case.

océan /ɔseɑ̃/ *nm* ocean.

Océanie /ɔseani/ *nf* Oceania.

ocre /ɔkʀ/ *a inv* ochre.

octante /ɔktɑ̃t/ *a* eighty.

octet /ɔktɛ/ *nm* byte.

octobre /ɔktɔbʀ/ *nm* October.

octogone /ɔktɔgɔn/ *nm* octagon.

octroyer /ɔktʀwaje/ [31] *vt* grant.

oculaire /ɔkylɛʀ/ *a* **témoin ~** eye-witness; **troubles ~s** eye trouble.

oculiste /ɔkylist/ *nmf* ophthalmologist.

odeur /ɔdœʀ/ *nf* smell.

O

odieux, -ieuse /ɔdjø, -z/ *a* odious.

odorant, ~e /ɔdɔrã, -t/ *a* sweet-smelling.

odorat /ɔdɔra/ *nm* sense of smell.

œil (*pl* **yeux**) /œj, jø/ *nm* eye; **à l'~** ⚀ for free; **à mes yeux** in my view; **faire de l'~ à** make eyes at; **faire les gros yeux à** glare at; **ouvrir l'~** keep one's eyes open; **~ poché** black eye; **fermer les yeux** shut one's eyes; (fig) turn a blind eye.

œillères /œjɛr/ *nfpl* blinkers.

œillet /œjɛ/ *nm* (plante) carnation; (trou) eyelet.

œuf (*pl* **~s**) /œf, ø/ *nm* egg; **~ à la coque/dur/sur le plat** boiled/hard-boiled/fried egg.

œuvre /œvr/ *nf* (ouvrage, travail) work; **~ d'art** work of art; **~ (de bienfaisance)** charity; **être à l'~** be at work; **mettre en ~** (*réforme, moyens*) implement; **mise en ~** implementation. ● *nm* (ensemble spécifié) **l'~ entier de Beethoven** the complete works of Beethoven.

œuvrer /œvre/ [1] *vi* work.

offense /ɔfãs/ *nf* insult.

offenser /ɔfãse/ [1] *vt* offend. □ **s'~** *vpr* take offence (**de** at).

offensive /ɔfãsiv/ *nf* offensive.

offert, ~e /ɔfɛr, -t/ ⇒OFFRIR [21].

office /ɔfis/ *nm* office; (Relig) service; (de cuisine) pantry; **faire ~ de** act as; **d'~** without consultation, automatically; **~ du tourisme** tourist information office.

officiel, ~le /ɔfisjɛl/ *a* official. ● *nm* official.

officier /ɔfisje/ [45] *vi* (Relig) officiate. ● *nm* officer.

officieux, -ieuse /ɔfisjø, -z/ *a* unofficial.

offre /ɔfr/ *nf* offer; (aux enchères) bid; **l'~ et la demande** supply and demand; **'~s d'emploi'** 'situations vacant'.

offrir /ɔfrir/ [21] *vt* offer (**de faire** to do); (*cadeau*) give; (acheter) buy; **~ à boire à** (chez soi) give a drink to; (au café) buy a drink for. □ **s'~** *vpr* (se proposer) offer oneself (**comme** as); (*solution*) present itself; (s'acheter) treat oneself to.

ogive /ɔʒiv/ *nf* **~ nucléaire** nuclear warhead.

OGM *abrév m* (**organisme génétiquement modifié**) GMO, genetically modified organism.

oie /wa/ *nf* goose.

oignon /ɔɲɔ̃/ *nm* (légume) onion; (de fleur) bulb.

oiseau (*pl* **~x**) /wazo/ *nm* bird.

oisif, -ive /wazif, -v/ *a* idle.

olive /ɔliv/ *nf* & *a inv* olive.

olivier *nm* olive tree.

olympique /ɔlɛ̃pik/ *a* Olympic.

ombrage /ɔ̃braʒ/ *nm* shade; **prendre ~ de** take offence at.

ombragé, ~e *a* shady.

ombre /ɔ̃br/ *nf* (pénombre) shade; (contour) shadow; (soupçon: fig) hint, shadow; **dans l'~** (*agir, rester*) behind the scenes; **faire de l'~ à qn** be in sb's light.

ombrelle /ɔ̃brɛl/ *nf* parasol.

omelette /ɔmlɛt/ *nf* omelette.

omettre /ɔmɛtr/ [42] *vt* omit, leave out.

omnibus /ɔmnibys/ *nm* stopping *ou* local train.

omoplate /ɔmɔplat/ *nf* shoulder blade.

on /ɔ̃/ *pron* (tu, vous) you; (nous) we; (ils, elles) they; (les gens) people, they; (quelqu'un) someone; (indéterminé) one, you; **~ dit** people say, they say, it is said; **~ m'a demandé mon avis** I was asked for my opinion.

oncle /ɔ̃kl/ *nm* uncle.

onctueux, -euse /ɔktɥø, -z/ a
smooth.

onde /ɔ̃d/ nf wave; ∼**s courtes/
longues** short/long wave; **sur les
∼s** on the air.

on-dit /ɔ̃di/ nm inv **les ∼** hearsay.

onduler /ɔ̃dyle/ [1] vi undulate;
(cheveux) be wavy.

onéreux, -euse /ɔnerø, -z/ a
costly.

ongle /ɔ̃gl/ nm (finger)nail; ∼ **de
pied** toenail; **se faire les ∼s** do
one's nails.

ont /ɔ̃/ ⇒AVOIR [5].

ONU abrév f (**Organisation des
Nations unies**) UN.

onze /ɔ̃z/ a & nm eleven.
onzième a & nmf eleventh.

OPA abrév f (**offre publique
d'achat**) takeover bid.

opéra /ɔpera/ nm opera; (édifice)
opera house. **opéra-comique** (pl
opéras-comiques) nm light
opera.

opérateur, -trice /ɔperatœr,
-tris/ nm, f operator.

opération /ɔperasjɔ̃/ nf
operation; (Comm) deal; (calcul)
calculation; ∼ **escargot** slow-
moving protest convoy.

opératoire /ɔperatwar/ a (Méd)
surgical; **bloc ∼** operating suite.

opérer /ɔpere/ [14] vt (personne)
operate on; (exécuter) carry out,
make; ∼ **qn d'une tumeur** operate
on sb to remove a tumour; **se
faire ∼** have surgery ou an
operation. ● vi (Méd) operate;
(faire effet) work. □ **s'∼** vpr (se
produire) occur.

opiniâtre /ɔpinjɑtr/ a tenacious.

opinion /ɔpinjɔ̃/ nf opinion.

opportuniste /ɔpɔrtynist/ nmf
opportunist.

opposant, -e /ɔpozã, -t/ nm, f
opponent.

opposé, ∼e /ɔpoze/ a (sens,
angle, avis) opposite; (factions)

opposing; (intérêts) conflicting;
être ∼ à be opposed to. ● nm
opposite; **à l'∼ de** (contrairement à)
contrary to, unlike.

opposer /ɔpoze/ [1] vt (objets)
place opposite each other;
(personnes) match, oppose;
(contraster) contrast; (résistance,
argument) put up. □ **s'∼** vpr
(personnes) confront each other;
(styles) contrast; **s'∼ à** oppose.

opposition /ɔpozisjɔ̃/ nf
opposition; **par ∼ à** in contrast
with; **entrer en ∼ avec** come into
conflict with; **faire ∼ à un chèque**
stop a cheque.

oppressant, ∼e /ɔpresã, -t/ a
oppressive.

opprimer /ɔprime/ [1] vt
oppress.

opter /ɔpte/ [1] vi ∼ **pour** opt for.

opticien, ∼ne /ɔptisjɛ̃, -ɛn/ nm, f
optician.

optimisme /ɔptimism/ nm
optimism.

optimiste /ɔptimist/ nmf
optimist. ● a optimistic.

option /ɔpsjɔ̃/ nf option.

optique /ɔptik/ a (verre) optical.
● nf (science) optics (+ sg);
(perspective) perspective.

or¹ /ɔr/ nm gold; **d'∼** golden; **en
∼** gold; (occasion) golden.

or² /ɔr/ conj now, well; (indiquant
une opposition) and yet.

orage /ɔraʒ/ nm (thunder)storm.
orageux, -euse a stormy.

oral, ∼e (mpl **-aux**) /ɔral, -o/ a
oral. ● nm (pl **-aux**) oral.

orange /ɔrãʒ/ a inv orange; (Aut)
(feu) amber; (US) yellow. ● nf
orange. **orangeade** nf
orangeade. **oranger** nm orange
tree.

orateur, -trice /ɔratœr, -tris/
nm, f speaker.

orbite /ɔrbit/ nf orbit; (d'œil)
socket.

O

orchestre /ɔʀkɛstʀ/ nm
orchestra; (de jazz) band; (parterre)
stalls.

ordinaire /ɔʀdinɛʀ/ a ordinary;
(habituel) usual; (qualité) standard;
(médiocre) very average. ●nm l'~
the ordinary; (nourriture) the
standard fare; **d'~, à l'~** usually.
ordinairement adv usually.

ordinateur /ɔʀdinatœʀ/ nm
computer; ~ **personnel/de bureau**
personal/desktop computer; ~
portable laptop (computer); ~
hôte (Internet) host.

ordonnance /ɔʀdɔnɑ̃s/ nf (ordre,
décret) order; (de médecin)
prescription.

ordonné, ~**e** /ɔʀdɔne/ a tidy.

ordonner /ɔʀdɔne/ [1] vt order (à
qn de sb to); (agencer) arrange;
(Méd) prescribe; (prêtre) ordain.

ordre /ɔʀdʀ/ nm order; (propreté)
tidiness; **aux ~s de qn** at sb's
disposal; **avoir de l'~** be tidy; **en**
~ tidy, in order; **de premier ~**
first-rate; **d'~ officiel** of an
official nature; **l'~ du jour**
(programme) agenda; **mettre de l' ~**
dans tidy up; **jusqu'à nouvel ~**
until further notice; **un ~ de**
grandeur an approximate idea.

ordure /ɔʀdyʀ/ nf filth; ~**s**
(détritus) rubbish; (US) garbage; ~**s**
ménagères household refuse.

oreille /ɔʀɛj/ nf ear.

oreiller /ɔʀeje/ nm pillow.

oreillons /ɔʀɛjɔ̃/ nmpl mumps.

orfèvre /ɔʀfɛvʀ/ nm goldsmith.

organe /ɔʀgan/ nm organ.

organigramme /ɔʀganigʀam/
nm organization chart; (Ordinat)
flowchart.

organique /ɔʀganik/ a organic.

organisateur, -trice
/ɔʀganizatœʀ, -tʀis/ nm, f
organizer.

organisation /ɔʀganizasjɔ̃/ nf
organization.

organiser /ɔʀganize/ [1] vt
organize. □ **s'~** vpr organize
oneself, get organized.

organisme /ɔʀganism/ nm body,
organism.

orge /ɔʀʒ/ nf barley.

orgelet /ɔʀʒɔlɛ/ nm sty.

orgue /ɔʀg/ nm organ; ~ **de**
Barbarie barrel-organ. **orgues**
nfpl organ.

orgueil /ɔʀgœj/ nm pride. **or-**
gueilleux, -euse a proud.

orient /ɔʀjɑ̃/ nm (direction) east;
l'O~ the Orient.

oriental, ~**e** (mpl -**aux**) /ɔʀjɑ̃tal,
-o/ a eastern; (de l'Orient) oriental.
O~, ~e (mpl -**aux**) nm, f Asian.

orientation /ɔʀjɑ̃tasjɔ̃/ nf
direction; (tendance politique)
leanings (+ pl); (de maison) aspect;
(Sport) orienteering; ~
professionnelle careers advice; ~
scolaire curriculum counselling.

orienter /ɔʀjɑ̃te/ [1] vt position;
(personne) direct. □ **s'~** vpr (se
repérer) find one's bearings; **s'~**
vers turn towards.

origan /ɔʀigɑ̃/ nm oregano.

originaire /ɔʀiʒinɛʀ/ a **être ~ de**
be a native of.

original, ~**e** (mpl -**aux**) /ɔʀiʒinal,
-o/ a original; (curieux) eccentric.
●nm (œuvre) original. ●nm, f
eccentric. **originalité** nf
originality; eccentricity.

origine /ɔʀiʒin/ nf origin; **à l'~**
originally; **d'~** (pièce, pneu)
original; **être d'~ noble** come
from a noble background.

originel, ~**le** /ɔʀiʒinɛl/ a
original.

orme /ɔʀm/ nm elm.

ornement /ɔʀnəmɑ̃/ nm
ornament.

orner /ɔʀne/ [1] vt decorate.

orphelin, ~**e** /ɔʀfəlɛ̃, -in/ nm, f
orphan. ●a orphaned.
orphelinat nm orphanage.

orteil /ɔʀtɛj/ nm toe.

orthodoxe /ɔʀtɔdɔks/ a orthodox.

orthographe /ɔʀtɔgʀaf/ nf spelling.

ortie /ɔʀti/ nf nettle.

os /ɔs, o/ nm inv bone.

OS abrév m ⇒OUVRIER SPÉCIALISÉ.

osciller /ɔsile/ [1] vi sway; (Tech) oscillate; (hésiter) waver; (fluctuer) fluctuate.

osé, ~e /oze/ a daring.

oseille /ozɛj/ nf (plante) sorrel.

oser /oze/ [1] vi dare.

osier /ozje/ nm wicker.

ossature /ɔsatyʀ/ nf skeleton, frame.

ossements /ɔsmɑ̃/ nmpl bones, remains.

osseux, -euse /ɔsø, -z/ a bony; (Méd) bone.

otage /ɔtaʒ/ nm hostage.

OTAN /ɔtɑ̃/ abrév f (Organisation du traité de l'Atlantique Nord) NATO.

otarie /ɔtaʀi/ nf eared seal.

ôter /ote/ [1] vt remove (à qn from sb); (déduire) take away.

otite /ɔtit/ nf ear infection.

ou /u/ conj or; ~ **bien** or else; ~ (**bien**)... ~ (**bien**)... either... or...; **vous ~ moi** either you or me.

où /u/ pron where; (dans lequel) in which; (sur lequel) on which; (auquel) at which; **d'~** from which; (pour cette raison) hence; **par ~** through which; ~ **qu'il soit** wherever he may be; **juste au moment ~** just as; **le jour ~** the day when. ● adv where; **d'~?** where from?

ouate /wat/ nf cotton wool; (US) absorbent cotton.

oubli /ubli/ nm forgetfulness; (trou de mémoire) lapse of memory; (négligence) oversight; **tomber dans l'~** sink into oblivion.

oublier /ublije/ [45] vt forget;

(omettre) leave out, forget. □ **s'~** vpr (chose) be forgotten.

ouest /wɛst/ nm a inv (façade, côte) west; (frontière, zone) western. ● nm west; **l'~ de l'Europe** western Europe; **vent d'~** westerly (wind); **aller vers l'~** go west; **l'O~** the West; **de l'O~** western.

oui /wi/ adv & nm inv yes.

ouï-dire: par ~ /parwidir/ loc by hearsay.

ouïe /wi/ nf hearing; (de poisson) gill.

ouragan /uʀagɑ̃/ nm hurricane.

ourlet /uʀlɛ/ nm hem.

ours /uʀs/ nm bear; ~ **blanc** polar bear; ~ **en peluche** teddy bear.

outil /uti/ nm tool. **outillage** nm tools (+ pl). **outiller** [1] vt equip.

outrage /utʀaʒ/ nm (grave) insult.

outrance /utʀɑ̃s/ nf **à ~** excessively. **outrancier, -ière** a extreme.

outre /utʀ/ prép besides. ● adv **passer ~** pay no heed; ~ **mesure** unduly; **en ~** in addition. **outre-mer** adv overseas.

outrepasser /utʀəpase/ [1] vt exceed.

outrer /utʀe/ [1] vt exaggerate; (indigner) incense.

ouvert, ~e /uvɛʀ, -t/ a open; (gaz, radio) on. ● ⇒OUVRIR [21].

ouverture /uvɛʀtyʀ/ nf opening; (Mus) overture; (Photo) aperture; ~**s** (offres) overtures; ~ **d'esprit** open-mindedness.

ouvrable /uvʀabl/ a **jour ~** working day; **aux heures ~s** during business hours.

ouvrage /uvʀaʒ/ nm (travail, livre) work; (couture) (piece of) needlework.

ouvre-boîtes /uvʀəbwat/ nm inv tin-opener.

O

ouvre-bouteilles /uvʀəbutɛj/ *nm inv* bottle-opener.

ouvreur, -euse /uvʀœʀ, -øz/ *nm, f* usherette.

ouvrier, -ière /uvʀije, -jɛʀ/ *nm, f* worker; **~ qualifié/spécialisé** skilled/unskilled worker. ●*a* working-class; (*conflit*) industrial; **syndicat ~** trade union.

ouvrir /uvʀiʀ/ [21] *vt* open (up); (*gaz, robinet*) turn on. ●*vi* open (up). □ **s'~** *vpr* open (up); **s'~ à qn** open one's heart to sb.

ovaire /ɔvɛʀ/ *nm* ovary.

ovale /ɔval/ *a & nm* oval.

ovni /ɔvni/ *abrév m* (**objet volant non-identifié**) UFO.

ovule /ɔvyl/ *nm* (à féconder) ovum; (gynécologique) pessary.

oxygène /ɔksiʒɛn/ *nm* oxygen.

oxygéner (s') /(s)ɔksiʒene/ [14] *vpr* get some fresh air.

ozone /ozon/ *nf* ozone; **la couche d'~** the ozone layer.

pacifique /pasifik/ *a* peaceful; (*personne*) peaceable; (Géog) Pacific. **P~** *nm* **le P~** the Pacific.

pacotille /pakɔtij/ *nf* junk, rubbish.

PACS /paks/ *abrév nm* (**pacte civil de solidarité**) contract of civil union.

pacser (se) /pakse/ [1] *vpr* sign a contract of civil union (PACS).

pagaie /pagɛ/ *nf* paddle.

pagaille /pagaj/ *nf* ▣ mess.

page /paʒ/ *nf* page; **mise en ~** layout; **tourner la ~** turn over a new leaf; **être à la ~** be up to date; **~ d'accueil** (Internet) home page.

paie /pɛ/ *nf* pay.

paiement /pemã/ *nm* payment.

païen, ~ne /pajɛ̃, -ɛn/ *a & nm, f* pagan.

paillasson /pajasɔ̃/ *nm* doormat.

paille /paj/ *nf* straw. ●*a* (*cheveux*) straw-coloured.

paillette /pajɛt/ *nf* (sur robe) sequin; (de savon) flake.

pain /pɛ̃/ *nm* bread; (miche) loaf (of bread); (de savon, cire) bar; **~ d'épices** gingerbread; **~ grillé** toast.

pair, ~e /pɛʀ/ *a* (*nombre*) even. ●*nm* (personne) peer; **aller de ~** go together (**avec** with); **au ~** (*jeune fille*) au pair. **paire** *nf* pair.

paisible /pezibl/ *a* peaceful.

paître /pɛtʀ/ [44] *vi* graze.

paix /pɛ/ *nf* peace; **fiche-moi la ~!** ▣ leave me alone!

Pakistan /pakistã/ *nm* Pakistan.

palace /palas/ *nm* luxury hotel.

palais /palɛ/ *nm* palace; (Anat) palate; **~ de Justice** law courts; **~ des sports** sports stadium.

pâle /pɑl/ *a* pale.

Palestine /palɛstin/ *nf* Palestine.

palier /palje/ *nm* (d'escalier) landing; (étape) stage.

pâlir /pɑliʀ/ [2] *vt/i* (turn) pale.

palissade /palisad/ *nf* fence.

pallier /palje/ [45] *vt* compensate for.

palmarès /palmaʀɛs/ *nm* list of prize-winners.

palme /palm/ *nf* palm leaf; (de nageur) flipper. **palmé, ~e** *a* (*patte*) webbed.

palmier /palmje/ *nm* palm (tree).

palper /palpe/ [1] *vt* feel.

palpiter /palpite/ [1] *vi* (battre) pound; (frémir) quiver.

paludisme /palydism/ *nm* malaria.

pamplemousse /pɑ̃pləmus/ *nm* grapefruit.

panaché, ∼e /panaʃe/ *a* (bariolé, mélangé) motley; **glace ∼e** mixed-flavour ice cream. ●*nm* shandy.

pancarte /pɑ̃kaʀt/ *nf* sign; (de manifestant) placard.

pané, ∼e /pane/ *a* breaded.

panier /panje/ *nm* basket; (de basket-ball) basket; **mettre au ∼** ⊞ throw out; **∼ à salade** salad shaker; (fourgon ⊞) police van.

panique /panik/ *nf* panic.
 paniquer [1] *vi* panic.

panne /pan/ *nf* breakdown; **être en ∼** have broken down; **être en ∼ sèche** have run out of petrol; **∼ d'électricité** *ou* **de courant** power failure.

panneau (*pl* ∼**x**) /pano/ *nm* sign; (publicitaire) hoarding; (de porte) panel; **∼ (d'affichage)** notice board; **∼ (de signalisation)** road sign.

panoplie /panɔpli/ *nf* (jouet) outfit; (gamme) range.

pansement /pɑ̃smɑ̃/ *nm* dressing; **∼ adhésif** plaster.
 panser [1] *vt* (plaie) dress; (*personne*) dress the wound(s) of; (*cheval*) groom.

pantalon /pɑ̃talɔ̃/ *nm* trousers (+ *pl*).

panthère /pɑ̃tɛʀ/ *nf* panther.

pantin /pɑ̃tɛ̃/ *nm* puppet.

pantomime /pɑ̃tɔmim/ *nf* mime; (spectacle) mime show.

pantoufle /pɑ̃tufl/ *nf* slipper.

paon /pɑ̃/ *nm* peacock.

papa /papa/ *nm* dad(dy).

pape /pap/ *nm* pope.

paperasse /papʀas/ *nf* (péj) bumf.

papeterie /papetʀi/ *nf* (magasin) stationer's shop.

papier /papje/ *nm* paper; (formulaire) form; **∼s (d'identité)** (identity) papers; **∼ absorbant** kitchen paper; **∼ aluminium** tin foil; **∼ buvard** blotting paper; **∼ cadeau** wrapping paper; **∼ calque** tracing paper; **∼ carbone** carbon paper; **∼ collant** adhesive tape; **∼ hygiénique** toilet paper; **∼ journal** newspaper; **∼ à lettres** writing paper; **∼ mâché** papier mâché; **∼ peint** wallpaper; **∼ de verre** sandpaper.

papillon /papijɔ̃/ *nm* butterfly; (contravention ⊞) parking-ticket; **∼ de nuit** moth.

papoter /papote/ [1] *vi* ⊞ chatter.

paquebot /pakbo/ *nm* liner.

pâquerette /pakʀɛt/ *nf* daisy.

Pâques /pak/ *nfpl & nm* Easter.

paquet /pakɛ/ *nm* packet; (de cartes) pack; (colis) parcel; **un ∼ de** (beaucoup ⊞) a mass of.

par /paʀ/ *prép* by; (à travers) through; (motif) out of, from; (provenance) from; **commencer/finir ∼ qch** begin/end with sth; **commencer/finir ∼ faire** begin by/ end up (by) doing; **∼ an/mois** a *ou* per year/month; **∼ jour** a day; **∼ personne** each, per person; **∼ avion** (lettre) (by) airmail; **∼-ci, ∼-là** here and there; **∼ contre** on the other hand; **∼ ici/là** this/that way.

parachute /paʀaʃyt/ *nm* parachute. **parachutiste** *nmf* parachutist; (Mil) paratrooper.

parader /paʀade/ [1] *vi* show off.

paradis /paʀadi/ *nm* (Relig) heaven; (lieu idéal) paradise; **∼ fiscal** tax haven.

paradoxal, ∼e (*mpl* **-aux**) /paʀadɔksal, -o/ *a* paradoxical.

paraffine /paʀafin/ *nf* paraffin wax.

parages /paʀaʒ/ *nmpl* **dans les ∼** around.

P

paragraphe /paʀagʀaf/ *nm* paragraph.

paraître /paʀɛtʀ/ [18] *vi* (se montrer) appear; (sembler) seem, appear; (ouvrage) be published, come out; **faire ∼** (ouvrage) bring out; **il paraît qu'ils…** apparently they…; **oui, il paraît** so I hear.

parallèle /paʀalɛl/ *a* parallel; (illégal) unofficial. ● *nm* parallel; **faire le ∼** make a connection. ● *nf* parallel (line).

paralyser /paʀalize/ [1] *vt* paralyse. **paralysie** *nf* paralysis.

parapente /paʀapɑ̃t/ *nm* paraglider; (activité) paragliding.

parapher /paʀafe/ [1] *vi* initial; (signer) sign.

parapluie /paʀaplɥi/ *nm* umbrella.

parasite /paʀazit/ *nm* parasite; **∼s** (radio) interference (+ *sg*).

parasol /paʀasɔl/ *nm* sunshade.

paratonnerre /paʀatɔnɛʀ/ *nm* lightning conductor *ou* rod.

paravent /paʀavɑ̃/ *nm* screen.

parc /paʀk/ *nm* park; (de bétail) pen; (de bébé) play-pen; (entrepôt) depot; **∼ relais** park and ride; **∼ de stationnement** car park.

parce que /paʀsk(ə)/ *conj* because.

parchemin /paʀʃəmɛ̃/ *nm* parchment.

parcmètre /paʀkmɛtʀ/ *nm* parking meter.

parcourir /paʀkuʀiʀ/ [20] *vt* travel *ou* go through; (distance) travel; (des yeux) glance at *ou* over.

parcours /paʀkuʀ/ *nm* route; (voyage) journey.

par-delà /paʀdəla/ *prép* beyond.

par-derrière /paʀdɛʀjɛʀ/ *adv* (attaquer) from behind; (critiquer) behind sb's back.

par-dessous /paʀdəsu/ *prép & adv* under(neath).

pardessus /paʀdəsy/ *nm* overcoat.

par-dessus /paʀdəsy/ *prép & adv* over; **∼ bord** overboard; **∼ le marché** 🇫 into the bargain; **∼ tout** above all.

par-devant /paʀdəvɑ̃/ *adv* (passer) by the front.

pardon /paʀdɔ̃/ *nm* forgiveness; (je vous demande) **∼!** (I am) sorry!; (pour demander qch) excuse me.

pardonner /paʀdɔne/ [1] *vt* forgive; **∼ qch à qn** forgive sb for sth.

pare-brise /paʀbʀiz/ *nm inv* windscreen.

pare-chocs /paʀʃɔk/ *nm inv* bumper.

pareil, ∼le /paʀɛj/ *a* similar (à to); (tel) such (a); **c'est ∼** it's the same; **ce n'est pas ∼** it's not the same thing. ● *nm, f* equal. ● *adv* 🇫 the same.

parent, ∼e /paʀɑ̃, -t/ *a* related (de to). ● *nm, f* relative, relation; **∼s** (père et mère) parents; **∼ isolé** single parent; **réunion de ∼s d'élèves** parents' evening.

parenté /paʀɑ̃te/ *nf* relationship.

parenthèse /paʀɑ̃tɛz/ *nf* bracket, parenthesis; (fig) digression.

parer /paʀe/ [1] *vt* (esquiver) parry; (orner) adorn. ● *vi* **∼ à** deal with; **∼ au plus pressé** tackle the most urgent things first.

paresse /paʀɛs/ *nf* laziness.

paresseux, -euse /paʀɛsø, -z/ *a* lazy. ● *nm, f* lazy person.

parfait, ∼e /paʀfɛ, -t/ *a* perfect. **parfaitement** *adv* perfectly; (bien sûr) absolutely.

parfois /paʀfwa/ *adv* sometimes.

parfum /paʀfœ̃/ *nm* (senteur) scent; (substance) perfume, scent; (goût) flavour. **parfumé, ∼e** *a* fragrant; (savon) scented; (thé) flavoured.

parfumer /paʀfyme/ [1] vt (embaumer) scent; (gâteau) flavour. □ se ~ vpr put on one's perfume.
parfumerie nf (produits) perfumes; (boutique) perfume shop.

pari /paʀi/ nm bet.

Paris /paʀi/ npr Paris.

parisien, **~ne** /paʀizjɛ̃, -ɛn/ a Parisian; (banlieue) Paris. **P~**, **~ne** nm, f Parisian.

parking /paʀkiŋ/ nm car park.

parlement /paʀləmɑ̃/ nm parliament.

parlementaire /paʀləmɑ̃tɛʀ/ a parliamentary. ● nmf Member of Parliament.

parlementer /paʀləmɑ̃te/ [1] vi negotiate.

parler /paʀle/ [1] vi talk (à to); ~ **de** talk about; **tu parles d'un avantage!** call that a benefit!; **de quoi ça parle?** what is it about? ● vt (langue) speak; (politique, affaires) talk. □ se ~ vpr (personnes) talk (to each other); (langue) be spoken. ● nm speech; (dialecte) dialect.

parmi /paʀmi/ prép among(st).

paroi /paʀwa/ nf wall; ~ **rocheuse** rock face.

paroisse /paʀwas/ nf parish.

parole /paʀɔl/ nf (mot, promesse) word; (langage) speech; **demander la** ~ ask to speak; **prendre la** ~ (begin to) speak; **tenir** ~ keep one's word; **croire qn sur** ~ take sb's word for it.

parquet /paʀkɛ/ nm (parquet) floor; **lame de** ~ floorboard; **le** ~ (Jur) prosecution.

parrain /paʀɛ̃/ nm godfather; (fig) sponsor.

parsemer /paʀsəme/ [6] vt strew (de with).

part /paʀ/ nf share, part; **à** ~ (de côté) aside; (séparément) separate; (excepté) apart from; **d'une** ~ on the one hand; **d'autre** ~ on the other hand; (de plus) moreover; **de la** ~ **de** from; **de toutes** ~s from all sides; **de** ~ **et d'autre** on both sides; **faire** ~ **à qn** inform sb (**de** of); **faire la** ~ **des choses** make allowances; **prendre** ~ **à** take part in; (joie, douleur) share; **pour ma** ~ as for me.

partage /paʀtaʒ/ nm (division) dividing; (répartition) sharing out; **recevoir qch en** ~ be left sth in a will.

partager /paʀtaʒe/ [40] vt divide; (distribuer) share out; (avoir en commun) share. □ se ~ **qch** vpr share sth.

partenaire /paʀtənɛʀ/ nmf partner.

parterre /paʀtɛʀ/ nm flower-bed; (Théât) stalls.

parti /paʀti/ nm (Pol) party; (décision) decision; (en mariage) match; ~ **pris** bias; **prendre** ~ get involved; **prendre** ~ **pour qn** side with sb; **j'en ai pris mon** ~ I've come to terms with that.

partial, **~e** (mpl **-iaux**) /paʀsjal, -jo/ a biased.

participe /paʀtisip/ nm (Gram) participle.

participant, **~e** /paʀtisipɑ̃, -t/ nm, f participant (**à** in).

participation /paʀtisipasjɔ̃/ nf participation; (financière) contribution; (d'un artiste) appearance.

participer /paʀtisipe/ [1] vi ~ **à** take part in, participate in; (profits, frais) share.

particule /paʀtikyl/ nf particle.

particulier, **-ière** /paʀtikylje, -jɛʀ/ a (spécifique) particular; (bizarre) unusual; (privé) private; **rien de** ~ nothing special. ● nm private individual; **en** ~ in particular, particularly. **particulièrement** adv particularly.

partie /paʀti/ nf part; (cartes, Sport)

P

game; (Jur) party; **une ~ de pêche**
a fishing trip; **en ~** partly, in
part; **en grande ~** largely; **faire ~
de** be part of; (adhérer à) be a
member of; **faire ~ intégrante de**
be an integral part of.

partiel, **~le** /paʀsjɛl/ a partial.
●*nm* (Univ) exam based on a
module.

partir /paʀtiʀ/ [46] *vi* (*aux être*)
go; (quitter un lieu) leave, go; (*tache*)
come out; (*bouton*) come off;
(*coup de feu*) go off; (commencer)
start; **~ pour le Brésil** leave for
Brazil; **~ du principe que** work on
the assumption that; **à ~ de** from;
à ~ de maintenant from now on.

partisan, **~e** /paʀtizã, -an/ *nm,f*
supporter. ●*nm* (Mil) partisan;
être ~ de be in favour of.

partition /paʀtisjɔ̃/ *nf* (Mus)
score.

partout /paʀtu/ *adv* everywhere;
~ où wherever.

paru /paʀy/ ⇒PARAÎTRE [18].

parure /paʀyʀ/ *nf* finery; (bijoux)
set of jewels; (de draps) set.

parution /paʀysjɔ̃/ *nf*
publication.

parvenir /paʀvəniʀ/ [58] *vi* (*aux
être*) **~ à** reach; **~ à faire** manage
to do; **faire ~** send.

parvenu, **~e** /paʀvəny/ *nm,f*
upstart.

- -

pas¹ /pɑ/

Pour les expressions comme
pas encore, pas mal, etc.
⇒**encore, mal**, etc.

●*adverbe*

····▸ not; **ne ~** not; **je ne sais ~** I
don't know; **je ne pense ~** I don't
think so; **il a aimé, moi ~** he
liked it, I didn't; **~ cher/poli**
cheap/impolite.

····▸ **~ du tout** not at all; **~ de
chance!** tough luck!

····▸ **on a bien ri, ~ vrai?** 🔲 we had
a good laugh, didn't we?

> ❗ In spoken colloquial French
> **ne... pas** is often shortened
> to **pas**. You will often hear
> **j'ai pas compris** instead of
> **je n'ai pas compris** (*I didn't
> understand*). Note that this
> would not be correct in
> written French.

- -

pas² /pɑ/ *nm* step; (bruit) footstep;
(trace) footprint; (vitesse) pace; **à
deux ~ (de)** a step away (from);
marcher au ~ march; **rouler au ~**
move very slowly; **à ~ de loup**
stealthily; **faire les cent ~** walk up
and down; **faire le premier ~** make
the first move; **~ de porte**
doorstep; **~ de vis** (Tech) thread.

passage /pɑsaʒ/ *nm* (traversée)
crossing; (visite) visit; (chemin) way,
passage; (d'une œuvre) passage; **de
~** (*voyageur*) visiting; (*amant*)
casual; **la tempête a tout emporté
sur son ~** the storm swept
everything away; **~ clouté**
pedestrian crossing; **~ interdit**
(panneau) no thoroughfare; **~ à
niveau** level crossing; **~ souterrain**
subway.

passager, **-ère** /pɑsaʒe, -ɛʀ/ *a*
temporary. ●*nm,f* passenger; **~
clandestin** stowaway.

passant, **~e** /pɑsã, -t/ *a* (rue)
busy. ●*nm,f* passer-by. ●*nm*
(anneau) loop.

passe /pɑs/ *nf* pass; **bonne/
mauvaise ~** good/bad patch; **en ~
de** on the road to.

passé, **~e** /pɑse/ *a* (révolu) past;
(dernier) last; (fané) faded; **~ de
mode** out of fashion. ●*nm* past.
●*prép* after.

passe-partout /pɑspaʀtu/ *nm*

inv master-key. ●*a inv* for all occasions.

passeport /paspɔʀ/ *nm* passport.

passer /pase/ [1] *vi (aux être ou avoir)* go past, pass; *(aller)* go; *(venir)* come; *(temps, douleur)* pass; *(film)* be on; *(couleur)* fade; **laisser** ~ let through; *(occasion)* miss; ~ **devant** (à pied) walk past; (en voiture) drive past; ~ **par** go through; **où est-il passé?** where did he get to?; ~ **outre** take no notice; **passons!** let's forget about it!; **passons aux choses sérieuses** let's turn to serious matters; ~ **dans la classe supérieure** go up a year; ~ **pour un idiot** look a fool. ●*vt (aux avoir)* (franchir) pass, cross; (donner) pass, hand; (temps) spend; (enfiler) slip on; *(vidéo, disque)* put on; (examen) take, sit; (commande) place; (faire) ~ **le temps** while away the time; ~ **l'aspirateur** hoover; ~ **un coup de fil à qn** give sb a ring; **je vous passe Mme X** (par le standard) I'll put you through to Mrs X; (en donnant l'appareil) I'll pass you over to Mrs X; ~ **qch en fraude** smuggle sth. □ **se** ~ *vpr* happen, take place; (s'écouler) go by; **se** ~ **de** go ou do without.

passerelle /pasʀɛl/ *nf* footbridge; (de navire) gangway; (d'avion) (passenger) footbridge; (Internet) gateway.

passe-temps /pastã/ *nm inv* pastime.

passif, -ive /pasif, -v/ *a* passive. ●*nm* (Comm) liabilities.

passion /pasjɔ̃/ *nf* passion. **passionnant, ~e** *a* fascinating.

passionné, ~e /pasjone/ *a* passionate; **être** ~ **de** have a passion for.

passionner /pasjone/ [1] *vt* fascinate. □ **se** ~ **pour** *vpr* have a passion for.

passoire /paswaʀ/ *nf* (à thé) strainer; (à légumes) colander.

pastèque /pastɛk/ *nf* watermelon.

pasteur /pastœʀ/ *nm* (Relig) minister.

pastille /pastij/ *nf* (médicament) pastille, lozenge.

patate /patat/ *nf* 🄸 spud; ~ **(douce)** sweet potato.

patauger /patoʒe/ [40] *vi* splash about.

pâte /pɑt/ *nf* paste; (à gâteau) dough; (à tarte) pastry; (à frire) batter; ~**s (alimentaires)** pasta (+ *sg*); ~ **à modeler** Plasticine®; ~ **d'amandes** marzipan.

pâté /pɑte/ *nm* (Culin) pâté; (d'encre) blot; (de sable) sandpie; ~ **en croûte** ≈ pie; ~ **de maisons** block (of houses).

pâtée /pɑte/ *nf* feed, mash.

patente /patãt/ *nf* trade licence.

paternel, ~le /patɛʀnɛl/ *a* paternal. **paternité** *nf* paternity.

pathétique /patetik/ *a* moving.

patience /pasjãs/ *nf* patience.

patient, ~e *a & nm,f* patient. **patienter** [1] *vi* wait.

patin /patɛ̃/ *nm* skate; ~ **à roulettes** roller-skate.

patinage /patinaʒ/ *nm* skating. **patiner** [1] *vi* skate; (roue) spin. **patinoire** *nf* ice rink.

pâtisserie /pɑtisʀi/ *nf* cake shop; (gâteau) pastry; (secteur) cake making. **pâtissier, -ière** *nm,f* confectioner, pastry-cook.

patrie /patʀi/ *nf* homeland.

patrimoine /patʀimwan/ *nm* heritage.

patriote /patʀijɔt/ *a* patriotic. ●*nmf* patriot.

patron, ~ne /patʀɔ̃, -ɔn/ *nm,f* employer, boss; (propriétaire) owner, boss; (saint) patron saint. ●*nm* (couture) pattern. **patronal,**

P

~**e** (*mpl* -**aux**) *a* employers'.
patronat *nm* employers (+ *pl*).
patrouille /patʀuj/ *nf* patrol.
patte /pat/ *nf* leg; (*pied*) foot; (*de chat*) paw; ~**s** (*favoris*) sideburns; **marcher à quatre** ~**s** walk on all fours; (*bébé*) crawl; ~**s de derrière** hind legs.
paume /pom/ *nf* (*de main*) palm.
paumé, ~**e** /pome/ *nm, f* 🔟 misfit.
paupière /popjɛʀ/ *nf* eyelid.
pause /poz/ *nf* pause; (*halte*) break.
pauvre /povʀ/ *a* poor. ● *nmf* poor man, poor woman. **pauvreté** *nf* poverty.
pavé /pave/ *nm* cobblestone.
pavillon /pavijɔ̃/ *nm* (*maison*) house; (*drapeau*) flag.
payant, ~**e** /pejɑ̃, -t/ *a* (*hôte*) paying; **c'est** ~ you have to pay to get in.
payer /peje/ [31] *vt/i* pay; (*service, travail*) pay for; ~ **qch à qn** buy sb sth; **faire** ~ **qn** charge sb; **il me le paiera!** he'll pay for this. □ **se** ~ *vpr* **se** ~ **qch** buy oneself sth; **se** ~ **la tête de** make fun of.
pays /pei/ *nm* country; (*région*) region; **du** ~ local.
paysage /peizaʒ/ *nm* landscape.
paysan, ~**ne** /peizã, -an/ *nm, f* farmer, country person; (*péj*) peasant. ● *a* (*agricole*) farming; (*rural*) country.
Pays-Bas /peibɑ/ *nmpl* **les** ~ the Netherlands.
PCV *abrév m* (**paiement contre vérification**) **téléphoner en** ~ reverse the charges.
PDG *abrév m* (**président-directeur général**) chairman and managing director.
péage /peaʒ/ *nm* toll; (*lieu*) tollgate.
peau (*pl* ~**x**) /po/ *nf* skin; (*cuir*)

hide; ~ **de chamois** shammy (leather); ~ **de mouton** sheepskin; **être bien/mal dans sa** ~ be/not be at ease with oneself.
pêche /pɛʃ/ *nf* (*fruit*) peach; (*activité*) fishing; (*poissons*) catch; ~ **à la ligne** angling.
péché /peʃe/ *nm* sin.
pêcher /peʃe/ *vt* (*poisson*) catch; (*dénicher* 🔟) dig up. ● *vi* fish.
pêcheur *nm* fisherman; (*à la ligne*) angler.
pécuniaire /pekynjɛʀ/ *a* financial.
pédagogie /pedagɔʒi/ *nf* education.
pédale /pedal/ *nf* pedal.
pédalo® /pedalo/ *nm* pedal boat.
pédant, ~**e** /pedã, -t/ *a* pedantic.
pédestre /pedɛstʀ/ *a* **faire de la randonnée** ~ go walking *ou* hiking.
pédiatre /pedjatʀ/ *nmf* paediatrician.
pédicure /pedikyʀ/ *nmf* chiropodist.
peigne /pɛɲ/ *nm* comb.
peigner /peɲe/ [1] *vt* comb; (*personne*) comb the hair of. □ **se** ~ *vpr* comb one's hair.
peignoir /pɛɲwaʀ/ *nm* dressing-gown.
peindre /pɛ̃dʀ/ [22] *vt* paint.
peine /pɛn/ *nf* sadness, sorrow; (*effort, difficulté*) trouble; (*Jur*) sentence; **avoir de la** ~ feel sad; **faire de la** ~ **à** hurt; **ce n'est pas la** ~ **de sonner** you don't need to ring the bell; **j'ai de la** ~ **à le croire** I find it hard to believe; **se donner** *ou* **prendre la** ~ **de faire** go to the trouble of doing; ~ **de mort** death penalty. ● *adv* **à** ~ hardly.
peiner /pene/ [1] *vi* struggle. ● *vt* sadden.
peintre /pɛ̃tʀ/ *nm* painter; ~ **en bâtiment** house painter.
peinture /pɛ̃tyʀ/ *nf* painting;

(matière) paint; ~ **à l'huile** oil painting.

péjoratif, -ive /peʒɔRatif, -v/ a pejorative.

pelage /pəlaʒ/ nm coat, fur.

pêle-mêle /pɛlmɛl/ adv in a jumble.

peler /pəle/ [6] vt/i peel.

pèlerinage /pɛlRinaʒ/ nm pilgrimage.

pelle /pɛl/ nf shovel; (d'enfant) spade.

pellicule /pelikyl/ nf film; ~**s** (cheveux) dandruff.

pelote /pəlɔt/ nf (of wool) ball.

peloton /p(ə)lɔtɔ̃/ nm platoon; (Sport) pack; ~ **d'exécution** firing squad.

pelotonner (se) /(sə)plɔtɔne/ [1] vpr curl up.

pelouse /p(ə)luz/ nf lawn.

peluche /p(ə)lyʃ/ nf (matière) plush; (jouet) cuddly toy; **en** ~ (lapin, chien) fluffy.

pénal, ~e (mpl -aux) /penal, -o/ a penal. **pénaliser** [1] vt penalize. **pénalité** nf penalty.

penchant /pɑ̃ʃɑ̃/ nm inclination; (goût) liking (**pour** for).

pencher /pɑ̃ʃe/ [1] vt tilt; ~ **pour** favour. ●vi lean (over), tilt. □ **se** ~ vpr lean (forward); **se** ~ **sur** (problème) examine.

pendaison /pɑ̃dɛzɔ̃/ nf hanging.

pendant[1] /pɑ̃dɑ̃/ prép (au cours de) during; (durée) for; ~ **que** while.

pendant[2], ~**e** /pɑ̃dɑ̃, -t/ a hanging; **jambes** ~**es** with one's legs dangling. ●nm (contrepartie) matching piece (**de** to); ~ **d'oreille** drop ear-ring.

pendentif /pɑ̃dɑ̃tif/ nm pendant.

penderie /pɑ̃dRi/ nf wardrobe.

pendre /pɑ̃dR/ [3] vt/i hang. □ **se** ~ vpr hang (**à** from); (se tuer) hang oneself.

pendule /pɑ̃dyl/ nf clock. ●nm pendulum.

pénétrer /penetRe/ [14] vi ~ (**dans**) enter; **faire** ~ **une crème** rub a cream in. ●vt penetrate.

pénible /penibl/ a (travail) hard; (nouvelle) painful; (enfant) tiresome.

péniche /peniʃ/ nf barge.

pénitence /penitɑ̃s/ nf (Relig) penance; (punition) punishment; **faire** ~ repent.

pénitentiaire /penitɑ̃sjɛR/ a (établissement) penal.

pénombre /penɔ̃bR/ nf half-light.

pensée /pɑ̃se/ nf (idée) thought; (fleur) pansy.

penser /pɑ̃se/ [1] vt/i think; ~ **à** (réfléchir à) think about; (se souvenir de, prévoir) think of; ~ **faire** think of doing; **faire** ~ **à** remind one of.

pensif, -ive /pɑ̃sif, -v/ a pensive.

pension /pɑ̃sjɔ̃/ nf (Scol) boarding school; (repas, somme) board; (allocation) pension; ~ (**de famille**) guest house; ~ **alimentaire** (Jur) alimony. **pensionnaire** nmf (Scol) boarder; (d'hôtel) guest.

pensionnat nm boarding school.

pente /pɑ̃t/ nf slope; **en** ~ sloping.

Pentecôte /pɑ̃tkot/ nf **la** ~ Whitsun.

pénurie /penyRi/ nf shortage.

pépin /pepɛ̃/ nm (graine) pip; (ennui []) hitch.

pépinière /pepinjɛR/ nf (tree) nursery.

perçant, ~e /pɛRsɑ̃, -t/ a (cri) shrill; (regard) piercing.

perce-neige /pɛRsənɛʒ/ nm or f inv snowdrop.

percepteur /pɛRsɛptœR/ nm tax inspector.

percer /pɛRse/ [10] vt pierce; (avec perceuse) drill; (mystère) penetrate. ●vi break through; (dent) come through. **perceuse** nf drill.

P

percevoir /pɛRsəvwaR/ [52] vt
perceive; (*impôt*) collect.

perche /pɛRʃ/ nf (*bâton*) pole.

percher (se) /(sə)pɛRʃe/ [1] vpr
perch.

percolateur /pɛRkɔlatœR/ nm
coffee machine.

percuter /pɛRkyte/ [1] vt
(*véhicule*) crash into.

perdant, **~e** /pɛRdɑ̃, -t/ a losing.
● nm, f loser.

perdre /pɛRdR/ [3] vt/i lose;
(*gaspiller*) waste; **~ ses poils** (*chat*)
moult. □ **se ~** vpr get lost; (*rester
inutilisé*) go to waste.

perdrix /pɛRdRi/ nf partridge.

perdu, **~e** /pɛRdy/ a lost;
(*endroit*) isolated; (*balle*) stray;
c'est du temps ~ it's a waste of
time.

père /pɛR/ nm father; **~ de famille**
father, family man; **~ spirituel**
father figure; **le ~ Noël** Santa
Claus.

perfection /pɛRfɛksjɔ̃/ nf
perfection.

perfectionner /pɛRfɛksjɔne/ [1]
vt (*technique*) perfect; (*art*) refine.
□ **se ~** vpr improve; **se ~ en
anglais** improve one's English.

perforer /pɛRfɔre/ [1] vt
perforate; (*billet, bande*) punch.

performance /pɛRfɔRmɑ̃s/ nf
performance.

perfusion /pɛRfyzjɔ̃/ nf drip; **sous
~** on a drip.

péridurale /peRidyRal/ nf
epidural.

péril /peRil/ nm peril; **à tes risques
et ~s** at your own risk.

périlleux, **-euse** /peRijø, -z/ a
perilous.

périmé, **~e** /peRime/ a (*produit*)
past its use-by date; (*désuet*)
outdated.

période /peRjɔd/ nf period.

périodique /peRjɔdik/ a period-
ic(al). ● nm (*journal*) periodical.

péripétie /peRipesi/ nf
(unexpected) event, adventure.

périphérique /peRifeRik/ a
peripheral. ● nm (**boulevard**) **~**
ring road.

périple /peRipl/ nm journey.

périr /peRiR/ [2] vi perish, die.

perle /pɛRl/ nf (d'huître) pearl; (de
verre) bead.

permanence /pɛRmanɑ̃s/ nf
permanence; (Scol) study room;
de ~ on duty; **en ~** permanently;
assurer une ~ keep the office
open.

permanent, **~e** /pɛRmanɑ̃, -t/ a
permanent; (*constant*) constant;
formation ~e continuous
education. **permanente** nf
(coiffure) perm.

permettre /pɛRmɛtR/ [42] vt
allow; **~ à qn de** allow sb to. □ **se
~** vpr (*achat*) afford; **se ~ de faire**
take the liberty of doing.

permis, **~e** /pɛRmi, -z/ a
allowed. ● nm licence, permit; **~
(de conduire)** driving licence.

permission /pɛRmisjɔ̃/ nf
permission; **en ~** (Mil) on leave.

Pérou /peRu/ nm Peru.

perpendiculaire /pɛRpɑ̃dikylɛR/
a & nf perpendicular.

perpétuité /pɛRpetɥite/ nf **à ~**
for life.

perplexe /pɛRplɛks/ a perplexed.

perquisition /pɛRkizisjɔ̃/ nf
(police) search.

perron /pɛRɔ̃/ nm (front) steps.

perroquet /pɛRɔke/ nm parrot.

perruche /pɛRyʃ/ nf budgerigar.

perruque /pɛRyk/ nf wig.

persécuter /pɛRsekyte/ [1] vt
persecute.

persévérance /pɛRseveRɑ̃s/ nf
perseverance. **persévérer** [14] vi
persevere.

persienne /pɛRsjɛn/ nf (outside)
shutter.

persil /pɛRsi/ nm parsley.

persistance /pɛʀsistɑ̃s/ *nf*
persistence. **persistant,** ~**e** *a*
persistent; (*feuillage*) evergreen.
persister /pɛʀsiste/ [1] *vi* persist
(à faire in doing).
personnage /pɛʀsɔnaʒ/ *nm*
character; (personne célèbre)
personality.
personnalité /pɛʀsɔnalite/ *nf*
personality.
personne /pɛʀsɔn/ *nf* person; ~**s**
people. ● *pron* nobody, no-one;
je n'ai vu ~ I didn't see anybody.
personnel, ~**le** /pɛʀsɔnɛl/ *a*
personal; (égoïste) selfish. ● *nm*
staff.
perspective /pɛʀspɛktiv/ *nf*
(art, point de vue) perspective; (vue)
view; (éventualité) prospect.
perspicace /pɛʀspikas/ *a*
shrewd. **perspicacité** *nf*
shrewdness.
persuader /pɛʀsɥade/ [1] *vt*
persuade (**de faire** to do).
persuasif, -ive /pɛʀsɥazif, -v/ *a*
persuasive.
perte /pɛʀt/ *nf* loss; (ruine) ruin; **à**
~ **de vue** as far as the eye can
see; ~ **de** (*temps, argent*) waste
of; ~ **sèche** total loss; ~**s** (Méd)
discharge.
pertinent, ~**e** /pɛʀtinɑ̃, -t/ *a*
pertinent.
perturbateur, -trice /pɛʀtyʀ-
batœʀ, -tʀis/ *nm, f* disruptive
element. **perturbation** *nf*
disruption. **perturber** [1] *vt*
disrupt; (*personne*) perturb.
pervers, ~**e** /pɛʀvɛʀ, -s/ *a*
(dépravé) perverted; (méchant)
wicked.
pervertir /pɛʀvɛʀtiʀ/ [2] *vt*
pervert.
pesant, ~**e** /pəzɑ̃, -t/ *a* heavy.
pesanteur /pəzɑ̃tœʀ/ *nf*
heaviness; **la** ~ (force) gravity.
pesée /pəze/ *nf* weighing; (effort)
pressure.

pèse-personne (*pl* ~**s**) /pɛzpɛʀ-
sɔn/ *nm* (bathroom) scales.
peser /pəze/ [6] *vt/i* weigh; ~ **sur**
bear upon.
pessimiste /pesimist/ *a*
pessimistic. ● *nmf* pessimist.
peste /pɛst/ *nf* plague; (personne
🖬) pest.
pet /pɛ/ *nm* 🖬 fart 🖬.
pétale /petal/ *nm* petal.
pétard /petaʀ/ *nm* banger.
péter /pete/ [14] *vi* 🖬 fart 🖬, go
bang; (casser) snap.
pétillant, ~**e** /petijɑ̃, -t/ *a*
(*boisson*) sparkling; (*personne*)
bubbly.
pétiller /petije/ [1] *vi* (*feu*)
crackle; (*champagne, yeux*)
sparkle; ~ **d'intelligence** sparkle
with intelligence.
petit, ~**e** /p(ə)ti, -t/ *a* small; (avec
nuance affective) little; (jeune) young,
small; (défaut) minor; (mesquin)
petty; **en** ~ in miniature; ~ **à** ~
little by little; **un** ~ **peu** a little
bit; ~ **ami** boyfriend; ~**e amie**
girlfriend; ~**es annonces** small
ads; ~**e cuillère** teaspoon; ~
déjeuner breakfast; ~ **pois** garden
pea. ● *nm, f* little child; (Scol)
junior; ~**s** (de chat) kittens; (de
chien) pups. **petite-fille** (*pl*
petites-filles) *nf* granddaughter.
petit-fils (*pl* **petits-fils**) *nm*
grandson.
pétition /petisjɔ̃/ *nf* petition.
petits-enfants /pətizɑ̃fɑ̃/ *nmpl*
grandchildren.
pétrin /petʀɛ̃/ *nm* **dans le** ~ 🖬 in
a fix 🖬.
pétrir /petʀiʀ/ [2] *vt* knead.
pétrole /petʀɔl/ *nm* oil; ~ **brut**
crude oil.
pétrolier, -ière /petʀɔlje, -jɛʀ/ *a*
oil. ● *nm* (navire) oil-tanker.
peu /pø/ *adv* ~ (**de**) (quantité) little,
not much; (nombre) few, not many;
~ **intéressant** not very interesting;

P

il mange ~ he doesn't eat very much. ●*pron* few. ●*nm* little; un ~ (de) a little; à ~ près more or less; de ~ only just; ~ à ~ gradually; ~ après/avant shortly after/before; ~ de chose not much; ~ nombreux few; ~ souvent seldom; pour ~ que if.

peuple /pœpl/ *nm* people.

peupler [1] *vt* populate.

peuplier /pøplije/ *nm* poplar.

peur /pœʀ/ *nf* fear; avoir ~ be afraid (de of); de ~ de for fear of; faire ~ à frighten. **peureux, -euse** *a* fearful.

peut /pø/ ⇒POUVOIR [49].

peut-être /pøtɛtʀ/ *adv* perhaps, maybe; ~ qu'il viendra he might come.

peux /pø/ ⇒POUVOIR [49].

phare /faʀ/ *nm* (tour) lighthouse; (de véhicule) headlight; ~ antibrouillard fog lamp.

pharmacie /faʀmasi/ *nf* (magasin) chemist's (shop), pharmacy; (science) pharmacy; (armoire) medicine cabinet. **pharmacien, ~ne** *nm, f* chemist, pharmacist.

phénomène /fenɔmɛn/ *nm* phenomenon; (personne 🄸) eccentric.

philosophe /filɔzɔf/ *nmf* philosopher. ●*a* philosophical. **philosophie** *nf* philosophy. **philosophique** *a* philosophical.

phobie /fɔbi/ *nf* phobia.

phonétique /fɔnetik/ *a* phonetic. ●*nf* phonetics.

phoque /fɔk/ *nm* (animal) seal.

photo /fɔto/ *nf* photo; (art) photography; prendre en ~ take a photo of; ~ d'identité passport photograph.

photocopie /fɔtɔkɔpi/ *nf* photocopy. **photocopier** [45] *vt* photocopy.

photographe /fɔtɔgʀaf/ *nmf* photographer. **photographie** *nf*

photograph; (art) photography. **photographier** [45] *vt* take a photo of.

phrase /fʀɑz/ *nf* sentence.

physicien, ~ne /fizisjɛ̃, -ɛn/ *nm, f* physicist.

physique /fizik/ *a* physical. ●*nm* physique; au ~ physically. ●*nf* physics (+ *sg*).

piano /pjano/ *nm* piano.

pianoter /pjanɔte/ [1] *vi* tinkle; ~ sur (*ordinateur*) tap at.

PIB *abrév m* (**produit intérieur brut**) GDP.

pic /pik/ *nm* (outil) pickaxe; (sommet) peak; (oiseau) woodpecker; à ~ (*falaise*) sheer; (*couler*) straight to the bottom; tomber à ~ 🄸 come just at the right time.

pichet /piʃɛ/ *nm* jug.

picorer /pikɔʀe/ [1] *vt/i* peck.

picotement /pikɔtmɑ̃/ *nm* tingling. **picoter** [1] *vt* sting; (*yeux*) sting.

pie /pi/ *nf* magpie.

pièce /pjɛs/ *nf* (d'habitation) room; (de monnaie) coin; (Théât) play; (pour raccommoder) patch; (écrit) document; (morceau) piece; ~ (de théâtre) play; dix francs (la) ~ ten francs each; ~ détachée part; ~ d'identité identity paper; ~s jointes enclosures; (courrier électronique) attachments; ~s justificatives written proof; ~ montée tiered cake; ~ de rechange spare part; un deux-~s a two-room flat.

pied /pje/ *nm* foot; (de meuble) leg; (de lampe) base; (de verre) stem; (d'appareil photo) stand; être ~s nus be bare-foot; à ~ on foot; au ~ de la lettre literally; avoir ~ be able to touch the bottom; jouer au tennis comme un ~ 🄸 be hopeless at tennis; mettre sur ~ set up; sur un ~ d'égalité on an equal footing; **mettre les ~s dans le plat** 🔲 put one's foot in it; **c'est le ~** 🔲 it's great. **pied-bot** (*pl* **pieds-bots**) *nm* club-foot.

piédestal /pjedɛstal/ *nm* pedestal.

piège /pjɛʒ/ *nm* trap.

piéger /pjeʒe/ [14] [40] *vt* trap; **lettre/voiture piégée** letter/car bomb.

piercing /piRsiŋ/ *nm* body piercing.

pierre /pjɛR/ *nf* stone; **~ précieuse** precious stone; **~ tombale** tombstone.

piétiner /pjetine/ [1] *vi* (*avancer lentement*) shuffle along; (*fig*) make no headway; **~ d'impatience** hop up and down with impatience. ●*vt* trample (on).

piéton /pjetɔ̃/ *nm* pedestrian.

pieu (*pl* **~x**) /pjø/ *nm* post, stake.

pieuvre /pjœvR/ *nf* octopus.

pieux, -ieuse /pjø, -z/ *a* pious.

pigeon /piʒɔ̃/ *nm* pigeon.

piger /piʒe/ [40] *vt/i* 🔲 understand, get (it).

pile /pil/ *nf* (*tas*) pile; (*Électr*) battery; **~ ou face?** heads or tails? ●*adv* (*s'arrêter* 🔲) dead; **à dix heures ~** 🔲 at ten on the dot

pilier /pilje/ *nm* pillar.

pillage /pijaʒ/ *nm* looting.

pillard, ~e *nm, f* looter. **piller** [1] *vt* loot.

pilote /pilɔt/ *nm* (*Aviat, Naut*) pilot; (*Auto*) driver. ●*a* pilot. **piloter** [1] *vt* (*Aviat, Naut*) pilot; (*Auto*) drive.

pilule /pilyl/ *nf* pill; **la ~** the pill.

piment /pimɑ̃/ *nm* hot pepper; (*fig*) spice. **pimenté, ~e** *a* spicy.

pin /pɛ̃/ *nm* pine.

pinard /pinaR/ *nm* 🔲 plonk 🔲, cheap wine.

pince /pɛ̃s/ *nf* (*outil*) pliers (+ *pl*); (*levier*) crowbar; (*de crabe*) pincer; (*à sucre*) tongs (+ *pl*); **~ à épiler** tweezers (+ *pl*); **~ à linge** clothes peg.

pinceau (*pl* **~x**) /pɛ̃so/ *nm* paintbrush.

pincée /pɛ̃se/ *nf* pinch (**de** of).

pincer /pɛ̃se/ [10] *vt* pinch; (*attraper* 🔲) catch. ▫ **se ~** *vpr* catch oneself; **se ~ le doigt** catch one's finger.

pince-sans-rire /pɛ̃ssɑ̃RiR/ *nmf inv* **c'est un ~** he has a deadpan sense of humour.

pingouin /pɛ̃gwɛ̃/ *nm* penguin.

pingre /pɛ̃gR/ *a* stingy.

pintade /pɛ̃tad/ *nf* guinea fowl.

piocher /pjɔʃe/ [1] *vt/i* dig; (*étudier* 🔲) study hard, slog away (at).

pion /pjɔ̃/ *nm* (*de jeu*) counter; (*aux échecs*) pawn; (*Scol* 🔲) supervisor.

pipe /pip/ *nf* pipe; **fumer la ~** smoke a pipe.

piquant, ~e /pikɑ̃, -t/ *a* (*barbe*) prickly; (*goût*) pungent; (*remarque*) cutting. ●*nm* prickle.

pique /pik/ *nm* (*aux cartes*) spades.

pique-nique (*pl* **~s**) /piknik/ *nm* picnic.

piquer /pike/ [1] *vt* (*épine*) prick; (*épice*) burn, sting; (*abeille, ortie*) sting; (*serpent, moustique*) bite; (*enfoncer*) stick; (*coudre*) (*machine-*) stitch; (*curiosité*) excite; (*voler* 🔲) pinch. ●*vi* (*avion*) dive; (*goût*) be hot. ▫ **se ~** *vpr* prick oneself.

piquet /pike/ *nm* stake; (*de tente*) peg; (*de parasol*) pole; **~ de grève** (strike) picket.

piqûre /pikyR/ *nf* prick; (*d'abeille*) sting; (*de serpent*) bite; (*point*) stitch; (*Méd*) injection, jab; **faire une ~ à qn** give sb an injection.

pirate /piRat/ *nm* pirate; **~ informatique** computer hacker; **~ de l'air** hijacker.

pire /piR/ *a* worse (**que** than); **les ~s mensonges** the most wicked lies. ●*nm* **le ~** the worst; **au ~** at worst.

pis /pi/ *nm* (*de vache*) udder. ●*a*

P

inv & adv worse; **aller de mal en ∼** go from bad to worse.

piscine /pisin/ *nf* swimming-pool; **∼ couverte** indoor swimming-pool.

pissenlit /pisãli/ *nm* dandelion.

pistache /pistaʃ/ *nf* pistachio.

piste /pist/ *nf* track; (de personne, d'animal) track, trail; (Aviat) runway; (de cirque) ring; (de ski) slope; (de danse) floor; (Sport) racetrack; **∼ cyclable** cycle lane.

pistolet /pistɔlɛ/ *nm* gun, pistol; (de peintre) spray-gun.

piteux, -euse /pitø, -z/ *a* pitiful.

pitié /pitje/ *nf* pity; **il me fait ∼** I feel sorry for him.

piton /pitɔ̃/ *nm* (à crochet) hook; (sommet pointu) peak.

pitoyable /pitwajabl/ *a* pitiful.

pitre /pitr/ *nm* clown; **faire le ∼** clown around.

pittoresque /pitɔrɛsk/ *a* picturesque.

pivot /pivo/ *nm* pivot. **pivoter** [1] *vi* revolve; (*personne*) swing round.

placard /plakaʀ/ *nm* cupboard; (affiche) poster. **placarder** [1] *vt* (*affiche*) post up; (*mur*) cover with posters.

place /plas/ *nf* place; (espace libre) room, space; (siège) seat, place; (prix d'un trajet) fare; (esplanade) square; (emploi) position; (de parking) space; **à la ∼ de** instead of; **en ∼, à sa ∼** in its place; **faire ∼ à** give way to; **sur ∼** on the spot; **remettre qn à sa ∼** put sb in his place; **ça prend de la ∼** it takes up a lot of room; **se mettre à la ∼ de qn** put oneself in sb's shoes *ou* place.

placement /plasmã/ *nm* (d'argent) investment.

placer /plase/ [10] *vt* place; (*invité, spectateur*) seat; (*argent*) invest. □ **se ∼** *vpr* (*personne*) take up a position.

plafond /plafɔ̃/ *nm* ceiling.

plage /plaʒ/ *nf* beach; **∼ horaire** time slot.

plagiat /plaʒja/ *nm* plagiarism.

plaider /plede/ [1] *vt/i* plead. **plaidoirie** *nf* (defence) speech. **plaidoyer** *nm* plea.

plaie /plɛ/ *nf* wound; (personne 🄸) nuisance.

plaignant, ∼e /plɛɲã, -t/ *nm, f* plaintiff.

plaindre /plɛ̃dr/ [22] *vt* pity. □ **se ∼** *vpr* complain (**de** about); **se ∼ de** (souffrir de) complain of.

plaine /plɛn/ *nf* plain.

plainte /plɛ̃t/ *nf* complaint; (gémissement) groan. **plaintif, -ive** *a* plaintive.

plaire /plɛʀ/ [47] *vi* **à** please; **ça lui plaît** he likes it; **elle lui plaît** he likes her; **ça me plaît de faire** I like *ou* enjoy doing; **s'il vous plaît** please. □ **se ∼** *vpr* **il se plaît ici** he likes it here.

plaisance /plɛzãs/ *nf* **la** (navigation de) **∼** boating.

plaisant, ∼e /plɛzã, -t/ *a* pleasant; (drôle) amusing.

plaisanter /plɛzãte/ [1] *vi* joke. **plaisanterie** *nf* joke. **plaisantin** *nm* joker.

plaisir /plezir/ *nm* pleasure; **faire ∼ à** please; **pour le ∼** for fun *ou* pleasure.

plan /plã/ *nm* plan; (de ville) map; (de livre) outline; **∼ d'eau** artificial lake; **∼ social** planned redundancy programme; **premier ∼** foreground.

planche /plãʃ/ *nf* board, plank; (gravure) plate; **∼ à repasser** ironing-board; **∼ à voile** windsurfing board; (Sport) windsurfing.

plancher /plãʃe/ *nm* floor.

planer /plane/ [1] *vi* glide; **∼ sur** (*mystère, danger*) hang over.

planète /planɛt/ *nf* planet.

planeur /planœR/ *nm* glider.

planifier /planifje/ [45] *vt* plan.

plant /plɑ̃/ *nm* seedling; (de légumes) patch.

plante /plɑ̃t/ *nf* plant; ~ d'appartement houseplant; ~ des pieds sole (of the foot).

planter /plɑ̃te/ [1] *vt* (*plante*) plant; (*enfoncer*) drive in; (*tente*) put up; **rester planté** 🖪 stand still.

plaque /plak/ *nf* plate; (de marbre) slab; (insigne) badge; ~ chauffante hotplate; ~ commémorative plaque; ~ minéralogique numberplate; ~ de verglas patch of ice.

plaquer /plake/ [1] *vt* (*bois*) veneer; (*aplatir*) flatten; (*rugby*) tackle; (*abandonner* 🖪) ditch 🖪; **tout** ~ chuck it all.

plastique /plastik/ *a & nm* plastic; **en** ~ plastic.

plastiquer /plastike/ [1] *vt* blow up.

plat, ~e /pla, -t/ *a* flat. ●*nm* (Culin) dish; (partie de repas) course; (de la main) flat. ●**à plat** *adv* (*poser*) flat; (*batterie, pneu*) flat; **à** ~ **ventre** flat on one's face.

platane /platan/ *nm* plane tree.

plateau (*pl* ~x) /plato/ *nm* tray; (de cinéma) set; (de balance) pan; (Géog) plateau; ~ de fromages cheeseboard; ~ de fruits de mer seafood platter. **plate-bande** (*pl* **plates-bandes**) *nf* flower-bed.

platine /platin/ *nm* platinum. ●*nf* (tourne-disque) turntable; ~ **laser** compact disc player.

plâtre /plɑtR/ *nm* plaster; (Méd) (plaster) cast.

plein, ~e /plɛ̃, -ɛn/ *a* full (de of); (total) complete. ●*nm* **faire le** ~ (d'essence) fill up (the tank); **à** ~ fully; **à** ~ **temps** full-time; **en** ~ **air** in the open air; **en** ~ **milieu**/

visage right in the middle/the face; **en** ~**e nuit** in the middle of the night. ●*adv* **avoir des idées** ~ **la tête** be full of ideas. **pleinement** *adv* fully.

pleurer /plœRe/ [1] *vi* cry, weep (**sur** over); (*yeux*) water. ●*vt* mourn.

pleurnicher /plœRniʃe/ [1] *vi* 🖪 snivel.

pleurs /plœR/ *nmpl* tears; **en** ~ in tears.

pleuvoir /pløvwaR/ [48] *vi* rain; (fig) rain *ou* shower down; **il pleut** it is raining; **il pleut à verse** *ou* **des cordes** it is pouring.

pli /pli/ *nm* fold; (de jupe) pleat; (de pantalon) crease; (lettre) letter; (habitude) habit; (**faux**) ~ crease.

pliant, ~e /plijɑ̃, -t/ *a* folding. ●*nm* folding stool, camp-stool.

plier /plije/ [45] *vt* fold; (courber) bend; (soumettre) submit (**à** to). ●*vi* bend. □ **se** ~ *vpr* fold; **se** ~ **à** submit to.

plinthe /plɛ̃t/ *nf* skirting-board.

plissé, ~e /plise/ *a* (jupe) pleated.

plisser /plise/ [1] *vt* crease; (*yeux*) screw up.

plomb /plɔ̃/ *nm* lead; (fusible) fuse; ~s (de chasse) lead shot; **de** *ou* **en** ~ lead. **plombage** *nm* filling.

plomberie /plɔ̃bRi/ *nf* plumbing. **plombier** *nm* plumber.

plongée /plɔ̃ʒe/ *nf* diving; **en** ~ (sous-marin) submerged.

plongeoir /plɔ̃ʒwaR/ *nm* diving-board.

plonger /plɔ̃ʒe/ [40] *vi* dive; (route) plunge. ●*vt* plunge. □ **se** ~ *vpr* plunge into; **se** ~ **dans** (fig) (lecture) bury oneself in.

plongeur, -euse *nm, f* diver; (de restaurant) dishwasher.

plu /ply/ ⇒PLAIRE [47], PLEUVOIR [48].

pluie /plɥi/ *nf* rain; (averse)

shower; ~ **battante/diluvienne** driving/torrential rain.

plume /plym/ *nf* feather; (pointe) nib.

plumeau (*pl* ~**x**) /plymo/ *nm* feather duster.

plumier /plymje/ *nm* pencil box.

plupart: la ~ /laplypaʀ/ *loc* **la** ~ **des** (*gens, cas*) most; **la** ~ **du temps** most of the time; **pour la** ~ for the most part.

pluriel, ~**le** /plyʀjɛl/ *a* & *nm* plural.

plus /ply, plys, plyz/

●*adverbe de comparaison*

••••▸ more (**que** than); ~ **âgé/tard** older/later; ~ **beau** more beautiful; ~ **j'y pense...** the more I think about it...; **deux fois** ~ twice as much; **deux fois** ~ **cher** twice as expensive.

••••▸ **le** ~ the most; **le** ~ **grand** the biggest; (de deux) the bigger.

••••▸ ~ **de** (*pain*) more; (*dix jours*) more than; **il est** ~ **de 8 heures** it is after 8 o'clock.

••••▸ **de** ~ more (**que** than); (en outre) moreover; **les enfants de** ~ **de 10 ans** children over 10 years old; **de** ~ **en** ~ more and more.

••••▸ **en** ~ on top of that; **c'est en** ~ it's extra; **en** ~ **de** in addition to.

••••▸ ~ **ou moins** more or less.

••••▸ **au** ~ **tard** at the latest.

●*adverbe de négation*

••••▸ **ne** ~ (*temps*) no longer, not any more; **je n'y vais** ~ I don't go there any longer *ou* any more.

••••▸ **ne** ~ **de** (*quantité*) no more; **il n'y a** ~ **de pain** there is no more bread.

••••▸ ~ **que deux jours!** only two days left!

●*préposition & nom masculin*

••••▸ (maths) plus.

plusieurs /plyzjœʀ/ *a* & *pron* several.

plus-value (*pl* ~**s**) /plyvaly/ *nf* (bénéfice) profit.

plutôt /plyto/ *adv* rather (**que** than).

pluvieux, -ieuse /plyvjø, -z/ *a* rainy.

PME *abrév f* (**petites et moyennes entreprises**) SME.

PNB *abrév m* (**produit national brut**) GNP.

pneu (*pl* ~**s**) /pnø/ *nm* tyre. **pneumatique** *a* inflatable.

poche /pɔʃ/ *nf* pocket; (sac) bag; ~**s** (sous les yeux) bags.

pocher /pɔʃe/ [1] *vt* (œuf) poach.

pochette /pɔʃɛt/ *nf* (de documents) folder; (sac) bag, pouch; (d'allumettes) book; (de disque) sleeve; (mouchoir) pocket handkerchief.

poêle /pwal/ *nf* ~ (à frire) frying-pan. ● *nm* stove.

poème /pɔɛm/ *nm* poem. **poésie** *nf* poetry; (poème) poem. **poète** *nm* poet. **poétique** *a* poetic.

poids /pwa/ *nm* weight; ~ **coq/lourd/plume** bantam/heavyweight/featherweight; ~ **lourd** (camion) lorry, juggernaut; (US) truck.

poignard /pwaɲaʀ/ *nm* dagger. **poignarder** [1] *vt* stab.

poigne /pwaɲ/ *nf* **avoir de la** ~ have a strong grip.

poignée /pwaɲe/ *nf* (de porte) handle; (quantité) handful; ~ **de main** handshake.

poignet /pwaɲɛ/ *nm* wrist; (de chemise) cuff.

poil /pwal/ *nm* hair; (pelage) fur; (de brosse) bristle; ~**s** (de tapis) pile; **à** ~ 🄙 naked; ~ **à gratter**

itching powder. **poilu**, ∼e a hairy.

poinçon /pwɛ̃sɔ̃/ nm awl; (marque) hallmark. **poinçonner** [1] vt (billet) punch.

poing /pwɛ̃/ nm fist.

point /pwɛ̃/ nm (endroit, Sport) point, (marque visible) spot, dot; (de couture) stitch; (pour évaluer) mark; enlever un ∼ par faute take a mark off for each mistake; à ∼ (Culin) medium; (arriver) at the right time; faire le ∼ take stock; mettre au ∼ (photo) focus; (technique) develop; mettre les choses au ∼ get things clear; Camille n'est pas encore au ∼ pour ses examens Camille is not ready for her exams; sur le ∼ de about to; au ∼ que to the extent that; ∼ (final) full stop, period; deux ∼s colon; ∼ d'interrogation/d'exclamation question/exclamation mark; ∼s de suspension suspension points; ∼ virgule semicolon; ∼ culminant peak; ∼ du jour daybreak; ∼ mort (Auto) neutral; ∼ de repère landmark; ∼ de suture (Méd) stitch; ∼ de vente point of sale; ∼ de vue point of view. ● adv (ne) ∼ not.

pointe /pwɛ̃t/ nf point, tip; (clou) tack; (de grille) spike; (fig) touch (de of); de ∼ (industrie) high-tech; en ∼ pointed; heure de ∼ peak hour; sur la ∼ des pieds on tiptoe.

pointer /pwɛ̃te/ [1] vt (cocher) tick off; (diriger) point, aim. ● vi (employé) (en arrivant) clock in; (en sortant) clock out. □ se ∼ vpr 🔟 turn up.

pointillé /pwɛ̃tije/ nm dotted line.

pointilleux, -euse /pwɛ̃tijø, -z/ a fastidious, particular.

pointu, ∼e /pwɛ̃ty/ a pointed; (aiguisé) sharp.

pointure /pwɛ̃tyʀ/ nf size.

poire /pwaʀ/ nf pear.

poireau (pl ∼x) /pwaʀo/ nm leek.

poirier /pwaʀje/ nm pear tree.

pois /pwa/ nm pea; (motif) dot; robe à ∼ polka dot dress.

poison /pwazɔ̃/ nm poison.

poisseux, -euse /pwasø, -z/ a sticky.

poisson /pwasɔ̃/ nm fish; ∼ rouge goldfish; ∼ d'avril April fool; les P∼s Pisces.
poissonnerie nf fish shop.
poissonnier, -ière nm, f fishmonger.

poitrine /pwatʀin/ nf chest; (seins) bosom.

poivre /pwavʀ/ nm pepper. **poivré**, ∼e a peppery. **poivrière** nf pepper-pot.

poivron /pwavʀɔ̃/ nm sweet pepper.

polaire /pɔlɛʀ/ a polar. ● nf (veste) fleece.

pôle /pol/ nm pole.

polémique /polemik/ nf debate. ● a controversial.

poli, ∼e /pɔli/ a (personne) polite.

police /pɔlis/ nf (force) police (+ pl), (discipline) (law and) order; (d'assurance) policy.

policier, -ière /pɔlisje, -jɛʀ/ a police; (roman) detective. ● nm policeman.

polir /pɔliʀ/ [2] vt polish.

politesse /pɔlitɛs/ nf politeness; (parole) polite remark.

politicien, ∼ne /pɔlitisjɛ̃, -ɛn/ nm, f (péj) politician.

politique /pɔlitik/ a political; homme ∼ politician. ● nf politics; (ligne de conduite) policy.

pollen /pɔlɛn/ nm pollen.

polluant, ∼e /pɔlɥɑ̃, -t/ a polluting. ● nm pollutant.

polluer /pɔlɥe/ [1] vt pollute. **pollution** nf pollution.

P

polo /polo/ *nm* (Sport) polo; (vêtement) polo shirt.

Pologne /pɔlɔɲ/ *nf* Poland.

polonais, ∼**e** /pɔlɔnɛ, -z/ *a* Polish. ●*nm* (Ling) Polish. **P**∼, ∼**e** *nm, f* Pole.

poltron, ∼**ne** /pɔltʀɔ̃, -ɔn/ *a* cowardly. ●*nm, f* coward.

polygame /pɔligam/ *nmf* polygamist.

polyvalent, ∼**e** /pɔlivalɑ̃, -t/ *a* varied; (*personne*) versatile.

pommade /pɔmad/ *nf* ointment.

pomme /pɔm/ *nf* apple; (d'arrosoir) rose; ∼ **d'Adam** Adam's apple; ∼ **de pin** pine cone; ∼ **de terre** potato; ∼**s frites** chips; (US) French fries; **tomber dans les** ∼**s** 🄘 pass out.

pommette /pɔmɛt/ *nf* cheekbone.

pommier /pɔmje/ *nm* apple tree.

pompe /pɔ̃p/ *nf* pump; (splendeur) pomp; ∼ **à incendie** fire-engine; ∼**s funèbres** undertaker's (+ *sg*).

pomper /pɔ̃pe/ [1] *vt* pump; (copier 🄘) copy, crib; ∼ **l'air à qn** 🄘 get on sb's nerves.

pompier /pɔ̃pje/ *nm* fireman.

pomponner (se) /(sə)pɔ̃pɔne/ [1] *vpr* get dolled up.

poncer /pɔ̃se/ [10] *vt* sand.

ponctuation /pɔ̃ktɥasjɔ̃/ *nf* punctuation.

ponctuel, ∼**le** /pɔ̃ktɥɛl/ *a* punctual.

pondre /pɔ̃dʀ/ [3] *vt/i* lay.

poney /pɔnɛ/ *nm* pony.

pont /pɔ̃/ *nm* bridge; (de navire) deck; (de graissage) ramp; **faire le** ∼ get an extended weekend; ∼ **aérien** airlift. **pont-levis** (*pl* **ponts-levis**) *nm* drawbridge.

populaire /pɔpylɛʀ/ *a* popular; (*expression*) colloquial; (*quartier, origine*) working-class.

popularité *nf* popularity.

population /pɔpylasjɔ̃/ *nf* population.

porc /pɔʀ/ *nm* pig; (viande) pork.

porcelaine /pɔʀsəlɛn/ *nf* china, porcelain.

porc-épic (*pl* **porcs-épics**) /pɔʀkepik/ *nm* porcupine.

porcherie /pɔʀʃəʀi/ *nf* pigsty.

pornographie /pɔʀnɔgʀafi/ *nf* pornography.

port /pɔʀ/ *nm* port, harbour; **à bon** ∼ safely; ∼ **maritime** seaport; (transport) carriage; (d'armes) carrying; (de barbe) wearing.

portable /pɔʀtabl/ *nm* (Ordinat) laptop (computer); (telephone) mobile (phone).

portail /pɔʀtaj/ *nm* gate.

portatif, **-ive** /pɔʀtatif, -v/ *a* portable.

porte /pɔʀt/ *nf* door; (passage) doorway; (de jardin, d'embarquement) gate; **mettre à la** ∼ throw out; ∼ **d'entrée** front door.

porté, ∼**e** /pɔʀte/ *a* ∼ **à** inclined to; ∼ **sur** keen on.

porte-avions /pɔʀtavjɔ̃/ *nm inv* aircraft carrier.

porte-bagages /pɔʀtbagaʒ/ *nm inv* (de vélo) carrier.

porte-bonheur /pɔʀtbɔnœʀ/ *nm inv* lucky charm.

porte-clefs /pɔʀtəkle/ *nm inv* key ring.

porte-documents /pɔʀtdɔkymɑ̃/ *nm inv* briefcase.

portée /pɔʀte/ *nf* (d'une arme) range; (de voûte) span; (d'animaux) litter; (impact) significance; (Mus) stave; **à** ∼ **de (la) main** within (arm's) reach; **hors de** ∼ **(de)** out of reach (of); **à la** ∼ **de qn** at sb's level.

porte-fenêtre (*pl* **portes-fenêtres**) /pɔʀtfənɛtʀ/ *nf* French window.

portefeuille /pɔʀtəfœj/ *nm* wallet; (de ministre) portfolio.

porte-jarretelles /pɔʀtʒaʀtɛl/ *nm inv* suspender belt.

portemanteau (*pl* ~x) /pɔʀtmɑ̃to/ *nm* coat *ou* hat stand.

porte-monnaie /pɔʀtmɔnɛ/ *nm inv* purse.

porte-parole /pɔʀtpaʀɔl/ *nm inv* spokesperson.

porter /pɔʀte/ [1] *vt* carry; (*vêtement, bague*) wear; (*fruits, responsabilité, coup*) bear; (*coup*) strike; (*amener*) bring; (*inscrire*) enter. ●*vi* (*bruit*) carry; (*coup*) hit home; ~ **sur** rest on; (*concerner*) be about. □ **se** ~ *vpr* **bien se** ~ be *ou* feel well; **se** ~ **candidat** stand as a candidate.

porteur, -euse /pɔʀtœʀ, -øz/ *nm, f* (de nouvelles) bearer; (Méd) carrier. ●*nm* (Rail) porter.

portier /pɔʀtje/ *nm* doorman.

portière /pɔʀtjɛʀ/ *nf* door.

porto /pɔʀto/ *nm* port (wine).

portrait /pɔʀtʀɛ/ *nm* portrait. **portrait-robot** (*pl* **portraits-robots**) *nm* identikit®, photofit®.

portuaire /pɔʀtɥɛʀ/ *a* port.

portugais, ~e /pɔʀtyɡɛ, -z/ *a* Portuguese. ●*nm* (Ling) Portuguese. **P~, ~e** *nm, f* Portuguese.

Portugal /pɔʀtyɡal/ *nm* Portugal.

pose /poz/ *nf* installation; (attitude) pose; (Photo) exposure.

posé, ~e /poze/ *a* calm, serious.

poser /poze/ [1] *vt* put (down); (installer) install, put in; (fondations) lay; (question) ask; (problème) pose; ~ **sa candidature** apply (à for). ●*vi* (modèle) pose. □ **se** ~ *vpr* (avion, oiseau) land; (regard) fall; (se présenter) arise.

positif, -ive /pozitif, -v/ *a* positive.

position /pozisjɔ̃/ *nf* position; **prendre** ~ take a stand.

posologie /pozɔlɔʒi/ *nf* dosage.

posséder /posede/ [14] *vt* (propriété) own, possess; (diplôme) have.

possessif, -ive /posesif, -v/ *a* possessive.

possession /posesjɔ̃/ *nf* possession; **prendre** ~ **de** take possession of.

possibilité /posibilite/ *nf* possibility.

possible /posibl/ *a* possible; **dès que** ~ as soon as possible; **le plus tard** ~ as late as possible. ●*nm* **le** ~ what is possible; **faire son** ~ do one's utmost.

postal, ~e (*mpl* **-aux**) /postal, -o/ *a* postal.

poste /post/ *nf* (service) post; (bureau) post office; ~ **aérienne** airmail; **mettre à la** ~ post; ~ **restante** poste restante. ●*nm* **le** (lieu, emploi) post; (de radio, télévision) set; (téléphone) extension (number); ~ **d'essence** petrol station; ~ **d'incendie** fire point; ~ **de pilotage** cockpit; ~ **de police** police station; ~ **de secours** first-aid post.

poster[1] /poste/ [1] *vt* (lettre, personne) post.

poster[2] /postɛʀ/ *nm* poster.

postérieur, ~e /posteʀjœʀ/ *a* later; (partie) back; ~ **à** after. ●*nm* ▣ posterior.

posthume /postym/ *a* posthumous.

postiche /postiʃ/ *a* false.

postier, -ière /postje, -jɛʀ/ *nm, f* postal worker.

post-scriptum /postskʀiptɔm/ *nm inv* postscript.

postuler /postyle/ [1] *vt/i* apply (à for); (principe) postulate.

pot /po/ *nm* pot; (en plastique) carton; (en verre) jar; (chance ▣) luck; (boisson ▣) drink; ~ **catalytique** catalytic converter; ~ **d'échappement** exhaust pipe.

P

potable /pɔtabl/ *a* eau ∼ drinking water.

potage /pɔtaʒ/ *nm* soup.

potager, -ère /pɔtaʒe, -ɛʀ/ *a* vegetable. ●*nm* vegetable garden.

pot-au-feu /pɔtofø/ *nm inv* (plat) stew.

pot-de-vin (*pl* pots-de-vin) /podvɛ̃/ *nm* bribe.

poteau (*pl* ∼x) /pɔto/ *nm* post; (télégraphique) pole; ∼ indicateur signpost.

potelé, ∼e /pɔtle/ *a* plump.

potentiel, ∼le /pɔtɑ̃sjɛl/ *a & nm* potential.

poterie /pɔtʀi/ *nf* pottery; (objet) piece of pottery. **potier** *nm* potter.

potins /pɔtɛ̃/ *nmpl* gossip (+ *sg*).

potiron /pɔtiʀɔ̃/ *nm* pumpkin.

pou (*pl* ∼x) /pu/ *nm* louse.

poubelle /pubɛl/ *nf* dustbin.

pouce /pus/ *nm* thumb; (de pied) big toe; (mesure) inch.

poudre /pudʀ/ *nf* powder; ∼ (à canon) gunpowder; en ∼ (lait) powdered; (chocolat) drinking.

poudrier /pudʀije/ *nm* (powder) compact.

pouf /puf/ *nm* pouffe.

poulailler /pulaje/ *nm* hen house.

poulain /pulɛ̃/ *nm* foal; (protégé) protégé.

poule /pul/ *nf* hen; (Culin) fowl; (femme 🖾) tart.

poulet /pulɛ/ *nm* chicken.

pouliche /puliʃ/ *nf* filly.

poulie /puli/ *nf* pulley.

pouls /pu/ *nm* pulse.

poumon /pumɔ̃/ *nm* lung.

poupe /pup/ *nf* stern.

poupée /pupe/ *nf* doll.

pour /puʀ/ *prép* for; (envers) to; (à la place de) on behalf of; (comme) as; ∼ cela for that reason; ∼ cent

per cent; ∼ de bon for good; ∼ faire (in order) to do; ∼ que so that; ∼ moi (à mon avis) as for me; trop poli ∼ too polite to; ∼ ce qui est de as for; être ∼ be in favour. ●*nm inv* le ∼ et le contre the pros and cons.

pourboire /puʀbwaʀ/ *nm* tip.

pourcentage /puʀsɑ̃taʒ/ *nm* percentage.

pourparlers /puʀpaʀle/ *nmpl* talks.

pourpre /puʀpʀ/ *a & nm* crimson; (violet) purple.

pourquoi /puʀkwa/ *conj & adv* why. ●*nm inv* le ∼ et le comment the why and the wherefore.

pourra, pourrait /puʀa, puʀɛ/ ⇒POUVOIR [49].

pourri, ∼e /puʀi/ *a* rotten. **pourrir** [2] *vt/i* rot. **pourriture** *nf* rot.

poursuite /puʀsɥit/ *nf* pursuit (de of); ∼s (Jur) legal action (+ *sg*).

poursuivre /puʀsɥivʀ/ [57] *vt* pursue; (continuer) continue (with); ∼ (en justice) take to court; (droit civil) sue. ●*vi* continue. □ se ∼ *vpr* continue.

pourtant /puʀtɑ̃/ *adv* yet.

pourvoir /puʀvwaʀ/ [63] *vi* ∼ à provide for; **pourvu de** supplied with.

pourvu que /puʀvyk(ə)/ *conj* (condition) provided (that); (souhait) let us hope (that).

pousse /pus/ *nf* growth; (bourgeon) shoot.

poussé, ∼e /puse/ *a* (études) advanced; (enquête) thorough.

poussée /puse/ *nf* pressure; (coup) push; (de prix) upsurge; (Méd) attack.

pousser /puse/ [1] *vt* push; (cri) let out; (soupir) heave; (continuer) continue; (exhorter) urge (à to); (forcer) drive (à to). ●*vi* push;

(grandir) grow; **faire ~** (cheveux) let grow; (plante) grow. □ **se ~** vpr move over ou up; **pousse-toi!** move over!

poussette /puset/ nf pushchair.

poussière /pusjɛʀ/ nf dust. **poussiéreux, -euse** a dusty.

poussin /pusɛ̃/ nm chick.

poutre /putʀ/ nf beam; (en métal) girder.

pouvoir /puvwaʀ/ [49] v aux (possibilité) can, be able; (permission, éventualité) may, can; **il peut/ pouvait/pourrait venir** he can/ could/might come; **je n'ai pas pu** I couldn't; **j'ai pu faire** (réussi à) I managed to do; **je n'en peux plus** I am exhausted; **il se peut que** it may be that. ● nm power; (gouvernement) government; **au ~ in** power; **~s publics** authorities.

prairie /pʀeʀi/ nf meadow.

praticien, ~ne /pʀatisjɛ̃, -ɛn/ nm, f practitioner.

pratiquant, ~e /pʀatikɑ̃, -t/ a practising. ● nm, f churchgoer.

pratique /pʀatik/ a practical. ● nf practice; (expérience) experience; **la ~ du golf/du cheval** golfing/riding. **pratiquement** adv (en pratique) in practice; (presque) practically.

pratiquer /pʀatike/ [1] vt/i practise; (Sport) play; (faire) make.

pré /pʀe/ nm meadow.

préalable /pʀealabl/ a preliminary, prior. ● nm precondition; **au ~** first.

préambule /pʀeɑ̃byl/ nm preamble.

préavis /pʀeavi/ nm notice.

précaire /pʀekɛʀ/ a precarious. **précarité** nf (d'emploi) insecurity.

précaution /pʀekosjɔ̃/ nf (mesure) precaution; (prudence) caution.

précédent, ~e /pʀesedɑ̃, -t/ a previous. ● nm precedent.

précéder /pʀesede/ [14] vt/i precede.

précepteur, -trice /pʀesɛptœʀ, -tʀis/ nm, f (private) tutor.

prêcher /pʀeʃe/ [1] vt/i preach.

précieux, -ieuse /pʀesjø, -z/ a precious.

précipitamment /pʀesipitamɑ̃/ adv hastily. **précipitation** nf haste.

précipiter /pʀesipite/ [1] vt throw, precipitate; (hâter) hasten. □ **se ~** vpr (se dépêcher) rush (**sur** at, on to); (se jeter) throw oneself; (s'accélérer) speed up.

précis, ~e /pʀesi, -z/ a precise, specific; (mécanisme) accurate; **dix heures ~es** ten o'clock sharp. ● nm summary.

préciser /pʀesize/ [1] vt specify; **précisez votre pensée** you be more specific. □ **se ~** vpr become clear(er). **précision** nf precision; (détail) detail.

précoce /pʀekɔs/ a (enfant) precocious.

préconiser /pʀekɔnize/ [1] vt advocate.

précurseur /pʀekyʀsœʀ/ nm forerunner.

prédicateur /pʀedikatœʀ/ nm preacher.

prédilection /pʀedilɛksjɔ̃/ nf preference.

prédire /pʀediʀ/ [37] vt predict.

prédominer /pʀedomine/ [1] vi predominate.

préface /pʀefas/ nf preface.

préfecture /pʀefɛktyʀ/ nf prefecture; **~ de police** police headquarters.

préféré, ~e /pʀefeʀe/ a & nm, f favourite.

préférence /pʀefeʀɑ̃s/ nf preference; **de ~** preferably.

préférentiel, ~le /pʀefeʀɑ̃sjɛl/ a preferential.

préférer /pʀefeʀe/ [14] vt prefer

P

(à to); ~ **faire** prefer to do; **je ne préfère pas** I'd rather not; **j'aurais préféré ne pas savoir** I wish I hadn't found out.

préfet /pʀefɛ/ nm prefect; ~ **de police** prefect ou chief of police.

préfixe /pʀefiks/ nm prefix.

préhistorique /pʀeistɔʀik/ a prehistoric.

préjudice /pʀeʒydis/ nm harm, prejudice; **porter** ~ **à** harm.

préjugé /pʀeʒyʒe/ nm prejudice; **être plein de** ~**s** be very prejudiced.

prélasser (se) /(sə)pʀelɑse/ [1] vpr loll (about).

prélèvement /pʀelɛvmɑ̃/ nm deduction; (de sang) sample. **prélever** [6] vt deduct (**sur** from); (sang) take.

préliminaire /pʀeliminɛʀ/ a & nm preliminary; ~**s** (sexuels) foreplay.

prématuré, ~e /pʀematyʀe/ a premature. ● nm premature baby.

premier, -ière /pʀəmje, -jɛʀ/ a first; (rang) front, first; (enfance) early; (nécessité, souci) prime; (qualité) top, prime; **de** ~ **ordre** first-rate; ~ **ministre** Prime Minister. ● nm, f first (one). ● nm (date) first; (étage) first floor; **en** ~ first. **première** nf (Rail) first class; (exploit jamais vu) first; (cinéma, Théât) première; (Aut) (vitesse) first (gear). **premièrement** adv firstly.

prémunir /pʀemyniʀ/ [2] vt protect (**contre** against).

prenant, ~e /pʀənɑ̃, -t/ a (activité) engrossing; (enfant) demanding.

prénatal, ~e (mpl ~s) /pʀenatal/ a antenatal.

prendre /pʀɑ̃dʀ/ [50] vt take; (attraper) catch, get; (acheter) get; (repas) have; (engager, adopter) take on; (poids) put on; (chercher) pick up; **qu'est-ce qui te prend?** what's the matter with you? ● vi (liquide) set; (feu) catch; (vaccin) take. □ **se** ~ vpr **se** ~ **pour** think one is; **s'en** ~ **à** attack; (rendre responsable) blame; **s'y** ~ set about (it).

preneur, -euse /pʀənœʀ, -øz/ nm, f buyer; **être** ~ be willing to buy; **trouver** ~ find a buyer.

prénom /pʀenɔ̃/ nm first name.

prénommer /pʀenɔme/ [1] vt call. □ **se** ~ vpr be called.

préoccupation /pʀeɔkypasjɔ̃/ nf (souci) worry; (idée fixe) preoccupation.

préoccuper /pʀeɔkype/ [1] vt worry; (absorber) preoccupy. □ **se** ~ **de** vpr think about.

préparation /pʀepaʀasjɔ̃/ nf preparation. **préparatoire** a preparatory.

préparer /pʀepaʀe/ [1] vt prepare; (repas, café) make; **plats préparés** ready-cooked meals. □ **se** ~ vpr prepare oneself (à for); (s'apprêter) get ready; (être proche) be brewing.

préposé, ~e /pʀepoze/ nm, f employee; (des postes) postman, postwoman.

préposition /pʀepozisjɔ̃/ nf preposition.

préretraite /pʀeʀətʀɛt/ nf early retirement.

près /pʀɛ/ adv near, close; ~ **de** near (to), close to; (presque) nearly; **à cela** ~ except that; **de** ~ closely.

présage /pʀezaʒ/ nm omen.

presbyte /pʀɛsbit/ a long-sighted, far-sighted.

prescrire /pʀɛskʀiʀ/ [30] vt prescribe.

préséance /pʀeseɑ̃s/ nf precedence.

présence /pʀezɑ̃s/ nf presence; (Scol) attendance.

présent, ~e /pʀezɑ̃, -t/ *a*
present. ● *nm* (temps, cadeau)
present; **à ~** now.

présentateur, -trice /pʀezɑ̃ta-
tœʀ, -tʀis/ *nm, f* presenter.

présentation /pʀezɑ̃tasjɔ̃/ *nf* (de
personne) introduction; (exposé)
presentation.

présenter /pʀezɑ̃te/ [1] *vt*
present; (*personne*) introduce (**à**
to); (montrer) show. ● *vi* **~ bien**
have a pleasing appearance. □ **se
~** *vpr* introduce oneself (**à** to);
(aller) go; (apparaître) appear;
(*candidat*) come forward;
(*occasion*) arise; **se ~ à** (*examen*)
sit for; (*élection*) stand for; **se ~
bien** look good.

préservatif /pʀezɛʀvatif/ *nm*
condom.

préserver /pʀezɛʀve/ [1] *vt*
protect.

présidence /pʀezidɑ̃s/ *nf* (d'État)
presidency; (de société)
chairmanship.

président, ~e /pʀezidɑ̃, -t/ *nm, f*
president; (de société, comité)
chairman, chairwoman;
~-directeur général managing
director.

présidentiel, ~le /pʀezidɑ̃sjɛl/ *a*
presidential.

présider /pʀezide/ [1] *vt* preside.

présomptueux, -euse /pʀezɔ̃p-
tɥø, -z/ *a* presumptuous.

presque /pʀɛsk(ə)/ *adv* almost,
nearly; **~ jamais** hardly ever; **~
rien** hardly anything; **~ pas (de)**
hardly any.

presqu'île /pʀɛskil/ *nf* peninsula.

pressant, ~e /pʀɛsɑ̃, -t/ *a*
pressing, urgent.

presse /pʀɛs/ *nf* (journaux, appareil)
press.

pressentiment /pʀɛsɑ̃timɑ̃/ *nm*
premonition. **pressentir** [46] *vt*
have a premonition of.

pressé, ~e /pʀese/ *a* in a hurry;
(*orange, citron*) freshly squeezed.

presser /pʀese/ [1] *vt* squeeze,
press; (appuyer sur, harceler) press;
(hâter) hasten; (inciter) urge (**de** to).
● *vi* (*temps*) press; (*affaire*) be
pressing. □ **se ~** *vpr* (se hâter)
hurry; (se grouper) crowd.

pressing /pʀesiŋ/ *nm* (teinturerie)
dry-cleaner's.

pression /pʀesjɔ̃/ *nf* pressure;
(bouton) press-stud.

prestance /pʀɛstɑ̃s/ *nf*
(imposing) presence.

prestation /pʀɛstasjɔ̃/ *nf*
allowance; (d'artiste) performance.

prestidigitation /pʀɛstidiʒita-
sjɔ̃/ *nf* conjuring.

prestige /pʀɛstiʒ/ *nm* prestige.
prestigieux, -ieuse *a*
prestigious.

présumer /pʀezyme/ [1] *vt*
presume; **~ que** assume that; **~
de** overrate.

prêt, ~e /pʀɛ, -t/ *a* ready (**à qch**
for sth, **à faire** to do). ● *nm* loan.
prêt-à-porter *nm inv* ready-to-
wear clothes.

prétendre /pʀetɑ̃dʀ/ [3] *vt* claim
(**que** that); (*vouloir*) intend; **on le
prétend riche** he is said to be very
rich. **prétendu, ~e** *a* so-called.
prétendument *adv* supposedly,
allegedly.

prétentieux, -ieuse /pʀetɑ̃sjø,
-z/ *a* pretentious.

prêter /pʀete/ [1] *vt* lend (**à** to);
(*attribuer*) attribute; **~ son aide à
qn** give sb some help; **~ attention**
pay attention; **~ serment** take an
oath. ● *vi* **~ à** lead to.

prêteur, -euse /pʀetœʀ, -øz/ *nm, f*
(money-)lender; **~ sur gages**
pawnbroker.

prétexte /pʀetɛkst/ *nm* pretext,
excuse.

prêtre /pʀɛtʀ/ *nm* priest.

preuve /pʀœv/ *nf* proof; **des ~s**

evidence (+ *sg*); **faire ~ de** show; **faire ses ~s** prove oneself.

prévaloir /pʀevalwaʀ/ [60] *vi* prevail.

prévenant, **~e** /pʀevnɑ̃, -t/ *a* thoughtful.

prévenir /pʀevniʀ/ [58] *vt* (*menacer*) warn; (*informer*) tell; (*médecin*) call; (*éviter, anticiper*) prevent.

préventif, **-ive** /pʀevɑ̃tif, -v/ *a* preventive.

prévention /pʀevɑ̃sjɔ̃/ *nf* prevention; **faire de la ~** take preventive action; **~ routière** road safety.

prévenu, **~e** /pʀevny/ *nm, f* defendant.

prévisible /pʀevizibl/ *a* predictable. **prévision** *nf* prediction; (*météorologique*) forecast.

prévoir /pʀevwaʀ/ [63] *vt* foresee; (*temps*) forecast; (*organiser*) plan (for), provide for; (*envisager*) allow (for); **prévu pour** (*jouet*) designed for; **comme prévu** as planned.

prévoyance /pʀevwajɑ̃s/ *nf* foresight. **prévoyant**, **~e** *a* far-sighted.

prier /pʀije/ [45] *vi* pray. ●*vt* pray to; (*demander à*) ask (**de** to); **je vous en prie** please; (*il n'y a pas de quoi*) don't mention it.

prière /pʀijɛʀ/ *nf* prayer; (*demande*) request; **~ de** (*vous êtes prié de*) will you please.

primaire /pʀimɛʀ/ *a* primary.

prime /pʀim/ *nf* free gift; (*d'employé*) bonus; (*subvention*) subsidy; (*d'assurance*) premium.

primé, **~e** /pʀime/ *a* prize-winning.

primeurs /pʀimœʀ/ *nfpl* early fruit and vegetables.

primevère /pʀimvɛʀ/ *nf* primrose.

primitif, **-ive** /pʀimitif, -v/ *a* primitive; (*d'origine*) original. ●*nm, f* primitive.

primordial, **~e** (*mpl* **-iaux**) /pʀimɔʀdjal, -jo/ *a* essential.

prince /pʀɛ̃s/ *nm* prince. **princesse** *nf* princess.

principal, **~e** (*mpl* **-aux**) /pʀɛ̃sipal, -o/ *a* main, principal. ●*nm* headmaster; (*chose*) main thing.

principe /pʀɛ̃sip/ *nm* principle; **en ~** in theory; (*d'habitude*) as a rule.

printanier, **-ière** /pʀɛ̃tanje, -jɛʀ/ *a* spring(-like).

printemps /pʀɛ̃tɑ̃/ *nm* spring.

prioritaire /pʀijɔʀitɛʀ/ *a* priority; **être ~** have priority. **priorité** *nf* priority; (Auto) right of way.

pris, **~e** /pʀi, -z/ *a* (*place*) taken; (*personne, journée*) busy; (*nez*) stuffed up; **~ de** (*peur, fièvre*) stricken with; **~ de panique** panic-stricken. ●⇒PRENDRE [50].

prise /pʀiz/ *nf* hold, grip; (*animal attrapé*) catch; (Mil) capture; **~ (de courant)** (*mâle*) plug; (*femelle*) socket; **~ multiple** multiplug adapter; **avoir ~ sur qn** have a hold over sb; **aux ~s avec** to grips with; **~ de conscience** awareness; **~ de contact** first contact, initial meeting; **~ de position** stand; **~ de sang** blood test.

prisé, **~e** /pʀize/ *a* popular.

prison /pʀizɔ̃/ *nf* prison, jail; (*réclusion*) imprisonment. **prisonnier**, **-ière** *nm, f* prisoner.

privation /pʀivasjɔ̃/ *nf* deprivation; (*sacrifice*) hardship.

privatiser /pʀivatize/ [1] *vt* privatize.

privé /pʀive/ *a* private. ●*nm* (Comm) private sector; (Scol) private schools (+ *pl*); **en ~** in private.

priver /pʀive/ [1] vt ~ de deprive of. □ se ~ (de) vpr go without.

privilège /pʀivilɛʒ/ nm privilege. **privilégié, ~e** nm, f privileged person.

prix /pʀi/ nm price; (récompense) prize; **à tout ~** at all costs; **au ~ de** (fig) at the expense of; ~ **coûtant, ~ de revient** cost price; **à ~ fixe** set price.

probabilité /pʀɔbabilite/ nf probability. **probable** a probable, likely. **probablement** adv probably.

probant, ~e /pʀɔbɑ̃, -t/ a convincing, conclusive.

problème /pʀɔblɛm/ nm problem.

procédé /pʀɔsede/ nm process; (manière d'agir) practice.

procéder /pʀɔsede/ [14] vi proceed; ~ **à** carry out.

procès /pʀɔsɛ/ nm (criminel) trial; (civil) lawsuit, proceedings (+ pl).

processus /pʀɔsesys/ nm process; ~ **de paix** peace process.

procès-verbal (pl **procès-verbaux**) /pʀɔsɛvɛʀbal, -o/ nm minutes (+ pl); (contravention) ticket.

prochain, ~e /pʀɔʃɛ̃, -ɛn/ a (suivant) next; (proche) imminent; (avenir) near. ● nm fellow man. **prochainement** adv soon.

proche /pʀɔʃ/ a near, close; (avoisinant) neighbouring; (parent, ami) close; ~ **de** close ou near to; **de ~ en ~** gradually; **dans un ~ avenir** in the near future; **être ~** (imminent) be approaching. ●nm close relative; (ami) close friend.

Proche-Orient /pʀɔʃɔʀjɑ̃/ nm Near East.

proclamation /pʀɔklamasjɔ̃/ nf declaration, proclamation. **proclamer** [1] vt declare, proclaim.

procuration /pʀɔkyʀasjɔ̃/ nf proxy.

procurer /pʀɔkyʀe/ [1] vt bring (à to). □ se ~ vpr obtain.

procureur /pʀɔkyʀœʀ/ nm public prosecutor.

prodige /pʀɔdiʒ/ nm (fait) marvel; (personne) prodigy; **enfant/musicien ~** child/musical prodigy. **prodigieux, -ieuse** a tremendous, prodigious.

prodigue /pʀɔdig/ a wasteful; **fils ~** prodigal son.

producteur, -trice /pʀɔdyktœʀ, -tʀis/ a producing. ● nm, f producer. **productif, -ive** a productive. **production** nf production; (produit) product. **productivité** nf productivity.

produire /pʀɔdɥiʀ/ [17] vt produce. □ se ~ vpr (survenir) happen; (acteur) perform.

produit /pʀɔdɥi/ nm product; ~s (de la terre) produce (+ sg); ~ **chimique** chemical; ~s **alimentaires** foodstuffs; ~ **de consommation** consumer goods; ~ **intérieur brut** gross domestic product; ~ **national brut** gross national product.

proéminent, ~e /pʀɔeminɑ̃, -t/ a prominent.

profane /pʀɔfan/ a secular. ●nmf lay person.

proférer /pʀɔfeʀe/ [14] vt utter.

professeur /pʀɔfesœʀ/ nm teacher; (Univ) lecturer; (avec chaire) professor.

profession /pʀɔfesjɔ̃/ nf occupation; ~ **libérale** profession. **professionnel, ~le** /pʀɔfesjɔnɛl/ a professional; (école) vocational. ●nm, f professional.

profil /pʀɔfil/ nm profile.

profit /pʀɔfi/ nm profit; **au ~ de** in aid of. **profitable** a profitable.

profiter /pʀɔfite/ [1] vi ~ **à** benefit; ~ **de** take advantage of.

profond, ~e /pʀɔfɔ̃, -d/ a deep; (sentiment, intérêt) profound;

P

(*causes*) underlying; au plus ~ de in the depths of. **profondément** *adv* deeply; (*différent, triste*) profoundly; (*dormir*) soundly. **profondeur** *nf* depth.

progéniture /pRɔʒenityR/ *nf* offspring.

progiciel /pRɔʒisjɛl/ *nm* (Ordinat) package.

programmation /pRɔgRamasjɔ̃/ *nf* programming.

programme /pRɔgRam/ *nm* programme; (Scol) (d'une matière) syllabus; (général) curriculum; (Ordinat) program. **programmer** [1] *vt* (*ordinateur, appareil*) program; (*émission*) schedule. **programmeur, -euse** *nm, f* computer programmer.

progrès /pRɔgRɛ/ *nm & nmpl* progress; **faire des ~** make progress. **progresser** [1] *vi* progress. **progressif, -ive** *a* progressive. **progression** *nf* progression.

prohibitif, -ive /pRɔibitif, -v/ *a* prohibitive.

proie /pRwa/ *nf* prey; **en ~ à** tormented by.

projecteur /pRɔʒɛktœR/ *nm* floodlight; (Mil) searchlight; (cinéma) projector.

projectile /pRɔʒɛktil/ *nm* missile.

projection /pRɔʒɛksjɔ̃/ *nf* projection; (*séance*) show.

projet /pRɔʒɛ/ *nm* plan; (*ébauche*) draft; **~ de loi** bill.

projeter /pRɔʒte/ [38] *vt* (*prévoir*) plan (**de** to); (*film*) project, show; (*jeter*) hurl, project.

prolétaire /pRɔletɛR/ *nmf* proletarian.

prologue /pRɔlɔg/ *nm* prologue.

prolongation /pRɔlɔ̃gasjɔ̃/ *nf* extension; **~s** (football) extra time.

prolonger /pRɔlɔ̃ʒe/ [40] *vt* extend. □ **se ~** *vpr* go on.

promenade /pRɔmnad/ *nf* walk;

(à bicyclette, à cheval) ride; (en auto) drive, ride; **faire une ~** go for a walk.

promener /pRɔmne/ [6] *vt* take for a walk; **~ son regard sur** cast an eye over. □ **se ~** *vpr* walk; (*aller*) **se ~** go for a walk.

promeneur, -euse *nm, f* walker.

promesse /pRɔmɛs/ *nf* promise.

prometteur, -euse /pRɔmɛtœR, -øz/ *a* promising.

promettre /pRɔmɛtR/ [42] *vt/i* promise. ● *vi* be promising. □ **se ~ de** *vpr* resolve to.

promoteur /pRɔmɔtœR/ *nm* (immobilier) property developer.

promotion /pRɔmɔsjɔ̃/ *nf* promotion; (Univ) year; (Comm) special offer.

prompt, ~e /pRɔ̃, -t/ *a* swift.

promu, ~e /pRɔmy/ *a* **être ~** be promoted.

prôner /pRone/ [1] *vt* extol.

pronom /pRɔnɔ̃/ *nm* pronoun. **pronominal, ~e** (*mpl* **-aux**) *a* pronominal.

prononcé, ~e /pRɔnɔ̃se/ *a* strong.

prononcer /pRɔnɔ̃se/ [10] *vt* pronounce; (*discours*) make. □ **se ~** *vpr* (*mot*) be pronounced; (*personne*) make a decision (**pour** in favour of). **prononciation** *nf* pronunciation.

pronostic /pRɔnɔstik/ *nm* forecast; (Méd) prognosis.

propagande /pRɔpagɑ̃d/ *nf* propaganda.

propager /pRɔpaʒe/ [40] *vt* spread. □ **se ~** *vpr* spread.

prophète /pRɔfɛt/ *nm* prophet. **prophétie** *nf* prophecy.

propice /pRɔpis/ *a* favourable.

proportion /pRɔpɔRsjɔ̃/ *nf* proportion; (en mathématiques) ratio; **toutes ~s gardées** relatively speaking. **proportionné, ~e** *a* proportionate (**à** to).

proportionnel, ∼**le** *a* proportional.

proportionnellement *adv* proportionately.

propos /pʀɔpo/ *nm* intention; (sujet) subject; **à** ∼ at the right time; (dans un dialogue) by the way; **à** ∼ **de** about; **à tout** ∼ at every possible occasion. ● *nmpl* (paroles) remarks.

proposer /pʀɔpoze/ [1] *vt* suggest, propose; (offrir) offer. □ **se** ∼ *vpr* volunteer (**pour** to).

proposition *nf* proposal; (affirmation) proposition; (Gram) clause.

propre /pʀɔpʀ/ *a* (non sali) clean; (soigné) neat; (honnête) decent; (à soi) own; (sens) literal; ∼ **à** (qui convient) suited to; (spécifique) particular to. ● *nm* **mettre au** ∼ write out again neatly; **c'est du** ∼! (ironique) well done!

proprement /pʀɔpʀəmã/ *adv* (avec soin) neatly; (au sens strict) strictly; **le bureau** ∼ **dit** the office itself.

propreté /pʀɔpʀəte/ *nf* cleanliness.

propriétaire /pʀɔpʀijetɛʀ/ *nmf* owner; (Comm) proprietor; (qui loue) landlord, landlady.

propriété /pʀɔpʀijete/ *nf* property; (droit) ownership.

propulser /pʀɔpylse/ [1] *vt* propel.

proroger /pʀɔʀɔʒe/ [40] *vt* (contrat) defer; (passeport) extend.

proscrire /pʀɔskʀiʀ/ [30] *vt* proscribe.

proscrit, ∼**e** /pʀɔskʀi, -t/ *a* proscribed. ● *nm, f* (exilé) exile.

prose /pʀoz/ *nf* prose.

prospectus /pʀɔspɛktys/ *nm* leaflet.

prospère /pʀɔspɛʀ/ *a* flourishing, thriving. **prospérer** [14] *vi* thrive,

prosper. **prospérité** *nf* prosperity.

prosterner (se) /(sə)pʀɔstɛʀne/ [1] *vpr* prostrate oneself; **prosterné devant** prostrate before.

prostituée /pʀɔstitɥe/ *nf* prostitute. **prostitution** *nf* prostitution.

protecteur, **-trice** /pʀɔtɛktœʀ, -tʀis/ *nm, f* protector. ● *a* protective.

protection /pʀɔtɛksjɔ̃/ *nf* protection.

protégé, ∼**e** /pʀɔteʒe/ *nm, f* protégé.

protéger /pʀɔteʒe/ [40] *vt* protect. □ **se** ∼ *vpr* protect oneself.

protéine /pʀɔtein/ *nf* protein.

protestant, ∼**e** /pʀɔtɛstã, -t/ *a & nm, f* Protestant.

protestation /pʀɔtɛstasjɔ̃/ *nf* protest. **protester** [1] *vt/i* protest.

protocole /pʀɔtɔkɔl/ *nm* protocol.

protubérant, ∼**e** /pʀɔtybeʀã/ *a* protruding.

proue /pʀu/ *nf* bow, prow.

prouesse /pʀuɛs/ *nf* feat, exploit.

prouver /pʀuve/ [1] *vt* prove.

provenance /pʀɔvnãs/ *nf* origin; **en** ∼ **de** from.

provençal, ∼**e** (*mpl* **-aux**) /pʀɔvãsal, -o/ *a & nm, f* Provençal.

provenir /pʀɔvniʀ/ [58] *vi* ∼ **de** come from.

proverbe /pʀɔvɛʀb/ *nm* proverb.

province /pʀɔvɛ̃s/ *nf* province; **de** ∼ provincial; **la** ∼ the provinces (+ *pl*). **provincial**, ∼**e** (*mpl* **-iaux**) *a & nm, f* provincial.

proviseur /pʀɔvizœʀ/ *nm* headmaster, principal.

provision /pʀɔvizjɔ̃/ *nf* supply, store; (sur un compte) credit (balance); (acompte) deposit; ∼**s** (vivres) food shopping.

P

provisoire /pʀɔvizwaʀ/ a provisional.

provocant, ~e /pʀɔvɔkã, -t/ a provocative. **provocation** nf provocation. **provoquer** [1] vt cause; (sexuellement) arouse; (défier) provoke.

proxénète /pʀɔksenɛt/ nm pimp, procurer.

proximité /pʀɔksimite/ nf proximity; **à ~ de** close to.

prude /pʀyd/ a prudish.

prudemment /pʀydamã/ adv (conduire) carefully; (attendre) cautiously. **prudence** nf caution. **prudent**, ~e a (au volant) careful; (à agir) cautious; (sage) wise.

prune /pʀyn/ nf plum.

pruneau (pl ~x) /pʀyno/ nm prune.

prunelle /pʀynɛl/ nf (pupille) pupil; (fruit) sloe.

prunier /pʀynje/ nm plum tree.

psaume /psom/ nm psalm.

pseudonyme /psødɔnim/ nm pseudonym.

psychanalyse /psikanaliz/ nf psychoanalysis. **psychanalyste** nmf psychoanalyst.

psychiatre /psikjatʀ/ nmf psychiatrist. **psychiatrie** nf psychiatry. **psychiatrique** a psychiatric.

psychique /psiʃik/ a mental, psychological.

psychologie /psikɔlɔʒi/ nf psychology. **psychologique** a psychological. **psychologue** nmf psychologist.

pu /py/ ⇒POUVOIR [49].

puant, ~e /pɥã, -t/ a stinking.

pub /pyb/ nf ⊞ la ~ advertising; **une ~** an advert.

puberté /pybɛʀte/ nf puberty.

public, **-que** /pyblik/ a public. ● nm public; (assistance) audience; (Scol) state schools (+ pl); **en ~** in public.

publication /pyblikasjɔ̃/ nf publication.

publicitaire /pyblisitɛʀ/ a publicity. **publicité** nf publicity, advertising; (annonce) advertisement.

publier /pyblije/ [45] vt publish.

publiquement /pyblikmã/ adv publicly.

puce /pys/ nf flea; (électronique) chip; **marché aux ~s** flea market.

pudeur /pydœʀ/ nf modesty.

pudibond, ~e /pydibɔ̃, -d/ a prudish.

pudique /pydik/ a modest.

puer /pɥe/ [1] vi stink. ● vt stink of.

puéricultrice /pɥeʀikyltʀis/ nf pediatric nurse.

puéril, ~e /pɥeʀil/ a puerile.

puis /pɥi/ adv then.

puiser /pɥize/ [1] vt draw (dans from). ● vi ~ **dans qch** dip into sth.

puisque /pɥisk(ə)/ conj since, as.

puissance /pɥisãs/ nf power; **en ~** potential.

puissant, ~e /pɥisã, -t/ a powerful.

puits /pɥi/ nm well; (de mine) shaft.

pull(-over) /pyl(ɔvɛʀ)/ nm pullover, jumper.

pulpe /pylp/ nf pulp.

pulsation /pylsasjɔ̃/ nf (heart-) beat.

pulvériser /pylveʀize/ [1] vt pulverize; (liquide) spray.

punaise /pynɛz/ nf (insecte) bug; (clou) drawing-pin.

punch[1] /pɔ̃ʃ/ nm (boisson) punch.

punch[2] /pœnʃ/ nm **avoir du ~** have drive.

punir /pyniʀ/ [2] vt punish. **punition** nf punishment.

pupille /pypij/ nf (de l'œil) pupil. ● nmf (enfant) ward.

pupitre /pypitʀ/ nm (Scol) desk; ~ à musique music stand.

pur /pyʀ/ a pure; (whisky) neat.

purée /pyʀe/ nf purée; (de pommes de terre) mashed potatoes (+ pl).

pureté /pyʀte/ nf purity.

purgatoire /pyʀgatwaʀ/ nm purgatory.

purge /pyʀʒ/ nf purge. **purger** [40] vt (Pol, Méd) purge; (peine: Jur) serve.

purifier /pyʀifje/ [45] vt purify.

puritain, ~e /pyʀitɛ̃, -ɛn/ nm, f puritan. ●a puritanical.

pur-sang /pyʀsɑ̃/ nm inv (cheval) thoroughbred.

pus /py/ nm pus.

putain /pytɛ̃/ nf ✕ whore.

puzzle /pœzl/ nm jigsaw (puzzle).

P-V abrév m (**procès-verbal**) ticket, traffic fine.

pyjama /piʒama/ nm pyjamas (+ pl); **un** ~ a pair of pyjamas.

pylône /pilon/ nm pylon.

Pyrénées /piʀene/ nfpl **les** ~ the Pyrenees.

pyromane /piʀɔman/ nmf arsonist.

Qq

QG abrév m (**quartier général**) HQ.

QI abrév m (**quotient intellectuel**) IQ.

qu' /k/ ⇒QUE.

quadriller /kadʀije/ [1] vt (armée) take control of; (police) spread one's net over; **papier quadrillé** squared paper.

quadrupède /kadʀypɛd/ nm quadruped.

quadruple /kadʀypl/ a quadruple. ●nm **le** ~ **de** four times. **quadrupler** [1] vt/i quadruple.

quai /ke/ nm (de gare) platform; (de port) quay; (de rivière) bank.

qualification /kalifikasjõ/ nf qualification; (compétence pratique) skills (+ pl).

qualifié, ~e /kalifje/ a (diplômé) qualified; (main-d'œuvre) skilled.

qualifier /kalifje/ [45] vt qualify; (décrire) describe (de as). □ **se** ~ vpr qualify (pour for).

qualité /kalite/ nf quality; (titre) occupation; (fonction) position; **en sa** ~ **de** in his ou her capacity as.

quand /kɑ̃/ adv when; ~ **même** all the same. ●conj when; (toutes les fois que) whenever; ~ **bien même** even if.

quant à /kɑ̃ta/ prép as for.

quantité /kɑ̃tite/ nf quantity; **une** ~ **de** a lot of; **des** ~s **(de)** masses ou lots (of).

quarantaine /kaʀɑ̃tɛn/ nf (Méd) quarantine; **une** ~ **(de)** about forty; **avoir la** ~ be in one's forties.

Q

quarante /kaʀɑ̃t/ a & nm forty.

quart /kaʀ/ nm quarter; (Naut) watch; **onze heures moins le** ~ quarter to eleven; ~ **(de litre)** quarter litre; ~ **de finale** quarter-final; ~ **d'heure** quarter of an hour; ~ **de tour** ninety-degree turn.

quartier /kaʀtje/ nm area, district; (zone ethnique) quarter; (de lune, pomme, bœuf) quarter; (d'une orange) segment; ~s (Mil) quarters; **de** ~, **du** ~ local; ~ **général** headquarters; **avoir** ~ **libre** be free.

quasiment /kazimɑ̃/ adv almost, practically.

quatorze /katɔʀz/ a & nm
fourteen.

quatre /katʀ(ə)/ a & nm four.
quatre-vingt(s) a & nm eighty.
quatre-vingt-dix a & nm ninety.

quatrième /katʀijɛm/ a & nmf
fourth. ● nf (Auto) fourth gear.

quatuor /kwatyɔʀ/ nm quartet.

que, qu' /kə, k/

qu' before vowel or mute h.

● *conjonction*

····➤ that; **je crains ~...** I'm worried
that...

····➤ (souhait, volonté) **je veux ~ tu
viennes** I want you to come; **~ tu
viennes ou non** whether you
come or not; **qu'il entre** let him
come in.

····➤ (comparaison) than; **plus grand
~ toi** taller than you.

● *pronom interrogatif*

····➤ what; **~ voulez-vous manger?**
what would you like to eat?

● *pronom relatif*

····➤ (personne) whom, that; **l'homme
~ j'ai rencontré** the man (whom)
I met.

····➤ (chose) that, which; **le cheval ~
Nick m'a offert** the horse (which)
Nick gave me.

● *adverbe*

····➤ **~ c'est joli!** it's so pretty!; **~
de monde!** what a lot of people!

Québec /kebɛk/ nm Quebec.

quel, quelle (*pl* **quel(le)s**) /kɛl/

● *adjectif interrogatif*

····➤ which, what; **~ auteur a
écrit...?** which writer wrote...?;
~ jour sommes-nous? what day
is it today?

● *adjectif exclamatif*

····➤ what; **~ idiot!** what an idiot!;
quelle horreur! that's horrible!

● *adjectif relatif*

····➤ **~ que soit son âge** whatever
his age; **quelles que soient tes
raisons** whatever your reasons;
~ que soit le gagnant whoever
the winner is.

quelconque /kɛlkɔ̃k/ a any,
some; (banal) ordinary; (médiocre)
poor, second rate.

quelque /kɛlkə/ a some; **~s** a
few, some. ● adv (environ) about,
some; **et ~** 🆔 and a bit; **~ chose**
something; (dans les phrases
interrogatives) anything; **~ part**
somewhere; **~ peu** somewhat.

quelquefois /kɛlkəfwa/ adv
sometimes.

quelques-uns, -unes /kɛlkəzœ̃,
-yn/ pron some, a few.

quelqu'un /kɛlkœ̃/ pron
someone, somebody; (dans les
phrases interrogatives) anyone,
anybody.

querelle /kəʀɛl/ nf quarrel.
quereller (se) [1] vpr quarrel.
querelleur, -euse a quarrelsome.

question /kɛstjɔ̃/ nf question;
(affaire) matter, question; **poser une
~** ask a question; **en ~** in
question; **il est ~ de** (cela concerne)
it is about; (on parle de) there is
talk of; **il n'en est pas ~** it is out
of the question; **pas ~!** no way!

questionnaire /kɛstjɔnɛʀ/ nm
questionnaire.

questionner /kɛstjɔne/ [1] vt
question.

quête /kɛt/ nf (Relig) collection;
(recherche) search; **en ~ de** in
search of.

queue /kø/ nf tail; (de poêle)
handle; (de fruit) stalk; (de fleur)
stem; (file) queue; (US) line; (de
train) rear; **faire la ~** queue (up);

(US) line up; ~ **de cheval** pony-tail; **faire une ~ de poisson à qn** (Auto) cut in front of sb.

qui /ki/

●*pronom interrogatif*

····▸ (sujet) who; ~ **a fait ça?** who did that?

····▸ (complément) whom; **à ~ est ce livre?** whose book is this?

●*pronom relatif*

····▸ (personne sujet) who; **c'est Isabelle qui vient d'appeler** it's Isabelle who's just called.

····▸ (autres cas) that, which; **qu'est-ce ~ te prend?** what is the matter with you?; **invite ~ tu veux** invite whoever you want; ~ **que ce soit** whoever it is, anybody.

quiche /kiʃ/ *nf* quiche.

quiconque /kikɔ̃k/ *pron* whoever; (n'importe qui) anyone.

quille /kij/ *nf* (de bateau) keel; (jouet) skittle.

quincaillerie /kɛ̃kajʀi/ *nf* hardware; (magasin) hardware shop. **quincaillier, -ière** *nm, f* hardware dealer.

quintal (*pl* **-aux**) /kɛ̃tal, -o/ *nm* quintal, one hundred kilos.

quinte /kɛ̃t/ *nf* ~ **de toux** coughing fit.

quintuple /kɛ̃typl/ *a* quintuple. ● *nm* **le ~ de** five times. **quintupler** [1] *vt/i* quintuple, increase fivefold.

quinzaine /kɛ̃zɛn/ *nf* **une ~ (de)** about fifteen.

quinze /kɛ̃z/ *a & nm inv* fifteen; ~ **jours** two weeks.

quiproquo /kipʀoko/ *nm* misunderstanding.

quittance /kitɑ̃s/ *nf* receipt.

quitte /kit/ *a* quits (**envers** with); ~ **à faire** even if it means doing.

quitter /kite/ [1] *vt* leave; (*vêtement*) take off; **ne quittez pas!** hold the line, please! □ **se ~** *vpr* part.

qui-vive /kiviv/ *nm inv* **être sur le ~** be alert.

quoi /kwa/ *pron* what; (après une préposition) which; **de ~ vivre** (assez) enough to live on; **de ~ écrire** something to write with; ~ **qu'il dise** whatever he says; ~ **que ce soit** anything; **il n'y a pas de ~** my pleasure; **il n'y a pas de ~ s'inquiéter** there's nothing to worry about.

quoique /kwak(ə)/ *conj* although, though.

quota /kɔta/ *nm* quota.

quote-part (*pl* **quotes-parts**) /kɔtpaʀ/ *nf* share.

quotidien, ~ne /kɔtidjɛ̃, -ɛn/ *a* daily; (banal) everyday. ● *nm* daily (paper); (vie quotidienne) everyday life. **quotidiennement** *adv* daily.

rabâcher /ʀabɑʃe/ [1] *vt* keep repeating.

rabais /ʀabɛ/ *nm* reduction, discount. **rabaisser** [1] *vt* (déprécier) belittle; (réduire) reduce.

rabat-joie /ʀabajwa/ *nm inv* killjoy.

rabattre /ʀabatʀ/ [11] *vt* (*chapeau, visière*) pull down; (refermer) shut; (diminuer) reduce; (déduire) take off; (*col, drap*) turn down. □ **se ~** *vpr* (se refermer) close; (*véhicule*) cut back in; **se ~ sur** make do with.

rabot /Rabo/ *nm* plane.

rabougri, ~e /RabugRi/ *a* stunted.

racaille /Rakaj/ *nf* rabble.

raccommoder /Rakɔmɔde/ [1] *vt* mend; (*personnes* 🔲) reconcile.

raccompagner /Rakɔ̃paɲe/ [1] *vt* see *ou* take back (*home*).

raccord /RakɔR/ *nm* link; (de papier peint) join; (retouche) touch-up. **raccorder** [1] *vt* connect, join.

raccourci /Rakursi/ *nm* short cut; **en ~** in short.

raccourcir /RakursiR/ [2] *vt* shorten. ● *vi* get shorter.

raccrocher /RakRɔʃe/ [1] *vt* hang back up; (*passant*) grab hold of; (relier) connect; **~ le combiné** *or* **le téléphone** hang up. ● *vi* hang up. □ **se ~ à** *vpr* cling to; (se relier à) be connected to *ou* with.

race /Ras/ *nf* race; (animale) breed; **de ~** (*chien*) pedigree; (*cheval*) thoroughbred.

racheter /Raʃte/ [6] *vt* buy (back); (acheter encore) buy more; (*nouvel objet*) buy another; (*société*) buy out; **~ des chaussettes** buy new socks. □ **se ~** *vpr* make amends.

racial, ~e (*mpl* **-iaux**) /Rasjal, -o/ *a* racial.

racine /Rasin/ *nf* root; **~ carrée/ cubique** square/cube root.

racisme /Rasism/ *nm* racism. **raciste** *a* & *nmf* racist.

racket /Raket/ *nm* racketeering.

raclée /Rakle/ *nf* 🔲 thrashing.

racler /Rakle/ [1] *vt* scrape. □ **se ~** *vpr* **se ~ la gorge** clear one's throat.

racolage /Rakɔlaʒ/ *nm* soliciting.

raconter /Rakɔ̃te/ [1] *vt* (*histoire*) tell; (*vacances*) tell about; (*vie, épisode*) describe; **~ à qn que** tell

sb that, say to sb that; **qu'est-ce que tu racontes?** what are you talking about?

radar /Radar/ *nm* radar.

radeau (*pl* **~x**) /Rado/ *nm* raft.

radiateur /RadjatœR/ *nm* radiator; (électrique) heater.

radiation /Radjasjɔ̃/ *nf* radiation.

radical, ~e (*mpl* **-aux**) /Radikal, -o/ *a* radical. ● *nm* (*pl* **-aux**) radical.

radieux, -ieuse /Radjø, -z/ *a* radiant.

radin, ~e /Radɛ̃, -in/ *a* 🔲 stingy 🔲.

radio /Radjo/ *nf* radio; **à la ~** on the radio; (radiographie) X-ray.

radioactif, -ive /Radjɔaktif, -v/ *a* radioactive. **radioactivité** *nf* radioactivity.

radiocassette /Radjɔkasɛt/ *nf* radio cassette player.

radiodiffuser /Radjɔdifyze/ [1] *vt* broadcast.

radiographie /RadjɔgRafi/ *nf* (photographie) X-ray.

radiomessageur /Radjɔmesa-ʒœR/ *nm* pager.

radis /Radi/ *nm* radish; **ne pas avoir un ~** 🔲 be broke.

radoter /Radɔte/ [1] *vi* 🔲 talk drivel.

radoucir (se) /(sə)RadusiR/ [2] *vpr* (*humeur*) improve; (*temps*) become milder.

rafale /Rafal/ *nf* (de vent) gust; (de mitraillette) burst.

raffermir /RafɛRmiR/ [2] *vt* strengthen. □ **se ~** *vpr* become stronger.

raffiné, ~e /Rafine/ *a* refined. **raffinement** *nm* refinement.

raffiner /Rafine/ [1] *vt* refine. **raffinerie** *nf* refinery.

raffoler /Rafɔle/ [1] *vt* 🔲 **~ de** be crazy about 🔲.

raffut /Rafy/ *nm* 🔲 din.

rafle /Rafl/ *nf* (police) raid.

rafraîchir /ʀafʀeʃiʀ/ [2] vt cool (down); (mur) give a fresh coat of paint to; (personne, mémoire) refresh. □ se ~ vpr (boire) refresh oneself; (temps) get cooler.
rafraîchissant, ~e a refreshing.
rafraîchissement /ʀafʀeʃismɑ̃/ nm (boisson) cold drink; ~s refreshments.

ragaillardir /ʀagajaʀdiʀ/ [2] vt 🄵 cheer up.

rage /ʀaʒ/ nf rage; (maladie) rabies; faire ~ (bataille, incendie) rage; (maladie) be rife; ~ de dents raging toothache. **rageant**, ~e a infuriating.

ragots /ʀago/ nmpl 🄵 gossip.

ragoût /ʀagu/ nm stew.

raid /ʀɛd/ nm (Mil) raid; (Sport) trek.

raide /ʀɛd/ a stiff; (côte) steep; (corde) tight; (cheveux) straight.
●adv (monter, descendre) steeply.
raideur nf stiffness; steepness.

raidir /ʀediʀ/ [2] vt (corps) tense.
□ se ~ vpr tense up; (position) harden; (corde) tighten.

raie /ʀɛ/ nf (ligne) line; (bande) strip; (de cheveux) parting; (poisson) skate.

raifort /ʀefɔʀ/ nm horseradish.

rail /ʀaj/ nm rail, track; le ~ (transport) rail.

raisin /ʀezɛ̃/ nm le ~ grapes; ~ sec raisin; un grain de ~ a grape.

raison /ʀezɔ̃/ nf reason; à ~ de at the rate of; avec ~ rightly; avoir ~ be right (de faire to do); avoir ~ de qn get the better of sb; donner ~ à prove right; en ~ de because of; ~ de plus all the more reason; perdre la ~ lose one's mind.

raisonnable /ʀezɔnabl/ a reasonable, sensible.

raisonnement /ʀezɔnmɑ̃/ nm reasoning; (propositions) argument.

raisonner /ʀezɔne/ [1] vi think.
●vt (personne) reason with.

rajeunir /ʀaʒœniʀ/ [2] vt ~ qn make sb (look) younger; (moderniser) modernize; (Méd) rejuvenate.
●vi (personne) look younger.

rajuster /ʀaʒyste/ [1] vt straighten; (salaires) (re)adjust.

ralenti, ~e /ʀalɑ̃ti/ a slow. ●nm (au cinéma) slow motion; tourner au ~ tick over, idle.

ralentir /ʀalɑ̃tiʀ/ [2] vt/i slow down. □ se ~ vpr slow down.

ralentisseur /ʀalɑ̃tisœʀ/ nm speed ramp.

râler /ʀɑle/ [1] vi groan; (protester 🄵) moan.

rallier /ʀalje/ [45] vt rally; (rejoindre) rejoin. □ se ~ vpr rally; se ~ à (avis) come round to; (parti) join.

rallonge /ʀalɔ̃ʒ/ nf (de table) leaf; (de fil électrique) extension lead.
rallonger [40] vt lengthen; (séjour, fil, table) extend.

rallumer /ʀalyme/ [1] vt (feu) relight; (lampe) switch on again; (ranimer: fig) revive.

rallye /ʀali/ nm rally.

ramassage /ʀamasaʒ/ nm (cueillette) gathering; (d'ordures) collection; ~ scolaire school bus service.

ramasser /ʀamase/ [1] vt pick up; (récolter) gather; (recueillir, rassembler) collect. □ se ~ vpr huddle up, curl up.

rame /ʀam/ nf (aviron) oar; (train) train.

ramener /ʀamne/ [1] vt (rapporter, faire revenir) bring back; (reconduire) take back; ~ à (réduire à) reduce to. □ se ~ vpr 🄵 turn up; se ~ à (problème) come down to.

ramer /ʀame/ [1] vi row.

ramollir /ʀamɔliʀ/ [2] vt soften.
□ se ~ vpr become soft.

R

ramoneur /Ramɔnœʀ/ *nm* (chimney) sweep.

rampe /Rɑ̃p/ *nf* banisters; (pente) ramp; **~ d'accès** (Auto) slip road; **~ de lancement** launching pad.

ramper /Rɑ̃pe/ [1] *vi* crawl.

rancard /Rɑ̃kaR/ *nm* ▣ date.

rancart /Rɑ̃kaR/ *nm* **mettre** *ou* **jeter au ~** ▣ scrap.

rance /Rɑ̃s/ *a* rancid.

rancœur /Rɑ̃kœR/ *nf* resentment.

rançon /Rɑ̃sɔ̃/ *nf* ransom. **ran-çonner** [1] *vt* rob, extort money from.

rancune /Rɑ̃kyn/ *nf* grudge; **sans ~!** no hard feelings! **rancunier, -ière** *a* vindictive.

randonnée /Rɑ̃dɔne/ *nf* walk, ramble; **la ~ à cheval** pony trekking; **faire une ~** go walking *ou* rambling.

rang /Rɑ̃/ *nm* row; (hiérarchie, condition) rank; **se mettre en ~** line up; **au premier ~** in the first row; (fig) at the forefront; **de second ~** (péj) second-rate.

rangée /Rɑ̃ʒe/ *nf* row.

rangement /Rɑ̃ʒmɑ̃/ *nm* (de pièce) tidying (up); (espace) storage space.

ranger /Rɑ̃ʒe/ [40] *vt* put away; (*chambre*) tidy (up); (disposer) place. □ **se ~** *vpr* (*véhicule*) park; (s'écarter) stand aside; (*conducteur*) pull over; (s'assagir) settle down; **se ~ à** (*avis*) accept.

ranimer /Ranime/ [1] *vt* revive; (Méd) resuscitate. □ **se ~** *vpr* come round.

rap /Rap/ *nm* rap (music).

rapace /Rapas/ *nm* bird of prey. ● *a* grasping.

rapatriement /Rapatʀimɑ̃/ *nm* repatriation. **rapatrier** [45] *vt* repatriate.

râpe /Rɑp/ *nf* (Culin) grater; (lime) rasp.

râpé, ~e /Rɑpe/ *a* (*vêtement*) threadbare; (*fromage*) grated.

râper /Rɑpe/ [1] *vt* grate; (*bois*) rasp.

rapide /Rapid/ *a* fast, rapid. ● *nm* (train) express (train); (cours d'eau) rapids (+ *pl*). **rapidement** *adv* fast, rapidly. **rapidité** *nf* speed.

rappel /Rapɛl/ *nm* recall; (deuxième avis) reminder; (de salaire) back pay; (Méd) booster; (de diplomate) recall; (de réservistes) call-up; (Théât) curtain call.

rappeler /Raple/ [38] *vt* (par téléphone) call back; (*réserviste*) call up; (*diplomate*) recall; (évoquer) recall; **~ qch à qn** remind sb of sth. □ **se ~** *vpr* remember, recall.

rappeur, -euse /Rapœʀ, øz/ *nmf* rapper.

rapport /RapɔR/ *nm* connection; (compte-rendu) report; (profit) yield; **~s** (relations) relations; **en ~ avec** (accord) in keeping with; **mettre/se mettre en ~ avec** put/get in touch with; **par ~ à** (comparé à) compared with; (vis-à-vis de) with regard to; **~s** (sexuels) intercourse.

rapporter /RapɔRte/ [1] *vt* (ici) bring back; (là-bas) take back, return; (*profit*) bring in; (dire, répéter) report. ● *vi* (Comm) bring in a good return; (moucharder ▣) tell tales. □ **se ~ à** *vpr* relate to.

rapporteur, -euse /RapɔRtœʀ, -øz/ *nm, f* (mouchard) tell-tale. ● *nm* protractor.

rapprochement /RapʀɔʃmÃ/ *nm* reconciliation; (Pol) rapprochement; (rapport) connection; (comparaison) parallel.

rapprocher /Rapʀoʃe/ *vt* move closer (**de** to); (réconcilier) bring together; (comparer) compare; (*date, rendez-vous*) bring forward. □ **se ~** *vpr* get *ou* come closer (**de** to); (*personnes, pays*) come together; (s'apparenter) be close (**de** to).

rapt /Rapt/ *nm* abduction.

raquette /Rakɛt/ *nf* (de tennis) racket; (de ping-pong) bat.

rare /RaR/ *a* rare; (insuffisant) scarce. **rarement** *adv* rarely, seldom. **rareté** *nf* rarity; scarcity.

ras, **~e** /Rɑ, Rɑz/ *adv* coupé **~** cut short. ●*a* (*herbe*, *poil*) short; **à ~ de terre** very close to the ground; **en avoir ~ le bol** 🔲 be really fed up; **~e campagne** open country; **à ~ bord** to the brim.

raser /Raze/ [1] *vt* shave; (*cheveux*, *barbe*) shave off; (frôler) skim; (abattre) raze. □ **se ~** *vpr* shave.

rasoir /Razwar/ *nm* razor. ●*a inv* 🔲 boring.

rassasier /Rasazje/ [45] *vt* satisfy, fill up; **être rassasié de** have had enough of.

rassemblement /Rasɑ̃bləmɑ̃/ *nm* gathering; (manifestation) rally.

rassembler /Rasɑ̃ble/ [1] *vt* gather; (*forces*, *courage*) summon up; (*idées*) collect. □ **se ~** *vpr* gather.

rassis, **~e** /Rasi, -z/ *a* (*pain*) stale.

rassurer /RasyRe/ [1] *vt* reassure. □ **se ~** *vpr* reassure oneself, **rassure-toi** don't worry.

rat /Ra/ *nm* rat.

rate /Rat/ *nf* spleen.

raté, **~e** /Rate/ *nm, f* (personne) failure. ●*nm* **avoir des ~s** (voiture) backfire.

râteau (*pl* **~x**) /Rɑto/ *nm* rake.

râtelier /Rɑtəlje/ *nm* hayrack; (dentier 🔲) dentures.

rater /Rate/ [1] *vt* (*train*, *rendez-vous*, *cible*) miss; (gâcher) make a mess of, spoil; (*examen*) fail. ●*vi* fail.

ratio /Rasjo/ *nm* ratio.

rationaliser /Rasjonalize/ [1] *vt* rationalize.

rationnel, **~le** /Rasjonɛl/ *a* rational.

rationnement /Rasjonmɑ̃/ *nm* rationing.

ratisser /Ratise/ [1] *vt* rake; (fouiller) comb.

rattacher /Rataʃe/ [1] *vt* (*lacets*) tie up again; (*ceinture de sécurité*, *collier*) refasten; (relier) link; (incorporer) join.

rattrapage /RatRapaʒ/ *nm* (Comm) adjustment; **cours de ~** remedial lesson.

rattraper /RatRape/ [1] *vt* catch; (rejoindre) catch up with; (*retard*, *erreur*) make up for. □ **se ~** *vpr* catch up; (se dédommager) make up for it; **se ~ à** catch hold of.

rature /RatyR/ *nf* deletion.

rauque /Rok/ *a* raucous, harsh.

ravager /Ravaʒe/ [40] *vt* devastate, ravage.

ravages /Ravaʒ/ *nmpl* **faire des ~** wreak havoc.

ravaler /Ravale/ [1] *vt* (*façade*) clean; (*colère*) swallow.

ravi, **~e** /Ravi/ *a* delighted (**que** that).

ravin /Ravɛ̃/ *nm* ravine.

ravir /RaviR/ [2] *vt* delight; **~ qch à qn** rob sb of sth.

ravissant, **~e** /Ravisɑ̃, -t/ *a* beautiful.

ravisseur, **-euse** /Ravisœʀ, -øz/ *nm, f* kidnapper.

ravitaillement /Ravitajmɑ̃/ *nm* provision of supplies (**de** to); (denrées) supplies; **~ en essence** refuelling.

ravitailler /Ravitaje/ [1] *vt* provide with supplies; (*avion*) refuel. □ **se ~** *vpr* stock up.

raviver /Ravive/ [1] *vt* revive; (*feu*, *colère*) rekindle.

rayé, **~e** /Reje/ *a* striped.

rayer /Reje/ [31] *vt* scratch; (biffer) cross out; **'~ la mention inutile'** 'delete as appropriate'.

R

rayon /REjɔ̃/ nm ray; (étagère) shelf; (de magasin) department; (de roue) spoke; (de cercle) radius; ~ d'action range; ~ de miel honeycomb; ~ X X-ray; en connaître un ~ 🆃 know one's stuff 🆃.

rayonnement /REjɔnmɑ̃/ nm (éclat) radiance; (influence) influence; (radiations) radiation.

rayonner [1] vi radiate; (de joie) beam; (se déplacer) tour around (from a central point).

rayure /REjyR/ nf scratch; (dessin) stripe; à ~s striped.

raz-de-marée /Radmare/ nm inv tidal wave; ~ électoral electoral landslide.

réacteur /Reaktœr/ nm jet engine; (nucléaire) reactor.

réaction /Reaksjɔ̃/ nf reaction; ~ en chaîne chain reaction; moteur à ~ jet engine.

réagir /Reaʒir/ [2] vi react; ~ sur have an effect on.

réalisateur, -trice /Realizatœr, -tris/ nm,f (au cinéma) director; (TV) producer.

réalisation /Realizasjɔ̃/ nf (de rêve) fulfilment; (œuvre) achievement; (TV, cinéma) production; projet en ~ project in progress.

réaliser /Realize/ [1] vt carry out; (effort, bénéfice, achat) make; (rêve) fulfil; (film) direct; (capital) realize; (se rendre compte de) realize. □ se ~ vpr be fulfilled.

réalisme /Realism/ nm realism.

réaliste /Realist/ a realistic. ● nmf realist.

réalité /Realite/ nf reality.

réanimation /Reanimasjɔ̃/ nf resuscitation; service de ~ intensive care. **réanimer** [1] vt resuscitate.

réarmement /Rearməmɑ̃/ nm rearmament.

rébarbatif, -ive /Rebarbatif, -v/ a forbidding, off-putting.

rebelle /Rəbɛl/ a rebellious; (soldat) rebel; ~ à resistant to. ● nmf rebel.

rébellion /Rebeljɔ̃/ nf rebellion.

rebondir /Rəbɔ̃dir/ [2] vi bounce; rebound; (fig) get moving again.

rebondissement /Rəbɔ̃dismɑ̃/ nm (new) development.

rebord /Rəbɔr/ nm edge; ~ de la fenêtre window ledge ou sill.

rebours: à ~ /aRəbuR/ loc (compter, marcher) backwards.

rebrousse-poil: à ~ /aRəbrus-pwal/ loc the wrong way; (fig) prendre qn à ~ rub sb up the wrong way.

rebrousser /Rəbruse/ [1] vt ~ chemin turn back.

rebut /Rəby/ nm mettre ou jeter au ~ scrap.

rebutant, ~e /Rəbytɑ̃, -t/ a off-putting.

recaler /Rəkale/ [1] vt 🆃 fail; se faire ~, être recalé fail.

recel /Rəsɛl/ nm receiving.

receler [6] vt (objet volé) receive; (cacher) conceal.

récemment /Resamɑ̃/ adv recently.

recensement /Rəsɑ̃smɑ̃/ nm census; (inventaire) inventory.

recenser [1] vt (population) take a census of; (objets) list.

récent, ~e /Resɑ̃, -t/ a recent.

récépissé /Resepise/ nm receipt.

récepteur /Reseptœr/ nm receiver.

réception /Resɛpsjɔ̃/ nf reception; (de courrier) receipt. **réceptionniste** nmf receptionist.

récession /Resesjɔ̃/ nf recession.

recette /Rəsɛt/ nf (Culin) recipe; (argent) takings; ~s (Comm) receipts.

receveur, -euse /Rəs(ə)vœR, -øz/ *nm, f* (de bus) conductor; ~ **des contributions** tax collector.

recevoir /Rəs(ə)vwaR/ [52] *vt* receive, get; (*client, malade*) see; (*invités*) welcome, receive; **être reçu à un examen** pass an exam.

rechange: de ~ /dəRəʃãʒ/ *loc* (*roue, vêtements*) spare; (*solution*) alternative.

réchapper /Reʃape/ [1] *vt/i* ~ **de** come through, survive.

recharge /RəʃaRʒ/ *nf* (de stylo) refill.

réchaud /Reʃo/ *nm* stove.

réchauffement /Reʃofmã/ *nm* (de température) rise (**de** in); **le** ~ **de la planète** global warming.

réchauffer /Reʃofe/ [1] *vt* warm up. □ **se** ~ *vpr* warm oneself up; (*temps*) get warmer.

rêche /Rεʃ/ *a* rough.

recherche /RəʃεRʃ/ *nf* search (**de** for); (raffinement) meticulousness; ~(**s**) (Univ) research; ~**s** (enquête) investigations; ~ **d'emploi** job-hunting.

recherché, ~e /RəʃεRʃe/ *a* in great demand; (*style*) original, recherché (péj); ~ **pour meurtre** wanted for murder.

rechercher /RəʃεRʃe/ [1] *vt* search for.

rechute /Rəʃyt/ *nf* (Méd) relapse; **faire une** ~ have a relapse.

récidiver /Residive/ [1] *vi* commit a second offence.

récif /Resif/ *nm* reef.

récipient /Resipjã/ *nm* container.

réciproque /ResipRɔk/ *a* mutual, reciprocal.

réciproquement /ResipRɔkmã/ *adv* each other; **et** ~ and vice versa.

récit /Resi/ *nm* (compte-rendu) account, story; (histoire) story.

réciter /Resite/ [1] *vt* recite.

réclamation /Reklamasjɔ̃/ *nf* complaint; (demande) claim.

réclame /Reklam/ *nf* advertisement; **faire de la** ~ advertise; **en** ~ on offer.

réclamer /Reklame/ [1] *vt* call for, demand. ● *vi* complain.

reclus, ~e /Rəkly, -z/ *nm, f* recluse. ● *a* reclusive.

réclusion /Reklyzjɔ̃/ *nf* imprisonment.

récolte /Rekɔlt/ *nf* (action) harvest; (produits) crop, harvest; (fig) crop. **récolter** [1] *vt* harvest, gather; (fig) collect, get.

recommandation /Rəkɔmãda-sjɔ̃/ *nf* recommendation.

recommandé /Rəkɔmãde/ *nm* registered letter; **envoyer en** ~ send by registered post.

recommander /Rəkɔmãde/ [1] *vt* recommend.

recommencer /Rəkɔmãse/ [10] *vt* (reprendre) begin *ou* start again; (refaire) repeat. ● *vi* start *ou* begin again; **ne recommence pas** don't do it again.

récompense /Rekɔ̃pãs/ *nf* reward; (prix) award. **récompenser** [1] *vt* reward (**de** for).

réconcilier /Rekɔ̃silje/ [45] *vt* reconcile. □ **se** ~ *vpr* become reconciled (**avec** with).

reconduire /Rəkɔ̃dɥiR/ [17] *vt* see home; (à la porte) show out; (renouveler) renew.

réconfort /Rekɔ̃fɔR/ *nm* comfort.

reconnaissance /Rekɔnεsãs/ *nf* gratitude; (fait de reconnaître) recognition; (Mil) reconnaissance. **reconnaissant, ~e** *a* grateful (**de** for).

reconnaître /RəkɔnεtR/ [18] *vt* recognize; (admettre) admit (**que** that); (Mil) reconnoitre; (*enfant, tort*) acknowledge. □ **se** ~ *vpr*

R

(s'orienter) know where one is; (l'un l'autre) recognize each other.

reconstituer /Rəkɔ̃stitɥe/ [1] vt reconstitute; (crime) reconstruct; (époque) recreate.

reconversion /Rəkɔ̃vɛRsjɔ̃/ nf (de main-d'œuvre) redeployment.

recopier /Rəkɔpje/ [45] vt copy out.

record /RəkɔR/ nm & a inv record.

recouper /Rəkupe/ [1] vt confirm. □ se ~ vpr check, tally, match up.

recourbé, ~e /RəkuRbe/ a curved; (nez) hooked.

recourir /RəkuRiR/ [20] vi ~ à (expédient, violence) resort to; (remède, méthode) have recourse to.

recours /RəkuR/ nm resort; avoir ~ à have recourse to, resort to; avoir ~ à qn turn to sb.

recouvrer /Rəkuvre/ [1] vt recover.

recouvrir /RəkuvRiR/ [21] vt cover.

récréation /RekReasjɔ̃/ nf recreation; (Scol) break; (US) recess.

recroqueviller (se) /(sə)RəkRɔkvije/ [1] vpr curl up.

recrudescence /RəkRydesɑ̃s/ nf new outbreak.

recrue /RəkRy/ nf recruit.

recrutement /RəkRytmɑ̃/ nm recruitment. **recruter** [1] vt recruit.

rectangle /Rɛktɑ̃gl/ nm rectangle. **rectangulaire** a rectangular.

rectifier /Rɛktifje/ [45] vt correct, rectify.

recto /Rɛkto/ nm au ~ on the front of the page.

reçu, ~e /Rəsy/ a accepted; (candidat) successful. ●nm receipt. ●⇒RECEVOIR [52].

recueil /Rəkœj/ nm collection.

recueillement /Rəkœjmɑ̃/ nm meditation.

recueillir /RəkœjiR/ [25] vt collect; (prendre chez soi) take in. □ se ~ vpr meditate.

recul /Rəkyl/ nm retreat; (éloignement) distance; (déclin) decline; avoir un mouvement de ~ recoil; être en ~ be on the decline; avec le ~ with hindsight.

reculé, ~e /Rəkyle/ a (région) remote.

reculer /Rəkyle/ [1] vt move back; (véhicule) reverse; (différer) postpone. ●vi move back; (voiture) reverse; (armée) retreat; (régresser) fall; (céder) back down; ~ devant (fig) shrink from. □ se ~ vpr move back.

récupération /RekypeRasjɔ̃/ nf (de l'organisme, de dette) recovery; (d'objets) salvage.

récupérer /RekypeRe/ [14] vt recover; (vieux objets) salvage. ●vi recover.

récurer /RekyRe/ [1] vt scour; poudre à ~ scouring powder.

récuser /Rekyze/ [1] vt challenge. □ se ~ vpr state that one is not qualified to judge.

recyclage /Rəsiklaʒ/ nm (de personnel) retraining; (de matériau) recycling.

recycler /Rəsikle/ [1] vt (personne) retrain; (chose) recycle. □ se ~ vpr retrain.

rédacteur, **-trice** /Redaktœr, -tris/ nm, f author, writer; (de journal, magazine) editor.

rédaction /Redaksjɔ̃/ nf writing; (Scol) essay, composition; (personnel) editorial staff.

redevable /Rədvabl/ a être ~ à qn de (argent) owe sb; (fig) be indebted to sb for.

redevance /Rədvɑ̃s/ nf (de

télévision) licence fee; (de téléphone) rental charge.

rédiger /Redize/ [40] vt write; (contrat) draw up.

redire /RədiR/ [27] vt repeat; **avoir ou trouver à ∼ à** find fault with.

redondant, **∼e** /Rədɔ̃dɑ̃, -t/ a superfluous.

redonner /Rədɔne/ [1] vt (rendre) give back; (donner davantage) give more; (donner de nouveau) give again.

redoubler /Rəduble/ [1] vt increase; (classe) repeat; **∼ de prudence** be even more careful. ● vi (Scol) repeat a year; (s'intensifier) intensify.

redoutable /Rədutabl/ a formidable.

redouter /Rədute/ [1] vt dread.

redressement /RədRɛsmɑ̃/ nm (reprise) recovery; **∼ judiciaire** receivership.

redresser /RədRese/ [1] vt straighten (out ou up); (situation) right, redress; (économie, entreprise) turn around. □ **se ∼** vpr (personne) straighten (oneself) up; (se remettre debout) stand up; (pays, économie) recover.

réduction /Redyksjɔ̃/ nf reduction.

réduire /RedɥiR/ [17] vt reduce (à to). □ **se ∼** vpr be reduced ou cut; **se ∼ à** (revenir à) come down to.

réduit, **∼e** /Redɥi, -t/ a (objet) small-scale; (limité) limited. ● nm cubbyhole.

rééducation /Reedykasjɔ̃/ nf (de handicapé) rehabilitation; (Méd) physiotherapy. **rééduquer** [1] vt (personne) rehabilitate; (membre) restore normal movement to.

réel, **∼le** /Reɛl/ a real. ● nm reality. **réellement** adv really.

réexpédier /Reɛkspedje/ [45] vt forward; (retourner) send back.

refaire /RəfɛR/ [33] vt do again; (erreur, voyage) make again; (réparer) do up, redo.

réfectoire /RefɛktwaR/ nm refectory.

référence /ReferɑdROs/ nf reference.

référendum /Referɛ̃dɔm/ nm referendum.

référer /Refere/ [14] vi **en ∼ à** consult. □ **se ∼ à** vpr refer to, consult.

refermer /RəfɛRme/ [1] vt close (again). □ **se ∼** vpr close (again).

réfléchi, **∼e** /Reflefi/ a (personne) thoughtful; (verbe) reflexive.

réfléchir /ReflefiR/ [2] vi think (à, sur about). ● vt reflect. □ **se ∼** vpr be reflected.

reflet /Rəflɛ/ nm reflection; (nuance) sheen.

refléter /Rəflete/ [14] vt reflect. □ **se ∼** vpr be reflected.

réflexe /Reflɛks/ a reflex. ● nm reflex; (réaction) reaction.

réflexion /Reflɛksjɔ̃/ nf (pensée) thought, reflection; (remarque) remark, comment; **à la ∼, on** second thoughts.

refluer /Rəflye/ [1] vi flow back; (foule) retreat; (inflation) go down.

reflux /Rəfly/ nm (marée) ebb, tide.

réforme /RefɔRm/ nf reform.

réformer [1] vt reform; (soldat) invalid out.

refouler /Rəfule/ [1] vt (larmes) hold back; (désir) repress; (souvenir) suppress.

refrain /RəfRɛ̃/ nm chorus; **le même ∼** the same old story.

réfréner /RefRene/ [14] vt curb, check.

réfrigérateur /RefRiʒeRatœR/ nm refrigerator.

refroidir /RəfRwadiR/ [2] vt/i cool

R

(down). □ **se ~** *vpr* (*personne,
temps*) get cold. **refroidissement**
nm cooling; (*rhume*) chill.

refuge /Rəfyʒ/ *nm* refuge; (*chalet*)
mountain hut.

réfugié, ~e /Refyʒje/ *nm,f*
refugee. **réfugier (se)** [45] *vpr*
take refuge.

refus /Rəfy/ *nm* refusal; **ce n'est
pas de ~** 🔲 I wouldn't say no.

refuser /Rəfyze/ [1] *vt* refuse (**de**
to); (*client, spectateur*) turn away;
(*recaler*) fail; (à un poste) turn down.
□ **se ~ à** *vpr* (*évidence*) reject; **se
~ à faire** refuse to do.

regain /Rəgɛ̃/ *nm* **~ de** renewal
ou revival of; (Comm) rise.

régal (*pl* **~s**) /Regal/ *nm* treat,
delight.

régaler /Regale/ [1] *vt* **~ qn de**
treat sb to. □ **se ~** *vpr* (de
nourriture) **je me régale** it's delicious.

regard /RəgaR/ *nm* (expression, coup
d'œil) look; (vue) eye; (yeux) eyes;
~ fixe stare; **au ~ de** with regard
to; **en ~ de** compared with.

regardant, ~e /RəgaRdɑ̃, -t/ *a* **~
avec son argent** careful with
money; **peu ~ (sur)** not fussy
(about).

regarder /RəgaRde/ [1] *vt* look at;
(observer) watch; (considérer)
consider; (concerner) concern; **~
fixement** stare at; **~ à** think about,
pay attention to. ● *vi* look. □ **se
~** *vpr* (*soi-même*) look at oneself;
(*personnes*) look at each other.

régate /Regat/ *nf* regatta.

régie /Reʒi/ *nf* **~ d'État** public
corporation; (radio, TV) control
room; (au cinéma) production;
(Théât) stage management.

régime /Reʒim/ *nm* (organisation)
system; (Pol) regime; (Méd) diet;
(de moteur) speed; (de bananes)
bunch; **se mettre au ~** go on a
diet; **à ce ~** at this rate.

régiment /Reʒimɑ̃/ *nm* regiment.

région /Reʒjɔ̃/ *nf* region.

régional, ~e (*mpl* **-aux**) *a*
regional.

régir /ReʒiR/ [2] *vt* govern.

régisseur /ReʒisœR/ *nm* (Théât)
stage manager; **~ de plateau** (TV)
floor manager; (au cinéma) studio
manager.

registre /RəgistR/ *nm* register.

réglage /Reglaʒ/ *nm* adjustment;
(de moteur) tuning.

règle /Rɛgl/ *nf* rule; (instrument)
ruler; **~s** (de femme) period; **en ~**
in order.

réglé, ~e /Regle/ *a* (vie) ordered;
(arrangé) settled; (papier) ruled.

règlement /Rɛgləmɑ̃/ *nm* (règles)
regulations; (solution) settlement;
(paiement) payment.
réglementaire *a* (uniforme)
regulation. **réglementation** *nf*
regulation, rules. **réglementer**
[1] *vt* regulate, control.

régler /Regle/ [14] *vt* settle;
(machine) adjust; (programmer) set;
(facture) settle; (personne) settle
up with; **~ son compte à** 🔲 settle
a score with.

réglisse /Reglis/ *nf* liquorice.

règne /Rɛɲ/ *nm* reign; (végétal,
animal, minéral) kingdom.

regret /RəgRɛ/ *nm* regret; **à ~**
with regret.

regretter /RəgRete/ [1] *vt* regret;
(personne) miss; (pour s'excuser) be
sorry.

regrouper /RəgRupe/ [1] *vt* group
ou bring together. □ **se ~** *vpr*
gather *ou* group together.

régularité /RegylaRite/ *nf*
regularity; (de rythme, progrès)
steadiness; (de surface, écriture)
evenness.

régulier, -ière /Regylje, -jɛR/ *a*
regular; (qualité, vitesse) steady,
even; (ligne, paysage) even; (légal)
legal; (honnête) honest.

rehausser /Rəose/ [1] *vt* raise; (faire valoir) enhance.

rein /Rɛ̃/ *nm* kidney; ~s (dos) small of the back.

reine /Rɛn/ *nf* queen.

réinsertion /Reɛ̃sɛRsjɔ̃/ *nf* reintegration.

réintégrer /Reɛ̃tegRe/ [14] *vt* (*lieu*) return to; (*Jur*) reinstate; (*personne*) reintegrate.

réitérer /Reitere/ [14] *vt* repeat.

rejaillir /RəʒajiR/ [2] *vi* ~ sur splash back onto; ~ sur qn (*succès*) reflect on sb.

rejet /Rəʒɛ/ *nm* rejection; ~s (déchets) waste.

rejeter /Rəʒte/ [38] *vt* throw back; (refuser) reject; (déverser) discharge; ~ une faute sur qn shift the blame for a mistake onto sb.

rejeton /Rəʒtɔ̃/ *nm* (enfant Ⓘ) offspring (*inv*).

rejoindre /Rəʒwɛ̃dR/ [22] *vt* go back to, rejoin; (rattraper) catch up with; (rencontrer) join, meet up with. □ **se** ~ *vpr* (*personnes*) meet up; (*routes*) join, meet.

réjoui, ~e /Reʒwi/ *a* joyful.

réjouir /ReʒwiR/ [2] *vt* delight. □ **se** ~ *vpr* be delighted (de at). **réjouissances** *nf/pl* festivities. **réjouissant**, ~e *a* cheering.

relâche /Rəlɑʃ/ *nm* (repos) break, rest; **faire** ~ (Théât) be closed.

relâcher /Rəlɑʃe/ [1] *vt* slacken; (*personne*) release; (*discipline*) relax. □ **se** ~ *vpr* slacken.

relais /Rəlɛ/ *nm* (Sport) relay; (hôtel) hotel; (intermédiaire) intermediary; **prendre le** ~ **de** take over from.

relancer /Rəlɑ̃se/ [10] *vt* boost, revive; (renvoyer) throw back.

relatif, **-ive** /Rəlatif, -v/ *a* relative; ~ **à** relating to.

relation /Rəlasjɔ̃/ *nf* relationship; (ami) acquaintance; (personne puissante) connection; ~s

relations; ~s **extérieures** foreign affairs; **en** ~ **avec qn** in touch with sb.

relativement /Rəlativmɑ̃/ *adv* relatively; ~ **à** in relation to.

relativité /Rəlativite/ *nf* relativity.

relax /Rəlaks/ *a inv* Ⓘ laid-back.

relaxer (se) /(sə)Rəlakse/ [1] *vpr* relax.

relayer /Rəleje/ [31] *vt* relieve; (*émission*) relay. □ **se** ~ *vpr* take over from one another.

reléguer /Rəlege/ [14] *vt* relegate.

relent /Rəlɑ̃/ *nm* stink; (fig) whiff.

relève /Rəlɛv/ *nf* relief; **prendre** *ou* **assurer la** ~ take over (de from).

relevé, ~e /Rəlve/ *a* spicy. ●*nm* (de compteur) reading; (facture) bill; ~ **bancaire**, ~ **de compte** bank statement; **faire le** ~ **de** list.

relever /Rəlve/ [6] *vt* pick up; (*personne tombée*) help up; (remonter) raise; (*col*) turn up; (*compteur*) read; (*défi*) accept; (relayer) relieve; (remarquer, noter) note; (*plat*) spice up; (rebâtir) rebuild; ~ **de** come within the competence of, (Méd) recover from. □ **se** ~ *vpr* (*personne*) get up (again); (*pays, économie*) recover.

relief /Rəljɛf/ *nm* relief; **mettre en** ~ highlight.

relier /Rəlje/ [45] *vt* link (up) (à to); (*livre*) bind.

religieux, **-ieuse** /Rəliʒjø, -z/ *a* religious. ●*nm*, *f* monk, nun.

religion /Rəliʒjɔ̃/ *nf* religion.

reliure /RəljyR/ *nf* binding.

reluire /RəlɥiR/ [17] *vi* shine.

remaniement /Rəmanimɑ̃/ *nm* revision; ~ **ministériel** cabinet reshuffle.

remarquable /RəmaRkabl/ *a* remarkable.

remarque /RəmaRk/ *nf* remark; (par écrit) comment.

remarquer /RəmaRke/ [1] *vt* notice; (*dire*) say; **faire ~** point out (à to); **se faire ~** draw attention to oneself; **remarque(z)** mind you.

remblai /Rɑ̃blɛ/ *nm* embankment.

remboursement /RɑbuRsəmɑ̃/ *nm* (d'emprunt, dette) repayment; (Comm) refund.

rembourser /RɑbuRse/ [1] *vt* (*dette, emprunt*) repay; (*billet, frais*) refund; (*client*) give a refund to; (*ami*) pay back.

remède /Rəmɛd/ *nm* remedy; (*médicament*) medicine.

remédier /Rəmedje/ [45] *vi* **~ à** remedy.

remerciements /RəmɛRsimɑ̃/ *nmpl* thanks. **remercier** /45/ *vt* thank (**de** for); (*licencier*) dismiss.

remettre /RəmɛtR/ [42] *vt* put back; (*vêtement*) put back on; (*donner*) hand over; (*devoir, démission*) hand in; (*faire fonctionner*) switch back on; (*restituer*) give back; (*différer*) put off; (*ajouter*) add; (*se rappeler*) remember; **~ en cause** *ou* **en question** call into question. □ **se ~** *vpr* (*guérir*) recover; **se ~ au tennis** take up tennis again; **se ~ au travail** get back to work; **se ~ à faire** start doing again; **s'en ~ à** leave it to.

remise /Rəmiz/ *nf* (abri) shed; (rabais) discount; (transmission) handing over; (ajournement) postponement; **~ en cause** *ou* **en question** calling into question; **~ des prix** prizegiving; **~ des médailles** medals ceremony; **~ de peine** remission.

remontant /Rəmɔ̃tɑ̃/ *nm* tonic.

remontée /Rəmɔ̃te/ *nf* ascent; (d'eau, de prix) rise; **~ mécanique** ski lift.

remonte-pente (*pl* **~s**) /Rəmɔ̃t-pɑ̃t/ *nm* ski tow.

remonter /Rəmɔ̃te/ [1] *vi* go *ou* come (back) up; (*prix, niveau*) rise (again); (*revenir*) go back (à to); **~ dans le temps** go back in time. ● *vt* (*rue, escalier*) go *ou* come (back) up; (*relever*) raise; (*montre*) wind up; (*objet démonté*) put together again; (*personne*) buck up.

remontoir /Rəmɔ̃twaR/ *nm* winder.

remords /RəmɔR/ *nm* remorse; **avoir du** *or* **des ~** feel remorse.

remorque /RəmɔRk/ *nf* trailer; **en ~** on tow. **remorquer** [1] *vt* tow.

remous /Rəmu/ *nm* eddy; (de bateau) backwash; (fig) turmoil.

rempart /RɑpaR/ *nm* rampart.

remplaçant, ~e /Rɑ̃plasɑ̃, -t/ *nm, f* replacement; (joueur) reserve, substitute.

remplacement /Rɑ̃plasmɑ̃/ *nm* replacement; **faire des ~s** do supply teaching. **remplacer** [10] *vt* replace.

rempli, ~e /Rɑ̃pli/ *a* full (**de** of); (*journée*) busy.

remplir /RɑpliR/ [2] *vt* fill (up); (*formulaire*) fill in *ou* out; (*condition*) fulfil; (*devoir, tâche, rôle*) carry out. □ **se ~** *vpr* fill (up). **remplissage** *nm* filling; (de texte) padding.

remporter /RɑpɔRte/ [1] *vt* take back; (*victoire*) win.

remuant, ~e /Rəmyɑ̃, -t/ *a* boisterous.

remue-ménage /Rəmymena3/ *nm inv* commotion, bustle.

remuer /Rəmye/ [1] *vt* move; (*thé, café*) stir; (*passé*) rake up. ● *vi* move; (*gigoter*) fidget. □ **se ~** *vpr* move.

rémunération /RemyneRasjɔ̃/ *nf* payment.

renaissance /Rənɛsɑ̃s/ *nf* rebirth.

renard /RənaR/ *nm* fox.

renchérir /Rɑ̃ʃeRiR/ [2] *vi* (dans une vente) raise the bidding; **~ sur** go one better than. ●*vt* increase, put up.

rencontre /Rɑ̃kɔ̃tR/ *nf* meeting; (de routes) junction; (Mil) encounter; (match) match; (US) game.

rencontrer /Rɑ̃kɔ̃tRe/ [1] *vt* meet; (heurter) hit; (trouver) find. □ **se ~** *vpr* meet.

rendement /Rɑ̃dmɑ̃/ *nm* yield; (travail) output.

rendez-vous /Rɑ̃devu/ *nm* appointment; (d'amoureux) date; (lieu) meeting-place; **prendre ~ (avec)** make an appointment (with).

rendormir (se) /(sə)Rɑ̃dɔRmiR/ [46] *vpr* go back to sleep.

rendre /Rɑ̃dR/ [3] *vt* give back, return; (donner en retour) return; (monnaie) give; (justice) dispense; (jugement) pronounce; **~ heureux/possible** make happy/possible; (vomir ⓘ) vomit; **~ compte de** report on; **~ service (à)** help; **~ visite à** visit. ●*vi* (terres) yield; (activité) be profitable. □ **se ~** *vpr* (capituler) surrender; (aller) go (à to); **se ~ utile** make oneself useful.

rêne /REn/ *nf* rein.

renfermé, **~e** /Rɑ̃fERme/ *a* withdrawn. ●*nm* **sentir le ~** smell musty.

renflé, **~e** /Rɑ̃fle/ *a* bulging.

renforcer /Rɑ̃fɔRse/ [10] *vt* reinforce.

renfort /Rɑ̃fɔR/ *nm* reinforcement; **à grand ~ de** with a great deal of.

renier /Rənje/ [45] *vt* (personne, œuvre) disown; (foi) renounce.

renifler /Rənifle/ [1] *vt/i* sniff.

renne /REn/ *nm* reindeer.

renom /Rənɔ̃/ *nm* renown; (réputation) reputation. **renommé**, **~e** *a* famous. **renommée** *nf* (célébrité) fame; (réputation) reputation.

renoncement /Rənɔ̃smɑ̃/ *nm* renunciation.

renoncer /Rənɔ̃se/ [10] *vi* **~ à** (habitude, ami) give up, renounce; (projet) abandon; **~ à faire** abandon the idea of doing.

renouer /Rənwe/ [1] *vt* tie up (again); (amitié) renew; **~ avec qn** get back in touch with sb; (après une dispute) make up with sb.

renouveau (*pl* **~x**) /Rənuvo/ *nm* revival.

renouveler /Rənuvle/ [38] *vt* renew; (réitérer) repeat; (remplacer) replace. □ **se ~** *vpr* be renewed; (incident) recur, happen again.

renouvellement /RənuvElmɑ̃/ *nm* renewal.

rénovation /Renɔvasjɔ̃/ *nf* (d'édifice) renovation; (d'institution) reform.

renseignement /Rɑ̃sɛɲ(ə)mɑ̃/ *nm* **~(s)** information; (bureau des) **~s** information desk; (service des) **~s téléphoniques** directory enquiries.

renseigner /Rɑ̃seɲe/ [1] *vt* inform, give information to. □ **se ~** *vpr* enquire, make enquiries, find out.

rentabilité /Rɑ̃tabilite/ *nf* profitability. **rentable** *a* profitable.

rente /Rɑ̃t/ *nf* (private) income; (pension) annuity. **rentier, -ière** *nm, f* person of private means.

rentrée /Rɑ̃tRe/ *nf* return; (revenu) income; **la ~ parlementaire** the reopening of Parliament; **la ~ (des classes)** the start of the new school year; **faire sa ~** make a comeback.

rentrer /Rɑ̃tRe/ [1] *vi* (aux être) go *ou* come back home, return home; (entrer) go *ou* come in;

R

(entrer à nouveau) go *ou* come back in; (*revenu*) come in; (*élèves*) go back (to school); ~ **dans** (heurter) smash into; **tout est rentré dans l'ordre** everything is back to normal; ~ **dans ses frais** break even. ● *vt* (*aux avoir*) bring in; (*griffes*) draw in; (*vêtement*) tuck in.

renverser /Rɑ̃vɛRse/ [1] *vt* knock over *ou* down; (*piéton*) knock down; (*liquide*) upset, spill; (mettre à l'envers) turn upside down; (*gouvernement*) overthrow; (inverser) reverse. □ **se** ~ *vpr* (*véhicule*) overturn; (*verre, vase*) fall over.

renvoi /Rɑ̃vwa/ *nm* return; (d'employé) dismissal; (d'élève) expulsion; (report) postponement; (dans un livre, fichier) cross-reference; (rot) burp.

renvoyer /Rɑ̃vwaje/ [32] *vt* send back, return; (*employé*) dismiss; (*élève*) expel; (ajourner) postpone; (référer) refer; (réfléchir) reflect.

repaire /RəpɛR/ *nm* den.

répandre /Repɑ̃dR/ [3] *vt* (liquide) spill; (étendre, diffuser) spread; (*odeur*) give off. □ **se** ~ *vpr* spread; (*liquide*) spill; **se** ~ **en injures** let out a stream of abuse.

répandu, ~**e** /Repɑ̃dy/ *a* widespread.

réparateur, -trice /RepaRatœR, -tRis/ *nm* engineer. **réparation** *nf* repair; (compensation) compensation. **réparer** [1] *vt* repair, mend; (*faute*) make amends for; (remédier à) put right.

repartie /Rəparti/ *nf* retort; **avoir de la** ~ always have a ready reply.

repartir /RəpartiR/ [46] *vi* start again; (*voyageur*) set off again; (s'en retourner) go back; (*secteur économique*) pick up again.

répartir /RepartiR/ [2] *vt* distribute; (partager) share out;

(étaler) spread. **répartition** *nf* distribution.

repas /Rəpɑ/ *nm* meal.

repassage /Rəpɑsaʒ/ *nm* ironing.

repasser /Rəpɑse/ [1] *vi* come *ou* go back; ~ **devant qch** go past sth again. ● *vt* (*linge*) iron; (*examen*) retake, resist; (*film*) show again.

repêcher /Rəpeʃe/ [1] *vt* recover, fish out; (*candidat*) allow to pass.

repentir¹ /Rəpɑ̃tiR/ *nm* repentance.

repentir² (**se**) /(sə)Rəpɑ̃tiR/ [2] *vpr* (Relig) repent (**de** of); **se** ~ **de** (regretter) regret.

répercuter /RepɛRkyte/ [1] *vt* (*bruit*) send back. □ **se** ~ *vpr* echo; **se** ~ **sur** have repercussions on.

repère /RəpɛR/ *nm* mark; (jalon) marker; (événement) landmark; (référence) reference point.

repérer /Rəpere/ [14] *vt* locate, spot. □ **se** ~ *vpr* get one's bearings.

répertoire /RepɛRtwaR/ *nm* (artistique) repertoire; (liste) directory; ~ **téléphonique** telephone directory; (personnel) telephone book. **répertorier** [45] *vt* index.

répéter /Repete/ [14] *vt* repeat; (Théât) rehearse. ● *vi* rehearse. □ **se** ~ *vpr* be repeated; (*personne*) repeat oneself.

répétition /Repetisjɔ̃/ *nf* repetition; (Théât) rehearsal.

répit /Repi/ *nm* respite, break.

replier /Rəplije/ [45] *vt* fold (up); (*ailes, jambes*) tuck in. □ **se** ~ *vpr* withdraw (**sur soi-même** into oneself).

réplique /Replik/ *nf* reply; (riposte) retort; (objection) objection; (Théât) line; (copie) replica. **répliquer** [1] *vt/i* reply; (riposter) retort; (objecter) answer back.

répondeur /Repɔ̃dœR/ *nm* answering machine.

répondre /RepɔdR/ [3] vt (injure, bêtise) reply with; ~ que answer ou reply that; ~ à (être conforme à) answer; (affection, sourire) return; (avances, appel, critique) respond to; ~ de answer for. ● vi answer, reply; (être insolent) answer back; (réagir) respond (à to).

réponse /Repɔs/ nf answer, reply; (fig) response.

report /RəpɔR/ nm (transcription) transfer; (renvoi) postponement.

reportage /RəpɔRtaʒ/ nm report; (par écrit) article.

reporter¹ /RəpɔRte/ [1] vt take back; (ajourner) put off; (transcrire) transfer. □ se ~ à vpr refer to.

reporter² /RəpɔRtɛR/ nm reporter.

repos /Rəpo/ nm rest; (paix) peace. **reposant, ~e** a restful.

reposer /Rəpoze/ [1] vt put down again; (délasser) rest. ● vi rest (sur on); **laisser ~** (pâte) leave to stand. □ se ~ vpr rest; se ~ sur rely on.

repousser /Rəpuse/ [1] vt push back; (écarter) push away; (dégoûter) repel; (décliner) reject; (ajourner) postpone, put back. ● vi grow again.

reprendre /RəpRɑ̃dR/ [50] vt take back; (confiance, conscience) regain; (souffle) get back; (évadé) recapture; (recommencer) resume; (redire) repeat; (modifier) alter; (blâmer) reprimand; ~ **du pain** take some more bread; **on ne m'y reprendra pas** I won't be caught out again. ● vi (recommencer) resume; (affaires) pick up. □ se ~ vpr (se ressaisir) pull oneself together; (se corriger) correct oneself.

représailles /RəpRezaj/ nfpl reprisals.

représentant, ~e /RəpRezɑ̃tɑ̃, -t/ nm, f representative.

représentation /RəpRezɑ̃tasjɔ̃/ nf representation; (Théât) performance.

représenter /RəpRezɑ̃te/ [1] vt represent; (figures) depict, show; (pièce de théâtre) perform. □ se ~ vpr (s'imaginer) imagine.

répression /RepResjɔ̃/ nf repression; (d'élan) suppression.

réprimande /RepRimɑ̃d/ nf reprimand.

réprimer /RepRime/ [1] vt (peuple) repress; (sentiment) suppress; (fraude) crack down on.

reprise /RəpRiz/ nf resumption; (Théât) revival; (TV) repeat; (de tissu) darn, mend; (essor) recovery; (Comm) part-exchange, trade-in; **à plusieurs ~s** on several occasions.

repriser /RəpRize/ [1] vt darn, mend.

reproche /RəpRɔʃ/ nm reproach; **faire des ~s à** find fault with.

reprocher /RəpRɔʃe/ [1] vt ~ **qch à qn** reproach ou criticize sb for sth.

reproducteur, -trice /RəpRɔdyktœR, -tRis/ a reproductive.

reproduire /RəpRɔdɥiR/ [17] vt reproduce; (répéter) repeat. □ se ~ vpr reproduce; (se répéter) recur.

reptile /Rɛptil/ nm reptile.

repu, ~e /Rəpy/ a satiated, replete.

républicain, ~e /Repyblikɛ̃, -ɛn/ a & nm, f republican.

république /Repyblik/ nf republic; ~ **populaire** people's republic.

répudier /Repydje/ [45] vt repudiate; (droit) renounce.

répugnance /Repyɲɑ̃s/ nf repugnance; (hésitation) reluctance; **avoir de la ~ pour** loathe.

répugnant, ~e a repulsive.

R

répugner /ʀepyɲe/ [1] vt be repugnant to, disgust; ~ à (effort, violence) be averse to; ~ à faire be reluctant to do.

répulsion /ʀepylsjɔ̃/ nf repulsion.

réputation /ʀepytasjɔ̃/ nf reputation.

réputé, ~e /ʀepyte/ a renowned (pour for); (école, compagnie) reputable; ~ pour être reputed to be.

requérir /ʀəkeʀiʀ/ [7] vt require, demand.

requête /ʀəkɛt/ nf request; (Jur) petition.

requin /ʀəkɛ̃/ nm shark.

requis, ~e /ʀəki, -z/ a (exigé) required; (nécessaire) necessary.

RER abrév m (réseau express régional) Parisian rapid transit rail system.

rescapé, ~e /ʀɛskape/ nm, f survivor. ● a surviving.

rescousse /ʀɛskus/ nf à la ~ to the rescue.

réseau (pl ~x) /ʀezo/ nm network; ~ local local area network, LAN; le ~ des ~x (Ordinat) Internet.

réservation /ʀezɛʀvasjɔ̃/ nf reservation, booking.

réserve /ʀezɛʀv/ nf reserve; (restriction) reservation, reserve; (indienne) reservation; (entrepôt) store-room; en ~ in reserve; les ~s (Mil) the reserves.

réserver /ʀezɛʀve/ [1] vt reserve; (place) book, reserve. □ se ~ vpr se ~ qch save sth for oneself; se ~ pour save oneself for; se ~ le droit de reserve the right to.

réservoir /ʀezɛʀvwaʀ/ nm tank; (lac) reservoir.

résidence /ʀezidɑ̃s/ nf residence; ~ secondaire second home; ~ universitaire hall of residence.

résident, ~e /ʀezidɑ̃, -t/ nm, f resident; (étranger) foreign resident.

résider /ʀezide/ [1] vi reside; ~ dans qch (difficulté) lie in.

résigner (se) /(sə)ʀeziɲe/ [1] vpr se ~ à faire resign oneself to doing.

résilier /ʀezilje/ [45] vt terminate.

résine /ʀezin/ nf resin.

résistance /ʀezistɑ̃s/ nf resistance; (fil électrique) element.

résistant, ~e a tough.

résister /ʀeziste/ [1] vi resist; ~ à (agresseur, assaut, influence, tentation) resist; (corrosion, chaleur) withstand.

résolu, ~e /ʀezɔly/ a resolute; ~ à faire determined to do. ● ⇒RÉSOUDRE [53].

résolution /ʀezɔlysjɔ̃/ nf (fermeté) resolution; (d'un problème) solving.

résonner /ʀezɔne/ [1] vi resound.

résorber /ʀezɔʀbe/ [1] vt reduce. □ se ~ vpr be reduced.

résoudre /ʀezudʀ/ [53] vt solve; (crise, conflit) resolve. □ se ~ à vpr (se décider) resolve to; (se résigner) resign oneself to.

respect /ʀɛspɛ/ nm respect.

respectabilité nf respectability.

respecter /ʀɛspɛkte/ [1] vt respect; faire ~ (loi, décision) enforce.

respectueux, -euse /ʀɛspɛktɥø, -z/ a respectful; ~ de l'environnement environmentally friendly.

respiration /ʀɛspiʀasjɔ̃/ nf breathing; (haleine) breath.

respiratoire a respiratory, breathing.

respirer /ʀɛspiʀe/ [1] vi breathe; (se reposer) catch one's breath. ● vt breathe (in); (exprimer) radiate.

resplendir /ʀɛsplɑ̃diʀ/ [2] vi

shine (de with). **resplendissant,**
~**e** *a* brilliant, radiant.

responsabilité /ʀɛspɔ̃sabilite/ *nf*
responsibility; (légale) liability.

responsable /ʀɛspɔ̃sabl/ *a*
responsible (**de** for); ~ **de** (chargé
de) in charge of. ●*nmf* person in
charge; (coupable) person
responsible.

resquiller /ʀɛskije/ [1] *vi* 🔲 (dans
le train) fare-dodge; (au spectacle)
get in without paying; (dans la
queue) jump the queue.

ressaisir (se) /(sə)ʀəseziʀ/ [2]
vpr pull oneself together; (équipe
sportive, valeurs boursières) make
a recovery.

ressemblance /ʀəsɑ̃blɑ̃s/ *nf*
resemblance.

ressemblant, ~**e** /ʀəsɑ̃blɑ̃, -t/ *a*
être ~ (portrait) be a good
likeness.

ressembler /ʀəsɑ̃ble/ [1] *vi* ~ **à**
resemble, look like. ◻ **se** ~ *vpr*
be alike; (physiquement) look alike.

ressentiment /ʀəsɑ̃timɑ̃/ *nm*
resentment.

ressentir /ʀəsɑ̃tiʀ/ [46] *vt* feel.
◻ **se** ~ **de** *vpr* feel the effects of.

resserrer /ʀəseʀe/ [1] *vt* tighten;
(contracter) compress; (vêtement)
take in. ◻ **se** ~ *vpr* tighten;
(route) narrow; (se regrouper) move
closer together.

ressort /ʀəsɔʀ/ *nm* (objet) spring;
(fig) energy; **être du** ~ **de** be the
province of; (Jur) be within the
jurisdiction of; **en dernier** ~ as a
last resort.

ressortir /ʀəsɔʀtiʀ/ [46] *vi* go *ou*
come back out; (se voir) stand out;
(film, disque) be re-released; **faire**
~ bring out; **il ressort que** it
emerges that. ●*vt* take out again;
(redire) come out with again;
(disque, film) re-release.

ressortissant, ~**e** /ʀəsɔʀtisɑ̃, -t/
nm, f national.

ressource /ʀəsuʀs/ *nf* resource;
~**s** resources; **à bout de** ~ at
one's wits' end.

ressusciter /ʀesysite/ [1] *vi*
come back to life. ●*vt* bring back
to life; (fig) revive.

restant, ~**e** /ʀɛstɑ̃, -t/ *a*
remaining. ●*nm* remainder.

restaurant /ʀɛstɔʀɑ̃/ *nm*
restaurant.

restauration /ʀɛstɔʀasjɔ̃/ *nf*
restoration; (hôtellerie) catering.

restaurer /ʀɛstɔʀe/ [1] *vt* restore.
◻ **se** ~ *vpr* eat.

reste /ʀɛst/ *nm* rest; (d'une
soustraction) remainder; ~**s**
remains (**de** of); (nourriture)
leftovers; **un** ~ **de poulet** some
left-over chicken; **au** ~, **du** ~
moreover, besides.

rester /ʀɛste/ [1] *vi* (aux être)
stay, remain; (subsister) be left,
remain; **il reste du pain** there is
some bread left (over); **il me reste
du pain** I have some bread left
(over); **il me reste à** it remains for
me to; **en** ~ **à** go no further than;
en ~ **là** stop there.

restituer /ʀɛstitɥe/ [1] *vt* (rendre)
return; (recréer) reproduce; (rétablir)
reconstruct.

restreindre /ʀɛstʀɛ̃dʀ/ [22] *vt*
restrict. ◻ **se** ~ *vpr* (dans les
dépenses) cut back.

résultat /ʀezylta/ *nm* result.

résulter /ʀezylte/ [1] *vi* ~ **de**
result from, be the result of.

résumé /ʀezyme/ *nm* summary;
en ~ in short; (pour finir) to sum
up. **résumer** [1] *vt* summarize.

résurrection /ʀezyʀɛksjɔ̃/ *nf*
resurrection; (renouveau) revival.

rétablir /ʀetabliʀ/ [2] *vt* restore;
(personne) restore to health. ◻ **se**
~ *vpr* (ordre, silence) be
restored; (guérir) recover.

rétablissement *nm* restoration;
(de malade, monnaie) recovery.

R

retard /Rətar/ nm lateness; (sur un programme) delay; (infériorité) backwardness; **avoir du ~** be late; (montre) be slow; **en ~** late; (retardé) behind; **en ~ sur l'emploi du temps** behind schedule; **rattraper** ou **combler son ~** catch up; **prendre du ~** fall behind.

retardataire /Rətardatɛr/ nmf latecomer. ● a late.

retarder /Rətarde/ [1] vt **~ qn/ qch** delay sb/sth, hold sb/sth up; (par rapport à une heure convenue) make sb/sth late; (montre) put back. ● vi (montre) be slow; (personne) be out of touch.

retenir /Rətnir/ [58] vt hold back; (souffle, attention, prisonnier) hold; (eau, chaleur) retain, hold; (larmes) hold back; (garder) keep; (retarder) detain, hold up; (réserver) book; (se rappeler) remember; (déduire) deduct; (accepter) accept. □ **se ~** vpr (se contenir) restrain oneself; **se ~ à** hold on to; **se ~ de faire** stop oneself from doing.

rétention /Retɑ̃sjɔ̃/ nf retention.

retentir /Rətɑ̃tir/ [2] vi ring out, resound; **~ sur** have an impact on. **retentissant**, **~e** a resounding. **retentissement** nm (effet) effect.

retenue /Rətny/ nf restraint; (somme) deduction; (Scol) detention.

réticent, **~e** /Retisɑ̃, -t/ a (hésitant) hesitant; (qui rechigne) reluctant; (réservé) reticent.

rétine /Retin/ nf retina.

retiré, **~e** /Rətire/ a (vie) secluded; (lieu) remote.

retirer /Rətire/ [1] vt (sortir) take out; (ôter) take off; (argent, offre, candidature) withdraw; (écarter) (main, pied) withdraw; (billet, bagages) collect, pick up; (avantage) derive; **~ à qn** take away from sb. □ **se ~** vpr withdraw, retire.

retombées /Rətɔ̃be/ nfpl (conséquences) effects; **~ radioactives** nuclear fall-out.

retomber /Rətɔ̃be/ [1] vi (faire une chute) fall again; (retourner au sol) land, come down; **~ dans** (erreur) fall back into.

retouche /Rətuʃ/ nf alteration; (de photo, tableau) retouch.

retour /Rətur/ nm return; **être de ~** be back (de from); **en arrière** flashback; **par ~ du courrier** by return of post; **en ~** in return.

retourner /Rəturne/ [1] vt (aux avoir) turn over; (vêtement) turn inside out; (maison) turn upside down; (lettre, compliment) return; (émouvoir ▣) shake, upset. ● vi (aux être) go back, return. □ **se ~** vpr turn round; (dans son lit) twist and turn; **s'en ~** go back; **se ~ contre** turn against.

retrait /Rətrɛ/ nm withdrawal; (des eaux) receding; **être** (situé) **en ~** (de) be set back (from).

retraite /Rətrɛt/ nf retirement; (pension) (retirement) pension; (fuite, refuge) retreat; **mettre à la ~** pension off; **prendre sa ~** retire.

retraité, **~e** /Rətrete/ a retired. ● nm, f (old-age) pensioner.

retrancher /Rətrɑ̃ʃe/ [1] vt remove; (soustraire) deduct, subtract. □ **se ~** vpr (Mil) entrench oneself; **se ~ derrière** take refuge behind.

retransmettre /Rətrɑ̃smɛtr/ [42] vt broadcast.

rétrécir /Retresir/ [2] vt make narrower; (vêtement) take in. ● vi (tissu) shrink. □ **se ~** vpr (rue) narrow.

rétribution /Retribysjɔ̃/ nf payment.

rétroactif, **-ive** /Retrɔaktif, -v/ a retrospective; **augmentation à effet ~** backdated pay rise.

retrousser /Rətruse/ [1] vt pull up; (*manche*) roll up.

retrouvailles /RətRuvɑj/ nfpl reunion.

retrouver /Rətruve/ [1] vt find (again); (rejoindre) meet (again); (*forces, calme*) regain; (*lieu*) be back in; (se rappeler) remember. □ se ∼ vpr find oneself (back); (se réunir) meet (again); (être présent) be found; s'y ∼ (s'orienter, comprendre) find one's way; (rentrer dans ses frais 🔟) break even.

rétroviseur /RetRɔvizœR/ nm (Auto) (rear-view) mirror.

réunion /Reynjɔ̃/ nf meeting; (rencontre) gathering; (après une séparation) réunion; (d'objets) collection.

réunir /Reynir/ [2] vt gather, collect; (rapprocher) bring together; (convoquer) call together; (raccorder) join; (*qualités*) combine. □ se ∼ vpr meet.

réussi, ∼e /Reysi/ a successful.

réussir /ReysiR/ [2] vi succeed, be successful; ∼ à faire succeed in doing, manage to do; ∼ à un examen pass an exam; ∼ à qn (*méthode*) work well for sb; (*climat, mode de vie*) agree with sb. ● vt (*vie*) make a success of.

réussite /Reysit/ nf success; (Jeu) patience.

revaloir /Rəvalwar/ [60] vt je vous revaudrai cela (en mal) I'll pay you back for this; (en bien) I'll repay you some day.

revanche /Rəvɑ̃ʃ/ nf revenge; (Sport) return *ou* revenge match; en ∼ on the other hand.

rêvasser /Revase/ [1] vi daydream.

rêve /REv/ nm dream; faire un ∼ have a dream.

réveil /Revɛj/ nm waking up, (fig) awakening; (pendule) alarm clock.

réveillé, ∼e /Reveje/ a awake.

réveille-matin /Revɛjmatɛ̃/ nm inv alarm clock.

réveiller /Reveje/ [1] vt wake (up); (*sentiment, souvenir*) awaken; (*curiosité*) arouse. □ se ∼ vpr wake up.

réveillon /Revɛjɔ̃/ nm (Noël) Christmas Eve; (nouvel an) New Year's Eve. **réveillonner** [1] vi see Christmas *ou* the New Year in.

révéler /Revele/ [14] vt reveal. □ se ∼ vpr be revealed; se ∼ facile turn out to be easy, prove easy.

revendeur, -euse /Rəvɑ̃dœR, -øz/ nm, f dealer, stockist; ∼ de drogue drug dealer.

revendication /Rəvɑ̃dikasjɔ̃/ nf claim. **revendiquer** [1] vt claim.

revendre /Rəvɑ̃dR/ [3] vt sell (again); avoir de l'énergie à ∼ have energy to spare.

revenir /RəvniR/ [58] vi (aux être) come back, return (à to); ∼ à (*activité*) go back to; (se résumer à) come down to; (échoir à) fall to; ∼ à 100 francs cost 100 francs; ∼ de (*maladie, surprise*) get over; ∼ sur ses pas retrace one's steps; faire ∼ (Culin) brown; ça me revient! now I remember!; je n'en reviens pas! 🔟 I can't get over it!

revenu /Rəvny/ nm income; (de l'État) revenue.

rêver /Reve/ [1] vt/i dream (à of; de faire of doing).

réverbère /RevɛRbɛR/ nm street lamp.

révérence /Reverɑ̃s/ nf reverence; (salut d'homme) bow; (salut de femme) curtsy.

rêverie /REvRi/ nf daydream; (activité) daydreaming.

revers /RəvER/ nm reverse; (de main) back; (d'étoffe) wrong side; (de veste) lapel; (de pantalon) turn-up;

R

(de manche) cuff; (tennis) backhand;
(fig) set-back.
revêtement /Rəvɛtmɑ̃/ *nm*
covering; (de route) surface; ~ **de
sol** floor covering. **revêtir** [61] *vt*
cover; (*habit*) put on; (prendre,
avoir) assume.
rêveur, -euse /Rɛvœʀ, -øz/ *a*
dreamy. ● *nm, f* dreamer.
réviser /Revize/ [1] *vt* revise;
(*machine, véhicule*) service.
révision *nf* revision; service.
revivre /Rəvivʀ/ [62] *vi* come
alive again. ● *vt* relive.
révocation /Revɔkasjɔ̃/ *nf*
repeal; (d'un fonctionnaire) dismissal.
revoir¹ /Rəvwaʀ/ [63] *vt* see
(again); (réviser) revise.
revoir² /Rəvwaʀ/ *nm* **au** ~
goodbye.
révolte /Revɔlt/ *nf* revolt.
révolté, ~e *nm, f* rebel.
révolter /Revɔlte/ [1] *vt* appal,
revolt. □ **se** ~ *vpr* revolt.
révolu, ~e /Revɔly/ *a* past; **avoir
21 ans** ~**s** be over 21 years of
age.
révolution /Revɔlysjɔ̃/ *nf*
revolution. **révolutionnaire** *a &
nmf* revolutionary. **révolutionner**
[1] *vt* revolutionize.
revolver /Revɔlvɛʀ/ *nm* revolver,
gun.
révoquer /Revɔke/ [1] *vt* repeal;
(*fonctionnaire*) dismiss.
revue /Rəvy/ *nf* (examen, défilé)
review; (magazine) magazine;
(spectacle) variety show.
rez-de-chaussée /Redʃose/ *nm
inv* ground floor; (US) first floor.
RF *abrév f* (**République
Française**) French Republic.
rhinocéros /RinɔseRɔs/ *nm*
rhinoceros.
rhubarbe /RybaRb/ *nf* rhubarb.
rhum /Rɔm/ *nm* rum.
rhumatisme /Rymatism/ *nm*
rheumatism.

rhume /Rym/ *nm* cold; ~ **des
foins** hay fever.
ri /Ri/ ⇒**RIRE** [54].
ricaner /Rikane/ [1] *vi* snigger.
riche /Riʃ/ *a* rich (**en** in). ● *nmf*
rich man, rich woman.
richesse /Riʃɛs/ *nf* wealth; (de sol,
décor) richness; ~**s** wealth;
(ressources) resources.
ride /Rid/ *nf* wrinkle; (sur l'eau)
ripple.
rideau (*pl* ~**x**) /Rido/ *nm* curtain;
(métallique) shutter; (fig) screen.
ridicule /Ridikyl/ *a* ridiculous.
● *nm* (d'une situation) absurdity; (le
grotesque) **le** ~ ridicule. **ridiculiser**
[1] *vt* ridicule.
rien /Rjɛ̃/ *pron* nothing; (quoi que ce
soit) anything; **de** ~! don't
mention it!; ~ **de bon** nothing
good; **elle n'a** ~ **dit** she didn't say
anything; ~ **d'autre/de plus**
nothing else/more; ~ **du tout**
nothing at all; ~ **que** (seulement)
just, only; **trois fois** ~ next to
nothing; **il n'y est pour** ~ he has
nothing to do with it; ~ **à faire!**
(c'est impossible) it's no good!; (refus)
no way! ⊡. ● *nm* **un** ~ **de** a touch
of; **être puni pour un** ~ be
punished for the slightest thing;
se disputer pour un ~ fight over
nothing; **en un** ~ **de temps** in next
to no time.
rieur, -euse /Rijœʀ, -øz/ *a*
cheerful; (*yeux*) laughing.
rigide /Riʒid/ *a* rigid.
rigolade /Rigɔlad/ *nf* fun.
rigoler /Rigɔle/ [1] *vi* laugh;
(s'amuser) have some fun;
(plaisanter) joke.
rigolo, ~te /Rigɔlo, -ɔt/ *a* ⊡
funny. ● *nm, f* ⊡ joker.
rigoureux, -euse /RiguRø, -z/ *a*
rigorous; (*hiver*) harsh; (*sévère*)
strict; (*travail, recherches*)
meticulous.
rigueur /RigœR/ *nf* rigour; **à la** ~

at a pinch; **être de** ∼ be obligatory; **tenir** ∼ **à qn de qch** bear sb a grudge for sth.

rime /ʀim/ *nf* rhyme.

rimer /ʀime/ [1] *vi* rhyme (**avec** with); **cela ne rime à rien** it makes no sense.

rinçage /ʀɛ̃saʒ/ *nm* rinse; (action) rinsing.

rincer /ʀɛ̃se/ [10] *vt* rinse.

riposte /ʀipɔst/ *nf* retort.

riposter /ʀipɔste/ [1] *vi* retaliate; ∼ **à** (*attaque*) counter; (*insulte*) reply to. ● *vt* retort (**que** that).

rire /ʀiʀ/ [54] *vi* laugh (**de** at); (*plaisanter*) joke; (*s'amuser*) have fun; **c'était pour** ∼ it was a joke. ● *nm* laugh; **des** ∼**s** laughter.

risée /ʀize/ *nf* **la** ∼ **de** the laughing-stock of.

risque /ʀisk/ *nm* risk. **risqué,** ∼**e** *a* risky; (*osé*) daring.

risquer /ʀiske/ [1] *vt* risk (**de faire** of doing); (*être passible de*) face; **il risque de pleuvoir** it might rain; **tu risques de te faire mal** you might hurt yourself. □ **se** ∼ **à/dans** *vpr* venture into/into.

ristourne /ʀistuʀn/ *nf* discount.

rite /ʀit/ *nm* rite; (*habitude*) ritual. **rituel,** ∼**le** *a & nm* ritual.

rivage /ʀivaʒ/ *nm* shore.

rival, ∼**e** (*mpl* **-aux**) /ʀival, -o/ *a & nm,f* rival. **rivaliser** [1] *vi* compete (**avec** with). **rivalité** *nf* rivalry.

rive /ʀiv/ *nf* (de fleuve) bank; (de lac) shore.

riverain, ∼**e** /ʀivʀɛ̃, -ɛn/ *a* riverside. ● *nm,f* riverside resident; (d'une rue) resident.

rivière /ʀivjɛʀ/ *nf* river.

riz /ʀi/ *nm* rice. **rizière** *nf* paddy field.

robe /ʀɔb/ *nf* (de femme) dress; (de juge) robe; (de cheval) coat; ∼ **de chambre** dressing-gown.

robinet /ʀɔbinɛ/ *nm* tap; (US) faucet.

robot /ʀɔbo/ *nm* robot; ∼ **ménager** food processor.

robuste /ʀɔbyst/ *a* robust.

roche /ʀɔʃ/ *nf* rock.

rocher /ʀɔʃe/ *nm* rock.

rock /ʀɔk/ *nm* (Mus) rock.

rodage /ʀɔdaʒ/ *nm* **en** ∼ (Auto) running in.

roder /ʀɔde/ [1] *vt* (Auto) run in; **être rodé** (*personne*) have got the hang of things.

rôder /ʀode/ [1] *vi* roam; (*suspect*) prowl.

rogne /ʀɔɲ/ *nf* 🖻 anger; **en** ∼ in a temper.

rogner /ʀɔɲe/ [1] *vt* trim; ∼ **sur** cut down on.

rognon /ʀɔɲɔ̃/ *nm* (Culin) kidney.

roi /ʀwa/ *nm* king; **les R**∼ **mages** the Magi; **la fête des R**∼ Twelfth Night.

rôle /ʀol/ *nm* role, part.

romain, ∼**e** /ʀɔmɛ̃, -ɛn/ *a* Roman. **R**∼, ∼**e** *nm,f* Roman. **romaine** *nf* (laitue) cos.

roman /ʀɔmɑ̃/ *nm* novel; (genre) fiction.

romance /ʀɔmɑ̃s/ *nf* ballad.

romancier, -ière /ʀɔmɑ̃sje, -jɛʀ/ *nm,f* novelist.

romanesque /ʀɔmanɛsk/ *a* romantic; (*fantastique*) fantastic; (*récit*) fictional; **œuvres** ∼**s** novels, fiction.

romantique /ʀɔmɑ̃tik/ *a & nmf* romantic. **romantisme** *nm* romanticism.

rompre /ʀɔ̃pʀ/ [3] *vt* break; (*relations*) break off. ● *vi* (se séparer) break up; ∼ **avec** (*fiancé*) break up with; (*parti*) break away from; (*tradition*) break with. □ **se** ∼ *vpr* break.

ronce /ʀɔ̃s/ *nf* bramble.

rond, ∼**e** /ʀɔ̃, -d/ *a* round; (*gras*) plump; (*ivre* 🖻) drunk. ● *nm*

R

(cercle) ring; (tranche) slice; **en ∼** in a circle; **il n'a pas un ∼** ⒠ he hasn't got a penny.

ronde /Rɔ̃d/ *nf* (de policier) beat; (de soldat, gardien) watch; (Mus) semibreve.

rondelle /Rɔ̃dɛl/ *nf* (Tech) washer; (tranche) slice.

rondement /Rɔ̃dmɑ̃/ *adv* promptly; (franchement) frankly.

rondeur /Rɔ̃dœR/ *nf* roundness; (franchise) frankness; (embonpoint) plumpness.

rondin /Rɔ̃dɛ̃/ *nm* log.

rond-point (*pl* **ronds-points**) /Rɔ̃pwɛ̃/ *nm* roundabout; (US) traffic circle.

ronfler /Rɔ̃fle/ [1] *vi* snore; (moteur) purr.

ronger /Rɔ̃ʒe/ [40] *vt* gnaw (at); (vers, acide) eat into. □ **se ∼** *vpr* **se ∼ les ongles** bite one's nails.

rongeur /Rɔ̃ʒœR/ *nm* rodent.

ronronner /Rɔ̃Rɔne/ [1] *vi* purr.

rosbif /Rɔsbif/ *nm* roast beef.

rose /Roz/ *nf* rose. ● *a & nm* pink.

rosé, **∼e** /Roze/ *a* pinkish. ● *nm* rosé.

roseau (*pl* **∼x**) /Rozo/ *nm* reed.

rosée /Roze/ *nf* dew.

rosier /Rozje/ *nm* rose bush.

rossignol /Rɔsiɲɔl/ *nm* nightingale.

rotatif, **-ive** /Rɔtatif, -v/ *a* rotary.

roter /Rɔte/ [1] *vi* ⒠ burp.

rôti /Roti/ *nm* joint; (cuit) roast; **∼ de porc** roast pork.

rotin /Rɔtɛ̃/ *nm* (rattan) cane.

rôtir /RɔtiR/ [2] *vt* roast.

rôtissoire /RɔtiswaR/ *nf* roasting spit.

rotule /Rɔtyl/ *nf* kneecap.

rouage /Rwaʒ/ *nm* (Tech) wheel; **les ∼s** the works; (d'une organisation: fig) wheels.

roucouler /Rukule/ [1] *vi* coo.

roue /Ru/ *nf* wheel; **∼ dentée**

cog(wheel); **∼ de secours** spare wheel.

rouer /Rwe/ [1] *vt* **∼ de coups** thrash.

rouge /Ruʒ/ *a* red; (fer) red-hot. ● *nm* red; (vin) red wine; (fard) blusher; **∼ à lèvres** lipstick. ● *nmf* (Pol) red. **rouge-gorge** (*pl* **rouges-gorges**) *nm* robin.

rougeole /Ruʒɔl/ *nf* measles (+ *sg*).

rouget /Ruʒɛ/ *nm* red mullet.

rougeur /RuʒœR/ *nf* redness; (tache) red blotch.

rougir /RuʒiR/ [2] *vi* turn red; (de honte) blush.

rouille /Ruj/ *nf* rust. **rouillé**, **∼e** *a* rusty.

rouiller /Ruje/ [1] *vi* rust. □ **se ∼** *vpr* get rusty.

rouleau (*pl* **∼x**) /Rulo/ *nm* roll; (outil, vague) roller; **∼ à pâtisserie** rolling pin; **∼ compresseur** steamroller.

roulement /Rulmɑ̃/ *nm* rotation; (bruit) rumble; (alternance) rotation; (de tambour) roll; **∼ à billes** ball-bearing; **travailler par ∼** work in shifts.

rouler /Rule/ [1] *vt* roll; (ficelle, manches) roll up; (pâte) roll out; (duper ⒠) cheat. ● *vi* (véhicule, train) go, travel; (conducteur) drive. □ **se ∼ dans** *vpr* (herbe) roll in; (couverture) roll oneself up in.

roulette /Rulɛt/ *nf* (de meuble) castor; (de dentiste) drill; (jeu) roulette; **comme sur des ∼s** very smoothly.

roulotte /Rulɔt/ *nf* caravan.

roumain, **∼e** /Rumɛ̃, -ɛn/ *a* Romanian. **R∼**, **∼e** *nm, f* Romanian.

Roumanie /Rumani/ *nf* Romania.

rouquin, **∼e** /Rukɛ̃, -in/ ⒠ *a* red-haired. ● *nm, f* redhead.

rouspéter /Ruspete/ [14] *vi* ⊡ grumble, moan.

rousse /Rus/ ⇨ROUX.

roussir /RusiR/ [2] *vt* scorch. ● *vi* turn brown.

route /Rut/ *nf* road; (Naut, Aviat) route; (direction) way; (voyage) journey; (chemin: fig) path; **en ~** on the way; **en ~!** let's go!; **mettre en ~** start; **~ nationale** trunk road, main road; **se mettre en ~** set out.

routier, -ière /Rutje, -jɛR/ *a* road. ● *nm* long-distance lorry *ou* truck driver; (restaurant) transport café; (US) truck stop.

routine /Rutin/ *nf* routine.

roux, rousse /Ru, Rus/ *a* red, russet; (*personne*) red-haired; (*chat*) ginger. ● *nm, f* redhead.

royal, ~e (*mpl* **-aux**) /Rwajal, -jo/ *a* royal; (*cadeau*) fit for a king.

royaume /Rwajom/ *nm* kingdom.

Royaume-Uni /Rwajomyni/ *nm* United Kingdom.

royauté /Rwajote/ *nf* royalty.

RTT *abrév f* (**réduction du temps de travail**) reduction in working hours.

ruban /Rybã/ *nm* ribbon; (de chapeau) band; **~ adhésif** sticky tape; **~ magnétique** magnetic tape.

rubéole /Rybeɔl/ *nf* German measles (+ *sg*).

rubis /Rybi/ *nm* ruby.

rubrique /RybRik/ *nf* heading; (article) column.

ruche /Ryʃ/ *nf* beehive.

rude /Ryd/ *a* (au toucher) rough; (pénible) tough; (grossier) coarse; (fameux ⊡) tremendous.

rudement /Rydmã/ *adv* (*frapper*) hard; (*traiter*) harshly; (très ⊡) really.

rudimentaire /RydimãtɛR/ *a* rudimentary.

rue /Ry/ *nf* street.

ruée /Rue/ *nf* rush.

ruer /Rue/ [1] *vi* (*cheval*) buck. □ **se ~** *vpr* rush (**dans** into; **vers** towards); **se ~ sur** pounce on.

rugby /Rygbi/ *nm* rugby.

rugir /RyʒiR/ [2] *vi* roar.

rugueux, -euse /Rygø, -z/ *a* rough.

ruine /Ruin/ *nf* ruin; **en ~(s)** in ruins. **ruiner** [1] *vt* ruin.

ruisseau (*pl* **~x**) /Ruiso/ *nm* stream; (rigole) gutter.

rumeur /RymœR/ *nf* (nouvelle) rumour; (son) murmur, hum.

ruminer /Rymine/ [1] *vi* (animal) ruminate; (méditer) meditate.

rupture /RyptyR/ *nf* break; (action) breaking; (de contrat) breach; (de pourparlers) breakdown; (de relations) breaking off; (de couple, coalition) break-up.

rural, ~e (*mpl* **-aux**) /RyRal, -o/ *a* rural.

ruse /Ryz/ *nf* cunning; **une ~** a trick, a ruse. **rusé, ~e** *a* cunning.

russe /Rys/ *a* Russian. ● *nm* (Ling) Russian. **R~** *nmf* Russian.

Russie /Rysi/ *nf* Russia.

rustique /Rystik/ *a* rustic.

rythme /Ritm/ *nm* rhythm; (vitesse) rate; (de la vie) pace.
rythmique *a* rhythmical.

s' /s/ ⇒SE.

sa /sa/ ⇨SON[1].

SA *abrév f* (**société anonyme**) PLC.

sabbatique /sabatik/ *a* (année) sabbatical year.

sable /sɑbl/ *nm* sand; **~s**

mouvants quicksands. **sabler** vt
[1] grit.
sablier /sablije/ nm (Culin)
eggtimer.
sablonneux, -euse /sablɔnø, -z/
a sandy.
sabot /sabo/ nm (de cheval) hoof;
(chaussure) clog; (de frein) shoe; ∼
de Denver® (wheel) clamp.
saboter /sabɔte/ [1] vt sabotage;
(bâcler) botch.
sac /sak/ nm bag; (grand, en toile)
sack; **mettre à** ∼ (maison)
ransack; (ville) sack; ∼ **à dos**
rucksack; ∼ **à main** handbag; ∼
de couchage sleeping-bag; **mettre
dans le même** ∼ lump together.
saccadé, ∼e /sakade/ a jerky.
saccager /sakaʒe/ [40] vt (abîmer)
wreck; (maison) ransack; (ville,
pays) sack.
saccharine /sakaʀin/ nf
saccharin.
sachet /saʃɛ/ nm (small) bag;
(d'aromates) sachet; ∼ **de thé** tea-
bag.
sacoche /sakɔʃ/ nf bag; (de vélo)
saddlebag.
sacre /sakʀ/ nm (de roi)
coronation; (d'évêque)
consecration. **sacré, ∼e** a
sacred; (maudit 🅟) damned.
sacrement nm sacrament.
sacrer [1] vt crown; consecrate.
sacrifice /sakʀifis/ nm sacrifice.
sacrifier /sakʀifje/ [45] vt
sacrifice; ∼ **à** conform to. □ **se** ∼
vpr sacrifice oneself.
sacrilège /sakʀilɛʒ/ nm
sacrilege. ● a sacrilegious.
sadique /sadik/ a sadistic. ● nmf
sadist.
sage /saʒ/ a wise; (docile) good,
well behaved. ● nm wise man.
sage-femme (pl **sages-
femmes**) /saʒfam/ nf midwife.
sagesse /saʒɛs/ nf wisdom.

Sagittaire /saʒitɛʀ/ nm le ∼
Sagittarius.
saignant, ∼e /sɛɲã, -t/ a (Culin)
rare.
saigner /seɲe/ [1] vt/i bleed; ∼
du nez have a nosebleed.
saillant, ∼e /sajã, -t/ a
prominent.
sain, ∼e /sɛ̃, sɛn/ a healthy;
(moralement) sane; ∼ **et sauf** safe
and sound.
saindoux /sɛ̃du/ nm lard.
saint, ∼e /sɛ̃, -t/ a holy; (bon, juste)
saintly. ● nm, f saint. **Saint-
Esprit** nm Holy Spirit. **sainteté**
nf holiness; (d'un lieu) sanctity.
Sainte Vierge nf Blessed Virgin.
Saint-Sylvestre nf New Year's
Eve.
sais /sɛ/ ⇒SAVOIR [55].
saisie /sezi/ nf (Jur) seizure;
(Comput) keyboarding; ∼ **de
données** data capture.
saisir /seziʀ/ [2] vt grab (hold of);
(proie) seize; (occasion, biens)
seize; (comprendre) grasp; (frapper)
strike; (Ordinat) keyboard, capture;
saisi de (peur) stricken by,
overcome by. □ **se** ∼ **de** vpr
seize. **saisissant, ∼e** a
(spectacle) gripping.
saison /sezõ/ nf season; **la morte**
∼ the off season. **saisonnier,
-ière** a seasonal.
sait /sɛ/ ⇒SAVOIR [55].
salade /salad/ nf (plat) salad;
(plante) lettuce. **saladier** nm salad
bowl.
salaire /salɛʀ/ nm wages (+ pl),
salary.
salarié, ∼e /salaʀje/ a wage-
earning. ● nm, f wage earner.
sale /sal/ a dirty; (mauvais) nasty.
salé, ∼e /sale/ a (goût) salty;
(plat) salted; (opposé à sucré)
savoury; (grivois 🅟) spicy; (excessif
🅟) steep. **saler** [1] vt salt.
saleté /salte/ nf dirtiness; (crasse)

dirt; (obscénité) obscenity; ~(s) (camelote) rubbish; (détritus) mess.

salir /saliʀ/ [2] vt (make) dirty; (réputation) tarnish. □ se ~ vpr get dirty. **salissant**, ~e a dirty; (étoffe) easily dirtied.

salive /saliv/ nf saliva.

salle /sal/ nf room; (grande, publique) hall; (de restaurant) dining room; (Théât, cinéma) auditorium; **cinéma à trois ~s** three-screen cinema; ~ **à manger** dining room; ~ **d'attente** waiting room; ~ **de bains** bathroom; ~ **de bavardage**, ~ **de causette** chatroom; ~ **de séjour** living room; ~ **de classe** classroom; ~ **d'embarquement** departure lounge; ~ **d'opération** operating theatre; ~ **des ventes** saleroom.

salon /salɔ̃/ nm lounge; (de coiffure, beauté) salon; (exposition) show; ~ **de thé** tea-room; ~ **virtuel** chatroom.

salopette /salɔpɛt/ nf dungarees (+ pl); (d'ouvrier) overalls (+ pl).

saltimbanque /saltɛ̃bɑ̃k/ nmf (street) acrobat.

salubre /salybʀ/ a healthy.

saluer /salɥe/ [1] vt greet; (en partant) take one's leave of; (de la tête) nod to; (de la main) wave to; (Mil) salute; (accueillir favorablement) welcome.

salut /saly/ nm greeting; (de la tête) nod; (de la main) wave; (Mil) salute; (rachat) salvation. ●interj (bonjour Ⓘ) hello; (au revoir Ⓘ) bye.

salutation /salytasjɔ̃/ nf greeting.

samedi /samdi/ nm Saturday.

SAMU /samy/ abrév m (**Service d'assistance médicale d'urgence**) ≈ mobile accident unit.

sanction /sɑ̃ksjɔ̃/ nf sanction. **sanctionner** [1] vt sanction; (punir) punish.

sandale /sɑ̃dal/ nf sandal.

sang /sɑ̃/ nm blood; **se faire du mauvais** ~ **ou un** ~ **d'encre** be worried stiff. **sang-froid** nm inv self-control. **sanglant**, ~e a bloody.

sangle /sɑ̃gl/ nf strap.

sanglier /sɑ̃glije/ nm wild boar.

sanglot /sɑ̃glo/ nm sob. **sangloter** [1] vi sob.

sanguin, ~e /sɑ̃gɛ̃, -in/ a (groupe) blood.

sanguinaire /sɑ̃ginɛʀ/ a bloodthirsty.

sanitaire /sanitɛʀ/ a (directives) health; (conditions) sanitary; (appareils, installations) bathroom, sanitary. **sanitaires** nmpl bathroom.

sans /sɑ̃/ prép without; ~ **ça**, ~ **quoi** otherwise; ~ **arrêt** nonstop; ~ **encombre/faute/tarder** without incident/fail/delay; ~ **fin/goût/ limite** endless/tasteless/limitless; ~ **importance/pareil/précédent/ travail** unimportant/unparalleled/ unprecedented/unemployed; **j'ai aimé mais** ~ **plus** it was good, it wasn't great.

sans-abri /sɑ̃zabʀi/ nmf inv homeless person.

sans-gène /sɑ̃ʒɛn/ a inv inconsiderate, thoughtless. ●nm inv thoughtlessness.

sans-papiers /sɑ̃papje/ nm inv illegal immigrant.

santé /sɑ̃te/ nf health; **à ta ou votre** ~! cheers!

saoul, ~e /su, sul/ ⇒SOÛL.

sapin /sapɛ̃/ nm fir(tree); ~ **de Noël** Christmas tree.

sarcasme /saʀkasm/ nm sarcasm. **sarcastique** a sarcastic.

sardine /saʀdin/ nf sardine.

sas /sɑs/ nm (Naut, Aviat) airlock.

satané, ~e /satane/ a Ⓘ damned.

satellite /satelit/ nm satellite.

S

satin /satɛ̃/ nm satin.

satire /satiʀ/ nf satire.

satisfaction /satisfaksjɔ̃/ nf satisfaction.

satisfaire /satisfɛʀ/ [33] vt satisfy. ● vi ~ à fulfil.

satisfaisant, **~e** a (acceptable) satisfactory. **satisfait**, **~e** a satisfied (de with).

saturer /satyʀe/ [1] vt saturate.

sauce /sos/ nf sauce; ~ **tartare** tartar sauce. **saucière** nf sauceboat.

saucisse /sosis/ nf sausage.

saucisson /sosisɔ̃/ nm (slicing) sausage.

sauf[1] /sof/ prép except; ~ **erreur** if I'm not mistaken; ~ **imprévu** unless anything unforeseen happens; ~ **avis contraire** unless otherwise stated.

sauf[2], **-ve** /sof, sov/ a safe, unharmed.

sauge /soʒ/ nf (Culin) sage.

saule /sol/ nm willow; ~ **pleureur** weeping willow.

saumon /somɔ̃/ nm salmon. ● a inv salmon-(pink).

sauna /sona/ nm sauna.

saupoudrer /sopudʀe/ [1] vt sprinkle (de with).

saut /so/ nm jump; **faire un ~ chez qn** pop round to sb's (place); **le ~** (Sport) jumping; ~ **en hauteur/longueur** high/long jump; ~ **périlleux** somersault; **au ~ du lit** on getting up.

sauté, **~e** /sote/ a & nm (Culin) sauté.

saute-mouton /sotmutɔ̃/ nm inv leap-frog.

sauter /sote/ [1] vi jump; (exploser) blow up; (fusible) blow; (se détacher) come off; **faire ~** (détruire) blow up; (fusible) blow; (casser) break; ~ **à la corde** skip; ~ **aux yeux** be obvious; ~ **au cou de qn** fling one's arms round sb; ~ **sur**

une occasion jump at an opportunity. ● vt jump (over); (page, classe) skip.

sauterelle /sotʀɛl/ nf grasshopper.

sautiller /sotije/ [1] vi hop.

sauvage /sovaʒ/ a wild; (primitif, cruel) savage; (farouche) unsociable; (illégal) unauthorized. ● nmf unsociable person; (brute) savage.

sauve /sov/ ⇒SAUF[2].

sauvegarder /sovgaʀde/ [1] vt safeguard; (Ordinat) back up.

sauver /sove/ [1] vt save; (d'un danger) rescue, save; (matériel) salvage. □ **se ~** vpr (fuir) run away; (partir [I]) be off. **sauvetage** nm rescue. **sauveteur** nm rescuer. **sauveur** nm saviour.

savant, **~e** /savɑ̃, -t/ a learned; (habile) skilful. ● nm scientist.

saveur /savœʀ/ nf flavour; (fig) savour.

savoir /savwaʀ/ [55] vt know; **elle sait conduire/nager** she can drive/ swim; **faire ~ à qn** inform sb that; **(pas) que je sache** (not) as far as I know; **à ~** namely. ● nm learning.

savon /savɔ̃/ nm soap; **passer un ~ à qn** [I] give sb a telling-off. **savonnette** nf bar of soap.

savourer /savuʀe/ [1] vt savour. **savoureux**, **-euse** a tasty; (fig) spicy.

scandale /skɑ̃dal/ nm scandal; (tapage) uproar; (en public) noisy scene; **faire ~** shock people; **faire un ~** make a scene. **scandaleux**, **-euse** a scandalous. **scandaliser** [1] vt scandalize, shock.

scander /skɑ̃de/ [1] vt (vers) scan; (slogan) chant.

scandinave /skɑ̃dinav/ a Scandinavian. **S~** nmf Scandinavian.

Scandinavie /skãdinavi/ *nf*
Scandinavia.

scarabée /skaʀabe/ *nm* beetle.

sceau (*pl* ∼x) /so/ *nm* seal.

scélérat /seleʀa/ *nm* scoundrel.

sceller /sele/ [1] *vt* seal.

scène /sɛn/ *nf* scene; (estrade, art
dramatique) stage; **mettre en** ∼
(*pièce*) stage; (*film*) direct; **mise
en** ∼ direction; ∼ **de ménage**
domestic dispute.

scepticisme /sɛptisism/ *nm*
scepticism.

sceptique /sɛptik/ *a* sceptical.
● *nmf* sceptic.

schéma /ʃema/ *nm* diagram.
schématique *a* schematic;
(sommaire) sketchy. **schématiser**
[1] *vt* simplify.

schizophrène /skizɔfʀɛn/ *a* &
nmf schizophrenic.

sciatique /sjatik/ *a* (*nerf*)
sciatic. ● *nf* sciatica.

scie /si/ *nf* saw.

sciemment /sjamã/ *adv*
knowingly.

science /sjãs/ *nf* science; (savoir)
knowledge.

science-fiction /sjãsfiksjõ/ *nf*
science fiction.

scientifique /sjãtifik/ *a*
scientific. ● *nmf* scientist.

scier /sje/ [45] *vt* saw.

scintiller /sɛ̃tije/ [1] *vi* glitter;
(*étoile*) twinkle.

scission /sisjõ/ *nf* split.

sclérose /skleʀoz/ *nf* sclerosis;
∼ **en plaques** multiple sclerosis.

scolaire /skɔlɛʀ/ *a* school.
scolarisé, ∼**e** *a* going to school.
scolarité *nf* schooling.

score /skɔʀ/ *nm* score.

scorpion /skɔʀpjõ/ *nm* scorpion;
le S∼ Scorpio.

scotch /skɔtʃ/ *nm* (boisson) Scotch
(whisky); (ruban adhésif)®
Sellotape®.

scout, ∼**e** /skut/ *nm & a* scout.

scrupule /skʀypyl/ *nm* scruple.
scrupuleux, **-euse** *a* scrupulous.

scruter /skʀyte/ [1] *vt* examine,
scrutinize.

scrutin /skʀytɛ̃/ *nm* (vote) ballot;
(élections) polls (+ *pl*).

sculpter /skylte/ [1] *vt* sculpt,
carve. **sculpteur** *nm* sculptor.
sculpture *nf* sculpture.

SDF *abrév mf* (**sans domicile
fixe**) homeless person.

se, **s'** /sə, s/

   s' before vowel or mute h.

● *pronom*
····▸ himself, (féminin) herself;
(indéfini) oneself; (non humain) itself;
(au pluriel) themselves; ∼ **laver les
mains** wash one's hands;
(réciproque) each other, one
another; **ils se détestent** they
hate each other.

! The translation of **se** will
   vary according to which
   verb it is associated with.
   You should therefore refer
   to the verb to find it. For
   example, **se promener, se
   taire** will be treated
   respectively under **promener**
   and **taire**.

séance /seãs/ *nf* session; (Théât,
cinéma) show; ∼ **de pose** sitting; ∼
tenante forthwith.

seau (*pl* ∼x) /so/ *nm* bucket,
pail.

sec, **sèche** /sɛk, sɛʃ/ *a* dry;
(*fruits*) dried; (*coup, bruit*) sharp;
(*cœur*) hard; (*whisky*) neat. ● *nm*
à ∼ (sans eau) dry; (sans argent)
broke; **au** ∼ in a dry place.

sèche-cheveux /sɛʃʃəvø/ *nm
inv* hairdrier.

sèchement /sɛʃmã/ *adv* drily

sécher /seʃe/ [14] *vt/i* dry;
(*cours*: 🔲) skip; (ne pas savoir

S

stumped. □ **se** ~ *vpr* dry oneself.
sécheresse /ʃɛʃʀɛs/ *nf* (de climat) dryness; (temps sec) drought. **séchoir** *nm* drier.

second, ~e /səɡɔ̃, -d/ *a & nm,f* second. ● *nm* (adjoint) second in command; (étage) second floor. **secondaire** *a* secondary. **seconde** *nf* (instant) second; (vitesse) second gear.

seconder /səɡɔ̃de/ [1] *vt* assist.

secouer /səkwe/ [1] *vt* shake; (poussière, torpeur) shake off. □ **se** ~ *vpr* Ⅱ (se dépêcher) get a move on; (réagir) shake oneself up.

secourir /səkuʀiʀ/ [20] *vt* assist, help. **secouriste** *nmf* first-aid worker.

secours /səkuʀ/ *nm* assistance, help; **au** ~! help!; **de** ~ (sortie) emergency; (équipe, opération) rescue. ● *nmpl* (Méd) first aid.

secousse /səkus/ *nf* jolt, jerk; (séisme) tremor.

secret, **-ète** /səkʀɛ, -t/ *a* secret. ● *nm* secret; (discrétion) secrecy; **le** ~ **professionnel** professional confidentiality; ~ **de Polichinelle** open secret; **en** ~ in secret, secretly.

secrétaire /səkʀetɛʀ/ *nmf* secretary; ~ **de direction** personal assistant. ● *nm* (meuble) writing-desk; ~ **d'État** junior minister.

secrétariat /səkʀetaʀja/ *nm* secretarial work; (bureau) secretariat.

sectaire /sɛktɛʀ/ *a* sectarian.

secte /sɛkt/ *nf* sect.

secteur /sɛktœʀ/ *nm* area; (Comm) sector; (circuit: Électr) mains (+ *pl*).

ection /sɛksjɔ̃/ *nf* section; (Scol) ~eam; (Mil) platoon. **sectionner** ~vt sever.

~riser /sekyʀize/ [1] *vt* ~re.

sécurité /sekyʀite/ *nf* security; (absence de danger) safety; **en** ~ safe, secure. **Sécurité sociale** *nf* social services, social security services.

sédatif /sedatif/ *nm* sedative.

sédentaire /sedɑ̃tɛʀ/ *a* sedentary.

séducteur, **-trice** /sedyktœʀ, -tʀis/ *a* seductive. ● *nm,f* seducer. **séduction** *nf* seduction; (charme) charm.

séduire /seduiʀ/ [17] *vt* charm; (plaire à) appeal to; (sexuellement) seduce. **séduisant**, ~e *a* attractive.

ségrégation /seɡʀeɡasjɔ̃/ *nf* segregation.

seigle /sɛɡl/ *nm* rye.

seigneur /sɛɲœʀ/ *nm* lord; **le S**~ the Lord.

sein /sɛ̃/ *nm* breast; **au** ~ **de** within.

séisme /seism/ *nm* earthquake.

seize /sɛz/ *a & nm* sixteen.

séjour /seʒuʀ/ *nm* stay; (pièce) living room. **séjourner** [1] *vi* stay.

sel /sɛl/ *nm* salt; (piquant) spice.

sélectif, **-ive** /selɛktif, -v/ *a* selective.

sélection /selɛksjɔ̃/ *nf* selection. **sélectionner** [1] *vt* select.

selle /sɛl/ *nf* saddle; ~**s** (Méd) stools.

sellette /sɛlɛt/ *nf* **sur la** ~ (personne) in the hot seat.

selon /səlɔ̃/ *prép* according to; ~ **que** depending on whether.

semaine /səmɛn/ *nf* week; **en** ~ during the week.

sémantique /semɑ̃tik/ *a* semantic. ● *nf* semantics.

semblable /sɑ̃blabl/ *a* similar (à to). ● *nm* fellow (creature).

semblant /sɑ̃blɑ̃/ *nm* **faire** ~ **de**

pretend to; un ~ de a semblance of.

sembler /sãble/ [1] *vi* seem (à to; que that); **il me semble que** it seems to me that.

semelle /səmɛl/ *nf* sole; ~ compensée wedge heel.

semence /s(ə)mãs/ *nf* seed.

semer /s(ə)me/ [6] *vt* (*graine, doute*) sow; (jeter, parsemer) strew; (*personne* 🔲) lose; ~ **la panique** spread panic.

semestre /səmɛstʀ/ *nm* half-year; (Univ) semester. **semestriel, ~le** *a* biannual; (examen) end-of-semester.

séminaire /seminɛʀ/ *nm* (Relig) seminary; (Univ) seminar.

semi-remorque /s(ə)miʀ(ə) mɔʀk/ *nm* articulated lorry.

semis /s(ə)mi/ *nm* (plant) seedling.

semoule /s(ə)mul/ *nf* semolina.

sénat /sena/ *nm* senate. **sénateur** *nm* senator.

sénile /senil/ *a* senile.

senior /senjɔʀ/ *a* (âgé) senior; (*mode, publication*) for senior citizens. ● *nmf* senior citizen.

sens /sãs/ *nm* (Méd) sense; (signification) meaning, sense; (direction) direction; **à mon ~** to my mind; **à ~ unique** (*rue*) one-way; **ça n'a pas de ~** it doesn't make sense; ~ **commun** common sense; ~ **giratoire** roundabout; ~ **interdit** no-entry sign; (rue) one-way street; **dans le ~ des aiguilles d'une montre** clockwise; **dans le ~ inverse des aiguilles d'une montre** anticlockwise; ~ **dessus dessous** upside down; ~ **devant derrière** back to front.

sensation /sãsasjɔ̃/ *nf* feeling, sensation; **faire ~** create a sensation. **sensationnel, ~le** *a* sensational.

sensé, ~e /sãse/ *a* sensible.

sensibiliser /sãsibilize/ [1] *vt* ~ l'opinion increase people's awareness (à qch to sth).

sensibilité /sãsibilite/ *nf* sensitivity. **sensible** *a* sensitive (à to); (appréciable) noticeable. **sensiblement** *adv* noticeably.

sensoriel, ~le /sãsɔʀjɛl/ *a* sensory.

sensualité /sãsɥalite/ *nf* sensuousness; sensuality. **sensuel, ~le** *a* sensual.

sentence /sãtãs/ *nf* sentence.

senteur /sãtœʀ/ *nf* scent.

sentier /sãtje/ *nm* path.

sentiment /sãtimã/ *nm* feeling; **faire du ~** sentimentalize; **j'ai le ~ que...** I get the feeling that...

sentimental, ~e (*mpl* -aux) *a* sentimental.

sentir /sãtiʀ/ [46] *vt* feel; (*odeur*) smell; (pressentir) sense; ~ **la lavande** smell of lavender; **je ne peux pas le ~** 🔲 I can't stand him. ● *vi* smell. □ **se ~** *vpr* **se ~ fier/mieux** feel proud/better.

séparation /separasjɔ̃/ *nf* separation.

séparatiste /separatist/ *a* & *nmf* separatist.

séparé, ~e /separe/ *a* separate; (conjoints) separated.

séparer /separe/ [1] *vt* separate; (en deux) split. □ **se ~** *vpr* separate, part (de from); (se détacher) split; **se ~ de** (se défaire de) part with.

sept /sɛt/ *a* & *nm* seven.

septante /sɛptãt/ *a* & *nm* seventy.

septembre /sɛptãbʀ/ *nm* September.

septentrional, ~e (*mpl* -aux) /sɛptãtʀijɔnal, -o/ *a* northern.

septième /sɛtjɛm/ *a* & *nmf* seventh.

sépulture /sepyltyʀ/ *nf* burial; (lieu) burial place.

séquelles /sekɛl/ *nfpl* (maladie) aftereffects; (fig) aftermath (+ *sg*).

S

séquence /sekɑ̃s/ *nf* sequence.

séquestrer /sekɛstʀe/ [1] *vt* confine (illegally).

sera, **serait** /səʀa, səʀɛ/ ⇒ÊTRE [4].

serbe /sɛʀb/ *a* Serbian. **S~** *nmf* Serbian.

Serbie /sɛʀbi/ *nf* Serbia.

serein, **~e** /səʀɛ̃, -ɛn/ *a* serene.

sérénité /seʀenite/ *nf* serenity.

sergent /sɛʀʒɑ̃/ *nm* sergeant.

série /seʀi/ *nf* series (+ *sg*); (*d'objets*) set; **de ~** (*véhicule etc.*) standard; **fabrication** *ou* **production en ~** mass production.

sérieusement /seʀjøzmɑ̃/ *adv* seriously.

sérieux, **-ieuse** /seʀjø, -z/ *a* serious; (*digne de confiance*) reliable; (*chances, raison*) good. ●*nm* seriousness; **garder son ~** keep a straight face; **prendre au ~** take seriously.

serin /səʀɛ̃/ *nm* canary.

seringue /səʀɛ̃g/ *nf* syringe.

serment /sɛʀmɑ̃/ *nm* oath; (*promesse*) vow.

sermon /sɛʀmɔ̃/ *nm* sermon.

sermonner /sɛʀmɔne/ [1] *vt* lecture.

séropositif, **-ive** /seʀɔpozitif, -v/ *a* HIV positive.

serpent /sɛʀpɑ̃/ *nm* snake; **~ à sonnettes** rattlesnake.

serpillière /sɛʀpijɛʀ/ *nf* floorcloth.

serre /sɛʀ/ *nf* (*de jardin*) greenhouse; (*griffe*) claw.

serré, **~e** /seʀe/ *a* (*habit, nœud, écrou*) tight; (*personnes*) packed, crowded; (*lutte, mailles*) close; (*écriture*) cramped; (*cœur*) heavy.

serrer /seʀe/ [1] *vt* (*saisir*) grip; (*presser*) squeeze; (*vis, corde, ceinture*) tighten; (*poing, dents*) clench; (*qn dans ses bras*) hug sb; **~ les rangs** close ranks; **~ qn** (*vêtement*) be tight on sb; **~ qn de près** follow sb closely; **~ la main à** shake hands with. ●*vi* **~ à droite** keep over to the right. □ **se ~** *vpr* (*se rapprocher*) squeeze (up).

serrure /seʀyʀ/ *nf* lock. **serrurier** *nm* locksmith.

servante /sɛʀvɑ̃t/ *nf* (maid) servant.

serveur, **-euse** /sɛʀvœʀ, -øz/ *nm, f* (homme) waiter; (femme) waitress. ●*nm* (Ordinat) server.

serviable /sɛʀvjabl/ *a* helpful.

service /sɛʀvis/ *nm* service; (fonction, temps de travail) duty; (pourboire) service (charge); (dans une société) department; **~ (non) compris** service (not) included; **être de ~** be on duty; **pendant le ~** (when) on duty; **rendre ~ à qn** be a help to sb; **~ à thé** tea set; **~ d'ordre** stewards (+ *pl*); **~ après-vente** after-sales service; **~ militaire** military service; **les ~s secrets** the secret service (+ *sg*).

serviette /sɛʀvjɛt/ *nf* (de toilette) towel; (cartable) briefcase; **~ (de table)** serviette, napkin; **~ hygiénique** sanitary towel.

servir /sɛʀviʀ/ [46] *vt/i* serve; (être utile) be of use, serve; **~ qn (à table)** wait on sb; **ça sert à** (outil, récipient) it is used for; **ça me sert à/de** I use it to/as; **ça ne sert à rien** (*action*) it's pointless; **~ de** serve as, be used as; **~ à qn de guide** act as a guide for sb. □ **se ~** *vpr* (à table) help oneself (**de** to); **se ~ de** use. **serviteur** *nm* servant.

ses /se/ ⇒SON¹.

session /sesjɔ̃/ *nf* session.

seuil /sœj/ *nm* doorstep; (entrée) doorway; (fig) threshold.

seul, **~e** /sœl/ *a* alone, on one's own; (unique) only; **un ~ exemple** only one example; **pas un ~ ami** not a single friend; **lui ~ le sait** only he knows; **dans le ~ but de** with the sole aim of; **parler tout ~**

talk to oneself; **faire qch tout ~** do sth on one's own. ● *nm, f* **le ~, la ~e** the only one. **seulement** *adv* only.

sève /sɛv/ *nf* sap.

sévère /sevɛʀ/ *a* severe. **sévérité** *nf* severity.

sévices /sevis/ *nmpl* physical abuse (+ *sg*).

sévir /seviʀ/ [2] *vi* (*fléau*) rage; **~ contre** punish.

sevrer /səvʀe/ [6] *vt* wean.

sexe /sɛks/ *nm* sex; (*organes*) genitals (+ *pl*). **sexiste** *a* sexist. **sexualité** *nf* sexuality. **sexuel, ~le** *a* sexual.

shampooing /ʃɑ̃pwɛ̃/ *nm* shampoo.

shérif /ʃeʀif/ *nm* sheriff.

short /ʃɔʀt/ *nm* shorts (+ *pl*).

si (**s'** before *il, ils*) /si, s/ *conj* if; (interrogation indirecte) if, whether; **~ on allait se promener?** what about a walk?; **s'il vous** *ou* **te plaît** please; **~ oui** if so; **~ seulement** if only; **~ bien que** (tellement) so; (oui) yes; **un ~ bon repas** such a good meal; **~ habile qu'il soit** however skilful he may be; **~ bien que** with the result that.

sida /sida/ *nm* (Méd) Aids.

sidérurgie /sideʀyʀʒi/ *nf* steel industry.

siècle /sjɛkl/ *nm* century; (époque) age.

siège /sjɛʒ/ *nm* seat; (Mil) siege; **~ éjectable** ejector seat; **~ social** head office, headquarters (+ *pl*). **siéger** [14] [40] *vi* (assemblée) sit.

sien, ~ne /sjɛ̃, -ɛn/ *pron* **le ~, la ~ne, les ~(ne)s** (homme) his; (femme) hers; (chose) its; **les ~s** (famille) one's family.

sieste /sjɛst/ *nf* nap, siesta.

sifflement /sifləmɑ̃/ *nm* whistling; **un ~ a** whistle.

siffler /sifle/ [1] *vi* whistle; (avec un sifflet) blow one's whistle;

(*serpent, gaz*) hiss. ● *vt* (*air*) whistle; (*chien*) whistle to *ou* for; (*acteur*) hiss.

sifflet /siflɛ/ *nm* whistle; **~s** (huées) boos.

sigle /sigl/ *nm* acronym.

signal (*pl* **-aux**) /siɲal, -o/ *nm* signal; **~ sonore** (de répondeur) tone.

signalement /siɲalmɑ̃/ *nm* description.

signaler /siɲale/ [1] *vt* indicate; (par une sonnerie, un écriteau) signal; (dénoncer, mentionner) report; (faire remarquer) point out.

signalisation /siɲalizasjɔ̃/ *nf* signalling, signposting; (signaux) signals (+ *pl*).

signataire /siɲatɛʀ/ *nmf* signatory.

signature /siɲatyʀ/ *nf* signature; (action) signing; **~ électronique** digital signature.

signe /siɲ/ *nm* sign; (de ponctuation) mark; **faire ~ à qn** wave at sb; (contacter) contact; **faire ~ à qn de** beckon sb to; **faire ~ que non** shake one's head; **faire ~ que oui** nod.

signer /siɲe/ [1] *vt* sign. □ **se ~** *vpr* (Relig) cross oneself.

signet /siɲɛ/ *nm* (pour livre, Internet) bookmark; **~s favoris** (Internet) hotlist.

significatif, -ive /siɲifikatif, -v/ *a* significant.

signification /siɲifikasjɔ̃/ *nf* meaning. **signifier** [45] *vt* mean, signify; (faire connaître) make known (**à** to).

silence /silɑ̃s/ *nm* silence; (Mus) rest; **garder le ~** keep silent.

silencieux, -ieuse /silɑ̃sjø, -z/ *a* silent. ● *nm* silencer.

silex /silɛks/ *nm inv* flint.

silhouette /silwɛt/ *nf* outline, silhouette.

sillon /sijɔ̃/ *nm* furrow; (de disque) groove.

S

sillonner /sijɔne/ [1] *vt*
crisscross.

similaire /similɛʀ/ *a* similar.
similitude *nf* similarity.

simple /sɛ̃pl/ *a* simple; (non double)
single. ●*nm* ~ **dames/messieurs**
ladies'/men's singles (+ *pl*).
simple d'esprit *nmf* simpleton.
simplement *adv* simply.
simplicité *nf* simplicity; (naïveté)
simpleness.

simplification /sɛ̃plifikasjɔ̃/ *nf*
simplification. **simplifier** [45] *vt*
simplify.

simpliste /sɛ̃plist/ *a* simplistic.

simulacre /simylakʀ/ *nm*
pretence, sham.

simulation /simylasjɔ̃/ *nf*
simulation. **simuler** [1] *vt*
simulate.

simultané, ~e /simyltane/ *a*
simultaneous.

sincère /sɛ̃sɛʀ/ *a* sincere.
sincérité *nf* sincerity.

singe /sɛ̃ʒ/ *nm* monkey; (grand)
ape. **singer** [40] *vt* mimic, ape.

singulier, -ière /sɛ̃gylje, -jɛʀ/ *a*
peculiar, remarkable; (Gram)
singular. ●*nm* (Gram) singular.

sinistre /sinistʀ/ *a* sinister. ●*nm*
disaster; (incendie) blaze;
(dommages) damage.

sinistré, ~e /sinistʀe/ *a*
stricken. ●*nm, f* disaster victim.

sinon /sinɔ̃/ *conj* (autrement)
otherwise; (sauf) except (**que**
that); **difficile** ~ **impossible**
difficult if not impossible.

sinueux, -euse /sinɥø, -z/ *a*
winding; (fig) tortuous.

sirène /siʀɛn/ *nf* (appareil) siren;
(femme) mermaid.

sirop /siʀo/ *nm* (de fruits, Méd)
syrup; (boisson) cordial.

sismique /sismik/ *a* seismic.

site /sit/ *nm* site; ~ **touristique**
place of interest; ~ **Internet** or
Web Web site.

sitôt /sito/ *adv* ~ **entré**
immediately after coming in; ~
que as soon as; **pas de** ~ not for a
while.

situation /sitɥasjɔ̃/ *nf* situation;
(emploi) job, position; ~ **de famille**
marital status.

situé, ~e /sitɥe/ *a* situated.

situer /sitɥe/ [1] *vt* situate,
locate. □ **se** ~ *vpr* (se trouver) be
situated.

six /sis/ (/si/ *before consonant*,
/siz/ *before vowel*) *a & nm* six.
sixième *a & nmf* sixth.

sketch (*pl* ~**es**) /skɛtʃ/ *nm*
(Théât) sketch.

ski /ski/ *nm* (matériel) ski; (Sport)
skiing; **faire du** ~ ski; ~ **de fond**
cross-country skiing; ~ **nautique**
water skiing. **skier** [45] *vi* ski.

slave /slav/ *a* Slav; (Ling)
Slavonic.

slip /slip/ *nm* (d'homme)
underpants (+ *pl*); (de femme)
knickers (+ *pl*); ~ **de bain**
(swimming) trunks (+ *pl*); (du
bikini) bikini bottom.

slogan /slɔgɑ̃/ *nm* slogan.

Slovaquie /slɔvaki/ *nf* Slovakia.

Slovénie /slɔveni/ *nf* Slovenia.

smoking /smɔkiŋ/ *nm* dinner
jacket.

SNCF *abrév f* (**Société nationale
des Chemins de fer français**)
French national railway company.

snob /snɔb/ *nmf* snob. ●*a*
snobbish. **snobisme** *nm*
snobbery.

sobre /sɔbʀ/ *a* sober.

social, ~e (*mpl* **-iaux**) /sɔsjal,
-jo/ *a* social.

socialisme /sɔsjalism/ *nm*
socialism. **socialiste** *nmf & a*
socialist.

société /sɔsjete/ *nf* society;
(entreprise) company; ~ **point com**
dot-com.

socle /sɔkl/ nm (de colonne, statue) plinth; (de lampe) base.

socquette /sɔkɛt/ nf ankle sock.

soda /sɔda/ nm fizzy drink.

sœur /sœʀ/ nf sister.

soi /swa/ pron oneself; **derrière ~** behind one; **en ~** in itself; **aller de ~** be obvious.

soi-disant /swadizɑ̃/ a inv so-called. ● adv supposedly.

soie /swa/ nf silk.

soif /swaf/ nf thirst; **avoir ~** be thirsty; **donner ~** make one thirsty.

soigné, ~e /swaɲe/ a (apparence) tidy, neat; (travail) carefully done.

soigner /swaɲe/ [1] vt (s'occuper de) look after, take care of; (tenue, style) take care over; (maladie) treat. □ **se ~** vpr look after oneself.

soigneusement /swaɲøzmɑ̃/ adv carefully. **soigneux, -euse** a careful (**de** about); (ordonné) tidy.

soi-même /swamɛm/ pron oneself.

soin /swɛ̃/ nm care; (ordre) tidiness; **~s** care; (Méd) treatment; **avec ~** carefully; **avoir ou prendre ~ de qn/de faire** take care of sb/to do; **premiers ~s** first aid (+ sg).

soir /swaʀ/ nm evening; **à ce ~** see you tonight.

soirée /swaʀe/ nf evening; (réception) party.

soit /swa/ conj (à savoir) that is to say; **~ ... ~** either … or. ● ⇒ÊTRE [4].

soixante /swasɑ̃t/ a & nm sixty. **soixante-dix** a & nm seventy.

soja /sɔʒa/ nm (graines) soya beans (+ pl); (plante) soya.

sol /sɔl/ nm ground; (de maison) floor; (terrain agricole) soil.

solaire /sɔlɛʀ/ a solar; (huile, filtre) sun.

soldat /sɔlda/ nm soldier.

solde¹ /sɔld/ nf (salaire) pay.

solde² /sɔld/ nm (Comm) balance; **les ~s** the sales; **~s** (écrit en vitrine) sale; **en ~** (acheter) at sale price.

solder /sɔlde/ [1] vt sell off at sale price; (compte) settle. □ **se ~ par** vpr (aboutir à) end in.

sole /sɔl/ nf (poisson) sole.

soleil /sɔlɛj/ nm sun; (fleur) sunflower; **il y a du ~** it's sunny.

solennel, ~le /sɔlanɛl/ a solemn.

solfège /sɔlfɛʒ/ nm musical theory.

solidaire /sɔlidɛʀ/ a (mécanismes) interdependent; (collègues) (mutually) supportive; **être ~ de qn** support sb. **solidarité** nf solidarity.

solide /sɔlid/ a solid; (personne) strong. ● nm solid.

solidifier /sɔlidifje/ [45] vt solidify. □ **se ~** vpr solidify.

solitaire /sɔlitɛʀ/ a solitary. ● nmf (personne) loner. **solitude** nf solitude.

solliciter /sɔlisite/ [1] vt seek; (faire appel à) call upon; **être très sollicité** be very much in demand. **sollicitude** /sɔlisityd/ nf concern.

solo /sɔlo/ nm & a inv (Mus) solo.

solution /sɔlysjɔ̃/ nf solution.

solvable /sɔlvabl/ a solvent.

solvant /sɔlvɑ̃/ nm solvent.

sombre /sɔ̃bʀ/ a dark; (triste) sombre.

sombrer /sɔ̃bʀe/ [1] vi sink (**dans** into).

sommaire /sɔmɛʀ/ a (exécution) summary; (description) rough. ● nm contents (+ pl); **au ~** on the programme.

sommation /sɔmasjɔ̃/ nf (Mil) warning; (Jur) notice.

somme /sɔm/ nf sum; **en ~, ~ toute** in short; **faire la ~ de** add (up), total (up). ● nm nap.

sommeil /sɔmɛj/ nm sleep; **avoir**

S

$\sim$ be *ou* feel sleepy; en $\sim$ (*projet*) put on ice. **sommeiller** [1] *vi* doze; (fig) lie dormant.

sommelier /sɔməlje/ *nm* wine steward.

sommer /sɔme/ [1] *vt* summon.

sommes /sɔm/ ⇒ÊTRE [4].

sommet /sɔmɛ/ *nm* top; (de montagne) summit; (de triangle) apex; (gloire) height.

sommier /sɔmje/ *nm* bed base.

somnambule /sɔmnãbyl/ *nm* sleepwalker.

somnifère /sɔmnifɛr/ *nm* sleeping pill.

somnolent, $\sim$e /sɔmnɔlã, -t/ *a* drowsy. **somnoler** [1] *vi* doze.

somptueux, -euse /sɔ̃ptɥø, -z/ *a* sumptuous.

son¹, sa (**son** *before vowel or mute h*) (*pl* **ses**) /sɔ̃, sa, sɔ̃, se/ *a* (homme) his; (femme) her; (chose) its; (indéfini) one's.

son² /sɔ̃/ *nm* (bruit) sound; (de blé) bran; **baisser le $\sim$** turn the volume down.

sondage /sɔ̃daʒ/ *nm* $\sim$ (**d'opinion**) (opinion) poll.

sonde /sɔ̃d/ *nf* (de forage) drill; (Méd) (d'évacuation) catheter; (d'examen) probe.

sonder /sɔ̃de/ [1] *vt* (*population*) poll; (*explorer*) sound; (*terrain*) drill; (*intentions*) sound out.

songe /sɔ̃ʒ/ *nm* dream.

songer /sɔ̃ʒe/ [40] *vt* $\sim$ **que** think that; $\sim$ **à** think about. **songeur, -euse** *a* pensive.

sonné, $\sim$e /sɔne/ *a* (étourdi) groggy; Ⅰ crazy.

sonner /sɔne/ [1] *vt/i* ring; (*clairon, glas*) sound; (*heure*) strike; (*domestique*) ring for; **midi sonné** well past noon; $\sim$ **de** (*clairon*) sound, blow.

sonnerie /sɔnri/ *nf* ringing; (de clairon) sounding; (sonnette) bell.

sonnet /sɔnɛ/ *nm* sonnet.

sonnette /sɔnɛt/ *nf* bell.

sonore /sɔnɔr/ *a* resonant; (*onde, effets*) sound; (*rire*) resounding.

sonorisation /sɔnɔrizasjɔ̃/ *nf* (matériel) public address system.

sonorité /sɔnɔrite/ *nf* resonance; (d'un instrument) tone.

sont /sɔ̃/ ⇒ÊTRE [4].

sophistiqué, $\sim$e /sɔfistike/ *a* sophisticated.

sorcellerie /sɔrsɛlri/ *nf* witchcraft. **sorcier** *nm* (guérisseur) witch doctor; (maléfique) sorcerer. **sorcière** *nf* witch.

sordide /sɔrdid/ *a* sordid; (lieu) squalid.

sort /sɔr/ *nm* (destin, hasard) fate; (condition) lot; (maléfice) spell; **tirer (qch) au $\sim$** draw lots (for sth).

sortant, $\sim$e /sɔrtã, -t/ *a* (*président etc.*) outgoing.

sorte /sɔrt/ *nf* sort, kind; **de $\sim$ que** so that; **en quelque $\sim$** in a way; **de la $\sim$** in this way; **faire en $\sim$ que** make sure that.

sortie /sɔrti/ *nf* exit; (promenade, dîner) outing; (déclaration Ⅰ) remark; (parution) publication; (de disque, film) release; (d'un ordinateur) output; $\sim$**s** (argent) outgoings.

sortilège /sɔrtilɛʒ/ *nm* (magic) spell.

sortir /sɔrtir/ [46] *vi* (aux être) go out, leave; (venir) come out; (aller au spectacle) go out; (*livre, film*) come out; (*plante*) come up; $\sim$ **de** (*pièce*) leave; (*milieu social*) come from; (*limites*) go beyond; $\sim$ **du commun** *ou* **de l'ordinaire** be out of the ordinary. ● *vt* (aux avoir) take out; (*livre, modèle*) bring out; (dire Ⅰ) come out with; $\sim$ **qn de** get sb out of; **être sorti d'affaire** be in the clear. □ **s'en $\sim$** *vpr* cope, manage.

sosie /sɔzi/ *nm* double.

sot, $\sim$te /so, sɔt/ *a* silly.

sottise /sɔtiz/ *nf* silliness; (action,

remarque) foolish thing; **faire des ~s** be naughty.

sou /su/ *nm* Ⅱ **~s** money; **sans le ~** without a penny; **près de ses ~s** tight-fisted.

soubresaut /subrəso/ *nm* (sudden) start.

souche /suʃ/ *nf* (d'arbre) stump; (de famille) stock; (de carnet) counterfoil.

souci /susi/ *nm* (inquiétude) worry; (préoccupation) concern; (plante) marigold; **se faire du ~** worry.

soucier (se) /(sə)susje/ [45] *vpr* **se ~ de** care about. **soucieux, -ieuse** *a* concerned (**de** about).

soucoupe /sukup/ *nf* saucer; **~ volante** flying saucer.

soudain, ~e /sudɛ̃, -ɛn/ *a* sudden. ●*adv* suddenly.

soude /sud/ *nf* soda.

souder /sude/ [1] *vt* weld, solder; **famille très soudée** close-knit family. □ **se ~** *vpr* (os) knit (together).

soudoyer /sudwaje/ [31] *vt* bribe.

souffle /sufl/ *nm* (haleine) breath; (respiration) breathing; (explosion) blast; (vent) breath of air; **le ~ coupé** out of breath; **à couper le ~** breathtaking.

souffler /sufle/ [1] *vi* blow; (haleter) puff. ●*vt* (bougie) blow out; (poussière, fumée) blow; (verre) blow; (par explosion) destroy; (chuchoter) whisper; **~ la réplique à** prompt. **souffleur, -euse** *nm, f* (Théât) prompter.

souffrance /sufrɑ̃s/ *nf* suffering; **en ~** (affaire) pending. **souffrant, ~e** *a* unwell.

souffrir /sufrir/ [21] *vi* suffer (**de** from). ●*vt* (endurer) suffer; **il ne peut pas le ~** he cannot stand *ou* bear him.

soufre /sufr/ *nm* sulphur.

souhait /swɛ/ *nm* wish; **à tes ~s!**

bless you!; **paisible à ~** incredibly peaceful. **souhaitable** *a* desirable.

souhaiter /swete/ [1] *vt* **~ qch à qn** wish sb sth; **~ que/faire** hope that/to do; **~ la bienvenue à qn** welcome sb.

soûl, ~e /su, sul/ *a* drunk. ●*nm* **tout son ~** as much as one can.

soulagement /sulaʒmɑ̃/ *nm* relief. **soulager** [40] *vt* relieve.

soûler /sule/ [1] *vt* make drunk. □ **se ~** *vpr* get drunk.

soulèvement /sulɛvmɑ̃/ *nm* uprising.

soulever /sulve/ [6] *vt* lift, raise; (question, poussière) raise; (enthousiasme) arouse; (foule) stir up. □ **se ~** *vpr* lift *ou* raise oneself up; (se révolter) rise up.

soulier /sulje/ *nm* shoe.

souligner /suliɲe/ [1] *vt* underline; (yeux) outline; (taille) emphasize.

soumettre /sumɛtr/ [42] *vt* (assujettir) subject (**à** to); (présenter) submit (**à** to). □ **se ~** *vpr* submit (**à** to). **soumis, ~e** *a* submissive. **soumission** *nf* submission.

soupape /supap/ *nf* valve.

soupçon /supsɔ̃/ *nm* suspicion; **un ~ de** (un peu de) a touch of. **soupçonner** [1] *vt* suspect. **soupçonneux, -euse** *a* suspicious.

soupe /sup/ *nf* soup.

souper /supe/ [6] *vi* have supper. ●*nm* supper.

soupeser /supəze/ [1] *vt* judge the weight of; (fig) weigh up.

soupière /supjɛr/ *nf* (soup) tureen.

soupir /supir/ *nm* sigh; **pousser un ~** heave a sigh.

soupirer /supire/ [1] *vi* sigh.

souple /supl/ *a* supple; (règlement, caractère) flexible.

S

souplesse *nf* suppleness; (de règlement) flexibility.

source /suRs/ *nf* (de rivière, origine) source; (eau) spring; **prendre sa ~ à** rise in; **de ~ sûre** from a reliable source; **~ thermale** hot spring.

sourcil /suRsi/ *nm* eyebrow.

sourciller /suRsije/ [1] *vi* **sans ~** without batting an eyelid.

sourd, **~e** /suR, -d/ *a* deaf; (bruit, douleur) dull; **faire la ~e oreille** turn a deaf ear. ●*nm, f* deaf person.

sourd-muet (*pl* **sourds-muets**), **sourde-muette** (*pl* **sourdes-muettes**) /suRmɥɛ, suRdmɥɛt/ *a* deaf and dumb. ●*nm, f* deaf-mute.

souricière /suRisjɛR/ *nf* mousetrap; (fig) trap.

sourire /suRiR/ [54] *vi* smile (à at); **~ à** (fortune) smile on. ●*nm* smile; **garder le ~** keep smiling.

souris /suRi/ *nf* mouse; **des ~** mice.

sournois, **~e** /suRnwa, -z/ *a* sly, underhand.

sous /su/ *prép* under, beneath; **~ la main** handy; **~ la pluie** in the rain; **~ peu** shortly; **~ terre** underground.

sous-alimenté, **~e** /suzalimɑ̃te/ *a* undernourished.

souscription /suskRipsjɔ̃/ *nf* subscription. **souscrire** [30] *vi* **~ à** subscribe to.

sous-entendre /suzɑ̃tɑ̃dR/ [3] *vt* imply. **sous-entendu** *nm* innuendo, insinuation.

sous-estimer /suzɛstime/ [1] *vt* underestimate.

sous-jacent, **~e** /suzasɑ̃, -t/ *a* underlying.

sous-marin, **~e** /sumaRɛ̃, -in/ *a* underwater; (plongée) deep-sea. ●*nm* submarine.

soussigné, **~e** /susiɲe/ *a & nm,f* undersigned.

sous-sol /susɔl/ *nm* (cave) basement.

sous-titre /sutitR/ *nm* subtitle.

soustraction /sustRaksjɔ̃/ *nf* (déduction) subtraction.

soustraire /sustRɛR/ [29] *vt* (déduire) subtract; (retirer) take away (à from). □ **se ~ à** *vpr* escape from.

sous-traitant /sutRɛtɑ̃/ *nm* subcontractor.

sous-verre /suvɛR/ *nm inv* glass mount.

sous-vêtement /suvɛtmɑ̃/ *nm* underwear.

soute /sut/ *nf* (de bateau) hold; **~ à charbon** coal-bunker.

soutenir /sutniR/ [59] *vt* support; (effort, rythme) sustain; (résister à) withstand; **~ que** maintain that.

soutenu, **~e** /sutny/ *a* (constant) sustained; (style) formal.

souterrain, **~e** /sutɛRɛ̃, -ɛn/ *a* underground. ●*nm* underground passage.

soutien /sutjɛ̃/ *nm* support.

soutien-gorge (*pl* **soutiens-gorge**) /sutjɛ̃gɔRʒ/ *nm* bra.

soutirer /sutiRe/ [1] *vt* **~ à qn** extract from sb.

souvenir¹ /suvniR/ *nm* memory, recollection; (objet) memento; (cadeau) souvenir; **en ~ de** in memory of.

souvenir² (**se**) /(sə)suvniR/ [59] *vpr* **se ~ de** remember; **se ~ que** remember that.

souvent /suvɑ̃/ *adv* often.

souverain, **~e** /suvRɛ̃, -ɛn/ *a* sovereign. ●*nm, f* sovereign.

soviétique /sɔvjetik/ *a* Soviet.

soyeux, **-euse** /swajø, -z/ *a* silky.

spacieux, **-ieuse** /spasjø, -z/ *a* spacious.

sparadrap /spaRadRa/ *nm* (sticking) plaster.

spatial, ~e (*mpl* -**iaux**) /spasjal, -jo/ *a* space.

speaker, ~**ine** /spikœr, -krin/ *nm, f* announcer.

spécial, ~e (*mpl* -**iaux**) /spesjal, -jo/ *a* special; (*bizarre*) odd. **spécialement** *adv* (*exprès*) specially; (*très*) especially.

spécialiser (se) /səspesjalize/ [1] *vpr* specialize (**dans** in). **spécialiste** *nmf* specialist. **spécialité** *nf* speciality; (US) specialty.

spécifier /spesifje/ [45] *vt* specify.

spécifique /spesifik/ *a* specific.

spécimen /spesimɛn/ *nm* specimen.

spectacle /spɛktakl/ *nm* show; (*vue*) sight, spectacle.

spectaculaire /spɛktakylɛr/ *a* spectacular.

spectateur, -**trice** /spɛktatœr, -tris/ *nm, f* (*Sport*) spectator; (*témoin oculaire*) onlooker; **les** ~**s** (Théât) the audience (+ *sg*).

spectre /spɛktr/ *nm* (*revenant*) spectre; (*images*) spectrum.

spéculateur, -**trice** /spekylatœr, -tris/ *nm, f* speculator. **spéculation** *nf* speculation. **spéculer** [1] *vi* speculate.

spéléologie /speleɔlɔʒi/ *nf* cave exploration, pot-holing.

spermatozoïde /spɛrmatɔzɔid/ *nm* spermatozoon. **sperme** *nm* sperm.

sphère /sfɛr/ *nf* sphere.

spirale /spiral/ *nf* spiral.

spirituel, ~**le** /spiritɥɛl/ *a* spiritual; (*amusant*) witty.

spiritueux /spiritɥø/ *nm* (*alcool*) spirit.

splendeur /splɑ̃dœr/ *nf* splendour. **splendide** *a* splendid.

sponsoriser /spɔ̃sɔrize/ [1] *vt* sponsor.

spontané, ~e /spɔ̃tane/ *a*

spontaneous. **spontanéité** *nf* spontaneity.

sport /spɔr/ *a inv* (*vêtements*) casual. ●*nm* sport; **veste/voiture de** ~ sports jacket/car.

sportif, -**ive** /spɔrtif, -v/ *a* (*personne*) sporty; (*physique*) athletic; (*résultats*) sports. ●*nm, f* sportsman, sportswoman.

spot /spɔt/ *nm* spotlight; ~ (**publicitaire**) ad.

square /skwar/ *nm* small public garden.

squatter /skwate/ [1] *vt* squat in.

squelette /skəlɛt/ *nm* skeleton. **squelettique** *a* skeletal.

SSII *abrév f* (**société de services et d'ingénierie informatiques**) computer services company.

stabiliser /stabilize/ [1] *vt* stabilize. **stable** *a* stable.

stade /stad/ *nm* (*Sport*) stadium; (*phase*) stage.

stage /staʒ/ *nm* (*cours*) course; (*professionnel*) placement. **stagiaire** *nmf* course member; (*apprenti*) trainee.

stagner /stagne/ [1] *vi* stagnate.

stand /stɑ̃d/ *nm* stand; (*de fête foraine*) stall.

standard /stɑ̃dar/ *nm* switchboard. ●*a inv* standard. **standardiser** [1] *vt* standardize. **standardiste** *nmf* switchboard operator.

standing /stɑ̃diŋ/ *nm* status, standing; **de** ~ (*hôtel*) luxury.

starter /startɛr/ *nm* (Auto) choke.

station /stasjɔ̃/ *nf* station; (*halte*) stop; ~ **debout** standing position; ~ **de taxis** taxi rank; ~ **balnéaire/ de ski** seaside/ski resort; ~ **thermale** spa.

stationnaire /stasjɔnɛr/ *a* stationary.

stationnement /stasjɔnmɑ̃/ *nm* parking. **stationner** [1] *vi* park.

station-service (*pl* **stations-**

S

service) /stasjɔ̃sɛʀvis/ nf service station.

statique /statik/ a static.

statistique /statistik/ nf statistic; (science) statistics (+ sg). ●a statistical.

statue /staty/ nf statue.

statuer /statɥe/ [1] vi ~ **sur** give a ruling on.

statut /staty/ nm status. **statutaire** a statutory.

sténo /steno/ nf (sténographie) shorthand. **sténodactylo** nf shorthand typist. **sténographie** nf shorthand.

stéréo /steʀeo/ nf & a inv stereo.

stéréotype /steʀeɔtip/ nm stereotype.

stérile /steʀil/ a sterile.

stérilet /steʀile/ nm coil, IUD.

stérilisation /steʀilizasjɔ̃/ nf sterilization. **stériliser** [1] vt sterilize.

stéroïde /steʀɔid/ a & nm steroid.

stimulant /stimylɑ̃/ nm stimulus; (médicament) stimulant.

stimulateur /stimylatœʀ/ nm ~ **cardiaque** (Méd) pacemaker.

stimuler /stimyle/ [1] vt stimulate.

stipuler /stipyle/ [1] vt stipulate.

stock /stɔk/ nm stock. **stocker** [1] vt stock.

stoïque /stɔik/ a stoical. ●nmf stoic.

stop /stɔp/ interj stop. ●nm stop sign; (feu arrière) brake light; **faire du ~** ⊞ hitch-hike. **stopper** [1] vt/i stop.

store /stɔʀ/ nm blind; (de magasin) awning.

strapontin /stʀapɔ̃tɛ̃/ nm folding seat, jump seat.

stratégie /stʀateʒi/ nf strategy. **stratégique** a strategic.

stress /stʀɛs/ nm stress. **stressant, ~e** a stressful.

stressé, ~e a stressed. **stresser** [1] vt put under stress.

strict /stʀikt/ a strict; (tenue, vérité) plain; **le ~ minimum** the bare minimum. **strictement** adv strictly.

strident, ~e /stʀidɑ̃, -t/ a shrill.

strophe /stʀɔf/ nf stanza, verse.

structure /stʀyktyʀ/ nf structure.

studieux, -ieuse /stydjø, -z/ a studious.

studio /stydjo/ nm (d'artiste, de télévision) studio; (logement) studio flat.

stupéfaction /stypefaksjɔ̃/ nf amazement. **stupéfait, ~e** a amazed.

stupéfiant, ~e /stypefjɑ̃, -t/ a astounding. ●nm drug, narcotic.

stupéfier /stypefje/ [45] vt amaze.

stupeur /stypœʀ/ nf amazement; (Méd) stupor.

stupide /stypid/ a stupid. **stupidité** nf stupidity.

style /stil/ nm style.

styliste /stilist/ nmf fashion designer.

stylo /stilo/ nm pen; ~ **(à) bille** ball-point pen; ~ **(à) encre** fountain pen.

su /sy/ ⇒SAVOIR [55].

suave /sɥav/ a sweet.

subalterne /sybaltɛʀn/ a & nmf subordinate.

subconscient /sypkɔ̃sjɑ̃/ nm subconscious.

subir /sybiʀ/ [2] vt be subjected to; (traitement, expériences) undergo.

subit, ~e /sybi, -t/ a sudden.

subjectif, -ive /sybʒɛktif, -v/ a subjective.

subjonctif /sybʒɔ̃ktif/ nm subjunctive.

subjuguer /sybʒyge/ [1] vt (charmer) captivate.

sublime /syblim/ a sublime.

submerger /sybmɛRʒe/ [40] *vt* submerge; (fig) overwhelm.

subordonné, **~e** /sybɔRdɔne/ *a* & *nm, f* subordinate.

subside /sybzid/ *nm* grant.

subsidiaire /sybzidjɛR/ *a* subsidiary; **question ~** tiebreaker.

subsistance /sybzistɑ̃s/ *nf* subsistence. **subsister** [1] *vi* subsist; (durer, persister) exist.

substance /sypstɑ̃s/ *nf* substance.

substantiel, **~le** /sypstɑ̃sjɛl/ *a* substantial.

substantif /sypstɑ̃tif/ *nm* noun.

substituer /sypstitɥe/ [1] *vt* substitute (à for). □ **se ~ à** *vpr* (remplacer) substitute for. **substitut** *nm* substitute; (Jur) deputy public prosecutor.

subtil, **~e** /syptil/ *a* subtle.

subtiliser /syptilize/ [1] *vt* **~ qch (à qn)** steal sth.

subvenir /sybvəniR/ [59] *vi* **~ à** provide for.

subvention /sybvɑ̃sjɔ̃/ *nf* subsidy. **subventionner** [1] *vt* subsidize.

subversif, **-ive** /sybvɛRsif, -v/ *a* subversive.

suc /syk/ *nm* juice.

succédané /syksedane/ *nm* substitute (de for).

succéder /syksede/ [14] *vi* **~ à** succeed. □ **se ~** *vpr* succeed one another.

succès /syksɛ/ *nm* success; **à ~** (film, livre,) successful; **avoir du ~** be a success.

successeur /syksesœR/ *nm* successor. **successif**, **-ive** *a* successive. **succession** *nf* succession; (Jur) inheritance.

succinct, **~e** /syksɛ̃, -t/ *a* succinct.

succomber /sykɔ̃be/ [1] *vi* die; **~ à** succumb to.

succulent, **~e** /sykylɑ̃, -t/ *a* delicious.

succursale /sykyRsal/ *nf* (Comm) branch.

sucer /syse/ [10] *vt* suck.

sucette /sysɛt/ *nf* (bonbon) lollipop; (tétine) dummy; (US) pacifier.

sucre /sykR/ *nm* sugar; **~ d'orge** barley sugar; **~ en poudre** caster sugar; **~ glace** icing sugar; **~ roux** brown sugar.

sucré /sykRe/ *a* sweet; (additionné de sucre) sweetened. **sucrer** [1] *vt* sugar, sweeten. **sucreries** *nfpl* sweets.

sucrier, **-ière** /sykRije, -jɛR/ *a* sugar. ● *nm* (récipient) sugar-bowl.

sud /syd/ *nm* south. ● *a inv* south; (partie) southern.

sud-est /sydɛst/ *nm* south-east.

sud-ouest /sydwɛst/ *nm* south-west.

Suède /sɥɛd/ *nf* Sweden.

suédois, **~e** /sɥedwa, -z/ *a* Swedish. ● *nm* (Ling) Swedish. **S~**, **~e** *nm, f* Swede.

suer /sɥe/ [1] *vt/i* sweat; **faire ~ qn** 🄯 get on sb's nerves.

sueur /sɥœR/ *nf* sweat; **en ~** covered in sweat.

suffire /syfiR/ [57] *vi* be enough (à qn for sb); **il suffit de compter** all you have to do is count; **une goutte suffit** a drop is enough; **~ à** (besoin) satisfy. □ **se ~ à soi-même** be self-sufficient.

suffisamment /syfizamɑ̃/ *adv* sufficiently; **~ de qch** enough of sth. **suffisance** *nf* (vanité) conceit. **suffisant**, **~e** *a* sufficient; (vaniteux) conceited.

suffixe /syfiks/ *nm* suffix.

suffoquer /syfɔke/ [1] *vt/i* choke, suffocate.

suffrage /syfRaʒ/ *nm* (voix: Pol) vote; (système) suffrage.

suggérer /sygʒeRe/ [14] *vt*

S

suggest. **suggestion** *nf* suggestion.

suicidaire /sɥisidɛʀ/ *a* suicidal. **suicide** *nm* suicide. **suicider (se)** [1] *vpr* commit suicide.

suinter /sɥɛ̃te/ [1] *vi* ooze.

suis /sɥi/ ⇒ÊTRE [4], SUIVRE [57].

Suisse /sɥis/ *nf* Switzerland. ● *nmf* Swiss. **suisse** *a* Swiss.

suite /sɥit/ *nf* continuation, rest; (d'un film) sequel; (série) series; (appartement, escorte) suite; (résultat) consequence; **à la ~, de ~** (successivement) in a row; **à la ~ de** (derrière) behind; **à la ~ de, par ~ de** (en conséquence) as a result of; **faire ~ (à)** follow; **par la ~** afterwards; **~ à votre lettre du** further to your letter of the; **des ~s de** as a result of.

suivant¹, **~e** /sɥivɑ̃, -t/ *a* following, next. ● *nm, f* following *ou* next person.

suivant² /sɥivɑ̃/ *prép* (selon) according to.

suivi, **~e** /sɥivi/ *a* (effort) steady, sustained; (cohérent) consistent; **peu/très ~** (cours) poorly/well attended.

suivre /sɥivʀ/ [57] *vt/i* follow; (comprendre) follow; **faire ~** (courrier) forward. □ **se ~** *vpr* follow each other.

sujet, **~te** /syʒɛ, -t/ *a* **~ à** liable *ou* subject to. ● *nm* (d'un royaume) subject; (question) subject; (motif) cause; (Gram) subject; **au ~ de** about.

super /sypɛʀ/ *nm* (essence) four-star. ● *a inv* 🄸 (très) great. ● *adv* 🄸 ultra, really.

superbe /sypɛʀb/ *a* superb.

supérette /sypeʀɛt/ *nf* minimarket.

superficie /sypɛʀfisi/ *nf* area.

superficiel, **~le** /sypɛʀfisjɛl/ *a* superficial.

superflu, **~e** /sypɛʀfly/ *a*

superfluous. ● *nm* (excédent) surplus.

supérieur, **~e** /sypeʀjœʀ/ *a* (plus haut) upper; (quantité, nombre) greater (à than); (études, principe) higher (à than); (meilleur, hautain) superior (à to). ● *nm, f* superior. **supériorité** *nf* superiority.

superlatif, **-ive** /sypɛʀlatif, -v/ *a & nm* superlative.

supermarché /sypɛʀmaʀʃe/ *nm* supermarket.

superposer /sypɛʀpoze/ [1] *vt* superimpose; **lits superposés** bunk beds.

superproduction /sypɛʀpʀɔdyksjɔ̃/ *nf* (film) blockbuster.

superpuissance /sypɛʀpɥisɑ̃s/ *nf* superpower.

superstitieux, **-ieuse** /sypɛʀstisjø, -z/ *a* superstitious.

superviser /sypɛʀvize/ [1] *vt* supervise.

suppléant, **~e** /sypleɑ̃, -t/ *nmf & a* (professeur) **~** supply teacher; (juge) **~** deputy (judge).

suppléer /syplee/ [15] *vt* (remplacer) fill in for. ● *vi* **~ à** (compenser) make up for.

supplément /syplemɑ̃/ *nm* (argent) extra charge; (de frites, légumes) extra portion; **en ~** extra; **un ~ de** (travail) additional; **payer un ~** pay a supplement. **supplémentaire** *a* extra, additional.

supplice /syplis/ *nm* torture.

supplier /syplije/ [45] *vt* beg, beseech (**de** to).

support /sypɔʀ/ *nm* support; (Ordinat) medium.

supportable /sypɔʀtabl/ *a* bearable.

supporter¹ /sypɔʀte/ [1] *vt* (privations) bear; (personne) put up with; (structure: Ordinat) support; **il ne supporte pas les enfants/de perdre** he can't stand children/losing.

supporter² /sypɔʀtɛʀ/ *nm* (Sport) supporter.

supposer /sypoze/ [1] *vt* suppose; (*impliquer*) imply; **à ~ que** supposing that.

suppression /sypʀɛsjɔ̃/ *nf* (de taxe) abolition; (de sanction) lifting; (de mot) deletion. **supprimer** [1] *vt* (*allocation*) withdraw; (*contrôle*) lift; (*train*) cancel; (*preuve*) suppress.

suprématie /sypʀemasi/ *nf* supremacy.

suprême /sypʀɛm/ *a* supreme.

sur /syʀ/ *prép* on, upon; (*par-dessus*) over; (au sujet de) about, on; (proportion) out of; (mesure) by; **~ la photo** in the photograph; **mettre/ jeter ~** put/throw on to; **~ mesure** made to measure; **~ place** on the spot; **~ ce, je pars** with that, I must go; **~ le moment** at the time.

sûr /syʀ/ *a* certain, sure; (sans danger) safe; (digne de confiance) reliable; (*main*) steady; (*jugement*) sound; **être ~ de soi** be self-confident; **j'en étais ~!** I knew it!

surabondance /syʀabɔ̃dɑ̃s/ *nf* overabundance.

surcharge /syʀʃaʀʒ/ *nf* overloading; (poids) excess load. **surcharger** [1] *vt* overload; (*texte*) alter.

surchauffer /syʀʃofe/ [1] *vt* overheat.

surcroît /syʀkʀwa/ *nm* increase (de in); **de ~** in addition.

surdité /syʀdite/ *nf* deafness.

surélever /syʀelve/ [6] *vt* raise.

sûrement /syʀmɑ̃/ *adv* certainly; (sans danger) safely; **il a ~ oublié** he must have forgotten.

surenchère /syʀɑ̃ʃɛʀ/ *nf* higher

bid. **surenchérir** [2] *vi* bid higher (**sur** than).

surestimer /syʀɛstime/ [1] *vt* overestimate.

sûreté /syʀte/ *nf* safety; (de pays) security; (d'un geste) steadiness; **être en ~** be safe; **S~ (nationale)** police (+ *pl*)

surexcité, ~e /syʀɛksite/ *a* very excited.

surf /sœʀf/ *nm* surfing.

surface /syʀfas/ *nf* surface; **faire ~** (*sous-marin*, fig) surface; **en ~** on the surface.

surfait, ~e /syʀfɛ, -t/ *a* overrated.

surfer /sœʀfe/ [1] *vi* go surfing; **~ sur l'Internet** surf the Internet.

surgelé, ~e /syʀʒəle/ *a* (deep-) frozen; **aliments ~s** frozen food (+ *sg*).

surgir /syʀʒiʀ/ [2] *vi* appear (suddenly); (*difficulté*) crop up.

sur-le-champ /syʀləʃɑ̃/ *adv* right away.

surlendemain /syʀlɑ̃dmɛ̃/ *nm* **le ~** two days later; **le ~ de** two days after.

surligneur /syʀliɲœʀ/ *nm* highlighter (pen).

surmenage /syʀmənaʒ/ *nm* overwork.

surmonter /syʀmɔ̃te/ [1] *vt* (*vaincre*) overcome, surmount; (être au-dessus de) surmount, top.

surnaturel, ~le /syʀnatyʀɛl/ *a* supernatural.

surnom /syʀnɔ̃/ *nm* nickname. **surnommer** [1] *vt* nickname.

surpeuplé, ~e /syʀpœple/ *a* overpopulated.

surplomber /syʀplɔ̃be/ [1] *vt/i* overhang.

surplus /syʀply/ *nm* surplus.

suprenant, ~e /syʀpʀənɑ̃, -t/ *a* surprising. **surprendre** [50] *vt* (étonner) surprise; (prendre au dépourvu) catch, surprise; (entendre)

overhear. **surpris**, ∼e *a* surprised (**de** at).
surprise /syRpRiz/ *nf* surprise.
surréaliste /syRRealist/ *a & nmf* surrealist.
sursaut /syRso/ *nm* start, jump; **en** ∼ with a start; ∼ **de** (*regain*) burst of. **sursauter** [1] *vi* start, jump.
sursis /syRsi/ *nm* reprieve; (Mil) deferment; **deux ans** (**de prison**) **avec** ∼ a two-year suspended sentence.
surtaxe /syRtaks/ *nf* surcharge.
surtout /syRtu/ *adv* especially; (*avant tout*) above all; ∼ **pas** certainly not.
surveillance /syRvɛjɑ̃s/ *nf* watch; (*d'examen*) supervision; (*de la police*) surveillance. **surveillant**, ∼e *nm, f* (*de prison*) warder; (*au lycée*) supervisor (in charge of discipline). **surveiller** [1] *vt* watch; (*travaux, élèves*) supervise.
survenir /syRvəniR/ [58] *vi* occur, take place; (*personne*) turn up.
survêtement /syRvɛtmɑ̃/ *nm* (Sport) tracksuit.
survie /syRvi/ *nf* survival.
survivant, ∼e /syRvivɑ̃, -t/ *a* surviving. ●*nm, f* survivor.
survivre /syRvivR/ [63] *vi* survive; ∼ **à** (*conflit*) survive; (*personne*) outlive.
survoler /syRvɔle/ [1] *vt* fly over; (*livre*) skim through.
sus: **en** ∼ /ɑ̃sys/ *loc* in addition.
susceptible /sysɛptibl/ *a* touchy; ∼ **de faire** likely to do.
susciter /sysite/ [1] *vt* (*éveiller*) arouse; (*occasionner*) create.
suspect, ∼e /syspɛ, -ɛkt/ *a* (*individu, faits*) suspicious; (*témoignage*) suspect; ∼ **de** suspected of. ●*nm, f* suspect.
suspecter [1] *vt* suspect.
suspendre /syspɑ̃dR/ [3] *vt* (*accrocher*) hang (up); (*interrompre, destituer*) suspend; **suspendu à** hanging from. □ **se** ∼ **à** *vpr* hang from.
suspens: **en** ∼ /ɑ̃syspɑ̃/ *loc* (*affaire*) outstanding; (*dans* l'indécision) in suspense.
suspense /syspɛns/ *nm* suspense.
suture /sytyR/ *nf* **point de** ∼ stitch.
svelte /svɛlt/ *a* slender.
S.V.P. *abrév* (**s'il vous plaît**) please.
syllabe /silab/ *nf* syllable.
symbole /sɛ̃bɔl/ *nm* symbol.
symboliser [1] *vt* symbolize.
symétrie /simetRi/ *nf* symmetry.
sympa /sɛ̃pa/ *a inv* 🄸 nice; **sois** ∼ be a pal.
sympathie /sɛ̃pati/ *nf* (*goût*) liking; (*compassion*) sympathy; **avoir de la** ∼ **pour** like. **sympathique** *a* nice, pleasant. **sympathisant**, ∼e *nm, f* sympathizer.
sympathiser [1] *vi* get on well (**avec** with).
symphonie /sɛ̃fɔni/ *nf* symphony.
symptôme /sɛ̃ptom/ *nm* symptom.
synagogue /sinagɔg/ *nf* synagogue.
synchroniser /sɛ̃kRɔnize/ [1] *vt* synchronize.
syncope /sɛ̃kɔp/ *nf* (Méd) blackout.
syndic /sɛ̃dik/ *nm* ∼ (**d'immeuble**) property manager.
syndicaliste /sɛ̃dikalist/ *nmf* (trade-)unionist. ●*a* (trade-) union.
syndicat /sɛ̃dika/ *nm* (trade) union; ∼ **d'initiative** tourist office.
syndiqué, ∼e /sɛ̃dike/ *a* **être** ∼ be a (trade-)union member.
synonyme /sinɔnim/ *a* synonymous. ●*nm* synonym.

syntaxe /sɛ̃taks/ *nf* syntax.

synthèse /sɛ̃tɛz/ *nf* synthesis.
synthétique *a* synthetic.

synthé(tiseur) /sɛ̃te(tizœʀ)/ *nm* synthesizer.

systématique /sistematik/ *a* systematic.

système /sistɛm/ *nm* system; **le ∼ D** Ⓣ resourcefulness.

t' /t/ ⇒TE.

ta /ta/ ⇒TON¹.

tabac /taba/ *nm* tobacco; (*magasin*) tobacconist's shop.

table /tabl/ *nf* table; **à ∼!** dinner is ready!; **∼ de nuit** bedside table; **∼ des matières** table of contents; **∼ à repasser** ironing board; **∼ roulante** (tea-)trolley; (US) (serving) cart.

tableau (*pl* ∼**x**) /tablo/ *nm* picture; (*peinture*) painting; (*panneau*) board; (*graphique*) chart; (*Scol*) blackboard; **∼ d'affichage** notice-board; **∼ de bord** dashboard.

tablette /tablɛt/ *nf* shelf; **∼ de chocolat** bar of chocolate.

tableur /tablœʀ/ *nm* spreadsheet.

tablier /tablije/ *nm* apron; (*de pont*) platform; (*de magasin*) shutter.

tabou /tabu/ *nm* & *a* taboo.

tabouret /tabuʀɛ/ *nm* stool.

tache /taʃ/ *nf* mark, spot; (*salissure*) stain; **faire ∼ d'huile** spread; **∼ de rousseur** freckle.

tâche /taʃ/ *nf* task, job.

tacher /taʃe/ [1] *vt* stain. ◻ **se ∼** *vpr* (*personne*) get oneself dirty.

tâcher /taʃe/ [1] *vi* **∼ de faire** try to do.

tacheté, ∼e /taʃte/ *a* spotted.

tact /takt/ *nm* tact.

tactique /taktik/ *a* tactical. ● *nf* (Mil) tactics; **une ∼** a tactic.

taie /tɛ/ *nf* **∼ (d'oreiller)** pillowcase.

taille /taj/ *nf* (*milieu du corps*) waist; (*hauteur*) height; (*grandeur*) size; **de ∼** sizeable; **être de ∼ à faire** be up to doing.

taille-crayons /tajkʀɛjɔ̃/ *nm inv* pencil-sharpener.

tailler /taje/ [1] *vt* cut; (*arbre*) prune; (*crayon*) sharpen; (*vêtement*) cut out. ◻ **se ∼** *vpr* ⊠ clear off.

tailleur /tajœʀ/ *nm* (*costume*) woman's suit; (*couturier*) tailor; **en ∼** cross-legged; **∼ de pierre** stone-cutter.

taire /tɛʀ/ [47] *vt* not to reveal; **faire ∼** silence. ◻ **se ∼** *vpr* be silent *ou* quiet; (*devenir silencieux*) fall silent.

talc /talk/ *nm* talcum powder.

talent /talɑ̃/ *nm* talent.
talentueux, -euse *a* talented, gifted.

talon /talɔ̃/ *nm* heel; (*de chèque*) stub.

tambour /tɑ̃buʀ/ *nm* drum; (*d'église*) vestibule.

Tamise /tamiz/ *nf* Thames.

tampon /tɑ̃pɔ̃/ *nm* (*de bureau*) stamp; (*ouate*) wad, pad; **∼ (hygiénique)** tampon.

tamponner /tɑ̃pɔne/ [1] *vt* (*document*) stamp; (*véhicule*) crash into; (*plaie*) swab.

tandem /tɑ̃dɛm/ *nm* (*vélo*) tandem; (*personnes*: fig) duo.

tandis que /tɑ̃di(ə)/ *conj* while.

tanière /tanjɛʀ/ *nf* den.

tant /tɑ̃/ *adv* (*travailler, manger*) so much; **∼ de** (*quantité*) so much; (*nombre*) so many; **∼ que** as long

T

as; **en ~ que** as; **~ mieux!** all the
better!; **~ pis!** too bad!

tante /tɑ̃t/ *nf* aunt.

tantôt /tɑ̃to/ *adv* sometimes.

tapage /tapaʒ/ *nm* din.

tape /tap/ *nf* slap. **tape-à-l'œil** *a
inv* flashy, tawdry.

taper /tape/ [1] *vt* hit; (prendre ▣)
scrounge; **~ (à la machine)** type.
● *vi* (cogner) bang; (soleil) beat
down; **~ dans** (puiser dans) dig
into; **~ sur** hit; **~ sur l'épaule de
qn** tap sb on the shoulder. ◻ **se ~**
vpr (corvée ▣) get stuck with ▣.

tapis /tapi/ *nm* carpet; (petit) rug;
~ de bain bathmat; **~ roulant** (pour
objets) conveyor belt; (pour piétons)
moving walkway.

tapisser /tapise/ [1] *vt* (wall)
paper; (fig) cover (**de** with).

tapisserie *nf* tapestry; (papier
peint) wallpaper.

taquin, ~e /takɛ̃, -in/ *a* fond of
teasing. ● *nm, f* tease(r).

tard /taʀ/ *adv* late; **au plus ~** at
the latest; **plus ~** later; **sur le ~**
late in life.

tarder /taʀde/ [1] *vi* (être lent à
venir) be a long time coming; **~ (à
faire)** take a long time (doing),
delay (doing); **sans (plus) ~**
without (further) delay; **il me
tarde de** I'm longing to.

tardif, -ive /taʀdif, -v/ *a* late.

tare /taʀ/ *nf* (défaut) defect.

tarif /taʀif/ *nm* rate; (de train, taxi)
fare; **plein ~** full price.

tarir /taʀiʀ/ [2] *vt/i* dry up. ◻ **se
~** *vpr* dry up.

tarte /taʀt/ *nf* tart. ● *a inv* (ridicule
▣) ridiculous.

tartine /taʀtin/ *nf* slice of bread;
~ de beurre slice of bread and
butter. **tartiner** [1] *vt* spread.

tartre /taʀtʀ/ *nm* (de bouilloire) fur,
scale; (sur les dents) tartar.

tas /tɑ/ *nm* pile, heap; **un ou des
~ de** ▣ lots of.

tasse /tɑs/ *nf* cup; **~ à thé**
teacup.

tasser /tɑse/ [1] *vt* pack,
squeeze; (terre) pack (down).
◻ **se ~** *vpr* (terrain) sink; (se
serrer) squeeze up.

tâter /tate/ [1] *vt* feel; (opinion: fig)
sound out. ● *vi* **~ de** try out.

tatillon, ~ne /tatijɔ̃, -jɔn/ *a*
finicky.

tâtonnements /tatɔnmɑ̃/ *nmpl*
(essais) trial and error (+ *sg*).

tâtons: **à ~** /atɑtɔ̃/ *loc* **avancer à
~** grope one's way along.

tatouage /tatwaʒ/ *nm* (dessin)
tattoo.

taupe /top/ *nf* mole.

taureau (*pl* ~**x**) /tɔʀo/ *nm* bull;
le T~ Taurus.

taux /to/ *nm* rate.

taxe /taks/ *nf* tax.

taxi /taksi/ *nm* taxi(-cab);
(personne ▣) taxi driver.

taxiphone® /taksifɔn/ *nm* pay
phone.

Tchécoslovaquie /tʃekɔslɔvaki/
nf Czechoslovakia.

tchèque /tʃɛk/ *a* Czech;
République ~ Czech Republic.
T~ *nmf* Czech.

te, t' /tə, t/ *pron* you; (indirect) (to)
you; (réfléchi) yourself.

technicien, ~ne /tɛknisjɛ̃, -ɛn/
nm, f technician.

technique /tɛknik/ *a* technical.
● *nf* technique.

techno /tɛkno/ *nf* (Mus) techno.

technologie /tɛknɔlɔʒi/ *nf*
technology.

teindre /tɛ̃dʀ/ [22] *vt* dye. ◻ **se ~**
vpr **se ~ les cheveux** dye one's
hair.

teint /tɛ̃/ *nm* complexion.

teinte /tɛ̃t/ *nf* shade. **teinter** [1]
vt (verre) tint; (bois) stain.

teinture /tɛ̃tyʀ/ *nf* (produit) dye.

teinturier, -ière /tɛ̃tyʀje, -jɛʀ/
nm, f dry-cleaner.

tel, ~**le** /tɛl/ *a* such; **un** ~ **livre** such a book; ~ **que** such as, like; (ainsi que) (just) as; ~ **ou** ~ such-and-such; ~ **quel** (just) as it is.

télé /tele/ *nf* 🔲 TV.

télécharger /teleʃaʀʒe/ [40] *vt* (Ordinat) download.

télécommande /telekɔmɑ̃d/ *nf* remote control.

télécommunications /telekɔmynikasjɔ̃/ *nfpl* telecommunications.

téléconférence /telekɔ̃feʀɑ̃s/ *nf* teleconferencing.

télécopie /telekɔpi/ *nf* fax. **télécopieur** *nm* fax machine.

téléfilm /telefilm/ *nm* TV film.

télégramme /telegʀam/ *nm* telegram.

télégraphier /telegʀafje/ [45] *vt/ i* ~ (à) cable.

téléguidé, ~**e** /telegide/ *a* radio-controlled.

télématique /telematik/ *nf* telematics (+ *sg*).

téléphérique /teleferik/ *nm* cable car.

téléphone /telefɔn/ *nm* (tele-)phone; ~ **à carte** cardphone.
téléphoner [1] *vt/i* ~ (à) (tele)phone.
téléphonie /telefɔni/ *nf* telephony; ~**mobile** mobile telephony.
téléphonique *a* (tele)phone.

télé-réalité /telerealite/ *nf* reality TV.

téléserveur /teleservœr/ *nm* (Internet) remote server.

télésiège /telesjɛʒ/ *nm* chairlift.

téléski /teleski/ *nm* ski tow.

téléspectateur, -**trice** /tele-spɛktatœr, -tris/ *nm, f* (television) viewer.

télévente /televɑ̃t/ *nf* telesales (+ *pl*).

télévisé, ~**e** /televize/ *a* (débat) televised; **émission** ~**e** television programme. **télévision** *nf* television.

télex /telɛks/ *nm* telex.

tellement /tɛlmɑ̃/ *adv* (tant) so much; (si) so; ~ **de** (quantité) so much; (nombre) so many.

téméraire /temerɛr/ *a* (*personne*) reckless.

témoignage /temwaɲaʒ/ *nm* testimony, evidence; (récit) account; ~ **de** (marque) token of.

témoigner /temwaɲe/ [1] *vi* testify (**de** to). ● *vt* (montrer) show; ~ **que** testify that.

témoin /temwɛ̃/ *nm* witness; (Sport) baton; **être** ~ **de** witness; ~ **oculaire** eyewitness.

tempe /tɑ̃p/ *nf* (Anat) temple.

tempérament /tɑ̃peramɑ̃/ *nm* temperament, disposition.

température /tɑ̃peratyr/ *nf* temperature.

tempête /tɑ̃pɛt/ *nf* storm; ~ **de neige** snowstorm.

temple /tɑ̃pl/ *nm* temple; (protes-tant) church.

temporaire /tɑ̃pɔrɛr/ *a* temporary.

temps /tɑ̃/ *nm* (notion) time; (Gram) tense; (étape) stage; **à** ~ **partiel/ plein** part-/full-time; **ces derniers** ~ lately; **dans le** ~ at one time; **dans quelque** ~ in a while; **de** ~ **en** ~ from time to time; ~ **d'arrêt** pause; **avoir tout son** ~ have plenty of time; (météo) weather; ~ **de chien** filthy weather; **quel** ~ **fait-il?** what's the weather like?

tenace /tɔnas/ *a* stubborn.

tenaille /tɔnaj/ *nf* pincers (+ *pl*).

tendance /tɑ̃dɑ̃s/ *nf* tendency; (évolution) trend; **avoir** ~ **à** tend to.

tendon /tɑ̃dɔ̃/ *nm* tendon.

tendre[1] /tɑ̃dr/ [3] *vt* stretch; (*piège*) set; (*bras*) stretch out; (*main*) hold out; (*cou*) crane; ~ **qch à qn** hold sth out to sb; ● ~ **l'oreille** prick up one's ears. ● *vi* ~ **à** tend to.

tendre[2] /tɑ̃dr/ *a* tender; (couleur, bois) soft. **tendresse** *nf* tenderness.

tendu, **~e** /tɑ̃dy/ a (corde) tight; (personne, situation) tense.

ténèbres /tenɛbʀ/ nfpl darkness (+ sg).

teneur /tənœʀ/ nf content.

tenir /təniʀ/ [59] vt hold; (pari, promesse, hôtel) keep; (place) take up; (propos) utter; (rôle) play; **~ de** (avoir reçu de) have got from; **~ pour** regard as; **~ chaud** keep warm; **~ compte de** take into account; **~ le coup** hold out; **~ tête à** stand up to. ● vi hold; **~ à** be attached to; **~ à faire** be anxious to do; **~ bon** stand firm; **~ dans** fit into; **~ de qn** take after sb; **tiens!** (surprise) hey! □ **se ~** vpr (debout) stand; (avoir lieu) be held; **se ~ à** hold on to; **s'en ~ à** (se limiter à) confine oneself to.

tennis /tenis/ nm tennis; **~ de table** table tennis. ● nmpl (chaussures) sneakers.

ténor /tenɔʀ/ nm tenor.

tension /tɑ̃sjɔ̃/ nf tension; **avoir de la ~** have high blood-pressure.

tentation /tɑ̃tasjɔ̃/ nf temptation.

tentative /tɑ̃tativ/ nf attempt.

tente /tɑ̃t/ nf tent.

tenter /tɑ̃te/ [1] vt (allécher) tempt; (essayer) try (**de faire** to do).

tenture /tɑ̃tyʀ/ nf curtain; **~s** draperies.

tenu, **~e** /təny/ a **bien ~** well kept; **~ de** required. ● **⇒TENIR** [58].

tenue /təny/ nf (habillement) dress; (de maison) upkeep; (conduite) (good) behaviour; (maintien) posture; **~ de soirée** evening dress.

Tergal® /tɛʀɡal/ nm Terylene®.

terme /tɛʀm/ nm (mot) term; (date limite) time-limit; (fin) end; **né avant ~** premature; **à long/court ~** long-/short-term; **en bons ~s** on good terms (**avec** with).

terminaison /tɛʀminɛzɔ̃/ nf (Gram) ending.

terminal, **~e** (mpl **-aux**) /tɛʀminal, -o/ a terminal. ● nm terminal. **terminale** nf (Scol) ≈ sixth form; (US) twelfth grade.

terminer /tɛʀmine/ [1] vt/i finish; (discours) end, finish. □ **se ~** vpr end (**par** with).

terne /tɛʀn/ a dull, drab.

ternir /tɛʀniʀ/ [2] vt/i tarnish. □ **se ~** vpr tarnish.

terrain /tɛʀɛ̃/ nm ground; (parcelle) piece of land; (à bâtir) plot; **~ d'aviation** airfield; **~ de camping** campsite; **~ de golf** golf course; **~ de jeu** playground; **~ vague** waste ground.

terrasse /tɛʀas/ nf terrace; **à la ~** (d'un café) outside (a café).

terrasser /tɛʀase/ [1] vt (adversaire) knock down; (maladie) strike down.

terre /tɛʀ/ nf (planète, matière) earth; (étendue, pays) land; (sol) ground; **à** (Naut) ashore; **par ~** (dehors) on the ground; (dedans) on the floor; **~ (cuite)** terracotta; **la ~ ferme** dry land; **~ glaise** clay. **terreau** (pl **~x**) nm compost. **terre-plein** (pl **terres-pleins**) nm platform; (de route) central reservation.

terrestre /tɛʀɛstʀ/ a (animaux) land; (de notre planète) of the Earth.

terreur /tɛʀœʀ/ nf terror.

terrible /tɛʀibl/ a terrible; (formidable 🄵) terrific.

terrier /tɛʀje/ nm (trou) burrow; (chien) terrier.

terrifier /tɛʀifje/ [45] vt terrify.

territoire /tɛʀitwaʀ/ nm territory.

terroir /tɛʀwaʀ/ nm land; **du ~** local.

terroriser /tɛʀɔʀize/ [1] vt terrorize.

terrorisme /tɛʀɔʀism/ nm

terrorism. **terroriste** *nmf* terrorist.

tertiaire /tɛRsjɛR/ *a* (*secteur*) service.

tes /te/ ⇒TON[1].

test /tɛst/ *nm* test.

testament /tɛstamɑ̃/ *nm* (Jur) will; (politique, artistique) testament; **Ancien/Nouveau T~** Old/New Testament.

tétanos /tetanos/ *nm* tetanus.

têtard /tɛtaR/ *nm* tadpole.

tête /tɛt/ *nf* head; (visage) face; (cheveux) hair; **à la ~ de** at the head of; **à ~ reposée** at one's leisure; **de ~** (*calculer*) in one's head; **faire la ~** sulk; **tenir ~ à qn** stand up to sb; **il n'en fait qu'à sa ~** he does just as he pleases; **en ~** (Sport) in the lead; **faire une ~** (au football) head the ball; **une forte ~** a rebel; **la ~ la première** head first; **de la ~ aux pieds** from head to toe.

tête-à-tête /tɛtatɛt/ *nm inv* tête-à-tête; **en ~** in private.

tétée /tete/ *nf* feed.

tétine /tetin/ *nf* (de biberon) teat; (sucette) dummy; (US) pacifier.

têtu, **~e** /tety/ *a* stubborn.

texte /tɛkst/ *nm* text; (de leçon) subject; (morceau choisi) passage.

texteur /tɛkstœR/ *nm* (Ordinat) word-processor.

textile /tɛkstil/ *nm & a* textile.

texto /tɛksto/ *nm* Ⓣ text message.

TGV *abrév m* (**train à grande vitesse**) TGV, high-speed train.

thé /te/ *nm* tea.

théâtre /teatR/ *nm* theatre; (d'un crime) scene; **faire du ~** act.

théière /tejɛR/ *nf* teapot.

thème /tɛm/ *nm* theme; (traduction: Scol) prose.

théorie /teɔRi/ *nf* theory. **théorique** *a* theoretical.

thérapie /teRapi/ *nf* therapy.

thermique /tɛRmik/ *a* thermal.

thermomètre /tɛRmɔmɛtR/ *nm* thermometer.

thermos® /tɛRmos/ *nm ou f* Thermos® (flask).

thermostat /tɛRmɔsta/ *nm* thermostat.

thèse /tɛz/ *nf* thesis.

thon /tɔ̃/ *nm* tuna.

thym /tɛ̃/ *nm* thyme.

tibia /tibja/ *nm* shinbone.

tic /tik/ *nm* (contraction) tic, twitch; (manie) habit.

ticket /tikɛ/ *nm* ticket.

tiède /tjɛd/ *a* lukewarm; (*nuit*) warm.

tiédir /tjediR/ [2] *vt/i* (faire) **~** warm up.

tien, **~ne** /tjɛ̃, -ɛn/ *pron* **le ~**, **la ~ne**, **les ~(ne)s** yours; **à la ~ne!** cheers!

tiens, **tient** /tjɛ̃/ ⇒TENIR [59].

tiercé /tjɛRse/ *nm* place-betting.

tiers, **tierce** /tjɛR, tjɛRs/ *a* third. ● *nm* (fraction) third; (personne) third party. **tiers-monde** *nm* Third World.

tige /tiʒ/ *nf* (Bot) stem, stalk; (en métal) shaft, rod.

tigre /tigR/ *nm* tiger.

tigresse /tigRɛs/ *nf* tigress.

tilleul /tijœl/ *nm* lime tree.

timbre /tɛ̃bR/ *nm* stamp; (sonnette) bell; (de voix) tone. **~ poste** (*pl* **~s poste**) *nm* postage stamp. **timbrer** [1] *vt* stamp.

timide /timid/ *a* shy, timid. **timidité** *nf* shyness.

timoré, **~e** /timɔRe/ *a* timorous.

tintement /tɛ̃tmɑ̃/ *nm* (de sonnette) ringing; (de clés) jingling.

tique /tik/ *nf* tick.

tir /tiR/ *nm* (Sport) shooting; (action de tirer) firing; (feu, rafale) fire; **~ à l'arc** archery; **~ au pigeon** clay pigeon shooting.

tirage /tiRaʒ/ *nm* (de photo)

T

printing; (de journal) circulation; (de livre) edition; (Ordinat) hard copy; (de cheminée) draught; ~ **au sort** draw.

tire-bouchon (pl ~s) /tiʀbuʃɔ̃/ nm corkscrew.

tirelire /tiʀliʀ/ nf piggy bank.

tirer /tiʀe/ [1] vt pull; (langue) stick out; (conclusion, trait, rideaux) draw; (coup de feu) fire; (gibier) shoot; (photo) print; ~ **de** (sortir) take ou get out of; (extraire) extract from; (plaisir, nom) derive from; ~ **parti de** take advantage of; ~ **profit de** profit from; **se faire** ~ **l'oreille** get told off. ● vi shoot, fire (**sur** at); ~ **sur** (corde) pull at; (couleur) verge on; ~ **à sa fin** be drawing to a close; ~ **au clair** clarify; ~ **au sort** draw lots (for). □ **se** ~ vpr 🄸 clear off; **se** ~ **de** get out of; **s'en** ~ (en réchapper) pull through; (réussir 🄸) cope.

tiret /tiʀɛ/ nm dash.

tireur /tiʀœʀ/ nm gunman; ~ **d'élite** marksman; ~ **isolé** sniper.

tiroir /tiʀwaʀ/ nm drawer. **tiroir-caisse** (pl tiroirs-caisses) nm till, cash register.

tisane /tizan/ nf herbal tea.

tissage /tisaʒ/ nm weaving. **tisser** [1] vt weave. **tisserand** nm weaver.

tissu /tisy/ nm fabric, material; (biologique) tissue; **un** ~ **de mensonges** (fig) a pack of lies. **tissu-éponge** (pl tissus-éponge) nm towelling.

titre /titʀ/ nm title; (diplôme) qualification; (Comm) bond; ~**s** (droits) claims; (gros) ~**s** headlines; **à** ~ **d'exemple** as an example; **à juste** ~ rightly; **à** ~ **privé** in a private capacity; **à double** ~ on two accounts; ~ **de propriété** title deed.

tituber /titybe/ [1] vi stagger.

titulaire /titylɛʀ/ a **être** ~ be a permanent staff member; **être** ~ **de** hold. ● nmf (de permis) holder. **titulariser** [1] vt give permanent status to.

toast /tost/ nm (pain) piece of toast; (canapé, allocution) toast.

toboggan /tɔbɔgɑ̃/ nm (de jeu) slide; (Auto) flyover.

toi /twa/ pron you; (réfléchi) yourself; **dépêche-** ~ hurry up.

toile /twal/ nf cloth; (tableau) canvas; ~ **d'araignée** cobweb; ~ **de fond** (fig) backdrop; **la** ~ (Internet) the Web.

toilette /twalɛt/ nf (habillement) outfit; ~**s** (cabinets) toilet(s); **de** ~ (articles, savon) toilet; **faire sa** ~ have a wash.

toi-même /twamɛm/ pron yourself.

toit /twa/ nm roof; ~ **ouvrant** (Auto) sunroof.

toiture /twatyʀ/ nf roof.

tôle /tol/ nf (plaque) iron sheet; ~ **ondulée** corrugated iron.

tolérant, ~e /tɔleʀɑ̃, -t/ a tolerant. **tolérer** [14] vt tolerate.

tomate /tɔmat/ nf tomato.

tombe /tɔ̃b/ nf grave; (pierre) gravestone.

tombeau (pl ~x) /tɔ̃bo/ nm tomb.

tomber /tɔ̃be/ [1] vi (aux être) fall; (fièvre, vent) drop; **faire** ~ knock over; (gouvernement) bring down; **laisser** ~ (objet, amoureux) drop; (collègue) let down; (activité) give up; **laisse** ~! 🄸 forget it!; ~ **à l'eau** (projet) fall through; ~ **bien** ou **à point** come at the right time; ~ **en panne** break down; ~ **en syncope** faint; ~ **sur** (trouver) run across.

tombola /tɔ̃bɔla/ nf tombola; (US) lottery.

tome /tɔm/ nm volume.

ton¹, ta (**ton** *before vowel or mute h*) (*pl* **tes**) /tɔ̃, ta, tɔn, te/ *a* your.

ton² /tɔ̃/ *nm* (hauteur de voix) pitch; **d'un ~ sec** drily; **de bon ~** in good taste.

tonalité /tɔnalite/ *nf* (Mus) key; (de téléphone) dialling tone; (US) dial tone.

tondeuse /tɔ̃døz/ *nf* (à moutons) shears (+ *pl*); (à cheveux) clippers (+ *pl*); **~ à gazon** lawn-mower.
tondre [3] *vt* (herbe) mow; (mouton) shear; (cheveux) clip.

tonne /tɔn/ *nf* tonne.

tonneau (*pl* **~x**) /tɔno/ *nm* barrel; (en voiture) somersault.

tonnerre /tɔnɛʀ/ *nm* thunder.

tonton /tɔ̃tɔ̃/ *nm* Ⓘ uncle.

tonus /tɔnys/ *nm* energy.

torche /tɔʀʃ/ *nf* torch.

torchon /tɔʀʃɔ̃/ *nm* (pour la vaisselle) tea towel.

tordre /tɔʀdʀ/ [3] *vt* twist. □ **se ~** *vpr* **se ~ la cheville** twist one's ankle; **se ~ de douleur** writhe in pain; **se ~ (de rire)** split one's sides.

tordu, ~e /tɔʀdy/ *a* twisted, bent; (esprit) warped, twisted.

torpille /tɔʀpij/ *nf* torpedo.

torrent /tɔʀɑ̃/ *nm* torrent.

torride /tɔʀid/ *a* torrid; (chaleur) scorching.

torse /tɔʀs/ *nm* chest; (Anat) torso.

tort /tɔʀ/ *nm* wrong; **avoir ~** be wrong (de faire to do); **donner ~ à** prove wrong; **être dans son ~** be in the wrong; **faire (du) ~ à** harm; **à ~** wrongly; **à ~ et à travers** without thinking.

torticolis /tɔʀtikɔli/ *nm* stiff neck.

tortiller /tɔʀtije/ [1] *vt* twist, twirl. □ **se ~** *vpr* wriggle.

tortionnaire /tɔʀsjɔnɛʀ/ *nm* torturer.

tortue /tɔʀty/ *nf* tortoise; (d'eau) turtle.

tortueux, -euse /tɔʀtɥø, -z/ *a* (chemin) twisting; (explication) tortuous.

torture /tɔʀtyʀ/ *nf* torture.
torturer [1] *vt* torture.

tôt /to/ *adv* early; **au plus ~** at the earliest; **le plus ~ possible** as soon as possible; **~ ou tard** sooner or later; **ce n'est pas trop ~!** it's about time!

total, ~e (*mpl* **-aux**) /tɔtal, -o/ *a* total. ● *nm* (*pl* **-aux**) total; **au ~** all in all. **totalement** *adv* totally. **totaliser** [1] *vt* total. **totalitaire** *a* totalitarian.

totalité /tɔtalite/ *nf* **la ~ de** all of.

touche /tuʃ/ *nf* (de piano) key; (de peinture) touch; (**ligne de**) **~** (Sport) touchline.

toucher /tuʃe/ [1] *vt* touch; (émouvoir) move, touch; (contacter) get in touch with; (cible) hit; (argent) draw; (chèque) cash; (concerner) affect. ● *vi* **~ à** touch; (question) touch on; (fin, but) approach; **je vais lui en ~ deux mots** I'll talk to him about it. □ **se ~** *vpr* (lignes) touch. ● *nm* (sens) touch.

touffe /tuf/ *nf* (de poils, d'herbe) tuft; (de plantes) clump.

toujours /tuʒuʀ/ *adv* always; (encore) still; (de toute façon) anyway; **pour ~** for ever; **~ est-il que** the fact remains that.

toupet /tupɛ/ *nm* (culot Ⓘ) cheek, nerve.

tour /tuʀ/ *nf* tower; (immeuble) tower block; (échecs) rook; **~ de contrôle** control tower. ● *nm* (mouvement, succession, tournure) turn; (excursion) trip; (à pied) walk; (en auto) drive; (artifice) trick; (circonférence) circumference; (Tech) lathe; **~ (de piste)** lap; **à ~ de rôle** in turn; **à mon ~** when it is my turn; **c'est mon ~ de** it is my turn to; **faire le ~ de** go round; (question) survey; **~ d'horizon**

T

survey; ~ **de potier** potter's
wheel; ~ **de taille** waist
measurement; (ligne) waistline.
tourbillon /tuʀbijɔ̃/ *nm*
whirlwind; (d'eau) whirlpool; (fig)
swirl.
tourisme /tuʀism/ *nm* tourism;
faire du ~ do some sightseeing.
touriste /tuʀist/ *nmf* tourist.
touristique *a* tourist; (route)
scenic.
tourmenter /tuʀmɑ̃te/ *vt*
torment. □ **se** ~ *vpr* worry.
tournant, ~**e** /tuʀnɑ̃, -t/ *a* (qui
pivote) revolving. ● *nm* bend; (fig)
turning-point.
tourne-disque (pl ~**s**)
/tuʀnədisk/ *nm* record-player.
tournée /tuʀne/ *nf* (de facteur, au
café) round; **c'est ma** ~ I'll buy
this round; (d'artiste) tour.
tourner /tuʀne/ [1] *vt* turn; (film)
shoot, make; ~ **le dos à** turn
one's back on; ~ **en dérision**
mock. ● *vi* turn; (toupie, tête)
spin; (moteur, usine) run; ~
autour de go round; (personne,
maison) hang around; (terre)
revolve round; (question) centre
on; ~ **de l'œil** 🔟 faint; **mal** ~
(affaire) turn out badly. □ **se** ~
vpr turn.
tournesol /tuʀnəsɔl/ *nm*
sunflower.
tournevis /tuʀnəvis/ *nm*
screwdriver.
tournoi /tuʀnwa/ *nm*
tournament.
tourte /tuʀt/ *nf* pie.
tourterelle /tuʀtəʀɛl/ *nf* turtle
dove.
Toussaint /tusɛ̃/ *nf* **la** ~ All
Saints' Day.
tousser /tuse/ [1] *vi* cough.
tout, ~**e** (pl **tous**, **toutes**) /tu,
tut/ *nm* (ensemble) whole; **en** ~ in
all; (n'importe quel) any; ~ **le pays**
the whole country, all the country;

~**e la nuit/journée** the whole
night/day; ~ **un paquet** a whole
pack; **tous les jours** every day;
tous les deux ans every two years;
~ **le monde** everyone; **tous les
deux, toutes les deux** both of
them; **tous les trois** all three (of
them). ● *pron* everything; all;
anything; **tous** /tus/, **toutes** all;
tous ensemble all together; **prends**
~ take everything; ~ **ce que tu
veux** everything you want. ● *adv*
(très) very; (entièrement) all; ~ **au
bout/début** right at the end/
beginning; ~ **en marchant** while
walking; ~ **à coup** all of a
sudden; ~ **à fait** quite,
completely; ~ **à l'heure** in a
moment; (passé) a moment ago; ~
au *ou* **le long de** throughout; ~ **au
plus/moins** at most/least; ~ **de
même** all the same; ~ **de suite**
straight away; ~ **entier** whole; ~
neuf brand new; ~ **nu** stark
naked. **tout-à-l'égout** *nm inv*
main drainage.
toutefois /tutfwa/ *adv* however.
tout(-)terrain /tuteʀɛ̃/ *a inv* all
terrain.
toux /tu/ *nf* cough.
toxicomane /tɔksikɔman/ *nmf*
drug addict.
toxique /tɔksik/ *a* toxic.
trac /tʀak/ *nm* **le** ~ nerves; (Théât)
stage fright.
traçabilité /tʀasabilite/ *nf*
traceability.
tracas /tʀaka/ *nm* worry.
trace /tʀas/ *nf* (traînée, piste) trail;
(d'animal, de pneu) tracks; ~**s de pas**
footprints.
tracer /tʀase/ [10] *vt* draw; (écrire)
write; (route) open up.
trachée-artère /tʀaʃeaʀtɛʀ/ *nf*
windpipe.
tracteur /tʀaktœʀ/ *nm* tractor.
tradition /tʀadisjɔ̃/ *nf* tradition.
traditionnel, ~**le** *a* traditional.
traducteur, **-trice** /tʀadyktœʀ,

-tris/ *nm, f* translator. **traduction** *nf* translation.

traduire /tradɥiʀ/ [17] *vt* translate; ~ **en justice** take to court.

trafic /trafik/ *nm* (commerce, circulation) traffic.

trafiquant, ~**e** /trafikɑ̃, -t/ *nm, f* trafficker; (d'armes, de drogues) dealer.

trafiquer /trafike/ [1] *vi* traffic. ● *vt* ⊞ (moteur) fiddle with.

tragédie /traʒedi/ *nf* tragedy. **tragique** *a* tragic.

trahir /traiʀ/ [2] *vt* betray. **trahison** *nf* betrayal; (Mil) treason.

train /trɛ̃/ *nm* (Rail) train; (allure) pace; **aller bon** ~ walk briskly; **en** ~ **de faire** (busy) doing; ~ **d'atterrissage** undercarriage; ~ **électrique** (jouet) electric train set; ~ **de vie** lifestyle.

traîne /trɛn/ *nf* (de robe) train; **à la** ~ lagging behind.

traîneau (*pl* ~**x**) /trɛno/ *nm* sleigh.

traînée /trɛne/ *nf* (trace) trail; (longue) streak; (femme: péj) slut.

traîner /trɛne/ [1] *vt* drag (along); ● **les pieds** drag one's feet. ● *vi* (pendre) trail; (rester en arrière) trail behind; (flâner) hang about; (*papiers, affaires*) lie around; ~ (**en longueur**) drag on. □ **se** ~ *vpr* (par terre) crawl.

traire /trɛʀ/ [29] *vt* milk.

trait /trɛ/ *nm* line; (en dessinant) stroke; (caractéristique) feature, trait; ~**s** (du visage) features; **avoir** ~ **à** relate to; **d'un** ~ (*boire*) in one gulp; ~ **d'union** hyphen; (fig) link.

traite /trɛt/ *nf* (de vache) milking; (Comm) draft; **d'une** (**seule**) ~ in one go, at a stretch.

traité /trɛte/ *nm* (pacte) treaty; (ouvrage) treatise.

traitement /trɛtmɑ̃/ *nm* treatment; (salaire) salary; ~ **de données** data processing; ~ **de texte** word processing.

traiter /trɛte/ [1] *vt* treat; (*affaire*) deal with; (données, produit) process; ~ **qn de lâche** call sb a coward. ● *vi* deal (**avec** with); ~ **de** (*sujet*) deal with.

traiteur /trɛtœʀ/ *nm* caterer; (boutique) delicatessen.

traître, **-esse** /trɛtʀ, -ɛs/ *a* treacherous. ● *nm, f* traitor.

trajectoire /traʒɛktwaʀ/ *nf* path.

trajet /traʒɛ/ *nm* (voyage) journey; (itinéraire) route.

trame /tram/ *nf* (de tissu) weft.

tramway /tramwɛ/ *nm* tram; (US) streetcar.

tranchant, ~**e** /trɑ̃ʃɑ̃, -t/ *a* sharp; (fig) cutting. ● *nm* cutting edge; **à double** ~ two-edged.

tranche /trɑ̃ʃ/ *nf* (rondelle) slice; (bord) edge; (d'âge, de revenu) bracket.

tranchée /trɑ̃ʃe/ *nf* trench.

trancher /trɑ̃ʃe/ [1] *vt* cut; (*question*) decide; (contraster) contrast (**sur** with).

tranquille /trɑ̃kil/ *a* quiet; (*esprit*) at rest; (*conscience*) clear; **être/laisser** ~ be/leave in peace; **tiens-toi** ~! be quiet!

tranquillisant *nm* tranquillizer. **tranquilliser** [1] *vt* reassure. **tranquillité** *nf* (peace and) quiet; (d'esprit) peace of mind.

transcription /trɑ̃skripsjɔ̃/ *nf* transcription; (copie) transcript. **transcrire** [30] *vt* transcribe.

transe /trɑ̃s/ *nf* **en** ~ in a trance.

transférer /trɑ̃sfere/ [14] *vt* transfer.

transfert /trɑ̃sfɛʀ/ *nm* transfer; ~ **d'appel** (au téléphone) call diversion.

T

transformation /trɑ̃sfɔrmasjɔ̃/
nf change; transformation.

transformer /trɑ̃sfɔrme/ [1] *vt*
change; (radicalement) transform;
(*vêtement*) alter. □ se ~ *vpr*
change; (radicalement) be
transformed; (se) ~ **en** turn into.

transgénique /trɑ̃sʒenik/ *a*
genetically modified.

transiger /trɑ̃siʒe/ [40] *vi*
compromise.

transiter /trɑ̃zite/ [1] *vt/i* ~ **par**
pass through.

transitif, -ive /trɑ̃zitif, -v/ *a*
transitive.

translucide /trɑ̃slysid/ *a*
translucent.

transmettre /trɑ̃smɛtr/ [42] *vt*
(*savoir, maladie*) pass on; (*ondes*)
transmit; (à la radio) broadcast.
transmission *nf* transmission;
(*radio*) broadcasting.

transparence /trɑ̃sparɑ̃s/ *nf*
transparency. **transparent**, ~**e** *a*
transparent.

transpercer /trɑ̃spɛrse/ [10] *vt*
pierce.

transpiration /trɑ̃spirasjɔ̃/ *nf*
perspiration. **transpirer** [1] *vi*
perspire.

transplanter /trɑ̃splɑ̃te/ [1] *vt*
(Bot, Méd) transplant.

transport /trɑ̃spɔr/ *nm* transport
(ation); **durant le** ~ in transit; **les**
~**s** transport (+ *sg*); **les** ~**s en**
commun public transport (+ *sg*).

transporter /trɑ̃spɔrte/ [1] *vt*
transport; (à la main) carry.
transporteur *nm* haulier; (US)
trucker.

transversal, ~**e** (*mpl* -**aux**)
/trɑ̃svɛrsal, -o/ *a* cross,
transverse.

trapu, ~**e** /trapy/ *a* stocky.

traumatisant, ~**e** /trɔmatizɑ̃, -t/
a traumatic. **traumatiser** *vt* [1]
traumatize. **traumatisme** *nm*
trauma.

travail (*pl* -**aux**) /travaj, -o/ *nm*
work; (emploi, tâche) job; (façonnage)
working; **travaux** work (+ *sg*);
(routiers) roadworks; ~ **à la chaîne**
production line work; **travaux**
dirigés (Scol) practical; **travaux**
forcés hard labour; **travaux**
manuels handicrafts; **travaux**
ménagers housework.

travailler /travaje/ [1] *vi* work;
(se déformer) warp. ● *vt* (façonner)
work; (étudier) work at *ou* on.

travailleur, -euse /travajœr,
-øz/ *nm, f* worker. ● *a*
hardworking.

travailliste /travajist/ *a* Labour.
● *nmf* Labour party member.

travers /travɛr/ *nm* (défaut)
failing; **à** ~ through; **au** ~ **(de)**
through; **de** ~ (*chapeau, nez*)
crooked; (*regarder*) askance; **j'ai**
avalé de ~ it went the wrong
way; **en** ~ **(de)** across.

traversée /travɛrse/ *nf* crossing.

traverser /travɛrse/ [1] *vt* cross;
(transpercer) go (right) through;
(*période, forêt*) go *ou* pass
through.

traversin /travɛrsɛ̃/ *nm* bolster.

travesti /travɛsti/ *nm*
transvestite.

trébucher /trebyʃe/ [1] *vi*
stumble, trip (over); **faire** ~ trip
(up).

trèfle /trɛfl/ *nm* (plante) clover;
(cartes) clubs.

treillis /treji/ *nm* trellis; (en métal)
wire mesh; (tenue militaire) combat
uniform.

treize /trɛz/ *a & nm* thirteen.

tréma /trema/ *nm* diaeresis.

tremblement /trɑ̃bləmɑ̃/ *nm*
shaking; ~ **de terre** earthquake.
trembler [1] *vi* shake, tremble;
(*lumière, voix*) quiver.

tremper /trɑ̃pe/ [1] *vt/i* soak;
(plonger) dip; (*acier*) temper; **faire**

~ soak; ~ **dans** (fig) be mixed up. □ **se** ~ *vpr* (se baigner) have a dip.

tremplin /tʀɑ̃plɛ̃/ *nm* springboard.

trente /tʀɑ̃t/ *a & nm* thirty; **se mettre sur son** ~ **et un** dress up; **tous les** ~**-six du mois** once in a blue moon.

trépied /tʀepje/ *nm* tripod.

très /tʀɛ/ *adv* very; ~ **aimé/estimé** much liked/esteemed.

trésor /tʀezɔʀ/ *nm* treasure; **le T**~ **public** the revenue department.

trésorerie /tʀezɔʀʀi/ *nf* (bureaux) accounts department; (du Trésor public) revenue office; (argent) funds (+ *pl*); (gestion) accounts (+ *pl*). **trésorier, -ière** *nm, f* treasurer.

tressaillement /tʀesajmɑ̃/ *nm* quiver; start.

tresse /tʀɛs/ *nf* braid, plait.

trêve /tʀɛv/ *nf* truce; (fig) respite; ~ **de plaisanteries** that's enough joking.

tri /tʀi/ *nm* (classement) sorting; (sélection) selection; **faire le** ~ **de** (classer) sort; (choisir) select; **centre de** ~ sorting office.

triangle /tʀijɑ̃gl/ *nm* triangle.

tribal, ~e (*mpl* **-aux**) /tʀibal, -o/ *a* tribal.

tribord /tʀibɔʀ/ *nm* starboard.

tribu /tʀiby/ *nf* tribe.

tribunal (*mpl* **-aux**) /tʀibynal, -o/ *nm* court.

tribune /tʀibyn/ *nf* (de stade) grandstand; (d'orateur) rostrum; (débat) forum; (d'église) gallery.

tribut /tʀiby/ *nm* tribute.

tributaire /tʀibytɛʀ/ *a* ~ **de** dependent on.

tricher /tʀiʃe/ [1] *vi* cheat. **tricheur, -euse** *nm, f* cheat.

tricolore /tʀikɔlɔʀ/ *a* three-coloured; (écharpe) red, white and blue; (équipe) French.

tricot /tʀiko/ *nm* (activité) knitting; (pull) sweater; **en** ~ knitted; ~ **de corps** vest; (US) undershirt. **tricoter** [1] *vt/i* knit.

trier /tʀije/ [45] *vt* (classer) sort; (choisir) select.

trimestre /tʀimɛstʀ/ *nm* quarter; (Scol) term. **trimestriel, ~le** *a* quarterly; (*bulletin*) end-of-term.

tringle /tʀɛ̃gl/ *nf* rail.

trinquer /tʀɛ̃ke/ [1] *vi* clink glasses.

triomphant, ~e /tʀijɔ̃fɑ̃, -t/ *a* triumphant. **triomphe** *nm* triumph. **triompher** [1] *vi* triumph (**de** over); (jubiler) be triumphant.

tripes /tʀip/ *nfpl* (mets) tripe (+ *sg*); (entrailles 🖫) guts.

triple /tʀipl/ *a* triple, treble. ● *nm* **le** ~ three times as much (**de** as). **triplés, -es** *nm, fpl* triplets.

tripot /tʀipo/ *nm* gambling den.

tripoter /tʀipɔte/ [1] *vt* 🖫 (*personne*) grope; (*objet*) fiddle with.

trisomique /tʀizɔmik/ *a* **être** ~ have Down's syndrome.

triste /tʀist/ *a* sad; (*rue, temps, couleur*) dreary; (lamentable) dreadful. **tristesse** *nf* sadness; dreariness.

trivial, ~e (*mpl* **-iaux**) /tʀivjal, -jo/ *a* coarse.

troc /tʀɔk/ *nm* exchange; (Comm) barter.

trognon /tʀɔɲɔ̃/ *nm* (de fruit) core.

trois /tʀwɑ/ *a & nm* three; **hôtel** ~ **étoiles** three-star hotel. **troisième** *a & nmf* third.

trombone /tʀɔ̃bɔn/ *nm* (Mus) trombone; (agrafe) paperclip.

trompe /tʀɔ̃p/ *nf* (d'éléphant) trunk; (Mus) horn.

tromper /tʀɔ̃pe/ [1] *vt* deceive, mislead; (déjouer) elude. □ **se** ~ *vpr* be mistaken; **se** ~ **de route**/

T

d'heure take the wrong road/get the time wrong.

trompette /tʀɔ̃pɛt/ *nf* trumpet.

trompeur, -euse /tʀɔ̃pœʀ, -øz/ *a* (*apparence*) deceptive.

tronc /tʀɔ̃/ *nm* trunk; (*boîte*) collection box.

tronçon /tʀɔ̃sɔ̃/ *nm* section.

tronçonneuse /tʀɔ̃sɔnøz/ *nf* chain saw.

trône /tʀon/ *nm* throne. **trôner** [1] *vi* (*vase*) have pride of place (**sur** on).

trop /tʀo/ *adv* (*grand, loin*) too; (*boire, marcher*) too much; ~ (**de**) (*quantité*) too much; (*nombre*) too many; **ce serait** ~ **beau** one should be so lucky; **de** ~, **en** ~ too much; too many; **il a bu un verre de** ~ he's had one too many; **se sentir de** ~ feel one is in the way.

trophée /tʀɔfe/ *nm* trophy.

tropical, ~e (*mpl* **-aux**) /tʀɔpikal, -o/ *a* tropical. **tropique** *nm* tropic.

trop-plein (*pl* ~**s**) /tʀɔplɛ̃/ *nm* excess; (*dispositif*) overflow.

troquer /tʀɔke/ [1] *vt* exchange; (Comm) barter (**contre** for).

trot /tʀo/ *nm* trot; **aller au** ~ trot. **trotter** [1] *vi* trot.

trotteuse /tʀɔtøz/ *nf* (de montre) second hand.

trottoir /tʀɔtwaʀ/ *nm* pavement; (US) sidewalk; ~ **roulant** moving walkway.

trou /tʀu/ *nm* hole; (*moment*) gap; (*lieu*: péj) dump; ~ (**de mémoire**) memory lapse; ~ **de serrure** keyhole; **faire son** ~ carve one's niche.

trouble /tʀubl/ *a* (*eau, image*) unclear; (*louche*) shady. ● *nm* (*émoi*) emotion; ~**s** (Pol) disturbances; (Méd) disorder (+ *sg*).

troubler /tʀuble/ [1] *vt* disturb;

(*eau*) make cloudy; (*inquiéter*) trouble. □ **se** ~ *vpr* (*personne*) become flustered.

trouer /tʀue/ [1] *vt* make a hole *ou* holes in; **mes chaussures sont trouées** my shoes have got holes in them.

troupe /tʀup/ *nf* troop; (d'acteurs) company.

troupeau (*pl* ~**x**) /tʀupo/ *nm* herd; (de moutons) flock.

trousse /tʀus/ *nf* case, bag; **aux** ~**s de** hot on sb's heels; ~ **de toilette** toilet bag.

trousseau (*pl* ~**x**) /tʀuso/ *nm* (de clefs) bunch; (de mariée) trousseau.

trouver /tʀuve/ [1] *vt* find; (*penser*) think; **il est venu me** ~ he came to see me. □ **se** ~ *vpr* (être) be; (*se sentir*) feel; **il se trouve que** it happens that; **si ça se trouve** maybe; **se** ~ **mal** faint.

truand /tʀyɑ̃/ *nm* gangster.

truc /tʀyk/ *nm* (*moyen*) way; (*artifice*) trick; (*chose* ▣) thing.

trucage *nm* (*cinéma*) special effect.

truffe /tʀyf/ *nf* (champignon, chocolat) truffle; (de chien) nose.

truffer /tʀyfe/ [1] *vt* (fig) fill, pack (**de** with).

truie /tʀyi/ *nf* (animal) sow.

truite /tʀyit/ *nf* trout.

truquer /tʀyke/ [1] *vt* fix, rig; (*photo*) fake; (*résultats*) fiddle.

tsar /tsaʀ/ *nm* tsar, czar.

tu /ty/ *pron* (parent, ami, enfant) you. ● ⇒TAIRE [47].

tuba /tyba/ *nm* (Mus) tuba; (Sport) snorkel.

tube /tyb/ *nm* tube.

tuberculose /tybɛʀkyloz/ *nf* tuberculosis.

tuer /tɥe/ [1] *vt* kill; (d'une balle) shoot, kill; (épuiser) exhaust; ~ **par balles** shoot dead. □ **se** ~ *vpr* kill oneself; (accident) be killed.

tuerie /tyʀi/ nf killing.

tue-tête: à ~ /atytɛt/ loc at the top of one's voice.

tuile /tɥil/ nf tile; (malchance ▯) (stroke of) bad luck.

tulipe /tylip/ nf tulip.

tumeur /tymœʀ/ nf tumour.

tumulte /tymylt/ nm commotion; (désordre) turmoil.

tunique /tynik/ nf tunic.

Tunisie /tynizi/ nf Tunisia.

tunnel /tynɛl/ nm tunnel.

turbo /tyʀbɔ/ a turbo. ● nf (voiture) turbo.

turbulent, ~e /tyʀbylã, -t/ a boisterous, turbulent.

turc, **-que** /tyʀk/ a Turkish. ● nm (Ling) Turkish. **T~**, **-que** Turk.

turfiste /tyʀfist/ nmf racegoer.

Turquie /tyʀki/ nf Turkey.

tutelle /tytɛl/ nf (Jur) guardianship; (fig) protection.

tuteur, **-trice** /tytœʀ, -tʀis/ nm, f (Jur) guardian. ● nm (bâton) stake.

tutoiement /tytwamã/ nm use of the 'tu' form. **tutoyer** [31] vt address using the 'tu' form.

tuyau (pl ~x) /tɥijo/ nm pipe; (conseil ▯) tip; ~ **d'arrosage** hosepipe.

TVA abrév f (**taxe à la valeur ajoutée**) VAT.

tympan /tɛ̃pã/ nm ear-drum.

type /tip/ nm (genre, traits) type; (individu ▯) bloke, guy; **le ~ même de** a classic example of ● a inv typical.

typique /tipik/ a typical.

tyran /tiʀã/ nm tyrant. **tyrannie** nf tyranny. **tyranniser** [1] vt oppress, tyrannize.

UE abrév f (**Union européenne**) European Union.

Ukraine /ykʀɛn/ nf Ukraine.

ulcère /ylsɛʀ/ nm (Méd) ulcer.

ULM abrév m (**ultraléger motorisé**) microlight.

ultérieur, ~e /ylteʀjœʀ/ a later. **ultérieurement** adv later.

ultime /yltim/ a final.

un, **une** /œ̃, yn/

●déterminant

····► a; (devant voyelle) an; ~ **animal** an animal; ~ **jour** one day; **pas ~ arbre** not a single tree; **il fait ~ froid!** it's so cold!

●pronom

····► one; **l'~ d'entre nous** one of us; **les ~ croient que...** some believe...

····► **la une** the front page.

····► **j'en veux une** I want one.

●adjectif

····► one, a, an; **j'ai ~ garçon et deux filles** I have a ou one boy and two girls; **il est une heure** it is one o'clock.

●nom masculin & féminin

····► ~ **par** ~ one by one.

unanime /ynanim/ a unanimous.

unanimité /ynanimite/ nf unanimity; **à l'~** unanimously.

uni, ~e /yni/ a united; (couple) close; (surface) smooth; (tissu) plain.

unième /ynjɛm/ *a* -first; **vingt et
~** twenty-first; **cent ~** one
hundred and first.

unifier /ynifje/ [45] *vt* unify.

uniforme /ynifɔʀm/ *nm* uniform.
● *a* uniform. **uniformiser** [1] *vt*
standardize. **uniformité** *nf*
uniformity.

unilatéral, **~e** (*mpl* **-aux**) /ynila-
teʀal, -o/ *a* unilateral.

union /ynjɔ̃/ *nf* union; **l'U~
européenne** the European Union.

unique /ynik/ *a* (seul) only; (*prix,
voie*) one; (*incomparable*) unique;
enfant ~ only child; **sens ~** one-
way street. **uniquement** *adv*
only, solely.

unir /yniʀ/ [2] *vt* unite. □ **s'~** *vpr*
unite, join.

unité /ynite/ *nf* unit; (*harmonie*)
unity.

univers /univɛʀ/ *nm* universe.

universel, **~le** /univɛʀsɛl/ *a*
universal.

universitaire /univɛʀsiteʀ/ *a*
(*résidence*) university; (*niveau*)
academic. ● *nmf* academic.

université /univɛʀsite/ *nf*
university.

uranium /yʀanjɔm/ *nm* uranium.

urbain, **~e** /yʀbɛ̃, -ɛn/ *a* urban.
urbanisme *nm* town planning.

urgence /yʀʒɑ̃s/ *nf* (cas)
emergency; (de situation, tâche)
urgency; **d'~** (*mesure*)
emergency; (*transporter*)
urgently; **les ~s** casualty (+ *sg*).
urgent, **~e** *a* urgent.

urine /yʀin/ *nf* urine. **urinoir** *nm*
urinal.

urne /yʀn/ *nf* (électorale) ballot
box; (vase) urn; **aller aux ~s** go to
the polls.

urticaire /yʀtikɛʀ/ *nf* hives (+
pl), urticar.

us /ys/ *nmpl* **les ~ et coutumes**
habits and customs.

usage /yzaʒ/ *nm* use; (coutume)
custom; (de langage) usage; **à l'~ de**
for; **d'~** (habituel) customary; **faire
~ de** make use of.

usagé, **~e** /yzaʒe/ *a* worn.

usager /yzaʒe/ *nm* user.

usé, **~e** /yze/ *a* worn (out); (banal)
trite.

user /yze/ [1] *vt* wear (out). ● *vi*
~ de use. □ **s'~** *vpr* (*tissu*) wear
(out).

usine /yzin/ *nf* factory, plant; **~
sidérurgique** ironworks (+ *pl*).

usité, **~e** /yzite/ *a* common.

ustensile /ystɑ̃sil/ *nm* utensil.

usuel, **~le** /yzɥɛl/ *a* ordinary,
everyday.

usure /yzyʀ/ *nf* (détérioration) wear
(and tear).

utérus /yteʀys/ *nm* womb,
uterus.

utile /ytil/ *a* useful.

utilisable /ytilizabl/ *a* usable.
utilisation *nf* use. **utiliser** [1] *vt*
use.

utopie /ytɔpi/ *nf* Utopia; (idée)
Utopian idea. **utopique** *a*
Utopian.

UV[1] *abrév f* (**unité de valeur**)
course unit.

UV[2] *abrév mpl* (**ultraviolets**)
ultraviolet rays; **faire des ~** use a
sunbed.

va /va/ ⇒ALLER [8].

vacance /vakɑ̃s/ *nf* (poste)
vacancy.

vacances /vakɑ̃s/ *nfpl* holiday
(s); (US) vacation; **en ~** on
holiday; **~ d'été, grandes ~**

summer holidays. **vacancier,**
-ière *nm, f* holidaymaker; (US)
vacationer.
vacant, ~**e** /vakɑ̃, -t/ *a* vacant.
vacarme /vakaRm/ *nm* din.
vaccin /vaksɛ̃/ *nm* vaccine.
vacciner [1] *vt* vaccinate.
vache /vaʃ/ *nf* cow. ● *a* (méchant
🈂) nasty.
vaciller /vasije/ [1] *vi* sway,
wobble; (*lumière*) flicker; (hésiter)
falter; (*santé, mémoire*) fail.
vadrouiller /vadRuje/ [1] *vi* 🈂
wander about.
va-et-vient /vaevjɛ̃/ *nm inv* toing
and froing; (de personnes) comings
and goings; **faire le** ~ go to and
fro; (interrupteur) two-way switch.
vagabond, ~**e** /vagabɔ̃, -d/ *nm, f*
vagrant.
vagin /vaʒɛ̃/ *nm* vagina.
vague /vag/ *a* vague. ● *nm*
regarder dans le ~ stare into
space; **il est resté dans le** ~ he
was vague about it. ● *nf* wave; ~
de fond ground swell; ~ **de froid**
cold spell; ~ **de chaleur** heatwave.
vaillant, ~**e** /vajɑ̃, -t/ *a* brave;
(vigoureux) strong.
vaille /vaj/ ⇒VALOIR [60].
vain, ~**e** /vɛ̃, vɛn/ *a* vain, futile;
en ~ in vain.
vaincre /vɛ̃kR/ [59] *vt* defeat;
(surmonter) overcome. **vaincu,** ~**e**
nm, f (Sport) loser. **vainqueur** *nm*
victor; (Sport) winner.
vais /vɛ/ ⇒ALLER [8].
vaisseau (*pl* ~**x**) /vɛso/ *nm* ship;
(veine) vessel; ~ **spatial** spaceship.
vaisselle /vɛsɛl/ *nf* crockery; (à
laver) dishes; **faire la** ~ do the
washing-up, wash the dishes;
liquide ~ washing-up liquid.
valable /valabl/ *a* valid; (de
qualité) worthwhile.
valet /valɛ/ *nm* (aux cartes) jack; ~
(de chambre) manservant.
valeur /valœR/ *nf* value; (mérite)

worth, value; ~**s** (Comm) stocks
and shares; **avoir de la** ~ be
valuable; **prendre/perdre de la** ~
go up/down in value; **objets de** ~
valuables; **sans** ~ worthless.
valide /valid/ *a* (*personne*) fit;
(*billet*) valid. **valider** [1] *vt*
validate.
valise /valiz/ *nf* (suit)case; **faire**
ses ~**s** pack (one's bags).
vallée /vale/ *nf* valley.
valoir /valwaR/ [60] *vi* (mériter) be
worth; (égaler) be as good as; (être
valable) (*règle*) apply; **faire** ~
(*mérite, qualité*) emphasize;
(*terrain*) cultivate; (*droit*) assert;
se faire ~ put oneself forward; ~
cher/100 francs be worth a lot/100
francs; **que vaut ce vin?** what's
this wine like?; **ne rien** ~ be
useless *ou* no good; **ça ne me dit**
rien qui vaille I don't like the
sound of that; ~ **la peine** *or* **le**
coup 🈂 be worth it; **il vaut/vaudrait**
mieux faire it is/would be better to
do. ● *vt* ~ **qch à qn** (*éloges,*
critiques) earn sb sth;
(*admiration*) win sb sth. □ **se** ~
vpr (être équivalents) be as good as
each other; **ça se vaut** it's all the
same.
valoriser /valɔRize/ [1] *vt* add
value to; (*produit*) promote;
(*profession*) make attractive;
(*région, ressources*) develop.
valse /vals/ *nf* waltz.
vandale /vɑ̃dal/ *nmf* vandal.
vanille /vanij/ *nf* vanilla.
vanité /vanite/ *nf* vanity.
vaniteux, -euse *a* vain,
conceited.
vanne /van/ *nf* (d'écluse) sluice-
gate; (propos 🈂) dig 🈂.
vantard, ~**e** /vɑ̃taR, -d/ *a*
boastful. ● *nm, f* boaster.
vanter /vɑ̃te/ [1] *vt* praise. □ **se**
~ *vpr* boast (**de** about); **se** ~ **de**
faire pride oneself on doing.

V

vapeur /vapœʀ/ *nf* (eau) steam; (brume, émanation) vapour; ~s fumes; **à** ~ (bateau, locomotive) steam; **faire cuire à la** ~ steam.

vaporisateur /vapɔʀizatœʀ/ *nm* spray, atomizer. **vaporiser** [1] *vt* spray.

varappe /vaʀap/ *nf* rock-climbing.

variable /vaʀjabl/ *a* variable; (temps) changeable.

varicelle /vaʀisɛl/ *nf* chickenpox.

varié, ~e /vaʀje/ *a* (non monotone, étendu) varied; (divers) various; **sandwichs ~s** a selection of sandwiches.

varier /vaʀje/ [45] *vt/i* vary.

variété /vaʀjete/ *nf* variety; **spectacle de ~s** variety show.

vase /vɑz/ *nm* vase. ● *nf* silt, mud.

vaseux, -euse /vɑzø, -z/ *a* (confus 🔟) woolly, hazy.

vaste /vast/ *a* vast, huge.

vaurien, ~ne /voʀjɛ̃, -ɛn/ *nm, f* good-for-nothing.

vautour /votuʀ/ *nm* vulture.

vautrer (se) /(sə)votʀe/ [1] *vpr* sprawl; **se ~ dans** (vice, boue) wallow in.

veau (*pl* ~x) /vo/ *nm* calf; (viande) veal; (cuir) calfskin.

vécu, ~e /veky/ *a* (réel) true, real. ● ⇒VIVRE [62].

vedette /vədɛt/ *nf* (artiste) star; **en** ~ (objet) in a prominent position; (personne) in the limelight; **joueur** ~ star player; (bateau) launch.

végétal (*mpl* -aux) /veʒetal, -o/ *a* plant. ● *nm* (*pl* -aux) plant.

végétalien, ~ne /veʒetaljɛ̃, -ɛn/ *a & nm,f* vegan.

végétarien, ~ne /veʒetaʀjɛ̃, -ɛn/ *a & nm,f* vegetarian.

végétation /veʒetasjɔ̃/ *nf* vegetation; ~s (Méd) adenoids.

véhicule /veikyl/ *nm* vehicle.

veille /vɛj/ *nf* (état) wakefulness; (jour précédent) **la** ~ (de) the day before; **la** ~ **de Noël** Christmas Eve; **à la** ~ **de** on the eve of; **la** ~ **au soir** the previous evening.

veillée /veje/ *nf* evening (gathering).

veiller /veje/ [1] *vi* stay up; (monter la garde) be on watch. ● *vt* (malade) watch over; ~ **à** attend to; ~ **sur** watch over.

veilleur /vɛjœʀ/ *nm* ~ **de nuit** night-watchman.

veilleuse /vɛjøz/ *nf* night light; (de véhicule) sidelight; (de réchaud) pilot light; **mettre qch en** ~ put sth on the back burner.

veine /vɛn/ *nf* (Anat) vein; (nervure, filon) vein; (chance 🔟) luck; **avoir de la** ~ 🔟 be lucky.

véliplanchiste /veliplɑ̃ʃist/ *nmf* windsurfer.

vélo /velo/ *nm* bike; (activité) cycling; **faire du** ~ go cycling; ~ **tout terrain** mountain bike.

vélomoteur /velɔmɔtœʀ/ *nm* moped.

velours /v(ə)luʀ/ *nm* velvet; ~ **côtelé** corduroy.

velouté, ~e /vəlute/ *a* smooth. ● *nm* (Culin) ~ **d'asperges** cream of asparagus soup.

vendanges /vɑ̃dɑ̃ʒ/ *nfpl* grape harvest.

vendeur, -euse /vɑ̃dœʀ, -øz/ *nm,f* shop assistant; (marchand) salesman, saleswoman; (Jur) vendor, seller.

vendre /vɑ̃dʀ/ [3] *vt* sell; **à** ~ for sale. □ **se** ~ *vpr* (être vendu) be sold; (trouver acquéreur) sell; **se** ~ **bien** sell well.

vendredi /vɑ̃dʀədi/ *nm* Friday; **V~ saint** Good Friday.

vénéneux, -euse /venenø, -z/ *a* poisonous.

vénérer /veneʀe/ [14] *vt* revere.

vénérien, ∼**ne** /venerjɛ̃, -ɛn/ a
maladie ∼**ne** venereal disease.

vengeance /vɑ̃ʒɑ̃s/ nf revenge,
vengeance.

venger /vɑ̃ʒe/ [40] vt avenge.
□ **se** ∼ vpr take ou get one's
revenge (**de qch** for sth; **de qn** on
sb).

vengeur, -eresse /vɑ̃ʒœʀ, -əʀɛs/
a vengeful. ● nm, f avenger.

venimeux, -euse /vənimø, -z/ a
poisonous, venomous.

venin /vənɛ̃/ nm venom.

venir /vəniʀ/ [58] vi (aux être)
come (**de** from); **faire** ∼ **qn** send
for sb, call sb; **en** ∼ **à** come to; **en**
∼ **aux mains** come to blows; **où**
veut-elle en ∼? what is she
driving at?; **il m'est venu à l'esprit**
or **à l'idée que** it occurred to me
that; **s'il venait à pleuvoir** if it
should rain; **dans les jours à** ∼ in
the next few days. ● v aux ∼ **de**
faire have just done; **il vient/venait**
d'arriver he has/had just arrived;
∼ **faire** come to do; **viens voir**
come and see.

vent /vɑ̃/ nm wind; **il fait du** ∼ it
is windy; **être dans le** ∼ 🔤 be
trendy.

vente /vɑ̃t/ nf sale; ∼ (**aux**
enchères) auction; **en** ∼ on ou for
sale; **mettre qch en** ∼ put sth up
for sale; ∼ **de charité** (charity)
bazaar; ∼ **au détail/en gros**
retailing/wholesaling; **équipe de**
∼ sales team.

ventilateur /vɑ̃tilatœʀ/ nm fan,
ventilator. **ventiler** [1] vt
ventilate.

ventouse /vɑ̃tuz/ nf suction pad;
(pour déboucher) plunger.

ventre /vɑ̃tʀ/ nm stomach;
(d'animal) belly; (utérus) womb; **avoir**
du ∼ have a paunch.

venu, -e /vəny/ a **bien** ∼ (à
propos) apt, timely; **mal** ∼ badly
timed; **il serait mal** ∼ **de faire** it

wouldn't be a good idea to do.
● ⇒VENIR [59].

venue /vəny/ nf coming.

ver /vɛʀ/ nm worm; (dans la
nourriture) maggot; (du bois)
woodworm; ∼ **luisant** glow-worm;
∼ **à soie** silkworm; ∼ **solitaire**
tapeworm; ∼ **de terre** earthworm.

verbal, -e (mpl **-aux**) /vɛʀbal,
-o/ a verbal.

verbe /vɛʀb/ nm verb.

verdir /vɛʀdiʀ/ [2] vi turn green.

véreux, -euse /veʀø, -z/ a
wormy; (malhonnête) shady.

verger /vɛʀʒe/ nm orchard.

verglas /vɛʀɡla/ nm black ice.

véridique /veʀidik/ a true.

vérification /veʀifikasjɔ̃/ nf
check(ing), verification.

vérifier /veʀifje/ [45] vt check,
verify; (confirmer) confirm.

véritable /veʀitabl/ a true, real;
(authentique) real.

vérité /veʀite/ nf truth; (de tableau,
roman) realism; **en** ∼ in fact,
actually.

vermine /vɛʀmin/ nf vermin.

verni, -e /vɛʀni/ a (chaussures)
patent (leather); (chanceux 🔤)
lucky.

vernir /vɛʀniʀ/ [2] vt varnish.
□ **se** ∼ vpr **se** ∼ **les ongles** apply
nail polish.

vernis /vɛʀni/ nm varnish; (de
poterie) glaze; ∼ **à ongles** nail
polish.

verra, verrait /veʀa, veʀɛ/ ⇒VOIR
[64].

verre /vɛʀ/ nm glass; (de lunettes)
lens; ∼ **à vin** wine glass; **prendre**
ou **boire un** ∼ have a drink; ∼ **de**
contact contact lens; ∼ **dépoli**
frosted glass.

verrière /veʀjɛʀ/ nf (toit) glass
roof; (paroi) glass wall.

verrou /veʀu/ nm bolt; **sous les**
∼**s** behind bars.

verrouillage /veʀujaʒ/ nm ∼

V

central or **centralisé** (**des portes**) central locking.

verrue /vɛʀy/ nf wart; ~ **plantaire** verruca.

vers[1] /vɛʀ/ prép towards; (aux environs de) (temps) about; (lieu) near, around; (période) towards; ~ **le soir** towards evening.

vers[2] /vɛʀ/ nm (poésie) line of verse.

versatile /vɛʀsatil/ a unpredictable, volatile.

verse: **à** ~ /avɛʀs/ loc in torrents.

Verseau /vɛʀso/ nm **le** ~ Aquarius.

versement /vɛʀsəmɑ̃/ nm payment; (échelonné) instalment.

verser /vɛʀse/ [1] vt/i pour; (larmes, sang) shed; (payer) pay. ●vi pour; (voiture) overturn; ~ **dans** (fig) lapse into.

version /vɛʀsjɔ̃/ nf version; (traduction) translation.

verso /vɛʀso/ nm back (of the page); **voir au** ~ see overleaf.

vert, ~**e** /vɛʀ, -t/ a green; (vieillard) sprightly. ●nm green; **les** ~**s** the Greens.

vertèbre /vɛʀtɛbʀ/ nf vertebra; **se déplacer une** ~ slip a disc.

vertical, ~**e** (mpl **-aux**) /vɛʀtikal, -o/ a vertical.

vertige /vɛʀtiʒ/ nm dizziness; ~**s** dizzy spells; **avoir le** ~ feel dizzy. **vertigineux**, **-euse** a dizzy; (très grand) staggering.

vertu /vɛʀty/ nf virtue; **en** ~ **de** in accordance with. **vertueux**, **-euse** a virtuous.

verveine /vɛʀvɛn/ nf verbena.

vessie /vesi/ nf bladder.

veste /vɛst/ nf jacket.

vestiaire /vɛstjɛʀ/ nm cloakroom; (Sport) changing-room; (US) locker-room.

vestibule /vɛstibyl/ nm hall; (Théât, d'hôtel) foyer.

vestige /vɛstiʒ/ nm (objet) relic; (trace) vestige.

veston /vɛstɔ̃/ nm jacket.

vêtement /vɛtmɑ̃/ nm article of clothing; ~**s** clothes, clothing.

vétéran /veteʀɑ̃/ nm veteran.

vétérinaire /veteʀinɛʀ/ nmf vet, veterinary surgeon, (US) veterinarian.

vêtir /vetiʀ/ [61] vt dress. □ **se** ~ vpr dress.

veto /veto/ nm inv veto.

vêtu, ~**e** /vety/ a dressed (**de** in).

veuf, **veuve** /vœf, -v/ a widowed. ●nm, f widower, widow.

veuille /vœj/ ⇒VOULOIR [64].

veut, **veux** /vø/ ⇒VOULOIR [64].

vexation /vɛksasjɔ̃/ nf humiliation.

vexer /vɛkse/ [1] vt upset, hurt. □ **se** ~ vpr be upset, be hurt.

viable /vjabl/ a viable; (projet) feasible.

viande /vjɑ̃d/ nf meat.

vibrer /vibʀe/ [1] vi vibrate; **faire** ~ (âme, foules) stir.

vicaire /vikɛʀ/ nm curate.

vice /vis/ nm (moral) vice; (physique) defect.

vicier /visje/ [45] vt contaminate; (air) pollute.

vicieux, **-ieuse** /visjø, -z/ a depraved. ●nm, f pervert.

victime /viktim/ nf victim; (d'un accident) casualty.

victoire /viktwaʀ/ nf victory; (Sport) win. **victorieux**, **-ieuse** a victorious; (équipe) winning.

vidange /vidɑ̃ʒ/ nf emptying; (Auto) oil change; (tuyau) waste pipe ou outlet.

vide /vid/ a empty. ●nm (absence, manque) vacuum, void; (espace) space; (trou) gap; (sans air) vacuum; **à** ~ empty; **emballé sous** ~ vacuum packed; **suspendu dans le** ~ dangling in space.

vidéo /video/ a inv video; **jeu** ~

video game. ●*nf* video.
vidéocassette *nf* video(tape).
vidéoclip *nm* music video.
vidéoconférence *nf*
videoconferencing; (séance)
videoconference. **vidéodisque**
nm videodisc. **vidéophone** *nm*
videophone.
vide-ordures /vidɔRdyR/ *nm inv*
rubbish chute.
vidéothèque /videotɛk/ *nf* video
library.
vider /vide/ [1] *vt* empty;
(*poisson*) gut; (expulser 🅘) throw
out. □ **se ~** *vpr* empty.
vie /vi/ *nf* life; (durée) lifetime; **à
~, pour la ~** for life; **donner la ~
à** give birth to; **en ~** alive; **la ~
est chère** the cost of living is
high.
vieil /vjɛj/ ⇨VIEUX.
vieillard /vjɛjaR/ *nm* old man.
vieille /vjɛj/ ⇨VIEUX.
vieillesse /vjɛjɛs/ *nf* old age.
vieillir /vjejiR/ [2] *vi* grow old,
age; (*mot, idée*) become old-
fashioned. ●*vt* age.
vieillissement *nm* ageing.
viens, vient /vjɛ̃/ ⇨VENIR [59].
vierge /vjɛRʒ/ *nf* virgin; **la V~**
Virgo. ●*a* virgin; (*feuille,
cassette*) blank; (*cahier, pellicule*)
unused, new.
vieux (**vieil** before vowel or mute
h), (*mpl* **vieux**) **vieille** /vjø, vjɛj/
a old. ●*nm, f* old man, old
woman; **petit ~** little old man; **les
~** old people; **vieille fille** (péj)
spinster; **~ garçon** old bachelor.
vieux jeu *a inv* old-fashioned.
vif, vive /vif, viv/ *a* (animé) lively;
(*émotion, vent*) keen; (*froid*)
biting; (*lumière*) bright; (*douleur,
contraste, parole*) sharp; (*souvenir, style, teint*) vivid; (*succès,
impatience*) great; **brûler/enterrer
~** burn/bury alive; **de vive voix**
personally. ●*nm* **à ~** (*plaie*)

open; **avoir les nerfs à ~** be on
edge; **blessé au ~** cut to the
quick.
vigie /viʒi/ *nf* lookout.
vigilant, ~e /viʒilɑ̃, -t/ *a* vigilant.
vigne /viɲ/ *nf* (plante) vine;
(vignoble) vineyard. **vigneron, ~ne**
nm, f wine-grower.
vignette /viɲɛt/ *nf* (étiquette) label;
(Auto) road tax disc.
vignoble /viɲɔbl/ *nm* vineyard.
vigoureux, -euse /viguRø, -z/ *a*
vigorous, sturdy.
vigueur /vigœR/ *nf* vigour; **être/
entrer en ~** (*loi*) be/come into
force; **en ~** current.
VIH *abrév m* (**virus immunodé-
ficitaire humain**) HIV.
vilain, ~e /vilɛ̃, -ɛn/ *a* (mauvais)
nasty; (laid) ugly. ●*nm, f* naughty
boy, naughty girl.
villa /villa/ *nf* detached house.
village /vilaʒ/ *nm* village.
villageois, ~e /vilaʒwa, -z/ *a*
village. ●*nm, f* villager.
ville /vil/ *nf* town; (importante) city;
~ d'eaux spa.
vin /vɛ̃/ *nm* wine; **~ d'honneur**
reception.
vinaigre /vinɛgR/ *nm* vinegar.
vinaigrette *nf* oil and vinegar
dressing, vinaigrette.
vingt /vɛ̃/ (/vɛ̃t/ *before vowel and
in numbers 22-29*) *a & nm* twenty.
vingtaine /vɛ̃tɛn/ *nf* **une ~** (**de**)
about twenty.
vingtième /vɛ̃tjɛm/ *a & nmf*
twentieth.
vinicole /vinikɔl/ *a* wine(-
producing).
viol /vjɔl/ *nm* (de femme) rape; (de
lieu, loi) violation.
violemment /vjɔlamɑ̃/ *adv*
violently.
violence /vjɔlɑ̃s/ *nf* violence;
(acte) act of violence. **violent, ~e**
a violent.

violer /vjɔle/ [1] vt rape; (*lieu, loi*) violate.

violet, ~**te** /vjɔlɛ, -t/ a purple. ● nm purple. **violette** nf violet.

violon /vjɔlɔ̃/ nm violin; ~ **d'Ingres** hobby.

violoncelle /vjɔlɔ̃sɛl/ nm cello.

vipère /vipɛʀ/ nf viper, adder.

virage /viʀaʒ/ nm bend; (en ski) turn; (*changement d'attitude*: fig) change of course.

virée /viʀe/ nf ▣ trip, tour; (en voiture) drive; (à vélo) ride.

virement /viʀmɑ̃/ nm (Comm) (credit) transfer; ~ **automatique** standing order.

virer /viʀe/ [1] vi turn; ~ **de bord** tack; (fig) do a U-turn; ~ **au rouge** turn red. ● vt (*argent*) transfer; (expulser ▣) throw out; (*élève*) expel; (licencier ▣) fire.

virgule /viʀgyl/ nf comma; (dans un nombre) (decimal) point.

viril, ~**e** /viʀil/ a virile.

virtuel, ~**le** /viʀtɥɛl/ a (potentiel) potential; (*mémoire, réalité*) virtual.

virulent, ~**e** /viʀylɑ̃, -t/ a virulent.

virus /viʀys/ nm virus.

vis¹ /vi/ ⇒VIVRE [62], VOIR [63].

vis² /vis/ nf screw.

visa /viza/ nm visa.

visage /vizaʒ/ nm face.

vis-à-vis /vizavi/ prép ~ **de** (en face de) opposite; (à l'égard de) in relation to; (comparé à) compared to, beside. ● nm inv (personne) person opposite; **en** ~ opposite each other.

visée /vize/ nf aim; **avoir des** ~**s sur** have designs on.

viser /vize/ [1] vt (*cible, centre*) aim at; (*poste, résultats*) aim for; (concerner) be aimed at; (*document*) stamp; ~ **à** aim at; (*mesure, propos*) be aimed at; ~ **à faire** aim to do. ● vi aim.

viseur /vizœʀ/ nm (d'arme) sights (+ pl); (Photo) viewfinder.

visière /vizjɛʀ/ nf (de casquette) peak; (de casque) visor.

vision /vizjɔ̃/ nf vision.

visite /vizit/ nf visit; (pour inspecter) inspection; (personne) visitor; **heures de** ~ visiting hours; ~ **guidée** guided tour; ~ **médicale** medical; **rendre** ~ **à**, **faire une** ~ **à** pay a visit; **être en** ~ (**chez qn**) be visiting (sb); **avoir de la** ~ have visitors.

visiter /vizite/ [1] vt visit; (*appartement*) view. **visiteur**, -**euse** nm, f visitor.

visser /vise/ vt screw (on).

visuel, ~**le** /vizɥɛl/ a visual. ● nm (Ordinat) visual display unit, VDU.

vit /vi/ ⇒VIVRE [62], VOIR [63].

vital, ~**e** (mpl -**aux**) /vital, -o/ a vital.

vitamine /vitamin/ nf vitamin.

vite /vit/ adv fast, quickly; (tôt) soon; ~! quick!; **faire** ~ be quick; **au plus** ~, **le plus** ~ **possible** as quickly as possible.

vitesse /vitɛs/ nf speed; (régime: Auto) gear; **à toute** ~ at top speed; **en** ~ in a hurry, quickly; **boîte à cinq** ~**s** five-speed gearbox.

viticole /vitikɔl/ a (*industrie*) wine; (*région*) wine-producing.

viticulteur nm wine-grower.

vitrage /vitʀaʒ/ nm (vitres) windows; **double** ~ double glazing.

vitrail (pl -**aux**) /vitʀaj, -o/ nm stained-glass window.

vitre /vitʀ/ nf (window) pane; (de véhicule) window.

vitrine /vitʀin/ nf (shop) window; (meuble) display cabinet.

vivace /vivas/ a (*plante*) perennial; (durable) enduring.

vivacité /vivasite/ nf liveliness; (agilité) quickness; (d'émotion, d'intelligence) keenness; (de souvenir, style, teint) vividness.

vivant, **~e** /vivɑ̃, -t/ *a* (*example, symbole*) living; (en vie) alive, living; (actif, vif) lively. ● *nm* un bon **~** a bon viveur; **de son ~** in his lifetime; **les ~s** the living.

vive¹ /viv/ ⇒VIF.

vive² /viv/ *interj* **~ le roi!** long live the king!

vivement /vivmɑ̃/ *adv* (fortement) strongly; (vite, sèchement) sharply; (avec éclat) vividly; (beaucoup) greatly; **~ la fin!** I'll be glad when it's the end!

vivier /vivje/ *nm* fish pond; (artificiel) fish tank.

vivifier /vivifje/ [45] *vt* invigorate.

vivre /vivʀ/ [62] *vi* live; **~ de** (*nourriture*) live on; **~ encore** be still alive; **faire ~** (*famille*) support. ● *vt* (vie) live; (*période, aventure*) live through.

vivres /vivʀ/ *nmpl* supplies.

VO *abrév f* (**version originale**) **en ~** in the original language.

vocabulaire /vɔkabylɛʀ/ *nm* vocabulary.

vocal, **~e** (*mpl* **-aux**) /vɔkal, -o/ *a* vocal.

vœu (*pl* **~x**) /vø/ *nm* (souhait) wish; (promesse) vow; **meilleurs ~x** best wishes.

vogue /vɔg/ *nf* fashion, vogue; **en ~** in fashion ou vogue.

voguer /vɔge/ [1] *vi* sail.

voici /vwasi/ *prép* here is, this is; (au pluriel) here are, these are; **me ~** here I am; **~ un an** (temps passé) a year ago; **~ un an que** it is a year since.

voie /vwa/ *nf* (route) road; (partie de route) lane; (chemin) way; (moyen) means, way; (rails) track; (quai) platform; **en ~ de** in the process of; **en ~ de développement** (*pays*)

developing; **espèce en ~ de disparition** endangered species; **par la ~ des airs** by air; **par ~ orale** orally; **sur la bonne/mauvaise ~** (fig) on the right/wrong track; **montrer la ~** lead the way; **~ de dégagement** slip-road; **~ ferrée** railway; (US) railroad; **V~ lactée** Milky Way; **~ navigable** waterway; **~ publique** public highway; **~ sans issue** (sur panneau) no through road; (fig) dead end.

voilà /vwala/ *prép* there is, that is; (au pluriel) there are, those are; (voici) here is, here are; **le ~** there he is; **~!** right!; (en offrant qch) there you are!; **~ un an** (temps passé) a year ago; **~ un an que** it is a year since; **tu en veux? en ~** do you want some? here you are; **en ~ des histoires!** what a fuss!; **et ~ que** and then.

voilage /vwalaʒ/ *nm* net curtain.

voile /vwal/ *nf* (de bateau) sail; (Sport) sailing. ● *nm* veil; (tissu léger) net.

voilé, **~e** /vwale/ *a* (allusion, femme) veiled; (flou) hazy.

voiler /vwale/ [1] *vt* (dissimuler) veil; (déformer) buckle. □ **se ~** *vpr* (devenir flou) become hazy; (se déformer) (roue) buckle.

voilier /vwalje/ *nm* sailing ship.

voir /vwaʀ/ [63] *vt* see; **faire ~ qch à qn** show sth to sb; **laisser ~** show; **avoir quelque chose à ~ avec** have something to do with; **ça n'a rien à ~** that's got nothing to do with it; **je ne peux pas le ~** I can't stand him. ● *vi* **y ~** be able to see; **je n'y vois rien** I cannot see; **~ trouble** have blurred vision; **voyons** let's see now; **voyons, soyez sages!** come on now, behave yourselves! □ **se ~** *vpr* (dans la glace) see oneself; (être visible) show; (se produire) be seen; (se trouver) find oneself; (se fréquenter, se rencontrer) see each other; (être vu) be seen.

voire /vwaʀ/ *adv* or even, not to say.

voirie /vwaʀi/ *nf* (service) highway maintenance.

voisin, ~e /vwazɛ̃, -in/ *a* (de voisinage) neighbouring; (proche) nearby; (adjacent) next (**de** to); (semblable) similar (**de** to). ● *nm, f* neighbour; **le ~** the man next door, the neighbour. **voisinage** *nm* neighbourhood; (proximité) proximity.

voiture /vwatyʀ/ *nf* (motor) car; (wagon) coach, carriage; **en ~!** all aboard!; **~ bélier** ramraiding car; **~ à cheval** horse-drawn carriage; **~ de course** racing car; **~ école** driving school car; **~ d'enfant** pram; (US) baby carriage; **~ de tourisme** saloon car.

voix /vwa/ *nf* voice; (suffrage) vote; **à ~ basse** in a whisper.

vol /vɔl/ *nm* (d'avion, d'oiseau) flight; (groupe d'oiseaux) flock, flight; (délit) theft; (hold-up) robbery; **~ à l'étalage** shoplifting; **~ à la tire** pickpocketing; **à ~ d'oiseau** as the crow flies; **de haut ~** high-ranking; **~ libre** hang-gliding; **~ à voile** gliding.

volaille /vɔlɑj/ *nf* **la ~** (poules) poultry; **une ~** a fowl.

volant /vɔlɑ̃/ *nm* (steering-) wheel; (de jupe) flounce; (de badminton) shuttlecock; **donner un coup de ~** turn the wheel sharply.

volcan /vɔlkɑ̃/ *nm* volcano.

volée /vɔle/ *nf* flight; (oiseaux) flight, flock; (de coups, d'obus, au tennis) volley; **à toute ~** hard; **à la ~** in flight, in mid-air.

voler /vɔle/ [1] *vi* (oiseau) fly; (dérober) steal ● *vt* steal; **~ qn** rob sb; **il ne l'a pas volé** he deserved it.

volet /vɔlɛ/ *nm* (de fenêtre) shutter; (de document) (folded *ou* tear-off) section; **trié sur le ~** hand-picked.

voleur, -euse /vɔlœʀ, -øz/ *nm, f* thief; **au ~!** stop thief! ● *a* thieving.

volley-ball /vɔlɛbol/ *nm* volleyball.

volontaire /vɔlɔ̃tɛʀ/ *a* (délibéré) voluntary; (opiniâtre) determined. ● *nmf* volunteer. **volontairement** *adv* voluntarily; (exprès) intentionally.

volonté /vɔlɔ̃te/ *nf* (faculté, intention) will; (souhait) wish; (énergie) will-power; **à ~** (comme on veut) as required; **du vin à ~** unlimited wine; **bonne ~** goodwill; **mauvaise ~** ill will.

volontiers /vɔlɔ̃tje/ *adv* (de bon gré) with pleasure, willingly, gladly; (admettre) readily.

volt /vɔlt/ *nm* volt.

volte-face /vɔltəfas/ *nf inv* (fig) U-turn; **faire ~** do a U-turn.

voltige /vɔltiʒ/ *nf* acrobatics (+ *pl*).

volume /vɔlym/ *nm* volume.

volumineux, -euse /vɔlyminø, -z/ *a* bulky; (livre, dossier) thick.

volupté /vɔlypte/ *nf* voluptuousness.

vomir /vɔmi/ *nm* vomit.

vomir /vɔmiʀ/ [2] *vt* vomit; (fig) belch out. ● *vi* be sick, vomit.

vomissement /vɔmismɑ̃/ *nm* vomiting; **~s du matin** morning sickness.

vont /vɔ̃/ ⇒ALLER [8].

vorace /vɔʀas/ *a* voracious.

vos /vo/ ⇒VOTRE.

votant, ~e /vɔtɑ̃, -t/ *nm, f* voter.

vote /vɔt/ *nm* (action) voting; (suffrage) vote; **~ d'une loi** passing of a bill; **~ par correspondance/ procuration** postal/proxy vote.

voter /vɔte/ [1] *vi* vote. ● *vt* vote for; (adopter) pass; (crédits) vote.

votre (*pl* **vos**) /vɔtʀ, vo/ *a* your.

vôtre /votʀ/ *pron* **le** *ou* **la ~, les ~s** yours.

vouer /vwe/ [1] *vt* (*vie, temps*) dedicate (à to); **voué à l'échec** doomed to failure.

vouloir /vulwaʀ/ [64] *vt* (*exiger*) want (**faire** to do); (*souhaiter*) want; **que veux-tu boire?** what would you like to drink?; **je voudrais bien y aller** I'd really like to go; **je veux bien venir** I'm happy to come; **comme tu voudras** as you wish; (*accepter*) **veuillez vous asseoir** please sit down; **veuillez patienter** (au téléphone) please hold the line; (*signifier*) **~ dire** mean; **qu'est-ce que cela veut dire?** what does that mean?; **en ~ à qn** bear a grudge against sb. □ **s'en ~** *vpr* regret; **je m'en veux de lui avoir dit** I really regret having told her.

voulu, ~e /vuly/ *a* (*délibéré*) intentional; (*requis*) required.

vous /vu/ *pron* (*sujet, complément*) you; (*indirect*) (to) you; (*réfléchi*) yourself; (*pluriel*) yourselves; (*l'un l'autre*) each other. **vous-même** *pron* yourself. **vous-mêmes** *pron* yourselves.

voûte /vut/ *nf* (*plafond*) vault; (*porche*) archway.

vouvoiement /vuvwamɑ̃/ *nm* use of the 'vous' form. **vouvoyer** [31] *vt* address using the 'vous' form.

voyage /vwajaʒ/ *nm* trip; (*déplacement*) journey; (*par mer*) voyage; **~(s)** (*action*) travelling; **~ d'affaires** business trip; **~ d'études** study trip; **~ de noces** honeymoon; **~ organisé** (package) tour.

voyager /vwajaʒe/ [40] *vi* travel.

voyageur, -euse /vwajaʒœʀ, -øz/ *nm, f* traveller; (*passager*) passenger; **~ de commerce** travelling salesman.

voyant, ~e /vwajɑ̃, -t/ *a* gaudy. ● *nm* (signal) (warning) light.

voyelle /vwajɛl/ *nf* vowel.

voyou /vwaju/ *nm* hooligan.

vrac: en ~ /ɑ̃vʀak/ *loc* (pêle-mêle) haphazardly; (sans emballage) loose; (en gros) in bulk.

vrai, ~e /vʀɛ/ *a* true; (*authentique*) real. ● *nm* truth; **à ~ dire** to tell the truth; **pour de ~** for real.

vraiment *adv* really.

vraisemblable /vʀɛsɑ̃blabl/ *a* (probable) likely; (*excuse, histoire*) plausible. **vraisemblablement** *adv* probably. **vraisemblance** *nf* likelihood, plausibility.

vrombir /vʀɔ̃biʀ/ [2] *vi* roar.

VRP *abrév m* (**voyageur représentant placier**) rep, representative.

VTT *abrév m* (**vélo tout terrain**) mountain bike.

vu, ~e /vy/ *a* **bien ~** well thought of; **ce serait plutôt mal ~** it wouldn't go down well; **bien ~!** good point! ● *prép* in view of; **~ que** seeing that. ● ⇒VOIR [63].

vue /vy/ *nf* (spectacle) sight; (vision) (eye)sight; (panorama, idée, image, photo) view; **avoir en ~** have in mind; **à ~** (tirer) on sight; (*payable*) at sight; **de ~** by sight; **perdre de ~** lose sight of; **en ~** (proche) in sight; (célèbre) in the public eye; **en ~ de faire** with a view to doing; **à ~ d'œil** visibly; **avoir des ~s sur** have designs on.

vulgaire /vylgɛʀ/ *a* (grossier) vulgar; (ordinaire) common.

vulnérable /vylneʀabl/ *a* vulnerable.

wagon /vagɔ̃/ *nm* (de voyageurs)
carriage; (de marchandises) wagon.
wagon-lit (*pl* **wagons-lits**)
nm sleeper. **wagon-restaurant** (*pl*
wagons-restaurants) *nm*
restaurant car.
walkman® /wokman/ *nm*
personal stereo, walkman®.
waters /watɛʀ/ *nmpl* toilets.
watt /wat/ *nm* watt.
wc /(dublə)vese/ *nmpl* toilet (+
sg).
Web /wɛb/ *nm* Web; **un site** ~ a
website; **une page** ~ web page.
webcam /wɛbkam/ *nf* webcam.
webmestre /wɛbmɛstʀ/ *nm*
webmaster.
week-end /wikɛnd/ *nm*
weekend.
whisky (*pl* **-ies**) /wiski/ *nm*
whisky.

xénophobe /gzenɔfɔb/ *a*
xenophobic. ●*nmf* xenophobe.
xérès /gzeʀɛs/ *nm* sherry.
xylophone /ksilɔfon/ *nm*
xylophone.

y /i/
●*adverbe*
••••► there; (dessus) on it; (pluriel) on
them; (dedans) in it; (pluriel) in
them; **j'**~ **vais** I'm on my way;
n'~ **va pas** don't go; **du lait? il
n'**~ **en a pas** milk? there's none;
tu n'~ **arriveras jamais** you'll
never manage it.

●*pronom*
••••► **s'**~ **habituer** get used to it.
••••► **s'**~ **attendre** expect it.
••••► ~ **penser** think about it.
••••► ~ **être pour qch** have sth to do
with it.

yaourt /'jauʀ(t)/ *nm* yoghurt.
yaourtière *nf* yoghurt-maker.
yard /'jaʀd/ *nm* yard (= *91,44 cm*).
yen /'jɛn/ *nm* yen.
yeux /jø/ ⇒ŒIL.
yoga /'jɔga/ *nm* yoga.
yougoslave /'jugɔslav/ *a*
Yugoslav. **Y**~ *nmf* Yugoslav.
Yougoslavie /'jugɔslavi/ *nf*
Yugoslavia.
yo-yo® /'jojo/ *nm inv* yo-yo®.

zapper /zape/ [1] *vi* (à la télévision) channel-hop.

zèbre /zɛbʀ/ *nm* zebra.

zèle /zɛl/ *nm* zeal.

zéro /zeʀo/ *nm* nought, zero; (température) zero; (Sport) nil; (tennis) love; (personne) nonentity; **partir de** ∼ start from scratch; **repartir à** ∼ start all over again.

zeste /zɛst/ *nm* peel; **un** ∼ **de** (fig) a touch of.

zézayer /zezeje/ [31] *vi* lisp.

zigzag /zigzag/ *nm* zigzag; **en** ∼ winding.

zinc /zɛ̃g/ *nm* (métal) zinc; (comptoir ⊞) bar.

zizanie /zizani/ *nf* discord; **semer la** ∼ put the cat among the pigeons.

zizi /zizi/ *nm* ⊞ willy.

zodiaque /zɔdjak/ *nm* zodiac.

zona /zona/ *nm* (Méd) shingles (+ *sg*).

zone /zon/ *nf* zone, area; (banlieue pauvre) slums; ∼ **bleue** restricted parking zone; ∼ **euro** euro zone.

zoo /zo(o)/ *nm* zoo.

zoom /zum/ *nm* zoom lens.

zut /zyt/ *interj* ⊞ damn ⊞.

Z

Test yourself with word games

This section contains a number of word games which will help
you to use your dictionary more effectively and to build up your
knowledge of French vocabulary and usage in an entertaining
way. You will find answers to all puzzles and games at the end of
the section.

1 Madame Irma

Madame Irma is very good at predicting the future, but she is
not very good at conjugating French verbs in the future tense.
Help her to replace all the verbs in brackets with the correct
future form.

Lion 23 juillet–22 août

Cette semaine, les Lions (être) à la fête.
Travail: Il ne (falloir) pas vous laisser
démoraliser par les problèmes et les
discussions qui (pouvoir) surgir en début de
semaine. Les 19 et 20 avril vous (offrir) la possibilité
d'un changement radical dans votre carrière. Pourquoi
ne pas saisir votre chance? **Santé**: Le stress ne vous
(épargner) pas, surtout le 18. Attention! Pour
décompresser, faites un peu de sport et tout (aller) bien.
Amitié: Vous êtes très sociable et cette semaine, vous
vous (faire) encore de nouveaux amis. **Côté cœur**:
Vénus (veiller) sur vous. Une nouvelle rencontre
(survenir) peut-être. Si vous avez un partenaire,
votre relation (être) au beau fixe.

2 Power cut

Unfortunately, there was a power cut while Jean was writing a computer manual for his office staff. He had just begun to label his diagram of a computer. Can you help Jean unscramble the letters and get on with his labelling?

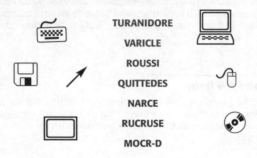

TURANIDORE

VARICLE

ROUSSI

QUITTEDES

NARCE

RUCRUSE

MOCR-D

3 The odd meaning out

Watch out: one word can have different meanings. In the following exercise, only two of the suggested translations are correct. Use the dictionary to spot the odd one out, then find the correct French translation for it.

example:

blindé   ❏ armoured

    ☑ blind

    ❏ immune

blind = aveugle

lentille   ❏ lentil

    ❏ lens

    ❏ lent

porte   ❏ door

    ❏ carry

    ❏ port (wine)

gauche   ❏ left

    ❏ gauge

    ❏ awkward

duvet   ❏ duvet

    ❏ down

    ❏ sleeping-bag

4 Word magnets

Antoine's brother took all his magnets off the fridge door to wipe it clean. He put them back the wrong way round. Can you help Antoine rewrite the correct sentences?

| heure | hier | suis | me | levé | bonne | de | je |

| dit | pourtant | je | fois | lui | plusieurs | ai | le |

| sur | sortant | table | les | prends | clés | en | la |

| ira | Portugal | elle | prochaine | au | vacances | l'année | en |

| film | voir | un | allés | cinéma | sommes | nous | au |

| voisine | de | là | frère | pas | le | la | n'est |

5 What are they like?

Here are two lists of adjectives you can use to describe people's characteristics. Each word in the second column is the opposite of one of the adjectives in the first column. Can you link them?

1. grand	A. intelligent
2. blond	B. méchant
3. bête	C. gros
4. énervé	D. petit
5. gentil	E. sympathique
6. timide	F. brun
7. patient	G. calme
8. désagréable	H. extraverti
9. poli	I. impatient
10. maigre	J. malpoli

example: 1.D. *grand* est le contraire de *petit*.

6 The odd one out

In each of the following series, all the words but one are related.
Find the odd one out and explain why. If there are words you
don't know, use your dictionary to find out what they mean.

example: stylo, agenda, livre, carnet scolaire, brosse à dents

The odd one out is 'brosse à dents', because you wouldn't find it in a
schoolbag.

1. voiture, avion, moteur, train, autocar

2. casserole, poêle, cafetière, cendrier, saladier

3. télévision, cassette, chaîne-hifi, magnétoscope, baladeur

4. ski nautique, natation, plongée, varappe, planche à voile

5. redoubler, courir, sauter, glisser, descendre, monter

6. chou, sou, caillou, genou, hibou, bijou

7 The shopping list

Paul has prepared a shopping list. When his friend sees the list, he realises that he needs exactly the same things. He asks Paul whether he would mind buying two of everything. Help Paul rewrite his list.

Watch out: the plurals of compound nouns are irregular. If in doubt, look them up in your dictionary.

Acheter:	Acheter:
- un taille-crayons	deux taille-crayons
- un bloc-notes	....
- un timbre-poste	....
- un abat-jour	....
- un couvre-lit	....
- un cache-nez	....
- un tire-bouchon	....
- un ouvre-boîtes	....
- un réveille-matin	....
- un chou-fleur	....

8 The mystery word

To fill in the grid, find the French words for all the musical instruments illustrated below. Once you have completed the grid, you'll discover the name of a famous classical composer.

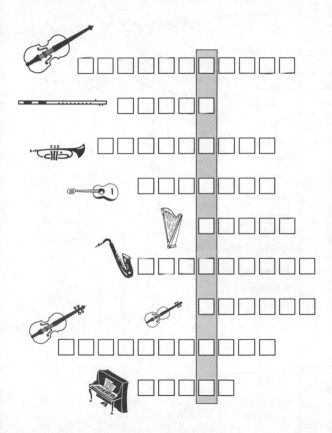

The composer is _ _ _ _ _ _ _ _ _ .

9 Body parts

Can you put the right number in the boxes next to the French words in the list?

- [ ] la bouche
- [ ] le bras
- [ ] la cheville
- [ ] le cou
- [ ] le coude
- [ ] la cuisse
- [ ] le doigt
- [ ] l'épaule
- [ ] le front
- [ ] le genou
- [ ] la hanche
- [ ] la jambe
- [ ] la joue
- [ ] la main
- [ ] le menton
- [ ] le mollet
- [ ] le nez
- [ ] le nombril
- [ ] l'œil
- [ ] l'oreille
- [ ] l'orteil
- [ ] le pied
- [ ] le poignet
- [ ] la tête

10 Liar liar!

Today, Sabine had a day off. She tells her mother what she has been up to:

> *« Ce matin, je me suis levée juste après ton départ. J'ai bu du café au lait et j'ai mangé des tartines. Après avoir fait ma toilette et m'être habillée, je suis allée au parc. Il faisait très beau et j'avais envie de me promener. Je suis revenue à la maison pour chercher mon maillot de bain et je suis allée à la piscine découverte. J'y suis restée pendant deux heures. En sortant, j'avais très faim, alors je me suis installée dans un café. J'ai commandé un sandwich. Après ça, je suis allée au cinéma. Le film était super! Je suis rentrée à la maison un peu avant que tu arrives. »*

What she doesn't say is that her little brother, Adrien, skipped school to spend the day with her. Rewrite her statement.

> *« Ce matin, nous nous sommes levés juste après ton départ... »*

Answers

1

seront	ira
faudra	ferez
pourront	veillera
offriront	surviendra
épargnera	sera

2

ordinateur	écran
clavier	curseur
souris	cd-rom
disquette	

3

lent = prêté
port = porto
gauge = jauge
duvet = couette

4

Hier, je me suis levé de bonne heure.
Pourtant, je le lui ai dit plusieurs fois.
Prends les clés sur la table en sortant.
L'année prochaine, elle ira en vacances au Portugal.
Nous sommes allés voir un film au cinéma.
Le frère de la voisine n'est pas là.

5

1.D. *grand* est le contraire de *petit*.
2.F. *blond* est le contraire de *brun*.
3.A. *bête* est le contraire d'*intelligent*.
4.G. *énervé* est le contraire de *calme*.
5.B. *gentil* est le contraire de *méchant*.
6.H. *timide* est le contraire d'*extraverti*.
7.I. *patient* est le contraire d'*impatient*.
8.E. *désagréable* est le contraire de *sympathique*.
9.J. *poli* est le contraire de *malpoli*.
10.C. *maigre* est le contraire de *gros*.

6

1. moteur—because it isn't a vehicle
2. cendrier—because it is not used for cooking
3. cassette—because it isn't an electrical device
4. varappe—because it is the only sport in the list which isn't a water-sport
5. redoubler—because it is the only verb in the list which doesn't describe a movement
6. sou—because it ends in "-s" in the plural, not in "-x" like the other five

7

deux taille-crayons
deux blocs-notes
deux timbres-poste
deux abat-jour
deux couvre-lits

deux cache-nez
deux tire-bouchons
deux ouvre-boîtes
deux réveille-matin
deux choux-fleurs

8

```
C O N T R E B A S S E
      F L U T E
   T R O M P E T T E
      G U I T A R E
         H A R P E
   S A X O P H O N E
         V I O L O N
V I O L O N C E L L E
      P I A N O
```

9

6. la bouche	15. le doigt	4. la joue	3. l'œil
11. le bras	10. l'épaule	14. la main	8. l'oreille
22. la cheville	2. le front	7. le menton	24. l'orteil
9. le cou	20. le genou	21. le mollet	23. le pied
12. le coude	17. la hanche	5. le nez	13. le poignet
18. la cuisse	19. la jambe	16. le nombril	1. la tête

10

*"Ce matin, nous nous sommes levés, juste après ton départ.
Nous avons bu du café au lait et nous avons mangé des tartines.
Après avoir fait notre toilette et nous être habillés, nous sommes
allés au parc. Il faisait très beau et nous avions envie de nous
promener. Nous sommes revenus à la maison pour chercher nos
maillots de bain et nous sommes allés à la piscine découverte.
Nous y sommes restés pendant deux heures. En sortant, nous
avions très faim, alors nous nous sommes installés dans un café.
Nous avons commandé des sandwichs. Après ça, nous sommes
allés au cinéma. Le film était super! Nous sommes rentrés à la
maison un peu avant que tu arrives."*

Calendar of French traditions, festivals, and holidays

January

1	8	15	22	29
2	9	16	23	30
3	10	17	24	31
4	11	18	25	
5	12	19	26	
6	13	20	27	
7	14	21	28	

February

1	8	15	22
2	9	16	23
3	10	17	24
4	11	18	25
5	12	19	26
6	13	20	27
7	**14**	21	28

March

1	8	15	22	29
2	9	16	23	30
3	10	17	24	31
4	11	18	25	
5	12	19	26	
6	13	20	27	
7	14	21	28	

April

1	8	15	22	29
2	9	16	23	30
3	10	17	24	31
4	11	18	25	
5	12	19	26	
6	13	20	27	
7	14	21	28	

May

1	**8**	15	22	29
2	9	16	23	30
3	10	17	24	31
4	11	18	25	
5	12	19	26	
6	13	20	27	
7	14	21	28	

June

1	8	15	22	29
2	9	16	23	30
3	10	17	**24**	
4	11	18	25	
5	12	19	26	
6	13	20	27	
7	14	21	28	

July

1	8	15	22	29
2	9	16	23	30
3	10	17	24	31
4	11	18	25	
5	12	19	26	
6	13	20	27	
7	**14**	21	28	

August

1	8	**15**	22	29
2	9	16	23	30
3	10	17	24	31
4	11	18	25	
5	12	19	26	
6	13	20	27	
7	14	21	28	

September

1	8	15	22	29
2	9	16	23	30
3	10	17	24	
4	11	18	25	
5	12	19	26	
6	13	20	27	
7	14	21	28	

October

1	8	15	22	29
2	9	16	23	30
3	10	17	24	31
4	11	18	25	
5	12	19	26	
6	13	20	27	
7	14	21	28	

November

1	8	15	22	29
2	9	16	23	30
3	10	17	24	
4	**11**	18	25	
5	12	19	26	
6	13	20	27	
7	14	21	28	

December

1	**8**	15	22	29
2	9	16	23	30
3	10	17	**24**	**31**
4	11	18	**25**	
5	12	19	**26**	
6	13	20	27	
7	14	21	28	

1 January

le jour de l'an (New Year's Day) is a public holiday and a day of family celebration, with a large lunch, traditionally featuring seafood of various kinds.

6 January

la Fête des Rois (Epiphany or Twelfth Night). Around this time, most families have a *galette des Rois*, a rich pastry cake filled with *frangipane* (almond paste). The cake contains a *fève*, literally a bean, as this is what was originally used. Nowadays the *fève* takes the form of a tiny plastic or ceramic figure. The person who gets the *fève* in their portion puts on the cardboard crown which comes with the cake.

2 February

la Chandeleur (Candlemas) is celebrated in the church but is not a public holiday. However, it is traditional to eat *crêpes* (pancakes) on this day.

14 February

la Saint Valentin (St Valentine's Day). As in many other countries, people celebrate a romantic relationship with gifts of flowers or chocolates.

1 April

le premier avril (April Fool's Day). The French also take advantage of this occasion to play tricks on one another, calling out *poisson d'avril!* (literally 'April fish').

1 May

La Fête du Travail (International Labour Day) is a public holiday.

8 May

le 8 mai or **la Fête de la Victoire** is a public holiday commemorating Victory in Europe on 8 May 1945.

24 June

la Saint-Jean (Midsummer's Day). In many areas, bonfires (*les feux de la Saint-Jean*) are lit on Midsummer's Night. People are supposed to jump over these, re-enacting a pagan custom intended to ward off the cold of winter.

14 July

la Fête Nationale or **le 14 juillet** is usually called Bastille Day in English and is a public holiday in France. It commemorates the taking of the Bastille prison in Paris and the liberation of its prisoners by the people of Paris in 1789, one of the first events of the Revolution. All over France there are parades on the day of the 14th and firework displays and *bals* (local dances) either on the night of the 13th or of the 14th.

15 August

l'Assomption (Feast of the Assumption) is a public holiday. Many people in France are either setting off on holiday around the 15th or else returning home, so this is traditionally a very busy time on the roads.

1 November

la Toussaint (All Saints' Day) is a public holiday and the day when people remember their dead relatives and friends, although properly speaking it is All Souls' Day the following day that is set aside for this in the church. People take flowers to the cemetery, particularly chrysanthemums, as these are in bloom at this time. Because of this association, it is best to avoid taking chrysanthemums as a gift for someone. Schoolchildren have a two-week holiday around this time.

11 November

le 11 novembre is a public holiday to commemorate the Armistice of 1918 and a day of remembrance for those who died in the two world wars and in subsequent conflicts. All towns and villages hold parades in which war veterans accompany local officials and a brass band to lay wreaths on the war memorial. In Paris, the President lays a wreath on the tomb of the unknown soldier beneath the *Arc de Triomphe* on the *Champs-Élysées*.

8 December

la fête de l'Immaculée Conception (Feast of the Immaculate Conception).
In the city of Lyons, this is celebrated as la Fête de la Lumière (Festival of Light) said to commemorate the Virgin's intervention to prevent the plague reaching Lyons in the Middle Ages. People put rows of candles in coloured glass jars on the outsides of their windowsills, so that all the buildings in the centre of the city are illuminated.

24 December

la veille de Noël (Christmas Eve) is the time when most people exchange presents. Many people go to *la messe de minuit* (midnight mass).

25 December

Noël (Christmas) is a public holiday and a day of eating and drinking. Lunch will often start with a variety of seafood, oysters being particularly popular. Turkey is often eaten as a main course, sometimes with chestnut stuffing. A variety of cheeses will be followed by *la bûche de Noël*, a rich chocolate cake in the form of a snow-covered log. French people do not usually send Christmas cards, the custom being to send wishes for the coming year to more distant friends and relatives during the month of January.

26 December

There is no particular name for the day after Christmas Day and it is not a public holiday.

31 December

la Saint-Sylvestre (New Year's Eve). Many people have parties to celebrate *le réveillon du Nouvel An* (New Year's Eve Party). Once again, food plays a major part and, as at Christmas, this is a time to splash out on luxury foods such as *foie gras*. There will often be dancing and the New Year will be welcomed in with champagne.

Movable feasts

Mardi gras

Shrove Tuesday, the last day of carnival before the beginning of Lent on Ash Wednesday. Traditionally, *crêpes* (pancakes) are eaten for supper. In many areas of France, sugared fritters called *bugnes* in and around Lyons and *oreillettes* farther south, are eaten between *la fête des Rois* and *mardi gras*.

le Vendredi saint

Good Friday is celebrated in the church, but is not a public holiday.

Pâques

Easter Sunday, *le dimanche de Pâques*, is for many people the occasion for a big family lunch. Easter hunts are organised for children, with chocolate eggs, rabbits, hens, or fish traditionally hidden in the family garden. *Le lundi de Pâques* (Easter Monday) is a public holiday.

l'Ascension the Thursday forty days after Easter is a public holiday in France.

la Pentecôte (Whitsun) on the seventh Sunday after Easter represents for many people the first long weekend of the summer, as *le lundi de la Pentecôte* (Whit Monday) is a public holiday. Many families go to stay with friends or relatives in the country.

la Fête des mères (Mother's Day) is the Sunday after *Pentecôte*. This is another occasion for a big family meal, with presents for the mother. **La fête des pères** (Father's Day) is celebrated in similar fashion two weeks later.

A–Z of French life and culture

Académie française
A learned body whose main role nowadays is to monitor new developments in the French language and to make decisions as to what is acceptable and what is not, although these decisions are not always taken entirely seriously by the public at large. Its 40 members are elected for life on the basis of their contribution to scholarship or literature.

Alliance Française
A private organization which aims to spread awareness of French language and culture. It has centres in cities throughout the world, providing classes and a variety of cultural activities.

année scolaire
The French school year starts with the **RENTRÉE** des classes in early September and ends in early July. There is a week's holiday in late October/early November around *la Toussaint* (All Saints' Day, 1 November), two weeks around Christmas and New Year, two weeks in February, and two weeks in April.

Antenne 2 ▸ FRANCE 2

arrondissement
The three largest cities in France – Paris, Lyons, and Marseilles – are divided into numbered administrative areas called *arrondissements*. Each has its own mayor and council, and the number of the *arrondissement* is usually part of the postcode. The system makes for a convenient way for people to talk about which part of the city they live in e.g. *'le neuvième arrondissement'* or simply *'le neuvième'*. An *arrondissement* is also a sub-division of a **DÉPARTEMENT**.

ARTE
A television channel, run jointly by France and Germany, which provides a high standard of cultural programmes.

Assemblée Nationale
The lower house of the French parliament, also called the *Chambre des députés*. There are 577 **DÉPUTÉS**, elected for a five-year term, often after two rounds of voting as at least 50% of the vote must be obtained.

Astérix

A hugely popular comic-book character invented by cartoonists Goscinny and Uderzo. *Astérix* is a tiny but invincible village leader in the ancient province of Gaul, whose fictional adventures with his fellow-villagers often involve fighting and outwitting the occupying Romans and make for gentle mockery of cultures outside Gaul. The *Astérix* books have been translated into 40 languages.

autoroute

France has an extensive motorway system, which is largely financed by tolls calculated according to the distance travelled and the vehicle type. Tickets are obtained and tolls paid at *péages* (tollgates). There is a speed limit for standard vehicles of 130 km/h (approx. 80 mph) and 110 km/h (approx. 70 mph) in wet weather.

baccalauréat

The *baccalauréat*, generally known informally as the *Bac*, is the examination sat in the final year of the LYCÉE (la *terminale*), so usually at age 17 or 18. Students sit exams in a fairly broad range of subjects in a particular category: the *Bac S* places emphasis on the sciences, for example, whilst the *Bac L* has a literary bias. Some categories cater for students specializing in more directly job-based subjects such as agriculture. The final result is given as a single overall mark or grade out of 20, although the scores for individual subjects are also given. It is common to use the *Bac* as a point of reference in job advertisements, so that *Bac + 4* would mean a person who had completed 4 years of fulltime study after the *Bac*, with appropriate diplomas to show for it.

bachelier

The holder of the BACCALAURÉAT, entitled to enrol for university courses.

bande dessinée (BD)

Comic books of all sorts and for a wide variety of age and interest groups are immensely popular in France and form an important part of French culture. Cartoon characters such as *Astérix*, *Lucky Luke*, and *Tintin* are household names and older comic books are often collectors' items.

Basque

The Basque country extends on both sides of the Pyrenees with about one quarter of a million Basques living in France and ten times that number in Spain. The French Basque region (*le Pays basque français*) does not have any autonomous status nor is

Basque recognized as an official language. It is, however, taught in some schools, and there are an estimated 40,000 Basque speakers in France.

boules

A type of bowls, also called PÉTANQUE, played all over France, using metal boules and a jack known as a *cochonnet*. Special areas (*terrains de boules*) are set aside for the game in towns and villages, although one of the obvious attractions of the game is that it can be played virtually anywhere. There are some regional variations, notably in the size and form of the playing area and the size of the bowls.

brasserie

The original meaning of *brasserie* is 'brewery', and although the word is still used in this sense, it has come also to mean a type of bar-restaurant, usually serving simple, traditional French food at reasonable prices. Most *brasseries* offer a fixed-price menu, especially at lunchtime.

Breton

The ancient Celtic language of Brittany (*Bretagne*). It is related to Welsh, Irish, Scottish Gaelic, and Cornish. Recent decades have seen a revival of interest in the language going hand in hand with the asser-

tion of a regional cultural identity and a movement for independence from France. Breton is fairly widely spoken and is taught in secondary schools in the region, although it is not recognized as an official language in France.

Brevet d'études professionnelles (BEP)

A vocational qualification awarded at the end of a two-year, practically-based course in a LYCÉE specializing in providing teaching directly related to the workplace.

Brevet de technicien (BT)

A vocational qualification awarded at the end of a three-year course in a special section of a LYCÉE. There is considerable competition for entry to courses, and the standards required result in a high dropout rate.

Brevet de technicien supérieur (BTS)

A vocational qualification awarded at the end of a two-year course after the BACCALAURÉAT in a specific professional field.

Brevet des collèges

A general educational qualification taken in a range of subjects by students aged around 15 in the final year of COLLÈGE.

bureau de tabac

Tobacconists are either individual shops or else are to be found in a *bar-tabac* or *café-tabac*. They are also often combined with a newsagents (*marchand de journaux*). As well as being licensed to sell tobacco and cigarettes, they have a state licence to sell stamps, LOTO tickets, the *vignette* (road tax disc for motor vehicles), and certain other official documents.

Canal Plus (Canal+)

A privately-owned French television channel broadcasting mainly feature films. Viewers pay a subscription and access the channel using a decoder.

CAPES - certificat d'aptitude au professorat de l'enseignement du second degré

The qualification normally required in order to teach in a secondary school. Qualification is by means of a competitive examination (CONCOURS) usually at the end of a two-year course in a specialist teacher-training institute (*IUFM: Institut universitaire pour la formation des maîtres*).

Carte bleue

A credit card issued by French banks as part of the international Visa network.

Carte grise

The registration document for a motor vehicle. It is an offence not to carry it when driving the vehicle, and police checks are frequent. Vehicle registration numbers depend on the DÉPARTEMENT in which the owner lives and have to be changed if the owner moves to a different one.

Carte nationale d'identité

Although not obligatory, most French citizens possess a *carte nationale d'identité* (national identity card), obtained from their local MAIRIE, PREFECTUR, or *commissariat de police* (police station), as proof of identity is often required, for example when paying by cheque. It is also accepted as a travel document by all EC countries.

Catalan

The language spoken by 25 per cent of people in Spain and by some people in the Perpignan area of southwest France. It is taught in schools in the area but is not recognized as an official language in France.

CDI - Centre de documentation et d'information

A resource and information centre providing library and IT facilities in a school or college. The term has largely replaced *bibliothèque* (library) in this context.

CE - cycle élémentaire

Also called *cours élémentaire*, this is the programme for the two years of primary school for children aged 7 to 9 (*CE1* and *CE2*).

Césars

Prizes awarded annually for achievements in the film industry, so the French equivalent of the Oscars.

Chambre des députés ▸ ASSEMBLÉE NATIONALE

champignons

The French use the word *champignons* (mushrooms) to refer to any of the types of mushroom-like fungi that are to be found in the countryside, whether edible or not. Cultivated button mushrooms are called *champignons de Paris*. Hunting for edible *champignons* is almost a national leisure activity, and many varieties are highly prized. Advice on whether a *champignon* is edible or not can usually be obtained in a PHARMACIE.

Champs-Élysées

The world-famous avenue in central Paris, known for its luxury shops, hotels, and clubs. At one end is the *Arc de Triomphe*, the scene of the remembrance ceremony each year for the Armistice of 1918 and under which is the tomb of an unknown soldier, killed in World War I.

charcuterie

A shop or supermarket counter selling a wide variety of pork products. As well as cuts of pork, *charcutiers* usually sell chicken, both raw and ready-cooked, and there will be various types of raw and cooked ham, a variety of pâtés, often homemade in small shops, and a selection of *saucissons*. Most *charcuteries* also offer a variey of salads, various types of savoury pastries, and a number of dishes, different every day, which can be reheated at home or on the premises. Some also offer a catering service, in which case the shop will probably call itself a *charcutier-traiteur*. The word *charcuterie* is also used to mean pork products such as ham and *saucisson*.

chasse

La chasse (hunting) is a widely practised sport in France. Legislation as to the rights of hunters to hunt over privately-owned land varies according to the region and the amount of land concerned. During the hunting season, hunting is permitted on Thursdays, Saturdays, and Sundays. It is advisable not to stray from public footpaths when walking in the countryside on these days. The hunters (*les chasseurs*) are a powerful political lobby and are represented in the ASSEMBLÉE NATIONALE.

Cinquième

La Cinquième is an educational television channel which broadcasts on the ARTE channel during the day.

Cinquième république

This is the present régime in France. The constitution was established in 1958 according to principles put forward by Charles de Gaulle.

classe de neige

A period, generally a week, which a school class, usually of under-twelves, spends in a mountain area. Ski tuition is integrated with normal school work.

classe préparatoire

An intensive two-year course, provided by some prestigious LYCÉES, which prepares students for the competitive examinations (CONCOURS) by means of which students are selected for the GRANDES ÉCOLES.

classes

In French schools, after CM, classes go in reverse order, starting at age 11-12 in *sixième* and progressing through *cinquième*, *quatrième*, *troisième*, *seconde*, *première*,

and ending in *terminale* at age 17 or 18, the year in which the BACCALAURÉAT is taken. Education in France is compulsory up to the end of *seconde*.

CM - Cycle moyen

Also called *Cours moyen* this is the programme for the two years of primary school for children aged 9 to 11 (*CM1* and *CM2*).

collège

A state school for pupils between the ages of 11 and 15, between the ÉCOLE PRIMAIRE and the LYCÉE. The organisation of the school and the curriculum followed are laid down at national level.

colonie de vacances

A holiday village or summer camp for children. Originally set up as a means of giving poorer city children a means of getting out into the countryside, these are still largely state-subsidized. The informal word for them is *colo*.

commune

The *commune* is the smallest administrative unit of French local government. Each has its own MAIRE (mayor).

concours

Entry into many areas of the public services, including the teaching profession, as well as the most prestigious institutes of higher education, depends on succeeding in a competitive examination or *concours*.

The number of candidates admitted depends on the number of posts or places available in a given year.

conduite accompagnée (CA)

A learner driver who has passed the theory part of the driving test (*code de la route*) in a state-approved driving school is allowed to practise driving a vehicle accompanied by a qualified driver over the age of 28. Such drivers are not allowed to drive on **AUTOROUTES** and are required to have a white sticker with a red 'A' displayed on the rear of their vehicle.

conseil de classe

A committee representing each class in a **COLLÈGE** or **LYCÉE** consisting of the class teachers, two elected parent members, and two elected class members. It is chaired by the head teacher. The *conseil de classe* meets regularly to discuss the progress of the class and any problems that have arisen.

CP - Cycle préparatoire

Also called *Cours préparatoire*, this is the first year of primary school, starting a child's formal education off at the statutory age of 6.

Most children will have already attended an **ÉCOLE MATERNELLE**.

CRS – compagnies républicaines de sécurité

Special police units trained in public order techniques and riot control. They also police the **AUTOROUTES** and support mountain rescue and lifeguard work.

département

An administrative unit of government in France. Each *département* has a number and this appears as the first two digits in postcodes for addresses within the département and as the two-digit number at the end of registration numbers on motor vehicles.

député

An elected member of the **ASSEMBLÉE NATIONALE**.

droguerie

As a shop or supermarket section, there seems little connection between the name, which might be literally translated as 'drugstore', and the merchandise displayed. However, *drogue* can also mean the raw ingredients of dyes, and *droguistes* were originally dye merchants. Nowadays you will find not only dyes but household products and cleaning utensils, candles, and a variey of other useful household items.

école libre
Private sector school education, provided predominantly by the Catholic Church.

école maternelle
A school providing free nursery education from age 2 to 6. Many children start at 2 and virtually all children attend between the ages of 4 and 6, which is the statutory school starting age and the time at which children move into the ÉCOLE PRIMAIRE.

école primaire
A primary school for children between the ages of 6, the statutory minimum age for starting school, and 11.

école secondaire
Secondary education in France consists of two phases. COLLÈGE (11–15 years) and LYCÉE (15/16 –17/18 years).

Élysée ▸ PALAIS DE L' ÉLYSÉE

Europe 1
A popular commercial French-language radio station, which broadcasts news, popular music, sport, and light entertainment from the Saarland in Germany.

Événement du jeudi - l'Événement du jeudi
A popular weekly news magazine.

Express - l'Express
A weekly news magazine offering in-depth coverage of political and cultural matters.

faculté
La faculté – and more usually and informally *la fac* – is the way that students refer to their university, particularly the location itself, so that *aller à la fac* would be the equivalent of 'to go into college'.

Figaro - le Figaro
A right-wing national daily newspaper with a wide circulation.

France 2
This is the main publicly-owned television channel and aims to provide a wide range of quality programmes.

France 3
A state-owned television channel which is regionally based and is required to promote regional diversity and to cover a wide range of beliefs and opinions.

France Culture
A 24-hour RADIO FRANCE radio station featuring serious talk programmes on a wide variety of cultural and social topics.

France Info
A 24-hour radio news station run by RADIO FRANCE.

France Inter

A RADIO FRANCE radio station broadcasting mainly light entertainment, including a considerable proportion of studio comedy shows, but also offering good news coverage.

France Musiques

A 24-hour RADIO FRANCE radio station. Its main focus is classical music but it also provides considerable coverage of jazz and world music.

Gendarmerie nationale

A section of the military which provides police services outside the major towns.

gîte rural

A farmhouse or other building in the country which has been turned into a holiday cottage. Houses displaying the official *gîte de France* sign must conform to certain standards.

grande école

A prestigious higher education establishment admitting students on the results of a CONCOURS. They have different areas of specialization, and competition for entry is fierce, as they are widely believed to offer the highest level of education available and thus a guarantee of subsequent career success.

hôtel de ville ▸ MAIRIE

Humanité - l'Humanité

The communist national daily newspaper.

Internet

A wealth of useful information on French culture, society, and current affairs can be obtained on the Internet. All the main French newspapers have websites (e.g. http://www.lemonde.fr), as do the television channels (e.g. http://www.france3.fr and http://www.tf1.fr). The *Louvre* museum has an interesting site at http://web.culture.fr/louvre.

immatriculation ▸ PLAQUE D'IMMATRICULATION

Libération

A left-wing national daily newspaper published in Paris. A separate edition is published for Lyons.

licence

A university degree awarded after a year's study following the DEUG.

Loto

The French national lottery. People play the *Loto* using special machines which can be found in BUREAUX DE TABAC throughout France.

Luxembourg ▸ PALAIS DU LUXEMBOURG

lycée

A school providing the last

three years of secondary education after **COLLÈGE**. The first year is *seconde* at the age of 15/16, going through *première*, and ending with *terminale* at age 17/18. As well as those which provide a conventional academic education, there are a number of different types of *lycée* offering a more vocationally-based education.

M6
A popular, privately-owned, commercial television channel.

magasins
Opening and closing times of shops (*les magasins*) vary according to the type of shop and the location. Department stores (*les grands magasins*) are generally open all day from 9 a.m. to 7 p.m. In larger towns, most other shops, with the exception of small food shops, are also open all day. Privately-owned food shops such as butchers and fishmongers generally open at 8 a.m. and do not close in the evening until 7 or 7.30. Most, however, are closed between midday and 2 or 3 p.m. In small towns, all the shops, with the exception of bakers, generally close for 2 or 3 hours in the middle of the day. In both small and large towns, it is always possible to find all types of food shops open on Sunday mornings until midday. In smaller towns, however, many of the shops are closed on Mondays.

maire
The chief officer of a **COMMUNE**, he or she represents state authority locally, officiates at marriages, and supervises local elections.

mairie
The *mairie* (town hall) is the administrative headquarters of the **CONSEIL MUNICIPAL**. In larger towns the *mairie* is often called the **HÔTEL DE VILLE**.

marchés
All towns in France have a weekly market with stalls selling a variety of produce, and some areas in big cities have a market every day. Many stalls are held by local people selling their own produce. Despite supermarkets, many people do much of their food shopping *au marché*.

Marianne
The symbolic female figure often used to represent the French Republic. There are statues of her in public places all over France, and she also appears on the standard French stamp. She is always depicted wearing the Phrygian bonnet, a pointed cap which became one of the symbols of liberty as represented

by the 1789 Revolution.

Marseillaise

The French national anthem, so called because it was the marching song of a group of republican volunteers from Marseilles a few years after the 1789 revolution.

Médecins du monde

A charitable organization which provides medical and humanitarian aid in areas stricken by war, famine, or natural disaster.

Médecins sans frontières

A charitable organisation which sends medical teams anywhere in the world where they are needed to cope with the effects on people of war and disaster.

Minitel

A computer terminal available in a variety of models to the subscribers of FRANCE TÉLÉCOM. It gives users access to the *Télétel* network, which has a huge variety of services, payable at different rates, including the telephone directory. It can now be accessed via the Internet.

MJC - Maison des jeunes et de la culture

A community youth centre offering a wide variety of services and activities.

Monde - le Monde

A national daily newspaper. Its political stance is left of centre, and it is entirely owned by its staff. It provides full coverage of national and international news and is known for its in-depth analysis of current issues. It is unusual in publishing virtually no photographs of current events.

Nouvel Observateur - le Nouvel Observateur

A left-wing weekly magazine providing in-depth articles on current political issues and good coverage of culture and the arts.

Palais Bourbon

A large eighteenth-century residence on the left bank of the Seine which is now the seat of the ASSEMBLÉE NATIONALE.

Palais de l'Élysée

The official residence and office of the French President, situated just off the CHAMPS-ÉLYSÉES in Paris.

Palais du Luxembourg

A seventeenth century palace in the jardin du Luxembourg in Paris. It is now the seat of the SÉNAT.

paysan

Since *paysan* can be used in French to mean both 'small farmer' and, more offensively, 'peasant', small farmers are generally referred to as *agriculteurs*. However, many small farmers take pride in their identity as *paysans*, particularly in the more remote areas of the country, where small farms are still the usual form of cultivation. The difficulty of making a living with a limited amount of land has, however, led to many such farms being abandoned or amalgamated into larger units and a general movement of the traditional rural population towards the towns.

permis de conduire

A driving licence can be issued to a person over the age of 18 who has passed both parts of the driving test. The first part is the theory test (*code de la route*) and consists of forty questions based on the highway code. This can be sat from the age of 16 onwards and gives the right to CON-DUITE ACCOMPAGNÉE. The practical driving test has to be taken within two years of the theory test. It is compulsory to carry your driving licence with you when you are driving a vehicle.

pétanque ▸ BOULES

pharmacie

Pharmacies in France generally sell only medicines and closely related products such as toiletries and some brands of make-up and perfume. The products of the major perfume houses are to be found in *parfumeries*. Pharmacists traditionally play an active paramedical role, and people will often consult them rather than a doctor in the case of minor ailments and accidents. Pharmacies are easily spotted by the green cross, which is lit up when the pharmacy is open. A *pharmacie de garde* (duty chemist) can dispense medicines outside normal opening hours as part of a local rota.

plaque d'immatriculation

A vehicle's registration plate. The last two figures indicate the number of the DÉPARTE-MENT in which the owner lives. If you move into another *département*, you are obliged by law to change your registration plate accordingly.

Point – le Point

A centre-right weekly news magazine offering in-depth coverage of politics and economics.

police

There are three principal police forces: the *police municipale* who are responsible for routine local policing such as traffic offences, who are locally organized and are not armed, the *police nationale* who are nationally organized and generally armed, and the *gendarmerie nationale* which is a branch of the military.

Poste – La Poste
The state monopoly postal service. Postboxes in France are yellow.

préfet
The most senior offical responsible for representing the state within the DÉPARTE-MENT.

préfecture
The administrative headquarters of a DÉPARTEMENT.

Premier ministre
The chief minister of the government, appointed by the PRÉSIDENT DE LA RÉPUBLIQUE and responsible for the overall management of government affairs.

Président de la République
The president is the head of state and is elected for a term of 7 years. Under the constitution of the CINQUIÈME RÉPUB-LIQUE the president plays a strong executive role in the governing of the country.

Quai d'Orsay
The *ministère des Affaires étrangères* (ministry of Foreign Affairs) is situated here, so *Quai d'Orsay* is often used by journalists to mean the ministry.

Radio France
The state-owned radio broadcasting company.

région
The largest administrative unit in France, consisting of a number of DÉPARTEMENTS. Each has its own *conseil régional* (regional council) which has responsibilities in education and economic planning.

rentrée
The week at the beginning of September when the new school year starts and around which much of French administrative life revolves. The preceding weeks see intensive advertising of associated merchandise, from books and stationery to clothes and sports equipment. *La rentrée littéraire* marks the start of the literary year and *la rentrée parlementaire* signals the reassembly of parliament after the recess.

repas
Traditionally the midday meal was the big meal of the day, and for people who live in country areas this is still largely the case. Even in big cities many people continue to eat a big meal in the middle of the day, though they are tending more and more to have a snack lunch and to eat their main meal in the

evening. In either case, the main meal virtually always consists of a number of courses, typically a starter such as pâté, *saucisson*, or salad, then meat or fish with a vegetable dish, followed by cheese and dessert. Cheese is virtually always eaten and is served before the dessert. In town and country alike, Sunday is the day for a big family meal in the middle of the day, and the **PÂTISSERIES** are usually crowded on Sunday mornings as people queue up to buy a large tart or cake for their hosts or guests.

restaurants

France is rightly famed for the quality of its restaurants. It is always possible to find restaurants and **BRASSERIES** offering fixed-price menus which are generally good value for money. A basket of bread is usually included in the price of the meal, and most restaurants will have several inexpensive house wines, available in *pichets* (jugs) of 1/4, 1/2, and 1 litre. Service is included in the bill, although many people do leave a tip if the meal and the service have been good.

route départementale

These are signalled on French road maps as 'D' followed by a number and are marked in

yellow. They are roads maintained by the **DÉPARTEMENT** and are secondary roads, not intended to be used for fast travel from place to place. Many of them have stretches marked in green on maps to highlight areas or views of particular beauty.

route nationale

A *route nationale* forms part of the state-maintained road network, outside the **AUTOROUTES** but providing fast roads for travel between towns and cities. They are signalled by 'N' followed by the road number and are marked in red on French road maps.

SAMU – service d'aide médicale d'urgence

A 24 hour service coordinated by each **DÉPARTEMENT** to provide mobile medical services and staff, ambulances, and helicopters to accident scenes and emergencies.

Sénat

The upper house of parliament which meets in the **PALAIS DU LUXEMBOURG**. It consists of 321 elected *sénateurs*. It votes laws and the state budget.

SNCF – Société nationale des chemins de fer français

The state-owned railway company, which also has access to private finance.

tabac ▸ BUREAU DE TABAC

télécarte
A phone card for use in telephone kiosks, widely available from *France Télécom* (the state owned telephone company), *bureaux de poste*, *tabacs* and *marchands de journaux*.

TF1 - Télévision française 1
Originally a state-controlled television channel, now privately-owned, *TF1* has an obligation to ensure that 50% of its programmes are of French origin.

TGV - train à grande vitesse
The new-generation high-speed electric train. It runs on special tracks and can reach speeds of up to 300 km/h.

Tintin
A comic-book character invented by the Belgian cartoonist Hergé in 1929. Tintin's adventures with the irrepressible Capitaine Haddock are still bestsellers and have been translated into more than 40 languages.

Tour de France
Probably the most famous cycle race in the world, the *Tour de France* takes place over a different route each year but always ends around July 14 on the CHAMPS ÉLYSÉES. The overall winner after each section of the race is entitled to wear *le maillot jaune* (yellow jersey).

Letter-writing in French

Holiday postcard

■ Address: On an envelope Mr, Mrs, and Miss can be abbreviated to *M.*, *Mme*, *Mlle*, although the full forms are considered preferable in more formal letters. There is no direct equivalent for Ms. If you do not know a woman's marital status use *Madame* (*Mme*).

■ Beginnings (informal): *Cher* is used for a man, *Chère* for a woman. A letter to two males or to a male and female begins with *Chers*. For two female correspondents *Chères Madeleine et Hélène*. For friends and relatives: *Chers amis*, *Chers cousins*, etc. For a family: *Chers tous*.

Road names such as *rue*, *avenue*, *place* are not generally given capital letters.

The name of the town comes after the postcode and on the same line.

14.7.2000

Cher Alexandre,

Grosses bises d'Edimbourg! Cela fait trois jours que nous sommes ici et nous n'avons pas encore vu la pluie! Espérons que ça va durer. La vieille ville est très belle et du château on a une vue splendide jusqu'à l'estuaire. Et en Normandie, comment ça va?

A bientôt pour des retrouvailles parisiennes.

Marie et Dominique

M. A. Pilnard

38 rue Glacière

75013 Paris

■ Endings (informal): *Bien amicalement*, *Amitiés*; *A bientôt* = see you soon.

Christmas and New Year wishes (informal)

■ On most personal letters French speakers do not put their address at the top of the letter. The date is given preceded by *le*. For the first day of the month *le 1er* is used. Generally, the name of the town in which the letter is written is placed before the date.

1 The tradition of Christmas cards is much less widespread in France than in Great Britain. While Christmas greetings may be sent, it is more customary to send best wishes for the New Year in January.

2 In the year 2000/2001 etc. = *en l'an 2000/2001* etc., but *bonne année 2000/2001* etc.

---

le 18 décembre 2000 **1**

Chers Steve et Michelle,

Nous vous souhaitons un Joyeux Noël **1** et une très bonne année 2001 **2**! En espérant que ce nouveau millénaire vous apportera tout ce que vous désirez et que nous trouverons une occasion pour nous revoir!

Bises à vous deux,

Gérard

New Year wishes (formal)

---

le 5 janvier 2001

Je vous **1** présente mes meilleurs vœux pour l'année 2001. Que cette année vous apporte, à vous et à votre famille, bonheur et prospérité.

Pierre Carlier

---

1 Note the use of the formal form *vous*.

Invitation (informal)

Invitations to parties are usually by word of mouth, but for more formal events such as weddings, invitations are sent out.

1 Note the use of the informal form *tu* betweeen good friends.

Paris, le 28/04/01

Cher Denis,

Que fais-tu **1** *cet été? Pascal et moi avons décidé d'inviter tous les copains d'Orléans à nous rejoindre dans notre maison de Dordogne pour le weekend du 14 juillet. Il y aura fête au village avec bal populaire et feu d'artifice. Le petit vin du pays n'est pas mal non plus!*

Nous comptons sur toi pour venir trinquer avec nous,

Bises,

Martine

■ Endings (informal): *Bises* (= lots of love) is very informal and is appropriate for very good friends and family. Alternatives for close friends and family include *Bien à toi, Bons baisers* or affectionately *Je t'embrasse*. If the letter is addressed to more than one person use *Bien à vous* or *Je vous embrasse*.

Invitation (formal)

Christine et Félix Prévost
81 rue Esque moise
59000 Lille

                        Lille, le 28 avril 2001

Chers amis,

Nous avons l'immense plaisir de vous
annoncer le mariage de notre fils Victor
et de mademoiselle Stéphanie Heusdens.

La cérémonie aura lieu à l'Hôtel de
Ville à 15 heures le samedi 5 juin. Vous
recevrez bientôt un faire-part et une
invitation à dîner mais nous tenions à
vous prévenir suffisamment tôt pour que
vous puissiez arranger votre voyage.
Nous espérons qu'il vous sera possible
de vous joindre à nous.

Amicalement,**1**

Christine et Félix

■ In a more formal letter, especially where a reply is generally
required, the sender's address is written on the left-hand side of the
page. An alternative is in the centre of the page, particularly on
printed stationery.

1 Endings: Alternatives could be *Amitiés*, *Bien amicalement*.

Accepting an Invitation

Emilie Joly
2 rue de la Pompe
75016 Paris

le 16 mars 2001

Chère Madame Dubois,

Je vous **1** remercie de bien vouloir me recevoir pour les deux premières semaines de juillet. Je serai très heureuse de vous revoir ainsi que Natalie, bien entendu. Nous avons passé un si bon séjour linguistique à Manchester l'été dernier que nous avions très envie de nous retrouver. Mes parents ne pouvant m'envoyer en Angleterre cette année, c'est avec un immense plaisir que j'accepte votre invitation.

Je vous prie de bien vouloir accepter, Madame, l'expression de mes sentiments les meilleurs.

Emilie

■ In a more formal social letter where the correspondent is known personally by name it can be used in the opening greeting.

■ The title of the person receiving the letter must be repeated in the closing formula. These formulas are more elaborate than in English, with a number of possible variations. Some of these are shown in the following letters in this section.

1 Since the letter is from a young person to the mother of a friend, she uses the formal *vous* form and writes to her as Madame Dubois. Madame Dubois would address Emilie using *tu*.

Seeking a job as an au pair

Sally Paledra
5 Avon Crescent
Kenilworth
Warwickshire
CV8 2PQ

le 3 mars 2001

Madame,

Vos coordonnées m'ont été communiquées par l'agence 'Au Pair International', qui m'a demandé de vous écrire directement. Je suis en effet à la recherche d'un emploi au pair pour une période de neuf à dix mois à partir de septembre prochain.

J'aime beaucoup les enfants et ils apprécient également ma compagnie. J'ai une grande expérience du baby-sitting. J'ai aussi fait un stage d'un mois dans une crèche privée **1**.

Je suis enthousiaste, discrète et je sais prendre des initiatives. J'ai étudié le français au lycée pendant cinq ans et je connais un peu la France pour y avoir passé des vacances à plusieurs reprises. J'ai aussi mon permis de conduire.

Dans l'espoir d'une réponse positive de votre part, je vous prie d'agréer, Madame, l'expression de mes salutations respectueuses.

S. Paledra

P.J. : un CV avec photo

---

1 Or be more specific, e.g. *pour des enfants de 3 mois à 3 ans.*

■ To supply references: *Vous trouverez également ci-joint les adresses de personnes pouvant fournir une lettre de recommandation* or *pouvant me recommander.*

Enquiry to a tourist office

M. et Mme Baude
13 La Faverolle
45000 Orléans

Syndicat d'initiative
de St Gervais
74170 Saint-Gervais-les-Bains

Orléans, le 24 mars 2001

Monsieur,

Nous vous serions reconnaissants de bien vouloir nous
faire parvenir toute la documentation dont vous disposez
sur les villas de location à proximité de la station thermale.
Nous désirons également recevoir des informations sur les
activités de loisirs durant l'été.
Vous trouverez ci-joint une enveloppe timbrée **1** pour la
réponse.

Dans l'attente de votre réponse, je vous prie d'agréer,
Monsieur, l'expression de nos salutations distinguées.

J. Baude

---

1 *enveloppe timbrée* = stamped addressed envelope.

■ Note that, unlike in English, a reference or the purpose of a
business letter is placed, where required, above the opening
greeting. e.g. *Objet: commande 99/08/21* or *Réf: 000/23*.

Booking a hotel room

Miss Sylvia Daley
The Willows
49 North Terrace
Kings Barton
Nottinghamshire
NG8 4LQ
England

Hôtel Beauséjour
Chemin des Mimosas
06100 Grasse

le 8 avril 2001

Madame,

J'ai bien reçu le dépliant de votre hôtel et je vous en remercie.

Je souhaite réserver une chambre calme avec salle de bains, en pension complète **1** pour la période du 7 au 18 juin. Pour les arrhes, je vous prie de m'informer de leur montant et des modalités de paiement possibles depuis la Grande-Bretagne.

En vous remerciant d'avance, je vous prie de croire, Madame, en mes sentiments les meilleurs.

S. Daley

---

1 Or *une chambre avec douche en demi-pension* or *avec petit déjeuner*. The term en suite does not exist for bathroom facilities in French.

Booking a campsite

Frances Good
22 Daniel Avenue
Caldwood
Leeds LS8 7RR
tel. 0113 2998767

Camping 'Les Embruns'
18 allée des Capucins
22116 Moëlan-sur-Mer

le 25 avril 2001

Monsieur,

Nous souhaitons réserver dans votre camping, pour la période du 2 au 15 juillet, deux emplacements de tente côte à côte**1** et, si possible, pas trop loin de la plage**2**. Il s'agit de deux tentes de deux personnes. Nous aurons également deux motos de 1000cc chacune.

Dès que nous aurons confirmation de votre part, nous vous adresserons le montant de la réservation.

Pouvez-vous nous indiquer à cet effet, les possibilités de paiement depuis l'étranger.

Veuillez croire, Monsieur, en l'expression de nos sentiments les meilleurs.

F. Good

1 Or if you have a caravan *un emplacement de caravane*.
2 Other requirements might be *ombragé* (shady), or *abrité* (sheltered).

Cancelling a reservation

Mrs J. Warrington
Downlands
Steyning
West Sussex

Hôtel des Voyageurs
BN44 6LZ
9 cours Gambetta
91949 Les Ulis

le 15 février 2001

Monsieur,

Je suis au regret de devoir annuler la réservation de chambre pour deux personnes pour la nuit du 24 au 25 mars, que j'avais effectuée par téléphone le 18 janvier dernier. **1**

Je vous remercie de votre compréhension et vous prie d'agréer, Monsieur, l'expression de mes sentiments distingués.

J. Warrington

1 If reasons for the cancellation are specified these could include: *pour raisons de santé/de famille, en raison d'un décès dans la famille*, etc.

sending an email

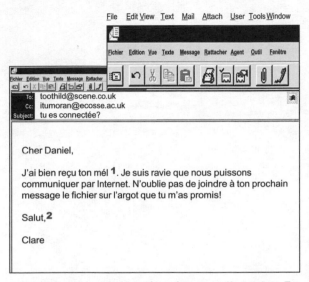

File Edit View Text Mail Attach User Tools Window

Fichier Edition Vue Texte Message Rattacher Agent Outil Fenêtre

Fichier Edition Vue Texte Message Rattacher

To: toothild@scene.co.uk
Cc: itumoran@ecosse.ac.uk
Subject: tu es connectée?

Cher Daniel,

J'ai bien reçu ton mél **1**. Je suis ravie que nous puissons communiquer par Internet. N'oublie pas de joindre à ton prochain message le fichier sur l'argot que tu m'as promis!

Salut,**2**

Clare

1 Note that *mél* is an abbreviated form of *message électronique*. To send an attachment = *joindre un fichier*.
2 Endings (informal): An alternative could be *A bientôt* or simply *Bises* to a close friend in an informal context.

Aa

a *determiner*

an avant voyelle ou h muet.

➡ For expressions such as **make a noise, make a fortune** ⇒**noise, fortune**.

⋯➤ un/une; ∼ **tree** un arbre; ∼ **chair** une chaise.

⋯➤ (*per*) **two euros** ∼ **kilo** deux euros le kilo; **three times** ∼ **day** trois fois par jour.

! When talking about what people do or are, **a** is not translated into French: **she's a teacher** *elle est professeur*; **he's a widower** *il est veuf*.

aback *adv* taken ∼ déconcerté.

abandon *vt* abandonner. ● *n* abandon *m*.

abate *vi* (*flood, fever*) baisser; (*storm*) se calmer. ● *vt* diminuer.

abbey *n* abbaye *f*.

abbot *n* abbé *m*.

abbreviate *vt* abréger. **abbreviation** *n* abréviation *f*.

abdicate *vt/i* abdiquer.

abdomen *n* abdomen *m*.

abduct *vt* enlever. **abductor** *n* ravisseur/-euse *m/f*.

abhor *vt* (*pt* **abhorred**) exécrer.

abide *vt* supporter; ∼ **by** respecter.

ability *n* capacité *f* (**to do** à faire); (*talent*) talent *m*.

abject *a* (*state*) misérable; (*coward*) abject.

ablaze *a* en feu.

able *a* (*skilled*) compétent; **be** ∼ **to do** pouvoir faire; (*know how to*)

savoir faire. **ably** *adv* avec compétence.

abnormal *a* anormal. **abnormality** *n* anomalie *f*.

aboard *adv* à bord. ● *prep* à bord de.

abode *n* demeure *f*; **of no fixed** ∼ sans domicile fixe.

abolish *vt* abolir.

Aborigine *n* aborigène *mf* (d'Australie).

abort *vt* faire avorter; (Comput) abandonner. ● *vi* avorter.

abortion *n* avortement *m*; **have an** ∼ se faire avorter.

abortive *a* (*attempt*) avorté; (*coup*) manqué.

about *adv* (approximately) environ; ∼ **the same** à peu près pareil; **there was no-one** ∼ il n'y avait personne; **it's** ∼ ... il s'agit de ...; **what I like** ∼ **her is** ce que j'aime chez elle c'est; **to wander** ∼ **the streets** errer dans les rues; **how/what** ∼ **some tea?** et si on prenait un thé?; **what** ∼ **you?** et toi? ● *adj* **be** ∼ **to do** être sur le point de faire; **be up and** ∼ être debout. ∼**-face**, ∼**-turn** *n* (fig) volte-face *f inv*.

above *prep* au-dessus de; **he is not** ∼ **lying** il n'est pas incapable de mentir; ∼ **all** surtout. ● *adv* **the apartment** ∼ l'appartement du dessus; **see** ∼ voir ci-dessus. ∼**-board** *a* honnête. ∼**-mentioned** *a* susmentionné.

abrasive *a* abrasif; (*manner*) mordant. ● *n* abrasif *m*.

abreast *adv* de front; **keep** ∼ **of** se tenir au courant de.

abroad *adv* à l'étranger.

abrupt *a* (sudden, curt) brusque; (steep) abrupt. **abruptly** *adv* (suddenly) brusquement; (curtly) avec brusquerie.

abscess *n* abcès *m*.

abseil *vi* descendre en rappel.

absence *n* absence *f*; (lack) manque *m*; **in the ~ of** faute de.

absent *a* absent.

absentee *n* absent/-e *m/f*.

absent-minded *a* distrait.

absolute *a* (monarch, majority) absolu; (chaos, idiot) véritable. **absolutely** *adv* absolument.

absolve *vt* **~ sb of sth** décharger qn de qch.

absorb *vt* absorber.

abstain *vi* s'abstenir (**from** de).

abstract¹ *a* abstrait. ●*n* (summary) résumé *m*; **in the ~** dans l'abstrait.

abstract² *vt* tirer.

absurd *a* absurde.

abundance *n* abondance *f*. **abundant** *a* abondant. **abundantly** *adv* (entirely) tout à fait.

abuse¹ *vt* (position) abuser de; (person) maltraiter; (insult) injurier.

abuse² *n* (misuse) abus *m* (**of** de); (cruelty) mauvais traitement *m*; (insults) injures *fpl*.

abusive *a* (person) grossier; (language) injurieux.

abysmal *a* épouvantable.

abyss *n* abîme *m*.

academic *a* (career) universitaire; (year) académique; (scholarly) intellectuel; (theoretical) théorique. ●*n* universitaire *mf*.

academy *n* (school) école *f*; (society) académie *f*.

accelerate *vi* (speed up) s'accélérer; (Auto) accélérer. **accelerator** *n* accélérateur *m*.

accent¹ *n* accent *m*.

accent² *vt* accentuer.

accept *vt* accepter. **acceptable** *a* acceptable. **acceptance** *n* (of offer) acceptation *f*; (of proposal) approbation *f*.

access *n* accès *m*. **accessible** *a* accessible.

accessory *a* accessoire. ●*n* (Jur) complice *mf* (**to** de).

accident *n* accident *m*; (chance) hasard *m*; **by ~** par hasard. **accidental** *a* (death) accidentel; (meeting) fortuit. **accidentally** *adv* accidentellement; (by chance) par hasard.

acclaim *vt* applaudir. ●*n* louanges *fpl*.

acclimatize *vt/i* (s')acclimater (**to** à).

accommodate *vt* loger; (adapt to) s'adapter à; (satisfy) satisfaire. **accommodating** *a* accommodant. **accommodation** *n* logement *m*.

accompaniment *n* accompagnement *m*. **accompany** *vt* accompagner.

accomplice *n* complice *mf* (**in, to** de).

accomplish *vt* accomplir; (objective) réaliser. **accomplished** *a* très compétent. **accomplishment** *n* (feat) réussite *f*; (talent) talent *m*.

accord *vi* concorder (**with** avec). ●*vt* accorder (**sb sth** qch à qn). ●*n* accord *m*; **of my own ~** de moi-même.

accordance *n* **in ~ with** conformément à.

according *adv* **~ to** (principle, law) selon; (person, book) d'après. **accordingly** *adv* en conséquence.

accordion *n* accordéon *m*.

accost *vt* aborder.

account *n* (Comm) compte *m*; (description) compte-rendu *m*; **on ~**

of à cause de; **on no ~** en aucun cas; **take into ~** tenir compte de; **it's of no ~** peu importe. □ **~ for** (explain) expliquer; (represent) représenter. **accountability** *n* responsabilité *f*. **accountable** *a* responsable (**for** de; **to** envers).

accountancy *n* comptabilité *f*. **accountant** *n* comptable *mf*. **accounts** *npl* comptabilité *f*, comptes *mpl*.

accumulate *vt/i* (s')accumuler.

accuracy *n* (of figures) justesse *f*; (of aim) précision *f*; (of forecast) exactitude *f*. **accurate** *a* juste, précis. **accurately** *adv* exactement, précisément.

accusation *n* accusation *f*.

accuse *vt* accuser; **the ~d** l'accusé/-e *m/f*.

accustomed *a* accoutumé; **become ~ to** s'accoutumer à.

ace *n* (card, person) as *m*.

ache *n* douleur *f*. ● *vi* (person) avoir mal; **my leg ~s** ma jambe me fait mal.

achieve *vt* (aim) atteindre; (result) obtenir; (ambition) réaliser. **achievement** *n* (feat) réussite *f*; (fulfilment) réalisation *f* (**of** de).

acid *a & n* acide (*m*). **acidity** *n* acidité *f*. **~ rain** *n* pluies *fpl* acides.

acknowledge *vt* (error, authority) reconnaître; (letter) accuser réception de. **acknowledgement** *n* reconnaissance *f*.

acne *n* acné *f*.

acorn *n* (Bot) gland *m*.

acoustic *a* acoustique. **acoustics** *npl* acoustique *f*.

acquaint *vt* **~ sb with sth** mettre qn au courant de qch; **be ~ed with** (person) connaître; (fact) savoir. **acquaintance** *n* connaissance *f*.

acquire *vt* acquérir; (habit) prendre.

acquit *vt* (*pt* **acquitted**) (Jur) acquitter. **acquittal** *n* acquittement *m*.

acre *n* acre *f*, ≈ demi-hectare *m*.

acrid *a* âcre.

acrimonious *a* acrimonieux.

acrobat *n* acrobate *mf*. **acrobatics** *npl* acrobaties *fpl*.

acronym *n* acronyme *m*.

across *adv & prep* (side to side) d'un côté à l'autre (de); (on other side) de l'autre côté (**from** de); **go** *or* **walk ~** traverser; **lie ~ the bed** se coucher en travers du lit; **~ the world** partout dans le monde.

act *n* acte *m*; (Jur, Pol) loi *f*; **put on an ~** jouer la comédie. ● *vi* agir; (Theat) jouer; **~ as** servir de. ● *vt* (*part, role*) jouer.

acting *n* (Theat) jeu *m*. ● *a* (temporary) intérimaire.

action *n* action *f*; (Mil) combat *m*; **out of ~** hors service; **take ~** agir.

activate *vt* (machine) faire démarrer; (alarm) déclencher.

active *a* actif; (volcano) en activité; **take an ~ interest in** s'intéresser activement à. **activist** *n* activiste *mf*. **activity** *n* activité *f*.

actor *n* acteur *m*. **actress** *n* actrice *f*.

actual *a* réel; **the ~ words** les mots exacts; **in the ~ house** (the house itself) dans la maison elle-même. **actuality** *n* réalité *f*. **actually** *adv* (in fact) en fait; (really) vraiment.

acute *a* (anxiety) vif; (illness) aigu; (shortage) grave; (mind) pénétrant.

ad *n* (TV) pub *f* 🄸; **small ~** petite annonce *f*.

AD *abbr* (**Anno Domini**) ap. J.-C.

adamant *a* catégorique.

adapt *vt/i* (s')adapter (**to** à).
adaptability *n* adaptabilité *f*.
adaptable *a* souple. **adaptation**
n adaptation *f*. **adaptor** *n* (Electr)
adaptateur *m*.

add *vt/i* ajouter (**to** à); (in maths)
additionner. □ ~ **up** (*facts,
figures*) s'accorder; ~ **sth up**
additionner qch; ~ **up to** s'élever
à.

adder *n* vipère *f*.

addict *n* toxicomane *mf*; (fig)
accro *mf* ▯.

addicted *a* **be** ~ avoir une
dépendance (**to** à); (fig) être accro
▯ (**to** à). **addiction** *n* (Med)
dépendance *f* (**to** à); passion *f* (**to**
pour). **addictive** *a* qui crée une
dépendance.

addition *n* (item) ajout *m*; (in maths)
addition *f*; **in** ~ en plus.
additional *a* supplémentaire.

additive *n* additif *m*.

address *n* adresse *f*; (speech)
discours *m*. ● *vt* (*letter*) mettre
l'adresse sur; (*crowd*) s'adresser
à; ~ **sth to** adresser qch à.
addressee *n* destinataire *mf*.

adequate *a* suffisant; (satisfactory)
satisfaisant.

adhere *vi* (lit, fig) adhérer (**to** à); ~
to (*policy*) observer.

adjacent *a* contigu; ~ **to** attenant
à.

adjective *n* adjectif *m*.

adjoin *vt* être contigu à.
adjoining *a* (*room*) voisin.

adjourn *vt* (*trial*) ajourner; **the
session was** ~**ed** la séance a été
levée. ● *vi* s'arrêter; (*Parliament*)
lever la séance; ~ **to** passer à.

adjust *vt* (*level, speed*) régler;
(*price*) ajuster; (*clothes*) rajuster.
● *vt/i* ~ (**oneself**) **to** s'adapter à.
adjustable *a* réglable.
adjustment *n* (of rates)
rajustement *m*; (of control) réglage
m; (of person) adaptation *f*.

ad lib *vt/i* (*pt* **ad libbed**)
improviser.

administer *vt* administrer.

administration *n* administration
f. **administrative** *a* administratif.
administrator *n* administrateur/
-trice *m/f*.

admiral *n* amiral *m*.

admiration *n* admiration *f*.
admire *vt* admirer. **admirer** *n*
admirateur/-trice *m/f*.

admission *n* (to a place) entrée *f*;
(confession) aveu *m*.

admit *vt* (*pt* **admitted**)
(acknowledge) reconnaître,
admettre; (*crime*) avouer; (*new
member*) admettre; ~ **to**
reconnaître. **admittance** *n*
entrée *f*. **admittedly** *adv* il est
vrai.

ado *n* **without more** ~ sans plus de
cérémonie.

adolescence *n* adolescence *f*.
adolescent *n* & *a* adolescent/-e
(*m/f*).

adopt *vt* adopter. **adopted** *a*
(*child*) adoptif. **adoption** *n*
adoption *f*. **adoptive** *a* adoptif.

adorable *a* adorable. **adoration**
n adoration *f*. **adore** *vt* adorer.

adorn *vt* orner.

adrift *a* & *adv* à la dérive.

adult *a* & *n* adulte (*mf*).

adultery *n* adultère *m*.

adulthood *n* âge *m* adulte.

advance *vt* (*sum*) avancer; (*tape,
career*) faire avancer; (*interests*)
servir. ● *vi* (lit) avancer; (progress)
progresser. ● *n* avance *f*; (progress)
progrès *m*; **in** ~ à l'avance.
advanced *a* avancé; (*studies*)
supérieur.

advantage *n* avantage *m*; **take** ~
of profiter de; (*person*) exploiter.
advantageous *a* avantageux.

adventure *n* aventure *f*.
adventurer *n* aventurier/-ière *m/
f*. **adventurous** *a* aventureux.

adverb n adverbe m.

adverse a défavorable.

advert n annonce f; (TV) pub f 🔲.

advertise vt faire de la publicité pour; (car, house, job) mettre une annonce pour. ● vi faire de la publicité; (for staff) passer une annonce. **advertisement** n publicité f; (in newspaper) annonce f. **advertiser** n annonceur m. **advertising** n publicité f.

advice n conseils mpl; **some ~, a piece of ~** un conseil.

advise vt conseiller; (inform) aviser; **~ against** déconseiller. **adviser** n conseiller/-ère m/f. **advisory** a consultatif.

advocate[1] n (Jur) avocat m; (supporter) partisan m.

advocate[2] vt recommander.

aerial a aérien. ● n antenne f.

aerobics n aérobic m.

aeroplane n avion m.

aerosol n bombe f aérosol.

aesthetic a esthétique.

afar adv **from ~** de loin.

affair n (matter) affaire f; (romance) liaison f.

affect vt affecter.

affection n affection f. **affectionate** a affectueux.

affinity n affinité f.

afflict vt affliger.

affluence n richesse f.

afford vt avoir les moyens d'acheter; (provide) fournir; **can you ~ the time?** avez-vous le temps?

afloat adj & adv (boat) à flot.

afoot adv **sth is ~** il se prépare qch.

afraid a **be ~** (frightened) avoir peur (of, to de; that que); (worried) craindre (that que); **I'm ~ I can't come** je suis désolé mais je ne peux pas venir.

Africa n Afrique f.

African n Africain/-e m/f. ● a africain.

after adv & prep après; **soon ~** peu après; **be ~ sth** rechercher qch; **~ all** après tout. ● conj après que; **~ doing** après avoir fait.

aftermath n conséquences fpl (of de).

afternoon n après-midi m or f inv; **in the ~** (dans) l'après-midi.

after: ~shave n après-rasage m. **~thought** n pensée f après coup.

afterwards adv après, par la suite.

again adv encore; **~ and ~** à plusieurs reprises; **start ~** recommencer; **she never saw him ~** elle ne l'a jamais revu.

against prep contre; **~ the law** illégal.

age n âge m; (era) ère f, époque f; **I've been waiting for ~s** j'attends depuis des heures. ● vt/i (pres p ageing) vieillir.

aged[1] a **~ six** âgé de six ans.

aged[2] a âgé.

ageism n discrimination f en raison de l'âge.

agency n agence f.

agenda n ordre m du jour; (fig) programme m.

agent n agent m.

aggravate vt (make worse) aggraver; (annoy) exaspérer. **aggravation** n (worsening) aggravation f; (annoyance) ennuis mpl.

aggression n agression f.

aggressive a agressif. **aggressiveness** n agressivité f. **aggressor** n agresseur m.

ago adv il y a; **a month ~** il y a un mois; **long ~** il y a longtemps; **how long ~?** il y a combien de temps?

agonize vi se tourmenter (**over** à

propos de). **agonized** *a* angoissé.
agonizing *a* déchirant. **agony** *n*
douleur *f* atroce; (mental) angoisse
f.

agree *vi* être d'accord (**on** sur;
with avec); ~ **to** consentir à; ~
with (approve of) approuver. ● *vt*
être d'accord (**that** sur le fait
que); (admit) convenir (**that** que);
(*date, solution*) se mettre d'accord
sur.

agreeable *a* agréable; **be** ~
(willing) être d'accord.

agreed *a* (*time, place*) convenu;
we're ~ nous sommes d'accord.

agreement *n* accord *m*; **in** ~
d'accord.

agricultural *a* agricole.
agriculture *n* agriculture *f*.

aground *adv* **run** ~ (*ship*)
s'échouer.

ahead *adv* (in front) en avant,
devant; (in advance) à l'avance; **be**
10 points ~ avoir 10 points
d'avance; ~ **of time** en avance; **go**
~! allez-y!

aid *vt* aider. ● *n* aide *f*; **in** ~ **of** au
profit de.

aide *n* aide *mf*.

Aids *n* (Med) sida *m*.

aim *vt* (*gun*) braquer (**at** sur); **be**
~**ed at sb** (*campaign, remark*)
viser qn. ● *vi* ~ **for/at sth** viser
qch; ~ **to do** avoir l'intention de
faire. ● *n* but *m*; **take** ~ viser.
aimless *a* sans but.

air *n* air *m*; **by** ~ par avion; **on the**
~ à l'antenne. ● *vt* aérer; (*views*)
exprimer. ● *a* (*base, disaster*)
aérien; (*pollution, pressure*)
atmosphérique. ~**bed** *n* matelas
m pneumatique. ~**conditioning**
n climatisation *f*. ~**craft** *n inv*
avion *m*. ~**craft carrier** *n* porte-
avions *m inv*. ~**field** *n* terrain *m*
d'aviation. ~ **force** *n* armée *f* de
l'air. ~ **freshener** *n* désodorisant
m d'atmosphère. ~ **hostess** *n*

hôtesse *f* de l'air. ~**lift** *vt*
transporter par pont aérien.
~**line** *n* compagnie *f* aérienne.
~**liner** *n* avion *m* de ligne.
~**lock** *n* (in pipe) bulle *f* d'air;
(chamber) sas *m*. ~**mail** *n* (by)
~**mail** par avion. ~**plane** *n* (US)
avion *m*. ~**port** *n* aéroport *m*. ~
raid *n* attaque *f* aérienne. ~**tight**
a hermétique. ~ **traffic**
controller *n* contrôleur/-euse *m/*
f aérien/-ne. ~**waves** *npl* ondes
fpl.

airy *a* (**-ier**, **-iest**) (*room*) clair et
spacieux.

aisle *n* (of church) allée *f* centrale;
(in train) couloir *m*.

ajar *adv & a* entrouvert.

akin *a* ~ **to** semblable à.

alarm *n* alarme *f*; (clock) réveil *m*;
(feeling) frayeur *f*. ● *vt* inquiéter.
~**-clock** *n* réveil *m*.

alas *interj* hélas!

Albania *n* Albanie *f*.

album *n* album *m*.

alcohol *n* alcool *m*.

alcoholic *a* alcoolique; (*drink*)
alcoolisé. ● *n* alcoolique *mf*.

ale *n* bière *f*.

alert *a* alerte; (watchful) vigilant.
● *n* alerte *f*; **on the** ~ sur le qui-
vive. ● *vt* alerter; ~ **sb to**
prévenir qn de. **alertness** *n*
vivacité *f*; vigilance *f*.

A-level *n* ≈ baccalauréat *m*.

algebra *n* algèbre *f*.

Algeria *n* Algérie *f*.

alias *n* (*pl* ~**es**) faux nom *m*.
● *prep* alias.

alibi *n* alibi *m*.

alien *n & a* étranger/-ère (*m/f*)
(**to** à).

alienate *vt* éloigner.

alight *a* en feu, allumé.

alike *a* semblable. ● *adv* de la
même façon; **look** ~ se
ressembler.

alive *a* vivant; ~ **to** conscient de; ~ **with** grouillant de.

all

● *pronoun*

····▶ (everything) tout; **is that** ~? c'est tout?; **that was** ~ (that) he said c'est tout ce qu'il a dit; **I ate it** ~ j'ai tout mangé.

! Use the translation **tous** for a group of masculine or mixed gender people or objects and **toutes** for a group of feminine gender: **we were all delighted** *nous étions tous ravis*; **'where are the cups?'—'they're all in the kitchen'** *'où sont les tasses?'—'elles sont toutes dans la cuisine'*.

● *determiner*

····▶ tout/toute/tous/toutes; ~ **the time** tout le temps; ~ **his life** toute sa vie; ~ **of us** nous tous; ~ **(the) women** toutes les femmes.

● *adverb*

····▶ (completely) tout; **they were** ~ **alone** ils étaient tout seuls; **tell me** ~ **about it** raconte-moi tout; ~ **for** tout à fait pour; **not** ~ **that well** pas si bien que ça; ~ **too** bien trop.

! When the adjective that follows is in the feminine and begins with a consonant, the translation is *toute/toutes*: **she was all alone** *elle était toute seule*.

allege *vt* prétendre. **allegedly** *adv* prétendument.

allergic *a* allergique (**to** à). **allergy** *n* allergie *f*.

alleviate *vt* alléger.

alley *n* (street) ruelle *f*.

alliance *n* alliance *f*.

allied *a* allié.

alligator *n* alligator *m*.

allocate *vt* (*funds*) affecter; (*time*) accorder; (*task*) assigner.

allot *vt* (*pt* **allotted**) (*money*) attribuer; (*task*) assigner. **allotment** *n* attribution *f*; (land) parcelle *f* de terre.

all-out *a* (*effort*) acharné; (*strike*) total.

allow *vt* (authorize) autoriser à; (let) laisser; (enable) permettre; (concede) accorder; ~ **for** tenir compte de.

allowance *n* allocation *f*; **make** ~**s for sth** tenir compte de qch; **make** ~**s for sb** essayer de comprendre qn.

alloy *n* alliage *m*.

all right *a* (not bad) pas mal; **are you** ~? ça va?; **is it** ~ **if …?** est-ce que ça va si …? ● *adv* (see) bien; (*function*) comme il faut. ● *interj* d'accord.

ally[1] *n* allié/-e *m/f*.

ally[2] *vt* allier; ~ **oneself with** s'allier avec.

almighty *a* tout-puissant; (very great) formidable.

almond *n* amande *f*. ~ **tree** *n* amandier *m*.

almost *adv* presque; **he** ~ **died** il a failli mourir.

alone *a & adv* seul.

along *prep* le long de; **walk** ~ **the beach** marcher sur la plage. ● *adv* **come** ~ venir; **walk** ~ marcher; **push/pull sth** ~ pousser/tirer qch; **all** ~ (time) depuis le début; ~ **with** avec.

alongside *adv* à côté; **come** ~ (Naut) accoster. ● *prep* (next to) à côté de; (all along) le long de.

aloof *a* distant.

aloud *adv* à haute voix.

alphabet n alphabet m.
 alphabetical a alphabétique.
alpine a (*landscape*) alpestre;
 (*climate*) alpin.
already adv déjà.
alright a & adv = ALL RIGHT.
Alsatian n (dog) berger m
 allemand.
also adv aussi.
altar n autel m.
alter vt/i changer; (*building*)
 transformer; (*garment*)
 retoucher. **alteration** n
 changement m; (to building)
 transformation f; (to garment)
 retouche f.
alternate[1] vt/i alterner.
alternate[2] a en alternance; **on ~
 days** un jour sur deux.
 alternately adv alternativement.
alternative a autre; (*solution*) de
 rechange. ● n (specified option)
 alternative f; (possible option) choix
 m. **alternatively** adv sinon.
alternator n alternateur m.
although conj bien que.
altitude n altitude f.
altogether adv (completely) tout à
 fait; (on the whole) tout compte fait.
aluminium n aluminium m.
always adv toujours.
am ⇒BE.
a.m. adv du matin.
amalgamate vt/i (merge)
 fusionner; (*metals*)
 (s')amalgamer.
amateur n & a amateur (m).
amaze vt stupéfaire. **amazed** a
 stupéfait. **amazement** n
 stupéfaction f. **amazing** a
 stupéfiant; (great) exceptionnel.
ambassador n ambassadeur m.
amber n ambre m; (Auto) orange
 m.
ambiguity n ambiguïté f.
 ambiguous a ambigu.

ambition n ambition f.
 ambitious a ambitieux.
ambulance n ambulance f.
ambush n embuscade f. ● vt
 tendre une embuscade à.
amenable a obligeant; **~ to**
 (responsive) sensible à.
amend vt modifier. **amendment**
 n (to rule) amendement m.
amends npl **make ~** réparer son
 erreur.
amenities npl équipements mpl.
America n Amérique f.
American n Américain/-e m/f.
 ● a américain.
amiable a aimable.
amicable a amical.
amid(st) prep au milieu de.
amiss a **there is something ~** il y
 a quelque chose qui ne va pas.
ammonia n (gas) ammoniac m;
 (solution) ammoniaque f.
ammunition n munitions fpl.
amnesty n amnistie f.
among(st) prep parmi; (affecting a
 group) chez; **be ~ the poorest** être
 un des plus pauvres; **be ~ the
 first** être dans les premiers.
amorous a amoureux.
amount n quantité f; (total)
 montant m; (sum of money) somme
 f. ● vi **~ to** (add up to) s'élever à;
 (be equivalent to) revenir à.
amp n ampère m.
amphibian n amphibie m.
ample a (*resources*) largement
 suffisant; (*proportions*) généreux.
amplifier n amplificateur m.
amputate vt amputer.
amuse vt amuser.
amusement n (mirth) amusement
 m; (diversion) distraction f. **~
 arcade** n salle f de jeux.
an ⇒A.
anaemia n anémie f.
anaesthetic n anesthésique m.

analyse vt analyser. **analysis** n (pl **-yses**) analyse f. **analyst** n analyste mf.

anarchist n anarchiste mf.

anatomical a anatomique. **anatomy** n anatomie f.

ancestor n ancêtre m.

anchor n ancre f. ● vt mettre à l'ancre. ● vi jeter l'ancre.

anchovy n anchois m.

ancient a ancien.

ancillary a auxiliaire.

and conj et; **two hundred ～ sixty** deux cent soixante; **go ～ see him** allez le voir; **richer ～ richer** de plus en plus riche.

anew adv (once more) encore, de nouveau; (in a new way) à nouveau.

angel n ange m.

anger n colère f. ● vt mettre en colère, fâcher.

angle n angle m. ● vi pêcher (à la ligne); **～ for** (fig) quêter. **angler** n pêcheur/-euse mf.

Anglo-Saxon a anglo-saxon. ● n Anglo-Saxon/-ne m/f.

angry a (**-ier, -iest**) fâché, en colère; **get ～** se fâcher, se mettre en colère (**with** contre); **make sb ～** mettre qn en colère.

anguish n angoisse f.

animal n & a animal (m).

animate¹ a (person) vivant; (object) animé.

animate² vt animer.

aniseed n anis m.

ankle n cheville f. **～ sock** n socquette f.

annex vt annexer.

anniversary n anniversaire m.

announce vt annoncer (**that** que). **announcement** n (spoken) annonce f; (written) avis m. **announcer** n (radio, TV) speaker/ -ine m/f.

annoy vt agacer, ennuyer. **annoyance** n contrariété f.

annoyed a fâché (**with** contre); **get ～ed** se fâcher. **annoying** a ennuyeux.

annual a annuel. ● n publication f annuelle. **annually** adv (earn, produce) par an; (do, inspect) tous les ans.

annul vt (pt **annulled**) annuler.

anonymity n anonymat m. **anonymous** a anonyme.

anorak n anorak m.

another det & pron un/-e autre; **～ coffee** (one more) encore un café; **～ ten minutes** encore dix minutes, dix minutes de plus; **can I have ～?** est-ce que je peux en avoir un autre?

answer n réponse f; (solution) solution f; (phone) **there's no ～** ça ne répond pas. ● vt répondre à; (prayer) exaucer; **～ the door** ouvrir la porte. ● vi répondre. □ **～ back** répondre; **～ for** répondre de; **～ to** (superior) dépendre de; (description) répondre à. **answerable** a responsable (**for** de; **to** devant).

answering machine n répondeur m.

ant n fourmi f.

antagonism n antagonisme m. **antagonize** vt provoquer l'hostilité de.

Antarctic n **the ～** l'Antarctique m. ● a antarctique.

antenatal a prénatal.

antenna n (pl **-ae**) (of insect) antenne f; (pl **-as**; aerial: US) antenne f.

anthem n (Relig) motet m; (of country) hymne m national.

anthrax n charbon m.

antibiotic n & a antibiotique (m).

antibody n anticorps m.

anticipate vt (foresee, expect) prévoir, s'attendre à.

anticipation n attente f; **in ～ of** en prévision or attente de.

anticlimax n (let-down) déception f.

anticlockwise adv & a dans le sens inverse des aiguilles d'une montre.

antics npl pitreries fpl.

antifreeze n antigel m.

antiquated a (idea) archaïque; (building) vétuste.

antique a (old) ancien; (old-style) à l'ancienne. ● n objet m ancien, antiquité f. ~ **dealer** n antiquaire mf. ~ **shop** n magasin m d'antiquités.

anti-Semitic a antisémite.

antiseptic a & n antiseptique (m).

antisocial a asocial, antisocial; (reclusive) sauvage.

antlers npl bois mpl.

anxiety n (worry) anxiété f; (eagerness) impatience f.

anxious a (troubled) anxieux; (eager) impatient (**to** de).

any det (some) du, de l', de la, des; (after negative) de, d'; (every) tout; (no matter which) n'importe quel; **at ~ moment** à tout moment; **have you ~ water?** avez-vous de l'eau? ● pron (no matter which one) n'importe lequel; (any amount of it or them) en; **I do not have ~** je n'en ai pas; **did you see ~ of them?** en avez-vous vu? ● adv (a little) un peu; **do you have ~ more?** en avez-vous encore?; **do you have ~ more tea?** avez-vous encore du thé?; **I don't do it ~ more** je ne le fais plus.

anybody pron (no matter who) n'importe qui; (somebody) quelqu'un; (after negative) personne; **he did not see ~** il n'a vu personne.

anyhow adv (anyway) de toute façon; (carelessly) n'importe comment.

anyone pron = ANYBODY.

anything pron (no matter what) n'importe quoi; (something) quelque chose; (after negative) rien; **he did not see ~** il n'a rien vu; ~ **but** nullement; ~ **you do** tout ce que tu fais.

anyway adv de toute façon.

anywhere adv (no matter where) n'importe où; (somewhere) quelque part; (after negative) nulle part; **he does not go ~** il ne va nulle part; ~ **you go** partout où tu vas, où que tu ailles; ~ **else** partout ailleurs.

apart adv (on or to one side) à part; (separated) séparé; (into pieces) en pièces; ~ **from** à part, excepté; **ten metres ~** à dix mètres l'un de l'autre; **come ~** (break) tomber en morceaux; (machine) se démonter; **legs ~** les jambes écartées; **keep ~** séparer; **take ~** démonter.

apartment n (US) appartement m.

ape n singe m. ● vt singer.

aperitif n apéritif m.

apex n sommet m.

apologetic a (tone) d'excuse; **be ~** s'excuser. **apologetically** adv en s'excusant.

apologize vi s'excuser (**for** de; **to** auprès de).

apology n excuses fpl.

apostrophe n apostrophe f.

appal vt (pt **appalled**) horrifier. **appalling** a épouvantable.

apparatus n appareil m.

apparent a apparent. **apparently** adv apparemment.

appeal n appel m; (attractiveness) attrait m, charme m. ● vi (Jur) faire appel; ~ **to sb** (beg) faire appel à qn; (attract) plaire à qn; ~ **to sb for sth** demander qch à qn. **appealing** a (attractive) attirant.

appear vi apparaître; (arrive) se présenter; (seem, be published)

paraître; (Theat) jouer; ~ **on TV**
passer à la télé. **appearance** n
apparition f; (aspect) apparence f.
appease vt apaiser.
appendix n (pl **-ices**) appendice
m.
appetite n appétit m.
appetizer n (snack) amuse-gueule
m inv; (drink) apéritif m.
appetizing a appétissant.
applaud vt/i applaudir; (decision)
applaudir à. **applause** n
applaudissements mpl.
apple n pomme f. ~**-tree** n
pommier m.
appliance n appareil m.
applicable a valable; **if** ~ le cas
échéant.
applicant n candidat/-e m/f (**for**
à).
application n application f;
(request, form) demande f; (for job)
candidature f.
apply vt appliquer. ● vi ~ **to**
(refer) s'appliquer à; (ask)
s'adresser à; ~ **for** (job) postuler
pour; (grant) demander; ~
oneself to s'appliquer à.
appoint vt (to post) nommer; (fix)
désigner; **well-~ed** bien équipé.
appointment n nomination f;
(meeting) rendez-vous m inv; (job)
poste m; **make an** ~ prendre
rendez-vous (**with** avec).
appraisal n évaluation f.
appraise vt évaluer.
appreciate vt (like) apprécier;
(understand) comprendre; (be grateful
for) être reconnaissant de. ● vi
prendre de la valeur.
appreciation n appréciation f;
(gratitude) reconnaissance f; (rise)
augmentation f. **appreciative** a
reconnaissant; (audience)
enthousiaste.
apprehend vt (arrest)
appréhender; (understand)
comprendre. **apprehension** n

(arrest) appréhension f; (fear)
crainte f.
apprehensive a inquiet; **be** ~ **of**
craindre.
apprentice n apprenti m. ● vt
mettre en apprentissage.
approach vt (s')approcher de;
(accost) aborder; (with request)
s'adresser à. ● vi (s')approcher.
● n approche f; **an** ~ **to** (problem)
une façon d'aborder; (person)
une démarche auprès de.
approachable a abordable.
appropriate¹ vt s'approprier.
appropriate² a approprié,
propre. **appropriately** adv à
propos.
approval n approbation f; **on** ~ à
or sous condition.
approve vt approuver. ● vi ~ **of**
approuver. **approving** a
approbateur.
approximate¹ vi ~ **to** se
rapprocher de.
approximate² a approximatif.
approximately adv environ.
approximation n approximation
f.
apricot n abricot m.
April n avril m. ~ **Fools Day** n le
premier avril.
apron n tablier m.
apt a (suitable) approprié; **be** ~ **to**
avoir tendance à.
aptitude n aptitude f.
aptly adv à propos.
Aquarius n Verseau m.
aquatic a aquatique; (Sport)
nautique.
Arab n Arabe mf. ● a arabe.
Arabian a d'Arabie.
Arabic a & n (Ling) arabe (m).
arbitrary a arbitraire.
arbitrate vi arbitrer. **arbitration**
n arbitrage m. **arbitrator** n
médiateur/-trice m/f.

arcade n (shops) galerie f; (arches) arcades fpl.

arch n arche f; (of foot) voûte f plantaire. ● vt/i (s')arquer. ● a (playful) malicieux.

archaeological a archéologique. **archaeologist** n archéologue mf. **archaeology** n archéologie f.

archbishop n archevêque m.

archery n tir m à l'arc.

architect n architecte mf; (of plan) artisan m. **architectural** a architectural. **architecture** n architecture f.

archives npl archives fpl.

archway n voûte f.

Arctic n the ~ l'Arctique m. ● a (climate) arctique; (expedition) polaire; (conditions) glacial.

ardent a ardent.

are ⇒BE.

area n (region) région f; (district) quartier m; (fig) domaine m; (in geometry) aire f; **parking/picnic** ~ aire f de parking/de pique-nique.

arena n arène f.

aren't = ARE NOT.

Argentina n Argentine f.

arguable a discutable. **arguably** adv selon certains.

argue vi (quarrel) se disputer; (reason) argumenter. ● vt (debate) discuter; ~ **that** alléguer que.

argument n dispute f; (reasoning) argument m; (discussion) débat m. **argumentative** a ergoteur.

Aries n Bélier m.

arise vi (pt **arose**; pp **arisen**) (problem) survenir; (question) se poser; ~ **from** résulter de.

aristocrat n aristocrate mf.

arithmetic n arithmétique f.

ark n (Relig) arche f.

arm n bras m; ~ **in arm** bras dessus bras dessous. ● vt armer; ~**ed robbery** vol m à main armée.

armament n armement m.

arm: ~**band** n brassard m. ~**chair** n fauteuil m.

armour n armure f. **armoured** a blindé. **armoury** n arsenal m.

armpit n aisselle f.

arms npl (weapons) armes fpl. ~ **dealer** n trafiquant m d'armes.

army n armée f.

aroma n arôme m. **aromatic** a aromatique.

arose ⇒ARISE.

around adv (tout) autour; (here and there) çà et là. ● prep autour de; ~ **here** par ici.

arouse vt (awaken, cause) éveiller; (excite) exciter.

arrange vt arranger; (time, date) fixer; ~ **to** s'arranger pour.

arrangement n arrangement m; (agreement) entente f; **make** ~**s** prendre des dispositions.

array n an ~ **of** (display) un étalage impressionnant de.

arrears npl arriéré m; **in** ~ (rent) arriéré; **he is in** ~ il a des retards dans ses paiements.

arrest vt arrêter; (attention) retenir. ● n arrestation f; **under** ~ en état d'arrestation.

arrival n arrivée f; **new** ~ nouveau venu m, nouvelle venue f.

arrive vi arriver; ~ **at** (destination) arriver à; (decision) parvenir à.

arrogance n arrogance f.

arrow n flèche f.

arse n ▣ cul m ▣.

arson n incendie m criminel. **arsonist** n incendiaire mf.

art n art m; (fine arts) beaux-arts mpl.

artery n artère f.

art gallery n (public) musée m (d'art); (private) galerie f (d'art).

arthritis n arthrite f.

artichoke n artichaut m.

article *n* article *m*; ~ **of clothing** vêtement *m*.

articulate *a* (*person*) capable de s'exprimer clairement; (*speech*) distinct.

articulated lorry *n* semi-remorque *m*.

artificial *a* artificiel.

artist *n* artiste *mf*.

arts *npl* the ~ les arts *mpl*; (Univ) lettres *fpl*.

artwork *n* (of book) illustrations *fpl*.

as *conj* comme; (while) pendant que; (over gradual period of time) au fur et à mesure que; ~ **she grew older** au fur et à mesure qu'elle vieillissait; **do** ~ **I say** fais ce que je dis; ~ **usual** comme d'habitude. ● *prep* ~ **a mother** en tant que mère; ~ **a gift** en cadeau; ~ **from Monday** à partir de lundi; ~ **for**, ~ **to** quant à; ~ **if** comme si; **you look** ~ **if you're tired** vous avez l'air (d'être) fatigué. ● *adv* ~ **tall** ~ aussi grand que; ~ **much** ~, ~ **many** ~ autant que; ~ **soon** ~ aussitôt que; ~ **well** ~ aussi bien que; ~ **wide** ~ **possible** aussi large que possible.

asbestos *n* amiante *f*.

ascend *vt* gravir. ● *vi* monter.

ascertain *vt* établir (**that** que).

ash *n* cendre *f*; ~(**-tree**) frêne *m*.

ashamed *a* be ~ avoir honte (**of** de).

ashore *adv* à terre.

ashtray *n* cendrier *m*.

Asia *n* Asie *f*.

Asian *n* Asiatique *mf*. ● *a* asiatique.

aside *adv* de côté; ~ **from** à part. ● *n* aparté *m*.

ask *vt/i* demander; (*invite*) inviter; ~ **sb sth** demander qch à qn; ~ **sb to do** demander à qn de faire; ~ **about**

(*thing*) se renseigner sur; (*person*) demander des nouvelles de; ~ **for** demander.

asleep *a* endormi; (numb) engourdi. ● *adv* **fall** ~ s'endormir.

asparagus *n* (plant) asperge *f*; (Culin) asperges *fpl*.

aspect *n* aspect *m*; (direction) orientation *f*.

asphyxiate *vt/i* (s')asphyxier.

aspire *vi* aspirer (**to** à; **to do** à faire).

aspirin *n* aspirine® *f*.

ass *n* âne *m*; (person 🆃) idiot/-e *m/f*.

assail *vt* attaquer. **assailant** *n* agresseur *m*.

assassin *n* assassin *m*. **assassinate** *vt* assassiner. **assassination** *n* assassinat *m*.

assault *n* (Mil) assaut *m*; (Jur) agression *f*. ● *vt* (*person*: Jur) agresser.

assemble *vt* (construct) assembler; (gather) rassembler. ● *vi* se rassembler.

assembly *n* assemblée *f*. ~ **line** *n* chaîne *f* de montage.

assent *n* assentiment *m*. ● *vi* consentir.

assert *vt* affirmer; (*rights*) revendiquer. **assertion** *n* affirmation *f*. **assertive** *a* assuré.

assess *vt* évaluer; (*payment*) déterminer le montant de. **assessment** *n* évaluation *f*. **assessor** *n* (valuer) expert *m*.

asset *n* (advantage) atout *m*; (financial) bien *m*; ~**s** (Comm) actif *m*.

assign *vt* (allot) assigner; ~ **sb to** (appoint) affecter qn à.

assignment *n* (task) mission *f*; (diplomatic) poste *m*; (academic) devoir *m*.

assist vt/i aider. **assistance** n aide f.

assistant n aide mf; (in shop) vendeur/-euse m/f. ● a (manager) adjoint.

associate¹ n & a associé/-e (m/f).

associate² vt associer. ● vi ~ **with** fréquenter. **association** n association f.

assorted a divers; (foods) assorti.

assortment n assortiment m; (of people) mélange m.

assume vt supposer; (power, attitude) prendre; (role, burden) assumer.

assurance n assurance f.

assure vt assurer.

asterisk n astérisque m.

asthma n asthme m.

astonish vt étonner.

astound vt stupéfier.

astray adv go ~ s'égarer; lead ~ égarer.

astride adv & prep à califourchon (sur).

astrologer n astrologue mf. **astrology** n astrologie f.

astronaut n astronaute mf.

astronomer n astronome mf.

asylum n asile m.

····································

at preposition

⟹ For expressions such as laugh at, look at ⇒laugh, look.

····► (in position or place) à; he's ~ his desk il est à son bureau; she's ~ work/school elle est au travail/à l'école.

····► (at someone's house or business) chez; ~ Mary's/the dentist's chez Mary/le dentiste.

····► (in times, ages) à; ~ four o'clock à quatre heures; ~ two years of age à l'âge de deux ans.

····································

ate ⇒EAT.

atheist n athée mf.

athlete n athlète mf. **athletic** a athlétique. **athletics** npl athlétisme m; (US) sports mpl.

Atlantic a atlantique. ● n the ~ (Ocean) l'Atlantique m.

atlas n atlas m.

atmosphere n (air) atmosphère f; (mood) ambiance f. **atmospheric** a atmosphérique; d'ambiance.

atom n atome m.

atrocious a atroce.

atrocity n atrocité f.

attach vt/i (s')attacher; (letter) joindre (to à).

attaché n (Pol) attaché/-e m/f. ~ **case** n attaché-case m.

attached a be ~ to (like) être attaché à; the ~ letter la lettre ci-jointe.

attachment n (accessory) accessoire m; (affection) attachement m; (e-mail) pièces fpl jointes.

attack n attaque f; (Med) crise f. ● vt attaquer.

attain vt atteindre (à); (gain) acquérir.

attempt vt tenter. ● n tentative f; an ~ on sb's life un attentat contre qn.

attend vt assister à; (class) suivre; (school, church) aller à. ● vi assister; ~ (to) (look after) s'occuper de. **attendance** n présence f; (people) assistance f.

attendant n employé/-e m/f. ● a associé.

attention n attention f; ~! (Mil) garde-à-vous!; pay ~ faire or prêter attention (to à).

attentive a attentif; (considerate)

attentionné. **attentively** *adv*
attentivement. **attentiveness** *n*
attention *f*.

attest *vt/i* ~ (**to**) attester.

attic *n* grenier *m*.

attitude *n* attitude *f*.

attorney *n* (US) avocat/-e *m/f*.

attract *vt* attirer. **attraction** *n*
attraction *f*; (*charm*) attrait *m*.

attractive *a* attrayant, séduisant.
attractively *adv* agréablement.
attractiveness *n* attrait *m*,
beauté *f*.

attribute¹ *vt* ~ **to** attribuer à.

attribute² *n* attribut *m*.

aubergine *n* aubergine *f*.

auction *n* vente *f* aux enchères.
● *vt* vendre aux enchères.
auctioneer *n* commissaire-
priseur *m*.

audacious *a* audacieux.

audience *n* (theatre, radio) public
m; (interview) audience *f*.

audiovisual *a* audiovisuel.

audit *n* vérification *f* des
comptes. ● *vt* vérifier.

audition *n* audition *f*. ● *vt/i*
auditionner (**for** pour).

auditor *n* commissaire *m* aux
comptes.

August *n* août *m*.

aunt *n* tante *f*.

auspicious *a* favorable.

Australia *n* Australie *f*.

Australian *n* Australien/-ne *m/f*.
● *a* australien.

Austria *n* Autriche *f*.

Austrian *n* Autrichien/-ne *m/f*.
● *a* autrichien.

authentic *a* authentique.

author *n* auteur *m*.

authoritarian *a* autoritaire.

authoritative *a* (credible) qui fait
autorité; (manner) autoritaire.

authority *n* autorité *f*; (permission)
autorisation *f*.

authorization *n* autorisation *f*.

authorize *vt* autoriser.

autistic *a* (*person*) autiste;
(*response*) autistique.

autograph *n* autographe *m*. ● *vt*
signer, dédicacer.

automate *vt* automatiser.

automatic *a* automatique. ● *n*
(Auto) voiture *f* automatique.

automobile *n* (US) auto(mobile)
f.

autonomous *a* autonome.

autumn *n* automne *m*.

auxiliary *a & n* auxiliaire (*mf*); ~
(**verb**) auxiliaire *m*.

avail *vt* ~ **oneself of** profiter de.
● *n* of no ~ inutile; **to no** ~ sans
résultat.

availability *n* disponibilité *f*.

available *a* disponible.

avenge *vt* venger; ~ **oneself** se
venger (**on** de).

avenue *n* avenue *f*; (line of approach:
fig) voie *f*.

average *n* moyenne *f*; **on** ~ en
moyenne. ● *a* moyen. ● *vt* faire
la moyenne de; (produce, do) faire
en moyenne.

aviary *n* volière *f*.

avocado *n* avocat *m*.

avoid *vt* éviter. **avoidance** *n* (of
injuries) prévention *f*; (of responsibility)
refus *m*.

await *vt* attendre.

awake *vt/i* (*pt* awoke; *pp*
awoken) (s')éveiller. ● *a* be ~ ne
pas dormir, être (r)éveillé.

award *vt* (grant) attribuer;
(prize) décerner; (points)
accorder. ● *n* récompense *f*, prix
m; (scholarship) bourse *f*; **pay** ~
augmentation *f* (de salaire).

aware *a* (well-informed) averti; be ~
of (danger) être conscient de;
(fact) savoir; **become** ~ **of**
prendre conscience de.
awareness *n* conscience *f*.

away adv (far) (au) loin; (absent)
absent, parti; ~ **from** loin de;
move ~ s'écarter; (to new home)
déménager; **six kilometres** ~ à six
kilomètres (de distance); **take** ~
emporter; **he was snoring** ~ il
ronflait. ● a & n ~ (**match**) match
m à l'extérieur.

awe n crainte f (révérencielle).

awe-inspiring a impressionnant.

awesome a redoutable.

awful a affreux. **awfully** adv
(badly) affreusement; (very ⊞)
rudement.

awkward a difficile; (inconvenient)
inopportun; (clumsy) maladroit;
(embarrassing) gênant; (embarrassed)
gêné. **awkwardly** adv
maladroitement; avec gêne.
awkwardness n maladresse f;
(discomfort) gêne f.

awning n auvent m; (of shop) store
m.

awoke, awoken ⇒AWAKE.

axe n hache f. ● vt (pres p **axing**)
réduire; (eliminate) supprimer;
(employee) renvoyer.

axis n (pl **axes**) axe m.

axle n essieu m.

BA abbr ⇒BACHELOR OF ARTS.

babble vi babiller; (stream)
gazouiller. ● n babillage m.

baby n bébé m. ~ **carriage** n
(US) voiture f d'enfant. ~-**sit** vi
faire du babysitting, garder des
enfants. ~-**sitter** n baby-sitter
mf.

bachelor n célibataire m. **B**~ **of
Arts** licencié/-e m/f ès lettres.

back n (of person, hand, page, etc.)
dos m; (of house) derrière m; (of
vehicle) arrière m; (of room) fond m;
(of chair) dossier m; (in football)
arrière m; **at the** ~ **of the book** à la
fin du livre; **in** ~ **of** (US) derrière.
● a (leg, wheel) arrière inv; (door,
gate) de derrière; (taxes) arriéré.
● adv en arrière; (returned) de
retour, rentré; **come** ~ revenir;
give ~ rendre; **take** ~ reprendre;
I want it ~ je veux le récupérer.
● vt (support) appuyer; (bet on)
miser sur; (vehicle) faire reculer.
● vi (of person, vehicle) reculer. □ ~
down céder; ~ **out** se désister;
(Auto) sortir en marche arrière; ~
up (support) appuyer. ~**ache** n
mal m de dos. ~-**bencher** n (Pol)
député m. ~**bone** n colonne f
vertébrale. ~**date** vt antidater.
~**fire** vi (Auto) pétarader; (fig) mal
tourner. ~**gammon** n trictrac m.

background n fond m, arrière-
plan m; (context) contexte m;
(environment) milieu m; (experience)
formation f. ● a (music, noise) de
fond.

backhand n revers m.
backhander n (bribe) pot-de-vin
m.

backing n soutien m.

back: ~**lash** n retour m de bâton;
réaction f violente (**against**
contre). ~**log** n retard m. ~
number n vieux numéro m.
~**pack** n sac m à dos. ~**side** n
(buttocks ⊞) derrière m. ~**stage** a
& adv dans les coulisses.
~**stroke** n dos m crawlé. ~**track**
vi rebrousser chemin; (change one's
opinion) faire marche arrière.

back-up n soutien m; (Comput)
sauvegarde f. ● a de secours;
(Comput) de sauvegarde.

backward a (step etc.) en
arrière; (retarded) arriéré.

backwards *adv* en arrière; (*walk*) à reculons; (*read*) à l'envers; **go ~ and forwards** aller et venir.

bacon *n* lard *m*; (in rashers) bacon *m*.

bacteria *npl* bactéries *fpl*.

bad *a* (**worse**, **worst**) mauvais; (wicked) méchant; (ill) malade; (*accident*) grave; (*food*) gâté; **feel ~** se sentir mal; **go ~** se gâter; **~ language** gros mots *mpl*; **too ~!** tant pis!; (I'm sorry) dommage!

badge *n* badge *m*; (coat of arms) insigne *m*.

badger *n* blaireau *m*. ● *vt* harceler.

badly *adv* mal; (*hurt*) gravement; **want ~** avoir grande envie de.

badminton *n* badminton *m*.

bad-tempered *a* irritable.

baffle *vt* déconcerter.

bag *n* sac *m*; **~s** (luggage) bagages *mpl*; (under eyes ⊞) valises *fpl*; **~s of** plein de.

baggage *n* bagages *mpl*; **~ reclaim** réception *f* des bagages.

baggy *a* large.

bagpipes *npl* cornemuse *f*.

bail *n* caution *f*; **on ~** sous caution; (cricket) bâtonnet *m*. ● *vt* mettre en liberté provisoire.

bailiff *n* huissier *m*.

bait *n* appât *m*. ● *vt* appâter; (fig) tourmenter.

bake *vt* faire cuire au four; **~ a cake** faire un gâteau. ● *vi* cuire; (*person*) faire du pain. **baked beans** *npl* haricots *mpl* blancs à la tomate. **baked potato** *n* pomme *f* de terre en robe des champs. **baker** *n* boulanger/-ère *m/f*. **bakery** *n* boulangerie *f*.

balance *n* équilibre *m*; (scales) balance *f*; (outstanding sum: Comm) solde *m*; (of payments, of trade) balance *f*; (remainder) restant *m*. ● *vt* mettre en équilibre; (weigh up

also Comm) balancer; (budget) équilibrer; (to compensate) contrebalancer. ● *vi* être en équilibre.

balcony *n* balcon *m*.

bald *a* chauve; (*tyre*) lisse; (fig) simple.

balk *vt* contrecarrer. ● *vi* **~ at** reculer devant.

ball *n* (golf, tennis, etc.) balle *f*; (football) ballon *m*; (billiards) bille *f*; (of wool) pelote *f*; (sphere) boule *f*; (dance) bal *m*.

ballet *n* ballet *m*.

balloon *n* ballon *m*.

ballot *n* scrutin *m*. ● *vt* consulter par vote (**on** sur). **~-box** *n* urne *f*. **~-paper** *n* bulletin *m* de vote.

ballpoint pen *n* stylo *m* (à) bille.

ban *vt* (*pt* **banned**) interdire; **~ sb from** exclure qn de; **~ sb from doing** interdire à qn de faire. ● *n* interdiction *f* (**on** de).

banal *a* banal.

banana *n* banane *f*.

band *n* (strip, group of people) bande *f*; (pop group) groupe *m*; (brass band) fanfare *f*. ● *vi* **~ together** se réunir.

bandage *n* bandage *m*. ● *vt* bander.

B and B *abbr* ⇒BED AND BREAKFAST.

bandit *n* bandit *m*.

bandstand *n* kiosque *m* à musique.

bang *n* (blow, noise) coup *m*; (explosion) détonation *f*; (of door) claquement *m*. ● *vt/i* taper; (*door*) claquer; **~ one's head** se cogner la tête. ● *interj* vlan. ● *adv* ⊞ **~ in the middle** en plein milieu; **~ on time** à l'heure pile.

banger *n* (*firework*) pétard *m*; (Culin) saucisse *f*; (old) **~** (*car* ⊞) guimbarde *f*.

banish *vt* bannir.

banister n rampe f d'escalier.

bank n (Comm) banque f; (of river) rive f; (of sand) banc m. ● vt mettre en banque. ● vi (Aviat) virer; ~ **with** avoir un compte à; ~ **on** compter sur. ~ **account** n compte m en banque. ~ **card** n carte f bancaire. ~ **holiday** n jour m férié.

banking n opérations fpl bancaires; (as career) la banque.

banknote n billet m de banque.

bankrupt a be ~ être en faillite; go ~ faire faillite. ● n failli/-e m/f. ● vt mettre en faillite. **bankruptcy** n faillite f.

bank statement n relevé m de compte.

banner n bannière f.

baptism n baptême m. **baptize** vt baptiser.

bar n (of metal) barre f; (on window, cage) barreau m; (of chocolate) tablette f; (pub) bar m; (counter) comptoir m; (Mus) mesure f; (fig) obstacle m; ~ **of soap** savonnette f; **the** ~ (Jur) le barreau. ● vt (pt **barred**) (obstruct) barrer; (prohibit) interdire; (exclude) exclure. ● prep sauf.

barbecue n barbecue m. ● vt faire au barbecue.

barbed wire n fil m de fer barbelé.

barber n coiffeur m (pour hommes).

bar code n code m (à) barres.

bare a nu; (cupboard) vide. ● vt mettre à nu. ~**foot** a nu-pieds inv, pieds nus. **barely** adv à peine.

bargain n (deal) marché m; (cheap thing) occasion f. ● vi négocier; (haggle) marchander; **not** ~ **for** ne pas s'attendre à.

barge n péniche f. ● vi ~ **in** interrompre; (into room) faire irruption.

bark n (of tree) écorce f; (of dog) aboiement m. ● vi aboyer.

barley n orge f.

bar: ~**maid** n serveuse f. ~**man** n (pl -**men**) barman m.

barn n grange f.

barracks npl caserne f.

barrel n tonneau m; (of oil) baril m; (of gun) canon m.

barren a stérile.

barricade n barricade f. ● vt barricader.

barrier n barrière f; **ticket** ~ guichet m.

barrister n avocat m.

bartender n (US) barman m.

barter n troc m. ● vt troquer (**for** contre).

base n base f. ● vt baser (**on** sur; **in** à). ● a ignoble. **baseball** n base-ball m.

basement n sous-sol m.

bash 🔲 vt cogner; ~**ed in** enfoncé. ● n coup m violent; **have a** ~ **at** s'essayer à.

basic a fondamental, élémentaire; **the** ~**s** l'essentiel m. **basically** adv au fond.

basil n basilic m.

basin n (for liquids) cuvette f; (for food) bol m; (for washing) lavabo m; (of river) bassin m.

basis n (pl **bases**) base f.

bask vi se prélasser (**in** à).

basket n corbeille f; (with handle) panier m. **basketball** n basket(-ball) m.

Basque n (person) Basque mf; (Ling) basque m. ● a basque.

bass[1] a (voice, part) de basse; (sound, note) grave. ● n (pl **basses**) basse f.

bass[2] n inv (freshwater fish) perche f; (sea) bar m.

bassoon n basson m.

bastard n (illegitimate) bâtard/-e m/f; (insult 🔲) salaud m 🔲.

bat n (cricket etc.) batte f; (table tennis) raquette f; (animal) chauve-souris f. ● vt (pt **batted**) (ball) frapper; **not ~ an eyelid** ne pas sourciller.

batch n (of cakes, people) fournée f; (of goods, text also Comput) lot m.

bath n (pl **-s**) bain m; (tub) baignoire f; **have a ~** prendre un bain; (swimming) **~s** piscine f. ● vt donner un bain à.

bathe vt baigner. ● vi se baigner; (US) prendre un bain.

bathing n baignade f. **~-costume** n maillot m de bain.

bath: **~robe** n (US) robe f de chambre. **~room** n salle f de bains.

baton n (policeman's) matraque f; (Mus) baguette f.

batter vt battre. ● n (Culin) pâte f (à frire).

battery n (Mil, Auto) batterie f; (of torch, radio) pile f.

battle n bataille f; (fig) lutte f. ● vi se battre. **~field** n champ m de bataille.

baulk vt/i = BALK.

bay n (Bot) laurier m; (Geog, Archit) baie f; (area) aire f; (bark) aboiement m; **keep or hold at ~** tenir à distance. ● vi aboyer. **~-leaf** n feuille f de laurier. **~ window** n fenêtre f en saillie.

bazaar n (shop, market) bazar m; (sale) vente f.

BC abbr (**before Christ**) avant J.-C.

BBS abbr (**Bulletin Board System**) (Internet) babillard m électronique, BBS m.

....

be

    present **am, is, are**; past **was, were**; past participle **been**.

● intransitive verb

••••➤ être; **I am tired** je suis fatigué; **it's me** c'est moi.

••••➤ (feelings) avoir; **I am hot** j'ai chaud; **he is hungry/thirsty** il a faim/soif; **her hands are cold** elle a froid aux mains.

••••➤ (age) avoir; **I am 15** j'ai 15 ans.

••••➤ (weather) faire; **it's warm** il fait chaud; **it's 25** il fait 25.

••••➤ (health) aller; **how are you?** comment allez-vous or comment vas-tu?

••••➤ (visit) aller; **I've never been to Italy** je ne suis jamais allé en Italie.

● auxiliary verb

••••➤ (in tenses) **I am working** je travaille; **he was writing to his mother** il écrivait à sa mère; **she is to do it at once** (obligation) elle doit le faire tout de suite.

••••➤ (in passives) **he was killed** il a été tué; **the window has been fixed** on a réparé la fenêtre.

••••➤ (in tag questions) **their house is lovely, isn't it?** leur maison est très jolie, n'est-ce pas?

••••➤ (in short answers) **'I am a painter'—'are you?'** 'je suis peintre'—'ah oui?'; **'are you a doctor?'—'yes, I am'** 'êtes-vous médecin?'—'oui'; **'you're not going out'—'yes I am'** 'tu ne sors pas'—'si'.

....

beach n plage f.

beacon n (lighthouse) phare m; (marker) balise f.

bead n perle f.

beak n bec m.

beaker n gobelet m.

beam n (timber) poutre f; (of light) rayon m; (of torch) faisceau m. ● vi rayonner. ● vt (broadcast) transmettre.

bean n haricot m.

bear n ours m. ● vt (pt **bore**; pp

borne) (carry, show, feel) porter; (endure, sustain) supporter; (*child*) mettre au monde. ● *vi* ~ **left** (go) prendre à gauche; ~ **in mind** tenir compte de. □ ~ **out** confirmer; ~ **up** tenir le coup. **bearable** *a* supportable.

beard *n* barbe *f*.

bearer *n* porteur/-euse *m/f*.

bearing *n* (behaviour) maintien *m*; (relevance) rapport *m*; **get one's ~s** s'orienter.

beast *n* bête *f*; (*person*) brute *f*.

beat *vt/i* (*pt* **beat**; *pp* **beaten**) battre; ~ **a retreat** battre en retraite; ~ **it!** dégage! 🄴; **it ~s me** 🄴 ça me dépasse. ● *n* (of drum, heart) battement *m*; (Mus) mesure *f*; (of policeman) ronde *f*. □ ~ **off** repousser; ~ **up** tabasser. **beating** *n* raclée *f*.

beautiful *a* beau.

beauty *n* beauté *f*. ~ **parlour** *n* institut *m* de beauté. ~ **spot** *n* grain *m* de beauté; (place) site *m* pittoresque.

beaver *n* castor *m*.

became ⇒BECOME.

because *conj* parce que; ~ **of** à cause de.

become *vt/i* (*pt* **became**; *pp* **become**) devenir; (befit) convenir à; **what has ~ of her?** qu'est-ce qu'elle est devenue?

bed *n* lit *m*; (layer) couche *f*; (of sea) fond *m*; (of flowers) parterre *m*; **go to ~** (aller) se coucher. ● *vi* (*pt* **bedded**) ~ **down** se coucher. **bed and breakfast** *n* chambre *f* avec petit déjeuner, chambre *f* d'hôte. ~**bug** *n* punaise *f*. ~**clothes** *npl* couvertures *fpl*.

bedding *n* literie *f*.

bed: ~**ridden** *a* cloué au lit. ~**room** *n* chambre *f* (à coucher). ~**side** *n* chevet *m*. ~**sit**, ~**sitter** *n* chambre *f* meublée, studio *m*.

~**spread** *n* dessus *m* de lit. ~**time** *n* heure *f* du coucher.

bee *n* abeille *f*; **make a ~-line for** aller tout droit vers.

beech *n* hêtre *m*.

beef *n* bœuf *m*. ~**burger** *n* hamburger *m*.

beehive *n* ruche *f*.

been ⇒BE.

beer *n* bière *f*.

beetle *n* scarabée *m*.

beetroot *n inv* betterave *f*.

before *prep* (time) avant; (place) devant; **the day ~ yesterday** avant-hier. ● *adv* avant; (already) déjà; **the day ~** la veille. ● *conj* ~ **leaving** avant de partir; ~ **I forget** avant que j'oublie. **beforehand** *adv* à l'avance.

beg *vt* (*pt* **begged**) (*food, money, favour*) demander (**from** à); ~ **sb to do** supplier qn de faire. ● *vi* mendier; **it is going ~ging** personne n'en veut.

began ⇒BEGIN.

beggar *n* mendiant/-e *m/f*.

begin *vt/i* (*pt* **began**, *pp* **begun**, *pres p* **beginning**) commencer (**to do** à faire). **beginner** *n* débutant/ -e *m/f*. **beginning** *n* commencement *m*, début *m*.

begun ⇒BEGIN.

behalf *n* **on ~ of** (*act, speak, campaign*) pour; (*phone, write*) de la part de.

behave *vi* se conduire; ~ **(oneself)** se conduire bien.

behaviour, (US) **behavior** *n* comportement *m* (**towards** envers).

behead *vt* décapiter.

behind *prep* derrière; (in time) en retard sur. ● *adv* derrière; (late) en retard; **leave ~** oublier. ● *n* (buttocks 🄴) derrière *m* 🄴.

beige *a & n* beige (*m*).

being *n* (person) être *m*.

belch vi avoir un renvoi. ● vt ~ **out** (smoke) s'échapper. ● n renvoi m.

Belgian n Belge mf. ● a belge. **Belgium** n Belgique f.

belief n conviction f; (trust) confiance f; (faith: Relig) foi f.

believe vt/i croire; ~ **in** croire à; (deity) croire en. **believer** n croyant/-e m/f.

bell n cloche f; (small) clochette f; (on door) sonnette f.

belly n ventre m. ~ **button** n nombril m.

belong vi ~ **to** appartenir à; (club) être membre de.

belongings npl affaires fpl.

beloved a & n bien-aimé/-e (m/f).

below prep sous, au-dessous de; (fig) indigne de. ● adv en dessous; (on page) ci-dessous.

belt n ceinture f; (Tech) courroie f; (fig) zone f. ● vt (hit 🆇) rosser. ● vi (rush 🆇) ~ **in/out** entrer/sortir à toute vitesse.

beltway n (US) périphérique m.

bemused a perplexe.

bench n banc m; the ~ (Jur) la magistrature (assise).

bend vt (pt **bent**) (knee, arm, wire) plier; (head, back) courber. ● vi (road) tourner; (person) ~ **down/over** se pencher. ● n courbe f; (in road) virage m; (of arm, knee) pli m.

beneath prep sous, au-dessous de; (fig) indigne de. ● adv en dessous.

benefactor n bienfaiteur/-trice m/f.

beneficial a bénéfique.

benefit n avantage m; (allowance) allocation f. ● vt (be useful to) profiter à; (do good to) faire du bien à. ● vi profiter; ~ **from** tirer profit de.

benign a (kindly) bienveillant; (Med) bénin.

bent ⇒BEND. ● n (talent) aptitude f; (inclination) penchant m. ● a tordu; 🆇 corrompu; ~ **on doing** décidé à faire.

bequest n legs m.

bereaved a endeuillé; the ~ la famille endeuillée. **bereavement** n deuil m.

berry n baie f.

berserk a fou furieux.

berth n (in train, ship) couchette f; (anchorage) mouillage m; **give a wide** ~ **to** éviter. ● vi mouiller.

beside prep à côté de; ~ **oneself** hors de soi; ~ **the point** sans rapport.

besides prep en plus de. ● adv en plus.

besiege vt assiéger.

best a meilleur; the ~ **book** le meilleur livre; the ~ **part of** la plus grande partie de; the ~ **thing is to** le mieux est de. ● adv (the) ~ (behave, play) mieux. ● n the ~ le meilleur, la meilleure; **do one's** ~ faire de son mieux; **make the** ~ **of** s'accommoder de. ~ **man** n témoin. ~**-seller** n bestseller m, livre m à succès.

bet n pari m. ● vt/i (pt **bet** or **betted**, pres p **betting**) parier (on sur).

betray vt trahir.

better a meilleur; the ~ **part of** la plus grande partie de; **get** ~ s'améliorer; (recover) se remettre. ● adv mieux; **I had** ~ **go** je ferais mieux de partir. ● vt (improve) améliorer; (do better than) surpasser. ● n **get the** ~ **of** l'emporter sur; **so much the** ~ tant mieux. ~ **off** a (richer) plus riche; **he is/would be** ~ **off at home** il est/serait mieux chez lui.

betting-shop n bureau m du PMU.

between prep entre. ● adv in ~ au milieu.

beverage n boisson f.

beware vi prendre garde (of à).

bewilder vt déconcerter.

beyond prep au-delà de; (control, reach) hors de; (besides) excepté. ● adv au-delà; **it is ~ me** ça me dépasse.

bias n (inclination) tendance f; (prejudice) parti m pris. ● vt (pt **biased**) influer sur. **biased** a partial.

bib n bavoir m.

Bible n Bible f.

biceps n biceps m.

bicycle n vélo m, bicyclette f. ● a (bell, chain) de vélo; (pump, clip) à vélo.

bid n (at auction) enchère f; (attempt) tentative f. ● vt/i (pt **bade**, pp **bidden** or **bid**, pres p **bidding**) (offer) offrir, mettre une enchère (de) (for pour); ~ **sb good morning** dire bonjour à qn; ~ **sb farewell** faire ses adieux à qn.

bidding n (at auction) enchères fpl; **he did my ~** il a fait ce que je lui ai dit.

bifocals npl verres mpl à double foyer.

big a (**bigger**, **biggest**) grand; (in bulk) gros.

bike n vélo m.

bikini n bikini m.

bilberry n myrtille f.

bilingual a bilingue.

bill n (invoice) facture f; (in hotel, for gas) note f; (in restaurant) addition f; (of sale) acte m; (Pol) projet m de loi; (banknote: US) billet m de banque; (Theat) **on the ~** à l'affiche; (of bird) bec m. ● vt (person: Comm) envoyer la facture à. ~**board** n panneau m d'affichage.

billet n cantonnement m. ● vt (pt **billeted**) cantonner (on chez).

billiards n billard m.

billion n billion m; (US) milliard m.

bin n (for rubbish) poubelle f; (for storage) casier m.

bind vt (pt **bound**) attacher; (book) relier; **be bound by** être tenu par. ● n (bore) corvée f.

binding n reliure f. ● a (agreement, contract) qui lie.

binge n (drinking) beuverie f; (eating) gueuleton m.

binoculars npl jumelles fpl.

biochemistry n biochimie f.

biodegradable a biodégradable.

biographer n biographe mf.

biography n biographie f.

biological a biologique.

biologist n biologiste mf.

biology n biologie f.

bioterrorism n bioterrorisme m.

birch n (tree) bouleau m; (whip) fouet m.

bird n oiseau m; (girl 🔲) nana f.

Biro® n stylo m à bille, bic® m.

birth n naissance f; **give ~** accoucher. ~ **certificate** n acte m de naissance. ~-**control** n contraception f. ~**day** n anniversaire m. ~**mark** n tache f de naissance. ~-**rate** n taux m de natalité.

biscuit n biscuit m; (US) petit pain m (au lait).

bishop n évêque m.

bit ⇒BITE. ● n morceau m; (of horse) mors m; (of tool) mèche f; **a ~** (a little) un peu; (Comput) bit m.

bitch n chienne f; (woman 🔲) garce f 🔲. ● vi dire du mal (about de).

bite vt/i (pt **bit**; pp **bitten**) mordre; ~ **one's nails** se ronger les ongles. ● n morsure f; (by insect) piqûre f; (mouthful) bouchée f; **have a ~** manger un morceau.

B

bitter a amer; (weather) glacial. ●n bière f. **bitterly** adv amèrement; **it is ~ly cold** il fait un temps glacial.

bizarre a bizarre.

black a noir; **~ and blue** couvert de bleus. ●n (colour) noir m; **B~** (person) Noir/-e m/f. ●vt noircir; (goods) boycotter. **~berry** n mûre f. **~bird** n merle m. **~board** n tableau m noir. **~currant** n cassis m.

blacken vt/i noircir.

black: **~ eye** n œil m poché. **~head** n point m noir. **~ ice** n verglas m. **~leg** n jaune m.

blacklist n liste f noire. ●vt mettre à l'index.

blackmail n chantage m. ●vt faire chanter. **blackmailer** n maître-chanteur m.

black: **~ market** n marché m noir. **~out** n panne f de courant; (Med) syncope f. **~ pudding** n boudin m. **~ sheep** n brebis f galeuse. **~smith** n forgeron m. **~ spot** n point m noir.

bladder n vessie f.

blade n (of knife) lame f; (of propeller, oar) pale f; **~ of grass** brin m d'herbe.

blame vt accuser; **~ sb for sth** reprocher qch à qn; **he is to ~** il est responsable (**for** de). ●n responsabilité f (**for** de).

bland a (insipid) fade.

blank a (page) blanc; (screen) vide; (cheque) en blanc; **to look ~** avoir l'air ébahi. ●n blanc m; ~ (**cartridge**) cartouche f à blanc.

blanket n couverture f; (layer) couche f.

blasphemous a blasphématoire; (person) blasphémateur.

blast n explosion f; (wave of air) souffle m; (of wind) rafale f; (noise from siren etc.) coup m. ●vt faire sauter. □ **~ off** décoller. **~**

furnace n haut-fourneau m. **~-off** n lancement m.

blatant a (obvious) flagrant; (shameless) éhonté.

blaze n feu m; (accident) incendie m. ●vt **~ a trail** faire œuvre de pionnier. ●vi (fire) brûler; (sky, eyes) flamboyer.

bleach n (for cleaning) eau f de Javel; (for hair, fabric) décolorant m. ●vt/i blanchir; (hair) décolorer.

bleak a (landscape) désolé; (outlook, future) sombre.

bleed vt/i (pt **bled**) saigner.

bleep n bip m.

blemish n imperfection f; (on fruit, reputation) tache f. ●vt entacher.

blend vt mélanger. ●vi se fondre ensemble; **to ~ with** se marier à. ●n mélange m. **blender** n mixeur n, mixer n.

bless vt bénir; **be ~ed with** jouir de; **~ you!** à vos souhaits! **blessed** a (holy) saint; (damned 🔢) sacré. **blessing** n bénédiction f; (benefit) avantage m; (stroke of luck) chance f.

blew ⇒BLOW.

blight n (disease: Bot) rouille f; (fig) plaie f.

blind a aveugle (**to** à); (corner, bend) sans visibilité. ●vt aveugler. ●n (on window) store m; **the ~** les aveugles mpl.

blindfold a be **~** avoir les yeux bandés. ●adv les yeux bandés. ●n bandeau m. ●vt bander les yeux à.

blindness n (Med) cécité f; (fig) aveuglement m.

blind spot n (Auto) angle m mort.

blink vi cligner des yeux; (light) clignoter.

bliss n délice m. **blissful** a délicieux.

blister n ampoule f; (on paint) cloque f. ●vi cloquer.

blitz n (Aviat) raid m éclair. ● vt bombarder.

blob n (drop) (grosse) goutte f; (stain) tache f.

block n bloc m; (buildings) pâté m de maisons; (in pipe) obstruction f; ~ **(of flats)** immeuble m; ~ **letters** majuscules fpl. ● vt bloquer.

blockade n blocus m. ● vt bloquer.

blockage n obstruction f.

block-buster n gros succès m.

bloke n 🄸 type m.

blond a & n blond (m).

blonde a & n blonde (f).

blood n sang m. ● a (donor, bath) de sang; (bank, poisoning) du sang; (group, vessel) sanguin. ~**-pressure** n tension f artérielle. ~**shed** n effusion f de sang. ~**shot** a injecté de sang. ~**stream** n sang m. ~ **test** n prise f de sang.

bloody a (-ier, -iest) sanglant; 🅧 sacré. ● adv 🅧 vachement 🄸. ~**-minded** a 🄸 hargneux, obstiné.

bloom n fleur f. ● vi fleurir; (person) s'épanouir.

blossom n fleur(s) f(pl). ● vi fleurir; (person) s'épanouir.

blot n tache f. ● vt (pt blotted) tacher; (dry) sécher; ~ **out** effacer.

blotch n tache f.

blouse n chemisier m.

blow vt/i (pt blew; pp blown) souffler; (fuse) (faire) sauter; (squander 🅧) claquer; (opportunity) rater; ~ **one's nose** se moucher; ~ **a whistle** siffler. ● n coup m. □ ~ **away** or **off** emporter; ~ **out** souffler; ~ **over** passer; ~ **up** (faire) sauter; (tyre) gonfler; (Photo) agrandir.

blow-dry n brushing m. ● vt faire un brushing à.

blown ⇒BLOW.

bludgeon n matraque f. ● vt matraquer.

blue a bleu; (movie) porno. ● n bleu m; **come out of the** ~ être inattendu; **have the** ~s avoir le cafard. ~**bell** n jacinthe f des bois. ~**print** n projet m.

bluff vt/i bluffer. ● n bluff m; **call sb's** ~ dire chiche à qn. ● a (person) carré.

blunder vi faire une bourde; (move) avancer à tâtons. ● n gaffe f.

blunt a (knife) émoussé; (person) brusque. ● vt émousser. **bluntly** adv carrément.

blur n image f floue. ● vt (pt blurred) brouiller.

blurb n résumé m publicitaire.

blush vi rougir. ● n rougeur f. **blusher** n fard m à joues.

blustery a ~ **wind** bourrasque f.

boar n sanglier m.

board n planche f; (for notices) tableau m; (food) pension f; **full** ~ pension f complète; **half** ~ demi-pension f; (committee) conseil m; ~ **of directors** conseil m d'administration; **go by the** ~ tomber à l'eau; **on** ~ à bord. ● vt/i (bus, train) monter dans; (Naut) monter à bord (de); ~ **with** être en pension chez.

boarding-school n école f privée avec internat.

boast vi se vanter (**about** de). ● vt s'enorgueillir de. ● n vantardise f.

boat n bateau m; (small) canot m; **in the same** ~ logé à la même enseigne.

bode vi ~ **well/ill** être de bon/ mauvais augure.

bodily a (need, well-being) physique; (injury) corporel. ● adv physiquement; (in person) en personne.

body n corps m; (mass) masse f;

(organization) organisme *m*; ~(work) (Auto) carrosserie *f*; **the main ~ of** le gros de. ~-**building** *n* culturisme *m*. ~**guard** *n* garde *m* du corps.

bog *n* marais *m*. ● *vt* (*pt* **bogged**) **get ~ged down** s'enliser dans.

bogus *a* faux.

boil *n* furoncle *m*; **bring to the ~** porter à ébullition. ● *vt/i* bouillir. □ ~ **down to** se ramener à; ~ **over** déborder. **boiled** *a* (*egg*) à la coque; (*potatoes*) à l'eau.

boiler *n* chaudière *f*; ~ **suit** bleu *m* (de travail).

boisterous *a* tapageur; (*child*) turbulent.

bold *a* hardi; (*cheeky*) effronté; (*type*) gras.

Bolivia *n* Bolivie *f*.

bollard *n* (on road) balise *f*.

bolt *n* (on door) verrou *m*; (for nut) boulon *m*; (lightning) éclair *m*. ● *vt* (*door*) verrouiller; (*food*) engouffrer. ● *vi* s'emballer.

bomb *n* bombe *f*; ~ **scare** alerte *f* à la bombe. ● *vt* bombarder.

bomber *n* (aircraft) bombardier *m*; (person) plastiqueur *m*.

bombshell *n* **be a ~** tomber comme une bombe.

bond *n* (agreement) engagement *m*; (link) lien *m*; (Comm) obligation *f*, bon *m*; **in ~** (entreposé) en douane.

bone *n* os *m*; (of fish) arête *f*. ● *vt* désosser. ~-**dry** *a* tout à fait sec.

bonfire *n* feu *m*; (for celebration) feu *m* de joie.

bonnet *n* (hat) bonnet *m*; (of vehicle) capot *m*.

bonus *n* prime *f*.

bony *a* (-**ier**, -**iest**) (thin) osseux; (*fish*) plein d'arêtes.

boo *interj* hou. ● *vt/i* huer. ● *n* huée *f*.

booby-trap *n* mécanisme *m* piégé. ● *vt* (*pt* -**trapped**) piéger.

book *n* livre *m*; (*exercise*) cahier *m*; (of tickets etc.) carnet *m*; ~**s** (Comm) comptes *mpl*. ● *vt* (reserve) réserver; (*driver*) dresser un PV à; (*player*) prendre le nom de; (write down) inscrire. ● *vi* retenir des places; (**fully**) ~**ed** complet. ~**case** *n* bibliothèque *f*.

booking-office *n* guichet *m*. ~**keeping** *n* comptabilité *f*.

booklet *n* brochure *f*. ~**maker** *n* bookmaker *m*. ~**mark** *n* (for book, Internet) signet *m*. ~**seller** *n* libraire *mf*. ~**shop** *n* librairie *f*. ~**stall** *n* kiosque *m* (à journaux).

boom *vi* (*gun, wind, etc.*) gronder; (*trade*) prospérer. ● *n* grondement *m*; (Comm) boom *m*, prospérité *f*.

boost *vt* stimuler; (*morale*) remonter; (*price*) augmenter; (publicize) faire de la réclame pour.

boot *n* (knee-length) botte *f*; (ankle-length) chaussure *f* (montante); (for walking) chaussure *f* de marche; (Sport) chaussure *f* de sport; (of vehicle) coffre *m*; **get the ~** ⊠ se faire virer. ● *vt/i* ~ **up** (Comput) amorcer.

booth *n* (for telephone) cabine *f*; (at fair) baraque *f*.

booze *vi* 🄃 boire (beaucoup). ● *n* 🄃 alcool *m*.

border *n* (edge) bord *m*; (frontier) frontière *f*; (in garden) bordure *f*. ● *vi* ~ **on** être voisin de, avoisiner.

bore *vt* ennuyer; **be ~d** s'ennuyer; ⇒BEAR. ● *vi* (Tech) forer. ● *n* raseur/-euse *m/f*; (thing) ennui *m*. **boredom** *n* ennui *m*. **boring** *a* ennuyeux.

born *a* né; **be ~** naître.

borne ⇒BEAR.

borough *n* municipalité *f*.

borrow *vt* emprunter (**from** à).

Bosnia *n* Bosnie *f*.

Bosnian *a* bosniaque. ●*n* Bosniaque.

bosom *n* poitrine *f*; ~ **friend** ami/ -e *m/f* intime.

boss *n* ⊞ patron/-ne *m/f*. ●*vt* ~ **(about)** ⊞ mener par le bout du nez.

bossy *a* autoritaire.

botch *vt* bâcler, saboter.

both *det* les deux; ~ **the books** les deux livres. ●*pron* tous/toutes (les) deux, l'un/-e et l'autre; **we ~ agree** nous sommes tous les deux d'accord; **I bought ~ (of them)** j'ai acheté les deux; **I saw ~ of you** je vous ai vus tous les deux; ~ **Paul and Anne** (et) Paul et Anne. ●*adv* à la fois.

bother *vt* (annoy, worry) ennuyer; (disturb) déranger. ●*vi* se déranger; **don't ~ (calling)** ce n'est pas la peine (d'appeler); **don't ~ about us** ne t'inquiète pas pour nous; **I can't be ~ed** j'ai la flemme ⊞. ●*n* ennui *m*; (effort) peine *f*; **it's no ~** ce n'est rien.

bottle *n* bouteille *f*; (for baby) biberon *m*. ●*vt* mettre en bouteille. □ ~ **up** contenir. ~ **bank** *n* collecteur *m* (*de verre usagé*). ~**neck** *n* (traffic jam) embouteillage *m*. ~**-opener** *n* ouvre-bouteilles *m inv*.

bottom *n* fond *m*; (of hill, page, etc.) bas *m*; (buttocks) derrière *m* ⊞. ●*a* inférieur, du bas.

bought ⇨BUY.

bounce *vi* rebondir; (person) faire des bonds, bondir; (cheques ⊠) être refusé. ●*vt* faire rebondir. ●*n* rebond *m*.

bound *vi* (leap) bondir; ~**ed by** limité par; ⇨BIND. ●*n* bond *m*. ●*a* **be** ~ **for** être en route pour, aller vers; ~ **to** (obliged) obligé de; (certain) sûr de.

boundary *n* limite *f*.

bounds *npl* limites *fpl*; **out of** ~ être interdit d'accès.

bout *n* période *f*; (Med) accès *m*; (boxing) combat *m*.

bow¹ *n* (weapon) arc *m*; (of violin) archet *m*; (knot) nœud *m*.

bow² *n* salut *m*; (of ship) proue *f*. ●*vt/i* (s')incliner.

bowels *npl* intestins *mpl*; (fig) profondeurs *fpl*.

bowl *n* (for washing) cuvette *f*; (for food) bol *m*; (for soup) assiette *f* creuse. ●*vt/i* (cricket) lancer; ~ **over** bouleverser.

bowler *n* (cricket) lanceur *m*; ~ **(hat)** (chapeau) melon *m*.

bowling *n* (ten-pin) bowling *m*; (on grass) jeu *m* de boules. ~**-alley** *n* bowling *m*.

bow-tie *n* nœud *m* papillon.

box *n* boîte *f*; (cardboard) carton *m*; (Theat) loge *f*; **the** ~ ⊞ la télé. ●*vt* mettre en boîte; (Sport) boxer; ~ **sb's ears** gifler qn; ~ **in** enfermer.

boxing *n* boxe *f*. ●*a* de boxe. **B~ Day** *n* le lendemain de Noël.

box office *n* guichet *m*.

boy *n* garçon *m*.

boycott *vt* boycotter. ●*n* boycottage *m*.

boyfriend *n* (petit) ami *m*.

bra *n* soutien-gorge *m*.

brace *n* (fastener) attache *f*; (dental) appareil *m*; (tool) vilbrequin *m*; ~**s** (for trousers) bretelles *fpl*. ●*vt* soutenir; ~ **oneself** rassembler ses forces.

bracket *n* (for shelf etc.) tasseau *m*, support *m*; (group) tranche *f*; **in** ~**s** entre parenthèses. ●*vt* mettre entre parenthèses *or* crochets.

braid *n* (trimming) galon *m*; (of hair) tresse *f*.

brain *n* cerveau *m*; ~**s** (fig) intelligence *f*. ●*vt* assommer.

brainless *a* stupide. ~**wash** *vt*

faire subir un lavage de cerveau à. **~wave** n idée f géniale, trouvaille f. **brainy** a (**-ier, -iest**) doué.

brake n (Auto also fig) frein m. ● vt/i freiner. **~ light** n feu m stop.

bran n son m.

branch n (of tree) branche f; (of road) embranchement m; (Comm) succursale f; (of bank) agence f. ● vi ~ (**off**) bifurquer.

brand n marque f. ● vt ~ sb as désigner qn comme qch.

brand-new a tout neuf.

brandy n cognac m.

brass n cuivre m; get down to ~ **tacks** en venir aux choses sérieuses; **the ~** (Mus) les cuivres mpl; **top ~** 🅸 galonnés mpl.

brat n 🅸 môme mf 🅸.

brave a courageux; (smile) brave. ● n (American Indian) brave m. ● vt braver. **bravery** n courage m.

brawl n bagarre f. ● vi se bagarrer.

Brazil n Brésil m.

breach n (of copyright, privilege) violation f; (in relationship) rupture f; (gap) brèche f. ● vt ouvrir une brèche dans.

bread n pain m; ~ **and butter** tartine f. **~bin**, (US) **~box** n boîte f à pain. **~crumbs** npl chapelure f.

breadth n largeur f.

bread-winner n soutien m de famille.

break vt (pt **broke**, pp **broken**) casser; (smash into pieces) briser; (vow, silence, rank, etc.) rompre; (law) violer; (a record) battre; (news) révéler; (journey) interrompre; (heart, strike, ice) briser; ~ **one's arm** se casser le bras. ● vi (se) casser; se briser. ● n cassure f, rupture f; (in relationship, continuity) rupture f;

(interval) interruption f; (at school) récréation f, récré f; (for coffee) pause f; (luck 🅸) chance f. □ ~ **away from** se détacher; ~ **down** vi (collapse) s'effondrer; (negotiations) échouer; (machine) tomber en panne; vt (door) enfoncer; (analyse) analyser; ~ **even** rentrer dans ses frais; ~ **into** cambrioler; ~ **off** (se) détacher; (suspend) rompre; (stop talking) s'interrompre; ~ **out** (fire, war, etc.) éclater; ~ **up** (end) (faire) cesser; (couple) rompre; (marriage) (se) briser; (crowd) (se) disperser; (schools) être en vacances. **breakable** a fragile. **breakage** n casse f.

breakdown n (Tech) panne f; (Med) dépression f; (of figures) analyse f. ● a (Auto) de dépannage.

breakfast n petit déjeuner m.

break: **~-in** n cambriolage m. **~through** n percée f.

breast n sein m; (chest) poitrine f. **~-feed** vt (pt **-fed**) allaiter. **~-stroke** n brasse f.

breath n souffle m, haleine f; out of ~ à bout de souffle; under one's ~ tout bas.

breathalyser® n alcootest m.

breathe vt/i respirer. □ ~ **in** inspirer; ~ **out** expirer.

breathless a à bout de souffle.

breathtaking a à vous couper le souffle.

bred ⇒BREED.

breed vt (pt **bred**) élever; (give rise to) engendrer. ● vi se reproduire. ● n race f.

breeze n brise f.

brew vt (beer) brasser; (tea) faire infuser. ● vi (beer) fermenter; (tea) infuser; (fig) se préparer. ● n décoction f. **brewer** n brasseur m. **brewery** n brasserie f.

bribe n pot-de-vin m. ● vt soudoyer. **bribery** n corruption f.

brick n brique f. ∼**layer** n maçon m.

bridal a (dress) de mariée; (car, chamber) des mariés.

bride n mariée f. ∼**groom** n marié m. ∼**smaid** n demoiselle f d'honneur.

bridge n pont m; (Naut) passerelle f; (of nose) arête f; (card game) bridge m. ● vt ∼ **a gap** combler une lacune.

bridle n bride f. ● vt brider. ∼**-path** n piste f cavalière.

brief a bref. ● n instructions fpl; (Jur) dossier m. ● vt donner des instructions à.

briefcase n serviette f.

briefs npl slip m.

bright a brillant, vif; (day, room) clair; (cheerful) gai; (clever) intelligent.

brighten vt égayer. ● vi (weather) s'éclaircir; (face) s'éclairer.

brilliant a (student, career) brillant; (light) éclatant; (very good 🅸) super.

brim n bord m. ● vi (pt brimmed); ∼ **over** déborder (with de).

bring vt (pt brought) (thing) apporter; (person, vehicle) amener; ∼ **to bear** (pressure etc.) exercer. □ ∼ **about** provoquer; ∼ **back** (return with) rapporter; (colour, shine) redonner; ∼ **down** faire tomber; (shoot down, knock down) abattre; ∼ **forward** avancer; ∼ **off** réussir; ∼ **out** (take out) sortir; (show) faire ressortir; (book) publier; ∼ **round** faire revenir à soi; ∼ **up** (child) élever; (Med) vomir; (question) aborder.

brink n bord m.

brisk a vif.

bristle n poil m. ● vi se hérisser; **bristling with** hérissé de.

Britain n Grande-Bretagne f.

British a britannique; **the** ∼ les Britanniques mpl.

Briton n Britannique mf.

Brittany n Bretagne f.

brittle a fragile.

broad a large; (choice, range) grand. ∼ **bean** n fève f.

broadcast vt/i (pt broadcast) diffuser; (person) parler à la télévision or à la radio. ● n émission f.

broadly adv en gros.

broad-minded a large d'esprit.

broccoli n inv brocoli m.

brochure n brochure f.

broke ⇒BREAK. ● a (penniless 🅸) fauché.

broken ⇒BREAK. ● a ∼ **English** mauvais anglais m.

bronchitis n bronchite f.

bronze n bronze m.

brooch n broche f.

brood n nichée f, couvée f. ● vi méditer tristement.

broom n balai m.

broth n bouillon m.

brothel n maison f close.

brother n frère m. ∼**hood** n fraternité f. ∼**-in-law** n (pl ∼**s-in-law**) beau-frère m.

brought ⇒BRING.

brow n front m; (of hill) sommet m.

brown a (object) marron; (hair) brun; ∼ **bread** pain m complet; ∼ **sugar** sucre m roux. ● n marron m; brun m. ● vt/i brunir; (Culin) (faire) dorer.

Brownie n jeannette f.

browse vi flâner; (animal) brouter. ● vt (Comput) naviguer. **browser** n (Comput) navigateur m.

bruise n bleu m. ● vt (knee, arm

etc.) faire un bleu à; (*fruit*) abîmer.

brush *n* brosse *f*; (skirmish) accrochage *m*; (bushes) broussailles *fpl*. ● *vt* brosser. □ ~ **against** frôler; ~ **aside** (dismiss) repousser; (move) écarter; ~ **up** (**on**) se remettre à.

Brussels *n* Bruxelles. ~ **sprouts** *npl* choux *mpl* de Bruxelles.

brutal *a* brutal.

brute *n* brute *f*; **by** ~ **force** par la force.

BSE *abbr* (**bovine spongiform encephalopathy**) encéphalopathie *f* spongiforme bovine, ESB *f*.

bubble *n* bulle *f*; **blow** ~**s** faire des bulles. ● *vi* bouillonner; ~ **over** déborder. ~ **bath** *n* bain *m* moussant.

buck *n* mâle *m*; (US, 🅰) dollar *m*; **pass the** ~ rejeter la responsabilité (**to** sur). ● *vi* (*horse*) ruer; ~ **up** 🅰 prendre courage; (hurry 🅰) se grouiller 🅰.

bucket *n* seau *m* (**of** de).

buckle *n* boucle *f*. ● *vt/i* (fasten) (se) boucler; (bend) voiler.

bud *n* bourgeon *m*. ● *vi* (*pt* **budded**) bourgeonner.

Buddhism *n* bouddhisme *m*.

budding *a* (*talent*) naissant; (*athlete*) en herbe.

budge *vt/i* (faire) bouger.

budgerigar *n* perruche *f*.

budget *n* budget *m*. ● *vi* ~ **for** prévoir (dans son budget).

buff *n* (colour) chamois *m*; 🅰 fanatique *mf*.

buffalo *n* (*pl* **-oes** *or* **-o**) buffle *m*; (US) bison *m*.

buffer *n* tampon *m*; ~ **zone** zone *f* tampon.

buffet¹ *n* (meal, counter) buffet *m*; ~ **car** buffet *m*.

buffet² *n* (blow) soufflet *m*. ● *vt* (*pt* **buffeted**) souffleter.

bug *n* (bedbug) punaise *f*; (any small insect) bestiole *f*; (germ) microbe *m*; (stomachache 🅰) ennuis *mpl* gastriques; (device) micro *m*; (defect) défaut *m*; (Comput) bogue *f*, bug *m*. ● *vt* (*pt* **bugged**) mettre des micros dans; 🅰 embêter.

buggy *n* poussette *f*.

build *vt/i* (*pt* **built**) bâtir, construire. ● *n* carrure *f*. □ ~ **up** (increase) augmenter, monter; (accumulate) (s')accumuler. **builder** *n* entrepreneur *m* en bâtiment; (workman) ouvrier *m* du bâtiment.

building *n* (structure) bâtiment *m*; (dwelling) immeuble *m*. ~ **society** *n* caisse *f* d'épargne.

build-up *n* accumulation *f*; (fig) publicité *f*.

built ⇒BUILD.

built-in *a* encastré.

built-up area *a* agglomération *f*, zone *f* urbanisée.

bulb *n* (Bot) bulbe *m*; (Electr) ampoule *f*.

Bulgaria *n* Bulgarie *f*.

Bulgarian *n* (person) Bulgare *mf*; (Ling) bulgare *m*. ● *a* bulgare.

bulge *n* renflement *m*. ● *vi* se renfler, être renflé; **be bulging with** être gonflé *a.* bourré de.

bulimia *n* boulimie *f*.

bulk *n* volume *f*; **in** ~ (*buy, sell*) en gros; (transport) en vrac; **the** ~ **of** la majeure partie de.

bull *n* taureau *m*. ~**dog** *n* bouledogue *m*. ~**doze** *vt* raser au bulldozer.

bullet *n* balle *f*.

bulletin *n* bulletin *m*.

bullet-proof *a* (*vest*) pare-balles *inv*; (*vehicle*) blindé.

bullfight *n* corrida *f*.

bullion *n* or *m or* argent *m* en lingots.

bullring *n* arène *f*.

bull's-eye *n* mille *m*.

bully *n* (child) petite brute *f*; (adult) tyran *m*. ● *vt* maltraiter.

bum n ⊠ derrière m ⬚; (US, ⊠) vagabond/-e m/f.

bumble-bee n bourdon m.

bump n (swelling) bosse f; (on road) bosse f. ● vt/i cogner, heurter. □ ~ **along** cahoter; ~ **into** (hit) rentrer dans; (meet) tomber sur.

bumper n pare-chocs m inv. ● a exceptionnel.

bumpy a (road) accidenté.

bun n (cake) petit pain m; (hair) chignon m.

bunch n (of flowers) bouquet m; (of keys) trousseau m; (of people) groupe m; (of bananas) régime m; ~ **of grapes** grappe f de raisin.

bundle n paquet m. ● vt mettre en paquet; (push) fourrer.

bung n bouchon m. ● vt (stop up) boucher; (throw ⊠) flanquer ⬚.

bunion n (Med) oignon m.

bunk n (on ship, train) couchette f. ~**-beds** npl lits mpl superposés.

buoy n bouée f. ● vt ~ **up** (hearten) soutenir, encourager.

buoyancy n (of floating object) flottabilité f; (cheerfulness) gaieté f.

burden n fardeau m. ● vt ennuyer (**with** de).

bureau n (pl **-eaux**) bureau m.

bureaucracy n bureaucratie f.

burglar n cambrioleur m; ~ **alarm** alarme f. **burglarize** vt (US) cambrioler. **burglary** n cambriolage m. **burgle** vt cambrioler.

Burgundy n (wine) bourgogne m.

burial n enterrement m.

burn vt/i (pt **burned** or **burnt**) brûler. ● n brûlure f. □ ~ **down** être réduit en cendres. **burning** a en flammes; (fig) brûlant.

burnt ⇒BURN.

burp n ⬚ rot m. ● vi ⬚ roter.

burrow n terrier m. ● vt creuser.

bursar n intendant/-e m/f.

bursary n bourse f.

burst vt/i (pt **burst**) (balloon, bubble) crever; (pipe) (faire) éclater. ● n explosion f; (of laughter) éclat m; (surge) élan m. □ ~ **into** (room) faire interruption dans; ~ **into tears** fondre en larmes; ~ **out** laughing éclater de rire; ~ **with** be ~ing with déborder de.

bury vt (person etc.) enterrer; (hide, cover) enfouir; (engross, thrust) plonger.

bus n (pl **buses**) (auto)bus m. ● vt transporter en bus. ● vi (pt **bussed**) prendre l'autobus.

bush n (shrub) buisson m; (land) brousse f.

business n (task, concern) affaire f; (commerce) affaires fpl; (line of work) métier m; (shop) commerce m; **he has no ~ to** il n'a pas le droit de; **mean ~** être sérieux; **that's none of your ~!** ça ne vous regarde pas! ~**like** a sérieux. ~**man** n homme m d'affaires.

busker n musicien/-ne m/f des rues.

bus-stop n arrêt m d'autobus.

bust n (statue) buste m; (bosom) poitrine f. ● vt/i (pt **busted** or **bust**) (burst ⊠) crever; (break ⊠) (se) casser. ● a (broken, finished ⊠) fichu; **go ~** ⊠ faire faillite.

bustle vi s'affairer. ● n affairement m, remue-ménage m.

busy a (**-ier**, **-iest**) (person) occupé; (street) animé; (day) chargé. ● vt ~ **oneself with** s'occuper à.

but conj mais. ● prep sauf; ~ **for** sans; **nobody ~** personne d'autre que; **nothing ~** rien que. ● adv (only) seulement.

butcher n boucher m. ● vt massacrer.

butler n maître m d'hôtel.

butt *n* (of gun) crosse *f*; (of cigarette) mégot *m*; (of joke) cible *f*; (barrel) tonneau *m*; (US, 🔲) derrière *m* 🔲. ● *vi* ~ **in** interrompre.

butter *n* beurre *m*. ● *vt* beurrer. ~**bean** *n* haricot *m* blanc. ~**cup** *n* bouton-d'or *m*.

butterfly *n* papillon *m*.

buttock *n* fesse *f*.

button *n* bouton *m*. ● *vt/i* ~ (**up**) (se) boutonner.

buttonhole *n* boutonnière *f*. ● *vt* accrocher.

buy *vt* (*pt* **bought**) acheter (**from** à); ~ **sth for sb** acheter qch à qn, prendre qch pour qn; (believe 🔲) croire, avaler.

buzz *n* bourdonnement *m*. ● *vi* bourdonner. **buzzer** *n* sonnerie *f*.

by *prep* par, de; (near) à côté de; (before) avant; (means) en, à, par; ~ **bike** à vélo; ~ **car** en auto; ~ **day** de jour; ~ **the kilo** au kilo; ~ **running** en courant; ~ **sea** par mer; ~ **that time** à ce moment-là; ~ **the way** à propos; ~ **oneself** tout seul. ● *adv* **close** ~ tout près; ~ **and large** dans l'ensemble.

bye(-bye) *interj* 🔲 au revoir, salut 🔲.

by-election *n* élection *f* partielle.

Byelorussia *n* Biélorussie *f*.

by-law *n* arrêté *m* municipal.

bypass *n* (Auto) rocade *f*; (Med) pontage *m*. ● *vt* contourner.

by-product *n* dérivé *m*; (fig) conséquence *f*.

byte *n* octet *m*.

cab *n* taxi *m*; (of lorry, train) cabine *f*.

cabbage *n* chou *m*.

cabin *n* (hut) cabane *f*; (in ship, aircraft) cabine *f*.

cabinet *n* petit placard *m*; (glass-fronted) vitrine *f*; (Pol) cabinet *m*.

cable *n* câble *m*. ● *vt* câbler. ~**-car** *n* téléphérique *m*. ~ **television** *n* télévision *f* par câble.

cache *n* (hoard) cache *f*; (place) cachette *f*.

cackle *n* (of hen) caquet *m*; (laugh) ricanement *m*. ● *vi* caqueter; (laugh) ricaner.

cactus *n* (*pl* **-ti** or ~**es**) cactus *m*.

cadet *n* élève *m* officier.

Caesarean *a* ~ (**section**) césarienne *f*.

café *n* café *m*, snack-bar *m*.

caffeine *n* caféine *f*.

cage *n* cage *f*. ● *vt* mettre en cage.

cagey *a* réticent.

cagoule *n* K-way® *m*.

cajole *vt* ~ **sb into doing sth** amener qn à faire qch par la cajolerie.

cake *n* gâteau *m*; (of soap) pain *m*. ● *vi* former une croûte (**on** sur).

calculate *vt* calculer; (estimate) évaluer. **calculated** *a* délibéré; (*risk*) calculé. **calculating** *a* calculateur. **calculation** *n* calcul *m*. **calculator** *n* calculatrice *f*.

calculus n (pl **-li** or **~es**) calcul m.

calendar n calendrier m.

calf n (pl **calves**) (young cow or bull) veau m; (of leg) mollet m.

calibre n calibre m.

call vt/i appeler; (loudly) crier; **he's ~ed John** il s'appelle John; **~ sb stupid** traiter qn d'imbécile. ● n appel m; (of bird) cri m; (visit) visite f; **make/pay a ~ on** rendre visite à; **be on ~** être de garde; **~ box** cabine f téléphonique. □ **~ back** rappeler; (visit) repasser; **~ for** (help) appeler à; (demand) demander; (require) exiger; (collect) passer prendre; **~ in** passer; **~ off** annuler; **~ on** (visit) rendre visite à; (urge) demander à (**to do** de faire); **~ out** (**to**) appeler; **~ round** venir; **~ up** appeler.

calling n vocation f.

callous a inhumain.

calm a calme. ● n calme m. ● vt/i **~ (down)** (se) calmer.

calorie n calorie f.

camcorder n caméscope® m.

came ⇒COME.

camel n chameau m.

camera n appareil(-photo) m; (TV, cinema) caméra f; **in ~** à huis clos. **~man** n (pl **-men**) cadreur m, cameraman m.

camouflage n camouflage m. ● vt camoufler.

camp n camp m. ● vi camper.

campaign n campagne f. ● vi faire campagne.

camper n campeur/-euse m/f. **~(-van)** n camping-car m.

camping n camping m; **go ~** faire du camping.

campsite n camping m.

campus n (pl **~es**) campus m.

can¹

infinitive **be able to**; present **can**; present negative **can't**, **cannot** (formal); past **could**; past participle **been able to**

● auxiliary verb

····▸ pouvoir; **where ~ I buy stamps?** où est-ce que je peux acheter des timbres?; **she can't come** elle ne peut pas venir.

····▸ (be allowed to) pouvoir; **~ I smoke?** est-ce que je peux fumer?

····▸ (know how to) savoir; **she ~ swim** elle sait nager; **he can't drive** il ne sait pas conduire.

····▸ (with verbs of perception) **I ~ hear you** je t'entends; **~ they see us?** est-ce qu'ils nous voient?

can² n (for food) boîte f; (of petrol) bidon m. ● vt (pt **canned**) mettre en conserve.

Canada n Canada m.

Canadian n Canadien/-ne m/f. ● a canadien.

canal n canal m.

canary n canari m.

cancel vt/i (pt **cancelled**) (call off, revoke) annuler; (cross out) barrer; (a stamp) oblitérer; **~ out** (se) neutraliser. **cancellation** n annulation f.

cancer n cancer m; **have ~** avoir un cancer.

Cancer n Cancer m.

cancerous a cancéreux.

candid a franc.

candidate n candidat/-e m/f.

candle n bougie f; (in church) cierge m. **~stick** n bougeoir m.

candy n (US) bonbon(s) m(pl). **~-floss** n barbe f à papa.

cane n canne f; (for baskets) rotin

m; (for punishment) badine f. ● vt
donner des coups de badine à.

canister n boîte f.

cannabis n cannabis m.

cannibal n cannibale mf.

cannon n (pl ~ or ~s) canon m.
~-**ball** n boulet m de canon.

cannot = CAN NOT.

canoe n canoë m. ● vi faire du
canoë. **canoeist** n canoéiste mf.

canon n (clergyman) chanoine m;
(rule) canon m.

can-opener n ouvre-boîtes m
inv.

canopy n dais m; (for bed)
baldaquin m.

can't = CAN NOT.

canteen n (restaurant) cantine f;
(flask) bidon m.

canter n petit galop m. ● vi aller
au petit galop.

canvas n toile f.

canvass vt/i (Comm, Pol) faire du
démarchage (auprès de); ~
opinion sonder l'opinion.

canyon n cañon m.

cap n (hat) casquette f; (of bottle,
tube) bouchon m; (of beer or milk
bottle) capsule f; (of pen) capuchon
m; (for toy gun) amorce f. ● vt (pt
capped) couronner.

capability n capacité f.

capable a (person) compétent; ~
of doing capable de faire.

capacity n capacité f; **in my ~ as
a doctor** en ma qualité de
médecin.

cape n (cloak) cape f; (Geog) cap m.

caper vi gambader. ● n (leap)
cabriole f; (funny film) comédie f;
(Culin) câpre f.

capital a (letter) majuscule;
(offence) capital. ● n (town)
capitale f; (money) capital m; ~
(letter) majuscule f.

capitalism n capitalisme m.

capitalize vi ~ **on** tirer parti de.

capitulate vi capituler.

Capricorn n Capricorne m.

capsize vt/i (faire) chavirer.

capsule n capsule f.

captain n capitaine m.

caption n (under photo) légende f;
(subtitle) sous-titre m.

captivate vt captiver.

captive a & n captif/-ive (m/f).
captivity n captivité f.

capture vt (person, animal)
capturer; (moment, likeness)
saisir. ● n capture f.

car n voiture f. ● a (industry,
insurance) automobile; (accident,
phone) de voiture; (journey,
chase) en voiture.

caravan n caravane f.

carbohydrate n hydrate m de
carbone.

carbon n carbone m.

carburettor n carburateur m.

card n carte f.

cardboard n carton m.

cardiac a cardiaque; ~ **arrest**
arrêt m du cœur.

cardigan n cardigan m.

cardinal a (sin) capital; (rule)
fondamental; (number) cardinal.
● n cardinal m.

card-index n fichier m.

care n (attention) soin m, attention
f; (worry) souci m; (looking after)
soins mpl; **take ~ of** (deal with)
s'occuper de; (be careful) faire
prendre soin de; **take ~ to do sth**
faire bien attention à faire qch.
● vi ~ **about** s'intéresser à; ~ **for**
s'occuper de; (invalid) soigner; ~
to do vouloir faire; **I don't ~** ça
m'est égal.

career n carrière f. ● vi ~ **in/out**
entrer/sortir à toute vitesse.

carefree a insouciant.

careful a prudent; (research,
study) méticuleux; (be careful) ~! (fais)

attention! **carefully** adv avec soin; (cautiously) prudemment.

careless a négligent; (work) bâclé.

caress n caresse f. ● vt caresser.

caretaker n concierge mf. ● a (president) par intérim.

car ferry n ferry m.

cargo n (pl ~es) chargement m; (Naut) cargaison f.

Caribbean a des Caraïbes, des Antilles. ● n the ~ (sea) la mer des Antilles; (islands) les Antilles fpl.

caring a affectueux.

carnation n œillet m.

carnival n carnaval m.

carol n chant m de Noël.

carp n inv carpe f. ● vi maugréer.

car-park n parc m de stationnement, parking m.

carpenter n (joiner) menuisier m; (builder) charpentier m. **carpentry** n menuiserie f; (structural) charpenterie f.

carpet n (fitted) moquette f; (loose) tapis m. ● vt (pt **carpeted**) mettre de la moquette dans.

carriage n (rail) wagon m; (ceremonial) carrosse m; (of goods) transport m; (cost) port m.

carriageway n chaussée f.

carrier n transporteur m; (Med) porteur/-euse m/f; ~ (**bag**) sac m en plastique.

carrot n carotte f.

carry vt/i porter; (goods) transporter; (involve) comporter; (motion) voter; **be carried away** s'emballer. □ ~ **off** emporter; (prize) remporter; ~ **on** (continue) continuer; (business) conduire; (conversation) mener; ~ **out** (order, plan) exécuter; (duty) remplir; (experiment, operation, repair) effectuer. ~-**cot** n porte-bébé m.

car sharing n covoiturage m.

cart n charrette f. ● vt (heavy bag ⊞) trimballer ⊞.

carton n (box) boîte f; (of yoghurt, cream) pot m; (of cigarettes) cartouche f.

cartoon n dessin m humoristique; (cinema) dessin m animé; (strip cartoon) bande f dessinée.

cartridge n cartouche f.

carve vt tailler; (meat) découper.

car-wash n lavage m automatique.

cascade n cascade f. ● vi tomber en cascade.

case n cas m; (Jur) affaire f; (suitcase) valise f; (crate) caisse f; (for spectacles) étui m; (just) **in** ~ au cas où; **in** ~ **he comes** au cas où il viendrait; **in** ~ **of fire** en cas d'incendie; **in any** ~ de toute façon; **the** ~ **for sth** les arguments mpl en faveur de qch; **the** ~ **for the defence** la défense.

cash n espèces fpl, argent m; **in** ~ en espèces. ● a (price) comptant. ● vt encaisser; ~ **in** (on) profiter (de). ~-**back** n retrait m d'argent à la caisse. ~ **desk** n caisse f. ~ **dispenser** n distributeur m de billets.

cashew n cajou m.

cash-flow n marge f brute d'auto-financement.

cashier n caissier/-ière m/f.

cashmere n cachemire m.

cash: ~ **point** n distributeur m de billets. ~ **point card** n carte f de retrait. ~ **register** n caisse f enregistreuse.

casino n casino m.

casket n (box) coffret m; (coffin) cercueil m.

casserole n (pan) daubière f; (food) ragoût m.

cassette n cassette f.

cast vt (pt **cast**) (object, glance) jeter; (shadow) projeter; (metal) couler; ~ (**off**) (shed) se dépouiller de; ~ **one's vote** voter; ~ **iron** fonte f. ● n (cinema, Theat, TV) distribution f; (Med) plâtre m.

castaway n naufragé/-e m/f.

cast-iron a de fonte; (fig) en béton.

castle n château m; (chess) tour f.

cast-offs npl vieux vêtements mpl.

castor n (wheel) roulette f.

castrate vt châtrer.

casual a (informal) décontracté; (remark) désinvolte; (acquaintance) de passage; (work) temporaire. **casually** adv (remark) d'un air détaché; (dress) simplement.

casualty n victime f; (part of hospital) urgences fpl.

cat n chat m; (feline) félin m.

catalogue n catalogue m. ● vt dresser un catalogue de.

catalyst n catalyseur m.

catalytic a ~ **converter** pot m catalytique.

catapult n lance-pierres m inv. ● vt projeter.

cataract n (Med, Geog) cataracte f.

catarrh n catarrhe m.

catastrophe n catastrophe f.

catch vt (pt **caught**) attraper; (bus, plane) prendre; (understand) saisir; ~ **sb doing** surprendre qn en train de faire; ~ **fire** prendre feu; ~ **sight of** apercevoir; ~ **sb's attention/eye** attirer l'attention de qn. ● vi (get stuck) se prendre (**in** dans); (start to burn) prendre. ● n (fastening) fermeture f; (drawback) piège m; (in sport) prise f. □ ~ **on** devenir populaire; ~ **out** prendre de court; ~ **up** rattraper

son retard; ~ **up with sb** rattraper qn.

catching a contagieux.

catchment n ~ **area** (School) secteur m.

catch-phrase n formule f favorite.

catchy a entraînant.

category n catégorie f.

cater vi organiser des réceptions; ~ **for/to** (guests) accueillir; (needs) pourvoir à; (reader) s'adresser à. **caterer** n traiteur m.

caterpillar n chenille f.

cathedral n cathédrale f.

catholic a éclectique. **Catholic** a & n catholique (mf). **Catholicism** n catholicisme m.

Catseye® n plot m rétroréfléchissant.

cattle npl bétail m.

caught ⇒CATCH.

cauliflower n chou-fleur m.

cause n cause f; (reason) raison f, motif m. ● vt causer; ~ **sth to grow/move** faire pousser/bouger qch.

causeway n chaussée f.

caution n prudence f; (warning) avertissement m. ● vt avertir.

cautious a prudent. **cautiously** adv prudemment.

cave n grotte f. ● vi ~ **in** s'effondrer; (agree) céder. ~**man** n (pl -**men**) homme m des cavernes.

cavern n caverne f.

caviare n caviar m.

caving n spéléologie f.

CCTV abbr (**closed circuit television**) télévision f en circuit fermé.

CD abbr (**compact disc**) disque m compact, CD m.

CD-ROM n disque m optique compact, CD-ROM m.

cease vt/i cesser. ~**-fire** n cessez-le-feu m inv.

cedar n cèdre m.

cedilla n cédille f.

ceiling n plafond m.

celebrate vt (occasion) fêter; (Easter, mass) célébrer. ● vi faire la fête. **celebrated** a célèbre. **celebration** n fête f.

celebrity n célébrité f.

celery n céleri m.

cell n cellule f; (Electr) élément m.

cellar n cave f.

cellist n violoncelliste mf. **cello** n violoncelle m.

Celt n Celte mf.

cement n ciment m. ● vt cimenter. **~-mixer** n bétonnière f.

cemetery n cimetière m.

censor n censeur m. ● vt censurer.

censure n censure f. ● vt critiquer.

census n recensement m.

cent n cent m.

centenary n centenaire m.

centigrade a centigrade.

centilitre, (US) **centiliter** n centilitre m.

centimetre, (US) **centimeter** n centimètre m.

centipede n millepattes m inv.

central a central; **~ heating** chauffage m central; **~ locking** fermeture f centralisée des portes. **centralize** vt centraliser. **centrally** adv (situated) au centre.

centre, (US) **center** n centre m. ● vt (pt **centred**) centrer. ● vi **~ on** tourner autour de.

century n siècle m.

ceramic a (art) céramique; (object) en céramique.

cereal n céréale f.

ceremonial n (dress) de cérémonie. ● n cérémonial m. **ceremony** n cérémonie f.

certain a certain; **for ~** avec

certitude; **make ~ of** s'assurer de.

certainly adv certainement.

certainty n certitude f.

certificate n certificat m.

certify vt certifier.

cesspit, cesspool n fosse f d'aisances.

chafe vt/i frotter (contre).

chagrin n dépit m.

chain n chaîne f; **~ reaction** réaction f en chaîne; **~ store** magasin m à succursales multiples. ● vt enchaîner. **~-smoke** vi fumer sans arrêt.

chair n chaise f; (armchair) fauteuil m; (Univ) chaire f; (chairperson) président/-e m/f. ● vt (preside over) présider. **~man** n (pl **-men**) président/-e m/f. **~woman** n (pl **-women**) présidente f.

chalk n craie f.

challenge n défi m; (opportunity) challenge m. ● vt (summon) défier (**to do** de faire); (question truth of) contester. **challenger** n (Sport) challenger m. **challenging** a stimulant.

chamber n (old use) chambre f. **~maid** n femme f de chambre. **~ music** n musique f de chambre. **~-pot** n pot m de chambre.

champagne n champagne m.

champion n champion/-ne m/f. ● vt défendre. **championship** n championnat m.

chance n (luck) hasard m; (opportunity) occasion f; (likelihood) chances fpl; (risk) risque m; **by ~** par hasard; **by any ~** par hasard; **~s are that** il est probable que. ● a fortuit. ● vt **~ doing** prendre le risque de faire; **~ it** tenter sa chance.

chancellor n chancelier m; **C~ of the Exchequer** Chancelier de l'Échiquier.

chandelier n lustre m.

C

change vt (alter) changer; (exchange) échanger (**for** contre); (money) changer; ~ **trains/one's dress** changer de train/de robe; ~ **one's mind** changer d'avis. ● vi changer; (change clothes) se changer; ~ **into** se transformer en; ~ **over** passer (**to** à). ● n changement m; (money) monnaie f; **a** ~ **for the better** une amélioration; **a** ~ **for the worse** un changement en pire; **a** ~ **of clothes** des vêtements de rechange; **for a** ~ pour changer. **changeable** a changeant. **changing room** n (in shop) cabine f d'essayage. (Sport) vestiaire m.

channel n (for liquid, information) canal m; (TV) chaîne f; (groove) rainure f. ● vt (pt **channelled**) canaliser. **C**~ n **the (English) C**~ la Manche; **the C**~ **tunnel** le tunnel sous la Manche; **the C**~ **Islands** les îles fpl Anglo-Normandes.

chant n (Relig) mélopée f; (of demonstrators) chant m scandé. ● vt/i scander; (Relig) psalmodier.

chaos n chaos m.

chap n (man 🄸) type m 🄸.

chapel n chapelle f.

chaplain n aumônier m.

chapped a gercé.

chapter n chapitre m.

char n (pt **charred**) carboniser.

character n caractère m; (in novel, play) personnage m; **of good** ~ de bonne réputation.

characteristic a & n caractéristique (f).

charcoal n charbon m de bois; (art) fusain m.

charge n (fee) frais mpl; (Mil) charge f; (Jur) inculpation f; (task, custody) charge f; **in** ~ **of** responsable de; **take** ~ **of** prendre en charge, se charger de. ● vt (customer) faire payer; (enemy, gun) charger; (Jur)

inculper (**with** de); ~ **£20 an hour** prendre 20 livres de l'heure; ~ **card** carte f d'achat. ● vi faire payer; (bull) foncer; (person) se précipiter.

charisma n charisme m.

charismatic a charismatique.

charitable a charitable. **charity** n charité f; (organization) organisation f caritative.

charm n charme m; (trinket) amulette f. ● vt charmer.

charming a charmant.

chart n (graph) graphique m; (table) tableau m; (map) carte f. ● vt (route) porter sur la carte.

charter n charte f; ~ **(flight)** charter m. ● vt affréter; ~**ed accountant** expert-comptable m.

chase vt poursuivre; ~ **away** or **off** chasser. ● vi courir (**after** après). ● n chasse f.

chassis n châssis m.

chastise vt châtier.

chat n conversation f; (on Internet) causette f, bavardage m, chat m; **have a** ~ bavarder; ~ **show** n talk-show m; ~**room** n salle f de causette, salle f de bavardage. ● vi (pt **chatted**) bavarder. 🄸 ~ **up** 🄸 draguer 🄸.

chatter n bavardage m. ● vi bavarder; **his teeth are** ~**ing** il claque des dents. ~**box** n bavard/-e m/f.

chatty a bavard.

chauffeur n chauffeur m.

chauvinist n chauvin/-e m/f; macho m.

cheap a bon marché inv; (fare, rate) réduit; (joke, gimmick) facile; ~**er** meilleur marché inv. **cheapen** vt déprécier. **cheaply** adv à bas prix.

cheat vi tricher. ● vt tromper. ● n tricheur/-euse m/f.

check vt/i vérifier; (tickets, rises, inflation) contrôler; (stop) arrêter;

(tick off: US) cocher. ● n contrôle m; (curb) frein m; (chess) échec m; (pattern) carreaux mpl; (bill: US) addition f; (cheque: US) chèque m. □ ~ **in** remplir la fiche; (at airport) enregistrer; ~ **out** partir; ~ **sth out** vérifier qch; ~ **up** vérifier; ~ **up on** (story) vérifier; (person) faire une enquête sur.

check: ~**-in** n enregistrement m. **checking account** n (US) compte m courant. ~**-list** n liste f de contrôle. ~**mate** n échec et mat. ~**-out** n caisse f. ~**-point** n contrôle m. ~**-up** n examen m médical.

cheek n joue f; (impudence) culot m ⊡. **cheeky** a effronté.

cheer n gaieté f; ~**s** acclamations fpl; (when drinking) à la vôtre. ● vt/i applaudir; ~ **sb** (**up**) (gladden) remonter le moral à qn; ~ **up** prendre courage. **cheerful** a joyeux. **cheerfulness** n gaieté f.

cheerio interj ⊡ salut ⊡.

cheese n fromage m.

cheetah n guépard m.

chef n chef m.

chemical a chimique. ● n produit m chimique.

chemist n pharmacien/-ne m/f; (scientist) chimiste mf; ~**'s** (shop) pharmacie f. **chemistry** n chimie f.

cheque n chèque m. ~**-book** n chéquier m. ~ **card** n carte f bancaire.

chequered a (pattern) à damiers; (fig) en dents de scie.

cherish vt chérir; (hope) caresser.

cherry n cerise f; (tree, wood) cerisier m.

chess n échecs mpl. ~**-board** n échiquier m.

chest n (Anat) poitrine f; (box) coffre m; ~ **of drawers** commode f.

chestnut n (nut) marron m,

châtaigne f; (tree) marronnier m; (sweet) châtaignier m.

chew vt mâcher.

chic a chic inv.

chick n poussin m.

chicken n poulet m. ● a ⊠ froussard. ● vi ~ **out** ⊠ se dégonfler. ~**-pox** n varicelle f.

chick-pea n pois m chiche.

chicory n (for salad) endive f; (in coffee) chicorée f.

chief n chef m. ● a principal. **chiefly** adv principalement.

chilblain n engelure f.

child n (pl children) enfant mf. ~**birth** n accouchement m. **childhood** n enfance f. **childish** a puéril. **childless** a sans enfants. **childlike** a enfantin. ~**-minder** n nourrice f.

Chile n Chili m.

chill n froid m; (Med) refroidissement m. ● a froid. ● vt (person) faire frissonner; (wine) rafraîchir; (food) mettre à refroidir.

chilli n (pl ~**es**) piment m.

chilly a froid; **it's** ~ il fait froid.

chime n carillon m. ● vt/i carillonner.

chimney n cheminée f. ~**-sweep** n ramoneur m.

chimpanzee n chimpanzé m.

chin n menton m.

china n porcelaine f.

China n Chine f.

Chinese n (person) Chinois/-e m/f; (Ling) chinois m. ● a chinois.

chip n (on plate) ébréchure f; (piece) éclat m; (of wood) copeau m; (Culin) frite f; (Comput) puce f; (potato) ~**s** (US) chips fpl. ● vt/i (pt **chipped**) (s')ébrécher; ~ **in** ⊡ dire son mot; (with money) contribuer.

chiropodist n pédicure mf.

chirp n pépiement m. ● vi pépier. **chirpy** a gai.

chisel n ciseau m. ● vt (pt **chiselled**) ciseler.

chit n note f; (voucher) bon m.

chitchat n 🖭 bavardage m.

chivalrous a galant.

chives npl ciboulette f.

chlorine n chlore m.

choc-ice n esquimau m.

chock-a-block a plein à craquer.

chocolate n chocolat m.

choice n choix m. ● a de choix.

choir n chœur m. **~boy** n jeune choriste m.

choke vt/i (s')étrangler; **~ (up)** boucher. ● n starter m.

cholesterol n cholestérol m.

choose vt/i (pt **chose**; pp **chosen**) choisir; **~ to do** décider de faire. **choosy** a difficile.

chop vt/i (pt **chopped**) (wood) couper; (food) hacher; **chopping board** planche f à découper; **~ down** abattre. ● n (meat) côtelette f. **chopper** n hachoir m; 🖭 hélico m 🖭.

choppy a (sea) agité.

chopstick n baguette f (chinoise).

chord n (Mus) accord m.

chore n (routine) tâche f; (unpleasant) corvée f.

chortle n gloussement m. ● vi glousser.

chorus n chœur m; (of song) refrain m.

chose, chosen ⇒CHOOSE.

Christ n le Christ.

christen vt baptiser. **christening** n baptême m.

Christian a & n chrétien/-ne (m/ f); **~ name** nom m de baptême. **Christianity** n christianisme m.

Christmas n Noël m; **~ Day/Eve** le jour/la veille de Noël. ● a (card, tree) de Noël.

chronic a (situation, disease) chronique; (bad 🖭) nul.

chronicle n chronique f.

chronological a chronologique.

chrysanthemum n chrysanthème m.

chubby a (-ier, -iest) potelé.

chuck vt 🖭 lancer; **~ away** or **out** 🖭 balancer.

chuckle n gloussement m. ● vi glousser.

chuffed a 🖭 vachement content 🖭.

chunk n morceau m. **chunky** a (sweater, jewellery) gros; (person) costaud.

church n église f. **~goer** n pratiquant/-e m/f. **~yard** n cimetière m.

churn n baratte f; (milk-can) bidon m. ● vt baratter; **~ out** produire en série.

chute n toboggan m; (for rubbish) vide-ordures m inv.

chutney n condiment m aigre-doux.

cider n cidre m.

cigar n cigare m.

cigarette n cigarette f; **~ end** mégot m.

cinder n cendre f.

cinema n cinéma m.

cinnamon n cannelle f.

circle n cercle m; (Theat) balcon m. ● vt (go round) tourner autour de; (word, error) encercler. ● vi tourner en rond.

circuit n circuit m. **~ board** n carte f de circuit imprimé. **~-breaker** n disjoncteur m.

circuitous a indirect.

circular a & n circulaire (f).

circulate vt/i (faire) circuler. **circulation** n circulation f; (of newspaper) tirage m.

circumcise vt circoncire.

circumference n circonférence f.

circumflex n circonflexe m.

circumstance n circonstance f; ~s (financial) situation f; **under no** ~s en aucun cas.

circus n cirque m.

cistern n réservoir m.

citizen n citoyen/-ne m/f; (of town) habitant/-e m/f. **citizenship** n nationalité f.

citrus a ~ **fruit(s)** agrumes mpl; ~ **tree** citrus m.

city n (grande) ville f.

civic a (official) municipal; (pride, duty) civique.

civil a civil. ~ **disobedience** n résistance f passive. ~ **engineer** n ingénieur m des travaux publics.

civilian a & n civil/-e (m/f).

civilization n civilisation f. **civilize** vt civiliser.

civil: ~ **law** n droit m civil. ~ **liberties** npl libertés fpl individuelles. ~ **rights** npl droits mpl civils. ~ **servant** n fonctionnaire mf. ~ **service** n fonction f publique. ~ **war** n guerre f civile.

claim vt (demand) revendiquer; (assert) prétendre. ● n revendication f; (assertion) affirmation f; (for insurance) réclamation f; (right) droit m. **claimant** n (of benefits) demandeur/-euse m/f.

clairvoyant n voyant/-e m/f.

clam n palourde f.

clamber vi grimper.

clammy a (-ier, -iest) moite.

clamour n clameur f. ● vi ~ **for** réclamer.

clamp n valet m; (Med) pince f; (wheel) ~ sabot m de Denver. ● vt cramponner; (jaw) serrer; (car) mettre un sabot de Denver à; ~ **down on** faire de la répression contre.

clan n clan m.

clang n son m métallique.

clap vt/i (pt clapped) applaudir; (put forcibly) mettre; ~ **one's hands** frapper dans ses mains. ● n applaudissement m; (of thunder) coup m.

claret n bordeaux m rouge.

clarification n clarification f. **clarify** vt/i (se) clarifier.

clarinet n clarinette f.

clarity n clarté f.

clash n choc m; (fig) conflit m. ● vi (metal objects) s'entrechoquer; (armies) s'affronter; (meetings) avoir lieu en même temps; (colours) jurer.

clasp n (fastener) fermoir m. ● vt serrer.

class n classe f. ● vt classer; ~ **sb/sth as** assimiler qn/qch à.

classic a & n classique (m); ~s (Univ) lettres fpl classiques. **classical** a classique.

classified a (information) secret; ~ (ad) petite annonce f.

classroom n salle f de classe.

clatter n cliquetis m. ● vi cliqueter.

clause n clause f; (Gram) proposition f.

claw n (of animal, small bird) griffe f; (of bird of prey) serre f; (of lobster) pince f. ● vt griffer.

clay n argile f.

clean a propre; (shape, stroke) net. ● adv complètement. ● vt nettoyer; ~ **one's teeth** se brosser les dents. ● vi ~ **up** faire le nettoyage. **cleaner** n (at home) femme f de ménage; (industrial) agent m de nettoyage; (of clothes) teinturier/-ière m/f. **cleanliness** n propreté f. **cleanly** adv proprement; (sharply) nettement.

cleanse vt nettoyer; (fig) purifier.

clean-shaven a glabre.

clear a (explanation) clair; (need, sign) évident; (glass) transparent; (profit) net; (road) dégagé; **make sth ~** être très clair sur qch; **~ of** (away from) à l'écart de. ● adv complètement; **stand ~ of** s'éloigner de. ● vt (free) dégager (**of** de); (table) débarrasser; (building) évacuer; (cheque) compenser; (jump over) franchir; (debt) liquider; (Jur) disculper. ● vi (fog) se dissiper; (cheque) être compensé. □ **~ away** or **off** (remove) enlever; **~ off** or **out** 🄸 décamper; **~ out** (clean) nettoyer; **~ up** (tidy) ranger; (weather) s'éclaircir.

clearance n (permission) autorisation f; (space) espace m; **~ sale** liquidation f.

clear-cut a net.

clearing n clairière f.

clearly adv clairement.

clef n (Mus) clé f.

cleft n fissure f.

clench vt serrer.

clergy n clergé m. **~man** n (pl **-men**) ecclésiastique m.

cleric n clerc m. **clerical** a (Relig) clérical; (staff, work) de bureau.

clerk n employé/-e m/f de bureau; (US (sales) **~** vendeur/ -euse m/f.

clever a intelligent; (skilful) habile.

click n déclic m; (Comput) clic m. ● vi faire un déclic; (people 🄸) sympathiser; (Comput) cliquer (**on** sur). ● vt (heels, tongue) faire claquer.

client n client/-e m/f.

clientele n clientèle f.

cliff n falaise f.

climate n climat m.

climax n (of story, contest) point m culminant; (sexual) orgasme m.

climb vt grimper; (steps) monter; (tree, ladder) grimper à; (mountain) faire l'ascension de. ● vi grimper; **~ into** (car) monter dans; **~ into bed** se mettre au lit. ● n (of mountain) escalade f; (steep hill, rise) montée f. □ **~ down** (fig) reculer. **climber** n (Sport) alpiniste mf.

clinch vt (deal) conclure; (victory, order) décrocher.

cling vi (pt **clung**) se cramponner (**to** à); (stick) coller. **~-film** n scellofrais® m.

clinic n centre m médical; (private) clinique f. **clinical** a clinique.

clink n tintement m. ● vt/i (faire) tinter.

clip n (for paper) trombone m; (for hair) barrette f; (for tube) collier m; (of film) extrait m. ● vt (pt **clipped**) (fasten) attacher (**to** à); (cut) couper.

clippers npl tondeuse f; (for nails) coupe-ongles m inv.

clipping n (from press) coupure f de presse.

cloak n cape f; (man's) houppelande f. **~room** n vestiaire m; (toilet) toilcttes fpl.

clobber n 🄸 attirail m. ● vt (hit 🄸) tabasser 🄸.

clock n pendule f; (large) horloge f. ● vi **~ on/in** or **off/out** pointer; **~ up** (miles) faire. **~-tower** n beffroi m. **~wise** a & adv dans le sens des aiguilles d'une montre.

clockwork n mécanisme m. ● a mécanique.

clog n sabot m. ● vt/i (pt **clogged**) (se) boucher.

cloister n cloître m.

clone n clone m. ● vt cloner.

close[1] a (friend, relative) proche (**to** de); (link, collaboration) étroit; (examination) minutieux; (result, match) serré; (weather) lourd; **~**

together (crowded) serrés; ~ **by,** ~ **at hand** tout près; **have a** ~ **shave** l'échapper belle; **keep a** ~ **watch on** surveiller de près. ● *adv* près. ● *n* (street) impasse *f*.

close² *vt* fermer; (*meeting, case*) mettre fin à. ● *vi* se fermer; (*shop*) fermer; (*meeting, play*) prendre fin. ● *n* fin *f*.

closely *adv* (follow) de près. **closeness** *n* proximité *f*.

closet *n* (US) placard *m*.

close-up *n* gros plan *m*.

closure *n* fermeture *f*.

clot *n* (of blood) caillot *m*; (in sauce) grumeau *m*. ● *vt/i* (*pt* **clotted**) (se) coaguler.

cloth *n* (fabric) tissu *m*; (duster) chiffon *m*; (table-cloth) nappe *f*.

clothe *vt* vêtir.

clothes *npl* vêtements *mpl*. ~**-hanger** *n* cintre *m*. ~**-line** *n* corde *f* à linge.

clothing *n* vêtements *mpl*.

cloud *n* nuage *m*. ● *vi* ~ (**over**) se couvrir (de nuages); (*face*) s'assombrir. **cloudy** *a* (sky) couvert; (*liquid*) trouble.

clout *n* (blow) coup *m* de poing; (power) influence *f*. ● *vt* frapper.

clove *n* clou *m* de girofle; ~ **of garlic** gousse *f* d'ail.

clover *n* trèfle *m*.

clown *n* clown *m*. ● *vi* faire le clown.

club *n* (group) club *m*; (weapon) massue *f*; (golf) ~ club *m* (de golf); ~**s** (cards) trèfle *m*. ● *vt/i* (*pt* **clubbed**) matraquer. □ ~ **together** cotiser.

cluck *vi* glousser.

clue *n* indice *m*; (in crossword) définition *f*; **I haven't a** ~ 🖭 je n'en ai pas la moindre idée.

clump *n* massif *m*.

clumsy *a* (**-ier, -iest**) maladroit; (*tool*) peu commode.

clung ⇒CLING.

cluster *n* (of people, islands) groupe *m*; (of flowers, berries) grappe *f*. ● *vi* se grouper.

clutch *vt* (hold) serrer fort; (grasp) saisir. ● *vi* ~ **at** (try to grasp) essayer de saisir. ● *n* (Auto) embrayage *m*; (of eggs) couveé *f*; (of people) groupe *m*.

clutter *n* désordre *m*. ● *vt* ~ (**up**) encombrer.

coach *n* autocar *m*; (of train) wagon *m*; (horse-drawn) carrosse *m*; (Sport) entraîneur/-euse *m/f*. ● *vt* (team) entraîner; (*pupil*) donner des leçons particulières à.

coal *n* charbon *m*. ~**field** *n* bassin *m* houiller. ~**-mine** *n* mine *f* de charbon.

coarse *a* grossier.

coast *n* côte *f*. ● *vi* (car, bicycle) descendre en roue libre. **coastal** *a* côtier.

coast: ~**guard** *n* (person) gardecôte *m*; (organization) gendarmerie *f* maritime. ~**line** *n* littoral *m*.

coat *n* manteau *m*; (of animal) pelage *m*; (of paint) couche *f*; ~ **of arms** armoiries *fpl*. ● *vt* enduire, couvrir; (with chocolate) enrober (**with** de). **coating** *n* couche *f*.

coax *vt* cajoler.

cob *n* (of corn) épi *m*.

cobbler *n* cordonnier *m*.

cobblestones *npl* pavés *mpl*.

cobweb *n* toile *f* d'araignée.

cocaine *n* cocaïne *f*.

cock *n* (rooster) coq *m*; (oiseau) mâle *m*. ● *vt* (*gun*) armer; (*ears*) dresser.

cockerel *n* jeune coq *m*.

cockle *n* (Culin) coque *f*.

cock: ~**pit** *n* poste *m* de pilotage. ~**roach** *n* cafard *m*. ~**tail** *n* cocktail *m*.

cocky *a* (**-ier, -iest**) trop sûr de soi.

cocoa *n* cacao *m*.

coconut *n* noix *f* de coco.

COD *abbr* (**cash on delivery**) envoi *m* contre remboursement.

cod *n inv* morue *f*; **~-liver oil** huile *f* de foie de morue.

code *n* code *m*. ● *vt* coder.

coerce *vt* contraindre.

coexist *vi* coexister.

coffee *n* café *m*. ● **bar** *n* café *m*. **~ bean** *n* grain *m* de café. **~-pot** *n* cafetière *f*. **~-table** *n* table *f* basse.

coffin *n* cercueil *m*.

cog *n* pignon *m*; (fig) rouage *m*.

cognac *n* cognac *m*.

coil *vt/i* (s')enrouler. ● *n* (of rope) rouleau *m*; (of snake) anneau *m*; (contraceptive) stérilet *m*.

coin *n* pièce *f* (de monnaie). ● *vt* (word) inventer.

coincide *vi* coïncider.

coincidence *n* coïncidence *f*.

coincidental *a* dû à une coïncidence.

colander *n* passoire *f*.

cold *a* froid; (person) be or feel **~** avoir froid; it is **~** il fait froid; get **~ feet** avoir les jetons Ⅲ; **~-blooded** (lit) à sang froid; (fig) sans pitié. ● *n* froid *m*; (Med) rhume *m*; **~ sore** bouton *m* de fièvre. **coldness** *n* froideur *f*.

coleslaw *n* salade *f* de chou cru.

colic *n* coliques *fpl*.

collaborate *vi* collaborer.

collapse *vi* s'effondrer; (person) s'écrouler; (fold) se plier. ● *n* effondrement *m*.

collar *n* col *m*; (of dog) collier *m*. **~-bone** *n* clavicule *f*.

collateral *n* nantissement *m*.

colleague *n* collègue *mf*.

collect *vt* rassembler; (pick up) ramasser; (call for) passer prendre; (money, fare) encaisser; (taxes, rent) percevoir; (as hobby) collectionner. ● *vi* se rassembler; (dust) s'amasser. ● *adv* call **~** (US) appeler en PCV. **collection** *n* collection *f*; (of money) collecte *f*; (in church) quête *f*; (of mail) levée *f*.

collective *a* collectif.

collector *n* (as hobby) collectionneur/-euse *m/f*; (of taxes) percepteur *m*; (of rent, debt) encaisseur *m*.

college *n* (for higher education) établissement *m* d'enseignement supérieur; (within university) collège *m*; be at **~** faire des études supérieures.

collide *vi* entrer en collision (with avec).

colliery *n* houillère *f*.

collision *n* collision *f*.

colloquial *a* familier.

colloquialism *n* expression *f* familière.

Colombia *n* Colombie *f*.

colon *n* (Gram) deux-points *m inv*; (Anat) côlon *m*.

colonel *n* colonel *m*.

colonial *a & n* colonial/-e (*m/f*).

colour, (US) **color** *n* couleur *f*; **~-blind** daltonien. ● *a* (photo) en couleur; (TV set) couleur *inv*. ● *vt* colorer; (with crayon) colorier. **coloured** *a* de couleur. **colourful** *a* aux couleurs vives; (fig) haut en couleur. **colouring** *n* (of skin) teint *m*; (in food) colorant *m*.

colt *n* poulain *m*.

column *n* colonne *f*.

coma *n* coma *m*.

comb *n* peigne *m*. ● *vt* peigner; **~ one's hair** se peigner; **~ a place** passer un lieu au peigne fin.

combat *n* combat *m*. ● *vt* (pt **combated**) combattre.

combination *n* combinaison *f*.

combine¹ *vt/i* (se) combiner, (s')unir.

combine² *n* (Comm) groupe *m*; ~ (*harvester*) moissonneuse-batteuse *f*.

come *vi* (*pt* came; *pp* come) venir; (*bus, letter*) arriver; (*postman*) passer; ~ and look! viens voir!; ~ in (*size, colour*) exister en; when it ~s to lorsqu'il s'agit de. □ ~ about survenir; ~ across (*meaning*) passer; ~ across sth tomber sur qch; ~ away (leave) partir; (come off) se détacher; ~ back revenir; ~ by obtenir; ~ down descendre; (*price*) baisser; ~ forward se présenter; ~ in entrer; ~ in useful être utile; ~ in for recevoir; ~ into (money) hériter de; ~ off (succeed) réussir; (fare) s'en tirer; (detach) se détacher; ~ on (actor) entrer en scène; (light) s'allumer; (improve) faire des progrès; ~ on! allez!; ~ out sortir; ~ round reprendre connaissance; (change mind) changer d'avis; ~ through s'en tirer; ~ to reprendre connaissance; ~ to sth (*amount*) revenir à qch; (*decision, conclusion*) arriver à qch; ~ up (*problem*) être soulevé; (*opportunity*) se présenter; (*sun*) se lever; ~ up against se heurter à qch; ~ up with trouver.

comedian *n* comique *m*.

comedy *n* comédie *f*.

comfort *n* confort *m*; (consolation) réconfort *m*. ● *vt* consoler. **comfortable** *a* (*chair, car*) confortable; (*person*) à l'aise; (wealthy) aisé.

comfortably *adv* confortablement; ~ off aisé.

comfy *a* 🄸 = COMFORTABLE.

comic *a* comique. ● *n* (person) comique *m*; ~ (book), ~ strip bande *f* dessinée.

coming *n* arrivée *f*; ~s and goings allées et venues *fpl*. ● *a* à venir.

comma *n* virgule *f*.

command *n* (authority) commandement *m*; (order) ordre *m*; (mastery) maîtrise *f*. ● *vt* ordonner à (**to do** de faire); (be able to use) disposer de; (*respect*) inspirer. **commandeer** *vt* réquisitionner. **commander** *n* commandant *m*. **commanding** *a* imposant. **commandment** *n* commandement *m*.

commando *n* commando *m*.

commemorate *vt* commémorer.

commence *vt/i* commencer.

commend *vt* (praise) louer; (entrust) confier.

commensurate *a* proportionné.

comment *n* commentaire *m*. ● *vi* faire des commentaires; ~ on commenter. **commentary** *n* commentaire *m*; (radio, TV) reportage *m*. **commentate** *vi* faire un reportage. **commentator** *n* commentateur/ -trice *m/f*.

commerce *n* commerce *m*.

commercial *a* commercial; (*traveller*) de commerce. ● *n* publicité *f*.

commiserate *vi* compatir (with avec).

commission *n* commission *f*; (order for work) commande *f*; out of ~ hors service. ● *vt* (order) commander; (Mil) nommer officier; ~ to do charger de faire. **commissioner** *n* préfet *m* (de police); (in EC) membre *m* de la Commission européenne.

commit *vt* (*pt* committed) commettre; (entrust) confier; ~ oneself s'engager; ~ perjury se parjurer; ~ suicide se suicider; ~

C

to **memory** apprendre par cœur.
commitment n engagement m.
committee n comité m.
commodity n article m.
common a (shared by all) commun
(to à); (usual) courant; (vulgar)
vulgaire, commun; **in** ~ en
commun; ~ **people** le peuple; ~
sense bon sens m. ● n terrain m
communal; **the C**~**s** Chambre f
des Communes.
commoner n roturier/-ière m/f.
common law n droit m
coutumier.
commonly adv communément.
commonplace a banal. ● n
banalité f.
common-room n salle f de
détente.
Commonwealth n **the** ~ le
Commonwealth m.
commotion n (noise) vacarme m;
(disturbance) agitation f.
communal a (shared) commun;
(life) collectif.
commune n (group) communauté
f.
communicate vt/i
communiquer. **communication** n
communication f.
communicative a communicatif.
communion n communion f.
Communism n communisme m.
Communist a & n communiste
(mf).
community n communauté f.
commute vi faire la navette. ● vt
(Jur) commuer. **commuter** n
navetteur/-euse m/f.
compact a compact; (lady's case)
poudrier m.
compact disc n disque m
compact. ~ **player** n platine f
laser.
companion n compagnon/-agne
m/f. **companionship** n
camaraderie f.

company n (companionship, firm)
compagnie f; (guests) invités/-es
m/fpl.
comparative a (study, form)
comparatif; (comfort) relatif.
compare vt comparer (with, to à);
~**d with** par rapport à. ● vi être
comparable. **comparison** n
comparaison f.
compartment n compartiment
m.
compass n (for direction) boussole
f; (scope) portée f; **a pair of** ~**es**
compas m.
compassionate a compatissant.
compatible a compatible.
compel vt (pt **compelled**)
contraindre. **compelling** a
irrésistible.
compensate vt/i (financially)
dédommager (for de); ~ **for sth**
compenser qch. **compensation** n
compensation f; (financial)
dédommagement m.
compete vi concourir; ~ **with**
rivaliser avec.
competent a compétent.
competition n (contest) concours
m; (Sport) compétition f; (Comm)
concurrence f.
competitive a (prices)
compétitif; (person) qui a l'esprit
de compétition.
competitor n concurrent/-e m/f.
compile vt (list) dresser; (book)
rédiger.
complacency n suffisance f.
complain vi se plaindre (about, of
de). **complaint** n plainte f; (official)
réclamation f; (illness) maladie f.
complement n complément m.
● vt compléter. **complementary**
a complémentaire.
complete a complet; (finished)
achevé; (downright) parfait. ● vt
achever; (a form) remplir.
completely adv complètement.
completion n achèvement m.

complex *a* complexe. ● *n* (Psych)
complexe *m*.

complexion *n* (of face) teint *m*;
(fig) caractère *m*.

compliance *n* (agreement)
conformité *f*.

complicate *vt* compliquer.
complicated *a* compliqué.
complication *n* complication *f*.

compliment *n* compliment *m*.
● *vt* complimenter.
complimentary *a* (offert) à titre
gracieux; (praising) flatteur.

comply *vi* ~ with se conformer à,
obéir à.

component *n* (of machine) pièce *f*;
(chemical substance) composant *m*;
(element: fig) composante *f*. ● *a*
constituant.

compose *vt* composer; ~ oneself
se calmer. **composed** *a* calme.
composer *n* (Mus) compositeur
m. **composition** *n* composition *f*.
composure *n* calme *m*.

compound *n* (substance, word)
composé *m*; (enclosure) enclos *m*.
● *a* composé.

comprehend *vt* comprendre.
comprehension *n*
compréhension *f*.

comprehensive *a* étendu,
complet; (*insurance*) tous risques
inv. ~ **school** *n* collège *m*
d'enseignement secondaire.

compress *vt* comprimer.

comprise *vt* comprendre,
inclure.

compromise *n* compromis *m*.
● *vt* compromettre. ● *vi* transiger,
arriver à un compromis.

compulsive *a* (Psych) compulsif;
(*liar, smoker*) invétéré.

compulsory *a* obligatoire.

computer *n* ordinateur *m*; ~
science informatique *f*.
computerize *vt* informatiser.

comrade *n* camarade *mf*.

con[1] *vt* (*pt* **conned**) ⊠ rouler ⊡,
escroquer (**out of** de). ● *n*
⊠ escroquerie *f*.

con[2] ⇒PRO.

conceal *vt* dissimuler (**from** à).

concede *vt* concéder. ● *vi* céder.

conceited *a* vaniteux.

conceive *vt/i* concevoir; ~ **of**
concevoir.

concentrate *vt/i* (se) concentrer.
concentration *n* concentration *f*.

concept *n* concept *m*.

conception *n* conception *f*.

concern *n* (interest, business) affaire
f; (worry) inquiétude *f*; (firm: Comm)
entreprise *f*, affaire *f*. ● *vt*
concerner; ~ oneself with, be ~ed
with s'occuper de. **concerned** *a*
inquiet. **concerning** *prep* en ce
qui concerne.

concert *n* concert *m*.

concession *n* concession *f*.

conciliation *n* conciliation *f*.

concise *a* concis.

conclude *vt* conclure. ● *vi* se
terminer. **conclusion** *n*
conclusion *f*. **conclusive** *a*
concluant.

concoct *vt* confectionner; (invent:
fig) fabriquer. **concoction** *n*
mélange *m*.

concourse *n* (Rail) hall *m*.

concrete *n* béton *m*. ● *a* de
béton; (fig) concret. ● *vt* bétonner.

concur *vi* (*pt* **concurred**) être
d'accord.

concurrently *adv*
simultanément.

concussion *n* commotion *f*
(cérébrale).

condemn *vt* condamner.

condensation *n* (on walls)
condensation *f*; (on windows) buée
f. **condense** *vt/i* (se) condenser.

condition *n* condition *f*; on ~ that
à condition que. ● *vt*

conditionner. **conditional** a conditionnel.

conditioner n après-shampooing m.

condolences npl condoléances fpl.

condom n préservatif m.

condone vt pardonner, fermer les yeux sur.

conducive a ~ **to** favorable à.

conduct[1] n conduite f.

conduct[2] vt conduire; (orchestra) diriger. **conductor** n chef m d'orchestre; (of bus) receveur m; (on train: US) chef m de train; (Electr) conducteur m. **conductress** n receveuse f.

cone n cône m; (of ice-cream) cornet m.

confectioner n confiseur/-euse m/f. **confectionery** n confiserie f.

confer vt/i (pt **conferred**) conférer.

conference n conférence f.

confess vt/i avouer; (Relig) (se) confesser. **confession** n confession f; (of crime) aveu m.

confide vt confier. ● vi ~ **in** se confier à.

confidence n (trust) confiance f; (boldness) confiance f en soi; (secret) confidence f; **in** ~ en confidence. **confident** a sûr.

confidential a confidentiel.

confine vt enfermer; (limit) limiter; ~**d space** espace m réduit; ~**d to** limité à.

confirm vt confirmer. **confirmed** a (bachelor) endurci; (smoker) invétéré.

confiscate vt confisquer.

conflict[1] n conflit m.

conflict[2] vi (statements, views) être en contradiction (**with** avec); (appointments) tomber en même

temps (**with** que). **conflicting** a contradictoire.

conform vt/i (se) conformer.

confound vt confondre.

confront vt affronter; ~ **with** confronter avec.

confuse vt (bewilder) troubler; (mistake, confound) confondre; **become** ~**d** s'embrouiller; **I am** ~**d** je m'y perds. **confusing** a déroutant. **confusion** n confusion f.

congeal vt/i (se) figer.

congested a (road) embouteillé; (passage) encombré; (Med) congestionné. **congestion** n (traffic) encombrement(s) m(pl); (Med) congestion f.

congratulate vt féliciter (**on** de). **congratulations** npl félicitations fpl.

congregate vi se rassembler. **congregation** n assemblée f.

congress n congrès m; **C**~ (US) le Congrès.

conjugate vt conjuguer. **conjugation** n conjugaison f.

conjunction n (Ling) conjonction f; **in** ~ **with** conjointement avec.

conjunctivitis n conjonctivite f.

conjure vi faire des tours de passe-passe. ● vt ~ **up** faire apparaître. **conjuror** n prestidigitateur/-trice m/f.

con man n ⊠ escroc m.

connect vt/i (se) relier; (in mind) faire le rapport entre; (install, wire up to mains) brancher; ~ **with** (of train) assurer la correspondance avec; ~**ed** (idea, event) lié; **be** ~**ed with** avoir rapport à.

connection n rapport m; (Rail) correspondance f; (phone call) communication f; (Electr) contact m; (joining piece) raccord m; ~**s** (Comm) relations fpl.

connive vi ~ **at** se faire le complice de.

C

conquer *vt* vaincre; (country) conquérir. **conqueror** *n* conquérant *m*.

conquest *n* conquête *f*.

conscience *n* conscience *f*. **conscientious** *a* consciencieux.

conscious *a* conscient; (deliberate) voulu. **consciously** *adv* consciemment. **consciousness** *n* conscience *f*; (Med) connaissance *f*.

conscript *n* appelé *m*.

consecutive *a* consécutif.

consensus *n* consensus *m*.

consent *vi* consentir (**to** à). ● *n* consentement *m*.

consequence *n* conséquence *f*. **consequently** *adv* par conséquent.

conservation *n* préservation *f*; ~ **area** zone *f* protégée. **conservationist** *n* défenseur *m* de l'environnement.

conservative *a* conservateur; (estimate) minimal.

Conservative Party *n* parti *m* conservateur.

conservatory *n* (greenhouse) serre *f*; (room) véranda *f*.

conserve *vt* conserver; (energy) économiser.

consider *vt* considérer; (allow for) tenir compte de; (possibility) envisager (**doing** de faire).

considerable *a* considérable; (much) beaucoup de.

considerate *a* prévenant, attentionné. **consideration** *n* considération *f*; (respect) égard(s) *m(pl)*.

considering *prep* compte tenu de.

consignment *n* envoi *m*.

consist *vi* consister (**of** en; **in doing** à faire).

consistency *n* (of liquids) consistance *f*; (of argument) cohérence *f*.

consistent *a* cohérent; ~ **with** conforme à.

consolation *n* consolation *f*.

consolidate *vt/i* (se) consolider.

consonant *n* consonne *f*.

conspicuous *a* (easily seen) en évidence; (showy) voyant; (noteworthy) remarquable.

conspiracy *n* conspiration *f*.

constable *n* agent *m* de police, gendarme *m*.

constant *a* (questions) incessant; (unchanging) constant; (friend) fidèle. ● *n* constante *f*. **constantly** *adv* constamment.

constellation *n* constellation *f*.

constipation *n* constipation *f*.

constituency *n* circonscription *f* électorale.

constituent *a* constitutif. ● *n* élément *m* constitutif; (Pol) électeur/-trice *m/f*.

constitution *n* constitution *f*.

constrain *vt* contraindre. **constraint** *n* contrainte *f*.

constrict *vt* (flow) comprimer; (movement) gêner.

construct *vt* construire. **construction** *n* construction *f*. **constructive** *a* constructif.

consulate *n* consulat *m*.

consult *vt* consulter. ● *vi* ~ **with** conférer avec. **consultant** *n* conseiller/-ère *m/f*; (Med) spécialiste *mf*. **consultation** *n* consultation *f*.

consume *vt* consommer; (destroy) consumer. **consumer** *n* consommateur/-trice *m/f*.

consummate *vt* consommer.

consumption *n* consommation *f*; (Med) phtisie *f*.

contact *n* contact *m*; (person) relation *f*. ● *vt* contacter. ~

lenses npl lentilles fpl (de contact).

contagious a contagieux.

contain vt contenir; ~ **oneself** se contenir. **container** n récipient m; (for transport) container m.

contaminate vt contaminer.

contemplate vt (gaze at) contempler; (think about) envisager.

contemporary a & n contemporain/-e (m/f).

contempt n mépris m. **contemptible** a méprisable. **contemptuous** a méprisant.

contend vt soutenir. ● vi ~ **with** (compete) rivaliser avec; (face) faire face à. **contender** n adversaire mf.

content¹ n (of letter) contenu m; (amount) teneur f; ~**s** contenu m.

content² a satisfait. ● vt contenter. **contented** a satisfait. **contentment** n contentement m.

contest¹ n (competition) concours m; (struggle) lutte f.

contest² vt contester; (compete for or in) disputer. **contestant** n concurrent/-e m/f.

context n contexte m.

continent n continent m; the C~ l'Europe f (continentale). **continental** a continental; européen. **continental quilt** n couette f.

contingency n éventualité f; ~ **plan** plan m d'urgence.

continual a continuel.

continuation n continuation f; (after interruption) reprise f; (new episode) suite f.

continue vt/i continuer; (resume) reprendre. **continued** a continu.

continuous a continu. **continuously** adv (without a break) sans interruption; (repeatedly) continuellement.

contort vt tordre; ~ **oneself** se contorsionner.

contour n contour m.

contraband n contrebande f.

contraception n contraception f. **contraceptive** a & n contraceptif (m).

contract¹ n contrat m.

contract² vt/i (se) contracter. **contraction** n contraction f.

contractor n entrepreneur/-euse m/f.

contradict vt contredire. **contradictory** a contradictoire.

contrary¹ a contraire (to à). ● n contraire m; on the ~ au contraire. ● adv ~ **to** contrairement à.

contrary² a entêté.

contrast¹ n contraste m.

contrast² vt/i contraster.

contravention n infraction f.

contribute vt donner. ● vi ~ **to** contribuer à; (take part) participer à; (newspaper) collaborer à. **contribution** n contribution f. **contributor** n collaborateur/-trice m/f.

contrive vt imaginer; ~ **to do** trouver moyen de faire.

control vt (pt **controlled**) (firm) diriger; (check) contrôler; (restrain) maîtriser. ● n contrôle m; (mastery) maîtrise f; ~**s** commandes fpl; (knobs) boutons mpl; **have under** ~ (event) avoir en main; **in** ~ **of** maître de. ~ **tower** n tour f de contrôle.

controversial a discutable, discuté. **controversy** n controverse f.

conurbation n agglomération f, conurbation f.

convalesce vi être en convalescence.

convene vt convoquer. ● vi se réunir.

convenience n commodité f; ~s toilettes fpl; all modern ~s tout le confort moderne; at your ~ quand cela vous conviendra, à votre convenance. ~ **foods** npl plats mpl tout préparés.

convenient a commode, pratique; (time) bien choisi; be ~ for convenir à.

convent n couvent m.

convention n (assembly, agreement) convention f; (custom) usage m. **conventional** a conventionnel.

conversation n conversation f. **conversational** a (tone) de la conversation; (French) de tous les jours.

converse[1] vi s'entretenir, converser (with avec).

converse[2] a & n inverse (m). **conversely** adv inversement.

conversion n conversion f.

convert[1] vt convertir; (house) aménager. ● vi ~ **into** se transformer en.

convert[2] n converti/-e m/f.

convertible a convertible. ● n (car) décapotable f.

convey vt (wishes, order) transmettre; (goods, people) transporter; (idea, feeling) communiquer. **conveyor belt** n tapis m roulant.

convict[1] vt déclarer coupable.

convict[2] n prisonnier/-ière m/f.

conviction n (Jur) condamnation f; (opinion) conviction f.

convince vt convaincre.

convoke vt convoquer.

convoy n convoi m.

convulse vt convulser; (fig) bouleverser; be ~d with laughter se tordre de rire.

cook vt/i (faire) cuire; (of person) faire la cuisine; ~ **up** ▣ fabriquer. ● n cuisinier/-ière

m/f. **cooker** n (stove) cuisinière f.

cookery n cuisine f.

cookie n (US) biscuit m.

cooking n cuisine f. ● a de cuisine.

cool a frais; (calm) calme; (unfriendly) froid; **●** n fraîcheur f; (calmness ▣) sang-froid m; in the ~ au frais. ● vt/i rafraîchir. ~ **box** n glacière f.

coolly adv calmement; froidement.

coop n poulailler m. ● vt ~ **up** enfermer.

co-operate vi coopérer.
co-operation n coopération f.

co-operative a coopératif. ● n coopérative f.

co-ordinate vt coordonner.

cop vt (pt **copped**) ▣ piquer. ● n (policeman ▣) flic m. □ ~ **out** ▣ se dérober.

cope vi s'en sortir ▣, se débrouiller; ~ **with** (problem) faire face à.

copper n cuivre m; (coin) sou m; ▣ flic m. ● a de cuivre.

copulate vi s'accoupler.

copy n copie f; (of book, newspaper) exemplaire m; (print: Photo) épreuve f. ● vt/i copier.

copyright n droit m d'auteur, copyright m.

copy-writer n rédacteur-concepteur m, rédactrice-conceptrice f.

cord n (petite) corde f; (of curtain, pyjamas) cordon m; (Electr) cordon m électrique; (fabric) velours m côtelé.

cordial a cordial. ● n (drink) sirop m.

corduroy n velours m côtelé.

core n (of apple) trognon m; (of problem) cœur m; (Tech) noyau m. ● vt (apple) évider.

cork n liège m; (for bottle) bouchon

m. ● *vt* boucher. **corkscrew** *n* tire-bouchon *m.*

corn *n* blé *m*; (maize: US) maïs *m*; (seed) grain *m*; (hard skin) cor *m.*

cornea *n* cornée *f.*

corner *n* coin *m*; (bend in road) virage *m*; (football) corner *m.* ● *vt* coincer, acculer; (market) accaparer. ● *vi* prendre un virage.

cornflour *n* farine *f* de maïs.

cornice *n* corniche *f.*

corny *a* (**-ier, -iest**) (*joke*) éculé.

corollary *n* corollaire *m.*

coronary *n* infarctus *m.*

coronation *n* couronnement *m.*

corporal *n* caporal *m.* ~ **punishment** *n* châtiment *m* corporel.

corporate *a* (*ownership*) en commun; (*body*) constitué.

corporation *n* (Comm) société *f.*

corpse *n* cadavre *m.*

corpuscle *n* globule *m.*

correct *a* (right) exact, juste, correct; (proper) correct; **you are ~** vous avez raison. ● *vt* corriger.

correction *n* correction *f.*

correlate *vt/i* (faire) correspondre.

correspond *vi* correspondre. **correspondence** *n* correspondance *f.*

corridor *n* couloir *m.*

corrode *vt/i* (se) corroder.

corrugated *a* ondulé; ~ **iron** tôle *f* ondulée.

corrupt *a* corrompu. ● *vt* corrompre. **corruption** *n* corruption *f.*

Corsica *n* Corse *f.*

cosh *n* matraque *f.* ● *vt* matraquer.

cosmetic *n* produit *m* de beauté. ● *a* cosmétique; (fig, pej) superficiel. ~ **surgery** *n* chirurgie *f* esthétique

cosmopolitan *a & n* cosmopolite (*mf*).

cosmos *n* cosmos *m.*

cost *vt* (*pt* cost) coûter; (*pt* costed) établir le prix de. ● *n* coût *m*; ~**s** (Jur) dépens *mpl*; **at all ~s** à tout prix; **to one's ~** à ses dépens; ~ **price** prix *m* de revient; ~ **of living** coût *m* de la vie. ~**-effective** *a* rentable.

costly *a* (**-ier, -iest**) coûteux; (valuable) précieux.

costume *n* costume *m*; (for swimming) maillot *m.* ~ **jewellery** *npl* bijoux *mpl* de fantaisie.

cosy *a* (**-ier, -iest**) confortable, intime.

cot *n* lit *m* d'enfant; (camp-bed: US) lit *m* de camp.

cottage *n* petite maison *f* de campagne; (thatched) chaumière *f.* ~ **pie** *n* hachis *m* Parmentier.

cotton *n* coton *m*; (for sewing) fil *m* (à coudre). ● *vi* ~ **on** ⊠ piger. ~ **wool** *n* coton *m* hydrophile.

couch *n* canapé *m.* ● *vt* (express) formuler.

cough *vi* tousser. ● *n* toux *f.* ▢ ~ **up** ⊠ cracher, payer.

could →CAN[1].

couldn't = COULD NOT.

council *n* conseil *m.* ~ **house** *n* maison *f* louée par la municipalité, ≈ H.L.M. *m or f.*

councillor *n* conseiller/-ère *m/f* municipal/-e.

counsel *n* conseil *m.* ● *n inv* (Jur) avocat/-e *m/f.* **counsellor** *n* conseiller/-ère *m/f.*

count *vt/i* compter. ● *n* (numerical record) décompte *m*; (nobleman) comte *m.* ▢ ~ **on** compter sur.

counter *n* comptoir *m*; (in bank) guichet *m*; (token) jeton *m.* ● *adv* ~ **to** à l'encontre de. ● *a* opposé. ● *vt* opposer; (blow) parer. ● *vi* riposter.

counteract *vt* neutraliser.

C

counterbalance n contrepoids m. ● vt contrebalancer.

counterfeit a & n faux (m). ● vt contrefaire.

counterfoil n souche f.

counter-productive a qui produit l'effet contraire.

countess n comtesse f.

countless a innombrable.

country n (land, region) pays m; (homeland) patrie f; (countryside) campagne f.

countryman n (pl -men) campagnard m; (fellow citizen) compatriote m.

countryside n campagne f.

county n comté m.

coup n (achievement) joli coup m; (Pol) coup m d'état.

couple n (people, animals) couple m; a ~ (of) (two or three) deux ou trois. ● vt/i (s')accoupler.

coupon n coupon m; (for shopping) bon m or coupon m de réduction.

courage n courage m.

courgette n courgette f.

courier n messager/-ère m/f; (for tourists) guide m.

course n cours m; (for training) stage m; (series) série f; (Culin) plat m; (for golf) terrain m; (at sea) itinéraire m; **change** ~ changer de cap; ~ (**of action**) façon f de faire; **during the** ~ **of** pendant; **in due** ~ en temps utile; **of** ~ bien sûr.

court n cour f; (tennis) court m; **go to** ~ aller devant les tribunaux. ● vt faire la cour à; (danger) rechercher.

courteous a courtois.

courtesy n courtoisie f; **by** ~ **of** avec la permission de.

court-house n (US) palais m de justice.

court-martial vt (pt -martialled)

faire passer en conseil de guerre. ● n cour f martiale.

court: ~**room** n salle f de tribunal. ~**shoe** n escarpin m. ~**yard** n cour f.

cousin n cousin/-e m/f; **first** ~ cousin/-e m/f germain/-e.

cove n anse f, crique f.

covenant n convention f.

cover vt couvrir. ● n (for bed, book) couverture f; (lid) couvercle m; (for furniture) housse f; (shelter) abri m; **take** ~ se mettre à l'abri. □ ~ **up** cacher; (crime) couvrir; ~ **up for** couvrir.

coverage n reportage m.

covering n enveloppe f; ~ **letter** lettre f d'accompagnement.

covert a (activity) secret; (threat) voilé; (look) dérobé.

cover-up n opération f de camouflage.

cow n vache f.

coward n lâche mf.

cowboy n cow-boy m.

cowshed n étable f.

coy a (faussement) timide, qui fait le or la timide.

cozy US = cosy.

crab n crabe m. ~**-apple** n pomme f sauvage.

crack n fente f; (in glass) fêlure f; (noise) craquement m; (joke 🖾) plaisanterie f. ● a 🗓 d'élite. ● vt/i (break partially) (se) fêler; (split) (se) fendre; (nut) casser; (joke) raconter; (problem) résoudre; **get** ~**ing** 🗓 s'y mettre. □ ~ **down on** 🗓 sévir contre; ~ **up** 🗓 craquer.

cracker n (Culin) biscuit m (salé); (for Christmas) diablotin f.

crackle vi crépiter. ● n crépitement m.

cradle n berceau m. ● vt bercer.

craft n métier m artisanal; (technique) art m; (boat) bateau m.

craftsman n (pl **-men**) artisan m. **craftsmanship** n art m.

crafty a (**-ier**, **-iest**) rusé.

crag n rocher m à pic.

cram vt/i (pt **crammed**); (for an exam) bachoter (**for** pour); ~ **into** (pack) (s')entasser dans; ~ **with** (fill) bourrer de.

cramp n crampe f.

cramped a à l'étroit.

cranberry n canneberge f.

crane n grue f. ● vt (neck) tendre.

crank n excentrique mf; (Tech) manivelle f.

crap n (nonsense ⊠) conneries fpl ⊠; (faeces ⊠) merde f ⊠.

crash n accident m; (noise) fracas m; (of thunder) coup m; (of firm) faillite f. ● vt/i avoir un accident (avec); (of plane) s'écraser; (two vehicles) se percuter; ~ **into** rentrer dans. ~ **course** n cours m intensif. ~**-helmet** n casque m (anti-choc). ~**-land** vi atterrir en catastrophe.

crate n cageot m.

cravat n foulard m.

crave vt/i ~ (**for**) désirer ardemment. **craving** n envie f irrésistible.

crawl vi (insect) ramper; (vehicle) se traîner; **be** ~**ing with** grouiller de. ● n (pace) pas m; (swimming) crawl m.

crayfish n inv écrevisse f.

crayon n craie f grasse.

craze n engouement m.

crazy a (**-ier**, **-iest**) fou; ~ **about** (person) fou de; (thing) fana or fou de.

creak n grincement m. ● vi grincer.

cream n crème f. ● a crème inv. ● vt écrémer.

crease n pli m. ● vt/i (se) froisser.

create vt créer. **creation** n

création f. **creative** a (person) créatif; (process) créateur.

creator n créateur/-trice m/f.

creature n créature f.

crèche n garderie f.

credentials npl (identity) pièces fpl d'identité; (competence) références fpl.

credibility n crédibilité f.

credit n (credence) crédit m; (honour) honneur m; **in** ~ créditeur; ~**s** (cinema) générique m. ● a (balance) créditeur. ● vt croire; (Comm) créditer; ~ **sb with** attribuer à qn. ~ **card** n carte f de crédit. ~ **note** n avoir m.

creditor n créancier/-ière m/f.

credit-worthy a solvable.

creed n credo m.

creek n (US) ruisseau m; **up the** ~ ⊠ dans le pétrin ⊡.

creep vi (pt **crept**) (insect, cat) ramper; (fig) se glisser. ● n (person ⊠) pauvre type m ⊡; **give sb the** ~**s** faire frissonner qn. **creeper** n liane f.

cremate vt incinérer. **cremation** n incinération f. **crematorium** n (pl **-ia**) crématorium m.

crêpe n crêpe m. ~ **paper** n papier m crêpon.

crept ⇒CREEP.

crescent n croissant m; (of houses) rue f en demi-lune.

cress n cresson m.

crest n crête f; (coat of arms) armoiries fpl.

cretin n crétin/-e m/f.

crevice n fente f.

crew n (of plane, ship) équipage m; (gang) équipe f. ~ **cut** n coupe f en brosse. ~ **neck** n (col) ras du cou m.

crib n lit m d'enfant. ● vt/i (pt **cribbed**) copier.

cricket n (Sport) cricket m; (insect) grillon m.

crime *n* crime *m*; (minor) délit *m*; (acts) criminalité *f*.

criminal *a* & *n* criminel/-le (*m/f*).

crimson *a* & *n* cramoisi (*m*).

cringe *vi* reculer; (fig) s'humilier.

crinkle *vt/i* (se) froisser. ● *n* pli *m*.

cripple *n* infirme *mf*. ● *vt* estropier; (fig) paralyser.

crisis *n* (*pl* **crises**) crise *f*.

crisp *a* (Culin) croquant; (air, reply) vif. **crisps** *npl* chips *fpl*.

criss-cross *a* entrecroisé. ● *vt/i* (s')entrecroiser.

criterion *n* (*pl* -**ia**) critère *m*.

critic *n* critique *m*. **critical** *a* critique. **critically** *adv* d'une manière critique; (*ill*) gravement.

criticism *n* critique *f*.

criticize *vt/i* critiquer.

croak *n* (bird) croassement *m*; (frog) coassement *m*. ● *vi* croasser; coasser.

Croatia *n* Croatie *f*.

Croatian *n* Croate *mf*. ● *a* Croate.

crochet *n* crochet *m*. ● *vt* faire du crochet.

crockery *n* vaisselle *f*.

crocodile *n* crocodile *m*.

crook *n* (criminal 🄰) escroc *m*; (stick) houlette *f*.

crooked *a* tordu; (winding) tortueux; (askew) de travers; (dishonest; fig) malhonnête.

crop *n* récolte *f*; (fig) quantité *f*. ● *vt* (*pt* **cropped**) couper. ● *vi* ~ up se présenter.

cross *n* croix *f*; (hybrid) hybride *m*. ● *vt/i* traverser; (legs, animals) croiser; (cheque) barrer; (paths) se croiser; ~ sb's mind venir à l'esprit de qn. ● *a* en colère, fâché (with contre); talk at ~ purposes parler sans se comprendre. □ ~ off or out rayer. ~-**check** *vt* vérifier (pour confirmer). ~-**country** (running)

n cross *m*. ~-**examine** *vt* faire subir un contre-interrogatoire à. ~-**eyed** *a* be ~-eyed loucher. ~-**fire** *n* feux *mpl* croisés.

crossing *n* (by boat) traversée *f*; (on road) passage *m* clouté.

crossly *adv* avec colère.

cross: ~-**reference** *n* renvoi *m*. ~-**roads** *n* carrefour *m*. ~-**word** *n* mots *mpl* croisés.

crotch *n* (of garment) entrejambes *m inv*.

crouch *vi* s'accroupir.

crow *n* corbeau *m*; as the ~ flies à vol d'oiseau. ● *vi* (of cock) chanter; (fig) jubiler. ~-**bar** *n* pied-de-biche *m*.

crowd *n* foule *f*. **crowded** *a* plein.

crown *n* couronne *f*; (top part) sommet *m*. ● *vt* couronner.

Crown Court *n* Cour *f* d'assises.

crucial *a* crucial.

crucifix *n* crucifix *m*.

crucify *vt* crucifier.

crude *a* (raw) brut; (rough, vulgar) grossier.

cruel *a* (**crueller**, **cruellest**) cruel.

cruise *n* croisière *f*. ● *vi* (ship) croiser; (tourists) faire une croisière; (vehicle) rouler; **cruising speed** vitesse *f* de croisière.

crumb *n* miette *f*.

crumble *vt/i* (s')effriter; (bread) (s')émietter; (collapse) s'écrouler.

crumple *vt/i* (se) froisser.

crunch *vt* croquer. ● *n* (event) moment *m* critique; **when it comes to the ~** quand ça devient sérieux.

crusade *n* croisade *f*. **crusader** *n* (knight) croisé *m*; (fig) militant/-e *m/f*.

crush *vt* écraser; (clothes) froisser. ● *n* (crowd) presse *f*; a ~ on 🄰 le béguin pour.

crust n croûte f. **crusty** a croustillant.

crutch n béquille f; (crotch) entrejambes m inv.

crux n the ∼ of (problem) le point crucial de.

cry n cri m. ● vi (weep) pleurer; (call out) crier. □ ∼ **off** se décommander.

crying a (need) urgent; a ∼ **shame** une vraie honte. ● n pleurs mpl.

cryptic a énigmatique.

crystal n cristal m. **∼-clear** a parfaitement clair.

cub n petit m; **Cub** (Scout) louveteau m.

Cuba n Cuba f.

cube n cube m. **cubic** a cubique; (metre) cube.

cubicle n (in room, hospital) box m; (at swimming-pool) cabine f.

cuckoo n coucou m.

cucumber n concombre m.

cuddle vt câliner. ● vi (kiss and) ∼ s'embrasser. ● n caresse f. **cuddly** a câlin; **cuddly toy** peluche f.

cue n signal m; (Theat) réplique f; (billiards) queue f.

cuff n manchette f; (US: on trousers) revers m; **off the ∼** impromptu. ● vt gifler. **∼-link** n bouton m de manchette.

cul-de-sac n (pl **culs-de-sac**) impasse f.

cull vt (select) choisir; (kill) massacrer.

culminate vi ∼ **in** se terminer par. **culmination** n point m culminant.

culprit n coupable mf.

cult n culte m.

cultivate vt cultiver. **cultivation** n culture f.

cultural a culturel.

culture n culture f. **cultured** a cultivé.

cumbersome a encombrant.

cunning a rusé. ● n astuce f, ruse f.

cup n tasse f; (prize) coupe f; **Cup final** finale f de la coupe.

cupboard n placard m.

cup-tie n match m de coupe.

curate n vicaire m.

curator n (of museum) conservateur m.

curb n (restraint) frein m; (of path) (US) bord m du trottoir. ● vt (desires) refréner; (price increase) freiner.

cure vt guérir; (fig) éliminer; (Culin) fumer; (in brine) saler. ● n (recovery) guérison f; (remedy) remède m.

curfew n couvre-feu m.

curiosity n curiosité f. **curious** a curieux.

curl vt/i (hair) boucler. ● n boucle f. □ ∼ **up** se pelotonner; (shrivel) se racornir.

curler n bigoudi m.

curly a (-ier, -iest) bouclé.

currant n raisin m de Corinthe.

currency n (money) monnaie f; (of word) fréquence f; **foreign ∼** devises fpl étrangères.

current a (term, word) usité; (topical) actuel; (year) en cours. ● n courant m. ∼ **account** n compte m courant. ∼ **events** npl l'actualité f.

currently adv actuellement.

curriculum n (pl **-la**) programme m scolaire. ∼ **vitae** n curriculum vitae m.

curry n curry m. ● vt ∼ **favour with** chercher les bonnes grâces de.

curse n (spell) malédiction f; (swearword) juron m. ● vt maudire. ● vi (swear) jurer.

C

cursor n curseur m.

curt a brusque.

curtain n rideau m.

curve n courbe f. ● vi (line) s'incurver; (edge) se recourber; (road) faire une courbe. ● vt courber.

cushion n coussin m. ● vt (a blow) amortir; (fig) protéger.

custard n crème f anglaise; (set) flan m.

custody n (of child) garde f; (Jur) détention f préventive.

custom n coutume f; (patronage: Comm) clientèle f. **customary** a habituel.

customer n client/-e m/f; (person 🔲) type m.

customize vt personnaliser.

custom-made a fait sur mesure.

customs npl douane f. ● a douanier. ∼ **officer** n douanier m.

cut vt/i (pt cut; pres p cutting) vt couper; (hedge) tailler; (prices) réduire. ● vi couper. ● n (wound) coupure f; (of clothes) coupe f; (in surgery) incision f; (share) part f; (in prices) réduction f. □ ∼ **back** vi faire des économies. vt réduire. ∼ **down** (on) réduire. ∼ **in** (in conversation) intervenir; ∼ **off** couper; (tide, army) isoler; ∼ **out** vt découper; (leave out) supprimer; vi (engine) s'arrêter. ∼ **short** (visit) écourter; ∼ **up** couper; (carve) découper.

cut-back n réduction f.

cute a 🔲 mignon.

cutlery n couverts mpl.

cutlet n côtelette f.

cut-price a à prix réduit.

cutting a cinglant. ● n (from newspaper) coupure f; (plant) bouture f.

CV abbr ⇒CURRICULUM VITAE.

cyanide n cyanure m.

cyberspace n cyberespace m.

cycle n cycle m; (bicycle) vélo m. ● vi aller à vélo.

cycling n cyclisme m. ∼ **shorts** npl cycliste m.

cyclist n cycliste mf.

cylinder n cylindre m.

cymbal n cymbale f.

cynic n cynique mf. **cynical** a cynique. **cynicism** n cynisme m.

cypress n cyprès m.

Cypriot n Cypriote mf. ● a cypriote.

Cyprus n Chypre f.

cyst n kyste m.

czar n tsar m.

Czech n (person) Tchèque mf; (Ling) tchèque m. ∼ **Republic** n République f tchèque.

dab vt (pt dabbed) tamponner; ∼ **sth on** appliquer qch par petites touches. ● n touche f.

dabble vi ∼ **in sth** faire qch en amateur.

dad n 🔲 papa m. **daddy** n 🔲 papa m.

daffodil n jonquille f.

daft a bête.

dagger n poignard m.

daily a quotidien. ● adv tous les jours. ● n (newspaper) quotidien m.

dainty a (-ier, -iest) (lace, food) délicat; (shoe, hand) mignon.

dairy n (on farm) laiterie f; (shop) crémerie f. ● a (farm, cow, product) laitier; (butter) fermier.

daisy n pâquerette f.

dam n barrage m.

damage n (to property) dégâts mpl; (Med) lésions fpl; **to do sth** ~ (cause, trade) porter atteinte à; ~**s** (Jur) dommages-intérêts mpl. ● vt (*property*) endommager; (*health*) nuire à; (*reputation*) porter atteinte à. **damaging** a (to health) nuisible; (to reputation) préjudiciable.

damn vt (Relig) damner; (condemn: fig) condamner. ● interj 🔲 zut 🔲, merde 🔲. ● n **not give/care a** ~ **about** se ficher de 🔲. ● a fichu 🔲. ● adv franchement.

damp n humidité f. ● a humide. **dampen** vt (lit) humecter; (fig) refroidir. **dampness** n humidité f.

dance vt/i danser. ● n danse f; (gathering) bal m; ~ **hall** dancing m. **dancer** n danseur/-euse m/f.

dandelion n pissenlit m.

dandruff n pellicules fpl.

Dane n Danois/-e m/f.

danger n danger m; (risk) risque m; **be in** ~ **of** risquer de. **dangerous** a dangereux.

dangle vt (*object*) balancer; (*legs*) laisser pendre. ● vi (*object*) se balancer (from à).

Danish n (Ling) danois m. ● a danois.

dare vt oser ((to) do faire); ~ **sb to do** défier qn de faire. ● n défi m. **daring** a audacieux.

dark a (day, colour, suit, mood, warning) sombre; (hair, eyes, skin) brun; (secret, thought) noir. ● n noir m; (nightfall) tombée f de la nuit; **in the** ~ (fig) dans le noir. **darken** vt/i (sky) (s')obscurcir; (mood) (s')assombrir. **darkness** n obscurité f. ~-**room** n chambre f noire.

darling a & n chéri/-e (m/f).

dart n fléchette f; ~**s** (game) fléchettes fpl. ● vi ~ **in/away** entrer/filer comme une flèche.

dash vi se précipiter; ~ **off** se sauver. ● vt (*hope*) anéantir; ~ **sth against** projeter qch contre. ● n course f folle; (of liquid) goutte f; (of colour) touche f; (in punctuation) tiret m.

dashboard n tableau m de bord.

data npl données fpl. ~-**base** n base f de données. ~ **capture** n saisie f de données. ~ **processing** n traitement m des données. ~ **protection** n protection f de l'information.

date n date f; (meeting) rendez-vous m; (fruit) datte f; **out of** ~ (old-fashioned) démodé; (*passport*) périmé; **to** ~ à ce jour; **up to** ~ (modern) moderne; (*list*) à jour. ● vt/i dater; (go out with) sortir avec; ~ **from** dater de. **dated** a démodé.

daughter n fille f. ~-**in-law** n (pl ~**s-in-law**) belle-fille f.

daunt vt décourager.

dawdle vi flâner, traînasser 🔲.

dawn n aube f. ● vi (day) se lever; **it** ~**ed on me that** je me suis rendu compte que.

day n jour m; (whole day) journée f; (period) époque f; **the** ~ **before** la veille; **the following** or **next** ~ le lendemain. ~**break** n aube f.

daydream n rêves mpl. ● vi rêvasser (about de).

day: ~**light** n jour m. ~**time** n journée f. ~ **trader** n spéculateur m à la journée, scalper m.

daze n **in a** ~ (from blow) étourdi; (from drug) hébété. **dazed** a (by blow) abasourdi; (by news) ahuri.

dazzle vt éblouir.

dead a mort; (numb) engourdi. ● adv complètement; **in** ~ **centre** au beau milieu; **stop** ~ s'arrêter net. ● n **in the** ~ **of** au cœur de; **the** ~ les morts. **deaden** vt (*sound, blow*) amortir; (*pain*)

calmer. ∼ **end** n impasse f.
∼**line** n date f limite. ∼**lock** n
impasse f.

deadly a (**-ier, -iest**) mortel;
(*weapon*) meurtrier.

deaf a sourd. **deafen** vt
assourdir. **deafness** n surdité f.

deal vt (*pt* **dealt**) donner; (*blow*)
porter. ● vi (trade) être en activité;
∼ **in** être dans le commerce de.
● n affaire f; (cards) donne f; **a
great** or **good** ∼ beaucoup (**of** de).
□ ∼ **with** (handle, manage)
s'occuper de; (be about) traiter de.
dealer n marchand/-e m/f; (agent)
concessionnaire mf. **dealings** npl
relations fpl.

dear a cher; ∼ **Sir/Madam**
Monsieur/Madame. ● n (**my**) ∼
mon chéri/ma chérie m/f. ● adv
cher. ● interj oh ∼! oh mon Dieu!

death n mort f; ∼ **penalty** peine f
de mort.

debatable a discutable.

debate n (formal) débat m; (informal)
discussion f. ● vt (formally)
débattre de; (informally) discuter.

debit n débit m. ● a (*balance*)
débiteur. ● vt (*pt* **debited**)
débiter.

debris n débris mpl; (rubbish)
déchets mpl.

debt n dette f; **be in** ∼ avoir des
dettes.

debug vt (Comput) déboguer.

decade n décennie f.

decadent a décadent.

decaffeinated a décaféiné.

decay vi (*vegetation*) pourrir;
(*tooth*) se carier; (fig) décliner. ● n
pourriture f; (of tooth) carie f; (fig)
déclin m.

deceased a décédé. ● n défunt/
-e m/f.

deceit n tromperie f. **deceitful** a
trompeur.

deceive vt tromper.

December n décembre m.

decent a (respectable) comme il
faut; (adequate) convenable; (good)
bon; (kind) gentil; (not indecent)
décent. **decently** adv
convenablement.

deception n tromperie f.
deceptive a trompeur.

decide vt/i décider (**to do** de
faire); (question) régler; ∼ **on** se
décider pour. **decided** a (firm)
résolu; (clear) net. **decidedly** adv
nettement.

decimal a décimal. ● n décimale
f; ∼ **point** virgule f.

decipher vt déchiffrer.

decision n décision f.

decisive a (conclusive) décisif; (firm)
décidé.

deck n pont m; (of cards: US) jeu
m; (of bus) étage m. ∼**-chair** n
chaise f longue.

declaration n déclaration f.
declare vt déclarer.

decline vt/i refuser; (fall) baisser.
● n (waning) déclin m; (drop) baisse
f; **in** ∼ sur le déclin.

decode vt décoder.

decommission vt (*arms*) mettre
hors service; (*reactor*)
démanteler.

decompose vt/i (se)
décomposer.

decor n décor m.

decorate vt décorer; (*room*)
refaire, peindre. **decoration** n
décoration f. **decorative** a
décoratif.

decorator n peintre m; (**interior**)
∼ décorateur/-trice m/f.

decoy n (person, vehicle) leurre m;
(for hunting) appeau m.

decrease[1] vt/i diminuer.

decrease[2] n diminution f.

decree n (Pol, Relig) décret m; (Jur)
jugement m. ● vt (*pt* **decreed**)
décréter.

decrepit a (building) délabré; (person) décrépit.

dedicate vt dédier; ~ **oneself to** se consacrer à.

dedicated a dévoué; ~ **line** (Internet) ligne f spécialisée.

dedication n dévouement m; (in book) dédicace f.

deduce vt déduire.

deduct vt déduire; (from wages) retenir.

deed n acte m.

deem vt considérer.

deep a profond; (mud, carpet) épais. ● adv profondément; ~ **in thought** absorbé dans ses pensées. **deepen** vt/i (admiration, concern) augmenter.

deep-freeze n congélateur m. ● vt congeler.

deep vein thrombosis n thrombose f veineuse profonde.

deer n inv cerf m; (doe) biche f.

deface vt dégrader.

default vi (Jur) (on payments) ne pas régler ses échéances. ● n (on payments) non-remboursement m; **by** ~ par défaut; **win by** ~ gagner par forfait. ● a (Comput) par défaut.

defeat vt vaincre; (thwart) faire échouer. ● n défaite f.

defect¹ n défaut m.

defect² vi faire défection; ~ **to** passer à.

defective a défectueux.

defector n transfuge mf.

defence n défense f.

defend vt défendre. **defendant** n (Jur) accusé/-e m/f. **defender** défenseur m.

defensive a défensif. ● n défensive f.

defer vt (pt **deferred**) (postpone) reporter; (judgement) suspendre; (payment) différer.

deference n déférence f. **deferential** a déférent.

defiance n défi m; **in** ~ **of** contre. **defiant** a rebelle. **defiantly** adv avec défi.

deficiency n insuffisance f; (fault) défaut m.

deficient a insuffisant; **be** ~ **in** manquer de.

deficit n déficit m.

define vt définir.

definite a (exact) précis; (obvious) net; (firm) ferme; (certain) certain. **definitely** adv certainement; (clearly) nettement.

definition n définition f.

deflate vt dégonfler.

deflect vt (missile) dévier; (criticism) détourner.

deforestation n déforestation f.

deform vt déformer.

defraud vt (client, employer) escroquer; (state, customs) frauder; ~ **sb of sth** escroquer qch à qn.

defrost vt dégivrer.

deft a adroit.

defunct a défunt.

defuse vt désamorcer.

defy vt défier; (attempts) résister à.

degenerate¹ vi dégénérer (into en).

degenerate² a & n dégénéré/-e (m/f).

degrade vt (humiliate) humilier; (damage) dégrader.

degree n degré m; (Univ) diplôme m universitaire; (Bachelor's degree) licence f; **to such a** ~ **that** à tel point que.

dehydrate vt/i (se) déshydrater.

deign vt ~ **to do** daigner faire.

dejected a découragé.

delay vt (flight) retarder; (decision) différer; ~ **doing**

attendre pour faire. ● *n* (of plane, post) retard *m*; (time lapse) délai *m*.

delegate¹ *n* délégué/-e *m/f*.

delegate² *vt* déléguer. **delegation** *n* délégation *f*.

delete *vt* supprimer; (Comput) effacer; (with pen) barrer. **deletion** *n* suppression *f*; (with line) rature *f*.

deliberate¹ *vi* délibérer.

deliberate² *a* délibéré; (*steps, manner*) mesuré. **deliberately** *adv* (*do, say*) exprès; (*sarcastically, provocatively*) délibérément.

delicacy *n* délicatesse *f*; (food) mets *m* raffiné.

delicate *a* délicat.

delicatessen *n* épicerie *f* fine.

delicious *a* délicieux.

delight *n* joie *f*, plaisir *m*. ● *vt* ravir. ● *vi* ~ **in** prendre plaisir à. **delighted** *a* ravi. **delightful** *a* charmant/-e.

delinquent *a & n* délinquant/-e (*m/f*).

delirious *a* délirant.

deliver *vt* (*message*) remettre; (*goods*) livrer; (*speech*) faire; (*baby*) mettre au monde; (*rescue*) délivrer. **delivery** *n* (of goods) livraison *f*; (of mail) distribution *f*; (of baby) accouchement *m*.

delude *vt* tromper; ~ **oneself** se faire des illusions.

deluge *n* déluge *m*. ● *vt* submerger (with de).

delusion *n* illusion *f*.

delve *vi* fouiller.

demand *vt* (request, require) demander; (forcefully) exiger. ● *n* (request) demande *f*; (pressure) exigence *f*; **in** ~ très demandé; **on** ~ à la demande. **demanding** *a* exigeant.

demean *vt* ~ **oneself** s'abaisser.

demeanour, (US) **demeanor** *n* comportement *m*.

demented *a* fou.

demise *n* disparition *f*.

demo *n* (demonstration 🆃) manif *f* 🆃.

democracy *n* démocratie *f*.

democrat *n* démocrate *mf*.

democratic *a* démocratique.

demolish *vt* démolir.

demon *n* démon *m*.

demonstrate *vt* démontrer; (*concern, skill*) manifester. ● *vi* (Pol) manifester. **demonstration** *n* démonstration *f*; (Pol) manifestation *f*. **demonstrative** *a* démonstratif. **demonstrator** *n* manifestant/-e *mf*.

demoralize *vt* démoraliser.

demote *vt* rétrograder.

den *n* (of lion) antre *m*; (room) tanière *f*.

denial *n* (of rumour) démenti *m*; (of rights) négation *f*; (of request) rejet *m*.

denim *n* jean *m*; ~**s** (jeans) jean *m*.

Denmark *n* Danemark *m*.

denomination *n* (Relig) confession *f*; (money) valeur *f*.

denounce *vt* dénoncer.

dense *a* dense. **densely** *adv* (*packed*) très. **density** *n* densité *f*.

dent *n* bosse *f*. ● *vt* cabosser.

dental *a* dentaire; ~ **floss** fil *m* dentaire; ~ **surgeon** chirurgien-dentiste *m*.

dentist *n* dentiste *mf*. **dentistry** *n* médecine *f* dentaire.

dentures *npl* dentier *m*.

deny *vt* nier (that que); (*rumour*) démentir; ~ **sb sth** refuser qch à qn.

deodorant *n* déodorant *m*.

depart *vi* partir; ~ **from** (deviate) s'éloigner de.

department *n* (in shop) rayon *m*; (in hospital, office) service *m*; (Univ) département *m*; **D**~ **of Health**

ministère *m* de la santé; ~ **store** grand magasin *m*.

departure *n* départ *m*; **a ~ from** (*custom, truth*) une entorse à.

depend *vi* dépendre (on de); ~ **on** (rely on) compter sur; **it** (all) ~s ça dépend; ~**ing on the season** suivant la saison. **dependable** *a* (*person*) digne de confiance. **dependant** *n* personne *f* à charge. **dependence** *n* dépendance *f*.

dependent *a* dépendant; **be ~ on** dépendre de.

depict *vt* (describe) dépeindre; (in picture) représenter.

deplete *vt* réduire.

deport *vt* expulser.

depose *vt* déposer.

deposit *vt* (*pt* **deposited**) déposer. ● *n* (in bank) dépôt *m*; (on house) versement *m* initial; (on holiday) acompte *m*; (against damage) caution *f*; (on bottle) consigne *f*; (of mineral) gisement *m*; ~ **account** compte *m* de dépôt. **depositor** *n* (Comm) déposant/-e *m/f*.

depot *n* dépôt *m*; (US) gare *f*.

depreciate *vt/i* (se) déprécier.

depress *vt* déprimer. **depressing** *a* déprimant. **depression** *n* dépression *f*; (Econ) récession *f*.

deprivation *n* privation *f*.

deprive *vt* ~ **of** priver de. **deprived** *a* démuni.

depth *n* profondeur *f*; (of knowledge, ignorance) étendue *f*; (of colour, emotion) intensité *f*.

deputize *vi* ~ **for** remplacer.

deputy *n* adjoint/-e *m/f*. ● *a* adjoint; ~ **chairman** vice-président *m*.

derail *vt* faire dérailler. **derailment** *n* déraillement *m*.

deranged *a* dérangé.

derelict *a* abandonné.

deride *vt* ridiculiser. **derision** *n*

moqueries *fpl*. **derisory** *a* dérisoire.

derivative *a & n* dérivé (*m*).

derive *vt* ~ **sth from** tirer qch de. ● *vi* ~ **from** découler de.

derogatory *a* (*word*) péjoratif; (*remark*) désobligeant.

descend *vt/i* descendre; **be ~ed from** descendre de. **descendant** *n* descendant/-e *m/f*. **descent** *n* descente *f*; (lineage) origine *f*.

describe *vt* décrire; ~ **sb as sth** qualifier qn de qch. **description** *n* description *f*. **descriptive** *a* descriptif.

desert[1] *n* désert *m*.

desert[2] *vt/i* abandonner; (*cause*) déserter. **deserted** *a* désert. **deserter** *n* déserteur *m*.

deserts *npl* **get one's ~** avoir ce qu'on mérite.

deserve *vt* mériter (**to** de). **deservedly** *adv* à juste titre. **deserving** *a* (*person*) méritant; (*action*) louable.

design *n* (sketch) plan *m*; (idea) conception *f*; (pattern) motif *m*; (art of designing) design *m*; (aim) dessein *m*. ● *vt* (sketch) dessiner; (devise, intend) concevoir.

designate *vt* désigner.

designer *n* concepteur/-trice *m/f*; (of fashion, furniture) créateur/-trice *m/f*. ● *a* (*clothes*) de haute couture; (*sunglasses, drink*) de dernière mode.

desirable *a* (*outcome*) souhaitable; (*person*) désirable.

desire *n* désir *m*. ● *vt* désirer.

desk *n* bureau *m*; (of pupil) pupitre *m*; (in hotel) réception *f*; (in bank) caisse *f*.

desolate *a* (place) désolé; (*person*) affligé.

despair *n* désespoir *m*. ● *vi* désespérer (**of** de).

desperate *a* désespéré; (criminal) prêt à tout; **be ~ for** avoir

désespérément besoin de.
desperately *adv* désespérément; (*worried*) terriblement; (*ill*) gravement.
desperation *n* désespoir *m*; in ∼ en désespoir de cause.
despicable *a* méprisable.
despise *vt* mépriser.
despite *prep* malgré.
despondent *a* découragé.
dessert *n* dessert *m*. ∼spoon *n* cuillère *f* à dessert.
destination *n* destination *f*.
destiny *n* destin *m*.
destitute *a* sans ressources.
destroy *vt* détruire; (*animal*) abattre. **destroyer** *n* (warship) contre-torpilleur *m*.
destruction *n* destruction *f*. **destructive** *a* destructeur.
detach *vt* détacher; ∼ed house maison *f* (individuelle).
detail *n* détail *m*; go into ∼ entrer dans les détails. ● *vt* (*plans*) exposer en détail.
detain *vt* retenir; (in prison) placer en détention. **detainee** *n* détenu/-e *m/f*.
detect *vt* (*error, trace*) déceler; (*crime, mine, sound*) détecter. **detection** *n* détection *f*. **detective** *n* inspecteur/-trice *m/f*; (private) détective *m*.
detention *n* détention *f*; (School) retenue *f*.
deter *vt* (*pt* **deterred**) dissuader (**from** de).
detergent *a & n* détergent (*m*).
deteriorate *vi* se détériorer.
determine *vt* déterminer; ∼ to do résoudre de faire. **determined** *a* (*person*) décidé; (*air*) résolu.
deterrent *n* moyen *m* de dissuasion. ● *a* (*effect*) dissuasif.
detest *vt* détester.
detonate *vt/i* (faire) détoner.

detonation *n* détonation *f*.
detonator *n* détonateur *m*.
detour *n* détour *m*.
detract *vi* ∼ **from** (*success, value*) porter atteinte à; (*pleasure*) diminuer.
detriment *n* to the ∼ of au détriment de. **detrimental** *a* nuisible (**to** à).
devalue *vt* dévaluer.
devastate *vt* (*place*) ravager; (*person*) accabler.
develop *vt* (*plan*) élaborer; (*mind, body*) développer; (*land*) mettre en valeur; (*illness*) attraper; (*habit*) prendre. ● *vi* (*child, country, plot, business*) se développer; (*hole, crack*) se former.
development *n* développement *m*; (**housing**) ∼ lotissement *m*; (**new**) ∼ fait *m* nouveau.
deviate *vi* dévier; ∼ **from** (*norm*) s'écarter de.
device *n* appareil *m*; (means) moyen *m*; (bomb) engin *m* explosif.
devil *n* diable *m*.
devious *a* (*person*) retors.
devise *vt* (*scheme*) concevoir; (*product*) inventer.
devoid *a* ∼ of dépourvu de.
devolution *n* (Pol) régionalisation *f*.
devote *vt* consacrer (**to** à). **devoted** *a* dévoué. **devotion** *n* dévouement *m*; (Relig) dévotion *f*.
devour *vt* dévorer.
devout *a* fervent.
dew *n* rosée *f*.
diabetes *n* diabète *m*.
diabolical *a* diabolique; (bad 🆃) atroce.
diagnose *vt* diagnostiquer. **diagnosis** *n* (*pl* **-oses**) diagnostic *m*.

diagonal a diagonal. ● n diagonale f.

diagram n schéma m.

dial n cadran m. ● vt (pt **dialled**) (number) faire; (person) appeler; **dialling code** indicatif m; **dialling tone** tonalité f.

dialect n dialecte m.

dialogue n dialogue m.

diameter n diamètre m.

diamond n diamant m; (shape) losange m; (baseball) terrain m; **~s** (cards) carreau m.

diaper n (US) couche f.

diaphragm n diaphragme m.

diarrhoea, (US) **diarrhea** n diarrhée f.

diary n (for appointments) agenda m; (journal) journal m intime.

dice n inv dé m. ● vt (food) couper en dés.

dictate vt/i dicter.

dictation n dictée f.

dictator n dictateur m. **dictatorship** n dictature f.

dictionary n dictionnaire m.

did ⇒DO.

didn't = DID NOT.

die vi (pres p **dying**) mourir; (plant) crever; **be dying to do** mourir d'envie de faire. □ **~ down** diminuer. **~ out** disparaître.

diesel n gazole m; **~ engine** moteur m diesel.

diet n (usual food) alimentation f; (restricted) régime m. ● vi être au régime. **dietary** a alimentaire. **dietician** n diététicien/-ne m/f.

differ vi différer (from de).

difference n différence f; (disagreement) différend m.

different a différent (from, to de).

differentiate vt différencier. ● vi faire la différence (between entre).

differently adv différemment (from de).

difficult a difficile. **difficulty** n difficulté f.

diffuse¹ a diffus.

diffuse² vt diffuser.

dig vt/i (pt **dug**; pres p **digging**) (excavate) creuser; (in garden) bêcher. ● n (poke) coup m de coude; (remark) pique f 🛙; (Archeol) fouilles fpl. □ **~ up** déterrer.

digest vt/i digérer. **digestible** a digestible. **digestion** n digestion f.

digger n excavateur m.

digit n chiffre m.

digital a (clock) à affichage numérique; (display, recording) numérique. **~ audio tape** n cassette f audionumérique. **~ camera** n appareil m photo numérique.

dignified a digne.

dignitary n dignitaire m.

dignity n dignité f.

digress vi faire une digression.

dilapidated a délabré.

dilate vt/i (se) dilater.

dilemma n dilemme m.

diligent a appliqué.

dilute vt diluer.

dim a (**dimmer**, **dimmest**) (weak) faible; (dark) sombre; (indistinct) vague; 🛙 stupide. ● vt/i (pt **dimmed**) (light) baisser.

dime n (US) (pièce f de) dix cents.

dimension n dimension f.

diminish vt/i diminuer.

dimple n fossette f.

din n vacarme m.

dine vi dîner. **diner** n dîneur/ -euse m/f; (US) restaurant m à service rapide.

dinghy n dériveur m.

dingy a (**-ier**, **-iest**) minable.

dining room n salle f à manger.

dinner n (evening meal) dîner m;

(lunch) déjeuner *m*; have ~ dîner. ~-**jacket** *n* smoking *m*. ~ **party** *n* dîner *m*.

dinosaur *n* dinosaure *m*.

dip *vt/i* (*pt* dipped) plonger; ~ **into** (*book*) feuilleter; (*savings*) puiser dans; ~ **one's headlights** se mettre en code. ● *n* (slope) déclivité *f*; (in sea) bain *m* rapide.

diploma *n* diplôme *m* (in en).

diplomacy *n* diplomatie *f*. **diplomat** *n* diplomate *mf*. **diplomatic** *a* (Pol) diplomatique; (tactful) diplomate.

dire *a* affreux; (*need, poverty*) extrême.

direct *a* direct. ● *adv* directement. ● *vt* diriger; (*letter, remark*) adresser; (*a play*) mettre en scène; ~ **sb to** indiquer à qn le chemin de; (*order*) signifier à qn de.

direction *n* direction *f*; (Theat) mise *f* en scène; ~**s** indications *fpl*; **ask** ~**s** demander le chemin; ~**s for use** mode *m* d'emploi.

directly *adv* directement; (at once) tout de suite. ● *conj* dès que.

director *n* directeur/-trice *m/f*; (Theat) metteur *m* en scène.

directory *n* (phone book) annuaire *m*. ~ **enquiries** *npl* renseignements *mpl* téléphoniques.

dirt *n* saleté *f*; (earth) terre *f*; ~ **cheap** ▣ très bon marché *inv*. ~-**track** *n* (Sport) cendrée *f*.

dirty *a* (-**ier**, -**iest**) sale; (word) grossier; **get** ~ se salir. ● *vt/i* (se) salir.

disability *n* handicap *m*.

disable *vt* rendre infirme. **disabled** *a* handicapé.

disadvantage *n* désavantage *m*. **disadvantaged** *a* défavorisé.

disagree *vi* ne pas être d'accord (with avec); ~ **with sb** (*food, climate*) ne pas convenir à qn.

disagreement *n* désaccord *m*; (quarrel) différend *m*.

disappear *vi* disparaître. **disappearance** *n* disparition *f* (of de).

disappoint *vt* décevoir. **disappointment** *n* déception *f*.

disapproval *n* désapprobation *f* (of de).

disapprove *vi* ~ (**of**) désapprouver.

disarm *vt/i* désarmer. **disarmament** *n* désarmement *m*.

disarray *n* désordre *m*.

disaster *n* désastre *m*. **disastrous** *a* désastreux.

disband *vi* disperser. ● *vt* dissoudre.

disbelief *n* incrédulité *f*.

disc *n* disque *m*; (Comput) = DISK.

discard *vt* se débarrasser de; (*beliefs*) abandonner.

discharge *vt* (unload) décharger; (*liquid*) déverser; (*duty*) remplir; (dismiss) renvoyer; (*prisoner*) libérer. ● *vi* (of pus) s'écouler.

disciple *n* disciple *m*.

disciplinary *a* disciplinaire.

discipline *n* discipline *f*. ● *vt* discipliner; (punish) punir.

disc jockey *n* disc-jockey *m*, animateur *m*.

disclaimer *n* démenti *m*.

disclose *vt* révéler. **disclosure** *n* révélation *f* (of de).

disco *n* (club ▣) discothèque *f*; (event) soirée *f* disco.

discolour *vt/i* (se) décolorer.

discomfort *n* gêne *f*.

disconcert *vt* déconcerter.

disconnect *vt* détacher; (unplug) débrancher; (cut off) couper.

discontent *n* mécontentement *m*.

discontinue *vt* (*service*) supprimer; (*production*) arrêter.

discord n discorde f; (Mus) discordance f.

discount[1] n remise f; (on minor purchase) rabais m.

discount[2] vt (advice) ne pas tenir compte de; (possibility) écarter.

discourage vt décourager.

discourse n discours m.

discourteous a peu courtois.

discover vt découvrir. **discovery** n découverte f.

discreet a discret.

discrepancy n divergence f.

discretion n discrétion f.

discriminate vt/i distinguer; ~ against faire de la discrimination contre. **discriminating** a qui a du discernement. **discrimination** n discernement m; (bias) discrimination f.

discus n disque m.

discuss vt (talk about) discuter de; (in writing) examiner. **discussion** n discussion f.

disdain n dédain m.

disease n maladie f.

disembark vt/i débarquer.

disenchanted a désabusé.

disentangle vt démêler.

disfigure vt défigurer.

disgrace n (shame) honte f; (disfavour) disgrâce f. ● vt déshonorer. **disgraced** a (in disfavour) disgracié. **disgraceful** a honteux.

disgruntled a mécontent.

disguise vt déguiser. ● n déguisement m; in ~ déguisé.

disgust n dégoût m. ● vt dégoûter.

dish n plat m; the ~es (crockery) la vaisselle. ● vt ~ out 🄸 distribuer; ~ up servir.

dishcloth n lavette f; (for drying) torchon m.

dishearten vt décourager.

dishevelled a échevelé.

dishonest a malhonnête.

dishonour, (US) **dishonor** n déshonneur m.

dishwasher n lave-vaisselle m inv.

disillusion vt désabuser. **disillusionment** n désillusion f.

disincentive n be a ~ to décourager.

disinclined a ~ to peu disposé à.

disinfect vt désinfecter. **disinfectant** n désinfectant m.

disintegrate vt/i (se) désintégrer.

disinterested a désintéressé.

disjointed a (talk) décousu.

disk n (US) = DISC; (Comput) disque m. ~ **drive** n drive m, lecteur m de disquettes.

diskette n disquette f.

dislike n aversion f. ● vt ne pas aimer.

dislocate vt (limb) disloquer.

dislodge vt (move) déplacer; (drive out) déloger.

disloyal a déloyal (to envers).

dismal a morne, triste.

dismantle vt démonter, défaire.

dismay n consternation f (at devant). ● vt consterner.

dismiss vt renvoyer; (appeal) rejeter; (from mind) écarter. **dismissal** n renvoi m.

dismount vi descendre, mettre pied à terre.

disobedient a désobéissant.

disobey vt désobéir à. ● vi désobéir.

disorder n désordre m; (ailment) trouble(s) m(pl). **disorderly** a désordonné.

disorganized a désorganisé.

disown vt renier.

disparaging a désobligeant.

dispassionate a impartial; (unemotional) calme.

dispatch vt (send, complete)

D

expédier; (troops) envoyer. ● n
expédition f; envoi m; (report)
dépêche f.

dispel vt (pt **dispelled**) dissiper.

dispensary n (in hospital)
pharmacie f, (in chemist's) officine
f.

dispense vt distribuer; (medicine)
préparer. ● vi ~ **with** se passer
de. **dispenser** n (container)
distributeur m.

disperse vt/i (se) disperser.

display vt montrer, exposer;
(feelings) manifester. ● n
exposition f; manifestation f;
(Comm) étalage m; (of computer)
visuel m.

displeased a mécontent (**with**
de).

disposable a jetable.

disposal n (of waste) évacuation f;
at sb's ~ à la disposition de qn.

dispose vt disposer. ● vi ~ **of** se
débarrasser de; **well** ~**d to** bien
disposé envers.

disposition n disposition f;
(character) naturel m.

disprove vt réfuter.

dispute vt contester. ● n
discussion f; (Pol) conflit m; **in** ~
contesté.

disqualify vt rendre inapte;
(Sport) disqualifier; ~ **from driving**
retirer le permis à.

disquiet n inquiétude f.
disquieting a inquiétant.

disregard vt ne pas tenir compte
de. ● n indifférence f (**for** à).

disrepair n délabrement m.

disreputable a peu
recommandable.

disrepute n discrédit m.

disrespect n manque m de
respect. **disrespectful** a
irrespectueux.

disrupt vt (disturb, break up)
perturber; (plans) déranger.

disruption n perturbation f.

disruptive a perturbateur.

dissatisfied a mécontent.

dissect vt disséquer.

disseminate vt diffuser.

dissent vi différer (**from** de). ● n
dissentiment m.

dissertation n mémoire m.

disservice n **do a** ~ **to sb** rendre
un mauvais service à qn.

dissident a & n dissident/-e (m/
f).

dissimilar a dissemblable,
différent.

dissipate vt/i (se) dissiper.
dissipated a (person) dissolu.

dissolve vt/i (se) dissoudre.

dissuade vt dissuader.

distance n distance f; **from a** ~
de loin; **in the** ~ au loin. **distant**
a éloigné, lointain; (relative)
éloigné; (aloof) distant.

distaste n dégoût m. **distasteful**
a désagréable.

distil vt (pt **distilled**) distiller.

distinct a distinct; (definite) net; **as**
~ **from** par opposition à.
distinction n distinction f; (in
exam) mention f très bien.
distinctive a distinctif.

distinguish vt/i distinguer.

distort vt déformer. **distortion** n
distorsion f; (of facts) déformation
f.

distract vt distraire. **distracted**
a (distraught) éperdu. **distracting** a
gênant. **distraction** n (lack of
attention, entertainment) distraction f.

distraught a éperdu.

distress n douleur f; (poverty,
danger) détresse f. ● vt peiner.
distressing a pénible.

distribute vt distribuer.

district n région f; (of town)
quartier m.

distrust n méfiance f. ● vt se
méfier de.

disturb vt déranger; (alarm, worry) troubler. **disturbance** n dérangement m (of de); (noise) tapage m. **disturbances** npl (Pol) troubles mpl. **disturbed** a troublé; (psychologically) perturbé. **disturbing** a troublant.

disused a désaffecté.

ditch n fossé m. ● vt ⊠ abandonner.

ditto adv idem.

dive vi plonger; (rush) se précipiter. ● n plongeon m; (of plane) piqué m; (place ⊠) bouge m. **diver** n plongeur/-euse m/f.

diverge vi diverger. **divergent** a divergent.

diverse a divers.

diversion n détournement m; (distraction) diversion f; (of traffic) déviation f. **divert** vt détourner; (traffic) dévier.

divide vt/i (se) diviser.

dividend n dividende m.

divine a divin.

diving: **∼-board** n plongeoir m. **∼-suit** n scaphandre m.

division n division f.

divorce n divorce m (from avec). ● vt/i divorcer (d'avec).

divulge vt divulguer.

DIY abbr ⇒DO-IT-YOURSELF.

dizziness n vertige m.

dizzy a (-ier, -iest) vertigineux; be or feel ∼ avoir le vertige.

....

do

present do, does; *present negative* don't, do not; *past* did; *past participle* done

● *transitive and intransitive verb*
····▶ faire; **she is doing her homework** elle fait ses devoirs.
····▶ (progress, be suitable) aller; **how are you doing?** comment ça va?

····▶ (be enough) suffire; **will five dollars ∼?** cinq dollars, ça suffira?

● *auxiliary verb*

····▶ (in questions) **∼ you like Mozart?** aimes-tu Mozart?, est-ce que tu aimes Mozart?; **did your sister phone?** est-ce que ta sœur a téléphoné?, ta sœur a-t-elle téléphoné?
····▶ (in negatives) **I don't like Mozart** je n'aime pas Mozart.
····▶ (emphatic uses) **I ∼ like your dress** j'aime beaucoup ta robe; **I ∼ think you should go** je pense vraiment que tu devrais y aller.
····▶ (referring back to another verb) **I live in Oxford and so does Lily** j'habite à Oxford et Lily aussi; **she gets paid more than I ∼** elle est payée plus que moi; '**I don't like carrots**'—'**neither ∼ I**' 'je n'aime pas les carottes'—'moi non plus'.
····▶ (imperatives) **don't shut the door** ne ferme pas la porte; **∼ be quiet** tais-toi!
····▶ (short questions and answers) **you like fish, don't you?** tu aimes le poisson, n'est-ce pas?; **Lola didn't phone, did she?** Lola n'a pas téléphoné par hasard?; '**does he play tennis?**'—'**no he doesn't/yes he does**' 'est-ce qu'il joue au tennis?'—'non/oui'; '**Marion didn't say that**'—'**yes she did**' 'Marion n'a pas dit ça'—'si'.
□ **do away with** supprimer; **do up** (fasten) fermer; (*house*) refaire; **do with** it's to ∼ with c'est à propos de; it's nothing to ∼ with ça n'a rien à voir avec; **do without** se passer de.

....

docile a docile.

dock n (Jur) banc m des accusés; dock m. ● vi arriver au port. ● vt mettre à quai; *(wages)* faire une retenue sur.

doctor *n* médecin *m*, docteur *m*; *(Univ)* docteur *m*. ● *vt (cat)* châtrer; *(fig)* altérer.

doctorate *n* doctorat *m*.

document *n* document *m*.
documentary *a & n* documentaire *(m)*.
documentation *n* documentation *f*.

dodge *vt* esquiver. ● *vi* faire un saut de côté. ● *n* mouvement *m* de côté.

dodgems *npl* autos *fpl* tamponneuses.

dodgy *a* (**-ier**, **-iest**) (🛑: difficult) épineux, délicat; (untrustworthy) louche 🛑.

doe *n* (deer) biche *f*.

does ⇒DO.

doesn't = DOES NOT.

dog *n* chien *m*. ● *vt* (pt **dogged**) poursuivre. ~**-collar** *n* col *m* romain. ~**-eared** *a* écorné.

dogged *a* obstiné.

dogma *n* dogme *m*. **dogmatic** *a* dogmatique.

dogsbody *n* bonne *f* à tout faire.

do-it-yourself *n* bricolage *m*.

doldrums *npl* be in the ~ (person) avoir le cafard.

dole *vt* ~ **out** distribuer. ● *n* 🛑 indemnité *f* de chômage; **on the** ~ 🛑 au chômage.

doll *n* poupée *f*. ● *vt* ~ **up** 🛑 bichonner.

dollar *n* dollar *m*.

dollop *n* (of food 🛑) gros morceau *m*.

dolphin *n* dauphin *m*.

domain *n* domaine *m*.

dome *n* dôme *m*.

domestic *a* familial; *(trade, flights)* intérieur; *(animal)* domestique. **domesticated** *a* *(animal)* domestiqué.

domestic science *n* arts *mpl* ménagers.

dominant *a* dominant.

dominate *vt/i* dominer.
domination *n* domination *f*.

domineering *a* dominateur.

domino *n* (pl ~**es**) domino *m*; ~**es** (game) dominos *mpl*.

donate *vt* faire don de. **donation** *n* don *m*.

done ⇒DO.

donkey *n* âne *m*. ~ **work** *n* travail *m* pénible.

donor *n* donateur/-trice *m/f*; (of blood) donneur/-euse *m/f*.

don't = DO NOT.

doodle *vi* griffonner.

doom *n* (ruin) ruine *f*; (fate) destin *m*. ● *vt* be ~ed to être destiné or condamné à; ~ed (**to failure**) voué à l'échec.

door *n* porte *f*; (of vehicle) portière *f*, porte *f*. ~**bell** *n* sonnette *f*. ~**man** *n* (pl -**men**) portier *m*. ~**mat** *n* paillasson *m*. ~**step** *n* pas *m* de (la) porte, seuil *m*. ~**way** *n* porte *f*.

dope *n* 🛑 cannabis *m*; (idiot 🛑) imbécile *mf*. ● *vt* doper. **dopey** *a* (foolish 🛑) imbécile.

dormant *a* en sommeil.

dormitory *n* dortoir *m*; (Univ, US) résidence *f*.

dosage *n* dose *f*; (on label) posologie *f*.

dose *n* dose *f*.

dot *n* point *m*; **on the** ~ 🛑 à l'heure pile.

dot-com *n* (société) point com *f*; ~ **millionaire** millionnaire *mf* de l'Internet. ~ **shares** actions *fpl* des sociétés point com.

dote *vi* ~ **on** adorer.

dotted *a* *(fabric)* à pois; ~ **line** pointillé *m*; ~ **with** parsemé de.

double *a* double; *(room, bed)* pour deux personnes; ~ **the size** deux fois plus grand. ● *adv* deux

fois; **pay** ~ payer le double. ● *n*
double *m*; (stuntman) doublure *f*;
~**s** (tennis) double *m*; **at** or **on the**
~ au pas de course. ● *vt/i*
doubler; (fold) plier en deux.
~**bass** *n* (Mus) contrebasse *f*.
~**check** *vt* revérifier. ~ **chin** *n*
double menton *m*. ~**cross** *vt*
tromper. ~**decker** *n* autobus *m*
à impériale.

doubt *n* doute *m*. ● *vt* douter de;
~ **if** or **that** douter que. **doubtful**
a incertain, douteux; (*person*) qui
a des doutes. **doubtless** *adv* sans
doute.

dough *n* pâte *f*; (money 🖾) fric *m*
🖾.

doughnut *n* beignet *m*.

douse *vt* arroser; (*light, fire*)
éteindre.

dove *n* colombe *f*.

Dover *n* Douvres *f*.

dowdy *a* (**-ier, -iest**) (*clothes*)
sans chic, monotone; (*person*)
sans élégance.

down *adv* en bas; (of sun) couché,
(lower) plus bas; **come** or **go** ~
descendre; **go** ~ **to the post office**
aller à la poste; ~ **under** aux
antipodes; ~ **with** à bas. ● *prep*
en bas de; (along) le long de. ● *vt*
(knock down, shoot down) abattre;
(drink) vider. ● *n* (fluff) duvet *m*.

down: ~**and-out** *n* clochard/-e
m/f. ~**cast** *a* démoralisé. ~**fall** *n*
chute *f*. ~**grade** *vt* déclasser.
~**hearted** *a* découragé.

downhill *adv* **go** ~ descendre;
(pej) baisser.

down: ~**load** *n* (Comput)
télécharger. ~**market** *a* bas de
gamme. ~ **payment** *n* acompte
m. ~**pour** *n* grosse averse *f*.

downright *a* (utter) véritable;
(honest) franc. ● *adv* carrément.

downsize *vt/i* dégraisser.

downstairs *adv* en bas. ● *a* d'en
bas.

down: ~**stream** *adv* en aval.
~**to-earth** *a* pratique.

downtown *a* (US) du centre-ville;
~ **Boston** le centre de Boston.

downward *a & adv*, **downwards**
adv vers le bas.

doze *vi* somnoler; ~ **off**
s'assoupir. ● *n* somme *m*.

dozen *n* douzaine *f*; **a** ~ **eggs** une
douzaine d'œufs; ~**s of** 🖾 des
dizaines de.

Dr *abbr* (**Doctor**) Docteur.

drab *a* terne.

draft *n* (outline) brouillon *m*;
(Comm) traite *f*; **the** ~ (Mil, US) la
conscription; **a** ~ **treaty** un projet
de traité; (US) = DRAUGHT. ● *vt*
faire le brouillon de; (draw up)
rédiger.

drag *vt/i* (*pt* **dragged**) traîner;
(*river*) draguer; (pull away)
arracher; ~ **on** s'éterniser. ● *n*
(task 🖾) corvée *f*; (person 🖾)
raseur/-euse *m/f*; **in** ~ en
travesti.

dragon *n* dragon *m*.

drain *vt* (*land*) drainer;
(*vegetables*) égoutter; (*tank, glass*)
vider; (use up) épuiser; ~ (**off**)
(*liquid*) faire écouler. ● *vi* ~ (**off**)
(of liquid) s'écouler. ● *n* (sewer)
égout *m*; ~(**-pipe**) tuyau *m*
d'écoulement; **a** ~ **on** une
ponction sur. **draining-board** *n*
égouttoir *m*.

drama *n* art *m* dramatique,
théâtre *m*; (play, event) drame *m*.
dramatic *a* (situation) dramatique;
(increase) spectaculaire. **dramatist**
n dramaturge *m*. **dramatize** *vt*
adapter pour la scène; (fig)
dramatiser.

drank ⇒DRINK.

drape *vt* draper. **drapes** *npl* (US)
rideaux *mpl*.

drastic *a* sévère.

draught *n* courant *m* d'air; ~**s**

(game) dames *fpl.* ~ **beer** *n* bière *f* pression.

draughty *a* plein de courants d'air.

draw *vt* (*pt* **drew**; *pp* **drawn**) (*picture*) dessiner; (*line*) tracer; (*pull*) tirer; (*attract*) attirer. ● *vi* dessiner; (*Sport*) faire match nul; (*come, move*) venir. ● *n* (*Sport*) match *m* nul; (in lottery) tirage *m* au sort. □ ~ **back** reculer; ~ **near** (s')approcher (**to** de); ~ **out** (*money*) retirer; ~ **up** *vi* (stop) s'arrêter; *vt* (*document*) dresser; (*chair*) approcher.

drawback *n* inconvénient *m*.

drawbridge *n* pont-levis *m*.

drawer *n* tiroir *m*.

drawing *n* dessin *m*. ~**-board** *n* planche *f* à dessin. ~**-pin** *n* punaise *f*. ~**-room** *n* salon *m*.

drawl *n* voix *f* traînante.

drawn ⇒DRAW. ● *a* (*features*) tiré; (*match*) nul.

dread *n* terreur *f*, crainte *f*. ● *vt* redouter. **dreadful** *a* épouvantable, affreux.

dreadfully *adv* terriblement.

dream *n* rêve *m*. ● *vt/i* (*pt* dreamed *or* dreamt) rêver; ~ **up** imaginer. ● *a* (ideal) de ses rêves.

dreary *a* (**-ier**, **-iest**) triste; (*boring*) monotone.

dredge *vt* (*river*) draguer; ~ **sth up** (fig) exhumer.

dregs *npl* lie *f*.

drench *vt* tremper.

dress *n* robe *f*; (*clothing*) tenue *f*. ● *vt/i* (s')habiller; (*food*) assaisonner; (*wound*) panser; ~ **up as** se déguiser en; **get** ~**ed** s'habiller. ~ **circle** *n* premier balcon *m*.

dresser *n* (*furniture*) buffet *m*; **be a stylish** ~ s'habiller avec chic.

dressing *n* (*sauce*) assaisonnement *m*; (*bandage*) pansement *m*. ~**-gown** *n* robe *f* de chambre. ~**-room** *n* (*Sport*) vestiaire *m*; (*Theat*) loge *f*. ~**-table** *n* coiffeuse *f*.

dressmaker *n* couturière *f*.

dressmaking *n* couture *f*.

dress rehearsal *n* répétition *f* générale.

dressy *a* (**-ier**, **-iest**) chic *inv*.

drew ⇒DRAW.

dribble *vi* (*liquid*) dégouliner; (*person*) baver; (football) dribbler.

dried *a* (fruit) sec.

drier *n* séchoir *m*.

drift *vi* aller à la dérive; (pile up) s'amonceler; ~ **towards** glisser vers. ● *n* dérive *f*; amoncellement *m*; (of events) tournure *f*; (meaning) sens *m*; **snow** ~ congère *f*.

driftwood *n* bois *m* flotté.

drill *n* (tool) perceuse *f*; (for teeth) roulette *f*; (training) exercice *m*; (procedure 🔲) marche *f* à suivre; (**pneumatic**) ~ marteau *m* piqueur. ● *vt* percer; (train) entraîner. ● *vi* être à l'exercice.

drink *vt/i* (*pt* **drank**; *pp* **drunk**) boire. ● *n* (liquid) boisson *f*; (glass of alcohol) verre *m*; **a** ~ **of water** un verre d'eau. **drinking water** *n* eau *f* potable.

drip *vi* (*pt* **dripped**) (é)goutter; (washing) s'égoutter. ● *n* goutte *f*; (person 🔲) lavette *f*.

drip-dry *vt* laisser égoutter. ● *a* sans essorage.

drive *vt* (*pt* **drove**; *pp* **driven**) (*vehicle*) conduire; (*sb somewhere*) chasser, pousser; (*machine*) actionner; ~ **mad** rendre fou. ● *vi* conduire. ● *n* promenade *f* en voiture; (private road) allée *f*; (fig) énergie *f*; (Psych) instinct *m*; (Pol) campagne *f*; (Auto) traction *f*; (golf, Comput) drive *m*; **it's a two-hour** ~ il y a deux heures de route; **left-hand** ~ conduite *f* à gauche. □ ~ **at** en venir à.

drivel *n* bêtises *fpl*.

driver n conducteur/-trice m/f, chauffeur m. ~'s **license** n (US) permis m de conduire.

driving n conduite f; **take one's ~ test** passer son permis. ● a (rain) battant; (wind) cinglant. ~ **licence** n permis m de conduire. ~ **school** n auto-école f.

drizzle n bruine f. ● vi bruiner.

drone n (of engine) ronronnement m; (of insects) bourdonnement m. ● vi ronronner; bourdonner.

drool vi baver (**over** sur).

droop vi pencher, tomber.

drop n goutte f; (fall, lowering) chute f. ● vt/i (pt **dropped**) (laisser) tomber; (decrease, lower) baisser; ~ (off) (person from car) déposer; ~ **a line** écrire un mot (**to** à). □ ~ **in** passer (**on** chez); ~ **off** (doze) s'assoupir; ~ **out** se retirer (**of** de); (of student) abandonner.

drop-out n marginal/-e m/f, raté/ -e m/f.

droppings npl crottes fpl.

drought n sécheresse f.

drove ⇒DRIVE.

droves npl foules fpl.

drown vt/i (se) noyer.

drowsy a somnolent; **be** or **feel ~** avoir envie de dormir.

drug n drogue f; (Med) médicament m. ● vt (pt **drugged**) droguer. ~ **addict** n drogué/-e m/f. **drugstore** n (US) drugstore m.

drum n tambour m; (for oil) bidon m; ~**s** batterie f. ● vi (pt **drummed**) tambouriner. ● vt ~ **into sb** répéter sans cesse à qn; ~ **up** (support) susciter; (business) créer. **drummer** n tambour m; (in pop group) batteur m.

drumstick n baguette f de tambour; (of chicken) pilon m.

drunk ⇒DRINK. ● a ivre; **get ~** s'enivrer. ● n ivrogne/-esse m/f. **drunkard** n ivrogne/-esse m/f.

drunken a ivre. **drunkenness** n ivresse f.

dry a (**drier, driest**) sec; (day) sans pluie; **be** or **feel ~** avoir soif. ● vt/i (faire) sécher; ~ **up** (dry dishes) essuyer la vaisselle; (of supplies) (se) tarir; (be silent 🞵) se taire. ~-**clean** vt nettoyer à sec. ~-**cleaner** n teinturier m. ~ **run** n galop m d'essai.

dual a double. ~ **carriageway** n route f à quatre voies. ~-**purpose** a qui fait double emploi.

dub vt (pt **dubbed**) (film) doubler (**into** en); (nickname) surnommer.

dubious a (pej) douteux; **be ~ about** avoir des doutes sur.

duck n canard m. ● vi se baisser subitement. ● vt (head) baisser; (person) plonger dans l'eau.

duct n conduit m.

dud a (tool 🞵) mal fichu; (coin 🞵) faux; (cheque 🞵) sans provision. ● n **be a ~** (not work 🞵) ne pas marcher.

due a (owing) dû; (expected) attendu; (proper) qui convient; ~ **to** à cause de; (caused by) dû à; **she's ~ to leave now** il est prévu qu'elle parte maintenant; **in ~ course** (at the right time) en temps voulu; (later) plus tard. ● adv ~ **east** droit vers l'est. ● n dû m; ~**s** droits mpl; (of club) cotisation f.

duel n duel m.

duet n duo m.

dug ⇒DIG.

duke n duc m.

dull a ennuyeux; (colour) terne; (weather) maussade; (sound) sourd. ● vt (pain) atténuer; (shine) ternir.

duly adv comme il convient; (as expected) comme prévu.

dumb a muet; (stupid 🞵) bête. □ ~ **down** (course, TV coverage) baisser le niveau intellectuel de.

D

dumbfound vt sidérer, ahurir.

dummy n (of tailor) mannequin m; (of baby) sucette f. ● a factice. **~ run** n galop m d'essai.

dump vt déposer; (get rid of 🗈) se débarrasser de. ● n tas m d'ordures; (refuse tip) décharge f; (Mil) dépôt m; (dull place 🗈) trou m 🗈; be in the **~s** 🗈 avoir le cafard.

dune n dune f.

dung n (excrement) bouse f, crotte f; (manure) fumier m.

dungarees npl salopette f.

dungeon n cachot.

duplicate[1] n double m. ● a identique.

duplicate[2] vt faire un double de; (on machine) polycopier.

durable a (tough) résistant; (enduring) durable.

duration n durée f.

during prep pendant.

dusk n crépuscule m.

dusky a (-ier, -iest) foncé.

dust n poussière f. ● vt/i épousseter; (sprinkle) saupoudrer (with de). **~bin** n poubelle f.

duster n chiffon m.

dust: **~man** n (pl -men) éboueur m. **~pan** n pelle f (à poussière).

dusty a (-ier, -iest) poussiéreux.

Dutch a néerlandais; go **~** partager les frais. ● n (Ling) néerlandais m. **~man** n Néerlandais m. **~woman** n Néerlandaise f.

dutiful a obéissant.

duty n devoir m; (tax) droit m; (of official) fonction f; on **~** de service. **~-free** a hors-taxe.

duvet n couette f.

dwarf n nain/-e m/f. ● vt rapetisser.

dwell vi (pt dwelt) demeurer; **~ on** s'étendre sur. **dweller** n habitant/-e m/f. **dwelling** n habitation f.

dwindle vi diminuer.

dye vt teindre. ● n teinture f.

dying a mourant; (art) qui se perd.

dynamic a dynamique.

dynamite n dynamite f.

dysentery n dysenterie f.

dyslexia n dyslexie f. **dyslexic** a & n dyslexique (mf).

each det chaque inv; **~ one** chacun/-e m/f. ● pron chacun/-e m/f; oranges at 30p **~** des oranges à 30 pence pièce.

each other pron l'un/l'une l'autre, les uns/les unes les autres; know **~** se connaître; love **~** s'aimer.

eager a impatient (**to** de); (person, acceptance) enthousiaste; **~ for** avide de.

eagle n aigle m.

ear n oreille f; (of corn) épi m. **~ache** n mal m à l'oreille. **~-drum** n tympan m.

earl n comte m.

early (-ier, -iest) adv tôt, de bonne heure; (ahead of time) en avance; **as I said earlier** comme je l'ai déjà dit. ● a (attempt, years) premier; (hour) matinal; (fruit) précoce; (retirement) anticipé; **have an ~ dinner** dîner tôt; **in ~ summer** au début de l'été; **at the earliest** au plus tôt.

earmark vt désigner (**for** pour).

earn vt gagner; (interest: Comm) rapporter.

earnest *a* sérieux; **in ~** sérieusement.

earnings *npl* salaire *m*; (profits) gains *mpl*.

ear: **~phones** *npl* casque *m*. **~-ring** *n* boucle *f* d'oreille. **~shot** *n* **within/in ~shot** à portée de voix.

earth *n* terre *f*; **why/how/where on ~...?** pourquoi/comment/où diable...? ● *vt* (Electr) mettre à la terre. **earthenware** *n* faïence *f*. **~quake** *n* tremblement *m* de terre.

ease *n* facilité *f*; (comfort) bien-être *m*; **at ~** à l'aise; (Mil) au repos; **with ~** facilement. ● *vt* (pain, pressure) atténuer; (congestion) réduire; (transition) faciliter. ● *vi* (pain, pressure) s'atténuer; (congestion, rain) diminuer.

easel *n* chevalet *m*.

east *n* est *m*; **the E~** (Orient) l'Orient *m*. ● *a* (side, coast) est; (wind) d'est. ● *adv* à l'est.

Easter *n* Pâques *m*; **~ egg** œuf *m* de Pâques.

easterly *a* (wind) d'est; (direction) de l'est.

eastern de l'est; **~ France** l'est de la France.

eastward *a* (side) est *inv*; (journey) vers l'est.

easy *a* (-ier, -iest) facile; **go ~ with** 🅸 y aller doucement avec; **take it ~** ne te fatigue pas. **~going** *a* accommodant.

eat *vt/i* (pt **ate**; pp **eaten**) manger; **~ into** ronger.

eavesdrop *vi* (pt **-dropped**) écouter aux portes.

ebb *n* reflux *m*. ● *vi* descendre; (fig) décliner.

EC *abbr* (**European Community**) CE *f*.

eccentric *a & n* excentrique (*mf*).

echo *n* (pl **-oes**) écho *m*. ● *vt* répercuter; (idea, opinion) reprendre. ● *vi* retentir, résonner (**to, with** de).

eclipse *n* éclipse *f*. ● *vt* éclipser.

ecological *a* écologique.

ecology *n* écologie *f*.

e-commerce *n* commerce *m* électronique, commerce *m* en ligne.

economic *a* économique; (profitable) rentable. **economical** *a* économique; (person) économe.

economics *n* économie *f*, sciences *fpl* économiques.

economist *n* économiste *mf*.

economize *vi* **~ (on)** économiser.

economy *n* économie *f*. **~-class syndrome** *n* syndrome *m* de la classe économique.

ecosystem *n* écosystème *m*.

ecstasy *n* extase *f*; (drug) ecstasy *m*.

edge *n* bord *m*; (of town) abords *mpl*; (of knife) tranchant *m*; **have the ~ on** 🅸 l'emporter sur; **on ~** énervé. ● *vt* (trim) border. ● *vi* **~ forward** avancer doucement.

edgeways *adv* **I can't get a word in ~** je n'arrive pas à placer un mot.

edgy *a* énervé.

edible *a* comestible.

edit *vt* (pt **edited**) (newspaper, page) être le rédacteur/la rédactrice de; (check) réviser; (cut) couper; (TV, cinema) monter.

edition *n* édition *f*.

editor *n* (writer) rédacteur/-trice *m/f*; (of works, anthology) éditeur/ -trice *m/f*; (TV, cinema) monteur/ -teuse *m/f*; **the ~ (in chief)** le rédacteur en chef.

editorial *a* de la rédaction. ● *n* éditorial *m*.

educate *vt* instruire; (mind, public) éduquer. **educated** *a* instruit.

education *n* éducation *f*; (schooling) études *fpl*. **educational**

a éducatif; (*establishment, method*) d'enseignement.

eel n anguille f.

eerie a (**-ier, -iest**) sinistre.

effect n effet m; **come into ∼** entrer en vigueur; **in ∼** effectivement; **take ∼** agir. ● vt effectuer.

effective a efficace; (*actual*) effectif. **effectively** adv efficacement; (*in effect*) en réalité. **effectiveness** n efficacité f.

effeminate a efféminé.

effervescent a effervescent.

efficiency n efficacité f; (*of machine*) rendement m. **efficient** a efficace. **efficiently** adv efficacement.

effort n efforts mpl; **make an ∼** faire un effort; **be worth the ∼** en valoir la peine. **effortless** a facile.

effusive a expansif.

e.g. abbr par ex.

egg n œuf m. ● vt **∼ on** pousser. **∼-cup** n coquetier m. **∼-plant** n (US) aubergine f. **∼shell** n coquille f d'œuf.

ego n amour-propre m; (Psych) moi m. **egotism** n égotisme m. **egotist** n égotiste mf.

Egypt n Égypte f.

eiderdown n édredon m.

eight a & n huit (m). **eighteen** a & n dix-huit (m). **eighth** a & n huitième (mf). **eighty** a & n quatre-vingts (m).

either det & pron l'un/une ou l'autre; (*with negative*) ni l'un/une ni l'autre; **you can take ∼** tu peux prendre n'importe lequel/ laquelle. ● adv non plus. ● conj **∼...or** ou (bien)...ou (bien); (*with negative*) ni...ni.

eject vt (*troublemaker*) expulser; (*waste*) rejeter.

elaborate[1] a compliqué.

elaborate[2] vt élaborer. ● vi préciser; **∼ on** s'étendre sur.

elastic a & n élastique (m); **∼ band** élastique m. **elasticity** n élasticité f.

elated a transporté de joie.

elbow n coude m; **∼ room** espace m vital.

elder a & n aîné/-e (m/f); (*tree*) sureau m.

elderly a âgé; **the ∼ les** personnes fpl âgées.

eldest a & n aîné/-e (m/f).

elect vt élire; **∼ to do** choisir de faire. ● a (president etc.) futur. **election** n élection f. **elector** n électeur/-trice m/f. **electoral** a électoral. **electorate** n électorat m.

electric a électrique; **∼ blanket** couverture f chauffante.

electrical a électrique.

electrician n électricien/-ne m/f.

electricity n électricité f.

electrify vt électrifier; (*excite*) électriser. **electrocute** vt électrocuter.

electronic a électronique. **∼ publishing** n éditique f. **electronics** n électronique f.

elegance n élégance f.

element n élément m; (*of heater etc.*) résistance f. **elementary** a élémentaire.

elephant n éléphant m.

elevate vt élever. **elevation** n élévation f. **elevator** n (US) ascenseur m.

eleven a & n onze (m). **eleventh** a & n onzième (mf).

elicit vt obtenir (**from** de).

eligible a admissible (**for** à); **be ∼ for** (*entitled to*) avoir droit à.

eliminate vt éliminer.

elm n orme m.

elongate vt allonger.

elope vi s'enfuir (**with** avec).

E

elopement n fugue f
(amoureuse).

eloquence n éloquence f.

else adv d'autre; **somebody/
nothing ~** quelqu'un/rien d'autre;
everybody ~ tous les autres;
somewhere/something ~ autre
part/chose; **or ~** ou bien.
elsewhere adv ailleurs.

elude vt échapper à.

elusive a insaisissable.

e-mail n (medium) courrier m
électronique; (item) e-mail m, mél
m. ● vt **~ sb** envoyer un e-mail
à qn; **~ sth** envoyer qch par
courrier électronique.

emancipate vt émanciper.

embankment n (of river) quai m;
(of railway) remblai m.

embark vt embarquer. ● vi (Naut)
embarquer; **~ on** (journey)
entreprendre; (campaign, career)
se lancer dans.

embarrass vt plonger dans
l'embarras; **be/feel ~ed** être/se
sentir gêné. **embarrassment** n
confusion f, gêne f.

embassy n ambassade f.

embed vt (pt **embedded**)
enfoncer (**in** dans).

embellish vt embellir.

embers npl braises fpl.

embezzle vt détourner (**from** de).
embezzlement n détournement
m de fonds.

emblem n emblème m.

embodiment n incarnation f.
embody vt incarner; (legally)
incorporer.

emboss vt (metal) repousser;
(paper) gaufrer.

embrace vt (person) étreindre;
(religion) embrasser; (include)
comprendre. ● n étreinte f.

embroider vt broder.
embroidery n broderie f.

embryo n embryon m.

emerald n émeraude f.

emerge vi (person) sortir (**from**
de); **it ~d that** il est apparu que.

emergence n apparition f.

emergency n (crisis) crise f; (urgent
case: Med) urgence f; **in an ~** en
cas d'urgence; **~** a d'urgence; **~
exit** n sortie f de secours. **~
landing** n atterrissage m forcé. **~
room** n (US) salle f des urgences.

emigrant n émigrant/-e m/f.

emigrate vi émigrer.

eminence n éminence f.

eminent a éminent.

emission n émission f.

emit vt (pt **emitted**) émettre.

emotion n émotion f. **emotional**
a (development) émotif; (reaction)
émotionel; (film, scene)
émouvant.

emotive a qui soulève les
passions.

emperor n empereur m.

emphasis n accent m; **lay ~ on**
mettre l'accent sur. **emphasize**
vt mettre l'accent sur. **emphatic**
a catégorique; (manner) énergique.

empire n empire m.

employ vt employer. **employee** n
employé/-e m/f. **employer** n
employeur/-euse m/f.

employment n emploi m; **find ~**
trouver du travail.

empower vt autoriser (**to do** à
faire).

empty a (-ier, -iest) vide; (street)
désert; (promise) vain; **on an ~
stomach** à jeun. ● vt/i (se) vider.
~-handed a les mains vides.

emulate vt imiter.

enable vt **~ sb to** permettre à qn
de.

enamel n émail m. ● vt (pt
enamelled) émailler.

encase vt revêtir, recouvrir (**in**
de).

enchant vt enchanter.

enclose vt entourer; (land) clôturer; (with letter) joindre. **enclosed** a (space) clos; (with letter) ci-joint. **enclosure** n enceinte f; (with letter) pièce f jointe.

encompass vt inclure.

encore interj & n bis (m).

encounter vt rencontrer. ● n rencontre f.

encourage vt encourager.

encroach vi ~ upon empiéter sur.

encyclopaedia n encyclopédie f. **encyclopaedic** a encyclopédique.

end n fin f; (farthest part) bout m; **come to an** ~ prendre fin; ~-**product** produit m fini; **in the** ~ finalement; **no** ~ **of** ⊞ énormément de; **on** ~ (upright) debout; (in a row) de suite; **put an** ~ **to** mettre fin à. ● vt (marriage) mettre fin à; ~ **one's days** finir ses jours. ● vi se terminer; ~ **up doing** finir par faire.

endanger vt mettre en danger.

endearing a attachant.

endeavour, (US) **endeavor** n (attempt) tentative f; (hard work) effort m. ● vi faire tout son possible (**to do** pour faire).

ending n fin f.

endive n chicorée f.

endless a interminable; (supply) inépuisable; (patience) infini.

endorse vt (candidate, decision) appuyer; (product, claim) approuver; (cheque) endosser.

endurance n endurance f.

endure vt supporter. ● vi durer. **enduring** a durable.

enemy n & a ennemi/-e (m/f).

energetic a énergique. **energy** n énergie f.

enforce vt (rule, law) appliquer, faire respecter; (silence, discipline) imposer (**on** à); ~d forcé.

engage vt (staff) engager; (attention) retenir; **be** ~d **in** se livrer à. ● vi ~ **in** se livrer à.

engaged a fiancé; (busy) occupé; **get** ~d se fiancer. **engagement** n fiançailles fpl; (meeting) rendezvous m; (undertaking) engagement m.

engaging a attachant, engageant.

engine n moteur m; (of train) locomotive f; (of ship) machines fpl. ~-**driver** n mécanicien m.

engineer n ingénieur m; (repairman) technicien m; (on ship) mécanicien m. ● vt (contrive) manigancer.

engineering n ingénierie f; (industry) mécanique f; **civil** ~ génie m civil.

England n Angleterre f.

English a anglais. ● n (Ling) anglais m; **the** ~ les Anglais mpl. ~**man** n Anglais m. ~-**speaking** a anglophone. ~**woman** n Anglaise f.

engrave vt graver.

engrossed a absorbé (**in** dans).

engulf vt engouffrer.

enhance vt (prospects, status) améliorer; (price, value) augmenter.

enjoy vt aimer (**doing** faire); (benefit from) jouir de; ~ **oneself** s'amuser; ~ **your meal!** bon appétit! **enjoyable** a agréable. **enjoyment** n plaisir m.

enlarge vt agrandir. ● vi s'agrandir; (pupil) se dilater; ~ **on** s'étendre sur. **enlargement** n agrandissement m.

enlighten vt éclairer (**on** sur). **enlightenment** n instruction f; (information) éclaircissement m.

enlist vt (person) recruter; (fig) obtenir. ● vi s'engager.

enmity n inimitié f.

enormous *a* énorme.
enormously *adv* énormément.

enough *adv & n* assez; **have ~ of** en avoir assez de. ● *det* assez de; **~ glasses/time** assez de verres/de temps.

enquire ⇒INQUIRE. **enquiry** ⇒INQUIRY.

enrage *vt* mettre en rage, rendre furieux.

enrol *vt/i* (*pt* **enrolled**) (s')inscrire. **enrolment** *n* inscription *f*.

ensure *vt* garantir; **~ that** (ascertain) s'assurer que.

entail *vt* entraîner.

entangle *vt* emmêler.

enter *vt* (*room, club, phase*) entrer dans; (note down, register) inscrire; (data) entrer, saisir. ● *vi* entrer (**into** dans); **~ for** s'inscrire à.

enterprise *n* entreprise *f*; (boldness) initiative *f*. **enterprising** *a* entreprenant.

entertain *vt* amuser, divertir; (guests) recevoir; (ideas) considérer. **entertainer** *n* artiste *mf*. **entertaining** *a* divertissant. **entertainment** *n* divertissement *m*; (performance) spectacle *m*.

enthral *vt* (*pt* **enthralled**) captiver.

enthusiasm *n* enthousiasme *m* (**for** pour).

enthusiast *n* passionné/-e *m/f* (**for** de). **enthusiastic** *a* (supporter) enthousiaste; **be ~ic about** être enthousiasmé par. **enthusiastically** *adv* avec enthousiasme.

entice *vt* attirer; **~ to do** entraîner à faire.

entire *a* entier. **entirely** *adv* entièrement. **entirety** *n* **in its ~ty** en entier.

entitle *vt* donner droit à (**to sth** à qch; **to do** de faire); **~d** (book)

intitulé; **be ~d to sth** avoir droit à qch.

entrance[1] *n* (entering, way in) entrée *f* (**to** de); (right to enter) admission *f*. ● *a* (charge, exam) d'entrée.

entrance[2] *vt* transporter.

entrant *n* (Sport) concurrent/-e *m/f*; (in exam) candidat/-e *m/f*.

entrenched *a* (opinion) inébranlable; (Mil) retranché.

entrepreneur *n* entrepreneur/ -euse *m/f*.

entrust *vt* confier; **~ sb with sth** confier qch à qn.

entry *n* entrée *f*; **~ form** fiche *f* d'inscription.

envelop *vt* (*pt* **enveloped**) envelopper.

envelope *n* enveloppe *f*.

envious *a* envieux (**of** de).

environment *n* (ecological) environnement *m*; (social) milieu *m*. **environmental** *a* du milieu; de l'environnement.

environmentalist *n* écologiste *mf*.

envisage *vt* prévoir (**doing** de faire).

envoy *n* envoyé/-e *m/f*.

envy *n* envie *f*. ● *vt* envier; **~ sb sth** envier qch à qn.

epic *n* épopée *f*. ● *a* épique.

epidemic *n* épidémie *f*.

epilepsy *n* épilepsie *f*.

episode *n* épisode *m*.

epitome *n* modèle *m*. **epitomize** *vt* incarner.

equal *a & n* égal/-e (*m/f*); **~ opportunities/rights** égalité *f* des chances/droits; **~ to** (task) à la hauteur de. ● *vt* (*pt* **equalled**) égaler. **equality** *n* égalité *f*. **equalize** *vt/i* égaliser. **equalizer** *n* (goal) but *m* égalisateur. **equally** *adv* (divide) en parts égales; (just as) tout aussi.

equanimity n sérénité f.

equate vt assimiler (**with** à). **equation** n équation f.

equator n équateur m.

equilibrium n équilibre m.

equip vt (pt **equipped**) équiper (**with** de). **equipment** n équipement m.

equity n équité f.

equivalence n équivalence f.

era n ère f, époque f.

eradicate vt éliminer; (disease) éradiquer.

erase vt effacer. **eraser** n (rubber) gomme f.

erect a droit. ● vt ériger. **erection** n érection f.

erode vt éroder; (fig) saper. **erosion** n érosion f.

erotic a érotique.

errand n commission f, course f.

erratic a (behaviour, person) imprévisible; (performance) inégal.

error n erreur f.

erupt vi (volcano) entrer en éruption; (fig) éclater.

escalate vt intensifier. ● vi (conflict) s'intensifier. **escalation** n intensification f. **escalator** n escalier m mécanique, escalator® m.

escapade n frasque f.

escape vt échapper à. ● vi s'enfuir, s'évader; (gas) fuir. ● n fuite f, évasion f; (of gas etc.) fuite f; **have a lucky** or **narrow** ~ l'échapper belle.

escapism n évasion f (du réel).

escort[1] n (guard) escorte f; (companion) compagnon/compagne m/f.

escort[2] vt escorter.

Eskimo n Esquimau/-de m/f.

especially adv en particulier.

espionage n espionnage m.

espresso n (café) express m.

essay n (in literature) essai m; (School) rédaction f; (Univ) dissertation f.

essence n essence f.

essential a essentiel; **the** ~**s** l'essentiel m. **essentially** adv essentiellement.

establish vt établir; (business) fonder.

establishment n (process) instauration f; (institution) établissement m; **the E**~ l'ordre m établi.

estate n (house and land) domaine m; (possessions) biens mpl; (housing estate) cité f. ~ **agent** n agent m immobilier. ~ **car** n break m.

esteem n estime f.

esthetic a (US) = AESTHETIC.

estimate[1] n (calculation) estimation f; (Comm) devis m.

estimate[2] vt évaluer; ~ **that** estimer que. **estimation** n (esteem) estime f; (judgment) opinion f.

Estonia n Estonie f.

estuary n estuaire m.

eternal a éternel.

eternity n éternité f.

ethic n éthique f; ~**s** moralité f. **ethical** a éthique.

ethnic a ethnique. ~ **cleansing** n nettoyage m ethnique.

EU abbr (**European Union**) UE f, Union f européenne.

euphoria n euphorie f.

euro n euro m. ~ **zone** n zone f euro.

euroland euroland m.

Europe n Europe f.

European a & n européen/-ne (m/f); ~ **Community** Communauté f Européenne.

eurosceptic n eurosceptique mf.

euthanasia n euthanasie f.

evacuate vt évacuer.

evade vt (*blow*) esquiver; (*question*) éluder.

evaporate vi s'évaporer; ∼**d milk** lait *m* condensé.

evasion n fuite *f* (of devant); (excuse) faux-fuyant *m*; **tax** ∼ évasion *f* fiscale. **evasive** a évasif.

eve n veille *f* (of de).

even a (*surface, voice, contest*) égal; (*teeth, hem*) régulier; (*number*) pair; **get** ∼ **with** se venger de. ● adv même; ∼ **better**/*etc.* (still) encore mieux/*etc.*; ∼ **so** quand même. □ ∼ **out** (*differences*) s'atténuer; ∼ **sth out** (*inequalities*) réduire qch; ∼ **up** équilibrer.

evening n soir *m*; (whole evening, event) soirée *f*.

evenly adv (spread, apply) uniformément; (*breathe*) régulièrement; (equally) en parts égales.

event n événement *m*; (Sport) épreuve *f*; **in the** ∼ **of** en cas de. **eventful** a mouvementé.

eventual a (outcome, decision) final; (aim) à long terme. **eventuality** n éventualité *f*. **eventually** adv finalement; (in future) un jour ou l'autre.

ever adv jamais; (at all times) toujours.

evergreen n arbre *m* à feuilles persistantes.

everlasting a éternel.

ever since prep & adv depuis.

every a ∼ **house/window** toutes les maisons/les fenêtres; ∼ **time/minute** chaque fois/minute; ∼ **day** tous les jours; ∼ **other day** tous les deux jours. **everybody** pron tout le monde. **everyday** a quotidien. **everyone** pron tout le monde. **everything** pron tout. **everywhere** adv partout; ∼**where he goes** partout où il va.

evict vt expulser (from de).

evidence n (proof) preuves *fpl* (that que; of, for de); (testimony) témoignage *m*; (traces) trace *f* (of de); **give** ∼ témoigner; **be in** ∼ être visible. **evident** a manifeste. **evidently** adv (apparently) apparemment; (obviously) manifestement.

evil a malfaisant. ● n mal *m*.

evoke vt évoquer.

evolution n évolution *f*.

evolve vi évoluer. ● vt élaborer.

ewe n brebis *f*.

ex- pref ex-, ancien.

exact a exact; **the** ∼ **opposite** exactement le contraire. ● vt exiger (from de). **exactly** adv exactement.

exaggerate vt/i exagérer.

exalted a élevé.

exam n 🆃 examen *m*.

examination n examen *m*.

examine vt examiner; (witness) interroger. **examiner** n examinateur/-trice *m/f*.

example n exemple *m*; **for** ∼ par exemple; **make an** ∼ **of** punir pour l'exemple.

exasperate vt exaspérer.

excavate vt fouiller. **excavations** npl fouilles *fpl*.

exceed vt dépasser. **exceedingly** adv extrêmement.

excel vi (pt **excelled**) exceller (at, in en; at doing à faire). ● vt surpasser.

excellence n excellence *f*. **excellent** a excellent.

except prep sauf, excepté; ∼ **for** à part. ● vt excepter. **excepting** prep sauf, excepté.

exception n exception *f*; **take** ∼ **to** s'offusquer. **exceptional** a exceptionnel.

excerpt n extrait *m*.

excess¹ n excès *m*.

excess² *a* ~ **weight** excès *m* de poids; ~ **baggage** excédent *m* de bagages.

excessive *a* excessif.

exchange *vt* échanger (**for** contre). ● *n* échange *m*; (between currencies) change *m*; ~ **rate** taux *m* de change; **telephone** ~ central *m* téléphonique.

Exchequer *n* (Pol) ministère *m* britannique des finances.

excise *n* excise *f*, taxe *f*.

excite *vt* exciter; (enthuse) enthousiasmer. **excited** *a* excité; **get** ~**d** s'exciter. **excitement** *n* excitation *f*. **exciting** *a* passionnant.

exclaim *vt* s'exclamer.

exclamation *n* exclamation *f*; ~ **mark** or **point** (US) point *m* d'exclamation.

exclude *vt* exclure.

exclusive *a* (club) fermé; (rights) exclusif; (news item) en exclusivité; ~ **of meals** repas non compris. **exclusively** *adv* exclusivement.

excruciating *a* atroce.

excursion *n* excursion *f*.

excuse¹ *vt* excuser; ~ **from** (exempt) dispenser de; ~ **me!** excusez-moi!, pardon!

excuse² *n* (reason) excuse *f*; (pretext) prétexte *m* (**for sth** à qch; **for doing** pour faire).

ex-directory *a* sur liste rouge.

execute *vt* exécuter. **executioner** *n* bourreau *m*.

executive *n* (person) cadre *m*; (committee) exécutif *m*. ● *a* exécutif.

exemplary *a* exemplaire.

exemplify *vt* illustrer.

exempt *a* exempt (**from** de). ● *vt* exempter.

exercise *n* exercice *m*; ~ **book** cahier *m*. ● *vt* exercer; (restraint, patience) faire preuve de. ● *vi* faire de l'exercice.

exert *vt* exercer; ~ **oneself** se fatiguer. **exertion** *n* effort *m*.

exhaust *vt* épuiser. ● *n* (Auto) pot *m* d'échappement.

exhaustive *a* exhaustif.

exhibit *vt* exposer; (fig) manifester. ● *n* objet *m* exposé.

exhibition *n* exposition *f*; (of skill) démonstration *f*. **exhibitionist** *n* exhibitionniste *mf*.

exhibitor *n* exposant/-e *m/f*.

exhilarate *vt* griser.

exile *n* exil *m*; (person) exilé/-e *m/f*. ● *vt* exiler.

exist *vi* exister. **existence** *n* existence *f*; **be in** ~**ence** exister. **existing** *a* actuel.

exit *n* sortie *f*. ● *vt/i* (also Comput) sortir (de).

exodus *n* exode *m*.

exonerate *vt* disculper.

exotic *a* exotique.

expand *vt* développer; (workforce) accroître. ● *vi* se développer; (population) s'accroître; (metal) se dilater.

expanse *n* étendue *f*.

expansion *n* développement *m*; (Pol, Comm) expansion *f*.

expatriate *a* & *n* expatrié/-e (*m/ f*).

expect *vt* s'attendre à; (suppose) supposer; (demand) exiger; (baby) attendre.

expectancy *n* attente *f*.

expectant *a* ~ **mother** future maman *f*.

expectation *n* (assumption) prévision *f*; (hope) aspiration *f*; (demand) exigence *f*.

expedient *a* opportun. ● *n* expédient *m*.

expedition *n* expédition *f*.

expel *vt* (pt **expelled**) expulser; (pupil) renvoyer.

expend vt consacrer.

expenditure n dépenses fpl.

expense n frais mpl; **at sb's ~** aux frais de qn; **~ account** frais mpl de représentation.

expensive a cher; (tastes) de luxe. **expensively** adv luxueusement.

experience n expérience f. ● vt (undergo) connaître; (feel) éprouver; ~**d** expérimenté.

experiment n expérience f. ● vi expérimenter, faire des essais.

expert n spécialiste mf. ● a spécialisé, expert. **expertise** n compétence f. **expertly** adv de manière experte.

expire vi expirer; ~**d** périmé. **expiry** n expiration f.

explain vt expliquer. **explanation** n explication f. **explanatory** a explicatif.

explicit a explicite.

explode vt/i (faire) exploser.

exploit[1] n exploit m.

exploit[2] vt exploiter.

exploration n exploration f. **exploratory** a (talks) exploratoire. **explore** vt explorer; (fig) étudier. **explorer** n explorateur/-trice m/f.

explosion n explosion f. **explosive** a & n explosif (m).

exponent n avocat/-e m/f (of de).

export[1] vt exporter.

export[2] n (process) exportation f; (product) produit m d'exportation.

expose vt exposer; (disclose) révéler.

exposure n révélation f; (Photo) pose f; **die of ~** mourir de froid.

express vt exprimer. ● a exprès. ● adv **send sth ~** envoyer qch en exprès. ● n (train) rapide m. **expression** n expression f. **expressive** a expressif. **expressly** adv expressément.

exquisite a exquis.

extend vt (visit) prolonger; (house) agrandir; (range) élargir; (arm, leg) étendre. ● vi (stretch) s'étendre; (in time) se prolonger.

extension n (of line, road) prolongement m; (of visa, loan) prorogation f; (building) addition f; (phone number) poste m; (cable) rallonge f.

extensive a vaste; (study) approfondi; (damage) considérable. **extensively** adv (much) beaucoup; (very) très.

extent n (size, scope) étendue f; (degree) mesure f; **to some ~** dans une certaine mesure; **to such an ~ that** à tel point que.

extenuating a atténuant.

exterior a & n extérieur (m).

exterminate vt exterminer.

external a extérieur; (cause, medical use) externe.

extinct a (species) disparu; (volcano, passion) éteint.

extinguish vt éteindre. **extinguisher** n extincteur m.

extol vt (pt extolled) louer, chanter les louanges de.

extort vt extorquer (from à). **extortion** n (Jur) extorsion f. **extortionate** a exorbitant.

extra a supplémentaire; **~ charge** supplément m; **~ time** (football) prolongation f; **~ strong** extra-fort. ● adv encore; plus. ● n supplément m; (cinema) figurant/-e m/f.

extract[1] vt sortir (from de); (tooth) extraire; (promise) arracher.

extract[2] n extrait m.

extra-curricular a parascolaire.

extradite vt extrader.

extramarital a extraconjugal.

extramural a (Univ) hors faculté.

extraordinary a extraordinaire.

extravagance n prodigalité f.
extravagant a (person)
dépenser; (claim) extravagant.
extreme a & n extrême (m).
extremely adv extrêmement.
extremist n extrémiste mf.
extremity n extrémité f.
extricate vt dégager.
extrovert n extraverti/-e m/f.
exuberance n exubérance f.
exude vt (charm) respirer; (smell)
exhaler.
eye n œil m (pl yeux); keep an ~
on surveiller. ● vt (pt eyed; pres
p eyeing) regarder. ~ball n
globe m oculaire. ~brow n
sourcil m. ~-catching a
attrayant. ~lash n cil m. ~lid n
paupière. ~-opener n
révélation f. ~-shadow n ombre
f à paupières. ~sight n vue f.
~sore n horreur f. ~witness n
témoin m oculaire.

fable n fable f.
fabric n (cloth) tissu m.
fabulous a fabuleux; (marvellous 🆃)
formidable.
face n visage m, figure f;
(expression) air m; (appearance, dignity)
face f; (of clock) cadran m; (Geol)
face f; (of rock) paroi f; in the ~ of
face à; make a (funny) ~ faire la
grimace; ~ to ~ face à face. ● vt
être en face de; (risk) devoir
affronter; (confront) faire face à;
(deal with) I can't ~ him je n'ai pas
le courage de le voir. ● vi
(person) regarder; (chair) être
tourné vers; (window) donner

sur; ~ up to faire face à; ~d with
face à.
face-lift n lifting m; give a ~ to
donner un coup de neuf à.
face value n valeur f nominale;
take sth at ~ prendre qch au pied
de la lettre.
facial a (hair) du visage; (injury)
au visage. ● n soin m du visage.
facility n (building) complexe m;
(feature) fonction f; facilities
(equipment) équipements mpl.
facsimile n fac-similé m.
fact n fait m; as a matter of ~, in
~ en fait; know for a ~ that savoir
de source sûre que; owing/due to
the ~ that étant donné que.
factor n facteur m.
factory n usine f.
factual a (account, description)
basé sur les faits; (evidence)
factuel.
faculty n faculté f.
fade vi (sound) s'affaiblir;
(memory) s'effacer; (flower) se
faner; (material) se décolorer;
(colour) passer.
fail vi échouer; (grow weak) (s'af)
faiblir; (run short) manquer;
(engine) tomber en panne. ● vt
(exam) échouer à; ~ to do (not do)
ne pas faire; (not be able) ne pas
réussir à faire; without ~ à coup
sûr.
failing n défaut m; ~ that/this
sinon.
failure n échec m; (person) raté/-e
m/f; (breakdown) panne f; ~ to do
(inability) incapacité f de faire.
faint a léger, faible; feel ~ (ill) se
sentir mal; I haven't the ~est idea
je n'en ai pas la moindre idée.
● vi s'évanouir. ● n
évanouissement m. ~-hearted a
timide.
fair n foire f. ● a (hair, person)
blond; (skin) clair; (weather)
beau; (amount, quality)

raisonnable; (just) juste, équitable.
● *adv* (*play*) loyalement.

fairground *n* champ *m* de foire.

fairly *adv* (justly) équitablement;
(rather) assez.

fairness *n* justice *f*.

fairy *n* fée *f*. ~ **story**, ~**-tale** *n*
conte *m* de fées.

faith *n* (belief) foi *f*; (confidence)
confiance *f*.

faithful *a* fidèle.

fake *n* (forgery) faux *m*; (person)
imposteur *m*; **it is a** ~ c'est un
faux. ● *a* faux. ● *vt* (*signature*)
contrefaire; (*results*) falsifier;
(*illness*) feindre.

falcon *n* faucon *m*.

fall *vi* (*pt* **fell**; *pp* **fallen**) tomber;
~ **short** être insuffisant. ● *n*
chute *f*; (autumn: US) automne *m*;
Niagara F~**s** chutes *fpl* du
Niagara. □ ~ **back on** se
rabattre sur; ~ **behind** prendre
du retard; ~ **down** *or* **off** tomber;
~ **for** (*person* 🔲) tomber
amoureux de; (*a trick* 🔲) se
laisser prendre à; ~ **in** (Mil) se
mettre en rangs; ~ **off** (decrease)
diminuer; ~ **out** se brouiller
(with avec); ~ **over** tomber (par
terre); ~ **through** (*plans*) tomber
à l'eau.

fallacy *n* erreur *f*.

false *a* faux. ~ **teeth** *npl* dentier
m.

falter *vi* (*courage*) faiblir; (when
speaking) bafouiller 🔲.

fame *n* renommée *f*. **famed** *a*
célèbre (**for** pour).

familiar *a* familier; **be** ~ **with**
connaître.

family *n* famille *f*.

famine *n* famine *f*.

famished *a* affamé.

famous *a* célèbre (**for** pour).

fan *n* (mechanical) ventilateur *m*;
(hand-held) éventail *m*; (of person)
fan *mf* 🔲, admirateur/-trice *m/f*;
(enthusiast) fervent/-e *m/f*,
passionné/-e *m/f*. ● *vt* (*pt*
fanned) (*face*) éventer; (fig)
attiser. ● *vi* ~ **out** se déployer en
éventail.

fanatic *n* fanatique *mf*.

fan belt *n* courroie *f* de
ventilateur.

fancy *n* (whim, fantasy) fantaisie *f*;
take a ~ **to sb** se prendre
d'affection pour qn; **it took my** ~
ça m'a plu. ● *a* (*buttons etc.*)
fantaisie *inv*; (*prices*)
extravagant; (*impressive*)
impressionnant. ● *vt* s'imaginer;
(*want* 🔲) avoir envie de; (*like* 🔲)
aimer. ~ **dress** *n* déguisement
m.

fang *n* (of dog) croc *m*; (of snake)
crochet *m*.

fantasize *vi* fantasmer.

fantastic *a* fantastique.

fantasy *n* fantaisie *f*; (daydream)
fantasme *m*.

fanzine *n* magazine *m* des fans,
fanzine *m*.

FAQ *abbr* (**Frequently Asked
Questions**) (Internet) FAQ *f*, foire *f*
aux questions.

far *adv* loin; (much) beaucoup;
(very) très; ~ **away**, ~ **off** au loin;
as ~ **as** (up to) jusqu'à; **as** ~ **as I
know** autant que je sache; **by** ~
de loin; ~ **from** loin de. ● *a*
lointain; (end, side) autre. ~**away**
a lointain.

farce *n* farce *f*.

fare *n* (prix du) billet *m*; (food)
nourriture *f*. ● *vi* (progress) aller;
(manage) se débrouiller.

Far East *n* Extrême-Orient *m*.

farewell *interj* & *n* adieu (*m*).

farm *n* ferme *f*. ● *vt* cultiver; ~
out céder en sous-traitance. ● *vi*
être fermier. **farmer** *n* fermier *m*.
~**house** *n* ferme *f*. **farming** *n*

agriculture *f*. ~**yard** *n* basse-cour *f*.

fart 🔲 *vi* péter 🔲. ● *n* pet *m* 🔲.

farther *adv* plus loin. ● *a* plus éloigné.

farthest *adv* le plus loin. ● *a* le plus éloigné.

fascinate *vt* fasciner.

Fascism *n* fascisme *m*.

fashion *n* (current style) mode *f*; (manner) façon *f*; **in ~** à la mode; **out of ~** démodé. ● *vt* façonner. **fashionable** *a* à la mode.

fast *a* rapide; (colour) grand teint *inv*; (firm) fixe, solide; **be ~** (of a clock) avancer. ● *adv* vite; (firmly) ferme; **be ~ asleep** dormir d'un sommeil profond. ● *vi* jeûner. ● *n* jeûne *m*.

fasten *vt/i* (s')attacher. **fastener**, **fastening** *n* attache *f*, fermeture *f*.

fast food *n* fast-food *m*; restauration *f* rapide.

fat *n* graisse *f*; (on meat) gras *m*. ● *a* (**fatter, fattest**) gros, gras; (meat) gras; (profit) gros; **a ~ lot** 🔲 bien peu (**of** de).

fatal *a* mortel; (fateful, disastrous) fatal. **fatality** *n* mort *m*. **fatally** *adv* mortellement.

fate *n* sort *m*. **fateful** *a* fatidique.

father *n* père *m*. ~**hood** *n* paternité *f*. ~**-in-law** *n* (*pl* ~**s-in-law**) beau-père *m*.

fathom *n* brasse *f* (*=1.8 m*). ● *vt* ~ (**out**) comprendre.

fatigue *n* épuisement *m*; (Tech) fatigue *f*. ● *vt* fatiguer.

fatten *vt/i* engraisser. **fattening** *a* qui fait grossir.

fatty *a* (*food*) gras; (*tissue*) adipeux.

faucet *n* (US) robinet *m*.

fault *n* (defect, failing) défaut *m*; (blame) faute *f*; (Geol) faille *f*; **at ~** fautif; **find ~ with** critiquer. ● *vt*

~ **sth/sb** prendre en défaut qn/ qch. **faulty** *a* défectueux.

favour, (US) **favor** *n* faveur *f*; **do sb a ~** rendre service à qn; **in ~ of** pour. ● *vt* favoriser; (support) être en faveur de; (prefer) préférer. **favourable** *a* favorable.

favourite *a & n* favori/-te (*m/f*).

fawn *n* (animal) faon *m*; (colour) beige *m* foncé. ● *vi* ~ **on** flagorner.

fax *n* fax *m*, télécopie *f*. ● *vt* faxer, envoyer par télécopie. ~ **machine** *n* fax *m*; télécopieur *m*; (for public use) Publifax® *m*.

FBI *abbr* (**Federal Bureau of Investigation**) (US) Police *f* judiciaire fédérale.

fear *n* crainte *f*, peur *f*; (fig) risque *m*; **for ~ of/that** de peur de/que. ● *vt* craindre.

feasible *a* faisable; (likely) plausible.

feast *n* festin *m*; (Relig) fête *f*. ● *vi* festoyer. ● *vt* régaler (**on** de).

feat *n* exploit *m*.

feather *n* plume *f*. ● *vt* ~ **one's nest** s'enrichir.

feature *n* caractéristique *f*; (of person, face) trait *m*; (film) long métrage *m*; (article) article *m* de fond. ● *vt* (advert) représenter; (give prominence to) mettre en vedette. ● *vi* figurer (**in** dans).

February *n* février *m*.

fed ⇒FEED. ● *a* **be ~ up** 🔲 en avoir marre 🔲 (**with** de).

federal *a* fédéral.

fee *n* (for entrance) prix *m*; ~(**s**) (of doctor) honoraires *mpl*; (of actor, artist) cachet *m*; (for tuition) frais *mpl*; (for enrolment) droits *mpl*.

feeble *a* faible.

feed *vt* (*pt* **fed**) nourrir, donner à manger à; (suckle) allaiter; (supply) alimenter. ● *vi* se nourrir (**on** de). ~ **in information** rentrer des données. ● *n* nourriture *f*; (of baby) tétée *f*.

feedback *n* réaction(s) *f(pl)*; (Med, Tech) feed-back *m*.

feel *vt* (*pt* felt) (touch) tâter; (be conscious of) sentir; (*emotion*) ressentir; (experience) éprouver; (think) estimer. ● *vi* (*tired, lonely*) se sentir; ~ hot/thirsty avoir chaud/soif; ~ awful (ill) se sentir malade; I ~ that avoir l'impression que; ~ like (want ▯) avoir envie de.

feeler *n* antenne *f*; put out ~s tâter le terrain.

feeling *n* (emotion) sentiment *m*; (physical) sensation *f*; (impression) impression *f*.

feet ⇒FOOT.

feign *vt* feindre.

fell ⇒FALL. ● *vt* (cut down) abattre.

fellow *n* compagnon *m*, camarade *m*; (of society) membre *m*; (man ▯) type *m* ▯. ~-**countryman** *n* compatriote *m*. ~-**passenger** *n* compagnon *m* de voyage.

fellowship *n* camaraderie *f*; (group) association *f*.

felony *n* crime *m*.

felt ⇒FEEL. ● *n* feutre *m*. ~-**tip** *n* feutre *m*.

female *a* (*animal*) femelle; (*voice, sex*) féminin. ● *n* femme *f*; (animal) femelle *f*.

feminine *a & n* féminin (*m*). **femininity** *n* féminité *f*. **feminist** *n* féministe *mf*.

fence *n* barrière *f*; sit on the ~ ne pas prendre position. ● *vt* ~ (in) clôturer. ● *vi* (Sport) faire de l'escrime. **fencing** *n* escrime *f*.

fend *vi* ~ for oneself se débrouiller tout seul. ● *vt* ~ off (blow, attack) parer.

fender *n* (for fireplace) garde-cendre *m*; (mudguard: US) garde-boue *m inv*.

ferment[1] *n* ferment *m*; (excitement: fig) agitation *f*.

ferment[2] *vt/i* (faire) fermenter.

fern *n* fougère *f*.

ferocious *a* féroce.

ferret *n* (animal) furet *m*. ● *vi* ~ about fureter. ● *vt* ~ out dénicher.

ferry *n* (long-distance) ferry *m*; (short-distance) bac *m*. ● *vt* transporter.

fertile *a* fertile; (*person, animal*) fécond. **fertilizer** *n* engrais *m*.

festival *n* festival *m*; (Relig) fête *f*.

festive *a* de fête, gai; ~ season période *f* des fêtes. **festivity** *n* réjouissances *fpl*.

fetch *vt* (go for) aller chercher; (bring person) amener; (bring thing) apporter; (be sold for) rapporter.

fête *n* fête *f*; (church) kermesse *f*. ● *vt* fêter.

fetish *n* (object) fétiche *m*; (Psych) obsession *f*.

feud *n* querelle *f*.

fever *n* fièvre *f*. **feverish** *a* fiévreux.

few *det* peu de; a ~ houses quelques maisons; quite a ~ people un bon nombre de personnes. ● *pron* quelques-uns/quelques-unes.

fewer *det* moins de; be ~ être moins nombreux (than que). **fewest** *det* le moins de.

fiancé *n* fiancé *m*. **fiancée** *n* fiancée *f*.

fibre, (US) **fiber** *n* fibre *f*. ~**glass** *n* fibre *f* de verre.

fiction *n* fiction *f*; (works of) ~ romans *mpl*. **fictional** *a* fictif.

fiddle *n* ▯ violon *m*; (swindle ▯) combine *f*. ● *vi* ▮ frauder. ● *vt* ▯ falsifier; ~ with ▯ tripoter ▯.

fidget *vi* gigoter sans cesse.

field *n* champ *m*; (Sport) terrain *m*; (fig) domaine *m*. ● *vt* (*ball*: cricket) bloquer.

fierce a féroce; (*storm, attack*) violent.

fiery a (**-ier, -iest**) (hot) ardent; (spirited) fougueux.

fifteen a & n quinze (*m*).

fifth a & n cinquième (*mf*).

fifty a & n cinquante (*m*).

fig n figue f.

fight vi (*pt* **fought**) se battre; (struggle: fig) lutter; (quarrel) se disputer. ● vt se battre avec; (*evil*: fig) lutter contre. ● n (struggle) lutte f; (quarrel) dispute f; (brawl) bagarre f; (Mil) combat m. □ ~ **back** se défendre (against contre); ~ **off** surmonter; ~ **over** se disputer qch. **fighter** n (determined person) lutteur/-euse m/f; (plane) avion m de chasse. **fighting** n combats mpl.

figment n a ~ **of the imagination** un produit de l'imagination.

figure n (number) chiffre m; (diagram) figure f; (shape) forme f; (body) ligne f; ~s arithmétique f. ● vt s'imaginer. ● vi (appear) figurer; **that** ~s (US, 🄸) c'est logique; ~ **out** comprendre. ~ **of speech** n façon f de parler.

file n (tool) lime f; dossier m, classeur m; (Comput) fichier m; (row) file f. ● vt limer; (*papers*) classer; (Jur) déposer. □ ~ **in** entrer en file; ~ **past** défiler devant.

filing cabinet n classeur m.

fill vt/i (se) remplir. ● n **have had one's** ~ en avoir assez. □ ~ **in** (*form*) remplir; ~ **out** prendre du poids; ~ **up** (Auto) faire le plein (de carburant); (*bath, theatre*) (se) remplir.

fillet n filet m. ● vt découper en filets.

filling n (of tooth) plombage m; (of sandwich) garniture f. ~ **station** n station-service f.

film n film m; (Photo) pellicule f.

● vt filmer. ~-**goer** n cinéphile mf. ~ **star** n vedette f de cinéma.

filter n filtre m; (traffic signal) flèche f. ● vt/i filtrer; (of traffic) suivre la flèche. ~ **coffee** n café m filtre.

filth n crasse f. **filthy** a crasseux.

fin n (of fish, seal) nageoire f; (of shark) aileron m.

final a dernier; (conclusive) définitif. ● n (Sport) finale f.

finale n (Mus) finale m.

finalize vt mettre au point, fixer.

finally adv (lastly, at last) enfin, finalement; (once and for all) définitivement.

finance n finance f. ● a financier. ● vt financer. **financial** a financier.

find vt (*pt* **found**) trouver; (*sth lost*) retrouver. ● n trouvaille f. ~ **out** vt découvrir; vi se renseigner (**about** sur). **findings** npl conclusions fpl.

fine a fin; (excellent) beau; ~ **arts** beaux-arts mpl. ● n amende f. ● vt condamner à une amende.

finger n doigt m. ● vt palper. ~-**nail** n ongle m. ~**print** n empreinte f digitale. ~**tip** n bout m du doigt.

finish vt/i finir; ~ **doing** finir de faire; ~ **up doing** finir par faire; ~ **up in** se retrouver à. ● n fin f; (of race) arrivée f; (appearance) finition f.

finite a fini.

Finland n Finlande f. **Finn** n Finlandais/-e m/f.

Finnish a finlandais. ● n (Ling) finnois m.

fir n sapin m.

fire n (element) feu m; (blaze) incendie m; (heater) radiateur m; **set** ~ **to** mettre le feu à. ● vt (bullet) tirer; (dismiss) renvoyer; (fig) enflammer. ● vi tirer (at sur); ~ **a gun** tirer un coup de revolver/de fusil. ~ **alarm** n alarme f

incendie. ~**arm** n arme f à feu.
~ **brigade** n pompiers mpl. ~
engine n voiture f de pompiers.
~ **escape** n escalier m de
secours. ~ **extinguisher** n
extincteur m. ~**man** n (pl -**men**)
pompier m. ~**place** n cheminée
f. ~ **station** n caserne f de
pompiers. ~**wall** n mur m
coupe-feu; (Internet) pare-feu m
inv. ~**wood** n bois m de
chauffage. ~**work** n feu m
d'artifice.

firing-squad n peloton m
d'exécution.

firm n entreprise f, société f. ● a
ferme; (belief) solide.

first a premier; **at ~ hand** de
première main; **at ~ sight** à
première vue; ~ **of all** tout
d'abord. ● n premier/-ière m/f.
● adv d'abord, premièrement;
(arrive) le premier, la première; **at
~** d'abord. ~ **aid** n premiers
soins mpl. ~**class** a de
première classe. ~ **floor** n
premier étage m; (US) rez-de-
chaussée m inv. ~ **gear** n
première (vitesse) f. **F~ Lady** n
(US) épouse f du Président.

firstly adv premièrement.

first name n prénom m.

fish n poisson m; ~ **shop**
poissonnerie f. ● vi pêcher; ~ **for**
(cod) pêcher; ~ **out** (from water)
repêcher; (take out ⌴) sortir.
fisherman n (pl -**men**) n pêcheur
m.

fishing n pêche f; **go ~** aller à la
pêche. ~ **rod** n canne f à pêche.

fishmonger n poissonnier/-ière
m/f.

fist n poing m.

fit n accès m, crise f; **be a good ~**
(dress) être à la bonne taille. ● a
(**fitter**, **fittest**) en bonne santé;
(proper) convenable; (good enough)
bon; (able) capable; **in no ~ state**

to do pas en état de faire. ● vt/i
(pt **fitted**) (into space) aller; (install)
poser. ⌴ ~ **in** vt caser; vi
(newcomer) s'intégrer; ~ **out**, ~
up équiper.

fitness n forme f; (of remark)
justesse f.

fitted a (wardrobe) encastré. ~
carpet n moquette f.

fitting a approprié. ● n essayage
m. ~ **room** n cabine f d'essayage.

five a & n cinq (m).

fix vt (make firm, attach, decide) fixer;
(mend) réparer; (deal with) arranger;
~ **sb up with sth** trouver qch à qn.

fixture n (Sport) match m; ~**s** (in
house) installations fpl.

fizz vi pétiller. ● n pétillement m.
fizzy a gazeux.

flabbergast vt sidérer.

flabby a flasque.

flag n drapeau m; (Naut) pavillon
m. ● vt (pt **flagged**) ~ (**down**)
faire signe de s'arrêter à. ● vi
(weaken) faiblir; (sick person)
s'affaiblir. ~**pole** n mât m.
~**stone** n dalle f.

flake n flocon m; (of paint, metal)
écaille f. ● vi s'écailler.

flamboyant a (colour) éclatant;
(manner) extravagant.

flame n flamme f; **burst into ~s**
exploser; **go up in ~s** brûler. ● vi
flamber.

flamingo n flamant m (rose).

flammable a inflammable.

flan n tarte f; (custard tart) flan m.

flank n flanc m. ● vt flanquer.

flannel n (material) flannelle f; (for
face) gant m de toilette.

flap vi (pt **flapped**) battre. ● vt ~
its wings battre des ailes. ● n (of
pocket) rabat m; (of table) abattant
m.

flare vi ~ **up** (fighting) éclater. ● n
flamboiement m; (Mil) fusée f

F

éclairante; (in skirt) évasement m.
flared a évasé.

flash vi briller; (on and off)
clignoter; ~ **past** passer à toute
vitesse. ● vt faire briller; (aim
torch) diriger (**at** sur); (flaunt) étaler;
~ **one's headlights** faire un appel
de phares. ● n (of news, camera)
flash m; **in a** ~ en un éclair.
~**back** n retour m en arrière.
~**light** n lampe f de poche.

flask n (for chemicals) flacon m; (for
drinks) thermos® m or f inv.

flat a (**flatter, flattest**) plat; (tyre)
à plat; (refusal) catégorique;
(fare, rate) fixe. ● adv (say)
carrément. ● n (rooms)
appartement m; (tyre ⬛) crevaison
f; (Mus) bémol m.

flat out adv (drive) à toute
vitesse; (work) d'arrache-pied.

flatten vt/i (s')aplatir.

flatter vt flatter.

flaunt vt étaler, afficher.

flavour, (US) **flavor** n goût m; (of
ice-cream) parfum m. ● vt parfumer
(**with** à), assaisonner (**with** de).
flavouring n arôme m artificiel.

flaw n défaut m.

flea n puce f. ~ **market** n marché
m aux puces.

fleck n petite tache f.

fled ⇒FLEE.

flee vt/i (pt **fled**) fuir.

fleece n toison f; (garment) polaire
f. ● vt plumer.

fleet n (Naut, Aviat) flotte f; **a** ~ **of
vehicles** (in reserve) parc m; (on road)
convoi m.

fleeting a très bref.

Flemish a flamand. ● n (Ling)
flamand m.

flesh n chair f; one's (own) ~ **and
blood** la chair de sa chair.

flew ⇒FLY.

flex vt (knee) fléchir; (muscle)
faire jouer. ● n (Electr) fil m.

flexible a flexible.

flexitime n horaire m variable.

flick n petit coup m. ● vt donner
un petit coup à; ~ **through**
feuilleter.

flight n (of bird, plane) vol m; ~ **of
stairs** escalier m; (fleeing) fuite f;
take ~ prendre la fuite. ~**-deck**
n poste m de pilotage.

flimsy a (**-ier, -iest**) (pej) mince,
peu solide.

flinch vi (wince) broncher; (draw
back) reculer.

fling vt (pt **flung**) jeter.

flint n (rock) silex m.

flip vt (pt **flipped**) donner un
petit coup à; ~ **through** feuilleter.
● n chiquenaude f.

flippant a désinvolte.

flipper n (of seal) nageoire f; (of
swimmer) palme f.

flirt vi flirter. ● n flirteur/-euse m/
f.

float vt/i (faire) flotter. ● n
flotteur m; (cart) char m.

flock n (of sheep) troupeau m; (of
people) foule f. ● vi affluer.

flog vt (pt **flogged**) (beat) fouetter;
(sell ⬛) vendre.

flood n inondation f; (fig) flot m.
● vt inonder. ● vi (building) être
inondé; (river) déborder; (people:
fig) affluer.

floodlight n projecteur m. ● vt
(pt **floodlit**) illuminer.

floor n sol m, plancher m; (for
dancing) piste f; (storey) étage m.
● vt (knock down) terrasser; (baffle)
stupéfier. ~**-board** n planche f.

flop vi (pt **flopped**) (drop) s'affaler;
(fail ⬛) échouer; (head) tomber.
● n ⬛ échec m, fiasco m.

floppy a lâche, flasque. ~ (**disk**)
n disquette f.

florist n fleuriste mf.

flounder vi (animal, person) se
débattre (**in** dans); (economy)

stagner. ● *n* flet *m*; (US) poisson *m* plat.

flour *n* farine *f*.

flourish *vi* prospérer. ● *vt* brandir. ● *n* geste *m* élégant.

flout *vt* se moquer de.

flow *vi* couler; (circulate) circuler; (*traffic*) s'écouler; (hang loosely) flotter; ~ **in** affluer; ~ **into** (of river) se jeter dans. ● *n* (of liquid, traffic) écoulement *m*; (of tide) flux *m*; (of orders, words: fig) flot *m*. ~ **chart** *n* organigramme *m*.

flower *n* fleur *f*. ● *vi* fleurir.

flown ⇒FLY.

flu *n* grippe *f*.

fluctuate *vi* varier.

fluent *a* (*style*) aisé; **be** ~ (**in a language**) parler (une langue) couramment.

fluff *n* peluche(s) *f(pl)*; (down) duvet *m*.

fluid *a* & *n* fluide (*m*).

fluke *n* coup *m* de chance.

flung ⇒FLING.

fluoride *n* fluor *m*.

flush *vi* rougir. ● *vt* nettoyer à grande eau; ~ **the toilet** tirer la chasse d'eau. ● *n* (blush) rougeur *f*; (fig) excitation *f*. ● *a* ~ **with** (level with) au ras de. □ ~ **out** chasser.

fluster *vt* énerver.

flute *n* flûte *f*.

flutter *vi* voleter; (of wings) battre. ● *n* (wings) battement *m*; (fig) agitation *f*; (bet 🔟) pari *m*.

flux *n* changement *m* continuel.

fly *n* mouche *f*; (of trousers) braguette *f*. ● *vi* (*pt* **flew**; *pp* **flown**) voler; (*passengers*) voyager en avion; (*flag*) flotter; (rush) filer. ● *vt* (*aircraft*) piloter; (*passengers, goods*) transporter par avion; (*flag*) arborer. □ ~ **off** s'envoler.

flyer *n* (person) aviateur *m*; (circular) prospectus *m*.

flying *a* (*saucer*) volant; **with** ~ **colours** haut la main; ~ **start** excellent départ *m*; ~ **visit** visite *f* éclair (*a inv*). ● *n* (activity) aviation *f*.

flyover *n* pont *m* (routier).

foal *n* poulain *m*.

foam *n* écume *f*, mousse *f*; ~ (**rubber**) caoutchouc *m* mousse. ● *vi* écumer, mousser.

focus *n* (*pl* ~**es** or **-ci**) foyer *m*; (fig) centre *m*; **be in/out of** ~ être/ ne pas être au point. ● *vt/i* (faire) converger; (*instrument*) mettre au point; (with camera) faire la mise au point (**on** sur); (fig) (se) concentrer. ~ **group** *n* groupe *m* de discussion.

fodder *n* fourrage *m*.

foe *n* ennemi/-e *m/f*.

foetus *n* fœtus *m*.

fog *n* brouillard *m*. ● *vt/i* (*pt* **fogged**) (*window*) (s')embuer.

foggy *a* brumeux; **it is** ~ il fait du brouillard.

foil *n* (tin foil) papier *m* d'aluminium; (deterrent) repoussoir *m*. ● *vt* (thwart) déjouer.

fold *vt/i* (*paper, clothes*) (se) plier; (*arms*) croiser; (fail) s'effondrer. ● *n* pli *m*; (for sheep) parc *m* à moutons; (Relig) bercail *m*. **folder** *n* (file) chemise *f*; (leaflet) dépliant *m*. **folding** *a* pliant.

foliage *n* feuillage *m*.

folk *n* gens *mpl*; ~**s** parents *mpl*. ● *a* (*dance*) folklorique; (*music*) folk.

folklore *n* folklore *m*.

follow *vt/i* suivre; **it** ~**s that** il s'ensuit que; ~ **suit** en faire autant; ~ **up** (*letter*) donner suite à. **follower** *n* partisan *m*.

following *n* partisans *mpl*. ● *a* suivant; ~ **day** lendemain. ● *prep* à la suite de.

fond *a* (loving) affectueux; (*hope*) cher; **be ~ of** aimer.

fondle *vt* caresser.

fondness *n* affection *f*; (for things) attachement *m*.

food *n* nourriture *f*; **French ~** la cuisine française. ● *a* alimentaire. **~ processor** *n* robot *m* (ménager).

fool *n* idiot/-e *m/f*. ● *vt* duper. ● *vi* **~ around** faire l'idiot. **foolish** *a* idiot.

foot *n* (*pl* **feet**) pied *m*; (measure) pied *m* (=30.48 cm); (*of stairs, page*) bas *m*; **on ~** à pied; **on** *or* **to one's feet** debout; **under sb's feet** dans les jambes de qn. ● *vt* (*bill*) payer. **foot-and-mouth disease** *n* fièvre *f* aphteuse.

football *n* (ball) ballon *m*; (game) football *m*. **footballer** *n* footballeur *m*.

foot: **~-bridge** *n* passerelle *f*. **~hold** *n* prise *f*.

footing *n* **on an equal ~** sur un pied d'égalité; **be on a friendly ~ with sb** avoir des rapports amicaux avec qn; **lose one's ~** perdre pied.

foot: **~note** *n* note *f* (*en bas de la page*). **~path** *n* (in countryside) sentier *m*; (in town) chemin *m*. **~print** *n* empreinte *f* (*de pied*). **~step** *n* pas *m*. **~wear** *n* chaussures *fpl*.

---

for

● *preposition*

····▸ pour; **~ me** pour moi; **music ~ dancing** de la musique pour danser; **what is it ~?** ça sert à quoi?

····▸ (with a time period that is still continuing) depuis; **I've been waiting ~ two hours** j'attends depuis deux heures; **I haven't seen him**

~ ten years je ne l'ai pas vu depuis dix ans.

····▸ (with a time period that has ended) pendant; **I waited ~ two hours** j'ai attendu pendant deux heures.

····▸ (with a future time period) pour; **I'm going to Paris ~ six weeks** je vais à Paris pour six semaines.

····▸ (with distances) pendant; **I drove ~ 50 kilometres** j'ai roulé pendant 50 kilomètres.

---

forbid *vt* (*pt* **forbade**; *pp* **forbidden**) interdire, défendre (**sb to do** à qn de faire); **~ sb sth** interdire *or* défendre qch à qn; **you are forbidden to leave** il vous est interdit de partir. **forbidding** *a* menaçant.

force *n* force *f*; **come into ~** entrer en vigueur; **the ~s** les forces *fpl* armées. ● *vt* forcer. □ **~ into** faire entrer de force; **~ on** imposer à. **forced** *a* forcé.

force-feed *vt* (*pt* **-fed**) (*person*) nourrir de force; (*animal*) gaver.

forceful *a* énergique.

ford *n* gué *m*. ● *vt* passer à gué.

forearm *n* avant-bras *m inv*.

forecast *vt* (*pt* **forecast**) prévoir. ● *n* **weather ~** météo *f*.

forecourt *n* (of garage) devant *m*; (of station) cour *f*.

forefinger *n* index *m*.

forefront *n* **at/in the ~ of** à la pointe de.

foregone *a* **it's a ~ conclusion** c'est couru d'avance.

foreground *n* premier plan *m*.

forehead *n* front *m*.

foreign *a* étranger; (*trade*) extérieur; (*travel*) à l'étranger. **foreigner** *n* étranger/-ère *m/f*.

foreman *n* (*pl* **-men**) contremaître *m*.

foremost a le plus éminent.
● adv first and ~ tout d'abord.

forensic a médico-légal; ~ medicine médecine f légale.

foresee vt (pt -saw; pp -seen) prévoir.

forest n forêt f. **forestry** n sylviculture f.

foretaste n avant-goût m.

forever adv toujours.

foreword n avant-propos m inv.

forfeit n (penalty) peine f; (in game) gage m. ● vt perdre.

forgave ⇒FORGIVE.

forge n forge f. ● vt (metal, friendship) forger; (copy) contrefaire, falsifier. ● vi ~ ahead aller de l'avant, avancer. **forger** n faussaire m. **forgery** n faux m, contrefaçon f.

forget vt/i (pt **forgot**; pp **forgotten**) oublier; ~ oneself s'oublier. **forgetful** a distrait. ~-**me-not** n myosotis m.

forgive vt (pt **forgave**; pp **forgiven**) pardonner (**sb for sth** qch à qn).

fork n fourchette f; (for digging) fourche f; (in road) bifurcation f. ● vi (road) bifurquer; ~ out ⬚ payer. **forked** a fourchu. ~-**lift truck** n chariot m élévateur.

form n forme f; (document) formulaire m; (School) classe f; on ~ en forme. ● vt/i (se) former.

formal a officiel, en bonne et due forme; (person) compassé, cérémonieux; (dress) de cérémonie; (denial, grammar) formel; (language) soutenu. **formality** n cérémonial m; (requirement) formalité f.

format n format m. ● vt (pt **formatted**) (disk) formater.

former a ancien; (first of two) premier. ● n the ~ celui-là, celle-là. **formerly** adv autrefois.

formula n (pl -ae or -as) formule f. **formulate** vt formuler.

fort n (Mil) fort m; **to hold the** ~ s'occuper de tout.

forth adv from this day ~ à partir d'aujourd'hui; **and so** ~ et ainsi de suite; **go back and** ~ aller et venir.

forthcoming a à venir, prochain; (sociable ⬚) communicatif.

forthright a direct.

forthwith adv sur-le-champ.

fortnight n quinze jours mpl, quinzaine f.

fortnightly a bimensuel. ● adv tous les quinze jours.

fortunate a heureux; **be** ~ avoir de la chance. **fortunately** adv heureusement.

fortune n fortune f; **make a** ~ faire fortune; **have the good** ~ **to** avoir la chance de. ~-**teller** n diseur/-euse m/f de bonne aventure.

forty a & n quarante (m); ~ **winks** un petit somme.

forward a en avant; (advanced) précoce; (bold) effronté. ● n (Sport) avant m. ● adv en avant; **come** ~ se présenter; **go** ~ avancer. ● vt (letter, e-mail) faire suivre; (goods) expédier; (fig) favoriser. **forwardness** n précocité f. **forwards** adv en avant.

fossil n & a fossile (m).

foster vt (promote) encourager; (child) élever. ● a (child, parent) adoptif; (family, home) de placement.

fought ⇒FIGHT.

foul a (smell, weather) infect; (place, action) immonde; (language) ordurier. ● n (football) faute f. ● vt souiller, encrasser; ~ **up** ⬚ gâcher. ~-**mouthed** a grossier.

found ⇒FIND. ● vt fonder.

foundation n fondation f; (basis)

fondement m; (make-up) fond m de teint. **founder** n fondateur/-trice m/f.

fountain n fontaine f. **~-pen** n stylo m à encre.

four a & n quatre (m).

fourteen a & n quatorze (m).

fourth a & n quatrième (mf).

four-wheel drive n (car) quatre-quatre m.

fowl n (one bird) poulet m; (group) volaille f.

fox n renard m. ● vt (baffle) mystifier; (deceive) tromper.

fraction n fraction f.

fracture n fracture f. ● vt/i (se) fracturer.

fragile a fragile.

fragment n fragment m.

fragrance n parfum m.

frail a frêle.

frame n (of building, boat) charpente f; (of picture) cadre m; (of window) châssis m; (of spectacles) monture f; **~ of mind** humeur f. ● vt encadrer; (fig) formuler; (Jur, ▣) monter un coup contre. **~work** n structure f; (context) cadre m.

France n France f.

franchise n (Pol) droit m de vote; (Comm) franchise f.

frank a franc. ● vt affranchir. **frankly** adv franchement.

frantic a frénétique; **~ with** fou de.

fraternity n (bond) fraternité f; (group, club) confrérie f.

fraud n (deception) fraude f; (person) imposteur m. **fraudulent** a frauduleux.

fray n the **~** la bataille. ● vt/i (s')effilocher.

freckle n tache f de rousseur.

free a libre; (gratis) gratuit; (lavish) généreux; **~ (of charge)** gratuit (ement); **a ~ hand** carte f

blanche. ● vt (pt **freed**) libérer; (clear) dégager.

freedom n liberté f.

free: **~ enterprise** n la libre entreprise. **~ kick** n coup m franc. **~lance** a & n free-lance (mf), indépendant/-e (m/f).

freely adv librement.

Freemason n franc-maçon m.

Freenet n (Comput) Libertel m.

free: **~ phone**, **~ number** n numéro m vert. **~-range** a (eggs) de ferme.

Freeware n (Comput) Gratuiciel m.

freeway n (US) autoroute f.

freeze vt/i (pt **froze**; pp **frozen**) geler; (Culin) (se) congeler; (wages) bloquer. ● n gel m; blocage m. **~-dried** a lyophilisé.

freezer n congélateur m.

freezing a glacial; **below ~** au-dessous de zéro.

freight n fret m.

French a français. ● n (Ling) français m; **the ~** les Français mpl. **~ bean** n haricot m vert. **~ fries** npl frites fpl. **~man** n Français m. **~-speaking** a francophone. **~ window** n porte-fenêtre f. **~woman** n Française f.

frenzied a frénétique. **frenzy** n frénésie f.

frequent[1] a fréquent.

frequent[2] vt fréquenter.

fresco n fresque f.

fresh a frais; (different, additional) nouveau; (cheeky ▣) culotté.

freshen vi (weather) fraîchir; **~ up** (person) se rafraîchir.

freshly adv nouvellement.

freshness n fraîcheur f.

freshwater a d'eau douce.

friction n friction f.

Friday n vendredi m.

fridge n frigo m.

fried ⇒FRY. ● *a* frit; ~ **eggs** œufs *mpl* sur le plat.

friend *n* ami/-e *m/f*. **friendly** *a* (**-ier, -iest**) amical, gentil. **friendship** *n* amitié *f*.

frieze *n* frise *f*.

fright *n* peur *f*; (person, thing) horreur *f*.

frighten *vt* effrayer; ~ **off** faire fuir; **frightened** *a* effrayé; **be** ~**ed** avoir peur (**of** de). **frightening** *a* effrayant.

frill *n* (trimming) fanfreluche *f*; **with no** ~**s** très simple.

fringe *n* (edging, hair) frange *f*; (of area) bordure *f*; (of society) marge *f*. ~ **benefits** *npl* avantages *mpl* sociaux.

frisk *vt* (search) fouiller.

fritter *n* beignet *m*. ● *vt* ~ **away** gaspiller.

frivolity *n* frivolité *f*.

frizzy *a* crépu.

fro ⇒TO AND FRO.

frog *n* grenouille *f*; **a** ~ **in one's throat** un chat dans la gorge.

frolic *vi* (*pt* **frolicked**) s'ébattre. ● *n* ébats *mpl*.

from *prep* de; (with time, prices) à partir de, de; (habit, conviction) par; (according to) d'après; **take** ~ **sb** prendre à qn; **take** ~ **one's pocket** prendre dans sa poche.

front *n* (of car, train) avant *m*; (of garment, building) devant *m*; (Mil, Pol) front *m*; (of book, pamphlet) début *m*; (appearance: fig) façade *f*. ● *a* de devant, avant *inv*; (first) premier; ~ **door** porte *f* d'entrée; **in** ~ (**of**) devant. **frontage** *n* façade *f*.

frontier *n* frontière *f*.

frost *n* gel *m*, gelée *f*; (on glass) givre *m*. ● *vt/i* (se) givrer. ~**-bite** *n* gelure *f*.

frosty *a* (weather, welcome) glacial; (window) givré.

froth *n* (on beer) mousse *f*; (on water) écume *f*. ● *vi* mousser, écumer.

frown *vi* froncer les sourcils; ~ **on** désapprouver. ● *n* froncement *m* de sourcils.

froze ⇒FREEZE.

frozen ⇒FREEZE. ● *a* congelé.

fruit *n* fruit *m*; (collectively) fruits *mpl*. **fruitful** *a* (discussions) fructueux. ~ **machine** *n* machine *f* à sous.

frustrate *vt* (plan) faire échouer; (person: Psych) frustrer; (upset 🅓) exaspérer. **frustration** *n* (Psych) frustration *f*; (disappointment) déception *f*.

fry *vt/i* (*pt* **fried**) (faire) frire. **frying-pan** *n* poêle *f* (à frire).

FTP *abbr* (**File Transfer Protocol**) (Internet) protocole *m* FTP.

fudge *n* caramel *m* mou. ● *vt* (issue) esquiver.

fuel *n* combustible *m*; (for car engine) carburant *m*. ● *vt* (*pt* **fuelled**) alimenter en combustible.

fugitive *n* & *a* fugitif/-ive (*m/f*).

fulfil *vt* (*pt* **fulfilled**) accomplir, réaliser; (condition) remplir; ~ **oneself** s'épanouir. **fulfilling** *a* satisfaisant. **fulfilment** *n* réalisation *f*; épanouissement *m*.

full *a* plein (**of** de); (bus, hotel) complet; (programme) chargé; (skirt) ample; **be** ~ (**up**) n'avoir plus faim; **at** ~ **speed** à toute vitesse. ● *n* **in** ~ intégralement; **to the** ~ complètement. ~ **back** *n* (Sport) arrière *m*. ~ **moon** *n* pleine lune *f*. ~ **name** *n* nom *m* et prénom *m*. ~**-scale** *a* (drawing etc.) grandeur nature *inv*; (fig) de grande envergure. ~ **stop** *n* point *m*. ~**-time** *a* & *adv* à plein temps.

fully *adv* complètement; ~ **fledged** (member, citizen) à part entière.

fume vi rager. **fumes** npl
émanations fpl, vapeurs fpl.

fun n amusement m; **be ~** être
chouette; **for ~** pour rire; **make ~
of** se moquer de.

function n (purpose, duty) fonction
f; (event) réception f. ● vi
fonctionner.

fund n fonds m. ● vt fournir les
fonds pour.

fundamental a fondamental.
fundamentalist n intégriste mf.

funeral n enterrement m. ● a
funèbre.

fun-fair n fête f foraine.

fungus n (pl **-gi**) (plant)
champignon m; (mould) moisissure
f.

funnel n (for pouring) entonnoir m;
(of ship) cheminée f.

funny a (**-ier**, **-iest**) drôle; (odd)
bizarre.

fur n (for garment) fourrure f; (on
animal) poils m; (in kettle) tartre m.

furious a furieux.

furnace n fourneau m.

furnish vt (room) meubler; (supply)
fournir. **furnishings** npl
ameublement m.

furniture n meubles mpl,
mobilier m.

furry a (animal) à fourrure; (toy)
en peluche.

further a plus éloigné; (additional)
supplémentaire. ● adv plus loin;
(more) davantage. ● vt avancer. **~
education** n formation f
continue.

furthermore adv en outre, de
plus.

furthest a le plus éloigné. ● adv
le plus loin.

fury n fureur f.

fuse vt/i (melt) fondre; (unite: fig)
fusionner; **~ the lights** faire
sauter les plombs. ● n (of plug)
fusible m; (of bomb) amorce f.

fuss n (when upset) histoire(s) f(pl);
(when excited) agitation f; **make a ~**
faire des histoires; s'agiter; (about
food) faire des chichis; **make a ~
of** faire grand cas de. ● vi
s'agiter. **fussy** a (finicky) tatillon;
(hard to please) difficile.

future a futur. ● n avenir m;
(Gram) futur m; **in ~** à l'avenir.

fuzzy a (hair) crépu; (photograph)
flou; (person Ⓣ) à l'esprit confus.

Gaelic n gaélique m.

gag n (on mouth) bâillon m; (joke)
blague f. ● vt (pt **gagged**)
bâillonner.

gain vt (respect, support) gagner;
(speed, weight) prendre. ● vi (of
clock) avancer. ● n (increase)
augmentation f (**in** de); (profit) gain
m.

galaxy n galaxie f.

gale n tempête f.

gallery n galerie f; (art) **~** musée
m.

Gallic a français.

gallon n gallon m (imperial =
4.546 litres; Amer. = 3.785 litres).

gallop n galop m. ● vi (pt
galloped) galoper.

galore adv (prizes, bargains) en
abondance; (drinks, sandwiches)
à gogo Ⓣ.

gamble vt/i jouer; **~ on** miser
sur. ● n (venture) entreprise f
risquée; (bet) pari m; (risk) risque
m. **gambling** n jeu m.

game n jeu m; (football) match m;
(tennis) partie f; (animals, birds)

gibier *m*. ● *a* (brave) courageux; ~
for prêt à. ~**keeper** *n* garde-
chasse *m*.

games console *n* console *f* de
jeux.

gammon *n* jambon *m*.

gang *n* (of youths) bande *f*; (of
workmen) équipe *f*. ● *vi* ~ up se
liguer (**on**, **against** contre).

gangway *n* passage *m*; (aisle)
allée *f*; (of ship) passerelle *f*.

gaol *n* & *vt* = JAIL.

gap *n* trou *m*, vide *m*; (in time)
intervalle *m*; (difference) écart *m*. ~
year *n* année *f* de coupure (*avant
d'entrer à l'université*).

gape *vi* rester bouche bée.
gaping *a* béant.

garage *n* garage *m*. ● *vt* mettre
au garage.

garbage *n* (US) ordures *fpl*.

garden *n* jardin *m*. ● *vi* jardiner.
gardener *n* jardinier/-ière *m/f*.
gardening *n* jardinage *m*.

gargle *vi* se gargariser.

garish *a* (clothes) tape-à-l'œil.

garland *n* guirlande *f*.

garlic *n* ail *m*.

garment *n* vêtement *m*.

garnish *vt* garnir (**with** de). ● *n*
garniture *f*.

garter *n* jarretière *f*.

gas *n* (*pl* ~**es**) gaz *m*; (Med)
anesthésie *m*; (petrol: US) essence
f. ● *a* (mask, pipe) à gaz. ● *vt*
asphyxier; (Mil) gazer.

gash *n* entaille *f*. ● *vt* entailler.

gasoline *n* (petrol: US) essence *f*.

gasp *vi* haleter; (in surprise: fig)
avoir le souffle coupé. ● *n*
halètement *m*.

gate *n* (in garden, airport) porte *f*; (of
field, level crossing) barrière *f*. ~**way**
n porte *f*; (Internet) passerelle *f*.

gather *vt* (*people, objects*)
rassembler; (pick up) ramasser;
(*flowers*) cueillir; (fig)
comprendre; ~ speed prendre de

la vitesse; (sewing) froncer. ● *vi*
(*people*) se rassembler; (pile up)
s'accumuler. **gathering** *n*
réunion *m*.

gauge *n* jauge *f*, indicateur *m*.
● *vt* (speed, distance) jauger;
(reaction, mood) évaluer.

gaunt *a* décharné.

gauze *n* gaze *f*.

gave ⇒GIVE.

gay *a* (joyful) gai; (homosexual) gay
inv. ● *n* gay *mf*.

gaze *vi* ~ (**at**) regarder
(fixement). ● *n* regard *m* (fixe).

GB *abbr* ⇒GREAT BRITAIN.

gear *n* (equipment) matériel *m*;
(Tech) engrenage *m*; (Auto) vitesse
f; **in** ~ en prise; **out of** ~ au point
mort. ● *vt* **to be geared to**
s'adresser à. ~**box** *n* (Auto) boîte *f*
de vitesses. ~**lever**, (US) ~**shift**
n levier *m* de vitesse.

geese ⇒GOOSE.

gel *n* (for hair) gel *m*.

gem *n* pierre *f* précieuse.

Gemini *n* Gémeaux *mpl*.

gender *n* (Ling) genre *m*; (of person)
sexe *m*.

gene *n* gène *m*. ~**library** *n*
génothèque *f*.

general *a* général. ● *n* général *m*;
in ~ en général.

general election *n* élections *fpl*
législatives.

generalization *n* généralisation
f. **generalize** *vt/i* généraliser.

general practitioner *n* (Med)
généraliste *m*.

generate *vt* produire.

generation *n* génération *f*.

generator *n* (Electr) groupe *m*
électrogène.

generosity *n* générosité *f*.
generous *a* généreux; (plentiful)
copieux.

genetics *n* génétique *f*.

Geneva n Genève.

genial a affable, sympathique.

genitals npl organes mpl génitaux.

genius n (pl ~es) génie m.

genome n génome m.

gentle a (mild, kind) doux; (pressure, breeze) léger; (reminder, hint) discret.

gentleman n (pl -men) (man) monsieur m; (well-bred) gentleman m.

gently adv doucement.

gents npl (toilets) toilettes fpl; (on sign) 'Messieurs'.

genuine a (reason, motive) vrai; (jewel, substance) véritable; (person, belief) sincère.

geography n géographie f.

geology n géologie f.

geometry n géométrie f.

geriatric a gériatrique.

germ n (Med) microbe m.

German n (person) Allemand/-e m/f; (Ling) allemand m. ● a allemand.

German measles n rubéole f.

Germany n Allemagne f.

gesture n geste m.

....

get

past **got**; *past participle* **got**, **gotten** (US); *present participle* **getting**

● *transitive verb*

····▸ recevoir; **we got a letter** nous avons reçu une lettre.

····▸ (obtain) **I got a job in Paris** j'ai trouvé un travail à Paris; **I'll ~ sth to eat at the airport** je mangerai qch à l'aéroport.

····▸ (buy) acheter; **~ sb a present** acheter un cadeau à qn.

····▸ (achieve) obtenir; **he got it right** il a obtenu le bon résultat; **~**

good grades avoir de bonnes notes.

····▸ (fetch) chercher; **go and ~ a chair** va chercher une chaise.

····▸ (transport) prendre; **we can ~ the bus** on peut prendre le bus.

····▸ (understand 🗊) comprendre; **now let me ~ this right** alors si je comprends bien...

····▸ (experience) **~ a surprise** être surpris; **~ a shock** avoir un choc.

····▸ (illness) **~ measles** attraper la rougeole; **~ a cold** s'enrhumer.

····▸ (ask or persuade) **~ him to call me** dis-lui de m'appeler; **I'll ~ her to help me** je lui demanderai de m'aider.

····▸ (cause to be done) **~ a TV repaired** faire réparer une télévision; **~ one's hair cut** se faire couper les cheveux.

● *intransitive verb*

····▸ devenir; **he's getting old** il vieillit; **it's getting late** il se fait tard.

····▸ (in passives) **~ married** se marier; **~ hurt** être blessé.

····▸ (arrive) arriver; **~ to the airport** arriver à l'aéroport.

□ **get about** (person) se déplacer.

get along (manage) se débrouiller; (progress) avancer.

get along with s'entendre avec.

get at (reach) atteindre; (imply) vouloir dire.

get away partir; (escape) s'échapper.

get back vi revenir. vt récupérer.

get by vi (manage) se débrouiller. vt (pass) passer.

get down vt/i descendre. vt (depress) déprimer.

get in entrer.

get into (car) monter dans; (dress) mettre.

get off vt (bus) descendre; (remove) enlever. vi (from bus) descendre; (leave) partir; (Jur) être acquitté.

get on vi (to bus) monter; (succeed) réussir. vt (bus) monter.

get on with (person) s'entendre avec; (job) attaquer.

get out sortir.

get out of (fig) se soustraire.

get over (illness) se remettre de.

get round (rule) contourner; (person) entortiller.

get through vi passer; (on phone) ~ **through to sb** avoir qn. vt traverser.

get up se lever.

get up to faire.

getaway n fuite f.

ghastly a (-ier, -iest) affreux.

gherkin n cornichon m.

ghetto n ghetto m.

ghost n fantôme m.

giant n & a géant (m).

gibberish n baragouin m, charabia m.

giblets npl abats mpl.

giddy a (-ier, -iest) vertigineux; be or feel ~ avoir le vertige.

gift n (present) cadeau m; (ability) don m.

gifted a doué.

gift-wrap n paquet-cadeau m.

gigantic a gigantesque.

giggle vi ricaner (sottement), glousser. ● n ricanement m; the ~s le fou rire.

gimmick n truc m.

gin n gin m.

ginger n gingembre m. ● a (hair) roux. ~ **beer** n boisson f gazeuse au gingembre. ~**bread** n pain m d'épices.

gingerly adv avec précaution.

giraffe n girafe f.

girl n (child) (petite) fille f; (young woman) (jeune) fille f. ~**friend** n amie f; (of boy) petite amie f.

giro n virement m bancaire; (cheque) mandat m.

gist n essentiel m.

give vt (pt **gave**; pp **given**) donner; (gesture) faire; (laugh, sigh) pousser; ~ **sb sth** donner qch à qn. ● vi donner; (yield) céder; (stretch) se détendre. ● n élasticité f. □ ~ **away** donner; (secret) trahir; ~ **back** rendre; ~ **in** (yield) céder (to à); ~ **off** (heat, fumes) dégager; (signal, scent) émettre; ~ **out** vt distribuer; ~ **over** (devote) consacrer; (stop ▯) cesser; ~ **up** vt/i (renounce) renoncer (à); (yield) céder; ~ **oneself up** se rendre; ~ **way** céder; (collapse) s'effondrer.

given ⇒GIVE. ● a donné. ~ **name** n prénom m.

glad a content. **gladly** adv avec plaisir.

glamorous a séduisant, ensorcelant.

glamour, (US) **glamor** n enchantement m, séduction f.

glance n coup m d'œil. ● vi ~ **at** jeter un coup d'œil à.

gland n glande f.

glare vi briller très fort; ~ **at** regarder d'un air furieux. ● n (of lights) éclat m (aveuglant); (stare; fig) regard m furieux. **glaring** a (dazzling) éblouissant; (obvious) flagrant.

glass n verre m. **glasses** npl (spectacles) lunettes fpl.

glaze vt (door) vitrer; (pottery) vernisser. ● n vernis m.

gleam n lueur f. ● vi luire.

glide vi glisser; (of plane) planer. **glider** n planeur m.

glimpse n (insight) aperçu m; **catch a ~ of** entrevoir.

G

glitter vi scintiller. ● n scintillement m.

global a (world-wide) mondial; (all-embracing) global. ~ **warming** n réchauffement m de la planète.

globalization n mondialisation f.

globe n globe m.

gloom n obscurité f; (sadness: fig) tristesse f. **gloomy** a triste; (pessimistic) pessimiste.

glorious a splendide; (deed, hero) glorieux.

glory n gloire f; (beauty) splendeur f. ● vi ~ **in** être très fier de.

gloss n lustre m, brillant m. ● a brillant. ● vi ~ **over** (make light of) glisser sur; (cover up) dissimuler.

glossary n glossaire m.

glossy a brillant.

glove n gant m. ~ **compartment** n (Auto) boîte f à gants.

glow vi (fire) rougeoyer; (person, eyes) rayonner. ● n rougeoiement m, éclat m. **glowing** a (report) enthousiaste.

glucose n glucose m.

glue n colle f. ● vt (pres p **gluing**) coller.

GM abbr (**genetically modified**) transgénique.

gnaw vt/i ronger.

GNP abbr (**Gross National Product**) produit m national brut, PNB m.

....

go

⇨ present **go**, **goes**; past **went**;
past participle **gone**

● intransitive verb

····➤ aller; ~ **to school/town/market** aller à l'école/en ville/au marché; ~ **for a swim/walk** aller nager/se promener.

····➤ (leave) s'en aller; **I must be** ~**ing** il faut que je m'en aille.

····➤ (vanish) **the money's gone** il n'y a plus d'argent; **my bike's gone** mon vélo n'est plus là.

····➤ (work, function) marcher; **is the car** ~**ing?** est-ce que la voiture marche?

····➤ (become) devenir; ~ **blind** devenir aveugle; ~ **pale/red** pâlir/rougir.

····➤ (turn out, progress) aller; **how's it going?** comment ça va?; **how did the exam** ~? comment s'est passé l'examen?

····➤ (in future tenses) **be** ~**ing to do** aller faire.

● noun

····➤ (turn) tour m; (try) essai m; **have a** ~! essaie!; **full of** ~ 🄸 dynamique.

▢ **go across** traverser.

go after poursuivre.

go away partir; ~ **away!** va-t'en!, allez-vous-en!

go back retourner; ~ **back in** rentrer; ~ **back to work** reprendre le travail.

go down (quality, price) baisser; (person) descendre; (sun) se coucher.

go in entrer.

go in for (exam) se présenter à.

go off (leave) partir; (bomb) exploser; (alarm clock) sonner; (milk) tourner; (light) s'éteindre.

go on (continue) continuer; (light) s'allumer; ~ **on doing** continuer à faire; **what's** ~**ing on?** qu'est-ce qui se passe?

go out sortir; (light, fire) s'éteindre.

go over vérifier.

go round (be enough) être assez; ~ **round to see sb** passer voir qn.

go through (check) examiner; (search) fouiller; ~ **through a difficult time** traverser une période difficile.

go **together** aller ensemble.

go **under** (sink) couler; (fail) échouer.

go **up** (*person*) monter; (*price, salary*) augmenter.

: go **without** se passer de.

go-ahead *n* feu *m* vert. ● *a* dynamique.

goal *n* but *m*. ~**keeper** *n* gardien *m* de but. ~**post** *n* poteau *m* de but.

goat *n* chèvre *f*.

gobble *vt* engouffrer.

go-between *n* intermédiaire *mf*.

god *n* dieu *m*. ~**child** *n* (*pl* -**children**) filleul/-e *m/f*. ~**daughter** *n* filleule *f*.

goddess *n* déesse *f*.

god: ~**father** *n* parrain *m*. ~**mother** *n* marraine *f*. ~**send** *n* aubaine *f*. ~**son** *n* filleul *m*.

goggles *npl* lunettes *fpl* (protectrices).

going *n* it is slow/hard ~ c'est lent/difficile. ● *a* (*price, rate*) actuel.

go-kart *n* kart *m*.

gold *n* or *m*. ● *a* en or, d'or.

golden *a* en or, d'or; (in colour) doré; (opportunity) unique.

gold: ~**fish** *n* poisson *m* rouge. ~**-plated** *a* plaqué or. ~**smith** *n* orfèvre *m*.

golf *n* golf *m*. ~**-course** *n* terrain *m* de golf.

gone ⇒GO. ● *a* parti; ~ six o'clock six heures passées; the butter's all ~ il n'y a plus de beurre.

good *a* (**better, best**) bon; (weather) beau; (well-behaved) sage; as ~ as (almost) pratiquement; that's ~ of you c'est gentil (de ta part); be ~ with savoir s'y prendre avec; feel ~ se sentir bien; it is ~ for you ça vous fait du bien. ● *n* bien *m*; do ~ faire

du bien; is it any ~? est-ce que c'est bien?; it's no ~ ça ne vaut rien; it is no ~ shouting ça ne sert à rien de crier; for ~ pour toujours. ~ **afternoon** *interj* bonjour. ~**bye** *interj* & *n* au revoir (*m inv*). ~ **evening** *interj* bonsoir. G~ **Friday** *n* Vendredi *m* saint. ~**-looking** *a* beau. ~ **morning** *interj* bonjour. ~**-natured** *a* gentil.

goodness *n* bonté *f*; my ~! mon Dieu!

good-night *interj* bonsoir, bonne nuit.

goods *npl* marchandises *fpl*.

goodwill *n* bonne volonté *f*.

goose *n* (*pl* **geese**) oie *f*.

gooseberry *n* groseille *f* à maquereau. ~**-pimples** *npl* chair *f* de poule.

gorge *n* (Geog) gorge *f*. ● *vt* ~ **oneself** se gaver (**on** de).

gorgeous *a* magnifique, splendide, formidable.

gorilla *n* gorille *m*.

gory *a* (-**ier, -iest**) sanglant; (horrific: fig) horrible.

gospel *n* évangile *m*; the G~ l'Évangile *m*.

gossip *n* bavardages *mpl*, commérages *mpl*; (person) bavard/ -e *m/f*. ● *vi* bavarder.

got ⇒GET. ● **have** ~ avoir; have ~ **to do** devoir faire.

govern *vt/i* gouverner.

governess *n* gouvernante *f*.

government *n* gouvernement *m*.

governor *n* gouverneur *m*.

gown *n* robe *f*; (of judge, teacher) toge *f*.

GP *abbr* ⇒GENERAL PRACTITIONER.

grab *vt* (*pt* **grabbed**) saisir.

grace *n* grâce *f*. ● *vt* (honour) honorer; (adorn) orner. **graceful** *a* gracieux.

gracious *a* (kind) bienveillant; (elegant) élégant.

G

grade n catégorie f; (of goods) qualité f; (on scale) grade m; (school mark) note f; (class: US) classe f. ● vt classer; (school work) noter. ~ **school** n (US) école f primaire.

gradual a progressif, graduel. **gradually** adv progressivement, peu à peu.

graduate[1] n (Univ) diplômé/-e m/f.

graduate[2] vi obtenir son diplôme. ● vt graduer. **graduation** n remise f des diplômes.

graffiti npl graffiti mpl.

graft n (Med, Bot) greffe f; (work) boulot m. ● vt greffer (**on to** sur); (work) trimer.

grain n (seed, quantity, texture) grain m; (in wood) fibre f.

gram n gramme m.

grammar n grammaire f.

grand a magnifique; (duke, chorus) grand.

grandad n 🔲 papy m.

grand: ~**child** n (girl) petite-fille f; (boy) petit-fils m; **her** ~**children** ses petits-enfants mpl. ~**daughter** n petite-fille f. ~**father** n grand-père m. ~**ma** n = GRANNY. ~**mother** n grand-mère f. ~**parents** npl grands-parents mpl. ~ **piano** n piano m à queue. ~**son** n petit-fils m. ~**stand** n tribune f.

granny n 🔲 mémé f, mamie f.

grant vt (permission) accorder; (request) accéder à; (admit) admettre (**that** que); **take sth for** ~**ed** considérer qch comme une chose acquise. ● n subvention f; (Univ) bourse f.

granule n (of sugar, salt) grain m; (of coffee) granulé m.

grape n grain m de raisin; ~**s** raisin(s) m(pl).

grapefruit n inv pamplemousse m.

graph n graphique m.

graphic a (arts) graphique; (fig) vivant, explicite. **graphics** npl (Comput) graphiques mpl.

grasp vt saisir. ● n (hold) prise f; (strength of hand) poigne f; (reach) portée f; (fig) compréhension f.

grass n herbe f. ~**hopper** n sauterelle f. ~**land** n prairie f.

grass roots npl peuple m. ● a (movement) populaire; (support) de base.

grate n (hearth) âtre m; (fire basket) grille f. ● vt râper. ● vi grincer.

grateful a reconnaissant.

grater n râpe f.

gratified a très heureux. **gratify** vt faire plaisir à.

grating n (bars) grille f; (noise) grincement m.

gratitude n reconnaissance f.

gratuity n (tip) pourboire m; (bounty: Mil) prime f.

grave[1] n tombe f. ● a (serious) grave.

grave[2] a ~ **accent** accent m grave.

gravel n graviers mpl.

grave: ~**stone** n pierre f tombale. ~**yard** n cimetière m.

gravity n (seriousness) gravité f; (force) pesanteur f.

gravy n jus m (de viande).

gray (US) a & n = GREY.

graze vi (eat) paître. ● vt (touch) frôler; (scrape) écorcher. ● n écorchure f.

grease n graisse f. ● vt graisser. **greasy** a graisseux.

great a grand; (very good 🔲) génial 🔲, formidable 🔲, (grandfather, grandmother) arrière.

Great Britain n Grande-Bretagne f.

greatly adv (very) très; (much) beaucoup.

Greece n Grèce f.

greed n avidité f; (for food) gourmandise f. **greedy** a avide; gourmand.

Greek n (person) Grec/-que m/f; (Ling) grec m. ● a grec.

green a vert; (fig) naïf. ● n vert m; (grass) pelouse f; (golf) green m; ~s légumes mpl verts. ~**grocer** n marchand/-e m/f de fruits et légumes.

green house n serre f; ~ **effect** effet m de serre.

greet vt (welcome) accueillir; (address politely) saluer. **greeting** n accueil m.

greetings interj salutations! ● npl (Christmas) vœux mpl. ~ **card** n carte f de vœux.

grew ⇒GROW.

grey a gris; (fig) triste; go ~ (hair, person) grisonner. ● n gris m. ~**hound** n lévrier m.

grid n grille f; (network: Electr) réseau m.

grief n chagrin m; come to ~ (person) avoir un malheur; (fail) tourner mal.

grievance n griefs mpl.

grieve vt/i (s')affliger; ~ **for** pleurer.

grill n (cooking device) gril m; (food) grillade f; (Auto) calandre f. ● vt/i (faire) griller; (interrogate) mettre sur la sellette.

grim a sinistre.

grimace n grimace f. ● vi grimacer.

grime n crasse f.

grin vi (pt **grinned**) sourire. ● n (large) sourire m.

grind vt (pt **ground**) (grain) écraser; (coffee) moudre; (sharpen) aiguiser; ~ **one's teeth** grincer des dents. ● vi ~ **to a halt** s'immobiliser. ● n corvée f.

grip vt (pt **gripped**) saisir; (interest) passionner. ● n prise f; (strength of hand) poigne f; **come to** ~**s with** en venir aux prises avec.

grisly a (-**ier**, -**iest**) (remains) macabre; (sight) horrible.

gristle n cartilage m.

grit n (for roads) sable m; (fig) courage m. ● vt (pt **gritted**) (road) sabler; (teeth) serrer.

groan vi gémir. ● n gémissement m.

grocer n (person) épicier/-ière m/f; (shop) épicerie f. **groceries** npl (shopping) courses fpl; (goods) épicerie f. **grocery** n (shop) épicerie f.

groin n aine f.

groom n marié m; (for horses) palefrenier/-ière m/f. ● vt (horse) panser; (fig) préparer.

groove n (for door etc.) rainure f; (in record) sillon m.

grope vi tâtonner; ~ **for** chercher à tâtons.

gross a (behaviour) vulgaire; (Comm) brut. ● n inv grosse f.

grotto n (pl ~**es**) grotte f.

grouch vi (grumble 🄸) rouspéter, râler.

ground[1] n terre f, sol m; (area) terrain m; (reason) raison f; (Electr, US) masse f; ~**s** terres fpl, parc m; (of coffee) marc m; **on the** ~ par terre; **lose** ~ perdre du terrain. ● vt/i (Naut) échouer; (aircraft) retenir au sol.

ground[2] ⇒GRIND. ● a a ~ **beef** (US) bifteck m haché.

ground: ~ **floor** n rez-de-chaussée m inv. ~**work** n travail m préparatoire.

group n groupe m. ● vt/i (se) grouper. ~**ware** n (Comput) logiciel m de groupe.

grovel vi (pt **grovelled**) ramper.

grow vi (pt **grew**; pp **grown**) (person) grandir; (plant) pousser; (become) devenir; (crime) augmenter. ● vt cultiver; ~ **up**

devenir adulte, grandir. **grower** *n* cultivateur/-trice *m/f*.

growl *vi* (*dog*) gronder; (*person*) grogner. ● *n* grognement *m*.

grown ⇒GROW. ● *a* adulte. **~-up** *a* & *n* adulte (*mf*).

growth *n* (of person, plant) croissance *f*; (in numbers) accroissement *m*; (of hair, tooth) pousse *f*; (Med) grosseur *f*, tumeur *f*.

grudge *vt* ~ doing faire à contrecœur; ~ sb sth (*success, wealth*) en vouloir à qn de qch. ● *n* rancune *f*; **have a ~ against** en vouloir à.

grumble *vi* ronchonner, grogner (**at** après).

grumpy *a* (**-ier, -iest**) grincheux, grognon.

grunt *vi* grogner. ● *n* grognement *m*.

guarantee *n* garantie *f*. ● *vt* garantir.

guard *vt* protéger; (watch) surveiller. ● *vi* ~ **against** se protéger contre. ● *n* (Mil) garde *f*; (person) garde *m*; (on train) chef *m* de train.

guardian *n* gardien/-ne *m/f*; (of orphan) tuteur/-trice *m/f*.

guess *vt/i* deviner; (suppose) penser. ● *n* conjecture *f*.

guest *n* invité/-e *m/f*; (in hotel) client/-e *m/f*. **~-house** *n* pension *f*. **~-room** *n* chambre *f* d'amis.

guidance *n* (advice) conseils *mpl*; (information) information *f*.

guide *n* (person, book) guide *m*; (girl) guide *f*. ● *vt* guider. **~-book** *n* guide *m*. **~-dog** *n* chien *m* d'aveugle. **~line** *n* indication *f*; (advice) conseils *mpl*.

guillotine *n* (for execution) guillotine *f*; (for paper) massicot *m*.

guilt *n* culpabilité *f*. **guilty** *a* coupable.

guinea-pig *n* (animal) cochon *m* d'Inde; (fig) cobaye *m*.

guitar *n* guitare *f*.

gulf *n* (part of sea) golfe *m*; (hollow) gouffre *m*.

gull *n* mouette *f*, (larger) goéland *m*.

gullible *a* crédule.

gully *n* (ravine) ravin *m*; (drain) rigole *f*.

gulp *vt* ~ (**down**) avaler en vitesse. ● *vi* (from fear etc.) avoir la gorge serrée. ● *n* gorgée *f*.

gum *n* (Anat) gencive *f*; (glue) colle *f*; (for chewing) chewing-gum *m*. ● *vt* (*pt* **gummed**) gommer.

gun *n* (pistol) revolver *m*; (rifle) fusil *m*; (large) canon *m*. ● *vt* (*pt* **gunned**) ~ **down** abattre. **~fire** *n* fusillade *f*. **~powder** *n* poudre *f* à canon. **~shot** *n* coup *m* de feu.

gurgle *n* (of water) gargouillement *m*; (of baby) gazouillis *m*. ● *vi* (*water*) gargouiller; (*baby*) gazouiller.

gush *vi* ~ (**out**) jaillir. ● *n* jaillissement *m*.

gust *n* rafale *f*; (of smoke) bouffée *f*.

gut *n* (belly 🔲) ventre *m*. ● *vt* (*pt* **gutted**) (*fish*) vider; (of fire) dévaster. **gutted** *a* 🔲 abattu.

guts *npl* 🔲 (insides of human) tripes *fpl* 🔲; (insides of animal, building) entrailles *fpl*; (courage) cran *m* 🔲.

gutter *n* (on roof) gouttière *f*; (in street) caniveau *m*.

guy *n* (man 🔲) type *m*.

gym *n* (place) gymnase *m*; (activity) gym(nastique) *f*.

gymnasium *n* gymnase *m*.

gymnastics *npl* gymnastique *f*.

gynaecologist *n* gynécologue *mf*.

gypsy *n* bohémien/-ne *m/f*.

habit n habitude f; (costume: Relig) habit m; **be in/get into the ~ of** avoir/prendre l'habitude de.

habitual a (usual) habituel; (*smoker, liar*) invétéré.

hack n (writer) écrivaillon m. ● vi (Comput) pirater; **~ into** s'introduire dans. ● vt tailler.

hacker n (Comput) pirate m informatique.

hackneyed a rebattu.

had ⇒HAVE.

haddock n inv églefin m.

haemorrhage n hémorragie f.

haggard a (*person*) exténué; (*face, look*) défait.

haggle vi marchander; **~ over sth** discuter du prix de qch.

hail n grêle f. ● vt (greet) saluer; (*taxi*) héler. ● vi grêler; **~ from** venir de. **~stone** n grêlon m.

hair n (on head) cheveux mpl; (on body, of animal) poils mpl; (single strand on head) cheveu m; (on body) poil m. **~brush** n brosse f à cheveux. **~cut** n coupe f de cheveux. **~do** n 🄸 coiffure f. **~dresser** n coiffeur/-euse m/f. **~drier** n séchoir m (à cheveux). **~pin** n épingle f à cheveux. **~ remover** n dépilatoire m. **~style** n coiffure f.

hairy a (-ier, -iest) poilu; (terrifying 🄸) horrifiant.

half n (pl **halves**) (part) moitié f; (fraction) demi m; **~ a dozen** une demi-douzaine; **~ an hour** une demi-heure; **four and a ~** quatre et demi; **an hour and a ~** une heure et demie; **~ and half** moitié moitié; **in ~** en deux. ● a demi; **~ price** à moitié prix. ● adv à moitié. **~-back** n (Sport) demi m. **~-hearted** a tiède. **~-mast** n **at ~-mast** en berne. **~-term** n vacances fpl de demi-trimestre. **~-time** n mi-temps f. **~-way** adv à mi-chemin. **~-wit** n imbécile mf.

hall n (in house) entrée f; (corridor) couloir m; (in airport) hall m; (for events) salle f; **~ of residence** résidence f universitaire.

hallmark n (on gold) poinçon m; (fig) caractéristique f.

hallo = HELLO.

Hallowe'en n la veille de la Toussaint.

halt n arrêt m; (temporary) suspension f; (Mil) halte f. ● vt (*proceedings*) interrompre; (*arms sales, experiments*) mettre fin à. ● vi (*vehicle*) s'arrêter; (*army*) faire halte.

halve vt (*time*) réduire de moitié; (*fruit*) couper en deux.

ham n jambon m.

hamburger n hamburger m.

hammer n marteau m. ● vt/i marteler; **~ sth into sth** enfoncer qch dans qch; **~ sth out** (*agreement*) parvenir à qch.

hammock n hamac m.

hamper n panier m. ● vt gêner.

hamster n hamster m.

hand n main f; (of clock) aiguille f; (writing) écriture f; (worker) ouvrier/ -ière m/f; (cards) jeu m; **give sb a ~** donner un coup de main à qn; **at ~** proche; **on ~** disponible; **on the one ~...on the other ~** d'une part...d'autre part; **to ~** à portée de la main. ● vt **~ sb sth**, **~ sth to sb** donner qch à qn. ▫ **~ in** or **over** remettre; **~ out** distribuer. **~bag** n sac m à main. **~-baggage** n bagages mpl à

main. ∼**book** n manuel m.
∼**brake** n frein m à main.
∼**cuffs** npl menottes fpl.

handicap n handicap m. ● vt (pt
handicapped) handicaper.

handkerchief n (pl ∼**s**)
mouchoir m.

handle n (of door, bag) poignée f;
(of implement) manche m; (of cup,
bucket) anse f; (of frying pan) queue
f. ● vt (manage) manier; (deal with)
traiter; (touch) manipuler.

handout n document m; (leaflet)
prospectus m; (money) aumône f.

hands-free kit n kit m mains
libres conducteur.

handshake n poignée f de main.

handsome a (good looking) beau;
(generous) généreux.

handwriting n écriture f.

handy a (-ier, -iest) (book, skill)
utile; (size, shape, tool) pratique;
(person) doué. ∼**man** n (pl
-**men**) bricoleur m.

hang vt (pt **hung**) (from hook,
hanger) accrocher; (from rope)
suspendre; (pt **hanged**) (person)
pendre. ● vi (from hook) être
accroché; (from rope) être
suspendu; (person) être pendu.
● n get the ∼ of doing 🅘 piger
comment faire 🅘. □ ∼**about**
traîner; ∼ **on** 🅘 (hold out) tenir;
(wait) attendre; ∼ **on to sth**
s'agripper à qch; ∼ **out** vi 🅘 (live)
crécher 🅘; (spend time) passer son
temps; ∼ (washing) étendre; ∼
up (telephone) raccrocher.

hanger n (for clothes) cintre m.

hang-gliding n vol m libre.

hangover n gueule f de bois 🅘.

hang-up n 🅘 complexe m.

haphazard a peu méthodique.

happen vi arriver, se passer; ∼ **to**
sb arriver à qn; **it so** ∼**s that** il se
trouve que.

happily adv joyeusement;
(fortunately) heureusement.

happiness n bonheur m.

happy a (-ier, -iest) heureux; **I'm**
not ∼ **about it** je ne suis pas
content; ∼ **with sth** satisfait de
qch; ∼ **medium** juste milieu m.

harass vt harceler. **harassment**
n harcèlement m.

harbour, (US) **harbor** n port m.
● vt (shelter) héberger.

hard a (difficult) difficile, dur;
(evidence, fact) solide; **find it** ∼ **to**
do avoir du mal à faire; ∼ **on sb**
dur envers qn. ● adv (work) dur;
(pull, hit, cry) fort; (think, study)
sérieusement. ∼**board** n
aggloméré m. ∼ **copy** n (Comput)
tirage m. ∼ **disk** n disque m dur.

hardly adv à peine; (expect, hope)
difficilement; ∼ **ever** presque
jamais.

hardship n (poverty) privations fpl;
(ordeal) épreuve f.

hard: ∼ **shoulder** n bande f
d'arrêt d'urgence. ∼ **up** a
🅘 fauché 🅘. ∼**ware** n (Comput)
matériel m, hardware m; (goods)
quincaillerie f. ∼**-working** a
travailleur.

hardy a (-ier, -iest) résistant.

hare n lièvre m.

harm n mal m; **there is no** ∼ **in** il
n'y a pas de mal à. ● vt (person)
faire du mal à; (object)
endommager. **harmful** a nuisible.
harmless a inoffensif.

harmony n harmonie f.

harness n harnais m. ● vt (horse)
harnacher; (use) exploiter.

harp n harpe f. ● vi ∼ **on** (about)
rabâcher.

harrowing a (experience) atroce;
(story) déchirant.

harsh a (punishment) sévère;
(person) dur; (light) cru; (voice)

rude; (*chemical*) corrosif.
harshness *n* dureté *f*.

harvest *n* récolte *f*; **the wine** ∼ les vendanges *fpl*. ● *vt* (*corn*) moissonner; (*vegetables*) récolter.

has ⇒HAVE.

hassle *n* complications *fpl*. ● *vt* Ⓤ talonner (**about** à propos de); (worry) stresser.

haste *n* hâte *f*; **in** ∼ à la hâte; **make** ∼ se dépêcher.

hasty *a* (**-ier, -iest**) précipité.

hat *n* chapeau *m*.

hatch *n* (Aviat) panneau *m* mobile; (Naut) écoutille *f*; (for food) passe-plats *m inv*. ● *vt/i* (*eggs*) (faire) éclore.

hate *n* haine *f*. ● *vt* détester; (violently) haïr; (*sport, food*) avoir horreur de.

hatred *n* haine *f*.

haughty *a* (**-ier, -iest**) hautain.

haul *vt* tirer. ● *n* (by thieves) butin *m*; (by customs) saisie *f*; **it will be a long** ∼ l'étape sera longue; **long/ short** ∼ (*transport*) long/court courrier *m*. **haulage** *n* transport *m* routier. **haulier** *n* (firm) société *f* de transports routiers.

haunt *vt* hanter. ● *n* lieu *m* de prédilection.

have

> present **have**, **has**; past **had**;
> past participle **had**

● *transitive verb*

····▶ (possess) avoir; **I** ∼ (**got**) **a car** j'ai une voiture; **they** ∼ (**got**) **problems** ils ont des problèmes.

····▶ (do sth) ∼ **a try** essayer; ∼ **a bath** prendre un bain.

····▶ ∼ **sth done** faire faire qch; ∼ **your hair cut** se faire couper les cheveux.

● *auxiliary verb*

····▶ (in perfect tenses) avoir; être; **I** ∼ **seen him** je l'ai vu; **she had fallen** elle était tombée.

····▶ (in tag questions) **you've seen her, haven't you?** tu l'as vue, n'est-ce pas?; **you haven't seen her,** ∼ **you?** tu ne l'as pas vue, par hasard?

····▶ (in short answers) '**you've never met him**'—'**yes I** ∼' 'tu ne l'as jamais rencontré'—'mais si!'

····▶ (must) ∼ **to** devoir; **I** ∼ **to go** je dois partir; **you don't** ∼ **to do it** tu n'es pas obligé de le faire.

⟹ For expressions such as **have a walk, have dinner** ⇒**walk, dinner.**

haven *n* refuge *m*; (fig) havre *m*.

havoc *n* dévastation *f*.

hawk *n* faucon *m*.

hay *n* foin *m*; ∼ **fever** rhume *m* des foins.

haywire *a* **go** ∼ (*plans*) dérailler; (*machine*) se détraquer.

hazard *n* risque *m*; ∼ (**warning**) **lights** feux *mpl* de détresse. ● *vt* hasarder.

haze *n* brume *f*.

hazel *n* (bush) noisetier *m*. ∼**nut** *n* noisette *f*.

hazy *a* (**-ier, -iest**) (misty) brumeux; (fig) vague.

he *pron* il; (emphatic) lui; **here** ∼ **is** le voici.

head *n* tête *f*; (leader) chef *m*; (of beer) mousse *f*; ∼**s or tails?** pile ou face? ● *vt* (list) être en tête de; (*team*) être à la tête de; (*chapter*) intituler; ∼ **the ball** faire une tête. ● *vi* ∼ **for** se diriger vers.

headache *n* mal *m* de tête; **have a** ∼ avoir mal à la tête.

heading *n* titre *m*; (subject category) rubrique *f*.

head: ∼**lamp,** ∼**light** *n* phare *m*. ∼**line** *n* gros titre *m*. ∼**master** *n*

H

directeur *m*. ~**mistress** *n* directrice *f*. ~ **office** *n* siège *m* social. ~**on** *a* & *adv* de front. ~**phones** *npl* casque *m*. ~**quarters** *npl* siège *m* social; (Mil) quartier *m* général. ~ **rest** *n* (Auto) repose-tête *m inv*. ~**strong** *a* têtu.

heal *vt/i* guérir.

health *n* santé *f*. ~ **centre** *n* centre *m* médico-social. ~ **food** *n* produits *mpl* diététiques. ~ **insurance** *a* assurance *f* maladie.

healthy *a* (*person, plant, skin, diet*) sain; (*air*) salutaire.

heap *n* tas *m*; ~s of 🔲 un tas de. ● *vt* ~ (**up**) entasser.

hear *vt* (*pt* **heard**) entendre; (*news, rumour*) apprendre; (*lecture, broadcast*) écouter. ● *vi* entendre; ~ **from** recevoir des nouvelles de; ~ **of** *or* **about** entendre parler de.

hearing *n* ouïe *f*; (of case) audience *f*; **give sb a** ~ écouter qn. ~**-aid** *n* prothèse *f* auditive.

hearse *n* corbillard *m*.

heart *n* cœur *m*; ~**s** (cards) cœur *m*; **at** ~ au fond; **by** ~ par cœur; **be** ~-**broken** avoir le cœur brisé; **lose** ~ perdre courage. ~ **attack** *n* crise *f* cardiaque. ~**burn** *n* brûlures *fpl* d'estomac. ~**felt** *a* sincère.

hearth *n* foyer *m*.

heartily *adv* (*greet*) chaleureusement; (*laugh, eat*) de bon cœur.

hearty *a* (-**ier**, -**iest**) (sincere) chaleureux; (*meal*) solide.

heat *n* chaleur *f*; (contest) épreuve *f* éliminatoire. ● *vt* (*house*) chauffer; ~ (**up**) (*food*) faire chauffer; (reheat) réchauffer. **heated** *a* (fig) passionné; (lit) (*pool*) chauffé. **heater** *n* appareil *m* de chauffage.

heather *n* bruyère *f*.

heating *n* chauffage *m*.

heave *vt* (lift) hisser; (pull) traîner péniblement; ~ **a sigh** pousser un soupir. ● *vi* (pull) tirer de toutes ses forces; (retch) avoir un haut-le-cœur.

heaven *n* ciel *m*.

heavily *adv* lourdement; (smoke, drink) beaucoup.

heavy *a* (-**ier**, -**iest**) lourd; (*cold, work*) gros; (*traffic*) dense. ~ **goods vehicle** *n* poids *m* lourd. ~**-handed** *a* maladroit. ~**weight** *n* poids *m* lourd.

Hebrew *n* (person) Hébreu *m*; (Ling) hébreu *m*. ● *a* hébreu; (Ling) hébraïque.

hectic *a* (activity) intense; (*period, day*) mouvementé.

hedge *n* haie *f*. ● *vi* (in answering) se dérober.

hedgehog *n* hérisson *m*.

heel *n* talon *m*.

hefty *a* (-**ier**, -**iest**) (*person*) costaud 🔲; (*object*) pesant.

height *n* hauteur *f*; (of person) taille *f*; (of plane, mountain) altitude *f*; (of fame, glory) apogée *m*; (of joy, folly, pain) comble *m*.

heir *n* héritier/-ière *m/f*. **heiress** *n* héritière *f*. **heirloom** *n* objet *m* de famille.

held ⇒HOLD.

helicopter *n* hélicoptère *m*.

hell *n* enfer *m*.

hello *interj* bonjour!; (on phone) allô!

helmet *n* casque *m*.

help *vt/i* aider (**to do** à faire); ~ (**sb**) **with a bag/the housework** aider qn à porter un sac/à faire le ménage; ~ **oneself** se servir; **he can't** ~ **it** ce n'est pas de sa faute. ● *n* aide *f*. ● *interj* au secours! **helper** *n* aide *mf*. **helpful** *a* utile; (*person*) serviable. **helping** *n* portion *f*. **helpless** *a* impuissant.

hem n ourlet m. ● vt (pt **hemmed**) faire un ourlet à; ~ **in** cerner.

hen n poule f.

hence adv (for this reason) d'où; (from now) d'ici. **henceforth** adv désormais.

hepatitis n hépatite f.

her pron la, l'; (indirect object) lui; it's ~ c'est elle; **for** ~ pour elle. ● a son, sa; pl ses.

herb n herbe f; ~**s** (Culin) fines herbes fpl.

herd n troupeau m.

here adv ici; ~**!** (take this) tiens!; tenez!; ~ **is**, ~ **are** voici; **I'm** ~ je suis là. **hereabouts** adv par ici. **hereafter** adv après; (in book) ci-après. **hereby** adv par le présent acte; (in letter) par la présente.

herewith adv ci-joint.

heritage n patrimoine m.

hernia n hernie f.

hero n (pl ~**es**) héros m.

heroic a héroïque.

heroin n héroïne f.

heroine n héroïne f.

heron n héron m.

herring n hareng m.

hers pron le sien, la sienne, les sien(ne)s; **it is** ~ c'est à elle or le sien or la sienne.

herself pron (emphatic) elle-même; (reflexive) se; **proud of** ~ fière d'elle; **by** ~ toute seule.

hesitate vi hésiter. **hesitation** n hésitation f.

heterosexual a & n hétérosexuel/-le (m/f).

hexagon n hexagone m.

heyday n apogée m.

HGV abbr ⇒HEAVY GOODS VEHICLE.

hi interj 🔲 salut! 🔲.

hiccup n hoquet m; (the) ~**s** le hoquet. ● vi hoqueter.

hide vt (pt **hid**; pp **hidden**) cacher (**from** à). ● vi se cacher (**from** de); **go into hiding** se cacher. ● n (skin) peau f.

hideous a (monster, object) hideux; (noise) affreux.

hiding n (go into) ~ se cacher; **give sb a** ~ administrer une correction à qn.

hierarchy n hiérarchie f.

hi-fi n (chaîne f) hi-fi f inv.

high a haut; (price, number) élevé; (priest, speed) grand; (voice) aigu; **in the** ~ **season** en pleine saison. ● n a (new) ~ un niveau record. ● adv haut. ~**brow** a & n intellectuel/-le (m/f). ~ **chair** n chaise f haute. ~ **court** n cour f suprême. **higher education** n enseignement m supérieur. ~-**jump** n saut m en hauteur. ~-**level** a à haut niveau.

highlight n (best moment) point m fort; ~**s** (in hair) reflet m; (artificial) mèches fpl; (Sport) résumé m. ● vt (emphasize) souligner.

highly adv extrêmement; (paid) très bien; **speak/think** ~ **of** dire/penser beaucoup de bien de.

Highness n Altesse f.

high: ~-**rise** (building) n tour f. ~ **school** n lycée m. ~-**speed** a (train) à grande vitesse; (film) ultrarapide. ~ **street** n rue f principale. ~-**tech** a de pointe.

highway n route f nationale; (US) autoroute f; ~ **code** code m de la route.

hijack vt détourner. ● n détournement m. **hijacker** n pirate m (de l'air).

hike n randonnée f; **price** ~ hausse f de prix. ● vi faire de la randonnée.

hilarious a désopilant.

hill n colline f; (slope) côte f. **hilly** a vallonné.

him *pron* le, l'; (indirect object) lui; it's ~ c'est lui; **for** ~ pour lui.

himself *pron* (emphatic) lui-même; (reflexive) se; **proud of** ~ fier de lui; **by** ~ tout seul.

hind *a* de derrière.

hinder *vt* (hamper) gêner; (prevent) empêcher. **hindrance** *n* obstacle *m*, gêne *f*.

hindsight *n* **with** ~ rétrospectivement.

Hindu *n* Hindou/-e *m/f*. ● *a* hindou.

hinge *n* charnière *f*. ● *vi* ~ **on** dépendre de.

hint *n* allusion *f*; (of spice, accent) pointe *f*; (of colour) touche *f*; (advice) conseil *m*. ● *vt* laisser entendre. ● *vi* ~ **at** faire allusion à.

hip *n* hanche *f*.

hippopotamus *n* (*pl* ~es) hippopotame *m*.

hire *vt* (thing) louer; (person) engager. ● *n* location *f*. ~-**car** *n* voiture *f* de location. ~-**purchase** *n* achat *m* à crédit.

his *a* son, sa, *pl* ses. ● *pron* le sien, la sienne, les sien(ne)s; **it is** ~ c'est à lui *or* le sien *or* la sienne.

hiss *n* sifflement *m*. ● *vt/i* siffler.

history *n* histoire *f*; **make** ~ entrer dans l'histoire.

hit *vt* (*pt* **hit**; *pres p* **hitting**) frapper; (collide with) heurter; (find) trouver; (affect, reach) toucher. ● *vi* ~ **on** (find) tomber sur; ~ **it off** s'entendre bien (**with** avec). ● *n* (blow) coup *m*; (fig) succès *m*; (song) tube *m* 🔲; (on Internet) (visit) visite *f*, accès *m*; (result) page *f* trouvée, résultat *m*.

hitch *vt* (fasten) accrocher; ~ **up** remonter. ● *n* (snag) anicroche *f*. ~-**hike** *vi* faire du stop 🔲. ~-**hiker** *n* auto-stoppeur/-euse *m/f*.

hi-tech *a* & *n* = HIGH-TECH.

HIV *abbr* (**human immunodeficiency virus**) VIH *m*.

hive *n* ruche *f*. ● *vt* ~ **off** séparer; (industry) céder.

HIV-positive *a* séropositif.

hoard *vt* amasser; (supplies) stocker. ● *n* trésor *m*; (of provisions) provisions *fpl*.

hoarse *a* enroué.

hoax *n* canular *m*.

hobby *n* passe-temps *m inv*.

hockey *n* hockey *m*.

hog *n* cochon *m*. ● *vt* (*pt* **hogged**) 🔲 monopoliser.

hold *vt* (*pt* **held**) tenir; (contain) contenir; (conversation, opinion) avoir; (shares, record, person) détenir; ~ (**the line**), please ne quittez pas. ● *vi* (rope, weather) tenir. ● *n* prise *f*; **get** ~ **of** attraper; (ticket) se procurer; (person) (by phone) joindre; **on** ~ en attente. ◻ ~ **back** (contain) retenir; (hide) cacher; ~ **down** (job) garder; (person) maîtriser; (costs) limiter; ~ **on** (stand firm) tenir bon; (wait) attendre; ~ **on to** (keep) garder; (cling to) se cramponner à; ~ **out** *vt* (offer) offrir; *vi* (resist) tenir le coup; ~ **up** (support) soutenir; (delay) retarder; (rob) attaquer.

holder *n* détenteur/-trice *m/f*; (of passport, post) titulaire *mf*; (for object) support *m*.

hold-up *n* retard *m*; (of traffic) embouteillage *m*; (robbery) hold-up *m inv*.

hole *n* trou *m*.

holiday *n* vacances *fpl*; (public) jour *m* férié; (time off) congé *m*. ● *vi* passer ses vacances. ● *a* de vacances. ~-**maker** *n* vacancier/ -ière *m/f*.

Holland *n* Hollande *f*.

hollow *a* creux; (fig) faux. ● *n* creux *m*. ● *vt* creuser.

holly *n* houx *m*.

holy *a* (**-ier, -iest**) saint; (water) bénit; **H~ Ghost, H~ Spirit** Saint-Esprit *m*.

homage *n* hommage *m*.

home *n* (place to live) logement *m*; maison *f*; (institution) maison *f*; (family base) foyer *m*; (country) pays *m*. ● *a* de la maison, du foyer; (of family) de famille; (Pol) intérieur; (*match, visit*) à domicile. ● *adv* (at) ~ à la maison, chez soi; **come** *or* **go** ~ rentrer; (from abroad) rentrer dans son pays; **feel at** ~ **with** être à l'aise avec. ~ **computer** *n* ordinateur *m*, PC *m*.

homeless *a* sans abri. ● *n* the ~ les sans-abri *mpl*.

homely *a* (**-ier, -iest**) (cosy) accueillant; (simple) sans prétention; (person: US) sans attraits.

home: ~**-made** *a* (fait) maison. **H~ Office** *n* ministère *m* de l'Intérieur. ~ **page** *n* (Internet) page *f* d'accueil. **H~ Secretary** *n* Ministre *m* de l'Intérieur. ~**sick** *a* **be** ~**sick** avoir le mal du pays. ~**work** *n* devoirs *mpl*.

homosexual *a & n* homosexuel/ -le (*m/f*).

honest *a* (truthful) intègre; (trustworthy) honnête; (sincere) franc. **honestly** *adv* honnêtement, franchement. **honesty** *n* honnêteté *f*.

honey *n* miel *m*; (person 🔲) chéri/ -e *m/f*. ~**moon** *n* voyage *m* de noces; (fig) lune *f* de miel.

honk *vi* klaxonner.

honorary *a* (person) honoraire; (degree) honorifique.

honour, (US) **honor** *n* honneur *m*. ● *vt* honorer.

hood *n* capuchon *m*; (on car, pram) capote *f*; (car engine cover: US) capot *m*.

hoof *n* (*pl* ~**s**) sabot *m*.

hook *n* crochet *m*; (on garment) agrafe *f*; (for fishing) hameçon *m*; **off the** ~ tiré d'affaire; (phone) décroché. ● *vt* accrocher.

hoot *n* (of owl) (h)ululement *m*; (of car) coup *m* de klaxon. ● *vi* (owl) (h)ululer; (car) klaxonner; (jeer) huer.

hoover *vt* ~ **a room** passer l'aspirateur dans une pièce.

Hoover® *n* aspirateur *m*.

hop *vi* (*pt* **hopped**) sauter (à cloche-pied); ~ **in!** 🔲 vas-y, monte! ● *n* bond *m*; ~**s** houblon *m*.

hope *n* espoir *m*. ● *vt/i* espérer; ~ **for** espérer avoir; **I** ~ **so** je l'espère.

hopeful *a* (news, sign) encourageant; (person) plein d'espoir; (mood) optimiste. **hopefully** *adv* (with luck) avec un peu de chance; (with hope) avec optimisme.

hopeless *a* désespéré; (useless: fig) nul 🔲.

horizon *n* horizon *m*.

horizontal *a* horizontal.

hormone *n* hormone *f*.

horn *n* corne *f*, (of car) klaxon® *m*; (Mus) cor *m*.

horoscope *n* horoscope *m*.

horrible *a* horrible.

horrid *a* horrible.

horrific *a* horrifiant.

horrify *vt* horrifier.

horror *n* horreur *f*. ● *a* (film, story) d'épouvante.

horse *n* cheval *m*. ~**back** *n* on ~**back** à cheval. ~**chestnut** *n* marron *m* (d'Inde). ~**man** *n* (*pl* **-men**) cavalier *m*. ~**power** *n* puissance *f* (en chevaux). ~**race** *n* course *f* de chevaux. ~**radish** *n* raifort *m*. ~**shoe** *n* fer *m* à cheval. ~**show** *n* concours *m* hippique.

H

hose *n* tuyau *m*. ● *vt* arroser.
~-**pipe** *n* tuyau *m*.

hospitable *a* hospitalier.

hospital *n* hôpital *m*.

host *n* (to guests) hôte *m*; (on TV)
animateur *m*; (Internet) ordinateur
m hôte; **a** ~ **of** une foule de;
(Relig) hostie *f*.

hostage *n* otage *m*; **hold sb** ~
garder qn en otage.

hostel *n* foyer *m*; (youth) ~
auberge *f* (de jeunesse).

hostess *n* hôtesse *f*.

hostile *a* hostile.

hot *a* (**hotter, hottest**) chaud;
(Culin) épicé; **be** *or* **feel** ~ avoir
chaud; **it is** ~ il fait chaud; **in** ~
water 🖭 dans le pétrin. ● *vt/i* (*pt*
hotted) ~ **up** 🖭 chauffer. ● **air
balloon** *n* montgolfière *f*. ~ **dog**
n hot-dog *m*.

hotel *n* hôtel *m*.

hot: ~**headed** *a* impétueux. ~
list *n* (Internet) signets *mpl* favoris.
~**plate** *n* plaque *f* chauffante. ~
water bottle *n* bouillotte *f*.

hound *n* chien *m* de chasse. ● *vt*
poursuivre.

hour *n* heure *f*.

hourly *a* horaire; **on an** ~ **basis** à
l'heure. ● *adv* toutes les heures.

house[1] *n* maison *f*; (Pol) Chambre
f; **on the** ~ aux frais de la
maison.

house[2] *vt* loger; (of building)
abriter.

household *n* (house, family)
ménage *m*. ● *a* ménager.

house: ~**keeper** *n* gouvernante
f. ~-**proud** *a* méticuleux.
~-**warming** *n* pendaison *f* de
crémaillère. ~**wife** *n* (*pl* -**wives**)
ménagère *f*. ~**work** *n* travaux
mpl ménagers.

housing *n* logement *m*; ~
association service *m* de
logement; ~ **development** cité *f*;
(smaller) lotissement *m*.

hover *vi* (*bird*) voleter; (vacillate)
vaciller. **hovercraft** *n*
aéroglisseur *m*.

how *adv* comment; ~ **are you?**
comment allez-vous?; ~ **long/tall
is...?** quelle est la longueur/
hauteur de...?; ~ **many?,** ~
much? combien?; ~ **pretty!**
comme *or* que c'est joli!; ~ **about
a walk?** si on faisait une
promenade?; ~ **do you do?**
(greeting) enchanté.

however *adv* (nevertheless)
cependant; ~ **hard I try** j'ai beau
essayer; ~ **much it costs** quel que
soit le prix; ~ **young/poor he is** si
jeune/pauvre soit-il; ~ **you like**
comme tu veux.

howl *n* hurlement *m*. ● *vi* hurler.

HP *abbr* ⇒HIRE-PURCHASE.

hp *abbr* ⇒HORSEPOWER.

HQ *abbr* ⇒HEADQUARTERS.

hub *n* moyeu *m*; (fig) centre *m*.

hug *vt* (*pt* **hugged**) serrer dans
ses bras. ● *n* étreinte *f*; **give sb a**
~ serrer qn dans ses bras.

huge *a* énorme.

hull *n* (of ship) coque *f*.

hum *vt/i* (*pt* **hummed**) (*person*)
fredonner; (*insect*) bourdonner;
(*engine*) ronronner. ● *n*
bourdonnement *m*;
ronronnement *m*.

human *a* humain. ● *n* humain *m*.
~ **being** *n* être *m* humain.

humane *a* (*person*) humain; (*act*)
d'humanité; (*killing*) sans
cruauté.

humanitarian *a* humanitaire.

humanity *n* humanité *f*.

humble *a* humble.

humid *a* humide.

humiliate *vt* humilier.

humorous *a* humoristique;
(*person*) plein d'humour.

humour, (US **humor**) *n* humour

m; (mood) humeur *f*. ● *vt*
amadouer.

hump *n* bosse *f*. ● *vt* 🇮 porter.

hunchback *n* bossu/-e *m/f*.

hundred *a & n* cent (*m*); **two ~
and one** deux cent un; **~s of** des
centaines de. **hundredth** *a & n*
centième (*mf*).

hung ⇒HANG.

Hungarian *n* (person) Hongrois/-e
m/f; (Ling) hongrois *m*. ● *a*
hongrois. **Hungary** *n* Hongrie *f*.

hunger *n* faim *f*. ● *vi* **~ for** avoir
faim de.

hungry *a* (**-ier, -iest**) affamé; **be
~** avoir faim.

hunt *vt/i* chasser; **~ for** chercher.
● *n* chasse *f*. **hunter** *n* chasseur
m. **hunting** *n* chasse *f*.

hurdle *n* (Sport) haie *f*; (fig)
obstacle *m*.

hurricane *n* ouragan *m*.

hurry *vi* se dépêcher; **~ out** sortir
précipitamment. ● *vt* (*work*)
terminer à la hâte; (*person*)
bousculer. ● *n* hâte *f*; **in a ~**
pressé.

hurt *vt/i* (*pt* hurt) faire mal (à);
(injure, offend) blesser. ● *a* blessé.
● *n* blessure *f*.

hurtle *vi* **~ down** dévaler; **~ along
a road** foncer sur une route.

husband *n* mari *m*.

hush *vt* faire taire; **~ up** (*news*)
étouffer. ● *n* silence *m*. ● *interj*
chut!

husky *a* (**-ier, -iest**) enroué. ● *n*
husky *m*.

hustle *vt* (push, rush) bousculer.
● *vi* (hurry) se dépêcher; (work: US)
se démener. ● *n* **~ and bustle**
agitation *f*.

hut *n* cabane *f*.

hyacinth *n* jacinthe *f*.

hydrant *n* (fire) **~** bouche *f*
d'incendie.

hydraulic *a* hydraulique.

hydroelectric *a* hydroélectrique.

hydrogen *n* hydrogène *m*; **~
bomb** bombe *f* à hydrogène.

hyena *n* hyène *f*.

hygiene *n* hygiène *f*. **hygienic** *a*
hygiénique.

hymn *n* cantique *m*; (fig) hymne
m.

hype *n* 🇮 battage *m* publicitaire.
● *vt* **~ (up)** (*film, book*) faire du
battage pour.

hyperactive *a* hyperactif.

hyperlink *n* hyperlien *m*.

hypermarket *n* hypermarché *m*.

hypertext *n* hypertexte *m*.

hyphen *n* trait *m* d'union.

hypnosis *n* hypnose *f*.

hypocrisy *n* hypocrisie *f*.
hypocrite *n* hypocrite *mf*.
hypocritical *a* hypocrite.

hypothesis *n* (*pl* **-ses**)
hypothèse *f*.

hysteria *n* hystérie *f*. **hysterical**
a hystérique.

hysterics *npl* crise *f* de nerfs; **be
in ~** rire aux larmes.

I *pron* je, j'; (stressed) moi.

ice *n* glace *f*; (on road) verglas *m*.
● *vt* (*cake*) glacer. ● *vi* **~ (up)**
(*window*) se givrer; (*river*) geler.
~box *n* (US) réfrigérateur *m*.
~-cream *n* glace *f*. **~-cube** *n*
glaçon *m*. **~ hockey** *n* hockey *m*
sur glace.

Iceland *n* Islande *f*. **Icelander** *n*
Islandais/-e *m/f*. **Icelandic** *a & n*
islandais (*m*).

ice: ~ lolly *n* glace *f* (sur

bâtonnet). ∼ **rink** *n* patinoire *f*. ∼
skate *n* patin *m* à glace.

icicle *n* stalactite *f* (de glace).

icing *n* (sugar) glaçage *m*.

icy *a* (**-ier, -iest**) (*hands, wind*)
glacé; (*road*) verglacé; (*manner,
welcome*) glacial.

ID *n* pièce *f* d'identité; ∼ **card**
carte *f* d'identité.

idea *n* idée *f*.

ideal *a* idéal. ● *n* idéal *m*.

identical *a* identique.

identification *n* identification *f*;
(*papers*) pièce *f* d'identité.

identify *vt* identifier. ● *vi* ∼ **with**
s'identifier à.

identikit *n* ∼ **picture** portrait-
robot *m*.

identity *n* identité *f*.

ideological *a* idéologique.

idiom *n* (phrase) idiome *m*;
(language) parler *m*, langue *f*.
idiomatic *a* idiomatique.

idiosyncrasy *n* particularité *f*.

idiot *n* idiot/-e *m/f*. **idiotic** *a*
idiot.

idle *a* (lazy) paresseux; (doing
nothing) oisif; (*boast, threat*) vain.
● *vi* (engine) tourner au ralenti.
● *vt* ∼ **away** gaspiller.

idol *n* idole *f*. **idolize** *vt* idolâtrer.

idyllic *a* idyllique.

i.e. *abbr* c-à-d, c'est-à-dire.

if *conj* si.

ignite *vt/i* (s')enflammer.

ignition *n* (Auto) allumage *m*; ∼
(switch) contact *m*; ∼ **key** clé *f* de
contact.

ignorance *n* ignorance *f*.
ignorant *a* ignorant (**of** de).
ignorantly *adv* par ignorance.

ignore *vt* (person) ignorer;
(mistake, remark) ne pas relever;
(feeling, fact) ne pas tenir
compte de.

ill *a* malade. ● *adv* mal. ● *n* mal
m. ∼**-advised** *a* malavisé. ∼ **at**

ease *a* mal à l'aise. ∼**-bred** *a*
mal élevé.

illegal *a* illégal.

illegible *a* illisible.

illegitimate *a* illégitime.

ill: ∼**-fated** *a* malheureux. ∼
feeling *n* ressentiment *m*.

illiterate *a* & *n* analphabète (*mf*).

illness *n* maladie *f*.

ill-treat *vt* maltraiter.

illuminate *vt* éclairer; (decorate with
lights) illuminer. **illumination** *n*
éclairage *m*; illumination *f*.

illusion *n* illusion *f*.

illustrate *vt* illustrer. **illustration**
n illustration *f*. **illustrative** *a* qui
illustre.

image *n* image *f*; (of firm, person)
image *f* de marque. **imagery** *n*
images *fpl*.

imaginable *a* imaginable.
imaginary *a* imaginaire.
imagination *n* imagination *f*.
imaginative *a* plein
d'imagination.

imagine *vt* (s')imaginer (**that**
que); ∼ **being rich** s'imaginer
riche.

imbalance *n* déséquilibre *m*.

imitate *vt* imiter.

immaculate *a* impeccable.

immaterial *a* sans importance
(**to** pour; **that** que).

immature *a* (person) immature;
(plant) qui n'est pas arrivé à
maturité.

immediate *a* immédiat.

immediately *adv*
immédiatement. ● *conj* dès que.

immense *a* immense.
immensely *adv* extrêmement,
immensément. **immensity** *n*
immensité *f*.

immerse *vt* plonger (**in** dans).
immersion *n* immersion *f*;
immersion heater chauffe-eau *m*
inv électrique.

immigrant n & a immigré/-e (m/ f); (newly-arrived) immigrant/-e (m/ f). **immigrate** vi immigrer. **immigration** n immigration f.

imminent a imminent.

immobilizer n système m antidémarrage.

immoral a immoral.

immortal a immortel.

immune a immunisé (**from, to** contre); (reaction, system) immunitaire. **immunity** n immunité f. **immunization** n immunisation f. **immunize** vt immuniser.

impact n impact m.

impair vt (performance) affecter; (ability) affaiblir.

impart vt communiquer, transmettre.

impartial a impartial.

impassable a (barrier) infranchissable; (road) impraticable.

impassive a impassible.

impatience n impatience f. **impatient** a impatient; **get impatient** s'impatienter. **impatiently** adv impatiemment.

impeccable a impeccable.

impede vt entraver.

impediment n entrave f; **speech ~** défaut m d'élocution.

impending a imminent.

imperative a urgent. ● n impératif m.

imperfect a incomplet; (faulty) défectueux. ● n (Gram) imparfait m. **imperfection** n imperfection f.

imperial a impérial; (measure) conforme aux normes britanniques. **imperialism** n impérialisme m.

impersonal a impersonnel.

impersonate vt se faire passer pour; (mimic) imiter.

impertinent a impertinent.

impervious a imperméable (**to** à).

impetuous a impétueux.

impetus n impulsion f.

impinge vi **~ on** affecter; (encroach) empiéter sur.

implement n instrument m; (tool) outil m. ● vt exécuter, mettre en application; (software) implanter.

implicit a (implied) implicite (**in** dans); (unquestioning) absolu.

imply vt (assume, mean) impliquer; (insinuate) laisser entendre.

impolite a impoli.

import[1] vt importer.

import[2] n (article) importation f; (meaning) signification f.

importance n importance f. **important** a important.

impose vt imposer (**on sb** à qn; **on sth** sur qch). ● vi s'imposer; **~ on sb** abuser de la bienveillance de qn. **imposing** a imposant.

impossible a impossible. ● n **the ~** l'impossible m.

impotent a impuissant.

impound vt confisquer, saisir.

impoverish vt appauvrir.

impractical a peu réaliste.

impregnable a imprenable.

impress vt impressionner; **~ sth on sb** faire bien comprendre qch à qn. **impression** n impression f. **impressionable** a impressionnable. **impressive** a impressionnant.

imprint[1] n empreinte f.

imprint[2] vt (fix) graver (**on** dans); (print) imprimer.

imprison vt emprisonner.

improbable a (not likely) improbable; (incredible) invraisemblable.

improper a (unseemly) malséant; (dishonest) irrégulier.

improve *vt/i* (s')améliorer.
improvement *n* amélioration *f*.

improvise *vt/i* improviser.

impudent *a* impudent.

impulse *n* impulsion *f*; on ~ sur un coup de tête. **impulsive** *a* impulsif. **impulsively** *adv* par impulsion.

impurity *n* impureté *f*.

in *prep* (inside, within) dans; (expressing place, position) à, en; (expressing time) en, dans; ~ **the box/garden** dans la boîte/le jardin; ~ **Paris/school** à Paris/ l'école; ~ **town** en ville; ~ **the country** à la campagne; ~ **English** en anglais; ~ **India** en Inde; ~ **Japan** au Japon; ~ **winter** en hiver; ~ **spring** au printemps; ~ **an hour** (at end of) au bout d'une heure; ~ **an hour('s time)** dans une heure; ~ **(the space of) an hour** en une heure; ~ **doing** en faisant; ~ **the evening** le soir; one ~ **ten** un sur dix; ~ **between** entre les deux; (time) entretemps; ~ **a firm voice** d'une voix ferme; ~ **blue** en bleu; ~ **ink** à l'encre; ~ **uniform** en uniforme; ~ **a skirt** en jupe; ~ **a whisper** en chuchotant; ~ **a loud voice** d'une voix forte; **the best** ~ le meilleur de; **we are** ~ **for** on va avoir; **have it** ~ **for sb** 𝕀 avoir qn dans le collimateur. ● *adv* (inside) dedans; (at home) là, à la maison; (in fashion) à la mode; **come** ~ entrer; **run** ~ entrer en courant.

inability *n* incapacité *f* (**to do** de faire).

inaccessible *a* inaccessible.

inaccurate *a* inexact.

inactive *a* inactif. **inactivity** *n* inaction *f*.

inadequate *a* insuffisant.

inadvertently *adv* par mégarde.

inadvisable *a* inopportun, à déconseiller.

inane *a* idiot, débile.

inanimate *a* inanimé.

inappropriate *a* inopportun; (*term*) inapproprié.

inarticulate *a* qui a du mal à s'exprimer.

inasmuch as *adv* dans la mesure où; (because) vu que.

inaugurate *vt* (open, begin) inaugurer; (*person*) investir.

inborn *a* inné.

inbred *a* (inborn) inné.

Inc. *abbr* (**incorporated**) S.A.

incapable *a* incapable (**of doing** de faire).

incapacitate *vt* immobiliser.

incense[1] *n* encens *m*.

incense[2] *vt* mettre en fureur.

incentive *n* motivation *f*; (payment) prime *f*.

incessant *a* incessant. **incessantly** *adv* sans cesse.

incest *n* inceste *m*. **incestuous** *a* incestueux.

inch *n* pouce *m* (=2.54 cm.). ● *vi* ~ **towards** se diriger petit à petit vers.

incidence *n* fréquence *f*.

incident *n* incident *m*. **incidental** *a* secondaire. **incidentally** *adv* à propos; (by chance) par la même occasion.

incinerate *vt* incinérer. **incinerator** *n* incinérateur *m*.

incite *vt* inciter, pousser.

inclination *n* (tendency) tendance *f*; (desire) envie *f*.

incline[1] *vt/i* (s')incliner; **be** ~**d to** avoir tendance à.

incline[2] *n* pente *f*.

include *vt* comprendre, inclure. **including** *prep* (y) compris. **inclusion** *n* inclusion *f*.

inclusive *a & adv* inclus; ~ **of delivery** livraison comprise.

income *n* revenus *mpl*; ~ **tax** impôt *m* sur le revenu.

incoming a (*tide*) montant; (*tenant, government*) nouveau; (*call*) qui vient de l'extérieur.

incompatible a incompatible.

incompetent a incompétent.

incomplete a incomplet.

incomprehensible a incompréhensible.

inconceivable a inconcevable.

inconclusive a peu concluant.

incongruous a déconcertant, surprenant.

inconsiderate a (*person*) peu attentif à autrui; (*act*) maladroit.

inconsistent a (*argument*) incohérent; (*performance*) inégal; (*behaviour*) changeant; ~ **with** en contradiction avec.

inconspicuous a qui passe inaperçu.

incontinent a incontinent.

inconvenience n dérangement m; (*drawback*) inconvénient m. ● vt déranger. **inconvenient** a incommode; **if it's not inconvenient for you** si cela ne vous dérange pas.

incorporate vt incorporer (**into** dans); (*contain*) comporter.

incorrect a incorrect.

increase[1] n augmentation f (**in**, **of** de); **be on the** ~ être en progression.

increase[2] vt/i augmenter. **increasing** a croissant. **increasingly** adv de plus en plus.

incredible a incroyable.

incriminate vt incriminer. **incriminating** a compromettant.

incubate vt (*eggs*) couver. **incubation** n incubation f. **incubator** n couveuse f.

incur vt (*pt* **incurred**) (*penalty, anger*) encourir; (*debts*) contracter.

indebted a ~ **to sb** redevable à

qn (**for** de); (*grateful*) reconnaissant à qn.

indecent a indécent.

indecisive a indécis; (*ending*) peu concluant.

indeed adv en effet; (*emphatic*) vraiment.

indefinite a vague; (*period, delay*) illimité. **indefinitely** adv indéfiniment.

indelible a indélébile.

indemnity n (*protection*) assurance f; (*payment*) indemnité f.

indent vt (*text*) renfoncer. **indentation** n (dent) marque f.

independence n indépendance f. **independent** a indépendant. **independently** adv de façon indépendante; **independently of** indépendamment de.

index n (*pl* ~**es**) (in book) index m; (in library) catalogue m; (in economy) indice m; ~ **card** fiche f; ~ (**finger**) index m. ● vt classer. ~**-linked** a indexé.

India n Inde f.

Indian n Indien/-ne m/f. ● a indien.

indicate vt indiquer. **indication** n indication f.

indicative a & n indicatif (m).

indicator n (pointer) aiguille f; (on vehicle) clignotant m; (board) tableau m.

indict vt inculper. **indictment** n accusation f.

indifferent a indifférent; (not good) médiocre.

indigenous a indigène.

indigestible a indigeste. **indigestion** n indigestion f.

indignant a indigné.

indirect a indirect. **indirectly** adv indirectement.

indiscreet a indiscret. **indiscretion** n indiscrétion f.

indiscriminate a sans

distinction. **indiscriminately** adv sans distinction.

indisputable a indiscutable.

individual a individuel; (tuition) particulier. ● n individu m.
individualist n individualiste mf.
individuality n individualité f.
individually adv individuellement.

indoctrinate vt endoctriner.
indoctrination n endoctrinement m.

indolent a indolent.

Indonesia n Indonésie f.

indoor a (clothes) d'intérieur; (pool, court) couvert. **indoors** adv à l'intérieur.

induce vt (influence) persuader; (stronger) inciter (to do à faire).
inducement n (financial) récompense f; (incentive) motivation f.

induction n (Electr) induction f; (inauguration) installation f.

indulge vt (person, whim) céder à; (child) gâter. ● vi ~ **in** se livrer à. **indulgence** n indulgence f; (treat) plaisir m. **indulgent** a indulgent.

industrial a industriel; (accident) du travail; ~ **action** grève f; ~ **dispute** conflit m social.
industrialist n industriel/-le m/f.
industrialized a industrialisé.
industrious a diligent.
industry n industrie f; (zeal) zèle m.

inebriated a ivre.

inedible a immangeable.

ineffective a inefficace.

inefficient a inefficace; (person) incompétent.

ineligible a inéligible; **be** ~ **for** ne pas avoir droit à.

inept a incompétent; (tactless) maladroit.

inequality n inégalité f.

inescapable a indéniable.

inevitable a inévitable.

inexcusable a inexcusable.

inexhaustible a inépuisable.

inexpensive a pas cher.

inexperience n inexpérience f.
inexperienced a inexpérimenté.

infallible a infaillible.

infamous a (person) tristement célèbre; (deed) infâme.

infancy n petite enfance f; **in its** ~ (fig) à ses débuts mpl. **infant** n (baby) bébé m; (at school) enfant m.

infantile a infantile.

infatuated a ~ **with** entiché de.
infatuation n engouement m.

infect vt contaminer; ~ **sb with sth** transmettre qch à qn.
infection n infection f.
infectious a contagieux.

infer vt (pt **inferred**) (deduce) déduire.

inferior a inférieur (to à); (work, product) de qualité inférieure.
● n inférieur/-e m/f. **inferiority** n infériorité f.

inferno n (hell) enfer m; (blaze) brasier m.

infertile a infertile.

infest vt infester (with de).

infidelity n infidélité f.

infighting n conflits mpl internes.

infinite a infini. **infinitely** adv infiniment. **infinitive** n infinitif m. **infinity** n infinité f.

infirm a infirme. **infirmary** n hôpital m; (sick-bay) infirmerie f.
infirmity n infirmité f.

inflame vt enflammer.
inflammable a inflammable.
inflammation n inflammation f.
inflammatory a incendiaire.

inflatable a gonflable. **inflate** vt (lit, fig) gonfler.

inflation n inflation f.

inflection n (of word root) flexion f; (of vowel, voice) inflexion f.

inflict vt infliger (**on** à).

influence n influence f; **under the ~** (drunk 🔲) éméché. ● vt (person) influencer; (choice) influer sur. **influential** a (powerful) influent; (theory, artist) très suivi.

influenza n grippe f.

influx n afflux m.

inform vt informer (**of** de); **keep ~ed** tenir au courant.

informal a (simple) simple, sans façons; (unofficial) officieux; (colloquial) familier. **informality** n simplicité f. **informally** adv (dress) en tenue décontractée; (speak) en toute simplicité.

informant n indicateur/-trice m/f.

information n renseignements mpl, informations fpl; **some ~** un renseignement. **~ superhighway** n autoroute f de l'information. **~ technology** n informatique f.

informative a (book) riche en renseignements; (visit) instructif.

informer n indicateur/-trice m/f.

infrequent a rare.

infringe vt (rule) enfreindre; (rights) ne pas respecter. **infringement** n infraction f.

infuriate vt exaspérer.

ingenuity n ingéniosité f.

ingot n lingot m.

ingrained a (hatred) enraciné; (dirt) bien incrusté.

ingratiate vt **~ oneself with** se faire bien voir de.

ingredient n ingrédient m.

inhabit vt habiter. **inhabitable** a habitable. **inhabitant** n habitant/-e m/f.

inhale vt inhaler; (smoke) avaler. **inhaler** n inhalateur m.

inherent a inhérent (**in** à). **inherently** adv en soi, par sa nature.

inherit vt hériter de; **~ sth from sb** hériter qch de qn. **inheritance** n héritage m.

inhibit vt (restrain) inhiber; (prevent) entraver.

inhospitable a inhospitalier.

inhuman a inhumain.

initial n initiale f. ● vt (pt **initialled**) parapher. ● a initial.

initiate vt (project) mettre en œuvre; (talks) amorcer; (person) initier (**into** à). **initiation** n initiation f; (start) amorce f.

initiative n initiative f.

inject vt injecter (**into** dans); (new element: fig) insuffler (**into** à). **injection** n injection f, piqûre f.

injure vt blesser; (damage) nuire à. **injury** n blessure f.

injustice n injustice f.

ink n encre f.

inkling n petite idée f.

inland a intérieur; **I~ Revenue** service m des impôts britannique.

in-laws npl (parents) beaux-parents mpl; (family) belle-famille f.

inlay[1] vt (pt **inlaid**) incruster (**with** de); (on wood) marqueter.

inlay[2] n incrustation f; (on wood) marqueterie f.

inlet n bras m de mer; (Tech) arrivée f.

inmate n (of asylum) interné/-e m/f; (of prison) détenu/-e m/f.

inn n auberge f.

innate a inné.

inner a intérieur; **~ city** quartiers mpl déshérités; **~ tube** chambre f à air.

innocent a & n innocent/-e (m/f).

innocuous a inoffensif.

innovate vi innover.

innuendo n (pl **~es**)

insinuations *fpl*; (sexual) allusions *fpl* grivoises.

innumerable *a* innombrable.

inoculate *vt* vacciner (**against** contre).

inopportune *a* inopportun.

in-patient *n* malade *mf* hospitalisé/-e.

input *n* (of energy) alimentation *f* (**of** en); (contribution) contribution *f*; (data) données *fpl*; (computer process) saisie *f* des données. ● *vt* (data) saisir.

inquest *n* enquête *f*.

inquire *vi* se renseigner (**about, into** sur). ● *vt* demander.

inquiry *n* demande *f* de renseignements; (inquest) enquête *f*.

inquisitive *a* curieux.

inroad *n* **make ~s into** faire une avancée sur.

insane *a* fou; (Jur) aliéné.
insanity *n* folie *f*; (Jur) aliénation *f* mentale.

inscribe *vt* inscrire. **inscription** *n* inscription *f*.

inscrutable *a* énigmatique.

insect *n* insecte *m*. **insecticide** *n* insecticide *m*.

insecure *a* (person) qui manque d'assurance; (job) précaire; (lock, property) peu sûr. **insecurity** *n* (of person) manque *m* d'assurance; (of situation) insécurité *f*.

insensitive *a* insensible; (remark) indélicat.

inseparable *a* inséparable (**from** de).

insert *vt* insérer (**in** dans).

in-service *a* (training) continu.

inshore *a* côtier.

inside *n* intérieur *m*; **~s** entrailles *fpl*. ● *a* intérieur.
● *adv* à l'intérieur; **go ~** entrer.
● *prep* à l'intérieur de; (of time) en

moins de; **~ out** à l'envers; (thoroughly) à fond.

insight *n* (perception) perspicacité *f*; (idea) aperçu *m*.

insignia *npl* insigne *m*.

insignificant *a* (cost, difference) négligeable; (person) insignifiant.

insincere *a* peu sincère.

insinuate *vt* insinuer.

insist *vt/i* insister (**that** pour que); **~ on** exiger; **~ on doing** vouloir à tout prix faire. **insistence** *n* insistance *f*. **insistent** *a* insistant.

insistently *adv* avec insistance.

insofar as *adv* dans la mesure où.

insolent *a* insolent.

insolvent *a* insolvable.

insomnia *n* insomnie *f*.
insomniac *n* insomniaque *mf*.

inspect *vt* (school, machinery) inspecter; (tickets) contrôler.
inspection *n* inspection *f*; (of passport, ticket) contrôle *m*.
inspector *n* inspecteur/-trice *m/f*; (on bus) contrôleur/-euse *m/f*.

inspiration *n* inspiration *f*.
inspire *vt* inspirer.

install *vt* installer.

instalment *n* (payment) versement *m*; (of serial) épisode *m*.

instance *n* exemple *m*; (case) cas *m*; **for ~** par exemple; **in the first ~** en premier lieu.

instant *a* immédiat; (food) instantané. ● *n* instant *m*.
instantaneous *a* instantané.
instantly *adv* immédiatement.

instead *adv* plutôt; **~ of doing** au lieu de faire; **~ of sb** à la place de qn.

instep *n* cou-de-pied *m*.

instigate *vt* (attack) lancer; (proceedings) engager.

instil *vt* (pt **instilled**) inculquer; (fear) insuffler.

instinct *n* instinct *m*. **instinctive** *a* instinctif.
institute *n* institut *m*. ● *vt* instituer; (*proceedings*) engager.
institution *n* institution *f*; (school, hospital) établissement *m*.
instruct *vt* (teach) instruire; (order) ordonner; ∼ **sb in sth** enseigner qch à qn; ∼ **sb to do** donner l'ordre à qn de faire. **instruction** *n* instruction *f*. **instructions** *npl* (for use) mode *m* d'emploi.
instructive *a* instructif.
instructor *n* (skiing, driving) moniteur/-trice *m/f*.
instrument *n* instrument *m*.
instrumental *a* instrumental; **be** ∼ **in** contribuer à. **instrumentalist** *n* instrumentaliste *mf*.
insubordinate *a* insubordonné.
insufficient *a* insuffisant.
insular *a* (Geog) insulaire; (mind, person: fig) borné.
insulate *vt* (room, wire) isoler.
insulin *n* insuline *f*.
insult[1] *vt* insulter.
insult[2] *n* insulte *f*.
insurance *n* assurance *f* (**against** contre).
insure *vt* assurer; ∼ **that** (US) s'assurer que.
intact *a* intact.
intake *n* (of food) consommation *f*; (School, Univ) admissions *fpl*.
integral *a* intégral (**to** à).
integrate *vt/i* (s')intégrer (**with** à; **into** dans).
integrity *n* intégrité *f*.
intellect *n* intelligence *f*. **intellectual** *a & n* intellectuel/-le (*m/f*).
intelligence *n* intelligence *f*; (Mil) renseignements *mpl*. **intelligent** *a* intelligent. **intelligently** *adv* intelligemment.
intend *vt* (*outcome*) vouloir; ∼ **to**

do avoir l'intention de faire.
intended *a* (*result*) voulu; (*visit*) projeté.
intense *a* intense; (person) sérieux. **intensely** *adv* (very) extrêmement.
intensify *vt/i* (s')intensifier.
intensive *a* intensif; **in** ∼ **care** en réanimation.
intent *n* intention *f*. ● *a* absorbé; ∼ **on doing** résolu à faire.
intention *n* intention *f*. **intentional** *a* intentionnel.
intently *adv* attentivement.
interact *vi* (*factors*) agir l'un sur l'autre; (*people*) communiquer. **interactive** *a* (*TV, video*) interactif.
intercept *vt* intercepter.
interchange *n* (road junction) échangeur *m*; (exchange) échange *m*.
interchangeable *a* interchangeable.
intercom *n* interphone® *m*.
interconnected *a* (*parts*) raccordé; (*problems*) lié.
intercourse *n* rapports *mpl*.
interest *n* intérêt *m*; ∼ **rate** taux *m* d'intérêt. ● *vt* intéresser (**in** à). **interested** *a* intéressé; **be** ∼**ed in** s'intéresser à. **interesting** *a* intéressant.
interfere *vi* se mêler des affaires des autres; ∼ **in** se mêler de; ∼ **with** (*freedom*) empiéter sur; (tamper with) toucher. **interference** *n* ingérence *f*; (sound, light waves) brouillage *m*; (radio) parasites *mpl*.
interim *n* **in the** ∼ **entre-temps**. ● *a* (*government*) provisoire; (*payment*) intermédiaire.
interior *n* intérieur *m*. ● *a* intérieur.
interjection *n* interjection *f*.
interlock *vt/i* (Tech) (s')emboîter, (s')enclencher.

I

interlude *n* intervalle *m*; (Theat, Mus) intermède *m*.

intermediary *a & n* intermédiaire (*mf*).

intermediate *a* intermédiaire; (*exam, level*) moyen.

intermission *n* (Theat) entracte *m*.

intermittent *a* intermittent.

intern[1] *vt* interner.

intern[2] *n* (US) stagiaire *mf*; (Med) interne *mf*.

internal *a* interne; (domestic: Pol) intérieur; I∼ Revenue (US) service *m* des impôts américain.

international *a* international.

Internet *n* Internet *m*; on the ∼ sur Internet; ∼ access accès à Internet; ∼ service provider fournisseur *m* d'accès Internet.

interpret *vt* interpréter (as comme). ● *vi* faire l'interprète.
interpretation *n* interprétation *f*.
interpreter *n* interprète *mf*.

interrelated *a* interdépendant, lié.

interrogate *vt* interroger.
interrogative *a & n* (Ling) interrogatif (*m*).

interrupt *vt/i* interrompre.
interruption *n* interruption *f*.

intersect *vt/i* (lines, roads) (se) croiser. **intersection** *n* intersection *f*.

interspersed *a* parsemé (with de).

intertwine *vt/i* (s')entrelacer.

interval *n* intervalle *m*; (Theat) entracte *m*.

intervene *vi* intervenir; (of time) s'écouler (**between** entre); (happen) arriver.

interview *n* (for job) entretien *m*; (by a journalist) interview *f*. ● *vt* (*candidate*) faire passer un entretien à; (*celebrity*) interviewer.

intestine *n* intestin *m*.

intimacy *n* intimité *f*.

intimate[1] *vt* (state) annoncer; (hint) laisser entendre.

intimate[2] *a* intime. **intimately** *adv* intimement.

intimidate *vt* intimider.

into *prep* (put, go, fall) dans; (divide, translate, change) en; **be** ∼ **jazz** être fana du jazz 🔟; **8** ∼ **24 is 3** 24 divisé par 8 égale 3.

intolerant *a* intolérant.

intonation *n* intonation *f*.

intoxicate *vt* enivrer.
intoxicated *a* ivre. **intoxication** *n* ivresse *f*.

intractable *a* (*person*) intraitable; (*problem*) rebelle.

Intranet *n* (Comput) Intranet *m*.

intransitive *a* intransitif.

intravenous *a* (Med) intraveineux.

intricate *a* complexe.

intrigue *vt* intriguer. ● *n* intrigue *f*. **intriguing** *a* fascinant; (curious) curieux.

intrinsic *a* intrinsèque (to à).

introduce *vt* (*person, idea, programme*) présenter; (*object, law*) introduire (**into** dans).
introduction *n* introduction *f*; (of person) présentation *f*.
introductory *a* (words) préliminaire.

introvert *n* introverti/-e *m/f*.

intrude *vi* (person) s'imposer (**on sb** à qn), déranger. **intruder** *n* intrus/-e *m/f*. **intrusion** *n* intrusion *f*.

intuition *n* intuition *f*. **intuitive** *a* intuitif.

inundate *vt* inonder (**with** de).

invade *vt* envahir.

invalid[1] *n* malade *mf*; (disabled) infirme *mf*.

invalid[2] *a* (*passport*) pas valable; (*claim*) sans fondement.

invalidate vt (*argument*) infirmer; (*claim*) annuler.

invaluable a inestimable.

invariable a invariable.
invariably adv invariablement.

invasion n invasion f.

invent vt inventer. **invention** n invention f. **inventive** a inventif. **inventor** n inventeur/-trice m/f.

inventory n inventaire m.

invert vt (*order*) intervertir; (*image, values*) renverser; ~ed commas guillemets mpl.

invest vt investir; (time, effort) consacrer. ● vi faire un investissement; ~ in (buy) s'acheter.

investigate vt examiner; (*crime*) enquêter sur. **investigation** n investigation f. **investigator** n (police) enquêteur/-euse m/f.

investment n investissement m; emotional ~ engagement m personnel. **investor** n investisseur/-euse m/f; (in shares) actionnaire mf.

invigilate vi (*exam*) surveiller. **invigilator** n surveillant/-e m/f.

invigorate vt revigorer.

invisible a invisible.

invitation n invitation f. **invite** vt inviter; (ask for) demander. **inviting** a engageant.

invoice n facture f. ● vt facturer.

involuntary a involontaire.

involve vt impliquer; (*person*) faire participer (in à). **involved** a (complex) compliqué; (at stake) en jeu; be ~d in (*work*) participer à; (*crime*) être mêlé à. **involvement** n participation f (in à).

inward a (*feeling*) intérieur. **inwardly** adv intérieurement. **inwards** adv vers l'intérieur.

iodine n iode m; (antiseptic) teinture f d'iode.

iota n iota m; not one ~ of pas un grain de.

IOU abbr (**I owe you**) reconnaissance f de dette.

IQ abbr (**intelligence quotient**) QI m.

Iran n Iran m.

Iraq n Irak m.

irate a furieux.

IRC abbrev (**Internet Relay Chat**) (Internet) conversation f IRC.

Ireland n Irlande f.

Irish n & a irlandais (m). ~man n Irlandais m. ~woman n Irlandaise f.

iron n fer m; (appliance) fer m (à repasser). ● a (will) de fer; (bar) en fer. ● vt repasser.

ironic(al) a ironique.

iron: **ironing-board** n planche f à repasser. ~**monger** n quincaillier m.

irony n ironie f.

irrational a irrationnel; (person) pas raisonnable.

irregular a irrégulier.

irrelevant a hors de propos.

irreplaceable a irremplaçable.

irresistible a irrésistible.

irrespective a ~ of sans tenir compte de.

irresponsible a irresponsable.

irreverent a irrévérencieux.

irrigate vt irriguer.

irritable a irritable.

irritate vt irriter. **irritating** a irritant.

is ⇒BE.

ISDN abbr (**integrated services digital network**) RNIS m, réseau m numérique à intégration de services.

Islam n (faith) islam m; (Muslims) Islam m. **Islamic** a islamique.

island n île f.

isle n île f.

isolate vt isoler. **isolation** n isolement m.

Israel n Israël m.

Israeli n Israélien/-ne m/f. ● a israélien.

issue n question f; (outcome) résultat m; (of magazine) numéro m; (of stamps) émission f; (offspring) descendance f; **at** ∼ en cause. ● vt distribuer; (stamps) émettre; (book) publier; (order) délivrer. ● vi ∼ **from** provenir de.

. . . .

it

● *pronoun*

····▸ (subject) il, elle; **'where's the book/chair?'—'**∼**'s in the kitchen'** 'où est le livre/la chaise?'—'il/elle est dans la cuisine'.

····▸ (object) le, la, l'; ∼**'s my book and I want** ∼ c'est mon livre et je le veux; **I liked his shirt, did you notice** ∼**?** sa chemise m'a plu, l'as-tu remarquée?; **give** ∼ **to me** donne-le-moi.

····▸ (with preposition) **we talked a lot about** ∼ on en a beaucoup parlé; **Elliott went to** ∼ Elliott y est allé.

····▸ (impersonal) il; ∼**'s raining** il pleut; ∼ **will snow** il va neiger.

. . . .

IT abbr ⇒INFORMATION TECHNOLOGY.

Italian n (person) Italien/-ne m/f; (Ling) italien m. ● a italien.

italics npl italique m.

Italy n Italie f.

itch n démangeaison f. ● vi démanger; **my arm** ∼**es** j'ai le bras qui me démange; **be** ∼**ing to do** mourir d'envie de faire.

item n article m; (on agenda) point m.

itemize vt détailler; ∼**d bill** facture f détaillée.

itinerary n itinéraire m.

its det son, sa; pl ses.

it's = IT IS, IT HAS.

itself pron lui-même, elle-même; (reflexive) se.

ivory n ivoire m; ∼ **tower** tour f d'ivoire.

ivy n lierre m.

jab vt (pt **jabbed**) ∼ **sth into sth** planter qch dans qch. ● n coup m; (injection) piqûre f.

jack n (Auto) cric m; (cards) valet m; (Electr) jack m. ● vt ∼ **up** soulever avec un cric.

jackal n chacal m.

jacket n veste f, veston m; (of book) jaquette f.

jack-knife n couteau m pliant. ● vi (lorry) se mettre en portefeuille.

jackpot n gros lot m; **hit the** ∼ gagner le gros lot.

jade n (stone) jade m.

jaded a (tired) fatigué; (bored) blasé.

jagged a (rock) déchiqueté; (knife) dentelé.

jail n prison f. ● vt mettre en prison.

jam n confiture f; (traffic) ∼ embouteillage m. ● vt/i (pt **jammed**) (wedge) (se) coincer; (cram) (s')entasser; (street) encombrer; (radio) brouiller.

Jamaica n Jamaïque f.

jam-packed a 🄸 bondé; ∼ **with** bourré de.

jangle n tintement m. ● vt/i (faire) tinter.

janitor n (US) gardien m.

January n janvier m.

Japan n Japon m.
Japanese n (person) Japonais/-e m/f; (Ling) japonais m. ● a japonais.
jar n pot m, bocal m. ● vi (pt **jarred**) rendre un son discordant; (colours) détonner. ● vt ébranler.
jargon n jargon m.
jaundice n jaunisse f.
javelin n javelot m.
jaw n mâchoire f.
jay n geai m.
jazz n jazz m. ● vt ~ up (dress) rajeunir; (event) ranimer.
jealous a jaloux. **jealousy** n jalousie f.
jeans npl jean m.
jeer vt/i ~ (at) huer. ● n huée f.
jelly n gelée f. ~**fish** n méduse f.
jeopardize vt (career, chance) compromettre; (lives) mettre en péril.
jerk n secousse f; (fool 🔲) crétin m 🔲. ● vt tirer brusquement. ● vi tressaillir. **jerky** a saccadé.
jersey n (garment) pull-over m; (fabric) jersey m.
jet n (plane, stream) jet m; (mineral) jais m; ~ **lag** décalage m horaire.
jettison vt jeter par-dessus bord; (Aviat) larguer; (fig) rejeter.
jetty n jetée f.
Jew n juif/juive m/f.
jewel n bijou m. **jeweller** n bijoutier/-ière m/f. **jeweller('s)** n (shop) bijouterie f. **jewellery** n bijoux mpl.
Jewish a juif.
jibe n moquerie f.
jigsaw n puzzle m.
jingle vt/i (faire) tinter. ● n tintement m; (advertising) refrain m publicitaire, sonal m.
jinx n (person) porte-malheur m inv; (curse) sort m.
jitters npl have the ~ 🔲 être nerveux. **jittery** a nerveux.

job n emploi m; (post) poste m; **out of a** ~ sans emploi; **it is a good** ~ **that** heureusement que; **just the** ~ tout à fait ce qu'il faut. ~ **centre** n bureau m des services nationaux de l'emploi. **jobless** a sans emploi.
jockey n jockey m.
jog n **go for a** ~ aller faire un jogging. ● vt (pt **jogged**) heurter; (memory) rafraîchir. ● vi faire du jogging. **jogging** n jogging m.
join vt (attach) réunir, joindre; (club) devenir membre de; (company) entrer dans; (army) s'engager dans; (queue) se mettre dans; ~ **sb** (in activity) se joindre à qn; (meet) rejoindre qn. ● vi (become member) adhérer; (pieces) se joindre; (roads) se rejoindre. ● n raccord m. □ ~ **in** participer; ~ **in sth** participer à qch; ~ **up** (Mil) s'engager; ~ **sth up** relier qch. **joiner** n menuisier/-ière m/f.
joint a (action) collectif; (measures, venture) commun; (winner) ex aequo inv; (account) joint; ~ **author** coauteur m. ● n (join) joint m; (Anat) articulation f; (Culin) rôti m, **out of** ~ déboîté.
joke n plaisanterie f; (trick) farce f; **it's no** ~ ce n'est pas drôle. ● vi plaisanter. **joker** n blagueur/ -euse m/f; (cards) joker m.
jolly a (-ier, -iest) (person) enjoué; (tune) joyeux. ● adv 🔲 drôlement.
jolt vt secouer. ● vi cahoter. ● n secousse f; (shock) choc m.
jostle vt/i (se) bousculer.
jot vt (pt **jotted**) ~ (**down**) noter.
journal n journal m. **journalism** n journalisme m. **journalist** n journaliste mf.
journey n (trip) voyage m; (short or habitual) trajet m. ● vi voyager.
joy n joie f. **joyful** a joyeux.

J

joy: ~**riding** n rodéo m à la voiture volée. ~**stick** n (Comput) manette f; (Aviat) manche m à balai.

jubilant a (*person*) exultant; (*mood*) réjoui.

Judaism n judaïsme m.

judge n juge m. ● vt juger; (*distance*) estimer; **judging by/from** à en juger par. **judg(e)ment** n jugement m.

judicial a judiciaire. **judiciary** n magistrature f.

judo n judo m.

jug n (glass) carafe f; (pottery) pichet m.

juggernaut n (lorry) poids m lourd.

juggle vt/i jongler (avec). **juggler** n jongleur/-euse m/f.

juice n jus m. **juicy** a juteux; (*details* 🖾) croustillant.

jukebox n juke-box m.

July n juillet m.

jumble vt mélanger. ● n (of objects) tas m; (of ideas) fouillis m; ~ **sale** vente f de charité.

jumbo n (also ~ **jet**) gros-porteur m.

jump vt sauter; ~ **the lights** passer au feu rouge; ~ **the queue** passer devant tout le monde. ● vi sauter; (in surprise) sursauter; (*price*) monter en flèche; ~ **at** (*opportunity*) sauter sur. ● n saut m, bond m; (increase) bond m.

jumper n pull(-over) m; (dress: US) robe f chasuble.

jump-leads npl câbles mpl de démarrage.

jumpy a nerveux.

junction n (of roads) carrefour m; (on motorway) échangeur m.

June n juin m.

jungle n jungle f.

junior a (young) jeune; (in rank) subalterne; (school) primaire. ● n cadet/-te m/f; (School) élève mf du primaire.

junk n bric-à-brac m inv; (poor quality) camelote f; ~ **food** nourriture f industrielle.

junkie n 🖾 drogué/-e m/f.

junk: ~ **mail** n prospectus mpl. ~**-shop** n boutique f de bric-à-brac.

jurisdiction n compétence f; (Jur) juridiction f.

juror n juré m.

jury n jury m.

just a (fair) juste. ● adv (immediately, slightly) juste; (simply) tout simplement; (exactly) exactement; **he has/had ~ left** il vient/venait de partir; **have ~ missed** avoir manqué de peu; **I'm ~ leaving** je suis sur le point de partir; **it's ~ a cold** ce n'est qu'un rhume; ~ **as tall/well as** tout aussi grand/bien que; ~ **listen!** écoutez donc!; **it's ~ ridiculous** c'est vraiment ridicule.

justice n justice f; **J~ of the Peace** juge m de paix.

justification n justification f. **justify** vt justifier.

jut vi (pt **jutted**) ~ (**out**) s'avancer en saillie.

juvenile a (childish) puéril; (*offender*) mineur; (*delinquent*) jeune. ● n jeune mf; (Jur) mineur/-e m/f.

juxtapose vt juxtaposer.

kangaroo n kangourou m.

karate n karaté m.

kebab n brochette f.

keel n (of ship) quille f. ● vi ∼ **over** (bateau) chavirer; (person) s'écrouler.

keen a (interest, wind, feeling) vif; (mind, analysis) pénétrant; (edge, appetite) aiguisé; (eager) enthousiaste; **be** ∼ **on** être passionné de; **be** ∼ **to do** or **on doing** tenir beaucoup à faire. **keenly** adv vivement. **keenness** n enthousiasme m.

keep vt (pt **kept**) garder; (promise, shop, diary) tenir; (family) faire vivre; (animals) élever; (rule) respecter; (celebrate) célébrer; (delay) retenir; ∼ **sth clean/warm** garder qch propre/au chaud; ∼ **sb in/out** empêcher qn de sortir/d'entrer; ∼ **sb from doing** empêcher qn de faire. ● vi (food) se conserver; ∼ **(on)** continuer (**doing** à faire). ● n pension f; (of castle) donjon m. □ ∼ **down** rester allongé; ∼ **sth down** limiter qch; ∼ **your voice down!** baisse la voix!; ∼ **to** (road) ne pas s'écarter de; (rules) respecter; ∼ **up** (car, runner) suivre; (rain) continuer; ∼ **up with sb** (in speed) aller aussi vite que; (class, inflation, fashion, news) suivre.

keeper n gardien/-ne m/f.

keepsake n souvenir m.

kennel n niche f.

kept ⇒KEEP.

kerb n bord m du trottoir.

kernel n amande f; ∼ **of truth** fond m de vérité.

kettle n bouilloire f.

key n clé f; (of computer, piano) touche f. ● a (industry, figure) clé (inv). ● vt ∼ **(in)** saisir. ∼**board** n clavier m. ∼**hole** n trou m de serrure. ∼**-pad** n (of telephone) clavier m numérique. ∼**-ring** n porte-clés m inv. ∼**stroke** n (Comput) frappe f.

khaki a kaki inv.

kick vt/i donner un coup de pied (à); (horse) botter. ● n coup m de pied; (of gun) recul m; **get a** ∼ **out of doing** 🔲 prendre plaisir à faire. □ ∼ **out** 🔲 virer 🔲.

kick-off n coup m d'envoi.

kid n (goat, leather) chevreau m; (child 🔲) gosse mf 🔲. ● vt/i (pt **kidded**) blaguer.

kidnap vt (pt **kidnapped**) enlever. **kidnapping** n enlèvement m.

kidney n rein m; (Culin) rognon m.

kill vt tuer; (rumour: fig) arrêter. ● n mise f à mort. **killer** n tueur/ -euse m/f. **killing** n meurtre m.

kiln n four m.

kilo n kilo m.

kilobyte n kilo-octet m.

kilogram n kilogramme m.

kilometre, (US) **kilometer** n kilomètre m.

kilowatt n kilowatt m.

kin n parents mpl.

kind n genre m, sorte f; **in** ∼ en nature; ∼ **of** (somewhat 🔲) assez. ● a gentil, bon.

kindergarten n jardin m d'enfants.

kindle vt/i (s')allumer.

kindly a (-**ier**, -**iest**) (person) gentil; (interest) bienveillant. ● adv avec gentillesse; **would you**

K

~ **do** auriez-vous l'amabilité de faire.

kindness n bonté f.

king n roi m. **kingdom** n royaume m; (Bot) règne m. ~**fisher** n martin-pêcheur m. ~-**size**(**d**) a géant.

kiosk n kiosque m; telephone ~ cabine f téléphonique; (Internet) borne f interactive, kiosque m.

kiss n baiser m. ● vt/i (s')embrasser.

kit n (clothing) affaires fpl; (set of tools) trousse f; (for assembly) kit m. ● vt (pt **kitted**) ~ **out** équiper.

kitchen n cuisine f.

kite n (toy) cerf-volant m; (bird) milan m.

kitten n chaton m.

kitty n (fund) cagnotte f.

knack n tour m de main (**of doing** pour faire).

knead vt pétrir.

knee n genou m. ~**cap** n rotule f.

kneel vi (pt **knelt**) ~ (**down**) se mettre à genoux; (in prayer) s'agenouiller.

knew ⇒KNOW.

knickers npl petite culotte f, slip m.

knife n (pl **knives**) couteau m. ● vt poignarder.

knight n chevalier m; (chess) cavalier m. ● vt anoblir. ~**hood** n titre m de chevalier.

knit vt/i (pt **knitted** or **knit**) tricoter; (bones) (se) souder. **knitting** n tricot m. **knitwear** n tricots mpl.

knob n bouton m.

knock vt/i cogner; (criticize 🅸) critiquer; ~ **sth off/out** faire tomber qch. ● n coup m. □ ~ **down** (chair, pedestrian) renverser; (demolish) abattre; (reduce) baisser; ~ **off** (stop work 🅸) arrêter de travailler; ~ **£10 off**

faire une réduction de 10 livres; ~ **it off!** 🅸 ça suffit!; ~ **out** assommer; ~ **over** renverser; ~ **up** (meal) préparer en vitesse.

knock-out n (boxing) knock-out m.

knot n nœud m. ● vt (pt **knotted**) nouer.

know vt/i (pt **knew**; pp **known**) (answer, reason, language) savoir (**that** que); (person, place, name, rule, situation) connaître; (recognize) reconnaître; ~ **how to do** savoir faire; ~ **about** (event) être au courant de; (subject) s'y connaître en; ~ **of** (from experience) connaître; (from information) avoir entendu parler de. ~-**how** n savoir-faire m inv.

knowingly adv (intentionally) délibérément; (meaningfully) d'un air entendu.

knowledge n connaissance f; (learning) connaissances fpl. **knowledgeable** a savant.

knuckle n jointure f, articulation f.

Koran n Coran m.

Korea n Corée f.

kosher a casher inv.

lab n 🅸 labo m.

label n étiquette f. ● vt (pt **labelled**) étiqueter.

laboratory n laboratoire m.

laborious a laborieux.

labour, (US) **labor** n travail m; (workers) main-d'œuvre f; **in** ~ en train d'accoucher. ● vi peiner (**to do** à faire). ● vt trop insister sur.

Labour *n* le parti travailliste. ● *a* travailliste.

laboured *a* laborieux.

labourer *n* ouvrier/-ière *m/f*; (on farm) ouvrier/-ière *m/f* agricole.

lace *n* dentelle *f*; (of shoe) lacet *m*. ● *vt* (*shoe*) lacer; (*drink*) arroser.

lacerate *vt* lacérer.

lack *n* manque *m*; **for ~ of** faute de. ● *vt* manquer de; **be ~ing** manquer (**in** de).

lad *n* garçon *m*, gars *m*.

ladder *n* échelle *f*; (in stocking) maille *f* filée. ● *vt/i* (*stocking*) filer.

laden *a* chargé (**with** de).

ladle *n* louche *f*.

lady *n* (*pl* **ladies**) dame *f*; **ladies and gentlemen** mesdames et messieurs; **young ~** jeune femme *or* fille *f*. **~bird** *n* coccinelle *f*.

ladylike *a* distingué.

lag *vi* (*pt* **lagged**) traîner. ● *vt* (*pipes*) calorifuger. ● *n* (interval) décalage *m*.

lager *n* bière *f* blonde.

lagoon *n* lagune *f*.

laid ⇒LAY[1]. **~ back** *a* décontracté.

lain ⇒LIE[2].

lake *n* lac *m*.

lamb *n* agneau *m*; **leg of ~** gigot *m* d'agneau.

lame *a* boiteux.

lament *n* lamentation *f*. ● *vt/i* se lamenter (sur).

laminated *a* laminé.

lamp *n* lampe *f*. **~post** *n* réverbère *m*. **~shade** *n* abat-jour *m inv*.

lance *vt* (Med) inciser.

land *n* terre *f*; (plot) terrain *m*; (country) pays *m*. ● *a* terrestre; (*policy, reform*) agraire. ● *vt/i* débarquer; (*aircraft*) (se) poser, (faire) atterrir; (fall) tomber;

(obtain) décrocher; (*a blow*) porter; **~ up** se retrouver.

landing *n* débarquement *m*; (Aviat) atterrissage *m*; (top of stairs) palier *m*. **~-stage** *n* débarcadère *m*.

land: ~lady *n* propriétaire *f*; (of pub) patronne *f*. **~lord** *n* propriétaire *m*; (of pub) patron *m*. **~mark** *n* (point de) repère *m*. **~mine** *n* mine *f* terrestre.

landscape *n* paysage *m*. ● *vt* aménager.

landslide *n* glissement *m* de terrain; (Pol) raz-de-marée *m inv* (électoral).

lane *n* (path, road) chemin *m*; (strip of road) voie *f*; (of traffic) file *f*; (Aviat) couloir *m*.

language *n* langue *f*; (speech, style) langage *m*. **~ engineering** *n* ingénierie *f* des langues. **~ laboratory** *n* laboratoire *m* de langue.

lank *a* (*hair*) plat.

lanky *a* (**-ier, -iest**) grand et maigre.

lantern *n* lanterne *f*.

lap *n* genoux *mpl*; (Sport) tour *m* (de piste). ● *vi* (*pt* **lapped**) (*waves*) clapoter. □ **~ up** laper.

lapel *n* revers *m*.

lapse *vi* (decline) se dégrader; (expire) se périmer; **~ into** retomber dans. ● *n* défaillance *f*, erreur *f*; (of time) intervalle *m*.

laptop *n* (Comput) portable *m*.

lard *n* saindoux *m*.

larder *n* garde-manger *m inv*.

large *a* grand, gros; **at ~** en liberté; **by and ~** en général.

largely *adv* en grande mesure.

lark *n* (bird) alouette *f*; (bit of fun 🔲) rigolade *f*. ● *vi* 🔲 rigoler.

larva *n* (*pl* **-vae**) larve *f*.

laryngitis *n* laryngite *f*.

laser *n* laser *m*. **~ printer** *n*

L

imprimante *f* laser. ~ **treatment**
n (Med) laserothérapie *f*.
lash *vt* fouetter. ● *n* coup *m* de
fouet; (eyelash) cil *m*. □ ~ **out**
(spend) dépenser follement; ~ **out**
against attaquer.
lass *n* jeune fille *f*.
lasso *n* lasso *m*.
last *a* dernier; **the** ~ **straw** le
comble; **the** ~ **word** le mot de la
fin; **on its** ~ **legs** sur le point de
rendre l'âme; ~ **night** hier soir.
● *adv* en dernier; (most recently) la
dernière fois. ● *n* dernier/-ière
m/f; (remainder) reste *m*; **at** (**long**) ~
enfin. ● *vi* durer. ~**-ditch** *a*
ultime. **lasting** *a* durable. **lastly**
adv en dernier lieu. ~**-minute** *a*
de dernière minute.
latch *n* loquet *m*.
late *a* (not on time) en retard;
(former) ancien; (hour, fruit) tardif;
the ~ **Mrs X** feu Mme X. ● *adv*
(not early) tard; (not on time) en
retard; **in** ~ **July** fin juillet; **of** ~
dernièrement. **lately** *adv*
dernièrement. **latest** *a* ⇒LATE;
(last) dernier.
lathe *n* tour *m*.
lather *n* mousse *f*. ● *vt* savonner.
● *vi* mousser.
Latin *n* (Ling) latin *m*. ● *a* latin. ~
America *n* Amérique *f* latine.
latitude *n* latitude *f*.
latter *a* dernier. ● *n* **the** ~
celui-ci, celle-ci.
Latvia *n* Lettonie *f*.
laudable *a* louable.
laugh *vi* rire (**at** de). ● *n* rire *m*.
laughable *a* ridicule.
laughing stock *n* risée *f*.
laughter *n* (act) rire *m*; (sound of
laughs) rires *mpl*.
launch *vt* (rocket) lancer; (boat)
mettre à l'eau; ~ (**out**) **into** se
lancer dans. ● *n* lancement *m*;
(boat) vedette *f*. **launching pad** *n*
aire *f* de lancement.

launderette *n* laverie *f*
automatique.
laundry *n* (place) blanchisserie *f*;
(clothes) linge *m*.
laurel *n* laurier *m*.
lava *n* lave *f*.
lavatory *n* toilettes *fpl*.
lavender *n* lavande *f*.
lavish *a* (person) généreux; (lush)
somptueux. ● *vt* prodiguer (**on** à).
lavishly *adv* luxueusement.
law *n* loi *f*; (profession, subject of study)
droit *m*; ~ **and order** l'ordre
public. ~**-abiding** *a* respectueux
des lois. ~**court** *n* tribunal *m*.
lawful *a* légal.
lawn *n* pelouse *f*, gazon *m*.
~**-mower** *n* tondeuse *f* à gazon.
lawsuit *n* procès *m*.
lawyer *n* avocat *m*.
lax *a* (government) laxiste;
(security) relâché.
laxative *n* laxatif *m*.
lay[1] *a* (non-clerical) laïque; (worker)
non-initié. ● *vt* (*pt* **laid**) poser,
mettre; (trap) tendre; (table)
mettre; (plan) former; (eggs)
pondre. ● *vi* pondre; ~ **waste**
ravager. □ ~ **aside** mettre de
côté; ~ **down** (dé)poser; (condition)
(im-)poser; ~ **off** *vt* (worker)
licencier; *vi* 🔢 arrêter; ~ **on**
(provide) fournir; ~ **out** (design)
dessiner; (display) disposer;
(money) dépenser.
lay[2] ⇒LIE[2].
lay-by *n* (*pl* ~s) aire *f* de repos.
layer *n* couche *f*.
layman *n* (*pl* **-men**) profane *m*.
layout *n* disposition *f*.
laze *vi* paresser. **laziness** *n*
paresse *f*. **lazy** *a* (**-ier**, **-iest**)
paresseux.
lead[1] *vt/i* (*pt* **led**) mener; (team)
diriger; (life) amener; (induce)
amener; ~ **to** conduire à, mener
à. ● *n* avance *f*; (clue) indice *m*;

(leash) laisse *f*; (Theat) premier rôle *m*; (wire) fil *m*; **in the ~** en tête. □ **~ away** emmener; **~ up to** (come to) en venir à; (precede) précéder.

lead² *n* plomb *m*; (of pencil) mine *f*.

leader *n* chef *m*; (of country, club) dirigeant/-e *m*/*f*; (leading article) éditorial *m*. **leadership** *n* direction *f*.

lead-free *a* (petrol) sans plomb.

leading *a* principal.

leaf *n* (*pl* **leaves**) feuille *f*; (of table) rallonge *f*. ● *vi* **~ through** feuilleter.

leaflet *n* prospectus *m*.

leafy *a* feuillu.

league *n* ligue *f*; (Sport) championnat *m*; **in ~ with** de mèche avec.

leak *n* fuite *f*. ● *vi* fuir; (news: fig) s'ébruiter. ● *vt* répandre; (fig) divulguer.

lean¹ *a* maigre. ● *n* (of meat) maigre *m*.

lean² *vt*/*i* (*pt* **leaned** *or* **leant**) (rest) (s')appuyer; (slope) pencher. □ **~ out** se pencher à l'extérieur; **~ over** (of person) se pencher.

leaning *a* penché. ● *n* tendance *f*.

leap *vi* (*pt* **leaped** *or* **leapt**) bondir. ● *n* bond *m*. **~ year** *n* année *f* bissextile.

learn *vt*/*i* (*pt* **learned** *or* **learnt**) apprendre (**to do** à faire).

learned *a* érudit. **learner** *n* débutant/-e *m*/*f*.

lease *n* bail *m*. ● *vt* louer à bail.

leash *n* laisse *f*.

least *a* **the ~** (smallest amount of) le moins de; (slightest) le *or* la moindre. ● *n* le moins. ● *adv* le moins; (with adjective) le *or* la moins; **at ~** au moins.

leather *n* cuir *m*.

leave *vt* (*pt* **left**) laisser; (depart from) quitter; (person) laisser

tranquille; **be left (over)** rester. ● *n* (holiday) congé *m*; (consent) permission *f*; **take one's ~** prendre congé (**of** de); **on ~** (Mil) en permission. □ **~ alone** (thing) ne pas toucher; (person) laisser tranquille; **~ behind** laisser; **~ out** omettre.

Lebanon *n* Liban *m*.

lecture *n* cours *m*, conférence *f*; (rebuke) réprimande *f*. ● *vt*/*i* faire un cours *or* une conférence (à); (rebuke) réprimander. **lecturer** *n* conférencier/-ière *m*/*f*; (Univ) enseignant/-e *m*/*f*.

led ⇒LEAD¹.

ledge *n* (window) rebord *m*; (rock) saillie *f*.

ledger *n* grand livre *m*.

leech *n* sangsue *f*.

leek *n* poireau *m*.

leer *vi* **~ (at)** lorgner. ● *n* regard *m* sournois.

leeway *n* (fig) liberté *f* d'action; (Naut) dérive *f*.

left ⇒LEAVE. ● *a* gauche. ● *adv* à gauche. ● *n* gauche *f*; **~-hand** *a* à *or* de gauche. **~-handed** *a* gaucher.

left luggage (office) *n* consigne *f*.

left-overs *npl* restes *mpl*.

left-wing *a* de gauche.

leg *n* jambe *f*; (of animal) patte *f*; (of table) pied *m*; (of chicken) cuisse *f*; (of lamb) gigot *m*; (of journey) étape *f*.

legacy *n* legs *m*.

legal *a* légal; (affairs) juridique.

legend *n* légende *f*.

leggings *npl* (for woman) caleçon *m*.

legible *a* lisible.

legionnaire *n* légionnaire *m*.

legislation *n* (body of laws) législation *f*; (law) loi *f*.

legislature *n* corps *m* législatif.

L

legitimate *a* légitime.

leisure *n* loisirs *mpl*; **at one's** à tête reposée. ● *a* (*centre*) de loisirs.

leisurely *a* lent. ● *adv* sans se presser.

lemon *n* citron *m*.

lemonade *n* (fizzy) limonade *f*; (still) citronnade *f*.

lend *vt* (*pt* **lent**) prêter; (*credibility*) conférer; ~ **itself to** se prêter à.

length *n* longueur *f*; (in time) durée *f*; (section) morceau *m*; **at** ~ (at last) enfin; **at** (great) ~ longuement.

lengthen *vt/i* (s')allonger.

lengthways *adv* dans le sens de la longueur.

lengthy *a* long.

lenient *a* indulgent.

lens *n* lentille *f*; (of spectacles) verre *m*; (Photo) objectif *m*.

lent ⇒LEND.

Lent *n* Carême *m*.

lentil *n* lentille *f*.

Leo *n* Lion *m*.

leopard *n* léopard *m*.

leotard *n* body *m*.

leprosy *n* lèpre *f*.

lesbian *n* lesbienne *f*. ● *a* lesbien.

less *a* (in quantity) moins de (**than** que). ● *adv, n & prep* moins; ~ **than** (with numbers) moins de; **work** ~ **than** travailler moins que; **ten pounds** ~ dix livres de moins; ~ **and** ~ de moins en moins.

lessen *vt/i* diminuer. **lesser** *a* moindre.

lesson *n* leçon *f*.

let *vt* (*pt* **let**; *pres p* **letting**) laisser; (lease) louer. ● *v aux* ~ **us do**, ~**'s do** faisons; ~ **him do** qu'il fasse; ~ **me know the results** informe-moi des résultats. ● *n* location *f*. □ ~ **down** baisser;

(deflate) dégonfler; (fig) décevoir; ~ **go** *vt* lâcher; *vi* lâcher prise; ~ **sb in/out** laisser *or* faire entrer/ sortir qn; ~ **a dress out** élargir une robe; ~ **oneself in for** (*task*) s'engager à; (*trouble*) s'attirer; ~ **off** (explode, fire) faire éclater *or* partir; (excuse) dispenser; (not punish) ne pas punir; ~ **up** 🔲 s'arrêter.

let-down *n* déception *f*.

lethal *a* mortel; (weapon) meurtrier.

letter *n* lettre *f*. ~**-bomb** *n* lettre *f* piégée. ~**-box** *n* boîte *f* à *or* aux lettres.

lettering *n* (letters) caractères *mpl*.

lettuce *n* laitue *f*, salade *f*.

let-up *n* répit *m*.

leukaemia *n* leucémie *f*.

level *a* plat, uni; (on surface) horizontal; (in height) au même niveau (**with** que); (in score) à égalité. ● *n* niveau *m*; (spirit) ~ niveau *m* à bulle; **be on the** ~ 🔲 être franc. ● *vt* (*pt* **levelled**) niveler; (aim) diriger. ~ **crossing** *n* passage *m* à niveau. ~**-headed** *a* équilibré.

lever *n* levier *m*. ● *vt* soulever au moyen d'un levier.

leverage *n* influence *f*.

levy *vt* (tax) prélever. ● *n* impôt *m*.

lexicon *n* lexique *m*.

liability *n* responsabilité *f*; 🔲 handicap *m*; **liabilities** (debts) dettes *fpl*.

liable *a* **be** ~ **to do** avoir tendance à faire, pouvoir faire; ~ **to** (illness) sujet à; (fine) passible de; ~ **for** responsable de.

liaise *vi* 🔲 faire la liaison. **liaison** *n* liaison *f*.

liar *n* menteur/-euse *m/f*.

libel *n* diffamation *f*. ● *vt* (*pt* **libelled**) diffamer.

liberal a libéral; (generous) généreux, libéral.

Liberal a & n (Pol) libéral/-e (m/ f).

liberate vt libérer.

liberty n liberté f; **at ~ to** libre de; **take liberties** prendre des libertés.

Libra n Balance f.

librarian n bibliothécaire mf.

library n bibliothèque f.

libretto n livret m.

lice ⇒LOUSE.

licence, (US) **license** n permis m; (for television) redevance f; (Comm) licence f; (liberty: fig) licence f. **~ plate** n plaque f minéralogique.

license vt accorder un permis à, autoriser.

lick vt lécher; (defeat 🔲) rosser; (fig) **a ~ of paint** un petit coup de peinture. ● n coup m de langue.

lid n couvercle m.

lie[1] n mensonge m. ● vi (pt lied; pres p lying) (tell lies) mentir.

lie[2] vi (pt lay; pp lain; pres p lying) s'allonger; (remain) rester; (be) se trouver, être; (in grave) reposer, **be lying** être allongé. □ **~ down** s'allonger; **~ in** faire la grasse matinée; **~ low** se cacher.

lieutenant n lieutenant m.

life n (pl lives) vie f. **~belt** n bouée f de sauvetage. **~boat** n canot m de sauvetage. **~buoy** n bouée f de sauvetage. **~ cycle** n cycle m de vie. **~-guard** n sauveteur m. **~ insurance** n assurance-vie f. **~-jacket** n gilet m de sauvetage.

lifeless a inanimé.

lifelike a très ressemblant.

life: **~long** a de toute la vie. **~ sentence** n condamnation f à perpétuité. **~-size(d)** a grandeur nature inv. **~ story** n vie f. **~-style** n style m de vie. **~ support machine** n appareil m de respiration artificielle.

lifetime n vie f; **in one's ~** de son vivant.

lift vt lever; (steal 🔲) voler. ● vi (of fog) se lever. ● n (in building) ascenseur m; **give a ~ to** emmener (en voiture). **~-off** n (Aviat) décollage m.

light n lumière f; (lamp) lampe f; (for fire, on vehicle) feu m; (headlight) phare m; **bring to ~** révéler; **come to ~** être révélé; **have you got a ~?** vous avez du feu? ● a (not dark) clair; (not heavy) léger. ● vt (pt lit or lighted) allumer; (room) éclairer; (match) frotter. □ **~ up** vi s'allumer; vt (room) éclairer. **~ bulb** n ampoule f.

lighten vt (give light to) éclairer; (make brighter) éclaircir; (make less heavy) alléger.

lighter n briquet m; (for stove) allume-gaz m inv.

light: **~-headed** a (dizzy) qui a un vertige; (frivolous) étourdi. **~-hearted** a gai. **~house** n phare m.

lighting n éclairage m.

lightly adv légèrement.

lightning n éclair m, foudre f. ● a (visit) éclair inv.

lightweight a léger. ● n (boxing) poids m léger.

light-year n année f lumière.

like[1] a semblable, pareil; **be ~-minded** avoir les mêmes sentiments. ● prep comme. ● conj 🔲 comme. ● n pareil m; **the ~s of you** les gens comme vous.

like[2] vt aimer (bien); **I should ~** je voudrais, j'aimerais; **would you ~?** voudriez-vous?, voudrais-tu?; **~s** goûts mpl. **likeable** a sympathique.

likelihood n probabilité f.

L

likely a (**-ier, -iest**) probable.
● adv probablement; he is ∼ to
do il fera probablement; not ∼!
▣ pas question!

likeness n ressemblance f.

likewise adv également.

liking n (for thing) penchant m; (for
person) affection f.

lilac n lilas m. ● a lilas inv.

Lilo® n matelas m pneumatique.

lily n lis m, lys m.

limb n membre m.

limber vi ∼ up faire des exercices
d'assouplissement.

limbo n be in ∼ (forgotten) être
tombé dans l'oubli.

lime n (fruit) citron m vert; ∼(-tree)
tilleul m.

limelight n in the ∼ en vedette.

limestone n calcaire m.

limit n limite f. ● vt limiter.

limited company n société f
anonyme.

limp vi boiter. ● n have a ∼
boiter. ● a mou.

line n ligne f; (track) voie f; (wrinkle)
ride f; (row) rangée f, file f; (of
poem) vers m; (rope) corde f; (of
goods) gamme f; (queue: US) queue
f; be in ∼ for avoir de bonnes
chances de; hold the ∼ ne quittez
pas; in ∼ with en accord avec;
stand in ∼ faire la queue. ● vt
(paper) régler; (streets) border;
(garment) doubler; (fill) remplir,
garnir. □ ∼ up (s')aligner; (in
queue) faire la queue; ∼ sth up
prévoir qch. ∼ dancing n danse
f en ligne.

linen n (sheets) linge m; (material)
lin m.

liner n paquebot m.

linesman n (football) juge m de
touche; (tennis) juge m de ligne.

linger vi s'attarder; (smells)
persister.

linguist n linguiste mf.

linguistics n linguistique f.

lining n doublure f.

link n lien m; (of chain) maillon m.
● vt relier; (relate) (re)lier; ∼ up (of
roads) se rejoindre. **linkage** n lien
m. **links** n inv terrain m de golf.
∼-up n liaison f.

lino n lino m.

lion n lion m. **lioness** n lionne f.

lip n lèvre f; (edge) rebord m; pay
∼-service to n'approuver que
pour la forme. ∼-read vt/i lire
sur les lèvres. ∼salve n baume
m pour les lèvres. ∼stick n
rouge m (à lèvres).

liquid n & a liquide (m).

liquidation n liquidation f; go
into ∼ déposer son bilan.

liquidize vt passer au mixeur.
liquidizer n mixeur m.

liquor n alcool m.

liquorice n réglisse f.

lisp n zézaiement m; with a ∼ en
zézayant. ● vi zézayer.

list n liste f. ● vt dresser la liste
de. ● vi (ship) gîter.

listen vi écouter; ∼ to, ∼ in (to)
écouter. **listener** n auditeur/
-trice m/f.

listless a apathique.

lit ⇒LIGHT.

liter ⇒LITRE.

literal a (meaning) littéral;
(translation) mot à mot. **literally**
adv littéralement; mot à mot.

literary a littéraire.

literate a qui sait lire et écrire.

literature n littérature f;
(brochures) documentation f.

Lithuania n Lituanie f.

litigation n litiges mpl.

litre, (US) **liter** n litre m.

litter n (rubbish) détritus mpl,
papiers mpl; (animals) portée f.
● vt éparpiller; (make untidy) laisser

des détritus dans; **~ed with** jonché de. **~-bin** *n* poubelle *f*.

little *a* petit; (not much) peu de. ● *n* peu *m*; **a ~** un peu (de). ● *adv* peu.

live[1] *a* vivant; (wire) sous tension; (broadcast) en direct; **be a ~ wire** être très dynamique.

live[2] *vt/i* vivre; (reside) habiter, vivre; **~ it up** mener la belle vie. □ **~ down** faire oublier; **~ on** (feed oneself on) vivre de; (continue) survivre; **~ up to** se montrer à la hauteur de.

livelihood *n* moyens *mpl* d'existence.

lively *a* (**-ier, -iest**) vif, vivant.

liven *vt/i* **~ up** (s')animer; (cheer up) (s')égayer.

liver *n* foie *m*.

livestock *n* bétail *m*.

livid *a* livide; (angry) furieux.

living *a* vivant. ● *n* vie *f*; **make a ~** gagner sa vie; **~ conditions** conditions *fpl* de vie. **~-room** *n* salle *f* de séjour.

lizard *n* lézard *m*.

load *n* charge *f*; (loaded goods) chargement *m*, charge *f*; (weight, strain) poids *m*; **~s of** 🅄 des tas de 🅄. ● *vt* charger.

loaf *n* (*pl* **loaves**) pain *m*. ● *vi* **~ (about)** fainéanter.

loan *n* prêt *m*; (money borrowed) emprunt *m*. ● *vt* prêter.

loathe *vt* détester (**doing** faire).

loathing *n* dégoût *m*.

lobby *n* entrée *f*, vestibule *m*; (Pol) lobby *m*, groupe *m* de pression. ● *vt* faire pression sur.

lobster *n* homard *m*.

local *a* local; (shops) du quartier; **~ government** administration *f* locale. ● *n* personne *f* du coin; (pub 🅄) pub *m* du coin.

locally *adv* localement; (nearby) dans les environs.

locate *vt* (situate) situer; (find) repérer.

location *n* emplacement *m*; **on ~** (cinema) en extérieur.

lock *n* (of door) serrure *f*; (on canal) écluse *f*; (of hair) mèche *f*. ● *vt/i* fermer à clef; (wheels: Auto) (se) bloquer. □ **~ in** *or* **up** (person) enfermer; **~ out** (by mistake) enfermer dehors.

locker *n* casier *m*.

locket *n* médaillon *m*.

locksmith *n* serrurier *m*.

locum *n* (doctor) remplaçant/-e *m/f*.

lodge *n* (house) pavillon *m* (de gardien *or* de chasse); (of porter) loge *f*. ● *vt* (accommodate) loger; (money, complaint) déposer. ● *vi* être logé (**with** chez); (become fixed) se loger. **lodger** *n* locataire *mf*, pensionnaire *mf*. **lodgings** *n* logement *m*.

loft *n* grenier *m*.

lofty *a* (**-ier, -iest**) (tall, noble) élevé; (haughty) hautain.

log *n* (of wood) bûche *f*; **~(-book)** (Naut) journal *m* de bord; (Auto) ≈ carte *f* grise. ● *vt* (*pt* **logged**) noter; (distance) parcourir. □ **~ on** (Comput) se connecter; **~ off** (Comput) se déconnecter.

logic *a* logique. **logical** *a* logique.

logistics *n* logistique *f*.

loin *n* (Culin) filet *m*; **~s** reins *mpl*.

loiter *vi* traîner.

loll *vi* se prélasser.

lollipop *n* sucette *f*.

London *n* Londres. **Londoner** *n* Londonien/-ne *m/f*.

lone *a* solitaire.

lonely (**-ier, -iest**) solitaire; (person) seul, solitaire.

long *a* long; **how ~ is?** quelle est la longueur de?; **how ~?** quelle est la durée de?; **how ~?** combien de temps?; **a ~ time**

longtemps. ● *adv* longtemps; **he will not be ~** il n'en a pas pour longtemps; **as** *or* **so ~ as** pourvu que; **before ~** avant peu; **I no ~er do** je ne fais plus. ● *vi* avoir bien *or* très envie (**for, to** de); **~ for sb** (pine for) se languir de qn.
~-distance *a* (*flight*) sur long parcours; (*phone call*) interurbain; (*runner*) de fond. **~ face** *n* grimace *f*. **~hand** *n* écriture *f* courante.

longing *n* envie *f* (**for** de); (nostalgia) nostalgie *f* (**for** de).

longitude *n* longitude *f*.

long: **~ jump** *n* saut *m* en longueur. **~-range** *a* (*missile*) à longue portée; (*forecast*) à long terme. **~-sighted** *a* presbyte. **~-standing** *a* de longue date. **~-term** *a* à long terme. **~ wave** *n* grandes ondes *fpl*. **~-winded** *a* verbeux.

loo *n* 🔲 toilettes *fpl*.

look *vi* regarder; (seem) avoir l'air; **~ like** ressembler à, avoir l'air de. ● *n* regard *m*; (appearance) air *m*, aspect *m*; (good) **~s** beauté *f*. 🔲 **~ after** s'occuper de, soigner; **~ at** regarder; **~ back on** repenser à; **~ down on** mépriser; **~ for** chercher; **~ forward to** attendre avec impatience; **~ in on** passer voir; **~ into** examiner; **~ out** faire attention; **~ out for** (*person*) guetter; (*symptoms*) guetter l'apparition de; **~ round** se retourner; **~ up** (*word*) chercher; (visit) passer voir; **~ up to** respecter.

look-out *n* (Mil) poste *m* de guet; (person) guetteur *m*; **be on the ~ for** rechercher.

loom *vi* surgir; (*war*) menacer; (*interview*) être imminent. ● *n* métier *m* à tisser.

loony *n* & *a* 🔲 fou, folle (*mf*).

loop *n* boucle *f*. ● *vt* boucler. **~hole** *n* lacune *f*.

loose *a* (*knot*) desserré; (*page*) détaché; (*clothes*) ample, lâche; (*tooth*) qui bouge; (lax) relâché; (not packed) en vrac; (inexact) vague; (pej) immoral; **at a ~ end** désœuvré; **come ~** bouger.

loosely *adv* sans serrer; (roughly) vaguement. **loosen** *vt* (slacken) desserrer; (untie) défaire.

loot *n* butin *m*. ● *vt* piller.

lord *n* seigneur *m*; (British title) lord *m*; **the L~** le Seigneur; (good) **L~!** mon Dieu!

lorry *n* camion *m*.

lose *vt/i* (*pt* **lost**) perdre; **get lost** se perdre. **loser** *n* perdant/-e *m/f*.

loss *n* perte *f*; **be at a ~** être perplexe; **be at a ~ to** être incapable de; **heat ~** déperdition *f* de chaleur.

lost ⇒LOSE. ● *a* perdu. **~ property** *n* objets *mpl* trouvés.

lot *n* **the ~** (le) tout *m*; (people) tous *mpl*, toutes *fpl*; **a ~ (of), ~s (of)** 🔲 beaucoup (de); **quite a ~ (of)** 🔲 pas mal (de); (fate) sort *m*; (at auction) lot *m*; (land) lotissement *m*.

lotion *n* lotion *f*.

lottery *n* loterie *f*.

loud *a* bruyant, fort. ● *adv* fort; **out ~** tout haut. **loudly** *adv* fort. **~speaker** *n* haut-parleur *m*.

lounge *vi* paresser. ● *n* salon *m*.

louse *n* (*pl* **lice**) pou *m*.

lousy *a* (**-ier, -iest**) 🔲 infect.

lout *n* rustre *m*.

lovable *a* adorable.

love *n* amour *m*; (tennis) zéro *m*; **in ~** amoureux (**with** de); **make ~** faire l'amour. ● *vt* (*person*) aimer; (like greatly) aimer (beaucoup) (**to do** faire). **~ affair** *n* liaison *f* amoureuse. **~ life** *n* vie *f* amoureuse.

lovely *a* (**-ier, -iest**) joli; (delightful 🇬🇧) très agréable.

lover *n* (male) amant *m*; (female) maîtresse *f*; (devotee) amateur *m* (**of** de).

loving *a* affectueux.

low *a & adv* bas; ~ **in sth** à faible teneur en qch. ● *n* (low pressure) dépression *f*; **reach a** (**new**) ~ atteindre son niveau le plus bas. ● *vi* meugler. ~**-calorie** *a* basses-calories. ~**-cut** *a* décolleté.

lower *a & adv* ⇒LOW. ● *vt* baisser; ~ **oneself** s'abaisser.

low: ~**-fat** *a* (*diet*) sans matières grasses; (*cheese*) allégé. ~**-key** *a* modéré; (discreet) discret. ~**lands** *npl* plaine(s) *f(pl)*. ~**-lying** *a* à faible altitude.

loyal *a* loyal (**to** envers).

loyalty *n* fidélité *f*. ~ **card** *n* carte *f* de fidélité.

lozenge *n* (shape) losange *m*; (tablet) pastille *f*.

LP *n* (disque *m*) 33 tours *m*.

Ltd. *abbr* (**Limited**) SA.

lubricant *n* lubrifiant *m*. **lubricate** *vt* lubrifier.

luck *n* chance *f*; **bad** ~ malchance *f*; **good** ~! bonne chance!

luckily *adv* heureusement.

lucky *a* (**-ier, -iest**) qui a de la chance, heureux; (event) heureux; (number) qui porte bonheur; **it's** ~ **that** heureusement que.

ludicrous *a* ridicule.

lug *vt* (*pt* **lugged**) traîner.

luggage *n* bagages *mpl*. ~**-rack** *n* porte-bagages *m inv*.

lukewarm *a* tiède.

lull *vt* **he** ~**ed them into thinking that** il leur a fait croire que. ● *n* accalmie *f*.

lullaby *n* berceuse *f*.

lumber *n* bois *m* de charpente. ● *vt* 🇬🇧 ~ **sb with** (*chore*) coller à qn 🇬🇧. ~**jack** *n* bûcheron *m*.

luminous *a* lumineux.

lump *n* morceau *m*; (swelling on body) grosseur *f*; (in liquid) grumeau *m*. ● *vt* ~ **together** réunir. ~ **sum** *n* somme *f* globale.

lunacy *n* folie *f*.

lunar *a* lunaire.

lunatic *n* fou/ folle *m/f*.

lunch *n* déjeuner *m*. ● *vi* déjeuner.

luncheon *n* déjeuner *m*. ~ **voucher** *n* chèque-repas *m*.

lung *n* poumon *m*.

lunge *vi* bondir (**at** sur; **forward** en avant).

lurch *n* **leave in the** ~ planter là, laisser en plan. ● *vi* (*person*) tituber.

lure *vt* appâter, attirer. ● *n* (attraction) attrait *m*, appât *m*.

lurid *a* choquant, affreux; (gaudy) voyant.

lurk *vi* se cacher; (in ambush) s'embusquer; (prowl) rôder; (*suspicion, danger*) menacer.

luscious *a* appétissant.

lush *a* luxuriant.

lust *n* luxure *f*.

Luxemburg *n* Luxembourg *m*.

luxurious *a* luxueux.

luxury *n* luxe *m*. ● *a* de luxe.

lying ⇒LIE[1], LIE[2]. ● *n* mensonges *mpl*.

lyric *a* lyrique. **lyrical** *a* lyrique. **lyrics** *npl* paroles *fpl*.

L

MA *abbr* ⇒MASTER OF ARTS.

mac *n* 🔲 *imper* m.

machine *n* machine *f*. ● *vt* (sew) coudre à la machine; (Tech) usiner. **~-gun** mitrailleuse *f*.

mackerel *n inv* maquereau *m*.

mackintosh *n* imperméable *m*.

mad *a* (**madder, maddest**) fou; (foolish) insensé; (*dog*) enragé; (angry 🔲) furieux; **be ~ about** se passionner pour; (*person*) être fou de; **drive sb ~** exaspérer qn; **like ~** comme un fou. **~ cow disease** *n* maladie *f* de la vache folle.

madam *n* madame *f*; (unmarried) mademoiselle *f*.

made ⇒MAKE.

madly *adv* (*interested, in love*) follement; (frantically) comme un fou.

madman *n* (*pl* -**men**) fou *m*.

madness *n* folie *f*.

magazine *n* revue *f*, magazine *m*; (of gun) magasin *m*.

maggot *n* (in fruit) ver *m*, (for fishing) asticot *m*.

magic *n* magie *f*. ● *a* magique.

magician *n* magicien/-ne *m/f*.

magistrate *n* magistrat *m*.

magnet *n* aimant *m*. **magnetic** *a* magnétique.

magnificent *a* magnifique.

magnify *vt* grossir; (*sound*) amplifier; (fig) exagérer. **magnifying glass** *n* loupe *f*.

magpie *n* pie *f*.

mahogany *n* acajou *m*.

maid *n* (servant) bonne *f*; (in hotel) femme *f* de chambre.

maiden *n* (old use) jeune fille *f*. ● *a* (*aunt*) célibataire; (*voyage*) premier. **~ name** *n* nom *m* de jeune fille.

mail *n* (postal service) poste *f*; (letters) courrier *m*; (armour) cotte *f* de mailles. ● *a* (bag, van) postal. ● *vt* envoyer par la poste. **~ box** *n* boîte *f* aux lettres; (Comput) boîte *f* aux lettres électronique. **mailing list** *n* liste *f* d'adresses. **~man** *n* (*pl* -**men**) (US) facteur *m*. **~ order** *n* vente *f* par correspondance. **~ shot** *n* publipostage *m*.

main *a* principal; **a ~ road** une grande route. ● *n* (water/gas) ~ conduite *f* d'eau/de gaz; **the ~s** (Electr) le secteur; **in the ~** en général. **~frame** *n* unité *f* centrale. **~land** *n* continent *m*. **~stream** *n* tendance *f* principale, ligne *f*.

maintain *vt* (continue, keep, assert) maintenir; (*house, machine, family*) entretenir; (*rights*) soutenir.

maintenance *n* (care) entretien *m*; (continuation) maintien *m*; (allowance) pension *f* alimentaire.

maisonette *n* duplex *m*.

maize *n* maïs *m*.

majestic *a* majestueux.

majesty *n* majesté *f*.

major *a* majeur. ● *n* commandant *m*. ● *vi* ~ **in** (Univ, US) se spécialiser en.

majority *n* majorité *f*; **the ~ of people** la plupart des gens. ● *a* majoritaire.

make *vt/i* (*pt* **made**) faire; (manufacture) fabriquer; (*friends*) se faire; (*money*) gagner; (*decision*) prendre; (*place, position*) arriver à; (cause to be) rendre; **~ sb do sth** faire faire qch à qn; (force) obliger qn à faire qch; **be made of** être fait de; ~ **oneself at home** se mettre à l'aise; ~ **sb happy** rendre qn heureux; ~ **it** arriver; (succeed) réussir; **I ~ it two o'clock** j'ai deux heures; **I ~ it 150** d'après moi, ça fait 150; **I cannot ~ anything of it** je n'y comprends rien; **can you ~ Friday?** vendredi, c'est possible?; ~ **as if to** faire mine de. ● *n* (brand) marque *f*. □ ~ **do** (manage) se débrouiller (**with** avec); ~ **for** se diriger vers; (cause) tendre à créer; ~ **good** *vi* réussir; *vt* compenser; (repair) réparer; ~ **off** filer (**with** avec); ~ **out** distinguer; (understand) comprendre; (draw up) faire; (assert) prétendre; ~ **up** *vt* faire, former; (story) inventer; (deficit) combler; *vi* se réconcilier; ~ **up for** compenser; (time) rattraper; ~ **up one's mind** se décider.

make-believe *a* feint, illusoire. ● *n* fantaisie *f*.

maker *n* fabricant *m*.

makeshift *a* improvisé.

make-up *n* maquillage *m*; (of object) constitution *f*; (Psych) caractère *m*.

malaria *n* paludisme *m*.

Malaysia *n* Malaisie *f*.

male *a* (voice, sex) masculin; (Bot, Tech) mâle. ● *n* mâle *m*.

malfunction *n* mauvais fonctionnement *m*. ● *vi* mal fonctionner.

malice *n* méchanceté *f*. **malicious** *a* méchant.

malignant *a* malveillant; (tumour) malin.

mall *n* (**shopping**) ~ (in suburbs) centre *m* commercial; (in town) galerie *f* marchande.

malnutrition *n* sous-alimentation *f*.

Malta *n* Malte *f*.

mammal *n* mammifère *m*.

mammoth *n* mammouth *m*. ● *a* (task) gigantesque; (organization) géant.

man *n* (*pl* **men**) homme *m*; (in sports team) joueur *m*; (chess) pièce *f*; ~ **to man** d'homme à homme. ● *vt* (*pt* **manned**) (desk) tenir; (ship) armer; (guns) servir; (be on duty at) être de service à.

manage *vt* (project, organization) diriger; (shop, affairs) gérer; (handle) manier; **I could ~ another drink** 🗊 je prendrais bien encore un verre; **can you ~ Friday?** vendredi, c'est possible? ● *vi* se débrouiller; ~ **to do** réussir à faire. **manageable** *a* (tool, size, person) maniable; (job) faisable.

management *n* (managers) direction *f*; (of shop) gestion *f*.

manager *n* directeur/-trice *m/f*; (of shop) gérant/-e *m/f*; (of actor) impresario *m*.

mandate *n* mandat *m*.

mandatory *a* obligatoire.

mane *n* crinière *f*.

mango *n* (*pl* ~**es**) mangue *f*.

manhandle *vt* maltraiter, malmener.

man: ~**hole** *n* regard *m*. ~**hood** *n* âge *m* d'homme; (quality) virilité *f*.

maniac *n* maniaque *mf*, fou *m*, folle *f*.

manicure *n* manucure *f*. ● *vt* soigner, manucurer.

manifest *a* manifeste. ● *vt* manifester.

manipulate *vt* (tool, person) manipuler.

mankind *n* genre *m* humain.

manly *a* viril.

man-made *a* (fibre) synthétique; (pond) artificiel; (disaster) d'origine humaine.

manned *a* (spacecraft) habité.

manner *n* manière *f*; (attitude)

M

attitude *f*; (kind) sorte *f*; ∼**s** (social behaviour) manières *fpl*.

mannerism *n* particularité *f*; (quirk) manie *f*.

manoeuvre *n* manœuvre *f*. ● *vt/i* manœuvrer.

manor *n* manoir *m*.

manpower *n* main-d'œuvre *f*.

mansion *n* (in countryside) demeure *f*; (in town) hôtel *m* particulier.

manslaughter *n* homicide *m* involontaire.

mantelpiece *n* (manteau *m* de) cheminée.

manual *a* (labour) manuel; (typewriter) mécanique. ● *n* (handbook) manuel *m*.

manufacture *vt* fabriquer. ● *n* fabrication *f*.

manure *n* fumier *m*.

many *a & n* beaucoup (de); **a great** *or* **good** ∼ un grand nombre (de); ∼ **a** bien des.

map *n* carte *f*; (of streets) plan *m*. ● *vt* (pt **mapped**) faire la carte de; ∼ **out** (route) tracer; (arrange) organiser.

mar *vt* (pt **marred**) gâcher.

marble *n* marbre *m*; (for game) bille *f*.

March *n* mars *m*.

march *vi* (Mil) marcher (au pas). ● *vt* ∼ **off** (lead away) emmener. ● *n* marche *f*.

margin *n* marge *f*.

marginal *a* marginal; (increase) léger, faible; (seat: Pol) disputé.

marinate *vt* faire mariner (in dans).

marine *a* marin. ● *n* (shipping) marine *f*; (sailor) fusilier *m* marin.

marital *a* conjugal. ∼ **status** *n* situation *f* de famille.

mark *n* (currency) mark *m*; (stain) tache *f*; (trace) marque *f*; (School) note *f*; (target) but *m*. ● *vt* marquer; (exam) corriger; ∼ **out**

délimiter; (person) désigner; ∼ **time** marquer le pas.

marker *n* (pen) marqueur *m*; (tag) repère *m*; (School, Univ) examinateur/-trice *m/f*.

market *n* marché *m*; **on the** ∼ en vente. ● *vt* (sell) vendre; (launch) commercialiser. ∼ **research** *n* étude *f* de marché.

marmalade *n* confiture *f* d'oranges.

maroon *n* bordeaux *m inv*. ● *a* bordeaux *inv*.

marooned *a* abandonné; (snowbound) bloqué.

marquee *n* grande tente *f*; (of circus) chapiteau *m*; (awning: US) auvent *m*.

marriage *n* mariage *m* (to avec).

married *a* marié (to à); (life) conjugal; **get** ∼ se marier (to avec).

marrow *n* (of bone) moelle *f*; (vegetable) courge *f*.

marry *vt* épouser; (give or unite in marriage) marier. ● *vi* se marier.

marsh *n* marais *m*.

marshal *n* maréchal *m*; (at event) membre *m* du service d'ordre. ● *vt* (pt **marshalled**) rassembler.

martyr *n* martyr/-e *m/f*. ● *vt* martyriser.

marvel *n* merveille *f*. ● *vi* (pt **marvelled**) s'émerveiller (at de).

marvellous *a* merveilleux.

marzipan *n* pâte *f* d'amandes.

masculine *a & n* masculin (m).

mash *n* (potatoes 🄳) purée *f*. ● *vt* écraser. **mashed potatoes** *npl* purée *f* (de pommes de terre).

mask *n* masque *m*. ● *vt* masquer.

Mason *n* franc-maçon *m*.

masonry *n* maçonnerie *f*.

mass *n* (Relig) messe *f*; masse *f*; **the** ∼**es** les masses *fpl*. ● *vt/i* (se) masser.

massacre *n* massacre *m*. ● *vt* massacrer.

massage *n* massage *m*. ● *vt* masser.

massive *a* (large) énorme; (heavy) massif.

mass media *n* médias *mpl*.

mass-produce *vt* fabriquer en série.

mast *n* (on ship) mât *m*; (for radio, TV) pylône *m*.

master *n* maître *m*; (in secondary school) professeur *m*; M~ **of Arts** titulaire *mf* d'une maîtrise ès lettres. ● *vt* maîtriser.

masterpiece *n* chef-d'œuvre *m*.

mastery *n* maîtrise *f*.

mat *n* (petit) tapis *m*; (at door) paillasson *m*.

match *n* (for lighting fire) allumette *f*; (Sport) match *m*; (equal) égal/-e *m/f*; (marriage) mariage *m*; (sb to marry) parti *m*; **be a ~ for** pouvoir tenir tête à. ● *vt* opposer; (go with) aller avec; (cups) assortir; (equal) égaler. ● *vi* (be alike) être assorti.

matchbox *n* boîte *f* à allumettes.

matching *a* assorti.

mate *n* camarade *mf*; (of animal) compagnon *m*, compagne *f*; (assistant) aide *mf*; (chess) mat *m*. ● *vt/i* (s')accoupler (**with** avec).

material *n* matière *f*; (fabric) tissu *m*; (documents, for building) matériau (x) *m(pl)*; ~**s** (equipment) matériel *m*. ● *a* matériel; (fig) important.

materialistic *a* matérialiste.

materialize *vi* se matérialiser, se réaliser.

maternal *a* maternel.

maternity *n* maternité *f*. ● *a* (clothes) de grossesse. ~ **hospital** *n* maternité *f*. ~ **leave** *n* congé *m* de maternité.

mathematics *n* & *npl* mathématiques *fpl*.

maths, (US) **math** *n* maths *fpl*.

mating *n* accouplement *m*.

matrimony *n* mariage *m*.

matron *n* (married, elderly) dame *f* âgée; (in hospital) infirmière *f* en chef.

matt *a* mat.

matter *n* (substance) matière *f*; (affair) affaire *f*; **as a ~ of fact** en fait; **what is the ~?** qu'est-ce qu'il y a? ● *vi* importer; **it does not ~** ça ne fait rien; **no ~ what happens** quoi qu'il arrive.

mattress *n* matelas *m*.

mature *a* (psychologically) mûr; (plant) adulte. ● *vt/i* (se) mûrir.

maturity *n* maturité *f*.

mauve *a* & *n* mauve (*m*).

maverick *n* non-conformiste *mf*.

maximize *vt* porter au maximum.

maximum *a* & *n* (*pl* -**ima**) maximum (*m*).

M

. . . .

may

> *past* **might**

● *auxiliary verb*

····▸ (possibility) **they ~ be able to come** ils pourront peut-être venir; **she ~ not have seen him** elle ne l'a peut-être pas vu; **it ~ rain** il risque de pleuvoir; **'will you come?'—'I might'** 'tu viendras?'—'peut-être'.

····▸ (permission) **you ~ leave** vous pouvez partir; **~ I smoke?** puis-je fumer?

····▸ (wish) **~ he be happy** qu'il soit heureux.

. . . .

May *n* mai *m*.

maybe *adv* peut-être.

mayhem *n* (havoc) ravages *mpl*.

mayonnaise *n* mayonnaise *f*.

mayor *n* maire *m*.

maze *n* labyrinthe *m*.

Mb *abbr* (**megabyte**) (Comput) Mo.

me *pron* me, m'; (after prep.) moi; (indirect object) me, m'; **he knows ~** il me connaît.

meadow *n* pré *m*.

meagre *a* maigre.

meal *n* repas *m*; (grain) farine *f*.

mean *a* (poor) misérable; (miserly) avare; (unkind) méchant; (average) moyen. ● *n* milieu *m*; (average) moyenne *f*; **in the ~ time** en attendant. ● *vt* (*pt* **meant**) vouloir dire, signifier; (involve) entraîner; **I ~ that!** je suis sérieux; **be meant for** être destiné à; **~ to do** avoir l'intention de faire.

meaning *n* sens *m*, signification *f*. **meaningful** *a* significatif. **meaningless** *a* dénué de sens.

means *n* moyen(s) *m(pl)*; **by ~ of sth** au moyen de qch. ● *npl* (wealth) moyens *mpl* financiers; **by all ~** certainement; **by no ~** nullement.

meant ⇒MEAN.

meantime, meanwhile *adv* en attendant.

measles *n* rougeole *f*.

measure *n* mesure *f*; (ruler) règle *f*. ● *vt/i* mesurer; **~ up to** être à la hauteur de.

meat *n* viande *f*. **meaty** *a* de viande; (fig) substantiel.

mechanic *n* mécanicien/-ne *m/f*.

mechanical *a* mécanique.

mechanism *n* mécanisme *m*.

medal *n* médaille *f*.

meddle *vi* (interfere) se mêler (**in** de); (tinker) toucher (**with** à).

media *n* ⇒MEDIUM. ● *npl* **the ~** les média *mpl*; **talk to the ~** parler à la presse.

median *a* médian. ● *n* médiane *f*.

mediate *vi* servir d'intermédiaire.

medical *a* médical; (student) en médecine. ● *n* visite *f* médicale.

medication *n* médicaments *mpl*.

medicine *n* (science) médecine *f*; (substance) médicament *m*.

medieval *a* médiéval.

mediocre *a* médiocre.

meditate *vt/i* méditer.

Mediterranean *a* méditerranéen. ● *n* **the ~** la Méditerranée *f*.

medium *n* (*pl* **media**) (mid-point) milieu *m*; (for transmitting data) support *m*; (*pl* **mediums**) (person) médium *m*. ● *a* moyen.

medley *n* mélange *m*; (Mus) pot-pourri *m*.

meet *vt* (*pt* **met**) rencontrer; (see again) retrouver; (be introduced to) faire la connaissance de; (face) faire face à; (requirement) satisfaire. ● *vi* se rencontrer; (see each other again) se retrouver; (in session) se réunir.

meeting *n* réunion *f*; (between two people) rencontre *f*.

megabyte *n* (Comput) mégaoctet *m*.

melancholy *n* mélancolie *f*. ● *a* mélancolique.

mellow *a* (fruit) mûr; (sound, colour) moelleux, doux; (person) mûri. ● *vt/i* (mature) mûrir; (soften) (s')adoucir.

melody *n* mélodie *f*.

melon *n* melon *m*.

melt *vt/i* (faire) fondre.

member *n* membre *m*. **M~ of Parliament** *n* député *m*.

membership *n* adhésion *f*; (members) membres *mpl*; (fee) cotisation *f*.

memento *n* (*pl* **~es**) (object) souvenir *m*.

memo *n* note *f*.

memoir *n* (record, essay) mémoire *m*.

memorandum *n* note *f*.

memorial *n* monument *m*. ● *a* commémoratif.

memorize *vt* apprendre par cœur.

memory *n* (mind, in computer) mémoire *f*; (thing remembered) souvenir *m*; **from ~** de mémoire; **in ~ of** à la mémoire de.

men ⇒MAN.

menace *n* menace *f*; (nuisance) peste *f*. ● *vt* menacer.

mend *vt* réparer; (darn) raccommoder; **~ one's ways** s'amender. ● *n* raccommodage *m*; **on the ~** en voie de guérison.

meningitis *n* méningite *f*.

menopause *n* ménopause *f*.

mental *a* mental; (*hospital*) psychiatrique.

mentality *n* mentalité *f*.

mention *vt* mentionner; **don't ~ it!** il n'y a pas de quoi!, je vous en prie! ● *n* mention *f*.

menu *n* (food, on computer) menu *m*; (list) carte *f*.

MEP *abbr* (**Member of the European Parliament**) député *m* au Parlement européen.

mercenary *a & n* mercenaire (*m*).

merchandise *n* marchandises *fpl*.

merchant *n* marchand *m*. ● *a* (*ship, navy*) marchand. **~ bank** *n* banque *f* de commerce.

merciful *a* miséricordieux.

mercury *n* mercure *m*.

mercy *n* pitié *f*; **at the ~ of** à la merci de.

mere *a* simple. **merest** *a* moindre.

merge *vt/i* (se) mêler (**with** à); (*companies*: Comm) fusionner. **merger** *n* fusion *f*.

mermaid *n* sirène *f*.

merrily *adv* (happily) joyeusement; (unconcernedly) avec insouciance.

merry *a* (**-ier, -iest**) gai; **make ~** faire la fête. **~-go-round** *n* manège *m*.

mesh *n* maille *f*; (fabric) tissu *m* à mailles; (network) réseau *m*.

mesmerize *vt* hypnotiser.

mess *n* désordre *m*, gâchis *m*; (dirt) saleté *f*; (Mil) mess *m*; **make a ~ of** gâcher. ● *vt* **~ up** gâcher. ● *vi* **~ about** s'amuser; (dawdle) traîner; **~ with** (tinker with) tripoter.

message *n* message *m*.

messenger *n* messager/-ère *m/f*.

messy *a* (**-ier, -iest**) en désordre; (dirty) sale.

met ⇒MEET.

metal *n* métal *m*. ● *a* de métal. **metallic** *a* métallique; (paint, colour) métallisé.

metallurgy *n* métallurgie *f*.

metaphor *n* métaphore *f*.

meteor *n* météore *m*.

meteorite *n* météorite *m*.

meteorology *n* météorologie *f*.

meter *n* compteur *m*; (US) = METRE.

method *n* méthode *f*.

methylated spirit(s) *n* alcool *m* à brûler.

meticulous *a* méticuleux.

metre, (US) **meter** *n* mètre *m*.

metric *a* métrique.

metropolis *n* métropole *f*. **metropolitan** *a* métropolitain.

mew *n* miaulement *m*. ● *vi* miauler.

mews *npl* appartements *mpl* chic aménagés dans d'anciennes écuries.

Mexico *n* Mexique *m*.

miaow *n & vi* = MEW.

mice ⇒MOUSE.

mickey *n* **take the ~ out of** 🄳 se moquer de.

M

microchip n puce f; circuit m intégré.

microlight n ULM m.

microprocessor n microprocesseur m.

microscope n microscope m.

microwave n micro-onde f; ~ (oven) four m à micro-ondes. ● vt passer au four à micro-ondes.

mid a in ~ air en plein ciel; in ~ March à la mi-mars; ~ afternoon milieu m de l'après-midi; he's in his ~ twenties il a environ vingt-cinq ans.

midday n midi m.

middle a (door, shelf) du milieu; (size) moyen. ● n milieu m; in the ~ of au milieu de. ~-aged a d'âge mûr. M~ Ages n Moyen Âge m. ~ class n classe f moyenne. M~ East n Moyen-Orient m.

midge n moucheron m.

midget n nain/-e m/f. ● a minuscule.

midnight n minuit f; it's ~ il est minuit.

midst n in the ~ of au beau milieu de; in our ~ parmi nous.

midsummer n milieu m de l'été; (solstice) solstice m d'été.

midway adv ~ between/along à mi-chemin entre/le long de.

midwife n (pl -wives) sage-femme f.

might¹ v aux I ~ have been killed! j'aurais pu être tué!; you ~ try doing sth vous pourriez faire qch; ⇒MAY.

might² n puissance f.

mighty a puissant; (huge 🗊) énorme. ● adv 🗊 vachement 🗊.

migrant a & n (bird) migrateur (m); (worker) migrant/-e (m/f).

migrate vi émigrer. **migration** n migration f.

mild a (surprise, taste, tobacco,

attack) léger; (weather, cheese, soap, person) doux; (case, infection) bénin.

mile n mile m (= 1.6 km); walk for ~s marcher pendant des kilomètres; ~s better 🗊 bien meilleur. **mileage** n nombre m de miles, kilométrage m.

milestone n (lit) borne f; (fig) étape f importante.

military a militaire.

militia n milice f.

milk n lait m. ● vt (cow) traire; (fig) pomper.

milkman n (pl -men) laitier m.

milky a (skin, colour) laiteux; (tea) au lait; M~ Way Voie f lactée.

mill n moulin m; (factory) usine f. ● vt moudre. ● vi ~ around grouiller.

millennium n (pl ~s) millénaire m.

millimetre, (US) **millimeter** n millimètre m.

million n million m; a ~ pounds un million de livres. **millionaire** n millionnaire m.

millstone n meule f; (fig) boulet m.

mime n (actor) mime mf; (art) mime m. ● vt/i mimer.

mimic vt (pt mimicked) imiter. ● n imitateur/-trice m/f.

mince vt hacher; not to ~ matters ne pas mâcher ses mots. ● n viande f hachée.

mind n esprit m; (sanity) raison f; (opinion) avis m; be on sb's ~ préoccuper qn; bear that in ~ ne l'oubliez pas; change one's ~ changer d'avis; make up one's ~ se décider (to à). ● vt (have charge of) s'occuper de; (heed) faire attention à; I do not ~ the noise le bruit ne me dérange pas; I don't ~ ça m'est égal; would you ~

checking? je peux vous demander de vérifier?

minder n (bodyguard) garde m de corps; (child) ~ nourrice f.

mindless a (programme) bête; (work) abrutissant; (vandalism) gratuit.

mine n mine f. ● vt extraire; (Mil) miner. ● pron le mien, la mienne, les mien(ne)s; **the blue car is** ~ la voiture bleue est la mienne or à moi.

minefield n (lit) champ m de mines; (fig) terrain m miné.

miner n mineur m.

mineral n & a minéral (m); ~ **water** eau f minérale.

minesweeper n (ship) dragueur m de mines.

mingle vt/i (se) mêler (with à).

minibus n minibus m.

minicab n taxi m (non agréé).

minimal a minimal.

minimize vt minimiser; (Comput) réduire.

minimum a & n (pl -ima) minimum (m).

minister n ministre m. **ministerial** a ministériel, **ministry** n ministère m.

mink n vison m.

minor a (change, surgery) mineur; (injury, burn) léger; (road) secondaire. ● n (Jur) mineur/-e m/f.

minority n minorité f; **in the** ~ en minorité. ● a minoritaire.

mint n (Bot, Culin) menthe f; (sweet) bonbon m à la menthe; (fortune ▥) fortune f. ● vt frapper; **in** ~ **condition** à l'état neuf.

minus prep moins; (without ▥) sans. ● n moins m; (drawback) inconvénient m.

minute[1] n minute f; ~**s** (of meeting) compte-rendu m.

minute[2] a (object) minuscule; (risk, variation) minime.

miracle n miracle m.

mirror n miroir m, glace f; (Auto) rétroviseur. ● vt refléter.

misbehave vi se conduire mal.

miscalculation n (lit) erreur f de calcul; (fig) mauvais calcul m.

miscarriage n fausse couche f; ~ **of justice** erreur f judiciaire.

miscellaneous a divers.

mischief n (playfulness) espièglerie f; (by children) bêtises fpl.

mischievous a espiègle; (malicious) méchant.

misconduct n mauvaise conduite f.

misconstrue vt mal interpréter.

misdemeanour, (US) **misdemeanor** n (Jur) délit m.

miser n avare mf.

miserable a (sad) malheureux; (wretched) misérable; (performance, result) lamentable.

misery n (unhappiness) souffrance f; (misfortune) misère f; (person ▥) rabat-joie mf inv.

misfit n inadapté/-e m/f.

misfortune n malheur m.

misgiving n (doubt) doute m; (apprehension) crainte f.

misguided a (foolish) imprudent; (mistaken) erroné; **be** ~ (person) se tromper.

mishap n incident m.

misjudge vt (distance, speed) mal évaluer; (person) mal juger.

mislay vt (pt **mislaid**) égarer.

mislead vt (pt **misled**) tromper. **misleading** a trompeur.

misplace vt mal ranger; (lose) égarer. **misplaced** a (fear, criticism) déplacé.

misprint n coquille f, faute f typographique.

misread vt (pt **misread**) mal lire; (intentions) mal interpréter.

M

miss vt/i manquer; (bus) rater; he ~es her/Paris elle/Paris lui manque; you're ~ing the point tu n'as rien compris; ~ sth out omettre qch; ~ out on sth laisser passer qch. ● n coup m manqué; it was a near ~ on l'a échappé belle.

Miss n Mademoiselle f; ~ Smith (written) Mlle Smith.

misshapen a difforme.

missile n (Mil) missile m; (thrown) projectile m.

mission n mission f. **missionary** n missionnaire mf.

misspell vt (pt **misspelt** or **misspelled**) mal écrire.

mist n brume f; (on window) buée f. ● vt/i (s')embuer.

mistake n erreur f; by ~ par erreur; make a ~ faire une erreur. ● vt (pt **mistook**; pp **mistaken**) (meaning) mal interpréter; ~ for prendre pour.

mistaken a (enthusiasm) mal placé; be ~ avoir tort.

mistletoe n gui m.

mistreat vt maltraiter.

mistress n maîtresse f.

misty a (-ier, -iest) brumeux; (window) embué.

misunderstanding n malentendu m.

misuse vt (word) mal employer; (power) abuser de; (equipment) faire mauvais usage de.

mitten n moufle f.

mix n mélange m. ● vt mélanger; (drink) préparer; (cement) malaxer. ● vi se mélanger (with avec, à); (socially) être sociable; ~ with sb fréquenter qn. □ ~ up (confuse) confondre; (jumble up) mélanger; get ~ed up in se trouver mêlé à.

mixed a (school) mixte; (collection, diet) varié; (nuts, sweets) assorti.

mixer n (Culin) batteur m électrique; be a good ~ être sociable; ~ tap mélangeur m.

mixture n mélange m.

mix-up n confusion f (over sur).

moan n gémissement m. ● vi gémir; (complain 🔲) râler 🔲.

mob n (crowd) foule f; (gang) gang m; the M~ la Mafia. ● vt (pt **mobbed**) assaillir.

mobile a mobile; ~ phone téléphone m portable. ● n mobile m.

mobilize vt/i mobiliser.

mock vt/i se moquer (de). ● a faux.

mockery n moquerie f; a ~ of une parodie de.

mock-up n maquette f.

mode n mode m.

model n (Comput, Auto) modèle m; (scale representation) maquette f; (person showing clothes) mannequin m. ● a modèle; (car) modèle réduit inv; (railway) miniature. ● vt (pt **modelled**) modeler; (clothes) présenter. ● vi être mannequin; (pose) poser. **modelling** n métier m de mannequin.

modem n modem m.

moderate a & n modéré/-e (m/f).

moderation n modération f; in ~ avec modération.

modern a moderne; ~ languages langues fpl vivantes. **modernize** vt moderniser.

modest a modeste. **modesty** n modestie f.

modification n modification f. **modify** vt modifier.

module n module m.

moist a (soil) humide; (skin, palms) moite; (cake) moelleux.

moisten vt humecter. **moisture** n humidité f. **moisturizer** n crème f hydratante.

molar n molaire f.

mold (US) = MOULD.

mole n grain m de beauté; (animal) taupe f.

molecule n molécule f.

molest vt (pester) importuner; (sexually) agresser sexuellement.

moment n (short time) instant m; (point in time) moment m.
momentarily adv momentanément; (soon: US) très bientôt. **momentary** a momentané.

momentum n élan m.

monarch n monarque m.
monarchy n monarchie f.

Monday n lundi m.

monetary a monétaire.

money n argent m; **make ~** (person) gagner de l'argent; (business) rapporter de l'argent. **~-box** n tirelire f. **~ order** n mandat m postal.

monitor n dispositif m de surveillance; (Comput) moniteur m.
● vt surveiller; (broadcast) être à l'écoute de.

monk n moine m.

monkey n singe m.

monopolize vt monopoliser.
monopoly n monopole m.

monotonous a monotone.
monotony n monotonie f.

monsoon n mousson f.

monster n monstre m.
monstrous a monstrueux.

month n mois m.

monthly a mensuel. ● adv (pay) au mois; (publish) tous les mois.
● n (periodical) mensuel m.

monument n monument m.

moo vi meugler.

mood n humeur f; **in a good/bad ~** de bonne/mauvaise humeur.
moody a d'humeur changeante.

moon n lune f.

moonlight n clair m de lune.

moonlighting n 🗓 travail m au noir.

moor n lande f. ● vt amarrer.

mop n balai m à franges; **~ of hair** crinière f 🗓. ● vt (pt **mopped**) **~ (up)** éponger.

moped n vélomoteur m.

moral a moral. ● n morale f; **~s** moralité f.

morale n moral m.

morbid a morbide.

more adv plus; **~ serious** plus sérieux; **work ~** travailler plus; **sleep ~ and ~** dormir de plus en plus; **once ~** une fois de plus; **I don't go there any ~** je n'y vais plus; **~ or less** plus ou moins.
● det plus de; **a little ~ wine** un peu plus de vin; **~ bread** encore un peu de pain; **there's no ~ bread** il n'y a plus de pain; **nothing ~** rien de plus. ● pron plus; **cost ~ than** coûter plus cher que; **I need ~ of it** il m'en faut davantage.

moreover adv de plus.

morning n matin m; (whole morning) matinée f.

Morocco n Maroc m.

morsel n morceau m.

mortal a & n mortel/-le (m/f).

mortgage n emprunt-logement m. ● vt hypothéquer.

mortuary n morgue f.

mosaic n mosaïque f.

mosque n mosquée f.

mosquito n (pl **~es**) moustique m.

moss n mousse f.

most det (nearly all) la plupart de; **~ people** la plupart des gens; **the ~ votes/money** le plus de voix/ d'argent. ● n le plus. ● pron la plupart; **~ of us** la plupart d'entre nous; **~ of the money** la plus grande partie de l'argent; **the ~ I can do is ...** tout ce que je

M

peux faire c'est … ●*adv* the ~ **beautiful house/hotel in Oxford** la maison la plus belle/l'hôtel le plus beau d'Oxford; ~ **interesting** très intéressant; **what I like ~ (of all) is** ce que j'aime le plus c'est.

mostly *adv* surtout.

moth *n* papillon *m* de nuit; (in cloth) mite *f*.

mother *n* mère *f*. ●*vt* (lit) materner; (fig) dorloter. **motherhood** *n* maternité *f*. ~**-in-law** *n* (*pl* ~**s-in-law**) belle-mère *f*. ~**-of-pearl** *n* nacre *f*. **M~'s Day** *n* la fête des mères. ~**-to-be** *n* future maman *f*. ~ **tongue** *n* langue *f* maternelle.

motion *n* mouvement *m*; (proposal) motion *f*; ~ **picture** (US) film *m*. ●*vt/i* ~ (**to**) **sb to** faire signe à qn de. **motionless** *a* immobile.

motivate *vt* motiver.

motive *n* motif *m*; (Jur) mobile *m*.

motor *n* moteur *m*; (car) auto *f*. ●*a* (*industry, insurance, vehicle*) automobile; (*activity, disorder*: Med) moteur. ~**bike** *n* moto *f*. ~ **car** *n* auto *f*. ~**-cyclist** *n* motocycliste *mf*. ~ **home** *n* auto-caravane *f*.

motorist *n* automobiliste *mf*.

motorway *n* autoroute *f*.

mottled *a* tacheté.

motto *n* (*pl* ~**es**) devise *f*.

mould *n* (shape) moule *m*; (fungus) moisissure *f*. ●*vt* mouler; (influence) former. **moulding** *n* moulure *f*. **mouldy** *a* moisi.

mount *n* (hill) mont *m*; (horse) monture *f*. ●*vt* (stairs) gravir; (*platform, horse, bike*) monter sur; (*jewel, picture, campaign, exhibit*) monter. ●*vi* monter; (*number, toll*) augmenter; (*concern*) grandir.

mountain *n* montagne *f*; ~ **bike** (vélo) tout terrain *m*, VTT *m*. **mountaineer** *n* alpiniste *mf*.

mourn *vt/i* ~ (**for**) pleurer. **mournful** *a* mélancolique. **mourning** *n* deuil *m*.

mouse *n* (*pl* **mice**) souris *f*. ~**trap** *n* souricière *f*.

mouth *n* bouche *f*; (of dog, cat) gueule *f*; (of cave, tunnel) entrée *f*. **mouthful** *n* bouchée *f*. ~**wash** *n* eau *f* dentifrice. ~**watering** *a* appétissant.

move *vt* (*object*) déplacer; (*limb, head*) bouger; (emotionally) émouvoir; ~ **house** déménager. ●*vi* bouger; (vehicle) rouler; (change address) déménager; (act) agir. ●*n* mouvement *m*; (in game) coup *m*; (player's turn) tour *m*; (step, act) manœuvre *f*; (house change) déménagement *m*; **on the** ~ en mouvement. □ ~ **back** reculer; ~ **in** emménager; ~ **in with** s'installer avec; ~ **on** (person) se mettre en route; (vehicle) repartir; (time) passer; ~ **sth on** faire avancer qch; ~ **sb on** faire circuler qn; ~ **over** or **up** se pousser.

movement *n* mouvement *m*.

movie *n* (US) film *m*; **the** ~**s** le cinéma.

moving *a* (vehicle) en marche; (*part, target*) mobile; (staircase) roulant; (touching) émouvant.

mow *vt* (*pp* **mowed** or **mown**) (lawn) tondre; (hay) couper; ~ **down** faucher. **mower** *n* tondeuse *f*.

MP *abbr* ⇒MEMBER OF PARLIAMENT.

Mr *n* (*pl* **Messrs**) ~ **Smith** Monsieur or M. Smith; ~ **President** Monsieur le Président.

Mrs *n* (*pl* **Mrs**) ~ **Smith** Madame or Mme Smith.

Ms *n* Mme.

much *adv* beaucoup; **too** ~ trop; **very** ~ beaucoup; **I like them as** ~ **as you (do)** je les aime autant que toi. ● *pron* beaucoup; **not ~** pas grand-chose; **he didn't say ~** il n'a pas dit grand-chose; **I ate so ~ that** j'ai tellement mangé que. ● *det* beaucoup de; **too ~ money** trop d'argent; **how ~ time is left?** combien de temps reste-t-il?

muck *n* saletés *fpl*; (manure) fumier *m*. □ **~ about** ⊡ faire l'imbécile. **mucky** *a* sale.

mud *n* boue *f*.

muddle *n* (mix-up) malentendu *m*; (mess) pagaille *f* ⊡; **get into a ~** s'embrouiller. □ **~ through** se débrouiller; **~ up** embrouiller.

muddy *a* couvert de boue.

muffle *vt* emmitoufler; (bell) assourdir; (voice) étouffer.

mug *n* grande tasse *f*; (for beer) chope *f*; (face ⊡) gueule *f* ⊠; (fool ⊡) poire *f* ⊡. ● *vt* (*pt* **mugged**) agresser. **mugger** *n* agresseur *m*.

muggy *a* lourd.

mule *n* mulet *m*.

multicoloured *a* multicolore.

multiple *a* & *n* multiple (*m*); **~ sclerosis** sclérose *f* en plaques.

multiplication *n* multiplication *f*.

multiply *vt/i* (se) multiplier.

multistorey *a* (car park) à niveaux multiples.

mum *n* ⊡ maman *f*.

mumble *vt/i* marmonner.

mummy *n* (mother ⊡) maman *f*; (embalmed body) momie *f*.

mumps *n* oreillons *mpl*.

munch *vt* mâcher.

mundane *a* terre-à-terre.

municipal *a* municipal.

mural *a* mural. ● *n* peinture *f* murale.

murder *n* meurtre *m*. ● *vt* assassiner. **murderer** *n* meurtrier *m*, assassin *m*.

murky *a* (**-ier**, **-iest**) (water) glauque; (past) trouble.

murmur *n* murmure *m*. ● *vt/i* murmurer.

muscle *n* muscle *m*. ● *vi* **~ in** ⊡ s'imposer (**on** dans).

muscular *a* (tissue, disease) musculaire; (body, person) musclé.

museum *n* musée *m*.

mushroom *n* champignon *m*. ● *vi* (town) proliférer; (demand) s'accroître rapidement.

music *n* musique *f*.

musical *a* (person) musicien; (voice) mélodieux; (accompaniment) musical; (instrument) de musique. ● *n* comédie *f* musicale.

musician *n* musicien/-ne *m/f*.

Muslim *n* Musulman/-e *m/f*. ● *a* musulman.

mussel *n* moule *f*.

must *v aux* devoir; **you ~ go** vous devez partir, il faut que vous partiez; **she ~ be consulted** il faut la consulter; **he ~ be old** il doit être vieux; **I ~ have done it** j'ai dû le faire. ● *n* **be a ~** ⊡ être indispensable.

mustard *n* moutarde *f*.

musty *a* (**-ier**, **-iest**) (room) qui sent le renfermé; (smell) de moisi.

mute *a* & *n* muet/-te (*m/f*). **muted** *a* (colour) sourd; (response) tiède; (celebration) mitigé.

mutilate *vt* mutiler.

mutter *vt/i* marmonner.

mutton *n* mouton *m*.

mutual *a* (reciprocal) réciproque; (common) commun; (consent) mutuel. **mutually** *adv* mutuellement.

muzzle *n* (snout) museau *m*; (device) muselière *f*; (of gun) canon *m*. ● *vt* museler.

my *a* mon, ma, *pl* mes.

M

myself *pron* (reflexive) me, m'; **I've hurt ~** je me suis fait mal; (emphatic) moi-même; **I did it ~** je l'ai fait moi-même; (after preposition) moi, moi-même; **I am proud of ~** je suis fier de moi.

mysterious *a* mystérieux.

mystery *n* mystère *m*.

mystic *a & n* mystique (*mf*). **mystical** *a* mystique.

myth *n* mythe *m*. **mythical** *a* mythique. **mythology** *n* mythologie *f*.

nag *vt/i* (*pt* **nagged**) critiquer; (pester) harceler. **nagging** *a* persistant.

nail *n* clou *m*; (of finger, toe) ongle *m*; **on the ~** sans tarder, tout de suite. ●*vt* clouer. **~ polish** *n* vernis *m* à ongles.

naïve *a* naïf.

naked *a* nu; **to the ~ eye** à l'œil nu.

name *n* nom *m*; (fig) réputation *f*. ●*vt* nommer; (*terms*) fixer; **be ~d after** porter le nom de.

namely *adv* à savoir.

nanny *n* nurse *f*.

nap *n* somme *m*.

nape *n* nuque *f*.

napkin *n* serviette *f*.

nappy *n* couche *f*.

narcotic *a & n* narcotique (*m*).

narrative *n* récit *m*. **narrator** *n* narrateur/-trice *m/f*.

narrow *a* étroit. ●*vt/i* (se) rétrécir; (limit) (se) limiter; **~ down the choices** limiter les choix.

~-minded *a* à l'esprit étroit; (*ideas*) étroit.

nasal *a* nasal.

nasty *a* (**-ier, -iest**) mauvais, désagréable; (malicious) méchant.

nation *n* nation *f*.

national *a* national. ●*n* ressortissant/-e *m/f*.

nationality *n* nationalité *f*.

nationalize *vt* nationaliser.

nationally *adv* à l'échelle nationale.

native *n* (local inhabitant) autochtone *mf*; (non-European) indigène *mf*; **be a ~ of** être originaire de. ●*a* indigène; (*country*) natal; (inborn) inné; **~ language** langue *f* maternelle; **~ speaker of French** personne *f* de langue maternelle française.

natural *a* naturel.

naturally *adv* (normally, of course) naturellement; (by nature) de nature.

nature *n* nature *f*.

naughty *a* (**-ier, -iest**) vilain, méchant; (indecent) grivois.

nausea *n* nausée *f*. **nauseous** *a* (*smell*) écœurant.

nautical *a* nautique.

naval *a* (*battle*) naval; (*officer*) de marine.

navel *n* nombril *m*.

navigate *vt* (*sea*) naviguer sur; (*ship*) piloter. ●*vi* naviguer. **navigation** *n* navigation *f*.

navy *n* marine *f*. ●*a* **~ (blue)** bleu *inv* marine.

near *adv* près; **draw ~** (s')approcher (**to** de). ●*prep* près de. ●*a* proche; **~ to** près de. ●*vt* approcher de.

nearby *a* proche. ●*adv* à proximité.

nearly *adv* presque; **I ~ forgot** j'ai failli oublier; **not ~ as pretty as** loin d'être aussi joli que.

nearness n proximité f.

nearside a (Auto) du côté du passager.

neat a soigné, net; (room) bien rangé; (clever) habile; (drink) sec. **neatly** adv avec soin; habilement.

necessarily adv nécessairement.

necessary a nécessaire.

necessitate vt nécessiter.

necessity n nécessité f; (thing) chose f indispensable.

neck n cou m; (of dress) encolure f. ∼ **and neck** a à égalité. ∼**lace** n collier m. ∼**line** n encolure f. ∼**tie** n cravate f.

nectarine n brugnon m, nectarine f.

need n besoin m. ● vt avoir besoin de; (demand) demander; **you** ∼ **not come** vous n'êtes pas obligé de venir.

needle n aiguille f.

needless a inutile.

needlework n couture f; (object) ouvrage m (à l'aiguille).

needy a (-ier, -iest) nécessiteux. ● n the ∼ les indigents.

negative a négatif. ● n (of photograph) négatif m; (word, Gram) négation f; **in the** ∼ (answer) par la négative; (Gram) à la forme négative.

neglect vt négliger, laisser à l'abandon; ∼ **to do** négliger de faire. ● n manque m de soins; (state of) ∼ abandon m.

negligent a négligent.

negotiate vt/i négocier.

negotiation n négociation f.

neigh n hennissement m. ● vi hennir.

neighbour, (US) **neighbor** n voisin/-e m/f. **neighbourhood** n voisinage m, quartier m; **in the** ∼**hood of** aux alentours de.

neighbouring a voisin.

neighbourly a amical.

neither a & pron aucun/-e des deux, ni l'un/-e ni l'autre. ● adv ni; ∼ **big nor small** ni grand ni petit. ● conj (ne) non plus; ∼ **am I coming** je ne viendrai pas non plus.

nephew n neveu m.

nerve n nerf m; (courage) courage m; (calm) sang-froid m; (impudence ⊞) culot m; ∼**s** (before exams) trac m. ∼-**racking** a éprouvant.

nervous a nerveux; **be** or **feel** ∼ (afraid) avoir peur; ∼ **breakdown** dépression f nerveuse.

nervousness n nervosité f; (fear) crainte f.

nest n nid m. ● vi nicher. ∼-**egg** n pécule m.

nestle vi se blottir.

net n filet m; (Comput) net m, Internet m. ● vt (pt **netted**) prendre au filet. ● a (weight) net. ∼**ball** n netball m.

Netherlands n the ∼ les Pays-Bas mpl.

netiquette n nétiquette f.

Netsurfer n Internaute mf.

nettle n ortie f.

network n réseau m.

neurotic a & n névrosé/-e (m/f).

neuter a & n neutre (m). ● vt (castrate) castrer.

neutral a neutre; ∼ (**gear**) (Auto) point m mort.

never adv (ne) jamais; **he** ∼ **refuses** il ne refuse jamais; **I** ∼ **saw him** ⊞ je ne l'ai pas vu; ∼ **again** plus jamais; ∼ **mind** (don't worry) ne vous en faites pas; (it doesn't matter) peu importe.

nevertheless adv néanmoins, toutefois.

new a nouveau; (brand-new) neuf. ∼-**born** a nouveau-né. ∼**comer** n nouveau venu m, nouvelle venue f.

N

newly adv nouvellement.
~-**weds** npl jeunes mariés mpl.
news n nouvelle(s) f(pl); (radio, press) informations fpl; (TV) actualités fpl, informations fpl. ~ **agency** n agence f de presse. ~**agent** n marchand/-e m/f de journaux. ~**caster** n présentateur/-trice m/f. ~**group** n (Internet) forum m de discussion. ~**letter** n bulletin m. ~**paper** n journal m.
new year n nouvel an m. **New Year's Day** n le jour de l'an. **New Year's Eve** n la Saint-Sylvestre.
New Zealand n Nouvelle-Zélande f.
next a prochain; (adjoining) voisin; (following) suivant; ~ **to** à côté de; ~ **door** à côté (**to** de). ●adv la prochaine fois; (afterwards) ensuite. ●n suivant/-e m/f; (e-mail) message m suivant. ~-**door** a d'à côté. ~ **of kin** n parent m le plus proche.
nib n plume f.
nibble vt/i grignoter.
nice a agréable, bon; (kind) gentil; (pretty) joli; (respectable) bien inv; (subtle) délicat. **nicely** adv agréablement; gentiment; (well) bien.
nicety n subtilité f.
niche n (recess) niche f; (fig) place f, situation f.
nick n petite entaille f; **be in good/bad** ~ être en bon/mauvais état. ●vt (steal, arrest ▣) piquer.
nickel n (metal) nickel m; (US) pièce f de cinq cents.
nickname n surnom m. ●vt surnommer.
nicotine n nicotine f.
niece n nièce f.
niggling a (person) tatillon; (detail) insignifiant.
night n nuit f; (evening) soir m. ●a

de nuit. ~-**cap** n boisson f (avant d'aller se coucher). ~-**club** n boîte f de nuit. ~-**dress** n chemise f de nuit. ~**fall** n tombée f de la nuit. **nightie** n chemise f de nuit.
nightingale n rossignol m.
nightly a & adv (de) chaque nuit or soir.
night: ~**mare** n cauchemar m. ~-**time** n nuit f.
nil n (Sport) zéro m. ●a (chances, risk) nul.
nimble a agile.
nine a & n neuf (m).
nineteen a & n dix-neuf (m).
ninety a & n quatre-vingt-dix (m).
ninth a & n neuvième (mf).
nip vt/i (pt **nipped**) (pinch) pincer; (rush ▣) courir; ~ **out/back** sortir/rentrer rapidement. ●n pincement m.
nipple n mamelon m; (of baby's bottle) tétine f.
nippy a (-**ier**, -**iest**) (air) piquant; (car) rapide.
nitrogen n azote m.
no det aucun/-e; pas de; ~ **man** aucun homme; ~ **money/time** pas d'argent/de temps; ~ **one** = NOBODY; ~ **smoking/entry** défense de fumer/d'entrer; ~ **way!** ▣ pas question! ●adv non. ●n(pl **noes**) non m inv.
nobility n noblesse f.
noble a noble. ~ **man** n (pl -**men**) noble m.
nobody pron (ne) personne; **he knows** ~ il ne connaît personne. ●n nullité f.
nocturnal a nocturne.
nod vt/i (pt **nodded**); ~ (**one's head**) faire un signe de tête; ~ **off** s'endormir. ●n signe m de tête.
noise n bruit m; **make a** ~ faire du bruit. **noisily** adv.

bruyamment. **noisy** *a* (**-ier, -iest**) bruyant.

no man's land *n* no man's land *m*.

nominal *a* symbolique, nominal; (*value*) nominal.

nominate *vt* nommer; (put forward) proposer.

none *pron* aucun/-e; ~ **of us** aucun/-e de nous; **I have** ~ je n'en ai pas.

non-existent *a* inexistant.

nonplussed *a* perplexe.

nonsense *n* absurdités *fpl*.

non-smoker *n* non-fumeur *m*.

non-stick *a* antiadhésif.

non-stop *a* (*train, flight*) direct. ● *adv* sans arrêt.

noodles *npl* nouilles *fpl*.

noon *n* midi *m*.

nor *adv* ni. ● *conj* (ne) non plus; ~ **shall I come** je ne viendrai pas non plus.

norm *n* norme *f*.

normal *a* normal.

Norman *n* Normand/-e *m/f*. ● *a* (*village*) normand; (*arch*) roman.

north *n* nord *m*. ● *a* nord *inv*, du nord. ● *adv* vers le nord.

North America *n* Amérique *f* du Nord.

north-east *n* nord-est *m*.

northerly *a* (*wind, area*) du nord; (*point*) au nord.

northern *a* (*accent*) du nord; (*coast*) nord. **northerner** *n* habitant/-e *m/f* du nord.

northward *a* (*side*) nord *inv*; (*journey*) vers le nord.

north-west *n* nord-ouest *m*.

Norway *n* Norvège *f*.

Norwegian *n* (*person*) Norvégien/-ne *m/f*; (*language*) norvégien *m*. ● *a* norvégien.

nose *n* nez *m*. ● *vi* ~ **about** fouiner.

nosedive *n* piqué *m*. ● *vi* descendre en piqué.

nostalgia *n* nostalgie *f*.

nostril *n* narine *f*; (of horse) naseau *m*.

nosy *a* (**-ier, -iest**) 🅸 curieux, indiscret.

not *adv* (ne) pas; **I do** ~ **know** je ne sais pas; ~ **at all** pas du tout; ~ **yet** pas encore; **I suppose** ~ je suppose que non.

notably *adv* notamment.

notch *n* entaille *f*. ● *vt* ~ **up** (score) marquer.

note *n* note *f*; (banknote) billet *m*; (short letter) mot *m*. ● *vt* noter; (notice) remarquer. ~**book** *n* carnet *m*.

nothing *pron* (ne) rien; **he eats** ~ il ne mange rien; ~ **else** rien d'autre; ~ **much** pas grand-chose; **for** ~ pour rien, gratis. ● *n* rien *m*; (person) nullité *f*. ● *adv* nullement.

notice *n* avis *m*, annonce *f*; (poster) affiche *f*; (advance) ~ préavis *m*; **at short** ~ dans des délais très brefs; **give in one's** ~ donner sa démission; **take** ~ faire attention (**of** à). ● *vt* remarquer, observer. **noticeable** *a* visible. ~**-board** *n* tableau *m* d'affichage.

notify *vt* (inform) aviser; (make known) notifier.

notion *n* idée *f*, notion *f*.

notorious *a* (*criminal*) notoire; (*district*) mal famé; (*case*) tristement célèbre.

notwithstanding *prep* malgré. ● *adv* néanmoins.

nought *n* zéro *m*.

noun *n* nom *m*.

nourish *vt* nourrir. **nourishing** *a* nourrissant. **nourishment** *n* nourriture *f*.

novel *n* roman *m*. ● *a* nouveau. **novelist** *n* romancier/-ière *m/f*. **novelty** *n* nouveauté *f*.

N

November n novembre m.

now adv maintenant. ● conj maintenant que; **just ∼** maintenant; (a moment ago) tout à l'heure; **∼ and again, ∼ and then** de temps à autre.

nowadays adv de nos jours.

nowhere adv nulle part.

nozzle n (tip) embout m; (of hose) jet m.

nuclear a nucléaire.

nude a nu. ● n nu/-e m/f; **in the ∼** tout nu.

nudge vt pousser du coude. ● n coup m de coude.

nudism n nudisme m. **nudity** n nudité f.

nuisance n (thing, event) ennui m; (person) peste f; **be a ∼** être embêtant.

null a nul.

numb a engourdi (**with** par). ● vt engourdir.

number n nombre m; (of ticket, house, page) numéro m; (written figure) chiffre m; **a ∼ of people** plusieurs personnes. ● vt numéroter; (count, include) compter. **∼-plate** n plaque f d'immatriculation.

numeral n chiffre m.

numerate a qui sait compter.

numerical a numérique.

numerous a nombreux.

nun n religieuse f.

nurse n infirmier/-ière m/f; (nanny) nurse f. ● vt soigner; (hope) nourrir.

nursery n (room) chambre f d'enfants; (for plants) pépinière f; (**day**) **∼** crèche f. **∼ rhyme** n comptine f. **∼ school** n (école) maternelle f.

nursing home n maison f de retraite.

nut n (walnut, Brazil nut) noix f; (hazelnut) noisette f; (peanut) cacahuète f; (Tech) écrou m. **∼crackers** npl casse-noix m inv.

nutmeg n muscade f.

nutrient n substance f nutritive.

nutritious a nutritif.

nuts a (crazy 🔲) cinglé.

nutshell n coquille f de noix; **in a ∼** en un mot.

nylon n nylon m.

oak n chêne m.

OAP abbr (**old-age pensioner**) retraité/-e m/f.

oar n rame f.

oath n (promise) serment m; (swear-word) juron m.

oats npl avoine f.

obedience n obéissance f. **obedient** a obéissant. **obediently** adv docilement.

obese a obèse.

obey vt/i obéir (à).

object[1] n (thing) objet m; (aim) but m; (Gram) complément m d'objet; **money is no ∼** l'argent n'est pas un problème.

object[2] vi protester. ● vt **∼ that** objecter que; **∼ to** (behaviour) désapprouver; (plan) protester contre. **objection** n objection f; (drawback) inconvénient m.

objective a & n objectif (m).

obligation n devoir m.

obligatory a obligatoire.

oblige vt obliger (**to do** à faire).

oblivion n oubli m. **oblivious** a inconscient (**to, of** de).

oblong a oblong. ● n rectangle m.

obnoxious *a* odieux.

oboe *n* hautbois *m*.

obscene *a* obscène.

obscure *a* obscur. ● *vt* obscurcir; (*conceal*) cacher.

observance *n* (of law) respect *m*; (of sabbath) observance *f*.

observant *a* observateur.

observation *n* observation *f*.

observe *vt* observer; (remark) remarquer.

obsess *vt* obséder. **obsession** *n* obsession *f*. **obsessive** *a* (*person*) maniaque; (*thought*) obsédant; (*illness*) obsessionnel.

obsolete *a* dépassé.

obstacle *n* obstacle *m*.

obstinate *a* obstiné.

obstruct *vt* (*road*) bloquer; (*view*) cacher; (*progress*) gêner. **obstruction** *n* (act) obstruction *f*; (thing) obstacle *m*; (in traffic) encombrement *m*.

obtain *vt* obtenir. ● *vi* avoir cours. **obtainable** *a* disponible.

obvious *a* évident. **obviously** *adv* manifestement.

occasion *n* occasion *f*; (big event) événement *m*; **on** ～ à l'occasion.

occasional *a* (*event*) qui a lieu de temps en temps; **the** ～ **letter** une lettre de temps en temps. **occasionally** *adv* de temps à autre.

occupation *n* (activity) occupation *f*; (job) métier *m*, profession *f*. **occupational therapy** *n* ergothérapie *f*.

occupier *n* occupant/-e *m/f*.

occupy *vi* occuper.

occur *vi* (*pt* occurred) se produire; (arise) se présenter; ～ **to sb** venir à l'esprit de qn.

occurrence *n* (event) fait *m*; (instance) occurrence *f*.

ocean *n* océan *m*.

Oceania *n* Océanie *f*.

o'clock *adv* it is six ～ il est six heures; **at one** ～ à une heure.

October *n* octobre *m*.

octopus *n* (*pl* ～es) pieuvre *f*.

odd *a* bizarre; (*number*) impair; (left over) qui reste; (*sock*) dépareillé; **write the** ～ **article** écrire un article de temps en temps; ～ **jobs** menus travaux *mpl*; **twenty** ～ vingt et quelques. **oddity** *n* bizarrerie *f*.

odds *npl* chances *fpl*; (in betting) cote *f* (**on** de); **at** ～ en désaccord; **it makes no** ～ ça ne fait rien; ～ **and ends** des petites choses.

odour, (US) **odor** *n* odeur *f*. **odourless** *a* inodore.

....

of

➡️ For expressions such as **of course, consist of** ⇒**course, consist.**

● *preposition*

⸱⸱⸱➤ de; **a photo** ～ **the dog** une photo du chien; **the king** ～ **the beasts** le roi des animaux; (made) ～ **gold** en or; **it's kind** ～ **you** c'est très gentil de votre part, **some** ⁱᵒ **us** quelques-uns d'entre nous; ～ **it/them** en; **have you heard** ～ **it?** est-ce que tu en as entendu parler?

....

off *adv* be ～ partir, s'en aller; **I'm** ～ je m'en vais; **30 metres** ～ à 30 mètres; **a month** ～ dans un mois. ● *a* (gas, water) coupé; (tap) fermé; (light, TV) éteint; (party, match) annulé; (bad) (food) avarié; (milk) tourné; **Friday is my day** ～ je ne travaille pas le vendredi; **25%** ～ 25% de remise. ● *prep* **3 metres** ～ **the ground** 3 mètres (au-dessus) du sol; **just** ～ **the kitchen** juste à côté de la cuisine; **that is** ～ **the point** là n'est pas la question.

O

offal n abats mpl.

offence n (Jur) infraction f; **give ~ to** offenser; **take ~** s'offenser (**at** de).

offend vt offenser; **be ~ed** s'offenser (**at** de). ● vi (Jur) commettre une infraction.

offender n délinquant/-e m/f.

offensive a (remark) injurieux; (language) grossier; (smell) repoussant; (weapon) offensif. ● n offensive f.

offer vt (pt **offered**) offrir. ● n offre f; **on ~** en promotion.

offhand a désinvolte. ● adv à l'improviste.

office n bureau m; (duty) fonction f; **in ~** au pouvoir. ● a de bureau.

officer n (army) officier m; (police) ~ policier m; (government) ~ fonctionnaire mf.

official a officiel. ● n (civil servant) fonctionnaire mf; (of party, union) officiel/-le m/f; (of police, customs) agent m.

off: ~**-licence** n magasin m de vins et spiritueux. ~**-line** a autonome; (switched off) déconnecté; (Comput) hors connexion. ~**-load** vt (stock) écouler; (Comput) décharger. ~**-peak** a (call) au tarif réduit; (travel) en période creuse. ~**-putting** a rebutant. ~**set** vt (pt **-set**; pres p **-setting**) compenser. ~**shore** a (waters) du large; (funds) hors-lieu inv. ~**side** a (Sport) hors jeu inv; (Auto) du côté du conducteur. ~**spring** n inv progéniture f.

often adv souvent; **how ~ do you meet?** vous vous voyez tous les combien?; **every so ~** de temps en temps.

oil n (for lubrication, cooking) huile f; (for fuel) pétrole m; (for heating) mazout m. ● vt huiler. ~**field** n gisement m pétrolifère.

~**-painting** n peinture f à l'huile. ~**skins** npl ciré m. ~**-tanker** n pétrolier m.

oily a graisseux.

ointment n pommade f.

OK, okay a d'accord; **is it ~ if...?** ça va si...?; **feel ~** aller bien.

old a vieux; (person) vieux, âgé; (former) ancien; **how ~ is he?** quel âge a-t-il?; **he is eight years ~** il a huit ans; ~**er**, ~**est** aîné. ~ **age** n vieillesse f. ~**-age pensioner** n retraité/-e m/f. ~**-fashioned** a démodé; (person) vieux jeu inv. ~ **man** n vieillard m, vieux m. ~ **woman** n vieille f.

olive n olive f; ~ **oil** huile f d'olive. ● a olive inv.

Olympic a olympique. ~ **Games** npl Jeux mpl olympiques.

omelette n omelette f.

omen n augure m.

ominous a (presence, cloud) menaçant; (sign) de mauvais augure.

omission n omission f. **omit** vt (pt **omitted**) omettre.

on prep sur; ~ **the table** sur la table; **put the key ~ it** mets la clé dessus; ~ **22 March** le 22 mars; ~ **Monday** lundi; ~ **TV** à la télé; ~ **video** en vidéo; **be ~ steroids** prendre des stéroïdes; ~ **arriving** en arrivant. ● a (TV, oven, light) allumé; (dishwasher, radio) en marche; (tap) ouvert; (lid) mis; **the match is still ~** le match aura lieu quand même; **the news is ~ in 10 minutes** les informations sont dans 10 minutes. ● adv have sth ~ porter qch; **20 years ~** 20 ans plus tard; **from that day ~** à partir de ce jour-là; **further ~** plus loin; ~ **and off** (occasionally) de temps en temps; **go ~ and ~** (person) parler pendant des heures.

once adv une fois; (formerly)

autrefois. ● *conj* une fois que; **all
at ~** tout d'un coup.

oncoming *a* (*vehicle*) qui
approche.

one *det & n* un/-e (*m/f*). ● *pron*
un/-e *m/f*; (impersonal) on; **~ (and
only)** seul (et unique); **a big ~** un
grand/une grande; **this/that ~**
celui-ci/-là, celle-ci/-là; **~
another** l'un/-e l'autre. **~-off** *a*
🄰 unique, exceptionnel. **~self**
pron soi-même; (reflexive) se.
~-way *a* (*street*) à sens unique;
(*ticket*) simple.

ongoing *a* (*process*) continu; **be
~** être en cours.

onion *n* oignon *m*.

on-line *a & adv* en ligne.

onlooker *n* spectateur/-trice *m/f*.

only *a* seul; **~ son** fils unique.
● *adv & conj* seulement; **he is ~
six** il n'a que six ans.

onset *n* début *m*.

onward(s) *adv* en avant.

open *a* ouvert; (*view*) dégagé; (*free
to all*) public; (*undisguised*)
manifeste; (*question*) en attente;
in the ~ air en plein air. ● *vt/i*
(*door*) (s')ouvrir; (*shop, play*)
ouvrir; **~ out** *or* **up** (s')ouvrir.
~-ended *a* (*stay*) de durée
indéterminée; (*debate, question*)
ouvert. **~-heart** *a* (*surgery*) à
cœur ouvert.

opening *n* (of book) début *m*; (of
exhibition, shop) ouverture *f*; (of film)
première *f*; (in market) débouché
m; (job) poste *m* (disponible).

open: ~-minded *a* **be ~-minded**
avoir l'esprit ouvert. **~-plan** *a*
paysagé.

opera *n* opéra *m*.

operate *vt/i* opérer; (Tech) (faire)
fonctionner; **~ on** (Med) opérer;
operating theatre salle *f*
d'opération.

operation *n* opération *f*; **have an**

~ se faire opérer; **in ~** (*plan*) en
vigueur; (*mine*) en service.

operative *n* employé/-e *m/f*. ● *a*
(*law*) en vigueur.

operator *n* opérateur/-trice *m/f*;
(telephonist) standardiste *mf*.

opinion *n* opinion *f*, avis *m*.

opinionated *a* qui a des avis sur
tout.

opponent *n* adversaire *mf*.

opportunity *n* occasion *f* (**to do**
de faire).

oppose *vt* s'opposer à; **as ~d to**
par opposition à. **opposing** *a*
opposé.

opposite *a* (*direction, side*)
opposé; (*building*) d'en face. ● *n*
contraire *m*. ● *adv* en face.
● *prep* **~ (to)** en face de.

opposition *n* opposition *f*.

oppress *vt* opprimer. **oppressive**
a (cruel) oppressif; (*heat*)
oppressant.

opt *vi* **~ for** opter pour; **~ out**
refuser de participer (**of** à); **~ to
do** choisir de faire.

optical *a* optique. **~ illusion** *n*
illusion *f* d'optique. **~ scanner** *n*
lecteur *m* optique.

optician *n* opticien/-ne *m/f*.

optimism *n* optimisme *m*.

optimist *n* optimiste *mf*.
optimistic *a* optimiste.

option *n* option *f*; (choice) choix *m*.

optional *a* facultatif; **~ extras**
accessoires *mpl* en option.

or *conj* ou; (with negative) ni.

oral *n & a* oral (*m*).

orange *n* (fruit) orange *f*; (*colour*)
orange *m*. ● *a* (colour) orange *inv*.

orbit *n* orbite *f*. ● *vt* décrire une
orbite autour de.

orchard *n* verger *m*.

orchestra *n* orchestre *m*.

orchid *n* orchidée *f*.

ordeal *n* épreuve *f*.

order *n* ordre *m*; (Comm)

O

commande *f*; in ~ (tidy) en ordre; (*document*) en règle; in ~ that pour que; in ~ to pour. ● *vt* ordonner; (*goods*) commander; ~ sb to ordonner à qn de.

orderly *a* (tidy) ordonné; (not unruly) discipliné. ● *n* (Mil) planton *m*; (Med) aide-soignant/-e *m/f*.

ordinary *a* (usual) ordinaire; (average) moyen.

ore *n* minerai *m*.

organ *n* organe *m*; (Mus) orgue *m*.

organic *a* organique; (*produce*) biologique.

organization *n* organisation *f*.

organize *vt* organiser.

organizer *n* organisateur/-trice *m/f*; **electronic** ~ agenda *m* électronique.

orgasm *n* orgasme *m*.

Orient *n* the ~ l'Orient *m*. **oriental** *a* oriental.

origin *n* origine *f*.

original *a* original; (*inhabitant*) premier; (*member*) originaire. **originality** *n* originalité *f*. **originally** *adv* (at the outset) à l'origine.

originate *vi* (plan) prendre naissance; ~ from provenir de; (person) venir de. ● *vt* être l'auteur de. **originator** *n* (of idea) auteur *m*; (of invention) créateur/-trice *m/f*.

ornament *n* (decoration) ornement *m*; (object) objet *m* décoratif.

orphan *n* orphelin/-e *m/f*. ● *vt* rendre orphelin. **orphanage** *n* orphelinat *m*.

orthopaedic *a* orthopédique.

ostentatious *a* tape-à-l'œil *inv*.

osteopath *n* ostéopathe *mf*.

ostrich *n* autruche *f*.

other *a* autre; the ~ one l'autre *mf*. ● *n & pron* autre *mf*; (some) ~s d'autres. ● *adv* ~ than (apart from) à part; (otherwise than)

autrement que. **otherwise** *adv* autrement.

otter *n* loutre *f*.

ouch *interj* aïe!

ought *v aux* devoir; **you** ~ **to stay** vous devriez rester; **he** ~ **to succeed** il devrait réussir; **I** ~ **to have done it** j'aurais dû le faire.

ounce *n* once *f* (= 28.35 g).

our *a* notre, *pl* nos.

ours *poss* le *or* la nôtre, les nôtres.

ourselves *pron* (reflexive) nous; (emphatic) nous-mêmes; (after preposition) **for** ~ pour nous, pour nous-mêmes.

out *adv* dehors; **he's** ~ il est sorti; **further** ~ plus loin; **be** ~ (*book*) être publié; (*light*) être éteint; (*sun*) briller; (*flower*) être épanoui; (*tide*) être bas; (*player*) être éliminé; ~ **of** hors de; **go/ walk/get** ~ **of** sortir de; ~ **of pity** par pitié; **made** ~ **of** fait de; **5** ~ **of 6** 5 sur 6. ~**break** *n* (of war) déclenchement *m*; (of violence, boils) éruption *f*. ~**burst** *n* explosion *f*. ~**cast** *n* paria *m*. ~**class** *vt* surclasser. ~**come** *n* résultat *m*. ~**cry** *n* tollé *m*. ~**dated** *a* démodé. ~**door** *a* (activity) de plein air; (*pool*) en plein air. ~**doors** *adv* dehors.

outer *a* extérieur; ~ **space** espace *m* extra-atmosphérique.

outfit *n* (clothes) tenue *f*.

outgoing *a* (minister, tenant) sortant; (sociable) ouvert. **outgoings** *npl* dépenses *fpl*.

outgrow *vt* (*pt* **-grew**; *pp* **-grown**) (*clothes*) devenir trop grand pour; (*habit*) dépasser.

outing *n* sortie *f*.

outlaw *n* hors-la-loi *m inv*. ● *vt* déclarer illégal.

outlet *n* (for water, gas) tuyau *m* de sortie; (for goods) débouché *m*; (for feelings) exutoire *m*.

outline n contour m; (of plan) grandes lignes fpl; (of essay) plan m. ● vt tracer le contour de; (summarize) exposer brièvement.

out: ~**live** vt survivre à. ~**look** n perspective f. ~**number** vt surpasser en nombre. ~ **of date** a démodé; (expired) périmé. ~ **of hand** a incontrôlable. ~ **of order** a en panne. ~ **of work** a sans travail. ~**patient** n malade mf externe.

output n rendement m; (Comput) sortie f. ● vt/i (Comput) sortir.

outrage n (anger) indignation f; (atrocity) attentat m; (scandal) outrage m. ● vt (morals) outrager; (person) scandaliser. **outrageous** a scandaleux.

outright adv (completely) catégoriquement; (killed) sur le coup. ● a (majority) absolu; (ban) catégorique; (hostility) pur et simple.

outset n début m.

outside n extérieur m. ● adv dehors. ● prep en dehors de; (in front of) devant. ● a extérieur. **outsider** n étranger/-ère m/f; (Sport) outsider m.

out: **~skirts** npl périphérie f. ~**spoken** a franc. ~**standing** a exceptionnel; (not settled) en suspens.

outward a & adv vers l'extérieur; (sign) extérieur; (journey) d'aller. **outwards** adv vers l'extérieur.

oval n & a ovale (m).

ovary n ovaire m.

oven n four m.

over prep (across) par-dessus; (above) au-dessus de; (covering) sur; (more than) plus de; **it's ~ the road** c'est de l'autre côté de la rue; ~ **here/there** par ici/là; **children ~ six** les enfants de plus de six ans; ~ **the weekend** pendant le week-end; **all ~ the house** partout dans la maison. ● a, adv (term) terminé; (war) fini; **get sth ~ with** en finir avec qch; **ask sb ~** inviter qn; ~ **and ~ (again)** à plusieurs reprises; **five times ~** cinq fois de suite.

overall a global, d'ensemble; (length) total. ~ adv globalement.

overalls npl combinaison f.

over: ~**board** adv par-dessus bord. ~**cast** a couvert. ~**charge** vt faire payer trop cher à. ~**coat** n pardessus m.

overcome vt (pt -**came**; pp -**come**) (enemy) vaincre; (difficulty, fear) surmonter; ~ **by** accablé de.

overcrowded a bondé; (country) surpeuplé.

overdo vt (pt -**did**; pp -**done**) (Culin) trop cuire; ~ **it** (overwork) en faire trop.

over: ~**dose** n surdose f, overdose f. ~**draft** n découvert m. ~**draw** vt (pt -**drew**; pp -**drawn**) faire un découvert sur. ~**due** a en retard; (bill) impayé.

overflow[1] vi déborder.

overflow[2] n (outlet) trop-plein m.

overhaul vt réviser.

overhead[1] adv au-dessus; (in sky) dans le ciel.

overhead[2] a aérien; ~ **projector** rétroprojecteur m. **overheads** npl frais mpl généraux.

over: ~**hear** vt (pt -**heard**) entendre par hasard. ~**lap** vt/i (pt -**lapped**) (se) chevaucher. ~**leaf** adv au verso. ~**load** vt surcharger. ~**look** vt (window) donner sur; (miss) ne pas voir.

overnight[1] adv dans la nuit; (instantly: fig) du jour au lendemain.

overnight[2] a (train) de nuit; (stay) d'une nuit; (fig) soudain.

over: ~**power** vt (thief) maîtriser; (army) vaincre; (fig) accabler. ~**priced** a trop cher.

O

~**rate** *vt* surestimer. ~**react** *vi*
réagir de façon excessive.
~**riding** *a* (*consideration*) numéro
un; (*importance*) primordial.
~**rule** *vt* (*decision*) annuler.

overrun *vt* (*pt* -**ran**; *pp* -**run**; *pres*
p -**running**) (*country*) envahir;
(*budget*) dépasser. ● *vi* (meeting)
durer plus longtemps que prévu.

overseas *a* étranger. ● *adv*
outre-mer, à l'étranger.

over: ~**see** *vt* (*pt* -**saw**; *pp*
-**seen**) surveiller. ~**sight** *n*
omission *f*. ~**sleep** *vi* (*pt* -**slept**)
se réveiller trop tard. ~**take** *vt/i*
(*pt* -**took**; *pp* -**taken**) dépasser;
(fig) frapper. ~**time** *n* heures *fpl*
supplémentaires. ~**turn** *vt/i* (se)
renverser. ~**weight** *a* trop gros.

overwhelm *vt* (*enemy*) écraser;
(*shame*) accabler. **overwhelmed**
a (with offers, calls) submergé (**with**,
by de); (with shame, work) accablé;
(by sight) ébloui. **overwhelming** *a*
(*heat, grief*) accablant; (*defeat,
victory*) écrasant; (*urge*)
irrésistible.

overwork *vt/i* (se) surmener. ● *n*
surmenage *m*.

owe *vt* devoir. **owing** *a* dû; **owing
to** en raison de.

owl *n* hibou *m*.

own *a* propre. ● *pron* my ~ le
mien, la mienne; **a house of one's
~** sa propre maison; **on one's ~**
tout seul. ● *vt* posséder; ~ **up (to)**
🔲 avouer. **owner** *n* propriétaire
mf. **ownership** *n* propriété *f*; (of
land) possession *f*.

oxygen *n* oxygène *m*.

oyster *n* huître *f*.

ozone *n* ozone *m*; ~ **layer** couche
f d'ozone.

PA *abbr* ⇨PERSONAL ASSISTANT.

pace *n* pas *m*; (speed) allure *f*;
keep ~ with suivre. ● *vt* (*room*)
arpenter. ● *vi* ~ **(up and down)**
faire les cent pas.

Pacific *n* ~ **(Ocean)** océan *m*
Pacifique.

pack *n* paquet *m*; (Mil) sac *m*; (of
hounds) meute *f*; (of thieves) bande *f*;
(of lies) tissu *m*. ● *vt* (into case)
mettre dans une valise; (into box,
crate) emballer; (for sale)
conditionner; (*crowd*) remplir
complètement; ~ **one's suitcase**
faire sa valise. ● *vi* faire ses
valises; ~ **into** (cram) s'entasser
dans; ~ **off** expédier; **send ~ing**
envoyer promener.

package *n* paquet *m*; (Comput)
progiciel *m*; ~ **deal** offre *f*
globale; ~ **holiday** voyage *m*
organisé. ● *vt* empaqueter.

packed *a* (crowded) bondé; ~
lunch repas *m* froid.

packet *n* paquet *m*.

packing *n* (action, material)
emballage *m*.

pad *n* (of paper) bloc *m*; (to protect)
protection *f*; (for ink) tampon *m*;
(**launch**) ~ rampe *f* de lancement.
● *vt* (*pt* **padded**) rembourrer;
(text: fig) délayer. ● *vi* (*pt* **padded**)
(walk) marcher à pas feutrés.
padding *n* rembourrage *m*.

paddle *n* pagaie *f*. ● *vt* ~ **a canoe**
pagayer. ● *vi* patauger.

padlock *n* cadenas *m*. ● *vt*
cadenasser.

paediatrician *n* pédiatre *mf*.

pagan a & n païen/-ne (m/f).

page n (of book) page f. ● vt (on pager) rechercher; (over speaker) faire appeler. **pager** n radiomessageur m.

pain n douleur f; ~s efforts mpl; **be in** ~ souffrir; **take** ~s **to** se donner du mal pour. ● vt (grieve) peiner. **painful** a douloureux; (laborious) pénible. ~-**killer** n analgésique m. **painless** a (operation) indolore; (death) sans souffrance; (trouble-free) sans peine. **painstaking** a minutieux.

paint n peinture f; ~s (in tube, box) couleurs fpl. ● vt/i peindre. ~**brush** n pinceau m. **painter** n peintre m. **painting** n peinture f. ~**work** n peintures fpl.

pair n paire f; (of people) couple m; **a** ~ **of trousers** un pantalon. ● vi ~ **off** former un couple.

pajamas npl (US) = PYJAMAS.

Pakistan n Pakistan m.

palace n palais m.

palatable a (food) savoureux; (solution) acceptable. **palate** n palais m.

pale a pâle. ● vi pâlir.

Palestine n Palestine f

pallid a pâle.

palm n (of hand) paume f; (tree) palmier m; (symbol) palme f. □ ~ **off** ⊡ ~ **sth off as** faire passer qch pour; ~ **sth off on sb** refiler qch à qn ⊡.

palpitate vi palpiter.

paltry a (-ier, -iest) dérisoire, piètre.

pamper vt choyer.

pamphlet n brochure f.

pan n casserole f; (for frying) poêle f.

pancake n crêpe f.

pandemonium n tohu-bohu m.

pander vi ~ **to** (person, taste) flatter bassement.

pane n carreau m, vitre f.

panel n (of door) panneau m; (of experts, judges) commission f; (on discussion programme) invités mpl; (**instrument**) ~ tableau m de bord.

pang n serrement m au cœur; ~s **of conscience** remords mpl.

panic n panique f. ● vt/i (pt **panicked**) (s')affoler. ~-**stricken** a pris de panique, affolé.

pansy n (Bot) pensée f.

pant vi haleter.

panther n panthère f.

pantomime n (show) spectacle m de Noël; (mime) mime m.

pantry n garde-manger m inv.

pants npl (underwear) slip m; (trousers: US) pantalon m.

paper n papier m; (newspaper) journal m; (exam) épreuve f; (essay) exposé m; (wallpaper) papier m peint; (identity) ~s papiers mpl (d'identité); **on** ~ par écrit. ● vt (room) tapisser. ~**back** n livre m de poche. ~-**clip** n trombone m. ~ **feed tray** n (Comput) bac m d'alimentation en papier. ~**work** n (work) travail m administratif; (documentation) documents mpl.

par n **be below** ~ ne pas être en forme; **on a** ~ **with** (performance) comparable à; (person) l'égal de; (golf) par m.

parachute n parachute m. ● vi descendre en parachute.

parade n (procession) parade f; (Mil) défilé m. ● vi défiler. ● vt faire étalage de.

paradise n paradis m.

paradox n paradoxe m.

paraffin n pétrole m (lampant); (wax) paraffine f.

paragliding n parapente m.

paragon n modèle m.

paragraph n paragraphe m.

parallel *a* parallèle. ● *n* parallèle *m*; (maths) parallèle *f*.

paralyse *vt* paralyser. **paralysis** *n* paralysie *f*.

paramedic *n* auxiliaire *mf* médical/-e.

paramount *a* suprême.

paranoia *n* paranoïa *f*. **paranoid** *a* paranoïaque; (Psych) paranoïde.

paraphernalia *n* attirail *m*.

parasol *n* ombrelle *f*; (on table, at beach) parasol *m*.

paratrooper *n* (Mil) parachutiste *mf*.

parcel *n* paquet *m*.

parchment *n* parchemin *m*.

pardon *n* pardon *m*; (Jur) grâce *f*; **I beg your ~** je vous demande pardon. ● *vt* (*pt* **pardoned**) pardonner (**sb for sth** qch à qn); (Jur) gracier.

parent *n* parent *m*.

parenthesis *n* (*pl* **-theses**) parenthèse *f*.

parenthood *n* (fatherhood) paternité *f*; (motherhood) maternité *f*.

Paris *n* Paris.

parish *n* (Relig) paroisse *f*; (municipal) commune *f*.

park *n* parc *m*. ● *vt/i* (se) garer; (remain parked) stationner. **~ and ride** *n* parc *m* relais.

parking *n* stationnement *m*; **no ~** stationnement interdit. **~-lot** *n* (US) parking *m*. **~-meter** *n* parcmètre *m*. **~ ticket** *n* (fine) contravention *f*, PV *m* 🄸.

parliament *n* parlement *m*. **parliamentary** *a* parlementaire.

parlour, (US) **parlor** *n* salon *m*.

parody *n* parodie *f*. ● *vt* parodier.

parole *n* **on ~** en liberté conditionnelle.

parrot *n* perroquet *m*.

parry *vt* (Sport) parer; (*question*) éluder. ● *n* parade *f*.

parsley *n* persil *m*.

parsnip *n* panais *m*.

part *n* partie *f*; (of serial) épisode *m*; (of machine) pièce *f*; (Theat) rôle *m*; (side in dispute) parti *m*; **in ~** en partie; **on the ~ of** de la part de; **take ~ in** participer à. ● *a* partiel. ● *adv* en partie. ● *vt/i* (separate) (se) séparer; **~ with** se séparer de.

part-exchange *n* reprise *f*; **take sth in ~** reprendre qch.

partial *a* partiel; (biased) partial; **be ~ to** avoir un faible pour.

participant *n* participant/-e *m/f*. **participate** *vi* participer (**in** à). **participation** *n* participation *f*.

participle *n* participe *m*.

particular *n* détail *m*; **~s** détails *mpl*; **in ~** en particulier. ● *a* particulier; (fussy) difficile; (careful) méticuleux; **that ~ man** cet homme-là. **particularly** *adv* particulièrement.

parting *n* séparation *f*; (in hair) raie *f*. ● *a* d'adieu.

partition *n* (of room) cloison *f*; (Pol) partition *f*. ● *vt* (*room*) cloisonner; (*country*) partager.

partly *adv* en partie.

partner *n* (professional) associé/-e *m/f*; (economic, sporting) partenaire *mf*; (spouse) époux/-se *m/f*; (unmarried) partenaire *mf*. **partnership** *n* association *f*.

partridge *n* perdrix *f*.

part-time *a & adv* à temps partiel.

party *n* fête *f*; (formal) réception *f*; (group) groupe *m*; (Pol) parti *m*; (Jur) partie *f*.

pass *vt/i* (*pt* **passed**) passer; (overtake) dépasser; (in exam) réussir; (approve) (*candidate*) admettre; (*invoice*) approuver; (*remark*) faire; (*judgement*) prononcer; (*law, bill*) adopter; **~ (by)** (*building*) passer devant;

(*person*) croiser. ● *n* (permit)
laisser-passer *m inv*; (ticket) carte
f d'abonnement; (Geog) col *m*;
(Sport) passe *f*; ~ (**mark**) (in exam)
moyenne *f*. □ ~ **away** mourir; ~
out (faint) s'évanouir; ~ **sth out**
distribuer qch; ~ **over** (overlook)
délaisser; ~ **up** (forego) laisser
passer.

passage *n* (way through, text)
passage *m*; (*voyage*) traversée *f*;
(corridor) couloir *m*.

passenger *n* (in car, plane, ship)
passager/-ère *m/f*; (in train, bus,
tube) voyageur/-euse *m/f*.

passer-by *n* (*pl* **passers-by**)
passant/-e *m/f*.

passing *a* (*motorist*) qui passe;
(*whim*) passager; (*reference*) en
passant.

passion *n* passion *f*. **passionate**
a passionné.

passive *a* passif.

passport *n* passeport *m*.

password *n* mot *m* de passe.

past *a* (*times, problems*) passé;
(*president*) ancien; **the ~ months**
ces derniers mois. ● *n* passé *m*.
● *prep* (beyond) après; **walk/go ~
sth** passer devant qch; **10 ~ 6** six
heures dix; **it's ~ 11** il est 11
heures passées. ● *adv* **go/walk ~**
passer.

pasta *n* pâtes *fpl* (alimentaires).

paste *n* (glue) colle *f*; (dough) pâte
f; (of fish, meat) pâté *m*; (jewellery)
strass *m*. ● *vt* coller.

pasteurize *vt* pasteuriser.

pastime *n* passe-temps *m inv*.

pastry *n* (dough) pâte *f*; (tart)
pâtisserie *f*.

pat *vt* (*pt* **patted**) tapoter. ● *n*
petite tape *f*.

patch *n* pièce *f*; (over eye) bandeau
m; (spot) tache *f*; (of snow, ice)
plaque *f*; (of vegetables) carré *m*;
bad ~ période *f* difficile. □ ~ **up**

(*trousers*) rapiécer; (*quarrel*)
résoudre.

patent *a* (obvious) manifeste;
(patented) breveté; ~ **leather** cuir *m*
verni. ● *n* brevet *m*. ● *vt* faire
breveter.

path *n* (*pl* **-s**) sentier *m*, chemin
m; (in park) allée *f*; (of rocket)
trajectoire *f*.

pathetic *a* misérable; (bad 🄵)
lamentable.

patience *n* patience *f*.

patient *a* patient. ● *n* patient/-e
m/f. **patiently** *adv* patiemment.

patriotic *a* patriotique; (*person*)
patriote.

patrol *n* patrouille *f*; ~ **car**
voiture *f* de police. ● *vt/i*
patrouiller (dans).

patron *n* (of the arts) mécène *m*;
(customer) client/-e *m/f*.

patronage *n* clientèle *f*; (support)
patronage *m*. **patronize** *vt*
(*person*) traiter avec
condescendance; (*establishment*)
fréquenter.

patter *n* (of steps) bruit *m*; (of rain)
crépitement *m*.

pattern *n* motif *m*, dessin *m*; (for
sewing) patron *m*; (for knitting)
modèle *f*.

paunch *n* ventre *m*.

pause *n* pause *f*. ● *vi* faire une
pause; (hesitate) hésiter.

pave *vt* paver; ~ **the way** ouvrir la
voie (**for** à).

pavement *n* trottoir *m*; (US)
chaussée *f*.

paving stone *n* pavé *m*.

paw *n* patte *f*. ● *vt* (*animal*)
donner des coups de patte à;
(touch 🄵) peloter 🄵.

pawn *n* pion *m*. ● *vt* mettre en
gage. ~**broker** *n* prêteur/-euse
m/f sur gages. ~**-shop** *n* mont-
de-piété *m*.

pay *vt* (*pt* **paid**) payer; (*interest*)
rapporter; (*compliment, attention*)

P

faire; (*visit, homage*) rendre. ● *vi*
payer; (*business*) rapporter; ~ **for**
sth payer qch. ● *n* salaire *m*; ~
rise augmentation *f* (*de salaire*).
□ ~ **back** rembourser; ~ **in**
déposer; ~ **off** (*loan*)
rembourser; (*worker*) congédier;
(succeed) être payant; ~ **out**
payer, débourser.

payable *a* payable; ~ **to** (*cheque*)
à l'ordre de.

payment *n* paiement *m*; (regular)
versement *m*; (reward) récompense
f.

payroll *n* fichier *m* des salaires;
be on the ~ **of** être employé par.

PC *abbr* ⇒PERSONAL COMPUTER.

PDA *abbr* (**personal digital**
assistant) assistant *m* personnel
numérique.

PE *abbr* (**physical education**)
éducation *f* physique, EPS *f*.

pea *n* (petit) pois *m*.

peace *n* paix *f*; ~ **of mind**
tranquillité *f* d'esprit. **peaceful** *a*
(tranquil) paisible; (peaceable)
pacifique.

peach *n* pêche *f*.

peacock *n* paon *m*.

peak *n* (of mountain) pic *m*; (of cap)
visière *f*; (maximum) maximum *m*;
(on graph) sommet *m*; (of career)
apogée *m*; (of fitness) meilleur *m*;
~ **hours** heures *fpl* de pointe.

peal *n* (of bells) carillon *m*; (of
laughter) éclat *m*.

peanut *n* cacahuète *f*; ~**s** (money
🖾) clopinettes *fpl* 🖾.

pear *n* poire *f*.

pearl *n* perle *f*.

peasant *n* paysan/-ne *m/f*.

peat *n* tourbe *f*.

pebble *n* caillou *m*; (on beach)
galet *m*.

peck *vt/i* (*food*) picorer; (attack)
donner des coups de bec (à). ● *n*
coup *m* de bec; a ~ **on the cheek**
une bise.

peckish *a* be ~ 🖾 avoir faim.

peculiar *a* (odd) bizarre; (special)
particulier (**to** à). **peculiarity** *n*
bizarrerie *f*.

pedal *n* pédale *f*. ● *vi* pédaler.

pedantic *a* pédant.

peddle *vt* colporter; (*drugs*) faire
du trafic de.

pedestrian *n* piéton *m*. ● *a*
(*precinct, street*) piétonnier; (fig)
prosaïque; ~ **crossing** passage *m*
pour piétons.

pedigree *n* (of animal) pedigree *m*;
(of person) ascendance *f*. ● *a* (*dog*)
de pure race.

pee *vi* 🖾 faire pipi 🖾.

peek *vi* & *n* = PEEP.

peel *n* (on fruit) peau *m*; (removed)
épluchures *fpl*. ● *vt* (*fruit,*
vegetables) éplucher; (*prawn*)
décortiquer. ● *vi* (of skin) peler; (of
paint) s'écailler.

peep *vi* jeter un coup d'œil
(furtif) (**at** à). ● *n* coup *m* d'œil
(furtif). ~**hole** *n* judas *m*.

peer *vi* ~ (**at**) regarder fixement.
● *n* (equal, noble) pair *m*. **peerage**
n pairie *f*.

peg *n* (for clothes) pince *f* à linge;
(to hang coats) patère *f*; (for tent)
piquet *m*. ● *vt* (*pt* **pegged**)
(*clothes*) accrocher avec des
pinces; (*prices*) indexer.

pejorative *a* péjoratif.

pelican *n* pélican *m*; ~ **crossing**
passage *m* pour piétons.

pellet *n* (round mass) boulette *f*; (for
gun) plomb *m*.

pelt *vt* bombarder (**with** de). ● *n*
(skin) peau *f*.

pelvis *n* (Anat) bassin *m*.

pen *n* stylo *m*; (for sheep) enclos *m*;
(for baby, cattle) parc *m*.

penal *a* pénal. **penalize** *vt*
pénaliser.

penalty *n* peine *f*; (fine) amende *f*;
(in football) penalty *m*.

penance n pénitence f.

pence ⇒PENNY.

pencil n crayon m. ●vt (pt **pencilled**) crayonner; ~ **in** noter provisoirement. ~**sharpener** n taille-crayons m inv.

pending a (matter) en souffrance; (Jur) en instance. ●prep (until) en attendant.

penetrate vt pénétrer; (silence, defences) percer; (organization) infiltrer. ●vi pénétrer. **penetrating** a pénétrant.

pen-friend n correspondant/-e m/f.

penguin n manchot m, pingouin m.

pen: ~**knife** n (pl -**knives**) canif m. ~**name** n pseudonyme m.

penniless a sans le sou.

penny n (pl **pennies** or **pence**) (unit of currency) penny m; (small amount) centime m.

pension n (from state) pension f; (from employer) retraite f; ~ **scheme** plan m de retraite. ●vt ~ **off** mettre à la retraite. **pensioner** n retraité/-e m/f.

pensive a songeur.

penthouse n appartement m de luxe (au dernier étage).

penultimate a avant-dernier.

people npl gens mpl, personnes fpl; English ~ les Anglais mpl; ~ **say** on dit. ●n peuple m. ●vt peupler. ~ **carrier** n monospace m.

pepper n poivre m; (vegetable) poivron m. ●vt (Culin) poivrer.

peppermint n (plant) menthe f poivrée; (sweet) bonbon m à la menthe.

per prep par; ~ **annum** par an; ~ **cent** pour cent; ~ **kilo** le kilo; **ten km** ~ **hour** dix km à l'heure.

percentage n pourcentage m.

perception n perception f.

perceptive a perspicace.

perch n (of bird) perchoir m. ●vi (se) percher.

perennial a perpétuel; (plant) vivace.

perfect[1] vt perfectionner.

perfect[2] a parfait. ●n (Ling) parfait m. **perfectly** adv parfaitement.

perfection n perfection f; **to** ~ à la perfection.

perforate vt perforer.

perform vt (task) exécuter; (function) remplir; (operation) procéder à; (play) jouer; (song) chanter. ●vi (actor, musician, team) jouer; ~ **well/badly** (candidate, business) avoir de bons/de mauvais résultats. **performance** n interprétation f; (of car, team) performance f; (show) représentation f; (fuss) histoire f. **performer** n artiste mf.

perfume n parfum m.

perhaps adv peut-être.

peril n péril m. **perilous** a périlleux.

perimeter n périmètre m.

period n période f; (era) époque f; (lesson) cours m; (Gram) point m; (Med) règles fpl. ●a d'époque. **periodical** n périodique m.

peripheral a (vision, suburb) périphérique; (issue) annexe. ●n (Comput) périphérique m.

perish vi périr; (rubber) se détériorer.

perjury n faux témoignage m.

perk n Ⓘ avantage m. ●vt/i ~ **up** Ⓘ (se) remonter. **perky** a Ⓘ gai.

perm n permanente f. ●vt **have one's hair** ~**ed** se faire faire une permanente.

permanent a permanent. **permanently** adv (happy) en permanence; (employed) de façon permanente.

permissible *a* permis.
permission *n* permission *f*.
permissive *a* libéral; (pej) permissif.
permit[1] *vt* (*pt* **permitted**) permettre (**sb to** à qn de), autoriser (**sb to** qn à).
permit[2] *n* permis *m*.
perpendicular *a* perpendiculaire.
perpetrator *n* auteur *m*.
perpetuate *vt* perpétuer.
perplexed *a* perplexe.
persecute *vt* persécuter.
perseverance *n* persévérance *f*.
persevere *vi* persévérer.
persist *vi* persister (**in doing** à faire). **persistence** *n* persistance *f*. **persistent** *a* (*cough, snow*) persistant; (obstinate) obstiné; (*noise, pressure*) continuel.
person *n* personne *f*; **in** ~ en personne.
personal *a* (*life, problem, opinion*) personnel; (*safety, freedom, insurance*) individuel. ~ **ad** *n* petite annonce *f*. ~ **assistant** *n* secrétaire *mf* de direction. ~ **computer** *n* ordinateur *m* (personnel), micro-ordinateur *m*.
personality *n* personnalité *f*; (star) vedette *f*.
personal: ~ **organizer** *n* agenda *m*. ~ **stereo** *n* baladeur *m*.
personnel *n* personnel *m*.
perspiration *n* (sweat) sueur *f*; (sweating) transpiration *f*. **perspire** *vi* transpirer.
persuade *vt* persuader (**to** de). **persuasion** *n* persuasion *f*. **persuasive** *a* persuasif.
pertinent *a* pertinent.
perturb *vt* troubler.
Peru *n* Pérou *m*.
pervasive *a* (*smell*) pénétrant; (*feeling*) envahissant.

perverse *a* (*desire*) pervers; (*refusal, attitude*) illogique.
perversion *n* perversion *f*.
pervert[1] *vt* (*truth*) travestir; (*values*) fausser; (*justice*) entraver.
pervert[2] *n* pervers/-e *m/f*.
pessimist *n* pessimiste *mf*.
pessimistic *a* pessimiste.
pest *n* (insect) insecte *m* nuisible; (animal) animal *m* nuisible; (person 🄸) enquiquineur/-euse *m/f* 🄸.
pester *vt* harceler.
pet *n* animal *m* de compagnie; (favourite) chouchou/-te *m/f*. ● *a* (*theory, charity*) favori; ~ **hate** bête *f* noire; ~ **name** petit nom *m*. ● *vt* (*pt* **petted**) caresser; (spoil) chouchouter 🄸.
petal *n* pétale *m*.
peter *vi* ~ **out** (*conversation*) tarir; (*supplies*) s'épuiser.
petite *a* (*woman*) menue.
petition *n* pétition *f*. ● *vt* adresser une pétition à.
petrol *n* essence *f*. ~ **bomb** *n* cocktail *m* molotov. ~ **station** *n* station-service *f*. ~ **tank** *n* réservoir *m* d'essence.
petticoat *n* jupon *m*.
petty *a* (**-ier, -iest**) (minor) petit; (mean) mesquin; ~ **cash** petite caisse *f*.
pew *n* banc *m* (d'église).
pharmacist *n* pharmacien/-ne *m/f*. **pharmacy** *n* pharmacie *f*.
phase *n* phase *f*. ● *vt* ~ **in/out** introduire/supprimer peu à peu.
PhD *abbr* (**Doctor of Philosophy**) doctorat *m*.
pheasant *n* faisan/-e *m/f*.
phenomenon *n* (*pl* **-ena**) phénomène *m*.
phew *interj* ouf.
philosopher *n* philosophe *mf*.
philosophical *a* philosophique;

(resigned) philosophe. **philosophy** *n* philosophie *f*.

phlegm *n* (Med) mucosité *f*.

phobia *n* phobie *f*.

phone *n* téléphone *m*; **on the ~** au téléphone. ●*vt* (person) téléphoner à; **~ England** téléphoner en Angleterre. ●*vi* téléphoner; **~ back** rappeler. **~ book** *n* annuaire *m*. **~ booth**, **~ box** *n* cabine *f* téléphonique. **~ call** *n* coup *m* de fil 🔲. **~card** *n* télécarte *f*. **~-in** *n* émission *f* à ligne ouverte. **~ number** *n* numéro *m* de téléphone.

phonetic *a* phonétique.

phoney *a* (**-ier**, **-iest**) 🔲 faux. ●*n* 🔲 (person) charlatan *m*; **it's a ~** c'est un faux.

photocopier *n* photocopieuse *f*.

photocopy *n* photocopie *f*. ●*vt* photocopier.

photograph *n* photographie *f*. ●*vt* photographier. **photographer** *n* photographe *mf*.

phrase *n* expression *f*; (idiom) locution *f*. ●*vt* exprimer, formuler. **~-book** *n* guide *m* de conversation.

physical *a* physique.

physicist *n* physicien/-ne *m/f*.

physics *n* physique *f*.

physiotherapist *n* kinésithérapeute *mf*. **physiotherapy** *n* kinésithérapie *f*.

physique *n* physique *m*.

piano *n* piano *m*.

pick *n* choix *m*; (best) meilleur/-e *m/f*; (tool) pioche *f*. ●*vt* choisir; (*flower*) cueillir; (*lock*) crocheter; **~ a quarrel with** chercher querelle à; **~ one's nose** se curer le nez. 🔲 **~ on** harceler; **~ out** choisir; (identify) distinguer; **~ up** *vt* ramasser; (*sth fallen*) relever; (*weight*) soulever; (*habit*,

passenger, speed) prendre; (learn) apprendre; *vi* s'améliorer.

pickaxe *n* pioche *f*.

picket *n* (striker) gréviste *mf*; (stake) piquet *m*; **~ (line)** piquet *m* de grève. ●*vt* (*pt* **picketed**) installer un piquet de grève devant.

pickle *n* conserves *fpl* au vinaigre; (gherkin) cornichon *m*. ●*vt* conserver dans du vinaigre.

pick-up *n* (stylus-holder) lecteur *m*; (on guitar) capteur *m*; (collection) ramassage *m*; (improvement) reprise *f*.

picnic *n* pique-nique *m*. ●*vi* (*pt* **picnicked**) pique-niquer.

pictorial *a* (*magazine*) illustré; (*record*) graphique.

picture *n* image *f*; (painting) tableau *m*; (photograph) photo *f*; (drawing) dessin *m*; (film) film *m*; (fig) description *f*; **the ~s** le cinéma. ●*vt* s'imaginer; **be ~d** (shown) être représenté.

picturesque *a* pittoresque.

pie *n* (sweet) tarte *f*; (savoury) tourte *f*.

piece *n* morceau *m*; (of string, ribbon) bout *m*; (of currency, machine) pièce *f*; **a ~ of advice/furniture** un conseil/meuble; **go to ~s** (fig) s'effondrer; **take to ~s** démonter.

pier *n* jetée *f*.

pierce *vt* percer.

pig *n* porc *m*, cochon *m*.

pigeon *n* pigeon *m*. **~-hole** *n* casier *m*.

pig-headed *a* entêté.

pigsty *n* porcherie *f*.

pigtail *n* natte *f*.

pike *n* *inv* (fish) brochet *m*.

pile *n* (heap) tas *m*; (stack) pile *f*; (of carpet) poil *m*; **~s of** 🔲 un tas de 🔲. ●*vt* **~ (up)** entasser. ●*vi* **~ into** s'engouffrer dans; **~ up** (*snow, leaves*) s'entasser; (*debts,* *work*) s'accumuler. **~-up** n (Auto) carambolage m.

pilgrim n pèlerin m. **pilgrimage** n pèlerinage m.

pill n pilule f.

pillar n pilier m. **~-box** n boîte f aux lettres.

pillion n siège m de passager; ride ~ monter en croupe.

pillow n oreiller m. **~case** n taie f d'oreiller.

pilot n pilote m. ● a pilote. ● vt (pt **piloted**) piloter. **~-light** n veilleuse f.

pimple n bouton m.

pin n épingle f; (of plug) fiche f; (for wood, metal) goujon m; (in surgery) broche f; have ~s and needles avoir des fourmis. ● vt (pt **pinned**) épingler, attacher; (trap) coincer; ~ **sb down** (fig) forcer qn à se décider; ~ **up** accrocher.

pinafore n tablier m.

pincers npl tenailles fpl.

pinch vt pincer; (steal 🔲) piquer. ● vi (be too tight) serrer. ● n (mark) pinçon m; (of salt) pincée f; at a ~ à la rigueur.

pine n (tree) pin m. ● vi ~ (**away**) dépérir; ~ **for** languir après.

pineapple n ananas m.

pinecone n pomme f de pin.

pink a & n rose (m).

pinpoint vt (problem, cause, location) indiquer; (time) déterminer.

pint n pinte f (GB = 0.57 litre; US = 0.47 litre).

pin-up n 🔲 pin-up f inv 🔲.

pioneer n pionnier m. ● vt ~ **the use of** être le premier à utiliser.

pious a pieux.

pip n (seed) pépin m; (sound) top m.

pipe n tuyau m; (to smoke) pipe f; (Mus) chalumeau m; **~s** cornemuse f. ● vt transporter par tuyau. ☐ ~ **down** se taire.

pipeline n oléoduc m; **in the ~** en cours.

piping n tuyauterie f; ~ **hot** fumant.

pirate n pirate m. ● vt pirater.

Pisces n Poissons mpl.

pistol n pistolet m.

pit n fosse f; (mine) puits m; (quarry) carrière f; (for orchestra) fosse f; (of stomach) creux m; (of cherry: US) noyau m. ● vt (pt **pitted**) marquer; (fig) opposer; ~ **oneself against** se mesurer à

pitch n (Sport) terrain m; (of voice, note) hauteur f; (degree) degré m; (Mus) ton m; (tar) brai m. ● vt jeter; (tent) planter. ● vi (ship) tanguer. ☐ ~ **in** 🔲 contribuer.

pitfall n écueil m.

pitiful a pitoyable. **pitiless** a impitoyable.

pit stop n arrêt m mécanique.

pittance n earn a ~ gagner trois fois rien.

pity n pitié f; (regrettable fact) dommage m; **take ~ on** avoir pitié de; **what a ~!** quel dommage! ● vt avoir pitié de.

pivot n pivot m. ● vi (pt **pivoted**) pivoter.

placard n affiche f.

place n endroit m, lieu m; (house) maison f; (seat, rank) place f; **at or to my ~** chez moi; **change ~s** changer de place; **in the first ~** d'abord; **out of ~** déplacé; **take ~** avoir lieu. ● vt placer; (order) passer; (remember) situer; **be ~d** (in race) se placer. **~-mat** n set m.

placid a placide.

plagiarism n plagiat m. **plagiarize** vt/i plagier.

plague n (bubonic) peste f; (epidemic) épidémie f; (of ants, locusts) invasion f. ● vt harceler.

plaice n inv carrelet m.

plain a (obvious) clair; (candid)

franc; (simple) simple; (not pretty)
sans beauté; (not patterned) uni; ~
chocolate chocolat *m* noir; **in ~
clothes** en civil. ●*adv*
franchement. ●*n* plaine *f.*
plainly *adv* clairement;
franchement; simplement.
plaintiff *n* plaignant/-e *m/f.*
plaintive *a* plaintif.
plait *vt* tresser. ●*n* natte *f.*
plan *n* projet *m,* plan *m;* (diagram)
plan *m.* ●*vt* (*pt* **planned**)
projeter (**to do** de faire);
(*timetable, day*) organiser;
(*economy, work*) planifier. ●*vi*
prévoir; ~ **on** s'attendre à.
plane *n* (level) plan *m;* (aeroplane)
avion *m;* (tool) rabot *m.* ●*a* plan.
●*vt* raboter.
planet *n* planète *f.*
plank *n* planche *f.*
planning *n* (of economy, work)
planification *f;* (of holiday, party)
organisation *f;* (of town) urbanisme
m; **family ~ planning** *m* familial;
~ **permission** permis *m* de
construire.
plant *n* plante *f;* (Tech) matériel
m; (factory) usine *f.* ●*vt* planter;
(bomb) placer.
plaster *n* plâtre *m;* (adhesive)
sparadrap *m.* ●*vt* plâtrer; (cover)
couvrir (**with** de).
plastic *a* en plastique; (*art,
substance*) plastique; ~ **surgery**
chirurgie *f* esthétique. ●*n*
plastique *m.*
plate *n* assiette *f;* (of metal) plaque
f; (silverware) argenterie *f;* (in book)
gravure *f.* ●*vt* (metal) plaquer.
plateau *n* (*pl* ~**x**) plateau *m;* (fig)
palier *m.*
platform *n* (stage) estrade *f;* (for
speaking) tribune *f;* (Rail) quai *m;*
(Pol) plate-forme *f.*
platoon *n* (Mil) section *f.*
play *vt/i* jouer; (*instrument*) jouer
de; (*record*) mettre; (*game*) jouer

à; (*opponent*) jouer contre;
(*match*) disputer; ~ **safe** ne pas
prendre de risques. ●*n* jeu *m;*
(Theat) pièce *f.* □ ~ **down**
minimiser; ~ **on** (*fears*)
exploiter; ~ **up** ⊡ commencer à
faire des siennes ⊡; ~ **up sth**
mettre l'accent sur qch.
playful *a* (*remark*) taquin; (*child*)
joueur.
play: ~**ground** *n* cour *f* de
récréation. ~**-group,** ~**-school** *n*
garderie *f.*
playing *n* (Sport) jeu *m;* (Theat)
interprétation *f.* ~**-card** *n* carte *f*
à jouer. ~**-field** *n* terrain *m* de
sport.
play: ~**-pen** *n* parc *m* (pour
bébé). ~**wright** *n* auteur *m*
dramatique.
plc *abbr* (**public limited
company**) SA.
plea *n* (for mercy, tolerance) appel *m;*
(for food, money) demande *f;* (reason)
excuse *f;* **make a ~ of guilty**
plaider coupable.
plead *vt/i* supplier; (Jur) plaider.
pleasant *a* agréable.
please *vt/i* plaire (à), faire plaisir
(à); ~ **oneself, do as one ~** n faire
ce qu'on veut. ●*adv* s'il vous *or*
te plaît. **pleased** *a* content (**with**
de). **pleasing** *a* agréable.
pleasure *n* plaisir *m;* **with ~** avec
plaisir; **my ~** je vous en prie.
pleat *n* pli *m.* ●*vt* plisser.
pledge *n* (token) gage *m;* (promise)
promesse *f.* ●*vt* promettre; (pawn)
mettre en gage.
plentiful *a* abondant.
plenty *n* abondance *f;* ~ **(of)** (a
great deal) beaucoup (de); (enough)
assez (de).
pliers *npl* pinces *fpl.*
plight *n* détresse *f.*
plinth *n* socle *m.*
plod *vi* (*pt* **plodded**) avancer
péniblement.

P

plonk n 🔲 pinard m 🔲.

plot n (*conspiracy*) complot m; (of novel) intrigue f; ~ **of land**) terrain m. ● vt/i (*pt* **plotted**) (*plan*) comploter; (*mark out*) tracer.

plough n charrue f. ● vt/i □ ~ **back** réinvestir; ~ **through** avancer péniblement dans.

plow n & vt/i (US) = PLOUGH.

ploy n stratagème m.

pluck vt (*flower, fruit*) cueillir; (*bird*) plumer; (*eyebrows*) épiler; (*strings*: Mus) pincer; ~ **up courage** prendre son courage à deux mains. **plucky** a courageux.

plug n (for sink) bonde f; (Electr) fiche f, prise f. ● vt (*pt* **plugged**) (*hole*) boucher; (publicize 🔲) faire du battage autour de. □ ~ **in** brancher. ~**hole** n bonde f.

plum n prune f; ~ **pudding** (plum-)pudding m.

plumber n plombier m.

plume n (of feathers) panache m.

plummet vi tomber, plonger.

plump a potelé, dodu.

plunge vt (dive, thrust) plonger; (fall) tomber. ● n plongeon m; (fall) chute f; **take the ~** se jeter à l'eau. **plunger** n (for sink) ventouse f.

plural a pluriel; (*noun*) au pluriel; (*ending*) du pluriel. ● n pluriel m.

plus prep plus; **ten ~** plus de dix. ● a (Electr & fig) positif. ● n signe m plus; (fig) atout m.

ply vt (*tool*) manier; (*trade*) exercer. ● vi faire la navette; ~ **sb with drink** offrir continuellement à boire à qn.

plywood n contreplaqué m.

p.m. adv de l'après-midi *or* du soir.

pneumatic drill n marteau-piqueur m.

pneumonia n pneumonie f.

PO abbr ⇒POST OFFICE.

poach vt/i (*game*) braconner; (*staff*) débaucher; (Culin) pocher.

PO Box n boîte f postale.

pocket n poche f; **be out of ~** avoir perdu de l'argent. ● a de poche. ● vt empocher. ~**book** n (notebook) carnet m; (wallet: US) portefeuille m; (handbag: US) sac m à main. ~**-money** n argent m de poche.

pod n (peas) cosse f; (vanilla) gousse f.

podgy a (**-ier, -iest**) dodu.

poem n poème m. **poet** n poète m. **poetic** a poétique. **poetry** n poésie f.

point n (position) point m; (tip) pointe f; (decimal point) virgule f; (remark) remarque f; **good ~s** qualités fpl; **on the ~ of** sur le point de; ~ **in time** moment m; ~ **of view** point m de vue; **to the ~** pertinent; **what is the ~?** à quoi bon? ● vt (aim) braquer; (show) indiquer; ~ **out** signaler. ● vi indiquer du doigt; ~ **out that, make the ~ that** faire remarquer que. ~**-blank** a & adv à bout portant.

pointed a (sharp) pointu; (window) en pointe; (remark) lourd de sens.

pointless a inutile.

poise n (confidence) assurance f; (physical elegance) aisance f.

poison n poison m. ● vt empoisonner. **poisonous** a (substance) toxique; (plant) vénéneux; (snake) venimeux.

poke vt/i (push) pousser; (fire) tisonner; (thrust) fourrer; ~ **fun at** se moquer de. ● n (petit) coup m. □ ~ **out** (head) sortir.

poker n (for fire) tisonnier m; (cards) poker m.

Poland n Pologne f.

polar a polaire.

pole n (stick) perche f; (for flag) mât m; (Geog) pôle m.

Pole n Polonais/-e m/f.

pole-vault n saut m à la perche.

police n police f. ● vt faire la police dans. ~ **constable** n agent m de police. ~**man** n (pl **-men**) agent m de police. ~ **station** n commissariat m de police. ~**woman** n (pl **-women**) femme-agent f.

policy n politique f; (insurance) police f (d'assurance).

polish vt polir; (shoes, floor) cirer. ● n (for shoes) cirage m; (for floor) encaustique f; (for nails) vernis m; (shine) poli m; (fig) raffinement m. □ ~ **off** finir en vitesse; ~ **up** (language) perfectionner.

Polish a polonais. ● n (Ling) polonais m.

polished a raffiné.

polite a poli.

political a politique.

politician n homme m politique, femme f politique.

politics n politique f.

poll n (vote casting) scrutin m; (survey) sondage m; **go to the ~s** aller aux urnes. ● vt (votes) obtenir.

pollen n pollen m.

polling booth n isoloir m.

polling station n bureau m de vote.

pollution n pollution f.

polo n polo m. ~ **neck** n col m roulé.

pomegranate n grenade f.

pomp n pompe f.

pompous a pompeux.

pond n étang m; (artificial) bassin m; (stagnant) mare f.

ponder vt/i réfléchir (à), méditer (sur).

pong n (stink 🔲) puanteur f. ● vi 🔲 puer.

pony n poney m. ~**tail** n queue f de cheval.

poodle n caniche m.

pool n (puddle) flaque f; (pond) étang m; (of blood) mare f; (for swimming) piscine f; (fund) fonds m commun; (of ideas) réservoir m; (snooker) billard m américain; ~**s** pari m mutuel sur le football. ● vt mettre en commun.

poor a (not wealthy) pauvre; (not good) médiocre, mauvais.

poorly a malade. ● adv mal.

pop n (noise) pan m; (music) pop m. ● a pop inv. ● vt/i (pt **popped**) (burst) crever; (put) mettre; ~ **in/ out/off** entrer/sortir/partir. □ ~ **up** surgir.

pope n pape m.

poppy n pavot m; (wild) coquelicot m.

popular a populaire; (in fashion) en vogue; **be ~ with** plaire à.

population n population f.

porcelain n porcelaine f.

porcupine n porc-épic m.

pork n porc m.

pornography n pornographie f.

port n (harbour) port m; (left: Naut) bâbord m; ~ **of call** escale f; (wine) porto m.

portable a portable.

porter n (carrier) porteur m; (door-keeper) portier m.

portfolio n (Pol, Comm) portefeuille m.

portion n (at meal) portion f; (part) partie f.

portrait n portrait m.

portray vt représenter.

Portugal n Portugal m.

Portuguese n (Ling) portugais m; (person) Portugais/-e m/f. ● a portugais.

P

pose vt/i poser; ~ **as** (*expert*) se poser en. ●n pose f.

poser n (person) frimeur/-euse m/f; (puzzle) colle f.

posh a 🔲 chic inv.

position n position f; (job, state) situation f. ●vt placer.

positive a positif; (sure) sûr, certain; (real) réel, vrai.

possess vt posséder.

possession n possession f; **take** ~ **of** prendre possession de.

possessive a possessif.

possible a possible.

possibly adv peut-être; **if I** ~ **can** si cela m'est possible; **I cannot** ~ **leave** il m'est impossible de partir.

post n (pole) poteau m; (station, job) poste m; (mail service) poste f; (letters) courrier m. ●a postal. ●vt (*letter*) poster; **keep** ~**ed** tenir au courant; ~ (**up**) (a notice) afficher; (appoint) affecter.

postage n affranchissement m; tarif m postal.

postal a postal. ~ **order** n mandat m.

post: ~**box** n boîte f aux lettres. ~**card** n carte f postale. ~ **code** n code m postal.

poster n (for information) affiche f; (for decoration) poster m.

postgraduate n étudiant/-e m/f de troisième cycle.

posthumous a posthume.

post: ~**man** n (pl -**men**) facteur m. ~**mark** n cachet m de la poste.

post-mortem n autopsie f.

post office n poste f.

postpone vt remettre.

postscript n (to letter) post-scriptum m inv.

posture n posture f. ●vi prendre des poses.

pot n pot m; (drug 🔲) hasch m; **go**

to ~ 🔲 aller à la ruine; **take** ~ **luck** tenter sa chance. ●vt (*plants*) mettre en pot.

potato n (pl ~**es**) pomme f de terre.

pot-belly n bedaine f.

potential a & n potentiel (m).

pot-hole n (in rock) caverne f; (in road) nid m de poule. **pot-holing** n spéléologie f.

potter n potier m. ●vi bricoler.

pottery n (art) poterie f; (objects) poteries fpl.

potty a (-**ier**, -**iest**) (crazy 🔲) toqué. ●n pot m.

pouch n poche f; (for tobacco) blague f.

poultry n volailles fpl.

pounce vi bondir (**on** sur). ●n bond m.

pound n (weight) livre f (= 454 g); (money) livre f; (for dogs, cars) fourrière f. ●vt (crush) piler; (bombard) pilonner. ●vi frapper fort; (of heart) battre fort; (walk) marcher à pas lourds.

pour vt verser. ●vi couler, ruisseler (**from** de); (rain) pleuvoir à torrents. □ ~ **in/out** (*people*) arriver/sortir en masse; ~ **off** or **out** vider. **pouring rain** n pluie f torrentielle.

pout vi faire la moue.

poverty n misère f, pauvreté f.

powder n poudre f. ●vt poudrer.

power n (strength) puissance f; (control) pouvoir m; (energy) énergie f; (Electr) courant m. ●vt (*engine*) faire marcher; (*plane*) propulser; ~**ed by** (*engine*) propulsé par; (*generator*) alimenté par. ~ **cut** n coupure f de courant.

powerful a puissant.

powerless a impuissant.

power: ~ **point** n prise f de courant. ~-**station** n centrale f électrique.

practical a pratique. ~ **joke** n farce f.

practice n (procedure) pratique f; (of profession) exercice m; (Sport) entraînement m; **in** ~ (in fact) en pratique; (well-trained) en forme; **out of** ~ rouillé; **put into** ~ mettre en pratique.

practise vt/i (musician, typist) s'exercer (à); (Sport) s'entraîner (à); (put into practice) pratiquer; (profession) exercer.

praise vt faire l'éloge de; (God) louer. ● n éloges mpl, louanges fpl.

pram n landau m.

prance vi caracoler.

prawn n crevette f rose.

pray vi prier. **prayer** n prière f.

preach vt/i prêcher; ~ **at** or **to** prêcher.

precarious a précaire.

precaution n précaution f.

precede vt précéder.

precedence n (in importance) priorité f; (in rank) préséance f.

precedent n précédent m.

precinct n quartier m commerçant; (pedestrian area) zone f piétonne; (district: US) circonscription f.

precious a précieux.

precipitate vt (person, event, chemical) précipiter.

précis n résumé m.

precise a précis; (careful) méticuleux. **precision** n précision f.

precocious a précoce.

preconceived a préconçu.

predator n prédateur m.

predicament n situation f difficile.

predict vt prédire. **predictable** a prévisible. **prediction** n prédiction f.

predispose vt prédisposer (**to do** à faire).

predominant a prédominant.

pre-empt vt (anticipate) anticiper; (person) devancer.

preface n (to book) préface f; (to speech) préambule m.

prefect n (pupil) élève m/f chargé/-e de la discipline; (official) préfet m.

prefer vt (pt **preferred**) préférer (**to do** faire). **preferably** adv de préférence. **preference** n préférence f. **preferential** a préférentiel.

prefix n préfixe m.

pregnancy n grossesse f. **pregnant** a (woman) enceinte; (animal) pleine; (pause) éloquent.

prehistoric a préhistorique.

prejudge vt (issue) préjuger de; (person) juger d'avance.

prejudice n préjugé(s) m(pl); (harm) préjudice m. ● vt (claim) porter préjudice à; (person) léser. **prejudiced** a partial; (person) qui a des préjugés.

premature a prématuré.

premeditated a prémédité.

premises npl locaux mpl; **on the** ~ sur les lieux.

premium n (insurance) prime f; **be at a** ~ être précieux.

preoccupied a préoccupé.

preparation n préparation f; ~**s** préparatifs mpl.

preparatory a préparatoire. ~ **school** n école f primaire privée; (US) école f secondaire privée.

prepare vt/i (se) préparer (**for** à); **be** ~**d for** (expect) s'attendre à; ~**d to** prêt à.

preposition n préposition f.

preposterous a absurde, ridicule.

P

prep school *n* = PREPARATORY SCHOOL.

prerequisite *n* condition *f* préalable.

prescribe *vt* prescrire.

prescription *n* (Med) ordonnance *f*.

presence *n* présence *f*; ∼ **of mind** présence *f* d'esprit.

present¹ *a* présent. ●*n* présent *m*; (gift) cadeau *m*; **at** ∼ à présent; **for the** ∼ pour le moment.

present² *vt* présenter; (*film, concert*) donner; ∼ **sb with** offrir à qn. **presentation** *n* présentation *f*. **presenter** *n* présentateur/-trice *m/f*.

preservation *n* (of food) conservation *f*; (of wildlife) préservation *f*.

preservative *n* (Culin) agent *m* de conservation.

preserve *vt* préserver; (Culin) conserver. ●*n* réserve *f*; (fig) domaine *m*; (jam) confiture *f*.

presidency *n* présidence *f*.

president *n* président/-e *m/f*.

press *vt/i* (button) appuyer (sur); (squeeze) presser; (iron) repasser; (pursue) poursuivre; **be** ∼**ed for** (*time*) manquer de; ∼ **for sth** faire pression pour avoir qch; ∼ **sb to do sth** pousser qn à faire qch; ∼ **on** continuer (**with sth** qch). ●*n* (newspapers, machine) presse *f*; (for wine) pressoir *m*. ∼ **cutting** *n* coupure *f* de presse.

pressing *a* pressant.

press: ∼ **release** *n* communiqué *m* de presse. ∼-**stud** *n* bouton-pression *m*. ∼-**up** *n* pompe *f*.

pressure *n* pression *f*. ●*vt* faire pression sur. ∼-**cooker** *n* cocotte-minute *f*. ∼ **group** *n* groupe *m* de pression.

pressurize *vt* (*cabin*) pressuriser; (*person*) faire pression sur.

prestige *n* prestige *m*.

presumably *adv* vraisemblablement.

presume *vt* (suppose) présumer.

pretence, (US) **pretense** *n* feinte *f*, simulation *f*; (claim) prétention *f*; (pretext) prétexte *m*.

pretend *vt/i* faire semblant (**to do** de faire); ∼ **to** (lay claim to) prétendre à.

pretentious *a* prétentieux.

pretext *n* prétexte *m*.

pretty *a* (**-ier, -iest**) joli. ●*adv* assez; ∼ **much** presque.

prevail *vi* (be usual) prédominer; (win) prévaloir; ∼ **on** persuader (**to do** de faire). **prevailing** *a* actuel; (*wind*) dominant.

prevalent *a* répandu.

prevent *vt* empêcher (**from doing** de faire). **prevention** *n* prévention *f*. **preventive** *a* préventif.

preview *n* avant-première *f*; (fig) aperçu *m*.

previous *a* précédent, antérieur; ∼ **to** avant. **previously** *adv* auparavant.

prey *n* proie *f*; **bird of** ∼ rapace *m*. ●*vi* ∼ **on** faire sa proie de; (worry) préoccuper.

price *n* prix *m*. ●*vt* fixer le prix de. **priceless** *a* inestimable; (amusing 🄸) impayable 🄸.

prick *vt* (with pin) piquer; ∼ **up one's ears** dresser l'oreille. ●*n* piqûre *f*.

prickle *n* piquant *m*.

pride *n* orgueil *m*; (satisfaction) fierté *f*; ∼ **of place** place *f* d'honneur. ●*vpr* ∼ **oneself on** s'enorgueillir de.

priest *n* prêtre *m*.

prim *a* (**primmer, primmest**) guindé, méticuleux.

primarily *adv* essentiellement.

primary *a* (*school, elections*) primaire; (chief, basic) premier, fondamental. ● n (Pol: US) primaire f.

prime a principal, premier; (first-rate) excellent. ● vt (pump, gun) amorcer; (surface) apprêter. **P~ Minister** n Premier Ministre m.

primitive a primitif.

primrose n primevère f (jaune).

prince n prince m. **princess** n princesse f.

principal a principal. ● n (of school) directeur/-trice m/f.

principle n principe m; **in/on ~** en/par principe.

print vt imprimer; (write in capitals) écrire en majuscules; **~ed matter** imprimés mpl. ● n (of foot) empreinte f; (letters) caractères mpl; (photograph) épreuve f; (engraving) gravure f; **in ~** disponible; **out of ~** épuisé. **printer** n (person) imprimeur m; (Comput) imprimante f.

prion n prion m.

prior a précédent. ● n (Relig) prieur m. **~ to** prep avant (de).

priority n priorité f; **take ~** avoir la priorité (over sur).

prise vt forcer; **~ open** ouvrir en forçant.

prison n prison f. **prisoner** n prisonnier/-ière m/f. **~ officer** n gardien/-ne m/f de prison.

pristine a **be in ~ condition** être comme neuf.

privacy n intimité f, solitude f.

private a privé; (confidential) personnel; (lessons, house) particulier; (ceremony) intime; **in ~** en privé; (of ceremony) dans l'intimité. ● n (soldier) simple soldat m. **privately** adv en privé; dans l'intimité; (inwardly) intérieurement.

privilege n privilège m. **privileged** a privilégié; **be ~d to** avoir le privilège de.

prize n prix m. ● vt (value) priser.

pro n **the ~s and cons** le pour et le contre.

probable a probable. **probably** adv probablement.

probation n (testing) essai m; (Jur) liberté f surveillée.

probe n (device) sonde f; (fig) enquête f. ● vt sonder. ● vi **~ into** sonder.

problem n problème m. ● a difficile. **problematic** a problématique.

procedure n procédure f; (way of doing sth) démarche f à suivre.

proceed vi (go) aller, avancer; (pass) passer (**to** à); (act) procéder; **~ (with)** continuer; **~ to do** se mettre à faire.

proceedings npl (discussions) débats mpl; (meeting) réunion f; (report) actes mpl; (Jur) poursuites fpl.

proceeds npl (profits) produit m, bénéfices mpl.

process n processus m; (method) procédé m; **in ~** en cours; **in the ~ of doing** en train de faire. ● vt (material, data) traiter.

procession n défilé m.

procrastinate vi différer, tergiverser.

procure vt obtenir.

prod vt/i (pt **prodded**) pousser doucement. ● n petit coup m.

prodigy n prodige m.

produce¹ n produits mpl.

produce² vt/i produire; (bring out) sortir; (show) présenter; (cause) provoquer; (Theat, TV) mettre en scène; (radio) réaliser; (cinema) produire. **producer** n metteur m en scène; réalisateur m; producteur m.

product n produit m.

production n production f; (Theat, TV) mise f en scène; (radio) réalisation f.

P

productive a productif.
  productivity n productivité f.
profession n profession f.
professional a professionnel; (of
  high quality) de professionnel;
  (*person*) qui exerce une
  profession libérale. ●n
  professionnel/-le m/f.
professor n professeur m
  (*titulaire d'une chaire*).
proficient a compétent.
profile n (of face) profil m; (of body,
  mountain) silhouette f; (by journalist)
  portrait m.
profit n profit m, bénéfice m. ●vi
  ~ **by** tirer profit de. **profitable** a
  rentable.
profound a profond.
profusely adv (*bleed*)
  abondamment; (*apologize*) avec
  effusion. **profusion** n profusion f.
program n (US) = PROGRAMME;
  (computer) ~ programme m. ●vt
  (pt **programmed**) programmer.
programme n programme m;
  (broadcast) émission f.
programmer n programmeur/
  -euse m/f.
programming n (Comput)
  programmation f.
progress[1] n progrès m(pl); **in** ~
  en cours; **make** ~ faire des
  progrès; ~ **report** compte-rendu
  m.
progress[2] vi (advance, improve)
  progresser.
progressive a progressif;
  (reforming) progressiste.
prohibit vt interdire (**sb from
  doing** à qn de faire).
project[1] vt projeter. ●vi (jut out)
  être en saillie.
project[2] n (plan) projet m;
  (undertaking) entreprise f; (School)
  dossier m.
projection n projection f; saillie
  f; (estimate) prévision f.

projector n projecteur m.
proliferate vi proliférer.
prolong vt prolonger.
prominent a (projecting)
  proéminent; (conspicuous) bien en
  vue; (fig) important.
promiscuous a de mœurs
  faciles.
promise n promesse f. ●vt/i
  promettre. **promising** a
  prometteur; (*person*) qui promet.
promote vt promouvoir; (advertise)
  faire la promotion de. **promotion**
  n promotion f.
prompt a rapide; (punctual) à
  l'heure, ponctuel. ●adv (on the
  dot) pile. ●vt inciter; (cause)
  provoquer; (Theat) souffler à. ●n
  (Comput) message m guide-
  opérateur. **prompter** n souffleur/
  -euse m/f. **promptly** adv
  rapidement; ponctuellement.
prone a ~ **to** sujet à.
pronoun n pronom m.
pronounce vt prononcer.
  pronunciation n prononciation f.
proof n (evidence) preuve f; (test, trial
  copy) épreuve f; (of alcohol) teneur f
  en alcool. ●a ~ **against** à
  l'épreuve de.
prop n support m; (Theat)
  accessoire m. ●vt (pt **propped**)
  ~ (**up**) (support) étayer; (lean)
  appuyer.
propaganda n propagande f.
propel vt (pt **propelled**) (vehicle,
  ship) propulser; (*person*)
  pousser.
propeller n hélice f.
proper a correct, bon; (adequate)
  convenable; (real) vrai; (thorough Ⓣ)
  parfait. **properly** adv
  correctement, comme il faut;
  (adequately) convenablement.
proper noun n nom m propre.
property n (house) propriété f;
  (things owned) biens mpl, propriété
  f. ●a immobilier, foncier.

prophecy n prophétie f.

prophet n prophète m.

proportion n (ratio, dimension) proportion f; (amount) partie f.

proposal n proposition f; (of marriage) demande f en mariage.

propose vt proposer. ● vi faire une demande en mariage; ~ **to do** se proposer de faire.

proposition n proposition f; (matter 🅣) affaire f. ● vt 🅣 faire des propositions malhonnêtes à.

proprietor n propriétaire mf.

propriety n (correct behaviour) bienséance f.

prose n prose f; (translation) thème m.

prosecute vt poursuivre en justice. **prosecution** n poursuites fpl. **prosecutor** n procureur m.

prospect[1] n (outlook) perspective f; (chance) espoir m.

prospect[2] vt/i prospecter.

prospective a (future) futur; (possible) éventuel.

prospectus n brochure f; (Univ) livret m de l'étudiant.

prosperity n prospérité f. **prosperous** a prospère.

prostitute n prostituée f.

prostrate a (prone) à plat ventre; (exhausted) prostré.

protect vt protéger. **protection** n protection f. **protective** a protecteur; (clothes) de protection.

protein n protéine f.

protest[1] n protestation f; **under** ~ en protestant.

protest[2] vt/i protester.

Protestant a & n protestant/-e (m/f).

protester n manifestant/-e m/f.

protocol n protocole m.

protrude vi dépasser.

proud a fier, orgueilleux.

prove vt prouver. ● vi ~ **(to be)**

easy se révéler facile; ~ **oneself** faire ses preuves. **proven** a éprouvé.

proverb n proverbe m.

provide vt fournir (sb with sth qch à qn). ● vi ~ **for** (allow for) prévoir; (guard against) parer à; (person) pourvoir aux besoins de.

provided conj ~ **that** à condition que.

providing conj = PROVIDED.

province n province f; (fig) compétence f.

provision n (stock) provision f; (supplying) fourniture f; (stipulation) dispositions fpl; ~**s** (food) provisions fpl.

provisional a provisoire.

provocative a provocant.

provoke vt provoquer.

prow n proue f.

prowess n prouesses fpl.

prowl vi rôder.

proxy n **by** ~ par procuration.

prudish a pudibond, prude.

prune n pruneau m. ● vt (cut) tailler.

pry vi ~ **into** mettre son nez dans.

psalm n psaume m.

pseudonym n pseudonyme m.

psychiatric a psychiatrique. **psychiatrist** n psychiatre mf. **psychiatry** n psychiatrie f.

psychic a (phenomenon) métapsychique; (person) doué de télépathie.

psychoanalyse vt psychanalyser.

psychological a psychologique. **psychologist** n psychologue mf. **psychology** n psychologie f.

PTO abbr **(please turn over)** TSVP.

pub n pub m.

puberty n puberté f.

P

public *a* public; (*library*) municipal; **in ~** en public.

publican *n* patron/-ne *m/f* de pub.

publication *n* publication *f*.

public house *n* pub *m*.

publicity *n* publicité *f*.

publicize *vt* faire connaître au public.

public: **~ relations** *n* relations *fpl* publiques. **~ school** *n* école *f* privée; (US) école *f* publique. **~ transport** *n* transports *mpl* en commun.

publish *vt* publier. **publisher** *n* éditeur *m*. **publishing** *n* édition *f*.

pudding *n* dessert *m*; (steamed) pudding *m*.

puddle *n* flaque *f* d'eau.

puff *n* (of smoke) bouffée *f*; (of breath) souffle *m*. ● *vt/i* souffler. □ **~ at** (*cigar*) tirer sur. **~ out** (swell) se gonfler.

pull *vt/i* tirer; (*muscle*) se froisser; **~ a face** faire une grimace; **~ one's weight** faire sa part du travail; **~ sb's leg** faire marcher qn. ● *n* traction *f*; (fig) attraction *f*; (influence) influence *f*; **give a ~** tirer. □ **~ away** (Auto) démarrer; **~ back** *or* **out** (withdraw) (se) retirer; **~ down** (*building*) démolir; **~ in** (enter) entrer; (stop) s'arrêter; **~ off** enlever; (fig) réussir; **~ out** (from bag) sortir; (extract) arracher; (Auto) déboîter; **~ over** (Auto) se ranger (sur le côté); **~ through** s'en tirer; **~ oneself together** se ressaisir.

pull-down menu *n* (Comput) menu *m* déroulant.

pulley *n* poulie *f*.

pullover *n* pull(-over) *m*.

pulp *n* (of fruit) pulpe *f*; (for paper) pâte *f* à papier.

pulpit *n* chaire *f*.

pulsate *vi* battre.

pulse *n* (Med) pouls *m*.

pump *n* pompe *f*; (plimsoll) chaussure *f* de sport. ● *vt/i* pomper; (*person*) soutirer des renseignements à; **~ up** gonfler.

pumpkin *n* citrouille *f*.

pun *n* jeu *m* de mots.

punch *vt* donner un coup de poing à; (*ticket*) poinçonner. ● *n* coup *m* de poing; (vigour 🔢) punch *m*; (device) poinçonneuse *f*; (drink) punch *m*. **~-line** *n* chute *f*.

punctual *a* à l'heure; (habitually) ponctuel.

punctuation *n* ponctuation *f*.

puncture *n* crevaison *f*. ● *vt/i* crever.

pungent *a* âcre.

punish *vt* punir (**for sth** de qch). **punishment** *n* punition *f*.

punk *n* (music, fan) punk *m*; (US: 🔢) voyou *m*.

punt *n* (boat) barque *f*; (Irish pound) livre *f* irlandaise.

puny *a* (**-ier, -iest**) chétif.

pupil *n* (person) élève *mf*; (of eye) pupille *f*.

puppet *n* marionnette *f*.

puppy *n* chiot *m*.

purchase *vt* acheter (**from sb** à qn). ● *n* achat *m*.

pure *a* pur.

purgatory *n* purgatoire *m*.

purge *vt* purger (**of** de). ● *n* purge *f*.

purification *n* (of water, air) épuration *f*; (Relig) purification *f*.

purify *vt* épurer; purifier.

puritan *n* puritain/-e *m/f*.

purity *n* pureté *f*.

purple *a* & *n* violet (*m*).

purpose *n* but *m*; (determination) résolution *f*; **on ~** exprès; **to no ~** sans résultat.

purr *n* ronronnement *m*. ● *vi* ronronner.

purse *n* porte-monnaie *m inv*;

(handbag: US) sac *m* à main. ● *vt*
(*lips*) pincer.

pursue *vt* poursuivre.

pursuit *n* poursuite *f*; (hobby)
activité *f*, occupation *f*.

pus *n* pus *m*.

push *vt/i* pousser; (*button*)
appuyer sur; (*thrust*) enfoncer;
(*recommend* 🔲) proposer avec
insistance; **be ~ed for** (*time*)
manquer de; **be ~ing thirty**
🔲 friser la trentaine; **~ sb around**
bousculer qn. ● *n* poussée *f*;
(*effort*) gros effort *m*; (*drive*)
dynamisme *m*; **give the ~ to**
🔲 flanquer à la porte 🔲. □ **~ in**
resquiller; **~ on** continuer; **~ up**
(lift) relever; (*prices*) faire monter.

pushchair *n* poussette *f*.

pusher *n* revendeur/-euse *m/f*
(de drogue).

push-up *n* pompe *f*.

put *vt/i* (*pt* put; *pres p* putting)
mettre, placer, poser; (*question*)
poser; **~ the damage at a million**
estimer les dégâts à un million;
~ sth tactfully dire qch avec tact.
□ **~ across** communiquer; **~
away** ranger; (in hospital, prison)
enfermer; **~ back** (postpone)
remettre; (delay) retarder; **~
down** (dé)poser; (write) inscrire;
(pay) verser; (suppress) réprimer; **~
forward** (*plan*) soumettre; **~ in**
(insert) introduire; (fix) installer;
(submit) soumettre; **~ in for** faire
une demande de; **~ off** (postpone)
renvoyer à plus tard; (disconcert)
déconcerter; (displease) rebuter; **~
sb off sth** dégoûter
qn de qch; **~ on** (*clothes, radio*)
mettre; (*light*) allumer; (*accent,
weight*) prendre; **~ out** sortir;
(stretch) (é)tendre; (extinguish)
éteindre; (disconcert) déconcerter;
(inconvenience) déranger; **~ up**
lever, remonter; (*building*)
construire; (*notice*) mettre;

(*price*) augmenter; (*guest*)
héberger; (*offer*) offrir; **~ up with**
supporter.

putty *n* mastic *m*.

puzzle *n* énigme *f*; (game) casse-
tête *m inv*; (jigsaw) puzzle *m*. ● *vt*
rendre perplexe. ● *vi* se creuser
la tête.

pyjamas *npl* pyjama *m*.

pylon *n* pylône *m*.

quack *n* (of duck) coin-coin *m inv*;
(doctor) charlatan *m*.

quadrangle (of college) *n* cour *f*.

quadruple *a & n* quadruple (*m*).
● *vt/i* quadrupler.

quail *n* (bird) caille *f*.

quaint *a* pittoresque; (old) vieillot;
(odd) bizarre.

qualification *n* diplôme *m*;
(ability) compétence *f*; (fig) réserve
f, restriction *f*.

qualified *a* diplômé; (able)
qualifié (**to do** pour faire); (fig)
conditionnel.

qualify *vt* qualifier; (modify) mettre
des réserves à; (*statement*)
nuancer. ● *vi* obtenir son
diplôme (**as** de); (Sport) se
qualifier; **~ for** remplir les
conditions requises pour.

quality *n* qualité *f*.

qualm *n* scrupule *m*.

quantity *n* quantité *f*.

quarantine *n* quarantaine *f*.

quarrel *n* dispute *f*, querelle *f*.
● *vi* (*pt* quarrelled) se disputer.

quarry *n* (excavation) carrière *f*;
(prey) proie *f*. ● *vt* extraire.

quart n ≈ litre m.

quarter n quart m; (of year) trimestre m; (25 cents: US) quart m de dollar; (district) quartier m; **~s** logement m; **from all ~s** de toutes parts. ● vt diviser en quatre; (troops) cantonner.

quarterly a trimestriel. ● adv tous les trois mois.

quartet n quatuor m.

quartz n quartz m. ● a (watch) à quartz.

quash vt (suppress) étouffer; (Jur) annuler.

quaver vi trembler, chevroter. ● n (Mus) croche f.

quay n (Naut) quai m.

queasy a feel ~ avoir mal au cœur.

queen n reine f; (cards) dame f.

queer a étrange; (dubious) louche; ▣ homosexuel.

quench vt éteindre; (thirst) étancher; (desire) étouffer.

query n question f. ● vt mettre en question.

quest n recherche f.

question n question f; **in ~** en question; **out of the ~** hors de question. ● vt interroger; (doubt) mettre en question, douter de. **~ mark** n point m d'interrogation.

questionnaire n questionnaire m.

queue n queue f. ● vi (pres p **queuing**) faire la queue.

quibble vi ergoter.

quick a rapide; (clever) vif/vive; **be ~** (hurry) se dépêcher. ● adv vite. ● n cut to the ~ piquer au vif. **quicken** vt/i (s')accélérer. **quickly** adv rapidement, vite. **~sand** n sables mpl mouvants.

quid n inv ▣ livre f sterling.

quiet a (calm, still) tranquille; (silent) silencieux; (gentle) doux; (discreet) discret; **keep ~** se taire. ● n tranquillité f; **on the ~** en cachette. **quieten** vt/i (se) calmer. **quietly** adv (speak) doucement; (sit) en silence.

quilt n édredon m; (continental) ~ couette f.

quirk n bizarrerie f.

quit vt (pt **quitted**) quitter; (smoking) arrêter de. ● vi abandonner; (resign) démissionner; **~ doing** (US) cesser de faire.

quite adv tout à fait, vraiment; (rather) assez; **~ a few** un bon nombre (de).

quits a quitte (with envers); **call it ~** en rester là.

quiver vi trembler.

quiz n (pl **quizzes**) test m; (game) jeu-concours m. ● vt (pt **quizzed**) questionner.

quotation n citation f; (price) devis m; (stock exchange) cotation f; **~ marks** guillemets mpl.

quote vt citer; (reference, number) rappeler; (price) indiquer; (share price) coter. ● vi **~ for** faire un devis pour; **~ from** citer. ● n (quotation) citation f; (estimate) devis m; **in ~s** ▣ entre guillemets.

rabbi n rabbin m.

rabbit n lapin m.

rabies n (disease) rage f.

race n (contest) course f; (group) race f. ● a racial; **~ relations**

relations *fpl* inter-raciales. ● *vt* (compete with) faire la course avec; (*horse*) faire courir. ● *vi* courir; (*pulse*) battre précipitamment; (*engine*) s'emballer. ~**course** *n* champ *m* de courses. ~**horse** *n* cheval *m* de course. ~**track** *n* piste *f*; (for horses) champ *m* de courses.

racing *n* courses *fpl*; ~ **car** voiture *f* de course.

racism *n* racisme *m*. **racist** *a & n* raciste (*mf*).

rack *n* (shelf) étagère *f*; (for clothes) portant *m*; (for luggage) compartiment *m* à bagages; (for dishes) égouttoir *m*. ● *vt* ~ **one's brains** se creuser la cervelle.

racket *n* (Sport) raquette *f*; (noise) vacarme *m*; (swindle) escroquerie *f*; (crime) trafic *m*.

radar *n & a* radar (*m*).

radial *n* ~ (**tyre**) pneu *m* radial.

radiate *vt* (*happiness*) rayonner de; (*heat*) émettre. ● *vi* rayonner (**from** de). **radiation** *n* (radioactivity) radiation *f*. **radiator** *n* radiateur *m*.

radical *n & a* radical/-e (*m/f*).

radio *n* radio *f*; **on the** ~ à la radio. ● *vt* (message) envoyer par radio; (*person*) appeler par radio.

radioactive *a* radioactif.

radiographer *n* manipulateur/-trice *m/f* radiographe.

radish *n* radis *m*.

radius *n* (*pl* **-dii**) rayon *m*.

raffle *n* tombola *f*.

rag *n* chiffon *m*; ~**s** loques *fpl*.

rage *n* rage *f*, colère *f*; **be all the** ~ faire fureur. ● *vi* (*person*) tempêter; (*storm, battle*) faire rage.

ragged *a* (*clothes*) en loques; (*person*) dépenaillé.

raid *n* (Mil, on stock market) raid *m*; (by police) rafle *f*; (by criminals) hold-up *m inv*. ● *vt* faire un raid

or une rafle or un hold-up dans. **raider** *n* (thief) pillard *m*; (Mil) commando *m*; (corporate) raider *m*.

rail *n* (on balcony) balustrade *f*; (stairs) rampe *f*; (for train) rail *m*; (for curtain) tringle *f*; **by** ~ par chemin de fer.

railing *n* (*also* ~**s**) grille *f*.

railway, (US) **railroad** *n* chemin *m* de fer. ~ **line** *n* voie *f* ferrée. ~ **station** *n* gare *f*.

rain *n* pluie *f*. ● *vi* pleuvoir. ~**bow** *n* arc-en-ciel *m*. ~**coat** *n* imperméable *m*. ~**fall** *n* précipitation *f*. ~ **forest** *n* forêt *f* tropicale.

rainy *a* (**-ier, -iest**) pluvieux; (*season*) des pluies.

raise *vt* (*barrier, curtain*) lever; (*child, cattle*) élever; (*question*) soulever; (*price, salary*) augmenter. ● *n* (US) augmentation *f*.

raisin *n* raisin *m* sec.

rake *n* râteau *m*. ● *vt* (*garden*) ratisser; (search) fouiller dans. □ ~ **in** (*money*) amasser; ~ **up** (*past*) remuer.

rally *vt/i* (se) rallier; (*strength*) reprendre; (after illness) aller mieux; ~ **round** venir en aide. ● *n* rassemblement *m*; (Auto) rallye *m*; (tennis) échange *m*.

ram *n* bélier *m*. ● *vt* (*pt* **rammed**) (thrust) enfoncer; (crash into) rentrer dans.

RAM *abbr* (**random access memory**) RAM *f*.

ramble *n* randonnée *f*. ● *vi* faire une randonnée. □ ~ **on** discourir.

ramp *n* (slope) rampe *f*; (in garage) pont *m* de graissage.

rampage[1] *vi* se déchaîner (**through** dans).

rampage[2] *n* **go on the** ~ tout saccager.

ran ⇒RUN.

R

rancid *a* rance.

random *a* (fait) au hasard. ● *n* at ~ au hasard.

rang ⇒RING².

range *n* (of prices, products) gamme *f*; (of people, beliefs) variété *f*; (of radar, weapon) portée *f*; (of aircraft) autonomie *f*; (of mountains) chaîne *f*. ● *vi* aller; (vary) varier.

rank *n* rang *m*; (Mil) grade *m*. ● *vt/i* ~ **among** (se) classer parmi.

ransack *vt* (search) fouiller; (pillage) mettre à sac.

ransom *n* rançon *f*.

rap *n* coup *m* sec; (Mus) rap *m*. ● *vi* (*pt* **rapped**) donner des coups secs (**on** sur).

rape *vt* violer. ● *n* viol *m*.

rapid *a* rapide.

rapist *n* violeur *m*.

rapturous *a* (*delight*) extasié; (*welcome*) enthousiaste.

rare *a* rare; (Culin) saignant. **rarely** *adv* rarement.

rascal *n* coquin/-e *m/f*.

rash *n* (Med) rougeurs *fpl*. ● *a* irréfléchi.

raspberry *n* framboise *f*.

rat *n* rat *m*. ● *vi* (*pt* **ratted**) ~ **on** (desert) lâcher; (inform on) dénoncer.

rate *n* (ratio, level) taux *m*; (speed) rythme *m*; (price) tarif *m*; (of exchange) taux *m*; **at any** ~ en tout cas. ● *vt* (value) estimer; (deserve) mériter; ~ **sth highly** admirer beaucoup qch. ● *vi* ~ **as** être considéré comme.

rather *adv* (by preference) plutôt; (fairly) assez, plutôt; (a little) un peu; **I would** ~ **go** j'aimerais mieux partir; ~ **than go** plutôt que de partir.

rating *n* (score, value) cote *f*; **the** ~**s** (TV) l'indice *m* d'écoute, l'audimat® *m*.

ratio *n* proportion *f*.

ration *n* ration *f*. ● *vt* rationner.

rational *a* rationnel; (*person*) sensé.

rationalize *vt* justifier; (organize) rationaliser.

rattle *vi* (bottles, chains) s'entrechoquer; (window) vibrer. ● *vt* (bottles, chains) faire s'entrechoquer; (fig, ▣) énerver. ● *n* cliquetis *m*; (toy) hochet *m*. ~**snake** *n* serpent *m* à sonnette, crotale *m*.

rave *vi* (enthuse) s'emballer; (in fever) délirer; (in anger) tempêter.

raven *n* corbeau *m*.

ravenous *a* **be** ~ avoir une faim de loup.

ravine *n* ravin *m*.

raving *a* ~ **lunatic** fou *m* furieux, folle *f* furieuse.

ravishing *a* ravissant.

raw *a* cru; (not processed) brut; (*wound*) à vif; (immature) inexpérimenté; **get a** ~ **deal** être mal traité; ~ **material** matière *f* première.

ray *n* (of light) rayon *m*; ~ **of hope** lueur *f* d'espoir.

razor *n* rasoir *m*. ~**-blade** *n* lame *f* de rasoir.

re *prep* au sujet de; (at top of letter) objet.

reach *vt* (*place, level*) atteindre; (*decision*) arriver à; (contact) joindre; (*audience, market*) toucher. ● *vi* ~ **up/down** lever/ baisser le bras; ~ **across** étendre le bras. ● *n* portée *f*; **within** ~ **of** à portée de; (close to) à proximité de.

react *vi* réagir. **reaction** *n* réaction *f*. **reactor** *n* réacteur *m*.

read *vt/i* (*pt* **read**) lire; (study) étudier; (*instrument*) indiquer; ~ **about sb** lire quelque chose sur qn; ~ **out** lire à haute voix. **reader** *n* lecteur/-trice *m/f*. **reading** *n* lecture *f*; (measurement)

readjust vt rajuster. ● vi se réadapter (**to** à).

read-only memory, ROM n mémoire f morte.

ready a (**-ier, -iest**) prêt; (quick) prompt. ~**-made** a tout fait. ~**-to-wear** a prêt-à-porter.

real a (not imaginary) véritable, réel; (not artificial) vrai; **it's a** ~ **shame** c'est vraiment dommage. ~ **estate** n biens mpl immobiliers.

realism n réalisme m. **realistic** a réaliste.

reality n réalité f ~ **TV** n téléréalité f.

realize vt se rendre compte de, comprendre; (fulfil, turn into cash) réaliser; (price) atteindre.

really adv vraiment.

reap vt (crop) recueillir; (benefits) récolter.

reappear vi reparaître.

rear n arrière m; (of person) derrière m 🄴. ● a (seat) arrière inv; (entrance) de derrière. ● vt élever. ● vi (horse) se cabrer. ~**-view mirror** n rétroviseur m.

reason n raison f (**to do, for doing** de faire); **within** ~ dans la limite du raisonnable.

reasonable a raisonnable.

reassurance n réconfort m.

reassure vt rassurer.

rebate n (refund) remboursement m; (discount) remise f.

rebel¹ n & a rebelle (mf).

rebel² vi (pt **rebelled**) se rebeller. **rebellion** n rébellion f.

rebound¹ vi rebondir; ~ **on** (backfire) se retourner contre.

rebound² n n rebond m.

rebuke vt réprimander. ● n réprimande f.

recall vt (remember) se souvenir de; (call back) rappeler. ● n

(memory) mémoire f; (Comput, Mil) rappel m.

recap vt/i (pt **recapped**) récapituler. ● n récapitulation f.

recede vi s'éloigner; **his hair is receding** son front se dégarnit.

receipt n (written) reçu m; (of letter) réception f; ~**s** (Comm) recettes fpl.

receive vt recevoir; (stolen goods) receler. **receiver** n (telephone) combiné m; (TV) récepteur m.

recent a récent. **recently** adv récemment.

receptacle n récipient m.

reception n réception f; **give sb a warm** ~ donner un accueil chaleureux à qn.

recess n (alcove) alcôve m; (for door) embrasure f; (Jur, Pol) vacances fpl; (School, US) récréation f.

recession n récession f.

recharge vt recharger.

recipe n recette f.

recipient n (of honour) récipiendaire mf; (of letter) destinataire mf.

reciprocate vt (compliment) retourner; (kindness) payer de retour. ● vi en faire autant.

recite vi réciter.

reckless a imprudent.

reckon vt/i calculer; (judge) considérer; (think) penser; ~ **on/ with** compter sur/avec. **reckoning** n (guess) estimation f; (calculation) calculs mpl.

reclaim vt récupérer; (flooded land) assécher.

recline vi s'allonger; (seat) s'incliner.

recluse n reclus/-e m/f.

recognition n reconnaissance f; **beyond** ~ méconnaissable; **gain** ~ être reconnu.

recognize vt reconnaître.

recollect vt se souvenir de, se rappeler. **recollection** n souvenir m.

recommend vt recommander. **recommendation** n recommandation f.

reconcile vt (*people*) réconcilier; (*facts*) concilier; ~ **oneself to** se résigner à.

recondition vt remettre à neuf.

reconsider vt réexaminer. ● vi réfléchir.

reconstruct vt reconstruire; (*crime*) faire une reconstitution de.

record¹ vt/i (in register, on tape) enregistrer; (in diary) noter; ~ **that** rapporter que.

record² n (of events) compte-rendu m; (official) procès-verbal m; (personal, administrative) dossier m; (historical) archives fpl; (past history) réputation f; (Mus) disque m; (Sport) record m; (**criminal**) ~ casier m judiciaire; **off the** ~ officieusement. ● a record inv.

recorder n (Mus) flûte f à bec.

recording n enregistrement m.

record-player n tourne-disque m.

recover vt récupérer. ● vi se remettre; (*economy*) se redresser. **recovery** n (Med) rétablissement m; (of economy) relance f.

recreation n récréation f.

recruit n recrue f. ● vt recruter. **recruitment** n recrutement m.

rectangle n rectangle m.

rectify vt rectifier.

recuperate vt récupérer. ● vi se rétablir.

recur vi (pt **recurred**) se reproduire.

recycle vt recycler.

red a (**redder**, **reddest**) rouge; (hair) roux. ● n rouge m; **in the** ~

en déficit. **R~ Cross** n Croix-Rouge f. ~**currant** n groseille f.

redecorate vt repeindre, refaire.

redeploy vt réorganiser; (*troops*) répartir.

red: ~**handed** a en flagrant délit. ~**hot** a brûlant.

redirect vt (*traffic*) dévier; (*letter*) faire suivre.

redness n rougeur f.

redo vt (pt **-did**; pp **-done**) refaire.

redress vt (*wrong*) redresser; (*balance*) rétablir. ● n réparation f.

reduce vt réduire; (*temperature*) faire baisser. **reduction** n réduction f.

redundancy n licenciement m.

redundant a superflu; (*worker*) licencié; **make** ~ licencier.

reed n (plant) roseau m.

reef n récif m, écueil m.

reel n (of thread) bobine f; (of film) bande f; (winding device) dévidoir m. ● vi chanceler. ● vt ~ **off** réciter.

refectory n réfectoire m.

refer vt/i (pt **referred**) ~ **to** (allude to) faire allusion à; (concern) s'appliquer à; (consult) consulter; (direct) renvoyer à.

referee n (Sport) arbitre m. ● vt (pt **refereed**) arbitrer.

reference n référence f; (mention) allusion f; (person) personne f pouvant fournir des références; **in** or **with** ~ **to** en ce qui concerne; (Comm) suite à.

referendum n (pl ~**s**) référendum m.

refill¹ vt (*glass*) remplir à nouveau; (*pen*) recharger.

refill² n recharge f.

refine vt raffiner.

reflect vt refléter; (*heat, light*) renvoyer. ● vi réfléchir (**on** à); ~

well/badly on sb faire honneur/du tort à qn.

reflection n réflexion f; (image) reflet m; (fig) à la réflexion.

reflective a (surface) réfléchissant; (person) réfléchi.

reflector n (on car) catadioptre m.

reflex a & n réflexe (m).

reflexive a (Gram) réfléchi.

reform vt réformer. ● vi (person) s'amender. ● n réforme f.

refrain n refrain m. ● vi s'abstenir (**from** de).

refresh vt (drink) rafraîchir; (rest) reposer. **refreshments** npl rafraîchissements mpl.

refrigerate vt réfrigérer. **refrigerator** n réfrigérateur m.

refuel vt/i (pt **refuelled**) (se) ravitailler.

refuge n refuge m; **take ∼** se réfugier. **refugee** n réfugié/-e m/f.

refund¹ vt rembourser.

refund² n remboursement m.

refurbish vt remettre à neuf.

refuse¹ vt/i refuser.

refuse² n ordures fpl.

regain vt retrouver; (lost ground) regagner.

regard vt considérer; **as ∼s** en ce qui concerne. ● n égard m, estime f; **in this ∼** à cet égard; **∼s** amitiés fpl. **regarding** prep en ce qui concerne.

regardless adv malgré tout; **∼ of** sans tenir compte de.

regime n régime m.

regiment n régiment m.

region n région f; **in the ∼ of** environ.

register n registre m. ● vt (record) enregistrer; (vehicle) faire immatriculer; (birth) déclarer; (letter) recommander; (indicate) indiquer; (express) exprimer. ● vi

(enrol) s'inscrire; (at hotel) se présenter; (fig) être compris.

registrar n officier m de l'état civil; (Univ) responsable m du bureau de la scolarité.

registration n (of voter, student) inscription f; (of birth) déclaration f; **∼ (number)** (Auto) numéro m d'immatriculation.

registry office n bureau m de l'état civil.

regret n regret m. ● vt (pt **regretted**) regretter (**to do** de faire). **regretfully** adv à regret.

regular a régulier; (usual) habituel. ● n habitué/-e m/f. **regularity** n régularité f. **regularly** adv régulièrement.

regulate vt régler. **regulation** n (rule) règlement m; (process) réglementation f.

rehabilitate vt (in public esteem) réhabiliter; (prisoner) réinsérer.

rehearsal n répétition f. **rehearse** vt/i répéter.

reign n règne m. ● vi régner (**over** sur).

reimburse vt rembourser.

reindeer n inv renne m.

reinforce vt renforcer. **reinforcement** n renforcement m; **∼s** renforts mpl.

reinstate vt (person) réintégrer; (law) rétablir.

reject¹ n marchandise f de deuxième choix.

reject² vt (offer, plea) rejeter; (goods) refuser. **rejection** n (personal) rejet m; (of candidate, work) refus m.

rejoice vi se réjouir.

relapse n rechute f. ● vi rechuter; **∼ into** retomber dans.

relate vt raconter; (associate) associer. ● vi **∼ to** se rapporter à; (get on with) s'entendre avec. **related** a (ideas) lié; **we are ∼d** nous sommes parents.

R

relation n rapport m; (person) parent/-e m/f. **relationship** n relations fpl; (link) rapport m.

relative n parent/-e m/f. ● a relatif; (respective) respectif.

relax vt (grip) relâcher; (muscle) décontracter; (discipline) assouplir. ● vi (person) se détendre; (grip) se relâcher. **relaxation** n détente f. **relaxing** a délassant.

relay¹ n (also ~ race) course f de relais.

relay² vt relayer.

release vt (prisoner) libérer; (fastening) faire jouer; (object, hand) lâcher; (film) faire sortir; (news) publier. ● n libération f; (of film) sortie f; (new record, film) nouveauté f.

relevance n pertinence f, intérêt m.

relevant a pertinent; be ~ to avoir rapport à.

reliability n (of firm) sérieux m; (of car) fiabilité f; (of person) honnêteté f. **reliable** a (firm) sérieux; (person, machine) fiable.

reliance n dépendance f.

relic n vestige m; (object) relique f.

relief n soulagement m (from à); (assistance) secours m; (outline) relief m; ~ **road** route f de délestage.

relieve vt soulager; (help) secourir; (take over from) relayer.

religion n religion f. **religious** a religieux.

relish n plaisir m; (Culin) condiment m. ● vt (food) savourer; (idea) se réjouir de.

relocate vt muter. ● vi (company) déménager; (worker) être muté.

reluctance n répugnance f.

reluctant a (person) peu enthousiaste; (consent) accordé à contrecœur; ~ **to** peu disposé à.

reluctantly adv à contrecœur.

rely vi ~ **on** (count) compter sur; (be dependent) dépendre de.

remain vi rester. **remainder** n reste m.

remand vt mettre en détention provisoire. ● n on ~ en détention provisoire.

remark n remarque f. ● vt remarquer. ● vi ~ **on** faire des remarques sur. **remarkable** a remarquable.

remedy n remède m. ● vt remédier à.

remember vt se souvenir de, se rappeler; ~ **to do** ne pas oublier de faire. **remembrance** n souvenir m.

remind vt rappeler (sb of sth qch à qn); ~ **sb to do** rappeler à qn de faire. **reminder** n rappel m.

reminisce vi évoquer ses souvenirs.

remission n (Med) rémission f; (Jur) remise f.

remnant n reste m; (trace) vestige m; (of cloth) coupon m.

remodel vt (pt **remodelled**) remodeler.

remorse n remords m.

remote a (place, time) lointain; (person) distant; (slight) vague; ~ **control** télécommande f.

removable a amovible.

removal n (of employee) renvoi m; (of threat) suppression f; (of troops) retrait m; (of stain) détachage m; (from house) déménagement m; ~ **men** déménageurs mpl.

remove vt enlever; (dismiss) renvoyer; (do away with) supprimer; (Comput) effacer.

remunerate vt rémunérer. **remuneration** n rémunération f.

render vt rendre.

renegade n renégat/-e m/f.

renew vt renouveler; (resume) reprendre. **renewable** a renouvelable.

renounce vt renoncer à; (disown) renier.

renovate vt rénover.

renown n renommée f.

rent n loyer m. ● vt louer; **for ∼** à louer. **rental** n prix m de location.

reopen vt/i rouvrir.

reorganize vt réorganiser.

rep n (Comm) représentant/-e m/f.

repair vt réparer. ● n réparation f; **in good/bad ∼** en bon/mauvais état.

repatriate vt rapatrier. **repatriation** n rapatriement m.

repay vt (pt repaid) rembourser; (reward) récompenser. **repayment** n remboursement m.

repeal vt abroger. ● n abrogation f.

repeat vt/i répéter; (renew) renouveler; **∼ itself, ∼ oneself** se répéter. ● n répétition f; (broadcast) reprise f.

repel vt (pt repelled) repousser.

repent vi se repentir (**of** de).

repercussion n répercussion f.

repetition n répétition f.

replace vt (put back) remettre; (take the place of) remplacer. **replacement** n remplacement m (**of** de); (person) remplaçant/-e m/f; (new part) pièce f de rechange.

replay n (Sport) match m rejoué; (recording) répétition f immédiate.

replenish vt (refill) remplir; (renew) renouveler.

replica n copie f exacte.

reply vt/i répondre. ● n réponse f.

report vt rapporter, annoncer (**that** que); (notify) signaler; (denounce) dénoncer. ● vi faire un rapport; **∼ (on)** (news item) faire un reportage sur; **∼ to** (go) se présenter chez. ● n rapport m; (in press) reportage m; (School) bulletin m. **reporter** n reporter m.

repossess vt reprendre.

represent vt représenter.

representation n représentation f; **make ∼s to** protester auprès de.

representative a représentatif, typique (**of** de). ● n représentant/-e m/f.

repress vt réprimer.

reprieve n (delay) sursis m; (pardon) grâce f. ● vt accorder un sursis à; gracier.

reprimand vt réprimander. ● n réprimande f.

reprisals npl représailles fpl.

reproach vt reprocher (**sb for sth** qch à qn). ● n reproche m.

reproduce vt/i (se) reproduire. **reproduction** n reproduction f. **reproductive** a reproducteur.

reptile n reptile m.

republic n république f. **republican** a & n républicain/-e (m/f).

repudiate vt répudier; (contract) refuser d'honorer.

reputable a honorable, de bonne réputation.

reputation n réputation f.

repute n réputation f.

request n demande f. ● vt demander (**of, from** à).

require vt (of thing) demander; (of person) avoir besoin de; (demand, order) exiger. **required** a requis. **requirement** n exigence f; (condition) condition f (requise).

rescue vt sauver. ● n sauvetage m (**of** de); (help) secours m.

research n recherche(s) f(pl). ● vt/i faire des recherches (sur). **researcher** n chercheur/-euse m/f.

R

resemblance n ressemblance f.
resemble vt ressembler à.

resent vt être indigné de, s'offenser de. **resentment** n ressentiment m.

reservation n (doubt) réserve f; (booking) réservation f; (US) réserve f (indienne); **make a** ~ réserver.

reserve vt réserver. ● n (stock, land) réserve f; (Sport) remplaçant/-e m/f; **in** ~ en réserve; **the** ~**s** (Mil) les réserves fpl. **reserved** a (person, room) réservé.

reshuffle vt (Pol) remanier. ● n (Pol) remaniement m (ministériel).

residence n résidence f; (of students) foyer m; **in** ~ (doctor) résidant.

resident a résidant; **be** ~ résider. ● n habitant/-e m/f; (foreigner) résident/-e m/f; (in hotel) pensionnaire mf. **residential** a résidentiel.

resign vt abandonner; (job) démissionner de. ● vi démissionner; ~ **oneself to** se résigner à. **resignation** n résignation f; (from job) démission f. **resigned** a résigné.

resilience n élasticité f; ressort m.

resin n résine f.

resist vt/i résister (à). **resistance** n résistance f. **resistant** a (Med) rebelle; (metal) résistant.

resolution n résolution f.

resolve vt résoudre (**to do** de faire). ● n résolution f.

resort vi ~ **to** avoir recours à. ● n (recourse) recours m; (place) station f; **in the last** ~ en dernier ressort.

resource n ressource f; ~**s** (wealth) ressources fpl. **resourceful** a ingénieux.

respect n respect m; (aspect) égard m; **with** ~ **to** à l'égard de, relativement à. ● vt respecter.

respectability n respectabilité f. **respectable** a respectable.

respectful a respectueux.

respective a respectif.

respite n répit m.

respond vi répondre (**to** à); ~ **to** (react to) réagir à. **response** n réponse f.

responsibility n responsabilité f. **responsible** a (job) qui comporte des responsabilités.

responsive a réceptif.

rest vt/i (se) reposer; (lean) (s')appuyer (**on** sur); (be buried, lie) reposer; (remain) demeurer. ● n repos m; (support) support m; **have a** ~ se reposer; **the** ~ (remainder) le reste (**of** de); (other people) les autres.

restaurant n restaurant m.

restless a agité.

restoration n rétablissement m; restauration f.

restore vt rétablir; (building) restaurer; ~ **sth to sb** restituer qch à qn.

restrain vt contenir; ~ **sb from** retenir qn de. **restrained** a (moderate) mesuré; (in control of self) maître de soi.

restrict vt restreindre.

rest room n (US) toilettes fpl.

result n résultat m. ● vi résulter; ~ **in** aboutir à.

resume vt/i reprendre.

résumé n résumé m; (of career: US) CV m, curriculum vitae m.

resurrect vt ressusciter.

resuscitate vt réanimer.

retail n détail m. ● a & adv au détail. ● vt/i (se) vendre (au détail). **retailer** n détaillant/-e m/f.

retain vt (hold back, remember) retenir; (keep) conserver.

retaliate vi riposter. **retaliation** n représailles fpl.

retch vi avoir un haut-le-cœur.

retire vi (from work) prendre sa retraite; (withdraw) se retirer; (go to bed) se coucher. **retired** a retraité. **retirement** n retraite f.

retort vt/i répliquer. ●n réplique f.

retrace vt ~ one's steps revenir sur ses pas.

retract vt/i (se) rétracter.

retrain vt/i (se) recycler.

retreat vi (Mil) battre en retraite. ●n retraite f.

retrieval n (Comput) extraction f.

retrieve vt (object) récupérer; (situation) redresser; (data) extraire.

retrospect n in ~ rétrospectivement.

return vi (come back) revenir; (go back) retourner; (go home) rentrer. ●vt (give back) rendre; (bring back) rapporter; (send back) renvoyer; (put back) remettre. ●n retour m; (yield) rapport m; ~s (Comm) bénéfices mpl; in ~ for en échange de. ~ ticket n aller-retour m.

reunion n réunion f.

reunite vt réunir.

rev n (Auto Ⅱ) tour m. ●vt/i (pt revved) ~ (up) (engine Ⅱ) (s')emballer.

reveal vt révéler; (allow to appear) laisser voir.

revelation n révélation f.

revenge n vengeance f. ●vt venger.

revenue n revenu m.

reverberate vi (sound, light) se répercuter.

reverend a révérend.

reversal n renversement m; (of view) revirement m.

reverse a contraire, inverse. ●n contraire m; (back) revers m, envers m; (gear) marche f arrière. ●vt (situation, bracket) renverser; (order) inverser; (decision) annuler; ~ the charges appeler en PCV. ●vi (Auto) faire marche arrière.

review n (inspection, magazine) revue f; (of book) critique f. ●vt passer en revue; (situation) réexaminer; faire la critique de. **reviewer** n critique m.

revise vt réviser; (text) revoir. **revision** n révision f.

revival n (of economy) reprise f; (of interest) regain m.

revive vt (person, hopes) ranimer; (custom) rétablir. ●vi se ranimer.

revoke vt révoquer.

revolt vt/i (se) révolter. ●n révolte f. **revolting** a dégoûtant.

revolution n révolution f.

revolve vi tourner.

revolver n revolver m.

revolving door n porte f à tambour.

reward n récompense f. ●vt récompenser (for de). **rewarding** a rémunérateur; (worthwhile) qui (en) vaut la peine.

rewind vt (pt rewound) rembobiner.

rewire vt refaire l'installation électrique de.

rhetorical a (de) rhétorique; (question) de pure forme.

rheumatism n rhumatisme m.

rhinoceros n (pl ~es) rhinocéros m.

rhubarb n rhubarbe f.

rhyme n rime f; (poem) vers mpl. ●vt/i (faire) rimer.

rhythm n rythme m. **rhythmic-(al)** a rythmique.

R

rib n côte f.

ribbon n ruban m; in ~s en lambeaux.

rice n riz m. ~ **pudding** n riz m au lait.

rich a riche.

rid vt (pt **rid**; pres p **ridding**) débarrasser (**of** de); **get** ~ **of** se débarrasser de.

ridden ⇒RIDE.

riddle n énigme f. ● vt ~ **with** (bullets) cribler de; (mistakes) bourrer de.

ride vi (pt **rode**; pp **ridden**) aller (à bicyclette, à cheval); (in car) rouler; (on a horse as sport) monter à cheval. ● vt (a particular horse) monter; (distance) parcourir. ● n promenade f, tour m; (distance) trajet m; **give sb a** ~ (US) prendre qn en voiture; **go for a** ~ aller faire un tour (à bicyclette, à cheval). **rider** n cavalier/-ière m/ f; (in horse race) jockey m; (cyclist) cycliste mf; (motorcyclist) motocycliste mf.

ridge n arête f, crête f.

ridiculous a ridicule.

riding n équitation f.

rifle n fusil m. ● vt (rob) dévaliser.

rift n (crack) fissure f; (between people) désaccord m.

rig vt (pt **rigged**) (equip) équiper; (election, match) truquer. ● n (for oil) derrick m. □ ~ **out** habiller; ~ **up** (arrange) arranger.

right a (morally) bon; (fair) juste; (best) bon, qu'il faut; (not left) droit; **be** ~ (person) avoir raison (**to** de); (calculation, watch) être exact; **put** ~ arranger, rectifier. ● n (entitlement) droit m; (not left) droite f; (not evil) le bien; **be in the** ~ avoir raison; **on the** ~ à droite. ● vt (a wrong, sth fallen) redresser. ● adv (not left) à droite; (directly) tout droit; (exactly) bien, juste; (completely) tout (à fait); ~ **away** tout de suite; ~ **now**

(at once) tout de suite; (at present) en ce moment.

righteous a vertueux.

rightful a légitime.

right-handed a droitier.

rightly adv correctement; (with reason) à juste titre.

right of way n (Auto) priorité f.

right wing a de droite.

rigid a rigide.

rigorous a rigoureux.

rim n bord m.

rind n (on cheese) croûte f; (on bacon) couenne f; (on fruit) écorce f.

ring¹ n (hoop) anneau m; (jewellery) bague f; (circle) cercle m; (boxing) ring m; (wedding) ~ alliance f. ● vt entourer; (word in text) entourer d'un cercle.

ring² vt/i (pt **rang**; pp **rung**) sonner; (of words) retentir; ~ **the bell** sonner. ● n sonnerie f; **give sb a** ~ donner un coup de fil à qn. □ ~ **back** rappeler; ~ **off** raccrocher; ~ **up** téléphoner (à).

ring road n périphérique m.

rink n patinoire f.

rinse vt rincer; ~ **out** rincer. ● n rinçage m.

riot n émeute f; (of colours) profusion f; **run** ~ se déchaîner. ● vi faire une émeute.

rip vt/i (pt **ripped**) (se) déchirer; **let** ~ (not check) laisser courir; ~ **off** ⊠ rouler. ● n déchirure f.

ripe a mûr. **ripen** vt/i mûrir.

rip-off n ⊠ vol m; arnaque f ⊠.

ripple n ride f, ondulation f. ● vt/i (water) (se) rider.

rise vi (pt **rose**; pp **risen**) (go upwards, increase) monter, s'élever; (stand up, get up from bed) se lever; (rebel) se soulever; (sun) se lever; (water) monter; ~ **up** se soulever. ● n (slope) pente f; (increase) hausse f; (in pay) augmentation f;

(progress, boom) essor m; **give ~ to** donner lieu à.

risk n risque m; **at ~** menacé. ●vt risquer; **~ doing** (venture) se risquer à faire. **risky** a risqué.

rite n rite m; **last ~s** derniers sacrements mpl.

rival n rival/-e m/f. ●a rival; (claim) opposé. ●vt (pt **rivalled**) rivaliser avec.

river n rivière f; (flowing into sea) fleuve m. ●a (fishing, traffic) fluvial.

rivet n (bolt) rivet m. ●vt (pt **riveted**) river, riveter.

Riviera n **the (French) ~** la Côte d'Azur.

road n route f; (in town) rue f; (small) chemin m; **the ~ to** (glory: fig) le chemin de. ●a (sign, safety) routier. **~-map** n carte f routière. **~ rage** n violence f au volant. **~worthy** a en état de marche.

roam vi errer. ●vt (streets, seas) parcourir.

roar n hurlement m; (of lion, wind) rugissement m; (of lorry, thunder) grondement m. ●vt/i hurler; (lion, wind) rugir; (lorry, thunder) gronder; **~ with laughter** rire aux éclats.

roast vt/i rôtir. ●n (meat) rôti m. ●a rôti. **~ beef** n rôti m de bœuf.

rob vt (pt **robbed**) voler (sb of sth qch à qn); (bank, house) dévaliser; (deprive) priver (of de). **robber** n voleur/-euse m/f. **robbery** n vol m.

robe n (of judge) robe f; (dressing-gown) peignoir m.

robin n rouge-gorge m.

robot n robot m.

robust a robuste.

rock n roche f; (rock face, boulder) rocher m; (hurled stone) pierre f; (sweet) sucre m d'orge; (Mus) rock m; **on the ~s** (drink) avec des glaçons; (marriage) en crise. ●vt/i (se) balancer; (shake) (faire) trembler; (child) bercer. **~-climbing** n varappe f.

rocket n fusée f.

rocking-chair n fauteuil m à bascule.

rocky a (-ier, -iest) (ground) rocailleux; (hill) rocheux; (shaky: fig) branlant.

rod n (metal) tige f; (wooden) baguette f; (for fishing) canne f à pêche.

rode ⇒RIDE.

roe n œufs mpl de poisson.

rogue n (dishonest) bandit m; (mischievous) coquin/-e m/f.

role n rôle m.

roll vt/i rouler; **~ (about)** (child, dog) se rouler; **be ~ing (in money)** 🔲 rouler sur l'or. ●n rouleau m; (list) liste f; (bread) petit pain m; (of drum, thunder) roulement m; (of ship) roulis m. □ **~ out** étendre; **~ over** se retourner; **~ up** (sleeves) retrousser.

roll-call n appel m.

roller n rouleau m. **R~blade**® n patin m en ligne, roller m. **~-coaster** n montagnes fpl russes. **~-skate** n patin m à roulettes.

ROM (abbr) (read-only memory) mémoire f morte.

Roman a & n romain/-e (m/f). **~ Catholic** a & n catholique (mf).

romance n (novel) roman m d'amour; (love) amour m; (affair) idylle f; (fig) poésie f.

Romania n Roumanie f.

Romanian a roumain. ●n (person) Roumain/-e m/f; (language) roumain m.

romantic a (love) romantique; (of the imagination) romanesque.

roof n toit m; (of mouth) palais m. ●vt recouvrir. **~-rack** n galerie f. **~-top** n toit m.

R

room n pièce f; (bedroom) chambre f; (large hall) salle f; (space) place f; ~ **for manoeuvre** marge f de manœuvre. ~**-mate** n camarade mf de chambre.

roomy a spacieux; (clothes) ample.

root n racine f; (source) origine f; **take** ~ prendre racine. ● vt/i (s')enraciner. □ ~ **about** fouiller; ~ **for** (US 🄵) encourager; ~ **out** extirper.

rope n corde f; **know the** ~**s** être au courant. ● vt attacher; ~ **in** (person) enrôler.

rose n rose f. ● ⇒RISE.

rosé n rosé m.

rosy a (-ier, -iest) rose; (hopeful) plein d'espoir.

rot vt/i (pt **rotted**) pourrir.

rota n liste f (de service).

rotary a rotatif.

rotate vt/i (faire) tourner; (change round) alterner.

rotten a pourri; (tooth) gâté; (bad 🄵) mauvais, sale.

rough a (manners) rude; (to touch) rugueux; (ground) accidenté; (violent) brutal; (bad) mauvais; (estimate) approximatif. ● adv (live) à la dure.

roughage n fibres fpl.

roughly adv rudement; (approximately) à peu près.

round a rond. ● n (circle) rond m; (slice) tranche f; (of visits, drinks) tournée f; (competition) partie f, manche f; (boxing) round m; (of talks) série f; ~ **of applause** applaudissements mpl; **go the** ~**s** circuler. ● prep autour de; **she lives** ~ **here** elle habite par ici; ~ **the clock** vingt-quatre heures sur vingt-quatre. ● adv autour; ~ **about** (nearby) par ici; (fig) à peu près; **go** or **come** ~ **to** (a friend) passer chez; **enough to go** ~ assez

pour tout le monde. ● vt (object) arrondir; (corner) tourner. □ ~ **off** terminer; ~ **up** rassembler

roundabout n (in fairground) manège m; (for traffic) rond-point m (à sens giratoire). ● a indirect.

round trip n voyage m aller-retour.

round-up n rassemblement m; (of suspects) rafle f.

route n itinéraire m, parcours m; (Naut, Aviat) route f.

routine n routine f. ● a de routine.

row¹ n rangée f, rang m; **in a** ~ (consecutive) consécutif. ● vi ramer; (Sport) faire de l'aviron. ● vt ~ **a boat up the river** remonter la rivière à la rame.

row² n (noise 🄵) tapage m; (quarrel 🄵) dispute f. ● vi 🄵 se disputer.

rowdy a (-ier, -iest) tapageur.

rowing n aviron m. ~**-boat** n bateau m à rames.

royal a royal. **royalty** n famille f royale; **royalties** droits mpl d'auteur.

RSI abbr (repetitive strain injury) TMS m, trouble m musculo-squelettique.

rub vt/i (pt **rubbed**) frotter; ~ **it in** insister, en rajouter. ● n friction f. □ ~ **out** (s')effacer.

rubber n caoutchouc m; (eraser) gomme f. ~ **band** n élastique m. ~ **stamp** n tampon m.

rubbish n (refuse) ordures fpl; (junk) saletés fpl; (fig) bêtises fpl.

rubble n décombres mpl.

ruby n rubis m.

rucksack n sac m à dos.

rude a impoli, grossier; (improper) indécent; (blow) brutal.

ruffle vt (hair) ébouriffer; (clothes) froisser; (person) contrarier. ● n (frill) ruche f.

rug n petit tapis m.

rugby n rugby m.

rugged a (*surface*) rude, rugueux; (*ground*) accidenté; (*character, features*) rude.

ruin n ruine f. ● vt (destroy) ruiner; (damage) abîmer; (spoil) gâter.

rule n règle f; (regulation) règlement m; (Pol) gouvernement m; **as a ~** en règle générale. ● vt gouverner; (master) dominer; (decide) décider; **~ out** exclure. ● vi régner. **ruler** n dirigeant/-e m/f, gouvernant m; (measure) règle f.

ruling a (*class*) dirigeant; (*party*) au pouvoir. ● n décision f.

rum n rhum m.

rumble vi gronder; (*stomach*) gargouiller. ● n grondement m; gargouillement m.

rumour, (US) **rumor** n bruit m, rumeur f; **there's a ~ that** le bruit court que.

rump n (of animal) croupe f; (of bird) croupion m; (steak) romsteck m.

run vi (pt **ran**; pp **run**; pres p **running**) courir; (flow) couler; (pass) passer; (function) marcher; (melt) fondre; (extend) s'étendre; (of bus) circuler; (of play) se jouer; (last) durer; (of colour in washing) déteindre; (in election) être candidat. ● vt (manage) diriger; (event) organiser; (risk, race) courir; (house) tenir; (temperature, errand) faire; (Comput) exécuter. ● n course f; (journey) parcours m; (outing) promenade f; (rush) ruée f; (series) série f; (for chickens) enclos m; (in cricket) point m; **in the long ~** avec le temps; **on the ~** en fuite. □ **~ across** rencontrer par hasard; **~ away** s'enfuir; **~ down**

descendre en courant; (of vehicle) renverser; (production) réduire progressivement; (belittle) dénigrer; **~ into** (hit) heurter; **~ off** (copies) tirer; **~ out** (be used up) s'épuiser; (of lease) expirer; **~ out of** manquer de; **~ over** (of vehicle) écraser; (details) revoir; **~ through** regarder qch rapidement; **~ sth through sth** passer qch à travers qch; **~ up** (bill) accumuler.

runaway n fugitif/-ive m/f. ● a fugitif; (horse, vehicle) fou; (inflation) galopant.

rung ⇒RING[2]. ● n (of ladder) barreau m.

runner n coureur/-euse m/f. **~ bean** n haricot m d'Espagne. **~-up** n second/-e m/f.

running n course f à pied; (of business) gestion f; (of machine) marche f; **be in the ~ for** être sur les rangs pour. ● a (commentary) suivi; (water) courant; **four days ~** quatre jours de suite.

runway n piste f.

rural a rural.

rush vi (move) se précipiter; (be in a hurry) se dépêcher. ● vt (person) bousculer; (Mil) prendre d'assaut; **~ to** envoyer d'urgence à. ● n ruée f; (haste) bousculade f; (plant) jonc m; **in a ~** pressé. **~-hour** n heure f de pointe.

Russia n Russie f.

Russian a russe. ● n (person) Russe mf; (language) russe.

rust n rouille f. ● vt/i rouiller.

rustle vt/i (papers) froisser.

rusty a rouillé.

ruthless a impitoyable.

rye n seigle m.

R

sabbath n (Jewish) sabbat m; (Christian) jour m du seigneur.
sabbatical a (Univ) sabbatique.
sabotage n sabotage m. ● vt saboter.
saccharin n saccharine f.
sack n (bag) sac m; **get the ~** Ⓕ être renvoyé. ● vt Ⓕ renvoyer; (plunder) saccager. **sacking** n (cloth) toile f à sac; (dismissal Ⓕ) renvoi m.
sacrament n sacrement m.
sacred a sacré.
sacrifice n sacrifice m. ● vt sacrifier.
sad a (**sadder**, **saddest**) triste.
saddle n selle f. ● vt (horse) seller.
sadist n sadique mf. **sadistic** a sadique.
sadly adv tristement; (unfortunately) malheureusement.
sadness n tristesse f.
safe a (not dangerous) sans danger; (reliable) sûr; (out of danger) en sécurité; (after accident) sain et sauf; **~ from** à l'abri de. ● n coffre-fort m.
safeguard n sauvegarde f. ● vt sauvegarder.
safely adv sans danger; (in safe place) en sûreté.
safety n sécurité f. **~-belt** n ceinture f de sécurité. **~-pin** n épingle f de sûreté. **~-valve** n soupape f de sûreté.
saffron n safran m.
sag vi (pt **sagged**) (beam,

mattress) s'affaisser; (flesh) être flasque.
sage n (herb) sauge f.
Sagittarius n Sagittaire m.
said ⇒SAY.
sail n voile f; (journey) tour m en bateau. ● vi (person) voyager en bateau; (as sport) faire de la voile; (set off) prendre la mer; **~ across** traverser. ● vt (boat) piloter; (sea) traverser. **sailing-boat**, **sailing-ship** n voilier m.
sailor n marin m.
saint n saint/-e m/f.
sake n **for the ~ of** pour.
salad n salade f.
salaried a salarié.
salary n salaire m.
sale n vente f; **for ~** à vendre; **on ~** en vente; (reduced) en solde; **~s** (reductions) soldes mpl; **~s assistant**, (US) **~s clerk** vendeur/ -euse m/f.
salesman n (pl **-men**) (in shop) vendeur m; (traveller) représentant m.
saline a salin. ● n sérum m physiologique.
saliva n salive f.
salmon n inv saumon m.
salon n salon m.
saloon n (on ship) salon m; **~ (car)** berline f.
salt n sel m. ● vt saler. **salty** a salé.
salutary a salutaire.
salute n salut m. ● vt saluer. ● vi faire un salut.
salvage n sauvetage m; (of waste) récupération f. ● vt sauver; (for re-use) récupérer.
same a même (**as** que). ● pron **the ~** le même, la même, les mêmes; **at the ~ time** en même temps; **the ~ (thing)** la même chose.
sample n échantillon m; (of blood)

prélèvement *m*. ● *vt* essayer; (*food*) goûter.

sanctimonious *a* (pej) supérieur.

sanction *n* sanction *f*. ● *vt* sanctionner.

sanctity *n* sainteté *f*.

sanctuary *n* (safe place) refuge *m*; (Relig) sanctuaire *m*; (for animals) réserve *f*.

sand *n* sable *m*; ~s (beach) plage *f*.

sandal *n* sandale *f*.

sandpaper *n* papier *m* de verre. ● *vt* poncer.

sandpit *n* bac *m* à sable.

sandwich *n* sandwich *m*; ~ **course** cours *m* avec stage pratique.

sandy *a* (beach) de sable; (soil) sablonneux; (hair) blond roux *inv*.

sane *a* (view) sensé; (person) sain d'esprit.

sang ⇒SING.

sanitary *a* (clean) hygiénique; (system) sanitaire; ~ **towel** serviette *f* hygiénique.

sanitation *n* installations *fpl* sanitaires.

sanity *n* équilibre *m* mental; (nnnn) bon sens *m*.

sank ⇒SINK.

Santa (**Claus**) *n* le père Noël.

sapphire *n* saphir *m*.

sarcasm *n* sarcasme *m*. **sarcastic** *a* sarcastique.

sash *n* (on uniform) écharpe *f*; (on dress) ceinture *f*.

sat ⇒SIT.

satchel *n* cartable *m*.

satellite *n* & *a* satellite (*m*); ~ **dish** antenne *f* parabolique.

satire *n* satire *f*. **satirical** *a* satirique.

satisfaction *n* satisfaction *f*.

satisfactory *a* satisfaisant.

satisfy *vt* satisfaire; (convince) convaincre.

saturate *vt* saturer. **saturated** *a* (wet) trempé.

Saturday *n* samedi *m*.

sauce *n* sauce *f*.

saucepan *n* casserole *f*.

saucer *n* soucoupe *f*.

Saudi Arabia *n* Arabie *f* saoudite.

sausage *n* (for cooking) saucisse *f*; (ready to eat) saucisson *m*.

savage *a* (blow, temper) violent; (attack) sauvage. ● *n* sauvage *mf*. ● *vt* attaquer sauvagement.

save *vt* sauver; (money) économiser; (time) gagner; (keep) garder; ~ (**sb**) **doing sth** éviter (à qn) de faire qch. ● *n* (football) arrêt *m*. **saver** *n* épargnant/-e *m/f*. **saving** *n* économie *f*. **savings** *npl* économies *fpl*.

saviour, (US) **savior** *n* sauveur *m*.

savour, (US) **savor** *n* saveur *f*. ● *vt* savourer. **savoury** *a* (tasty) savoureux; (Culin) salé.

saw ⇒SEE. ● *n* scie *f*. ● *vt* (*pt* **sawed**; *pp* **sawn** *or* **sawed**) scier.

sawdust *n* sciure *f*.

saxophone *n* saxophone *m*

say *vt/i* (*pt* **said**) dire; (prayer) faire. ● *n* **have a** ~ dire son mot; (in decision) avoir voix au chapitre.

saying *n* proverbe *m*.

scab *n* croûte *f*.

scaffolding *n* échafaudage *m*.

scald *vt* (injure, cleanse) ébouillanter. ● *n* brûlure *f*.

scale *n* (for measuring) échelle *f*; (extent) étendue *f*; (Mus) gamme *f*; (on fish) écaille *f*; **on a small** ~ sur une petite échelle; ~ **model** maquette *f*. ● *vt* (climb) escalader; ~ **down** réduire. **scales** *npl* (for weighing) balance *f*.

scallop *n* coquille *f* Saint-Jacques.

scalp *n* cuir *m* chevelu.

S

scampi npl (fresh) langoustines fpl; (breaded) scampi mpl.

scan vt (pt **scanned**) scruter; (quickly) parcourir. ● n (ultrasound) échographie f; (CAT) scanner m.

scandal n scandale m; (gossip) potins mpl ▣.

Scandinavia n Scandinavie f.

scanty a (-ier, -iest) maigre; (clothing) minuscule.

scapegoat n bouc m émissaire.

scar n cicatrice f. ● vt (pt **scarred**) marquer.

scarce a rare. **scarcely** adv à peine.

scare vt faire peur à; **be ∼d** avoir peur. ● n peur f; **bomb ∼** alerte f à la bombe. **scarecrow** n épouvantail m.

scarf n (pl **scarves**) écharpe f; (over head) foulard m.

scarlet a écarlate; **∼ fever** scarlatine f.

scary a (-ier, -iest) ▣ qui fait peur.

scathing a cinglant.

scatter vt (throw) éparpiller, répandre; (disperse) disperser. ● vi se disperser.

scavenge vi fouiller (dans les ordures). **scavenger** n (animal) charognard m.

scene n scène f; (of accident, crime) lieu m; (sight) spectacle m; **behind the ∼s** en coulisse. **scenery** n paysage m; (Theat) décors mpl. **scenic** a panoramique.

scent n (perfume) parfum m; (trail) piste f. ● vt flairer; (make fragrant) parfumer.

sceptic n sceptique mf. **sceptical** a sceptique. **scepticism** n scepticisme m.

schedule n horaire m; (for job) planning m; **behind ∼** en retard; **on ∼** dans les temps. ● vt prévoir; **∼d flight** vol m régulier.

scheme n projet m; (dishonest) combine f; **pension ∼** plan m de retraite. ● vi comploter.

schizophrenic a & n schizophrène (mf).

scholar n érudit/-e m/f.

school n école f; **go to ∼** aller à l'école. ● a (age, year, holidays) scolaire. **∼boy** n élève m. **∼girl** n élève f. **schooling** n scolarité f. **∼teacher** n (primary) instituteur/ -trice m/f; (secondary) professeur m.

science n science f; **teach ∼** enseigner les sciences. **scientific** a scientifique. **scientist** n scientifique mf.

scissors npl ciseaux mpl.

scold vt gronder.

scoop n (shovel) pelle f; (measure) mesure f; (for ice cream) cuillère f à glace; (news) exclusivité f.

scooter n (child's) trottinette f; (motor cycle) scooter m.

scope n étendue f; (competence) compétence f; (opportunity) possibilité f.

scorch vt brûler; (iron) roussir.

score n score m; (Mus) partition f; **on that ∼** à cet égard. ● vt marquer; (success) remporter. ● vi marquer un point; (football) marquer un but; (keep score) marquer les points. **scorer** n (Sport) marqueur m.

scorn n mépris m. ● vt mépriser.

Scorpio n Scorpion m.

Scot n Écossais/-e m/f.

Scotland n Écosse f.

Scottish a écossais.

scoundrel n gredin m.

scour vt (pan) récurer; (search) parcourir. **scourer** n tampon m à récurer.

scourge n fléau m.

scout n éclaireur m. ● vi ∼ **around for** rechercher.

scowl n air m renfrogné. ● vi prendre un air renfrogné.

scramble vi (clamber) grimper. ● vt (eggs) brouiller. ● n (rush) course f.

scrap n petit morceau m; ~s (of metal, fabric) déchets mpl; (of food) restes mpl; (fight 🄸) bagarre f. ● vt (pt scrapped) abandonner; (car) détruire.

scrape vt gratter; (damage) érafler. ● vi ~ against s'érafler. □ ~ through réussir de justesse.

scrap: ~-paper n papier m brouillon. ~ yard n casse f.

scratch vt/i (se) gratter; (with claw, nail) griffer; (graze) érafler; (mark) rayer. ● n (on body) égratignure f; (on surface) éraflure f; **start from** ~ partir de zéro; **up to** ~ à la hauteur. ~ **card** n jeu m de grattage.

scrawl n gribouillage m. ● vt/i gribouiller.

scrawny a (-ier, -iest) décharné.

scream vt/i crier. ● n cri m (perçant).

screech vi (scream) hurler; (tyres) crisser. ● n cri m strident; (of tyres) crissement m.

screen n écran m, (folding) paravent m. ● vt masquer; (protect) protéger; (film) projeter; (candidates) filtrer; (Med) faire subir un test de dépistage.
screening n (cinema) projection f; (Med) dépistage m.

screen: ~play n scénario m. ~ saver n protecteur m d'écran.

screw n vis f. ● vt visser; ~ **up** (eyes) plisser; (ruin 🄸) cafouiller 🄸. ~**driver** n tournevis m.

scribble vt/i griffonner. ● n griffonnage m.

script n script m; (of play) texte m.

scroll n rouleau m. ● vt/i (Comput) (faire) défiler. ~**bar** n barre f de défilement.

scrounge 🄸 vt (favour) quémander; (cigarette) piquer 🄸; ~ **money from sb** taper de l'argent à qn. ● vi ~ **off sb** vivre sur le dos de qn.

scrub n (land) broussailles fpl. ● vt/i (pt scrubbed) nettoyer (à la brosse), frotter.

scruffy a (-ier, -iest) 🄸 dépenaillé.

scrum n (rugby) mêlée f.

scruple n scrupule m.

scrutinize vt scruter. **scrutiny** n examen m minutieux.

scuba-diving n plongée f sous-marine.

scuffle n bagarre f.

sculpt vt/i sculpter. **sculptor** n sculpteur m.

sculpture n sculpture f.

scum n (on liquid) mousse f; (people: pej) racaille f.

scurry vi se précipiter, courir (for pour chercher); ~ **off** se sauver.

sea n mer f; **at** ~ en mer; **by** ~ par mer. ● a (air) marin; (bird) de mer; (voyage) par mer. ~**food** n fruits mpl de mer. ~**gull** n mouette f.

seal n (animal) phoque m; (insignia) sceau m; (with wax) cachet m. ● vt sceller; cacheter; (stick down) coller. □ ~ **off** (area) boucler.

seam n (in cloth) couture f; (of coal) veine f.

search vt/i (examine) fouiller; (seek) chercher; (study) examiner; (Comput) rechercher. ● n fouille f; (quest) recherches fpl; (Comput) recherche f; **in** ~ **of** à la recherche de. ~ **engine** n (Internet) moteur m de recherche. ~**light** n projecteur m. ~**-warrant** n mandat m de perquisition.

sea: ~**shell** n coquillage m. ~**shore** n (coast) littoral m; (beach) plage f.

seasick a be ~ avoir le mal de mer.

seaside n bord m de la mer.

season n saison f; ~ **ticket** carte f d'abonnement. ● vt assaisonner. **seasonal** a saisonnier.

seasoning n assaisonnement m.

seat n siège m; (place) place f; (of trousers) fond m; **take a** ~ asseyez-vous. ● vt (put) placer; **the room** ~**s 30** la salle peut accueillir 30 personnes. ~**-belt** n ceinture f (de sécurité).

seaweed n algue f marine.

secluded a retiré.

seclusion n isolement m.

second[1] a deuxième, second; **a** ~ **chance** une nouvelle chance; **have** ~ **thoughts** avoir des doutes. ● n deuxième mf, second/-e m/f; (unit of time) seconde f; ~**s** (food) rab ▣. ● adv (in race) deuxième; (secondly) deuxièmement. ● vt (proposal) appuyer.

second[2] vt (transfer) détacher (**to** à).

secondary a secondaire; ~ **school** lycée m, école f secondaire.

second-best n pis-aller m.

second-class a (Rail) de deuxième classe; (post) au tarif lent.

second hand n (on clock) trotteuse f.

second-hand a & adv (article) d'occasion; (information) de seconde main.

secondly adv deuxièmement.

second-rate a médiocre.

secrecy n secret m.

secret a secret. ● n secret m; **in** ~ en secret.

secretarial a (work) de secrétaire.

secretary n secrétaire mf; **S~ of**

State ministre m; (US) ministre m des Affaires étrangères.

secrete vt (Med) sécréter; (hide) cacher.

secretive a secret. **secretly** adv secrètement.

sect n secte f. **sectarian** a sectaire.

section n partie f; (in store) rayon m; (of newspaper) rubrique f; (of book) passage m.

sector n secteur m.

secular a (school) laïque; (art, music) profane.

secure a (safe) sûr; (job, marriage) stable; (knot, lock) solide; (window) bien fermé; (feeling) de sécurité; (person) sécurisé. ● vt attacher; (obtain) s'assurer; (ensure) assurer.

security n (safety) sécurité f; (for loan) caution f; ~ **guard** vigile m.

sedate a calme. ● vt donner un sédatif à. **sedative** n sédatif m.

seduce vt séduire. **seducer** n séducteur/-trice m/f. **seduction** n séduction f. **seductive** a séduisant.

see vt/i (pt **saw**; pp **seen**) voir; **see you** (soon)! à bientôt!; ~**ing that** vu que. □ ~ **out** (person) raccompagner à la porte; ~ **through** (deception) déceler; (person) percer à jour; ~ **sth through** mener qch à bonne fin; ~ **to** s'occuper de; ~ **to it that** veiller à ce que.

seed n graine f; (collectively) graines fpl; (origin: fig) germe m; (tennis) tête f de série. **seedling** n plant m.

seek vt (pt **sought**) chercher.

seem vi sembler; **he** ~**s to think** il a l'air de croire.

seen ⇒SEE.

seep vi suinter; ~ **into** s'infiltrer dans.

see-saw *n* tapecul *m*. ● *vt* osciller.

seethe *vi* ~ **with** (*anger*) bouillir de; (*people*) grouiller de.

segment *n* segment *m*; (of orange) quartier *m*.

segregate *vt* séparer.

seize *vt* saisir; (*territory, prisoner*) s'emparer de. ● *vi* ~ **on** (*chance*) saisir; ~ **up** (*engine*) se gripper.

seizure *n* (Med) crise *f*.

seldom *adv* rarement.

select *vt* sélectionner. ● *a* privilégié. **selection** *n* sélection *f*. **selective** *a* sélectif.

self *n* (*pl* selves) moi *m*; (on cheque) moi-même. ~**-assured** *a* plein d'assurance. ~**-catering** *a* (*holiday*) en location. ~**-centred**, (US) ~**-centered** *a* égocentrique. ~**-confident** *a* sûr de soi. ~**-conscious** *a* timide. ~**-contained** *a* (*flat*) indépendant. ~**-control** *n* sang-froid *m*. ~**-defence** *n* autodéfense *f*; (Jur) légitime défense *f*. ~**-employed** *a* qui travaille à son compte. ~**-esteem** *n* amour-propre *m*. ~**-governing** *a* autonome. ~**-indulgent** *a* complaisant. ~**-interest** *n* intérêt *m* personnel.

selfish *a* égoïste.

selfless *a* désintéressé.

self: ~**-portrait** *n* autoportrait *m*. ~**-reliant** *a* autosuffisant. ~**-respect** *n* respect *m* de soi. ~**-righteous** *a* satisfait de soi. ~**-sacrifice** *n* abnégation *f*. ~**-satisfied** *a* satisfait de soi. ~**-seeking** *a* égoïste. ~**-service** *n* & *a* libre-service (*m*).

sell *vt/i* (*pt* sold) vendre; ~ **well** se vendre bien. □ ~ **off** liquider; ~ **out** (*items*) se vendre; **have sold out** avoir tout vendu.

Sellotape® *n* scotch® *m*.

sell-out *n* (betrayal) ▯ revirement *m*; **be a** ~ (*show*) afficher complet.

semester *n* (Univ) semestre *m*.

semicircle *n* demi-cercle *m*.

semicolon *n* point-virgule *m*.

semi-detached *a* ~ **house** maison *f* jumelée.

semifinal *n* demi-finale *f*.

seminar *n* séminaire *m*.

semolina *n* semoule *f*.

senate *n* sénat *m*. **senator** *n* sénateur *m*.

send *vt/i* (*pt* sent) envoyer. □ ~ **away** (dismiss) renvoyer; ~ (**away** **or off**) **for** commander (par la poste); ~ **back** renvoyer; ~ **for** (*person, help*) envoyer chercher; ~ **up** ▯ parodier.

senile *a* sénile.

senior *a* plus âgé (**to** que); (in rank) haut placé; **be** ~ **to sb** être le supérieur de qn. ● *n* aîné/-e *m/f*. ~ **citizen** *n* personne *f* âgée. ~ **school** *n* lycée *m*.

sensation *n* sensation *f*. **sensational** *a* sensationnel.

sense *n* sens *m*; (mental impression) sentiment *m*; (common sense) bon sens *m*; ~**s** (mind) raison *f*; **there's no** ~ **in doing** cela ne sert à rien de faire; **make** ~ avoir un sens; **make** ~ **of** comprendre. ● *vt* (pres)sentir. **senseless** *a* insensé; (Med) sans connaissance.

sensible *a* raisonnable; (*clothing*) pratique.

sensitive *a* sensible (**to** à); (*issue*) difficile.

sensory *a* sensoriel.

sensual *a* sensuel. **sensuality** *n* sensualité *f*.

sensuous *a* sensuel.

sent ⇒SEND.

sentence *n* phrase *f*; (punishment:

S

Jur) peine f. ● vt ~ **to** condamner à.

sentiment n sentiment m.
sentimental a sentimental.

sentry n sentinelle f.

separate[1] a (piece) à part; (issue) autre; (sections) différent; (organizations) distinct.

separate[2] vt/i (se) séparer.

separately adv séparément.

separation n séparation f.

September n septembre m.

septic a (wound) infecté; ~ **tank** fosse f septique.

sequel n suite f.

sequence n (order) ordre m; (series) suite f; (in film) séquence f.

Serb a serbe. ● n (person) Serbe mf; (Ling) serbe m.

Serbia n Serbie f.

sergeant n (Mil) sergent m; (policeman) brigadier m.

serial n feuilleton m. ● a (Comput) série inv.

series n inv série f.

serious a sérieux; (accident, crime) grave.

seriously adv sérieusement; (ill) gravement; **take** ~ prendre au sérieux.

sermon n sermon m.

serpent n serpent m.

serrated a dentelé.

serum n sérum m.

servant n domestique mf.

serve vt/i servir; faire; (transport, hospital) desservir; ~ **as/to** servir de/à; ~ **a purpose** être utile; ~ **a sentence** (Jur) purger une peine. ● n (tennis) service m.

server n serveur m; **remote** ~ téléserveur m.

service n service m; (maintenance) révision f; (Relig) office m; ~**s** (Mil) forces fpl armées. ● vt (car) réviser. ~ **area** n (Auto) aire f de

services. ~ **charge** n service m. ~ **station** n station-service f.

session n séance f; **be in** ~ (Jur) tenir séance.

set vt (pt **set**; pres p **setting**) placer; (table) mettre; (limit) fixer; (clock) mettre à l'heure; (example, task) donner; (TV, cinema) situer; ~ **fire to** mettre le feu à; ~ **free** libérer; ~ **to music** mettre en musique. ● vi (sun) se coucher; (jelly) prendre; (TV, radio) poste m; (Theat) décor m; (tennis) set m; (mathematics) ensemble m. ● a (time, price) fixe; (procedure) bien déterminé; (meal) à prix fixe; (book) au programme; ~ **against sth** opposé à; **be** ~ **on doing** tenir absolument à. □ ~ **about** se mettre à; ~ **back** (delay) retarder; (cost ▯) coûter; ~ **in** (take hold) s'installer, commencer; ~ **off** or **out** partir; ~ **off** (panic, riot) déclencher; (bomb) faire exploser; ~ **out** (state) présenter; (arrange) disposer; ~ **out to do sth** chercher à faire qch; ~ **up** (stall) monter; (equipment) assembler; (experiment) préparer; (company) créer; (meeting) organiser. ~**-back** n revers m.

settee n canapé m.

setting n cadre m; (on dial) position f.

settle vt (arrange, pay) régler; (date) fixer; (nerves) calmer. ● vi (come to rest) (bird) se poser; (dust) se déposer; (live) s'installer. □ ~ **down** se calmer; (marry etc.) se ranger; ~ **for** accepter; ~ **in** s'installer; ~ **up (with)** régler.

settlement n règlement m (of de); (agreement) accord m; (place) colonie f.

settler n colon m.

seven _a & n_ sept (_m_).

seventeen _a & n_ dix-sept (_m_).

seventh _a & n_ septième (_mf_).

seventy _a & n_ soixante-dix (_m_).

sever _vt_ (cut) couper; (_relations_) rompre.

several _a & pron_ plusieurs; ~ of us plusieurs d'entre nous.

severe _a_ (harsh) sévère; (serious) grave.

sew _vt/i_ (_pt_ sewed; _pp_ sewn _or_ sewed) coudre.

sewage _n_ eaux _fpl_ usées.

sewer _n_ égout _m_.

sewing _n_ couture _f_. ~-machine _n_ machine _f_ à coudre.

sewn ⇒SEW.

sex _n_ sexe _m_; have ~ avoir des rapports (sexuels). ● _a_ sexuel. **sexist** _a & n_ sexiste (_mf_). **sexual** _a_ sexuel.

shabby _a_ (-ier, -iest) (_place_, _object_) miteux; (_person_) habillé de façon miteuse; (_treatment_) mesquin.

shack _n_ cabane _f_.

shade _n_ ombre _f_; (of colour, opinion) nuance _f_; (for lamp) abat-jour _m_ _inv_; a ~ bigger légèrement plus grand ● _vt_ (_tree_) ombrager; (_hat_) projeter une ombre sur.

shadow _n_ ombre _f_. ● _vt_ (follow) filer. S~ Cabinet _n_ cabinet _m_ fantôme.

shady _a_ (-ier, -iest) ombragé; (dubious) véreux.

shaft _n_ (of tool) manche _m_; (of arrow) tige _f_; (in machine) axe _m_; (of mine) puits _m_; (of light) rayon _m_.

shake _vt_ (_pt_ shook; _pp_ shaken) secouer; (_bottle_) agiter; (_belief_) ébranler; ~ hands with serrer la main à; ~ one's head dire non de la tête. ● _vi_ trembler. ● _n_ secousse _f_; give sth a ~ secouer qch. □ ~ off se débarrasser de. ~-up _n_ (Pol) remaniement _m_.

shaky _a_ (-ier, -iest) (_hand, voice_) tremblant; (_ladder_) branlant; (weak: fig) instable.

shall _v aux_ I ~ do je ferai; we ~ see nous verrons; ~ we go...? si on allait...?

shallow _a_ peu profond; (fig) superficiel.

shame _n_ honte _f_; it's a ~ c'est dommage. ● _vt_ faire honte à.

shampoo _n_ shampooing _m_. ● _vt_ faire un shampooing à.

shandy _n_ panaché _m_.

shan't = SHALL NOT.

shanty _n_ (shack) baraque _f_; ~ town bidonville _m_.

shape _n_ forme _f_. ● _vt_ (_clay_) modeler; (_rock_) façonner; (_future_: fig) déterminer; ~ sth into balls faire des boules avec qch. ● _vi_ ~ up (_plan_) prendre tournure; (_person_) faire des progrès.

share _n_ part _f_; (Comm) action _f_. ● _vt/i_ partager; (_feature_) avoir en commun. ~holder _n_ actionnaire _mf_. ~ware _n_ (Comput) logiciel _m_ contributif.

shark _n_ requin _m_.

sharp _a_ (_knife_) tranchant; (_pin_) pointu; (_point, angle, cry_) aigu; (_person, mind_) vif; (_tone_) acerbe. ● _adv_ (stop) net; (_sing, play_) trop haut; six o'clock ~ six heures pile. ● _n_ (Mus) dièse _m_.

sharpen _vt_ aiguiser; (_pencil_) tailler.

shatter _vt_ (_glass_) fracasser; (_hope_) briser. ● _vi_ (_glass_) voler en éclats.

shave _vt/i_ (se) raser. ● _n_ have a ~ se raser. **shaver** _n_ rasoir _m_ électrique.

shaving _n_ (of wood) copeau _m_. ● _a_ (cream, foam, gel) à raser.

shawl _n_ châle _m_.

she _pron_ elle. ● _n_ (animal) femelle _f_.

S

shear vt (pp **shorn** or **sheared**) (sheep) tondre; ~ **off** se détacher.

shears npl cisaille f.

shed n remise f. ● vt (pt **shed**; pres p **shedding**) perdre; (light, tears) répandre.

sheen n lustre m.

sheep n inv mouton m. ~-**dog** n chien m de berger.

sheepish a penaud.

sheepskin n peau f de mouton.

sheer a pur; (steep) à pic; (fabric) très fin. ● adv à pic.

sheet n drap m; (of paper) feuille f; (of glass, ice) plaque f.

shelf n (pl **shelves**) étagère f; (in shop, fridge) rayon m; (in oven) plaque f.

shell n coquille f; (on beach) coquillage m; (of building) carcasse f; (explosive) obus m. ● vt (nut) décortiquer; (peas) écosser; (Mil) bombarder.

shellfish npl (lobster etc.) crustacés mpl; (mollusc) coquillages mpl.

shelter n abri m. ● vt/i (s')abriter; (give lodging to) donner asile à.

shelve vt (plan) mettre en suspens.

shepherd n berger m; ~'s **pie** hachis m Parmentier. ● vt (people) guider.

sherry n xérès m.

shield n bouclier m; (screen) écran m. ● vt protéger.

shift vt/i (se) déplacer, bouger; (exchange, alter) changer de. ● n changement m; (workers) équipe f; (work) poste m; ~ **work** travail m posté, travail m par roulement.

shifty a (-ier, -iest) louche.

shimmer vi chatoyer. ● n chatoiement m.

shin n tibia m.

shine vt (pt **shone**) (torch) braquer (**on** sur). ● vi (light, sun,

hair) briller; (brass) reluire. ● n lustre m.

shingle n (pebbles) galets mpl; (on roof) bardeau m.

shingles npl (Med) zona m.

shiny a (-ier, -iest) brillant.

ship n bateau m, navire m. ● vt (pt **shipped**) transporter.

shipment n (by sea) cargaison f; (by air, land) chargement m.

shipping n (ships) navigation f. ~**wreck** n épave f; (event) naufrage m.

shirt n chemise f; (woman's) chemisier m.

shiver vi frissonner. ● n frisson m.

shock n choc m; (Electr) décharge f; **in** ~ en état de choc; ~ **absorber** amortisseur m. ● a (result) choc inv; (tactics) de choc. ● vt choquer.

shoddy a (-ier, -iest) mal fait; (behaviour) mesquin.

shoe n chaussure f; (of horse) fer m; (brake) ~ sabot m (de frein). ● vt (pt **shod**; pres p **shoeing**) (horse) ferrer. ~**lace** n lacet m. ~ **size** n pointure f.

shone ⇒SHINE.

shook ⇒SHAKE.

shoot vt (pt **shot**) (gun) tirer un coup de; (bullet) tirer; (missile, glance) lancer; (person) tirer sur; (kill) abattre; (execute) fusiller; (film) tourner. ● vi tirer (**at** sur). ● n (Bot) pousse f. □ ~ **down** abattre; ~ **out** (rush) sortir en vitesse; ~ **up** (spurt) jaillir; (grow) pousser vite.

shooting n (killing) meurtre m (par arme à feu); **hear** ~ entendre des coups de feu.

shop n magasin m; (small) boutique f; (workshop) atelier m. ● vi (pt **shopped**) faire ses courses; ~ **around** comparer les prix. ~ **assistant** n vendeur/

-euse *m/f*. ~**-floor** *n* (workers) ouvriers *mpl*. ~**keeper** *n* commerçant/-e *m/f*. ~**lifter** *n* voleur/-euse *m/f* à l'étalage.

shopper *n* acheteur/-euse *m/f*.

shopping *n* (goods) achats *mpl*; go ~ (for food) faire les courses; (for clothes etc.) faire les magasins. ~ **bag** *n* sac *m* à provisions. ~ **centre**, (US) ~ **center** *n* centre *m* commercial.

shop window *n* vitrine *f*.

shore *n* côte *f*, rivage *m*; on ~ à terre.

short *a* court; (*person*) petit; (brief) court, bref; (curt) brusque; be ~ (of) manquer (de); **everything** ~ **of** tout sauf; **nothing** ~ **of** rien de moins que; **cut** ~ écourter; **cut sb** ~ interrompre qn; **fall** ~ **of** ne pas arriver à; **he is called Tom for** ~ son diminutif est Tom; **in** ~ en bref. ● *adv* (stop) net. ● *n* (Electr) court-circuit *m*; (film) court-métrage *m*; ~**s** (trousers) short *m*.

shortage *n* manque *m*.

short: ~**bread** *n* sablé *m*. ~**-change** *vt* (cheat) rouler 🔲. ~ **circuit** *n* court-circuit *m*. ~**coming** *n* défaut *m*. ~ **cut** *n* raccourci *m*.

shorten *vt* raccourcir.

shortfall *n* déficit *m*.

shorthand *n* sténographie *f*; ~ **typist** sténodactylo *f*.

short: ~ **list** *n* liste *f* des candidats choisis. ~**-lived** *a* de courte durée.

shortly *adv* bientôt.

short: ~**-sighted** *a* myope. ~**-staffed** *a* à court de personnel; ~ **story** *n* nouvelle *f*. ~**-term** *a* à court terme.

shot ⇒SHOOT. ● *n* (firing, attempt) coup *m* de feu; (person) tireur *m*; (bullet) balle *f*; (photograph) photo *f*; (injection) piqûre *f*; **like a** ~ sans

hésiter. ~**-gun** *n* fusil *m* de chasse.

should *v aux* devoir; **you** ~ **help me** vous devriez m'aider; **I** ~ **have stayed** j'aurais dû rester; **I** ~ **like to** j'aimerais bien; **if he** ~ **come** s'il venait.

shoulder *n* épaule *f*. ● *vt* (*responsibility*) endosser; (*burden*) se charger de. ~**-bag** *n* sac *m* à bandoulière. ~**-blade** *n* omoplate *f*.

shout *n* cri *m*. ● *vt/i* crier (at après); ~ **sth out** lancer qch à haute voix.

shove *n* give sth a ~ pousser qch. ● *vt/i* pousser; ~ **off**! 🔲 tire-toi! 🔲.

shovel *n* pelle *f*. ● *vt* (*pt* **shovelled**) pelleter.

show *vt* (*pt* **showed**; *pp* **shown**) montrer; (*dial, needle*) indiquer; (put on display) exposer; (*film*) donner; (conduct) conduire; ~ **sb in/out** faire entrer/sortir qn. ● *vi* (be visible) se voir. ● *n* (exhibition) exposition *f*, salon *m*; (Theat) spectacle *m*; (cinema) séance *f*; (of strength) démonstration *f*; **for** ~ pour l'effet; **on** ~ exposé. □ ~ **off** faire le fier/la fière; ~ **sth/sb off** exhiber qch/qn; ~ **up** se voir; (appear) se montrer; ~ **sb up** 🔲 faire honte à qn.

shower *n* douche *f*; (of rain) averse *f*. ● *vt* ~ **with** couvrir de. ● *vi* se doucher.

showing *n* performance *f*; (cinema) séance *f*.

show-jumping *n* concours *m* hippique.

shown ⇒SHOW.

show: ~**-off** *n* m'as-tu-vu *mf inv* 🔲. ~**room** *n* salle *f* d'exposition.

shrank ⇒SHRINK.

shrapnel *n* éclats *mpl* d'obus.

shred *n* lambeau *m*; (least amount:

S

fig) parcelle f. ● vt (pt **shredded**) déchiqueter; (Culin) râper.

shrewd a (person) habile; (move) astucieux.

shriek n hurlement m. ● vt/i hurler.

shrill a (voice) perçant; (tone) strident.

shrimp n crevette f.

shrine n (place) lieu m de pèlerinage.

shrink vt/i (pt **shrank**; pp **shrunk**) rétrécir; (lessen) diminuer; ~ **from** reculer devant.

shrivel vt/i (pt **shrivelled**) (se) ratatiner.

shroud n linceul m. ● vt (veil) envelopper.

Shrove Tuesday n mardi m gras.

shrub n arbuste m.

shrug vt (pt **shrugged**) ~ one's **shoulders** hausser les épaules; ~ **sth off** ignorer qch.

shrunk ⇒SHRINK.

shudder vi frémir. ● n frémissement m.

shuffle vt (feet) traîner; (cards) battre. ● vi traîner les pieds.

shun vt (pt **shunned**) fuir.

shut vt (pt **shut**; pres p **shutting**) fermer. ● vi (door) se fermer; (shop) fermer. □ ~ **in** or **up** enfermer; ~ **up** 🔳 se taire; ~ **sb up** faire taire qn.

shutter n volet m; (Photo) obturateur m.

shuttle n (bus) navette f; ~ **service** navette f. ● vi faire la navette. ● vt transporter.

shuttlecock n (badminton) volant m.

shy a timide. ● vi ~ **away from** se tenir à l'écart de.

sibling n frère/sœur m/f.

sick a malade; (humour) macabre; (mind) malsain; **be** ~

(vomit) vomir; **be** ~ **of** 🔳 en avoir assez or marre de 🔳; **feel** ~ avoir mal au cœur. ~-**leave** n congé m de maladie.

sickly a (-ier, -iest) (person) maladif; (taste, smell) écœurant.

sickness n maladie f.

sick-pay n indemnité f de maladie.

side n côté m; (of road, river) bord m; (of hill, body) flanc m; (Sport) équipe f; (TV 🔳) chaîne f; ~ **by** ~ côte à côte. ● a latéral. ● vi ~ **with** se ranger du côté de. ~**board** n buffet m. ~-**effect** n effet m secondaire. ~**light** n (Auto) feu m de position. ~**line** n activité f secondaire. ~-**show** n attraction f. ~-**step** vt (pt -**stepped**) éviter. ~-**street** n rue f latérale. ~-**track** vt fourvoyer. ~**walk** n (US) trottoir m.

sideways a (look) de travers. ● adv (move) latéralement; (look at) de travers.

siding n voie f de garage.

sidle vi s'avancer furtivement (up to vers).

siege n siège m.

siesta n sieste f.

sieve n tamis m; (for liquids) passoire f. ● vt tamiser.

sift vt tamiser. ● vi ~ **through** examiner.

sigh n soupir m. ● vt/i soupirer.

sight n vue f; (scene) spectacle m; (on gun) mire f; **at** or **on** ~ à vue; **catch** ~ **of** apercevoir; **in** ~ visible; **lose** ~ **of** perdre de vue. ● vt apercevoir.

sightseeing n tourisme m.

sign n signe m; (notice) panneau m. ● vt/i signer. □ ~ **on** (as unemployed) pointer au chômage; ~ **up** (s')engager.

signal n signal m. ● vt (pt **signalled**) (gesture) faire signe (that que); (indicate) indiquer.

signatory n signataire mf.

signature n signature f; ~ **tune** indicatif m.

significance n importance f; (meaning) signification f.

significant a important; (meaningful) significatif.

significantly adv (much) sensiblement.

signify vt signifier.

signpost n panneau m indicateur.

silence n silence m. ● vt faire taire.

silent a silencieux; (film) muet. **silently** adv silencieusement.

silhouette n silhouette f. ● vt be ~d **against** se profiler contre.

silicon n silicium m; ~ **chip** puce f électronique.

silk n soie f.

silly a (-ier, -iest) bête, idiot.

silver n argent m; (silverware) argenterie f. ● a en argent.

similar a semblable (**to** à). **similarity** n ressemblance f. **similarly** adv de même.

simile n comparaison f.

simmer vt/i (soup) mijoter; (water) (laisser) frémir.

simple a simple.

simplicity n simplicité f.

simplify vt simplifier.

simplistic a simpliste.

simply adv simplement; (absolutely) absolument.

simulate vt simuler.

simultaneous a simultané.

sin n péché m. ● vi (pt **sinned**) pécher.

....

since

● **preposition**

····▸ depuis; **I haven't seen him ~ Monday** je ne l'ai pas vu depuis lundi; **I've been waiting ~ yesterday** j'attends depuis hier; **she had been living in Paris ~ 1985** elle habitait Paris depuis 1985.

● **conjunction**

····▸ (in time expressions) depuis que; ~ **she's been working here** depuis qu'elle travaille ici; ~ **she left** depuis qu'elle est partie or depuis son départ.

····▸ (because) comme; ~ **he was ill, he couldn't go** comme il était malade, il ne pouvait pas y aller.

● **adverb**

····▸ depuis; **he hasn't been seen ~** on ne l'a pas vu depuis.

....

sincere a sincère. **sincerely** adv sincèrement. **sincerity** n sincérité f.

sinful a immoral; ~ **man** pécheur m.

sing vt/i (pt **sang**; pp **sung**) chanter.

singe vt (pres p **singeing**) brûler légèrement; (with iron) roussir.

singer n chanteur/-euse m/f.

single a seul; (not double) simple; (unmarried) célibataire; (room, bed) pour une personne; (ticket) simple; **in ~ file** en file indienne. ● n (ticket) aller simple m; (record) 45 tours m inv; ~**s** (tennis) simple m. ● vt ~ **out** choisir. ~**-handed** a tout seul. ~**-minded** a tenace. ~ **parent** n parent m isolé.

singular n singulier m. ● a (strange) singulier; (noun) au singulier.

sinister a sinistre.

sink vt (pt **sank**; pp **sunk**) (boat) couler; (well) forer; (post) enfoncer. ● vi (boat) couler; (sun, level) baisser; (wall) s'effondrer. ● n (in kitchen) évier m; (wash-basin)

S

lavabo *m*. □ ~ **in** (*news*) faire son chemin.

sinner *n* pécheur/-eresse *m/f*.

sip *n* petite gorgée *f*. ● *vt* (*pt* **sipped**) boire à petites gorgées.

siphon *n* siphon *m*. ● *vt* ~ **off** siphonner.

sir *n* Monsieur *m*; **Sir** (title) Sir *m*.

siren *n* sirène *f*.

sirloin *n* aloyau *m*.

sister *n* sœur *f*; (nurse) infirmière *f* en chef. ~**-in-law** *n* (*pl* ~**s-in-law**) belle-sœur *f*.

sit *vt/i* (*pt* **sat**; *pres p* **sitting**) (s')asseoir; (*committee*) siéger; ~ (**for**) (exam) se présenter à; **be** ~**ting** être assis. □ ~ **around** ne rien faire; ~ **down** s'asseoir.

site *n* emplacement *m*; (building) ~ chantier *m*. ● *vt* construire.

sitting *n* séance *f*; (in restaurant) service *m*. ~**-room** *n* salon *m*.

situate *vt* situer; **be** ~**d** être situé. **situation** *n* situation *f*.

six *a & n* six (*m*).

sixteen *a & n* seize (*m*).

sixth *a & n* sixième (*mf*).

sixty *a & n* soixante (*m*).

size *n* dimension *f*; (of person, garment) taille *f*; (of shoes) pointure *f*; (of sum, salary) montant *m*; (extent) ampleur *f*. □ ~ **up** (*person*) se faire une opinion de; (*situation*) évaluer. **sizeable** *a* assez grand.

skate *n* patin *m*; (fish) raie *f*. ● *vi* patiner.

skateboard *n* skateboard *m*, planche *f* à roulettes. ● *vi* faire du skateboard.

skating *n* patinage *m*.

skeleton *n* squelette *m*; ~ **staff** effectifs *mpl* minimums.

sketch *n* esquisse *f*; (hasty) croquis *m*; (Theat) sketch *m*. ● *vt* faire une esquisse *or* un croquis de. ● *vi* faire des esquisses.

sketchy *a* (**-ier, -iest**) (*details*) insuffisant; (*memory*) vague.

skewer *n* brochette *f*.

ski *n* ski *m*. ● *a* de ski. ● *vi* (*pt* **ski'd** or **skied**; *pres p* **skiing**) skier; (go skiing) faire du ski.

skid *vi* (*pt* **skidded**) déraper. ● *n* dérapage *m*.

skier *n* skieur/-euse *m/f*.

skiing *n* ski *m*.

ski jump *n* saut *m* à ski.

skilful *a* habile.

ski lift *n* remontée *f* mécanique.

skill *n* habileté *f*; (craft) compétence *f*; ~**s** connaissances *fpl*. **skilled** *a* (*worker*) qualifié; (talented) consommé.

skim *vt* (*pt* **skimmed**) écumer; (*milk*) écrémer; (pass over) effleurer. ● *vi* ~ **through** parcourir.

skimpy *a* (*clothes*) étriqué.

skin *n* peau *f*. ● *vt* (*pt* **skinned**) (*animal*) écorcher; (*fruit*) éplucher.

skinny *a* (**-ier, -iest**) 🅸 maigre.

skip *vi* (*pt* **skipped**) sautiller; (with rope) sauter à la corde. ● *vt* (*page, class*) sauter. ● *n* petit saut *m*; (container) benne *f*.

skipper *n* capitaine *m*.

skirmish *n* escarmouche.

skirt *n* jupe *f*. ● *vt* contourner. **skirting-board** *n* plinthe *f*.

skittle *n* quille *f*.

skull *n* crâne *m*.

sky *n* ciel *m*. ~**-blue** *a & n* bleu ciel *m inv*. ~**scraper** *n* gratte-ciel *m inv*.

slab *n* (of stone) dalle *f*.

slack *a* (not tight) détendu; (*person*) négligent; (*period*) creux. ● *n* (in rope) mou *m*. ● *vi* se relâcher.

slacken *vt* (*rope*) donner du mou à; (*grip*) relâcher; (*pace*) réduire. ● *vi* (*grip, rope*) se relâcher;

(*activity*) ralentir; (*rain*) se
calmer.

slam vt/i (pt **slammed**) (*door*)
claquer; (throw) flanquer; (criticize
🗊) critiquer. ● n (noise)
claquement m.

slander n (offence) diffamation f;
(statement) calomnie f. ● vt
calomnier; (Jur) diffamer.
slanderous a diffamatoire.

slang n argot m.

slant vt/i (faire) pencher; (*news*)
présenter sous un certain jour.
● n inclinaison f; (bias) angle m.
slanted a (biased) orienté; (sloping)
en pente.

slap vt (pt **slapped**) (strike)
donner une tape à; (*face*) gifler;
(put) flanquer 🗊. ● n claque f; (on
face) gifle f. ● adv tout droit.

slapdash a (*person*) brouillon 🗊;
(*work*) bâclé 🗊.

slash vt (*picture, tyre*) taillader;
(*face*) balafrer; (*throat*) couper;
(fig) réduire (radicalement). ● n
lacération f.

slat n (in blind) lamelle f; (on bed)
latte f.

slate n ardoise f. ● vt 🗊 taper sur
🗊.

slaughter vt massacrer; (*animal*)
abattre. ● n massacre m; abattage
m.

slave n esclave mf. ● vi trimer 🗊.
slavery n esclavage m.

sleazy a (-ier, -iest) 🗊 (*story*)
scabreux; (*club*) louche.

sledge n luge f; (horse-drawn)
traîneau m.

sleek a (*hair*) lisse, brillant;
(*shape*) élégant.

sleep n sommeil m; go to ~
s'endormir. ● vi (pt **slept**)
dormir; (spend the night) coucher; ~
in faire la grasse matinée. ● vt
loger.

sleeper n (Rail) (berth) couchette f;
(on track) traverse f.

sleeping-bag n sac m de
couchage.

sleeping-pill n somnifère m.

sleep-walker n somnambule mf.

sleepy a (-ier, -iest) somnolent;
be ~ avoir sommeil.

sleet n neige f fondue.

sleeve n manche f; (of record)
pochette f; up one's ~ en réserve.

sleigh n traîneau m.

slender a (*person*) mince;
(*majority*) faible.

slept ⇒SLEEP.

slice n tranche f. ● vt couper (en
tranches).

slick a (adept) habile; (insincere)
roublard 🗊. ● n (oil) ~ marée f
noire.

slide vt/i (pt **slid**) glisser; ~ into
(go silently) se glisser dans. ● n
glissade f; (fall: fig) baisse f; (in
playground) toboggan m; (for hair)
barrette f; (Photo) diapositive f.

sliding a (*door*) coulissant; ~
scale échelle f mobile.

slight a petit, léger; (slender)
mince; (frail) frêle. ● vt (insult)
offenser. ● n affront m. **slightest**
a moindre. **slightly** adv
légèrement, un peu.

slim a (**slimmer, slimmest**)
mince. ● vi (pt **slimmed**)
maigrir.

slime n dépôt m gluant; (on river-
bed) vase f. **slimy** a visqueux; (fig)
servile.

sling n (weapon, toy) fronde f;
(bandage) écharpe f. ● vt (pt **slung**)
jeter, lancer.

slip vt/i (pt **slipped**) glisser;
~ped disc hernie f discale; ~ sb's
mind échapper à qn. ● n (mistake)
erreur f; (petticoat) combinaison f;
(paper) bout m de papier; ~ of the
tongue lapsus m. □ ~ away
s'esquiver; ~ into (go) se glisser
dans; (clothes) mettre; ~ up
🗊 faire une gaffe 🗊.

S

slipper n pantoufle f.

slippery a glissant.

slip road n bretelle f.

slit n fente f. ● vt (pt **slit**; pres p **slitting**) déchirer; ~ **sth open** ouvrir qch; ~ **sb's throat** égorger qn.

slither vi glisser.

sliver n (of glass) éclat m; (of soap) reste m.

slobber vi 🔲 baver.

slog 🔲 vt (pt **slogged**) (hit) frapper dur. ● vi (work) bosser 🔲. ● n (work) travail m dur.

slogan n slogan m.

slope vi être en pente; (handwriting) pencher. ● n pente f; (of mountain) flanc m.

sloppy a (-ier, -iest) (food) liquide; (work) négligé; (person) négligent.

slosh vt 🔲 répandre; (hit 🔲) frapper. ● vi clapoter.

slot n fente f. ● vt/i (pt **slotted**) (s')insérer.

sloth n paresse f.

slot-machine n distributeur m automatique; (for gambling) machine f à sous.

slouch vi être avachi.

Slovakia n Slovaquie f.

Slovenia n Slovénie f.

slovenly a débraillé.

slow a lent; **be** ~ (clock) retarder; **in** ~ **motion** au ralenti. ● adv lentement. ● vt/i ralentir. **slowly** adv lentement. **slowness** n lenteur f.

sludge n vase f.

slug n (mollusc) limace f; (bullet 🔲) balle f; (blow 🔲) coup m.

sluggish a (person) léthargique; (circulation) lent.

slum n taudis m.

slump n (Econ) effondrement m; (in support) baisse f. ● vi (demand, trade) chuter; (economy) s'effondrer; (person) s'affaler.

slung ⇒SLING.

slur vt/i (pt **slurred**) (words) mal articuler. ● n calomnie f (on sur).

slush n (snow) neige f fondue. ~ **fund** n caisse f noire.

sly a (crafty) rusé; (secretive) sournois. ● n on the ~ en cachette.

smack n tape f; (on face) gifle f. ● vt donner une tape à; gifler. ● vi ~ **of sth** sentir qch. ● adv 🔲 tout droit.

small a petit. ● n ~ **of the back** creux m des reins. ● adv (cut) menu. ~ **ad** n petite annonce f. ~ **business** n petite entreprise f. ~ **change** n petite monnaie f. ~ **pox** n variole f. ~ **print** n petits caractères mpl. ~ **talk** n banalités fpl.

smart a élégant; (clever 🔲) malin, habile; (restaurant) chic inv; (Comput) intelligent. ● vi (wound) brûler.

smarten vt/i ~ (up) embellir; ~ (oneself) up s'arranger.

smash vt/i (se) briser, (se) fracasser; (opponent, record) pulvériser. ● n (noise) fracas m; (blow) coup m; (car crash) collision f; (hit record 🔲) tube m 🔲.

smashing a 🔲 épatant.

SME abbr (**small and medium enterprises**) PME.

smear vt (stain) tacher; (coat) enduire; (discredit: fig) diffamer. ● n tache f; (effort to discredit) propos m diffamatoire; ~ (test) frottis m.

smell n odeur f; (sense) odorat m. ● vt/i (pt **smelt** or **smelled**) sentir; ~ **of** sentir. **smelly** a qui sent mauvais.

smelt ⇒SMELL.

smile n sourire m. ● vi sourire.

smiley n (Internet) binette f.

smirk n petit sourire m satisfait.

smitten *a* (in love) fou d'amour.

smog *n* smog *m*.

smoke *n* fumée *f*; **have a ~** fumer. ● *vt/i* fumer. **smoked** *a* fumé. **smokeless** *a* (*fuel*) non polluant. **smoker** *n* fumeur/-euse *m/f*. **smoky** *a* (*air*) enfumé.

smooth *a* lisse; (*movement*) aisé; (*manners*) onctueux; (*flight*) sans heurts. ● *vt* lisser; (*process*) faciliter.

smoothly *adv* (*move, flow*) doucement; (*brake, start*) en douceur; **go ~** marcher bien.

smother *vt* (stifle) étouffer; (cover) couvrir.

smoulder *vi* (lit) se consumer; (fig) couver.

smudge *n* trace *f*. ● *vt/i* (*ink*) (s')étaler.

smug *a* (**smugger, smuggest**) suffisant.

smuggle *vt* passer (en contrebande). **smuggler** *n* contrebandier/-ière *m/f*. **smuggling** *n* contrebande *f*.

smutty *a* grivois.

snack *n* casse-croûte *m inv*.

snag *n* inconvénient *m*; (in cloth) accroc *m*

snail *n* escargot *m*.

snake *n* serpent *m*.

snap *vt/i* (*pt* **snapped**) (*whip, fingers*) (faire) claquer; (break) (se) casser net; (say) dire sèchement. ● *n* claquement *m*; (Photo) photo *f*. ● *a* soudain. □ **~ up** (buy) sauter sur.

snapshot *n* photo *f*.

snare *n* piège *m*.

snarl *vi* gronder (en montrant les dents). ● *n* grondement *m*. **~-up** *n* embouteillage *m*.

snatch *vt* (grab) attraper; (steal) voler; (*opportunity*) saisir; **~ sth from sb** arracher qch à qn. ● *n*

(theft) vol *m*; (short part) fragment *m*.

sneak *vi* aller furtivement. ● *n* Ⓔ rapporteur/-euse *m/f*.

sneer *n* sourire *m* méprisant. ● *vi* sourire avec mépris.

sneeze *n* éternuement *m*. ● *vi* éternuer.

snide *a* narquois.

sniff *vt/i* renifler. ● *n* reniflement *m*.

snigger *n* ricanement *m*. ● *vi* ricaner.

snip *vt* (*pt* **snipped**) couper.

sniper *n* tireur *m* embusqué.

snippet *n* bribe *f*.

snivel *vi* (*pt* **snivelled**) pleurnicher.

snob *n* snob *mf*.

snooker *n* snooker *m*.

snoop *vi* Ⓔ fourrer son nez partout.

snooty *a* (**-ier, -iest**) Ⓔ snob *inv*, hautain.

snooze *n* petit somme *m*. ● *vi* sommeiller.

snore *n* ronflement *m*. ● *vi* ronfler.

snorkel *n* tuba *m*.

snort *n* grognement *m*. ● *vi* (*person*) grogner; (*horse*) s'ébrouer.

snout *n* museau *m*.

snow *n* neige *f*. ● *vi* neiger; **be ~ed under with** être submergé de.

snowball *n* boule *f* de neige. ● *vi* faire boule de neige.

snow: **~boarding** *n* surf *m* des neiges. **~-bound** *a* bloqué par la neige. **~-drift** *n* congère *f*. **~drop** *n* perce-neige *m or f inv*. **~flake** *n* flocon *m* de neige. **~man** *n* (*pl* **-men**) bonhomme *m* de neige. **~-plough** *n* chasse-neige *m inv*.

snub *vt* (*pt* **snubbed**) rembarrer. ● *n* rebuffade *f*.

snuffle *vi* renifler.

S

snug *a* (**snugger**, **snuggest**) (cosy) confortable; (tight) bien ajusté.

snuggle *vi* se pelotonner.

so *adv* si, tellement; (*thus*) ainsi; ∼ am I moi aussi; ∼ good as aussi bon que; **that is** ∼ c'est ça; **I think** ∼ je pense que oui; **five or** ∼ environ cinq; ∼ **as to** de manière à; ∼ **far** jusqu'ici; ∼ **long!** 🄸 à bientôt!; ∼ **many**, ∼ **much** tant (de); ∼ **that** pour que. ● *conj* donc, alors.

soak *vt/i* (faire) tremper (**in** dans). □ ∼ **in** pénétrer; ∼ **up** absorber. **soaking** *a* trempé.

soap *n* savon *m*. ● *vt* savonner. ∼ **opera** *n* feuilleton *m*. ∼ **powder** *n* lessive *f*.

soar *vi* monter (en flèche).

sob *n* sanglot *m*. ● *vi* (*pt* **sobbed**) sangloter.

sober *a* qui n'a pas bu d'alcool; (*serious*) sérieux. ● *vi* ∼ **up** dessoûler.

soccer *n* football *m*.

sociable *a* sociable.

social *a* social. ● *n* réunion *f* (amicale), fête *f*.

socialism *n* socialisme *m*. **socialist** *a* & *n* socialiste (*mf*).

socialize *vi* se mêler aux autres; ∼ **with** fréquenter.

socially *adv* socialement; (*meet*) en société.

social: ∼ **security** *n* aide *f* sociale. ∼ **worker** *n* travailleur/ -euse *m/f* social/-e.

society *n* société *f*.

sociological *a* sociologique. **sociologist** *n* sociologue *mf*. **sociology** *n* sociologie *f*.

sock *n* chaussette *f*. ● *vt* (hit 🄸) flanquer un coup (de poing) à.

socket *n* (for lamp) douille *f*; (Electr) prise *f* (de courant); (of eye) orbite *f*.

soda *n* soude *f*; ∼(-**water**) eau *f* de Seltz.

sodden *a* détrempé.

sofa *n* canapé *m*. ∼ **bed** *n* canapé-lit *m*.

soft *a* (gentle, lenient) doux; (not hard) doux, mou; (*heart, wood*) tendre; (silly) ramolli. ∼ **drink** *n* boisson *f* non alcoolisée.

soften *vt/i* (se) ramollir; (tone down, lessen) (s')adoucir.

soft spot *n* **to have a** ∼ **for sb** avoir un faible pour qn.

software *n* logiciel *m*.

soggy *a* (-ier, -iest) (*ground*) détrempé; (*food*) ramolli.

soil *n* sol *m*, terre *f*. ● *vt/i* (se) salir.

sold ⇒SELL. ● *a* ∼ **out** épuisé.

solder *n* soudure *f*. ● *vt* souder.

soldier *n* soldat *m*. ● *vi* ∼ **on** 🄸 persévérer.

sole *n* (of foot) plante *f*; (of shoe) semelle *f*; (fish) sole *f*. ● *a* unique, seul. **solely** *adv* uniquement.

solemn *a* solennel.

solicitor *n* notaire *m*; (for court and police work) ≈ avocat/-e *m/f*.

solid *a* solide; (not hollow) plein; (*gold*) massif; (*mass*) compact; (*meal*) substantiel. ● *n* solide *m*; ∼**s** (food) aliments *mpl* solides.

solidarity *n* solidarité *f*.

solidify *vt/i* (se) solidifier.

solitary *a* (alone) solitaire; (only) seul.

solo *n* solo *m*. ● *a* (Mus) solo *inv*; (*flight*) en solitaire.

soluble *a* soluble.

solution *n* solution *f*.

solve *vt* résoudre.

solvent *a* (Comm) solvable. ● *n* (dis)solvant *m*.

some
● *determiner*

····▸ (unspecified amount) du/de l'/de la/des; **I have to buy ~ bread** je dois acheter du pain; **have ~ water** prenez de l'eau; **~ sweets** des bonbons.

····▸ (certain) certains/certaines; **~ people say that** certains disent que.

····▸ (unknown) un/une; **~ man came to the house** un homme est venu à la maison.

····▸ (considerable amount) **we stayed there for ~ time** nous sommes restés là assez longtemps; **it will take ~ doing** ça ne va pas être facile à faire.

> ! In front of a plural adjective *des* changes to *de*: **some pretty dresses** *de jolies robes*.

● *pronoun*

····▸ en; **he wants ~** il en veut; **have ~ more** reprenez-en.

····▸ (certain) certains/certaines; **~ are expensive** certains sont chers.

● *adverb*

····▸ environ; **~ 20 people** environ 20 personnes.

somebody *pron* quelqu'un. ● *n* **be a ~** être quelqu'un.

somehow *adv* d'une manière ou d'une autre; (for some reason) je ne sais pas pourquoi.

someone *pron & n* = SOMEBODY.

someplace *adv* (US) = SOMEWHERE.

somersault *n* roulade *f*. ● *vi* faire une roulade.

something *pron & n* quelque chose (*m*); **~ good** quelque chose de bon; **~ like** un peu comme.

sometime *adv* un jour; **~ in June** en juin. ● *a* (former) ancien.

sometimes *adv* quelquefois, parfois.

somewhat *adv* quelque peu, un peu.

somewhere *adv* quelque part.

son *n* fils *m*.

song *n* chanson *f*; (of bird) chant *m*.

son-in-law *n* (*pl* **sons-in-law**) gendre *m*.

soon *adv* bientôt; (early) tôt; **I would ~er stay** j'aimerais mieux rester; **~ after** peu après; **~er or later** tôt ou tard.

soot *n* suie *f*.

soothe *vt* calmer.

sophisticated *a* raffiné; (*machine*) sophistiqué.

sopping *a* trempé.

soppy *a* (**-ier, -iest**) 🔲 sentimental.

sorcerer *n* sorcier *m*.

sordid *a* sordide.

sore *a* douloureux; (vexed) en rogne (**at, with** contre). ● *n* plaie *f*.

sorely *adv* fortement.

sorrow *n* chagrin *m*.

sorry *a* (**-ier, -iest**) (regretful) désolé (**to** de; **that** que); (wretched) triste; **feel ~ for** plaindre; **~!** pardon!

sort *n* genre *m*, sorte *f*, espèce *f*; (person 🔲) type *m*; **what ~ of?** quel genre de?; **be out of ~s** ne pas être dans son assiette. ● *vt* **~ (out)** (classify) trier; **~ out** (tidy) ranger; (arrange) arranger; (*problem*) régler.

so-so *a & adv* comme ci comme ça.

sought ⇒SEEK.

soul *n* âme *f*.

sound *n* son *m*, bruit *m*. ● *a* solide; (healthy) sain; (sensible) sensé. ● *vt/i* sonner; (seem) sembler (**as if** que); (test) sonder; **~ out** sonder; **~ a horn** klaxonner; **~ like** sembler être. **~**

S

asleep a profondément endormi. ~ **barrier** n mur m du son.

soundly adv (sleep) à poings fermés; (built) solidement.

sound-proof a insonorisé. ● vt insonoriser.

sound-track n bande f sonore.

soup n soupe f, potage m.

sour a aigre. ● vt/i (s')aigrir.

source n source f.

south n sud m. ● a sud inv, du sud. ● adv vers le sud.

South Africa n Afrique f du Sud.

South America n Amérique f du Sud.

south-east n sud-est m.

southern a du sud. **southerner** n habitant/-e m/f du sud.

southward a (side) sud inv; (journey) vers le sud.

south-west n sud-ouest m.

souvenir n souvenir m.

sovereign n & a souverain/-e (m/f).

sow¹ vt (pt sowed; pp sowed or sown) (seed) semer; (land) ensemencer.

sow² n (pig) truie f.

soya n soja m. ~ **sauce** n sauce f soja.

spa n station f thermale.

space n espace m; (room) place f; (period) période f. ● a (research) spatial. ● vt ~ (out) espacer. ~**craft** n inv, ~**ship** n engin m spatial. ~**suit** n combinaison f spatiale.

spacious a spacieux.

spade n (for garden) bêche f; (child's) pelle f; (cards) pique m. ~**work** n (fig) travail m préparatoire.

spaghetti n spaghetti mpl.

Spain n Espagne f.

spam n (Comput) multipostage m abusif.

span n (of arch) portée f; (of wings) envergure f; (of time) durée f. ● vt (pt spanned) enjamber; (in time) embrasser.

Spaniard n Espagnol/-e m/f.

spaniel n épagneul m.

Spanish a espagnol. ● n espagnol m.

spank vt donner une fessée à.

spanner n (tool) clé f (plate); (adjustable) clé f à molette.

spare vt (treat leniently) épargner; (do without) se passer de; (afford to give) donner, accorder. ● a en réserve; (surplus) de trop; (tyre, shoes) de rechange; (room, bed) d'ami; are there any ~ **tickets?** y a-t-il encore des places? ● n ~ (part) pièce f de rechange. ~ **time** n loisirs mpl.

sparing a frugal. **sparingly** adv en petite quantité.

spark n étincelle f. ● vt ~ **off** (initiate) provoquer.

sparkle vi étinceler. ● n étincellement m. **sparkling** a (wine) mousseux; (eyes) brillant.

spark-plug n bougie f.

sparrow n moineau m.

sparse a clairsemé. **sparsely** adv (furnished) peu.

spasm n (of muscle) spasme m; (of coughing, anger) accès m.

spat ⇒SPIT.

spate n a ~ **of** (letters) une avalanche de.

spatter vt éclabousser (with de).

spawn n frai m, œufs mpl. ● vt pondre. ● vi frayer.

speak vi (pt spoke; pp spoken) parler. ● vt (say) dire; (language) parler. ▢ ~ **up** parler plus fort.

speaker n (in public) orateur m; (Pol) président m; (loudspeaker) baffle m; be a French/a good ~ parler français/bien.

spear n lance f.

spearmint n menthe f verte.

special *a* spécial; (exceptional) exceptionnel.

specialist *n* spécialiste *mf*.

speciality, (US) **specialty** *n* spécialité *f*.

specialize *vi* se spécialiser (**in** en).

specially *adv* spécialement.

species *n inv* espèce *f*.

specific *a* précis, explicite.

specification *n* (of design) spécification *f*; (of car equipment) caractéristiques *fpl*. **specify** *vt* spécifier.

specimen *n* spécimen *m*, échantillon *m*.

speck *n* (stain) (petite) tache *f*; (particle) grain *m*.

specs *npl* 🄴 lunettes *fpl*.

spectacle *n* spectacle *m*. **spectacles** *n* lunettes *fpl*.

spectacular *a* spectaculaire.

spectator *n* spectateur/-trice *m/f*.

spectrum *n* (*pl* **-tra**) spectre *m*; (of ideas) gamme *f*.

speculate *vi* s'interroger (**about** sur); (Comm) spéculer. **speculation** *n* conjectures *fpl*; (Comm) spéculation *f*. **speculator** *n* spéculateur/-trice *m/f*.

speech *n* (faculty) parole *f*; (diction) élocution *f*; (dialect) langage *m*; (address) discours *m*. **speechless** *a* muet (**with** de).

speed *n* (of movement) vitesse *f*; (swiftness) rapidité *f*. ● *vi* (*pt* **sped**) aller vite; (*pt* **speeded**) (drive too fast) aller trop vite. □ ~ **up** accélérer; (of pace) s'accélérer.

speedboat *n* vedette *f*.

speeding *n* excès *m* de vitesse.

speed limit *n* limitation *f* de vitesse.

speedometer *n* compteur *m* (de vitesse).

spell *n* (magic) charme *m*, sortilège *m*; (curse) sort *m*; (of time) (course) période *f*. ● *vt/i* (*pt* **spelled** or **spelt**) écrire; (mean) signifier; ~ **out** épeler; (explain) expliquer. ~**checker** *n* correcteur *m* orthographique.

spelling *n* orthographe *f*. ● *a* (mistake) d'orthographe.

spend *vt* (*pt* **spent**) (money) dépenser (**on** pour); (time, holiday) passer; (energy) consacrer (**on** à). ● *vi* dépenser.

spent ⇒SPEND. ● *a* (used) utilisé; (person) épuisé.

sperm *n* (*pl* **sperms** or **sperm**) sperme *m*.

sphere *n* sphère *f*.

spice *n* épice *f*; (fig) piquant *m*.

spick-and-span *a* impeccable.

spicy *a* épicé; piquant.

spider *n* araignée *f*.

spike *n* pointe *f*.

spill *vt* (*pt* **spilled** or **spilt**) renverser, répandre. ● *vi* se répandre; ~ **over** déborder.

spin *vt/i* (*pt* **spun**; *pres p* **spinning**) (wool, web) filer; (turn) (faire) tourner; (story) débiter; ~ **out** faire durer. ● *n* (movement, excursion) tour *m*.

spinach *n* épinards *mpl*.

spinal *a* vertébral. ~ **cord** *n* moelle *f* épinière.

spin-drier *n* essoreuse *f*.

spine *n* colonne *f* vertébrale; (prickle) piquant *m*.

spin-off *n* avantage *m* accessoire; (by-product) dérivé *m*.

spinster *n* célibataire *f*; (pej) vieille fille *f*.

spiral *a* en spirale; (staircase) en colimaçon. ● *n* spirale *f*. ● *vi* (*pt* **spiralled**) (prices) monter (en flèche).

spire *n* flèche *f*.

spirit *n* esprit *m*; (boldness) courage *m*; ~**s** (morale) moral *m*;

(drink) spiritueux *mpl*. ● *vt* ~ **away**
faire disparaître. **spirited** *a*
fougueux. ~-**level** *n* niveau *m* à
bulle.

spiritual *a* spirituel.

spit *vt/i* (*pt* **spat** *or* **spit**; *pres p*
spitting) cracher; (of rain)
crachiner; ~ **out** cracher; **the**
~**ting image of** le portrait craché
or vivant de. ● *n* crachat(s) *m(pl)*;
(for meat) broche *f*.

spite *n* rancune *f*; **in** ~ **of** malgré.
● *vt* contrarier.

splash *vt* éclabousser. ● *vi* faire
des éclaboussures; ~ (**about**)
patauger. ● *n* (act, mark)
éclaboussure *f*; (sound) plouf *m*; (of
colour) tache *f*.

spleen *n* (Anat) rate *f*.

splendid *a* magnifique,
splendide.

splint *n* (Med) attelle *f*.

splinter *n* éclat *m*; (in finger)
écharde *f*. ~ **group** *n* groupe *m*
dissident.

split *vt/i* (*pt* **split**; *pres p*
splitting) (se) fendre; (tear) (se)
déchirer; (divide) (se) diviser;
(share) partager; ~ **one's sides** se
tordre (de rire). ● *n* fente *f*;
déchirure *f*; (share 🄸) part *f*,
partage *m*; (quarrel) rupture *f*; (Pol)
scission *f*. □ ~ **up** (*couple*)
rompre. ~ **second** *n* fraction *f*
de seconde.

splutter *vi* crachoter; (stammer)
bafouiller; (*engine*) tousser.

spoil *vt* (*pt* **spoilt** *or* **spoiled**)
(pamper) gâter; (ruin) abîmer; (mar)
gâcher, gâter. ● *n* ~(**s**) butin *m*.
~-**sport** *n* trouble-fête *mf inv*.

spoke[1] *n* rayon *m*.

spoke[2], **spoken** ⇒SPEAK.

spokesman *n* (*pl* **-men**) porte-
parole *m inv*.

sponge *n* éponge *f*. ● *vt* éponger.
● *vi* ~ **on** vivre aux crochets de.

~-**bag** *n* trousse *f* de toilette.
~-**cake** *n* génoise *f*.

sponsor *n* (of concert) parrain *m*,
sponsor *m*; (surety) garant *m*; (for
membership) parrain *m*, marraine *f*.
● *vt* parrainer, sponsoriser;
(*member*) parrainer.

sponsorship *n* patronage *m*;
parrainage *m*.

spontaneous *a* spontané.

spoof *n* 🄸 parodie *f*.

spoon *n* cuiller *f*, cuillère *f*.

spoonful *n* (*pl* ~**s**) cuillerée *f*.

sport *n* sport *m*; (**good**) ~ (person
🄸) chic type *m*; ~**s car/coat**
voiture/veste *f* de sport. ● *vt*
(display) exhiber, arborer.

sporting *a* sportif; **a** ~ **chance**
une assez bonne chance.

sportsman *n* (*pl* **-men**) sportif
m.

sporty *a* 🄸 sportif.

spot *n* (mark, stain) tache *f*; (dot)
point *m*; (in pattern) pois *m*; (drop)
goutte *f*; (place) endroit *m*; (pimple)
bouton *m*; **a** ~ **of** 🄸 un peu de; **on
the** ~ sur place; (without delay) sur
le coup. ● *vt* (*pt* **spotted**)
🄸 apercevoir. ~-**check** *n*
contrôle *m* surprise.

spotless *a* impeccable.

spotlight *n* (lamp) projecteur *m*,
spot *m*.

spotty *a* (skin) boutonneux.

spouse *n* époux *m*, épouse *f*.

spout *n* (of teapot) bec *m*; (of liquid)
jet *m*; **up the** ~ (ruined 🄸) fichu.
● *vi* jaillir.

sprain *n* entorse *f*, foulure *f*. ● *vt*
~ **one's wrist** se fouler le poignet.

sprang ⇒SPRING.

sprawl *vi* (*town, person*) s'étaler.
● *n* étalement *m*.

spray *n* (of flowers) gerbe *f*; (water)
gerbe *f* d'eau; (from sea) embruns
mpl; (device) bombe *f*, atomiseur
m. ● *vt* (*surface, insecticide, plant*)

vaporiser; (*person*) asperger; (*crops*) traiter.

spread *vt/i* (*pt* spread) (stretch, extend) (s')étendre; (*news, fear*) (se) répandre; (*illness*) (se) propager; (*butter*) (s')étaler. ● *n* propagation *f*; (of population) distribution *f*; (paste) pâte *f* à tartiner; (food) belle table *f*. **∼-eagled** *a* bras et jambes écartés. **∼sheet** *n* tableur *m*.

spree *n* go on a ∼ (have fun 🄳) faire la noce.

sprig *n* petite branche *f*.

sprightly *a* (-ier, -iest) alerte, vif.

spring *vi* (*pt* sprang; *pp* sprung) bondir. ● *vt* ∼ sth on sb annoncer qch de but en blanc à qn. ● *n* bond *m*; (device) ressort *m*; (season) printemps *m*; (of water) source *f*. □ ∼ from provenir de; ∼ up surgir. **∼board** *n* tremplin *m*. **∼ onion** *n* oignon *m* blanc.

springy *a* (-ier, -iest) élastique.

sprinkle *vt* (with liquid) arroser (**with** de); (with salt, flour) saupoudrer (**with** de); (*sand*) répandre. **sprinkler** *n* (in garden) arroseur *m*; (for fires) extincteur *m* (à déclenchement) automatique.

sprint *vi* (Sport) sprinter. ● *n* sprint *m*.

sprout *vt/i* pousser. ● *n* (on plant) pousse *f*; (**Brussels**) **∼s** choux *mpl* de Bruxelles.

spruce *a* pimpant. ● *vt* ∼ oneself up se faire beau. ● *n* (tree) épicéa *m*.

sprung ⇒SPRING.

spud *n* 🄳 patate *f*.

spun ⇒SPIN.

spur *n* (of rider) éperon *m*; (stimulus) aiguillon *m*; **on the ∼ of the moment** sous l'impulsion du moment. ● *vt* (*pt* spurred) éperonner.

spurious *a* faux.

spurn *vt* repousser.

spurt *vi* jaillir; (fig) accélérer. ● *n* jet *m*; (of energy) sursaut *m*.

spy *n* espion/-ne *m/f*. ● *vi* espionner. ● *vt* apercevoir.

squabble *vi* se chamailler. ● *n* chamaillerie *f*.

squad *n* (of soldiers) escouade *f*; (Sport) équipe *f*.

squadron *n* (Mil) escadron *m*; (Aviat) escadrille *f*.

squalid *a* sordide.

squander *vt* (*money, time*) gaspiller.

square *n* carré *m*; (open space in town) place *f*. ● *a* carré; (honest) honnête; (*meal*) solide; (boring 🄳) ringard; (all) (quits) quitte; ∼ **metre** mètre *m* carré. ● *vt* (settle) régler; ∼ up to faire face à.

squash *vt* écraser; (crowd) serrer. ● *n* (game) squash *m*; (marrow: US) courge *f*; **lemon** ∼ citronnade *f*; **orange** ∼ orangeade *f*.

squat *vi* (*pt* squatted) s'accroupir; ∼ **in a house** squatteriser une maison. ● *a* (dumpy) trapu. **squatter** *n* squatter *m*.

squawk *n* cri *m* rauque. ● *vi* pousser un cri rauque.

squeak *n* petit cri *m*; (of door) grincement *m*. ● *vi* crier; grincer.

squeal *n* cri *m* aigu. ● *vi* pousser un cri aigu; ∼ **on** (inform on 🄳) dénoncer.

squeamish *a* (trop) délicat.

squeeze *vt* presser; (*hand, arm*) serrer; (extract) exprimer (**from** de); (extort) soutirer (**from** à). ● *vi* (force one's way) se glisser. ● *n* pression *f*; (Comm) restrictions *fpl* de crédit.

squid *n* calmar *m*.

squint *vi* loucher; (with half-shut eyes) plisser les yeux. ● *n* (Med) strabisme *m*.

squirm *vi* se tortiller.

squirrel *n* écureuil *m*.

S

squirt vt/i (faire) jaillir. ● n jet m.

stab vt (pt **stabbed**) (with knife) poignarder. ● n coup m (de couteau); **have a ~ at sth** essayer de faire qch.

stability n stabilité f. **stabilize** vt stabiliser.

stable a stable. ● n écurie f. **~-boy** n lad m.

stack n tas m. ● vt ~ (**up**) entasser, empiler.

stadium n stade m.

staff n personnel m; (in school) professeurs mpl; (Mil) état-major m; (stick) bâton m. ● vt pourvoir en personnel.

stag n cerf m.

stage n (Theat) scène f; (phase) stade m, étape f; (platform in hall) estrade f; **go on the ~** faire du théâtre. ● vt mettre en scène; (fig) organiser. ~ **door** n entrée f des artistes. ~ **fright** n trac m.

stagger vi chanceler. ● vt (shock) stupéfier; (payments) échelonner. **staggering** a stupéfiant.

stagnate vi stagner.

stag night n soirée f pour enterrer une vie de garçon.

staid a sérieux.

stain vt tacher; (wood) colorer. ● n tache f; (colouring) colorant m. **stained glass window** n vitrail m.

stainless steel n acier m inoxydable.

stain remover n détachant m.

stair n marche f; **the ~s** l'escalier m. ~**case**, ~**way** n escalier m.

stake n (post) pieu m; (wager) enjeu m; **at ~** en jeu. ● vt (area) jalonner; (wager) jouer; ~ **a claim to** revendiquer.

stale a pas frais; (bread) rassis; (smell) de renfermé.

stalk n (of plant) tige f. ● vi marcher de façon guindée. ● vt

(hunter) chasser; (murderer) suivre.

stall n (in stable) stalle f; (in market) éventaire m; ~**s** (Theat) orchestre m. ● vt/i (Auto) caler; ~ (**for time**) temporiser.

stallion n étalon m.

stamina n résistance f.

stammer vt/i bégayer. ● n bégaiement m.

stamp vt/i ~ (**one's foot**) taper du pied. ● vt (letter) timbrer. ● n (for postage, marking) timbre m; (mark: fig) sceau m. □ ~ **out** supprimer. ~**-collecting** n philatélie f.

stampede n fuite f désordonnée; (rush: fig) ruée f. ● vi s'enfuir en désordre; se ruer.

stand vi (pt **stood**) être or se tenir (debout); (rise) se lever; (be situated) se trouver; (Pol) être candidat (**for** à); ~ **in line** (US) faire la queue; ~ **to reason** être logique. ● vt mettre (debout); (tolerate) supporter; ~ **a chance** avoir une chance. ● n (stance) position f; (Mil) résistance f; (for lamp) support m; (at fair) stand m; (in street) kiosque m; (for spectators) tribune f; (Jur, US) barre f; **make a ~** prendre position. □ ~ **back** reculer; ~ **by** or **around** ne rien faire; ~ **by** (be ready) se tenir prêt; (promise, person) rester fidèle à; ~ **down** se désister; ~ **for** représenter; Ⓔ supporter; ~ **in for** remplacer; ~ **out** ressortir; ~ **up** se lever; ~ **up for** défendre; ~ **up to** résister à.

standard n norme f; (level) niveau m (voulu); (flag) étendard m; ~ **of living** niveau m de vie; ~**s** (morals) principes mpl. ● a ordinaire.

standard of living n niveau m de vie.

stand-by a de réserve. ● n **be a ~** être de réserve.

stand-in n remplaçant/-e m/f.

standing *a* debout *inv.* ● *n* réputation *f*; (duration) durée *f*. **~ order** *n* prélèvement *m* bancaire.

standpoint *n* point *m* de vue.

standstill *n* **at a ~** immobile; **bring/come to a ~** (s')immobiliser.

stank ⇒STINK.

staple *n* agrafe *f*. ● *vt* agrafer. ● *a* principal, de base. **stapler** *n* agrafeuse *f*.

star *n* étoile *f*; (person) vedette *f*. ● *vt* (*pt* **starred**) (*film*) avoir pour vedette. ● *vi* **~ in** être la vedette de.

starch *n* amidon *m*; (in food) fécule *f*. ● *vt* amidonner.

stardom *n* célébrité *f*.

stare *vi* **~ at** regarder fixement. ● *n* regard *m* fixe.

starfish *n* étoile *f* de mer.

stark *a* (desolate) désolé; (severe) austère; (utter) complet; (*fact*) brutal. ● *adv* complètement.

starling *n* étourneau *m*.

start *vt/i* commencer; (*machine*) (se) mettre en marche; (*fashion*) lancer; (cause) provoquer; (jump) sursauter; (of vehicle) démarrer; **~ to do** commencer *or* se mettre à faire; **~ing tomorrow** à partir de demain. ● *n* commencement *m*, début *m*; (of race) départ *m*; (lead) avance *f*; (jump) sursaut *m*. □ **~ off** commencer (**doing** par faire); **~ out** partir; **~ up** (*business*) lancer. **starter** *n* (Auto) démarreur *m*; (runner) partant *m*; (Culin) entrée *f*.

starting point *n* point *m* de départ.

startle *vt* (make jump) faire tressaillir; (shock) alarmer.

starvation *n* faim *f*.

starve *vi* mourir de faim. ● *vt* affamer; (deprive) priver.

stash *vt* cacher.

state *n* état *m*; (pomp) apparat *m*; **S~** État *m*; **the S~s** les États-Unis; **get into a ~** s'affoler. ● *a* d'État, de l'État; (school) public. ● *vt* affirmer (**that** que); (*views*) exprimer; (fix) fixer.

stately *a* (**-ier, -iest**) majestueux. **~ home** *n* château *m*.

statement *n* déclaration *f*; (of account) relevé *m*.

statesman *n* (*pl* **-men**) homme *m* d'État.

static *a* statique. ● *n* (radio, TV) parasites *mpl*.

station *n* (Rail) gare *f*; (TV) chaîne *f*; (Mil) poste *m*; (rank) condition *f*. ● *vt* poster, placer; **~ed at** *or* **in** (Mil) en garnison à.

stationary *a* immobile, stationnaire; (*vehicle*) à l'arrêt.

stationery *n* papeterie *f*.

station wagon *n* (US) break *m*.

statistic *n* statistique *f*; **~s** statistique *f*.

statue *n* statue *f*.

status *n* (*pl* **~es**) situation *f*, statut *m*; (prestige) standing *m*.

statute *n* loi *f*; **~s** (rules) statuts *mpl*. **statutory** *a* statutaire; (holiday) légal.

staunch *a* (*friend*) loyal, fidèle.

stave *n* (Mus) portée *f*. ● *vt* **~ off** éviter, conjurer.

stay *vi* rester; (spend time) séjourner; (reside) loger. ● *vt* (*hunger*) tromper. ● *n* séjour *m*. □ **~ away from** (school) ne pas aller à; **~ behind** *or* **~ on** rester; **~ in** rester à la maison; **~ up** veiller, se coucher tard.

stead *n* **stand sb in good ~** être utile à qn.

steadfast *a* ferme.

steady *a* (**-ier, -iest**) stable; (*hand, voice*) ferme; (regular) régulier; (staid) sérieux. ● *vt* maintenir, assurer; (calm) calmer.

steak *n* steak *m*, bifteck *m*; (of fish) darne *f*.

S

steal vt/i (pt **stole**; pp **stolen**)
voler (**from sb** à qn).

steam n vapeur f; (on glass) buée
f. ● vt (cook) cuire à la vapeur.
● vi fumer. ~**-engine** n
locomotive f à vapeur

steamer n (Culin) cuit-vapeur m;
(boat) (bateau à) vapeur f.

steel n acier m; ~ **industry**
sidérurgie f. ● vpr ~ **oneself**
s'endurcir, se cuirasser.

steep a raide, rapide; (price: ▯)
excessif. ● vt (soak) tremper; ~**ed**
in (fig) imprégné de.

steeple n clocher m.

steer vt diriger; (ship) gouverner;
(fig) guider. ● vi (in ship)
gouverner; ~ **clear of** éviter.

steering-wheel n volant m.

stem n tige f; (of glass) pied m.
● vi (pt **stemmed**) ~ **from**
provenir de. ● vt (pt **stemmed**)
(check, stop) endiguer, contenir. ~
cell n cellule f souche.

stench n puanteur f.

stencil n pochoir m. ● vt (pt
stencilled) décorer au pochoir.

step vi (pt **stepped**) marcher,
aller. ● n pas m; (stair) marche f;
(of train) marchepied m; (action)
mesure f; ~**s** (ladder) escabeau m;
in ~ au pas; (fig) conforme (**with**
à). □ ~ **down** (resign)
démissionner; (from ladder)
descendre; ~ **forward** faire un
pas en avant; ~ **in** (intervene)
intervenir; ~ **up** (pressure)
augmenter. ~**brother** n demi-
frère m. ~**daughter** n belle-fille
f. ~**father** n beau-père m.
~**-ladder** n escabeau m.
~**mother** n belle-mère f.
stepping-stone n (fig) tremplin
m. ~**sister** n demi-sœur f. ~**son**
n beau-fils m.

stereo n stéréo f; (record-player)
chaîne f stéréo. ● a stéréo inv.

stereotype n stéréotype m.

sterile a stérile. **sterility** n
stérilité f.

sterilize vt stériliser.

sterling n livre(s) f(pl) sterling.
● a sterling inv; (silver) fin; (fig)
excellent.

stern a sévère. ● n (of ship) arrière
m.

steroid n stéroïde m.

stew vt/i cuire à la casserole;
~**ed** fruit compote f; ~**ed tea** thé
m trop infusé. ● n ragoût m.

steward n (of club) intendant m;
(on ship) steward m. **stewardess**
n hôtesse f.

stick vt (pt **stuck**) (glue) coller;
(put ▯) mettre; (endure ▯)
supporter. ● vi (adhere) coller,
adhérer; (to pan) attacher; (remain
▯) rester; (be jammed) être coincé;
be stuck with sb ▯ se farcir qn.
● n bâton m; (for walking) canne f.
□ ~ **at** persévérer dans; ~ **out** vt
(head) sortir; (tongue) tirer; vi
(protrude) dépasser; ~ **to**
(promise) rester fidèle à; ~ **up**
for ▯ défendre.

sticker n autocollant m.

sticky a (-ier, -iest) poisseux;
(label, tape) adhésif.

stiff a raide; (limb, joint)
ankylosé; (tough) dur; (drink) fort;
(price) élevé; (manner) guindé; ~
neck torticolis m.

stifle vt/i étouffer.

stiletto a & n ~**s**, ~ **heels** talons
mpl aiguille.

still a immobile; (quiet) calme,
tranquille; **keep** ~! arrête de
bouger! ● n silence m. ● adv
encore, toujours; (even) encore;
(nevertheless) tout de même.

stillborn a mort-né.

still life n nature f morte.

stimulate vt stimuler.

stimulation n stimulation f.

stimulus n (pl **-li**) (spur) stimulant
m.

sting n piqûre f; (of insect) aiguillon m. ● vt/i (pt **stung**) piquer.

stingy a (**-ier**, **-iest**) avare (**with** de).

stink n puanteur f. ● vi (pt **stank** or **stunk**; pp **stunk**) ~ (**of**) puer.

stipulate vt stipuler.

stir vt/i (pt **stirred**) (move) remuer; (excite) exciter; ~ **up** (trouble) provoquer. ● n agitation f.

stirrup n étrier m.

stitch n point m; (in knitting) maille f; (Med) point m de suture; (muscle pain) point m de côté; **be in ~es** Ⓣ avoir le fou rire. ● vt coudre.

stock n réserve f; (Comm) stock m; (financial) valeurs fpl; (family) souche f; (soup) bouillon m; **we're out of ~** il n'y en a plus; **take ~** (fig) faire le point; **in ~** en stock. ● a (goods) courant. ● vt (shop) approvisionner; (sell) vendre. ● vi ~ **up** s'approvisionner (**with** de). ~ **broker** n agent m de change. ~ **cube** n bouillon-cube m. **S~ Exchange** n Bourse f.

stocking n bas m.

stock market n Bourse f.

stockpile n stock m. ● vt stocker; (arms) amasser.

stock-taking n (Comm) inventaire m.

stocky a (**-ier**, **-iest**) trapu.

stodgy a lourd.

stole, **stolen** ⇒STEAL.

stomach n estomac m; (abdomen) ventre m. ● vt (put up with) supporter. ~**-ache** n mal m à l'estomac or au ventre.

stone n pierre f; (pebble) caillou m; (in fruit) noyau m; (weight) 6,350 kg. ● a de pierre; ~**-cold/-deaf** complètement froid/sourd. ● vt (throw stones) lapider; (fruit) dénoyauter.

stony a pierreux.

stood ⇒STAND.

stool n tabouret m.

stoop vi (bend) se baisser; (condescend) s'abaisser. ● n **have a ~** être voûté.

stop vt/i (pt **stopped**) arrêter (**doing** de faire); (moving, talking) s'arrêter; (prevent) empêcher (**from** de); (hole, leak) boucher; (pain, noise) cesser; (stay Ⓣ) rester. ● n arrêt m; (full stop) point m; ~**(-over)** halte f; (port of call) escale f. □ ~ **off** s'arrêter; ~ **up** boucher.

stopgap n bouche-trou m. ● a intérimaire.

stoppage n arrêt m; (of work) arrêt m de travail; (of pay) retenue f.

stopper n bouchon m.

stop-watch n chronomètre m.

storage n (of goods, food) emmagasinage m. ~ **heater** n radiateur m électrique à accumulation.

store n réserve f; (warehouse) entrepôt m; (shop) grand magasin m; (US) magasin m; **have in ~ for** réserver à; **set ~ by** attacher du prix à. ● vt (for future) mettre en réserve; (in warehouse, mind) emmagasiner. ~**-room** n réserve f.

storey n étage m.

stork n cigogne f.

storm n tempête f, orage m. ● vt prendre d'assaut. ● vi (rage) tempêter.

story n histoire f; (in press) article m; (storey: US) étage m. ~**-teller** n conteur/-euse m/f.

stout a corpulent; (strong) solide. ● n bière f brune.

stove n cuisinière f.

stow vt ~ **away** (put away) ranger; (hide) cacher. ● vi voyager clandestinement.

straddle vt être à cheval sur, enjamber.

straggler n traînard/-e m/f.

S

straight a droit; (tidy) en ordre;
(frank) franc; ～ **face** visage m
sérieux; **get sth** ～ mettre qch au
clair. ● adv (in straight line) droit;
(direct) tout droit; ～ **ahead** or **on**
tout droit; ～ **away** tout de suite;
～ **off** ▣ sans hésiter. ● n (Sport)
ligne f droite.

straighten vt (nail, situation)
redresser; (tidy) arranger.

straightforward a honnête;
(easy) simple.

straight off a ▣ sans hésiter.

strain vt (rope, ears) tendre;
(limb) fouler; (eyes) fatiguer;
(muscle) froisser; (filter) passer;
(vegetables) égoutter; (fig) mettre
à l'épreuve. ● vi fournir des
efforts. ● n tension f; (fig) effort
m; (breed) race f; (of virus) variété f;
～**s** (tune: Mus) accents mpl.
strained a forcé; (relations)
tendu. **strainer** n passoire f.

strait n détroit m; ～**s** détroit m;
be in dire ～**s** être aux abois.
～**jacket** n camisole f de force.

strand n (thread) fil m, brin m; (of
hair) mèche f.

stranded a (person) en rade;
(ship) échoué.

strange a étrange; (unknown)
inconnu. **stranger** n inconnu/-e
m/f.

strangle vt étrangler.

stranglehold n **have a** ～ **on** tenir
à la gorge.

strap n (of leather) courroie f; (of
dress) bretelle f; (of watch) bracelet
m. ● vt (pt **strapped**) attacher.

strategic a stratégique. **strategy**
n stratégie f.

straw n paille f; **the last** ～ le
comble.

strawberry n fraise f.

stray vi s'égarer; (deviate)
s'écarter. ● a perdu; (isolated)
isolé. ● n animal m perdu.

streak n raie f, bande f; (trace)

trace f; (period) période f; (tendency)
tendance f. ● vt (mark) strier. ● vi
filer à toute allure.

stream n ruisseau m; (current)
courant m; (flow) flot m; (in school)
classe f (de niveau). ● vi ruisseler
(**with** de); (eyes, nose) couler.

streamline vt rationaliser.
streamlined a (shape)
aérodynamique.

street n rue f. ～**car** n (US)
tramway m. ～ **lamp** n réverbère
m. ～ **map** n indicateur m des
rues.

strength n force f; (of wall, fabric)
solidité f; **on the** ～ **of** en vertu de.
strengthen vt renforcer, fortifier.

strenuous a (exercise)
énergique; (work) ardu.

stress n (emphasis) accent m;
(pressure) pression f; (Med) stress
m. ● vt souligner, insister sur.

stretch vt (pull taut) tendre; (arm,
leg) étendre; (neck) tendre;
(clothes) étirer; (truth) forcer; ～
one's legs se dégourdir les
jambes. ● vi s'étendre; (person)
s'étirer; (clothes) se déformer. ● n
étendue f; (period) période f; (of
road) tronçon m; **at a** ～ d'affilée.
● a (fabric) extensible.

stretcher n brancard m.

strew vt (pt **strewed**; pp
strewed or **strewn**) (scatter)
répandre; (cover) joncher.

strict a strict.

stride vi (pt **strode**; pp **stridden**)
faire de grands pas. ● n grand
pas m.

strife n conflit(s) m(pl).

strike vt (pt **struck**) frapper;
(blow) donner; (match) frotter;
(gold) trouver. ● vi faire grève;
(attack) attaquer; (clock) sonner.
● n (of workers) grève f; (Mil)
attaque f; (find) découverte f; **on** ～
en grève. ▢ ～ **off** or **out** rayer; ～
up (a friendship) lier amitié (**with**

avec). **striker** n gréviste mf; (football) attaquant/-e m/f. **striking** a frappant.

string n ficelle f; (of violin, racket) corde f; (of pearls) collier m; (of lies) chapelet m; **the ~s** (Mus) les cordes; **pull ~s** faire jouer ses relations. ● vt (pt **strung**) (thread) enfiler. **stringed** a (instrument) à cordes.

stringent a rigoureux, strict.

stringy a filandreux.

strip vt/i (pt **stripped**) (undress) (se) déshabiller; (deprive) dépouiller. ● n bande f.

stripe n rayure f, raie f. **striped** a rayé.

strip light n néon m.

stripper n strip-teaseur/-euse m/f; (solvent) décapant.

strip-tease n strip-tease m.

strive vi (pt **strove**, pp **striven**) s'efforcer (**to** de).

strode ⇒STRIDE.

stroke vt (with hand) caresser. ● n coup m; (of pen) trait m; (swimming) nage f; (Med) attaque f, congestion f; **at a ~** d'un seul coup.

stroll vi flâner; **~ in** entrer tranquillement. ● n petit tour m.

stroller n (US) poussette f.

strong a fort; (shoes, fabric) solide; **be fifty ~** être fort de cinquante personnes. **~hold** n bastion m.

strongly adv (greatly) fortement; (with energy) avec force; (deeply) profondément.

strove ⇒STRIVE.

struck ⇒STRIKE.

structure n (of cell, poem) structure f; (building) construction f.

struggle vi lutter, se battre. ● n lutte f; (effort) effort m; **have a ~ to** avoir du mal à.

strum vt (pt **strummed**) gratter de.

strung ⇒STRING. ● a **~ up** (tense) nerveux.

strut n (support) étai m. ● vi (pt **strutted**) se pavaner.

stub n bout m; (counterfoil) talon m. ● vt (pt **stubbed**) **~ one's toe** se cogner le doigt de pied. □ **~ out** écraser.

stubble n (on chin) barbe f de plusieurs jours; (remains of wheat) chaume m.

stubborn a obstiné.

stuck ⇒STICK. ● a (jammed) coincé; **I'm ~** (for answer) je sèche. **~-up** a 🄳 prétentieux.

stud n (on jacket) clou m; (for collar) bouton m; (stallion) étalon m; (horse farm) haras m. ● vt (pt **studded**) clouter.

student n (Univ) étudiant/-e m/f; (School) élève mf. ● a (restaurant, life) universitaire.

studio n studio m.

studious a (person) studieux; (deliberate) étudié.

study n étude f; (office) bureau m. ● vt/i étudier.

stuff n substance f; 🄳 chose(s) f(pl). ● vt rembourrer; (animal) empailler; (cram) bourrer; (Culin) farcir; (block up) boucher; (put) fourrer. **stuffing** n bourre f; (Culin) farce f.

stuffy a (-ier, -iest) mal aéré; (dull 🄳) vieux jeu inv.

stumble vi trébucher; **~ across** or **on** tomber sur. **stumbling-block** n obstacle m.

stump n (of tree) souche f; (of limb) moignon m; (of pencil) bout m.

stumped a embarrassé.

stun vt (pt **stunned**) étourdir; (bewilder) stupéfier.

stung ⇒STING.

stunk ⇒STINK.

stunning a (delightful 🄳) sensationnel.

S

stunt vt (*growth*) retarder. ● n
(feat 🆃) tour m de force; (trick 🆃)
truc m; (dangerous) cascade f.

stupid a stupide, bête. **stupidity**
n stupidité f.

sturdy a (**-ier, -iest**) robuste.

stutter vi bégayer. ● n
bégaiement m.

sty n (pigsty) porcherie f; (on eye)
orgelet m.

style n style m; (fashion) mode f;
(sort) genre m; (pattern) modèle m;
do sth in ∼ faire qch avec classe.
● vt (design) créer; ∼ **sb's hair**
coiffer qn.

stylish a élégant.

stylist n (of hair) coiffeur/-euse m/
f.

suave a (urbane) courtois; (smooth:
pej) doucereux.

subconscious a & n inconscient
(m), subconscient (m).

subcontract vt sous-traiter.

subdue vt (*feeling*) maîtriser;
(country) subjuguer. **subdued** a
(person, mood) morose; (light)
tamisé; (criticism) contenu.

subject[1] a (state) soumis; ∼ **to**
soumis à; (liable to, dependent on)
sujet à. ● n sujet m; (focus) objet
m; (School, Univ) matière f; (citizen)
ressortissant/-e m/f, sujet/-te m/
f.

subject[2] vt soumettre.

subjective a subjectif.

subject-matter n contenu m.

subjunctive a & n subjonctif (m).

sublet vt sous-louer.

submarine n sousmarin m.

submerge vt submerger. ● vi
plonger.

submissive a soumis.

submit vt/i (pt **submitted**) (se)
soumettre (**to** à).

subordinate a subalterne; (Gram)
subordonné. ● n subordonné/-e
m/f.

subpoena n (Jur) citation f,
assignation f.

subscribe vt/i verser (de
l'argent) (**to** à); ∼ **to** (loan, theory)
souscrire à; (newspaper)
s'abonner à, être abonné à.

subscriber n abonné/-e m/f.

subscription n abonnement m;
(membership dues) cotisation f.

subsequent a (later) ultérieur;
(next) suivant. **subsequently** adv
par la suite.

subside vi (land) s'affaisser;
(flood, wind) baisser.

subsidiary a accessoire. ● n
(Comm) filiale f.

subsidize vt subventionner.
subsidy n subvention f.

substance n substance f.

substandard a de qualité
inférieure.

substantial a considérable;
(meal) substantiel.

substitute n succédané m;
(person) remplaçant/-e m/f. ● vt
substituer (**for** à).

subtitle n sous-titre m.

subtle a subtil.

subtract vt soustraire.

suburb n faubourg m, banlieue f;
∼**s** banlieue f. **suburban** a de
banlieue. **suburbia** n la banlieue.

subway n passage m souterrain;
(US) métro m.

succeed vi réussir (**in doing** à
faire). ● vt (follow) succéder à.

success n succès m, réussite f.

successful a réussi, couronné
de succès; (favourable) heureux; (in
exam) reçu; **be** ∼ **in doing** réussir à
faire.

succession n succession f; **in** ∼
de suite.

successive a successif; **six** ∼
days six jours consécutifs.

successor n successeur m.

such det & pron tel(le), tel(le)s;

(so much) tant (de). ● *adv* si; ~ **a book** un tel livre; ~ **books** de tels livres; ~ **courage** tant de courage; ~ **a big house** une si grande maison; ~ **as** comme, tel que; **as ~ en** tant que tel; **there's no ~ thing** ça n'existe pas. **~-and-~** *a* tel ou tel.

suck *vt* sucer. □ ~ **in** *or* **up** aspirer. **sucker** *n* (rubber pad) ventouse *f*; (person 🏴) dupe *f*.

suction *n* succion *f*.

sudden *a* soudain, subit; **all of a ~** tout à coup. **suddenly** *adv* subitement, brusquement.

sue *vt* (*pres p* **suing**) poursuivre (en justice).

suede *n* daim *m*.

suffer *vt/i* souffrir; (loss, attack) subir. **sufferer** *n* victime *f*, malade *mf*. **suffering** *n* souffrance(s) *f(pl)*.

sufficient *a* (enough) suffisamment de; (big enough) suffisant.

suffix *n* suffixe *m*.

suffocate *vt/i* suffoquer.

sugar *n* sucre *m*. ● *vt* sucrer.

suggest *vt* suggérer. **suggestion** *n* suggestion *f*.

suicidal *a* suicidaire.

suicide *n* suicide *m*; **commit ~** se suicider.

suit *n* (man's) costume *m*; (woman's) tailleur *m*; (cards) couleur *f*. ● *vt* convenir à; (garment, style) aller à; (adapt) adapter.

suitable *a* qui convient (for à), convenable. **suitably** *adv* convenablement.

suitcase *n* valise *f*.

suite *n* (rooms) suite *f*; (furniture) mobilier *m*.

suited *a* (well) ~ (matched) bien assorti; ~ **to** fait pour, apte à.

sulk *vi* bouder.

sullen *a* maussade.

sultana *n* raisin *m* de Smyrne, raisin *m* sec.

sultry *a* (-ier, -iest) étouffant, lourd; (fig) sensuel.

sum *n* somme *f*; (in arithmetic) calcul *m*. ● *vt/i* (*pt* **summed**) ~ **up** résumer, récapituler; (assess) évaluer.

summarize *vt* résumer.

summary *n* résumé *m*. ● *a* sommaire.

summer *n* été *m*. ● *a* d'été. **~time** *n* (season) été *m*.

summery *a* estival.

summit *n* sommet *m*; ~ (**conference**) (Pol) (conférence *f* au) sommet *m*.

summon *vt* appeler; ~ **sb to a meeting** convoquer qn à une réunion; ~ **up** (strength, courage) rassembler.

summons *n* (Jur) assignation *f*. ● *vt* assigner.

sun *n* soleil *m*. ● *vt* (*pt* **sunned**) ~ **oneself** se chauffer au soleil. **~burn** *n* coup *m* de soleil.

Sunday *n* dimanche *m*. ~ **school** *n* catéchisme *m*.

sundry *a* divers; **sundries** articles *mpl* divers; **all and ~** tout le monde.

sunflower *n* tournesol *m*.

sung ⇒SING.

sun-glasses *npl* lunettes *fpl* de soleil.

sunk ⇒SINK.

sunken *a* (ship) submergé; (eyes) creux.

sunlight *n* soleil *m*.

sunny *a* (-ier, -iest) ensoleillé.

sun: ~**rise** *n* lever *m* du soleil. ~**roof** *n* toit *m* ouvrant. ~ **screen** *n* filtre *m* solaire. ~**set** *n* coucher *m* du soleil. ~**shine** *n* soleil *m*. ~**stroke** *n* insolation *f*.

sun-tan *n* bronzage *m*. ~ **lotion**

S

n lotion *f* solaire. ∼ **oil** *n* huile *f* solaire.

super *a* ⊞ formidable.

superb *a* superbe.

superficial *a* superficiel.

superfluous *a* superflu.

superimpose *vt* superposer (on à).

superintendent *n* directeur/ -trice *m/f*; (of police) commissaire *m*.

superior *a & n* supérieur/-e (*m/ f*).

superlative *a* suprême. ● *n* (Gram) superlatif *m*.

supermarket *n* supermarché *m*.

supersede *vt* remplacer, supplanter.

superstition *n* superstition *f*. **superstitious** *a* superstitieux.

superstore *n* hypermarché *m*.

supervise *vt* surveiller, diriger. **supervision** *n* surveillance *f*. **supervisor** *n* surveillant/-e *m/f*; (shop) chef *m* de rayon; (firm) chef *m* de service.

supper *n* dîner *m*; (late at night) souper *m*.

supple *a* souple.

supplement[1] *n* supplément *m*. **supplementary** *a* supplémentaire.

supplement[2] *vt* compléter.

supplier *n* fournisseur *m*.

supply *vt* fournir; (equip) pourvoir; (feed) alimenter (with en). ● *n* provision *f*; (of gas) alimentation *f*; **supplies** (food) vivres *mpl*; (material) fournitures *fpl*.

support *vt* soutenir; (*family*) assurer la subsistance de. ● *n* soutien *m*, appui *m*; (Tech) support *m*. **supporter** *n* partisan/ -e *m/f*; (Sport) supporter *m*. **supportive** *a* qui soutient et encourage.

suppose *vt/i* supposer; **be** ∼**d to**

do être censé faire, devoir faire; **supposing he comes** supposons qu'il vienne. **supposedly** *adv* soi-disant, prétendument.

suppress *vt* (put an end to) supprimer; (restrain) réprimer; (stifle) étouffer.

supreme *a* suprême.

surcharge *n* supplément *m*; (tax) surtaxe *f*.

sure *a* sûr; **make** ∼ **of** s'assurer de; **make** ∼ **that** vérifier que. ● *adv* (US ⊞) pour sûr. **surely** *adv* sûrement.

surf *n* ressac *m*. ● *vi* faire du surf; (*Internet*) surfer.

surface *n* surface *f*. ● *a* superficiel. ● *vt* revêtir. ● *vi* faire surface; (fig) réapparaître.

surfer *n* surfeur/-euse *m/f*; (*Internet*) internaute *mf*.

surge *vi* (*waves, crowd*) déferler; (increase) monter. ● *n* (wave) vague *f*; (rise) montée *f*.

surgeon *n* chirurgien *m*.

surgery *n* chirurgie *f*; (office) cabinet *m*; (session) consultation *f*; **need** ∼ devoir être opéré.

surgical *a* chirurgical. ∼ **spirit** *n* alcool *m* à 90 degrés.

surly *a* (**-ier**, **-iest**) bourru.

surname *n* nom *m* de famille.

surplus *n* surplus *m*. ● *a* en surplus.

surprise *n* surprise *f*. ● *vt* surprendre. **surprised** *a* surpris (at de). **surprising** *a* surprenant.

surrender *vi* se rendre. ● *vt* (hand over) remettre; (Mil) rendre. ● *n* (Mil) reddition *f*; (of passport) remise *f*.

surround *vt* entourer; (Mil) encercler. **surrounding** *a* environnant. **surroundings** *npl* environs *mpl*; (setting) cadre *m*.

surveillance *n* surveillance *f*.

survey[1] *vt* (review) passer en

revue; (inquire into) enquêter sur; (*building*) inspecter.

survey² *n* (inquiry) enquête *f*; inspection *f*; (general view) vue *f* d'ensemble.

surveyor *n* expert *m* (géomètre).

survival *n* survie *f*.

survive *vt/i* survivre (à). **survivor** *n* survivant/-e *m/f*.

susceptible *a* sensible (**to** à); ~ **to** (prone to) prédisposé à.

suspect¹ *vt* soupçonner; (doubt) douter de.

suspect² *n & a* suspect/-e (*m/f*).

suspend *vt* (hang, stop) suspendre; (*licence*) retirer provisoirement.

suspended sentence *n* condamnation *f* avec sursis.

suspender *n* jarretelle *f*; ~**s** (braces: US) bretelles *fpl*. ~ **belt** *n* porte-jarretelles *m*.

suspension *n* suspension *f*; retrait *m* provisoire.

suspicion *n* soupçon *m*; (distrust) méfiance *f*.

suspicious *a* soupçonneux; (causing suspicion) suspect; **be** ~ **of** se méfier de. **suspiciously** *adv* de façon suspecte.

sustain *vt* supporter; (*effort*) soutenir; (suffer) subir.

sustenance *n* (food) nourriture *f*; (nourishment) valeur *f* nutritive.

swallow *vt/i* avaler; ~ **up** (absorb, engulf) engloutir. ● *n* hirondelle *f*.

swam ⇒SWIM.

swamp *n* marais *m*. ● *vt* (flood, overwhelm) submerger.

swan *n* cygne *m*.

swap *vt/i* (*pt* **swapped**) ▣ échanger. ● *n* ▣ échange *m*.

swarm *n* essaim *m*. ● *vi* fourmiller; ~ **into** *or* **round** (*crowd*) envahir.

swat *vt* (*pt* **swatted**) (*fly*) écraser.

sway *vt/i* (se) balancer; (influence)

influencer. ● *n* balancement *m*; (rule) empire *m*.

swear *vt/i* (*pt* **swore**; *pp* **sworn**) jurer (**to sth** de qch); ~ **at** injurier; ~ **by sth** ▣ ne jurer que par qch. ~**-word** *n* juron *m*.

sweat *n* sueur *f*. ● *vi* suer.

sweater *n* pull-over *m*.

sweat-shirt *n* sweat-shirt *m*.

swede *n* rutabaga *m*.

Swede *n* Suédois/-e *m/f*. **Sweden** *n* Suède *f*.

Swedish *a* suédois. ● *n* (Ling) suédois *m*.

sweep *vt/i* (*pt* **swept**) (*floor*) balayer; (carry away) emporter, entraîner; (*chimney*) ramoner. ● *n* coup *m* de balai; (curve) courbe *f*; (mouvement) geste *m*, mouvement *m*; (for chimneys) ramoneur *m*. □ ~ **by** passer rapidement *or* majestueusement.

sweeper *n* (for carpet) balai *m* mécanique; (football) libero *m*.

sweet *a* (not sour, pleasant) doux; (not savoury) sucré; (charming ▣) gentil; **have a** ~ **tooth** aimer les sucreries. ● *n* bonbon *m*; (dish) dessert *m*. ~**corn** *n* maïs *m*.

sweeten *vt* sucrer; (fig) adoucir. **sweetener** *n* édulcorant *m*.

sweetheart *n* petit/-e ami/-e *m/f*; (term of endearment) chéri/-e *m/f*.

sweetly *adv* gentiment.

sweetness *n* douceur *f*; goût *m* sucré.

sweet pea *n* pois *m* de senteur.

swell *vt/i* (*pt* **swelled**; *pp* **swollen** *or* **swelled**) (increase) grossir; (expand) (se) gonfler; (*hand, face*) enfler. ● *n* (of sea) houle *f*. **swelling** *n* (Med) enflure *f*.

sweltering *a* étouffant.

swept ⇒SWEEP.

swerve *vi* faire un écart.

swift *a* rapide. ● *n* (bird) martinet *m*.

swim *vi* (*pt* swam; *pp* swum; *pres p* swimming) nager; (be dizzy) tourner. ● *vt* traverser à la nage; (*distance*) nager. ● *n* baignade *f*; **go for a ~** aller se baigner. **swimmer** *n* nageur/ -euse *m/f*. **swimming** *n* natation *f*.

swimming-pool *n* piscine *f*.

swim-suit *n* maillot *m* (de bain).

swindle *vt* escroquer. ● *n* escroquerie *f*.

swine *npl* (pigs) pourceaux *mpl*. ● *n inv* (person 🗊) salaud *m*.

swing *vt/i* (*pt* swung) (se) balancer; (turn round) tourner; (*pendulum*) osciller. ● *n* balancement *m*; (seat) balançoire *f*; (of opinion) revirement *m* (**towards** en faveur de); (Mus) rythme *m*; **be in full ~** battre son plein. □ **~ round** (*person*) se retourner.

swipe *vt* (hit 🗊) frapper; (steal 🗊) piquer.

swirl *vi* tourbillonner. ● *n* tourbillon *m*.

Swiss *a* suisse. ● *n inv* Suisse *mf*.

switch *n* bouton *m* (électrique), interrupteur *m*; (shift) changement *m*, revirement *m*. ● *vt* (transfer) transférer; (exchange) échanger (**for** contre); (reverse positions of) changer de place; **~ trains** (change) changer de train. ● *vi* changer. □ **~ off** éteindre; **~ on** mettre, allumer.

switchboard *n* standard *m*.

Switzerland *n* Suisse *f*.

swivel *vt/i* (*pt* swivelled) (faire) pivoter.

swollen ⇒SWELL.

swoop *vi* (bird) fondre; (*police*) faire une descente, foncer. ● *n* (police raid) descente *f*.

sword *n* épée *f*.

swore ⇒SWEAR.

sworn ⇒SWEAR. ● *a* (*enemy*) juré; (*ally*) dévoué.

swot *vt/i* (*pt* swotted) (study 🗊) bûcher 🗊. ● *n* 🗊 bûcheur/-euse *m/f* 🗊.

swum ⇒SWIM.

swung ⇒SWING.

syllabus *n* (*pl* ~es) (School, Univ) programme *m*.

symbol *n* symbole *m*.
symbolic(al) *a* symbolique.
symbolize *vt* symboliser.

symmetrical *a* symétrique.

sympathetic *a* compatissant; (fig) compréhensif.

sympathize *vi* **~ with** (pity) plaindre; (fig) comprendre les sentiments de. **sympathizer** *n* sympathisant/-e *m/f*.

sympathy *n* (pity) compassion *f*; (fig) compréhension *f*; (solidarity) solidarité *f*; (condolences) condoléances *fpl*; (affinity) affinité *f*; **be in ~ with** comprendre, être en accord avec.

symptom *n* symptôme *m*.

synagogue *n* synagogue *f*.

synonym *n* synonyme *m*.

synopsis *n* (*pl* -opses) résumé *m*.

syntax *n* syntaxe *f*.

synthesis *n* (*pl* -theses) synthèse *f*.

synthetic *a* synthétique.

syringe *n* seringue *f*.

syrup *n* (liquid) sirop *m*; (treacle) mélasse *f* raffinée.

system *n* système *m*; (body) organisme *m*; (order) méthode *f*.
systematic *a* systématique.
systems analyst *n* analyste-programmeur/-euse *m/f*.

tab 563 **talk**

tab n (on can) languette f; (on garment) patte f; (label) étiquette f; (US ▦) addition f; (Comput) tabulatrice f; (setting) tabulation f.

table n table f; **at (the)** ~ à table; **lay** or **set the** ~ mettre la table. ● vt (motion) présenter. ~**cloth** n nappe f. ~**mat** n set m de table. ~**spoon** n cuillère f de service.

tablet n (of stone) plaque f; (drug) comprimé m.

table tennis n tennis m de table; ping-pong® m.

taboo n & a tabou (m).

tacit a tacite.

tack n (nail) clou m; (stitch) point m de bâti; (course of action) voie f. ● vt (nail) clouer; (stitch) bâtir; (add) ajouter. ● vi (Naut) louvoyer.

tackle n équipement m; (in soccer) tacle m, (in rugby) plaquage m. ● vt (problem) s'attaquer à; (player) tacler, plaquer.

tact n tact m. **tactful** a plein de tact.

tactics npl tactique f.

tadpole n têtard m.

tag n (label) étiquette f. ● vt (pt tagged) (label) étiqueter. ● vi ~ **along** ▦ suivre.

tail n queue f; ~**s** (coat) habit m; ~**s!** (on coin) pile! ● vt (follow) filer. ● vi ~ **away** or **off** diminuer. ~**back** n bouchon m. ~**gate** n hayon m.

tailor n tailleur m. ● vt (garment) façonner; (fig) adapter. ~**made** a fait sur mesure.

take vt/i (pt **took**; pp **taken**) prendre (**from sb** à qn); (carry) emporter, porter (**to** à); (escort) emmener; (contain) contenir; (tolerate) supporter; (accept) accepter; (prize) remporter; (exam) passer; (precedence) avoir; (view) adopter; ~ **sb home** ramener qn chez lui; **be taken by** or **with** être impressionné par; **be taken ill** tomber malade; **it** ~**s time** il faut du temps pour. □ ~ **after** tenir de; ~ **apart** démonter; (fig) descendre en flammes ▦; ~ **away** (object) enlever; (person) emmener; (pain) supprimer; ~ **back** reprendre; (return) rendre; (accompany) raccompagner; (statement) retirer; ~ **down** (object) descendre; (notes) prendre; ~ **in** (object) rentrer; (include) inclure; (cheat) tromper; ~ **off** (Aviat) décoller; ~ **sth off** enlever qch; ~ **sb off** imiter qn; ~ **on** (task, staff, passenger) prendre; (challenger) relever le défi de; ~ **out** sortir; (stain) enlever; ~ **over** vt (country, firm) prendre le contrôle de; vi prendre le pouvoir; ~ **over from** remplacer, ~ **part** participer (**in** à); ~ **place** avoir lieu; ~ **to** se prendre d'amitié pour; (activity) prendre goût à; ~ **to doing** se mettre à faire; ~ **up** (object) monter; (hobby) se mettre à; (occupy) prendre; (resume) reprendre; ~ **up with** se lier avec. ~**away** n (meal) repas m à emporter. ~**off** n (Aviat) décollage m. ~**over** n (Pol) prise f de pouvoir; (Comm) rachat m.

tale n conte m; (report) récit m; (lie) histoire f.

talent n talent m. **talented** a doué.

talk vt/i parler; (chat) bavarder; ~ **sb into doing** persuader qn de faire; ~ **sth over** discuter de qch.

T

● *n* (talking) propos *mpl*;
(conversation) conversation *f*;
(lecture) exposé *m*.

talkative *a* bavard.

tall *a* (high) haut; (*person*) grand.

tame *a* apprivoisé; (dull) insipide.
● *vt* apprivoiser; (*lion*) dompter.

tamper *vi* ∼ **with** (*lock, machine*)
tripoter; (*accounts, evidence*)
trafiquer.

tan *vt/i* (*pt* tanned) bronzer;
(*hide*) tanner. ● *n* bronzage *m*.

tangerine *n* mandarine *f*.

tangle *vt/i* ∼ (**up**) s'emmêler. ● *n*
enchevêtrement *m*.

tank *n* réservoir *m*; (vat) cuve *f*;
(for fish) aquarium *m*; (Mil) char *m*
(de combat).

tanker *n* (lorry) camion-citerne *m*;
(ship) navire-citerne *m*; **oil/petrol**
∼ pétrolier *m*.

tantrum *n* crise *f* (de colère).

tap *n* (for water) robinet *m*; (knock)
petit coup *m*; **on** ∼ disponible.
● *vt* (*pt* tapped) (knock) taper
(doucement); (*resources*)
exploiter; (*phone*) mettre sur
écoute.

tape *n* bande *f* (magnétique);
(cassette) cassette *f*; (video) cassette
f vidéo; (fabric) ruban *m*; (sticky)
scotch® *m*. ● *vt* (record)
enregistrer; ∼ **sth to sth** coller
qch à qch. ∼**-measure** *n* mètre
m ruban. ∼ **recorder** *n*
magnétophone *m*.

tapestry *n* tapisserie *f*.

tar *n* goudron *m*. ● *vt* (*pt* tarred)
goudronner.

target *n* cible *f*; (objective) objectif
m. ● *vt* (*city*) prendre pour cible;
(*weapon*) diriger; (in marketing)
viser.

tariff *n* (price list) tarif *m*; (on imports)
droit *m* de douane.

tarmac, Tarmac® *n* macadam *m*;
(runway) piste *f*.

tarpaulin *n* bâche *f*.

tarragon *n* estragon *m*.

tart *n* tarte *f*. ● *a* aigrelet.

task *n* tâche *f*.

taste *n* goût *m*; (experience) aperçu
m. ● *vt* (eat, enjoy) goûter à; (try)
goûter; (perceive taste of) sentir (le
goût de). ● *vi* ∼ **of** *or* **like** avoir
un goût de. **tasteful** *a* de bon
goût.

tattoo *vt* tatouer. ● *n* tatouage *m*.

tatty *a* (**-ier, -iest**) Ⅲ miteux.

taught ⇒TEACH.

taunt *vt* railler. ● *n* raillerie *f*.

Taurus *n* Taureau *m*.

tax *n* (on goods, services) taxe *f*; (on
income) impôt *m*. ● *vt* imposer; (put
to test: fig) mettre à l'épreuve.
taxable *a* imposable. **taxation** *n*
imposition *f*; (taxes) impôts *mpl*.

tax: ∼**-collector** *n* percepteur *m*.
∼**-deductible** *a* déductible des
impôts. ∼ **disc** *n* vignette *f*.
∼**-free** *a* exempt d'impôts. ∼
haven *n* paradis *m* fiscal.

taxi *n* taxi *m*. ∼ **rank** *n* station *f*
de taxi.

tax: ∼**payer** *n* contribuable *mf*. ∼
relief *n* dégrèvement *m* fiscal. ∼
return *n* déclaration *f* d'impôts.

tea *n* (drink, meal) thé *m*; (children's
snack) goûter *m*; ∼ **bag** sachet *m*
de thé.

teach *vt* (*pt* taught) apprendre
(**sb sth** qch à qn); (in school)
enseigner (**sb sth** qch à qn). ● *vi*
enseigner. **teacher** *n* enseignant/
-e *m/f*; (secondary) professeur *m*;
(primary) instituteur/-trice *m/f*.

team *n* équipe *f*; (of animals)
attelage *m*. ● *vi* ∼ **up** faire équipe
(**with** avec).

teapot *n* théière *f*.

tear¹ *vt/i* (*pt* tore; *pp* torn) (se)
déchirer; (snatch) arracher (**from**
à); (rush) aller à toute vitesse. ● *n*
déchirure *f*.

tear² *n* larme *f*; **in** ∼**s** en larmes.
∼**-gas** *n* gaz *m* lacrymogène.

tease vt taquiner. ● n taquin/-e m/f.

tea: ~**-shop** n salon m de thé. ~**spoon** petite cuillère f.

teat n tétine f.

tea-towel n torchon m.

technical a technique.

technician n technicien/-ne m/f.

technique n technique f.

techno n (Mus) techno f.

technology n technologie f.

teddy a ~ **bear** ours m en peluche.

tedious a ennuyeux.

tee n (golf) tee m.

teenage a (*girl, boy*) adolescent; (*fashion*) des adolescents.

teenager n jeune mf, adolescent/ -e m/f.

teens npl in one's ~ adolescent.

teeth ⇒TOOTH.

teethe vi faire ses dents.

teetotaller n personne f qui ne boit pas d'alcool.

telecommunications npl télécommunications fpl.

telecommuting n télétravail m.

teleconferencing n téléconférence f.

telegram n télégramme m.

telegraph n télégraphe m. ● a télégraphique.

telephone n téléphone m. ● vt (*person*) téléphoner à; (*message*) téléphoner. ● vi téléphoner. ~ **book** annuaire m. ~ **booth**, ~**-box** n cabine f téléphonique. ~ **call** n coup m de téléphone. ~ **number** n numéro m de téléphone.

telephoto a ~ **lens** téléobjectif m.

telescope n télescope m. ● vt/i (se) télescoper.

teletext n télétexte m.

televise vt téléviser.

television n télévision f; ~ **set** poste m de télévision, téléviseur m.

teleworking n télétravail m.

telex n télex m. ● vt envoyer par télex.

tell vt (*pt* told) dire (**sb sth** qch à qn); (*story*) raconter; (distinguish) distinguer; ~ **sb to do sth** dire à qn de faire qch; ~ **sth from sth** voir la différence entre qch et qch. ● vi (show) avoir un effet; (know) savoir. □ ~ **off** ⊡ gronder.

temp n intérimaire mf. ● vi faire de l'intérim.

temper n humeur f; (anger) colère f; **lose one's** ~ se mettre en colère.

temperament n tempérament m.

temperamental a capricieux.

temperature n température f; **have a** ~ avoir de la fièvre or de la température.

temple n temple m; (of head) tempe f.

temporary a temporaire, provisoire.

tempt vt tenter; ~ **sb to do** donner envie à qn de faire.

ten a & n dix (m)

tenacious a tenace.

tenancy n location f. **tenant** n locataire mf.

tend vt s'occuper de. ● vi ~ **to** (be apt to) avoir tendance à; (look after) s'occuper de. **tendency** n tendance f.

tender a tendre; (sore, painful) sensible. ● vt offrir, donner. ● vi faire une soumission. ● n (Comm) soumission f; **be legal** ~ (money) avoir cours.

tendon n tendon m.

tennis n tennis m. ● a (*court, match*) de tennis.

tenor n (meaning) sens m général; (Mus) ténor m.

tense n (Gram) temps m. ● a

T

tendu. ● vt (*muscles*) tendre, raidir. ● vi (*face*) se crisper.

tension n tension f.

tent n tente f.

tentative a provisoire; (hesitant) timide.

tenth a & n dixième (*mf*).

tepid a tiède.

term n (word, limit) terme m; (of imprisonment) temps m; (School) trimestre m; ~s conditions *fpl*; on good/bad ~s en bons/mauvais termes; in the short/long ~ à court/long terme; come to ~s with sth accepter qch; ~ of office (Pol) mandat m. ● vt appeler.

terminal a (point) terminal; (*illness*) incurable. ● n (oil, computer) terminal m; (Rail) terminus m; (Electr) borne f; (air) ~ aérogare f.

terminate vt mettre fin à. ● vi prendre fin.

terminus n (pl **-ni**) (station) terminus m.

terrace n terrasse f; (houses) rangée f de maisons contiguës; the ~s (Sport) les gradins *mpl*.

terracotta n terre f cuite.

terrible a affreux, atroce.

terrific a (huge) énorme; (great 🄸) formidable.

terrify vt terrifier; be terrified of avoir très peur de.

territory n territoire m.

terror n terreur f.

terrorism n terrorisme m.

terrorist n terroriste mf.

test n épreuve f; (written exam) contrôle m; (of machine, product) essai m; (of sample) analyse f; driving ~ examen m du permis de conduire. ● vt évaluer; (School) contrôler; (machine, product) essayer; (*sample*) analyser; (*patience, strength*) mettre à l'épreuve. ● vi ~ for faire une recherche de.

testament n testament m; Old/New T~ Ancien/Nouveau Testament m.

testicle n testicule m.

testify vt/i témoigner (to de; that que).

testimony n témoignage m.

test tube n éprouvette f.

tetanus n tétanos m.

text n texte m. ● vt ~ sb envoyer un message texte à qn. ~book n manuel m ~ message n message m texte.

texture n (of paper) grain m; (of fabric) texture f.

than conj que, qu'; (with numbers) de; more/less ~ ten plus/moins de dix.

thank vt remercier; ~ you!, ~s! merci! thankful a reconnaissant (for de). thanks *npl* remerciements *mpl*; ~s to grâce à. Thanksgiving (Day) n (US) jour m d'Action de Grâces

....

that pl those

● *determiner*

····▸ ce, cet, cette, ces; ~ dog ce chien; ~ man cet homme; ~ woman cette femme; those books ces livres; at ~ moment à ce moment-là.

❗ To distinguish from this and these, you need to add *-là* after the noun: I prefer that car *je préfère cette voiture-là*.

● *pronoun*

····▸ cela, ça, ce; what's ~?, what are those? qu'est-ce que c'est (que ça)?; who's ~? qui est-ce?; ~ is my brother c'est *or* voilà mon frère; those are my parents ce sont mes parents.

····▸ (emphatic) celui-là, celle-là, ceux-là, celles-là; all the dresses

are nice but I like ∼/those best
toutes les robes sont jolies mais
je préfère celle-là/celles-là.

● *relative pronoun*

····> (for subject) qui; **the man ∼ stole
the car** l'homme qui a volé la
voiture.

····> (for object) que; **the girl ∼ I met**
la fille que j'ai rencontrée.

! With a preposition, use
*lequel/laquelle/lesquels/
lesquelles*: **the chair ∼ I
was sitting on** *la chaise sur
laquelle j'étais assis.*

! With a preposition that
translates as *à*, use *auquel/
à laquelle/auxquels/
auxquelles*: **the girls ∼ I
was talking to** *les filles
auxquelles je parlais.*

! With a preposition that
translates as *de*, use *dont*:
**the people ∼ I've talked
about** *les personnes dont
j'ai parlé.*

● *conjunction* que; **she said ∼
she would do it** elle a dit
qu'elle le ferait.

thatched *a* de chaume; ∼ **cottage**
chaumière *f*.

thaw *vt/i* (faire) dégeler; (*snow*)
(faire) fondre. ● *n* dégel *m*.

the *determiner*

····> le, l', la, les; ∼ **dog** le chien;
∼ **tree** l'arbre; ∼ **chair** la chaise;
to ∼ shops aux magasins.

! With a preposition that
translates as *à*: *à* + *le* = *au*
and *à* + *les* = *aux*.

theatre *n* théâtre *m*.

theft *n* vol *m*.

their *a* leur, *pl* leurs.

theirs *pron* le *or* la leur, les leurs.

them *pron* les; (after preposition) eux,
elles; (**to**) ∼ leur; **phone ∼!**
téléphone-leur!; **I know ∼** je les
connais; **both of ∼** tous/toutes les
deux.

themselves *pron* eux-mêmes,
elles-mêmes; (reflexive) se; (after
preposition) eux, elles.

then *adv* alors; (next) ensuite,
puis; (therefore) alors, donc. ● *a*
d'alors; **from ∼ on** dès lors.

theology *n* théologie *f*.

theory *n* théorie *f*.

therapy *n* thérapie *f*.

there *adv* là; (with verb) y; (over
there) là-bas; **he goes** ∼ il y va; **on
∼** là-dessus; ∼ **is**, ∼ **are** il y a;
(pointing) voilà. ● *interj* ∼, ∼!
allons, allons!

therefore *adv* donc.

thermal *a* thermique.

thermometer *n* thermomètre *m*.

Thermos® *n* thermos® *m or f
inv*.

thermostat *n* thermostat *m*.

thesaurus *n* (*pl* **-ri**) dictionnaire
m de synonymes.

these ⇒THIS

thesis *n* (*pl* **theses**) thèse *f*.

they *pron* ils, elles; (emphatic) eux,
elles; (people in general) on.

thick *a* épais; (stupid) bête; **be 6 cm
∼** avoir 6 cm d'épaisseur.

thief *n* (*pl* **thieves**) voleur/-euse
m/f.

thigh *n* cuisse *f*.

thin *a* (**thinner, thinnest**) mince;
(*person*) maigre, mince; (sparse)
clairsemé; (fine) fin. ● *vt/i* (*pt
thinned) ∼ (**down**) (*paint*) diluer;
(*soup*) allonger.

thing *n* chose *f*; ∼**s** (belongings)
affaires *fpl*; **the best ∼ is to** le
mieux est de; **the (right) ∼** ce qu'il
faut (**for sb** à qn).

think *vt/i* (*pt **thought**) penser

T

(about, of à); (carefully) réfléchir
(about, of à); (believe) croire; **I ~ so**
je crois que oui; **~ of doing**
envisager de faire. □ **~ over** bien
réfléchir à; **~ up** inventer.

third *a* troisième. ● *n* troisième
mf; (fraction) tiers *m*. **T~ World** *n*
tiers-monde *m*.

thirst *n* soif *f*.

thirsty *a* **be ~** avoir soif; **make ~**
donner soif à.

thirteen *a & n* treize (*m*).

thirty *a & n* trente (*m*).

this *pl* **these**

● *determiner*

····▶ ce/cet/cette/ces; **~ dog** ce
chien; **~ man** cet homme; **~
woman** cette femme; **these books**
ces livres.

! To distinguish from **that** and
those, you need to add *-ci*
after the noun: **I prefer this
car** *je préfère cette
voiture-ci.*

● *pronoun*

····▶ ce; **what's ~?, what are these?**
qu'est-ce que c'est?; **who is ~?**
qui est-ce?; **~ is the kitchen** voici
la cuisine; **~ is Sophie** je te *or*
vous présente Sophie; **these are
your things** ce sont tes affaires.

····▶ (emphatic) celui-ci/
celle-ci/ceux-ci/celles-ci; **all the
dresses are nice but I like ~/these
best** toutes les robes sont jolies
mais je préfère celle-ci/celles-ci.

thistle *n* chardon *m*.

thorn *n* épine *f*.

thorough *a* (detailed) approfondi;
(meticulous) minutieux. **thoroughly**
adv (*clean, study*) à fond; (very)
tout à fait.

those ⇒THAT.

though *conj* bien que. ● *adv*
quand même.

thought ⇒THINK. ● *n* pensée *f*,
idée *f*. **thoughtful** *a* pensif; (kind)
prévenant.

thousand *a & n* mille (*m inv*); **~s
of** des milliers de. **thousandth** *a
& n* millième (*mf*).

thread *n* (yarn & fig) fil *m*; (of screw)
pas *m*. ● *vt* enfiler; **~ one's way**
se faufiler.

threat *n* menace *f*. **threaten** *vt/i*
menacer (with de).

three *a & n* trois (*m*).

threw ⇒THROW.

thrill *n* frisson *m*; (pleasure) plaisir
m. ● *vt* transporter (de joie); **be
~ed** être ravi. ● *vi* frissonner (de
joie).

thrive *vi* (*pt* **thrived** *or* **throve**;
pp **thrived** *or* **thriven**) prospérer;
he ~s on it cela lui réussit.

throat *n* gorge *f*; **have a sore ~**
avoir mal à la gorge.

throb *vi* (*pt* **throbbed**) (*heart*)
battre; (*engine*) vibrer. ● *n* (pain)
élancement *m*; (of engine) vibration
f. **throbbing** *a* (*pain*) lancinant.

throne *n* trône *m*.

through *prep* à travers; (during)
pendant; (by means or way of, out of)
par; (by reason of) grâce à, à cause
de. ● *adv* à travers; (entirely)
jusqu'au bout. ● *a* (*train*) direct;
be ~ (finished) avoir fini; **come** *or*
go ~ (cross, pierce) traverser; **I'm
putting you ~** je vous passe votre
correspondant.

throughout *prep* **~ the country**
dans tout le pays; **~ the day**
pendant toute la journée. ● *adv*
(place) partout; (time) tout le
temps.

throw *vt* (*pt* **threw**; *pp* **thrown**)
jeter, lancer; (baffle) déconcerter;
~ a party faire une fête. ● *n* jet
m; (of dice) coup *m*. □ **~ away**
jeter; **~ off** (get rid of) se

débarrasser de; ~ **out** jeter; (*person*) expulser; (reject) rejeter; ~ **up** (*arms*) lever; (vomit 🔲) vomir.

thrust *vt* (*pt* **thrust**) pousser. ● *n* poussée *f*.

thud *n* bruit *m* sourd.

thug *n* voyou *m*.

thumb *n* pouce *m*. ● *vt* (*book*) feuilleter; ~ **a lift** faire de l'auto-stop. ~**-index** *n* répertoire *m* à onglets.

thump *vt/i* cogner (sur); (*heart*) battre fort. ● *n* coup *m*.

thunder *n* tonnerre *m*. ● *vi* (*weather, person*) tonner. ~**storm** *n* orage *m*.

Thursday *n* jeudi *m*.

thus *adv* ainsi.

thwart *vt* contrecarrer.

thyme *n* thym *m*.

tick *n* (sound) tic-tac *m*; (mark) coche *f*; (moment 🔲) instant *m*; (insect) tique *f*. ● *vi* faire tic-tac. ● *vt* ~ (**off**) cocher. ☐ ~ **over** tourner au ralenti.

ticket *n* billet *m*; (for bus, cloakroom) ticket *m*; (label) étiquette *f*. ~**-collector** *n* contrôleur/-euse *m/f*. ~**-office** *n* guichet *m*.

tickle *vt* chatouiller; (amuse: fig) amuser. ● *n* chatouillement *m*.

tidal *a* (*river*) à marées; ~ **wave** raz-de-marée *m inv*.

tide *n* marée *f*; (of events) cours *m*.

tidy *a* (**-ier, -iest**) (*room*) bien rangé; (*appearance, work*) soigné; (methodical) ordonné; (amount 🔲) joli. ● *vt/i* ~ (**up**) faire du rangement; ~ **sth** (**up**) ranger qch; ~ **oneself up** s'arranger.

tie *vt* (*pres p* **tying**) attacher; (*knot*) faire; (*scarf*) nouer; (*link*) lier. ● *vi* (in football) faire match nul; (in race) être ex aequo. ● *n* (necktie) cravate *f*; (fastener) attache *f*; (link) lien *m*; (draw) match *m* nul. ☐ ~ **down** attacher; ~ **in with**

être lié à; ~ **up** attacher; (*money*) immobiliser; (*occupy*) occuper.

tier *n* étage *m*, niveau *m*; (in stadium) gradin *m*.

tiger *n* tigre *m*.

tight *a* (*clothes, budget*) serré; (*grip*) ferme; (*rope*) tendu; (*security*) strict; (*angle*) aigu. ● *adv* (hold, sleep) bien; (squeeze) fort.

tighten *vt/i* (se) tendre; (*bolt*) (se) resserrer; (*control*) renforcer.

tights *npl* collant *m*.

tile *n* (on wall, floor) carreau *m*; (on roof) tuile *f*. ● *vt* carreler; couvrir de tuiles.

till *n* caisse *f* (enregistreuse). ● *vt* (*land*) cultiver. ● *prep & conj* = UNTIL.

timber *n* bois *m* (de construction); (trees) arbres *mpl*.

time *n* temps *m*; (moment) moment *m*; (epoch) époque *f*; (by clock) heure *f*; (occasion) fois *f*; (rhythm) mesure *f*; ~**s** (multiplying) fois *fpl*; **any** ~ n'importe quand; **for the** ~ **being** pour le moment; **from** ~ **to** ~ de temps en temps; **have a good** ~ n'amuser; **in no** ~ en un rien de temps; **in** ~ à temps; (eventually) avec le temps; **a long** ~ longtemps; **on** ~ à l'heure; **what's the** ~? quelle heure est-il?; ~ **off** du temps libre. ● *vt* choisir le moment de; (measure) minuter; (Sport) chronométrer. ~**-limit** *n* délai *m*.

timer *n* minuterie *f*; (for cooker) minuteur *m*.

time: ~**-scale** *n* délais *mpl*. ~**table** *n* horaire *m*. ~ **zone** *n* fuseau *m* horaire.

timid *a* timide; (fearful) peureux.

tin *n* étain *m*; (container) boîte *f*; ~(**plate**) fer-blanc *m*. ● *vt* (*pt* **tinned**) mettre en boîte. ~ **foil** *n* papier *m* d'aluminium.

T

tingle vi picoter. ● n picotement m.

tin-opener n ouvre-boîtes m inv.

tint n teinte f; (for hair) shampooing m colorant. ● vt teinter.

tiny a (-ier, -iest) tout petit.

tip n (of stick, pen, shoe, ski) pointe f; (of nose, finger, wing) bout m; (gratuity) pourboire m; (advice) tuyau m; (for rubbish) décharge f. ● vt/i (pt tipped) (tilt) pencher; (overturn) (faire) basculer; (pour) verser; (empty) déverser; (give money) donner un pourboire à. □ ∼ off prévenir.

tiptoe n on ∼ sur la pointe des pieds.

tire vt/i (se) fatiguer; ∼ of se lasser de. ● n (US) pneu m.

tired a fatigué; be ∼ of en avoir assez de.

tiring a fatigant.

tissue n tissu m; (handkerchief) mouchoir m en papier; ∼ (paper) papier m de soie.

tit n (bird) mésange f; give ∼ for tat rendre coup pour coup.

title n titre m. ∼ deed n titre m de propriété.

....

to

● preposition

····▶ à; ∼ **Paris** à Paris; **give the book** ∼ **Jane** donne le livre à Jane; ∼ **the office** au bureau; ∼ **the shops** aux magasins.

····▶ (with feminine countries) en; ∼ **France** en France.

····▶ (to + personal pronoun) me/te/lui/ nous/vous/leur; **she gave it** ∼ **them** elle le leur a donné; **I'll say it** ∼ **her** je vais le lui dire.

! à + le = au
! à + les = aux.

● in infinitive

to is not normally translated (**to go** aller; **to sing** chanter)

····▶ (in order to) pour; **he's gone into town** ∼ **buy a shirt** il est parti en ville pour acheter une chemise.

····▶ (after adjectives) à; de; **be easy/ difficult** ∼ **read** être facile/ difficile à lire; **it's easy/difficult to read her writing** c'est facile/ difficile de lire son écriture.

➡ For verbal expressions using the infinitive 'to' such as **tell sb to do sth**, **help sb to do sth** ⇒tell, help.

....

toad n crapaud m.

toast n pain m grillé, toast m; (drink) toast m. ● vt (bread) faire griller; (drink to) porter un toast à.

toaster n grille-pain m inv.

tobacco n tabac m.

tobacconist n marchand/-e m/f de tabac; ∼'s (**shop**) tabac m.

toboggan n toboggan m, luge f.

today n & adv aujourd'hui (m).

toddler n bébé m (qui fait ses premiers pas).

toe n (of foot) orteil m; (of shoe) bout m; **on one's** ∼**s** vigilant. ● vt ∼ **the line** se conformer.

together adv ensemble; (at same time) à la fois; ∼ **with** avec.

toilet n toilettes fpl.

toiletries npl articles mpl de toilette.

token n (symbol) témoignage m; (voucher) bon m; (coin) jeton m. ● a symbolique.

told ⇒TELL.

tolerance n tolérance f.

tolerate vt tolérer.

toll n péage m; **death** ∼ nombre m de morts; **take its** ∼ faire des ravages. ● vi (bell) sonner.

tomato n (pl ∼es) tomate f.

tomb n tombeau m.

tomorrow n & adv demain (m); ~ **morning/night** demain matin/soir; **the day after** ~ après-demain.

ton n tonne f (= 1016 kg); (**metric**) ~ tonne f (= 1000 kg); ~**s of** 🔲 des masses de.

tone n ton m; (of radio, telephone) tonalité f. ● vt ~ **down** atténuer. ● vi ~ (**in**) s'harmoniser (**with** avec).

tongs npl (for coal) pincettes fpl; (for sugar) pince f; (for hair) fer m.

tongue n langue f.

tonic n (Med) tonique m. ● a (effect, accent) tonique; ~ (**water**) tonic m, Schweppes® m.

tonight n & adv (evening) ce soir; (night) cette nuit.

tonsil n amygdale f.

too adv trop; (also) aussi; ~ **many people** trop de gens; **I've got** ~ **much/many** j'en ai trop; **me** ~ moi aussi.

took ⇒TAKE.

tool n outil m. ~**bar** n barre f d'outils. ~**box** n boîte f à outils.

toot n coup m de klaxon®. ● vt/i ~ (**the horn**) klaxonner.

tooth n (pl **teeth**) dent f. ~**ache** n mal m de dents. ~**brush** n brosse f à dents. ~**paste** n dentifrice m. ~**pick** n cure-dents m inv.

top n (highest point) sommet m; (upper part) haut m; (upper surface) dessus m; (lid) couvercle m; (of bottle, tube) bouchon m; (of beer bottle) capsule f; (of list) tête f; **on** ~ **of** sur; (fig) en plus de. ● a (shelf) du haut; (step, floor) dernier; (in rank) premier; (best) meilleur; (distinguished) éminent; (maximum) maximum. ● vt (pt **topped**) (exceed) dépasser; (list) venir en tête de; ~ **up** remplir; ~**ped with**

(dome) surmonté de; (cream) recouvert de.

topic n sujet m.

topless a aux seins nus.

torch n (electric) lampe f de poche; (flaming) torche f.

tore ⇒TEAR[1].

torment vt tourmenter.

torn ⇒TEAR[1].

torrent n torrent m.

tortoise n tortue f. ~**shell** n écaille f.

torture n torture f; (fig) supplice m. ● vt torturer.

Tory n & a tory (mf), conservateur/-trice (m/f).

toss vt lancer; (salad) tourner; (pancake) faire sauter. ● vi se retourner; ~ **a coin**, ~ **up** tirer à pile ou face (**for** pour).

tot n petit/-e enfant m/f; (drink) petit verre m.

total n & a total (m). ● vt (pt **totalled**) (add up) additionner; (amount to) se monter à.

touch vt toucher; (tamper with) toucher à. ● vi se toucher. ● n (sense) toucher m; (contact) contact m; (of artist, writer) touche f; **a** ~ **of** (small amount) un petit peu de; **get in** ~ **with** se mettre en contact avec; **out of** ~ **with** déconnecté de. ▢ ~ **down** (Aviat) atterrir; ~ **up** retoucher. ~**down** n atterrissage m; (Sport) essai m. ~**-line** n ligne f de touche. ~**-tone** a (phone) à touches.

tough a (negotiator) coriace; (law) sévère; (time) difficile; (robust) robuste.

tour n voyage m; (visit) visite f; (by team) tournée f; **on** ~ en tournée. ● vt visiter.

tourist n touriste mf. ● a touristique. ~ **office** n syndicat m d'initiative.

tournament n tournoi m.

tout vi ~ (**for**) racoler 🔲. ● vt (sell)

T

revendre. ● *n* racoleur/-euse *m/f*; revendeur/-euse *m/f*.

tow *vt* remorquer. ● *n* remorque *f*; **on** ∼ en remorque.

toward(s) *prep* vers; (*of attitude*) envers.

towel *n* serviette *f*.

tower *n* tour *f*. ● *vi* ∼ **above** dominer.

town *n* ville *f*; **in** ∼ en ville. ∼ **council** *n* conseil *m* municipal. ∼ **hall** *n* mairie *f*.

tow: ∼**-path** *n* chemin *m* de halage. ∼ **truck** *n* dépanneuse *f*.

toxic *a* toxique.

toy *n* jouet *m*. ● *vi* ∼ **with** (*object*) jouer avec; (*idea*) caresser.

trace *n* trace *f*. ● *vt* (*person*) retrouver; (*cause*) déterminer; (*life*) retracer; (*draw*) tracer; (*with tracing paper*) décalquer.

track *n* (*of person, car*) traces *fpl*; (*of missile*) trajectoire *f*; (*path*) sentier *m*; (*Sport*) piste *f*; (*Rail*) voie *f*; (*on disc*) morceau *m*; **keep** ∼ **of** suivre. ● *vt* suivre la trace *or* la trajectoire de. □ ∼ **down** retrouver. ∼ **suit** *n* survêtement *m*.

tractor *n* tracteur *m*.

trade *n* commerce *m*; (*job*) métier *m*; (*swap*) échange *m*. ● *vi* faire du commerce; ∼ **on** exploiter. ● *vt* échanger. ● *a* (*route, deficit*) commercial. ∼**-in** *n* reprise *f*. ∼ **mark** *n* marque *f* (de fabrique); (*registered*) marque *f* déposée.

trader *n* commerçant/-e *m/f*; (*on stockmarket*) opérateur/-trice *m/f*.

trade union *n* syndicat *m*.

trading *n* commerce *m*; (*on stockmarket*) transactions *fpl* (boursières).

tradition *n* tradition *f*.

traffic *n* trafic *m*; (*on road*) circulation *f*. ● *vi* (*pt* **trafficked**) faire du trafic (**in** de). ∼ **jam** *n* embouteillage *m*. ∼**-lights** *npl*

feux *mpl* (de circulation). ∼ **warden** contractuel/-le *m/f*.

trail *vt/i* traîner; (*plant*) ramper; (*track*) suivre; ∼ **behind** traîner. ● *n* (*of powder*) traînée *f*; (*track*) piste *f*; (*path*) sentier *m*.

trailer *n* remorque *f*; (*caravan*) caravane *f*; (*film*) bande-annonce *f*.

train *n* (Rail) train *m*; (*underground*) rame *f*; (*procession*) file *f*; (*of dress*) traîne *f*. ● *vt* (*instruct, develop*) former; (*sportsman*) entraîner; (*animal*) dresser; (*ear*) exercer; (*aim*) braquer. ● *vi* être formé, étudier; (Sport) s'entraîner.

trained *a* (*skilled*) qualifié; (*doctor*) diplômé. **trainee** *n* stagiaire *mf*.

trainer *n* (Sport) entraîneur/-euse *m/f*. **trainers** *npl* (*shoes*) chaussures *fpl* de sport. **training** *n* formation *f*; (Sport) entraînement *m*.

tram *n* tram(way) *m*.

tramp *vi* marcher (d'un pas lourd). ● *vt* parcourir. ● *n* (*vagrant*) clochard/-e *m/f*; (*sound*) bruit *m*.

trample *vt/i* ∼ (**on**) piétiner; (fig) fouler aux pieds.

tranquil *a* tranquille.

tranquillizer *n* tranquillisant *m*.

transact *vt* négocier.

transaction *n* transaction *f*.

transcript *n* transcription *f*.

transfer[1] *vt* (*pt* **transferred**) transférer; (*power*) céder; (*employee*) muter. ● *vi* être transféré; (*employee*) être muté.

transfer[2] *n* transfert *m*; (*of employee*) mutation *f*; (*image*) décalcomanie *f*.

transform *vt* transformer.

transitive *a* transitif.

translate *vt* traduire. **translation** *n* traduction *f*. **translator** *n* traducteur/-trice *m/f*.

transmit *vt* (*pt* **transmitted**)

transmettre. **transmitter** n
émetteur m.
transparency n transparence f;
(Photo) diapositive f.
transplant n transplantation f;
(Med) greffe f.
transport¹ vt transporter.
transport² n transport m.
trap n piège m. ● vt (pt **trapped**)
(jam, pin down) coincer; (cut off)
bloquer; (snare) prendre au piège.
trash n (refuse) ordures fpl;
(nonsense) idioties fpl. **~can** n
(US) poubelle f.
trauma n traumatisme m.
traumatic a traumatisant.
travel vi (pt **travelled**, US
traveled) voyager; (vehicle,
bullet) aller. ● vt parcourir. ● n
voyages mpl. **~ agency** n agence
f de voyages.
traveller, (US) **traveler** n
voyageur/-euse m/f; **~'s cheque**
chèque m de voyage.
trawler n chalutier m.
tray n plateau m; (on office desk)
corbeille f.
treacle n mélasse f.
tread vi (pt **trod**; pp **trodden**)
marcher (on sur). ● vt fouler. ● n
(sound) pas m; (of tyre) chape f.
treasure n trésor m. ● vt (gift,
memory) chérir; (friendship,
possession) tenir beaucoup à.
treasury n trésorerie f; **the T~** le
ministère des Finances.
treat vt traiter; **~ sb to sth** offrir
qch à qn. ● n (pleasure) plaisir m;
(food) gâterie f. **treatment** n
traitement m.
treaty n traité m.
treble a triple; **~ clef** clé f de sol.
● vt/i tripler. ● n (voice) soprano
m.
tree n arbre m.
trek n randonnée f. ● vi (pt
trekked) **~ across/through**

traverser péniblement; **go ~king**
faire de la randonnée.
tremble vi trembler.
tremendous a énorme; (excellent)
formidable.
tremor n tremblement m; (earth)
~ secousse f.
trench n tranchée f.
trend n tendance f; (fashion) mode
f. **trendy** a 🔲 branché 🔲.
trespass vi s'introduire
illégalement (on dans).
trespasser n intrus/-e m/f.
trial n (Jur) procès m; (test) essai
m; (ordeal) épreuve f; **go on ~**
passer en jugement; **by ~ and
error** par expérience.
triangle n triangle m.
tribe n tribu f.
tribunal n tribunal m.
tributary n affluent m.
tribute n tribut m; **pay ~ to**
rendre hommage à.
trick n tour m; (dishonest) combine
f; (knack) astuce f; **do the ~** 🔲 faire
l'affaire. ● vt tromper. **trickery** n
ruse f.
trickle vi dégouliner; **~ in/out**
arriver ou partir en petit nombre.
● n filet m; (fig) petit nombre m.
tricky a (task) difficile; (question)
épineux; (person) malin.
trifle n bagatelle f; (cake)
diplomate m; **a ~** (small amount) un
peu. ● vi **~ with** jouer avec.
trigger n (of gun) gâchette f; (of
machine) manette f. ● vt **~ (off)**
(initiate) déclencher.
trim a (**trimmer, trimmest**)
soigné; (figure) svelte. ● vt (pt
trimmed) (hair, grass) couper;
(budget) réduire; (decorate)
décorer. ● n (cut) coupe f
d'entretien; (decoration) garniture f;
in ~ en forme.
trinket n babiole f.
trip vt/i (pt **tripped**) (faire)

T

trébucher. ● *n* (journey) voyage *m*; (outing) excursion *f*.

triple *a* triple. ● *vt/i* tripler.
 triplets *npl* triplés/-es *m/fpl*.

tripod *n* trépied *m*.

trite *a* banal.

triumph *n* triomphe *m*. ● *vi*
 triompher (**over** de).

trivial *a* insignifiant.

trod, trodden ⇒TREAD.

trolley *n* chariot *m*.

trombone *n* (Mus) trombone *m*.

troop *n* bande *f*; ~s (Mil) troupes
 fpl. ● *vi* ~ **in/out** entrer/sortir en
 bande.

trophy *n* trophée *m*.

tropic *n* tropique *m*; ~s
 tropiques *mpl*.

trot *n* trot *m*; **on the** ~ 🄳 coup sur
 coup. ● *vi* (*pt* **trotted**) trotter.

trouble *n* problèmes *mpl*; ennuis
 mpl; (pains, effort) peine *f*; **be in** ~
 avoir des ennuis; **go to a lot of** ~
 se donner du mal; **what's the** ~?
 quel est le problème? ● *vt* (bother)
 déranger; (worry) tracasser. ● *vi* ~
 (oneself) **to do** se donner la peine
 de faire. ~**maker** *n* provocateur/
 -trice *m/f*. ~**shooter** *n*
 conciliateur/-trice *m/f*; (Tech)
 expert *m*.

troublesome *a* ennuyeux.

trousers *npl* pantalon *m*; **short** ~
 short *m*.

trout *n inv* truite *f*.

trowel *n* (garden) déplantoir *m*; (for
 mortar) truelle *f*.

truant *n* (School) élève *mf* qui fait
 l'école buissonnière; **play** ~
 sécher les cours.

truce *n* trêve *f*.

truck *n* (lorry) camion *m*; (cart)
 chariot *m*; (Rail) wagon *m* de
 marchandises. ~**-driver** *n* routier
 m.

true *a* vrai; (accurate) exact; (faithful)
 fidèle.

truffle *n* truffe *f*.

truly *adv* vraiment; (faithfully)
 fidèlement; (truthfully) sincèrement.

trumpet *n* trompette *f*.

trunk *n* (of tree, body) tronc *m*; (of
 elephant) trompe *f*; (box) malle *f*;
 (Auto, US) coffre *m*; ~s (for
 swimming) slip *m* de bain.

trust *n* confiance *f*; (association)
 trust *m*; **in** ~ en dépôt. ● *vt* avoir
 confiance en; ~ **sb with** confier à
 qn. ● *vi* ~ **in** or **to** s'en remettre
 à. **trustee** *n* administrateur/-trice
 m/f. **trustworthy** *a* digne de
 confiance.

truth *n* (*pl* -**s**) vérité *f*. **truthful** *a*
 (account) véridique; (person) qui
 dit la vérité.

try *vt/i* (*pt* **tried**) essayer; (be a
 strain on) éprouver; (Jur) juger; ~
 on or **out** essayer; ~ **to do** essayer
 de faire. ● *n* (attempt) essai *m*;
 (rugby) essai *m*.

T-shirt *n* tee-shirt *m*.

tub *n* (for flowers) bac *m*; (of ice
 cream) pot *m*; (bath) baignoire *f*.

tube *n* tube *m*; **the** ~ 🄳 le métro.

tuberculosis *n* tuberculose *f*.

tuck *n* pli *m*. ● *vt* (put away, place)
 ranger; (hide) cacher. ● *vi* ~ **in** or
 into 🄳 attaquer; ~ **in** (shirt)
 rentrer; (blanket, person) border.

Tuesday *n* mardi *m*.

tug *vt* (*pt* **tugged**) tirer. ● *vi* ~ **at**/
 on tirer sur. ● *n* (boat)
 remorqueur *m*.

tuition *n* cours *mpl*; (fee) frais *mpl*
 pédagogiques.

tulip *n* tulipe *f*.

tumble *vi* (fall) dégringoler. ● *n*
 chute *f*. ~**-drier** *n* sèche-linge *m*
 inv.

tumbler *n* verre *m* droit.

tummy *n* 🄳 ventre *m*.

tumour *n* tumeur *f*.

tuna *n inv* thon *m*.

tune *n* air *m*; **be in** ~/**out of** ~

(instrument) être/ne pas être en accord; (singer) chanter juste/faux. ● vt (engine) régler; (Mus) accorder. ● vi ~ **in** (**to**) (radio, TV) écouter. □ ~ **up** s'accorder.

Tunisia n Tunisie f.

tunnel n tunnel m; (in mine) galerie f. ● vi (pt **tunnelled**) creuser un tunnel (**into** dans).

turf n (pl **turf** or **turves**) gazon m; the ~ (racing) le turf. ● vt ~ **out** 🄸 jeter dehors.

Turk n Turc m, Turque f. **Turkey** n Turquie f.

turkey n dinde f.

Turkish a turc. ● n (Ling) turc m.

turn vt/i tourner; (person) se tourner; (to other side) retourner; (change) (se) transformer (**into** en); (become) devenir; (deflect) détourner; (milk) tourner. ● n tour m; (in road) tournant m; (of mind, events) tournure f; **do a good** ~ rendre service; **in** ~ à tour de rôle; **take** ~**s** se relayer. □ ~ **against** se retourner contre; ~ **away** vi se détourner; vt (avert) détourner; (refuse) refuser; (send back) renvoyer; ~ **back** vi (return) retourner; (vehicle) faire demi-tour; vt (fold) rabattre; ~ **down** refuser; (fold) rabattre; (reduce) baisser; ~ **off** (light) éteindre; (engine) arrêter; (tap) fermer; (of driver) tourner; ~ **on** (light) allumer; (engine) allumer; (tap) ouvrir; ~ **out** vt (light) éteindre; (empty) vider; (produce) produire; vi **it** ~**s out that** il se trouve que; ~ **out well/badly** bien/mal se terminer; ~ **over** (se) retourner; ~ **round** (person) se retourner; ~ **up** vi arriver; (be found) se retrouver; vt (find) déterrer; (collar) remonter.

turning n rue f; (bend) virage m.

turnip n navet m.

turn: ~**-out** n assistance f. ~**over**

n (pie) chausson m; (money) chiffre m d'affaires. ~**table** n (for record) platine f.

turquoise a turquoise inv.

turtle n tortue f (de mer). ~**-neck** n col m montant.

tutor n (private) professeur m particulier; (Univ) (GB) chargé/-e m/f de travaux dirigés.

tutorial n (Univ) classe f de travaux dirigés.

tuxedo n (US) smoking m.

TV n télé f.

tweezers npl pince f (à épiler).

twelfth a & n douzième (mf).

twelve a & n douze (m); ~ (**o'clock**) midi m or minuit m.

twentieth a & n vingtième (mf).

twenty a & n vingt (m).

twice adv deux fois.

twig n brindille f.

twilight n crépuscule m. ● a crépusculaire.

twin n & a jumeau/-elle (m/f). ● vt (pt **twinned**) jumeler.

twinge n (of pain) élancement m; (of conscience, doubt) accès m.

twinkle vi (star) scintiller; (eye) pétiller. ● n scintillement m; pétillement m.

twinning n jumelage m.

twist vt tordre; (weave together) entortiller; (roll) enrouler; (distort) déformer. ● vi (rope) s'entortiller; (road) zigzaguer. ● n torsion f; (in rope) tortillon m; (in road) tournant m; (in play, story) coup m de théâtre.

twitch vi (person) trembloter; (mouth) trembler; (string) vibrer. ● n (tic) tic m; (jerk) secousse f.

two a & n deux (m); **in** ~**s** par deux; **break in** ~ casser en deux.

tycoon n magnat m.

type n type m, genre m; (print) caractères mpl. ● vt/i (write) taper (à la machine). ~**face** n police f

T

(de caractères). ~**writer** *n*
machine *f* à écrire.

typical *a* typique.

typist *n* dactylo *mf*.

tyrant *n* tyran *m*.

tyre *n* pneu *m*.

udder *n* pis *m*, mamelle *f*.

UFO *n* OVNI *m inv*.

UHT *abbr* (**ultra heat treated**) ~
milk lait *m* longue conservation.

ugly *a* (**-ier, -iest**) laid.

UK *abbr* ⇒UNITED KINGDOM.

Ukraine *n* Ukraine *f*.

ulcer *n* ulcère *m*.

ulterior *a* ultérieur; ~ **motive**
arrière-pensée *f*.

ultimate *a* dernier, ultime;
(definitive) définitif; (basic)
fondamental.

ultrasound *n* ultrason *m*.

umbilical cord *n* cordon *m*
ombilical.

umbrella *n* parapluie *m*.

umpire *n* arbitre *m*. ● *vt* arbitrer.

umpteenth *a* ▯ énième.

UN *abbr* (**United Nations**) ONU
f.

unable *a* incapable; (through
circumstances) dans l'impossibilité
(**to do** de faire).

unacceptable *a* (*suggestion*)
inacceptable; (*behaviour*)
inadmissible.

unanimous *a* unanime.
unanimously *adv* à l'unanimité.

unattended *a* sans surveillance.

unattractive *a* (*idea*) peu
attrayant; (*person*) peu attirant.

unauthorized *a* non autorisé.

unavoidable *a* inévitable.

unbearable *a* insupportable.

unbelievable *a* incroyable.

unbiased *a* impartial.

unblock *vt* déboucher.

unborn *a* (*child*) à naître;
(*generation*) à venir.

uncalled-for *a* injustifié, déplacé.

uncanny *a* (**-ier, -iest**) étrange,
troublant.

uncivilized *a* barbare.

uncle *n* oncle *m*.

uncomfortable *a* (*chair*)
inconfortable; (*feeling*) pénible;
feel *or* **be** ~ (person) être mal à
l'aise.

uncommon *a* rare.

unconscious *a* sans
connaissance, inanimé; (not aware)
inconscient (**of** de). ● *n*
inconscient *m*.

unconventional *a* peu
conventionnel.

uncouth *a* grossier.

uncover *vt* découvrir.

undecided *a* indécis.

under *prep* sous; (less than) moins
de; (according to) selon. ● *adv*
au-dessous; ~ **it/there** là-dessous.
~ **age** *a* mineur. ~**cover** *a*
secret. ~**cut** *vt* (*pt* **-cut**; *pres p*
-cutting) (Comm) vendre moins
cher que. ~**dog** *n* (Pol) opprimé/
-e *m/f*; (socially) déshérité/-e *m/f*.
~**done** *a* pas assez cuit.
~**estimate** *vt* sous-estimer.
~**fed** *a* sous-alimenté. ~**go** *vt*
(*pt* -**went**; *pp* **-gone**) subir.
~**graduate** *n* étudiant/-e *m/f*
(*qui prépare la licence*).

underground *a* souterrain;
(secret) clandestin. ● *adv* sous
terre. ● *n* (rail) métro *m*.

under: ~**line** vt souligner. ~**mine** vt saper.

underneath prep sous. ● adv (en) dessous.

under: ~**pants** npl slip m. ~**rate** vt sous-estimer.

understand vt/i (pt **-stood**) comprendre.

understanding a compréhensif. ● n compréhension f; (agreement) entente f.

undertake vt (pt **-took**; pp **-taken**) entreprendre. ~**taker** n entrepreneur m de pompes funèbres. ~**taking** n (task) entreprise f; (promise) promesse f.

underwater a sous-marin. ● adv sous l'eau.

under: ~**wear** n sous-vêtements mpl. ~**world** n (of crime) milieu m, pègre f.

undo vt (pt **-did**; pp **-done**) défaire, détacher; (wrong) réparer; (Comput) annuler.

undress vt/i (se) déshabiller; **get** ~**ed** se déshabiller.

undue a excessif.

unearth vt déterrer.

uneasy a (ill at ease) mal à l'aise; (worried) inquiet; (situation) difficile.

uneducated a (person) inculte; (speech) populaire.

unemployed a en chômage. ● npl **the** ~ les chômeurs mpl.

unemployment n chômage m; ~ **benefit** allocations fpl de chômage.

uneven a inégal.

unexpected a inattendu, imprévu. **unexpectedly** adv (arrive) à l'improviste; (small, fast) étonnamment.

unfair a injuste.

unfaithful a infidèle.

unfit a (Med) pas en forme; (ill) malade; (unsuitable) impropre (**for** à); ~ **to** (unable) pas en état de.

unfold vt déplier; (expose) exposer. ● vi se dérouler.

unforeseen a imprévu.

unforgettable a inoubliable.

unfortunate a malheureux; (event) fâcheux.

ungrateful a ingrat.

unhappy a (**-ier**, **-iest**) (person) malheureux; (face) triste; (not pleased) mécontent (**with** de).

unharmed a indemne, sain et sauf.

unhealthy a (**-ier**, **-iest**) (climate) malsain; (person) en mauvaise santé.

unheard-of a inouï.

unhurt a indemne.

uniform n uniforme m. ● a uniforme.

unify vt unifier.

unintentional a involontaire.

uninterested a indifférent (**in** à).

union n union f; (trade union) syndicat m; **U**~ **Jack** drapeau m du Royaume-Uni.

unique a unique.

unit n unité f; (of furniture) élément m; ● **trust** ≈ SICAV f.

unite vt/i (s')unir.

United Kingdom n Royaume-Uni m.

United Nations npl Nations fpl Unies.

United States (of America) npl États-Unis mpl (d'Amérique).

unity n unité f.

universal a universel.

universe n univers m.

university n université f. ● a universitaire; (student, teacher) d'université.

unkind a pas gentil, méchant.

unknown a inconnu. ● n **the** ~ l'inconnu m.

unleaded a sans plomb.

U

unless *conj* à moins que.

unlike *a* différent. ● *prep* contrairement à; (*different from*) différent de.

unlikely *a* improbable.

unload *vt* décharger.

unlock *vt* ouvrir.

unlucky *a* (**-ier, -iest**) malheureux; (*number*) qui porte malheur.

unmarried *a* célibataire.

unnatural *a* pas naturel, anormal.

unnecessary *a* inutile.

unnoticed *a* inaperçu.

unofficial *a* officieux.

unpack *vt* (*suitcase*) défaire; (*contents*) déballer. ● *vi* défaire sa valise.

unpleasant *a* désagréable (**to** avec).

unplug *vt* débrancher.

unpopular *a* impopulaire; **~ with** mal vu de.

unprofessional *a* peu professionnel.

unqualified *a* non diplômé; (*success*) total; **be ~ to** ne pas être qualifié pour.

unravel *vt* (*pt* **unravelled**) démêler.

unreasonable *a* irréaliste.

unrelated *a* sans rapport (**to** avec).

unreliable *a* peu sérieux; (*machine*) peu fiable.

unrest *n* troubles *mpl*.

unroll *vt* dérouler.

unruly *a* indiscipliné.

unsafe *a* (*dangerous*) dangereux; (*person*) en danger.

unscheduled *a* pas prévu.

unscrupulous *a* sans scrupules, malhonnête.

unsettled *a* instable.

unsightly *a* laid.

unskilled *a* (*worker*) non qualifié.

unsound *a* (*roof*) en mauvais état; (*investment*) douteux.

unsteady *a* (*step*) chancelant; (*ladder*) instable; (*hand*) mal assuré.

unsuccessful *a* (*result, candidate*) malheureux; (*attempt*) infructueux; **be ~** ne pas réussir (**in doing** à faire).

unsuitable *a* inapproprié; **be ~** ne pas convenir.

unsure *a* incertain.

untidy *a* (**-ier, -iest**) (*person*) désordonné; (*room*) en désordre; (*work*) mal soigné.

untie *vt* (*knot, parcel*) défaire; (*person*) détacher.

until *prep* jusqu'à; **not ~** pas avant. ● *conj* jusqu'à ce que; **not ~** pas avant que.

untrue *a* faux.

unused *a* (*new*) neuf; (not in use) inutilisé.

unusual *a* exceptionnel; (*strange*) insolite, étrange.

unwanted *a* (*useless*) superflu; (*child*) non désiré.

unwelcome *a* fâcheux; (*guest*) importun.

unwell *a* souffrant.

unwilling *a* peu disposé (**to** à); (*accomplice*) malgré soi.

unwind *vt/i* (*pt* **unwound**) (se) dérouler; (relax 🄵) se détendre.

unwise *a* imprudent.

unwrap *vt* déballer.

up *adv* en haut, en l'air; (*sun, curtain*) levé; (out of bed) levé, debout; (finished) fini; **be ~** (*level, price*) avoir monté. ● *prep* (a hill) en haut de; (a tree) dans; (a ladder) sur; **come** *or* **go ~** monter; **~ in the bedroom** là-haut dans la chambre; **~ there** là-haut; **~ to** jusqu'à; (*task*) à la hauteur de; **it is ~ to you** ça dépend de vous (**to**

de); **be ~ to sth** (able) être capable de qch; (plot) préparer qch; **be ~ to** (in book) en être à; **be ~ against** faire face à; **~ to date** moderne; (news) récent. ● n **~s and downs** les hauts et les bas mpl.

up-and-coming a prometteur.

upbringing n éducation f.

update vt mettre à jour.

upgrade vt améliorer; (person) promouvoir.

upheaval n bouleversement m.

uphill a qui monte; (fig) difficile. ● adv **go ~** monter.

upholstery n rembourrage m; (in vehicle) garniture f.

upkeep n entretien m.

up-market a haut-de-gamme.

upon prep sur.

upper a supérieur; **have the ~ hand** avoir le dessus. ● n (of shoe) empeigne f. **~ class** n aristocratie f. **~most** a (highest) le plus haut.

upright a droit. ● n (post) montant m.

uprising n soulèvement m.

uproar n tumulte m.

uproot vt déraciner.

upset[1] vt (pt **upset**; pres p **upsetting**) (overturn) renverser; (plan, stomach) déranger; (person) contrarier, affliger. ● a peiné.

upset[2] n dérangement m; (distress) chagrin m.

upside-down adv (lit) à l'envers; (fig) sens dessus dessous.

upstairs adv en haut. ● a (flat) du haut.

uptight a ▣ tendu, coincé ▣.

up-to-date a à la mode; (records) à jour.

upward a & adv, **upwards** adv vers le haut.

urban a urbain.

urge vt conseiller vivement (to do de faire); **~ on** encourager. ● n forte envie f.

urgency n urgence f; (of request, tone) insistance f. **urgent** a urgent; (request) pressant.

urinal n urinoir m.

urine n urine f.

us pron nous; **(to) ~** nous; **both of ~** tous/toutes les deux.

US abbr ⇒UNITED STATES.

USA abbr ⇒UNITED STATES OF AMERICA.

use[1] vt se servir de, utiliser; (consume) consommer; **~ up** épuiser.

use[2] n usage m, emploi m; **in ~** en usage; **it is no ~ doing** ça ne sert à rien de faire; **make ~ of** se servir de; **of ~** utile.

used[1] a (car) d'occasion.

used[2] v aux **he ~ to smoke** il fumait (autrefois). ● a **~ to** habitué à.

useful a utile.

useless a inutile; (person) incompétent.

user n (of road, service) usager m; (of product) utilisateur/-trice m/f. **~-friendly** a facile d'emploi; (Comput) convivial.

usual a habituel, normal; **as ~** comme d'habitude. **usually** adv d'habitude.

utility n utilité f; (public) **~** service m public.

utmost a (furthest, most intense) extrême; **the ~ care** le plus grand soin. ● n **do one's ~** faire tout son possible.

utter a complet, absolu. ● vt prononcer.

U-turn n demi-tour m; (fig) volte-face f inv.

U

vacancy n (post) poste m vacant; (room) chambre f disponible.

vacant a (post) vacant; (seat) libre; (look) vague.

vacate vt quitter.

vacation n vacances fpl.

vaccinate vt vacciner.

vacuum n vide m. ~ **cleaner** n aspirateur m. ~**-packed** a emballé sous vide.

vagina n vagin m.

vagrant n vagabond/-e m/f.

vague a vague; (outline) flou; **be ~ about** ne pas préciser.

vain a (conceited) vaniteux; (useless) vain; **in ~** en vain.

valentine n ~ (**card**) carte f de la Saint-Valentin.

valid a (argument, ticket) valable; (passport) valide.

valley n vallée f.

valuable a (object) de valeur; (help) précieux. **valuables** npl objets mpl de valeur.

valuation n (of painting) expertise f; (of house) évaluation f.

value n valeur f; ~ **added tax** taxe f à la valeur ajoutée, TVA f. ● vt (appraise) évaluer; (cherish) attacher de la valeur à.

valve n (Tech) soupape f; (of tyre) valve f; (Med) valvule f.

van n camionnette f.

vandal n vandale mf.

vanguard n **in the ~ of** à l'avant-garde f de.

vanilla n vanille f.

vanish vi disparaître.

vapour n vapeur f.

variable a variable.

varicose a ~ **veins** varices fpl.

varied a varié.

variety n variété f; (entertainment) variétés fpl.

various a divers.

varnish n vernis m. ● vt vernir.

vary vt/i varier.

vase n vase m.

vast a (space) vaste; (in quantity) énorme.

vat n cuve f.

VAT abbr (value added tax) TVA f.

vault n (roof) voûte f; (in bank) chambre f forte; (tomb) caveau m; (jump) saut m. ● vt/i sauter.

VCR abbr ⇒VIDEO CASSETTE RECORDER.

VDU abbr ⇒VISUAL DISPLAY UNIT.

veal n veau m.

vegan a & n végétalien/-ne (m/f).

vegetable n légume m. ● a végétal.

vegetarian a & n végétarien/-ne (m/f).

vehicle n véhicule m.

veil n voile m.

vein n (in body, rock) veine f; (on leaf) nervure f.

velvet n velours m.

vending-machine n distributeur m automatique.

veneer n (on wood) placage m; (fig) vernis m.

venereal a vénérien.

venetian a ~ **blind** jalousie f.

vengeance n vengeance f; **with a ~** de plus belle.

venison n venaison f.

venom n venin m.

vent n bouche f, conduit m; (in coat) fente f. ● vt (anger) décharger (**on** sur).

ventilate vt ventiler. **ventilator** n ventilateur m.

venture n entreprise f. ● vt/i (se) risquer.

venue n lieu m.

verb n verbe m.

verbal a verbal.

verdict n verdict m.

verge n bord m; on the ∼ of doing sur le point de faire. ● vi ∼ on friser, frôler.

verify vt vérifier.

vermin n vermine f.

versatile a (person) aux talents variés; (mind) souple.

verse n strophe f; (of Bible) verset m; (poetry) vers mpl.

version n version f.

versus prep contre.

vertebra n (pl **-brae**) vertèbre f.

vertical a vertical.

vertigo n vertige m.

very adv très. ● a (actual) même; the ∼ day le jour même; at the ∼ end tout à la fin; the ∼ first le tout premier; ∼ much beaucoup.

vessel n vaisseau m.

vest n maillot m de corps; (waistcoat: US) gilet m.

vet n vétérinaire mf. ● vt (pt **vetted**) (candidate) examiner (de près).

veteran n vétéran m; (war) ∼ ancien combattant m.

veterinary a vétérinaire; ∼ **surgeon** vétérinaire mf.

veto n (pl ∼**es**) veto m; (right) droit m de veto. ● vt mettre son veto à.

vibrate vt/i (faire) vibrer.

vicar n pasteur m.

vice n (depravity) vice m; (Tech) étau m.

vicinity n environs mpl; in the ∼ of à proximité de.

vicious a (spiteful) méchant; (violent) brutal; ∼ **circle** cercle m vicieux.

victim n victime f.

victor n vainqueur m. **victory** n victoire f.

video a (game, camera) vidéo inv. ● n (recorder) magnétoscope m; (film) vidéo f; ∼ (**cassette**) cassette f vidéo. ● vt enregistrer. ∼ **game** n jeu m vidéo. ∼**phone** n vidéophone m.

videotape n bande f vidéo. ● vt (programme) enregistrer; (wedding) filmer avec une caméra vidéo.

view n vue f; in my ∼ à mon avis; in ∼ of compte tenu de; on ∼ exposé; with a ∼ to dans le but de. ● vt (watch) regarder; (consider) considérer (as comme); (house) visiter. **viewer** n (TV) téléspectateur/-trice m/f.

view: ∼**finder** n viseur m. ∼**point** n point m de vue.

vigilant a vigilant.

vigour, (US) **vigor** n vigueur f.

vile a (base) vil; (bad) abominable.

villa n pavillon m; (for holiday) villa f.

village n village m.

villain n scélérat m, bandit m; (in story) méchant m.

vindictive a vindicatif.

vine n vigne f.

vinegar n vinaigre m.

vineyard n vignoble m.

vintage n (year) année f, millésime m. ● a (wine) de grand cru; (car) d'époque.

viola n (Mus) alto m.

violate vt violer.

violence n violence f. **violent** a violent.

violet n (Bot) violette f; (colour) violet m.

violin n violon m.

VIP abbr (**very important person**) personnalité f, VIP m.

virgin *n* (woman) vierge *f*.
Virgo *n* Vierge *f*.
virtual *a* quasi-total; (Comput) virtuel. **virtually** *adv* pratiquement.
virtue *n* vertu *f*; (advantage) mérite *m*; **by ~ of** en raison de.
virus *n* virus *m*.
visa *n* visa *m*.
visibility *n* visibilité *f*. **visible** *a* visible.
vision *n* vision *f*.
visit *vt* (*pt* **visited**) (*person*) rendre visite à; (*place*) visiter. ● *vi* être en visite. ● *n* (tour, call) visite *f*; (stay) séjour *m*. **visitor** *n* visiteur/-euse *m/f*; (guest) invité -e *m/f*.
visual *a* visuel. **~ display unit** *n* visuel *m*, console *f* de visualisation.
visualize *vt* se représenter; (foresee) envisager.
vital *a* vital.
vitamin *n* vitamine *f*.
vivacious *a* plein de vivacité.
vivid *a* (*colour, imagination*) vif; (*description, dream*) frappant.
vivisection *n* vivisection *f*.
vocabulary *n* vocabulaire *m*.
vocal *a* vocal; (*person*) qui s'exprime franchement. **~ cords** *npl* cordes *fpl* vocales.
vocation *n* vocation *f*. **vocational** *a* professionnel.
voice *n* voix *f*. ● *vt* (express) formuler. **~ mail** *n* messagerie *f* vocale.
void *a* vide (**of** de); (not valid) nul. ● *n* vide *m*.
volatile *a* (*person*) versatile; (*situation*) explosif.
volcano *n* (*pl* **~es**) volcan *m*.
volley *n* (of blows, in tennis) volée *f*; (of gunfire) salve *f*.
volt *n* (Electr) volt *m*. **voltage** *n* tension *f*.

volume *n* volume *m*.
voluntary *a* volontaire; (unpaid) bénévole.
volunteer *n* volontaire *mf*. ● *vi* s'offrir (**to do** pour faire); (Mil) s'engager comme volontaire. ● *vt* offrir.
vomit *vt/i* (*pt* **vomited**) vomir. ● *n* vomi *m*.
vote *n* vote *m*; (right) droit *m* de vote. ● *vt/i* voter; **~ sb in** élire qn. **voter** *n* électeur/-trice *m/f*. **voting** *n* vote *m* (**of** de); (poll) scrutin *m*.
vouch *vi* **~ for** se porter garant de.
voucher *n* bon *m*.
vowel *n* voyelle *f*.
voyage *n* voyage *m* (en mer).
vulgar *a* vulgaire.
vulnerable *a* vulnérable.

wad *n* (pad) tampon *m*; (bundle) liasse *f*.
wade *vi* **~ through** (*mud*) patauger dans; (*book*: fig) avancer péniblement dans.
wafer *n* (biscuit) gaufrette *f*.
waffle *n* (talk 🔲) verbiage *m*; (cake) gaufre *f*. ● *vi* 🔲 divaguer.
wag *vt/i* (*pt* **wagged**) (tail) remuer.
wage *vt* (campaign) mener; **~ war** faire la guerre. ● *n* (weekly, daily) salaire *m*; **~s** salaire *m*. **~-earner** *n* salarié/-e *m/f*.
wagon *n* (horse-drawn) chariot *m*; (Rail) wagon *m* (de marchandises).

wail *vi* gémir. ● *n* gémissement *m*.

waist *n* taille *f*. ∼**coat** *n* gilet *m*.

wait *vt/i* attendre; **I can't ∼ to start** j'ai hâte de commencer; **let's ∼ and see** attendons voir; ∼ **for** attendre; ∼ **on** servir. ● *n* attente *f*.

waiter *n* garçon *m*, serveur *m*.

waiting-list *n* liste *f* d'attente.

waiting-room *n* salle *f* d'attente.

waitress *n* serveuse *f*.

waive *vt* renoncer à.

wake *vt/i* (*pt* **woke**; *pp* **woken**) ∼ **(up)** (se) réveiller. ● *n* (track) sillage *m*; **in the ∼ of** (after) à la suite de. ∼ **up call** *n* réveil *m* téléphoné.

Wales *n* pays *m* de Galles.

walk *vi* marcher; (not ride) aller à pied; (stroll) se promener. ● *vt* (streets) parcourir; (distance) faire à pied; (dog) promener. ● *n* promenade *f*, tour *m*; (gait) démarche *f*; (pace) marche *f*, pas *m*; (path) allée *f*; **have a ∼** faire une promenade. □ ∼ **out** (go away) partir; (worker) faire grève; ∼ **out on** abandonner.

walkie-talkie *n* talkie-walkie *m*.

walking *n* marche *f* (à pied). ● *a* (corpse, dictionary: fig) ambulant.

walkman® *n* walkman® *m*, baladeur *m*.

walk: ∼**-out** *n* grève *f* surprise. ∼**-over** *n* victoire *f* facile.

wall *n* mur *m*; (of tunnel, stomach) paroi *f*. ● *a* mural. **walled** *a* (city) fortifié.

wallet *n* portefeuille *m*.

wallpaper *n* papier *m* peint. ● *vt* tapisser.

walnut *n* (nut) noix *f*; (tree) noyer *m*.

waltz *n* valse *f*. ● *vi* valser.

wander *vi* errer; (stroll) flâner;

(digress) s'écarter du sujet; (in mind) divaguer.

wane *vi* décroître.

want *vt* vouloir (**to do** faire); (need) avoir besoin de (**doing** d'être fait); (ask for) demander; **I ∼ you to do it** je veux que vous le fassiez. ● *vi* ∼ **for** manquer de. ● *n* (need, poverty) besoin *m*; (desire) désir *m*; (lack) manque *m*; **for ∼ of** faute de. **wanted** *a* (*criminal*) recherché par la police.

war *n* guerre *f*; **at ∼** en guerre; **on the ∼path** sur le sentier de la guerre.

ward *n* (in hospital) salle *f*; (minor: Jur) pupille *mf*; (Pol) division *f* électorale. ● *vt* ∼ **off** (*danger*) prévenir.

warden *n* directeur/-trice *m/f*; (of park) gardien/-ne *m/f*; (*traffic*) ∼ contractuel/-le *m/f*.

wardrobe *n* (furniture) armoire *f*; (clothes) garde-robe *f*.

warehouse *n* entrepôt *m*.

wares *npl* marchandises *fpl*.

warfare *n* guerre *f*.

warm *a* chaud; (hearty) chaleureux; **be** *or* **feel ∼** avoir chaud; **it is ∼** il fait chaud. ● *vt/i* ∼ **(up)** (se) réchauffer; (*food*) chauffer; (liven up) (s')animer; (exercise) s'échauffer.

warmth *n* chaleur *f*.

warn *vt* avertir, prévenir; ∼ **sb off sth** (advise against) mettre qn en garde contre qch; (forbid) interdire qch à qn.

warning *n* avertissement *m*; (notice) avis *m*; **without ∼** sans prévenir. ∼ **light** *n* voyant *m*. ∼ **triangle** *n* triangle *m* de sécurité.

warp *vt/i* (*wood*) (se) voiler; (pervert) pervertir; (*judgment*) fausser.

warrant *n* (for arrest) mandat *m* (d'arrêt); (Comm) autorisation *f*. ● *vt* justifier.

warranty n garantie f.

wart n verrue f.

wartime n in ~ en temps de guerre.

wary a (-ier, -iest) prudent.

was ⇒BE.

wash vt/i (se) laver; (flow over) baigner; ~ one's hands of se laver les mains de. ● n lavage m; (clothes) lessive f; have a ~ se laver. □ ~ up faire la vaisselle; (US) se laver. ~-basin n lavabo m.

washer n rondelle f.

washing n lessive f. ~-machine n machine f à laver. ~-powder n lessive f.

washing-up n vaisselle f. ~ liquid n liquide m vaisselle.

wash: ~-out n 🄸 fiasco m. ~-room n (US) toilettes fpl.

wasp n guêpe f.

wastage n gaspillage m.

waste vt gaspiller; (time) perdre. ● vi ~ away dépérir. ● a superflu; ~ products or matter déchets mpl. ● n gaspillage m; (of time) perte f; (rubbish) déchets mpl; lay ~ dévaster. **wasteful** a peu économique; (person) gaspilleur.

waste: ~ land n (desolate) terre f désolée; (unused) terre f inculte; (in town) terrain m vague. ~ paper n vieux papiers mpl. ~-paper basket n corbeille f (à papier).

watch vt/i (television) regarder; (observe) observer; (guard, spy on) surveiller; (be careful about) faire attention à. ● n (for telling time) montre f; (Naut) quart m; be on the ~ guetter; keep ~ on surveiller. □ ~ out faire attention (for à); ~ out for (keep watch) guetter.

water n eau f; by ~ en bateau. ● vt arroser. ● vi (eyes) larmoyer; my/his mouth ~s l'eau me/lui vient à la bouche. □ ~ down

couper (d'eau); (tone down) édulcorer. ~-colour n (painting) aquarelle f. ~-cress n cresson m (de fontaine). ~fall n chute f d'eau, cascade f. ~ heater n chauffe-eau m. watering-can n arrosoir m. ~-lily n nénuphar m. ~-melon n pastèque f. ~proof a (material) imperméable. ~shed n (in affairs) tournant m décisif. ~-skiing n ski m nautique. ~tight a étanche. ~way n voie f navigable.

watery a (colour) délavé; (eyes) humide; (soup) trop liquide.

wave n vague f; (in hair) ondulation f; (radio) onde f; (sign) signe m. ● vt agiter. ● vi faire signe (de la main); (move in wind) flotter.

waver vi vaciller.

wavy a (line) onduleux; (hair) ondulé.

wax n cire f; (for skis) fart m. ● vt cirer; farter; (car) lustrer.

way n (road, path) chemin m (to de); (distance) distance f; (direction) direction f; (manner) façon f; (means) moyen m; ~s (habits) habitudes fpl; be in the ~ bloquer le passage; (hindrance: fig) gêner (qn); be on one's or the ~ être sur son or le chemin; by the ~ à propos; by the ~side au bord de la route; by ~ of comme; (via) par; go out of one's ~ se donner du mal; in a ~ dans un sens; make one's ~ somewhere se rendre quelque part; push one's ~ through se frayer un passage; that ~ par là; this ~ par ici; ~ in entrée f; ~ out sortie f. ● adv 🄸 loin.

we pron nous.

weak a faible; (delicate) fragile.

weakness n faiblesse f; (fault) point m faible; a ~ for (liking) un faible pour.

wealth *n* richesse *f*; (riches, resources) richesses *fpl*; (quantity) profusion *f*.

wealthy *a* (**-ier, -iest**) riche. ● *n* the ~ les riches *mpl*.

weapon *n* arme *f*.

wear *vt* (*pt* **wore**; *pp* **worn**) porter; (put on) mettre; (*expression*) avoir. ● *vi* (last) durer; ~ (**out**) (s')user. ● *n* (use) usage *m*; (damage) usure *f*. □ ~ **down** user; ~ **off** (*colour, pain*) passer; ~ **out** (exhaust) épuiser.

weary *a* (**-ier, -iest**) fatigué, las. ● *vi* ~ **of** se lasser de.

weather *n* temps *m*; **under the** ~ patraque. ● *a* météorologique. ● *vt* (survive) réchapper de *or* à. ~ **forecast** *n* météo *f*.

weave *vt/i* (*pt* **wove**; *pp* **woven**) tisser; (*basket*) tresser; (move) se faufiler. ● *n* (style) tissage *m*.

web *n* (of spider) toile *f*; (on foot) palmure *f*. ~**cam** *n* webcam *f*. ~**master** *n* administrateur *m* de site Internet. ~ **page** *n* page *f* Web. ~ **search** *n* recherche *f* sur le Web. ~**site** *n* site *m* Internet. **Web** *n* (Comput) Web *m*.

wedding *n* mariage *m*. ~**ring** *n* alliance *f*.

wedge *n* (of wood) coin *m*; (under wheel) cale *f*. ● *vt* caler; (push) enfoncer; (crowd) coincer.

Wednesday *n* mercredi *m*.

weed *n* mauvaise herbe *f*. ● *vt/i* désherber; ~ **out** extirper.

week *n* semaine *f*; **a** ~ **today/ tomorrow** aujourd'hui/demain en huit. ~**day** *n* jour *m* de semaine. ~**end** *n* week-end *m*, fin *f* de semaine.

weekly *adv* toutes les semaines. ● *a & n* (periodical) hebdomadaire (*m*).

weep *vt/i* (*pt* **wept**) pleurer (**for sb** qn).

weigh *vt/i* peser; ~ **anchor** lever l'ancre. □ ~ **down** lester (avec un poids); (bend) faire plier; (fig) accabler; ~ **up** calculer.

weight *n* poids *m*; **lose/put on** ~ perdre/prendre du poids. ~**-lifting** *n* haltérophilie *f*. ~ **training** *n* musculation *f* en salle.

weird *a* bizarre.

welcome *a* agréable; (timely) opportun; **be** ~ être le *or* la bienvenu(e), être les bienvenu (e)s; **you're** ~! il n'y a pas de quoi!; ~ **to do** libre de faire. ● *interj* soyez le *or* la bienvenu (e), soyez les bienvenu(e)s. ● *vt* accueil *m*. ● *vt* accueillir; (as greeting) souhaiter la bienvenue à; (fig) se réjouir de.

weld *vt* souder. ● *n* soudure *f*.

welfare *n* bien-être *m*; (aid) aide *f* sociale. **W~ State** *n* État-providence *m*.

well¹ *n* puits *m*.

well² *adv* (**better, best**) bien; **do** ~ (succeed) réussir; ~ **done!** bravo! ● *a* bien *inv*; **as** ~ aussi; **be** ~ (healthy) aller bien. ● *interj* eh bien; (surprise) tiens.

well: ~ **behaved** *a* sage. ~**being** *n* bien-être *m inv*.

wellington *n* (boot) botte *f* de caoutchouc.

well: ~**-known** *a* (bien) connu. ~**-meaning** *a* bien intentionné. ~ **off** aisé, riche. ~**-read** *a* instruit. ~**-to-do** *a* riche. ~**-wisher** *n* admirateur/-trice *m/ f*.

Welsh *a* gallois. ● *n* (Ling) gallois *m*.

went ⇒GO.

wept ⇒WEEP.

were ⇒BE.

west *n* ouest *m*; **the W~** (Pol) l'Occident *m*. ● *a* d'ouest. ● *adv* vers l'ouest.

western *a* de l'ouest; (Pol)
occidental. ● *n* (film) western *m*.
westerner *n* occidental/-e *m/f*.
West Indies *n* Antilles *fpl*.
westward *a* (side) ouest *inv*;
(journey) vers l'ouest.
wet *a* (wetter, wettest) mouillé;
(damp, rainy) humide; (paint) frais;
get ~ se mouiller. ● *vt* (pt
wetted) mouiller. ● *n* **the ~**
l'humidité *f*; (rain) la pluie *f*. **~
suit** *n* combinaison *f* de plongée.
whale *n* baleine *f*.
wharf *n* quai *m*.

what

● *pronoun*

····➤ (in questions as object pronoun)
qu'est-ce que?; **~ are we going to
do?** qu'est-ce que nous allons
faire?

····➤ (in questions as subject pronoun)
qu'est-ce qui?; **~ happened?**
qu'est-ce qui s'est passé?

····➤ (introducing clause as object) ce
que; **I don't know ~ he wants** je
ne sais pas ce qu'il veut.

····➤ (introducing clause as subject) ce
qui; **tell me ~ happened** raconte-
moi ce qui s'est passé.

····➤ (with prepositions) quoi; **~ are
you thinking about?** à quoi
penses-tu?

● *determiner*

····➤ quel/quelle/quels/quelles; **~
train did you catch?** quel train
as-tu pris?; **~ time is it?** quelle
heure est-il?

whatever *a* **~ book** quel que
soit le livre. ● *pron* (no matter what) quoi
que, quoi qu'; (anything that) tout ce
qui; (object) tout ce que *or* qu'; **~
happens** quoi qu'il arrive; **~
happened?** qu'est-ce qui est
arrivé?; **~ the problems** quels que

soient les problèmes; **~ you want**
tout ce que vous voulez; **nothing
~** rien du tout.
whatsoever *a & pron* =
WHATEVER.
wheat *n* blé *m*, froment *m*.
wheel *n* roue *f*; **at the ~** (of vehicle)
au volant; (helm) au gouvernail.
● *vt* pousser. ● *vi* tourner; **~ and
deal** faire des combines.
~barrow *n* brouette *f*. **~chair** *n*
fauteuil *m* roulant.
when *adv & pron* quand. ● *conj*
quand, lorsque; **the day/moment
~** le jour/moment où.
whenever *conj & adv* (at whatever
time) quand; (every time that) chaque
fois que.
where *adv, conj & pron* où;
(whereas) alors que; (the place that) là
où.
whereabouts *adv* (à peu près)
où. ● *n* **sb's ~** l'endroit où se
trouve qn.
whereas *conj* alors que.
wherever *conj & adv* où que;
(everywhere) partout où; (anywhere)
(là) où; (emphatic where) où donc.
whether *conj* si; **not know ~** ne
pas savoir si; **~ I go or not** que
j'aille ou non.

which

● *pronoun*

····➤ (in questions) lequel/laquelle/
lesquels/lesquelles; **there are
three peaches, ~ do you want?** il
y a trois pêches, laquelle
veux-tu?

····➤ (in questions with superlative
adjective) quel/quelle/quels/
quelles; **~ (apple) is the biggest?**
quelle est la plus grosse?

····➤ (in relative clauses as subject) qui;
the book ~ is on the table le livre
qui est sur la table.

····▸ (in relative clauses as object) que;
the book ~ Tina is reading le livre
que lit Tina.

● *determiner*

····▸ quel/quelle/quels/quelles; **~
car did you choose?** quelle
voiture as-tu choisie?

whichever *a* **~ book** quel que
soit le livre que *or* qui; **take ~
book you wish** prenez le livre que
vous voulez. ● *pron* celui/celle/
ceux/celles qui *or* que.

while *n* moment *m*. ● *conj* (when)
pendant que; (although) bien que;
(as long as) tant que. ● *vt* **~ away**
(*time*) passer.

whilst *conj* = WHILE.

whim *n* caprice *m*.

whine *vi* gémir, se plaindre. ● *n*
gémissement *m*.

whip *n* fouet *m*. ● *vt* (*pt
whipped*) fouetter; (Culin)
fouetter, battre; (seize) enlever
brusquement. ● *vi* (move) aller en
vitesse. □ **~ up** exciter; (cause)
provoquer; (*meal* ▣) préparer.

whirl *vt/i* (faire) tourbillonner.
● *n* tourbillon *m*. **~pool** *n*
tourbillon *m*. **~wind** *n* tourbillon
m (de vent).

whisk *vt* (snatch) enlever *or*
emmener brusquement; (Culin)
fouetter. ● *n* (Culin) fouet *m*.

whiskers *npl* (of animal)
moustaches *fpl*; (of man) favoris
mpl.

whisper *vt/i* chuchoter. ● *n*
chuchotement *m*; (rumour: fig)
rumeur *f*, bruit *m*.

whistle *n* sifflement *m*; (instrument)
sifflet *m*. ● *vt/i* siffler; **~ at** *or* **for**
siffler.

white *a* blanc. ● *n* blanc *m*;
(person) blanc/-che *m/f*. **~ coffee**
n café *m* au lait. **~-collar worker**
n employé/-e *m/f* de bureau. **~
elephant** *n* projet *m* coûteux et

peu rentable. **~ lie** *n* pieux
mensonge *m*. **W~ Paper** *n* livre
m blanc.

whitewash *n* blanc *m* de chaux.
● *vt* blanchir à la chaux; (*person*:
fig) blanchir.

Whitsun *n* la Pentecôte.

whiz *vi* (*pt* **whizzed**) (through air)
fendre l'air; (hiss) siffler; (rush)
aller à toute vitesse. **~-kid** *n*
jeune prodige *m*.

who *pron* qui.

whoever *pron* (no matter who) qui
que ce soit qui *or* que; (the one
who) quiconque; **tell ~ you want**
dites-le à qui vous voulez.

whole *a* entier; (intact) intact; **the
~ house** toute la maison. ● *n*
totalité *f*; (unit) tout *m*; **on the ~**
dans l'ensemble. **~foods** *npl*
aliments *mpl* naturels et
diététiques. **~-hearted** *a* sans
réserve. **~meal** *a* complet.

wholesale *a* (*firm*) de gros; (fig)
systématique. ● *adv* (in large
quantities) en gros; (fig) en masse.

wholesome *a* sain.

wholly *adv* entièrement.

whom *pron* (that) que, qu'; (after
prepositions & in questions) qui, *or* **~**
dont; **with ~** avec qui.

whooping cough *n* coqueluche
f.

whose *pron & a* à qui, de qui; **~
hat is this?**, **~ is this hat?** à qui est
ce chapeau?; **~ son are you?** de
qui êtes-vous le fils?; **the man ~
hat I see** l'homme dont je vois le
chapeau.

why *adv* pourquoi; **the reason ~** la
raison pour laquelle.

wicked *a* méchant, mauvais,
vilain.

wide *a* large; (*ocean*) vaste. ● *adv*
(*fall*) loin du but; **open ~** ouvrir
tout grand; **~ open** grand ouvert;
~ awake éveillé. **widely** *adv*
(*spread, space*) largement;

(*travel*) beaucoup; (generally) généralement; (extremely) extrêmement.

widespread *a* très répandu.

widow *n* veuve *f*. **widowed** *a* (*man*) veuf; (*woman*) veuve. **widower** *n* veuf *m*.

width *n* largeur *f*.

wield *vt* (*axe*) manier; (*power*: fig) exercer.

wife *n* (*pl* **wives**) femme *f*, épouse *f*.

wig *n* perruque *f*.

wiggle *vt/i* remuer; (*hips*) tortiller; (*worm*) se tortiller.

wild *a* sauvage; (*sea, enthusiasm*) déchaîné; (*mad*) fou; (*angry*) furieux. ● *adv* (*grow*) à l'état sauvage.

wildlife *n* faune *f*.

will¹

present will; *present negative* won't, will not; *past* would

● *auxiliary verb*

····► (in future tense) **he'll come** il viendra; **it ~ be sunny tomorrow** il va faire du soleil demain.

····► (inviting and requesting) **~ you have some coffee?** est-ce que vous voulez du café?

····► (making assumptions) **they won't know what's happened** ils ne doivent pas savoir ce qui s'est passé.

····► (in short questions and answers) **you'll come again, won't you?** tu reviendras, n'est-ce pas?; **'they won't forget'—'yes they ~'** 'ils n'oublieront pas'—'si'.

····► (capacity) **the lift ~ hold 12** l'ascenseur peut transporter 12 personnes.

····► (ability) **the car won't start** la voiture ne veut pas démarrer.

● *transitive verb*

····► **~ sb's death** souhaiter ardemment la mort de qn.

will² *n* volonté *f*; (*document*) testament *m*; **at ~** quand *or* comme on veut.

willing *a* (*help, offer*) spontané; (*helper*) bien disposé; **~ to** disposé à. **willingly** *adv* (with pleasure) volontiers; (not forced) volontairement. **willingness** *n* empressement *m* (**to do** à faire).

willow *n* saule *m*.

will-power *n* volonté *f*.

win *vt/i* (*pt* **won**; *pres p* **winning**) gagner; (*victory, prize*) remporter; (*fame, fortune*) acquérir, trouver; **~ round** convaincre. ● *n* victoire *f*.

winch *n* treuil *m*. ● *vt* hisser au treuil.

wind¹ *n* vent *m*; (*breath*) souffle *m*; **get ~ of** avoir vent de; **in the ~** dans l'air. ● *vt* essouffler. **~ farm** *n* ferme *f* d'éoliennes.

wind² *vt/i* (*pt* **wound**) (s')enrouler; (*of path, river*) serpenter; **~ (up)** (*clock*) remonter; **~ (up)** (*end*) (se) terminer; **~ up in hospital** finir à l'hôpital.

windmill *n* moulin *m* à vent.

window *n* fenêtre *f*; (*glass pane*) vitre *f*; (in vehicle, train) vitre *f*; (in shop) vitrine *f*; (counter) guichet *m*; (Comput) fenêtre *f*. **~-box** *n* jardinière *f*. **~-cleaner** *n* laveur *m* de carreaux. **~-dresser** *n* étalagiste *mf*. **~-ledge** *n* rebord *m* de (la) fenêtre. **~-shopping** *n* lèche-vitrines *m*. **~-sill** *n* (inside) appui *m* de (la) fenêtre; (outside) rebord *m* de (la) fenêtre.

windscreen *n* pare-brise *m inv*. **~ wiper** *n* essuie-glace *m*.

windshield *n* (US) = WINDSCREEN.

windsurfing *n* planche *f* à voile.

windy *a* (**-ier, -iest**) venteux; **it is ~** il y a du vent.

wine *n* vin *m*. **~-cellar** *n* cave *f* (à vin). **~glass** *n* verre *m* à vin. **~-grower** *n* viticulteur *m*. **~ list** *n* carte *f* des vins. **~-tasting** *n* dégustation *f* de vins.

wing *n* aile *f*; **~s** (Theat) coulisses *fpl*; **under one's ~** sous son aile. **~ mirror** *n* rétroviseur *m* extérieur.

wink *vi* faire un clin d'œil; (*light, star*) clignoter. ● *n* clin *m* d'œil; clignotement *m*.

winner *n* (of game) gagnant/-e *m/f*; (of fight) vainqueur *m*.

winning ⇒WIN. ● *a* (*number, horse*) gagnant; (*team*) victorieux; (*smile*) engageant. **winnings** *npl* gains *mpl*.

winter *n* hiver *m*.

wipe *vt* essuyer. ● *vi* **~ up** essuyer la vaisselle. ● *n* coup *m* de torchon *or* d'éponge. □ **~ out** (destroy) anéantir; (remove) effacer.

wire *n* fil *m*; (US) télégramme *m*.

wiring *n* (Electr) installation *f* électrique.

wisdom *n* sagesse *f*.

wise *a* prudent, sage; (*look*) averti.

wish *n* (specific) souhait *m*, vœu *m*; (general) désir *m*; **best ~es** (in letter) amitiés *fpl*; (on greeting card) meilleurs vœux *mpl*. ● *vt* souhaiter, vouloir, désirer (**to do** faire); (bid) souhaiter. ● *vi* **~ for** souhaiter; **I ~ he'd leave** je voudrais bien qu'il parte.

wishful *a* **it's ~ thinking** c'est prendre ses désirs pour des réalités.

wistful *a* mélancolique.

wit *n* intelligence *f*; (humour) esprit *m*; (person) homme *m* d'esprit, femme *f* d'esprit.

witch *n* sorcière *f*.

with *prep* avec; (having) à; (because of) de; (at house of) chez; **the man ~** the beard l'homme à la barbe; **fill ~** remplir de; **pleased/shaking ~** content/frémissant de.

withdraw *vt/i* (*pt* withdrew; *pp* withdrawn) (se) retirer.

withdrawal *n* retrait *m*.

wither *vt/i* (se) flétrir.

withhold *vt* (*pt* withheld) refuser (de donner); (retain) retenir; (conceal) cacher (**from** à).

within *prep & adv* à l'intérieur (de); (in distances) à moins de; **~ a month** (before) avant un mois; **~ sight** en vue.

without *prep* sans; **~ my knowing** sans que je sache.

withstand *vt* (*pt* withstood) résister à.

witness *n* témoin *m*; (evidence) témoignage *m*; **bear ~ to** témoigner de. ● *vt* être le témoin de, voir. **~ box**, **~ stand** *n* barre *f* des témoins.

witty *a* (**-ier, -iest**) spirituel.

wives ⇒WIFE.

wizard *n* magicien *m*; (genius: fig) génie *m*.

woke, woken ⇒WAKE.

wolf *n* (*pl* wolves) loup *m*. ● *vt* (*food*) engloutir.

woman *n* (*pl* women) femme *f*; **~ doctor** femme *f* médecin; **~ driver** femme *f* au volant.

women ⇒WOMAN.

won ⇒WIN.

wonder *n* émerveillement *m*; (thing) merveille *f*; **it is no ~** ce *or* il n'est pas étonnant (**that** que). ● *vt* se demander (**if** si). ● *vi* s'étonner (**at** de); (reflect) songer (**about** à).

wonderful *a* merveilleux.

won't = WILL NOT.

wood *n* bois *m*.

wooden *a* en *or* de bois; (stiff: fig) raide, comme du bois.

wood: ~wind *n* (Mus) bois *mpl*.

~**work** n (craft, objects) menuiserie f.

wool n laine f. **woollen** a de laine. **woollens** npl lainages mpl.

woolly a laineux; (vague) nébuleux. ● n (garment ⬚) lainage m.

word n mot m; (spoken) parole f, mot m; (promise) parole f; (news) nouvelles fpl; **by ~ of mouth** de vive voix; **give/keep one's ~** donner/tenir sa parole; **have a ~ with** parler à; **in other ~s** autrement dit. ● vt rédiger. **wording** n termes mpl.

word processing n traitement m de texte. **word processor** n machine f à traitement de texte.

wore ⇒WEAR.

work n travail m; (product, book) œuvre f, ouvrage m; (building work) travaux mpl; **~s** (Tech) mécanisme m; (factory) usine f. ● vi (person) travailler; (drug) agir; (Tech) fonctionner, marcher. ● vt (Tech) faire fonctionner, faire marcher; (land, mine) exploiter; (shape, hammer) travailler; **~ sb** (make work) faire travailler qn. □ **~ out** vt (solve) résoudre; (calculate) calculer; (elaborate) élaborer; vi (succeed) marcher; (Sport) s'entraîner; **~ up** vt développer; vi (to climax) monter vers; **~ed up** (person) énervé.

workaholic n ⬚ bourreau m de travail.

worker n travailleur/-euse m/f; (manual) ouvrier/-ière m/f.

work-force n main-d'œuvre f.

working a (day, lunch) de travail; **~s** mécanisme m; **in ~ order** en état de marche.

working class n classe f ouvrière. ● a ouvrier.

workman n (pl **-men**) ouvrier m.

work: ~ out n séance f de mise

en forme. **~shop** n atelier m. **~-station** n poste m de travail.

world n monde m; **best in the ~** meilleur au monde. ● a (power) mondial; (record) du monde.

world-wide a universel.

World Wide Web, WWW n World Wide Web m, réseau m des réseaux.

worm n ver m. ● vt **~ one's way into** s'insinuer dans.

worn ⇒WEAR. ● a usé. **~-out** a (thing) complètement usé; (person) épuisé.

worried a inquiet.

worry vt/i (s')inquiéter. ● n souci m.

worse a pire, plus mauvais; **be ~ off** perdre. ● adv plus mal. ● n pire m. **worsen** vt/i empirer.

worship n (adoration) culte m. ● vt (pt **worshipped**) adorer. ● vi faire ses dévotions.

worst a pire, plus mauvais. ● adv (the) **~** (sing) le plus mal. ● n the **~** (one) (person, object) le or la pire; the **~** (thing) le pire.

worth a **be ~** valoir; **it is ~ waiting** la peine d'attendre; **it is ~** (one's) **while** ça (en) vaut la peine. ● n valeur f; **ten pence ~ of** (pour) dix pence de. **worthless** a qui ne vaut rien. **worthwhile** a qui (en) vaut la peine.

worthy a (**-ier, -iest**) digne (of de); (laudable) louable.

would v aux **he ~ do/you ~ sing** (conditional tense) il ferait/tu chanterais; **he ~ have done** il aurait fait; **I ~ come every day** (used to) je venais chaque jour; **I ~ like some tea** je voudrais du thé; **~ you come here?** voulez-vous venir ici?; **he wouldn't come** il a refusé de venir. **~-be** a soi-disant.

wound¹ *n* blessure *f*. ● *vt* blesser; **the ~ed** les blessés *mpl*.

wound² ⇒WIND².

wove, woven ⇒WEAVE.

wrap *vt* (*pt* **wrapped**) **~ (up)** envelopper. ● *vi* **~ up** (dress warmly) se couvrir; **~ped up in** (engrossed) absorbé dans.

wrapping *n* emballage *m*.

wreak *vt* **~ havoc** faire des ravages.

wreath *n* (of flowers, leaves) couronne *f*.

wreck *n* (sinking) naufrage *m*; (ship, remains, person) épave *f*; (vehicle) voiture *f* accidentée *or* délabrée. ● *vt* détruire; (*ship*) provoquer le naufrage de. **wreckage** *n* (pieces) débris *mpl*; (wrecked building) décombres *mpl*.

wrestle *vi* lutter, se débattre (**with** contre).

wrestling *n* lutte *f*; (**all-in**) **~ catch** *m*.

wriggle *vt/i* (se) tortiller.

wring *vt* (*pt* **wrung**) (twist) tordre; (*clothes*) essorer; **~ out of** (obtain from) arracher à.

wrinkle *n* (crease) pli *m*; (on skin) ride *f*. ● *vt/i* (se) rider.

wrist *n* poignet *m*.

write *vt/i* (*pt* **wrote**; *pp* **written**) écrire. □ **~ back** répondre; **~ down** noter; **~ off** (*debt*) passer aux profits et pertes; (*vehicle*) considérer bon pour la casse; **~ up** (from notes) rédiger.

write-off *n* perte *f* totale.

writer *n* auteur *m*, écrivain *m*; **~ of** auteur de.

write-up *n* compte-rendu *m*.

writing *n* écriture *f*; **~(s)** (works) écrits *mpl*; **in ~** par écrit. **~-paper** *n* papier *m* à lettres.

written ⇒WRITE.

wrong *a* (incorrect, mistaken) faux, mauvais; (unfair) injuste; (amiss) qui ne va pas; (*clock*) pas à l'heure; **be ~** (*person*) avoir tort (**to** de); (be mistaken) se tromper; **go ~** (err) se tromper; (turn out badly) mal tourner; **it is ~ to** (morally) c'est mal de; **what's ~?** qu'est-ce qui ne va pas?; **what is ~ with you?** qu'est-ce que vous avez? ● *adv* mal. ● *n* injustice *f*; (evil) mal *m*; **be in the ~** avoir tort. ● *vt* faire (du) tort à. **wrongful** *a* injustifié, injuste. **wrongfully** *adv* à tort. **wrongly** *adv* mal; (blame) à tort.

wrote ⇒WRITE.

wrought iron *n* fer *m* forgé.

wrung ⇒WRING.

Xmas *n* Noël *m*.

X-ray *n* rayon *m* X; (photograph) radio(graphie) *f*. ● *vt* radiographier.

yank *vt* tirer brusquement. ● *n* coup *m* brusque.

yard *n* (measure) yard *m* (= *0.9144 metre*); (of house) cour *f*; (garden: US) jardin *m*; (for storage) chantier *m*, dépôt *m*. **~stick** *n* mesure *f*.

yawn *vi* bâiller. ● *n* bâillement *m*.

year *n* an *m*, année *f*; **school/tax**

~ année scolaire/fiscale; **be ten ~s old** avoir dix ans.

yearly a annuel. ● adv annuellement.

yearn vi avoir bien or très envie (**for, to** de).

yeast n levure f.

yell vt/i hurler. ● n hurlement m.

yellow a jaune; (cowardly 🆎) froussard. ● n jaune m.

yes adv oui; (as answer to negative question) si. ● n oui m inv.

yesterday n & adv hier (m).

yet adv encore; (already) déjà. ● conj pourtant, néanmoins.

yew n if m.

yield vt (produce) produire, rendre; (profit) rapporter; (surrender) céder. ● n rendement m.

yoga n yoga m.

yoghurt n yaourt m.

yolk n jaune m (d'œuf).

you pron (familiar form) tu, pl vous; (polite form) vous; (object) te, t', pl vous; (polite) vous; (after prep.) toi, pl vous; (polite) vous; (indefinite) on; (object) vous; (**to**) ~ te, t', pl vous; (polite) vous; **I gave ~ a pen** je vous ai donné un stylo; **I know ~** je te connais or je vous connais.

young a jeune. ● n (people) jeunes mpl; (of animals) petits mpl.

your a (familiar form) ton, ta, pl tes; (polite form, & familiar form pl.) votre, pl vos.

yours pron (familiar form) le tien, la tienne, les tien(ne)s; (polite form, & familiar form pl.) le or la vôtre, les vôtres; ~ **faithfully/sincerely** je vous prie d'agréer mes salutations les meilleures.

yourself pron (familiar form) toi-même; (polite form) vous-même; (reflexive & after prepositions) te, t'; vous; **proud of ~** fier de toi.

yourselves pron vous-mêmes; (reflexive) vous.

youth n jeunesse f; (young man) jeune m. ~ **hostel** n auberge f de jeunesse.

Yugoslav a yougoslave. ● n Yougoslave mf.

Yugoslavia n Yougoslavie f.

zap vt 🆎 (kill) descendre; (Comput) enlever.

zeal n zèle m.

zebra n zèbre m. ~ **crossing** n passage m pour piétons.

zero n zéro m.

zest n (gusto) entrain m; (spice: fig) piment m; (of orange or lemon peel) zeste m.

zip n (vigour) allant m; ~(**-fastener**) fermeture f éclair®. ● vt (pt **zipped**) fermer avec une fermeture éclair®; (Comput) compresser. **Zip code** (US) n code m postal.

zodiac n zodiaque m.

zone n zone f.

zoo n zoo m.

zoom vi (rush) se précipiter. □ ~ **off** or **past** filer (comme une flèche). ~ **lens** n zoom m.

zucchini n inv (US) courgette f.

Summary of French grammar

Grammar provides a useful description of the patterns which make up a language. The following pages offer a summary for reference.

1 NOUNS and GENDER

- All nouns are either *masculine* or *feminine* in French
- The gender is an important feature of each noun
- The gender is shown by the article (*definite* or *indefinite*)

1.1 The definite article (= THE)

	Singular	Plural
Masculine	*le*	*les*
Feminine	*la*	*les*

- *le* and *la* are reduced to *l'* before:
  a singular noun starting with a vowel (*école* → *l'école*)
  a singular noun starting with a silent h (*hôtel* → *l'hôtel*)
- *les* is the plural in all cases

1.2 The indefinite article (= A or AN; plural = SOME)

	Singular	Plural
Masculine	*un*	*des*
Feminine	*une*	*des*

- *un* and *une* also indicate the number 1 in counting:
  e.g. *une pomme* = one apple [*see* NUMBERS *section 9.1*]
- *des* is the plural in all cases

⚠ *Note:* Articles are rarely omitted:
e.g. *les enfants aiment les bonbons* = children like sweets
BUT when specifying someone's occupation, the article is dropped:
e.g. *il est boucher* = he is a butcher,
ma soeur est avocat = my sister is a lawyer

2 NOUNS and NUMBER

- number means *singular* or *plural*
- nouns in most cases add an ending in the plural

2.1 Typical nouns:

Most nouns add *-s* in the plural:
e.g. *chaise → chaises* (= chairs) *chien → chiens* (= dogs)

2.2 Nouns ending in -eu or -eau:

These nouns usually add *-x* in the plural:
e.g. *jeu → jeux* (= games)   *bureau → bureaux* (= desks)

2.3 Nouns ending in -ou:

These nouns usually add *-s* in the plural.
BUT there are 6 common exceptions which add *-x*:
bijou → bijoux (= jewels)   *genou → genoux* (= knees)
caillou → cailloux (= pebbles) *hibou → hiboux* (= owls)
chou → choux (= cabbages)   *joujou → joujoux* (= toys)

2.4 Nouns ending in -al:

These nouns usually change from *-al* to *-aux*:
e.g. *rival → rivaux* (= rivals); *cheval → chevaux* (= horses)
BUT there are exceptions: e.g. *bal → bals* (= dances)

2.5 Nouns ending in -ail:

These nouns usually add *-s*:
   e.g. *détail → détails* (= details)
BUT there are exceptions:
   e.g. *travail → travaux* (= works)

2.6 Some nouns have unusual plurals:

These plurals need to be learnt individually:
e.g. *ciel → cieux* (= skies)   *oeil → yeux* (= eyes)

⚠ *Note*: the group: monsieur ‡ messieurs; madame ‡ mesdames;
mademoiselle ‡ mesdemoiselles; mon-, ma- in these words meant 'my'
originally (as in 'my lord', 'my lady')
[*See* POSSESSIVE ADJECTIVES *section 6*]

2.7 Hyphenated nouns

■ The plurals of this group of nouns vary and depend
   on how the word is formed (*adjective + noun*,
   verb + noun, etc.)

■ In cases where there is an ADJECTIVE + NOUN,
   it is normal for both words in the compound to change:
   e.g. *beau-père* → *beaux-pères* (= fathers-in-law)

■ It is often helpful to translate the compound and find
   which word will logically become plural:
   e.g. *arc-en-ciel* (= rainbow) → *arcs-en-ciel* (= rainbows)
   (literally 'arc in the sky' → 'arcs in the sky')

⚠ *Note:* sometimes it is logical to leave the word unchanged in the
plural because no noun is present in the make-up of the compound:
e.g. *un passe-partout* = skeleton key ‡ *des passe-partout* = skeleton
keys (literally 'a go-everywhere' : VERB + ADVERB)

2.8 Nouns showing no change between singular and plural

Nouns already ending in *-s*: e.g. *bois* → *bois* (= woods)
Nouns already ending in *-x*: e.g. *voix* → *voix* (= voices)
Nouns already ending in -*z*: e.g. *nez* → *nez* (= noses)

3 NOUNS and QUANTITY

■ There are many nouns which indicate quantity
   e.g. *un kilo de* = a kilo of...; *une livre de* = a pound of...;
   une bouteille de = a bottle of...

■ The word *de* is important in quantity expressions

■ Sometimes *de* combines with *le / la / l' / les* to mean
   'some'

3.1 The partitive article (= SOME)

```
de + NOUNS
de + le → du     e.g. le pain → du pain = some bread
de + la → de la  e.g. la crème → de la crème = some cream
de + l' → de l'  e.g. l'huile → de l'huile = some oil
de + les → des   e.g. les oranges → des oranges = some
                                                  oranges
```

⚠ *Note:* After a negative (*not, no more*, etc.: *see* NEGATIVES *section 12*), only use *de* or *d'*: e.g. *je n'ai plus de pain* = I haven't got any more bread; *il ne prend pas d'huile* = he's not buying any oil
After a quantity expression such as *un kilo de*, do not change *de* to *des*: e.g. *un kilo de pommes* = a kilo of apples

4 NOUNS replaced by PRONOUNS

4.1 Subject pronouns

- Subject pronouns (*I, we, they*, etc.) replace nouns
- They refer to people or things
- They govern verbs (e.g. *je chante* = I sing)
  [*see* VERBS *section 10.1*]

Singular	Plural
je = I	*nous* = we
tu = you	*vous* = you
il = he /it	*ils* = they [*masculine*]
elle = she / it	*elles* = they [*feminine*]
on = one*	

• *on* is used as a less specific subject pronoun to mean 'one', 'you', 'people', 'we', 'they':
e.g. *on mange ici?* = shall we eat here?
on n'aime pas refuser = one doesn't like to refuse
on parle français là? = do they speak French there?

4.2 Object pronouns

4.2.a Direct object pronouns

- Direct object pronouns (*it, him, us*, etc.) replace nouns
- They refer to people or things
- They are the object (= affected by the action) of verbs:
  e.g. hit the ball; go on, hit it! = *frappe la balle; allez, frappe-la!*

French	English
me / m'	me
te / t'	you [*singular*]
le / l'	him /it
la / l'	her / it
se / s'	himself/ herself/ itself
nous	us
vous	you [*plural*]
les	them
se / s'	themselves

- *m' / t' / l' / s'* are used if the word that follows starts with a vowel or a silent h:
  e.g. *ils l'aiment* = they love her
  elles l'ont humidifié = they sprayed it with water
- object pronouns affect the ending of a past participle [*see* VERBS *section 10.1.f*] if the object is feminine or plural:
  e.g. *elle a poli la table → elle l'a polie* (she polished it)

4.2.b Indirect object pronouns

- Indirect object pronouns (*to it, to him, to us*, etc.) replace nouns
- They refer to people or things
- They are the indirect object (= *indirectly* affected by the action) of verbs:
  e.g. *donnez-lui la balle!* = give the ball to him (or to her)!
  il m'a montré la photo = he showed me the photo

French	English
me / m'	(to) me
te / t'	(to) you [*singular*]
lui	(to) him or it
lui	(to) her or it
nous	(to) us
vous	(to) you [*plural*]
leur	(to) them

- (to) shows that the word 'to' is understood in the sentence even though it may not actually be said:
  e.g. give them that! = give that to them! = *donne-le*-leur!

4.2.c Indirect object pronouns: places and quantities

- The indirect object pronoun referring to a place is:
  y (= there) e.g. *j'y vais* = I'm going there
- The indirect object pronoun referring to a quantity is:
  en (= of it, of them, some) e.g. *j'en voudrais 3* = I'd like 3 (of them); *offrez-leur-en* = offer them some

4.3 Order of object pronouns in the sentence

- Object pronouns come before most verb parts:
  e.g. *elle leur rend les livres* = she returns the books to them
- Object pronouns come before an infinitive:
  e.g. *elle va leur rendre les livres* = she is going to return the books to them
- Object pronouns come before the first part of a compound tense (= conjugated with *avoir* or *être*: *see* VERBS *section 10.1.f*)
  e.g. *elle leur a rendu les livres* = she returned the books to them
- Object pronouns follow the imperative form of the verb and are linked to it by a hyphen:
  e.g. *rends-leur les livres!* = return the books to them!
- Object pronouns return to normal order even with an imperative if it is negative:
  e.g. *ne les rendez pas!* = don't return them!
- When they occur in multiples in a sentence, object pronouns have a fixed order

OBJECT PRONOUN ORDER (see above tables for meanings):

me					
te	le	lui	y	en	
se*	la	leur			
nous	les				
vous					
se*					

- the first column (me, te, se) is also used with reflexive verbs [*see* VERBS *section 10.1*]
- *se* means: (to) himself, (to) herself, (to) oneself, (to) themselves

⚠️ *Note:* any combination of object pronouns will fall in this order:
e.g. *ils y en ont mis 6* = they put 6 of them there
il le lui a payé = he bought it for her
ils le leur y ont expliqué = they explained it to them there

4.4 Disjunctive or emphatic pronouns

■ Pronouns are sometimes used for emphasis:

Disjunctive Pronouns	
moi	*nous*
toi	*vous*
lui	*eux*
elle	*elles*

■ They take on these spellings:
* after prepositions:
e.g. *avec moi* = with me
* after *que* or *qu'* in comparative sentences [*see* COMPARISON *section 8.1*]:
e.g. *plus petit que lui* = smaller than him
* to emphasize the subject:
e.g. *lui, il n'aime pas le vin rouge mais elle, elle l'adore*
= he doesn't like red wine but she loves it
* with *même* meaning 'self' (*myself*, *yourself*, etc.):
e.g. *toi-même* = yourself
vous-mêmes = yourselves

⚠ *Note:* that *-s* is added to *même* in the plural

⚠ *Note:* *moi* and *toi* are also used as 'emphatics' in imperatives when pronouns follow the verb: e.g. *donnez-le-moi*! = give it to me! *mettez-toi là*! = sit yourself there!

5 ADJECTIVES

- Adjectives qualify nouns
- They usually follow the noun in French
- They reflect the noun in both gender and number
- Many determiners (*this, my, all, three*, etc.) are adjectival
- Some adjectives are used alone as nouns
  e.g. *il est intelligent, le petit* = the little one (= boy) is bright

5.1 Common adjectival endings:

- The masculine form is that given in the dictionary
- Add *-e* to form the feminine:
  e.g. *une jupe courte* = a short skirt
- Add *-s* to the masculine to form the masculine plural:
  e.g. *des voyages intéressants* = interesting journeys
- Add *-s* to the feminine to form the feminine plural
  e.g. *des histoires amusantes* = funny stories

5. 2 Adjectives ending in -e

These stay the same in the feminine:
e.g. *aimable* → feminine *aimable*

⚠ *Note:* unless the *-e* has an acute accent:
e.g. *aimé* → feminine *aimée*

-s is added in the normal way in the plural:
e.g. *aimable* → plural *aimables*

⚠ *Note:* this is true of all adjectives:
unless the ending is *-x* (e.g. *curieux* → masculine plural *curieux*)
unless there is already a final *-s* (*bas* → masculine plural *bas*)

5.3 Table of adjectives showing typical endings and their feminines:

Typical ending	Adjective	Feminine	English
The following double the last letter and add an -e			
-as	*bas*	*basse*	low
-eil	*pareil*	*pareille*	similar
-el	*mortel*	*mortelle*	fatal
-en	*ancien*	*ancienne*	ancient
-et	*muet*	*muette*	mute
! sometimes !	*inquiet*	*inquiète*	anxious
-on	*bon*	*bonne*	good
-ul	*nul*	*nulle*	no good
The following add a final -e and lengthen the syllable by adding an accent or changing a consonant or consonant group			
-er	*premier*	*première*	first
-ef	*bref*	*brève*	brief
-if	*actif*	*active*	active
-eux	*fameux*	*fameuse*	infamous
-eur	*menteur*	*menteuse*	untruthful
-nc	*blanc*	*blanche*	white
-ic	*public*	*publique*	public
-gu	*aigu*	*aiguë*	acute

The following are examples of irregular adjectives which show additional variations

doux → douce (= sweet); *faux → fausse* (= false)
favori → favorite (= favourite); *frais → fraîche* (= fresh)
gentil → gentille (= kind); *jaloux → jalouse* (= jealous)
malin → maligne (= cunning); *roux → rousse* (= red)
sot → sotte (=silly)

5.4 Position of adjectives

- Most adjectives follow the noun; this is because an adjective distinguishes the noun in some way (colour, shape, etc.) and this position gives more emphasis in French: e.g. *un chocolat chaud* (= a hot chocolate).
- Some adjectives go before the noun: these are usually common adjectives where a distinguishing feature is less pronounced:
  e.g. *un vieil ami de la famille* (= an old family friend)

These may almost become part of the noun as
a compound:

e.g. *un jeune homme* (= a young man)
les petits enfants (= the little children;
the grandchildren)

■ Some adjectives change meaning if they go before
the noun: e.g. *la pauvre fille* (= the poor girl!)
la fille pauvre (= the girl with little money)
la mauvaise clé (= the wrong key)
un animal mauvais (= a vicious animal)
un seul président (= only one president)
elle, seule, le sait (= she alone knows that)

5.4.a beau, nouveau, vieux

■ These 3 adjectives go before the noun
■ They form a group because they have an extra spelling:

Masculine	Masculine with vowel*	Masculine Plural	Feminine	Feminine Plural	English
beau	*bel*	*beaux*	*belle*	*belles*	beautiful
nouveau	*nouvel*	*nouveaux*	*nouvelle*	*nouvelles*	new
vieux	*vieil*	*vieux*	*vieille*	*vieilles*	old

• The extra spelling is used if the noun is masculine and
starts with a vowel:
e.g. *arbre* → *un bel arbre* (= a lovely tree)

Examples: *une belle femme* (= a beautiful woman)
de nouveaux livres (= new books)
de vieilles histoires (= old stories)

 Note: des changes to *de* in front of a plural adjective

6 POSSESSION

■ Possession is commonly expressed by using *de*
■ The style used is:
'the dog of Paul' = *le chien de Paul* = Paul's dog
'the clothes of Sophie' = *les vêtements de Sophie*
= Sophie's clothes

■ Possession is also shown by possessive adjectives
  (*my*, *your*, etc.):

POSSESSIVE ADJECTIVES

Masculine	Feminine	Plural	English
mon	*ma*	*mes*	my
ton	*ta*	*tes*	your
son	*sa*	*ses*	his/her/its/one's
notre	*notre*	*nos*	our
votre	*votre*	*vos*	your
leur	*leur*	*leurs*	their

• The word matches the gender and number of the 'thing'
  possessed NOT the speaker:
  e.g. *ma soeur* = my sister (the speaker may be male)
• *ma*, *ta*, and *sa* end in vowels; therefore they are not used
  before a vowel:
  e.g. NOT *sa amie* BUT *son amie* = his girlfriend

6.1 mine, yours, etc.

■ These are expressed by possessive pronouns
■ They reflect the gender and number of the 'thing'
  possessed:

POSSESSIVE PRONOUNS

		Masculine	Feminine	
Masculine	Feminine	Plural	Plural	English
le mien	*la mienne*	*les miens*	*les miennes*	mine
le tien	*la tienne*	*les tiens*	*les tiennes*	yours
le sien	*la sienne*	*les siens*	*les siennes*	his/hers/its
le nôtre	*la nôtre*	*les nôtres*	*les nôtres*	ours
le vôtre	*la vôtre*	*les vôtres*	*les vôtres*	yours
le leur	*la leur*	*les leurs*	*les leurs*	theirs

• The word matches the gender and number of the 'thing'
  possessed NOT the speaker:
  e.g. *cette chaise est la mienne* = this chair is mine (*the
  speaker may be male*)

7 ADVERBS

- Adverbs usually give additional information about a verb's action: i.e. they say 'how' (= in what way or manner), 'when', 'where' something happens
- Most adverbs are formed from the feminine adjective by adding *-ment*
  e.g. *heureux* → *heureuse* → *heureusement* (= happily, fortunately)

Exceptions include:

7.1 masculine adjectives ending in a vowel

The feminine *-e* is dropped:
e.g. *hardi* → *hardiment* (= robustly)
résolu → *résolument* (= resolutely)

7.2 adjectives ending in -ant or -ent

The *-nt* is dropped and the *-m-* is doubled:
e.g. *constant* → *constamment* (= constantly)
intelligent → *intelligemment* (= intelligently)
Note however *lent* → *lentement* (= slowly)

8 COMPARISON

8.1 Comparative of adjectives and adverbs

- The comparative in English is usually expressed by:
  'more...' (e.g. *more interesting*)
  'as...'   (e.g. *as big*)
  'less...' (e.g. *less intelligent*)
  or the suffix '-er'   (e.g. *bigger*)
- The comparative in French is expressed in most cases by: 'plus...' (e.g. *plus intéressant*)
  'aussi...' (e.g. *aussi grand*)
  'moins...' (e.g. *moins intelligent*)
- The word for 'than' in French is *que* (or *qu'*)
- The adjective reflects the gender and number of the noun described. Examples:
  il est plus grand que toi = he is taller than you
  cette rue est moins longue que celui-là = this road is shorter than that one

SOME IRREGULAR COMPARATIVES

Adjective	Comparative	English
bon = good	***meilleur***	better
mauvais = bad	***pire***	worse
petit = small	***moindre***	lesser, less great,
! *sometimes* !	***plus petit***	smaller
bien = well	***mieux***	better
mal = badly	***pis***	worse
! *sometimes* !	***plus mal***	
peu = little	***moins***	less

8.2 Superlative of adjectives and adverbs

- The superlative in English is usually expressed by
  'most...' (e.g. *most interesting*)
  or the suffix '-est' (e.g. *biggest*)
- The superlative in French is expressed in most cases by:
  '*le/la/les plus*...' (e.g. ***le plus intéressant***)
- The article is repeated reflecting the gender and number
  of the noun described:
  e.g. ***la ville la plus belle*** = the most beautiful city
- The superlative is often followed by 'in' which is translated by ***de***...:
  e.g. ***la ville la plus belle*** ***du monde*** = the most beautiful
  city in the world

9 TIMES

- Time phrases begin with ***il est***... (= it is...)
- The French equivalent of 'o' clock' is ***heures***
  BUT 1 o' clock = ***une heure*** (i.e. no -*s* required in the
  singular)
- The 24 hour clock is often used to make a.m. and p.m.
  clear
- The number of hours is stated first before any minutes
  are detailed:
    minutes 'past' the hour are simply added to the end of
    the phrase: e.g. ***il est sept heures*** ***dix***

'quarter past' is expressed by *et quart*:

e.g. *il est sept heures et quart*

minutes 'to' the hour follow the word *moins* (= minus):

e.g. *il est quatre heures moins cinq* (= five to four)

'quarter to' is expressed by *moins le quart*:

e.g. *il est quatre heures moins le quart*

'half past' is expressed by *et demie*:

e.g. *il est trois heures et demie*

⚠️ *Note: midi* (= midday) and *minuit* (= midnight) are masculine; therefore *et demie* changes to *et demi*: e.g. *il est midi et demi*

9.1 The cardinal numbers 1-24

[*see* ORDINAL NUMBERS *section 9.5*]

1 un/e	7 sept	13 treize	19 dix-neuf
2 deux	8 huit	14 quatorze	20 vingt
3 trois	9 neuf	15 quinze	21 vingt et un/e
4 quatre	10 dix	16 seize	22 vingt-deux
5 cinq	11 onze	17 dix-sept	23 vingt-trois
6 six	12 douze	18 dix-huit	24 vingt-quatre

Examples:

1.00 = *il est une heure*

2.00 = *il est deux heures*

2.10 = *il est deux heures dix*

2.15 = *il est deux heures et quart*
　　　　[also *il est deux heures quinze*]

2.30 = *il est deux heures et demie*
　　　　[also *il est deux heures trente*]

2.35 = *il est trois heures moins vingt-cinq*
　　　　[also *il est deux heures trente-cinq*]

9.2 The numbers 30-100 (in 10s)

30	trente	
40	quarante	70 soixante-dix
50	cinquante	80 quatre-vingts
60	soixante	90 quatre-vingt-dix
		100 cent

9.3 Numbers: norms and exceptions

■ Numbers normally count up by linking each digit to 20, 30, etc. by a hyphen: e.g. *vingt-deux, vingt-trois*...

Exceptions worthy of note include:

■ Numbers ending in 1 (*31, 41,* etc.) add *et un* (= and one) to the main number: e.g. 61 = *soixante et un* EXCEPT for: 81 (*quatre-vingt-un*); 91 (*quatre-vingt-onze*); 101 (*cent un*):

■ Numbers 70-79 are unusual in that they count literally as:

sixty-ten (*soixante-dix*) = 70
sixty-eleven (*soixante et onze*) = 71
sixty-twelve (*soixante-douze*) = 72 etc.

■ Numbers 80-100 are unusual in that they count literally as:

four-twenties (*quatre-vingts*) = 80
four-twenties-one (*quatre-vingt-un*) = 81
four-twenties-two (*quatre-vingt-deux*) = 82 etc.
and over 90...
four-twenties-seventeen (*quatre-vingt-dix-sept*) = 97 etc.

 Note: the final *-s* of *vingts* is dropped if any digit follows

■ Over 100, there is no hyphen linking the 100, 200, etc. with following digits: e.g. *trois cent dix-huit* = 318

 Note: the final *-s* of *cents* is dropped if any digit follows

0.4 1000 and year dates

The number 1000 = *mille*. However, in written dates, *mille* changes to *mil*:
e.g. 1914 = *mil neuf cent quatorze*

 Note: the word *cent* is not omitted

9.4.a Other dates

■ The article *le* is used to specify the day of the month: e.g. *c'est aujourd'hui le six septembre* = today is the 6th of September

■ The cardinal numbers (*un, deux,* ...) are used (NOT the ordinal numbers as in English style: *1st, 2nd,* etc.)

- sometimes the article *le* goes before the day :
  e.g. *c'est le mardi deux juillet* = it's Tuesday 2 July

9.5 Ordinal numbers

- The ordinal numbers count focusing on sequence or priority (*first, second, third,* etc.)
- Ordinal numbers in French are usually formed by adding *-ième* to the cardinal number:
  e.g. *deuxième* (= 2nd), *troisième* (= 3rd), etc.
  BUT there are exceptions:
  e.g. *premier* = 1st

⚠️ *Note:* numbers like 21st do not follow this change:
e.g. 31st = *trente-et-unième*

- There is sometimes a spelling change:
  e.g. *neuvième* = 9th (*-f-* changes to *-v-*)
  onzième = 11th (*onze* drops the final *-e*)

10 VERBS

- Verbs add action to a phrase (*he kicks the ball*) or they describe a state (*she is lazy*)
- A sentence needs a verb for it to make sense
  (*he... the dog* → *he strokes the dog*)
- An infinitive is a verb preceded by 'to' (*I want to go*)
- A finite verb indicates tense (*will go; went*)
- Tense is the time at which something happens, exists, etc.

10.1 Regular verbs

- Some verbs belong to 'regular' groups where they follow the same pattern
- Regular patterns are identified by the endings *-er, -ir*, and *-re*
- Some regular verbs are REFLEXIVE which means the action involves *oneself*:
  e.g. *je me lave* = I wash myself [*see* PRONOUNS *section 4.3*]

10.1.a Regular verbs in the present tense

The present tense describes what is happening now (*it is raining*) or what regularly happens (*he plays football on Tuesdays*) or a current truth (*she does love chips*)

---

parler 'to speak' AN EXAMPLE OF AN -ER VERB

je parle = I speak	*nous parlons* = we speak
tu parles = you speak	*vous parlez* = you speak
il parle = he speaks	*ils (masc) parlent* = they speak
elle parle = she speaks	*elles (fem) parlent* = they speak

- *tu* is used to speak to a child or someone known well
- *vous* is used in polite speech or to more than one person
- *ils* also means 'they' referring to a mixed male and female group
- the translation *I speak*, etc., may also be *I am speaking* and *I do speak*

---

finir 'to finish' AN EXAMPLE OF AN -IR VERB

je finis = I finish	*nous finissons* = we finish
tu finis = you finish	*vous finissez* = you finish
il finit = he finishes	*ils (masc) finissent* = they finish
elle finit = she finishes	*elles (fem) finissent* = they finish

- note the lengthened stem *iss-* in the plural

---

vendre 'to sell' AN EXAMPLE OF AN -RE VERB

je vends = I sell	*nous vendons* = we sell
tu vends = you sell	*vous vendez* = you sell
il vend = he sells	*ils (masc) vendent* = they sell
elle vend = she sells	*elles (fem) vendent* = they sell

- note the dropped verb ending with *il* and *elle*

Other present tense patterns are individual to each verb or to a small number of verbs; these are known as 'irregular' verbs. [*see* VERB TABLES]

10.1.b Regular verbs in the imperative

- The imperative is a way of ordering, suggesting strongly
- 3 parts of the present tense are used: *tu, nous, vous*

- The *-s* is dropped from the *tu* part of the verb:
  e.g. *parle!* (= talk!); *parlons!* (= let's talk!); *parlez!*
  (= talk!)
BUT there are exceptions [*see* VERB TABLES]:
  e.g. *aie!* (= have!); *ayons!* (= let's have!); *ayez!* (= have!)
  sois! (= be!); *soyons!* (= let's be!); *soyez!* (= be!)
  sache! (= know!); *sachons!* (= let's know!); *sachez!*
  (= know!)

10.1.c Regular verbs in the imperfect tense

The imperfect tense describes what was happening in the
past (*it was raining*) or what used to be a fact or occurrence
(*he used to like chocolate*; *he used to go to classes*); in French
it also expresses what happened regularly (*il jouait au
football tous les jeudis* = he played football every
Tuesday)

Imperfect tense endings	
-ais	*-ions*
-ais	*-iez*
-ait	*-aient*
-ait	*-aient*

- these endings apply to all verbs
- they are added to a stem
- the stem is taken from the *nous* part of the
  present tense
  e.g. *nous finissons → finiss- → je finissais*
- the only irregular stem is *ét-* from *être*:
  e.g. *j'étais* (= I was), *tu étais* (= you were)...etc.

10.1.d Regular verbs in the future tense

The future tense describes what will happen (*it will rain*) or
what is expected to be a fact (*it will be easy*)

Future tense endings	
-ai	*-ons*
-as	*-ez*
-a	*-ont*
-a	*-ont*

- these endings apply to all verbs
- they are added to a stem: the stem is the infinitive
  e.g. *finir* → *je finirai* (= I shall finish)
  BUT *-re* verbs drop the final *-e*:
  e.g. *vendre* → *je vendrai* (= I shall sell)
- some irregular stems have to be learnt
- the future may also be expressed by:
  the verb ALLER + INFINITIVE = *je vais finir*...
  (I am going to finish...)

TABLE of irregular future stems: [*see* VERB TABLES]

Infinitive	Future Stem	Infinitive	Future Stem
avoir	*j'aurai* = I shall have	tenir	*je tiendrai* = I shall hold
être	*je serai* = I shall be	vouloir	*je voudrai* = I shall want
faire	*je ferai* = I shall make	pouvoir	*je pourrai* = I shall be able
savoir	*je saurai* = I shall know	recevoir	*je recevrai* = I shall get
voir	*je verrai* = I shall see	devoir	*je devrai* = I shall have to
envoyer	*j'enverrai* = I shall send	courir	*je courrai* = I shall run
venir	*je viendrai* = I shall come	mourir	*je mourrai* = I shall die

- compounds of the above have the same stem:
  e.g. *retenir* (= to hold back) → *je retiendrai*

10.1.e Regular verbs in the conditional tense

The conditional tense describes what would happen (*it would make him angry*) or what would be a fact (*it would be easy*)

Formation: = FUTURE STEM + CONDITIONAL ENDINGS

Conditional tense endings	
-ais	*-ions*
-ais	*-iez*
-ait	*-aient*
-ait	*-aient*

■ these endings apply to all verbs
  e.g. *il commencerait* (= he would begin)
  tu devrais (= you ought to)
■ the word *si* (= if) is often present or understood in the
  meaning: e.g. *il le ferait si tu le lui demandais*
  (= he'd do it if you asked him)

10.1.f Regular verbs in the perfect tense

The perfect tense describes what has happened (*it has
snowed*; *they have written*). In French it is also used for
what happened and remained the case until a specific point
in time (*ils y sont restés jusqu'à mardi* = they stayed
there until Tuesday) or to state an action as part of a
series, each action being complete in itself (*je me suis
approché de la maison, j'ai sonné à la porte*... = I went
up to the house, rang the doorbell...)

Formation of the perfect tense:
■ Two common verbs are important in the formation
  of this tense: AVOIR and ÊTRE

avoir = to have	
j'ai	*nous avons*
tu as	*vous avez*
il a	*ils ont*
elle a	*elles ont*

être = to be	
je suis	*nous sommes*
tu es	*vous êtes*
il est	*ils sont*
elle est	*elles sont*

■ 3 parts are needed to make the perfect tense:
  SUBJECT + AVOIR/ÊTRE + PAST PARTICIPLE
■ The past participle of regular verbs is made by removing
  the last syllable of the infinitive (*regarder, choisir,*

rendre) and by replacing it with *é, -i, -u* respectively:
e.g. *regarder → regardé → j'ai regardé* (= I have
watched)
choisir → choisi → tu as choisi (= you have chosen)
rendre → rendu → il a rendu (= he has given back)
BUT some past participles have to be learnt [*see* VERB
TABLES].

**TABLE giving common irregular past participles
following the auxiliary (= 'helper') verb *avoir*:**

Infinitive	Past Participle	Infinitive	Past Participle
avoir	*j'ai eu* = I have had	croire	*j'ai cru* = I have believed
être	*j'ai été* = I have been	savoir	*j'ai su* = I have known
faire	*j'ai fait* = I have made	voir	*j'ai vu* = I have seen
boire	*j'ai bu* = I have drunk	pleuvoir	*il a plu* = it has rained
pouvoir	*j'ai pu* = I have been able	dire	*j'ai dit* = I have said
devoir	*j'ai dû* = I have had to	écrire	*j'ai écrit* = I have written
lire	*j'ai lu* = I have read	mettre	*j'ai mis* = I have put
vouloir	*j'ai voulu* = I have wanted	prendre	*j'ai pris* = I have taken

• the past participle does not change its spelling after *avoir*
  unless there is a direct object preceding it: e.g. *j'ai vendu
  la table* (= I sold the table)
  BUT *où est la table que tu as vendue*? (= where is the
  table you've sold?)

■ Most verbs make their perfect tense with *avoir* but
the exceptions are: 1 reflexive verbs and 2 a small group
of verbs of 'motion'. These take *être* and the past
participle behaves like an adjective.

---

1 *se laver* = to get washed / to wash oneself

je me suis lavé(e) = I got washed
tu t'es lavé(e) = you got washed
il s'est lavé = he got washed
elle s'est lavée = she got washed
nous nous sommes lavé(e)s = we got washed
vous vous êtes lavé(e)(s) = you got washed
ils se sont lavés = they got washed
elles se sont lavées = they got washed

• The alternatives in brackets depend on gender (masculine
or feminine) and number (singular or plural)

---

2 VERBS OF MOTION WHICH TAKE ÊTRE

arriver	*je suis arrivé(e)*	= I arrived
partir	*je suis parti(e)*	= I left
retourner	*je suis retourné(e)*	= I returned
rester	*je suis resté(e)*	= I stayed
tomber	*je suis tombé(e)*	= I fell
mourir	*je suis mort(e)*	= I died
naître	*je suis né(e)*	= I was born
monter	*je suis monté(e)*	= I went up
descendre	*je suis descendu(e)*	= I went down
entrer	*je suis entré(e)*	= I entered
aller	*je suis allé(e)*	= I went
sortir	*je suis sorti(e)*	= I went out
venir	*je suis venu(e)*	= I came
revenir	*je suis revenu(e)*	= I came back

• compounds of the above also take *être* e.g. *devenir*
(= to become) → *je suis devenu(e)*

10.1.g Regular verbs in the pluperfect tense

The pluperfect tense describes what had happened
(*it had snowed; they had written*) or what had been the case
(*it had been easy*).
Formation: = IMPERFECT TENSE OF AVOIR OR ÊTRE +
PAST PARTICIPLE [*see* VERB TABLES]

Examples:
j'avais fini = I had finished
nous avions vendu l'appartement = we had sold the flat
elle s'était réveillée = she had woken up
nous étions partis = we had left

⚠️ *Note:* past participles after *être* behave in the same way as
they do for the perfect tense: i.e. they look like adjectives reflecting
the gender and number of the subject

10.1.h Regular verbs in the future perfect tense

The future perfect tense describes what will have happened
(*he will have arrived*) or what will have been the case
(*it will not have been easy*)

Formation: = FUTURE TENSE OF AVOIR OR ÊTRE +
PAST PARTICIPLE [*see* VERB TABLES]

Examples:
j'aurai fini = I shall have finished
nous aurons vendu la voiture = we shall have sold the car
nous serons descendus = we shall have gone down

⚠️ *Note:* past participles after *être* behave in the same way as
they do for the perfect tense: i.e. they look like adjectives reflecting
the gender and number of the subject

10.2 Irregular verbs [*see* VERB TABLES]

11 NEGATIVES

- The negative expresses *not, never, no-one*, etc.
- In French the negative usually has 2 parts:
  e.g. *ne... pas* (= not), *ne... jamais* (= never),
  ne...personne (= nobody), etc.
- If the negative is the SUBJECT (*nobody knows*), then
  the negative reverses:
  i.e. *ne...personne → personne ne...*
  e.g. *personne ne sait*!
- Usually however with verbs, the 2 parts 'sandwich'
  the finite verb: e.g. *il ne mange pas* = he is not eating
BUT if an infinitive is present, they exclude the infinitive
from the 'sandwich':
  e.g. *il ne veut pas manger* = he doesn't want to eat
AND in a compound tense (e.g. *perfect, pluperfect*), they
only sandwich the first verb:
  e.g. *il n'est pas allé* = he didn't go
ALSO if object pronouns are present, these 'cling' to the
verb within the 'sandwich':
  e.g. *elle l'a acheté → elle ne l'a pas acheté*
  (= she didn't buy it)
- If no verb is present, as in a short response, then
  the *ne...* is omitted:
  e.g. '*Qui a frappé*?' - '*Personne!*' (= 'Who knocked ?'
  'Nobody!')

French verbs

1 chanter

Present indicative

je	chante
tu	chantes
il	chante
nous	chantons
vous	chantez
ils	chantent

Present subjunctive

(que)	je	chante
(que)	tu	chantes
(qu')	il	chante
(que)	nous	chantions
(que)	vous	chantiez
(qu')	ils	chantent

Future indicative

je	chanterai
tu	chanteras
il	chantera
nous	chanterons
vous	chanterez
ils	chanteront

Present conditional

je	chanterais
tu	chanterais
il	chanterait
nous	chanterions
vous	chanteriez
ils	chanteraient

Imperfect indicative

je	chantais
tu	chantais
il	chantait
nous	chantions
vous	chantiez
ils	chantaient

Past participle

chanté/chantée

Perfect indicative

j'	ai	chanté
tu	as	chanté
il	a	chanté
elle	a	chanté
nous	avons	chanté
vous	avez	chanté
ils	ont	chanté
elles	ont	chanté

Pluperfect indicative

j'	avais	chanté
tu	avais	chanté
il	avait	chanté
elle	avait	chanté
nous	avions	chanté
vous	aviez	chanté
ils	avaient	chanté
elles	avaient	chanté

2 finir

Present indicative

je	finis
tu	finis
il	finit
nous	finissons
vous	finissez
ils	finissent

Present subjunctive

(que)	je	finisse
(que)	tu	finisses
(qu')	il	finisse
(que)	nous	finissions
(que)	vous	finissiez
(qu')	ils	finissent

Future indicative

je	finirai
tu	finiras
il	finira
nous	finirons
vous	finirez
ils	finiront

Present conditional

je	finirais
tu	finirais
il	finirait
nous	finirions
vous	finiriez
ils	finiraient

Imperfect indicative

je	finissais
tu	finissais
il	finissait
nous	finissions
vous	finissiez
ils	finissaient

Past participle

fini/finie

Perfect indicative

j'	ai	fini
tu	as	fini
il	a	fini
elle	a	fini
nous	avons	fini
vous	avez	fini
ils	ont	fini
elles	ont	fini

Pluperfect indicative

j'	avais	fini
tu	avais	fini
il	avait	fini
elle	avait	fini
nous	avions	fini
vous	aviez	fini
ils	avaient	fini
elles	avaient	fini

3 attendre

Present indicative

j'	attends
tu	attends
il	attend
nous	attendons
vous	attendez
ils	attendent

Present subjunctive

(que)	j'	attende
(que)	tu	attendes
(qu')	il	attende
(que)	nous	attendions
(que)	vous	attendiez
(qu')	ils	attendent

Future indicative

j'	attendrai
tu	attendras
il	attendra
nous	attendrons
vous	attendrez
ils	attendront

Present conditional

j'	attendrais
tu	attendrais
il	attendrait
nous	attendrions
vous	attendriez
ils	attendraient

Imperfect indicative

j'	attendais
tu	attendais
il	attendait
nous	attendions
vous	attendiez
ils	attendaient

Past participle

attendu/attendue

Perfect indicative

j'	ai	attendu
tu	as	attendu
il	a	attendu
elle	a	attendu
nous	avons	attendu
vous	avez	attendu
ils	ont	attendu
elles	ont	attendu

Pluperfect indicative

j'	avais	attendu
tu	avais	attendu
il	avait	attendu
elle	avait	attendu
nous	avions	attendu
vous	aviez	attendu
ils	avaient	attendu
elles	avaient	attendu

4 être

Present indicative

je	suis
tu	es
il	est
nous	sommes
vous	êtes
ils	sont

Present subjunctive

(que)	je	sois
(que)	tu	sois
(qu')	il	soit
(que)	nous	soyons
(que)	vous	soyez
(qu')	ils	soient

Future indicative

je	serai
tu	seras
il	sera
nous	serons
vous	serez
ils	seront

Present conditional

je	serais
tu	serais
il	serait
nous	serions
vous	seriez
ils	seraient

Imperfect indicative

j'	étais
tu	étais
il	était
nous	étions
vous	étiez
ils	étaient

Past participle

été (*invariable*)

Pluperfect indicative

j'	avais	été
tu	avais	été
il	avait	été
elle	avait	été
nous	avions	été
vous	aviez	été
ils	avaient	été
elles	avaient	été

Perfect indicative

j'	ai	été
tu	as	été
il	a	été
elle	a	été
nous	avons	été
vous	avez	été
ils	ont	été
elles	ont	été

5 avoir

Present indicative

j'	ai
tu	as
il	a
nous	avons
vous	avez
ils	ont

Future indicative

j'	aurai
tu	auras
il	aura
nous	aurons
vous	aurez
ils	auront

Imperfect indicative

j'	avais
tu	avais
il	avait
nous	avions
vous	aviez
ils	avaient

Perfect indicative

j'	ai	eu
tu	as	eu
il	a	eu
elle	a	eu
nous	avons	eu
vous	avez	eu
ils	ont	eu
elles	ont	eu

Present subjunctive

(que)	j'	aie
(que)	tu	aies
(qu')	il	ait
(que)	nous	ayons
(que)	vous	ayez
(qu')	ils	aient

Present conditional

j'	aurais
tu	aurais
il	aurait
nous	aurions
vous	auriez
ils	auraient

Past participle

eu/eue

Pluperfect indicative

j'	avais	eu
tu	avais	eu
il	avait	eu
elle	avait	eu
nous	avions	eu
vous	aviez	eu
ils	avaient	eu
elles	avaient	eu

[6] **acheter**
1 j'achète 2 j'achèterai
3 j'achetais 4 que j'achète
5 acheté

[7] **acquérir**
1 j'acquiers, nous acquérons,
ils acquièrent 2 j'acquerrai
3 j'acquérais 4 que
j'acquière 5 acquis

[8] **aller**
1 je vais, tu vas, il va, nous
allons, vous allez, ils vont
2 j'irai 3 j'allais 4 que
j'aille, que nous allions,
qu'ils aillent 5 allé

[9] **asseoir**
1 j'assois, tu assois, il assoit,
nous assoyons, vous assoyez,
ils assoient 2 j'assoirai
3 j'assoyais 4 que j'assoie,
que nous assoyions, qu'ils
assoient 5 assis

[10] **avancer**
1 nous avançons 3 j'avançais

[11] **battre**
1 je bats, il bat, nous battons
2 je battrai 3 je battais
4 que je batte 5 battu

[12] **boire**
1 je bois, il boit, nous
buvons, ils boivent 2 je
boirai 3 je buvais 4 que je
boive 5 bu

[13] **bouillir**
1 je bous, il bout, nous
bouillons, ils bouillent
2 je bouillirai 3 je bouillais
4 que je bouille 5 bouilli

[14] **céder**
1 je cède, nous cédons,
ils cèdent 2 je céderai 3 je
cédais 4 que je cède 5 cédé

[15] **créer**
1 je crée, nous créons 2 je
créerai 3 je créais 4 que je
crée 5 créé

[16] **conclure**
1 je conclus, il conclut, nous
concluons, ils concluent
2 je conclurai 3 je concluais
4 que je conclue 5 conclu
(*but* inclus)

[17] **conduire**
1 je conduis, nous
conduisons 2 je conduirai
3 je conduisais 4 que je
conduise 5 conduit (*but* lui,
nui)

[18] **connaître**
1 je connais, il connaît, nous
connaissons 2 je connaîtrai
3 je connaissais 4 que je
connaisse 5 connu

[19] **coudre**
1 je couds, il coud, nous
cousons, ils cousent 2 je
coudrai 3 je cousais 4 que
je couse 5 cousu

[20] **courir**
1 je cours, il court, nous
courons, ils courent 2 je
courrai 3 je courais 4 que
je coure 5 couru

[21] **couvrir**
1 je couvre 2 je couvrirai

---

1 Present Indicative 2 Future Indicative 3 Imperfect Indicative 4 Present Subjunctive 5 Past Participle

3 je couvrais 4 que je couvre
5 couvert

[22] craindre
1 je crains, il craint, nous
craignons, ils craignent
2 je craindrai 3 je craignais
4 que je craigne 5 craint

[23] croire
1 je crois, il croit, nous
croyons, ils croient 2 je
croirai 3 je croyais, nous
croyions 4 que je croie, que
nous croyions 5 cru

[24] croître
1 je crois, il croît, nous
croissons 2 je croîtrai 3 je
croissais 4 que je croisse
5 crû/crue (*but* accru, décru)

[25] cueillir
1 je cueille 2 je cueillerai
3 je cueillais 4 que je cueille
5 cueilli

[26] devoir
1 je dois, il doit, nous devons,
ils doivent 2 je devrai 3 je
devais 4 que je doive, que
nous devions 5 dû/due

[27] dire
1 je dis, il dit, nous disons,
vous dites, ils disent 2 je
dirai 3 je disais 4 que je
dise 5 dit

[28] dissoudre
1 je dissous, il dissout, nous
dissolvons, ils dissolvent
2 je dissoudrai 3 je dissolvais
4 que je dissolve 5 dissous/
dissoute

[29] distraire
1 je distrais, il distrait, nous
distrayons 2 je distrairai
3 je distrayais 4 que je
distraie 5 distrait

[30] écrire
1 j'écris, il écrit, nous
écrivons 2 j'écrirai
3 j'écrivais 4 que j'écrive
5 écrit

[31] employer
1 j'emploie, nous employons,
ils emploient 2 j'emploierai
3 j'employais, nous
employions 4 que j'emploie,
que nous employions
5 employé

[32] envoyer
1 j'envoie, nous envoyons,
ils envoient 2 j'enverrai
3 j'envoyais, nous envoyions
4 que j'envoie, que nous
envoyions 5 envoyé

[33] faire
1 je fais, nous faisons (*say*
/fəzɔ̃/), vous faites, ils font
2 je ferai 3 je faisais (*say*
/fəzɛ/) 4 que je fasse, que
nous fassions 5 fait

[34] falloir (*impersonal*)
1 il faut 2 il faudra 3 il
fallait 4 qu'il faille 5 fallu

[35] fuir
1 je fuis, nous fuyons
2 je fuirai 3 je fuyais, nous
fuyions 4 que je fuie, que
nous fuyions 5 fui

---

1 Present Indicative 2 Future Indicative 3 Imperfect Indicative 4 Present Subjunctive 5 Past Participle

[36] haïr
1 je hais, il hait, nous haïssons, ils haïssent 2 je haïrai 3 je haïssais 4 que je haïsse 5 haï

[37] interdire
1 j'interdis, vous interdisez 2 j'interdirai 3 j'interdisais 4 que j'interdise 5 interdit

[38] jeter
1 je jette, nous jetons, ils jettent 2 je jetterai 3 je jetais 4 que je jette 5 jeté

[39] lire
1 je lis, il lit, nous lisons 2 je lirai 3 je lisais 4 que je lise 5 lu

[40] manger
1 je mange, nous mangeons 2 je mangerai 3 je mangeais 4 que je mange, que nous mangions 5 mangé

[41] maudire
1 je maudis, il maudit, nous maudissons 2 je maudirai 3 je maudissais 4 que je maudisse 5 maudit

[42] mettre
1 je mets, tu mets, nous mettons 2 je mettrai 3 je mettais 4 que je mette 5 mis

[43] mourir
1 je meurs, il meurt, nous mourons 2 je mourrai 3 je mourais 4 que je meure 5 mort

[44] naître
1 je nais, il naît, nous naissons 2 je naîtrai 3 je naissais 4 que je naisse 5 né

[45] oublier
1 j'oublie, nous oublions, ils oublient 2 j'oublierai 3 j'oubliais, nous oubliions, vous oubliiez 4 que nous oubliions, que vous oubliiez 5 oublié

[46] partir
1 je pars, nous partons 2 je partirai 3 je partais 4 que je parte 5 parti

[47] plaire
1 je plais, il plaît (*but* il tait), nous plaisons 2 je plairai 3 je plaisais 4 que je plaise 5 plu

[48] pleuvoir (*impersonal*)
1 il pleut 2 il pleuvra 3 il pleuvait 4 qu'il pleuve 5 plu

[49] pouvoir
1 je peux, il peut, nous pouvons, ils peuvent 2 je pourrai 3 je pouvais 4 que je puisse, que nous puissions 5 pu

[50] prendre
1 je prends, il prend, nous prenons 2 je prendrai 3 je prenais 4 que je prenne 5 pris

[51] prévoir
1 je prévois, il prévoit, nous prévoyons, ils prévoient 2 je prévoirai 3 je prévoyais,

nous prévoyions 4 que je prévoie, que nous prévoyions 5 prévu

[52] **recevoir**
1 je reçois, il reçoit, nous recevons, ils reçoivent 2 je recevrai 3 je recevais 4 que je reçoive, que nous recevions 5 reçu

[53] **résoudre**
1 je résous, il résout, nous résolvons, ils résolvent 2 je résoudrai 3 je résolvais 4 que je résolve 5 résolu

[54] **rire**
1 je ris, nous rions, ils rient 2 je rirai 3 je riais, nous riions 4 que je rie, que nous riions 5 ri

[55] **savoir**
1 je sais, il sait, nous savons, ils savent 2 je saurai 3 je savais 4 que je sache, que nous sachions 5 su

[56] **suffire**
1 il suffit, ils suffisent 2 il suffira 3 il suffisait 4 qu'il suffise 5 suffi (*but* frit)

[57] **suivre**
1 je suis, il suit, nous suivons 2 je suivrai 3 je suivais 4 que je suive 5 suivi

[58] **tenir**
1 je tiens, il tient, nous

tenons, ils tiennent 2 je tiendrai 3 je tenais 4 que je tienne, que nous tenions 5 tenu

[59] **vaincre**
1 je vaincs, il vainc, nous vainquons, ils vainquent 2 je vaincrai 3 je vainquais 4 que je vainque 5 vaincu

[60] **valoir**
1 je vaux, il vaut, nous valons 2 je vaudrai 3 je valais 4 que je vaille, que nous valions 5 valu

[61] **vêtir**
1 je vêts, il vêt, nous vêtons 2 je vêtirai 3 je vêtais 4 que je vête 5 vêtu

[62] **vivre**
1 je vis, il vit, nous vivons, ils vivent 2 je vivrai 3 je vivais 4 que je vive 5 vécu

[63] **voir**
1 je vois, nous voyons, ils voient 2 je verrai 3 je voyais, nous voyions 4 que je voie, que nous voyions 5 vu

[64] **vouloir**
1 je veux, il veut, nous voulons, ils veulent 2 je voudrai 3 je voulais 4 que je veuille, que nous voulions 5 voulu

---

1 Present Indicative 2 Future Indicative 3 Imperfect Indicative 4 Present Subjunctive 5 Past Participle

What are the equivalent tenses in English

Present indicative
je chante = *I sing, I'm singing*

Future indicative
je chanterai = *I will sing*

Imperfect indicative
je chantais = *I was singing*

Perfect indicative
j'ai chanté
= *I sang, I have sung*

Pluperfect indicative
j'avais chanté = *I had sung*

Present subjunctive
bien que je chante
= *although I sing*

Present conditional
si je pouvais, je chanterais
= *if I could, I would sing*

Past participle
chanté/chantée = *sung*

How to conjugate a reflexive verb

Present indicative and other simple tenses
je me lave
tu te laves
il se lave
elle se lave
nous nous lavons
vous vous lavez
ils se lavent
elles se lavent

in the negative form
je ne me lave pas
tu ne te laves pas
il ne se lave pas
elle ne se lave pas
nous ne nous lavons pas
vous ne vous lavez pas
ils ne se lavent pas
elles ne se lavent pas

Perfect indicative and other compound tenses
(always with auxiliary être)
je me suis lavé
tu t'es lavé
il s'est lavé
elle s'est lavée
nous nous sommes lavés
vous vous êtes lavés
ils se sont lavés
elles se sont lavées

in the negative form
je ne me suis pas lavé
tu ne t'es pas lavé
il ne s'est pas lavé
elle ne s'est pas lavée
nous ne nous sommes pas lavés
vous ne vous êtes pas lavés
ils ne se sont pas lavés
elles ne se sont pas lavées